COGNITIVE PSYCHOLOGY

To Christine with love
(M.W.E.)

To Ruth and Alicia
(M.K.)

If you know, to recognise that you know,
if you don't know, to realise that you
don't know: That is knowledge.

Confucius

Cognitive Psychology
A Student's Handbook

Fifth Edition

Michael W. Eysenck
Royal Holloway University of London, UK

Mark Keane
University College Dublin, Ireland

HOVE AND NEW YORK

This edition first published 2005 by Psychology Press Ltd
27 Church Road, Hove, East Sussex, BN3 2FA

http://www.psypress.co.uk

Simultaneously published in the USA and Canada
by Taylor & Francis Inc
270 Madison Avenue, New York, NY 10016

Psychology Press is part of the Taylor & Francis Group

British Library Cataloguing in Publication Data
A catalogue record for this book is available from the British Library

Library of Congress Cataloging-in-Publication Data
Eysenck, Michael W.
Cognitive psychology : a student's handbook / Michael W. Eysenck & Mark T. Keane.—5th ed.
p. cm.
Includes bibliographical references and index.
ISBN 1-84169-358-8 (hardcover) — ISBN 1-84169-359-6 (pbk.)
1. Cognition—Textbooks. 2. Cognitive psychology—Textbooks.
I. Keane, Mark T., 1961– II. Title.

BF311.E935 2005
153—dc22

2005001750

ISBN 1-84169-358-8 (hbk)
ISBN 1-84169-359-6 (pbk)

Cover design and image by Anú Design
Typeset in Hong Kong by Graphicraft Limited
Printed and bound in Italy by Legoprint

Contents

Preface

Cognitive psychology has continued to change in several exciting ways since the fourth edition of this textbook was written five years ago. The number of studies of human cognition using brain-imaging techniques has increased dramatically over that period of time. Much more importantly, however, the quality of such studies has increased much more than the sheer quantity. We have finally reached the point at which brain-imaging research is making genuine theoretical contributions to our understanding of human cognition rather than simply providing us with attractive coloured pictures of the brain. This entire approach (often known as cognitive neuroscience) deservedly receives much more coverage in this edition than in previous ones.

Several other approaches to human cognition have also made considerable progress in the last five years. In brief, these approaches are experimental cognitive psychology based mainly on laboratory studies on normals; cognitive neuropsychology focusing on the effects of brain damage on cognition; and computational cognitive science focusing on developing computational models of human cognition.

We have done our level best in this book to identify the most significant research and theorising stemming from the above approaches and to integrate all of this information. Whether we have succeeded is up to our readers to decide. As ever, our busy professional lives have made it essential for us to work hard to avoid chaos. For example, the first author wrote several parts of the book in Argentina, and other parts were written in Brazil, Chile, Beijing, Australia, Bali, South Africa, and Thailand.

I (Michael Eysenck) would like to express my profound gratitude to my wife Christine, to whom this book (in common with the previous two editions) is appropriately dedicated. What she and our three children (Fleur, William, and Juliet) have added to my life is more profound than mere words can express.

I (Mark Keane) would like to express my thanks to all my colleagues at University College Dublin.

We would also like to thank David Andrewes, Marc Brysbaert, Gérard Emilien, Jonathan St. B.T. Evans, John Field, Mark Georgeson, Vittorio Girotto, Ian Gordon, Jonathan Grainger, Patrick Green, Trevor Harley, Ashok Jansari, Ken Manktelow, David Pearson, and Gerry Quinn who commented on various chapters.

Michael Eysenck and Mark Keane

Approaches to Cognitive Psychology

INTRODUCTION

We are now several years into the third millennium, and there is more interest than ever in trying to unravel the mysteries of the human brain. This interest is reflected in the recent upsurge of scientific research within cognitive psychology. What is cognitive psychology? It is concerned with the internal processes involved in making sense of the environment, and deciding what action might be appropriate. These processes include attention, perception, learning, memory, language, problem solving, reasoning, and thinking. Scientific interest in the brain is mirrored in the popular media —there are numerous books, films, and television programmes devoted to the more accessible and/or dramatic aspects of cognitive research. Increasingly, media coverage includes coloured pictures of the brain, showing clearly which parts of the brain are most activated when people perform various tasks.

It is almost as pointless to ask "When did cognitive psychology start?" as it is to inquire about the length of a piece of string. However, the year 1956 was of critical importance. At a meeting at the Massachusetts Institute of Technology, Noam Chomsky gave a paper on his theory of language, George Miller presented a paper on the magic number seven in short-term memory (Miller, 1956), and Newell and Simon discussed their extremely influential model called the General Problem Solver (discussed in Newell, Shaw, & Simon, 1958). In addition, the first systematic attempt to consider concept formation from a cognitive perspective was reported (Bruner, Goodnow, & Austin, 1956).

Artificial intelligence was also founded in 1956, at the Dartmouth Conference, which was attended by Chomsky, McCarthy, Minsky, Newell, Simon, and Miller (see Gardner, 1985). Thus, 1956 witnessed the emergence of both cognitive psychology and cognitive science as major disciplines.

Historically, most cognitive psychologists have adopted the information-processing approach. Some of the main assumptions of this approach are as follows:

- Information made available by the environment is processed by a series of processing systems (e.g., attention, perception, short-term memory).

- These processing systems transform or alter the information in various systematic ways (e.g., three connected lines are presented to our eyes, but we see a triangle).
- The major goal of research is to specify the processes and structures (e.g., long-term memory) that underlie cognitive performance.
- Information processing in people resembles that in computers.

A version of the information-processing approach that was popular at one time is shown in Figure 1.1. According to this version, a stimulus (an environmental event such as a problem or task) is presented to an individual, causing various internal cognitive processes to occur. These processes finally produce the required response or answer. Processing directly affected by the stimulus input is known as **bottom-up processing**. In addition, it was assumed that only one process occurs at any given moment in time. This is known as **serial processing**, meaning that one process is completed before the next begins.

This version of the information-processing approach has been abandoned because it is grossly oversimplified. For example, it ignores **top-down processing**, which is processing influenced by the individual's knowledge and expectations rather than simply by the stimulus itself. Look at Figure 1.2, and read what it says in the triangle. Unless you are familiar with the trick, you will probably have read "Paris in the spring". Look again, and you will see that the word "the" is repeated. Your expectation that it is the well-known phrase (i.e., top-down processing) dominated the information available in the stimulus (i.e., bottom-up processing).

FIGURE 1.1

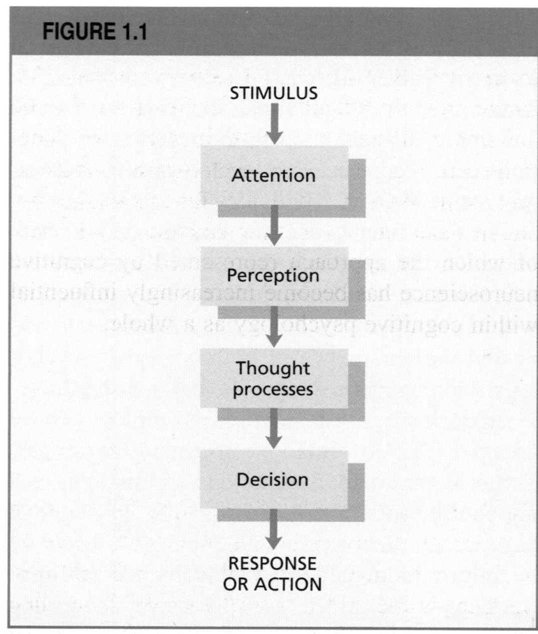

An early version of the information-processing approach.

FIGURE 1.2

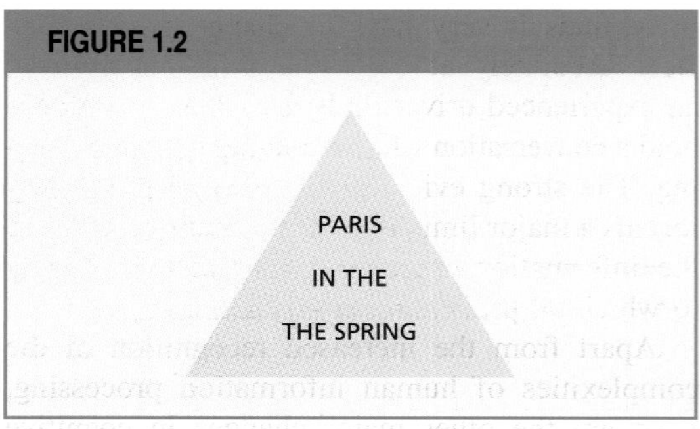

Diagram to demonstrate top-down processing.

Most human cognition involves a mixture of bottom-up and top-down processing. For example, Bruner, Postman, and Rodrigues (1951) carried out a study in which participants expected to see conventional playing cards presented very briefly. When black hearts were presented, some of them claimed to have seen purple or brown hearts. What we have here is an almost literal blending of the black colour, stemming from bottom-up processing, and of the red colour, stemming from top-down processing (i.e., the expectation that hearts will be red).

Processing in which some or all of the processes involved in a cognitive task occur at the same time is known as **parallel processing**. A common form of parallel processing is called **cascade processing**, in which later processes begin before some of the earlier processes have been completed. As we will see in Chapter 5, parallel processing occurs much more often when people are highly skilled and practised in performing a task than when they first encounter it. For example, someone just starting to learn to drive finds it very hard to change gear and to steer accurately at the same time. In contrast, an experienced driver finds it easy, and can even hold a conversation while changing gear and steering. The strong evidence for parallel processing reveals a major limitation in the simple version of the information-processing approach, according to which all processing is serial.

Apart from the increased recognition of the complexities of human information processing, what are the other major changes in cognitive psychology in recent decades? The most dramatic change is the huge increase in the number of weapons available to cognitive psychologists trying to conquer the citadel of the human brain. Cognitive psychology used to consist almost exclusively of laboratory studies on normal individuals. Nowadays, however, many cognitive psychologists study brain-damaged individuals, others construct elaborate computer-based models of human cognition, and still others make use of numerous brain-scanning techniques. More specifically, four major approaches to human cognition have been developed (discussed below), and it is generally accepted that combining information from all four approaches will eventually allow us to attain a full understanding of human cognition. These four approaches are as follows:

- **Experimental cognitive psychology**: This approach involves carrying out experiments on healthy individuals, typically under laboratory conditions.
- **Cognitive neuropsychology**: This approach involves studying patterns of cognitive impairment shown by brain-damaged patients to provide valuable information about normal human cognition.
- **Computational cognitive science**: This approach involves developing computational models to further our understanding of human cognition.
- **Cognitive neuroscience**: This approach (which has become of major importance within the last 15 years) involves using numerous brain-imaging techniques to study aspects of brain functioning and structure relevant to human cognition. This definition of "cognitive neuroscience" is relatively narrow, and a more general definition is considered shortly. This sounds confusing; indeed, it *is* confusing. However, in this book it will nearly always be obvious from the context whether the narrow or the general definition is intended.

The actual distinctions among approaches are less neat and tidy than suggested so far. There has been a rapid increase in the number of studies in which two or more of the four approaches have been combined (some relevant examples are considered later in the chapter). Many of those carrying out such studies regard themselves as cognitive neuroscientists, defining "cognitive neuroscience" in a broad sense. According to Rugg (1997, p. 1), "Cognitive neuroscience aims to understand how cognitive functions, and their manifestations in behaviour and subjective experience, arise from the activity of the brain." The central assumption of cognitive neuroscience is that understanding human cognition requires that we consider evidence about behaviour *and* about brain functioning, and about how brain functioning influences behaviour. This assumption seems very reasonable, given that virtually all human cognition depends on activity in various areas of the brain.

Why has the rise of cognitive neuroscience in this broad sense been relatively recent? The single most important reason is that it used to be extremely difficult to record in detail the functioning of the brain. The development of increasingly sophisticated techniques for assessing brain activity has transformed the situation, as a result of which the approach represented by cognitive neuroscience has become increasingly influential within cognitive psychology as a whole.

EXPERIMENTAL COGNITIVE PSYCHOLOGY

For many years, nearly all research in cognitive psychology involved carrying out experiments on healthy individuals under laboratory conditions. Such experiments are typically tightly controlled and "scientific". Researchers have shown great ingenuity in designing experiments revealing the processes involved in attention, perception, learning, memory, and so on. As a result, the findings obtained by experimental cognitive psychologists have played a major role in the development and subsequent testing of most theories in cognitive psychology.

Experimental cognitive psychology was for many years the engine room of progress in cognitive psychology as a whole, and all three of the newer approaches have derived some benefit from it. For example, cognitive neuropsychology became a significant discipline about 20 years after cognitive psychology. It was only when cognitive psychologists had developed reasonable accounts of normal human cognition that the performance of brain-damaged patients could be understood properly. Before that, it was hard to decide which patterns of cognitive impairment were of theoretical importance. Similarly, the computational modelling activities of computational cognitive scientists are often informed to a large extent by pre-computational psychological theories. Finally, the selection of tasks by cognitive neuroscientists (narrow definition) for their brain-imaging studies is influenced in part by the theoretical and empirical efforts of experimental cognitive psychologists.

A striking success of experimental cognitive psychology has been the way its approach has influenced several areas of psychology. For example, social, developmental, and clinical psychology have all become decidedly more "cognitive" in recent years. Many of the experimental tasks used by researchers in those areas were initially developed in the research laboratories of experimental cognitive psychologists.

Finally, the methodological contributions of experimental cognitive psychology should not be under-emphasised. Experimental cognitive psychologists possess many well-worked-out empirical methods built up over 100 years of experimentation. In computational cognitive science and the neurosciences, in contrast, the methodologies for studying phenomena are still being developed (unsurprising in view of their more recent development). As a result, cognitive modellers are often accused of being unprincipled in their use of models (e.g., Cooper & Shallice, 1995), and in brain imaging there are still many issues about the methods used to rule out "noise" and exclude activity in brain regions that are merely by-products of the focus of a study.

Limitations

In spite of its numerous successes, experimental cognitive psychology possesses various limitations, six of which will be considered here. First, how people behave in the laboratory may differ from how they behave in everyday life. The concern is that laboratory research lacks **ecological validity**, which refers to the extent to which the findings of laboratory studies are applicable to everyday life.

Wachtel (1973) identified an important way in which much research lacks ecological validity. In the real world, people are constantly behaving so as to have an impact on the environment (e.g., turning on the television to watch a favourite programme). Thus, the responses that people make typically change the stimulus situation. In contrast, most of the research of cognitive psychologists involves what Wachtel (1973) referred to as the "implacable [unyielding] experimenter". That is to say, the sequence of stimuli the experimenter presents to the participant is *not* influenced by the participant's behaviour, but rather is determined by the experimenter's predetermined plan.

The problems raised by the implacable experimenter can be seen with respect to attention (see Chapter 5). Fundamental aspects of attention have been de-emphasised, because the participants' focus of attention in most research is determined by the experimenter's instructions. As a result, relatively little is known of the factors normally influencing the focus of attention: relevance of stimuli to current goals; unexpectedness of stimuli; threateningness of stimuli; intensity of stimuli; and so on. This is an important limitation, because we could not predict someone's cognitive processes and behaviour in most situations without detailed knowledge of the factors determining attentional focus.

Second, experimental cognitive psychologists obtain measures of the speed and accuracy of task performance. These measures provide only *indirect* evidence about the internal processes involved in cognition and about their relationship to each other. For example, suppose a researcher believes that four processes underlie performance on a complex task. However, he/she may well be unable to decide whether these processes occurred one at a time (serial processing), with some overlap in time (cascade processing), or all at the same time (parallel processing).

Third, if we are to understand human cognition fully, we need to know what is happening in the brain. This cannot be achieved by experimental cognitive psychology on its own, because it lacks the techniques to study the brain directly. This limitation is, of course, being overcome by the development of numerous technological advances in equipment designed to measure brain activity. This helps to explain the rapid growth in cognitive neuroscience (broad definition).

Fourth, experimental cognitive psychologists have often put forward theories expressed only in verbal terms. As a result, these theories tend to be somewhat vague, making it hard to know precisely what predictions follow from them. This limitation of experimental cognitive psychology can largely be overcome by developing computer models specifying in detail the assumptions of any given theory. This is how computational cognitive scientists (and before them developers of mathematical models) have contributed to the development of cognitive psychology.

Fifth, a puzzling feature of experimental cognitive psychology is the reluctance to take individual differences seriously. The typical research strategy involves using analysis of variance to assess statistically the effects of various experimental manipulations on cognitive performance, with individual differences being relegated to the error term. This might be defensible if everyone used the same processes to deal with a given cognitive task. However, as we will see at various points in this book (e.g., Chapter 16), this is often not the case.

Sixth, the emphasis within experimental cognitive psychology has been on relatively specific theories applicable only to a narrow range of cognitive tasks. What has been lacking is an overarching theoretical architecture. Such an architecture would clarify the interrelationships among different components of the cognitive system. Various candidate cognitive architectures have been proposed, e.g., Anderson's (1993) ACT [Adaptive Control of Thought] model (see Chapter 13). However, the research community has not abandoned specific theories in favour of using cognitive architectures, because researchers are not convinced that any of them is the "one true cognitive architecture".

COGNITIVE NEUROPSYCHOLOGY

Cognitive neuropsychology is concerned with the patterns of cognitive performance (intact and impaired) shown by brain-damaged patients. According to cognitive neuropsychologists, the study of brain-damaged patients can tell us much about normal human cognition. Indeed, according to Coltheart (2001, p. 7), "The essence of cognitive neuropsychology [is] building a theory about normal cognition from a study of abnormal cognition." We can go even further. As McCloskey (2001, p. 594) pointed out, "Complex systems often reveal their inner workings more clearly when they are malfunctioning than when they are running smoothly." As an example, he describes how he only began to discover much about his laser printer when it started misprinting things.

We can gain some insight into the cognitive neuropsychological approach by considering a brain-damaged patient (known as AC), who was studied by Coltheart, Inglis, Cupples, Michie, Bates, and Budd (1998) and discussed by Coltheart (2001). AC was a 67-year-old man who had suffered several strokes, as a result of which he had severe problems with object knowledge. Suppose that we all possess a *single* system for object knowledge. It would then seem to follow that someone like AC would have severe impairment for *all* aspects of object recognition. However, that is not what Coltheart et al. (1998) found. AC was at chance level at deciding whether or not various species of animals possess legs, and his performance was as poor when asked to indicate whether various species possess tails, have a round shape, or are coloured versus black and white.

However, AC was very good at answering other kinds of questions about animals. For example, he was right 95% of the time when asked to classify animals as dangerous or not, he had a 96% success rate when deciding which animals are normally eaten, and a 90% success when deciding which animals live in water. Finally, AC was correct 92% of the time when given a test of auditory perceptual knowledge of animals ("Does it make a sound?"), and his success rate was 95% when given a test of olfactory perceptual knowledge ("Does it have a smell?").

What can we conclude from the above findings? As Coltheart (2001, p. 6) argued:

> If everything we know about objects is represented in a single object knowledge system, it is hard to see how one particular form of knowledge (e.g., visual knowledge) could be lost while other forms of knowledge are essentially intact. We are therefore led to the view that there is a system of knowledge about what objects look like which is quite separate from other stores of knowledge about other kinds of properties of objects.

Thus, the study of a single brain-damaged patient has provided support for a theory of object knowledge in intact individuals (see Chapter 7).

One other general point needs to be made before considering the theoretical assumptions underlying cognitive neuropsychology. The patients studied by cognitive neuropsychologists have all suffered damage to various parts of the brain, and it is of potential importance to relate each patient's cognitive impairments to his/her pattern of brain damage. However, this has *not* been of central concern to cognitive neuropsychology, even though it is to the related area of neuropsychology. As Coltheart (2001, p. 4) pointed out, "Cognitive neuropsychology is not a kind of neuropsychology . . . because . . . cognitive neuropsychology is about the mind, while neuropsychology is about the brain." We can see what this means in practice by returning to the case of AC. He provided evidence that visual perceptual knowledge is stored separately from other kinds of object knowledge. Thus, we may have discovered something important about the cognitive organisation of object knowledge without locating the parts of the brain involved in object recognition.

Coltheart's comments are becoming less applicable as time goes by, for two reasons. First, it is now relatively easy to identify which areas of the brain are damaged in any given patient by using magnetic resonance imaging (MRI) or some similar technique. In years gone by, in contrast, there was much more reliance on post-mortem examination. As a result, accurate identification of the precise scope of a patient's brain damage often occurred several years after his/her cognitive abilities had been assessed. Second, there has been a rapid increase in the number of brain-imaging studies carried out on brain-damaged patients (see Humphreys & Price, 2001, for a review). This combination of cognitive neuropsychology and cognitive neuroscience (narrow definition) is discussed in more detail later in this chapter.

Theoretical assumptions

Coltheart (2001) has described very clearly the main theoretical assumptions of cognitive neuropsychologists, and his analysis will form the basis of our account. One key assumption is that of functional **modularity**. In order to understand the meaning of this assumption, we must consider the term module, which in this context means a processor within the cognitive system functioning to some extent in an independent or separate fashion. In the words of Coltheart (1999, p. 118), a module is

> a "cognitive system whose application is domain specific" . . . a cognitive system is domain-specific if it only responds to stimuli of a particular class . . . to say that there is a domain-specific face recognition module is to say that there is a cognitive system which responds when its input is a face, but does not respond when its input is, say, a written word, or a visually-presented object, or someone's voice.

The assumption of functional modularity implies that cognitive systems consist of sets of modules. This assumption may or may not be correct. Fodor (1983) argued that humans possess various input modules involved in encoding and recognising perceptual inputs. However, he also argued that the central system (which is involved in higher-level processes such as thinking and reasoning) is non-modular. Much of the evidence relevant to Fodor's position is inconsistent.

The second major assumption of cognitive neuropsychology is that of *anatomical modularity*, according to which each module is located in a specific and potentially identifiable area of the brain. Why is this assumption important? In essence, cognitive neuropsychologists make most progress when they study patients having brain damage limited to a single module. Such patients may not exist if the assumption of anatomical modularity is incorrect. For example, suppose all modules were distributed across large areas of the brain. If that were the case, then the great majority of brain-damaged patients would suffer damage to most modules, and it would be impossible to use data from them to work out the number and nature of modules they possessed. In fact, there is very little support for the notion of anatomical modularity. For example, Duncan and Owen (2000) pointed out that the same areas within the frontal lobes are activated when very different tasks are being performed, provided that the tasks are relatively difficult. This finding strongly suggests an absence of anatomical modularity. Alternatively, there may be various modules in the same area of the brain.

The third major assumption is what Coltheart (2001, p. 10) called "uniformity of functional architecture across people". Suppose this assumption is actually false, and there are substantial individual differences in the arrangement of modules. We would be unable to use the findings from individual patients to draw conclusions about other people's functional architecture. We must certainly hope that the assumption of uniformity of functional architecture across people is correct, because, as Coltheart (2001, p. 10) noted, "This assumption is not peculiar to cognitive neuropsychology; it is widespread throughout the whole of cognitive psychology. Thus, if this assumption is false, that's not just bad news for cognitive neuropsychology; it is bad news for all of cognitive psychology."

The fourth (and final) assumption of cognitive neuropsychology is that of *subtractivity*: "Brain damage can impair or delete existing boxes or arrows in the system, but cannot introduce new ones: that is, it can subtract from the system, but cannot add to it" (Coltheart, 2001, p. 10). (In case you are wondering, "boxes" refers to modules and "arrows" to the connections between modules.) Why is the subtractivity assumption important? Suppose patients develop their own modules to compensate for the cognitive impairments caused by the brain damage. If that were the case, it would be very difficult to learn much about intact cognitive systems by studying brain-damaged patients, or at least the task of cognitive neuropsychologists would become more difficult.

How confident can we be that most or all of the theoretical assumptions discussed here are essentially correct? The greatest reason for confidence is the overall success of cognitive neuropsychology based on these assumptions. As Coltheart (2001, p. 11) expressed it, "If any of these four assumptions were false, that would have soon become apparent, because cognitive-neuropsychological research would soon have run into severe difficulties." However, there are real doubts about the assumption of anatomical modularity, and so Coltheart's conclusions may be too optimistic.

Cognitive neuropsychological evidence

How do cognitive neuropsychologists set about understanding how the cognitive system functions? A crucial goal is the discovery of a **dissociation**, which occurs when a patient performs normally on one task (task X) but is impaired on a second task (task Y). For example, the patient AC discussed earlier performed at normal levels on non-perceptual object knowledge (task X) but was severely impaired on perceptual object knowledge (task Y). It is tempting to use such findings to argue that the two tasks involve different processing modules, and that the module or modules needed to perform task Y have been damaged by brain injury.

There is a potential problem in drawing sweeping conclusions from dissociations. A patient may perform poorly on one task and well on a second task simply because the first task is more complex than the second, rather than because the first involves specific modules affected by brain damage. As McCloskey (2001, p. 598) pointed out, one way of interpreting a dissociation is by assuming that "Both tasks require the same processing mechanisms, but one task demands more from these mechanisms than the other, and consequently shows greater impairment when these mechanisms are damaged."

The agreed solution to the above problem is to look for double dissociations. A **double dissociation** between two tasks (X and Y) is shown when one patient performs normally on task X and at an impaired level on task Y, whereas another patient performs normally on task Y and at an impaired level on task X. If a double dissociation can be shown, then we cannot explain the findings away as occurring because one task is harder than the other.

It is generally accepted that the existence of double dissociations provides reasonable evidence that two systems are at work, one of which is required for task X and the other of which is needed for task Y. However, Baddeley (2003) identified two limitations of this approach. First, double dissociations can provide evidence of the existence of *two* separate systems, but are of little or no use when trying to demonstrate the existence of three or four systems. Second, "Even if one accepts the double dissociation as evidence for two systems, this does not necessarily imply that the systems are those proposed by the theorist" (Baddeley, 2003, p. 131).

For the sake of completeness, we will briefly consider associations. An **association** occurs when a patient is impaired on task X *and* is also impaired on task Y. Historically, there was much emphasis on associations of symptoms. It was regarded as of central importance to identify **syndromes**, which are certain sets of symptoms or impairments usually found together. It was typically assumed that performance on two tasks (X and Y) was impaired because they made use of the same mechanisms or modules.

A syndrome-based approach allows us to impose some order on the numerous brain-damaged patients who have been studied by assigning them to a fairly small number of categories. However, there is a fatal flaw with the syndrome-based approach and a reliance on associations to reveal the structure of the cognitive system: associations can occur even if tasks X and Y depend on entirely separate processing mechanisms or modules, if these mechanisms happen to be adjacent in the brain. Thus, associations often tell us nothing at all about the functional organisation of the brain.

Gerstmann's syndrome provides a convincing example of the limitations of evidence based on associations. This syndrome is defined by four very different symptoms: problems of finger identification; problems in calculation; impaired spelling; and left–right disorientation. It seems improbable that any cognitive modules or mechanisms are involved in all four tasks. Instead, it is virtually certain that these four symptoms co-occur because they depend on different modules which happen to be anatomically adjacent in the brain.

Groups vs. individuals

An issue that used to be regarded as highly controversial concerns the relative advantages (and disadvantages) of carrying out group studies (in which patients with the same symptoms or syndrome are considered together) versus single-case studies. In most of psychological research, it is argued that we can have more confidence in our findings if they are based on fairly large groups of participants. However, the group-based approach is very problematic when applied to cognitive neuropsychological research, because different patients typically do not show a uniform pattern of impairments. More specifically, according to McCloskey (2001, pp. 597–598), the key problems are "(a) that aggregating [combining] data over patients requires the assumption that the patients are homogeneous [uniform] with respect to the nature of their deficits, but (b) that regardless of how patients are selected, homogeneity of deficits cannot be assumed a priori (and indeed is unlikely when deficits are characterised at the levels of detail required for addressing issues of current interest in the study of normal cognition)."

If there are convincing reasons for not combining brain-damaged patients into groups, then we must use single-case studies, as has been argued by numerous cognitive neuropsychologists (e.g., Caramazza, 1984). This approach is also not without its problems. As Shallice (1991, p. 433) argued, "A selective impairment found in a particular task in some patient could just reflect: the patient's idiosyncratic strategy, the greater difficulty of that task compared with the others, a premorbid lacuna [gap] in that patient, or the way a reorganised system but not the original system operates."

In most areas of cognitive neuropsychology, it has proved possible to find a number of patients exhibiting rather similar patterns of impairment. It is then possible to replicate the findings from a single case or patient by using further single cases. This approach (the multiple single-patient study method) provides more convincing evidence than can be obtained from a single patient.

The reader may still doubt the desirability of leaning so heavily on data from single patients. However, an important justification for doing precisely that was offered by Coltheart (1984). According to him, cognitive neuropsychologists claim that "there exists a single theory of the relevant cognitive system which can offer interpretations of the various sets of symptoms exhibited by various different patients" (p. 6). Thus, the findings from individual patients can be used to test the researcher's theory. The fact that patients differ from each other is an advantage in some ways, because it means that the underlying theory is exposed to different tests.

We can clarify the above argument with an analogy. The theory being tested is like a very large and complicated jigsaw puzzle, and the individual patients are like very small jigsaw pieces. If the theory is correct, then patients with very different symptoms will nevertheless all fit into the jigsaw puzzle. Conversely, if the theory is incorrect, then there will be some patients (jigsaw pieces) that simply do not fit the theory (jigsaw puzzle). However, most of the jigsaw pieces are very small, and it may be a very long time before we see a coherent picture.

Limitations

What are the limitations of the cognitive neuropsychological approach? First, it is typically assumed that the cognitive performance of brain-damaged patients provides reasonably direct evidence of the impact of brain damage on previously normal cognitive systems. However, some brain-damaged patients may have had somewhat unusual cognitive systems prior to brain damage. In addition, some of the impact of brain damage on cognitive functioning may be camouflaged because patients develop *compensatory strategies* to help them cope with their brain damage. For example, consider patients with pure alexia, a condition in which there are severe reading problems. Such patients do manage to read words by using the compensatory strategy of identifying each letter individually.

Second, in order for cognitive neuropsychology to make rapid progress, it would be ideal to find patients in whom brain damage had affected only *one* module. In practice, however, brain damage is typically much more extensive than that. When several different processing modules are damaged, it is often hard to interpret the findings.

Third, the modular approach may exaggerate the extent to which cognitive functions are localised within the brain (Farah, 1994b). As Banich (1997, p. 52) noted, "The brain is composed of about 50 billion *interconnected* neurons. Therefore, even complex cognitive functions for which a modular description seems apt rely on a number of interconnected brain regions or systems."

Fourth, the entire cognitive neuropsychological approach is very complex, because there are often large differences among individuals having broadly similar brain damage. As Banich (1997, p. 55) pointed out, such individuals "typically vary widely in age, socioeconomic status, and educational background. Prior to brain damage, these individuals may have had diverse life experiences. Afterward, their life experiences likely vary too, depending on the type of rehabilitation they receive, their attitudes toward therapy and recovery and their social support network."

Fifth, cognitive neuropsychology has often been applied to relatively *specific* aspects of cognitive functioning. For example, consider the study of language, which may be regarded as the "jewel in the crown" of cognitive neuropsychology. There has been a substantial amount of work on the reading and spelling of individual words by brain-damaged patients, but rather little on the comprehension of texts.

COMPUTATIONAL COGNITIVE SCIENCE

We will start by drawing a distinction between computational modelling and artificial intelligence. **Computational modelling** involves programming computers to model or mimic some aspects of human cognitive functioning. In contrast, **artificial intelligence** involves constructing computer systems that produce intelligent outcomes, but the processes involved may bear little resemblance to those used by humans. For example, a chess program known as Deep Blue considers approximately 9 billion moves per second, which bears no resemblance to the processing engaged in by human chess players (see Chapter 13). Note that the distinction between computational modelling and artificial intelligence is often blurred in practice.

Computational cognitive scientists develop computational models to understand human cognition. A good computational model can show us that a given theory can be specified and allows us to predict behaviour in new situations. Mathematical models were used in experimental psychology long before the emergence of the information-processing paradigm (e.g., in IQ testing). These models can be used to make predictions, but often lack an explanatory component. For example, having three traffic violations is a good predictor of whether a person is a bad risk for car insurance, but it is not clear why. One of the major benefits of the computational models developed in computational cognitive science is that they can provide an explanatory and a predictive basis for a phenomenon (e.g., Costello & Keane, 2000; Keane, Ledgeway, & Duff, 1994).

Computational modelling: From flowcharts to simulations

In the past, many experimental cognitive psychologists stated their theories in vague verbal statements. This made it hard to decide whether the evidence fitted the theory. In contrast, cognitive scientists produce computer programs to represent cognitive theories with all the details made explicit. In the 1960s and 1970s, cognitive psychologists tended to use flowcharts rather than programs to characterise their theories. Computer scientists use flowcharts as a sort of plan or blueprint for a program, before they write the detailed code for it. Flowcharts are more specific than verbal descriptions, but can still be under-specified.

An example of a very inadequate flowchart is shown in Figure 1.3. This is a flowchart of a bad theory about how we understand sentences. It assumes that a sentence is encoded in some form and then stored. After that, a decision process (indicated by a diamond) determines if the sentence is too long. If it is too long, then it is broken up and we return to the encode stage to re-encode the sentence. If it is ambiguous, then its two senses are distinguished, and we return to the encode stage. If it is not ambiguous, then it is stored in long-term memory. After one sentence is stored, we return to the encode stage to consider the next sentence.

In the days when cognitive psychologists only used flowcharts, sarcastic questions abounded, such as, "What happens in the boxes?" or "What goes down the arrows?". Such comments point to genuine criticisms. For example, after deciding that only a certain length of sentence is acceptable, it may be impossible to decide whether the sentence portions are ambiguous without considering the entire sentence. Thus, real problems may appear when the contents of the boxes are specified.

In similar fashion, exactly what goes down the arrows is critical. If one examines all the arrows converging on the "encode sentence" box, it is clear that more needs to be specified. There are four different kinds of thing entering this box: an encoded sentence from the environment;

FIGURE 1.3

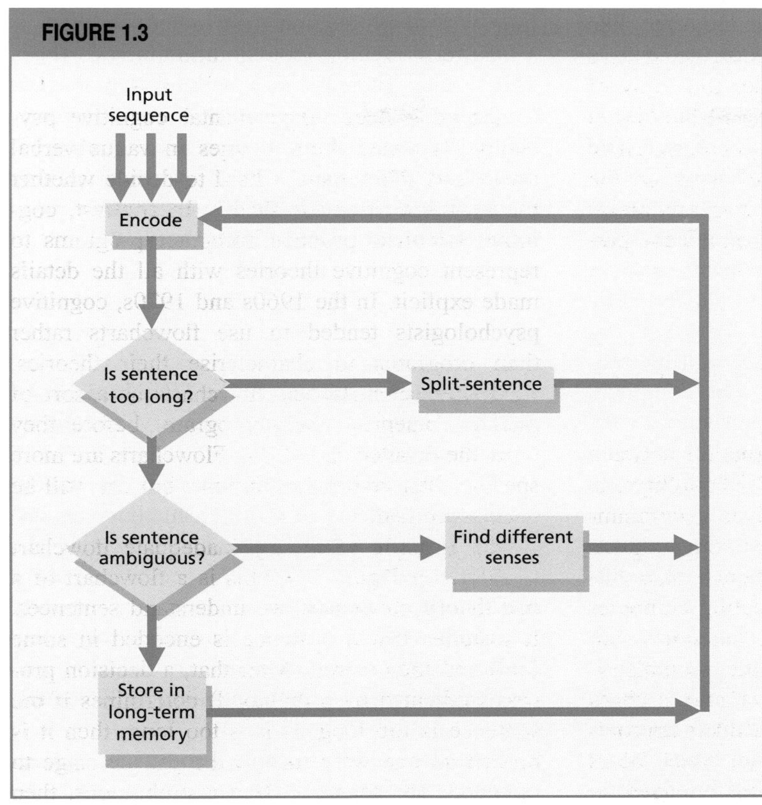

A flowchart of a bad theory about how we understand sentences.

a sentence that has been broken up into bits by the "split-sentence" box; a sentence that has been broken up into several senses; and a command to consider the next sentence. Thus, the "encode" box has to perform several specific operations, but the flowchart sadly fails to consider precisely how this is done.

Implementing a theory as a program is a good method for checking that it contains no hidden assumptions or vague terms. In the previous example, this would involve specifying the form of the input sentences, the nature of the storage mechanisms, and the various decision processes (e.g., those about sentence length and ambiguity). These computer programs are written in artificial intelligence programming languages.

Many issues surround the use of computer simulations and the ways in which they mimic cognitive processes (Cooper, Fox, Farringdon, & Shallice, 1996; Costello & Keane, 2000; Palmer & Kimchi, 1986). Palmer and Kimchi (1986) argued that it should be possible to decompose a theory successively through a number of levels (from descriptive statement to flowchart to specific functions in a program) until one reaches a written program. They also argued it should be possible to draw a line at some level of decomposition, and say that everything above that line is psychologically plausible or meaningful, whereas everything below it is not. This issue of separating psychological aspects of the program from other aspects arises because parts of the program have little to do with the psychological theory, and are there simply because of the particular programming language being used and the machine on which the program is running. For example, to see what the program is doing, it is necessary to have print commands in the program showing the outputs of various stages on the computer's screen. However, such print commands do not form part of the psychological model. Cooper et al. (1996) argued that a formal specification language should be used. This would be a very precise language, like a logic, that would be directly executable as a program.

Other issues arise about the relationship between the performance of the program and human performance (Costello & Keane, 2000). For example, it is seldom meaningful to relate the speed of the program doing a simulated task to the reaction time taken by human participants, because the processing times of programs are affected by psychologically irrelevant features. Programs run faster on more powerful computers, or if the program's code is interpreted rather than compiled. However, the various materials presented to the program should result in differences in program operation time correlating closely with differences in participants' reaction times in processing the same materials. At the very least, the program should reproduce the same outputs as participants given the same inputs.

Computational modelling techniques

It is now time to deal with some of the main types of computational model. Two main types are of special importance, and are outlined briefly here: production systems and connectionist networks.

Production systems

Production systems consist of productions, where a production is an "IF . . . THEN" rule. These rules can take many forms, but an everyday example is "If the green man is lit up, then cross the road." In a typical production system model, there is a long-term memory containing numerous IF . . . THEN rules. There is also a working memory (i.e., a system holding information that is currently being processed). If information from the environment that "green man is lit up" reaches working memory, it will match the IF-part of the rule in long-term memory, and trigger the THEN-part of the rule (i.e., cross the road).

Production systems have the following characteristics:

- They have numerous IF . . . THEN rules.
- They have a working memory containing information.
- The production system operates by matching the contents of working memory against the IF-parts of the rules and executing the THEN-parts.
- If some information in working memory matches the IF-part of many rules, there may be a *conflict-resolution strategy* selecting one of these rules as the best one to be executed.

Consider a very simple production system operating on lists of letters involving As and Bs (see Figure 1.4). The system has two rules:

(1) IF a list in working memory has an A at the end
THEN replace the A with AB.
(2) IF a list in working memory has a B at the end
THEN replace the B with an A.

FIGURE 1.4

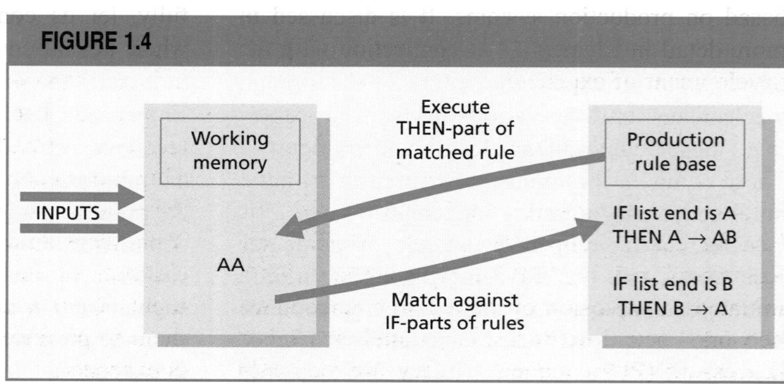

A schematic diagram of a simple production system.

If we give this system different inputs in the form of different lists of letters, then different things happen. If we give it CCC, this will be stored in working memory but will remain unchanged, because it does not match either of the IF-parts of the two rules. If we give it A, then it will be notified by the rules after the A is stored in working memory. This A is a list of one item and as such it matches rule 1. Rule 1 has the effect of replacing the A with AB, so that when the THEN-part is executed, working memory will contain an AB. On the next cycle, AB does not match rule 1 but it does match rule 2. As a result, the B is replaced by an A, leaving an AA in working memory. The system will next produce AAB, then AAAB, and so on.

Many aspects of cognition can be specified as sets of IF . . . THEN rules. For example, chess knowledge can readily be represented as a set of productions based on rules such as "If the Queen is threatened, then move the Queen to a safe square." In this way, people's basic knowledge of chess can be modified as a collection of productions, and gaps in this knowledge as the absence of some productions.

Newell and Simon (1972) first established the usefulness of production system models in characterising cognitive processes like problem solving and reasoning (see Chapter 13). However, these models have a wider applicability. For example, Anderson (1993) put forward his ACT-R theory [Adaptive Control of Thought—Rational], which can account for a wide range of findings (see Anderson & Lebiere, 2003, for a review). ACT-R, developed further by Anderson and Lebiere (1998), is one of the most influential theories based on production systems. It is discussed in more detail in Chapter 13 in connection with the development of expertise.

Connectionist networks

Books by Rumelhart, McClelland, and the PDP Research Group (1986), and by McClelland, Rumelhart, and the PDP Research Group (1986), initiated an explosion of interest in connectionist networks, neural networks, or parallel distributed processing (PDP) models as they are variously called. **Connectionist networks** make use of elementary units or nodes connected together, and consist of various structures or layers (e.g., input; intermediate or hidden; output). Connectionist networks typically have the following characteristics (see Figure 1.5):

- The network consists of elementary or neuron-like *units* or *nodes* connected together so that a single unit has many links to other units.
- Units affect other units by exciting or inhibiting them.
- The unit usually takes the weighted sum of all of the input links, and produces a single output to another unit if the weighted sum exceeds some threshold value.
- The network as a whole is characterised by the properties of the units that make it up, by the way they are connected together, and by the rules used to change the strength of connections among units.
- Networks can have different structures or layers; they can have a layer of input links, intermediate layers (of so-called "hidden units"), and a layer of output units.
- A representation of a concept can be stored in a distributed manner by a pattern of activation throughout the network.
- The same network can store many patterns without them necessarily interfering with each other if they are sufficiently distinct.
- An important learning rule used in networks is called *backward propagation of errors* (*BackProp*) (see below).

In order to understand connectionist networks fully, let us consider how individual units act when activation impinges on them. Any given unit can be connected to several other units (see Figure 1.6). Each of these other units can send an excitatory or an inhibitory signal to the first unit. This unit generally takes a weighted sum of all these inputs. If this sum exceeds some threshold, it produces an output. Figure 1.6 shows a simple diagram of just such a unit, which takes the inputs from a number of other units and sums them to produce an output if a certain threshold is exceeded.

FIGURE 1.5

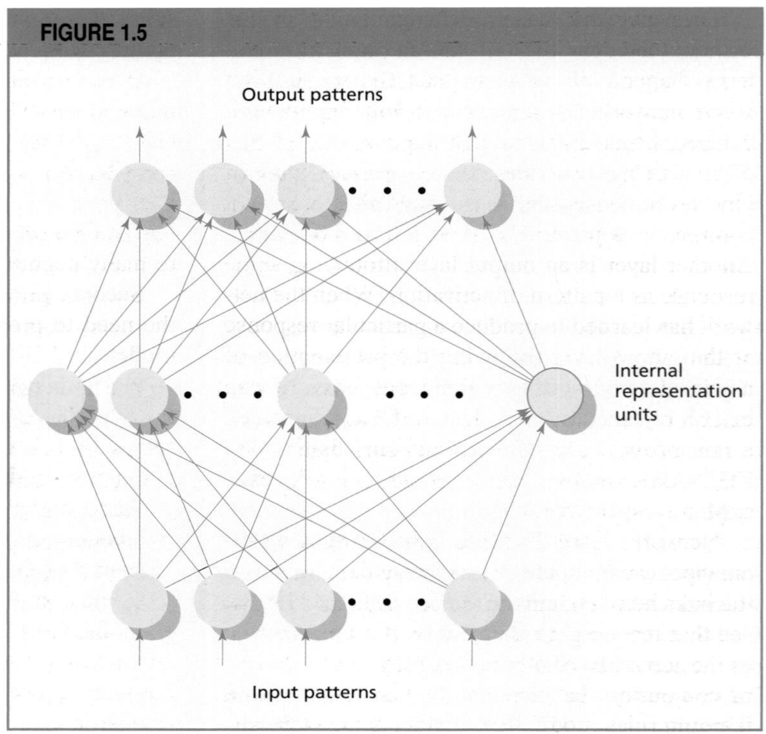

A multi-layered connectionist network with a layer of input units, a layer of internal representation units or hidden units, and a layer of output units. Input patterns can be encoded, if there are enough hidden units, in a form that allows the appropriate output pattern to be generated from a given input pattern. Reproduced with permission from David E. Rumelhart and James L. McClelland, *Parallel distributed processing: Explorations in the microstructure of cognition (Vol. 1)*, published by The MIT Press, © 1986, The Massachusetts Institute of Technology.

FIGURE 1.6

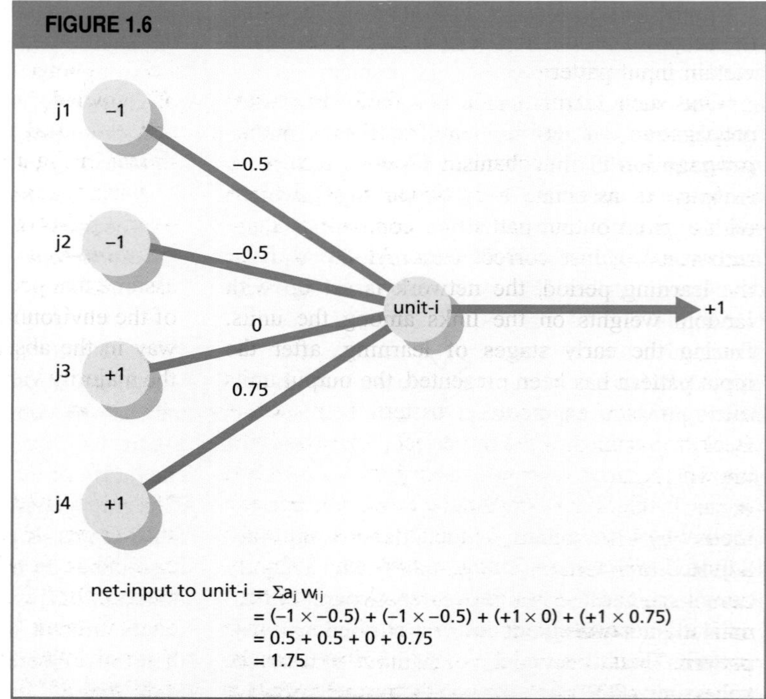

Diagram showing how the inputs from a number of units are combined to determine the overall input to unit-i. Unit-i has a threshold of 1; so if its net input exceeds 1 then it will respond with +1, but if the net input is less than 1 then it will respond with –1.

These networks can model cognitive behaviour without the explicit rules found in production systems. They do this by storing patterns of activation in the network that associate various inputs with certain outputs. The models typically make use of several layers to deal with complex behaviour. One layer consists of input units that encode a stimulus as a pattern of activation in those units. Another layer is an output layer producing some response as a pattern of activation. When the network has learned to produce a particular response at the output layer following the presentation of a particular stimulus at the input layer, it can exhibit behaviour that looks "as if" it had learned a rule of the form "IF such-and-such is the case THEN do so-and-so." However, no such rules exist explicitly in the model.

Networks learn the association between different inputs and outputs by modifying the weights on the links between units in the net. In Figure 1.6, we see that the weight on the links to a unit, as well as the activation of other units, plays a crucial role in computing the response of that unit. Various learning rules modify these weights in systematic ways. When we apply such learning rules to a network, the weights on the links are modified until the net produces the required output patterns given certain input patterns.

One such learning rule is called "backward propagation of errors" or BackProp. **Back-propagation** is a mechanism allowing a network to learn to associate a particular input pattern with a given output pattern by comparing actual responses against correct ones. At the start of the learning period, the network is set up with random weights on the links among the units. During the early stages of learning, after the input pattern has been presented, the output units often produce an incorrect pattern or response. BackProp compares the imperfect pattern with the known required response, noting the errors that occur. It then back-propagates activation through the network so the weights between the units are adjusted to produce the required pattern. This process is repeated with a particular stimulus pattern until the network produces the required response pattern. Thus, the model can be made to learn the behaviour with which the computational cognitive scientist is concerned, rather than being explicitly programmed to do so.

Why has the connectionist approach been so influential (and controversial)? First, as Bowers (2002, p. 438) pointed out, "The key theoretical contribution of connectionist models is . . . that they have introduced a fundamental set of learning and processing principles that apply broadly to many cognitive domains."

Second, previous techniques were marked by the need to program explicitly all aspects of the model, and by their use of explicit symbols to represent concepts. Connectionist networks, on the other hand, can to some extent program themselves, in that they can "learn" to produce specific outputs when certain inputs are given to them.

Third, many (but by no means all) connectionist models are based on the assumption that knowledge (e.g., about a word or concept) is represented in a *distributed* fashion rather than in a given location. In the words of McLeod, Plunkett, and Rolls (1998, p. 3), "Traditional models of cognitive processing usually assume a local representation of knowledge. That is, knowledge about different things is stored in different, independent locations . . . In connectionist models information storage is not local, it is distributed. There is no one place where a particular piece of knowledge can be located." The distinction between local and distributed representations is shown in Figure 1.7.

Fourth, those who devise connectionist networks typically assume that human cognition does not involve the use of explicit rules. Instead, they assume that people are responsive to the structure of the environment and so behave in a "rule-like" way in the absence of rules. This contrasts with the majority view (e.g., Fodor, 2000; Pinker, 1999) that human cognition depends on various rules.

Evidence

Networks have been used to produce very interesting results. For example, Sejnowski and Rosenberg (1987) produced a connectionist network called NETtalk, which was given 50,000 trials to learn the spelling–sound relationships of a set of 1000 words. After this training, NETtalk achieved 95% success with the words on which it

FIGURE 1.7

John	1	0	0	0
Paul	0	1	0	0
George	0	0	1	0
Ringo	0	0	0	1

(a)

John	1	1	0	0
Paul	0	1	1	0
George	0	0	1	1
Ringo	1	0	0	1

(b)

There are four nodes which can take one or two values (0 or 1). In (a), the four names are represented in a *local* fashion, since activity in a single node identifies each name. In (b), the four names are represented in a *distributed* fashion, since it is the *pattern* of activity across nodes that identifies each name. From Page (2000) with permission from Cambridge University Press.

had been trained, and was also 77% correct on a further 20,000 words. Thus, the network seemed to have learned the "rules of English pronunciation" without having explicit rules that combine and encode sounds.

Connectionist models such as NETtalk have great "gee-whiz" value, and have been the subject of much research interest. However, there are important differences between NETtalk and human word reading. For example, NETtalk processes words in a serial fashion from left to right, whereas people typically process short words in a parallel fashion.

Page (2000) and Bowers (2002) identified various problems with the distributed representations often found in connectionist networks. For example, distributed connectionist theories have great difficulty in explaining how we can encode two words at the same time. As Bowers (2002, p. 430) pointed out, "Distributed systems can only represent one thing at a time. A pattern of activation across all the units defines a single item, and overlapping patterns over the same set of units results in a blend that is ambiguous given that there is no way to determine which features belong to which item." Refer back to Figure 1.7. If the names John and George were both encoded at the same time, all four nodes would be activated. Precisely the same pattern of activity would be found if the names Paul and Ringo were encoded at the same time. Thus, it would be impossible to tell which pair of names was being encoded.

Contrary to what is often believed, there is actually no need for connectionist models to assume that representations are distributed. Indeed, several connectionist models assume there is local representation of knowledge. Examples include the reading model of Coltheart, Rastle, Perry, Langdon, and Ziegler (2001; see Chapter 10), the TRACE model of word recognition (McClelland & Elman, 1986; see Chapter 10), and the models of speech production proposed by Dell (1986; see Chapter 12) and by Levelt, Roelofs, and Meyer (1999a; see Chapter 12). Problems plaguing distributed connectionist models (e.g., representing two things at once) are largely avoided by localist connectionist models. In Chapter 10, we consider a direct comparison between a distributed connectionist model of reading (Plaut, McClelland, Seidenberg, & Patterson, 1996) and a localist connectionist model (Coltheart et al., 2001). The localist model predicts human reading performance much more accurately than does the distributed model.

Production systems vs. connectionism

Anderson and Lebiere (2003) had the interesting idea of evaluating connectionism and production systems as exemplified by ACT-R with respect to several criteria suggested by Newell (1980). The 12 criteria they used are shown in Table 1.1, together with their ratings. Note that these ratings are *within-theory*: they indicate how well a theory has done on a given criterion relative to its performance on other criteria. Thus, the ratings are not relative to the other theory, and so do *not* provide a direct comparison of the two theories.

In spite of the fact that the ratings are within-theory, it is of interest to consider those criteria for which the ratings differ substantially between the two theories: operates in human time; uses language; accounts for developmental phenomena; and theoretical components map onto the brain. We will start with operating in human time. Within

Table 1.1

Within-theory ratings of classical connectionism and ACT-R with respect to Newell's 12 criteria.

Criterion	*Connectionism*	*ACT-R*
1. Computationally universal (copes with very diverse environmental changes)	3	4
2. Operates in human time	2	5
3. Produces effective and adaptive behaviour	4	4
4. Uses vast amounts of knowledge	2	3
5. Copes with unexpected errors	3	4
6. Integrates diverse knowledge	2	3
7. Uses language	4	2
8. Exhibits sense of self	2	2
9. Learns from environment	4	4
10. Accounts for developmental phenomena	4	2
11. Relates to evolutionary considerations	1	1
12. Theoretical components map onto the brain	5	2

Scores range from 1 = worst to 5 = best. Based on Anderson and Lebiere (2003).

ACT-R, every processing step has a time associated with it. In contrast, most connectionist models do not account for the timing effects produced by perceptual or motor aspects of a task. In addition, the number of trials taken to acquire an ability is typically very much greater in connectionist models than in human learning (Schneider & Oliver, 1991).

So far as the criterion of using language is concerned, several major connectionist theories are in the area of language as mentioned above. In contrast, as Anderson and Lebiere (2003, p. 599) admit, "ACT-R's treatment of natural language is fragmentary." With respect to accounting for developmental phenomena, connectionist models assume that development is basically a learning process constrained by brain architecture and by the timing of brain development. In contrast, "Language development is an area that has seen spotty efforts from ACT-R . . . there is not a well-developed ACT-R position on how cognition develops."

Finally, there is the criterion of the mapping between theoretical components and the brain. This is a weakness in ACT-R, although there have been some recent attempts to take more account of how ACT-R might be instantiated in the brain (see Anderson & Lebiere, 1998). In contrast, connectionist theorists often claim that connectionist processing units resemble biological neurons. However, this claim is hotly disputed (see below under Limitations).

In sum, the pattern of strengths and weaknesses differs between connectionist models and ACT-R. The focus in many connectionist models is on language and cognitive development, and there have been systematic attempts to take some account of actual brain functioning. In contrast, ACT-R has emphasised the importance of predicting human processing time as well as human behaviour.

Limitations

What are the main limitations of the computational cognitive science approach? First, computational models are rarely used to make new predictions. For any given theory, there are numerous possible models (probably an infinite number), and these variations are rarely explored. To quote Gazzaniga, Ivry, and Mangun (1998, p. 102), "Unlike experimental work which by its nature is cumulative, modelling research tends to occur in isolation. There may be lots of ways to model a particular phenomenon, but less effort has been devoted to devising critical tests that pit one theory against another." Computational cognitive scientists typically develop *one* model of a phenomenon rather than exploring many models, which could then be distinguished by critical empirical testing. However, some exceptions refer to Hummel and Holyoak (1997) and Keane (1997).

One of the reasons for the above state of affairs may be the lack of any definite methodology for relating a computational model's behaviour to human behaviour. As Costello and Keane (2000) pointed out, there are many levels of detail at which a model can simulate people. For example, a model can capture the direction of a difference in correct responses between two groups of people in an experiment, the specific correct and error responses of groups, general trends in response times for all response types, response times and types for specific individuals, and so on. Many models operate at the more general end of these possible parallels, and so may always be weak predictively.

Second, connectionist models that are claimed to have neural plausibility do not really resemble the human brain. For example, it is assumed in many connectionist models that the basic processing units are like biological neurons, and that these processing units resemble neurons in being massively interconnected. However, the resemblances are fairly superficial. There are 12 different kinds of neuron in the human neocortex (Churchland & Sejnowski, 1994), and it is unclear which type or types of neurons most resemble the processing units. In addition, each cortical neuron is connected to only about 3% of neurons in the surrounding square millimetre of cortex (Churchland & Sejnowski, 1994), which does not even approximate to massive interconnectivity. Furthermore, as Garson (2002, p. 5) pointed out, "It is far from clear that the brain contains the kind of reverse connections that would be needed if the brain were to learn by a process such as backpropagation."

Third, numerous models can generally be found to "explain" any sets of findings. As Carey and Milner (1994, p. 66) pointed out, "any neural net which produces a desired output from a specified input is hugely under-constrained; an infinitely large number of solutions can be found for each problem addressed."

Fourth, computational models often fail to capture the scope of cognitive phenomena. Human cognition is influenced by several potentially conflicting motivational and emotional factors, many of which may be operative at the same time. Most models do not try to capture these wider aspects of cognition. For example, most language processing models focus on the process of understanding a sentence or phrase—for instance, a metaphor like "surgeons are butchers"—without considering its emotional import. However, if you were a surgeon, and this was said to you by a patient, the negative implications of the metaphor would be your main concern (see Veale & Keane, 1994). Similar arguments have been made about the failure to capture the moral and social dimensions of cognitive behaviour (Shotter, 1991).

Norman (1980) pointed out that human functioning involves an interplay between a cognitive system (the Pure Cognitive System) and a biological system (the Regulatory System). Much of the activity of the Pure Cognitive System is determined by the various needs of the Regulatory System, including the need for survival, for food and water, and for protection of oneself and one's family. Computational cognitive science (like most of cognitive psychology) focuses on the Pure Cognitive System and virtually ignores the key role played by the Regulatory System.

Fifth, computational cognitive science may fail to deliver on its greatest promise, namely, the provision of a general unified theory of cognition to weld the fragmentary theories of cognitive psychology together. One of the greatest developments in computational cognitive science has been the proposal and elaboration of unified theories of cognition (e.g., ACT-R; connectionism). However, such unified theories have not had a substantial impact within cognitive psychology, and there is some scepticism concerning their fundamental potential (Cooper & Shallice, 1995).

COGNITIVE NEUROSCIENCE

Technological advances mean we now have numerous new and exciting ways of obtaining detailed information about the brain's structure and functioning. In principle, we can now establish *where*

FIGURE 1.8

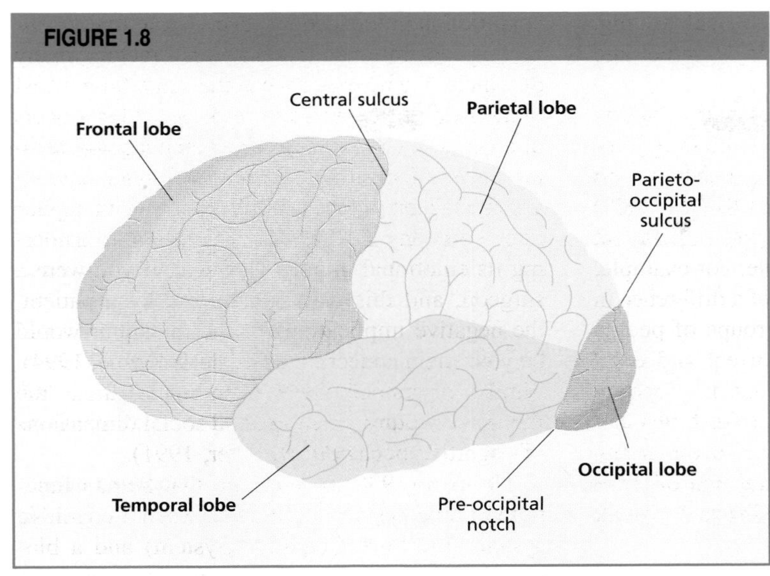

The four lobes, or divisions, of the cerebral cortex in the left hemisphere. From Gazzaniga et al. (1998). Reproduced with permission from the author.

in the brain specific cognitive processes occur, and *when* these processes occur. Such information can allow us to determine the order in which different parts of the brain become active when someone is performing a task. It also allows us to find out whether two tasks involve the same parts of the brain in the same way, or whether there are important differences.

Since our focus here is on the brain, we need to consider how different areas of the brain are described. Alas, the brain is complicated (an understatement!), and various ways of describing specific areas are used. We will briefly mention two of the main ways. First, the cerebral cortex is divided into four main divisions or lobes (see Figure 1.8). There are four lobes in each brain hemisphere: frontal, parietal, temporal, and occipital. The frontal lobes are divided from the parietal lobes by the central sulcus (**sulcus** means furrow or groove), the lateral fissure separates the temporal lobes from the parietal and frontal lobes, and the parieto-occipital sulcus and pre-occipital notch divide the occipital lobes from the parietal and temporal lobes. The main **gyri** (or ridges; gyrus is the singular) within the cerebral cortex are shown in Figure 1.9.

Researchers often use various terms to describe more precisely the area of the brain activated during the performance of some task. Some of the main terms are as follows:

dorsal: superior or on top;
ventral: inferior or at the bottom;
lateral: situated at the side;
medial: situated in the middle.

Second, the German neurologist Korbinian Brodmann (1868–1918) produced a **cytoarchitectonic map** of the brain based on variations in the cellular structure of the tissues (see Figure 1.10). Many (but by no means all) of the areas identified by Brodmann have subsequently been found to correspond to functionally distinct areas. In this text, you will come upon reference to areas such as BA17, which simply means Brodmann Area 17.

The rest of this section of the chapter is divided into two main sections. First, we consider the major techniques used by cognitive neuroscientists, including an assessment of the strengths and limitations of those techniques. Second, we discuss challenging (and controversial) issues relating to the value of functional imaging in understanding human cognition, issues that are also considered in detail in Chapter 17.

FIGURE 1.9

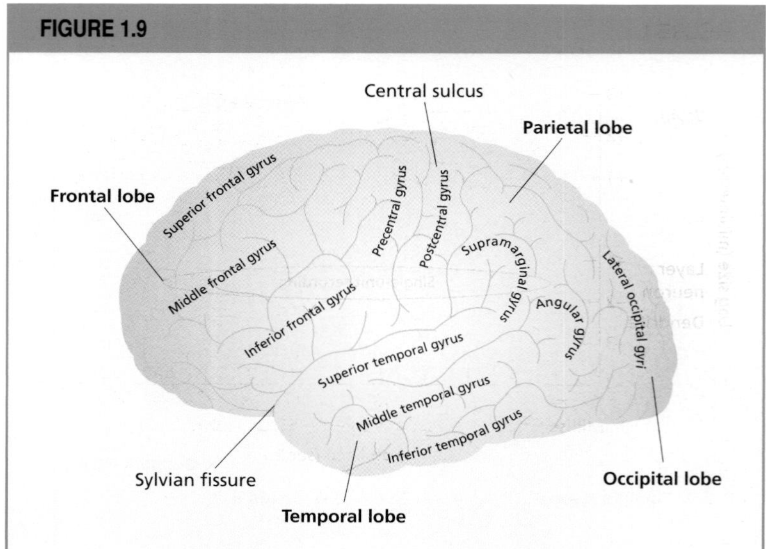

The four lobes within the left hemisphere including some of the main gyri or ridges. From Gazzaniga et al. (1998). Reproduced with permission from the author.

FIGURE 1.10

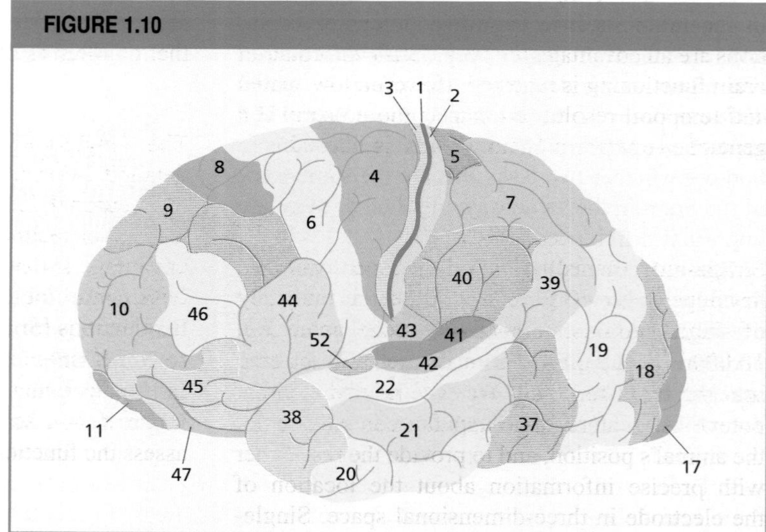

The main areas of the brain identified by Brodmann. From *Cognitive Neuroscience: The biology of the mind* by Michael S. Gazzaniga, Richard Ivry, and George R. Mangun. Copyright © 1998 by W.W. Norton & Company, Inc. Used by permission of W.W. Norton & Company, Inc.

Techniques for study brain functioning

Cognitive neuroscientists use various techniques to study the functioning of the brain with a view to understanding how the brain works. These techniques vary in the precision with which they identify which areas of the brain are active when a task is being performed (spatial resolution) and the time course of such activation (temporal resolution). Some techniques provide information at the single-cell level, whereas others tell us about activity over much larger groups of cells. In terms of temporal resolution, some techniques provide information about brain activity on a millisecond-by-millisecond basis (corresponding to the timescale for thinking), whereas others indicate brain activity only over much larger time periods such as minutes or hours.

FIGURE 1.11

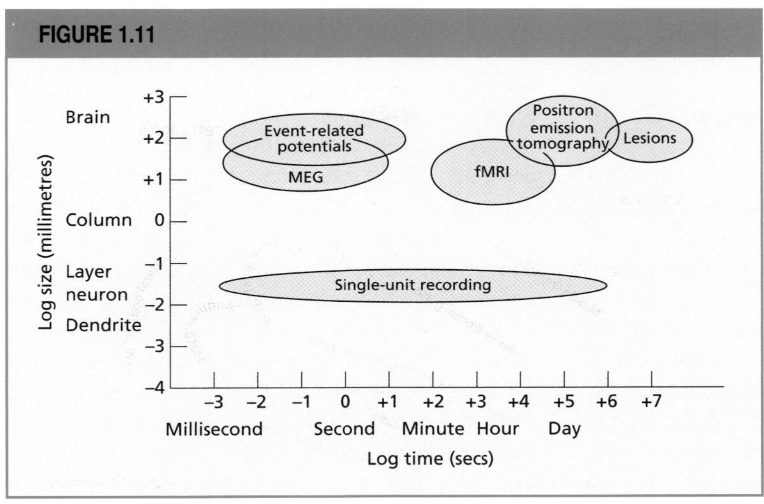

The spatial and temporal ranges of some techniques used to study brain functioning. Adapted from Churchland and Sejnowski (1991).

The spatial and temporal resolutions of some of the main techniques are shown in Figure 1.11. In general terms, high spatial and temporal resolutions are an advantage if a very detailed account of brain functioning is required. However, low spatial and temporal resolutions can be more useful if a general overview of brain activity is needed.

Single-unit recording

Single-unit recording is a fine-grain technique developed over 40 years ago to permit the study of single neurons. A micro-electrode about one 10,000th of a millimetre in diameter is inserted into the brain to obtain a record of extracellular potentials. A stereotaxic apparatus is used to fix the animal's position, and to provide the researcher with precise information about the location of the electrode in three-dimensional space. Single-unit recording is a very sensitive technique, since electrical charges of as little as one-millionth of a volt can be detected.

The best-known application of this technique was by Hubel and Wiesel (1962, 1979), who studied the neurophysiology of basic visual processes in cats and monkeys. They found simple and complex cells in the primary visual cortex, but there were many more complex cells. These two types of cells both respond maximally to straight-line stimuli in a particular orientation (see Chapter 2). The findings of Hubel and Wiesel were so clear-cut that they constrained several subsequent theories of visual perception, including that of Marr (1982; see Chapter 3).

Evaluation

The single-unit recording technique provides detailed information about brain functioning at the neuronal level, and is thus more fine-grain than other techniques (see Figure 1.11). Another advantage is that information about neuronal activity can be obtained over a very wide range of time periods from small fractions of a second up to several hours or days. However, it can only provide information about activity at the level of single neurons, and so other techniques are needed to assess the functioning of larger areas of the cortex.

Event-related potentials (ERPs)

The electroencephalogram (EEG) is based on recordings of electrical brain activity measured at the surface of the scalp. Very small changes in electrical activity within the brain are picked up by scalp electrodes. These changes can be shown on the screen of a cathode-ray tube by means of an oscilloscope. A key problem with the EEG is that spontaneous or background brain activity sometimes obscures the impact of stimulus processing on the EEG recording.

A solution to the above problem is to present the same stimulus several times. After that, the segment of EEG following each stimulus is extracted and lined up with respect to the time of stimulus onset. These EEG segments are then simply averaged together to produce a single waveform. This method produces **event-related potentials** (ERPs) from EEG recordings, and allows us to distinguish genuine effects of stimulation from background brain activity.

ERPs are particularly useful for assessing the timing of certain cognitive processes. For example, some attention theorists have argued that attended and unattended stimuli are processed differently at an early stage of processing, whereas others claim they are both analysed fully in a similar way (see Chapter 5). Studies using ERPs have provided good evidence in favour of the former position. For example, Woldorff et al. (1993) found ERPs were greater to attended than unattended auditory stimuli about 20–50 milliseconds after stimulus onset.

Evaluation

ERPs provide more detailed information about the time course of brain activity than most other techniques, and have many medical applications (e.g., diagnosis of multiple sclerosis). However, ERPs do not indicate with any precision which regions of the brain are most involved in processing. This is due in part to the fact that the presence of skull and brain tissue distorts the electrical fields emerging from the brain. Furthermore, ERPs are mainly of value when the stimuli are simple and the task involves basic processes (e.g., target detection) occurring at a certain time after stimulus onset. As a result of these constraints (and the necessity of presenting the same stimulus several times) it would not be feasible to study most complex forms of cognition (e.g., problem solving, reasoning) with ERPs.

Positron emission tomography (PET)

Positron emission tomography or the PET scan is based on the detection of positrons, which are the atomic particles emitted by some radioactive substances. Radioactively labelled water is injected into the body, and rapidly gathers in the brain's blood vessels. When part of the cortex becomes active, the labelled water moves rapidly to that place. A scanning device next measures the positrons emitted from the radioactive water. A computer then translates this information into pictures of the activity levels in different brain areas. It may sound dangerous to inject a radioactive substance into someone, but only tiny amounts of radioactivity are involved.

Raichle (1994b) has described the typical way in which PET has been used by cognitive neuroscientists. It is based on a subtractive logic. Brain activity is assessed during an experimental task, and also during some control or baseline condition (e.g., before the task is presented). The brain activity during the control condition is then subtracted from that during the experimental task. It is assumed that this allows us to identify those parts of the brain active only during the performance of the task. This technique has been used in several studies designed to locate the parts of the brain most involved in **episodic memory**, which is long-term memory involving conscious recollection of the past (see Chapter 7). There is more activity in the right prefrontal cortex when participants are trying to retrieve episodic memories than when trying to retrieve other kinds of memories (see Wheeler, Stuss, & Tulving, 1997, for a review).

Evaluation

PET has reasonable spatial resolution, in that any active area within the brain can be located to within about 3 or 4 millimetres. It is also a fairly versatile technique, in that it can be used to identify the brain areas involved in a wide range of different cognitive activities.

PET has several limitations. First, the temporal resolution is very poor. PET scans indicate the total amount of activity in each region of the brain over a period of 60 seconds or longer, and so cannot reveal the rapid changes in brain activity accompanying most cognitive processes.

Second, PET provides only an indirect measure of neural activity. As Anderson, Holliday, Singh, and Harding (1996, p. 423) pointed out, "changes in regional cerebral blood flow, reflected by changes in the spatial distribution of intravenously administered positron emitted radioisotopes, are assumed to reflect changes in neural activity." This assumption may be more applicable at early stages of processing.

Third, it is an invasive technique, because participants have to be injected with radioactively labelled water. This makes it unacceptable to some potential participants in PET studies.

Fourth, it can be hard to interpret the findings from use of the subtraction technique. For example, it may seem plausible to assume that those parts of the brain active during retrieval of episodic memories but not other kinds of memories are directly involved in episodic memory retrieval. However, the participants may have been more motivated to retrieve such memories than other memories, and so some brain activity may reflect the involvement of motivational rather than memory systems.

Fifth, the number of brain areas apparently involved in performance of a task depends very much on the level of statistical significance set by the experimenter. As Savoy (2001) showed, the same PET data may show very few brain areas active during task performance if a very stringent criterion is set, but may show numerous brain areas active if a much more lenient criterion is adopted.

FIGURE 1.12

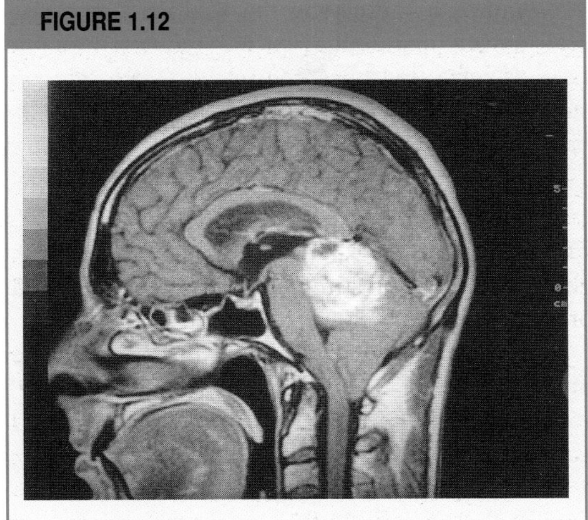

MRI scan showing a brain tumour. The tumour appears in bright contrast to the surrounding brain tissue. Photo credit: Simon Fraser/Neuroradiology Department, Newcastle General Hospital/Science Photo Library.

Magnetic resonance imaging (MRI and fMRI)

In **magnetic resonance imaging** (MRI), radio waves are used to excite atoms in the brain. This produces magnetic changes detected by a very large magnet (weighing up to 11 tons) surrounding the patient. These changes are then interpreted by a computer and turned into a very precise three-dimensional picture. MRI scans (Figure 1.12) can be used to detect very small brain tumours. MRI scans can be obtained from numerous different angles. However, they only tell us about the *structure* of the brain rather than about its *functions*.

The MRI technology has also been applied to the measurement of brain activity to provide functional magnetic resonance imaging (fMRI). Neural activity in the brain produces increased blood flow in the active areas, and there is oxygen and glucose within the blood. According to Raichle (1994b, p. 41), "the amount of oxygen carried by haemoglobin (the molecule that transports oxygen . . .) affects the magnetic properties of the haemoglobin . . . MRI can detect the functionally induced changes in blood oxygenation in the human brain." The approach based on fMRI provides three-dimensional images of the brain with areas of high activity clearly indicated. It is more useful than PET, because it provides more precise spatial information, and shows changes over shorter periods of time. As a result, fMRI has largely superseded PET. However, it shares with PET a reliance on the subtraction technique in which brain activity during a control task or situation is subtracted from brain activity during the experimental task.

A study showing the usefulness of fMRI was reported by Tootell et al. (1995b). It involved the so-called waterfall illusion, in which lengthy viewing of a stimulus moving in one direction (e.g., a waterfall) is followed by the illusion that stationary objects are moving in the opposite direction. There were two key findings. First, the gradual reduction in the size of the waterfall illusion over the first

60 seconds of observing the stationary stimulus was closely paralleled by the reduction in the area of activation observed in the fMRI. Second, most of the brain activity produced by the waterfall illusion was in V5, an area of the visual cortex much involved in motion perception (see Chapter 2). Thus, the basic brain processes underlying the waterfall illusion resemble those underlying normal motion perception.

Evaluation

Raichle (1994a, p. 350) argued that fMRI has several advantages over other techniques:

> The technique has no known biological risk except for the occasional subject who suffers claustrophobia in the scanner (the entire body must be inserted into a relatively narrow tube). MRI provides both anatomical and functional information, which permits an accurate anatomical identification of the regions of activation in each subject. The spatial resolution is quite good, approaching the 1–2 millimetre range.

However, fMRI provides only an *indirect* measure of neural activity. As Anderson et al. (1996, p. 423) pointed out, "With fMRI, neural activity is reflected by changes in the relative concentrations of oxygenated and deoxygenated haemoglobin in the vicinity of the activity." Another limitation is that it has poor temporal resolution of the order of a few seconds, so we cannot track the detailed time course of cognitive processes. A further limitation is that it relies on the subtraction technique, and this may not accurately assess brain activity directly involved in the experimental task.

Finally, as with PET, the number of brain areas apparently involved in performing any given task depends very much on the stringency or leniency of the criteria used to evaluate the data. As Savoy (2001, p. 30) argued, "Will area A in the cortex show a change in activity (an increase or decrease) in response to task X, compared to its response to task Y? If our imaging system is powerful enough . . . then the answer will almost always be Yes, for any A, X, and Y."

Magneto-encephalography (MEG)

Magneto-encephalography or MEG was developed during the 1990s. It involves using a superconducting quantum interference device (SQUID) to measure the magnetic fields produced by electrical brain activity. It can be regarded as "a direct measure of cortical neural activity" (Anderson et al., 1996, p. 423). MEG provides very accurate measurement of brain activity, in part because the skull is virtually transparent to magnetic fields. Thus, magnetic fields are little distorted by intervening tissue, which is an advantage over the electrical activity assessed by the EEG.

Anderson et al. (1996) used MEG in combination with MRI to study the properties of an area of the visual cortex known as V5 (see Chapter 2). MEG revealed that motion-contrast patterns produced large responses from V5, but that V5 was unresponsive to colour. These data, in conjunction with previous findings from PET and fMRI studies, led Anderson et al. (1996, p. 429) to conclude that "these findings provide strong support for the hypothesis that a major function of human V5 is the rapid detection of objects moving relative to their background." In addition, Anderson et al. (1996) obtained evidence that V5 was active approximately 20 milliseconds after V1 (the primary visual cortex) in response to motion-contrast patterns. This is more valuable information than simply establishing that V1 and V5 are both active during this task, because it suggests that activity in V1 *preceded* that in V5.

Evaluation

MEG possesses several valuable features. First, the magnetic signals reflect neural activity reasonably directly. In contrast, PET and fMRI signals reflect blood flow, which is assumed in turn to reflect neural activity. Second, MEG supplies detailed information at the millisecond level about the time course of cognitive processes. This matters because it makes it possible to work out the sequence of activation in different areas of the cortex. There have been developments in MEG technology in recent years, with the result that the spatial resolution of MEG now resembles that of fMRI.

Initially, there were some technical problems associated with the use of MEG, but these problems have been largely (or entirely) resolved. Accordingly, MEG is a valuable tool for assessing brain activation during performance of cognitive tasks.

Transcranial magnetic stimulation

Transcranial magnetic stimulation (TMS) is a technique in which a coil (or pair of coils) is placed close to the participant's head, and a very brief but large magnetic pulse of current is run through it. As a result, there is a short-lived magnetic field, which inhibits processing activity in the area affected. In practice, several magnetic pulses are usually administered in a fairly short period of time; this is known as repetitive transcranial magnetic stimulation (rTMS).

Why are TMS and rTMS useful? In essence, TMS or rTMS creates a "temporary lesion", so that the role of some brain area in performing a given task can be assessed. If TMS applied to a particular brain area leads to impairment of performance on a task, it is reasonable to conclude that that brain area is necessary for normal task performance. Conversely, if TMS has no effects on task performance, then the brain area affected by it is not needed to perform the task effectively.

We will briefly consider one study to show how useful rTMS can be. There has been much controversy concerning the degree of similarity between visual perception and visual imagery. Everyone agrees that primary visual cortex (also known as Area 17) plays a crucial role in visual perception (see Chapter 2), and so it is of interest to find out whether it is also involved in visual imagery. Kosslyn et al. (1999), using PET, found that Area 17 was activated during a visual imagery task. This makes it likely that Area 17 is necessary for visual imagery, but does not definitely establish the point. However, Kosslyn et al. also found when applying rTMS to Area 17 that performance on the imagery task was impaired, which is strong evidence that that area is necessary for good performance on the task (see Chapter 3).

Evaluation

TMS is a technique with exciting potential. Of special importance, it can be used to show that activity in a particular area of the brain is necessary for normal levels of performance on some task. Thus, we are often in a stronger position to make *causal* statements about the brain areas underlying performance when we use TMS than when we use most other techniques. TMS is perhaps of particular importance when used in conjunction with other techniques. For example, fMRI or PET can be used to identify the brain areas that are active when a given task is performed. TMS can then be used to decide which of these brain areas is essential for task performance (as in Kosslyn et al., 1999).

Savoy (2001) identified three major limitations with TMS. First, there are some concerns about safety, especially when magnetic pulses are presented repeatedly in rapid succession. For example, seizures have been induced in normal individuals when a presentation rate of 5–10 pulses per second has been used (Savoy, 2001). In practice, however, magnetic pulses are typically spaced sufficiently in time to ensure that participants will *not* suffer from seizures. Even when this is done, there can nevertheless be minor physical discomfort if TMS activates muscles in the head or face.

Second, TMS has limited spatial resolution. It is hard to ascertain the precise spatial resolution, but it is clear that the area affected by TMS is fairly large (Pascual-Leone, Bartres-Faz, & Keenan, 1999). The peak brain activity triggered by TMS may cover about 0.5–1.0 cm, but activation may extend well beyond this area (Savoy, 2001). Third, the length of time for which TMS affects brain activity is not known with any precision.

There is an additional limitation that should be mentioned. TMS is much more effective when applied to some brain areas than to others. More specifically, it does not work well in areas where there is overlying muscle.

Summary

We have discussed some of the main techniques, all of which possess strengths and limitations. As a result, it is often desirable to combine different techniques to study any given aspect of human cognition. If similar findings are obtained from two techniques, this is known as *converging evidence*. Such evidence is of special value, because it suggests the techniques are not providing distorted information. For example, studies using PET, fMRI, and MEG (e.g., Anderson et al., 1996; Tootell et al., 1995a, 1995b) all indicate clearly that a region of the brain called area V5 is much involved in motion perception (see Chapter 2).

It can be of value to use two techniques differing in their particular strengths. For example, the ERP technique has good temporal resolution but poor spatial resolution, whereas the opposite is the case with fMRI. Accordingly, it is often useful to use both techniques at the same time so that good temporal and spatial resolution can both be obtained.

Limitations

We will now consider some of the general limitations of functional-imaging techniques. First, such techniques are typically most useful when applied to areas of the brain organised in functionally discrete [separate] ways (S. Anderson, personal communication). For example, as we have seen, there is evidence that area V5 is specialised for motion perception. Higher-order cognitive functions are probably not organised in a similarly neat and tidy way. For example, as was mentioned earlier, areas within the frontal lobes are activated across a wide range of complex tasks (Duncan & Owen, 2000). Thus, there is not always a simple relationship between specific processing activities and areas of brain activation.

Second, in most neuroimaging studies, data are collected from several individuals and then averaged. Concern has been expressed about such averaging, because of the existence of significant individual differences. In practice, however, the evidence suggests that the organisation of cognitive functions within the brain is broadly similar for most people.

Third, too many studies in cognitive neuroscience have lacked any clear theoretical basis. There is generally no particular value in discovering that brain areas x and y are activated when individuals perform a given task unless we already have a theoretical understanding of those brain areas. As Tulving (1998, p. 275) pointed out in his typically trenchant way, "The single most critical piece of equipment is still the researcher's own brain . . . What is badly needed now, with all those scanners whirring away, is an understanding of exactly what we are observing, and seeing, and measuring."

Fourth, consider the coloured maps you will have seen showing which areas of the brain were activated when a given task was performed. All the coloured areas are those where the amount of activity exceeded some threshold level determined arbitrarily by the experimenter. The problem here is that the number of brain areas active during performance of a task can vary wildly depending on the threshold level which is set (Savoy, 2001). To make matters worse, we generally have no very convincing arguments as to the appropriate setting of the threshold level.

Theoretical value of functional imaging

The sceptical reader may wonder whether cognitive neuroscientists are right when they claim it is important to know which parts of the brain are active when we are performing a given task. We can develop psychological theories of human cognition *without* considering neurophysiological processes within the brain, and it could be argued that cognitive psychology does not need a contribution from functional-imaging research. Precisely this point was made by Coltheart (2004, p. 22): "Facts about the brain do not constrain the possible natures of mental information-processing systems . . . no facts about the activity of the brain could be used to confirm or refute some information-processing model of cognition." In contrast, Shallice (2004) argued that functional imaging has proved very useful in contributing to our understanding of the major subsystems involved in human cognition and the connections among them.

The basic position adopted here is a consensual one. On the one hand, it remains the case that there are several major questions in cognitive psychology to which cognitive neuroscience has as yet contributed little by way of an answer. Examples of such questions include "Is human cognition rule based?" and "What processes are involved in reading?". On the other hand, as is discussed below, functional imaging is starting to provide important evidence on a range of important issues (see below and Chapter 17). That said, it is indisputable that there is a very long way to go before our understanding of human cognition is transformed by cognitive neuroscience.

Evidence

Humphreys and Price (2001, pp. 119–120) have provided plausible reasons why cognitive neuroscience is of real relevance to theories of human cognition: "Imaging studies can contribute directly to functional-level theories, by providing converging evidence on the neural locus of cognition—knowing 'where' can allow new inferences about 'how' a given task is performed." Their central point is as follows: it can be of great importance to know which areas of the brain are activated during performance of a given task *provided that we already have a reasonably clear idea from previous research of the specific types of processing associated with those areas of the brain.*

We can illuminate the above point by considering a concrete example. People can name objects more rapidly when coloured drawings of objects are presented rather than black-and-white drawings. There are two possible explanations of these findings. First, colour may speed up *perceptual* recognition of objects. Second, colour information may directly influence the process of name *retrieval*, if there is a direct association between a colour and an object's name (e.g., yellow and banana). Moore and Price (1999) carried out a PET study involving the naming of coloured and black-and-white drawings of objects. There was less activation in posterior cortical areas (especially in the right hemisphere) around the occipito-temporal junction with coloured drawings than with black-and-white ones. Previous research had indicated that this area is involved in high-level visual analysis of objects. Thus, it is highly probable that colour speeds up the perceptual recognition of objects. Name retrieval primarily involves areas within the left hemisphere, and so the PET findings provided no support for the view that colour speeds up the processes of name retrieval.

Functional imaging has been combined successfully with other approaches. We will illustrate this by considering two concrete examples in which the cognitive neuropsychology and cognitive neuroscience approaches have been used together. First, we will discuss a study by Price et al. (1998) on **deep dyslexia**. This is a condition in which there are severe problems in reading words, including the making of so-called "semantic errors" (e.g., reading "ship" as "boat"). How can we account for deep dyslexia? According to Coltheart (1980, 2000), deep dyslexics rely very largely on the right hemisphere for language processing as a result of serious damage to the left hemisphere. This causes the poor reading of deep dyslexics, because language processing in most intact individuals is based primarily in the left hemisphere.

Weekes, Coltheart, and Gordon (1997) used various reading tasks with a participant with deep dyslexia (LH), and three other participants. Regional cerebral blood flow during visual word recognition was greater in the right hemisphere than in the left hemisphere. This supports the right-hemisphere hypothesis of deep dyslexia, although other evidence does not (see Chapter 10).

Our second example concerns a brain-damaged condition known as **extinction** (see Chapter 5). Patients with this condition can generally detect a single visual stimulus when it is presented to the contralesional side of space (the side opposite the site of the brain damage). However, they fail to detect the same stimulus when a second stimulus is presented at the same time to the ipsilateral side (i.e., the same side as the brain damage). This failure to detect a contralesional stimulus is known as extinction.

A key issue is to determine the extent to which extinguished stimuli are processed by the visual system. This issue was addressed by Rees, Wojciulik, Clarke, Husain, Frith, and Driver (2000). They used fMRI, and found that extinguished stimuli produced reasonable levels of activation in various areas within the visual cortex. Thus, as Humphreys and Price (2001, p. 147) pointed out, "The patient cannot detect the contralesional stimulus, but the evidence from functional imaging is that the stimulus is processed normally at early stages of vision."

Summary

There will be a substantial increase in the number of studies combining the cognitive neuroscience approach with other approaches in the future. Among other advantages, this will serve to reduce the number of incorrect conclusions that are reached. For example, there is a tendency for the cognitive neuropsychological approach to *underestimate* the brain areas necessary to perform a given cognitive function, whereas the brain-imaging approach tends to *overestimate* them. If both approaches are applied to the same task, then there are reasonable prospects of the true state of affairs revealing itself. More generally, the goal of achieving a complete understanding of human cognition will almost certainly require the four approaches to cognitive psychology to be combined (see discussion in Chapter 17).

OUTLINE OF THIS BOOK

One problem with writing a textbook of cognitive psychology is that virtually all the processes and structures of the cognitive system are interdependent. Consider, for example, the case of a student *reading* a book to prepare for an examination. The student is *learning*, but there are several other processes going on as well. *Visual perception* is involved in the intake of information from the printed page, and there is *attention* to the content of the book (although attention may be captured by irrelevant stimuli). In order for the student to profit from the book, he or she must possess considerable *language skills*, and must also have rich *knowledge representations* that are relevant to the material in the book. There may be an element of *problem solving* in the student's attempts to relate what is in the book to the possibly conflicting information he or she has learned elsewhere. Furthermore, what the student learns will depend on his or her *emotional state*. Finally, the acid test of whether the learning has been effective and produced *long-term memory* comes during the examination itself, when the material contained in the book must be *retrieved*.

The words italicised in the previous paragraph indicate some of the main ingredients of human cognition, and form the basis of our coverage of cognitive psychology. In view of the interdependent functioning of all aspects of the cognitive system, there is an emphasis in this book on the ways in which each process (e.g., perception) depends on other processes and structures (e.g., attention, long-term memory, stored representations). This should aid the task of making sense of the complexities of the human cognitive system.

CHAPTER SUMMARY

- Introduction
  Historically, cognitive psychology was unified by a common approach based on an analogy between the mind and the computer. This information-processing approach viewed the mind as a general-purpose, symbol-processing system of limited capacity. Today there are four main approaches within cognitive psychology: experimental cognitive psychology; cognitive neuropsychology; computational cognitive science; and cognitive neuroscience (focusing on brain imaging). However, the four approaches are increasingly combined, with information from behaviour and from brain activity being integrated. This integrative approach is often referred to as cognitive neuroscience in the broad sense.

- Experimental cognitive psychology
  Experimental cognitive psychology has been of great importance historically. Well-controlled laboratory studies have revealed much about the processes and structures involved in human cognition. However, such studies sometimes lack ecological validity, and provide no direct evidence of brain functioning. Experimental cognitive psychologists typically ignore individual differences. Their theories tend to apply only to a narrow range of cognitive tasks, and to be expressed in rather vague terms.

- Cognitive neuropsychology
  Cognitive neuropsychologists assume that the cognitive system is modular, that there is isomorphism between the organisation of the physical brain and the mind, and that the study of brain-damaged patients can tell us much about normal human cognition. Cognitive neuropsychologists used to pay little attention to the brain, but this is much less so nowadays. Double dissociations are typically much more informative than associations of symptoms and syndromes. It can be hard to interpret the findings from brain-damaged patients for various reasons: they may develop compensatory strategies after brain damage; the brain damage may affect several modules; they may have had specific cognitive impairments *before* the brain damage.

- Computational cognitive science
  Computational cognitive scientists focus on computational models, in which theoretical assumptions have to be made explicit. These models are expressed in computer programs, which should produce the same outputs as people when given the same inputs. Production systems and connectionist networks are important types of computational models having somewhat different patterns of strengths and limitations. Production systems consist of productions in the form of "IF . . . THEN" rules. Connectionist networks differ from previous approaches in that they can "learn" from experience (e.g., through the backward propagation of errors) and they lack explicit rules. Such networks often have several structures or layers (e.g., input units, intermediate or hidden units, and output units). Representations in connectionist networks are often distributed, but localist connectionist networks are generally more successful. Computational models rarely make new predictions, they lack neural plausibility in several ways, and motivational and emotional influences on cognitive processing are ignored.

- Cognitive neuroscience
  Cognitive neuroscientists use various techniques for studying the brain, with these techniques varying in their spatial and temporal resolution. It is often useful to combine two techniques differing in their strengths. Transcranial magnetic stimulation has the advantage that it can potentially be used to show that a given brain area is necessarily involved in a particular cognitive function. Functional imaging is generally most useful when the focus is on brain areas organised in functionally discrete ways. Limitations include ignoring individual differences, the atheoretical nature of much research, and the use of arbitrary criteria to decide how many brain areas are activated during a given task. There is much controversy concerning the potential value of functional-imaging data to an understanding of human cognition. However, there are encouraging signs that cognitive neuroscience can contribute to the resolution of important theoretical issues. Progress has been greatly assisted by our increased understanding of the roles in human cognitive processing played by numerous brain areas.

FURTHER READING

- Anderson, J.R., & Lebiere, C. (2003). The Newell Test for a theory of cognition. *Behavioral and Brain Sciences*, *26*, 587–640. The authors assess the relative strengths and weaknesses of the connectionist and ACT-R production system approaches in terms of several criteria.
- D'Esposito, M. (2003). *Neurological foundations of cognitive neuroscience*. Cambridge, MA: MIT Press. The contributors to this edited book focus on understanding various disorders of language, memory, and attention from the cognitive neuropsychology and cognitive neuroscience perspectives.
- Garson, J. (2002). Connectionism. In E.N. Zalta (Ed.), *The Stanford Encyclopedia of Philosophy* (winter 2002 edition). Retrieved September 28, 2004 from http://plato.stanford.edu.archives/entries/connectionism This article provides a good overall account of connectionism including an account of its strengths and limitations.
- Gazzaniga, M.S., Ivry, R.B., & Mangun, G.R. (2002). *Cognitive neuroscience: The biology of the mind* (2nd Ed.). New York: Norton. This book provides a good account of the ways in which studying the brain has increased our understanding of human behaviour.
- Harley, T.A. (2004). Does cognitive neuropsychology have a future? *Cognitive Neuropsychology*, *21*, 3–16. This article (and replies to it in the same issue of the journal by Caplan, McCloskey, Dell, Coltheart, Vallar, Shallice and Lambon Ralph) provides interesting views on many key issues relating to cognitive neuropsychology, connectionism, and cognitive neuroscience. Be warned that the experts often have very different views from each other!
- Humphreys, G.W., & Price, C.J. (2001). Cognitive neuropsychology and functional brain imaging: Implications for functional and anatomical models of cognition. *Acta Psychologica*, *107*, 119–153. The theoretical value of neuroimaging and the important relationship between cognitive neuropsychology and cognitive neuroscience are discussed thoroughly.

Part I

Visual Perception and Attention

Visual perception is of enormous importance in our everyday lives. It allows us to move around freely, to see people with whom we are interacting, to read magazines and books, to admire the wonders of nature, and to watch films and television. It is also enormously important because we depend on visual perception being accurate to ensure our survival. For example, if we misperceived how close we were to the edge of a cliff or how close cars were to us as we tried to cross the road, the consequences could easily be fatal. Thus, it comes as no surprise to discover that far more of the cortex is devoted to vision than to any other sensory modality.

We should probably make a start by considering what is meant by *perception*: "The acquisition and processing of sensory information in order to see, hear, taste, or feel objects in the world; also guides an organism's actions with respect to those objects" (Sekuler & Blake, 2002, p. 621). Visual perception seems so simple and effortless that we typically take it for granted. In fact, it is very complex, and numerous processes are involved in transforming and interpreting sensory information. Some of the complexities of visual perception only became clear when researchers in artificial intelligence tried to program computers to "perceive" the environment. Even when the environment was artificially simplified (e.g., consisting only of white solids) and the task was apparently easy (e.g., deciding how many objects there are), computers required very complicated programming to succeed. It is still the case that no computer can match more than a fraction of the skills of visual perception possessed by nearly every adult human.

As the authors have discovered to their cost, there is a vast literature on visual perception. What we have endeavoured to do over the next three chapters is to provide reasonably detailed coverage of the main issues. In Chapter 2, our coverage of visual perception focuses on a discussion of basic processes, emphasising the enormous advances that have been made in understanding the various brain systems involved. In addition, there is detailed consideration of important aspects of visual perception including colour perception, perception without awareness, and depth and size perception.

One of the major achievements of perceptual processing is object recognition, which involves identifying the objects in the world around us.

The central focus of Chapter 3 is on the processes underlying this achievement. Initially, we discuss perceptual organisation, and the ways in which we decide which parts of the visual information presented to us belong together and thus form an object. We then move onto other, related issues. Are the same processes used regardless of the type of object? This is a controversial issue, but many experts have argued that face recognition differs in important ways from ordinary object recognition. Accordingly, face recognition is discussed separately. The final part of Chapter 3 is devoted to another major controversial issue, namely whether the processes involved in visual imagery are the same as those involved in visual perception. As we will see, there are good grounds for arguing that this controversy has recently been resolved (turn to Chapter 3 to find out how!).

When people think about visual perception, they naturally think in terms of object recognition and our conscious awareness of our environment. However, it could well be argued that that is not the only important function of visual perception. Perception is also vitally important in guiding our actions, helping to make sure we don't knock into objects or trip over when walking on rough surfaces. It is perhaps natural to assume that the same processes that lead to object recognition also guide perception for action. However, we will see in Chapter 4 that somewhat different processes are involved. In that chapter, we start by considering the views of James Gibson, who argued more than 50 years ago that perception and action are very closely connected. We also discuss various issues related to perception for action, including visually guided action, the processes involved in reaching and grasping, and motion perception.

There are clearly important links between visual perception and attention. Indeed, the final topic discussed in Chapter 4 is concerned with the notion that we may need to *attend* to an object in order to perceive it consciously. Issues relating directly to attention are considered in detail in Chapter 5. In that chapter, we start by considering the processes involved in focused attention in the visual and auditory modalities. After that, we consider how we use visual processes when engaged in the everyday task of searching for some object (e.g., a pair of socks in a drawer). There has been a dramatic increase in the amount of research concerned with disorders of visual attention, and this research has greatly increased our understanding of visual attention in healthy individuals. Finally, as we all know to our cost, it can be very hard to do two things at once. We conclude Chapter 5 by considering the factors determining the extent to which we do this successfully or unsuccessfully.

In sum, the area spanning visual perception and attention is among the most exciting and important ones within cognitive psychology. There has been tremendous progress in unravelling the complexities of perception and attention over the past decade, and some of the choicest fruits of that endeavour are set before you in the four chapters forming this section of the book.

2

Basic Processes in Visual Perception

INTRODUCTION

There has been considerable progress in understanding visual perception in recent years. Much of this is due to the efforts of cognitive neuroscientists, thanks to whom we now have reasonable knowledge of the brain systems involved in visual perception. We will begin by considering the main areas of the brain involved in vision and the functions served by each area. After that, some of the main theories of brain systems in vision are discussed. Finally, there is a detailed consideration of some of the basic aspects of visual perception (e.g., colour processing, motion processing, depth processing).

BRAIN SYSTEMS

In this section, we focus mainly on some of the main brain systems involved in visual perception. However, in order to understand fully visual processing in the brain, it is useful to consider what happens between the eye and the cortex. Accordingly, we start with that before moving on to discuss cortical processing.

From eye to cortex

What happens when a visual stimulus reaches receptors in the retina of the eye? There are *three* major consequences (Kalat, 2001). First, there is *reception*, which involves absorption of physical energy by the receptors. Second, there is *transduction*, in which the physical energy is converted into an electrochemical pattern in the neurons. Third, there is *coding*, meaning there is a direct one-to-one correspondence between aspects of the physical stimulus and aspects of the resultant nervous system activity.

Light waves from objects in the environment pass through the transparent cornea at the front of the eye and proceed to the iris (see Figure 2.1). It is just in behind the cornea and gives the eye its distinctive colour. The amount of light entering the eye is determined by the pupil, which is an opening in the iris. The lens focuses light onto the retina at the back of the eye. Each lens adjusts in shape by a process of accommodation to bring images into focus on the retina.

FIGURE 2.1

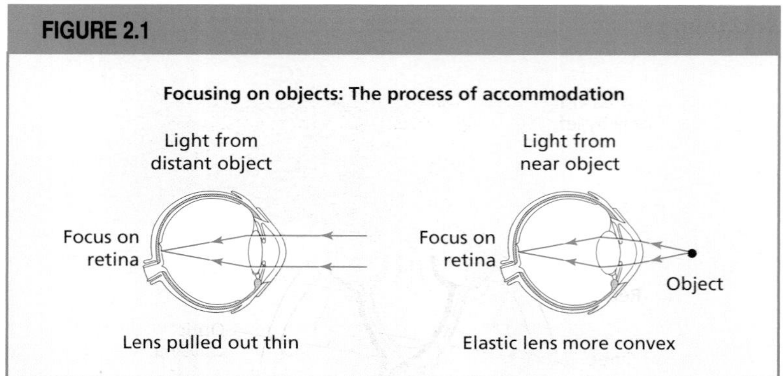

The process of accommodation.

The retina itself is complex, consisting of five different layers of cells. The arrangement of these cells is slightly odd. Light from the lens goes through all the layers of cells until it reaches the receptor cells at the back, after which the neural message goes back through the layers. Impulses from the retina leave the eye via the optic nerve, which is at the front of the retina.

There are two types of visual receptor cells in the retina: cones and rods. There are six million cones, mostly in the fovea or central part of the retina. The cones are specialised for colour vision and for sharpness of vision (see later section on colour perception). There are 125 million rods concentrated in the outer regions of the retina. Rods are specialised for vision in dim light and for movement detection. Many of these differences between cones and rods stem from the fact that a retinal ganglion cell receives input from only a few cones but from hundreds of rods. Thus, only rods produce much activity in retinal ganglion cells in poor lighting conditions.

The main pathway between the eye and the cortex is the retina-geniculate-striate pathway. This transmits information from the retina to the primary visual cortex or striate cortex via the lateral geniculate nuclei of the thalamus. The entire retina-geniculate-striate system is organised in a similar way to the retinal system. Thus, for example, two stimuli adjacent to each other in the retinal image will also be adjacent to each other at higher levels within that system.

Each eye has its own optic nerve, and the two optic nerves meet at the optic chiasma. At this point, the axons from the outer halves of each retina proceed to the hemisphere on the same side, whereas the axons from the inner halves cross over and go to the other hemisphere. Signals then proceed along two optic tracts within the brain. One tract contains signals from the left half of each eye, and the other signals from the right half (see Figure 2.2).

After the optic chiasma, the optic tract proceeds to the lateral geniculate nucleus (LGN), which is part of the thalamus. Nerve impulses finally reach the primary visual cortex within the occipital lobe before spreading out to nearby secondary visual cortical areas.

There is another important feature of the retina-geniculate-striate system. There are two relatively independent channels or pathways within this system:

(1) The parvocellular (or P) pathway: this pathway is most sensitive to colour and to fine detail; most of its input comes from cones.
(2) The magnocellular (or M) pathway: this pathway is most sensitive to information about movement; most of its input comes from rods.

Brain systems

As mentioned above, neurons from the P and M pathways mainly project to the primary visual cortex or V1 (see Figure 2.3). The P and M pathways are not totally segregated, because there is an input from the M pathway into the P pathway (Nealey & Maunsell, 1994). The P pathway has

FIGURE 2.2

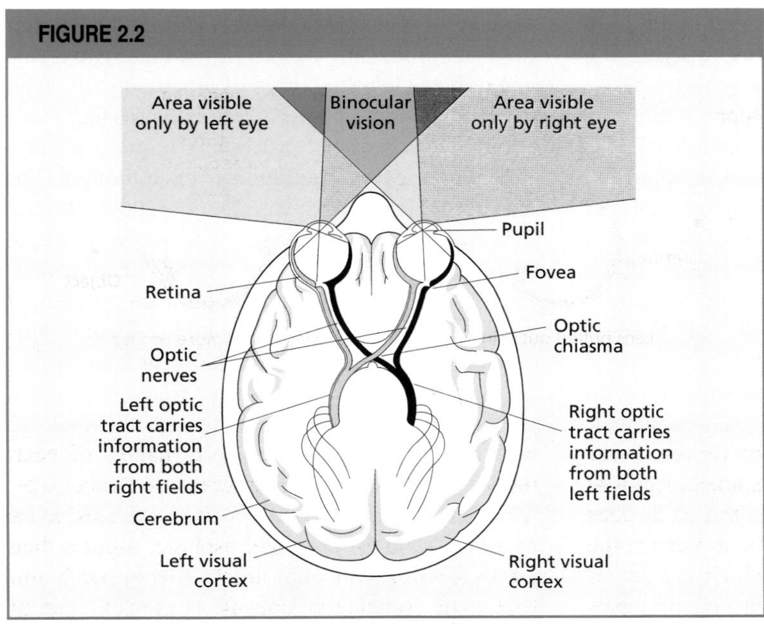

Route of visual signals. Note that all light from the fields left of centre of both eyes (blue) falls on the right sides of the two retinas; and information about these fields goes to the right visual cortex. Information about the right fields of vision (grey) goes to the left cortex. Data about the binocular vision go to both cortices.

FIGURE 2.3

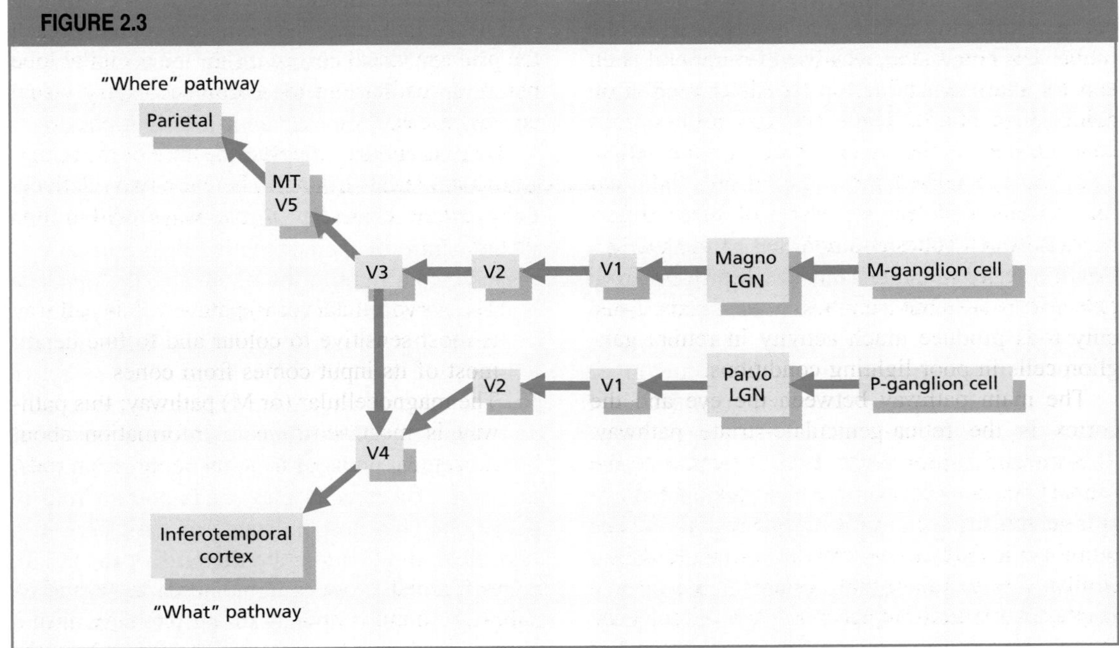

A very simplified illustration of the pathways and brain areas involved in vision. There is much more interconnectivity within the brain (VI onwards) than is shown, and there are additional unshown brain areas involved in vision. Adapted from Goldstein (1996).

two divisions. The areas associated with high metabolic activity are called **blobs**, whereas the areas of lower activity are called **interblobs**. These areas correspond to separate divisions within the P pathway. Cells in all three pathways (the M pathway; blob regions of the P pathway; interblob regions of the P pathway) respond strongly to contrast. Cells in the M pathway also respond strongly to motion, those in the blob regions of the P pathway respond strongly to colour, and those in the interblob regions respond strongly to location and orientation.

There are three repeating substructures in area V2, consisting of thick stripes, thin stripes, and interstripes. The thick stripes represent the continuation of the M pathway, the thin stripes are a continuation of the P-blob pathway, and the interstripes are an extension of the P-interblob pathway.

After V2, there are two visual pathways proceeding further into the cortex. These are the parietal and temporal pathways, respectively (see Figure 2.3). We will be considering these pathways in more detail shortly. For now, note that the parietal pathway is mainly concerned with movement processing, whereas the temporal pathway is more concerned with colour and form processing.

V1 and V2

We will start with three important general points. First, in order to understand visual processing in primary visual cortex (V1) and in secondary visual cortex (V2), we must consider the notion of **receptive field**. The receptive field for any given neuron is that region of the retina in which light affects its activity.

Second, neurons often have effects on each other. For example, there is the phenomenon of **lateral inhibition**, a reduction of activity in one neuron caused by activity in a neighbouring neuron. Lateral inhibition is useful, because it increases the contrast at the edges of objects, thus making it easier to identify the dividing line between one object and another.

Third, the primary visual cortex (V1) and the secondary visual cortex (V2) occupy relatively large areas within the cortex. A substantial amount of visual processing occurs within these two areas, and only some of the types of processing involved will be considered here. There is increasing evidence that early visual processing in areas V1 and V2 is more extensive than was once thought. For example, Hegde and Van Essen (2000) studied neuronal responses to complex shapes in macaque monkeys. They found that "approximately one-third of the V2 cells showed significant differential responsiveness to various complex shape characteristics, and many were also selective for the orientation, size, and/or spatial frequency of the preferred shape. These results indicate that V2 cells explicitly represent complex shape information" (Hegde & Van Essen, 2000, p. RC61).

Much of our knowledge of neurons (and their receptive fields) in primary and secondary visual cortex comes from the Nobel-Prize-winning research of Hubel and Wiesel. They used single-unit recordings to study individual neurons, and found that many cells responded in two different ways to a spot of light depending on which part of the cell was affected:

(1) An "on" response, with an increased rate of firing while the light was on.
(2) An "off" response, with the light causing a decreased rate of firing.

On-centre cells produce the on-response to a light in the centre of their receptive field and an off-response to a light in the periphery; the opposite is the case with off-centre cells.

Hubel and Wiesel (e.g., 1979) discovered the existence of two types of neurons in the receptive fields of the primary visual cortex: simple cells and complex cells. Simple cells have "on" and "off" regions, with each region being rectangular in shape. These cells play an important role in detection. They respond most to dark bars in a light field, light bars in a dark field, or to straight edges between areas of light and dark. Any given simple cell only responds strongly to stimuli of a particular orientation, and so the responses of these cells could be relevant to feature detection.

Complex cells resemble simple cells in that they respond maximally to straight-line stimuli in a particular orientation. However, complex cells have large receptive fields, and they respond more to moving contours. Each complex cell is driven by several simple cells having the same orientation preference and closely overlapping receptive fields (Alonso & Martinez, 1998).

Finally, there are hypercomplex cells. These cells respond most to rather more complex patterns than do simple or complex cells. Of key importance, hypercomplex cells produce a stronger response to a line ending within the field than to one crossing it.

Cortical cells provide *ambiguous* information, because they respond in the same way to different stimuli. For example, a cell responding maximally to a horizontal line moving slowly may respond moderately to a horizontal line moving rapidly and to a nearly horizontal line moving slowly. We need to *combine* information from numerous neurons in order to remove ambiguities.

Another important feature of primary visual cortex is that it is organised as a **retinotopic map**, which is defined as "an array of nerve cells that have the same positions relative to one another as their receptive fields have on the surface of the retina" (Bruce, Green, & Georgeson, 2003, pp. 462–463). Thus, the spatial organisation within early visual cortex resembles that on the retina. However, the retinotopic map is inverted compared to the arrangement on the retina, and the cortical area devoted to the centre of the visual field is much larger than that devoted to its periphery.

There is a final key point concerning primary visual cortex. We have focused so far on the notion that V1 and V2 are involved in the early stages of visual processing. That is correct, but it is not the complete story. According to Lamme and Roelfsema (2000), there is an initial "feedforward sweep" proceeding systematically through the visual areas in the way shown in Figure 2.3. After that, however, there is a second phase of processing in which feedback signals proceed in the opposite direction.

Evidence for the above view was reported by Lee, Mumford, Romero, and Lamme (1998). Complex cells in V1 responded selectively to orientation of line segments during the initial feedforward sweep. After 60 ms, these cells started responding to a boundary between two regions of differently oriented line segments, provided that the boundary was aligned with their preferred orientation. Thus, there was a shift from "low-level" filtering of orientation of local image elements to "high-level" filtering of boundaries.

Warnings

Two key points need to be made before proceeding. First, a very oversimplified view of brain functioning is presented in this chapter. There are more than 30 visual areas in the visual cortex, and approximately 25% of the cortex is devoted to vision. Second, as Preuss, Qi, and Kaas (1999, p. 11601) pointed out, "Our current understanding of the structure and function of the human visual system depends critically on experimental studies of non-human primates, especially macaque monkeys." The assumption that the visual systems of humans and non-human primates are basically similar is not entirely correct. For example, Preuss et al. (1999, p. 11605) discovered important differences between humans and monkeys in the organisation of primary visual cortex (V1), and there are major differences between those two species in the brain areas devoted to motion processing (Orban et al., 2003; see later).

Functional specialisation theory

Zeki (1992, 1993) put forward a functional specialisation theory, according to which different parts of the cortex are specialised for different visual functions. By analogy, the visual system resembles a team of workers each of whom works on his/her own to solve part of a complex problem. The results of their labours are then combined to produce the solution (i.e., coherent visual perception).

Some of the main areas of the visual cortex in the macaque monkey are shown in Figure 2.4. The retina connects primarily to what is known as the primary visual cortex or area V1. The importance of area V1 is shown by the fact that lesions at any point along the pathway to it from the retina lead to virtually total blindness within the affected part of V1. However, areas V2 to V5

FIGURE 2.4

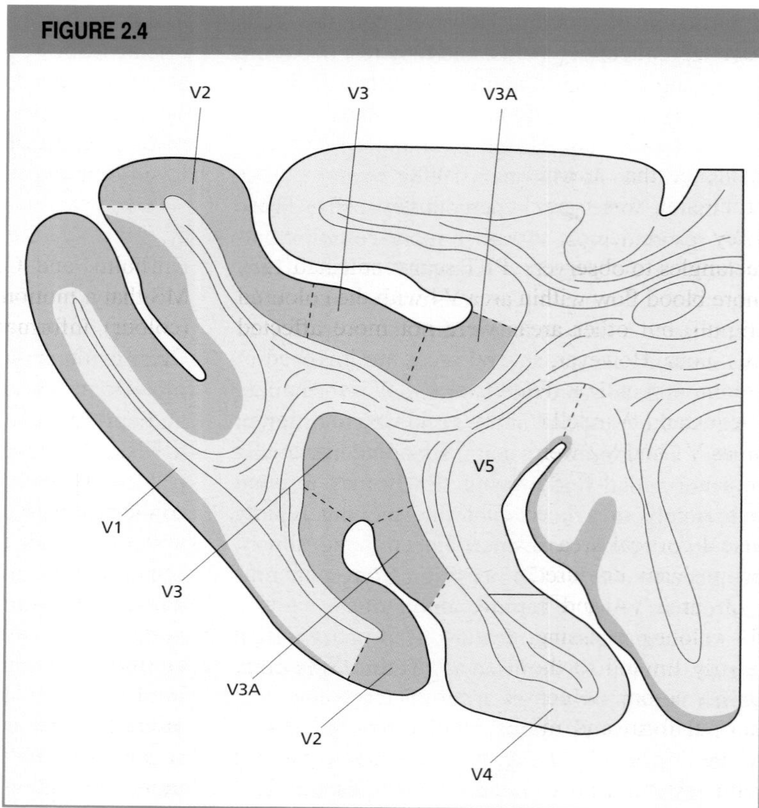

A cross-section of the visual cortex of the macaque monkey. From Zeki (1992). Reproduced with permission from Carol Donner.

are also of major significance in visual perception. As mentioned earlier, it is generally assumed that the organisation of the human visual system closely resembles that of the macaque, and so reference is often made to human brain areas such as V1, V2, and so on. Technically, however, they should be referred to as analogue V1, analogue V2, and so on, because these areas are identified by analogy with the macaque brain. Here are the main functions Zeki (1992, 1993) ascribed to these areas:

- V1 and V2: These areas are involved at an early stage of visual perception. They contain different groups of cells responsive to colour and form, and "contain pigeonholes into which the different signals are assembled before being relayed to the specialised visual areas" (Zeki, 1992, p. 47).
- V3 and V3A: Cells in these areas are responsive to form (especially the shapes of objects in motion) but not to colour.
- V4: The overwhelming majority of cells in this area are responsive to colour; many are also responsive to line orientation. This area in monkeys is unusual in that there is much mixing of connections from temporal and parietal cortex (Baizer, Ungerleider, & Desimone, 1991).
- V5: This area is specialised for visual motion (in studies with macaque monkeys Zeki found that all the cells in this area are responsive to motion, but are not to colour).

A central assumption made by Zeki (1992, 1993) was that colour, form, and motion are processed in anatomically separate parts of the visual cortex. Much of the original evidence came from studies of monkeys. Relevant human evidence is considered below.

Colour processing

Evidence that area V4 is specialised for colour processing was reported by Lueck et al. (1989). They presented coloured or grey squares and rectangles to observers. PET scans indicated 13% more blood flow within area V4 with the coloured stimuli, but other areas were not more affected by colour. However, several areas are involved in colour processing. For example, Wade, Brewer, Rieger, and Wandell (2002) used fMRI, and found areas V1 and V2 were actively involved in colour processing in addition to the involvement of area V4. Hadjikhani et al. (1998) found that human visual cortical area V8 is activated when normal people view coloured patterns.

If area V4 and related areas are specialised for colour processing, then patients with damage mostly limited to those areas should show little or no colour perception, combined with fairly normal form and motion perception and ability to see fine detail. This is the case in some patients with **achromatopsia**, also known as cerebral achromatopsia to indicate that the problems are due to brain damage rather than abnormal cone functioning in the retina. Heywood and Cowey (1999, p. 21) reviewed the relevant evidence, and concluded that "the brain areas that are compromised in achromatopsia are located in the ventromedial occipital cortex in the region of the lingual and fusiform gyri." Thus, achromatopsia often involves some damage to areas V2 and V3 even though typically area V4 is most damaged.

Some aspects of colour processing are often preserved in patients with achromatopsia. Heywood, Cowey, and Newcombe (1994) studied MS, a patient with achromatopsia. He performed very poorly on an oddity task, on which he had to select the odd colour from a set of stimuli having the same shape. However, he performed well on a similar task in which the shapes of hidden figures could only be identified by means of colour processing. On this task, he was able to select the odd form out of a set of stimuli (e.g., one cross and two squares). As Köhler and Moscovitch (1997, p. 326) concluded, "M.S. is able to process information about colour implicitly when the actual perceptual judgement concerns form, but is unable to use this information explicitly when the judgement concerns colour."

Further evidence that achromatopsics can process colour in spite of a loss of colour experience was reported by Cole, Heywood, Kentridge, Fairholm, and Cowey (2003). They found with MS that a motion signal based only on chromatic (colour) information could guide his attention. Other evidence suggested that this effect occurred because MS has intact chromatic opponent processes (red–green, blue–yellow, and white–black neurons).

In sum, area V4 is undoubtedly involved in colour processing, as has been found in brain-imaging studies and studies on people with achromatopsia. However, the association between colour processing and activation of area V4 is not perfect. First, studies on normals and achromatopsics indicate that colour processing is not limited to area V4. Second, some implicit colour processing occurs in achromatopsics with extensive damage to V4 and other related areas. Third, monkeys with lesions to V4 can still perform various tasks involving colour perception (Heywood & Cowey, 1999). Fourth, "The size of V4 (it is substantially the largest area beyond V2) and its anatomical position (it is the gateway to the temporal lobe) necessitate that it do more than just support colour vision" (Lennie, 1998, p. 920).

Form processing

Several areas are involved in form processing in humans, including areas V3, V4, and IT (see Figure 2.3). However, the cognitive neuroscience approach to form perception has focused mainly on IT (inferotemporal cortex). For example, Sugase, Yamane, Ueno, and Kawano (1999) presented human faces, monkey faces, and simple geometrical objects (e.g., squares, circles) to monkeys. Neural activity occurring about 50 ms after the presentation of a stimulus varied as a function of the type of stimulus presented (e.g., human face vs. monkey face). Neural activity occurring several hundred milliseconds after stimulus presentation was influenced by more detailed characteristics of the stimulus (e.g., facial expression).

Kobatake and Tanaka (1994) found in monkeys that cells detecting complex object properties are most common in anterior IT. In contrast, cells responding to intermediate complexity are mostly found in posterior IT and V4. Young and Yamane (1992) reported that a fairly small population of face-selective cells in IT can produce a pattern of activity uniquely coding a given face.

It might be expected that some brain-damaged patients would suffer from severely impaired form vision but fairly normal colour and motion processing. However, Zeki (1992, p. 47) claimed that, "no one has ever reported a complete and specific loss of form vision". He argued that the reason for this might be that a lesion large enough to destroy areas V3, V4, and IT would probably destroy area V1 as well. As a result, the patient would suffer from total blindness rather than simply loss of form perception.

Motion processing

Area V5 (also known as MT, standing for middle temporal) is heavily involved in motion processing. Anderson et al. (1996) used magneto-encephalography (MEG) and MRI to assess brain activity in response to motion stimuli (see Chapter 1). They reported that "human V5 is located near the occipito-temporal border in a minor sulcus [groove] immediately below the superior temporal sulcus" (Anderson et al., 1996, p. 428). This finding was consistent with previous findings using other techniques. For example, the special involvement of V5 in motion processing has been found in PET studies (e.g., Zeki et al., 1991) and in studies using functional MRI (e.g., Tootell et al., 1995a).

The importance of area V5 in motion processing is shown in studies on brain-damaged patients suffering from **akinetopsia**. In this condition, stationary objects are generally perceived fairly normally but objects in motion become invisible. Zihl, von Cramon, and Mai (1983) studied LM, a woman with akinetopsia who had suffered brain damage in both hemispheres. Shipp et al. (1994) used a high-resolution MRI scan to show that LM has bilateral damage to V5. She was good at locating stationary objects by sight, she had good colour discrimination, and her binocular visual functions (e.g., stereoscopic depth perception) were normal, but her motion perception was grossly deficient. According to Zihl et al. (1983):

> She had difficulty . . . in pouring tea or coffee into a cup because the fluid appeared to be frozen, like a glacier. In addition, she could not stop pouring at the right time since she was unable to perceive the movement in the cup (or a pot) when the fluid rose . . . In a room where more than two people were walking she felt very insecure . . . because "people were suddenly here or there but I have not seen them moving".

LM's condition did not improve over time. However, she developed various ways of coping with her lack of motion perception. For example, she stopped looking at people talking to her, because she found it disturbing that their lips did not seem to move (Zihl et al., 1991).

Striking evidence of the involvement of V5 in motion perception was reported by Beckers and Zeki (1995). They used transcranial magnetic stimulation (see Chapter 1) to produce a temporary lesion in V5. The result was what appeared to be complete akinetopsia, in that no motion perception was possible. Additional evidence was provided by Salzman et al. (1992). They applied tiny amounts of electrical stimulation to directionally selective neurons in V5 or MT of monkeys. Then they presented random-dot displays, and obtained evidence about the perceived direction of these displays from the monkeys' eye movements. The display was perceived to move in the direction preferred by the neurons that had been electrically stimulated.

V5 or MT is not the only area implicated in motion processing. Another area that is involved is area MST (which stands for medial superior temporal). This area is adjacent to and just above V5 or MT. For example, Vaina (1998) reported findings from two patients with damage to MST. Both patients performed at normal levels on several tests of motion perception, including discrimination of direction and judgements of speed. However, they both had problems relating to motion perception. One of the patients (RR) "frequently bumped into people, corners and things in his way, particularly into moving targets (e.g., people walking)" (Vaina, 1998, p. 498). According to Sekuler and Blake (2002, p. 385), such evidence suggests that "signals from various MST neurons probably make crucial contributions to the visual guidance of locomotion."

Vaina et al. (2000) found evidence that V2 is also involved in motion perception. They studied a 60-year-old man with a very small area of brain damage in V2. In spite of the fact that V5 or MT was totally intact, this patient performed poorly on a range of motion tasks.

There is increasing evidence that more brain areas are involved in motion processing in humans than in monkeys. For example, Orban et al. (2003) carried out an fMRI study on humans and monkeys, finding that motion stimuli caused activation in MT/V5 and surrounding areas in both species. However, area V3A and several regions in the intraparietal sulcus were much more activated by motion stimuli in humans than in monkeys. Why do these species' differences exist? Speculatively, Orban et al. (2003, p. 1766) suggested the following answer: "The use of tools requires the control of motion (e.g., primitive ways of making fire). To a large degree this is also true for hunting with primitive weapons . . . it may well be that motion processing became behaviourally much more important when humans emerged from the primate family millions of years ago."

Evaluation

Zeki's functional specialisation theory is an interesting attempt to provide a relatively simple overview of a remarkably complex reality. There are grounds for agreeing with Zeki that analysis of motion does proceed somewhat independently of other types of visual processing (see discussion below). However, there are three limitations with this theoretical approach. First, the various brain areas involved in visual processing are not nearly as specialised and limited in their processing as implied by the theory. This can be seen clearly if we follow Heywood and Cowey (1999) in considering the percentage of cells in each visual cortical area that respond selectively to various stimulus characteristics (see Figure 2.5). Cells in several areas respond to orientation, disparity, and colour, and there is reasonable evidence for specialisation only with respect to responsiveness to direction of stimulus motion.

Second, early visual processing in the cortex in areas V1 and V2 is more extensive than suggested by Zeki. For example, Hegde and Van Essen (2000) studied neuronal responses to complex shapes in macaque monkeys. They found that "approximately one-third of the V2 cells showed significant differential responsiveness to various complex shape characteristics, and many were also selective for the orientation, size, and/or spatial frequency of the preferred shape. These results indicate that V2 cells explicitly represent complex shape information" (Hegde & Van Essen, 2000, p. RC61).

Third, the functional specialisation proposed by Zeki poses difficulties of integration, in that information about an object's motion, colour, and form needs to be combined. The task of integrating information about objects in the visual field is known as the **binding problem**. As yet, little is known of how the brain solves the binding problem.

Alternative view: Hierarchical model

According to Zeki's (1993) theoretical position, "Visual perception is a divide-and-conquer strategy. Rather than have each visual area represent all attributes of an object, each area provides its own limited analysis. Processing is distributed and specialised" (Gazzaniga, Ivry, & Mangun, 1998). An alternative view was presented by Lennie (1998, p. 894): "Cortex is organised so that perceptually relevant information can be recovered at every level in the hierarchy, and, with one rather special exception, through all stages of analysis all dimensions of the image remain intimately coupled." Thus, Lennie (1998) argued that visual processing is hierarchical, with analyses in successive brain areas becoming more detailed and

FIGURE 2.5

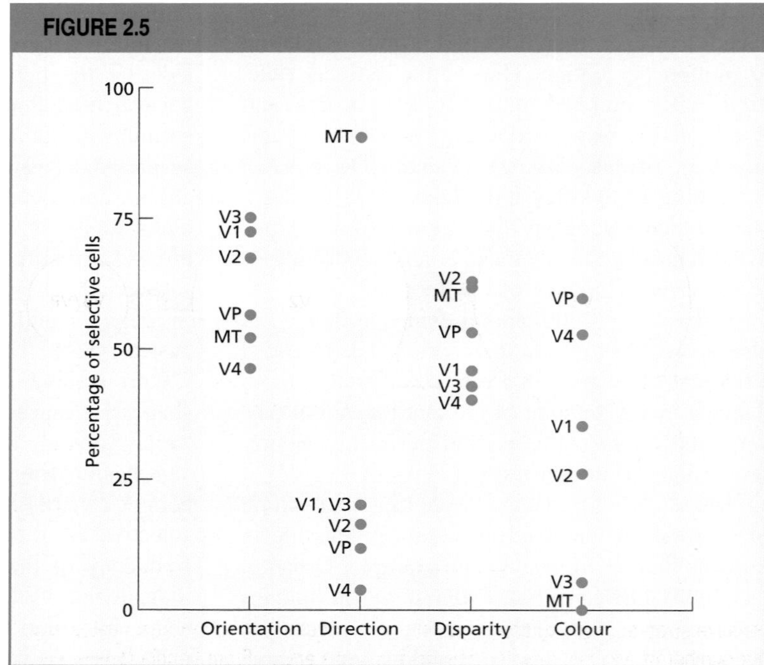

The percentage of cells in six different visual cortical areas responding selectively to orientation, direction of motion, disparity, and colour. From Heywood and Cowey (1999). Reprinted with permission from Lawrence Erlbaum Associates Inc.

precise. The "rather special exception" is motion processing, which is assumed to be dealt with by V5 or MT somewhat independently of other areas involved in visual processing.

Lennie (1998) argued that his views are supported by a consideration of the size and organisation of the visual areas. The approximate relative sizes of the visual areas and the strengths of the connections among them in macaque cortex are shown in Figure 2.6. What can we learn from this figure? First, it suggests that a considerable amount of visual processing occurs in V1 and V2 given that they are relatively much larger than any other areas. Second, it appears that most visual processing in the cortex is based on the strongly interconnected V1, V2, and V4. According to Lennie (1998, p. 895), "The preponderance of this stream [of processing] prompts one to ask whether or not visual analysis really is best conceived as a distributed task, in which the results of different component analysis undertaken separately are ultimately brought together."

Third, the tendency for later visual areas to be smaller than earlier ones "implies that a lot of information is discarded at each level in the hierarchy, which in turn implies that perceptual decisions have been made" (Lennie, 1998, p. 896). Fourth, area V5 or MT is separate from the main processing stream, and so it is plausible that its processing activities (revolving around motion) are largely independent of those occurring in other visual areas.

Evaluation

Lennie's (1998) hierarchical model is broadly consistent with most of the evidence. For example, the fact that areas V1 and V2 are much larger than any subsequent visual areas supports Lennie's (1998) view that they are involved in a wide range of processing activities. This view is also supported by the evidence summarised in Figure 2.5, which shows that V1 and V2 both contain numerous cells responding selectively to orientation,

FIGURE 2.6

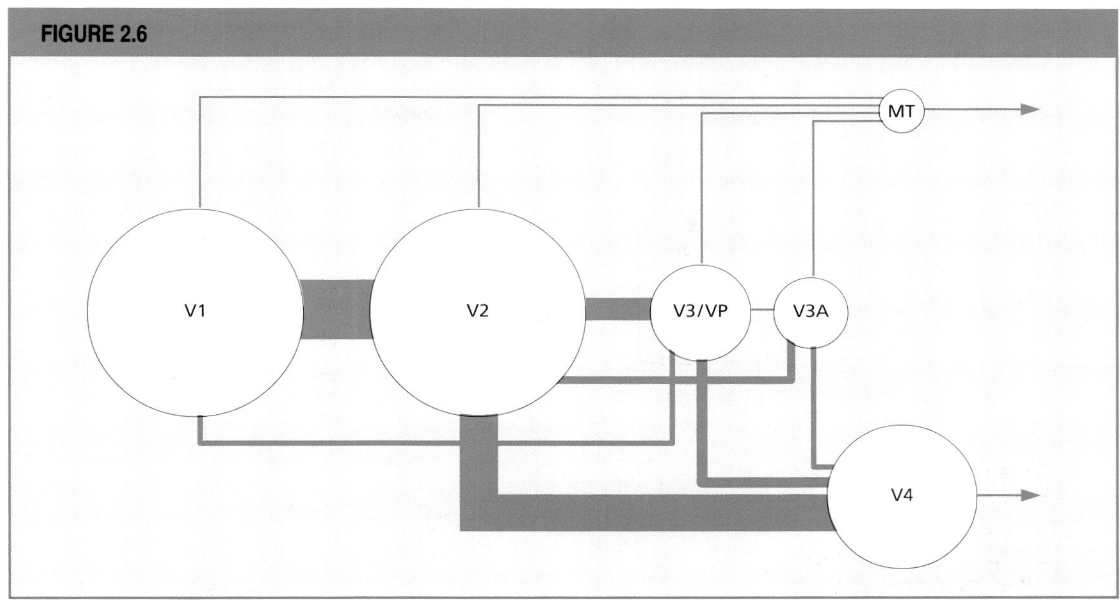

Relative sizes of major cortical areas in the macaque involved in visual processing. The thicknesses of the lines indicate the number of ascending projections among these areas. From Lennie (1998). Reprinted with permission from Pion Limited, London.

to disparity, and to colour. Lennie's (1998) view that motion processing occurs largely independently of other forms of visual processing has also received much support (discussed below).

There is another significant strength of Lennie's theoretical approach, in that the binding problem may be less than with Zeki's approach. Why is that? It would presumably be very difficult to integrate the outcomes of different visual analyses if these analyses are distributed throughout the visual cortex as assumed by Zeki. On Lennie's hierarchical model, processing is organised hierarchically rather than in a distributed way, and so any problems with integrating information are likely to be reduced.

The main limitation of Lennie's hierarchical model is that it is speculative. It is very difficult to prove that visual processing proceeds in the hierarchical way proposed, and we are a long way from doing so. In addition, as Lennie (1998, p. 922) admitted, "Perhaps the most troublesome objection to the picture I have developed is that an enormous amount of cortex is used to achieve remarkably little. Nearly 60% of known visual cortex lies in the areas I have discussed, yet all that has been achieved is to articulate surfaces and their positions." It is hard to evaluate this objection, but Lennie (1998, p. 922) dismissed it as follows: "We underestimate the importance of what is achieved by recovering surface structure, and we overestimate the work that remains to be done."

"What and where" or "what and how" systems

Several theorists (e.g. Mishkin & Ungerleider, 1982) have argued that vision is used for two crucial functions (refer back to Figure 2.3). First, there is object perception (*what* is it?). Second, there is spatial perception (*where* is it?). There is good evidence (at least in macaque monkeys) that rather different brain systems underlie each of these functions:

(1) There is a ventral pathway running from the primary visual area in the cortex to the inferior temporal cortex; this pathway is specialised for object perception (i.e., what is it?).
(2) There is a dorsal pathway running from the primary visual area in the cortex to the posterior parietal cortex; this pathway is specialised for spatial perception (i.e., where is it?).

Some of the original research in this area was reported by Mishkin and Ungerleider (1982). They used a situation with two food wells, each of which was covered by a lid. There was food in one of the wells, and monkeys were allowed to lift one lid to find it. Food was associated either with a specific lid pattern (object information) or with whichever food well was closer to a small model tower (spatial information). Monkeys whose inferior temporal lobes were removed had problems in using object information but not spatial information. In contrast, monkeys whose parietal lobes were removed experienced difficulty in using spatial information but not object information.

Neuroimaging evidence was reported by Haxby et al. (1994). They used two tasks with normal participants. There was an object-recognition task that involved deciding which of two faces matched a target face. There was also a spatial task that involved deciding which of two figures consisting of a dot and two lines was a rotated version of the target figure. PET data indicated that the occipital region of the cortex was activated as participants performed both tasks. However, the pattern of activation differed elsewhere in the cortex. The object-recognition task produced heightened activation in the inferior and medial temporal cortex, whereas the spatial task led to increased activation in the parietal cortex. These patterns of activation are as predicted by the theory.

Perception–action model

Milner and Goodale (1995, 1998) provided an alternative to Ungerleider and Mishkin's theoretical ideas in their perception–action model. They drew a distinction between vision for perception and vision for action. Both these systems use object and spatial information. However, they do so in different ways, with different representations being used for recognition and for visually guided action. According to Milner and Goodale (1995, 1998), the dorsal pathway may be of greatest value in providing an answer to the question, "How do I interact with that object?" That contrasts with Mishkin and Ungerleider (1982), who claimed the dorsal pathway provides information to answer the question, "Where is that object?"

According to the perception–action model, vision for action makes use of rather different information from vision for perception. Vision for action (based on the dorsal pathway) uses short-lasting, viewpoint-dependent representations (i.e., the representations are influenced by the angle of viewing). In contrast, vision for perception (based on the ventral pathway) may use long-lasting, viewpoint-independent representations (i.e., the representations rely on stored knowledge and are not influenced by the angle of viewing). According to Milner and Goodale (1998, p. 12), the dorsal system "is designed to guide actions purely in the here and now, and its products are consequently useless for later reference . . . it is only through knowledge gained via the ventral stream that we can exercise insight, hindsight and foresight about the visual world."

Evidence

Some of the most convincing evidence for the notion of separate visual systems for perception and for action has come from the study of brain-damaged patients. It was predicted there would be a **double dissociation**: some patients would have reasonably intact vision for perception but severely impaired vision for action, and others would show the opposite pattern.

Half of the above double dissociation consists of patients with **optic ataxia**. According to Georgopoulos (1997, p. 142), such patients "do not usually have impaired vision or impaired hand or arm movements, but show a severe impairment in visually guided reaching in the absence of perceptual disturbance in estimating distance." For example, consider a study by Perenin and Vighetto (1988). Patients with optic ataxia experienced great difficulty in rotating their hands appropriately when given the task of reaching towards and into a large oriented slot in front of them.

Which brain areas are damaged in optic ataxia? The answer varies from patient to patient. However, there is typically damage in the posterior parietal lobe, especially in the superior area (Perenin & Vighetto, 1988). This forms part of the dorsal pathway.

The other half of the double dissociation consists of some patients with **visual agnosia** (see Chapter 3). This is a condition involving severe problems with object recognition. DF is the most studied patient having visual agnosia coupled with fairly good spatial perception. In spite of having reasonable visual acuity, DF was unable to identify any of a series of drawings of common objects. However, as pointed out by Milner et al. (1991), DF "had little difficulty in everyday activity such as opening doors, shaking hands, walking around furniture, and eating meals . . . she could accurately reach out and grasp a pencil orientated at different angles."

In a study by Goodale and Milner (1992), DF held a card in her hand, and looked at a circular block into which a slot had been cut. When she was asked to orient the card so it would fit into the slot, she was unable to do so, suggesting that she has very poor perceptual skills. However, DF performed well when asked to move her hand forward and insert the card into the slot.

Carey, Harvey, and Milner (1996) obtained additional evidence of DF's ability to use visual information to guide her actions. She was given the task of picking up rectangular shapes differing in width and orientation. She could do this as well as normal individuals. However, DF had impaired performance when trying to pick up more complex objects (e.g., crosses) in which two different orientations are present together.

Dijkerman, Milner, and Carey (1998) assessed DF's performance on various tasks when presented with several differently coloured objects. There were three main findings. First, DF could not distinguish accurately between the coloured objects. Second, DF reached out and touched the objects as accurately as normals using information about their positions relative to her own body. Third, DF was relatively poor at copying the objects in their correct spatial positions. The third finding is of most theoretical importance. It is predicted by the perception–action model but is inconsistent with the views of Ungerleider and Mishkin (1982).

According to Milner and Goodale (1998), many visual illusions occur because of the processing of the visual input by the ventral system. According to Milner and Goodale (1998, p. 10), "the dorsal system, by and large, is not deceived by such optical illusions." Thus, the dorsal pathway system allows us to make accurate eye and hand movements with respect to illusory figures that we misperceive. There is a large literature addressing this issue (reviewed by Glover, 2004). There are many complexities in the findings (see Chapter 4 for a full discussion and Glover's rival planning–control model), but many studies have reported results supportive of the perception–action model. Below we consider one illustrative study.

Haart, Carey, and Milne (1999) considered a three-dimensional version of the Müller-Lyer illusion (see Figure 2.7). The vertical lines in the two figures are the same length. However, the vertical line on the left looks longer than the one on the right. There were two tasks: (1) a matching task, in which participants indicated the length of the shaft on one figure by the size of the gap between their index finger and thumb; (2) a grasping task, in which participants rapidly grasped

FIGURE 2.7

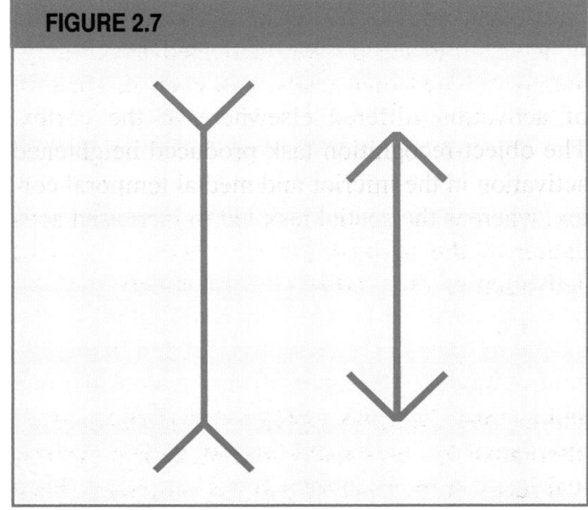

The Müller-Lyer illusion.

FIGURE 2.8

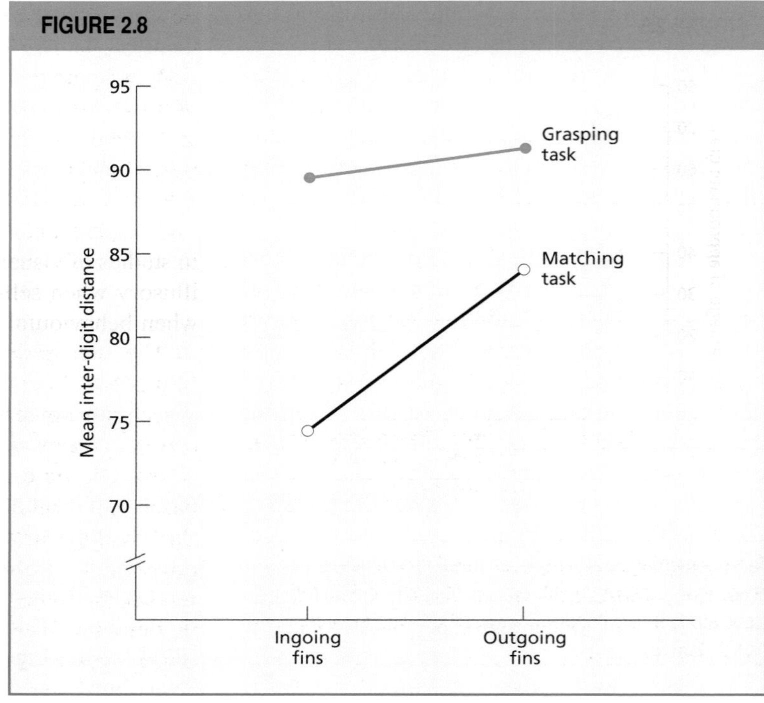

Performance on a three-dimensional version of the Müller-Lyer illusion as a function of task (grasping vs. matching) and type of stimulus (ingoing fins vs. outgoing fins). Based on data in Haart et al. (1999).

the target figure lengthwise using their index finger and thumb. It was assumed that the matching task (which emphasises perceptual processing) would involve the ventral system, whereas the grasping task (which emphasises action) would involve the dorsal system.

Haart et al. (1999) found there was a strong illusory effect with the matching task but no illusory effect at all with the grasping task (see Figure 2.8). The findings were as predicted by the perception–action model. As Haart et al. (1999, p. 1442) concluded, "These data suggest separate systems of processing involved in perception and the visual control of action."

Much of the evidence indicating that the perception–action model is oversimplified is discussed in Chapter 4 (see section headed Planning–control model). Here we will simply consider one study suggesting that perception for action sometimes depends on the ventral pathway as well as the dorsal one. According to Creem and Proffitt (2001a), when we consider someone seeing and grasping an object, we should distinguish between *effective* and *appropriate* grasping. For example, we can grasp a toothbrush effectively by its bristles, but appropriate grasping involves picking it up by the handle. The key assumption is that appropriate grasping involves accessing stored knowledge about the object, with the consequence that appropriate grasping depends in part on the ventral stream.

Creem and Proffitt (2001b) tested the above hypothesis by asking participants to pick up various familiar objects with distinct handles (e.g., toothbrush, hammer, knife). The handle always pointed away from the participant, and the measure of interest was the percentage of occasions on which the objects were grasped appropriately. The grasping task was performed on its own (control condition), at the same time as learning a list of paired associates, or at the same time as performing a spatial imagery task.

What was predicted by Creem and Proffitt (2001b)? If appropriate grasping requires the retrieval of object knowledge from long-term memory, then paired-associate learning (which

FIGURE 2.9

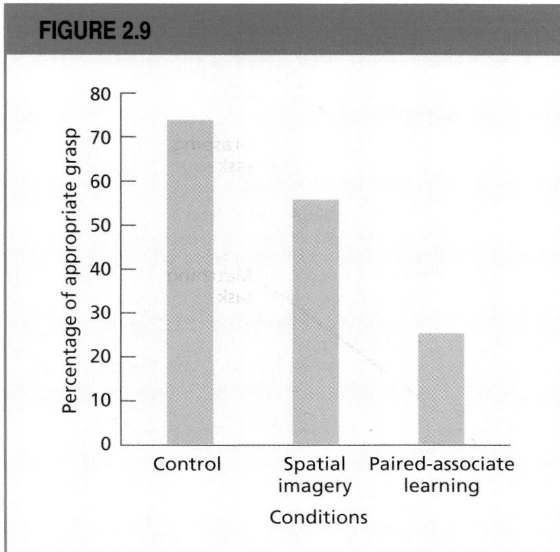

Mean percentages of objects grasped appropriately in the control (grasping only), spatial imagery, and paired-associate learning conditions. Based on data in Creem and Proffitt (2001b).

also involves retrieving words from memory) should greatly impair people's ability to grasp objects appropriately. That is precisely what was found (see Figure 2.9). You might very well argue that these findings simply show that paired-associate learning is much more demanding than spatial imagery. However, when participants were asked to track a moving dot on a computer screen, the spatial imagery task impaired performance much more than the paired-associate learning task; indeed, the latter task had no adverse effect on performance. Thus, we can conclude that retrieval of object knowledge (*not* involving the dorsal stream) is necessary for appropriate grasping.

Evaluation

The arrival of the perception–action model has led to several exciting consequences. First, as Milner and Goodale (1998, p. 2) pointed out, "Standard accounts of vision implicitly assume that the purpose of the visual system is to construct some sort of internal model of the world outside." Their perception–action model has corrected the balance and increased the focus on perception for action (which is the main topic in Chapter 4). Second, the central theoretical assumption that there are somewhat separate visual systems underlying perception for recognition and perception for action is probably broadly correct. Third, and related to the second point, the accuracy of visual perception assessed by self-report and behavioural measures (e.g., grasping) is often surprisingly discrepant. This has been found repeatedly in studies of visual illusions, which are often more illusory when self-report measures are used than when behavioural measures are used.

The perception–action model has various limitations. First, the division into rather separate perception-for-recognition and perception-for-action systems is clearly oversimplified. Second, we need to be careful when interpreting findings based on visual illusions (e.g., Haart et al., 1999). Such findings provide strong support for the model provided we assume that the *only* important difference between the two versions of the task is that one involves a perceptual judgement and the other involves a motor action. In fact, the tasks are so different that this is a dangerous assumption to make (see Vishton, Rea, Cutting, & Nuñez, 1999, for further discussion of this point).

Third, our actions (e.g., grasping) are often influenced by object knowledge as well as by processing in the dorsal pathway (e.g., Creem & Proffitt, 2001b). Fourth, more generally, the model fails to provide an adequate account of the numerous *interactions* between the dorsal and ventral systems. Fifth, there is evidence that processing within the dorsal pathway is more diverse than assumed by Milner and Goodale (1995, 1998). For example, Creem and Proffitt (2001a) reviewed evidence suggesting that the views of Ungerleider and Mishkin (1982) and of Milner and Goodale are both partially correct. According to them, there are separate dorsal systems for spatial perception (as assumed by Ungerleider & Mishkin) and for visually guided action (as assumed by Milner and Goodale) (see below).

Dual-process approach

Norman (2002) proposed a dual-process approach resembling the perception–action model. He agreed with Milner and Goodale (1995, 1998)

Table 2.1

Eight main differences between the ventral and dorsal systems (based on Norman, 2002).

Factor	Ventral system	Dorsal system
1. Function	Recognition/identification	Visually guided behaviour
2. Sensitivity	High spatial frequencies: details	High temporal frequencies: motion
3. Memory	Memory-based (stored representations)	Only very short-term storage
4. Speed	Relatively slow	Relatively fast
5. Consciousness	Typically high	Typically low
6. Frame of reference	Allocentric or object-centred	Egocentric or body-centred
7. Visual input	Mainly foveal or parafoveal	Across retina
8. Monocular vision	Generally reasonably small effects	Often large effects (e.g., motion parallax)

that there are separate ventral and dorsal pathways. He also agreed that the functions of each pathway were basically those proposed by Milner and Goodale. In broad terms, the functions of the two pathways or systems are as follows: "The dorsal system deals mainly with the utilisation of visual information for the guidance of behaviour in one's environment. The ventral system deals mainly with the utilisation of visual information for 'knowing' one's environment, that is, identifying and recognising items previously encountered and storing new visual information for later encounters" (Norman, 2002, p. 95).

We can understand the essence of the dual-process approach if we consider the various differences assumed by Norman (2002) to exist between the two visual processing systems (see Table 2.1).

Norman's (2002) dual-process approach provides a more detailed account of differences between the ventral and dorsal systems than is contained within Milner and Goodale's (1995) perception–action model. However, the strengths and limitations of Norman's dual-process approach are similar to those of Milner and Goodale's model, and so do not require detailed discussion here. The most serious limitation of the dual-process approach is fairly obvious: "The proposed integrative theory and its concomitant dual-process approach are clearly an oversimplified view of what transpires in visual perception" (Norman, 2002, p. 96).

Where and how systems

Creem and Proffitt (2001a) suggested a way of resolving the differences between those (e.g., Ungerleider & Mishkin, 1982) arguing that the dorsal pathway is a "where" or spatial system and those (e.g., Milner & Goodale, 1995; Norman, 2002) claiming it is a "how" or action-related system. In essence, Creem and Proffitt (2001a, p. 60) claimed that we do not need to choose between "where" and "how" systems: "Distinct portions in the posterior parietal lobe subserve functionally different spatial tasks. In humans, the traditional dorsal stream [superior parietal area] may process egocentric 'how' information in preparation for action, whereas inferior areas of the parietal cortex may play a role in more global spatial 'where' processing involving multiple frames of reference."

Much of the support for Creem and Proffitt's views comes from studies on brain-damaged patients. It follows from the theory that patients whose main problems revolve around visually guided action (e.g., patients with optic ataxia) should have damage to the superior part of the posterior parietal cortex. Perenin and Vighetto (1988) found in a review of 10 cases of optic ataxia that most of them had damage to that area, and all of them had damage to the intraparietal sulcus [groove] at the boundary between the superior and inferior regions of the posterior parietal cortex.

It also follows from the theory that patients whose main problems involve deficient perceptions of space should have damage to the inferior part of the posterior parietal cortex. We will consider patients with **unilateral visual neglect**, which is a condition in which the left half of the visual field is neglected or ignored (this condition is discussed more fully in Chapter 5). Various accounts of unilateral neglect have been offered, but in it there is a disrupted conscious representation of the left side of space. As predicted, most patients with unilateral neglect have damage to inferior parietal lobe (e.g., Perenin, 1997).

In sum, reasonable evidence suggests that there are somewhat separate "where" and "how" systems within the posterior parietal cortex. What is needed in future is a more detailed account of the functioning of the two systems.

COLOUR PERCEPTION

Why has colour vision developed? After all, if you see an old black-and-white film on television, you can easily make sense of the moving images presented to your eyes. According to Sekuler and Blake (2002), there are two main reasons. First, "One of colour's important contributions is to promote figure/ground segmentation, causing an object to stand out from its background" (Sekuler & Blake, 2002, p. 264). Second, "Besides aiding our ability to detect the presence of objects, colour also helps us recognise (identification) and distinguish (discrimination) them from among various objects in the environment." For example, colour perception helps us to decide whether a piece of fruit is under-ripe, ripe, or over-ripe.

Before going any further, we need to consider the meaning of the word "colour". There are three qualities associated with colour. First, there is *hue*, which is what distinguishes red from yellow or blue. Second, there is *brightness*, which is the perceived intensity of light. Third, there is *saturation*, which allows us to determine whether a colour is vivid or pale. We saw earlier that the cones in the retina are specialised for colour vision, and we turn now to a more detailed consideration of their role.

Young–Helmholtz theory

Cone receptors contain light-sensitive photopigment which allows them to respond to light. According to the trichromatic [three-coloured] theory put forward by Thomas Young and developed by Hermann von Helmholtz, there are three distinct sets of nervous fibres differing in the light wavelengths to which they respond most strongly. Subsequent research led to these sets of fibres becoming identified with three different kinds of cone receptors. One type of cone receptor is most sensitive to short-wavelength light, and responds most to stimuli perceived as blue. A second type of cone receptor is most sensitive to medium-wavelength light, and responds greatly to stimuli seen as yellow-green. The third type of cone receptor responds most to long-wavelength light such as that coming from stimuli distinguished as orange-red.

How do we see other colours? According to the theory, most stimuli activate two or even all three cone types. The colour we perceive is determined by the relative levels of stimulation of each cone type, with activation of all three cone types leading to the perception of whiteness.

Dartnall, Bowmaker, and Mollon (1983) obtained support for this theory using a technique known as **microspectrophotometry**. This revealed three types of cones or receptors responding maximally to different wavelengths of light (see Figure 2.10). Each cone type absorbs a wide range of wavelengths, and so it would be wrong to equate one cone type directly with perception of blue, one with yellow-green, and one with orange-red. There are about 4 million long-wavelength cones, over 2 million medium-wavelength cones, and under 1 million short-wavelength cones (Cicerone & Nerger, 1989).

Roorda and Williams (1999) discovered that all three types of cones are distributed fairly randomly within the human eye, except that there are few cones responsive to short-wavelength light within the fovea or central area of the retina. More surprisingly, there were substantial

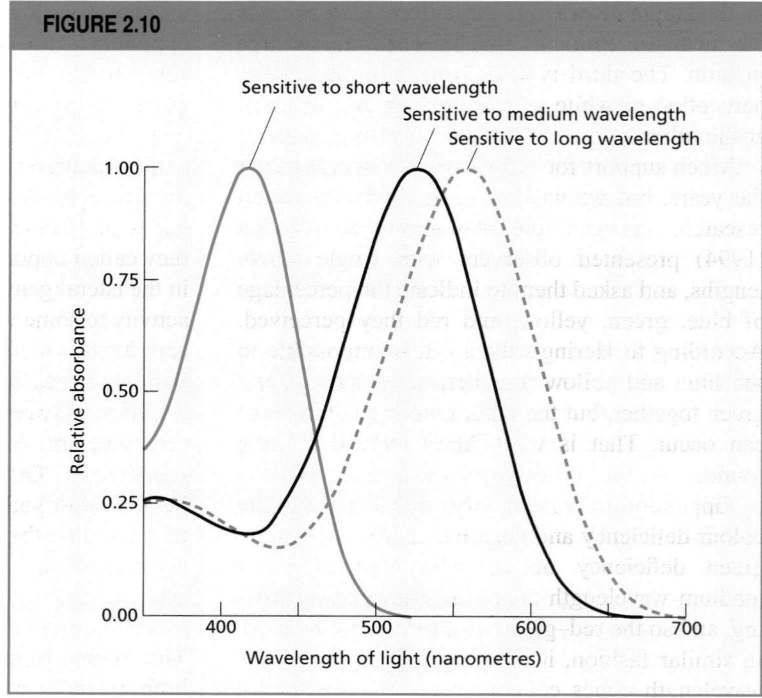

Three types of colour receptors or cones identified by microspectrophotometry. From Bowmaker and Dartnall (1980) with permission from the Royal Society.

individual differences in the distribution of the three types of cones.

Most individuals with colour deficiency are not completely colour-blind, because they can distinguish some colours. The most common type of colour-blindness is *red–green deficiency*. There are other, rarer forms of colour deficiency, such as *blue–yellow deficiency*. Red–green deficiency is the commonest form of colour blindness because the medium- and long-wavelength cone types are more likely to be damaged or missing than the short-wavelength cones. There are rarer cases in which the short-wavelength cones are missing, and this disrupts perception of blue and yellow. However, this is not a complete account of colour deficiency, as we will see shortly.

Why has evolution equipped us with three types of cones? According to Sekuler and Blake (2002, p. 284), "Trichromacy . . . represents a very efficient means for representing the behaviourally important surface colours in our natural environment. Just look at how many different colours we can distinguish!"

The Young–Helmholtz theory fails to explain **negative afterimages**. If you stare at a square of a given colour for several seconds, and then shift your gaze to a white surface, you will see a negative afterimage in the complementary colour. For example, a green square produces a red afterimage, whereas a blue square produces a yellow afterimage.

Opponent-process theory

The Young–Helmholz theory provides a reasonable account of the early stages of colour processing based on three cone types. However, it does not indicate clearly how activity in these cone types is organised so that we perceive colour. Ewald Hering (1878) put forward an opponent-process theory, handling some findings not explained by the Young–Helmholtz theory. Hering's key assumption was that there are three types of opponent processes in the visual system. One type of process produces perception of green when it responds in one way and of red when it responds in the opposite way. A second type of process produces perception of blue or yellow in the same fashion. The third type of process produces the perception of white at one extreme and of black at the other.

Much support for this theory has accrued over the years, but we will focus on relatively recent research. For example, Abramov and Gordon (1994) presented observers with single wavelengths, and asked them to indicate the percentage of blue, green, yellow, and red they perceived. According to Hering's theory, it is impossible to see blue and yellow together, or to see red and green together, but the other colour combinations can occur. That is what Abramov and Gordon found.

Opponent-process theory helps to explain colour deficiency and negative afterimages. Red–green deficiency occurs when the high- or medium-wavelength cones are damaged or missing, and so the red–green channel cannot be used. In similar fashion, individuals lacking the short-wavelength cones cannot make effective use of the yellow–blue channel, and so their perception of these colours is disrupted. Negative afterimages can be explained by assuming that prolonged viewing of a given colour (e.g., red) produces one extreme of activity in the relevant opponent processes. When attention is then directed to a white surface, the opponent process moves to its other extreme, thus producing the negative afterimage.

DeValois and DeValois (1975) obtained physiological evidence in monkeys broadly consistent with Hering's theory. They discovered what they called opponent cells. These are cells located in the lateral geniculate nucleus showing increased activity to some wavelengths of light but decreased activity to others. For some cells, the transition point between increased and decreased activity occurred between the green and the red parts of the spectrum. As a result, they were called red–green cells. Other cells had a transition point between the yellow and blue parts of the spectrum, and so they were called blue–yellow cells.

Synthesis

The Young–Helmholtz and Hering theories are both partially correct, and have been combined into a two-stage theory (Sekuler & Blake, 2002). According to this theory, signals from the three cone types identified by the Young–Helmholtz theory are sent to the opponent cells described

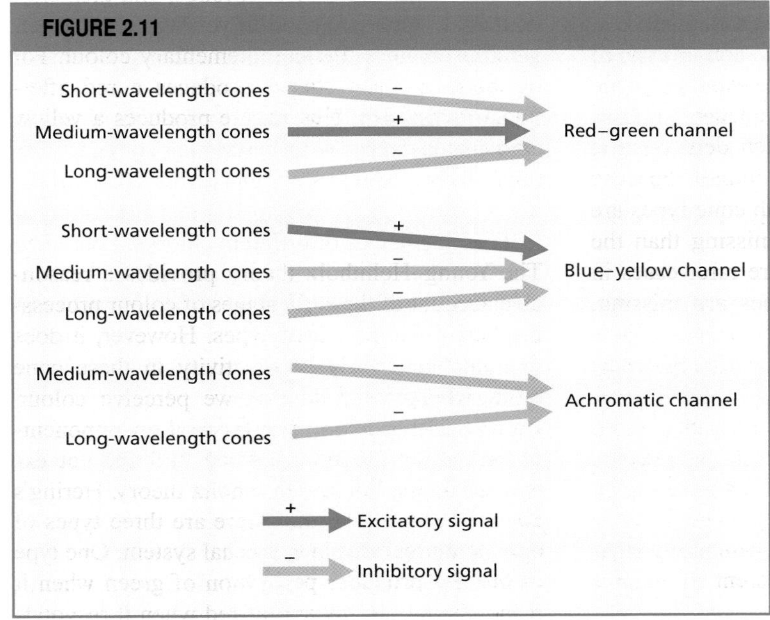

Two-stage theory of colour vision.

within the opponent-process theory (see Figure 2.11). There are three channels. The achromatic [non-colour] channel combines the activity of the medium- and long-wavelength cones. The blue–yellow channel represents the difference between the sum of the medium- and long-wavelength cones on the one hand and the short-wavelength cones on the other. The direction of difference determines whether blue or yellow is seen. Finally, the red–green channel represents the difference between activity levels in the medium- and long-wavelength cones. The direction of this difference determines whether red or green is perceived.

Colour constancy

Colour constancy is the tendency for a surface or object to appear to have the same colour when there is a change in the wavelengths contained in the illuminant (the light illuminating the surface or object). The phenomenon of colour constancy indicates that colour vision does *not* depend only on the wavelengths of the light reflected from objects. If that were the case, then the same object would appear redder in artificial light than in natural light. In fact, we often show reasonable colour constancy in such circumstances. However, as Hurlbert (1999, p. R558) pointed out, "The ugly fact is that, in previous laboratory studies, colour constancy typically has not measured up to our everyday, subjective experience." One reason why colour constancy is often far from complete is because of limitations in the method of asymmetric matching by adjustment typically used. With this method, participants view two scenes under different lighting conditions, and adjust the colour of part of one scene to match that of the other scene. This is an unnatural task, because in everyday life we tend simply to decide whether a colour is the same as (or different from) that seen under different lighting conditions. Bramwell and Hurlbert (1996) devised a more natural task involving same–different judgements of colour, and obtained greater colour constancy than normally found.

Zeki (1993, p. 12) argued forcefully that colour constancy is very important: "It [colour constancy] has been treated as a departure from the general rule, although it is in fact the central problem of colour vision . . . That general rule supposes that there is a precise and simple relationship between the wavelength composition of the light reaching the eye from every point on a surface and the colour of that point."

Evidence

Why do we show colour constancy? One factor is **chromatic adaptation**, in which sensitivity to light of any given colour decreases over time. For example, if you are standing outside after dark, you may be struck by the yellowness of the artificial lights in people's houses. However, if you have been in a room illuminated by artificial light for some time, the light does not seem yellow. Chromatic adaptation reduces the distorting effects of any given illumination on colour constancy.

Another reason we show colour constancy is because of familiarity. People living in England know that post boxes are bright red, and so they look the same colour whether illuminated by the sun or by artificial street lighting. Delk and Fillenbaum (1965) presented various shapes cut out of the same orange-red cardboard. The shapes of objects that are typically red (e.g., heart, apple) were perceived as slightly redder than the shapes of other objects (e.g., mushrooms). However, it is hard with such evidence to distinguish between genuine perceptual effects and response or reporting bias.

Some insight into the factors involved in colour constancy with unfamiliar objects was obtained by Land (1977). Observers saw two displays (known as Mondrian stimuli) consisting of rectangular shapes of different colours. Land then adjusted the lighting of the displays so that two differently coloured rectangles (one from each display) reflected exactly the same wavelengths of light. However, the two rectangles were seen by the observers in their actual colours, showing strong evidence of colour constancy in the absence of familiarity. Finally, Land (1977) found that the two rectangles looked exactly the same (and so colour constancy broke down) when everything else in the two displays was blocked out.

What was happening in Land's study? According to Land's (1977, 1986) retinex theory, we decide the colour of a surface by *comparing* its ability to reflect short, medium, and long wavelengths against that of adjacent surfaces. Colour constancy breaks down when such comparisons cannot be made effectively.

Hurlbert (1999) noted that Mondrian stimuli such as those used by Land (1977), "do not . . . resemble real surfaces, which are typically curved or angled, shaded and textured and so neither uniformly coloured nor uniformly bright." Kraft and Brainard (1999) constructed a more natural visual environment in a box, which included a tube wrapped in tin foil, a pyramid, and a cube in addition to a Mondrian stimulus. When all the objects were visible, colour constancy was as high as 83% even with large changes in illumination. However, colour constancy decreased when the various cues were progressively eliminated.

What factors were responsible for colour constancy in the study by Kraft and Brainard (1999)? The most important factor was *local contrast*, which involves comparing the retinal cone responses from the target surface with those from the immediate background. When local contrast could not be used, colour constancy dropped from 83% to 53%. Another important factor was *global contrast*, in which retinal cone responses from the target surface are compared with the average cone responses across the whole visual scene. When the observers could not use global contrast, colour constancy dropped from 53% to 39%. When all the non-target objects were removed, the observers were denied valuable information in the form of reflected highlights from glossy surfaces (e.g., tube wrapped in tin foil). As a result, colour constancy dropped to 11%. The fact that it did not drop to zero probably occurred because of mutual reflections between the sides of the box and the back wall.

Bloj, Kersten, and Hurlbert (1999) found colour constancy can be greatly reduced by top-down influences (effects based on knowledge). Observers viewed folded cards with the left side painted magenta (a deep purplish red) and the right side painted white. Each card was actually concave or curved inwards so that light from the magenta side was reflected onto the white side. The viewing conditions were such that the folded cards appeared either concave or convex (curved outwards), but note that the retinal stimulation from the cards was the same in both conditions. The perceived colour of the white side of the card was pale pink when the card appeared concave but it was deep magenta when it appeared convex. Thus, there was much less colour constancy in the convex condition than the concave one.

What do the above findings mean? In the concave condition, observers used their knowledge of the effects of light reflection between surfaces to produce reasonable colour constancy. In the convex condition, they mistakenly assumed that the magenta side of the card did not influence the white side of the card, and so they showed a considerable divergence from constancy. Thus, our perception of three-dimensional shape can have a major impact on colour constancy.

Zeki (1983) found in a study on monkeys that certain cells in area V4 (discussed earlier in the chapter) responded strongly to a red patch in a multicoloured display illuminated mainly by red light. These cells did *not* respond when the red patch was replaced by a green, blue, or white patch, even though the dominant reflected wavelength was red. Thus, these cells responded to the *actual* colour of a surface rather than simply to the wavelengths reflected from it, and so may play a significant role in colour constancy. Further evidence that V4 is important in colour constancy comes in studies on macaque monkeys with lesions in that area (see Heywood & Cowey, 1999). These monkeys showed a lack of colour constancy even though they retained many aspects of colour vision.

Evaluation

Several factors are involved in colour constancy. This can be seen clearly in the study by Kraft and Brainard (1999), in which local contrast, global contrast, reflected highlights, and mutual reflections all contributed to colour constancy. Local contrast operates at early levels within the visual system, whereas global contrast operates at higher levels (see Hulbert, 1999), suggesting that different mechanisms underlie these two forms of contrast. Other evidence (e.g., Bloj et al., 1999) shows colour constancy can be greatly affected by top-down processes based on our perception of three-dimensional shape.

Much research is limited in that colour constancy is often lower in the laboratory than in real life. It may well be that observers under laboratory conditions often lack information from reflected highlights and mutual reflections (Kraft & Brainard, 1999). Another major limitation is that we still lack a comprehensive theory indicating how the various factors combine to produce colour constancy.

PERCEPTION WITHOUT AWARENESS

It is easy to assume that visual perception is a conscious process, at least in the sense that we are consciously aware of the object or objects at which we are looking. However, there is substantial evidence that that is not always the case. For example, there are patients with severe damage to V1 (primary visual cortex) who suffer from a condition known as **blindsight**. In essence, blindsight involves the ability to respond appropriately to visual stimuli in the absence of conscious visual experience. After we have considered findings on patients with blindsight, we will consider evidence from normals relating to **subliminal perception** (perception occurring below the level of conscious awareness).

Blindsight

Several patients with severe brain damage to V1 (primary visual cortex) have a loss of conscious perception in some areas of the visual field. This is not surprising considering that primary visual cortex is important for visual processing (see earlier discussion), and also connects to the other main areas involved in visual processing. What is more surprising is that such patients can still make accurate judgements and discriminations about visual stimuli presented to the "blind" area. Farah (2001, p. 162) described the abilities of blindsight patients: "Detection and localisation of light, and detection of motion are invariably preserved to some degree. In addition, many patients can discriminate orientation, shape, direction of movement, and flicker. Colour vision mechanisms also appear to be preserved in some cases." Before proceeding, note that blindsight patients vary considerably in the extent of their visual abilities and in the probable underlying neural mechanisms.

According to Milner and Goodale (1995), patients with blindsight may have a relatively intact dorsal pathway, which is used to process motion. Evidence supporting that view was reported by Morland (1999). He found that a patient with blindsight, GY, could match the speed of moving stimuli in his blind field to those in his seeing field. However, the fact that blindsight patients can process shape and orientation indicates that their abilities extend beyond processing information about motion.

The most thoroughly studied patient with blindsight was DB, who had undergone surgical removal of the right occipital cortex including most of V1. Weiskrantz (e.g., 1986) discovered that DB had an area of blindness in the lower left quadrant of the visual field. He could detect whether or not a visual stimulus had been presented to the blind area and could also identify its location.

In spite of DB's performance, he reported no conscious visual experience. According to Weiskrantz et al. (1974, p. 721), "When he was shown his results [by presenting them to the right visual field] he expressed surprise and insisted several times that he thought he was just 'guessing.' When he was shown a video film of his reaching and judging orientation of lines, he was openly astonished." However, it is hard to be sure that DB had no conscious visual experience, and the reports of other patients are sometimes confused. For example, EY "sensed a definite pinpoint of light", although "it does not actually look like a light. It looks like nothing at all" (Weiskrantz, 1980).

Suppose you fixate on a red square for several seconds, after which you look away at a white surface. The surface will appear to have the complementary colour (i.e., green). This is known as a negative aftereffect (see earlier in chapter). Weiskrantz (2002) found to his considerable surprise that DB showed this negative aftereffect. This finding is surprising because there was conscious perception of the afterimage but not of the stimulus responsible for producing the afterimage! DB showed other afterimages found in normal individuals. For example, he reported an apparent increase in the size of visual afterimages when viewed against a nearby surface and then against a surface farther away (this is **Emmert's law**). The existence of these afterimages indicates that DB's perceptual processing is more varied and thorough than previously believed.

Weiskrantz, Barbur, and Sahraie (1995) argued that any residual conscious vision in blindsight patients is very different from conscious vision in normal individuals. They argued that it is characterised by "a contentless kind of awareness, a feeling of something happening, albeit not normal seeing" (Weiskrantz et al., 1995, p. 6122). They asked their patient to detect the direction of motion of a stimulus, and also to indicate whether he had any awareness of what was being presented. On "aware" trials, his detection performance was better when the stimulus was moving faster. However, his performance on "unaware" trials did not depend on stimulus speed. As Weiskrantz (1995, p. 149) concluded, the patient's "unaware mode is not just a pale shadow of his aware mode."

Support for the notion that blindsight differs greatly from near-threshold normal vision was obtained by Kentridge, Heywood, and Weiskrantz (1999). A blindsight patient (GY) could discriminate the location of low-contrast targets in his blind field in the absence of a cue indicating approximately when the target would appear. However, GY performed at chance level when given a similar task in his spared visual field, in spite of the fact that he reported more awareness of these low-contrast stimuli in the spared field than the blind one. Kentridge et al. (1999, p. 479) concluded that, "GY's blindsight is qualitatively different from near-threshold normal vision."

An important study was reported by Rafal et al. (1990). Blindsight patients performed at chance when trying to detect a light presented to the blind area of the visual field. However, their speed of reaction to a light presented to the intact part of the visual field was slowed down when a light was presented to the blind area at the same time. Thus, a light not producing any conscious awareness nevertheless received sufficient processing to disrupt visual performance on another task. This latter finding is noteworthy, because it provides strong evidence for blindsight without making use of patients' reports on the "unseen" stimulus.

Brain regions

Three main suggestions have been made concerning the brain regions involved in blindsight. First, there may be residual functioning within primary visual cortex (V1). For example, Wessinger, Fendrich, and Gazzaniga (1997) found that blindsight patients could report visual stimuli presented to certain small regions of the visual field. They concluded that their patients had preserved "islands" of function within the primary visual cortex. However, fMRI studies on other blindsight patients (e.g., Stoerig, Kleinschmidt, & Frahm, 1998) have failed to detect activation of primary visual cortex.

Second, blindsight may depend on the subcortical visual system. This visual system is specialised for abilities (e.g., the detection and localisation of moving stimuli) typically preserved in blindsight patients. Köhler and Moscovitch (1997) discussed findings from several patients who had had an entire cerebral hemisphere removed, and thus could presumably only make use of subcortical mechanisms. These patients showed evidence of blindsight for stimulus detection, stimulus localisation, form discrimination, and motion detection.

Third, blindsight may depend on the cortical visual system even though the primary visual cortex is destroyed. Cowey and Stoerig (1989) reviewed evidence indicating that there are direct links between the lateral geniculate nucleus and areas of visual cortex (e.g., V4, V5), with these links bypassing primary visual cortex. Some support was reported by Zeki and ffytche (1998). They found with GY that stimulation of his blind field activated left extrastriate cortex including V5. We can compare blindsight patients having a cortical visual system (apart from primary visual cortex) with blindsight patients lacking this visual system (due to removal of a cerebral hemisphere). Patients in the former group can perform a wider range of perceptual tasks (e.g., making judgements about colour) than those in the latter group (Stoerig & Cowey, 1997). These findings suggest that the cortical visual system plays a role in blindsight.

Evaluation

There is solid experimental evidence that blindsight is a genuine phenomenon. According to Umiltà (2001, pp. 163–164), "Blindsight is not the result of degraded normal vision, if 'normal' is taken to mean relying on primary visual cortex. It is also clearly not a single homogeneous [uniform] phenomenon: at the level of preserved visual abilities, subjective experience, and neural mechanisms, there is apparently much variation from subject to subject."

The precise brain mechanisms involved in blindsight remain unclear. However, the remaining perceptual abilities of some blindsight patients probably depend on subcortical mechanisms, whereas those of other patients probably involve direct projections from the lateral geniculate nucleus to extrastriate areas (e.g., V4, V5). Still other blindsight patients probably have islands of spared cortex.

Subliminal perception

In 1957, it was reported in the press that James Vicary flashed the words EAT POPCORN and DRINK COCA-COLA for 1/300th of a second numerous times during the cinema showing of a film. This subliminal advertising allegedly led to an 18% increase in the cinema sales of Coca-Cola and a 58% increase in popcorn sales. However, the film (*Picnic*) contained scenes of eating and drinking, and the increased sales were probably due to the film itself rather than the subliminal advertising. This conclusion is based on the fact that there is very little evidence from over 200 studies that subliminal advertising is effective in changing behaviour (Pratkanis & Aronson, 1992).

Even though subliminal advertising does not change people's *behaviour*, it is entirely possible that subliminal perception exists. Before considering the evidence, we need to discuss the threshold or criterion used to decide whether there is conscious awareness of visual stimuli. There is an important distinction between two thresholds (Merikle, Smilek, & Eastwood, 2001):

(1) *Subjective threshold*: This is defined by an individual's failure to report conscious awareness of a stimulus.
(2) *Objective threshold*: This is defined by an individual's inability to make accurate forced-choice decisions about a stimulus (e.g., guess at above chance level whether it is a word or not).

Observers often show "awareness" of a stimulus assessed by the objective threshold, even when the stimulus does not exceed the subjective threshold. Thus, what appears to be subliminal perception using the subjective threshold is often no longer subliminal when the objective threshold is used. Which threshold is preferable? It is hard to say. However, as Merikle et al. (2001, p. 120) pointed out:

> A widely held view is that objective measures of perceptual discriminations provide a more accurate method for determining whether or not perception is accompanied by an awareness of perceiving than is provided by subjective measures of conscious experiences . . . statements indicating an absence of an awareness of perceiving may reflect preconceived ideas regarding the value of particular conscious experiences for making decisions rather than a true absence of relevant conscious experiences.

Evidence

The fact that objective measures of awareness are more stringent than subjective measures means we can have more confidence that subliminal perception has been demonstrated in studies using objective measures. Bar and Biederman (1998) presented drawings of objects very rapidly. Observers who failed to name an object performed at chance level on a forced-choice test containing four object names (objective measure). However, 21% of these non-identified objects were named correctly when presented very briefly for a second time. Thus, perceptual information must have been obtained from the drawings on their initial presentation.

Dehaene et al. (1998) found initially that participants could not distinguish between trials on which a masked digit was or was not presented very briefly (objective measure). After that, participants on each trial were presented with a masked digit followed by a clearly visible target digit. The task was to decide whether this target digit was larger or smaller than 5. The masked digit was either congruent with the target (both numbers on the same side of 5) or incongruent. The key finding was that performance was slower on incongruent trials than on congruent ones, because information from the masked digit had been processed.

Dehaene et al. (1998) obtained additional information about the subliminal processing of the masked primes by using event-related potentials and fMRI. Semantic analysis of these primes involved various brain areas associated with sensory processing. In addition, masked primes activated brain areas involved in the motor programming of responses. As Dehaene et al. (1998, p. 599) concluded, these findings indicate that "a large amount of cerebral processing, including perception, semantic categorisation, and task execution, can be performed in the absence of consciousness."

Any reader still sceptical about the existence of subliminal perception may be convinced by findings from a different approach. Suppose information perceived with awareness allows us to control our actions, whereas information perceived without awareness does not. In that case, there should be situations in which perceiving with or without awareness has very different effects on behaviour. Supporting evidence was reported by Debner and Jacoby (1994). On each trial, a word was presented for either 50 or 150 ms followed by a mask. Immediately after that, the first three letters of the word were presented again, and the participants were instructed to think of the first word that came to mind starting with those letters, except for the word that had just been masked (exclusion instructions). There was also a control

FIGURE 2.12

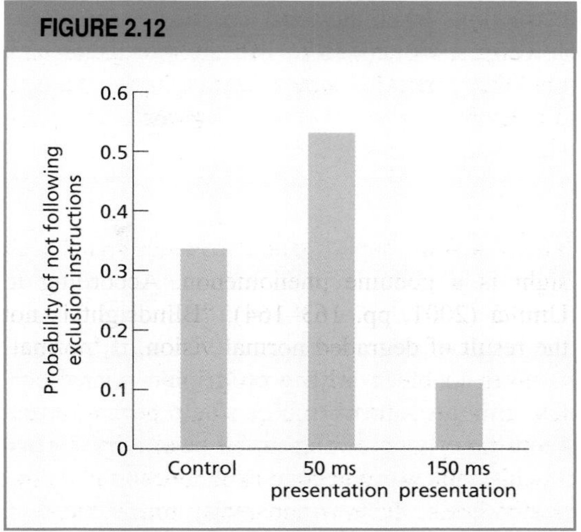

Probability of not following exclusion instructions in control (no relevant preceding word), 50ms word presentation, and 150ms word presentation conditions. Based on data in Debner and Jacoby (1994).

condition, in which each word stem was preceded by an unrelated word.

The findings obtained by Debner and Jacoby (1994) are shown in Figure 2.12. When the masked word was presented for 150 ms, the participants followed instructions to avoid using that word on the word-stem completion task. Presumably this occurred because they perceived the masked word consciously, and so deliberately avoided using it. In contrast, when the masked word was presented for 50 ms, it was often used to complete the word. Presumably there was perception of the masked word without awareness, and this produced relatively automatic reactions to its activation in semantic memory.

It could be that the studies we have considered are very artificial, in that we very rarely attend to stimuli that are only present for 50 ms or so. Subliminal perception would be most likely to occur in everyday life when we fail to attend to a stimulus. Smith and Merikle (1999) used a situation in which participants attended to (or did not attend to) words. This was followed by a word-stem completion test on which the participants were told to avoid the word that had just been presented. The participants successfully followed instructions when they had attended to the word. However, they tended to use the word that had just been presented when they had not attended to it, indicating that the word had been perceived without awareness.

Evaluation

According to Merikle et al. (2001, p. 131), "After more than a century of research studies investigating perception without awareness, it is possible to conclude with considerable confidence that stimulus information can be perceived even when there is no awareness of perceiving." This conclusion is warranted, given that subliminal perception has been shown in studies with subjective and with objective measures of awareness, in artificial and more naturalistic conditions, and with a variety of behavioural measures of perception. In addition, there is brain-imaging evidence (e.g., Dehaene et al., 1998) that there can be sensory, semantic, and motor processing of stimuli for which there is no conscious awareness.

DEPTH AND SIZE PERCEPTION

One of the major accomplishments of visual perception is the transformation of the two-dimensional retinal image into perception of a three-dimensional world. The term "depth perception" is used in two rather different senses (Sekuler & Blake, 2002). First, there is *absolute distance*, the distance away from the observer at which an object is located. Second, there is *relative distance*, which refers to the distance between two objects. It is used, for example, when fitting a slice of bread into a toaster. Judgements of relative distance are generally more accurate than judgements of absolute distance.

In real life, cues to depth are often provided by movement either of the observer or of objects in the visual environment. However, the major focus here will be on depth cues available even if the observer and the objects in the environment are static. These cues can conveniently be divided into monocular, binocular, and oculomotor cues. **Monocular cues** are those requiring only the use of one eye, although they can be used readily when someone has both eyes open. Such cues clearly exist, because the world still retains a sense of depth with one eye closed. **Binocular cues** are those involving both eyes being used together. Finally, **oculomotor cues** are kinaesthetic, depending on sensations of muscular contraction of the muscles around the eye.

Monocular cues

There are various monocular cues to depth. They are sometimes called *pictorial cues*, because they have been used by artists trying to create the impression of three-dimensional scenes while painting on two-dimensional canvases. One such cue is *linear perspective*. Parallel lines pointing directly away from us seem progressively closer together as they recede into the distance (e.g., railway tracks or the edges of a motorway). This convergence of lines creates a powerful impression of depth in a two-dimensional drawing.

Another aspect of perspective is *aerial perspective*. Light is scattered as it travels through the atmosphere, especially if the atmosphere is dusty. As a result, more distant objects lose contrast and seem somewhat hazy. O'Shea, Blackburn, and Ono (1994) mimicked the effects of aerial perspective. Reducing the contrast of features within a picture led those features to appear more distant. Thus, reduced contrast from aerial perspective is an effective cue to distance.

Another cue related to perspective is *texture*. Most objects (e.g., cobble-stoned roads, carpets) possess texture, and textured objects slanting away from us have what Gibson (e.g., 1979) described as a **texture gradient**. This is a gradient (rate of change) of texture density as you look from the front to the back of a slanting object. If you were unwise enough to stand between the rails of a railway track and look along it, the details would become less clear as you looked into the distance. In addition, the distance between the connections would appear to reduce.

Sinai, Ooi, and He (1998) showed that texture is an important cue to distance. Observers were good at judging the distance of objects within

FIGURE 2.13

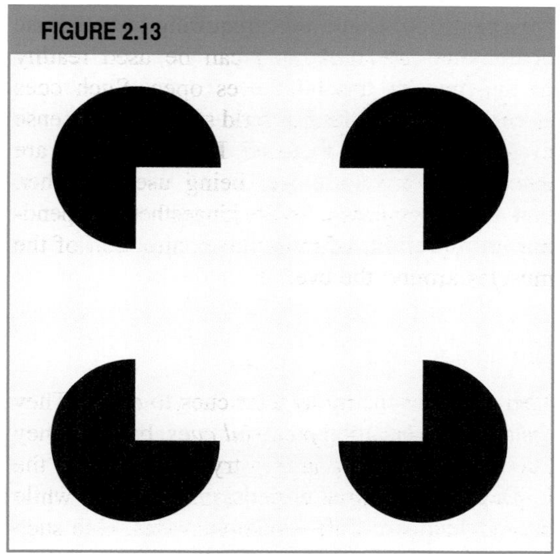

Kanizsa's (1976) illusory square.

seven metres of them, provided the ground in between was uniformly textured. However, distances were systematically overestimated when there was a gap (e.g., a ditch) in the texture pattern. Distance judgements were also prone to error when the ground between the observer and the object was divided into two regions having very different textures (e.g., concrete; grass).

A further cue is *interposition*, in which a nearer object hides part of a more distant object from view. Some evidence of how powerful interposition can be is provided by Kanizsa's (1976) illusory square (see Figure 2.13). There is a strong impression of a white square in front of four black circles, in spite of the fact that most of the contours of the white square are missing. Thus, the visual system makes sense of the four sectored black discs by perceiving an illusory interpolated white square.

Another cue to depth is provided by *shading*. Flat, two-dimensional surfaces do not cast shadows, and so the presence of shading generally provides good evidence for the presence of a three-dimensional object. Ramachandran (1988) presented observers with a visual display consisting of numerous very similar shaded circular patches, some illuminated by one light source and the remainder illuminated by a different light source. The observers incorrectly assumed that the visual display was lit by a single light source above the display, which led them to assign different depths to different parts of the display (i.e., some "dents" were seen as bumps).

The sun was easily the major source of light until fairly recently in our evolutionary history, and this might explain why people assume that visual scenes are generally illuminated from above. Howard, Bergstrom, and Masao (1990) pointed out that the notion of "above" is ambiguous, in that it can be above with reference to gravity (as is assumed in the explanation just given), or it can be above with reference to the position of the head. Accordingly, they persuaded their participants to view displays like those of Ramachandran (1988) with their heads upside down! The perceived source of light was determined with reference to head position rather than gravity, indicating that the location of the sun is *not* relevant to decisions about the direction of illumination.

Shadows can provide surprisingly powerful depth cues. Kersten, Mamassian, and Knill (1997) presented observers with a grey ball and a dark ellipse (shadow) moving together in a box. In one condition, the shadow remained in contact with the bottom of the object, whereas in a second condition there was an increasing gap between the ball and its shadow followed by a decreasing gap. In the first condition, the ball seemed to slide forwards and backwards across the box, whereas it seemed to rise and fall in the second condition.

Another cue to depth is provided by *familiar size*. We can use the retinal image size of an object to provide an accurate estimate of its distance, but only when we know its actual size. Ittelson (1951) had participants look at playing cards through a peephole restricting them to monocular vision and largely eliminated cues to depth other than familiar size. There were three playing cards (normal size, half size, and double size) presented one at a time at a distance of 2.28 metres from the observer. On the basis of familiar size, the judged distance of the normal card should have been 2.28 metres, that of the half-size card 4.56 metres, and that of the double-size card 1.14 metres. The actual judged distances were

2.28 metres, 4.56 metres, and 1.38 metres, indicating that familiar size can be a powerful determinant of distance judgements.

Another cue to depth is *image blur*. As Mather (1997, p. 1147) pointed out, "if one image region contains sharply focused texture, and another contains blurred texture, then the two regions may be perceived at different depths, even in the absence of other depth cues." He discussed his findings on ambiguous stimuli consisting of two regions of texture (one sharp and one blurred) separated by a wavy boundary. When the boundary was sharp, the sharp texture was seen as nearer, whereas the opposite was the case when the boundary was blurred. Thus, the boundary is seen as part of the nearer region.

The final monocular cue we will discuss is **motion parallax**, which refers to the movement of an object's image over the retina due to movement of the observer's head. Consider, for example, a situation in which there are two stationary objects at different distances from an observer, and he/she moves sideways. The image of the nearer object would travel a greater distance across the retina. Some properties of motion parallax can be seen through the windows of a moving train. Look into the far distance, and you will notice that the apparent speed of objects passing by seems faster the nearer they are to you.

Convincing evidence that motion parallax can generate depth information in the absence of all other cues was obtained by Rogers and Graham (1979). Observers looked with only one eye at a display containing about 2000 random dots. When there was relative motion of part of the display (motion parallax) to simulate the movement produced by a three-dimensional surface, the participants reported a three-dimensional surface standing out in depth from its surroundings. As Rogers and Graham (1979, p. 134) concluded, "Parallax information can be a subtle and powerful cue to the shape and relative depth of three-dimensional surfaces."

Binocular and oculomotor cues

The pictorial cues we have discussed could all be used as well by one-eyed people as by those with normal vision. Depth perception also depends on oculomotor cues, based on perceiving contractions of the muscles around the eyes. One such cue is **convergence**, which refers to the fact that the eyes turn inwards to focus on an object to a greater extent with a very close object than with one that is farther away. Another oculomotor cue is **accommodation**, which refers to the variation in optical power produced by a thickening of the lens of the eye when focusing on a close object. Each of these cues only produces a *single* value in any given situation, and so they cannot possibly do more than provide information about the distance of one object at a time (Bruce et al., 2003).

Depth perception also depends on binocular cues, which are only available when both eyes are used. **Stereopsis** involves binocular cues. It is stereoscopic vision depending on the difference or disparity in the images projected on the retinas of the two eyes. Convergence, accommodation, and stereopsis are only effective in facilitating depth perception over relatively short distances. The usefulness of convergence as a cue to distance has been disputed. However, it is clearly of no use at distances greater than a few metres, and the findings have been negative when real objects are used (Wade & Swanston, 2001). Accommodation is also of limited use. Its potential value as a depth cue is limited to the region of space immediately in front of you. However, distance judgements based on accommodation are rather inaccurate even with nearby objects (e.g., Künnapas, 1968). So far as stereopsis is concerned, the disparity or discrepancy in the retinal images of an object decreases by a factor of 100 as its distance increases from 2 to 20 metres (Bruce et al., 2003). As a consequence, stereopsis rapidly becomes less effective at greater distances.

The importance of stereopsis was shown clearly by Wheatstone (1838), who probably invented the stereoscope. In a stereoscope, separate pictures or drawings are presented to an observer so that each eye receives essentially the information it would receive if the object or objects depicted were actually presented. The simulation of the disparity or difference in the images presented to the two eyes produces a strong depth effect.

In general terms, stereopsis involves two stages. First, matched features in the input to the two eyes need to be identified. Second, the retinal disparities between these sets of features need to be calculated. There are many binocular neurons that receive input from both eyes, and which typically respond maximally when the two eyes view matched features. These binocular neurons are of use in calculating retinal disparities or differences. Some of them respond most to features giving rise to zero disparity, whereas others respond most to features imaged on different areas of the two eyes. Evidence that these binocular neurons are actually used in stereoscopic depth perception was reported by Blakemore (1976). Kittens had an opaque contact lens placed over one eye on one day and on the other eye on the following day. When the cats were tested as adults, they were unable to perform simple tasks involving binocular depth discriminations. In essence, the cats' binocular neurons had turned into monocular ones.

It has proved very hard to work out in detail how two separate images turn into a single percept. At one time, it was believed that the forms or objects presented to one eye were recognised independently, and that they were then fused into a single percept. However, this does not seem likely. Crucial evidence was obtained by Julesz (1971) using stereograms (two slightly different images which appear three-dimensional when seen through a stereoscope). Julesz used random-dot stereograms, in which both images were identical except that part of one (e.g., a central square) was shifted sideways to change its disparity relative to the background. Each image seemed to consist of a random mixture of black and white dots. However, when the stereogram was viewed in a stereoscope, an object (e.g., a square) was clearly visible.

Cells in area MT are involved in stereopsis. DeAngelis, Cumming, and Newsome (1998) initially identified cells in this area that responded more strongly to some disparities than to others. After that, they stimulated electrically clusters of cells in monkey MT. The monkey's depth perception in a stereo display was biased towards the preferred disparity of the cells that were stimulated. Thus, disparity-selective cells seem to be involved directly in depth perception. Backus, Fleet, Parker, and Heeger (2001) found using fMRI that several areas of the brain (including V2, V3, and V3A) in addition to MT are involved in stereo depth perception.

It has often been assumed that depth information (e.g., based on stereoscopic processing) is available early in visual perception, and is of use in object recognition. However, Bülthoff, Bülthoff, and Sinha (1998) argued that these assumptions are incorrect. They found that observers' recognition of familiar objects was not adversely affected when stereoscopic information was scrambled and thus incongruous. Indeed, the observers seemed unaware that the depth information was scrambled! What was going on here? According to Bülthoff et al. (1998, p. 254), processes associated with object recognition influence how depth information is interpreted: "Expectations about a familiar object's 3-dimensional structure override the true stereoscopic information."

Integrating cue information

We generally have access to several depth cues. What do we do if two depth cues provide conflicting evidence? Bruno and Cutting (1988) identified three strategies that may be used by observers having information available from two or more depth cues:

- *Additivity*: All the information from different cues is simply added together.
- *Selection*: Information from a single cue is used, with information from the other cue or cues being ignored.
- *Multiplication*: Information from different cues interacts in a multiplicative fashion.

Bruno and Cutting (1988) studied relative distance in studies in which three untextured parallel flat surfaces were arranged in depth. The observers viewed the displays monocularly, and there were four sources of information about depth: relative size; height in the projection plane; interposition; and motion parallax. The findings supported the additivity notion (Bruno & Cutting, 1988, p. 161).

Bruno and Cutting (1988) did not study what happens when two cues provide *conflicting* information about depth. However, it follows from their general theoretical orientation that observers should combine information from both cues. Support for this position was obtained by Rogers and Collett (1989). When binocular disparity and motion parallax cues provided conflicting information about depth, the conflict was resolved by taking both cues into account. Bradshaw and Rogers (1996) went further and found that the effects of binocular disparity and motion parallax on depth perception involved a common mechanism.

According to Sekuler and Blake (2002, p. 346), "The strategy of pitting cues against one another has been employed in many . . . experiments . . . In essentially all cases, depth perception is degraded when cues conflict, implying that no single source of information dominates." It could be argued that this is a reasonable strategy. Any depth cue may provide inaccurate information under some circumstances, and so relying exclusively on any one cue would often lead to error.

Selection

There are several situations in which depth perception is influenced mainly (or exclusively) by one cue. For example, Bruce et al. (2003) discussed evidence based on "pseudoscopic" viewing in which the information presented to the left and right eyes is reversed by using optical means. If stereoscopic information is all-important, pseudoscopic viewing should reverse perceived depth. This is what happens with random-dot stereograms and with pictures of wire-frame objects. However, pseudoscopic viewing of photographed scenes rarely produces reversed depth for the objects (e.g., cars, buildings) shown in the photograph. In this case, other cues (e.g., knowledge of objects, perspective, occlusion) dominate over stereoscopic cues.

The "hollow face" illusion (Gregory, 1973) is another example of stereoscopic information being ignored (see Figure 2.14). When a hollow mask of a face is seen from a few feet away, it is perceived as a normal face. This illusion is influenced by the familiarity of faces and our preference for convexity (Hill & Bruce, 1993).

There are other circumstances in which depth perception is influenced by the cues present, but some cues have more impact than others. For example, Johnston, Cumming, and Parker (1993) examined depth perception in textured stereograms of curved, cylindrical surfaces. The stereo depth cue was five to six times more important than the texture cue in determining the perceived depth of the cylinder.

Conclusions

Information from different depth cues is typically combined to produce accurate depth perception, and this often occurs in an additive fashion. However, there are several situations in which one cue is dominant over others, and still other situations in which one cue is selected in preference to others. As yet, we have no clear theoretical understanding of these diverse findings. However, depth perception is most likely to be based almost entirely on one cue when different cues provide very conflicting information. This is sensible. If, for example, one cue suggests an object is 10 metres away and another cue suggests it is 90 metres away, it is unlikely to be correct to split the difference and decide it is 50 metres away! Note that, as Bruce et al. (2003, p. 201) pointed out, "Natural vision does not generally involve such gross conflict of cues, and the study of concordant [in agreement] cues may be more informative." It may well be that additivity is the norm in such circumstances.

Size constancy

Size constancy is the tendency for objects to appear the same size whether their size in the retinal image is large or small. For example, if someone walks towards you, their retinal image increases progressively, but their size seems to remain the same.

Most research on size constancy has been carried out in the laboratory, but Brunswik (1956) argued that it was important to study size constancy in the external environment. Accordingly, he asked a student to walk around outdoors and

FIGURE 2.14

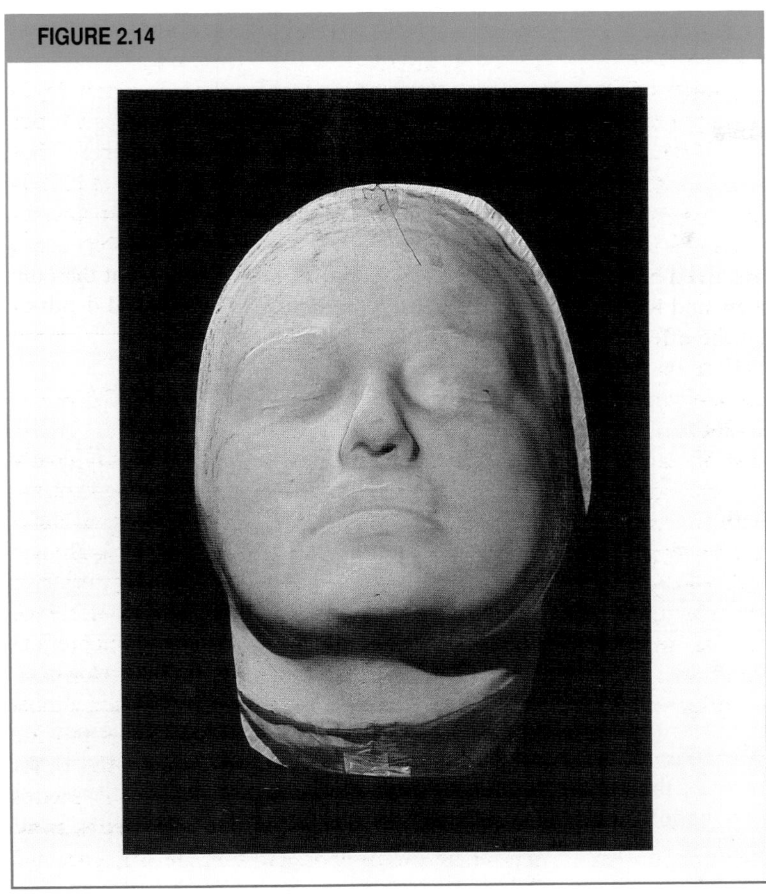

This is a picture of a hollow mask, illuminated from behind. In real life, as in this photograph, we see a normal face, with the tip of the nose nearer to us than the eyelids. Photograph by Sam Grainger.

to provide estimates of the sizes of numerous objects. She did this very successfully, and there was a correlation of +.99 between actual size and judged size. This high level of performance did not depend simply on information about retinal size. The correlation between actual object size and retinal image size was +.7 across all objects, but was only +.1 when small objects were excluded. Familiar size probably had a strong influence on the student's performance, because she produced very similar judgements when estimating size from memory alone.

Why do we show size constancy? Part of the reason is that we take account of an object's apparent distance when judging its size. For example, an object may be judged to be large even though its retinal image is very small if it is a long way away. The fact that size constancy is often not shown when we look at objects on the ground from the top of a tall building or from a plane may be because it is hard to judge distance accurately. These ideas were incorporated into the size–distance invariance hypothesis (Kilpatrick & Ittelson, 1953), according to which for a given size of retinal image, the perceived size of an object is proportional to its perceived distance. As we will see, this hypothesis is more applicable to unfamiliar objects than to familiar ones.

Evidence consistent with the size–distance invariance hypothesis was reported by Holway and Boring (1941). Participants sat at the intersection of two hallways. The test circle was presented in one hallway, and the comparison circle was presented in the other one. The test circle could be

FIGURE 2.15

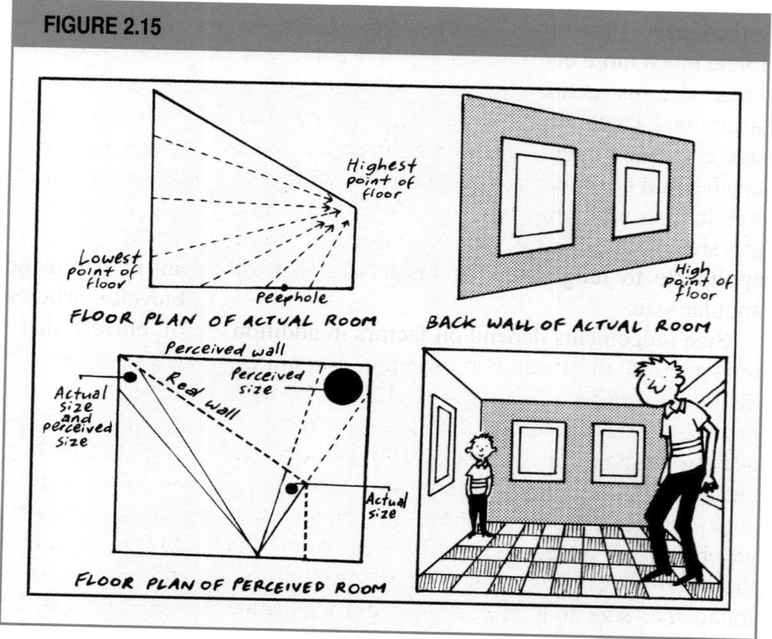

The Ames room.

of various sizes and at various distances, and the participants' task was to adjust the comparison circle so that it was the same size as the test circle. Their performance was very good when depth cues were available. However, it became poor when depth cues were removed by placing curtains in the hallway and requiring the participants to look through a peephole. Lichten and Lurie (1950) removed all depth cues, and found that observers relied totally on retinal image size in their judgements of object size.

If size judgements depend on perceived distance, then size constancy should not be found when the perceived distance of an object is very different from its actual distance. The Ames room provides a good example (see Figure 2.15). It has a peculiar shape: the floor slopes, and the rear wall is not at right angles to the adjoining walls. In spite of this, the Ames room creates the same retinal image as a normal rectangular room when viewed through a peephole. The fact that one end of the rear wall is much farther from the viewer is disguised by making it much higher. The cues suggesting that the rear wall is at right angles to the viewer are so strong that observers mistakenly assume that two adults standing in the corners by the rear wall are at the same distance from them. This leads them to estimate the size of the nearer adult as being much greater than that of the adult who is farther away.

The illusion effect with the Ames room is so great that an individual who walks backwards and forwards in front of the rear wall appears to grow and shrink as he/she moves! However, it has been argued that observers are more likely to realise what is going on if the person walking backwards and forwards is someone they know very well. There is an anecdote about a researcher's wife who arrived at the laboratory to find him inside the Ames room. Her immediate reaction was to call out, "Gee, honey, that room's distorted!" (Ian Gordon, personal communication).

Perceived size and size constancy generally depend in part on perceived distance. However, the relationship between perceived distance and perceived size is influenced by the kind of size judgements made by observers. Kaneko and Uchikawa (1997) distinguished between perceived linear size (what the actual size of the object seems to be) and perceived angular size (the apparent retinal size of the object). Kaneko and Uchikawa found much more evidence for size constancy with linear-size instructions than with angular-size instructions. There was a closer approximation to size constancy with linear-size instructions when depth could be perceived more accurately, but this was less so with angular-size instructions. Thus, the size–distance invariance hypothesis is more applicable to judgements of linear size than of angular size.

Size judgements depend on factors in addition to perceived distance. For example, Bertamini, Yang, and Proffitt (1998) argued that the horizon provides useful information, because the line connecting the point of observation to the horizon is virtually parallel to the ground. For example, if your eyes are 1.5 metres above the ground, then an object that appears to be the same height as the horizon is 1.5 metres tall. Bertamini et al. found that size judgements were most accurate when objects were at about eye level, and this was the case regardless of whether observers were standing or sitting.

Haber and Levin (2001) argued strongly that size perception of objects typically depends on *memory* of their familiar size rather than on perceptual information concerning their distance from the observer. In their first experiment, participants estimated the sizes of common objects with great accuracy purely on the basis of memory. Haber and Levin (2001) then tested their argument by presenting observers with various objects at close viewing range (0–50 metres) or distant viewing range (50–100 metres), and asking them to make size judgements. Some of these stimuli belonged to categories of objects that are almost invariant in size or height (e.g., tennis racquet, guitar, bicycle), whereas others belonged to categories of objects that vary in size (e.g., house plant, television set, Christmas tree). Finally, there were some unfamiliar stimuli (ovals, rectangles, and triangles of various sizes).

What findings would we expect? If familiar size is of major importance, then size judgements should be better for objects of invariant size than those of variable size, with size judgements worst for unfamiliar objects. Suppose that distance perception is all-important. Distances are estimated more accurately for nearby objects than for more distant ones, so size judgements for all categories of objects should be better at close than at distant viewing range. The actual findings indicate the importance of familiar size to accuracy of size judgements (see Figure 2.16). However, we obviously cannot account for the fairly high accuracy of size judgements of unfamiliar objects in terms

FIGURE 2.16

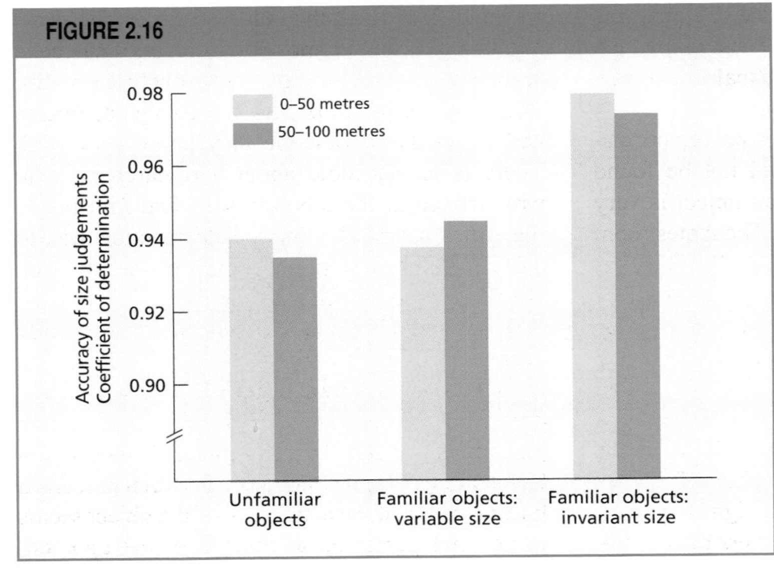

Accuracy of size judgements as a function of object type (unfamiliar; familiar variable size; familiar invariant size) and viewing distance (0–50 metres vs. 50–100 metres). Based on data in Haber and Levin (2001).

of familiar size. Haber and Levin (2001, p. 1150) admitted, "We do not know how the subjects arrived at the size estimations for the unfamiliar objects in this experiment."

Evaluation

Size perception and size constancy depend mainly on perceived distance and familiarity. As yet, we do not have a coherent account of *how* these (and other) factors combine to produce size judgements. As Haber and Levin (2001, p. 1140) pointed out, "Explanations of the sources of information and processing mechanisms that human observers depend on for the perception of size have been very unsatisfying and share nothing of the complexity and completeness of the comparable descriptions for distance perception."

CHAPTER SUMMARY

- Brain systems
  In the retina, there are cones (specialised for colour vision) and rods (specialised for movement detection). The main route between the eye and the cortex is the retina-geniculate-striate pathway, which is divided into fairly separate P and M pathways. There are two main pathways in the visual cortex, one terminating in the parietal cortex and the other terminating in the inferotemporal cortex. According to Zeki's functional specialisation theory, different parts of the cortex are specialised for different visual functions. There is some support for this view from patients with selective visual deficits (e.g., patients with achromatopsia or akinetopsia), but there is much less specialisation than claimed by Zeki. Lennie proposed a hierarchical model, according to which analyses in successive brain areas become more detailed and precise. This model is supported by the fact that the early cortical areas (V1 and V2) are much larger than later ones. Lennie's model is speculative, and implies that a large area of visual cortex achieves surprisingly little. Mishkin and Ungerleider (1982) distinguished between a ventral system specialised for object perception and a dorsal system specialised for spatial perception. In contrast, Milner and Goodale (1995) argued in their perception–action model that the dorsal system is used to guide action. This model is oversimplified and de-emphasises the numerous interactions between the two systems. Creem and Proffitt (2001a) argued in favour of a synthesis of the perception–action model and the views of Mishkin and Ungerleider, proposing that the dorsal pathway contains separate spatial and action-related systems.

- Colour perception
  Colour vision helps us to detect objects and to make fine discriminations among objects. According to the Young–Helmholtz theory, there are three types of nervous fibres (now known as cone receptors) differing in the light wavelengths to which they respond most strongly. This theory does not account fully for deficient colour vision or for negative after-images. Hering argued that there are three types of opponent processes in the visual system: green–red, blue–yellow, and white–black. A synthesis of the Young–Helmholtz and Hering theories accounts reasonably well for colour perception. Colour constancy occurs when a surface seems to have the same colour when there is a change in the illuminant. Chromatic adaptation and familiar colour are two factors involved in colour constancy, but there are several others. Local contrast and global contrast are of particular importance, but reflected highlights from glossy objects and mutual reflections are additional factors. Colour constancy is lower in the laboratory than in real life because some cues to colour constancy (e.g., reflected highlights) are not available in the laboratory.

- Perception without awareness
  Blindsight probably depends on subcortical mechanisms in some cases, whereas in others it mainly depends on direct connections between the lateral geniculate nucleus and extrastriate areas (e.g., V4, V5). Subliminal perception can be assessed using a subjective threshold or a more stringent objective threshold. There is strong evidence for subliminal perception in studies using either type of threshold. Neuroimaging evidence indicates that there can be extensive sensory, semantic, and motor processing of subliminal stimuli. Most studies of subliminal perception have presented masked stimuli very briefly. However, subliminal perception has also been shown in more naturalistic situations in which individuals fail to attend to certain areas of the visual field, but can make accurate judgements and discriminations about those stimuli.

- Depth and size perception
  Monocular cues to depth include linear perspective, aerial perspective, texture, shading, shadows, familiar size, and motion parallax. Convergence and accommodation are oculomotor cues of limited usefulness. Stereopsis involves binocular cues, and is based on establishing correspondences between the information presented to one eye and that presented to the other eye. Information from depth cues is often combined, but combination is less common when there are gross differences in the depth information supplied by different cues. Size constancy depends mainly on perceived distance, but familiar size and horizon information can both be used to estimate size.

FURTHER READING

- Bruce, V., Green, P.R., & Georgeson, M.A. (2003). *Visual perception: Physiology, psychology and ecology (4th Ed.)*. Hove, UK: Psychology Press. Several parts of this excellent textbook (e.g., Chapters 3, 5, and 6) provide good discussions of topics considered in this chapter.
- Healy, A.F., & Proctor, R.W. (2003). *Handbook of psychology: Experimental psychology*. New York: Wiley & Sons. This edited book contains relevant chapters by Kubovy, Epstein, and Gepshtein on foundations of visual perception, and by Proffitt and Caudek on depth perception.
- Lamberts, K., & Goldstone, R. (2004). *Handbook of cognition*. London: Sage. This edited book has coverage of basic visual processes, especially in the chapter by Wagemans, Wichmann, and Op de Beeck.
- Morgan, M. (2003). *The space between our ears: How the brain represents visual space*. London: Weidenfeld & Nicolson. This book provides entertaining coverage of most of the topics discussed in this chapter.
- Sekuler, R., & Blake, R. (2002). *Perception (4th Ed.)*. New York: McGraw-Hill. There is good introductory coverage of numerous topics in perception in this American textbook.

3

Object Recognition

INTRODUCTION

Throughout the waking day we are bombarded with information from the visual environment. Mostly we make sense of that information, which usually involves identifying or recognising the objects that surround us. Object recognition typically occurs so effortlessly that it is hard to believe it is actually a rather complex achievement.

The complexities of object recognition can be grasped by discussing the processes involved. First, there are usually numerous different overlapping objects in the visual environment, and we must somehow decide where one object ends and the next starts. This is difficult, as can be seen if we consider the visual environment of the author word-processing these words. There are over 100 objects visible in the room in front of him and in the garden outside. Over 90% of these objects overlap (and are overlapped by) other objects.

Second, objects can be recognised accurately over a wide range of viewing distances and orientations. For example, there is a small table directly in front of the author. He is confident the table is round, although its retinal image is elliptical. The term "constancy" refers to the fact that the apparent size and shape of an object do not change despite large variations in the size and shape of the retinal image (see Chapter 2).

Third, we recognise an object is, say, a chair without any apparent difficulty. Chairs vary enormously in their visual properties (e.g., colour, size, shape), and it is not immediately obvious how we manage to allocate such diverse visual stimuli to the same category. The discussion of the representation of concepts in Chapter 9 is relevant here.

In spite of the complexities of object recognition, we can generally go beyond simply identifying objects in the visual environment. For example, we can normally describe what an object would look like if viewed from a different angle, and we know its uses and functions.

All in all, there is more to object recognition than might initially be supposed (than meets the eye?). This chapter is devoted to the task of unravelling some of the mysteries of object recognition in normal and brain-damaged individuals. Note that some of the issues relating to object recognition (e.g., depth perception, size constancy) were discussed in Chapter 2.

PERCEPTUAL ORGANISATION

A basic issue in visual perception is **perceptual segregation**, i.e., our ability to work out accurately which parts of presented visual information belong together and thus form separate objects. One of the first systematic attempts to study perceptual segregation (and the perceptual organisation to which it gives rise) was made by the Gestaltists. They were German psychologists (including Koffka, Köhler, and Wertheimer) who emigrated to the United States between the two World Wars. Their fundamental principle of perceptual organisation was the law of Prägnanz: "Of several geometrically possible organisations that one will actually occur which possesses the best, simplest and most stable shape" (Koffka, 1935, p. 138).

Although the law of Prägnanz was their key organisational principle, the Gestaltists also proposed several other laws, most of which can be subsumed under the law of Prägnanz (see Figure 3.1). The fact that three horizontal arrays of dots rather than vertical groups are perceived in Figure 3.1a indicates that visual elements tend to be grouped together if they are close to each other (the law of proximity). Figure 3.1b illustrates the law of similarity, which states that elements will be grouped together perceptually if they are similar. Vertical columns rather than horizontal rows are seen because the elements in the vertical columns are the same, whereas those in the horizontal rows are not. We see two crossing lines in Figure 3.1c, because according to the law of good continuation we group together those elements requiring the fewest changes or interruptions in straight or smoothly curving lines. Figure 3.1d illustrates the law of closure, according to which missing parts of a figure are filled in to complete the figure. Thus, a circle is seen, even though it is incomplete.

The Gestaltists relied heavily on introspective reports, or the "look at the figure and see for yourself" method. More convincing evidence was provided by Pomerantz (1981). Observers were presented with four-item visual arrays, and had to identify rapidly the one differing from the others. When the array was simple but could not easily be organised, it took an average of 1.9 seconds to perform the task. However, when the array was more complex but more easily organised, it took only 0.75 seconds on average. This beneficial effect of organisation is known as the configural superiority effect.

FIGURE 3.1

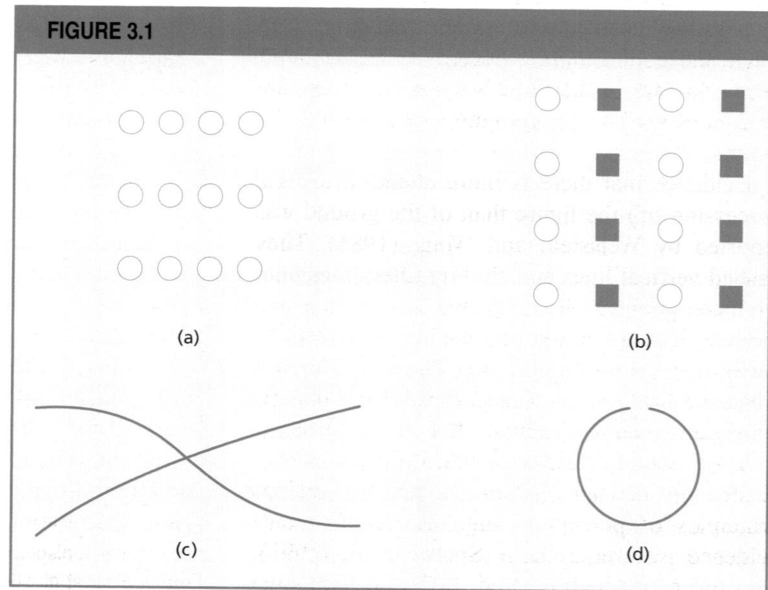

Examples of some of the Gestalt laws of perceptual organisation: (a) the law of proximity; (b) the law of similarity; (c) the law of good continuation; and (d) the law of closure.

Most Gestalt laws were derived from the study of static two-dimensional figures. However, they also proposed the law of common fate, according to which visual elements apparently moving together are grouped together. This was shown by Johansson (1973; see Chapter 4). He attached lights to the joints of an actor wearing dark clothes, and then filmed him moving around a dark room. Observers saw only a meaningless display of lights when the actor was at rest. However, they perceived a moving human figure when he walked around, although they could actually see only the lights. Other Gestalt-like phenomena (e.g., perceived causality) are also discussed in Chapter 4.

The Gestaltists emphasised the importance of **figure–ground segregation** in perceptual organisation. One object or part of the visual field is identified as the figure, whereas the rest of the visual field is less important and so forms the ground. The laws of perceptual organisation permit this segregation into figure and ground to happen. According to the Gestaltists, the figure is perceived as having a distinct form or shape, whereas the ground lacks form. In addition, the figure is perceived as being in front of the ground, and the contour separating the figure from the ground is seen as belonging to the figure.

You can check the validity of these claims about figure and ground by looking at reversible figures such as the faces–goblet figure (see Figure 3.2). When the goblet is the figure, it seems to be in front of a dark background, whereas the faces are in front of a white background when forming the figure.

Evidence that there is more attention to (and processing of) the figure than of the ground was reported by Weisstein and Wong (1986). They flashed vertical lines and slightly tilted lines onto the faces–goblet figure, and gave their participants the task of deciding whether the line was vertical. Performance on this task was three times better when the line was presented to what the participants perceived as the figure than to the ground.

The Gestaltists assumed that no learning was needed for newborn infants to use the various principles of perceptual organisation. Contrary evidence was reported by Spelke et al. (1993), who presented infants aged 3, 5, and 9 months and adults with simple but unfamiliar visual displays. Each display could be perceived as a single object or as two joined objects (see Figure 3.3). Adults typically used the Gestalt principles of good continuation, form, and colour and texture similarity. In contrast, nearly all the infants saw most of the displays as single objects. They used the law of proximity but largely ignored the other

FIGURE 3.2

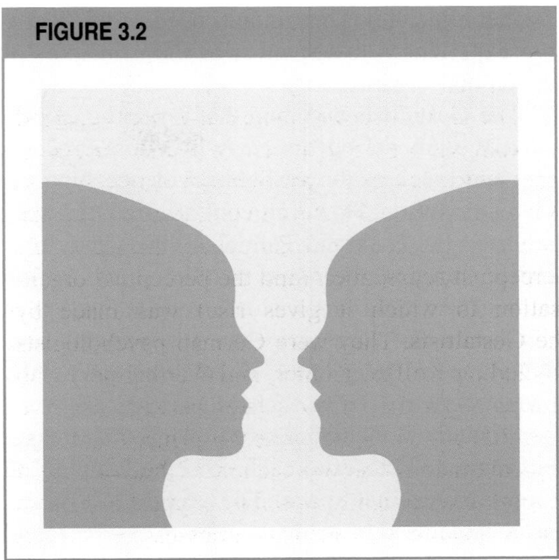

An ambiguous drawing which can be seen either as two faces or as a goblet.

FIGURE 3.3

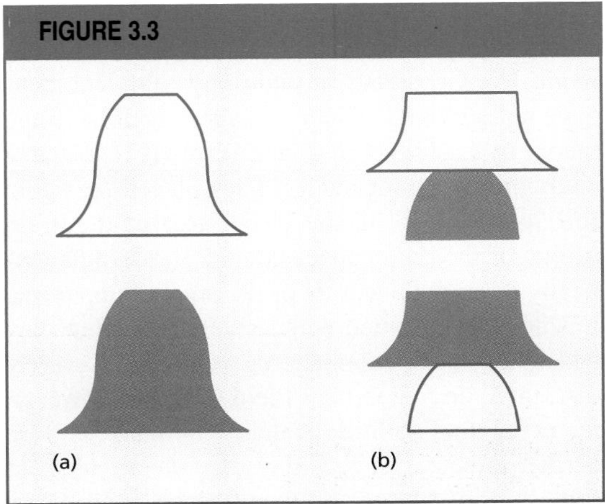

Schematic depiction of two types of displays: (a) homogeneous displays and (b) heterogeneous displays. From Spelke et al. (1993) with permission from Elsevier.

Gestalt principles. Thus, infants need certain learning experiences to use most of the principles of perceptual organisation.

The Gestaltists assumed that grouping of perceptual elements occurs *early* in visual processing, and much of the available evidence supports that assumption. However, contrary findings were reported by Rock and Palmer (1990). They presented luminous beads on parallel strings in the dark. The beads were closer to each other in the horizontal direction than the vertical one. When the display was tilted backwards, the beads were closer to each other vertically than horizontally in the two-dimensional retinal image, but remained closer to each other horizontally in three-dimensional space. The observers saw the beads organised in vertical columns. As Rock and Palmer (1990, p. 51) concluded, "Grouping was based on perceived proximity in three-dimensional space rather than on actual proximity on the retina. Grouping by proximity must therefore occur after depth perception." Thus, grouping can occur later in processing than assumed by the Gestaltists.

The Gestaltists tried to explain perceptual organisation by their doctrine of **isomorphism**, according to which the experience of visual organisation is mirrored by a precisely corresponding process in the brain. It was assumed there are electrical "field forces" in the brain helping to produce the experience of a stable perceptual organisation when we look at our visual environment. The Gestaltists' pseudo-physiological ideas have not survived. Much damage was done to the theory by Lashley, Chow, and Semmes (1951) in a study on two chimpanzees. They placed four gold foil "conductors" in the visual area of the brain of one of the chimpanzees, and 23 gold pins vertically through the cortex of the other chimpanzee. Lashley et al. argued persuasively that what they had done to these chimpanzees would have severely disrupted any electrical field forces. However, the perceptual abilities of their chimpanzees were hardly affected, suggesting that electrical field forces are of little or no significance.

According to the Gestaltists, the various laws of grouping operate in a bottom-up (or stimulus-driven) way to produce perceptual organisation.

FIGURE 3.4

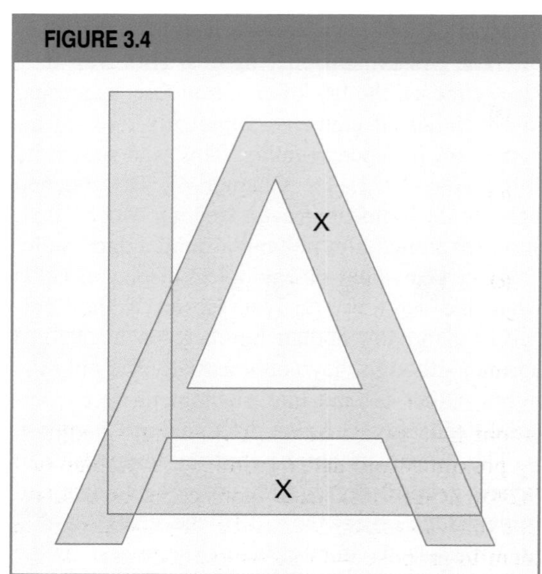

Overlapping transparent letters of the type used by Vecera and Farah (1997).

Thus, information about objects in the visual field is *not* used to determine how the visual field is segmented. Contrary evidence was reported by Vecera and Farah (1997), who presented two overlapping transparent letters (see Figure 3.4). The participants' task was to decide rapidly whether two *x*s in the figure were on the same shape. The key manipulation was whether the letters were presented in the upright position or upside down.

Vecera and Farah (1997) found that performance was significantly faster with upright letters than with upside-down ones, because the two shapes to be segmented were much more familiar in the upright condition. Thus, as Vecera and Farah (1997, p. 1293) concluded, "top-down [knowledge-driven] activation can partly guide the segmentation process." This suggests the Gestaltists exaggerated the role of bottom-up processes in segmentation.

The Gestaltists de-emphasised the complexities involved when laws of grouping are in conflict. This issue was addressed by Quinlan and Wilton (1998). For example, they presented a display such as the one shown in Figure 3.5a, in which there is a conflict between proximity and similarity.

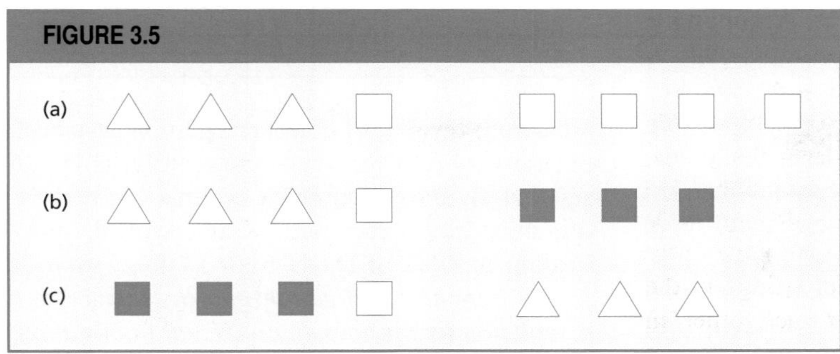

(a) Display involving a conflict between proximity and similarity; (b) display with a conflict between shape and colour; (c) a different display with a conflict between shape and colour. All adapted from Quinlan and Wilton (1998).

About half the participants grouped the stimuli by proximity and half by similarity. Quinlan and Wilton (1998) also used more complex displays like those in Figure 3.5b and c. Their findings led them to propose the following notions:

- The visual elements in a display are initially grouped or clustered on the basis of proximity.
- Additional processes are used if elements provisionally clustered together differ in one or more features (within-cluster mismatch).
- If there is a within-cluster mismatch on features but a between-cluster match (e.g., Figure 3.5a), then participants choose between grouping based on proximity or on similarity.
- If there are within-cluster and between-cluster mismatches, then proximity is ignored, and grouping is often based on colour. In the case of the displays shown in Figure 3.5b and c, most participants grouped on the basis of common colour rather than common shape.

Quinlan and Wilton (1998) have made an interesting contribution. However, we still need a detailed theoretical account of the processes involved when conflicts between laws of grouping need to be resolved.

Evaluation

The Gestaltists discovered several important aspects of perceptual organisation. As Rock and Palmer (1990, p. 50) pointed out, "the laws of grouping have withstood the test of time. In fact, not one of them has been refuted." In addition, the Gestaltists focused on key issues. For example, it is generally accepted that an understanding of perceptual organisation (e.g., figure–ground segregation) is of fundamental importance.

There are many limitations with the Gestalt approach. First, nearly all the evidence the Gestaltists provided for their principles of perceptual organisation was based on two-dimensional line drawings. Second, the Gestaltists produced *descriptions* of interesting perceptual phenomena, but failed to provide adequate *explanations*. Third, they assumed that observers use the various laws of perceptual grouping without the need for relevant perceptual learning. However, they did not provide any supporting evidence, and the assumption is incorrect (e.g., Spelke et al., 1993).

Fourth, while grouping undoubtedly occurs relatively early in processing, it does not always happen as early as assumed by the Gestaltists (Rock & Palmer, 1990). Fifth, top-down processes can play a greater role in perceptual grouping than was assumed by the Gestaltists (Vecera & Farah, 1997). Sixth, the speculative neurophysiological ideas of the Gestaltists have been discarded. Seventh, the Gestaltists did not consider fully enough what happens when different perceptual laws are in conflict (Quinlan & Wilton, 1998).

Subsequent theories

Geisler, Perry, Super, and Gallogly (2001) were interested in how we achieve good continuation, i.e., deciding accurately on the contours forming the outline shapes of objects. They argued that a good starting point is to consider the contours of actual objects in the visual world. Accordingly, they examined in great detail the contours of flowers, trees, a mountain, a river, and so on. Two key principles emerged: (1) adjacent segments of any contour typically have very similar orientations, and (2) segments of any given contour that are further apart generally have somewhat different orientations.

Geisler et al. (2001) presented observers with two complex patterns at the same time, giving them the task of deciding which pattern contained a winding contour. Performance on this task was predicted very well from the two key principles described above. These findings suggest that, "Development of contour integration mechanisms . . . is driven by the occurrence statistics of images encountered in the natural world" (Sekuler & Blake, 2002, p. 211). Thus, we use our extensive knowledge of real objects when making decisions about contours.

Palmer and Rock (1994) proposed a new principle of visual organisation termed **uniform connectedness**. According to this principle, any connected region having uniform visual properties (e.g., colour, texture, lightness) tends to be organised as a single perceptual unit. Palmer and Rock argued that uniform connectedness can be more powerful than Gestalt grouping principles such as proximity and similarity, and that it occurs prior to the operation of those other principles. Palmer and Rock (1994) showed that grouping by uniform connectedness could dominate over proximity and similarity by putting these grouping principles in conflict.

Uniform connectedness may be less important than assumed by Palmer and Rock (1994). Han, Humphreys, and Chen (1999) assessed discrimination speed for visual stimuli, with the elements of the stimuli being grouped by proximity, by similarity, or by uniform connectedness. Their key findings were as follows: "Grouping by similarity of shapes is perceived slower than grouping by UC [uniform connectedness], but grouping by proximity can be as fast and efficient as that by UC" (Han et al., 1999, p. 661). Thus, uniform connectedness is an important organisational principle, but is not necessarily more important than organisation on the basis of proximity.

THEORIES OF OBJECT RECOGNITION

Numerous theories of object recognition have been put forward over the years. However, it is fair to say that the most significant landmark in theorising about object recognition came with the publication in 1982 of David Marr's book *Vision: A computational investigation into the human representation and processing of visual information*. That was followed a few years later by Irving Biederman's (1987) recognition-by-components theory, which represents a development and extension of Marr's theory. Both of these influential theories are discussed here in some detail.

Unsurprisingly, it has become increasingly clear in the years since Marr and Biederman proposed their theories that object recognition is more complex than they had imagined. Accordingly, towards the end of this section we discuss some of the main limitations of their theoretical approaches. Finally, we consider various more recent theoretical approaches which grapple with the complexities not addressed by Marr or Biederman.

Marr's theory

Marr (1982) put forward a computational theory of the processes involved in object recognition. He proposed a series of *representations* (i.e., descriptions) providing increasingly detailed information about the visual environment:

- *Primal sketch*: This provides a two-dimensional description of the main light-intensity changes in the visual input, including information about edges, contours, and blobs.
- *$2\frac{1}{2}$-D sketch*: This incorporates a description of the depth and orientation of visible surfaces, making use of information provided by shading, texture, motion, binocular disparity, and so on; like the primal sketch, it is observer centred or viewpoint dependent.
- *3-D model representation*: This describes three-dimensionally the shapes of objects and their relative positions independent of the observer's viewpoint (it is thus viewpoint invariant).

Primal sketch

According to Marr (1982), we can identify two versions of the primal sketch: the raw primal sketch and the full primal sketch. Both sketches are symbolic, meaning they represent the image as a list of symbols. The **raw primal sketch** contains information about light-intensity changes in the visual scene, and the full primal sketch makes use of this information to identify the number and outline shapes of visual objects. Why are *two* separate primal sketches created? Part of the answer is that light-intensity changes can occur for various reasons. The intensity of light reflected from a surface depends on the angle at which light strikes it, and is reduced by shadows falling on the surface. In addition, there can be substantial differences in light intensity reflected from an object due to variations in its texture. As a result, the light-intensity changes incorporated into the raw primal sketch provide a *fallible* guide to object shapes and edges.

The raw primal sketch is formed from what is known as a *grey-level representation* of the retinal image. This representation is based on the light intensities in each very small area of the image; these areas are called *pixels* (picture elements). The intensity of light reflecting from any given pixel fluctuates continuously, and so there is a danger the grey-level representation will be distorted by these momentary fluctuations. One approach is to average the light-intensity values of neighbouring pixels. This smoothing process eliminates "noise" but can produce a blurring effect in which valuable information is lost.

One answer to the above problem is to assume that several representations of the image are formed, varying in their degree of blurring. Information from these image representations is then combined to form the raw primal sketch. According to Marr and Hildreth (1980), the raw primal sketch consists of four different tokens: edge-segments, bars, terminators, and blobs. Each of these tokens is based on a different pattern of light-intensity change in the blurred representations. Within Marr and Hildreth's theory, "The key idea was that edges in an image are those points at which the luminance is changing most steeply across space" (Bruce, Green, & Georgeson, 2003, p. 89).

Some support for Marr and Hildreth's (1980) theory was reported by Georgeson and Freeman (1997). They asked participants to identify the positions of edges within a one-dimensional pattern formed of sine-wave gratings. Edges were typically identified at those places predicted by the theory. However, these patterns were much simpler than the two-dimensional images typically forming the basis of visual perception, and the theory works less well with such images (Bruce et al., 2003). More generally, the theory has not fared well when confronted by our increasing knowledge of what happens in the visual cortex. As Bruce et al., 2003, p. 103) pointed out, "Marr and Hildreth's (1980) theory does not provide a role for the spatial filtering properties of many cortical cells, especially those responsive to fine detail." For example, Smallman, MacLeod, He, and Kentridge (1996) found that there are visual channels in the fovea (centre of the retina) having receptive field centres only one or two cone receptors across.

Full primal sketch

Various processes are applied to the raw primal sketch to identify its underlying structure or organisation. This is needed, because the information contained in the raw primal sketch is typically ambiguous and compatible with several underlying structures. Marr (1976) found it was valuable to use two general principles when designing a program to achieve perceptual organisation:

(1) The *principle of explicit naming.*
(2) The *principle of least commitment.*

According to the former principle, it is useful to give a name or symbol to a set of grouped elements. The reason is that the name or symbol can be used over and over again to describe other sets of grouped elements, all of which can then form a much larger grouping. According to the principle of least commitment, ambiguities are resolved only when there is convincing evidence as to the appropriate solution. This principle is useful, because mistakes at an early stage of processing can lead on to several other mistakes.

With respect to the principle of explicit naming, Marr's program assigned place tokens to small regions of the raw primal sketch, such as the position of a blob or edge, or the termination of a longer blob or edge. Various edge points in the raw primal sketch are incorporated into a single place token on the basis of Gestalt-like notions such as proximity, figural continuity, and closure (see earlier in this chapter). Place tokens are then grouped together in various ways, in part on the basis of the grouping principles advocated by the Gestaltists. Some examples of the ways in which place tokens are combined are as follows:

- Clustering: Place tokens close together can be combined to form higher-order place tokens.
- Curvilinear aggregation: Place tokens aligned in the same direction will be joined to produce a contour.

Marr provided one of the first detailed accounts of the initial processes in visual perception. As such, it has been very influential. Marr's (1976, 1982) visual processing program for the full primal sketch was reasonably successful. One reason why the grouping principles applied to place tokens work is because they reflect what is generally the case in the real world. For example, visual elements close together are likely to belong to the same object, as are elements that are similar. The program works well although it typically does not rely on object knowledge or expectations when deciding what goes with what. However, there were cases of ambiguity when the program could not specify the contour or perceptual organisation until supplied with additional information. Other complications and limitations are discussed by Bruce et al. (2003).

Marr (1982) assumed that grouping is based on two-dimensional representations. However, grouping can also be based on three-dimensional representations (e.g., Rock & Palmer, 1990, discussed earlier). Enns and Rensick (1990) found that their participants immediately perceived which in a display of block figures was the "odd man out". They were able to do this even though the figures differed only in their three-dimensional orientation. Thus, three-dimensional or depth information can be used to group stimuli.

$2\frac{1}{2}$-D sketch

According to Marr (1982), various stages are involved in the transformation of the primal sketch into the $2\frac{1}{2}$-D sketch. The first stage involves the construction of a *range map* ("local point-by-point depth information about surfaces in the scene", Frisby, 1986, p. 164). After this, higher-level descriptions (e.g., of convex and concave junctions between two or more surfaces) are produced by combining information from related parts of the range map. More is known of the processes involved in constructing a range map than in proceeding from that to the $2\frac{1}{2}$-D sketch itself.

What kinds of information are used in changing the primal sketch into the $2\frac{1}{2}$-D sketch? Use is made of shading, motion, texture, shape, and binocular disparity (see Chapter 2).

3-D model representation

The $2\frac{1}{2}$-D sketch apparently provides a poor basis for identifying an object, mainly because it is observer centred or viewpoint dependent. This means an object's representation will vary considerably depending on the angle from which it is viewed, and this variability greatly complicates object recognition. As a result, the 3-D model representation (which contains viewpoint-invariant information) is produced. This representation remains the same regardless of the viewing angle.

Marr and Nishihara (1978) identified three desirable criteria for a 3-D representation:

- Accessibility: The representation can be constructed easily.
- Scope and uniqueness: "Scope" is the extent to which the representation is applicable to all the shapes in a given category, and "uniqueness" means that all the different views of an object produce the same standard representation.
- Stability and sensitivity: "Stability" indicates that a representation incorporates the similarities among objects, and "sensitivity" means it incorporates salient differences.

Marr and Nishihara (1978) proposed that the primitive units for describing objects should be cylinders having a major axis. These primitive units are hierarchically organised, with high-level units providing information about object shape and low-level units providing more detailed information. Why did Marr and Nishihara adopt this axis-based approach? They argued the main axes of an object are usually easy to establish regardless of the viewing position, whereas other object characteristics (e.g., precise shape) are not.

We can illustrate Marr and Nishihara's (1978) theoretical approach by considering the hierarchical organisation of the human form (see Figure 3.6). The human form can be decomposed into a series of generalised cones at different levels of generality. A **generalised cone** can be defined as "the surface created by moving a cross-section of constant shape but variable size along an axis" (Bruce et al., 2003, p. 276). Spheres, pyramids, arms, and legs are all examples of generalised cones. It was assumed that this overall 3-D description is stored in memory, and enables us to recognise appropriate visual stimuli as humans regardless of the angle of viewing.

According to Marr and Nishihara (1978), object recognition involves matching the 3-D model representation constructed from a visual stimulus against a catalogue of 3-D model representations stored in memory. To do this, we must identify the major axes of the visual stimulus. Marr and Nishihara (1978) proposed that concavities (areas where the contour points into the object) are identified first. With the human form, for example, there is a concave area in each armpit. These concavities are used to divide the visual image into segments (e.g., arms, legs, torso, head). Finally, the main axis of each segment is found.

There are some advantages associated with this emphasis on concavities and axis-based representations. First, the identification of concavities plays an important role in object recognition. Consider, for example, the faces–goblet ambiguous figure (look back at Figure 3.2) studied by Hoffman and Richards (1984). When one of the faces is seen, the concavities help the identification of the forehead, nose, lips, and chin. In contrast, when the goblet is seen, the concavities serve to define its base, stem, and bowl.

Second, we can calculate the lengths and arrangement of axes of most visual objects regardless of the viewing angle. Third, information about axes can help object recognition. As Humphreys and Bruce (1989) pointed out, humans can be readily distinguished from gorillas on the basis of the relative lengths of the axes of the segments or cones corresponding to arms and legs: our legs are longer than our arms, whereas the opposite is true of gorillas.

Third, there is some experimental support for the notion that an object's axes play an important role in object recognition. For example, Lawson and Humphreys (1996) presented participants with

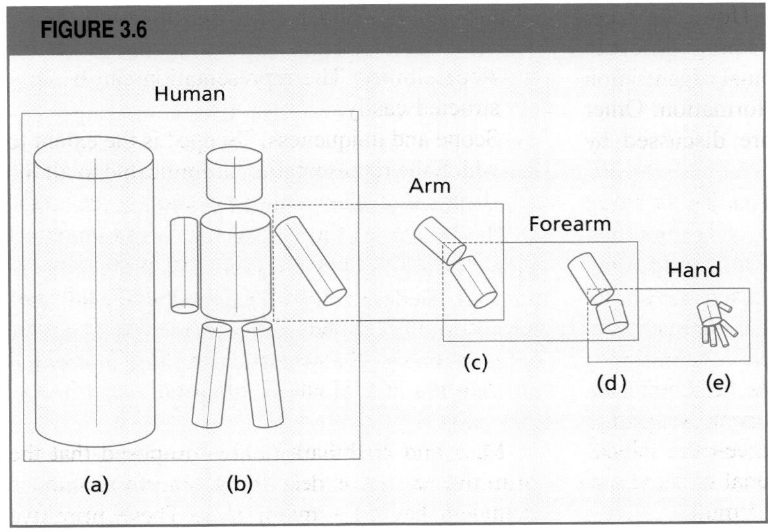

The hierarchical organisation of the human figure (from Marr & Nishihara, 1978) at various levels: (a) axis of the whole body; (b) axes at the level of arms, legs, and head; (c) arm divided into upper and lower arm; (d) a lower arm with separate hand; and (e) the palm and fingers of a hand. Reproduced with permission from The Royal Society.

line drawings of objects rotated in depth. Two line drawings were presented at varying intervals, and the task involved deciding whether they represented the same object. Performance was impaired when the to-be-matched line drawing had its main axis foreshortened.

There are several problems with Marr's theoretical approach. In general terms, those problems are rather similar to the ones characterising Biederman's theory. Accordingly, we will defer a consideration of these limitations until Biederman's approach has been described in detail.

Biederman's recognition-by-components theory

Biederman (1987, 1990) put forward a theory of object recognition extending that of Marr and Nishihara (1978). The central assumption of his recognition-by-components theory is that objects consist of basic shapes or components known as "geons" (geometric ions). Examples of geons are blocks, cylinders, spheres, arcs, and wedges. According to Biederman (1987), there are about 36 different geons. This may seem suspiciously few to provide descriptions of *all* the objects we can recognise and identify. However, we can identify enormous numbers of spoken English words even though there are only about 44 phonemes in the English language. The reason is that these phonemes can be arranged in almost endless different orders. The same is true of geons. Part of the reason for the richness of the object descriptions provided by geons stems from the different possible spatial relationships among them. For example, a cup can be described by an arc connected to the side of a cylinder, and a pail can be described by the same two geons, but with the arc connected to the top of the cylinder.

In order to understand recognition-by-components theory more fully, you should refer to Figure 3.7. The stage we have discussed so far is that of the determination of the components or geons of a visual object and their relationships. When this information is available, it is matched with stored object representations or structural models containing information about the nature of the relevant geons, their orientations, sizes, and so on. In general terms, the identification of any given visual object is determined by whichever stored object representation provides the best fit with the component- or geon-based information obtained from the visual object.

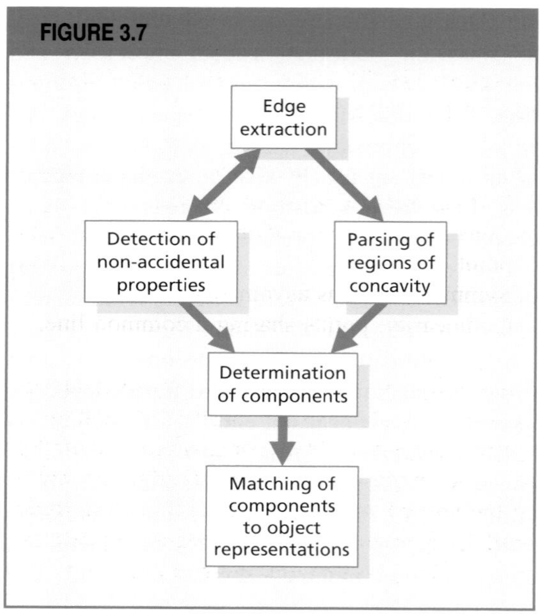

An outline of Biederman's recognition-by-components theory. Adapted from Biederman (1987).

As can be seen in Figure 3.7, only part of Biederman's theory has been presented so far. What has been omitted is any discussion of how an object's components or geons are determined. The first step is edge extraction, described by Biederman (1987, p. 117) in the following way: "[There is] an early edge extraction stage, responsive to differences in surface characteristics namely, luminance, texture, or colour, providing a line drawing description of the object."

The next step is to decide how a visual object should be segmented to establish its parts or components. Biederman (1987) agreed with Marr and Nishihara (1978) that the concave parts of an object's contour are of particular value in accomplishing the task of segmenting the visual image into parts.

The other major element is to decide which edge information from an object possesses the important characteristic of remaining *invariant* across different viewing angles. According to Biederman (1987), there are five such invariant properties of edges:

- Curvature: points on a curve.
- Parallel: sets of points in parallel.
- Cotermination: edges terminating at a common point.
- Symmetry: versus asymmetry.
- Collinearity: points sharing a common line.

According to the theory, the components or geons of a visual object are constructed from these invariant properties. Thus, for example, a cylinder has curved edges and two parallel edges connecting the curved edges, whereas a brick has three parallel edges and no curved edges. Biederman (1987, p. 116) argued that the five properties:

> have the desirable properties that they are invariant over changes in orientation and can be determined from just a few points on each edge. Consequently, they allow a primitive [component or geon] to be extracted with great tolerance for variations of viewpoint, occlusion [obstruction], and noise.

This part of the theory leads to one of the key (but controversial) predictions of the theory: object recognition is typically viewpoint invariant, meaning an object can be recognised equally easily from nearly all viewing angles. Why is this prediction made? In essence, object recognition depends crucially on the identification of geons, and geons can be identified from a great variety of viewpoints. It follows that object recognition from a given viewing angle would be difficult only when one or more geons were hidden from view.

An important part of Biederman's theory with respect to the invariant properties is what he called the "non-accidental" principle. According to this principle, regularities in the visual image reflect actual (or non-accidental) regularities in the world rather than depending on accidental characteristics of a given viewpoint. Thus, for example, a two-dimensional symmetry in the visual image is assumed to indicate symmetry in the three-dimensional object.

Use of the non-accidental principle helps object recognition, but occasionally leads to error. For example, a straight line in a visual image usually reflects a straight edge in the world, but it might not (e.g., a bicycle viewed end-on). Some visual illusions can be explained by assuming that we use the non-accidental principle. For example, consider the Ames distorted room (see Chapter 2). It is actually of a most peculiar shape, but when viewed from a particular point it gives rise to the same retinal image as a conventional rectangular room. Of particular relevance here, misleading properties such as symmetry and parallelism can be derived from the visual image of the Ames room, and may underlie the illusion.

Biederman's (1987) theory makes it clear how objects can be recognised in normal viewing conditions. However, we can generally recognise objects when the conditions are suboptimal (e.g., an intervening object obscures part of the target object). According to Biederman (1987), the following factors explain how we achieve object recognition in such conditions:

- The invariant properties (e.g., curvature, parallel lines) of an object can still be detected even when only parts of edges can be seen.
- Provided the concavities of a contour are visible, there are mechanisms allowing the missing parts of a contour to be restored.
- There is normally a considerable amount of redundant information available for recognising complex objects, and so they can still be identified when some geons or components are missing (e.g., a giraffe could be identified from its neck even if its legs were hidden from view).

Any adequate theory of object recognition must address the **binding problem** (how do we integrate different kinds of information to produce object recognition?). A version of this problem arises when we are presented with several objects at the same time, and have to decide which features or geons belong to which object. An attempt to solve this problem was made by Hummel and

Biederman (1992), who proposed a connectionist model of Biederman's (1987) geon theory (connectionist networks are discussed at length in Chapter 1). This model is a seven-layer connectionist network taking as its input a line drawing of an object and producing as its output a unit representing its identity. According to Ellis and Humphreys (1999, p. 157), "The binding mechanism they employ . . . depends on synchrony in the activation of units in the network . . . units whose activation varies together are bound together, therefore so are the features they represent." More specifically, units that typically belong to the same object are connected by fast links, which help to ensure that related units are all activated at the same time.

Hummel and Biederman (1992) carried out various simulation studies with their connectionist model, and showed that it provided an efficient and accurate mechanism for binding. For example, the model was trained to recognise 10 objects presented from a single viewpoint. After that, it could recognise accurately new instances of these objects presented from different viewpoints, as can human observers. The model's performance deteriorated when objects were presented in different orientations, which is also in line with human performance. The major limitation of Hummel and Biederman's connectionist model is that it has only been tested with a small number of objects.

FIGURE 3.8

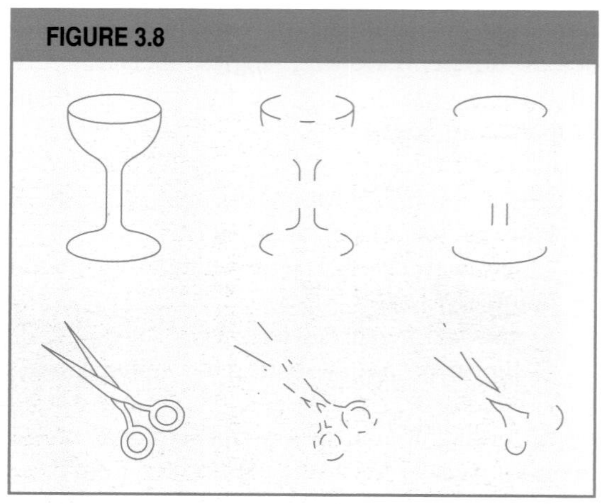

Intact figures (left-hand side), with degraded line drawings either preserving (middle column) or not preserving (far-right column) parts of the contour providing information about concavities. Adapted from Biederman (1987).

Experimental evidence

Biederman (1987) discussed one of his studies in which participants were presented with degraded line drawings of objects (see Figure 3.8). Object recognition was much harder to achieve when parts of the contour providing information about concavities were omitted than when other parts of the contour were deleted. This confirms the assumption that information about concavities is important for object recognition.

According to Biederman's theory, object recognition depends on edge information rather than on surface information (e.g., colour). To test this, participants were presented with line drawings or full-colour photographs of common objects for between 50 and 100 ms (Biederman & Ju, 1988). Performance was comparable with the two types of stimuli: mean identification times were 11 ms faster with the coloured objects, but the error rate was slightly higher. Even objects for which colour is important (e.g., yellow for bananas) showed no benefit from being presented in colour.

Joseph and Proffitt (1996) pointed out that many studies have found that colour helps object recognition, especially for objects (e.g., cherries) having a characteristic colour. They replicated this finding. They also found that colour *knowledge* can be more important than colour *perception* in object recognition. For example, their participants took a relatively long time to decide that an orange-coloured asparagus was not celery, because the stored colours for asparagus and celery are very similar.

According to Biederman's theory, the detection of geons is of crucial importance in object recognition. Evidence supporting this assumption was reported by Cooper and Biederman (1993). Participants had to decide whether two objects presented in rapid succession had the same name (e.g., hat). There were two conditions in which the two objects shared the same name but were not identical: (1) one of the geons was changed (e.g.,

FIGURE 3.9

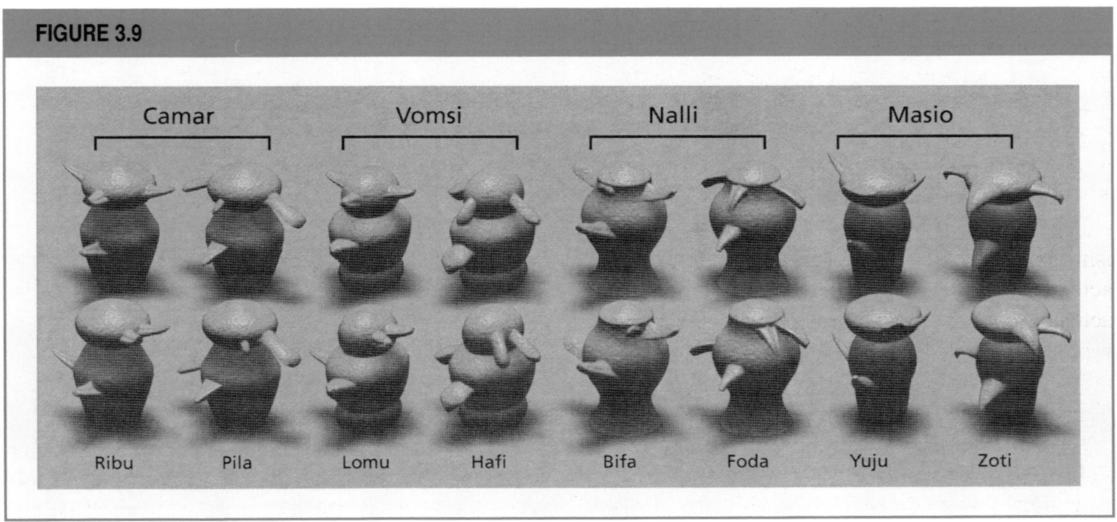

Examples of "Greebles". In the top row, four different "families" (Camar, Vomsi, Nalli, Masio) are represented. For each family, two members of different "genders" are shown (e.g., Ribu is one gender and Pila is the other). The bottom row shows a new set of Greeble figures constructed on the same logic but asymmetrical in structure. Images provided courtesy of Michael J. Tarr (Brown University, Providence, RI), see www.tarrlab.org

from a top hat to a bowler hat); (2) the second object was larger or smaller than the first. The key finding was that task performance was significantly worse when a geon changed than when it did not.

Interesting evidence suggesting that some cortical neurons in monkeys are sensitive to geons was reported by Vogels, Biederman, Bar, and Lorincz (2001). They assessed the response of individual neurons in inferior temporal cortex to changes in a geon compared to changes in the size of an object with no change in the geon. Some neurons responded more to geon changes than to changes in object size, thus providing some support for the reality of geons.

Biederman (1987, 1990) assumed that object recognition typically involves matching an object-centred representation *independent* of the observer's viewpoint with object information stored in long-term memory. Biederman and Gerhardstein (1993) argued that object naming would be primed as well by two different views of an object as by two identical views, provided the same object-centred structural description could be constructed from both views. Their findings supported the prediction even when there was an angular change of 135°. However, these findings are the exception rather than the rule. For example, Tarr and Bülthoff (1995) gave their participants extensive practice at recognising novel objects from certain specified viewpoints. The findings across several studies were very consistent (but opposed to predictions from Biederman's theory): "Response times and error rates for naming a familiar object in an unfamiliar viewpoint increased with rotation distance between the unfamiliar viewpoint and the nearest familiar viewpoint" (Tarr & Bülthoff, 1995, p. 1500). Thus, object recognition was viewpoint dependent.

We could try to reconcile the divergent findings on object recognition by assuming that developing expertise with given objects produces a shift from viewpoint-dependent to viewpoint-invariant recognition. However, there was no evidence of such a shift in a study by Gauthier and Tarr (2002). They gave participants 7 hours of practice in learning to identify Greebles (artificial objects belonging to various "families"; see Figure 3.9). Two Greebles were presented in rapid succession, and participants had to decide whether the second

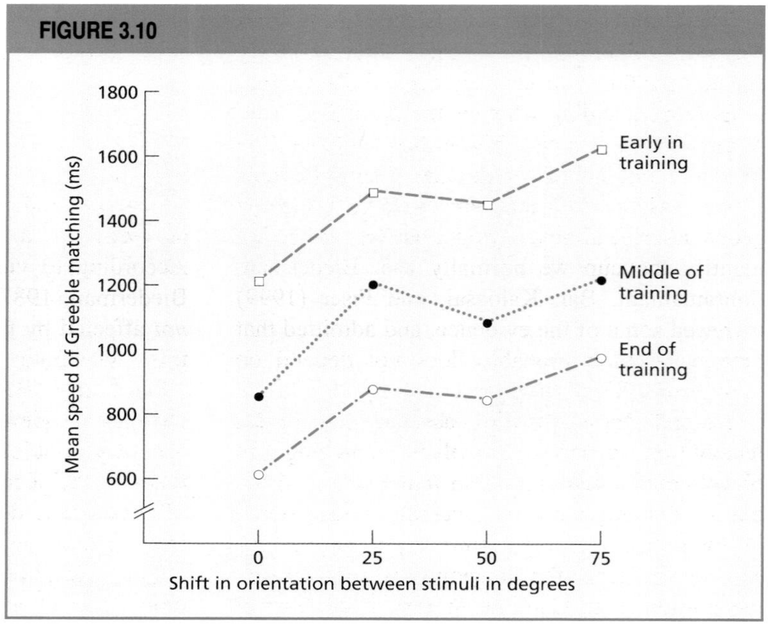

Speed of Greeble matching as a function of stage training and difference in orientation between successive Greeble stimuli. Based on data in Gauthier and Tarr (2002).

Greeble was the same as the first. The second Greeble was presented at the same orientation as the first, or at various other orientations up to 75°.

Gauthier and Tarr's (2002) findings are shown in Figure 3.10. There was a general increase in speed as expertise developed, but performance remained strongly viewpoint dependent throughout the course of the experiment. Such findings are hard to reconcile with Biederman's emphasis on viewpoint-invariant recognition.

As we have seen, Biederman's (1987) argument that edge-based extraction processes provide enough information to permit object recognition was supported by Biederman and Ju (1988), who found that object recognition was as good with line drawings as with colour photographs. However, Sanocki et al. (1998) pointed out that line drawings should contain *all* the edges present in the original stimulus to provide strong evidence for the hypothesis. In fact, line drawings are usually idealised versions of the original edge information (e.g., edges irrelevant to the object are often omitted). Sanocki et al. (1998) also pointed out that edge-extraction processes are more likely to lead to accurate object recognition when objects are presented on their own rather than in the context of other objects. The reason is that it can be hard to decide which edges belong to which objects when several objects are presented together.

Sanocki et al. (1998) obtained strong support for the view that edge information is often insufficient to allow object recognition. Their participants were presented for 1 second each with objects in the form of edge drawings or full-colour photographs, and these objects were presented in isolation or in context. Object recognition was much worse with the edge drawings than with the colour photographs, especially when objects were presented in context.

Evaluation

Theories such as those of Marr and Biederman have the advantage over earlier theories of being more realistic about the complexities of object recognition. For example, the assumption that the identification of concavities and edges is of major importance in object recognition seems justified. There is also much evidence (e.g., Cooper & Biederman, 1993; Vogels et al., 2001) that geons or geon-like components are involved in visual object recognition.

The theories of Marr and Biederman possess various limitations. First, these theories only account for fairly unsubtle perceptual discriminations (e.g., deciding whether the animal in front of us is a dog or a cat). These theories have little to say about subtle perceptual discriminations *within* classes of objects. For example, the same geons describe almost any cup, but we can readily identify the cup we normally use. Biederman, Subramaniam, Bar, Kalocsai, and Fiser (1999) reviewed some of the evidence, and admitted that face recognition probably does not depend on descriptions based on geons.

Second, these theories assume that object recognition generally involves matching an object-centred representation *independent* of the observer's viewpoint with object information stored in long-term memory. However, there is considerable evidence for viewpoint-dependent object recognition (e.g., Gauthier & Tarr, 2002; Tarr & Bülthoff, 1995), indicating that the theories are oversimplified. This issue is discussed further below.

Third, the theories de-emphasise the role played by context in object recognition. For example, Palmer (1975) presented a picture of a scene (e.g., a kitchen), followed by the very brief presentation of the picture of an object. This object was either appropriate to the context (e.g., a loaf) or inappropriate (e.g., mailbox or drum). There was also a further condition in which no contextual scene was presented. The probability of identifying the object correctly was greatest when the object was appropriate to the context, intermediate with no context, and lowest when the object was inappropriate to the context. However, context seems to affect only the later stages of object recognition. Ganis and Kutas (2003) recorded event-related potentials while participants were presented with objects in a context that was either congruous (e.g., a pot in a kitchen) or incongruous (e.g., a desk in a river). The event-related potentials for these two conditions did not differ for the first 300 ms after presentation, suggesting that contextual effects do not influence the early stages of object recognition.

Fourth, these theories are reasonably effective when applied to objects having readily identifiable constituent parts, but are much less so when applied to objects that do not (e.g., clouds).

Viewpoint-dependent and viewpoint-invariant theories

Theories of object recognition can be categorised as viewpoint invariant or viewpoint dependent. According to viewpoint-invariant theories (e.g., Biederman, 1987), ease of object recognition is *not* affected by the observer's viewpoint. In contrast, viewpoint-dependent theories (e.g., Tarr, 1995; Tarr & Bülthoff, 1995, 1998) assume that changes in viewpoint reduce the speed and/or accuracy of object recognition. According to such theories, "object representations are collections of views that depict the appearance of objects from specific viewpoints" (Tarr & Bülthoff, 1995). Object recognition is easier when the view of an object seen by an observer corresponds to one of the stored views of that object than when it does not. As we have seen, there is empirical support for the predictions of this theory (e.g., Gauthier & Tarr, 2002; Tarr & Bülthoff, 1995).

The evidence suggests that viewpoint-invariant mechanisms are used sometimes in object recognition, whereas viewpoint-dependent mechanisms are used at other times. According to Tarr and Bülthoff (1995), viewpoint-invariant mechanisms are typically used when the task involves making easy categorical discriminations (e.g., between cars and bicycles). In contrast, viewpoint-dependent mechanisms are more important when the task requires difficult within-category discriminations (e.g., between different makes of car). Indeed, Tarr and Bülthoff (1998, pp. 4–5) concluded that, "almost every behavioural study that has reported viewpoint-dependent recognition has also used tasks in which subjects must discriminate between visually-similar objects, not object classes."

Evidence consistent with the above general approach was reported by Tarr et al. (1998). They considered recognition of the same 3-D objects under various conditions across nine experiments. Performance was close to viewpoint invariant when the recognition task was easy (e.g., detailed feedback on each trial), but it was viewpoint

FIGURE 3.11

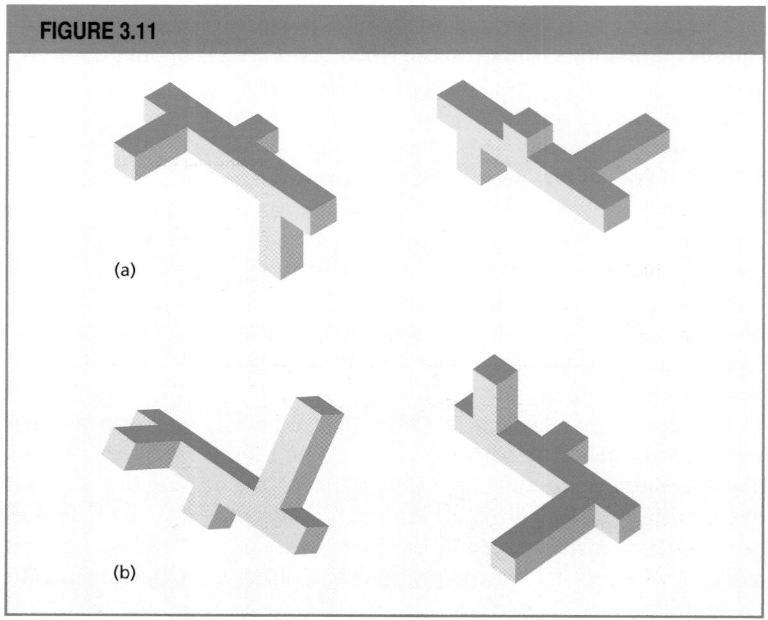

Non-matching stimuli in (a) the invariance condition and (b) the rotation condition. From Vanrie et al. (2002) with permission from Elsevier.

dependent when the task was difficult (e.g., no feedback provided).

Milner and Goodale (1995) put forward a rather different account (see Chapter 2). According to their theory, there is an important distinction between two pathways. First, there is the dorsal pathway or stream. This pathway is involved in the visual control of action, and makes use of viewpoint-dependent information to do so. Second, there is the ventral pathway or stream. This pathway is involved in conscious visual recognition, and makes use of viewpoint-invariant information.

Evidence consistent with Milner and Goodale's theory was reported by Vanrie, Béatse, Wagemans, Sunaert, and van Hecke (2002). They presented participants with pairs of three-dimensional block figures in different orientations, and asked them to decide whether they represented the same figure (i.e., matching vs. non-matching). There were two conditions differing in terms of how non-matches were produced: (1) an invariance condition, in which the side components were tilted upward or downward by 10°; (2) a rotation condition, in which one object was a mirror image of the other (see Figure 3.11). Vanrie et al. selected these conditions in the expectation that object recognition would be viewpoint invariant in the much simpler invariance condition, but would be viewpoint dependent in the more complex rotation condition.

What did Vanrie et al. (2002) find? First, performance in the invariance condition was viewpoint invariant, because performance was not influenced by altering the angular difference between the two objects (see Figure 3.12). Second, performance in the rotation condition was strongly viewpoint dependent, because performance was greatly affected by alteration in angular difference (see Figure 3.12). Third, consistent with Milner and Goodale's (1995) theory, fMRI revealed that there was more activation of parietal brain areas than occipito-temporal areas in the rotation condition, suggesting greater involvement of the dorsal stream in that task. Fourth, there was greater activation of occipito-temporal areas than parietal areas in the invariance condition, suggesting greater involvement of the ventral stream in that task.

In sum, as Vanrie et al. (2002, p. 917) pointed out, "The key question is no longer *if* object recognition is viewpoint-dependent or viewpoint-independent, but rather *when*, i.e., under which circumstances." It appears that viewpoint-dependent mechanisms are typically used when complex within-category decisions have to be made and/or

FIGURE 3.12

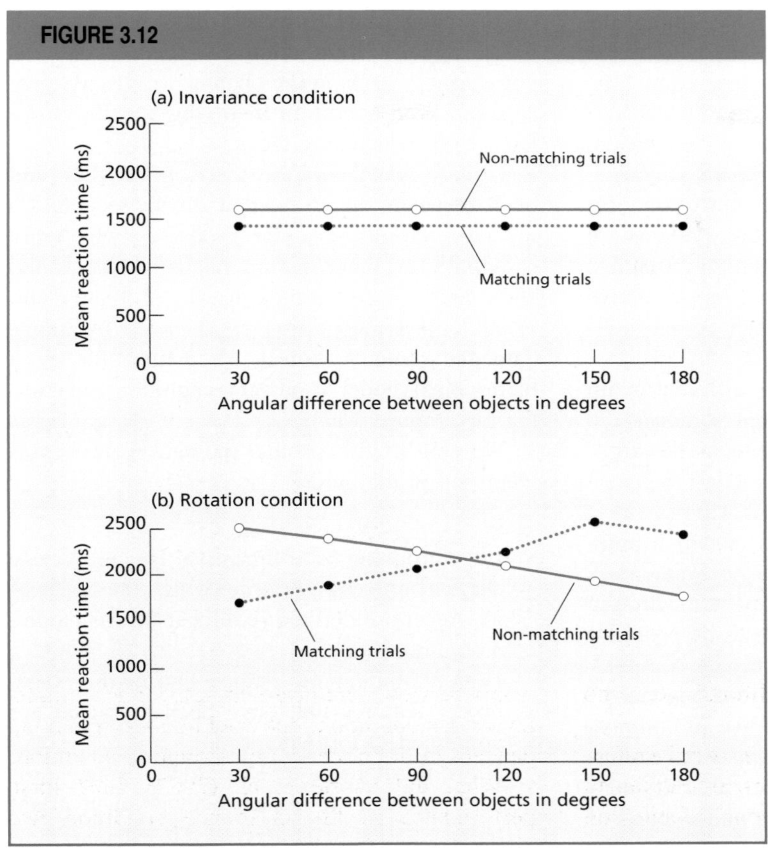

Speed of performance in (a) the invariance condition and (b) the rotation condition as a function of angular difference and trial type (matching vs. non-matching). Based on data in Vanrie et al. (2002).

the dorsal stream is involved (e.g., because visual control of action is needed). In contrast, viewpoint-invariant mechanisms are more likely to be used when easy categorical decisions need to be made and/or the ventral stream is involved because conscious visual object recognition is needed. It is probable that clarification of the precise conditions producing viewpoint-dependent or viewpoint-invariant object recognition will rapidly emerge from future research.

BRAIN SYSTEMS IN OBJECT RECOGNITION

Information from brain-damaged patients and from brain-imaging studies has enhanced our understanding of the processes involved in object recognition. In this section, we will focus on **visual agnosia**, which is "the impairment of visual object recognition in people who possess sufficiently preserved visual fields, acuity and other elementary forms of visual ability to enable object recognition, and in whom the object recognition impairment cannot be attributed to . . . loss of knowledge about objects . . . [Agnosics'] impairment is one of visual recognition rather than naming, and is therefore manifest on naming and non-verbal tasks alike" (Farah, 1999, p. 181).

Historically, a distinction was often made between two forms of visual agnosia:

(1) **Apperceptive agnosia**: Object recognition is impaired because of deficits in perceptual processing.
(2) **Associative agnosia**: Perceptual processes are essentially intact, but object recognition is impaired partly or mainly because of difficulties in accessing relevant knowledge about objects from memory.

How can we distinguish between apperceptive and associative agnosia? One way is to assess patients' ability to copy objects that cannot be recognised (Humphreys, 1999). Patients who can copy objects are said to have associative agnosia, and those who cannot have apperceptive agnosia. A test often used to assess apperceptive agnosia is the Gollin picture test. In this test, patients are presented with a series of increasingly complete drawings of an object. Those with apperceptive agnosia require more drawings than normal individuals to identify the objects.

There is some evidence that different brain areas are damaged in apperceptive agnosia and associative agnosia, which strengthens the argument that there is a valid distinction between the two disorders. Jankowiak and Albert (1994) considered findings from studies in which brain scanning was used to work out the brain areas affected. They concluded that "Lesion location in apperceptive visual agnosia tends to be posterior in the cerebral hemispheres, involving occipital, parietal, or posterior temporal regions bilaterally" (Jankowiak & Albert, 1994, p. 436). In contrast, associative agnosics typically have posterior lesions in those parts of the posterior cerebral artery supplying blood to the temporal lobe and to parts of the visual cortex. According to Jankowiak and Albert, such damage may disrupt pathways sending visual information to brain areas containing stored visual information about objects.

The distinction between apperceptive and associative agnosia has various limitations. First, while the perceptual abilities of associative agnosics are greatly superior to those of apperceptive agnosics, those of associative agnosics are typically not at normal level. For example, associative agnosics produce normal copies of objects, but "the process by which [they] produce their good copies is invariably characterised as slow, slavish, and line-by-line" (Farah, 1999, p. 191).

Second, the distinction between apperceptive and associative agnosia is oversimplified. As we will see, patients suffering from various different problems can all be categorised as having apperceptive agnosia.

Third, patients with apperceptive agnosia and associative agnosia have fairly *general* deficits in object recognition. However, many patients with visual agnosia have relatively *specific* deficits. For example, later in the chapter we discuss prosopagnosia, a condition involving specific problems with recognising faces.

Our discussion of the theories of Marr and of Biederman suggested that object recognition involves various separate processes which are essentially arranged hierarchically. Riddoch and Humphreys (2001) argued that the problems with visual object recognition experienced by brain-damaged patients can be accounted for by a hierarchical model of object recognition and naming (see Figure 3.13).

We will briefly consider the various processes identified in the model:

- Edge grouping by collinearity: This is an early stage of processing during which the edges of an object are derived (collinear means having a common line).
- Feature binding into shapes: During this stage, object features that have been extracted are combined to form shapes.
- View normalisation: During this stage, processing occurs to allow a viewpoint-invariant representation to be derived. This stage is controversial, since much evidence suggests that object recognition does not always involve viewpoint-invariant representations (see earlier in chapter).
- Structural description: During this stage, individuals gain access to stored knowledge about the structural descriptions of objects.
- Semantic system: The final stage in object recognition involves gaining access to stored knowledge of semantic information relevant to an object.

What predictions follow from this model? The most obvious one is that we might expect to find different patients with visual agnosia having problems in object recognition at each of these stages of processing. If so, that would indicate very clearly the limitations in drawing only a distinction between apperceptive and associative agnosia.

FIGURE 3.13

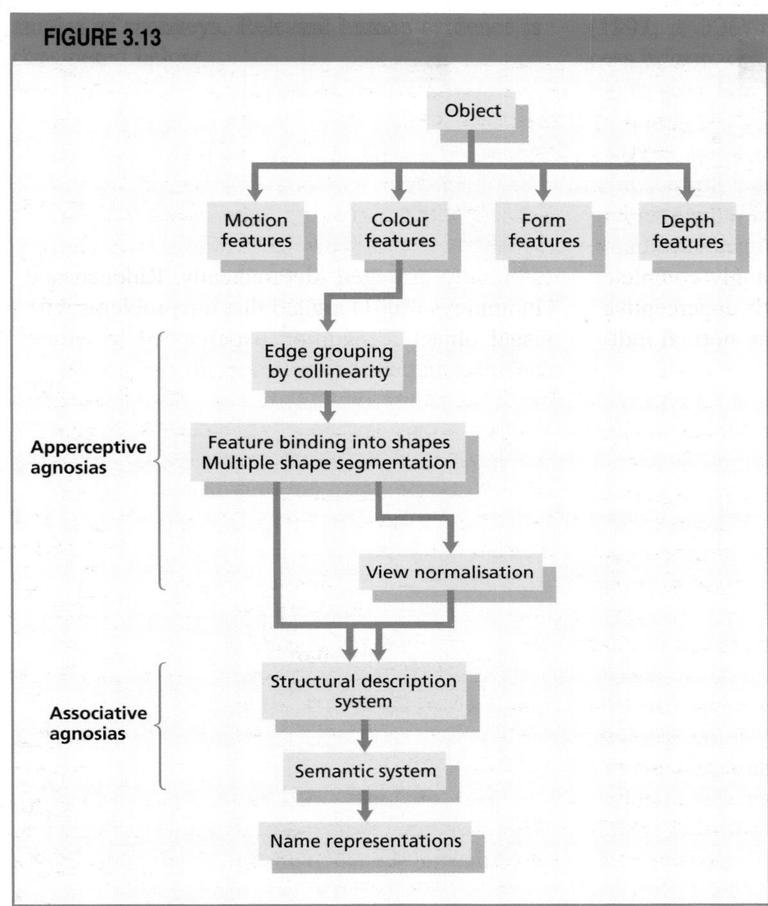

A hierarchical model of object recognition and naming, specifying different component processes which, when impaired, can produce varieties of apperceptive and associative agnosia. From Riddoch and Humphreys (2001).

Evidence

In our discussion of the evidence, we will follow Riddoch and Humphreys (2001) in considering each stage in the model separately. We will work through progressively from the first stage (edge grouping) to the last stage (semantic system).

Edge grouping

Some patients seem to have problems with edge grouping. For example, Milner et al. (1991) studied a patient, DF, who had very severely impaired object recognition. She recognised only a few real objects and could not recognise any objects shown in line drawings. DF also performed poorly when making judgements about simple patterns grouped on the basis of various properties (e.g., collinearity, proximity). Other patients have shown similar problems with edge grouping (see Riddoch & Humphreys, 2001).

In view of her severe problems with the early stages of object recognition, it is surprising that DF could use visual information to guide her actions. This pattern of impaired object recognition but reasonable perception for action is of theoretical importance, and was discussed in Chapter 2.

Feature binding

Humphreys (1999) discussed what he termed **integrative agnosia**, a condition in which the patient has great difficulty in combining or integrating features of an object in the process of recognition. Humphreys and Riddoch (1987) studied HJA, who produced accurate drawings of objects he could not recognise, and who could draw objects from memory. However, he found it very hard to *integrate* visual information. In HJA's own words: "I have come to cope with recognising many common objects, if they are standing alone. When objects are placed together, though, I have more difficulties. To recognise one sausage on its own is far from picking one out from a dish of cold foods in a salad" (Humphreys & Riddoch, 1987).

Evidence that HJA had a serious problem in grouping or organising visual information was obtained by Humphreys et al. (1992). The task of searching for an inverted T target among a set of upright Ts is easy for most people. However, HJA's performance was very slow and error prone, presumably because he found it very hard to group the distractors together.

The problems of patients whose ability to bind features is impaired can be seen most clearly when there is *competition* in assigning elements to different shapes. HJA was relatively good at doing this when only one item was present, but not when multiple shapes were present. For example, Giersch, Humphreys, Boucart, and Kovacs (2000) presented HJA with an array of three geometric shapes that were spatially separated or superimposed or occluded (see Figure 3.14). Then a second visual array was presented, which was either the original array or a distractor array in which the positions of the shapes had been rearranged. HJA performed reasonably well with separated shapes but not with superimposed or occluded shapes. Thus, HJA has poor ability for shape segregation.

Behrmann and Kimchi (2003) studied two patients (RN and SM), both of whom suffered from integrative agnosia. Both patients had severe problems with object recognition, since they failed to identify more than one-third of simple objects presented to them. However, they possessed knowledge of these objects, because they performed normally when naming objects they touched while blindfolded.

Which aspects of perceptual organisation are intact in these patients and which ones are not? They could group objects by collinearity, proximity, and similarity (see earlier in the chapter). However, they were poor at shape formation or configuring the elements of a stimulus into a coherent whole. Consider when they had to decide whether two stimuli were the same or different. Normals performed this task equally rapidly whether the stimuli contained a few or many elements (see Figure 3.15). However, the two patients were about 30–40% slower with stimuli consisting of many elements.

What conclusions follow from these findings? According to Behrmann and Kimchi (2003, p. 39):

> Perceptual organisation . . . involves a multiplicity of processes, some of which are simpler, operate earlier, and are instantiated in lower areas of visual cortex, such as grouping by collinearity. In contrast, other processes are more complex, operate later, and rely on higher order visual areas, such as grouping by closure and shape formation. It is these latter processes that are critical for object recognition.

FIGURE 3.14

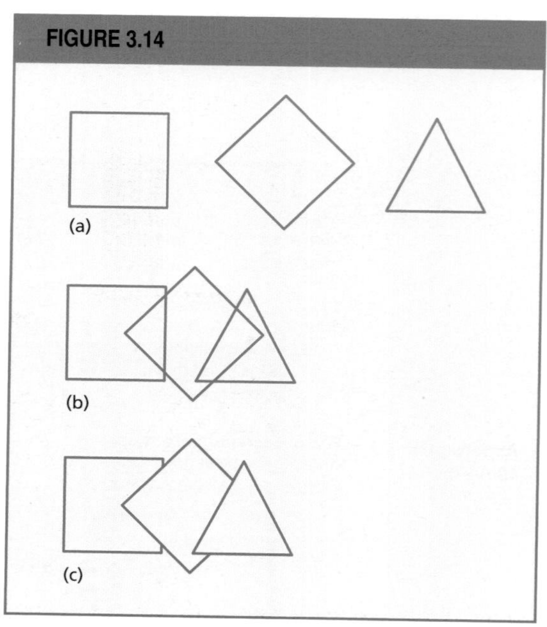

Examples of (a) separated, (b) superimposed, and (c) occluded shapes used by Giersch et al. (2000). From Riddoch and Humphreys (2001).

FIGURE 3.15

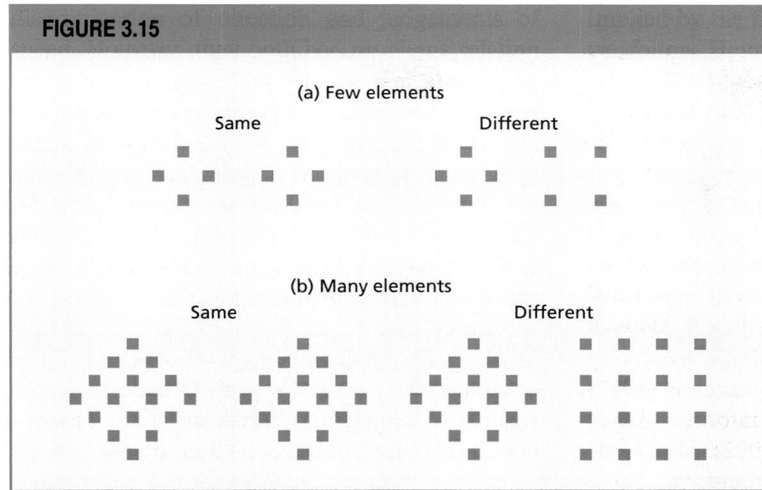

Examples of pairs of stimuli that are the same or different consisting of (a) few elements or (b) many elements. Based on information contained in Behrmann and Kimchi (2003).

View normalisation

Patients having problems with view normalisation would find it difficult to recognise that two objects are the same because of differences in the angle from which they are viewed. Warrington and Taylor (1978) found evidence for such problems. They presented pairs of photographs, one of which was a conventional or usual view and the other of which was an unusual view. For example, the usual view of a flat-iron was photographed from above, whereas the unusual view showed only the base of the iron and part of the handle. When the photographs were shown one at a time, the patients were reasonably good at identifying the objects when shown in the usual or conventional view. However, they were very poor at identifying the same objects shown from an unusual angle.

Warrington and Taylor (1978) obtained more dramatic evidence of the perceptual problems of these patients when they presented pairs of photographs together, and asked the patients to decide whether the same object was depicted in both photographs. The patients performed poorly on this task. Thus, they found it hard to identify an object shown from an unusual angle even when they had already identified it from the accompanying usual view.

Humphreys and Riddoch (1984, 1985) argued that the view of an object can be unusual in at least two ways:

(1) The object is foreshortened, thus making it hard to determine its principal axis of elongation.
(2) A distinctive feature of the object is hidden from view.

They used photographs in which some unusual views were based on obscuring a distinctive feature, whereas others were based on foreshortening. The patients either named the object in a photograph, or decided which two out of three photographs were of the same object.

In four patients having right posterior cerebral lesions, Humphreys and Riddoch (1984, 1985) found they performed poorly with the foreshortened photographs, but not with those lacking a distinctive feature. Marr and Nishihara (1978) argued that foreshortening makes it especially hard to attain a 3-D model representation, and so the findings are generally consistent with their theoretical position.

How important is view normalisation for object recognition? As you can see in Figure 3.13, it is suggested within the model that object recognition can occur *without* view normalisation. Relevant evidence was reported by Warrington and James (1988). They studied three patients with right-hemisphere damage. All three had severe problems on tasks involving *perceptual categorisation* in which they had to categorise different versions of the same object as equivalent. However, they performed surprisingly well on various tasks involving *semantic categorisation*. For example, they knew which object in a display is found in the kitchen and could match pairs of drawings having the same function and names (e.g., two types of boat).

The patients studied by Warrington and James (1988) had no significant problems in everyday life in spite of having apparently severe problems with view normalisation. Thus, view normalisation as measured by perceptual categorisation is of less importance in object recognition than might have been supposed. Rudge and Warrington (1991) proposed there is a perceptual categorisation system in the right hemisphere and a semantic categorisation system in the left hemisphere. There is a route from basic visual analysis to semantic categorisation that does not involve the perceptual categorisation system, and this may be the route used by the patients.

Structural descriptions

One way of determining whether a given patient can produce structural descriptions of objects is to give him/her an object-decision task. On this task, patients are presented with pictures or drawings of objects and non-objects, and decide which are the real objects. Some patients perform poorly on this task even though they can perform tasks designed to assess earlier stages of object recognition (e.g., matching objects presented from different viewing angles; see Riddoch & Humphreys, 2001, for a review).

There are other patients who perform well on object-decision tasks, but who nevertheless have severe problems with object recognition. For example, Riddoch and Humphreys (1987) studied a patient, JB, who performed as well as normals on an object-decision task. However, he could not tell from visual information which two of three objects (e.g., nail, hammer, spanner) would be used together. However, he could do this easily when given the names of the objects, indicating that the necessary semantic information was stored in memory. Thus, JB was impaired in his ability to use visual information to access semantic knowledge.

A similar case was reported by Fery and Morais (2003). DJ recognised only 16% of common objects when presented visually, but his performance was normal when recognising objects presented verbally. He performed well on tasks involving shape processing, integration of parts, and copying and matching objects. Of greatest relevance here, DJ was correct on 93% of trials on a difficult animal-decision task in which the non-animals were actual animals with one part added, deleted, or substituted (see Figure 3.16). As Fery and Morais (2003, p. 615) pointed out, "This case constitutes evidence that associative agnosia may arise subsequent to contacting stored structural descriptions." DJ's problem is that he finds it very difficult to use the information in structural descriptions to access semantic knowledge about objects.

Semantic system

Some patients have **category-specific deficits**, meaning they have special problems in recognising certain categories of objects. The most typical pattern is for patients to have more severe problems with recognising living things than non-living things (see Shelton & Caramazza, 2001, for a review). However, a few patients show the opposite pattern. For example, Hillis and Caramazza (1991) studied two patients. PS could name only 39% of animals and 25% of vegetables, but averaged 95% correct across several categories of non-living things. In contrast, JJ named 91% of animals correctly, but only averaged 20% correct across all other categories. Another patient showing the same pattern as JJ was EW, who was much better at naming animate than inanimate objects (Caramazza & Shelton, 1998).

Why do more patients have problems with recognising living things than non-living things? Perhaps living things are visually more similar to each other than are non-living things, and are thus harder to recognise (see Humphreys & Forde, 2001). Gaffan and Heywood (1993) asked normal individuals to name pictures of living and non-living things presented for only 20 ms each. The participants performed much worse on living than on non-living things, indicating that living things are harder to recognise.

FIGURE 3.16

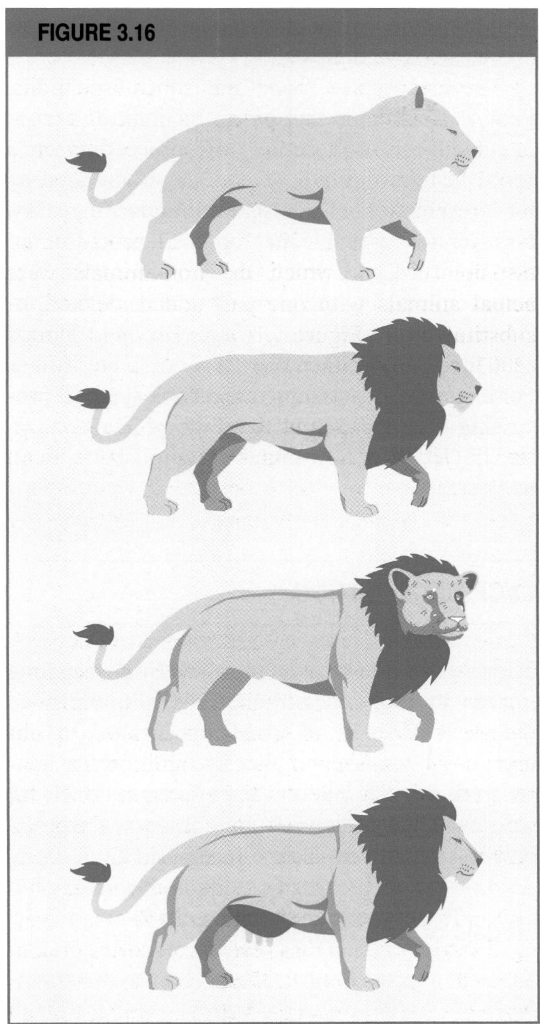

Examples of animal stimuli with (from top to bottom) a part missing, the intact animal, with a part substituted, and a part added. From Fery and Morais (2003).

How can we account for category-specific deficits? There has been much controversy and disagreement about the answer to that question (see Humphreys & Forde, 2001). One intriguing notion is that these impairments provide valuable information about the organisation of **semantic memory**, a form of long-term memory consisting of general knowledge about the world (see discussion in Chapter 7). More specifically, our knowledge of living things may be stored in one part of the brain, with our knowledge of non-living things stored in another part. According to Shelton and Caramazza (2001, p. 441), "There may be non-overlapping areas of the brain that are important for processing different categories of items. The inferior areas of the temporal lobe appear to be especially important for processing living things and the posterior area of the temporal lobe and fronto-parietal areas appear more important for processing non-living things." Alternative theoretical views are discussed at some length in Chapter 7.

Evidence

Damasio et al. (1996) gave brain-damaged participants the task of naming famous faces, animals, and tools. Different areas of the left hemisphere of the brain were associated with impaired object recognition for the three types of objects. Problems with naming famous faces were associated with damage in the left temporal pole, whereas poor naming of animals was associated with damage in the left inferotemporal region, and deficient naming of tools was associated with damage in the posterolateral inferotemporal region.

Similar findings to those of Damasio et al. (1996) were reported by Tranel, Logan, Frank, and Damasio (1997). Patients having problems of object recognition with tools had damage to the left occipito-temporal-parietal junction. In contrast, patients having problems of object recognition with animals had medial occipito-temporal lesions. This area is posterior to the area associated with naming difficulties for animals in Damasio et al.

The findings from brain-imaging studies on normals provide less support for the notion that different brain regions are involved in object recognition for living and non-living things (see Chapter 7). For example, Price and Friston (2002) found that there was considerable variability across PET studies in the brain areas activated by naturally occurring and man-made objects. Devlin et al. (2002) carried out several experiments, and found that there was widespread activation of temporal cortex for both natural and man-made items.

Evaluation

Patients with much worse object recognition for living than for non-living things typically have brain damage to different areas from patients having the opposite pattern (see Shelton & Caramazza, 2001). On the face of it, that is strong evidence for the hypothesis that semantic memory is organised in such a way that knowledge of living things is stored separately from knowledge of non-living things. However, there are real limitations with that hypothesis. First, the crucial distinction may *not* be between living and non-living things. For example, Farah and McClelland (1991) argued that living things are distinguished from each other mainly on the basis of their visual or perceptual properties, whereas non-living things are distinguished from each other primarily by their functional properties (i.e., what they are used for). Thus, semantic knowledge may be organised on the basis of visual vs. functional properties rather than living vs. non-living things (see Chapter 7).

Second, the findings from brain-imaging studies on normals provide very inconsistent support for the hypothesis. As we have seen, the same brain areas tend to be activated regardless of whether living or non-living things are being recognised.

Third, some patients have more specific impairments of object recognition than the ones discussed so far. For example, Hillis and Caramazza (1991) studied patients having impairments in visual recognition of living things. Some of them could name pictures of plants accurately but had severe problems in naming pictures of animals, whereas others had the opposite pattern.

Overall evaluation

The hierarchical model proposed by Riddoch and Humphreys (2001) is based in large measure on Marr's (1982) theoretical approach. Probably the greatest strength of the model is that it provides a useful framework within which to discuss the various problems with object recognition shown by visual agnosics. The evidence from brain-damaged patients is broadly consistent with the predictions of the model. The model may well be deficient in some details, but it certainly offers a more realistic account of visual agnosia than the simple-minded distinction between apperceptive and associative agnosia.

The hierarchical model has some limitations. First, it is assumed that object recognition occurs in an entirely bottom-up way, proceeding in a serial fashion through several stages initiated by the presentation of a visual stimulus. In reality, however, it is probable that top-down processes are also involved, with processes associated with later stages influencing the processing at earlier stages. Second, the model should probably be regarded as a framework rather than as a complete theory. For example, it is assumed that each stage of processing uses the output from the previous stage, but the details of how this is accomplished remain unclear.

FACE RECOGNITION

There are various reasons for devoting a separate section to face recognition. First, the ability to recognise faces is of great significance in our everyday lives. Second, face recognition may differ from other forms of object recognition. Third, we now know a considerable amount about the processes involved in face recognition.

Models of face recognition

Bruce and Young's model

Influential models of face recognition were put forward by Bruce and Young (1986) and Burton and Bruce (1993). There are eight components in the Bruce and Young (1986) model (see Figure 3.17):

- *Structural encoding*: this produces various representations or descriptions of faces.
- *Expression analysis*: people's emotional states can be inferred from their facial features.
- *Facial speech analysis*: speech perception can be aided by observing a speaker's lip movements.
- *Directed visual processing*: specific facial information may be processed selectively.

FIGURE 3.17

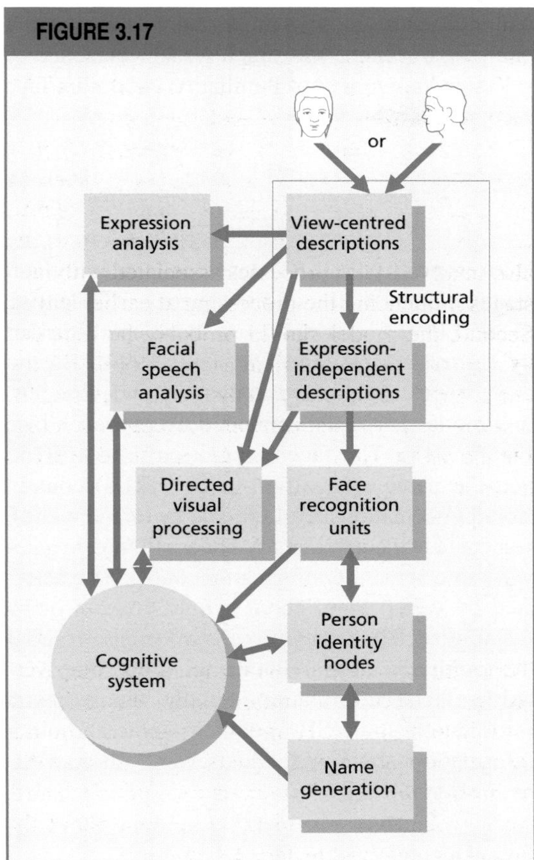

The model of face recognition put forward by Bruce and Young (1986).

- *Face recognition units*: they contain structural information about known faces.
- *Person identity nodes*: they provide information about individuals (e.g., their occupation, interests).
- *Name generation*: a person's name is stored separately.
- *Cognitive system*: this contains additional information (e.g., that actors and actresses tend to have attractive faces), and influences which other components receive attention.

The recognition of familiar faces depends mainly on structural encoding, face recognition units, person identity nodes, and name generation. In contrast, the processing of unfamiliar faces involves structural encoding, expression analysis, facial speech analysis, and directed visual processing.

Experimental evidence

Bruce and Young (1986) assumed that familiar and unfamiliar faces are processed differently, and there is much support for this assumption (see Schweinberger & Burton, 2003). For example, if we could find patients showing good recognition of familiar faces but poor recognition of unfamiliar faces, and other patients showing the opposite pattern, this double dissociation would suggest that the processes involved in the recognition of familiar and unfamiliar faces are different.

Malone et al. (1982) tested one patient with reasonable ability to recognise photographs of famous statesmen (14 out of 17 correct), but who was very impaired at matching unfamiliar faces. A second patient performed normally at matching unfamiliar faces, but had great difficulty in recognising photographs of famous people (only 5 out of 22 correct).

According to the model, the name generation component can be accessed only via the appropriate person identity node. As a result, we should never be able to put a name to a face without at the same time having available other information about that person (e.g., his/her occupation). Young, Hay, and Ellis (1985) asked participants to keep a diary record of problems they experienced in face recognition. There were 1008 incidents altogether, but participants never reported putting a name to a face while knowing nothing else about that person. In contrast, there were 190 occasions on which a participant could remember a fair amount of information about a person, but not their name.

Practically no brain-damaged patients can put names to faces without knowing anything else about the person, but several patients show the opposite pattern. For example, Flude, Ellis, and Kay (1989) studied a patient, EST, who could retrieve the occupations for 85% of very familiar people when presented with their faces, but could recall only 15% of their names.

According to the model, if the appropriate face recognition unit is activated, but the person identity node is not, a feeling of familiarity should be coupled with an inability to think of any relevant information about the person. In the incidents collected by Young et al. (1985), this was reported on 233 occasions.

Reference back to Figure 3.17 suggests further predictions. When we look at a familiar face, familiarity information from the face recognition unit should be accessed first, followed by information about that person (e.g., occupation) from the person identity node, followed by that person's name from the name generation component. Thus, familiarity decisions about a face should be made faster than decisions based on person identity nodes. As predicted, Young et al. (1986b) found that the decision as to whether a face was familiar was made faster than the decision as to whether it was the face of a politician.

According to the model, decisions based on person identity nodes should be made faster than those based on the name generation component. Young et al. (1986a) found that participants were much faster to decide whether a face belonged to a politician than they were to produce the person's name.

Evaluation

The model of Bruce and Young (1986) provides a coherent account of the various kinds of information about faces, and the ways in which these kinds of information are related. Another significant strength is that differences in the processing of familiar and unfamiliar faces are spelled out.

There are various limitations with the model. First, the account of the processing of unfamiliar faces is much less detailed than that of familiar faces. Second, the cognitive system is vaguely specified. Third, the theory predicts that some patients should show better recognition for familiar faces than unfamiliar ones, whereas others show the opposite pattern. This double dissociation was obtained by Malone et al. (1982), but has proved difficult to replicate. For example, Young et al. (1993) studied 34 brain-damaged men, and assessed their familiar face identification, unfamiliar face matching, and expression analysis. Five patients had a selective impairment of expression analysis, but there was much weaker evidence of selective impairment of familiar or unfamiliar face recognition.

Interactive activation and competition model

Burton and Bruce (1993) developed the Bruce and Young (1986) model and the theory of Valentine et al. (1991), and this was developed further by Burton, Bruce, and Hancock (1999). Burton and Bruce's interactive activation and competition model adopted a connectionist approach (see Figure 3.18). The face recognition units (FRUs) and the name recognition units (NRUs) contain stored information about specific faces and names, respectively. Person identity nodes (PINs) are gateways into semantic information, and can be activated by verbal input about people's names or by facial input. Thus, they provide information about the familiarity of individuals based on either verbal or facial information. Finally, the semantic information units (SIUs) contain name and other information about individuals (e.g., occupation, nationality).

Experimental evidence

The model has been applied to associative priming effects found with faces. For example, the time taken to decide whether a face is familiar is reduced when the face of a related person is shown immediately beforehand (e.g., Bruce & Valentine, 1986). According to the model, the first face activates SIUs, which feed back activation to the PIN of that face and related faces. This then speeds up the familiarity decision for the second face. Since PINs can be activated by both names and faces, it follows that associative priming for familiarity decisions on faces should be found when the name of a person (e.g., Prince Philip) is followed by the face of a related person (e.g., Queen Elizabeth). Precisely this has been found (e.g., Bruce & Valentine, 1986).

One difference between the interactive activation and competition model and Bruce and Young's (1986) model concerns the storage of name and autobiographical information. These

FIGURE 3.18

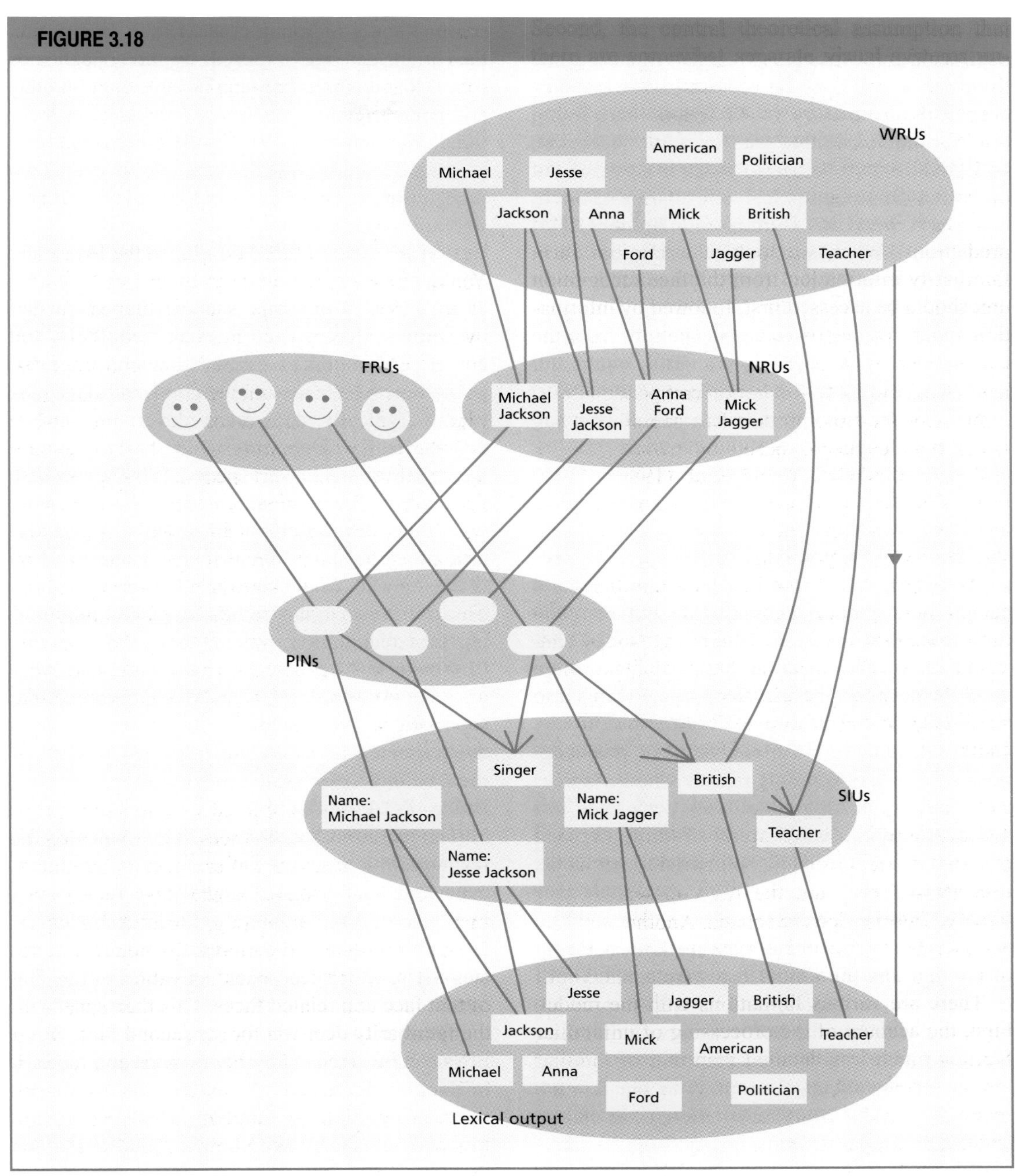

The interactive activation and competition model put forward by Burton and Bruce (1993). WRUs = word recognition units; FRUs = face recognition units; NRUs = name recognition units; PINs = person identity nodes; SIUs = semantic information units.

kinds of information are both stored in SIUs in the Burton and Bruce (1993) model, whereas name information can only be accessed *after* autobiographical information in the Bruce and Young (1986) model. The fact that the amnesic patient, ME could match names to faces in spite of not accessing autobiographical information is more consistent with the Burton and Bruce (1993) model (de Haan, Young, & Newcombe, 1991). In similar fashion, Cohen (1990) found that faces produced better recall of names than of occupations when the names were meaningful and the occupations were meaningless. This could not happen according to the Bruce and Young (1986) model, but poses no problems for the Burton and Bruce (1993) model.

Covert face recognition

We turn now to patients suffering from **prosopagnosia**, a condition in which familiar faces cannot be recognised consciously but common objects are recognised. In spite of the lack of conscious recognition of faces, prosopagnosics often show evidence of covert recognition which can be assessed in various ways. For example, Young, Hellawell, and de Haan (1988) gave prosopagnosics the task of deciding rapidly whether names were familiar or unfamiliar. They performed this task more rapidly when presented with a related priming face immediately before the target name, even though they could not recognise the face overtly. That is an example of covert recognition assessed by a behavioural measure. Covert recognition can also be assessed physiologically. For example, when people with prosopagnosia are presented with familiar and unfamiliar faces, there are larger skin conductance responses (reflecting a state of physiological arousal) to the familiar faces even when overt recognition is at chance level (e.g., Tranel & Damasio, 1988).

Schweinberger and Burton (2003) developed the previous models of Burton and Bruce (1993) and Burton et al. (1999) (see Figure 3.19). One of their key assumptions was that the same functional system is used in overt recognition (involving conscious recognition) and covert recognition as assessed by behavioural measures (as in the priming study of Young et al., 1988). In essence, the brain damage suffered by prosopagnosics means that the links between face recognition units and person identity nodes are weakened at location A (see Figure 3.19). Covert face recognition is less affected by this damage than is overt face recognition, because measures of covert recognition are more sensitive.

Evidence

Three kinds of evidence support the notion that the same system is used in overt recognition and covert recognition assessed behaviourally. First, patients who have reasonably good overt face perception typically show more covert recognition than patients with very poor overt face perception (see Schweinberger & Burton, 2003). Second, there are no cases in which patients show intact overt face recognition but impaired covert recognition as assessed by behavioural measures. This is exactly what would be expected from the theory. Third, if prosopagnosics have a weakly functioning face recognition system, they might be able to recognise faces overtly if the task were very easy. As predicted, overt face recognition can be produced in prosopagnosics when several faces are presented and they are informed that all of them belong to the same category (e.g., Morrison, Bruce, & Burton, 2003).

The picture is somewhat different when covert recognition is assessed physiologically. We might expect that no patients would have intact overt face recognition combined with impaired covert recognition assessed by skin conductance responses reflecting increased arousal. In fact, that expectation has been disproved in patients with **Capgras delusion**, who believe that very familiar people have been replaced by impostors, aliens, or doubles. Patients with Capgras delusion show overt recognition of familiar faces, but do not produce enhanced skin conductance responses to such faces (Ellis, Lewis, Moselhy, & Young, 2000; Hirstein & Ramachandran, 1997). However, they do show covert face recognition assessed by behavioural measures (Ellis et al., 2000).

What is going on here? According to Schweinberger and Burton (2003), skin conductance responses to familiar faces are produced via

FIGURE 3.19

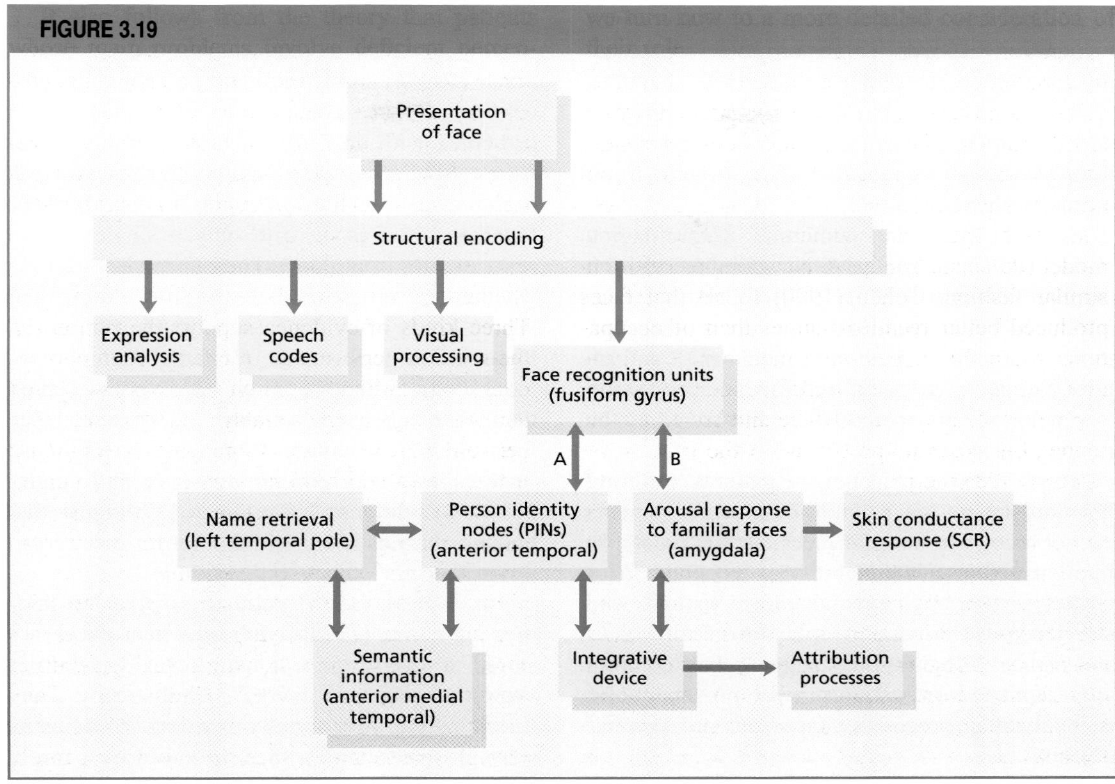

Model of face recognition proposed by Schweinberger and Burton (2003).

an arousal response in the amygdala, and patients with Capgras delusion have damage at location B (see Figure 3.19). In contrast, covert recognition assessed behaviourally and overt recognition both involve person identity nodes. This two-pathway assumption neatly fits the data.

Evaluation

Schweinberger and Burton's (2003) model provides a satisfactory account of covert face recognition in prosopagnosics. There is reasonable evidence that covert recognition assessed behaviourally involves the same functional system as overt recognition, whereas covert recognition assessed physiologically does not. These findings are as predicted by the model. In future research, it may be worth investigating the assumption that the two pathways from face recognition units are totally separate from each other.

Are faces special? Yes!

It has often been assumed there is something special about face recognition. Three main reasons have been put forward to support this assumption. First, it is argued that faces are processed differently from objects. For example, Farah (1990, 1994a) put forward a two-process model of object recognition in which two processes or forms of analysis were distinguished:

(1) Holistic analysis, in which the configuration or overall structure of an object is processed.
(2) Analysis by parts, in which processing focuses on the constituent parts of an object.

Farah (1990, 1994a) argued that holistic analysis and analysis by parts are involved in the recognition of most objects, and reading words or text mostly involves analytic processing. However, face recognition depends mainly on holistic processing. According to Farah et al. (1998, p. 484), "[Holistic processing] involves relatively little part decomposition", meaning that explicit representations of parts of the face (e.g., face, mouth) are of minor importance.

Second, there are numerous brain-imaging studies investigating whether face recognition involves different brain areas from object recognition. It has been found in many studies that there is an area of the brain (mainly the fusiform gyrus) apparently specialised for face processing (see below). This area is often referred to as the fusiform face area.

Third, there is research on patients suffering from prosopagnosia, a condition in which patients cannot recognise familiar faces but can recognise familiar objects. This inability to recognise faces occurs even though prosopagnosic patients can still recognise familiar people from their voices and names. These findings suggest that the brain area damaged in patients with prosopagnosia is involved in processing faces but not familiar objects.

Evidence

Farah (1994a) studied holistic or configural processing of faces and objects. Participants were presented with drawings of faces or houses, and were told to associate a name with each face and each house. Then they were presented with whole faces and houses or with only a single feature (e.g., mouth, front door). Their task was to decide whether a given feature belonged to the individual whose name they had been given previously. Recognition performance for facial features was much better when the whole face was presented than when only a single feature was presented (see Figure 3.20). In contrast, recognition for house features was very similar in whole and single-feature conditions. These findings suggest that holistic analysis is more important for face recognition than for object recognition

Farah et al. (1998) pointed out that the findings of Farah (1994a) indicated that faces are stored in *memory* in a holistic form, but did not show that faces are *perceived* holistically. They filled this gap in a series of studies. Participants were presented with a face, followed by a mask,

FIGURE 3.20

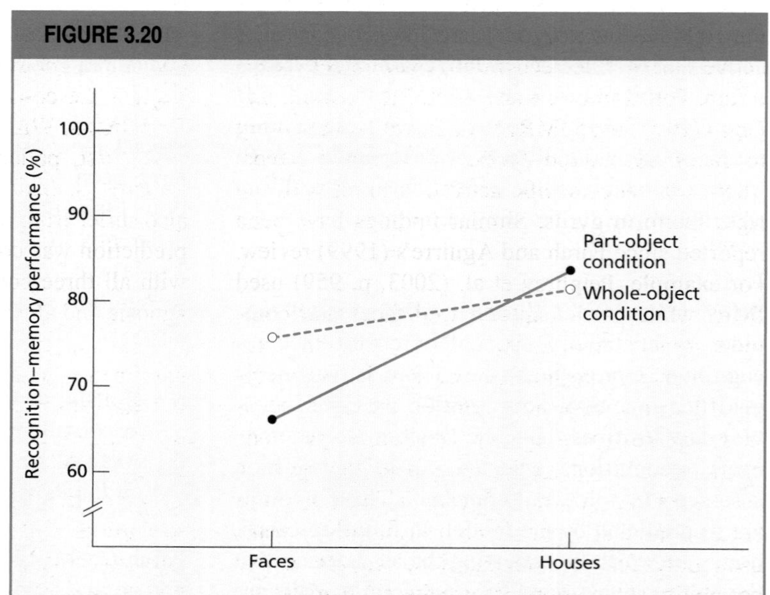

Recognition memory for features of houses and faces when presented with whole houses or faces or with only features. Data from Farah (1994a).

followed by a second face. The task was to decide whether the second face was the same as the first. The key manipulation was the nature of the mask, which consisted either of a face arranged randomly or of a whole face. The crucial prediction was as follows: "If faces are recognised as a whole and part representation plays a relatively small role in face recognition, then a mask made up of face parts should be less detrimental than a mask consisting of a whole face" (Farah et al., 1998, p. 485).

What did Farah et al. (1998) find? As predicted, face-recognition performance was better when part masks were used than when whole masks were used. This finding suggests that faces were processed holistically. In other conditions, the effects of part and whole masks on word and house recognition were assessed. The beneficial effects of part masks over whole masks were less with house stimuli than with faces, and there were no beneficial effects at all with word stimuli. Thus, there seemed to be less holistic processing of object (house) and word stimuli than of faces.

Farah and Aguirre (1999) carried out a meta-analysis of PET and fMRI studies designed to see whether separate brain regions are associated with face and object recognition. The findings were somewhat inconsistent. However, parts of the right fusiform gyrus were more likely to be active during face recognition than object recognition. For example, Kanwisher, McDermott, and Chun (1997) used fMRI to compare brain activity to faces, scrambled faces, houses, and hands. There was face-specific activation in parts of the right fusiform gyrus. Similar findings have been reported since Farah and Aguirre's (1999) review. For example, Pelphrey et al. (2003, p. 959) used fMRI while participants viewed faces and common objects, finding that "Face activated areas were localised to the fusiform and inferior temporal gyri and adjacent cortex."

As we have seen, patients with prosopagnosia cannot recognise familiar faces even though they can recognise familiar objects. This may occur because there are specific processing mechanisms used only for face recognition. An alternative possibility is that more precise discriminations are required to distinguish between two specific faces than to distinguish between familiar objects (e.g., a chair and a table). Farah (1994a) obtained evidence that prosopagnosic patients can be good at making precise discriminations for objects. LH (a patient with prosopagnosia) and control participants were presented with various faces and pairs of spectacles, and were then given a recognition-memory test. LH was at a great disadvantage to the controls on face recognition, but performed comparably on spectacle recognition.

Evidence that the fusiform face area is damaged in prosopagnosics was reported by Hadjikhani and de Gelder (2002). They found with fMRI that prosopagnosics showed similar activation of the mid-fusiform gyrus and the inferior occipital gyrus to faces and to objects. These findings suggest that damage to these areas played a role in their problems with face processing.

Earlier we mentioned Farah's (1990) theory, according to which face recognition involves primarily holistic processing, reading involves primarily analytic processing, and object recognition involves holistic and analytic processing. We can test this theory by considering brain-damaged patients falling into the following categories: prosopagnosia; visual agnosia (deficient object recognition); and **alexia** (problems with reading in spite of good ability to comprehend spoken language and good object recognition). Farah (1990) studied the co-occurrence of these conditions in 87 patients. What would we expect from her theory? First, patients with visual agnosia (having impaired holistic and analytic processing) should also suffer from prosopagnosia and/or alexia. This prediction was confirmed. There were 21 patients with all three conditions, 15 patients with visual agnosia and alexia, 14 patients with visual agnosia and prosopagnosia, but only 1 patient who may have had visual agnosia on its own. However, a few cases of visual agnosia without prosopagnosia or alexia have been reported subsequently. For example, Humphreys and Rumiati (1998) tested a 72-year-old woman with visual agnosia. Her face recognition and visual word recognition were both within normal limits, which is contrary to Farah's theory.

Second, and most importantly, there was a double dissociation between prosopagnosia and alexia. There were 35 patients who had prosopagnosia but not alexia, and there are numerous reports of patients with alexia without prosopagnosia. These findings suggest that the brain mechanisms underlying face recognition differ from those underlying word recognition.

Third, it is assumed that reading and object recognition both involve analytic processing. Thus, patients with alexia (who have problems with analytic processing) should be impaired in their object recognition. This contrasts with the conventional view that patients with "pure" alexia have impairments only to reading abilities. Behrmann, Nelson, and Sekuler (1998) studied six patients who seemed to have "pure" alexia. Five of these patients were significantly slower than normal participants to name visually complex pictures.

Fourth, patients with severe deficits in both holistic and analytic processing should also have greatly impaired object recognition. In Farah's (1990) data, there were no patients who had prosopagnosia and alexia without visual agnosia. However, this pattern was observed by Buxbaum, Glosser, and Coslett (1999). Their patient, WB, had severe prosopagnosia and alexia, but nevertheless performed reasonably well on tests of object recognition. This is inconsistent with Farah's theory.

Evaluation

Several differences have been found between face and object recognition. Such findings suggest that separate processes are involved in face and object recognition. However, as we will see shortly, most of the findings lend themselves to an alternative interpretation. Farah's (1990, 1994a) theory was an ambitious and influential attempt to identify the processes involved in face, object, and word processing. The theory has some successes to its credit but offers an oversimplified viewpoint. The existence of impairments of object recognition combined with normal face and word recognition (Humphreys & Rumiati, 1998) and of intact object recognition combined with severely impaired face and word recognition (Buxbaum et al., 1999) is particularly damaging for the theory.

Are faces special? No!

The evidence discussed above seems to provide strong evidence that there are major differences between face processing and object processing. However, the findings should not be taken at face value (no pun intended!). Gauthier and Tarr (2002) argued there are two reasons why faces appear special even though they are not. First, faces are typically recognised at the individual level (e.g., "That's our William!") far more often than is the case with members of other categories (e.g., cars, birds). Second, we have considerably more *experience* (and thus *expertise*) in recognising faces than in recognising individual members of most other categories. The key predictions following from this theoretical position are as follows: the processes and brain mechanisms allegedly specific to faces are also involved in recognising individual members of any object category for which we possess expertise.

Evidence

Is holistic or configural processing specific to faces? Contrary evidence was obtained by Gauthier and Tarr (2002) using families of artificial objects they called "Greebles" (see Figure 3.9). They gave participants several hours of expertise training in learning to identify Greebles at the individual and family levels in a study discussed earlier. There was a progressive increase in sensitivity to configural changes in Greebles as a function of developing expertise. The implication is that our holistic processing of faces reflects a general tendency for holistic processing to occur with any objects with which we have great familiarity and expertise.

Is the fusiform face area specific to face processing? Negative evidence was provided by Gauthier et al. (1999) and by Gauthier, Skudlarski, Gore, and Anderson (2000). Gauthier et al. (1999) gave participants several hours' practice in recognising Greebles. The fusiform face area was activated when participants recognised Greebles, and this was especially the case as their expertise with Greebles increased. Gauthier et al. (2000) used fMRI to assess activation of the fusiform face area during recognition tasks involving faces, familiar objects, birds, and cars. Some of the participants were experts on birds, and the others were experts on cars. Expertise influenced activation of the fusiform face area: there was more activation to cars when recognised by car experts than by bird experts, and to birds when recognised by bird experts than by car experts.

Do prosopagnosics have *specific* problems with face recognition? Gauthier, Behrmann, and Tarr (1999) reported evidence suggesting the answer is "No". They presented faces and non-face objects (e.g., synthetic snowflakes). Prosopagnosics showed inferior recognition compared to normals with objects as well as faces, and their problems were especially great compared to normals when they had to recognise objects as belonging to a specific category rather than to a more general category. Henke, Schweinberger, Grigo, Klos, and Sommer (1998) studied two prosopagnosics. One of them had difficulty in recognising exemplars in living (e.g., fruit, vegetables) and non-living (e.g., cars) categories of objects, whereas the other prosopagnosic did not. These findings suggest that at least some prosopagnosics have general problems with complex object recognition regardless of whether faces are involved.

Overall evaluation

There is general agreement that face recognition involves holistic or configural processing, that face processing is associated with activation of the fusiform face area, and that prosopagnosics have great problems in recognising faces. Several theorists (e.g., Farah, 1990; Farah et al., 1998) have interpreted these findings by assuming that face recognition depends on different processes and brain areas from object recognition. However, there is increasing evidence suggesting that that may *not* be an appropriate interpretation of the evidence. Gauthier and her colleagues have found that expertise with objects (whether acquired in the laboratory or over the years) is associated with holistic processing and with activation of the so-called fusiform face area. They have also found that prosopagnosics' problems extend beyond face recognition to the recognition of complex objects. It is probably premature to conclude that face recognition does not involve any special processes, but the evidence is certainly trending in that direction.

VISUAL IMAGERY

This section of the chapter is concerned with visual imagery. According to Kosslyn and Thompson (2003, p. 723), "Visual mental imagery occurs when a visual short-term memory (STM) representation is present but the stimulus is not actually being viewed; visual imagery is accompanied by the experience of 'seeing with the mind's eye'." Visual imagery has been studied for a long time. Over 2000 years ago, Aristotle regarded imagery as the main medium of thought. Others in ancient Greece used imagery-based mnemonic techniques to memorise speeches (see Yates, 1966). For example, there is the method of loci, in which someone giving a speech associates successive points in his/her speech with locations ("loci") along a favourite walk (see Chapter 8). When it comes to giving the talk, he/she uses the locations on the walk as cues to assist recall of the key points.

The first systematic research on visual imagery was carried out in 1883 by the British scientist, Francis (later Sir Francis) Galton. He distributed a questionnaire to eminent scientific colleagues, asking them to imagine various situations (e.g., their breakfast table that morning). He was surprised to discover some of his colleagues reported no conscious imagery at all. Most early research on imagery (including Galton's) relied on **introspection**, a technique in which individuals report their conscious experience. During the behaviourist era, introspection fell into disrepute and mental representations were "banned". As a result, research on imagery was neglected for many years. However, with the emergence of cognitive psychology, the study of imagery became respectable again. Nevertheless, there is an important difference between modern research and the pioneer studies of Galton. As we have seen, Galton's approach involved the use of introspection. In contrast, most recent research has involved behavioural measures (e.g., reaction time).

Throughout recorded history, the most popular notion about mental imagery has been that it is very similar to perception. As you will probably agree, our introspections seem consistent with this notion. However, if visual images closely resemble perceptions, why do we not confuse images and perceptions? People *are* occasionally confused, as happens in the case of hallucinations, which produce a very similar pattern of brain activity to that occurring in visual perception (ffytche et al., 1998). Thankfully, most of us rarely experience hallucinations, and anyone suffering from many of them is unlikely to remain at liberty for long! One likely reason why we rarely confuse imagery with perception is because images typically contain less detail than perceptions. In addition, we are often aware that we have constructed images deliberately, which is not the case with perceptions.

Some support for the general notion that there are close links between imagery and perception comes from studies on mental rotation (discussed below). After that, we turn to Stephen Kosslyn's important theory of visual imagery.

Mental scanning

We will consider a study by Cooper and Shepard (1973) to show what is involved in research on mental rotation. Participants were presented with letters (test figures) in either their normal form or in reversed mirror-image form (see Figure 3.21). They had to judge whether a test figure was the normal or reversed version of the standard figure. The test figures were presented in various orientations (see Figure 3.22).

The key finding was that the farther the test figure was rotated from the upright standard figure, the more time the participants took to make their decisions (see Figure 3.22). There is some generality to these findings, because they have been replicated with various other kinds of stimuli such as digits and block-like forms (see Shepard, 1978, for a review).

The impression we obtain from studies on mental rotation is that visual images have virtually all the attributes of actual objects in the world.

FIGURE 3.21

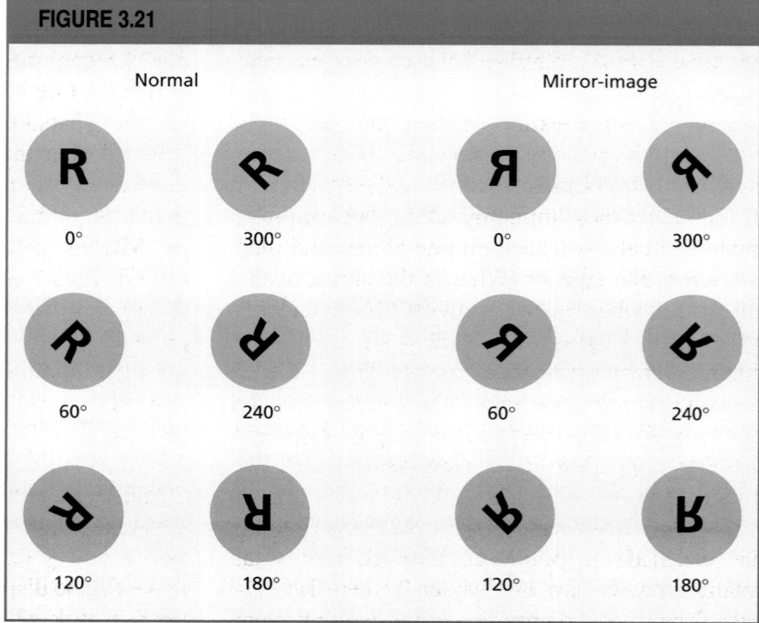

The different degrees of rotations performed on the materials in Cooper and Shepard (1973) for mirror-imaged letters (on the right) and normal letters (on the left).

FIGURE 3.22

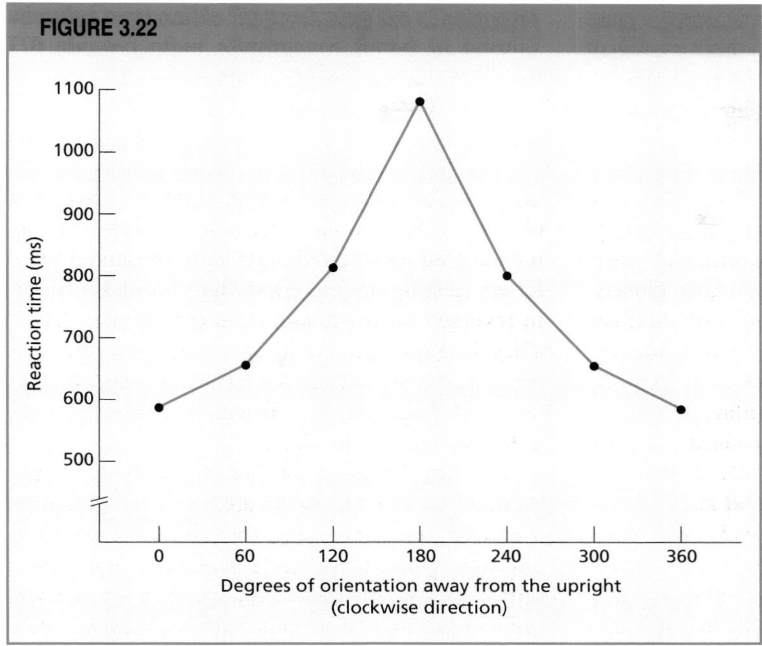

The mean time to decide whether a visual stimulus was in the normal or mirror-image version as a function of orientation. Data from Cooper and Shepard (1973).

However, this view is not wholly justified, because there are conditions in which mental rotation effects differ from physical rotation. If the imagined object is complex, participants are less able to make correct judgements about its appearance when rotated (Rock, 1973). Such a problem would not arise with the physical rotation of a physical object.

Another complication with mental rotation is that people's capacity to imagine objects (even simple cubes) depends crucially on the description of the object they implicitly adopt. For example, imagine a cube balanced on one corner and then cut across the equator. What is the shape of the cut surface when the top is cut off? Most students say that it is a square (Ian Gordon, personal communication), but the actual answer is that it is a regular hexagon. The implication is that images often consist of simplified structural descriptions that omit important aspects of the object being imagined.

More recent research involving brain imaging has clarified the processes involved in mental rotation. As we saw in Chapter 2, there is evidence from studies on perception for two somewhat separate pathways in the brain, one concerned mainly with visual object recognition (*what* is it?) and the other concerned mainly with spatial and movement perception (*where* is it?). The parietal cortex (especially the posterior area) is much more involved in visuo-spatial processing than in object recognition, whereas the inferior temporal cortex is more involved in object recognition than in visuo-spatial processing. Which brain areas are active during mental rotation? The answer from most studies is that the parietal cortex is of particular importance. For example, consider a study by Muthukumaraswamy, Johnson, and Hamm (2003). They found using event-related potentials (ERP) that posterior parietal cortex was activated early in mental rotation, followed by activation of the right anterior parietal cortex.

Evidence that posterior parietal cortex is necessary for mental rotation was reported by Harris and Miniussi (2003). Repetitive transcranial magnetic stimulation (rTMS) was delivered to that area while participants engaged in mental rotation. The key finding was that rTMS to the right parietal lobe disrupted performance on the mental rotation task when it was delivered 400–600 ms after the presentation of the mental rotation task. Finally, there is evidence from brain-damaged patients. Morton and Morris (1995) studied a patient, MG, who had damage to the left parietal lobe. She performed poorly on mental rotation, but had intact visual imagery for form, faces, and colour.

In sum, involvement of posterior parietal cortex is necessary for mental rotation, and this is an area associated with visuo-spatial perception. Thus, research on mental rotation provides suggestive evidence for links between aspects of visual imagery and aspects of visual perception. However, there are limits to mental rotation, especially when people try to imagine rotating complex objects.

Perceptual anticipation theory

Kosslyn (e.g., 1980, 1994; Kosslyn & Thompson, 2003) has put forward an extremely influential theory of mental imagery. This theory is sometimes referred to as perceptual anticipation theory, because the mechanisms used to generate images involve processes used to anticipate perceiving stimuli. The essence of Kosslyn's theory is that there are close similarities between visual imagery and visual perception, with visual images being depictive or "quasi-pictorial" representations. According to Kosslyn (1994, p. 5):

> A depictive representation is a type of picture, which specifies the locations and values of configurations of points in a space. For example, a drawing of a ball on a box would be a depictive representation . . . In a depictive representation, each part of an object is represented by a pattern of points, and the spatial relations among these patterns in the functional space correspond to the spatial relations among the parts themselves. Depictive representations convey meaning via their resemblance to an object, with parts of the representation corresponding to parts of the object.

Where in the brain are these depictive representations formed? Kosslyn argued that such representations must be formed in a topographically organised brain area, meaning that the spatial organisation of brain activity resembles that of the object being imagined. According to Kosslyn and Thompson (2003), depictive representations are created in early visual cortex, which consists of primary visual cortex (also known as Area 17 or V1) and secondary visual cortex (also known as Area 18 or V2).

Of central importance within the theory is the notion of a visual buffer, which is where the depictive representations of imagery are formed. This visual buffer is used in visual perception as well as visual imagery. In perception, processing in the visual buffer depends primarily on external stimulation, whereas visual images in the visual buffer depend on non-pictorial, propositional information stored in long-term memory. Visual long-term memories of shapes are stored in the inferior temporal lobe, whereas spatial representations are stored in posterior parietal cortex. A sketch-map of the theory is shown in Figure 3.23.

We can compare Kosslyn's perceptual anticipation theory against the propositional theory proposed by Pylyshyn (e.g., 2002, 2003). According to propositional theory, performance on mental imagery tasks does *not* depend on depictive or

FIGURE 3.23

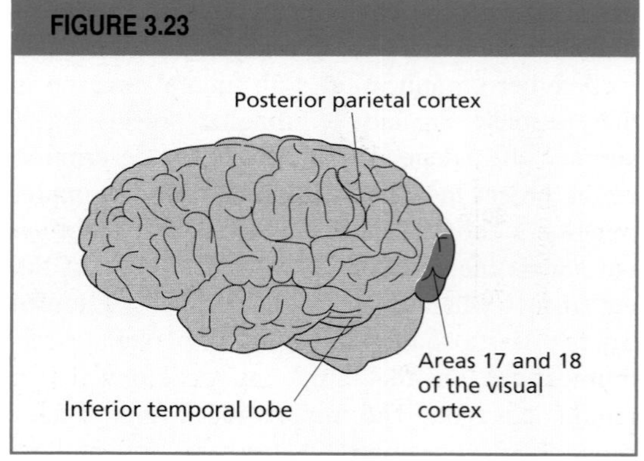

This figure shows the approximate locations of the visual buffer in Areas 17 and 18, of long-term memories of shapes in the inferior temporal lobe, and of spatial representations in posterior parietal cortex according to Kosslyn and Thompson's (2003) perceptual anticipation theory.

quasi-pictorial representations. Instead, what is involved is tacit knowledge, which is often not consciously accessible. More specifically, the type of tacit knowledge used in imagery tasks is "knowledge of *what things would look like* to subjects in situations like the ones in which they are to imagine themselves" (Pylyshyn, 2002, p. 161). This knowledge is in the form of propositions, which are abstract symbolic representations embodying meaning.

Evidence

Finke and Kosslyn (1980) assessed the fields of resolution within the visual buffer in perception and in imagery. Participants were initially presented with dots 6, 12, and 18 millimetres apart. They indicated how far into the visual periphery the dots could move until it was no longer possible to tell the dots were separate. This task was performed either while looking at the dots or while imaging them, and it was performed in the vertical and horizontal directions.

Under both perception and imagery conditions, the fields of resolution increased at less than a constant rate as the distance separating the two dots increased (see Figure 3.24). Participants with vivid imagery produced fields of resolution remarkably similar in size to the fields of resolution obtained in perception, whereas non-vivid imagers produced somewhat smaller fields of resolution in imagery than in perception. There was a general tendency in both perception and imagery for the fields to be elongated along the horizontal axis, with the upper half of the field being longer than the lower half.

Were the participants in the above study simply guessing the characteristics of the various fields of resolution in the imagery conditions? This seems very unlikely. Finke (1980) found that participants asked to guess mistakenly argued that field size would increase in direct proportion to increasing dot size and that the field of resolution would be symmetrical above and below the horizontal axis.

If visual perception and visual imagery both depend on the same visual buffer, then we would expect perception and imagery to influence each other. More specifically, there should be *facilitation* effects if the content of the perception and

FIGURE 3.24

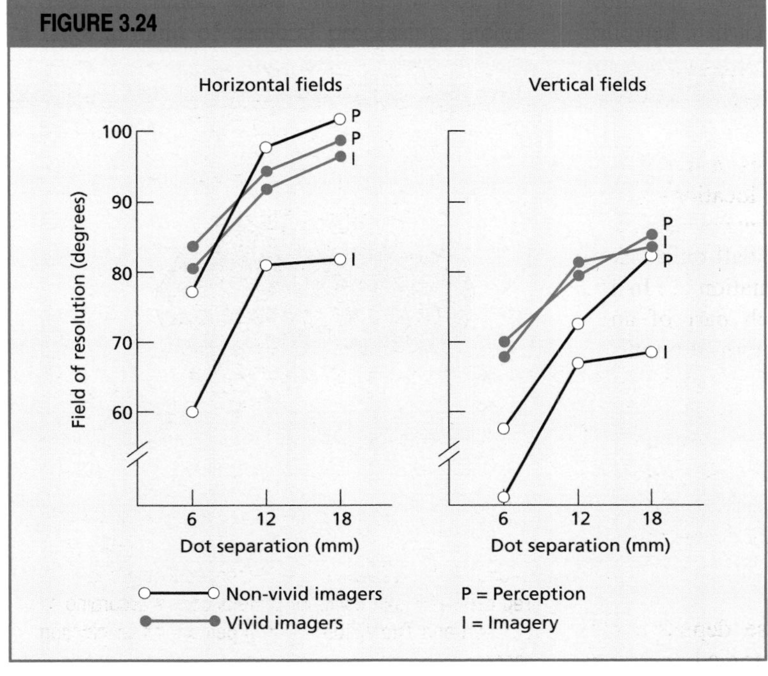

Horizontal and vertical fields of resolution in perception and imagery as a function of dot separation and vividness of imagery. Data from Finke and Kosslyn (1980).

the image is the same, but there should be *interference* effects if the content is different. Both predictions have been supported. So far as facilitation is concerned, McDermott and Roediger (1994) initially asked participants to form visual images of objects (e.g., "apple") or the object names themselves were presented. After that, participants identified degraded pictures of those objects. The key finding was that there was a facilitation effect, with participants in the imagery condition being better at identifying these pictures.

Baddeley and Andrade (2000) obtained an interference effect. Their participants rated the vividness of visual or auditory images under control conditions (no additional task) or while performing a second task. This second task either involved the visuo-spatial sketchpad (tapping a pattern on a keypad) or it involved the phonological loop (counting aloud repeatedly from 1 to 10). There are accounts of the visuo-spatial sketchpad and the phonological loop in Chapter 6.

What would be predicted in this study by Baddeley and Andrade (2000)? According to Kosslyn's theory, visual imagery and the spatial tapping task both involve use of the visual buffer, and so there would be an interference effect. This is precisely what was found (see Figure 3.25), since spatial tapping reduced the vividness of visual imagery more than the vividness of auditory imagery. The counting task reduced the vividness of auditory imagery more than it did the vividness of visual imagery, presumably because auditory perception and auditory imagery use the same mechanisms.

It will be remembered that Kosslyn has attempted to identify the brain areas underlying visual perception and visual imagery (see Figure 3.23). This can be done by carrying out brain-imaging studies on normals or by studying brain-damaged patients. Clearer evidence has been obtained from brain-imaging studies, and so we will start by considering such studies.

Do brain-imaging studies indicate that the same brain areas are activated in visual perception and imagery? According to perceptual anticipation theory, the processing underlying visual imagery occurs in early visual cortex (Areas 17 and 18), although several other brain areas are also involved. Kosslyn and Thompson (2003) considered a total of 59 brain-imaging studies in which activation of early visual cortex had been investigated. Tasks involving visual imagery were

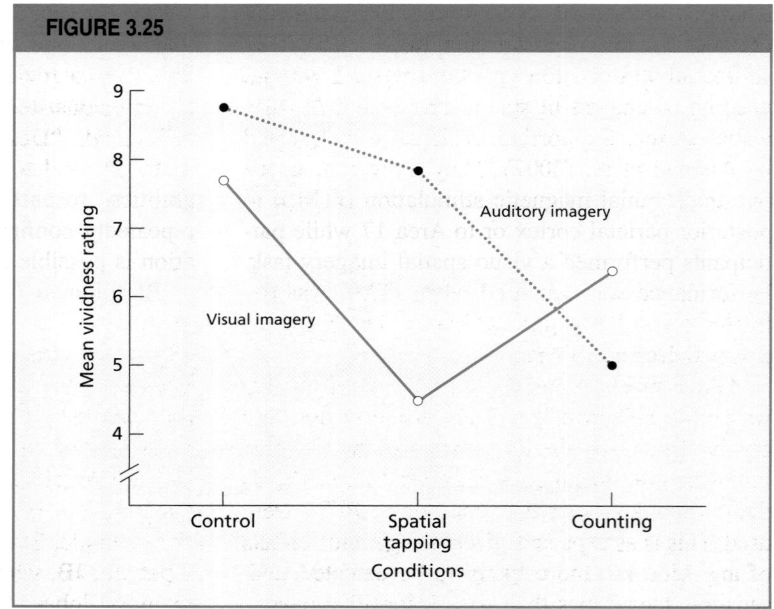

Vividness of auditory and visual imagery as a function of additional task (none in the control condition, spatial tapping, or counting). Data from Baddeley and Andrade (2000).

associated with activation of early visual cortex in about half of the studies reviewed.

There are issues of concern with the brain-imaging findings we have discussed so far. First, as we have seen, the findings are rather inconsistent and leave some doubt as to the validity of Kosslyn's theory. Second, there is the issue of whether brain activity in early visual cortex (when it is found) is necessary for the production of visual images. We consider the first issue now and will shortly discuss the second issue. Kosslyn and Thompson (2003) reviewed the literature, and identified three factors determining the probability that early visual cortex was activated. First, studies in which it was necessary for the participants to inspect high-resolution details of their images were much more likely to be associated with activity in early visual cortex than studies lacking this requirement. This makes theoretical sense if we assume that detailed visual information about objects is only implicit in long-term memory representations, and needs to be made explicit by processing in early visual cortex.

Second, early visual cortex was more often activated in studies in which the imagery task put an emphasis on shape-based processing rather than spatial processing. Why is this? According to Kosslyn and Thompson (2003), spatial representations are stored spatially in topographically organised areas of posterior parietal cortex, and so spatial information can be accessed without needing to engage in spatial processing in early visual cortex. Supporting evidence was reported by Aleman et al. (2002). They delivered repetitive transcranial magnetic stimulation (rTMS) to posterior parietal cortex or to Area 17 while participants performed a visuo-spatial imagery task. Performance was impaired when rTMS was delivered to posterior parietal cortex, but *not* when it was delivered to Area 17.

Third, and least interesting theoretically, there was more evidence that early visual cortex was involved in visual imagery when more sensitive brain-imaging techniques were used (e.g., fMRI) than when less sensitive ones (e.g., PET) were used. This is as expected, given that genuine effects of any kind are more likely to be detected with sensitive techniques than with insensitive ones.

How do we know that activation in early visual cortex plays a functional role in the processing involved in visual imagery? As Kosslyn and Thompson (2003, p. 738) pointed out, the findings discussed so far provide no guarantee that early visual cortex is *essential* for visual imagery: "Activation in early visual cortex could be analogous to the heat from a light bulb used for reading, which plays no role in accomplishing the task." Convincing evidence that early visual cortex is of functional importance in imagery was reported by Kosslyn et al. (1999; see Chapter 1). In the first study, they asked participants to memorise a stimulus containing four sets of stripes, after which they formed a visual image of it and compared the stripes (e.g., in terms of their relative width). Immediately before performing the task, some participants received repetitive transcranial magnetic stimulation (rTMS; see Chapter 1) applied to Area 17 or V1, which has the effect of producing a temporary "lesion" in that area. The key finding was rTMS significantly impaired performance on the imagery task, thus showing that Area 17 is causally involved in imagery.

We turn now to studies on brain-damaged patients. If visual perception and visual imagery involve the same mechanisms, then brain damage should often have similar effects on perception and on imagery. There are several studies in which that was found to be the case (see Bartolomeo, 2002, for a review), but the evidence overall is rather inconsistent. As Bartolomeo (2002, p. 372) concluded, "Despite the great variety of the methods used to assess perceptual and imagery abilities, recently published case studies have repeatedly confirmed that every type of dissociation is possible between these functions."

Bartolomeo (2002) discussed several studies in which brain-damaged patients had essentially intact visual perception but impaired visual imagery. What brain areas were associated with this pattern? According to Bartolomeo (2002, p. 362), "In the available cases of (relatively) isolated deficits of visual mental imagery, the left temporal lobe seems always extensively damaged." For example, Sirigu and Duhamel (2001) studied a patient, JB, who had extensive damage to both temporal lobes. JB initially had severe problems with visual perception, but these problems disappeared subsequently. However, JB continued to have a profound impairment of visual imagery.

How can we account for intact visual perception combined with impaired visual imagery? According to Kosslyn (1994), patients with that pattern have problems in generating visual images from information about objects stored in long-term memory. It is hard to evaluate this view, but there is good evidence that much object information is stored in the temporal lobes. For example, Lee et al. (2000) applied electrical cortical stimulation to epileptic patients. The patients only had conscious visual experience of complex visual forms (e.g., animals, people, landscapes) when the temporal lobe was stimulated.

The opposite pattern of intact visual imagery but impaired visual perception has also been reported (Bartolomeo, 2002). Servos and Goodale (1995) studied a patient, DF, with damage to Area 18 in early visual cortex and to Area 19. He had severely impaired visual object recognition, but his visual imagery was apparently preserved. In similar fashion, Bartolomeo et al. (1998) studied a patient, D, who had extensive brain damage to parts of early visual cortex (Area 18) and to temporal cortex. She had severe perceptual impairments for object recognition, colour identification, and face recognition, but intact visual imagery for all of these abilities. According to Bartolomeo (2002, p. 365), "Madame D. performed the imagery tasks . . . in such a rapid and easy way as to suggest that her imagery resources were relatively spared by the lesions."

How can we account for intact visual imagery combined with impaired visual perception? There is no clear answer to this question. One possibility is that such patients actually have impairments of visual imagery which would become apparent if they were given imagery tasks requiring focusing on high-resolution details. If that is the case, then that would preserve Kosslyn's theory. However, at present we simply do not know why some patients have much worse perception than imagery.

Evaluation

Considerable progress has been made in understanding the relationship between visual imagery and visual perception. The central assumption of Kosslyn's perceptual anticipation theory, namely that very similar processes are involved in imagery and perception, has attracted considerable support. The predictions that perceptual and imagery tasks will have facilitatory effects on each other if the content is the same, but will interfere with each other otherwise, have been confirmed. Of most importance, visual imagery involving attention to high-resolution details consistently involves early visual cortex, a finding that is much more in line with Kosslyn's theory than with Pylyshyn's propositional theory.

On the negative side, the evidence from brain-damaged patients is harder to evaluate. In particular, the existence of patients with intact visual imagery but severely impaired visual perception is puzzling from the perspective of Kosslyn's theory. More generally, we need to develop more of an understanding of why dissociations occur between perception and imagery. Finally, there is convincing evidence that different brain areas are involved in imagery for object shapes and imagery for movement and spatial relationships. However, these forms of imagery are presumably often used together, and we have little understanding of how that happens.

CHAPTER SUMMARY

- Perceptual organisation
  The Gestaltists put forward several laws of perceptual organisation, including the laws of proximity, similarity, good continuation, closure, and common fate. These laws assist in figure–ground segregation. The Gestaltists tried unsuccessfully to explain visual organisation in terms of electrical field forces in the brain. The Gestaltists provided descriptions rather than explanations, and

their laws of perceptual organisation are only approximately correct. The Gestaltists argued that the principles of visual organisation do not depend on learning, but the evidence suggests this is incorrect. Perceptual grouping can involve top-down processing, and a new principle of uniform connectedness seems to be important in perceptual grouping.

- Object recognition
  According to Marr, three main kinds of representation are involved in object recognition. The primal sketch makes use of information about light-intensity changes to identify the outline shapes of visual objects. This is followed by the $2\frac{1}{2}$-D sketch, which incorporates a description of the depth and orientation of visible surfaces. It is observer centred or viewpoint dependent, whereas the subsequent 3-D model representation is viewpoint invariant and provides a three-dimensional description of objects. Biederman assumed that objects consist of basic shapes known as geons. An object's geons are determined by edge extraction processes focusing on invariant properties of edges (e.g., curvature), and the resulting geonal description is viewpoint invariant. Edge information is often insufficient to permit object recognition, and surface information (e.g., colour) is often more involved in object recognition than predicted by Biederman. The theories of Marr and of Biederman were designed to account for easy categorical discriminations, and the viewpoint-invariant processes emphasised by them are less important for hard within-category discriminations. Viewpoint-dependent recognition may be particularly important when perception is being used for action.

- Brain systems in object recognition
  Visual agnosia can be subdivided into apperceptive agnosia and associative agnosia. However, this is an oversimplification. Most of the evidence can be incorporated into a hierarchical model in which object recognition proceeds through stages, including edge grouping, feature binding into shapes, view normalisation, structural descriptions, and finally contact with relevant information in the semantic system. As predicted by the model, there are patients with impairments at most levels of the hierarchy. There is controversy about the underlying problem in patients with category-specific deficits. However, damage to parts of the brain storing visual or functional properties of objects may often be involved. The hierarchical model is based on the assumption that processing stages occur in a serial, bottom-up fashion, but it is likely that there are some top-down influences during object recognition.

- Face recognition
  Several kinds of information can be extracted from faces, with important differences existing between familiar and unfamiliar faces. It is very rare for anyone to put a name to a face without knowing anything else about the person. There is good evidence for configural processing of faces. Prosopagnosic patients do not recognise familiar faces overtly, but often show evidence of covert recognition. Overt recognition and covert recognition assessed behaviourally involve the same functional system. It has often been argued that faces are special because they involve holistic or configural processing, there is a brain area (fusiform face area) specifically associated with face processing, and prosopagnosics have recognition problems only with faces. However, the evidence increasingly suggests that faces are not special, and that they only appear special because we have much expertise with them.

- Visual imagery
  Studies of mental rotation suggest there are strong links between visual imagery and perception, although the links are weaker when the imagined object is complex. The brain areas involved in mental rotation are those associated with visuo-spatial perception. According to Kosslyn's

perceptual anticipation theory, there are close similarities between visual imagery and perception, with images being depictive or "quasi-pictorial" representations. Pylyshyn has put forward a propositional theory, according to which people asked to form images make use of tacit knowledge in the form of propositions. Evidence from brain-damaged patients and from brain-imaging studies supports Kosslyn's theory. Of particular importance, early visual cortex (Areas 17 and 18) is generally active during visual imagery, provided participants have to imagine high-resolution details and the emphasis is on shape-based processing. The finding that transcranial magnetic stimulation of early visual cortex impairs visual imagery indicates that it plays a functional role in imagery. Many brain-damaged patients have comparable impairments of perception and imagery, but the existence of dissociations between perception and imagery poses problems for Kosslyn's theory.

FURTHER READING

- Bruce, V., Green, P.R., & Georgeson, M.A. (2003). *Visual perception: Physiology, psychology and ecology (4th Ed.)*. Hove, UK: Psychology Press. Issues relating to vision and action are dealt with thoroughly in Chapters 10, 11, and 12 of this renowned textbook.
- Healy, A.F., & Proctor, R.W. (2003). *Handbook of psychology: Experimental psychology, Vol. 4*. New York: Wiley & Sons. There is an informative chapter on visual perception of objects by Stephen Palmer in this edited book, and other chapters deal with key topics in visual perception.
- Kimchi, R., Behrmann, M., et al. (2003). *Perceptual organisation in vision: Behavioural and neural perspectives*. Mahwah, NJ: Lawrence Erlbaum Associates Inc. Several chapters in this edited book (including one by Kellman on visual perception of objects and boundaries) are relevant to the themes dealt with in this chapter.
- Lamberts, K., & Goldstone, R. (2004). *Handbook of cognition*. London: Sage. There is advanced coverage of many topics in visual perception, with the chapter by Hayward and Tarr being of most relevance to object recognition.
- Morgan, M. (2003). *The space between our ears: How the brain represents visual space*. London: Weidenfeld & Nicolson. Much of this well-written book is devoted to the topics discussed in this chapter.
- Purves, D., & Lotto, R.B. (2003). *Why we see what we do*. Sunderland, MA: Sinauer Associates Inc. The authors present interesting new ideas on visual perception, some of which are based on their empirical theory of vision.
- Sekuler, R., & Blake, R. (2002). *Perception (4th Ed.)*. New York: McGraw-Hill. Chapter 6 of this American textbook provides good coverage of topics relating to object recognition.

4

Perception, Motion, and Action

INTRODUCTION

Several issues considered in this chapter hark back to earlier discussions in Chapter 2. The first major theme addressed in this chapter is perception for action, or how we manage to act appropriately on the environment and the objects within it. Of some relevance here are theories (e.g., the perception–action model; the dual-process approach) distinguishing between processes and systems involved in perception-for-recognition and those involved in perception-for-action. These theories are discussed in Chapter 2. Here we will consider theories providing more detailed accounts of perception-for-action and/or of the workings of the dorsal pathway allegedly underlying perception-for-action.

The second major theme addressed in this chapter is perception of movement. Again, this issue was considered to some extent in Chapter 2, to which reference should be made. In this chapter, we have more detailed coverage, which includes specific topics such as apparent movement, perceived causality, and biological movement.

Finally, we consider the extent to which visual perception depends on attention. We will see there is convincing evidence that attention plays an important role in determining which aspects of the environment are consciously perceived. This issue is discussed at the end of the chapter because it provides a useful bridge between the areas of visual perception and of attention (the subject of the next chapter).

DIRECT PERCEPTION

James Gibson (1950, 1966, 1979) put forward a theoretical approach to visual perception regarded as so radical that it was largely ignored for many years. At the risk of oversimplifying matters, we can say that 30–50 years ago most perception theorists (e.g., Gregory, 1973; Neisser, 1967) assumed the central function of visual perception was to allow us to identify or recognise objects in the world around us. In order to do that, we engage in extensive cognitive processing, including relating information extracted from the visual environment with stored information about objects. Gibson argued that this approach was basically wrong, in part because it is of limited relevance to visual perception in the real world. In our everyday lives, perceptual information is used primarily in the organisation of action, and so perception and action are closely intertwined. As Wade and Swanston (2001, p. 4) pointed out, Gibson "incorporated the time dimension in perception, so that all perception becomes motion perception."

There are other important differences between Gibson's views and those of most other theorists. According to him, perception influences our actions without any need for complex cognitive processing to occur. This is possible because the information available from environmental stimuli is much greater than other theorists had assumed.

Gibson regarded his theoretical approach as an *ecological* one, to emphasise that the central function of perception is to facilitate interactions between the individual and his/her environment. More specifically, Gibson's theory is known as a direct theory of perception for the following reasons (Gibson, 1979, p. 147):

> When I assert that perception of the environment is direct, I mean that it is not mediated by *retinal* pictures, *neural* pictures, or *mental* pictures. *Direct perception* is the activity of getting information from the ambient array of light. I call this a process of *information pickup* that involves the exploratory of looking around, getting around, and looking at things.

It is now time to consider some of the more specific theoretical assumptions made by Gibson:

- The pattern of light reaching the eye is an **optic array**; this structured light contains all the visual information from the environment striking the eye.
- This optic array provides unambiguous or invariant information about the layout of objects in space. This information comes in many forms, including texture gradients, optic flow patterns, and affordances (all described later).
- Perception involves "picking up" the rich information provided by the optic array directly via resonance with little or no information processing involved.

Gibson was given the task in the Second World War of preparing training films describing the problems experienced by pilots taking off and landing. This led him to wonder exactly what information pilots have available to them while performing these manoeuvres. There is **optic flow** (Gibson, 1950), which consists of the changes in the pattern of light reaching an observer created when he/she moves or parts of the visual environment move. The typical perceptual experience produced by optic flow can be illustrated by considering a pilot approaching the landing strip. The point towards which the pilot is moving (the **focus of expansion** or **pole**) appears motionless, with the rest of the visual environment apparently moving away from that point (see Figure 4.1). The further away any part of the landing strip is

FIGURE 4.1

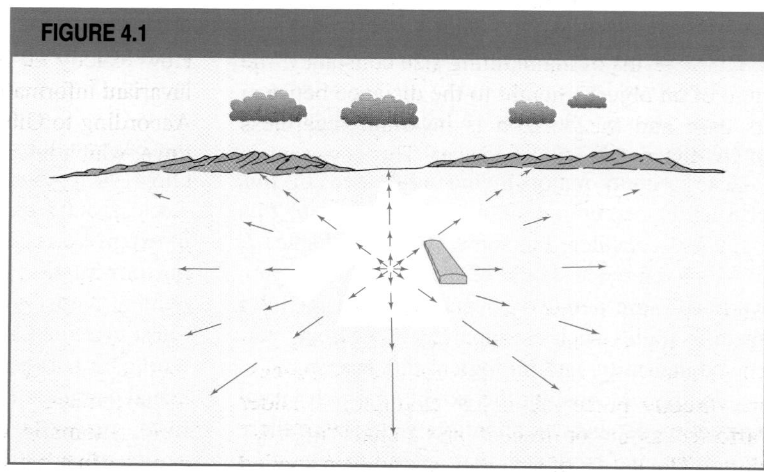

The optic flow field as a pilot comes in to land, with the focus of expansion in the middle. From Gibson (1950). Copyright © 1950 by Houghton Mifflin Company. Used with permission.

from that point, the greater is its apparent speed of movement. Over time, aspects of the environment at some distance from the pole pass out of the visual field and are replaced by new aspects emerging at the pole. A shift in the centre of the outflow indicates a change in the plane's direction.

According to Gibson (1950), optic flow provides pilots with unambiguous information about their direction, speed, and altitude. Gibson was so impressed by the wealth of sensory information available to pilots in optic flow fields that he devoted himself to an analysis of the information available in sensory data under other conditions. For example, **texture gradients** provide very useful information. As we saw in Chapter 2, objects slanting away from you have a gradient (rate of change) of texture density as you look from the near edge to the far edge. Gibson (1966, 1979) claimed that observers "pick up" this information from the optic array, and so some aspects of depth are perceived directly.

Optic flow and texture density illustrate some of the information providing observers with an unambiguous spatial layout of the environment. In more general terms, Gibson (1966, 1979) argued that certain higher-order characteristics of the visual array (**invariants**) remain unaltered when observers move around their environment. The fact that they remain the same over different viewing angles makes invariants of particular importance. The lack of apparent movement of the point towards which we are moving (the focus of expansion or pole) is one invariant feature of the optic array (discussed earlier). Another invariant is useful in terms of maintaining size constancy: the ratio of an object's height to the distance between its base and the horizon is invariant regardless of its distance from the viewer. This invariant is known as the horizon ratio relation.

Meaning: Affordances

How can the Gibsonian approach handle the problem of meaning? Gibson (1979) claimed that all potential uses of objects (their **affordances**) are directly perceivable. For example, a ladder "affords" ascent or descent, and a chair "affords" sitting. The notion of affordances was even applied (implausibly) to postboxes (Gibson, 1979, p. 139): "The postbox . . . affords letter-mailing to a letter-writing human in a community with a postal system. This fact is perceived when the postbox is identified as such." Most objects give rise to more than one affordance, with the particular affordance influencing behaviour depending on the perceiver's current psychological state. Thus, a hungry person will perceive the affordance of edibility when presented with an orange and so eat it, whereas an angry person may detect the affordance of a projectile and throw the orange at someone.

Gibson assumed that considerable perceptual learning has occurred during the history of mankind, and so does not need to occur during the individual's lifetime. However, we have to learn which affordances will satisfy particular goals, and we need to learn to attend to the appropriate aspects of the visual environment. According to Gibson's theory (Gordon, 1989, p. 161), "The most important contribution of learning to perception is to educate attention."

The notion of affordances forms part of Gibson's attempt to show that all the information needed to make sense of the visual environment is directly present in the visual input, and it illustrates the close relationship between perception and action. If he had not proposed the notion of affordances, then Gibson would have been forced to admit that the meaning of objects is stored in long-term memory.

Resonance

How exactly do human perceivers "pick up" the invariant information supplied by the visual world? According to Gibson, there is a process of **resonance**, which he explained by analogy to the workings of a radio. When a radio set is turned on, there may be only a hissing sound. However, if it is tuned properly, speech or music will be clearly audible. In Gibson's terms, the radio is now resonating with the information contained in the electromagnetic radiation.

This analogy suggests that perceivers can pick up information from the environment in a relatively automatic way if attuned to it. The radio operates in a holistic way, in the sense that damage to any part of its circuitry would prevent it from working. In a similar way, Gibson assumed that the nervous system works in a holistic way when perceiving.

Evaluation

The ecological approach to perception has proved successful in some ways. First, Gibson's views have had a major impact at the philosophical level. According to Gibson (1979, p. 8), "The words 'animal' and 'environment' make an inseparable pair. Each term implies the other. No animal could exist without an environment surrounding it. Equally, though not so obvious, an environment implies an animal (or at least an organism) to be surrounded." Gibson was right to emphasise that visual perception evolved in large part to allow us to move successfully around the environment.

Second, Gibson was correct that visual stimuli provide much more information than had previously been thought to be the case. Traditional laboratory research had generally involved static observers looking at impoverished visual displays, often with chin rests being used to prevent head movements. Not surprisingly, such research failed to reveal the richness of the information available in the everyday environment. In contrast, Gibson correctly emphasised that we spend much of our time in motion, and that the consequent moment-by-moment changes in the optic array provide much useful information (discussed more fully in the next section).

Third, Gibson was correct in arguing that inaccurate perception often depends on the use of very artificial situations and a failure to focus on the important role of visual perception in guiding behaviour. For example, many powerful illusory effects present when observers make judgements about visual stimuli disappear when observers grasp the stimuli in question (see later section on the planning–control model).

Fourth, as Norman (2002) pointed out (see Chapter 2), many of Gibson's views are currently reflected in our understanding of visual processing driven by the dorsal stream. For example, Gibson argued that our perceptual system allows us to respond rapidly and accurately to environmental stimuli without making use of memory, and it has been claimed (e.g., by Norman) that these are all features of dorsal-stream processing. Thus, Gibson's theoretical approach is of considerable historical importance and current relevance.

What are the limitations of Gibson's approach? First, the processes involved in identifying invariants in the environment, in discovering affordances, in "resonance", and so on, are much more complicated than implied by Gibson. In the words of Marr (1982, p. 30), the major shortcoming of Gibson's analysis, "results from a failure to realise two things. First, the detection of physical invariants, like image surfaces, is exactly and precisely an information-processing problem, in modern terminology. And second, he vastly under-rated the sheer difficulty of such detection."

Second, Gibson's theoretical approach virtually ignored important aspects of perception, especially those dependent on the ventral stream of processing. The distinction between "seeing" and "seeing as" is useful in addressing this issue (Bruce, Green, & Georgeson, 2003). According to Fodor and Pylyshyn (1981, p. 189), "What you see when you see a thing depends upon what the thing you see is. But what you see the thing as depends upon what you know about what you are seeing." This sounds like mumbo jumbo. However, Fodor and Pylyshyn illustrated the point by considering someone called Smith who is lost at sea. Smith sees the Pole Star, but what matters for his survival is whether he sees it as the Pole Star or as simply an ordinary star. If it is the former, then this will be useful for navigational purposes; if it is the latter, then he remains as lost as ever. Gibson's approach is relevant to "seeing", but has little to say about "seeing as".

Third, Gibson's argument that there is no need to postulate internal representations (e.g., memories; $2\frac{1}{2}$-D sketches) to understand perception is seriously flawed. For example, Creem and Proffitt (2001b) found objects can be grasped effectively without observers gaining access to stored object knowledge, but cannot be grasped *appropriately* (e.g., by the handle). More generally, it follows from the logic of Gibson's position that, "There are invariants specifying a friend's face, a performance of Hamlet, or the sinking of the Titanic, and no knowledge of the friend, of the play, or of maritime history is required to perceive these things" (Bruce et al., 2003, p. 410).

Fourth, as discussed in the next section, Gibson's views are oversimplified when applied to central issues with which he was concerned. For example, when moving towards a goal, we use many more sources of information than suggested by Gibson. As we will see, he was right to emphasise the importance of optic flow to guide our direction of movement, but other factors are also involved.

VISUALLY GUIDED MOVEMENT

From an ecological perspective, it is of central importance to focus on how we move around the environment. For example, what information do we use when walking towards a given target? If we are to avoid premature death, we have to ensure we are not hit by cars when crossing the road; we must avoid falling over the edges of cliffs; and when driving we must avoid hitting cars coming the other way. Visual perception plays a major role in facilitating human locomotion and ensuring our safety. Some of the main processes involved are discussed below.

Heading and steering: Optic flow

When we want to reach some goal (e.g., a gate at the end of a field), we need to use visual information to ensure that we move directly towards it. Gibson (1950) emphasised the importance of optic flow. When someone is moving forwards, the point towards which he/she is looking (the focus of expansion) appears motionless. In contrast, the visual field around that point seems to be expanding. Various aspects of optic flow might be of crucial importance to an observer's perception of heading, which is the point towards which he/she is moving. Gibson (1950) proposed a global radial outflow hypothesis, according to which it is the overall or global outflow pattern that specifies an observer's heading. If we happen not to be moving directly towards our goal, we can resolve the problem simply by using the focus of expansion and optic flow to bring our heading into alignment with our goal.

It will make it easier to understand the evidence if we anticipate a little the overall verdict on Gibson's approach. His views are ingenious and original, and we could in principle control our movements as we go straight from point A to point B as he suggests. However, complications occur when we start considering what happens when we cannot move directly to our goal (e.g., going around a bend in the road). There is also the issue of head and eye movements. What is typically the case is that the **retinal flow field** (changes in the pattern of light on the retina) is determined by two factors: (1) linear flow containing a focus of expansion: and (2) rotary flow produced by following a curved path and by eye and head movements, and generally more important when we are moving indirectly to our goal. Thus, in practice, it is likely to prove difficult for us to use information from retinal flow to determine our direction of heading. One possible way of doing this would be by using extra-retinal information about eye and head movements (e.g., signals from stretch receptors in the eye muscles) to remove the effects of rotary flow.

Evidence

There have been several attempts to locate the brain area centrally involved in processing optic-flow information. Most relevant studies (e.g., Bradley, Maxwell, Andersen, Banks, & Shenoy, 1996) have involved primates, and have implicated area MST (middle superior temporal area). Britten and van Wezel (1998) found they could produce biases in heading perception in monkeys by stimulating parts of MST. The implication of this finding is that areas within MST play an important role in processing direction of heading. Morrone et al. (2000) carried out an fMRI study in humans focusing on responsiveness to various kinds of pattern motion. They identified a region within MT+ (see later) responsive to expanding patterns, and expansion is a key aspect of optic flow.

Warren and Hannon (1988) produced two films consisting of patterns of moving dots, with each film simulating the optic flow that would be produced if someone were moving in a given direction. In one condition, observers generated retinal flow by making an eye movement to pursue a target in the display. In the other condition, observers fixated a point in the display and rotary flow was added to the display. The same retinal flow information was available in both conditions, but additional extra-retinal information to calculate rotary flow was only available in the first condition. The accuracy of heading judgements was unaffected by the extra-retinal information, suggesting that observers may use optic flow on its own.

Subsequent research has indicated that extra-retinal information about eye and head movements often influences heading judgements. For example, Wilkie and Wann (2003) had observers watch films simulating brisk walking or steady cycling/slow driving along a linear path while fixating a target offset from the direction of movement. Extra-retinal information consistently influenced heading judgements. Similar findings were obtained by Wilkie and Wann (2002), who found that steering on a simulated driving task was affected by extra-retinal information.

Our heading judgements are often influenced by factors over and above optic-flow information, which is unsurprising given the typical richness of the available environmental information. For example, van den Berg and Brenner (1994) pointed out that we only need one eye to use optic-flow information. However, heading judgements were more accurate when observers used two eyes rather than only one, probably because binocular disparity provided useful additional information about the relative depths of objects in the display. Beusmans (1998) set up a situation in which two sources of information (centre of expansion of optic flow and perspective changes to an object) provided conflicting information about heading. Observers' heading judgements were determined more by perspective changes than by optic flow.

Gibson assumed that optic-flow patterns generated by motion are of fundamental importance for the perception and control of our movements through the environment. However, Hahn, Andersen, and Saidpour (2003) provided evidence that motion is *not* essential for accurate perception of heading. Observers were presented with two photographs of a real-world scene in rapid succession. In one condition, the two photographs were presented only 50 ms apart and apparent motion was perceived. In another condition, they were presented 1000 ms apart and no apparent motion was perceived. The camera position moved by 7.5, 15, 22.5, or 30 cm between photographs, and the observers' task in each case was to identify the direction of heading.

Hahn et al.'s (2003) findings are shown in Figure 4.2. Judgements of heading direction were generally more accurate when the change in camera position between photographs was relatively great. However, the key finding was that performance was reasonably good even when apparent motion information was *not* available (1000 ms conditions). Indeed, the absence of apparent motion had no effect on accuracy of heading judgements when the change in camera position was 22.5 or 30 cm. As Hahn et al. (2003, p. 548) concluded, "Subjects could judge the direction of locomotion accurately from two static frames of a real-world scene, that is, without optic-flow information."

Evaluation

Optic flow patterns generally, and the focus of expansion specifically, probably contribute towards our ability to head in the right direction. However, Gibson's approach does not fully acknowledge that movement on the retina is determined by eye and head movements as well as by optic flow. More generally, observers often use various kinds of information (e.g., depth, perspective) in addition to, or instead of, optic flow. As Bruce et al. (2003, p. 343) pointed out, "The control of direction . . . cannot be regarded as a single task, based on a general-purpose visual mechanism. Instead, we are able to use a variety of control mechanisms, according to the demands of different tasks." Alternative theoretical views are discussed next.

FIGURE 4.2

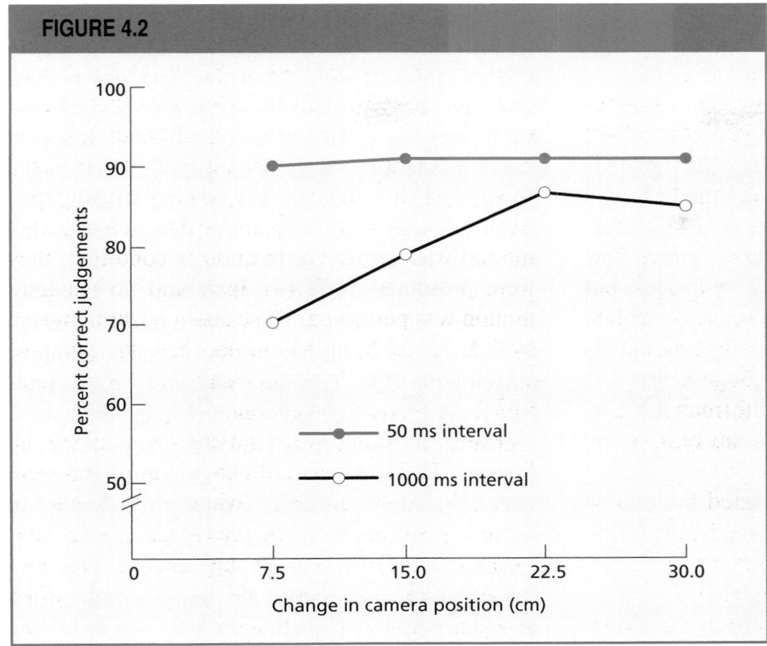

Percent correct judgements on heading direction as a function of extent of change in camera position (7.5, 15, 22.5, and 30 cm) and of time interval between photographs (50 vs. 1000 ms). Based on data in Hahn et al. (2003).

Heading and steering: Object-based approach

Cutting, Wang, Fluckiger, and Baumberger (1999) and Wang and Cutting (1999) proposed an object-based approach to the perception of heading. They contrasted their approach with the field-based approach stemming from Gibson (1950), according to which heading judgements depend on motion information contained in retinal flow. However, the differences between the two approaches are less extreme than implied by Cutting, given that the object-based approach involves use of information contained in the optic flow.

Some of the main assumptions of the object-based approach are as follows:

(1) Pedestrians' perception of heading is based on information indicating that the direction of self-motion is to the left or right of various environmental objects. Thus, in contrast to the Gibsonian approach, heading is *not* generally perceived as being towards a given point in the visual field.

(2) Pedestrians use information about the relative motions of environmental objects in the retinal flow field when perceiving heading. More specifically, there are three possibilities with respect to the relative motion of two objects as we move forwards (see Figure 4.3):

- *Convergence*: The object images move closer together with accelerating velocity; this is an invariant cue because it always means the direction of heading is outside the nearer object.
- *Accelerating divergence*: The object images move further apart with accelerating velocity; this generally (but not always) means the direction of heading is to the outside of the further object.
- *Decelerating divergence*: The object images move further apart with decelerating velocity; this is an invariant cue because it always means the direction of heading is outside the nearer object.

(3) Static depth is involved in heading perception, because it is important to establish which of any pair of objects is closer to the observer.

FIGURE 4.3

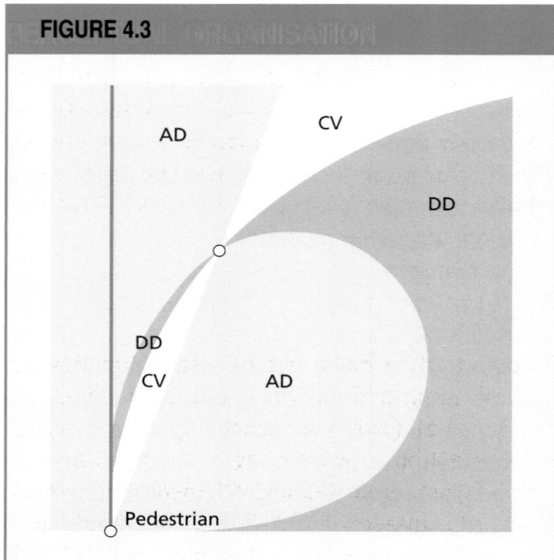

The relative motion between pairs of objects as a pedestrian moves straight up the page looking off to the right. CV = convergence, AD = accelerating divergence, and DD = decelerating divergence (see text for more details). From Wang and Cutting (1999) with permission from Blackwell Publishing.

(4) In practice, observers will generally use information from several pairs of objects to obtain a precise assessment of their direction of heading.

Evidence

There is mixed support for Cutting's object-based approach. For example, Best, Day, and Crassini (2003) found that convergence was an effective cue for heading judgements as predicted by the theory. However, decelerating divergence was significantly less effective than accelerating divergence, even though theoretically it is supposed to be more informative.

Cutting and Readinger (2002) used computer-generated simulations of an observer moving towards 10 randomly placed poles, one of which was moving. Two of their findings supported the object-based approach. First, observers' heading judgements were accurate 79% of the time. In similar previous research in which only two poles were present, accuracy was only 66%. This difference probably occurred because relative motion can be assessed for far more pairs of objects when ten objects are present rather than two. Second, consider observers' ability to detect the moving pole. Observers should have found it easier to identify the pole that had moved when its movement produced misleading information about the direction of heading than when it did not. That is precisely what was found.

According to the theory, it is essential to assess the relative depth of objects when using information about their relative motion to make heading judgements. Best, Crassini, and Day (2002) presented observers with computer-generated displays simulating self-movement through an environment containing two objects. They held retinal-image motion constant across conditions while manipulating static depth information by varying the apparent depth of one of the objects. The key finding was that perceived heading was influenced by static depth information.

Evaluation

Information about the relative motion of pairs of objects is often used when making heading judgements. There is also support for the assumption that heading judgements frequently use information about the relative depth of objects. However, the object-based approach is not radically different from that of Gibson, in that the information emphasised by Cutting is available from optic flow. Another limitation is that decelerating divergence is a much less effective cue than assumed theoretically. Finally, the theory is limited because it ignores the important cue of visual direction.

Heading and steering: Visual direction

Perhaps the simplest explanation of how we move towards a particular goal is that we use information about perceived target location. More specifically, we use the cue of **visual direction** (the angle between a target and the front–back body axis) to try to walk directly to the target. In the real world, optic flow and visual direction are typically both present, and it is hard to know which source of information is actually being used.

Evidence

Wilkie and Wann (2002) used a simulated driving task in which participants had to steer a smooth, curved path to approach a gate under various lighting conditions designed to resemble daylight, twilight, and night. This is a task in which participants rotate their gaze from the direction in which they are heading to fixate the target (i.e., the gate). Wilkie and Wann argued that three sources of information might be used to produce accurate steering: (1) visual direction (the direction of the gate with respect to the front–back body axis); (2) extra-retinal information in the form of head- and eye-movement signals to take account of gaze rotation; (3) retinal flow.

What did Wilkie and Wann (2002) find? First, all three sources of information identified above were used in steering. Second, when information about visual direction was available, it was generally the dominant source of information. Third, there was less reliance on retinal flow information and more on head- and eye-movement signals when the lighting conditions were poor.

Rushton, Harris, Lloyd, and Wann (1998) carried out a fascinating experiment designed to put optic-flow information and visual direction in conflict. Observers walked towards a target about 10 metres away while wearing prisms displacing the apparent location of the target and thus providing misleading information about visual direction. However, the prisms should have had no effect on optic-flow information. The observers tried to walk directly to the target, but the displacing prisms caused them to walk along a curved path as predicted if they were using the misleading information about visual direction available to them. The findings are at variance with the prediction from the optic-flow hypothesis that the prisms would have no effect on the direction of walking. The findings are also at variance with predictions from Cutting's object-based approach, given that useful information about the relative motion of objects was available.

It could be argued that Rushton et al.'s (1998) findings are less conclusive than they appear. For example, prisms greatly reduce the observer's visual field and thus limit access to optic-flow information. Harris and Carré (2001) replicated Rushton et al.'s findings, and did not obtain any direct evidence that limited access to optic-flow information influenced walking direction. However, observers wearing displacing prisms moved more directly to the target when required to crawl rather than walk, indicating that visual direction is not always the sole cue used.

Evaluation

Observers often make use of visual direction to guide heading and steering, and the findings of Rushton et al. (1998) are especially impressive in that connection. However, there may be problems in generalising from studies with displacing prisms to real life. In addition, as Lappe, Bremmer, and van den Berg (1999) pointed out, we can still walk towards a target even when it is temporarily hidden from view by a passing object or obstacle. Thus, other sources of information can be used successfully to guide locomotion.

Time to contact

There are numerous situations in which we want to know when we are going to reach some object. These situations include ones in which we are moving towards some object (e.g., a wall) and those in which an object (e.g., a ball, a car) is approaching us. We could calculate the *time to contact* by estimating the initial distance away of the object, estimating our speed, and then combining these two estimates into an overall estimate of the time to contact by dividing distance by speed. However, there are two possible sources of error in such calculations, and it is fairly complex to combine the two kinds of information.

Lee (1980) argued that it is unnecessary to perceive either the distance or speed of an approaching object to work out the time to contact, provided we are approaching it (or it is approaching us) with constant velocity. Time to contact can be calculated using only a *single* variable, namely, the rate of expansion of the object's retinal image: the faster the image is expanding, the less time there is to contact. Lee (1980) used this notion to propose a measure of time to contact called T or tau, which is defined as the size of the retinal image divided by its rate of expansion. According to the tau hypothesis, tau is used to estimate time to contact. This hypothesis is in agreement with Gibson's approach, because it is assumed that information about time to contact is directly available from optic flow.

We will shortly turn to a consideration of the relevant experimental evidence. Before doing so, however, we need to consider basic limitations of tau as a source of information about time to contact. Tresilian (1999) identified four factors limiting the informativeness of tau. First, it ignores accelerations in object velocity. Second, it can only provide information about time to contact with the eyes. In many situations (e.g., driving a car), this information is insufficient. For example, a driver using tau to brake to avoid an obstacle might find the front of his/her car has been smashed in! Third, it is only accurate when applied to objects that are spherically symmetrical. Fourth, it requires that the image size and expansion of the object are both detectable.

Tresilian (1999) argued for a position very different from Lee's emphasis on the direction detection of the invariant tau as the main way of assessing time to contact. According to Tresilian, time to contact is actually determined by combining information from several different cues (probably including tau). The extent to which any particular cue is used depends on the observer's task.

Evidence

Schiff and Detwiler (1979) obtained evidence that tau, rather than perceived distance or perceived velocity, is used to calculate time to contact. Adults were reasonably accurate at predicting when an object shown in a film would have hit them. Their accuracy was little affected by whether the object was filmed against a blank or a textured background, suggesting that information about the rate of expansion of the retinal image is sufficient to decide when an object will arrive.

According to Lee (1976), drivers make use of tau when braking to a stop. More specifically, we brake so as to hold constant the rate of change of tau. Kaiser and Phatak (1993) discussed relevant evidence, which indicated that the time course of deceleration is variable. Sometimes it increases progressively as predicted by Lee, but often it rises and then falls. Yilmaz and Warren (1995) obtained some support for Lee's position. Participants were asked to stop at a stop sign in a simulated driving task. There was generally a linear reduction in tau during braking, but sometimes there were large changes in tau shortly before stopping. However, the fact that participants were told not to apply the brake repeatedly or at the last moment may have distorted their behaviour.

Lee (1980) assumed that the rate of expansion of an object's retinal image crucially influences judgements of time to contact. It would thus be valuable to manipulate the rate of expansion as directly as possible. Savelsbergh, Whiting, and Bootsma (1991) achieved this by requiring participants to catch a deflating ball swinging towards them on a pendulum. The rate of expansion of the retinal image is less for a deflating than a non-deflating ball. Thus, on Lee's theory, participants should assume the deflating ball would take longer to reach them than was actually the case.

Savelsbergh et al. (1991) found the peak grasp closure was 5 milliseconds later with the deflating ball, and Savelsbergh, Pijpers, and van Santvoord (1993) obtained similar results. These findings are apparently in line with prediction. However, Wann (1996) argued persuasively this is *not* the case. Strict application of the tau hypothesis to the data of Savelsbergh et al. (1993) indicated that the peak grasp closure should have occurred about 230 milliseconds later to the deflating ball than to the non-deflating ball. In fact, the average difference was only about 30 milliseconds.

According to the tau hypothesis, people do not make use of information about the rate of acceleration of an object when estimating time to contact. In fact, this assumption is sometimes wrong. For example, Lacquaniti, Carozzo, and Borghese (1993) studied observers catching balls dropped from heights of under 1.5 metres. Their performance was better than predicted by the tau hypothesis because they took account of the ball's acceleration.

In contrast, consider the findings of Benguigui, Ripoli, and Broderick (2003). Their participants were presented with a horizontal moving stimulus which was accelerating or decelerating. The stimulus was hidden from view shortly before reaching a specified position, and they estimated its time of arrival. The prediction from the tau hypothesis (according to which observers assume stimulus velocity is constant) is that time to contact should be *overestimated* when the stimulus accelerates and *underestimated* when it decelerates. That is precisely what Benguigui et al. found.

How can we account for the different findings of Lacquaniti et al. (1993) and of Benguigui et al. (2003)? We have probably learned through experience to take account of acceleration when it is due to gravity but not otherwise. Some support for that explanation comes from an interesting study by McIntyre, Zago, Berthoz, and Lacquaniti (2001). Astronauts showed better timing when catching falling balls on earth than in zero-gravity conditions during a space flight. This difference may well have occurred because the astronauts used knowledge of earth's gravity in the former condition.

According to the tau hypothesis, the rate of expansion of an object's retinal image is estimated from changes in optic flow. However, as Schrater, Knill, and Simoncelli (2001) pointed out, rate of expansion could also be estimated from changes in the size or scale of an object's features. They devised stimuli in which there were gradual increases in the scale of object features but the optic-flow pattern was random. Their key finding was that expansion rates could be estimated fairly accurately from scale-change information in the *absence* of useful optic-flow information. Thus, the importance of optic flow to assess rate of expansion may have been exaggerated by Lee (1980).

What factors other than tau influence estimated time to contact? Peper, Bootsma, Mestre, and Bakker (1994) had participants judge whether a ball had passed within arm's reach. The judgements were usually accurate, except when the ball was larger or smaller than expected. In those circumstances, the observers systematically misjudged the distance between themselves and the ball. Thus, familiar size can influence judgements of object motion relevant to an individual observer.

Binocular information is often used when estimating time to contact. For example, Gray and Regan (1998) found that binocular information produced more accurate time-to-contact estimates when the approaching object was small, but there was no difference in accuracy between binocular and monocular conditions when the approaching object was large. Gray and Regan (2000) found that estimates of time to contact were influenced more by binocular information when a simulated object was non-spherical and rotating than when it was not spherical.

Strong evidence that binocular disparity influences estimates of time to contact was reported by Wann and Rushton (1995). They used a virtual reality set-up, which allowed them to manipulate tau and binocular disparity separately. The participants' task was to grasp a moving virtual ball with their hand. Tau and binocular disparity were both used to determine the timing of the participants' grasping movements.

Similar findings were reported by Rushton and Wann (1999). They also used a virtual reality situation involving catching balls, and manipulated tau and binocular disparity independently. When tau indicated contact with the ball 100 ms before binocular disparity, observers responded about 75 ms earlier. When tau indicated contact 100 ms after disparity, the response was delayed by about 35 ms. Thus, information about tau is combined with information about binocular disparity. According to Rushton and Wann, the source of information specifying the shortest time to contact is given the greatest weight in this combination process.

Evaluation

The tau hypothesis is appealingly simple, and is applicable to numerous situations (e.g., hitting a falling object; avoiding a stationary object; braking to a stop). Tau is often used to assist in making decisions about time to contact. In addition, observers sometimes assume that accelerating or decelerating objects are moving with constant velocity as predicted by the tau hypothesis.

There are several problems with the tau-based approach. First, time-to-contact estimates are often based on various factors other than tau. These factors include binocular disparity, size familiarity, and information about object acceleration or deceleration.

Second, the notion that tau is an invariant always providing accurate information about time to contact is erroneous. As Tresilian (1999, p. 306) pointed out, "No stimulus correlate of TTC [time to contact] yet identified is completely specific – it would be misleading to call any of them 'invariants'. They are more properly described by the traditional term 'cue'."

Third, it is an oversimplification to claim that observers always assume that moving objects have constant velocity. This may be the case in some situations, but observers take account of object acceleration caused by gravity (e.g., Lacquaniti et al., 1993; McIntyre et al., 2001).

Fourth, the assumption that an object's rate of expansion is estimated from optic flow may be only partially correct. There is evidence (e.g., Schrater et al., 2001) that scale-change information can also be used to estimate expansion rate.

In sum, it will be important in future to develop a theoretical understanding of the processes involved in combining different sources of information when estimating time to contact. It will also be important to focus on the reasons why the precise cues used to estimate time to contact vary depending on the nature of the task.

PLANNING–CONTROL MODEL

Glover (2004) was interested in explaining how visual information is used in the production of human action (e.g., reaching for a pint of beer; grasping a book). In his planning–control model, he argued we initially use a planning system followed by a control system, but with the two systems overlapping somewhat in time. This model is in part a development of Milner and Goodale's perception–action model (discussed in Chapter 2), but it makes some different predictions. Here are the key characteristics of the planning and control systems identified within the model:

(1) Planning system
- This system is used mostly *before* the initiation of movement, but is also used early during the movement.
- The functions of this system include selecting an appropriate target (e.g., pint of beer), deciding how it should be grasped, and the timing of the movement.
- This system is influenced by several factors (e.g., the individual's goals; the nature of the target object; visual context; various cognitive processes). More generally, this system uses both spatial and non-spatial (e.g., weight, fragility) information.
- This system is relatively slow because it uses a wide range of information and is susceptible to conscious influence.
- Planning depends on a visual representation located in the inferior parietal lobe, together with motor processes in the frontal lobes and basal ganglia (see Figure 4.4).

(2) Control system
- This system is used after the planning system and operates during the carrying out of a movement.
- The functions of this system are to ensure that movements are accurate and to make adjustments if required.
- This system is influenced *only* by the target object's spatial characteristics (e.g., size, shape, orientation).
- This system is relatively fast because it makes use of little information and is not susceptible to conscious influence.
- Control depends on a visual representation located in the superior parietal lobe combined with motor processes in the cerebellum (see Figure 4.4).

As you can see, Glover (2004) argued that different brain regions are involved in planning and in control. His views differ from those of most previous theorists, and we need to consider some relevant issues here. Milner and Goodale (1995) argued (in part on the basis of evidence obtained from monkey studies) that the roles of the ventral and dorsal pathways are "what" and "how", respectively. According to this

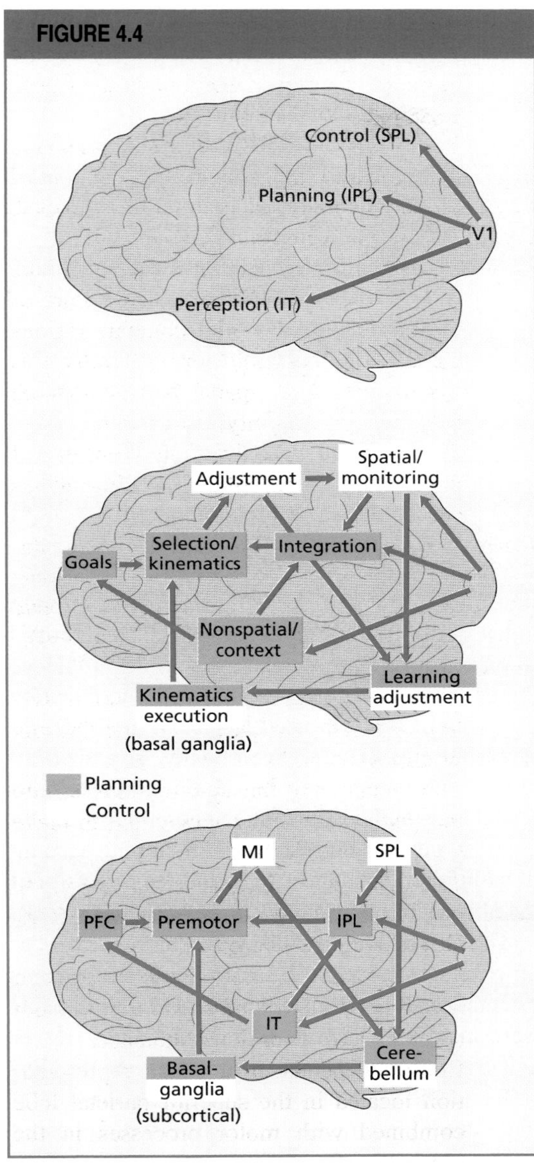

Brain areas involved in the planning and control systems within Glover's theory. IPL = inferior parietal lobe; IT = inferotemporal lobe; M1 = primary motor; PFC = prefrontal cortex; SPL = superior parietal lobe. From Glover (2004) with permission from Cambridge University Press.

position, the dorsal pathway is of crucial importance to reaching and grasping, with the underlying mechanisms being located in the superior parietal lobe.

Glover (2004) argued that there are important differences between monkey and human brain organisation and function. More specifically, Glover (2004, p. 16) claimed that "The evolution of the human brain has resulted in the localisation of planning processes in the newer cortex of the inferior parietal lobule [sub-division of a lobe]. Tool and object use in particular has required that human motor planning processes integrate ventral stream functions related to object identification and context. I hypothesise that this integration occurs in the IPL [inferior parietal lobe]." Accordingly, Glover's theory predicts that the inferior posterior lobe (and the ventral pathway) will be much more involved during motor behaviour than does Milner and Goodale's theory.

Glover's planning–control model is of relevance to an understanding of the factors determining whether perception is accurate or inaccurate. Of crucial importance, most errors and inaccuracies in perception and action stem from the planning system, whereas the control system typically ensures that human action is accurate and achieves its goal. So far as visual illusions are concerned, many of them occur because of the influence of the surrounding visual context. According to the planning–control model, information about visual context is used by the planning system but not by the control system. Accordingly, responses to visual illusions should typically be inaccurate if they depend on the planning system but should be accurate if they depend on the control system.

Evidence

One of the central assumptions of the model is that planning is subject to conscious influence whereas control is not. We certainly feel we have conscious influence over most aspects of planning (e.g., deciding how to cross the road in safety), although our feelings of control may be illusory (see Chapter 17). What evidence is there that the mechanisms underlying control are immune from conscious influence? Pisella et al. (2000) carried out a study in which the participants had to make fast movements to target objects that remained stationary or that jumped to a different location. The participants were instructed to respond to

FIGURE 4.5

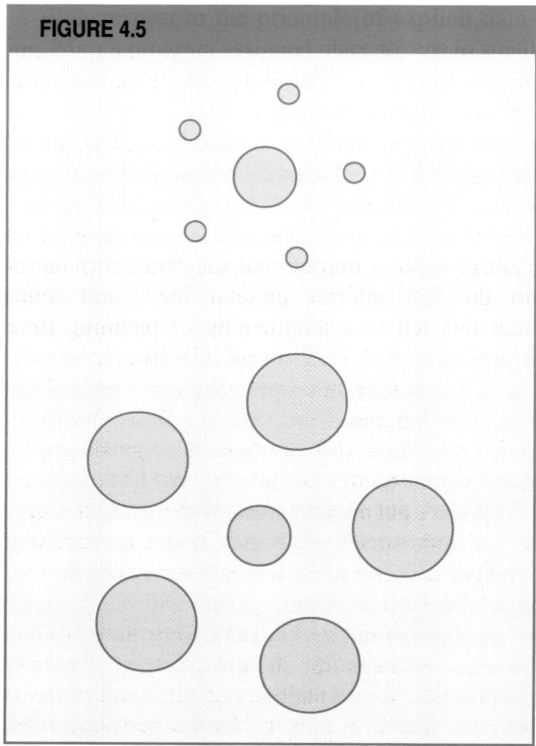

The Ebbinghaus illusion: The two central circles are the same size, but the top one looks larger.

FIGURE 4.6

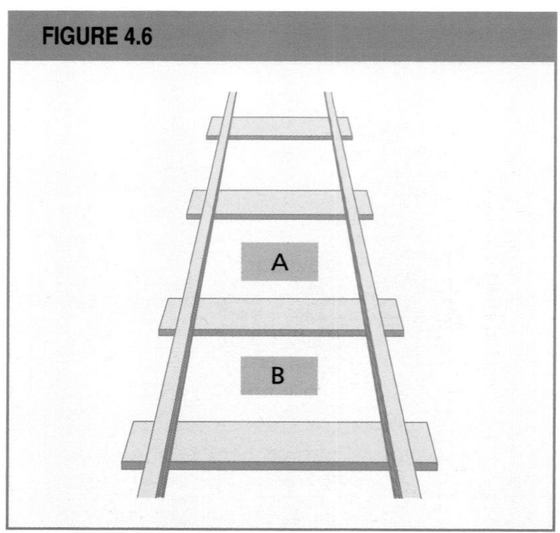

The Ponzo illusion.

target jumping *either* by correcting their movement *or* by stopping their movement. When the participants' movement times were under 250 ms, participants often corrected their movement towards an object that had moved even when they had been told to stop their movement. This key finding suggests that fast control mechanisms are generally not influenced by conscious control.

There is much support for the planning–control model from studies of visual illusions. Glover and Dixon (2002a) found the Ebbinghaus illusion (see Figure 4.5) as assessed by grip aperture (trying to adjust one's grip so that it is appropriate for grasping the target) decreased as the hand approached the target. According to the model, this happened because the initial planning process is influenced by the illusion but the subsequent control process is not.

Jackson and Shaw (2000) used the Ponzo illusion (see Figure 4.6), and asked participants to grasp an object and lift it into the air. The illusion had no effect on the grip aperture between index finger and thumb as the participants moved to pick it up. However, the illusion did influence the perceived weight of the object as assessed by the force of the grip used to pick it up. What do these findings mean? Theoretically, grip aperture close to the object is based on perception of object size, and depends on the control system. In contrast, perceived weight involves taking account of additional kinds of information (e.g., density of the object), and thus involves the planning system.

Glover and Dixon (2001) presented a small bar on a background grating which caused the bar's orientation to be misperceived. The participants were instructed to pick up the bar. What Glover and Dixon found was that the effects of the illusion on hand orientation were relatively large early in the reaching movement, but almost disappeared as the hand approached the bar (see Figure 4.7). This is predicted by the model: initially the movement is influenced by the error-prone planning system, but it is influenced by the more accurate control system as the movement continues.

Glover and Dixon (2002b) used a task in which participants reached for an object that had either the word "LARGE" or the word "SMALL" written on it. According to the planning–control model, the cognitive processes involved in understanding word meaning are associated with the planning system rather than the control system. Early in

FIGURE 4.7

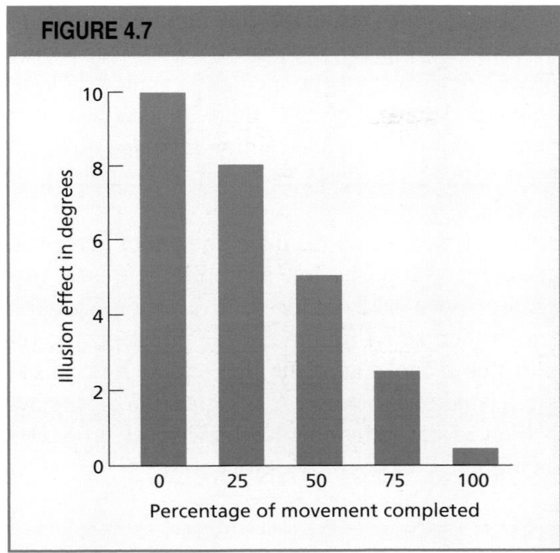

Magnitude of the orientation illusion as a function of time into the movement. Based on data in Glover and Dixon (2001).

the reach (when movement was directed by the planning system), the participants showed an illusion effect in that their grip aperture was greater for objects with the word "LARGE" on them. Later in the reach (when movement was directed by the control system), the illusion effect decreased.

We turn now to evidence concerning the brain regions involved in planning and in control. The findings from several brain-imaging studies (mostly using PET) provide reasonable support for the prediction that planning involves the inferior parietal lobe whereas control involves the superior parietal lobe. For example, Krams et al. (1998) used a task in which participants had to copy a hand posture shown on a screen. There were three conditions varying in the involvement of planning and control: (1) control only: participants copied the movement immediately; (2) planning and control: participants had to pause before copying the movement; and (3) planning only: participants prepared the movement but did not carry it out.

What did Krams et al. (1998) find? When they compared conditions, they discovered there was increased activity in the inferior parietal lobe, the premotor cortex, and the basal ganglia in the condition with more emphasis on planning (e.g., planning and control vs. control only). In contrast, there was some evidence of increased activity in the superior parietal lobe and cerebellum in conditions emphasising control (planning and control vs. planning only).

Relevant evidence has also come from studies using transcranial magnetic stimulation (see Chapter 1), which produces "temporary lesions" in a given brain area. Rushworth, Ellison, and Walsh (2001) applied transcranial magnetic stimulation to the left inferior parietal lobe, and found that this led to a lengthening of planning time. Desmurget et al. (1999) applied transcranial magnetic stimulation to an area bordering the inferior parietal lobe and the superior parietal lobe. There were no effects of this stimulation on the accuracy of movements to stationary targets, but there was significant disruption when movements needed to be corrected because the target moved. This finding suggests there was interference with control but not with planning.

Additional relevant information about the areas involved in planning and control has come from studies on brain-damaged patients. Patients with damage to the inferior parietal lobe should have problems mainly with the planning of actions. Damage to the left inferior parietal lobe often produces **ideomotor apraxia**, in which patients find it hard to carry out learned movements. Clark et al. (1994) studied three patients with ideomotor apraxia. They showed some impairment when asked to carry out the action of slicing bread even when both bread and knife were present. However, such patients are often reasonably proficient at simple pointing and grasping movements. This pattern of performance is consistent with the view that they have impaired planning (as shown by their inability to slice bread properly) combined with a reasonably intact control system (as shown by adequate pointing and grasping).

Patients with damage to the superior parietal lobe should have problems mainly with the control of action. Damage to the superior parietal lobe often produces optic ataxia, in which there are severe impairments in the ability to make accurate movements in spite of intact visual perception (see Chapter 2). Some optic ataxics have relatively intact velocity and grip aperture early in the making of a reaching and grasping movement but not thereafter (e.g., Binkofski et al.,

1998; Jakobson, Archibald, Carey, & Goodale, 1991), a pattern suggesting greater problems with control than with planning.

Grea et al. (2002) studied a patient with optic ataxia, IG. She performed as well as healthy controls when reaching out and grasping a stationary object. However, IG had much poorer performance when the target suddenly jumped to a new location. These findings suggest damage to the planning system rather than to the control system.

Evaluation

The notion that separate planning and control systems are involved in reaching for and grasping objects is supported by many experimental findings. As predicted by the theory, the errors involved in starting to reach for objects seem to be due primarily to the planning system rather than to the control system. In addition, findings from brain-imaging studies, from studies using transcranial stimulation, and from brain-damaged patients indicate that somewhat separate brain regions are involved in planning and in control. More specifically, planning processes involve mainly the inferior parietal lobe, whereas control processes focus around the superior parietal lobe and the cerebellum.

The planning–control model has various limitations. First, in spite of convincing evidence for separate planning and control systems, it is probable that the two systems interact in very complex ways in performing many kinds of action. Second, the precise number and nature of the processing activities carried out within the planning system are unclear. Third, the model considers body movements but not eye movements, in spite of the fact that coordination of eye and body movements is important.

MOTION PERCEPTION

The focus in this section is on the perception of object motion. Three issues are discussed. First, there is an analysis of basic processes involved in motion detection.

Second, the issue of how we are able to perceive biological movement even when only provided with impoverished information is considered. As we will see, there is evidence that perception of biological motion involves different brain areas from those involved in perception of motion in general.

Third, we discuss the phenomenon of perceived causality. Suppose, for example, you see one square move and collide with a second square, which then starts to move away. Most people report that it looks as if the first square has caused the second one to move. A key question is whether perceived causality involves low-level processes or higher-level cognitive processes.

Motion detection

There is general agreement that certain areas of the brain are specialised for motion detection and perception. Part of the supporting evidence comes from patients with akinetopsia, a condition in which objects in motion cannot be perceived even though stationary objects are perceived reasonably well (see Chapter 2). We will consider in some detail those parts of the brain involved in motion perception, as well as the complexities posed by trying to decide whether movement of the retinal image is due to object movement or to eye movement.

There is good evidence from monkey research that an area known as MT (middle temporal area) is much involved in motion detection (see Chapter 2). In humans, the equivalent area is sometimes called MT+, and the term V5 is also used to describe the brain area most involved in motion detection. Note that there is no precise equivalence between monkey and human brains. There is increasing evidence (e.g., Orban et al., 2003) that several brain regions outside MT (e.g., in the intraparietal sulcus) are much more sensitive to motion in humans than in monkeys (see Chapter 2).

Some of the earliest evidence suggesting there are brain cells that are direction selective in their responding came from studies on the **motion aftereffect**. You can observe the motion aftereffect by looking at a moving pattern for several seconds or longer. When the moving pattern stops, it seems to move in the opposite direction for some time thereafter, with the illusory motion being slower than the preceding actual motion. What is going on here? Suppose you initially observe for some time a pattern (e.g., a waterfall) moving downwards. This will produce a short-lasting desensitisation of motion detectors that are specialised for detection of downward movement. As a result, observing the pattern when it is stationary will be associated with more activation of motion detectors specialised for detection of upward movement than those specialised for detection of downward movement. This causes us to see the motion aftereffect.

Evidence supporting the above account was reported by Tolhurst (1973). He found that inspection of a stimulus moving in one direction reduced observers' contrast sensitivity for another stimulus moving in the same direction. However, it had only a small effect on contrast sensitivity for a stimulus moving in the opposite direction. Presumably these findings were obtained because the initial inspection of a stimulus reduced the sensitivity of motion detectors specialised for detection of movement in the direction in which the stimulus was moving.

Most cells in area MT not only respond to moving images, but are also direction selective. Relevant evidence has been obtained in studies on monkeys who are presented with visual displays containing hundreds of moving dots, most of which are moving randomly but a few of which are moving in a given direction. Newsome and Paré (1988) found that small lesions in the middle temporal area reduced monkeys' ability to detect the direction of movement of dots. Salzman, Britten, and Newsome (1990) investigated the effects of micro-stimulation of clusters of direction-selective cells especially responsive to motion in a particular direction (e.g., downwards). The effect of stimulating downward-sensitive MT cells was the same as increasing the number of downward-moving dots in the visual display.

Object movement or eye movement?

The information in the retinal image is often ambiguous, in that image movement could be due either to object movement or to eye movement. However, we rarely have any problem in interpreting image movement accurately. Presumably we use information from eye movements to assist us in this interpretive task. This could be achieved in various ways. Sherrington (1906) proposed an inflow theory, according to which the visual system monitors changes in the eye muscles controlling eye movements, and then uses that information to interpret changes in the retinal image.

Helmholtz (1866) proposed an outflow theory, according to which image movement is interpreted by using information about intended movement sent to the eye muscles. The fact that the visual world seems to move when the side of the eyeball is pressed supports this theory. There is movement within the retinal image unaccompanied by commands to the eye muscles, and so it is perceived as genuine. The earlier discussion of the role of extra-retinal information in heading is of relevance to this theory.

Stevens et al. (1976) carried out an experiment in which a participant (John Stevens himself) was subjected to paralysis of his entire body to prevent any eye movements from occurring. When he attempted to make a saccadic eye movement, he reported there was a kind of relocation of the visual world but without any experience of movement. This finding provides some support for Helmholtz's outflow theory and against inflow theory.

Other sources of information can be used to decide whether it is the eyes or an attended object that is moving. For example, movement of the entire retinal image suggests there has been an eye movement, whereas movement of only part of the image suggests an object is moving. When a visual display contains a structured background, observers generally make much use of information about an object's motion relative to that background and relative little of information about eye position (Pelz & Hayhoe, 1995).

As we perceive the world around us, we often move our head as well as our eyes, and this adds additional complications. As Tresilian (1994, p. 336) pointed out, outflow theory "predicts that if the eyes are stationary in the head, as the head rotates, the resulting image motion will be interpreted as motion of the environment, yet everyone knows that this does not happen." What probably happens is that we use information about head movements to interpret movement in the retinal image. In addition, we realise that movement of the entire retinal image implies movement of the head or eyes, whereas movement of only part of the retinal image implies object movement. Andersen, Snyder, Bradley, and Xing (1997) reviewed evidence indicating that activity in various brain areas (e.g., MST, 7a) along the dorsal pathway (discussed in Chapter 2) is influenced by head and eye position. The implication is that these areas are involved in integrating information from eye and head movements with information from the retinal image.

Suppose you are asked to estimate the speed of an object that you are following by making pursuit eye movements. As Bruce et al. (2003) pointed out, you probably combine information from retinal image velocity and eye-movement velocity. There is support for this position, but research has revealed some unexpected complexities. In order to make sense of the various findings, Freeman and Banks (1998) assumed that information derived from eye movements indicates the eyes are moving at only 60% of their actual speed. As we will see, this underestimate allows us to interpret two phenomena.

First, there is the **Aubert–Fleischl effect**, which is that the perceived speed of a moving object is slower (and so underestimated) when tracked by the eyes than when the eyes remain stationary. Why does this underestimate occur? The retinal image of the moving object is stationary, and so the object's perceived speed depends solely on information about eye velocity. If Freeman and Banks (1998) are correct in assuming we underestimate eye velocity, this would account for the Aubert–Fleischl effect.

Second, there is the **Filehne illusion**, in which a stationary background object is perceived as moving in the opposite direction to another object tracked by the eyes. In this case, observers use information from image velocity *and* from eye velocity. If both velocities were calculated accurately, then the background object would appear stationary. In fact, eye velocity is underestimated, and so the background appears to move away from the direction in which the eyes are moving.

Haarmeier, Thier, Repnow, and Petersen (1997) studied a patient, RW. He has bilateral damage in extrastriate cortex, and is totally unable to use information about eye velocity. His motion perception is fine when his eyes are stationary, and he can track a moving pattern. However, a moving target appears stationary when he tracks it. In addition, he has a complete Filehne illusion, with a stationary background appearing to move in the opposite direction to his eyes at the same speed as his eyes are moving.

Biological motion

Most people are very good at interpreting the movements of other people, and can decide very rapidly whether someone is walking, running, or limping. How successful would we be at interpreting biological movement if the visual information available to us were greatly reduced? Johansson (1975) addressed this issue by attaching lights to actors' joints (e.g., wrists, knees, ankles). The actors were dressed entirely in black so only the lights were visible, and they were then filmed moving around (see Figure 4.8). Reasonably accurate perception of a moving person was achieved even with only six lights and a short segment of film. Most observers described accurately the posture and movements of the actors, and it almost seemed as if their arms and legs could be seen.

Observers can make very precise discriminations when viewing point-light displays. Cutting and Kozlowski (1977) found that observers were reasonably good at identifying themselves and others known to them from point-light displays. Kozlowski and Cutting (1978) discovered that observers were correct about 65% of the time when guessing the sex of someone walking. Judgements were better when joints in both the upper and lower body were illuminated, presumably because good judgements depend on some overall bodily feature or features.

Interesting findings with point-light displays were reported by Runeson and Frykholm (1983). In one experiment, they asked actors to lift a box

FIGURE 4.8

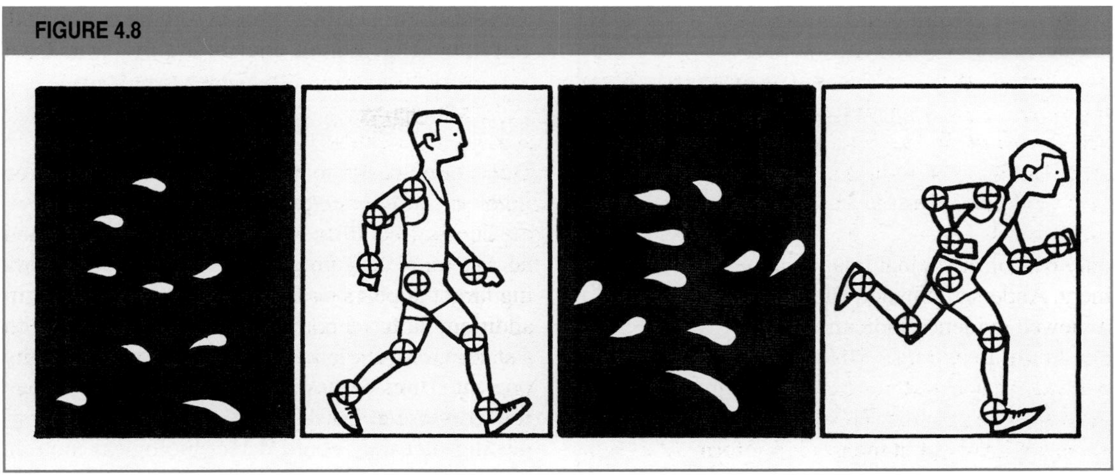

Johansson (1975) attached lights to an actor's joints. While the actor stood still in a darkened room, observers could not make sense of the arrangement of lights. However, as soon as he started to move around, they were able to perceive the lights as defining a human figure.

weighing 4 kilograms and to carry it to a table, while trying to give the impression that the box weighed 6.5, 11.5, or 19 kilograms. Observers detected the actors' deceptive intentions from the pattern of lights, and so their perception of the weight of the box did not vary across conditions.

In another experiment, Runeson and Frykholm (1983) showed films of actors throwing sandbags to targets at different distances. The observers judged accurately how far the actors had intended to throw the bags, even though there were no lights on the bags. Finally, Runeson and Frykholm (1983) asked actors to carry out a sequence of actions naturally or as if they were a member of the opposite sex. Observers guessed the gender of the actor correctly 85.5% of the time when he/she acted naturally, and there was only a modest reduction to 75.5% correct in the deception condition.

Is there anything special about the perception of biological motion? There is increasing evidence that the answer is "Yes". For example, consider studies on "motion-blind" patients with damage to area MT/V5 who have severely impaired ability to perceive motion in general. Such patients are reasonably good at detecting biological motion (e.g., McLeod, Dittrich, Driver, Perrett, & Zihl, 1996; Vaina, Cowey, LeMay, Bienfang, & Kinkinis, 2002). Perhaps what is of central importance in the detection of biological motion is the ability to integrate information from the moving points of light, and that integration process does not involve area MT/V5.

Brain-imaging studies also suggest that the perception of biological motion involves different areas from that of motion in general. Grossman et al. (2000) found that point-light displays of biological motion activated an area in the superior temporal sulcus, whereas displays of other patterns of motion did not (see Figure 4.9). This area is also activated by other forms of human motion, including movements of the head, face, and hands (Allison, Puce, & McCarthy, 2000). Servos, Osu, Santi, and Kawato (2002) presented observers with motion displays, some of which showed biological motion and some of which did not. There was evidence of selective activation of the superior temporal gyrus when observers saw biological motion, which was consistent with the findings of Grossman et al. (2000). However, the key finding was that activation specific to biological motion was located within area VP (see Figure 4.9). It is noteworthy that perception of biological motion did *not* involve selective activation of area MT, which is specialised for motion detection.

FIGURE 4.9

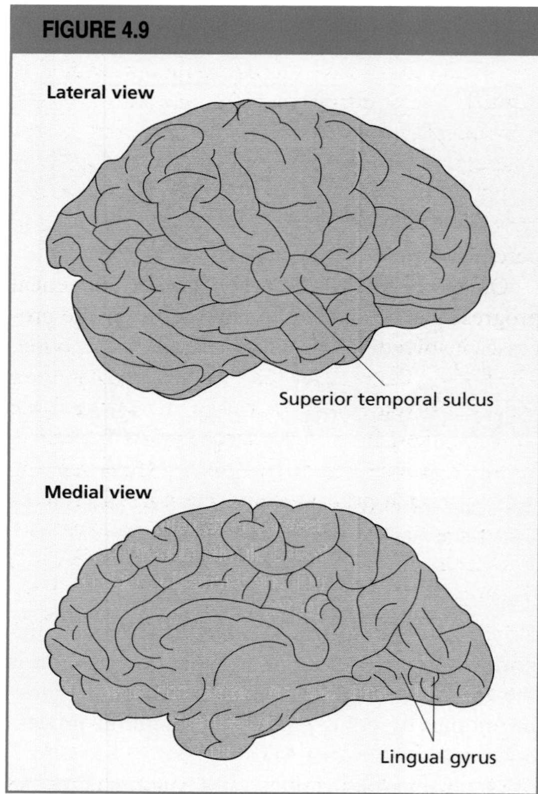

Brain areas involved in perception of biological motion. Based on Grossman et al. (2000).

Why are two different brain areas heavily involved in perception of biological motion? According to Servos et al. (2002, p. 780), "The STS [superior temporal sulcus] may be involved in providing the social meaning of biological motion stimuli (Allison et al., 2000), whereas the lingual gyrus (specifically area VP) may be involved in deriving biological forms from the motion information."

Observation of human movement generally also activates areas of the primary motor cortex and elsewhere associated with the control of bodily movements. More specifically, those areas in motor and premotor cortex activated when we observe a given biological movement are also activated when we perform the same movement ourselves (Nishitani & Hari, 2000). This internal simulation of another person's movements may assist us in predicting their future movements.

Theoretical accounts

Does our ability to perceive biological motion involve complex cognitive processes? Some evidence suggests it does not. For example, Fox and McDaniel (1982) presented two different motion displays side by side to infants. One display consisted of dots representing someone running on the spot, and the other showed the same activity presented upside down. Infants 4 months of age looked more at the display the right way up, suggesting that they could detect biological motion. In addition, Johansson, von Hofsten, and Jansson (1980) found that observers who saw moving lights for only one-fifth of a second perceived biological motion with no apparent difficulty.

The above findings are consistent with Johansson's (1975) view that the ability to perceive biological motion is innate. However, 4-month-old infants may have learned from experience how to perceive biological motion. Runeson and Frykholm (1983) argued for a Gibsonian position, according to which aspects of biological motion provide invariant information. These invariants can be perceived with the impoverished information available from point-light displays, and can be identified even when there are deliberate attempts to deceive observers.

What invariants are involved? Cutting, Proffitt, and Kozlowski (1978) pointed out that men tend to show relatively greater side-to-side motion (or swing) of the shoulders than of the hips, whereas women show the opposite. This happens because men typically have broad shoulders and narrow hips in comparison to women. The shoulders and hips move in opposition to each other, i.e., when the right shoulder is forward, the left hip is forward. One can identify the **centre of moment** in the upper body, which is the neutral reference point around which the shoulders and hips swing. The position of the centre of moment is determined by the relative sizes of the shoulders and hips, and is typically lower in men than in women. Cutting et al. found the centre of moment correlated well with observers' sex judgements.

Cutting (1978) extended the above findings. He used artificial moving dot displays (i.e., the lights were not attached to people) in which only the centre of moment was varied. Judgements of the sex of "male" and "female" walkers were correct over 80% of the time, suggesting the importance of centre of moment. However, Cutting used a greater range of variation in the centre of moment than is found in real human beings, and the general artificiality of his situation suggests caution in generalising his findings to real-life situations.

Mather, Radford, and West (1992) considered the effects of omitting different dots from artificial point-light displays. Omitting the shoulder and hip points had very little effect on the accuracy with which the motions of "walkers" were detected. However, performance was greatly impaired when the wrist and ankle points were omitted. According to Mather et al., the wrists and ankles move more than other parts of the body when we walk, and so provide more information about our movements.

Mather and Murdoch (1994) also used artificial point-light displays. Most previous studies had involved movement across the line of sight, but the "walkers" in their displays appeared to walk either towards or away from the camera. There are two correlated cues that may be used by observers to decide whether they are looking at a man or a woman in point-light displays:

(1) Structural cues based on the tendency of men to have broad shoulders and narrow hips, whereas women have the opposite tendency; these structural cues form the basis of the centre of moment.
(2) Dynamic cues based on the tendency for men to show relatively greater body sway with the upper body than with the hips when walking, whereas women show the opposite.

Sex judgements were based much more on dynamic cues than on structural ones when the two cues were in conflict. Thus, the centre of moment may be less important than assumed by Cutting (e.g., 1978).

Evaluation

Our ability to perceive biological motion with very limited visual information is impressive. There is reasonably convincing evidence from brain-imaging studies and from brain-damaged patients that the brain areas involved in perception of biological motion are different from those used in perceiving motion in general.

On the negative side, only limited theoretical progress has been made in understanding the processes involved in perception of biological motion. The finding that we can perceive biological motion accurately even when presented with moving lights for only one-fifth of a second suggests that fairly low-level processes are involved. However, the nature of such processes and the possible role of invariants in perceiving biological motion remain somewhat unclear. Finally, we lack definitive research on the roles played by the superior temporal gyrus and area VP in perception of biological motion.

Perception of causality

Michotte (1946) carried out several studies on **perceived causality** in which the stimuli he presented were shapes displayed in films. In some studies, observers watched as one square moved towards a second square, with the first square stopping and the second square moving off at a slower rate than the first one as they came into contact. According to Michotte (1946), observers perceived that the first square had caused the motion of the second square (the "launching effect"). The perception of causality disappeared when there was a time interval between the contact and the second square moving off, or if the second square moved off in a different direction from that of the first square.

Another effect observed by Michotte (1946) was termed "entraining". This occurred when one object moved towards a second object, and then the two objects moved off together at the same speed until they stopped together. It seemed to the observers as if the first object were carrying the second one or pushing it. The launching and entraining effects were not affected by the nature of the objects involved. In addition, the effects were observed even when the two objects were very different from each other.

Michotte (1946) put forward a Gestaltist view of perceived causality, according to which it occurs naturally when specific motion sequences are seen. He argued that causality is perceived directly, and is not reliant on inferences or other cognitive processes. In addition, Michotte claimed that the perception of causality is probably innately determined.

Evidence

If the perception of causality is direct, we might expect to find it even in infants. Leslie and Keeble (1987) found 6-month-old infants could perceive the launching effect. This finding suggests that fairly basic processes are involved in the perception of causality. Oakes (1994) obtained similar findings from 7-month-olds using simple displays. However, the same infants failed to perceive causality in more complex displays.

Michotte's (1946) assumption that the perception of causality does not involve the use of inferences was tested by Schlottmann and Shanks (1992). They arranged matters so that a change of colour by the second object *always* predicted its movement, whereas impact of the first object on the second object was less predictive. The participants learned to draw the correct inference that the change of colour in the second object was necessary for its movement, but this did not influence their causal impressions. However, when the first object collided with the second object, which changed colour and moved off, the observers claimed that it looked as if the first object caused the second one to move.

What do these findings mean? Schlottmann and Shanks (1992, p. 340) concluded as follows: "The results support the distinction that Michotte advocated between causal knowledge that arises from inference and that which is directly given in perception." This conclusion was supported by finding that 85% of the participants regarded their inference judgements and their ratings of perceived causality as *independent* of each other.

Schlottmann and Anderson (1993) studied the launching effect. They manipulated the gap between the two objects, the time period between the collision and the second object moving, and the ratio of the speeds of the two objects. They identified two successive processes, which they termed "valuation" and "integration". Valuation involves assigning weights to the various aspects of the moving display, and there were substantial individual differences in this form of processing. Integration involves combining or integrating information from these various aspects, and there were great similarities in this process across participants. Schlottmann and Anderson (1993, p. 797) concluded as follows: "The averaging integration model may correspond to the invariant perceptual structure of phenomenal causality, as proposed by Michotte. The valuation operation, on the other hand, can accommodate individual differences that may have experiential components, as suggested by his critics."

More support for Michotte's theoretical position was reported by Blakemore et al. (2001) in an fMRI study. Observers watched one ball colliding with another ball, having been given instructions leading them either to direct attention to (or away from) the causal nature of the stimuli. The key finding was that activity in MT/V5 and related brain areas involved in processing motion was significantly greater when the presented visual event produced perceived causality than when it did not. In contrast, direction of attention to or away from causality had no effect on brain activation, suggesting that higher-level attentional processes are not relevant to the detection of perceived causality. Blakemore et al. concluded that perceived causality depends on low-level perceptual processes, as was proposed by Michotte (1946).

Evaluation

The available evidence suggests Michotte was correct in assuming that causality is often perceived fairly directly. However, the perception of causality is sometimes more complex than he assumed. The existence of substantial individual differences in the perception of causality suggests that learning and experience play a greater role than admitted by Michotte. It is hard to disagree with the conclusion of Schlottmann and Anderson (1993, p. 799): "In adult cognition . . . the perceptual illusion of phenomenal causality must function together with acquired knowledge about causality in the physical world. Thus, ways are needed that can make effective progress on the innate-*plus*-learned question."

CHANGE BLINDNESS

We feel we have a clear and detailed visual representation of the world around us as we go about our daily business. In other words, "Our subjective impression of a coherent and richly detailed world leads most of us to assume that we see what there is to be seen by merely opening our eyes and looking" (Mack, 2003, p. 180). As a result, we are confident we could immediately detect any change in the visual environment provided it was sufficiently great (Levin, Momen, Drivdahl, & Simons, 2000). In fact, as we will see, our ability to detect such changes is often far less impressive than we think it is.

Suppose you are watching a film in which students are passing a ball to each other. At some point a woman in a gorilla suit walks right into camera shot, looks at the camera, thumps her chest, and then walks off. Altogether she is on the screen for 9 seconds. Imagine yourself in that situation: wouldn't you be very confident of spotting the woman dressed up as a gorilla almost immediately? Surprisingly, when an experiment along the lines just described was carried out (Simons & Chabris, 1999; see Figure 4.10), 50% of observers did not notice the woman's presence at all! It should be noted that the observers had been given the task of counting the number of passes made by members of one of the teams of students. Many observers failed to spot the gorilla because they were attending to movements of the ball and to members of the relevant team.

FIGURE 4.10

Frame showing a woman in a gorilla suit in the middle of a game of passing the ball. From Simons and Chabris (1999). Reproduced with permission from D.J. Simons.

The phenomenon described above, in which observers do not notice an unexpected object appearing in a visual display, is **inattentional blindness**. It is closely related to another, broader phenomenon known as change blindness. In essence, **change blindness** is a failure to detect that an object has moved or disappeared, and is the opposite of change detection. The phenomenon of change blindness can be demonstrated even when the change in question is large. For example, Simons and Levin (1998) carried out studies in which participants started to have a conversation with a stranger. This stranger was then replaced by a different stranger during a brief interruption (e.g., a large object coming between them). Many participants simply did not realise that their conversational partner had changed! However, it should be pointed out that participants' attention was closely focused on a written set of directions during the time the switch occurred.

Consider an experiment on change blindness in which two pictures are presented in rapid succession, with the second picture differing from the first in having an object removed. It is likely that participants would notice a change by detecting image motion even if they did not know how the second picture differed from the first. Accordingly, various techniques have been used to ensure that the ability to detect visual changes is *not* simply due to the detection of motion (Rensink, 2002):

(1) Occlusion-contingent change: the change is made when there is an occlusion or obstruction hiding the change itself from view (as in the study by Simons & Levin, 1998).
(2) Saccade-contingent change: the change is made during a saccade (rapid movement of the eyes).
(3) Gap-contingent change: the change is made during a short temporal gap between the original and altered stimuli.
(4) Blink-contingent change: the change is made during an eyeblink.

How can we explain change blindness? Rensink (2000, 2002) proposed coherence theory, which is based on a small number of assumptions:

(1) Prior to focused attention, there is an early stage of processing extending across the visual field. This processing produces representations of several objects, but these representations lack stability and are rapidly replaced by new stimuli at their location.
(2) Focused attention produces a very detailed and longer-lasting representation of one object, which allows the object's representation to withstand a brief interruption. An object that is the focus of attention will be perceived as transformed when a new stimulus replaces it.
(3) When focused attention is removed from an object, its representation disintegrates and returns to the state it was in prior to becoming the focus of attention.

It follows from the above assumptions that only visual changes to a currently attended object will be detected. Thus, change blindness is a fairly common occurrence, because changes to any unattended object will not be detected. The general notion that attentional processes are of crucial importance in determining whether change blindness (and inattentional blindness) occurs is a common one, and is a point of agreement among most theorists (e.g., Hollingworth & Henderson, 2002; Simons, 2000).

Hollingworth and Henderson (2002) proposed an alternative theory of scene perception. They argued that fairly detailed visual representations are formed of objects that are the focus of attention. These representations are incorporated within a mental map coding the spatial layout of the scene. Information about these visual representations and spatial layout is stored in long-term memory. As a result, "Over multiple fixations on a scene, local object information accumulates in LTM [long-term memory] from previously fixated and attended regions and is indexed within the scene map, forming a detailed representation of the scene as a whole" (Hollingworth & Henderson, 2002, p. 132).

There are three main differences between Hollingworth and Henderson's theory and Rensink's coherence theory. First, consider objects that change some time after they were attended to. According to Hollingworth and Henderson, the visual representations of such objects continue to exist over time, and so there is a reasonable chance the change will be detected. In contrast, it is predicted by coherence theory that the representations of non-attended objects disintegrate rapidly, and so there should be change blindness for such objects.

Second, Hollingworth and Henderson assume that fairly detailed representations of most scenes are stored in long-term memory, whereas that is not assumed within coherence theory. As a result, observers should often be able to detect changes in visual displays that were initially seen several minutes previously.

Third, Rensink assumed that focused attention to an object produces a very detailed point-by-point representation of that object, which can survive a brief interruption (e.g., a saccade). In Hollingworth and Henderson's theory, on the other hand, it is assumed that more abstract and less detailed visual representations are formed when objects are the focus of attention.

Evidence

The extent to which observers show change blindness or inattentional blindness depends on several factors. One such factor is the observer's intention. At one extreme, there is the intentional approach in which observers are told to expect a change in the visual display. At the other extreme, there are studies involving the incidental approach (e.g., Simons & Chabris, 1999; Simons & Levin, 1998) in which there is no mention at all of a possible change, and it is only afterwards that observers are asked whether they noticed a change. Not surprisingly, many more observers show change blindness or inattentional blindness with the incidental approach (see Rensink, 2002, for a review).

An important factor in inattentional blindness is the *similarity* between an unexpected object and other objects in the visual display. For example, Most et al. (2001) asked observers to count either the number of white shapes or the number of black shapes bouncing off the edges of the display window. What was of interest was the percentage of observers noticing an unexpected object which could be white, light grey, dark grey, or black. The detection rates for unexpected objects were much higher when they were similar in luminance or brightness to the target objects (see Figure 4.11), presumably because those resembling target objects were most likely to receive attention.

Earlier we discussed the surprising finding of Simons and Chabris (1999) that 50% of observers failed to detect a woman dressed as a gorilla. Similarity was a factor, in that the gorilla was black whereas the members of the team whose passes the observers were counting were dressed in white. Simons and Chabris carried out a further experiment in which observers either counted the passes made by members of the team dressed in white or the one dressed in black. The gorilla's presence was detected by only 42% of observers when the attended team was the one dressed in white, thus replicating the previous findings. However, the gorilla's presence was detected by 83% of observers when the attended team was the one dressed in black, thus showing the impact of similarity between the unexpected stimulus (gorilla) and task-relevant stimuli (members of attended team).

As we saw earlier, most theorists assume that failures of attention are responsible for change blindness. One of the oddities of the research literature is that attentional processes were not assessed in most studies on change blindness. However, an important exception is the research of Hollingworth and Henderson (2002). Eye movements were recorded while participants looked at a visual scene (e.g., kitchen, living room), and pressed a button if they detected any change in the scene. There were two possible kinds of change: *type* change in which the object was replaced by an object from a different category (e.g., knife replaced by fork) and *token* change, in which the object was replaced by another object from the same category (e.g., one knife replaced by a different knife). Finally, there was a test of long-term memory occurring between 5 and 30 minutes

FIGURE 4.11

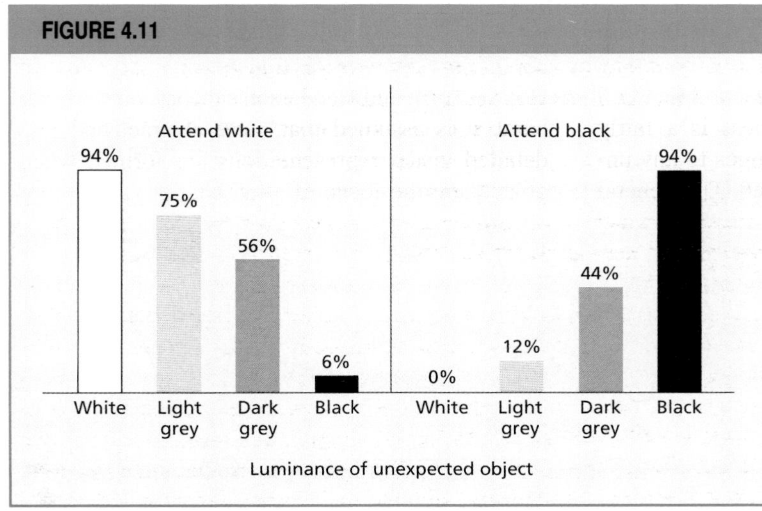

Percent of participants detecting unexpected objects as a function of similarity between their luminance or brightness and that of target objects. From Most et al. (2001) with permission from Blackwell Publishing.

after each scene had been viewed. On this test, participants saw two scenes: (1) the original scene with a target object marked with a green arrow; (2) a distractor scene identical to the original scene except that there was a different object in the location of the target object. The task was to decide which was the original object.

What did Hollingworth and Henderson (2002) find? First, they considered the probability of reporting a change as a function of whether the changed object had been fixated prior to the change. Change detection was much greater when the changed object had been fixated before the change (see Figure 4.12a). Since observers mistakenly claimed to have detected a change on 9% of trials on which there was no change (false alarm rate), there was no real evidence that observers could accurately detect changes in objects not fixated prior to change. These findings suggest that attention to the to-be-changed object is necessary (but not sufficient) for change detection, because there was change blindness for about 60% of changed objects fixated before they were changed.

Second, Hollingworth and Henderson (2002) studied the fate of objects fixated some time prior to being changed. As can be seen in Figure 4.12b, the number of fixations on other objects occurring after the last fixation on the to-be-changed object had *no* systematic effect on change detection. This finding is consistent with Hollingworth and Henderson's theory. However, it is not consistent

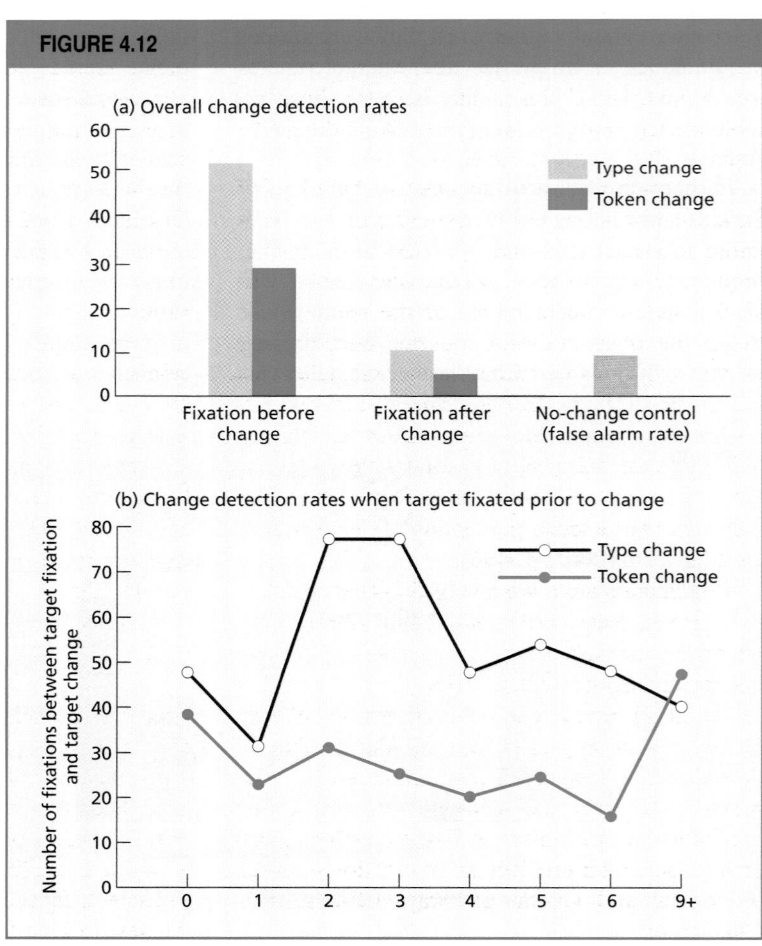

(a) Percent correct change detection as a function of form of change (type vs. token) and time of fixation (before vs. after change); also false alarm rate when there was no change. From Hollingworth and Henderson (2002). (b) Mean percent correct change detection as a function of the number of fixations between target fixation and change of target and form of change (type vs. token). From Hollingworth and Henderson (2002). Copyright © 2002 by the American Psychological Association. Reprinted with permission.

with coherence theory, which predicts very poor ability to detect change when the changed object is not being attended to at the time of the change.

Third, as can be seen in Figure 4.12a and b, change detection was much better when there was a change in the type of object rather than merely swapping one member of a category for another (token change). This makes sense, because type changes are more dramatic and obvious than token changes.

Fourth, long-term memory for objects presented in the visual scenes was assessed. Reasonable long-term object memory is predicted by Hollingworth and Henderson (2002), whereas essentially no long-term memory is predicted by coherence theory. In fact, Hollingworth and Henderson found that 93% of type changes were detected as well as 81% of token changes.

Henderson and Hollingworth (2003) addressed the issue of whether focused attention leads to the creation of highly detailed point-by-point representations of visual scenes as predicted by Rensink (2000, 2002). Observers were presented with complex real-world scenes in which half of each scene was hidden by vertical grey bars. The entire scene changed during a saccade so that the previously visible parts of the scene were now hidden and the hidden parts became visible. Even though the observers were told the precise nature of the changes that might occur, they detected very few of them (2.7%). These findings disconfirm the prediction from coherence theory, and "indicate that point-by-point representations are not functional across saccades during complex real-world scene perception" (Henderson & Hollingworth, 2003, p. 496).

Which brain areas are involved in change detection? Beck, Rees, Frith, and Lavie (2001) gave observers the task of detecting a visual change occurring during a screen flicker. They used fMRI to identify differences in brain activation between change detection and change blindness. Change detection was associated with more activation in parietal and right dorsolateral prefrontal cortex than was change blindness. They concluded that change detection involves an interaction between the dorsal and ventral pathways (discussed in Chapter 2).

Turatto, Angrilli, Mazza, Umiltà, and Driver (2002) compared change detection and change blindness using event-related potentials (ERPs). P300 (a positive wave occurring about 300 ms after stimulus presentation) was only present in frontal and parietal areas when a change was detected. P300 has been found in other research to be associated with conscious identification of targets, and so it makes sense that it was present only when change was detected.

A final issue needs to be addressed. Change blindness and inattentional blindness have generally been assessed by asking observers to indicate whether they saw any changes in a scene. Perhaps observers who deny detecting any changes might reveal evidence of detection if more sensitive measures were used. For example, Hollingworth, Williams, and Henderson (2001) used eye-movement data as well as self-report. They compared gaze duration on changed objects when the change had not been reported by observers with gaze duration on unchanged objects. Gaze duration was 250 ms longer on the former objects than on the latter ones. Thus, the change was actually detected in some sense, even though conscious awareness of the change was lacking. Similar findings were reported by Hollingworth and Henderson (2002).

Additional evidence that self-report measures of change detection may underestimate our ability to detect change was reported by Fernandez-Duque and Thornton (2000). Observers failing to detect a change at the level of conscious awareness were nevertheless asked to guess the location at which the change had occurred. Their guesses were accurate more often than chance would allow.

Evaluation

Inattentional blindness and change blindness are important phenomena, and several relevant factors (e.g., whether or not observers expect a change) have been identified. Prior attention to the object that is subsequently changed is necessary to prevent change blindness. However, it is often not sufficient, especially when the change is relatively modest (e.g., a token change).

Theoretically, the approach taken by Hollingworth and Henderson (2002) is more in line with the available evidence than is Rensink's (2000, 2002) coherence theory. According to coherence theory, observers have available very detailed information about objects currently being attended, but very imprecise information about objects attended a short time ago. In fact, the evidence suggests (in line with Hollingworth and Henderson's prediction) that moderately detailed information about previously attended objects is available for at least a few seconds after they cease to receive attention. In addition, and also as predicted by Hollingworth and Henderson, some information about previously attended objects is stored in long-term memory.

In sum, our belief that we have a clear, detailed representation of our visual environment is exaggerated but not entirely wrong. What we actually have is a fairly clear and detailed representation of those parts of the visual environment to which we have paid attention in the recent past.

CHAPTER SUMMARY

- Direct perception
  Gibson argued that perception and action are closely intertwined, with the main purpose of visual perception being to assist in the organisation of action. According to his direct theory, movement of an observer creates optic flow, which provides useful information. Of particular importance are invariants, which remain the same as people move around the environment, and which are detected by a process of resonance. The uses of objects (their affordances) were claimed to be perceived directly. Gibson's approach was very original and focused on important interactions between vision and action previously ignored. However, he underestimated the complexity of visual processing, he minimised the importance of stored object knowledge in grasping objects appropriately, and he de-emphasised those aspects of visual perception concerned with object recognition.

- Visually guided action
  According to Gibson, our perception of heading depends on optic-flow information. However, the retinal flow field is determined by eye and head movements as well as by our movement through the environment. Heading judgements are also influenced by binocular disparity, and optic-flow information is not essential for accurate judgements. Alternative approaches have emphasised relative motion of pairs of objects and static depth or visual direction as sources of information influencing heading judgements. According to the tau hypothesis, observers assume that moving objects have constant velocity, and use tau to estimate time to contact. In fact, observers sometimes take account of accelerating or decelerating object velocity, and time-to-contact estimates use information about binocular disparity and familiar size. Time-to-contact estimates typically depend on combining information from various sources.

- Planning–control model
  In Glover's planning–control model, he distinguished between a slow planning system used mostly before the initiation of movement and a fast control system used during the carrying out of a movement. According to the model, planning depends on a visual representation in the inferior parietal lobe, whereas control depends on the superior parietal lobe. As predicted by the model, action errors typically stem from the planning system rather than the control system. Evidence from brain-damaged patients and from brain imaging in normals supports the proposed locations of the planning and control systems. The processes of the planning system need to be spelled out in more detail, as do the complex interactions between the two systems.

- Motion perception
  Motion detection involves MT and other brain regions, with many cells in MT being direction selective. We can decide whether movement in the retinal image is due to object movement or eye movement by using information about intended eye movement sent to the eye muscles. In addition, eye movement produces movement of the entire retinal image, whereas object movement produces movement of only part of it. We underestimate the speed of our pursuit eye movements, which produces errors in perceiving the speed of moving objects. Biological motion is perceived even when impoverished visual information is available. The perception of biological motion involves different brain areas (e.g., superior temporal sulcus; VP) from those used to detect motion in general. Perception of biological motion may involve the use of invariant information. Structural and dynamic cues are used to decide whether we are looking at a man or a woman in point-light displays. Perceived causality generally depends on low-level processes, and involves brain areas specialised for motion processing. However, inferential processes can also be involved.

- Change blindness
  There is convincing evidence for the existence of inattentional blindness and change blindness. The percentage of observers showing these effects depends on several factors, including the observer's intention, the sensitivity of measurement, the similarity between the unexpected object and attended objects (inattentional blindness), and the extent of change (change blindness). However, the single most important factor with change blindness is whether the changed object was attended to prior to change. Reasonably detailed (but not point-by-point representations) of attended parts of a visual display are accessible for some time after being formed, and assist in change detection. The findings generally favour the theory proposed by Hollingworth and Henderson (2002) over Rensink's coherence theory.

FURTHER READING

- Bruce, V., Green, P.R., & Georgeson, M.A. (2003). *Visual perception: Physiology, psychology, and ecology (4th Ed.)*. Hove, UK: Psychology Press. Chapters 7, 8, and 9 of this well-written and informative British textbook amplify the coverage of various topics dealt with in this chapter.
- Lamberts, K., & Goldstone, R. (2004). *Handbook of cognition*. London: Sage. Several chapters in this edited book are devoted to visual perception, including vision for action.
- Morgan, M. (2003). *The space between our ears: How the brain represents visual space*. London: Weidenfeld & Nicolson. Michael Morgan discusses some of the key research on vision for action in this witty book.
- Rensink, R.A. (2002). Change detection. *Annual Review of Psychology*, *53*, 245–277. This article provides a good overview of theory and research on the increasingly important topic of change blindness.
- Sekuler, R., & Blake, R. (2002). *Perception (4th Ed.)*. New York: McGraw-Hill. Several issues relating to motion perception and perception for action are discussed in an accessible way in this American textbook.

5

Attention and Performance Limitations

INTRODUCTION

As Pashler (1998, p. 1) pointed out, "Attention has long posed a major challenge for psychologists." Historically, the concept of "attention" fell into disrepute in the early twentieth century, because the behaviourists regarded all internal processes with the utmost suspicion. Attention became fashionable again following the publication of Broadbent's book *Perception and communication* in 1958, and has remained so ever since.

Attention typically refers to selectivity of processing, as was emphasised by William James (1890, pp. 403–404):

> Everyone knows what attention is. It is the taking possession of the mind, in clear and vivid form, of one out of what seem several simultaneously possible objects or trains of thought. Focalisation, concentration, of consciousness are of its essence.

William James (1890) distinguished between "active" and "passive" modes of attention. Attention is active when controlled in a top-down way by the individual's goals or expectations, whereas it is passive when controlled in a bottom-up way by external stimuli (e.g., a loud noise). This distinction, which remains important in recent research and theorising (e.g., Corbetta & Shulman, 2002), is discussed in detail later in the chapter.

There is a crucial distinction between focused and divided attention (see Figure 5.1). **Focused attention** (or selective attention) is studied by presenting people with two or more stimulus inputs at the same time, and instructing them to respond only to one. Work on focused attention can tell us how effectively people select certain inputs rather than others, and it enables us to study the nature of the selection process and the fate of unattended stimuli. **Divided attention** is also studied by presenting at least two stimulus inputs at the same time, but with instructions that participants must attend to and respond to *all* stimulus inputs. Studies of divided attention provide useful information about an individual's processing limitations, and may tell us something about attentional mechanisms and their capacity.

There are three important limitations with much attentional research. First, although we can attend to *either* the external environment *or* the internal

FIGURE 5.1

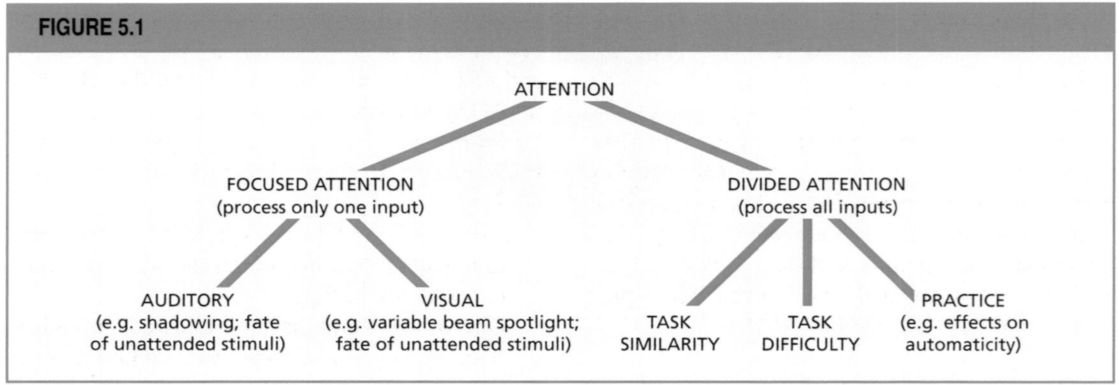

The ways in which different topics in attention are related to each other.

environment (i.e., our own thoughts and information in long-term memory), most research has been concerned only with the former. The reason is that it is much easier to identify and control environmental stimuli than internal determinants of attention.

Second, what we attend to in the real world is largely determined by our current goals. As Allport (1989, p. 664) pointed out, "What is important to recognise . . . is not the location of some imaginary boundary between the provinces of attention and motivation but, to the contrary, their essential interdependence." In most research, however, what participants attend to is determined by the experimenter's instructions rather than by their motivational states.

Third, in the real world we generally attend to three-dimensional people and objects, and decide what actions might be suitable with respect to them. In the laboratory, the emphasis is on "experiments that briefly present static 2D displays and require arbitrary responses . . . such experimental situations are rarely encountered in our usual interactions with the environment" (Tipper, Lortie, & Baylis, 1992, p. 902).

There has been a large increase in the amount of research devoted to attention in recent years. Accordingly, this chapter is longer than in previous editions of this book. Nevertheless, two important topics related to attention are to be found in other chapters. First, there is the phenomenon of change blindness, which indicates that visual attention and perception are closely related (see Chapter 4). More specifically, change blindness occurs when changes in an object are not perceived when that object was not previously the focus of attention. Second, there is the vexed topic of consciousness. It has often been argued that there are close links between attention and consciousness. For example, it may be that the contents of consciousness are determined by focal attention. The topic of consciousness (including an analysis of its relationship with attention) is discussed in Chapter 17.

FOCUSED AUDITORY ATTENTION

The British scientist Colin Cherry became fascinated by the "cocktail party" problem, i.e., how are we able to follow just one conversation when several people are all talking at once? Cherry (1953) found that this ability involves using physical differences (e.g., sex of speaker, voice intensity, speaker location) to maintain attention to a chosen auditory message. When Cherry presented two messages in the same voice to both ears at once (thereby eliminating these physical differences), listeners found it very hard to separate out the two messages on the basis of meaning alone.

Cherry also carried out studies in which one auditory message had to be shadowed (i.e., repeated back out loud) while a second auditory message was played to the other ear. Very little information seemed to be extracted from the second or non-attended message. Listeners seldom noticed when that message was spoken in a foreign language or in reversed speech. In contrast, physical changes (e.g., a pure tone) were nearly always detected. The conclusion that unattended auditory information receives practically no processing was supported by the finding that there was very little memory for unattended words even when presented 35 times each (Moray, 1959).

Broadbent's theory

Broadbent (1958) argued that the findings from the shadowing task were important. He was also impressed by data from a memory task in which three pairs of digits were presented dichotically, i.e., three digits were heard one after the other by one ear, at the same time as three different digits were presented to the other ear. Most participants chose to recall the digits ear by ear rather than pair by pair. Thus, if 496 were presented to one ear and 852 to the other ear, recall would be 496852 rather than 489562.

Broadbent (1958) accounted for the various findings as follows (see Figure 5.2):

- Two stimuli or messages presented at the same time gain access in parallel (at the same time) to a sensory buffer.
- One of the inputs is then allowed through a filter on the basis of its physical characteristics, with the other input remaining in the buffer for later processing.
- This filter prevents overloading of the limited-capacity mechanism beyond the filter; this mechanism processes the input thoroughly (e.g., in terms of its meaning).

This theory handles Cherry's basic findings, with unattended messages being rejected by the

FIGURE 5.2

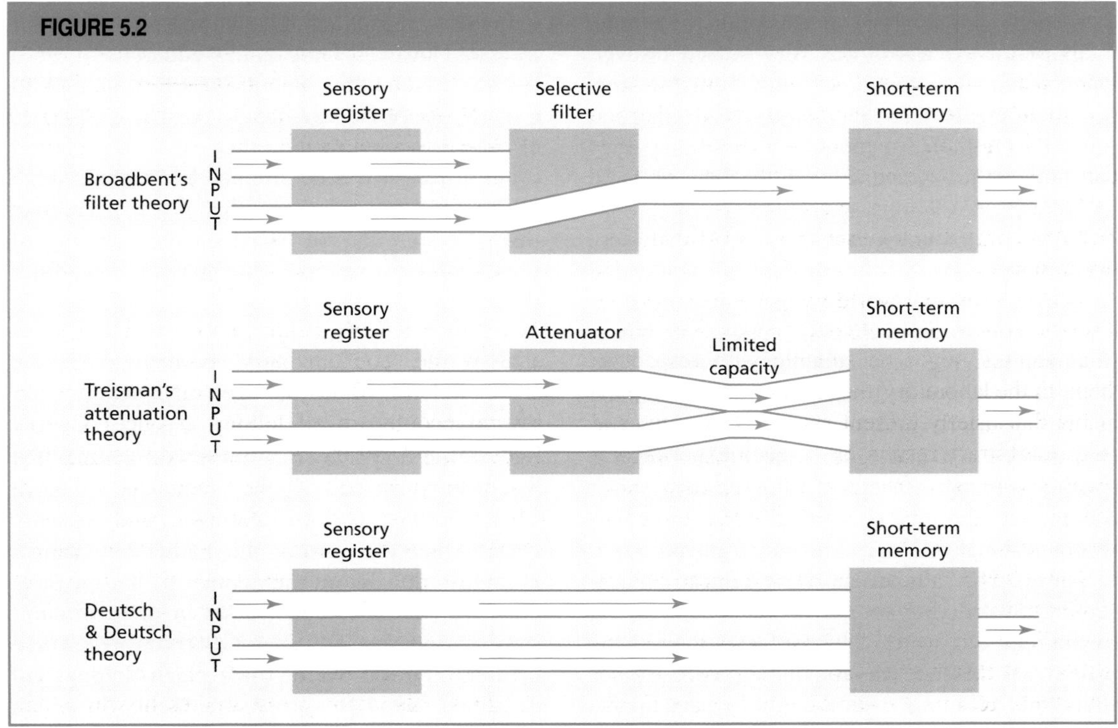

A comparison of Broadbent's theory (top); Treisman's theory (middle); and Deutsch and Deutsch's theory (bottom).

filter and thus receiving minimal processing. It also accounts for performance on Broadbent's dichotic task, because the filter selects one input on the basis of the most prominent physical characteristic distinguishing the two inputs (i.e., the ear of arrival). However, it was assumed incorrectly that the unattended message is *always* rejected at an early stage of processing. The original shadowing experiments used participants with very little experience of shadowing messages, so nearly all their available processing resources had to be allocated to shadowing. Underwood (1974) found that naive participants detected only 8% of the digits on the non-shadowed message, but an experienced researcher in the area (Neville Moray) detected 67% of them.

In most early work on the shadowing task, the two messages were rather similar (i.e., auditorily presented verbal messages). Allport, Antonis, and Reynolds (1972) found that the degree of *similarity* between the two messages had a major impact on memory for the non-shadowed message. When shadowing of auditorily presented passages was combined with auditory presentation of words, memory for the words was very poor. However, when shadowing was combined with picture presentation, memory for the pictures was very good (90% correct). If two inputs are dissimilar, they can both be processed more fully than assumed by Broadbent.

In the early studies, it was assumed that there was no processing of the meaning of unattended messages because the participants had no conscious awareness of hearing them. However, meaning may be processed without awareness. Von Wright, Anderson, and Stenman (1975) presented two lists of words auditorily, with instructions to shadow one list and ignore the other. When a word previously associated with electric shock was presented on the non-attended list, there was sometimes a physiological reaction (galvanic skin response). The same effect was produced by presenting a word very similar in sound or meaning to the shocked word. Thus, information on the unattended message was sometimes processed for sound and meaning, even though the participants were not consciously aware that a word related to the previously shocked word had been presented.

When the participant's own name is presented in the unattended message, approximately one-third of them report hearing it (e.g., Moray, 1959). This finding is hard to account for on Broadbent's theory. Conway, Cowan, and Bunting (2001) found the probability of detecting one's own name on the unattended message depended on individual differences in working memory capacity (see Chapter 6). More specifically, individuals with low working memory capacity were most likely to detect their own name, presumably because they lack the processing capacity to block out distracting information.

Evaluation

Broadbent's (1958) *inflexible* system of selective attention cannot account for the great variability in the amount of analysis of the non-shadowed message. The same inflexibility of the filter theory is shown in its assumption that the filter selects information on the basis of physical features. This assumption is supported by the tendency of participants to recall dichotically presented digits ear by ear. However, Gray and Wedderburn (1960) used a version of the dichotic task in which "Who 6 there" might be presented to one ear, as "4 goes 1" was presented to the other ear. The preferred order of report was determined by meaning (e.g., "Who goes there" followed by "4 6 1"). The fact that selection can be based on the meaning of presented information is inconsistent with filter theory.

Alternative theories

Treisman (1960) found with the shadowing task that the participants sometimes said a word that had been presented on the unattended channel. This is known as "breakthrough", and typically occurs when the word on the unattended channel is highly probable in the context of the message on the attended channel. Even in those circumstances, however, Treisman (1960) only observed breakthrough on 6% of trials. Such findings led Treisman (1964) to propose a theory in which the filter reduces or attenuates the analysis of unattended information (see Figure 5.2). Treisman claimed that the location of the bottleneck was more flexible than Broadbent had suggested. She proposed that stimulus analysis proceeds systematically through a hierarchy starting with analyses based on physical cues, syllabic pattern, and specific words, and moving on to analyses based on individual words, grammatical structure, and meaning. If there is insufficient processing capacity to permit full stimulus analysis, then tests towards the top of the hierarchy are omitted.

Treisman (1964) argued that the thresholds of all stimuli (e.g., words) consistent with current expectations are lowered. As a result, partially processed stimuli on the unattended channel sometimes exceed the threshold of conscious awareness. This aspect of the theory helps to account for the phenomenon of breakthrough.

Treisman's theory accounted for the extensive processing of unattended sources of information that had proved embarrassing for Broadbent. However, the same facts were also explained by Deutsch and Deutsch (1963). They argued that all stimuli are fully analysed, with the most important or relevant stimulus determining the response (see Figure 5.2). This theory places the bottleneck in processing much nearer the response end of the processing system than did Treisman's attenuation theory.

Treisman and Geffen (1967) had participants shadow one of two auditory messages, and tap when they detected a target word in either message. According to Treisman's theory, there should be attenuated analysis of the non-shadowed message, and so fewer targets should be detected on that message. According to Deutsch and Deutsch, there is complete perceptual analysis of all stimuli, and so there should be no difference in detection rates between the two messages. In fact, detection rates were much higher on the shadowed than the non-shadowed message (87% vs. 8%, respectively).

According to Deutsch and Deutsch (1967), only important inputs lead to responses. As the task used by Treisman and Geffen (1967) required their participants to make two responses (i.e., shadow and tap) to target words in the shadowed message, but only one response (i.e., tap) to targets in the non-shadowed message, the shadowed targets were more important than the non-shadowed ones.

Treisman and Riley (1969) responded by carrying out a study in which exactly the same response was made to all targets. Participants stopped shadowing and tapped when they detected a target in either message. Many more target words were detected on the shadowed message than the non-shadowed one.

Neurophysiological studies support Triesman's theory (see Luck, 1998, for a review). Woldorff et al. (1993) used the task of detecting auditory targets presented to the attended ear, with fast trains of non-targets being presented to each ear. Event-related potentials (ERPs; see Chapter 1) were recorded from attended and unattended stimuli. There were greater ERPs to attended stimuli as early as 20–50 milliseconds after stimulus onset. According to Umiltà (2001, p. 139), such findings indicate that "attentional modulation affects the primary auditory cortex".

Perceptual load theory

Lavie (e.g., 1995, 2000) argued that sometimes there is early selection (as claimed by Broadbent, 1958) and sometimes there is late selection (as claimed by Deutsch and Deutsch, 1963). She argued in her perceptual load theory that the following factors determine when selection occurs:

- Everyone has limited attentional capacity.
- The amount of attentional capacity allocated to the main task depends on its perceptual load, which is determined by "the number of units in the display and the nature of processing required for each unit" (Lavie & Tsal, 1994, p. 185).
- "Any spare capacity beyond that taken by the high-priority relevant stimuli is automatically allocated to the irrelevant stimuli" (Lavie, 1995, p. 452). Thus, the total available attentional capacity is always allocated to processing.

It follows from these assumptions that there will be early selection when perceptual load is high. In contrast, there will be late selection when

FIGURE 5.3

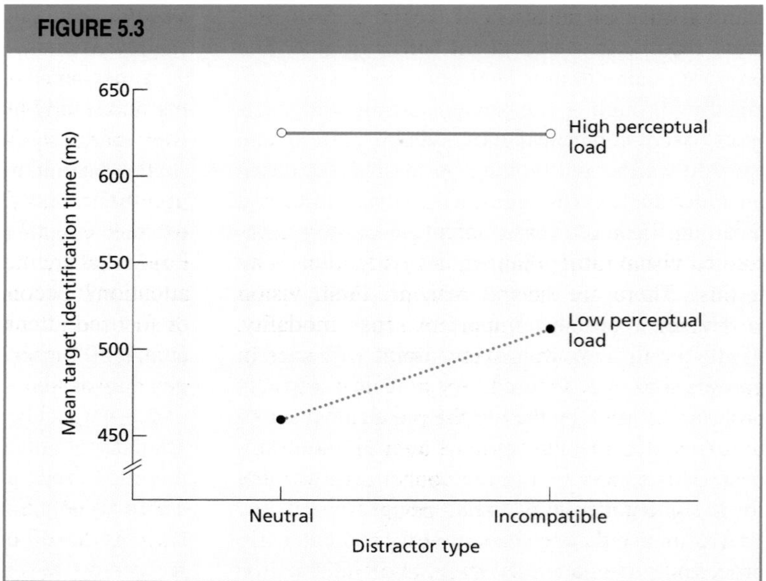

Mean target identification time as a function of distractor type (neutral vs. incompatible) and perceptual load (low vs. high). Based on data in Lavie (1995).

perceptual load is low. Perceptual load theory is discussed here because it is potentially applicable to auditory as well as to visual attention, and because it is very relevant to the controversy about early versus late selection. However, nearly all of the tests of the theory have involved visual attention.

Evidence

There is much support for perceptual load theory. For example, Lavie (1995) carried out an experiment in which the participants had to detect a target letter (an x or a z) appearing in one of six positions arranged in a row. In the high perceptual load condition, the other five positions were occupied by non-target letters, whereas none of those positions was occupied in the low perceptual load condition. Finally, a large distractor letter was also presented. On some trials, this letter was incompatible (i.e., it was x when the target was z or vice versa), and on other trials it was neutral. According to the theory, the nature of the distractor should have more effect on time to identify target stimuli when perceptual load is low than when it was high. As can be seen in Figure 5.3, that is precisely what happened.

Evaluation

The central notion behind perceptual load theory, namely that the extent to which task-irrelevant stimuli are processed is flexible, is an important one. It also seems reasonable that the extent of such processing should depend on the perceptual load associated with relevant stimuli. This theoretical approach also has the advantage that it reduces the earlier mistaken emphasis on trying to identify the location of a bottleneck in processing. As Styles (1997, p. 28) pointed out, "Discovering precisely where selection occurs is only one small part of the issues surrounding attention, and finding *where* selection takes place may not help us to understand *why* or *how* this happens."

There are two limitations with perceptual load theory. First, its applicability to auditory attention has not been clearly demonstrated, although it is assumed that the theory is relevant to auditory attention as well as to visual attention. Second, the concept of "perceptual load" is somewhat vague and no ways of measuring perceptual load precisely have been developed as yet.

FOCUSED VISUAL ATTENTION

Over the past 25 years, most researchers have studied visual rather than auditory attention. Why is this? There are several reasons. First, vision is probably our most important sense modality. Second, we can study a wider range of issues in the visual than in the auditory modality. Third, it is easier to control precisely the presentation times of visual stimuli than those of auditory stimuli.

Visual attention has been considered from the cognitive neuropsychological perspective. Three attentional disorders have been studied fairly thoroughly: neglect, extinction, and Balint's syndrome (see Driver, 1998, for a review). **Neglect** is typically found after brain damage in the right parietal lobe, and is often the result of a stroke. Neglect patients with right-hemisphere damage do not notice (or fail to respond to) objects presented to the left (or contralesional) side. For example, when neglect patients draw an object or copy a drawing, they typically leave out everything on the left side of it.

Extinction is a phenomenon frequently found in neglect patients. However, the disorders are distinct, and mainly co-occur because they involve damage to anatomically close brain areas (Karnath, Himmelbach, & Küker, 2003). A *single* stimulus on either side of the visual field can be judged normally. However, when *two* stimuli are presented together, the one further towards the side of the visual field away from the damage tends to go undetected. Some patients only show extinction when the two objects presented simultaneously are the same.

Balint's syndrome is associated with lesions in both hemispheres involving the posterior parietal lobe or parieto-occipital junction. It is characterised by various attentional problems. These include fixed gazing, gross misreaching for objects, and a strong tendency to attend to (and perceive) only one stimulus at a time (this is known as **simultagnosia**). As Martin (1998, p. 228) noted, "A patient with Balint's syndrome might focus quite narrowly on the tip of a cigarette in his or her mouth and be unable to see a match offered a short distance away."

There are more studies on focused visual attention than you can shake a stick at. Accordingly, we will consider only a few of the key issues. First, what are the major systems involved in visual attention? Second, what is selected in selective or focused attention? Third, what happens to unattended stimuli? Fourth, what has the study of visual disorders taught us about visual attention?

Major attentional systems

Several theorists (e.g., Corbetta & Shulman, 2002; Posner, 1980; Posner & Petersen, 1990; Yantis & Jonides, 1990) have argued that there are two major attentional systems (Posner's views are discussed below in the section headed "What is selected?"). In essence, one attentional system has variously been described as voluntary, endogenous, or goal directed, whereas the other system is regarded as involuntary, exogenous, or stimulus driven. In this section, we will focus mainly on the theoretical views of Corbetta and Shulman, which have the advantage that the main brain areas associated with each attentional system are identified. They distinguished between a goal-directed or top-down system involved in the selection of sensory information and responses and a stimulus-driven or bottom-up system involved in the detection of salient or conspicuous unattended visual stimuli.

The functioning of the goal-directed system is influenced by expectation, knowledge, and current goals. Thus, this system would be involved if participants were given a cue predicting the location, motion, or other characteristic of a forthcoming visual stimulus. According to Corbetta and Shulman (2002) this system consists of a dorsal fronto-parietal network (see Figure 5.4). In contrast, the stimulus-driven attentional system is used when an unexpected and potentially important stimulus (e.g., flames appearing under the door of your room) is presented. This system has a "circuit-breaking" function, meaning that visual

FIGURE 5.4

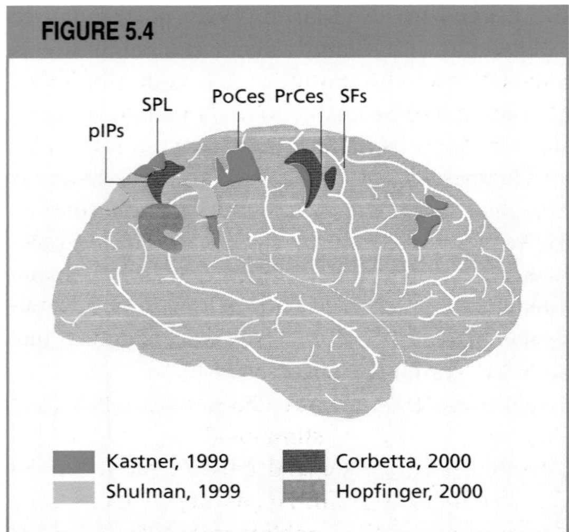

The brain network involved in the goal-directed attentional system, based on findings from various brain-imaging studies in which participants were expecting certain visual stimuli. The full names of the brain areas are in the text. From Corbetta and Shulman (2002). Copyright © 2002 by Nature Publishing Group. Reproduced with permission.

FIGURE 5.5

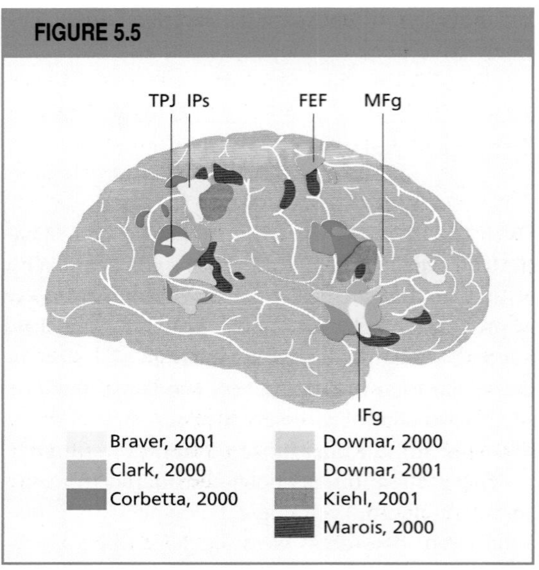

The brain network involved in the stimulus-driven attentional system, based on findings from various brain-imaging studies in which participants detected low-frequency target stimuli. The full names of the brain areas are in the text. From Corbetta and Shulman (2002). Copyright © 2002 by Nature Publishing Group. Reproduced with permission.

attention is redirected from its current focus. According to Corbetta and Shulman (2002), this system consists of a right-hemisphere ventral fronto-parietal network (see Figure 5.5).

We have seen that Corbetta and Shulman (2002) identified two rather separate attentional systems. However, in line with many other theorists, they assumed that these two systems interact and influence each other in most situations. Corbetta and Shulman (2002) addressed the issue of how the two attentional systems interact with each other. There is little directly relevant evidence, but they speculated that connections between the temporo-parietal junction and the intraparietal sulcus serve to interrupt goal-directed attention when unattended stimuli are detected. More specifically, the intraparietal sulcus provides the temporo-parietal junction with information concerning the significance of unexpected stimuli.

Evidence

Corbetta and Shulman (2002) carried out meta-analyses of brain-imaging studies of the goal-directed system. As can be seen in Figure 5.4, the brain areas most often activated while expecting a stimulus that has not yet been presented are the posterior intraparietal sulcus (pIPs), the superior parietal lobule (SPL), the postcentral sulcus (PoCes), the precentral sulcus (PrCes), and the superior frontal sulcus (SFs).

It can be seen in Figure 5.4 that somewhat different brain areas were activated from one study to the next. This probably reflects the fact that what participants expected varied across studies. They were expecting a stimulus at a given location in the Corbetta and Hopfinger studies, they expected a given direction of motion in the Shulman study, and they expected a complex visual array in the Kastner study. As Corbetta and Shulman (2002, p. 205) concluded, "The dorsal fronto-parietal network that is recruited when subjects expect to see object features other than location clearly overlaps with regions that are recruited by attending to location, but the exact overlap between regions recruited by different kinds of advance information is unclear, and many visual features have yet to be tested."

Corbetta and Shulman (2002) also carried out a meta-analysis of brain-imaging studies focusing on the stimulus-driven system, in which low-frequency targets were detected (see Figure 5.5). The brain areas in this attentional network include the temporo-parietal junction (TPJ), the intraparietal sulcus (IPs), the frontal eye field (FEF), and the middle frontal gyrus (Mfg). In spite of several differences in the precise tasks used from study to study, there is substantial overlap in the areas activated across studies, especially in areas like the temporo-parietal junction. Note that activation was primarily present in the right hemisphere in all of the studies contributing to the meta-analysis.

As was mentioned earlier, patients suffering from neglect generally ignore or neglect visual stimuli presented to the left side. According to Corbetta and Shulman (2002), neglect patients typically have damage to the stimulus-driven attentional system. This is supported by several findings. First, many neglect patients have damage to the right temporo-parietal junction (Vallar & Perani, 1987), which is an important part of the stimulus-driven system. Second, neglect is more common after damage to the right hemisphere than to the left one, and the stimulus-driven system is located in the right hemisphere. Third, neglect patients can voluntarily attend to the left side, and can use cues to direct attention to that side during rehabilitation (see Corbetta & Shulman, 2002). Additional support for the view that neglect mainly involves impairment to the stimulus-driven system is discussed later in the section on visual disorders.

We now consider the view (by no means unique to Corbetta & Shulman, 2002) that the two attentional systems typically interact with each other. It might seem as if there are many situations in which that is *not* the case. For example, stimulus-driven or involuntary processes would appear to be dominant when a flash of lightning causes us to look up at the sky. It is generally assumed that stimuli changing rapidly over time (especially those having abrupt onsets) attract attention, as do stimuli whose properties are very different from all other nearby stimuli. Strong evidence for involuntary or stimulus-driven attentional processes was reported by Remington, Johnston, and Yantis (1992). The participants carried out a task involving abrupt-onset target stimuli, and abrupt-onset distractors were also presented. The distractors were always presented at non-target locations, so attending to them was almost guaranteed to impair task performance. Remington et al. found that task performance was worse when the abrupt-onset distractors were presented, indicating that they captured attention.

Folk, Remington, and Johnston (1992) argued that involuntary or stimulus-driven capture of attention does *not* depend only on the nature of the distracting stimuli. According to them, only distracting stimuli resembling task stimuli in some way will capture attention. They used targets defined either in terms of colour or abrupt onset and the same was true of the distractors. When the participants looked for abrupt-onset targets, abrupt-onset distractors captured attention but colour distractors did not. In contrast, when the participants looked for colour targets, colour distractors captured attention but abrupt-onset distractors did not. Thus, involuntary capture depends on the relationship between the target and distractor stimuli rather than simply on the nature of the distracting stimuli themselves. These findings reflect the combined influence of the goal-directed and stimulus-driven systems.

Pashler (2001) extended the above findings. Participants searched for a given red digit in a display containing 30 stationary red digits and 30 green distractors. These green distractors either remained stationary or they twinkled and flashed. It would seem likely that all this twinkling and flashing would capture attention. However, search times for the red digit were no longer when the green distractors twinkled and flashed than when they did not. Presumably these twinkling and flashing distractors did not capture attention because their characteristics did not resemble those of the target stimuli.

The old idea that some visual stimuli will always attract attention to themselves is incorrect. What appears to be the case is that distractor stimuli sharing some property or characteristic with target stimuli capture attention in an involuntary or stimulus-driven way. As Pashler, Johnston, and Ruthroff (2001, p. 637) concluded, "Though the ability of the distractor stimuli themselves to draw attention is unwanted in a local sense, it is properly understood as an inevitable by-product of what the subject *is* voluntarily trying to attend." In other words, we need to consider interactions between the two attentional systems in order to understand the conditions in which distractor stimuli capture attention.

Evaluation

The theoretical views of Corbetta and Shulman (2002) represent a development and extension of pre-existing theoretical ideas. The assumption that there are separate goal-directed and stimulus-driven systems is strengthened by the accumulating evidence that distinct brain areas are involved in each system. In addition, the notion that neglect patients have damage to the stimulus-driven system is supported by much of the evidence (discussed further below). Furthermore, there is much support for the assumption that the two attentional systems generally function together and interact with each other.

Corbetta and Shulman's assumption that there are two attentional systems will probably be shown to be oversimplified as our knowledge of attention increases. We have seen in this chapter that attentional processes are involved in the performance of an extremely wide range of tasks, and it is unlikely that all these processes can be neatly assigned to one or other of Corbetta and Shulman's systems. Another limitation is that relatively little is known of the ways in which the two attentional systems interact with each other. Such interactions are undoubtedly complex, but need to be studied in detail if we are to develop a complete theory of visual attention.

What is selected?

There are three major answers to the question of what is selected in focused visual attention. First, we may selectively attend to an area or region of space, as when we look behind us to identify the source of a sound. Second, we may attend to a given object or objects. This seems reasonable in view of the fact that visual perception is mainly concerned with specific objects of interest to us (see Chapters 2 and 3). Third, our processing systems may be so flexible that we can attend either to an area of space *or* to a given object. These possibilities will be considered in turn.

Location-based attention

In some ways, focused visual attention seems to resemble a spotlight. Everything within a fairly small region of the visual field can be seen clearly, but it is much harder to see anything not falling within the beam of the attentional spotlight. A more complex view of focused visual attention was put forward by Eriksen and St. James (1986). According to their zoom-lens model, attention is directed to a given region of the visual field. However, the area of focal attention can be increased or decreased in line with task demands.

Evidence

Posner (1980) favoured the spotlight notion. He argued there can be **covert attention**, in which the attentional spotlight shifts to a different spatial location in the absence of an eye movement. In his studies, the participants responded as rapidly as possible when they detected the onset of a light. Shortly before the onset of the light, they were presented with a central cue (arrow pointing to the left or right) or a peripheral cue (brief illumination of a box outline). These cues were mostly valid (i.e., they indicated where the target light would appear), but sometimes they were invalid (i.e., they provided misleading information about the location of the target light).

Posner's (1980) key findings were that valid cues produced faster responding to light onset than did neutral cues (a central cross), whereas invalid cues produced slower responding than neutral cues. The findings were comparable for central and peripheral cues, and were obtained in the absence of eye movements. When the cues were valid on only a small fraction of trials, they were ignored when they were central cues, but affected performance when they were peripheral cues. These findings led Posner (1980) to distinguish between two systems:

(1) An endogenous system, controlled by the participant's intentions and involved when central cues are presented; this resembles Corbetta and Shulman's (2002) goal-directed system.
(2) An exogenous system, which automatically shifts attention and is involved when uninformative peripheral cues are presented; this resembles Corbetta and Shulman's (2002) stimulus-driven system.

How different are the endogenous and exogenous attention systems? Rosen et al. (1999) found in an fMRI study that similar brain areas (e.g., the superior parietal regions) were activated by both systems. However, there was greater activation over a larger brain area with endogenous than with exogenous orienting. As Umiltà (2001, p. 147) noted, "This is consistent with the notion that endogenous orienting is controlled and effortful, whereas exogenous orienting is automatic and reflexive."

O'Craven, Downing and Kanwisher (2000) obtained findings supporting the notion that attention can be location based. The participants were presented with two ovals of different colours, one to the left of fixation and one to the right. They had to indicate the orientation of the one in a given colour. Each oval was superimposed on a task-irrelevant face or house. O'Craven, Downing and Kanwisher (2000) used fMRI, making use of the fact that the fusiform face area is selectively activated when faces are processed, whereas the parahippocampal place area is selectively activated when houses are processed. As predicted on the basis that attention is location based, fMRI indicated that there was more processing of the stimulus superimposed on the attended oval than of the stimulus superimposed on the unattended oval.

Evidence in favour of the zoom-lens model was reported by LaBerge (1983). Five-letter words were presented. A probe requiring rapid response was occasionally presented instead of (or immediately after) the word. The probe could appear in the spatial position of any of the five letters of the word. In one condition, an attempt was made to focus the participants' attention on the middle letter of the five-letter word by asking them to categorise that letter. In another condition, the participants were required to categorise the entire word. It was expected that this would lead the participants to adopt a broader attentional beam.

The findings on speed of detection of the probe are shown in Figure 5.6. LaBerge (1983) assumed the probe was responded to faster when it fell within the central attentional beam than when it

FIGURE 5.6

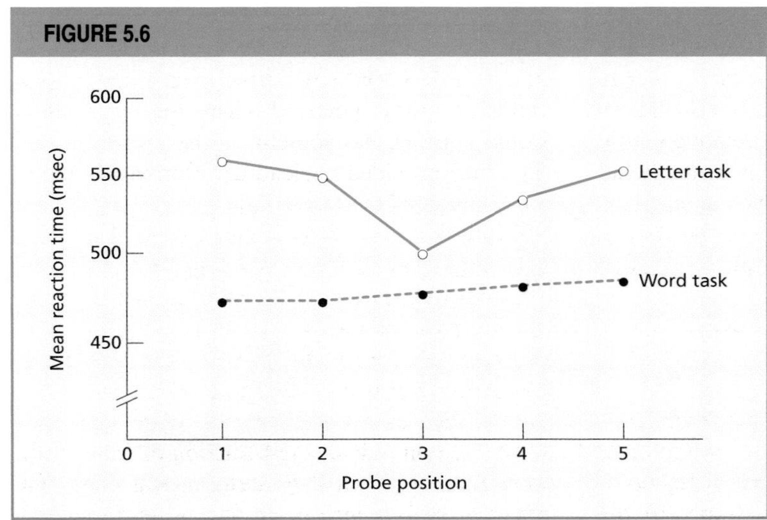

Mean reaction time to the probe as a function of probe position. The probe was presented at the time that a letter string would have been presented. Data from LaBerge (1983).

did not. On this assumption, the attentional spotlight can have either a very narrow beam (letter task) or rather broad beam (word task).

Eriksen and St. James (1986) also obtained support for the zoom-lens model. Their participants performed a task on a target stimulus whose location was indicated beforehand. Performance was impaired by the presence of distracting visual stimuli. However, the area over which interference effects were found was less when the participants had longer forewarning of the target stimulus. Presumably visual attention zoomed in more precisely on the area around the target stimulus over time.

According to the zoom-lens model, it should not be possible for people to show **split attention**, in which attention is directed to two regions of space not adjacent to each other. Awh and Pashler (2000) carried out a study on split attention. The participants were presented with a 5 × 5 visual display containing 23 letters and 2 digits, and had to report the identity of the digits. Just before the display was presented, the participants were given two cues indicating the likely locations of the two digits. However, these cues were invalid on 20% of trials. Part of what was involved can be seen in Figure 5.7a. The crucial condition was the one in which the cues were invalid, with one of the digits being presented in between the cued locations. If attention is directed to an area of space, performance should be high for this digit. In contrast, if split attention is possible, performance should be low. In fact, performance was much lower than

FIGURE 5.7

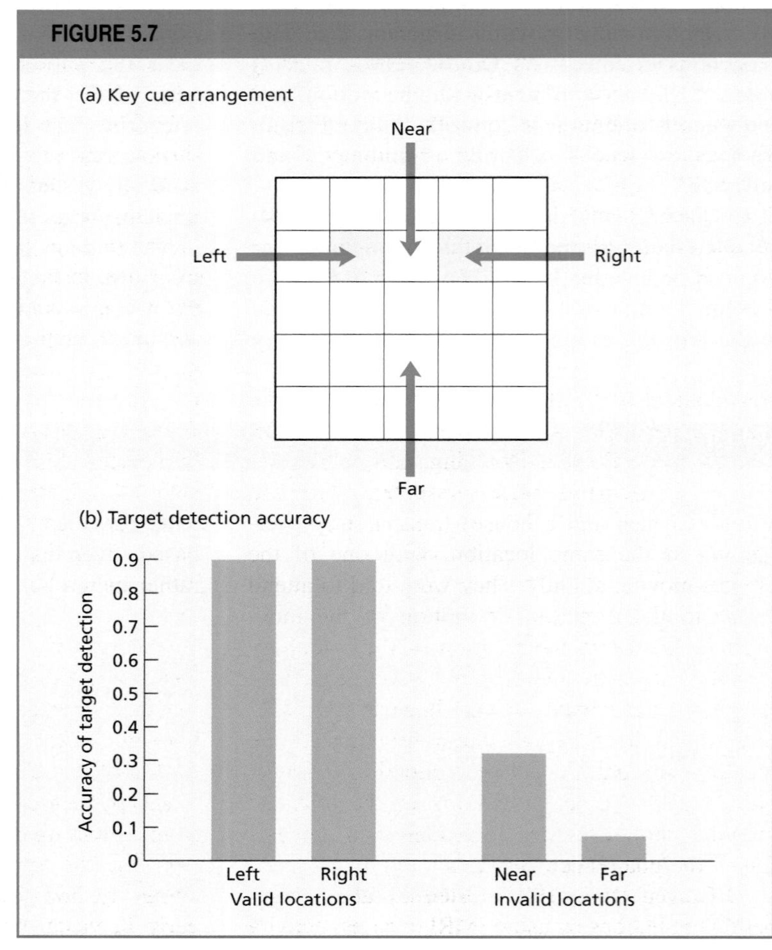

(a) Shaded areas indicate the cued locations and the near and far locations are not cued. Based on information in Awh and Pashler (2000). (b) Probability of target detection at valid (left or right) and invalid (near or far) locations. Based on information in Awh and Pashler (2000).

for digits presented to cued locations, indicating split attention is possible (see Figure 5.7b).

Evaluation

Visual attention can be directed to a given region of space, which is in line with the spotlight and zoom-lens models. As the zoom-lens model predicts, the size of the visual field within focal attention can vary substantially. However, there are four major limitations with such theoretical approaches to visual attention. First, there is convincing evidence that attention can be split between two non-adjacent regions of space. Second, as we will see shortly, there is good evidence that visual attention can be directed to objects rather than to a region of space. Third, the zoom-lens model implies that there is little processing of visual stimuli not in the attended region of space. However, as we will see, there is convincing evidence that unattended visual stimuli can be processed reasonably thoroughly. Fourth, it is assumed theoretically that the area surrounding the spotlight or zoom lens is simply ignored. In fact, Slotnick, Hopfinger, Klein, and Sutter (2002), using event-related potentials (ERPs; see Chapter 1), found that there is an area of attentional inhibition around the spotlight or zoom lens.

Object-based attention

Visual attention is often directed to *objects* rather than to a particular *region*. Consider, for example, a study by O'Craven, Downing, and Kanwisher (1999). Participants were presented with two stimuli (a face and a house) transparently overlapping at the same location, with one of the objects moving slightly. They were told to attend *either* to the direction of motion of the moving stimulus *or* to the position of the stationary stimulus. Suppose attention is location based. In that case, participants would have to attend to both stimuli, because both stimuli were in the same location. In contrast, suppose attention is object based. In that case, processing of the attended stimulus should be more thorough than processing of the unattended stimulus.

O'Craven et al. (1999) tested the above competing predictions by using fMRI to assess activity in brain areas selectively involved in processing faces (fusiform face area) or houses (parahippocampal place area). There was more activity in the fusiform face area when the face stimulus was attended than unattended, and more activity in the parahippocampal place area when the house stimulus was attended than unattended. Thus, attention was object based rather than location based.

There is also evidence for object-based selection from studies on patients with neglect. For example, Marshall and Halligan (1994) presented a patient with neglect in the left visual field with ambiguous displays, each of which could be seen as a black shape against a white background or as a white shape on a black background. There was a jagged edge dividing the two shapes at the centre of each display. The patient copied this jagged edge when asked to draw the shape on the left side of the display, but could not copy exactly the same edge when asked to draw the shape on the right side. Thus, the patient attended to objects rather than simply to a region of visual space.

Halligan and Marshall (1993) asked a neglect patient to copy a drawing of a plant in a pot. The plant consisted of a stem from which emerged two branches, each of which had a flower on it. The patient only copied the right branch, leaving out the left branch altogether. The drawing was then altered by omitting the common stem and the pot, so that only two unconnected branches with flowers on remained. The patient copied both branches and flowers, but failed to include the left sides of the objects. This patient's attentional problems were clearly object based rather than location based, given that the omissions centred on objects rather than a particular part of visual space.

Evaluation

Visual attention can be object based, with some of the most convincing findings coming from neglect patients. It is not surprising that visual attention is often object based, given that the goal of visual perception is generally to identify objects in the environment. It is also relevant to remember that the grouping processes (e.g., law of similarity, law of proximity) that occur relatively early in visual perception help to segregate the visual environment into figure (central object) and ground (see Chapter 2). The major limitation of object-based accounts of visual attention is that (as we have seen) attention can also be location based. Accordingly, object-based views fail to provide a complete explanation of visual attention.

Location- and object-based attention

The evidence discussed so far suggests strongly that visual attention can be either location based or object based. The notion that visual attention can operate in either way is strengthened by the existence of studies obtaining evidence for both location-based and object-based attention. For example, consider a study by Egly, Driver, and Rafal (1994). They used displays like those shown in Figure 5.8. The task was to detect a target stimulus as quickly as possible. A cue was presented before the target, and this cue was either valid (same location as target) or invalid (different location from target). Of key importance, invalid cues were either in the same object as the target or in a different object. Target detection was slower on invalid trials than on valid ones. On invalid trials, target detection was slower when the cue was in a different object, suggesting that attention was at least partially object based.

Egly et al. (1994) also used the same displays to test patients suffering from brain damage to either the right or the left parietal area. There were two key findings. When the cue was presented to the same side as the brain damage, but the target was presented to the opposite side, right-parietal patients showed a greater slowing of target detection than did left-parietal patients. This occurred because the right-parietal patients had greater impairment to the location-based component of visual attention, and so could not switch attention from one part of visual space to another as rapidly as the left-parietal patients. The other key finding was that only left-parietal patients had particular problems in dealing with the situation in which the cue and target were in different objects. This suggests that the object-based component of visual attention is based in the left hemisphere.

When we are searching the visual environment, it would be inefficient if we repeatedly attended to any given location. This could be avoided if we possess inhibitory processes reducing the probability of that happening. Thus, we may possess a bias favouring the processing of novel locations and objects. Of direct relevance here is the phenomenon of **inhibition of return**, which is "a reduced perceptual priority for information in a region that recently enjoyed a higher priority"

FIGURE 5.8

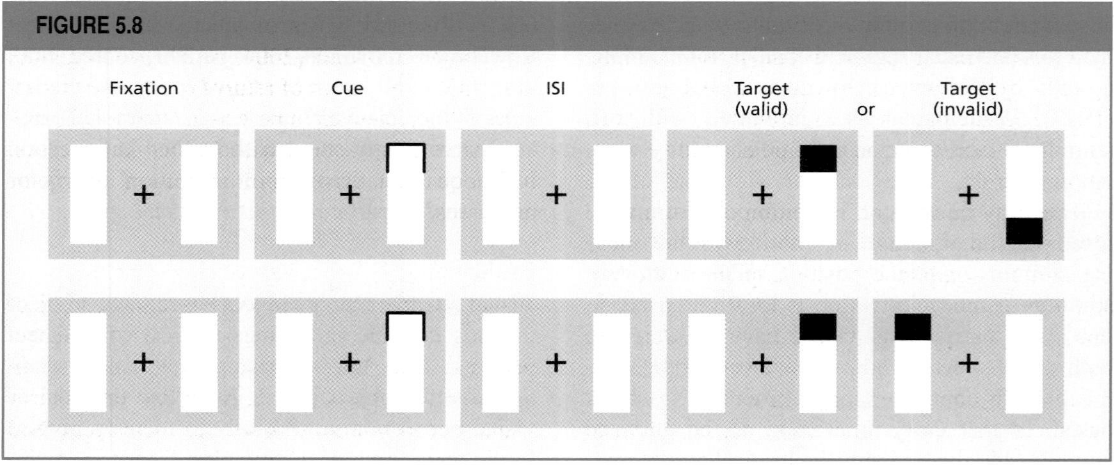

Examples of the displays used by Egly et al. (1994). The heavy black lines in the panels of the second column represent the cue. The filled squares in the panels of the fourth and fifth columns represent the target stimulus. In the fifth column, the top row shows a within-object invalid trial, whereas the bottom row shows a between-object invalid trial. From Umiltà (2001).

(Samuel & Kat, 2003, p. 897). One of the central issues here is whether inhibition of return applies to locations or to objects. To anticipate a little, we will see that inhibition of return (involving exogenous attention) is location based *and* object based.

Posner and Cohen (1984) provided the original demonstration of inhibition of return. There were two boxes, one on each side of the fixation point. An uninformative cue was presented in one of the boxes (e.g., its outline brightened). This was followed by the presentation of a target stimulus (e.g., an asterisk) in one of the boxes, with the participant's task being to respond as rapidly as possible when it was detected. When the time interval between cue and target was under 300 ms, targets in the cued location were detected faster than targets in the non-cued location. However, when the time interval exceeded about 300 ms, there was inhibition of return, with targets in the cued location being responded to more slowly than those in the non-cued location.

Samuel and Kat (2003) carried out a meta-analysis to explore the time course of inhibition of return. The amount of inhibition of return was fairly constant for cue–target intervals of between 300 and 1600 ms, and was still clearly present up to about 3000 ms. However, there was an important change in one key aspect of inhibition of return over this time period: degree of inhibition was greater when there was little spatial distance between cue and target with cue–target intervals up to 1 second, but this effect disappeared thereafter. Thus, the processes underlying inhibition of return vary depending on the time interval between cue and target.

The early findings on inhibition of return were somewhat ambiguous, in that it was not clear whether the inhibitory effects applied to a given *location* or to a given *object*. Leek, Reppa, and Tipper (2003) proposed a two-component model according to which object-based and location-based inhibition of return both exist. It follows that the magnitude of inhibitory effect observed under standard conditions (with an object present as in Posner & Cohen, 1984) is a summation of location- and object-based inhibition of return. Leek et al. compared inhibition of return under conditions in which an object was absent or present. According to the model, an inhibitory effect should be present in the object-absent condition (due to location-based inhibition of return), but should be stronger in the object-present condition (due to location-based + object-based inhibition of return). As predicted, inhibition of return was obtained in both conditions but was stronger in the object-present than the object-absent condition (40 ms vs.18 ms, respectively).

What inhibitory processes underlie inhibition of return? Two major types of answer have been proposed to that question. According to Posner (e.g., Posner & Cohen, 1984) the phenomenon is due to inhibition of perceptual and/or attentional processes. In contrast, Taylor and Klein (1998) argued that it is due to inhibition of motor processes. Of course, it is entirely possible that inhibition of return depends on multiple mechanisms including both perceptual and motor ones, but the available evidence is inconclusive.

Prime and Ward (2004) reported an interesting study using event-related potentials (ERPs) to clarify the processes involved in inhibition of return. Their most important ERP finding was that early visual processing of targets presented to the location previously cued was reduced (or inhibited) compared to that of targets presented to a different location. In contrast, the ERP evidence failed to indicate any difference in motor processes between the two types of target. These findings led Prime and Ward (2004, p. 272) to conclude that, "IOR [inhibition of return] must arise at least in part from changes in perceptual processes, and, at least when measured with manual key presses, IOR does not arise from inhibition of motor processes."

Evaluation

Visual attention can be location based or object based, and there is some evidence that different regions of the brain may be mainly involved in these two forms of attention. What remains unclear is the precise relationship between location-based and object-based visual attention. There are really two issues here. First, are these two types of attentional selection mutually exclusive, in the sense that only one can operate at any one time? Second, if they are not mutually exclusive, does one type of attentional selection precede the other or do they occur at the same time in an interactive process? Mozer and Sitton (1998) argued that object-based selection operates either before or at the same time as location-based selection, but the evidence is inconclusive.

The notion that visual attention can be location based or object based is strengthened by research on inhibition of return. There is some controversy concerning the mechanisms responsible for inhibition of return, and several mechanisms may play a role. However, the findings of Prime and Ward (2004) suggest that inhibition of return is mainly associated with reduced sensory processing.

What happens to unattended visual stimuli?

Neurophysiological evidence indicates that there is reduced processing of unattended visual stimuli (see Umiltà, 2001, for a review). For example, Wojciulik, Kanwisher, and Driver (1998) presented participants with displays containing two faces and two houses. There was a same–different judgement task that applied in separate blocks to the faces or to the houses, with the other type of stimulus being unattended. An area of the brain (the fusiform face area), which apparently responds selectively to faces, was assessed by fMRI (see Chapter 1). Activity in the fusiform face area was significantly greater when the faces needed to be attended to than when they did not, indicating that they received less processing when unattended.

Event-related potentials (ERPs) are generally greater to attended than to unattended stimuli. For example, Martinez et al. (1999) compared ERPs to attended and unattended visual displays. The attended displays produced a greater first positive wave (P1) approximately 70–75 ms after stimulus presentation and a greater first negative wave (N1) about 130–140 ms after stimulus presentation. However, there was no effect of attention on ERPs 50–55 ms after stimulus presentation, indicating that attentional processes do not influence the very early stages of processing. Martinez et al. also made use of fMRI. Attention was associated with increased activation of visual areas V2, V3, and V4 (see Chapter 2), supporting the notion that intermediate stages of processing are influenced by attention.

Earlier in the chapter we discussed Lavie's (1995, 2000) perceptual load theory. She argued that there is more processing of unattended stimuli when the perceptual load associated with processing relevant stimuli is low than when it is high. Findings supporting this theory were reported by Lavie (1995; see Figure 5.3).

Evidence that there can be more processing of unattended visual stimuli than initially seems to be the case has been reported with neglect patients. McGlinchey-Berroth et al. (1993) asked such patients to decide which of two drawings matched a drawing presented immediately beforehand to the left or the right visual field. Neglect patients performed well when the initial drawing was presented to the right visual field but at chance level when it was presented to the left visual field (see Figure 5.9). The latter finding suggests that stimuli in the left visual field were not processed. However, a very different conclusion emerged from a second study, in which neglect patients decided whether letter strings formed words. Decision times were faster on "yes" trials when the letter string was preceded by a semantically related object rather than an unrelated object. This effect was the same size regardless of whether the object was presented to the left or the right visual field (see Figure 5.9), indicating some semantic processing of left-field stimuli by neglect patients.

In sum, studies on neglect and extinction patients and neuroimaging studies on intact individuals both reveal some processing of unattended stimuli, although less than for attended stimuli. However, studies on brain-damaged patients suggest there is greater processing of unattended visual stimuli than appears from neuroimaging studies. Umiltà (2001, p. 153) offered a speculative interpretation of this apparent difference: "Facilitation of attended information occurs at early stages, which are tapped by neurophysiological methods, whereas inhibition of unattended information occurs at later stages, which are tapped by neuropsychological tasks." Thus, there may be a reasonable amount of processing of unattended visual stimuli even though they produce less

FIGURE 5.9

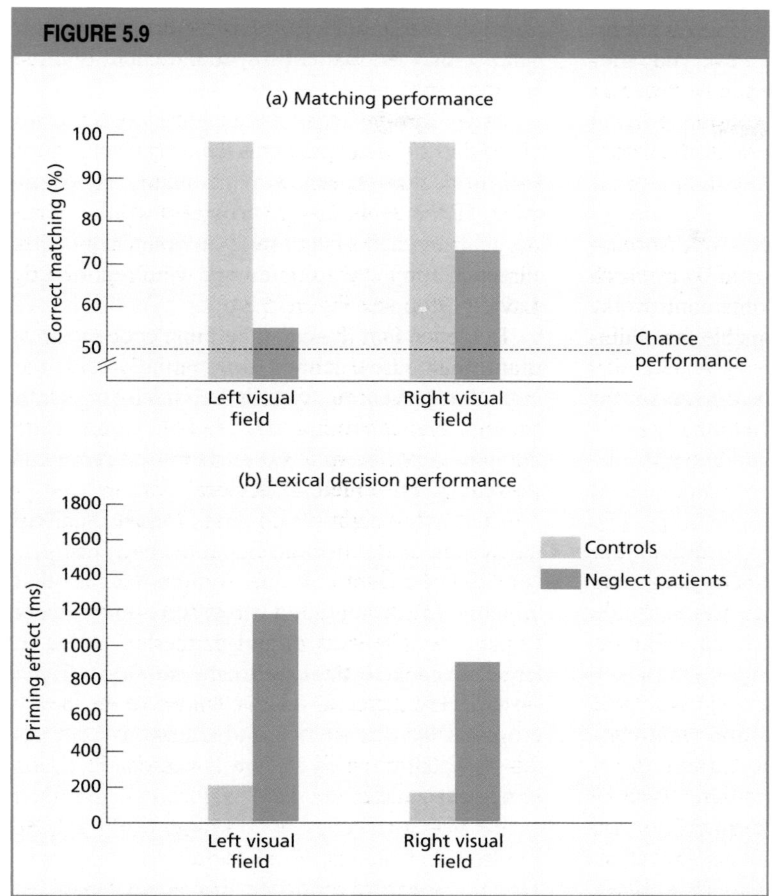

Effects of prior presentation of a drawing to the left or right visual field on matching performance and lexical decision in neglect patients. Data from McGlinchey-Berroth et al. (1993).

activation of the visual cortical areas than attended visual stimuli.

Disorders of visual attention

As was mentioned earlier, cognitive neuropsychologists have studied several disorders of visual attention. The most investigated of such disorders are neglect and extinction, and that is where we start our coverage.

Neglect and extinction

Neglect (also known as unilateral neglect) is a condition in which there is a lack of awareness of stimuli presented to the side of space on the opposite side to the brain damage (the contralesional side). In the great majority of patients, the brain damage is in the right hemisphere (involving the inferior parietal lobe), and there is little awareness of stimuli on the left side of the visual field. This occurs because of the nature of the visual system, with information from the left side of the visual field proceeding to the right hemisphere of the brain. According to Driver and Vuilleumier (2001, p. 40), "Neglect patients often behave as if half of their world no longer exists. In daily life, they may be oblivious to objects and people on the neglected side of the room, may eat from only one side of their plate, . . . and make-up or shave only one side of their face."

Neglect patients sometimes detect a single stimulus presented to their left visual field, but fail to detect the same stimulus when another stimulus is presented to the right of it. This phenomenon is known as extinction. Extinction is important because we are typically confronted by multiple stimuli at the same time in everyday life.

There are clear similarities between neglect and extinction, in that they both involve a tendency to ignore stimuli presented to the contralesional side combined with a good ability to attend to stimuli presented to the same side as the brain damage (the ipsilesional side). However, the two disorders are separate, and some patients suffer only from neglect or only from extinction (Karnath et al., 2003). In addition, neglect is a more serious disorder than extinction.

Neglect is of theoretical interest because "so many of the neural pathways conventionally associated with conscious perception (including primary sensory areas) remain intact in many neglect patients" (Driver & Vuilleumier, 2001, p. 45). Neglect is also of importance because stimuli that are unattended and of which there is no conscious awareness can nevertheless receive a reasonable amount of processing (e.g., McGlinchey-Beroth et al., 1993, discussed earlier).

How can we explain neglect? Driver and Vuilleumier (2001, p. 40) argued that what happens in neglect patients is a more extreme form of what happens in healthy individuals: "Perceptual awareness is not determined solely by the stimuli impinging on our senses, but also by which of these stimuli we choose to attend. This choice seems pathologically restricted in neglect patients, with their attention strongly biased towards events on the ipsilesional side [same side as the lesion]." Thus, there are important similarities between neglect in patients and inattention in healthy individuals.

How can we explain extinction? Marzi et al. (2001, p. 1354) offered the following explanation: "The presence of extinction only during bilateral stimulation is strongly suggestive of a competition mechanism, whereby the presence of a more salient stimulus presented on the same side of space as that of the brain lesion (ipsilesional side) captures attention and hampers the perception of a less salient stimulus on the opposite (contralesional) side." Driver and Vuilleumier (2001, p. 50) provided a similar account of neglect: "While extinction is by no means the whole story for neglect, it encapsulates a critical general principle that applies for most aspects of neglect, namely that the patient's spatial deficit is most apparent in *competitive* situations."

As we saw earlier in the chapter, Corbetta and Shulman (2002) argued that the attentional problems of neglect patients are due mainly to impairment of the stimulus-driven system rather than the goal-directed system (relevant evidence is discussed below). Bartolomeo and Chokron (2002, p. 217) proposed a very similar hypothesis: "A basic mechanism leading to left neglect behaviour is an impaired exogenous [originating outside the individual] orienting towards left-sided targets. In contrast, endogenous processes [originating inside the individual] seem to be relatively preserved, if slowed, in left unilateral neglect."

There is a reasonable amount of overlap among the various theoretical accounts we have just discussed. For example, it may well be the case that impaired functioning of a competition mechanism in patients with neglect and extinction is due in large measure to damage to the stimulus-driven system. However, a distinctive feature of the theory proposed by Bartolomeo and Chokron (2002) is that the goal-directed system is reasonably intact in neglect patients.

Evidence

There is plentiful evidence that neglect patients do process stimuli on the neglected side of the visual field. For example, Marshall and Halligan (1988) presented a neglect patient with two drawings of a house that were identical, except that the house presented to the left visual field had flames coming out of one of its windows. The patient could not report any differences between the two drawings, but indicated that she would prefer to live in the house on the right.

Vuilleumier and Rafal (1999) discovered that extinguished stimuli can be processed to some extent. Neglect patients tried to identify the location of a target stimulus. In one condition, a single target was presented to the right visual field; in another condition, two targets were presented together, one to each visual field. The participants reported the same conscious perception in both cases (i.e., a single target presented to the right visual field). However, the patients took longer to detect the right-field target when a second, undetected target was presented to the left visual field.

Further evidence that extinguished stimuli are processed was reported by Rees et al. (2000) in an fMRI study. Extinguished stimuli produced moderate levels of activation in the primary visual cortex and some nearby areas, suggesting that these stimuli of which the patient was unaware were nonetheless processed reasonably thoroughly.

The notion that neglect and extinction involve an exaggerated form of the attentional limitations found in healthy individuals has received some support. Duncan (1980) found that normal individuals sometimes missed one of two targets presented simultaneously for a very brief period of time, even though they practically never missed either target when presented on its own. This seems very similar to extinction.

Duncan (1984) found in a subsequent study that healthy individuals showed much better detection of two simultaneous targets when they were both attributes of the same objects. In these circumstances, the two targets did not compete with each other for attention. A similar finding with an extinction patient was reported by Mattingley, Davis, and Driver (1997). There was extinction for black circles with quarter-segments removed which were presented to the contralesional side at the same time as similar stimuli were presented to the ipsilesional side. However, there was very much less evidence for extinction when the stimuli were altered slightly to form Kanizsa's illusory square (see Figure 2.13). Rather similar findings were found with neglect patients by Vuilleumier and Landis (1998). Thus, patients with neglect and extinction can group visual stimuli from both sides of the visual field, thereby reducing attentional competition and allowing them to gain conscious access to stimuli presented to the contralesional side.

As was mentioned earlier, it has been argued that a competition mechanism plays an important role in extinction. Relevent evidence was reported by Marzi et al. (1997). They found that extinction patients detected contralesional stimuli more slowly than ipsilesional ones when only one stimulus was presented at a time. Those patients showing the greatest difference in detecting contralesional and ipsilesional stimuli had the greatest severity of extinction. What do these findings mean? According to Marzi et al., extinction occurs in part because the contralesional stimuli cannot *compete* successfully for attention. The greater the slowness of processing contralesional stimuli compared to ipsilesional stimuli, the less their ability to compete for attention.

Some theorists (e.g., Bartolomeo & Chokron, 2002) have claimed that neglect is due to impaired exogenous orienting (or stimulus-driven processing) rather than endogenous orienting (or goal-directed attention). We will consider three studies providing evidence that neglect patients have reasonably good endogenous orienting. First, Smania et al. (1998) compared the time to detect stimuli when the side on which they would appear was predictable (thus permitting endogenous orienting) and when presented randomly (thus not permitting endogenous orienting). Neglect patients responded faster in *both* visual fields when presentation side was predictable, thus showing evidence for endogenous orienting.

Second, Bartolomeo, Siéroff, Decaix, and Chokron (2001) carried out an experiment in which a visual cue presented to one side of visual space predicted that the target would probably be presented to the other side. Endogenous orienting or goal-directed attention is required to shift attention away from the cue to the probable target location. Neglect patients resembled normals in that they responded rapidly when the cue was presented to the right side and the target to the left side.

Third, Duncan et al. (1999) presented arrays of letters briefly, and asked neglect patients either to recall all the letters or to recall only those letters in a pre-specified colour. It was assumed that endogenous orienting was possible only in the latter condition. As expected, recall of letters presented to the left side was much worse than that of letters presented to the right side when all letters had to be reported. However, neglect patients resembled normal controls in showing approximately equal recall of letters presented to each side of visual space when target letters were defined by colour. Thus, neglect patients have reasonable endogenous or top-down attentional control.

Evaluation

The study of neglect and extinction patients has proved of relevance to several key theoretical issues in visual attention. First, such patients have problems with both location-based and object-based attention. Second, there is convincing evidence that neglect and extinction patients can process unattended stimuli, and sometimes this processing is at the semantic level (e.g., McGlinchey-Berroth et al., 1993). Third, such patients provide evidence about the range of preattentive processing, which can include grouping of visual stimuli (e.g., Mattingley et al., 1997). Fourth, there is accumulating evidence that neglect patients have severe impairments of exogenous orienting but much milder impairment of endogenous orienting.

On the negative side, there remains theoretical controversy about the precise differences in attentional processing between neglect and extinction patients. In addition, as Driver and Vuilleumier (2001, p. 49) pointed out, "Attentional accounts for neglect are not universally popular. Sceptics point out that little explanation is offered until the concept of attention is fleshed out in mechanistic terms."

Three attentional abilities

Posner and Petersen (1990) proposed a theoretical framework, according to which three separate abilities are involved in controlling the attentional spotlight:

- *Disengagement* of attention from a given visual stimulus.
- *Shifting* of attention from one target stimulus to another.
- *Engaging* or locking attention on a new visual stimulus.

These three abilities are all functions of the posterior attention system (resembling the stimulus-driven system of Corbetta & Shulman, 2002). In addition, there is an anterior attention system (resembling the goal-directed system of Corbetta & Shulman, 2002). This is involved in coordinating the different aspects of visual attention, and resembles the central executive component of the working memory system (see Chapter 6). According to Posner and Petersen (1990, p. 40), there is "a hierarchy of attentional systems in which the anterior system can pass control to the posterior system when it is not occupied with processing other material."

Posner (1995) developed these ideas. The anterior attentional system based in the frontal lobes was regarded as controlling stimulus selection and the allocation of mental resources. The posterior attentional system is influenced by the anterior system and controls lower-level aspects of attention, such as the disengagement of attention.

Disengagement of attention

As we have seen, patients with neglect have suffered damage to the parietal region of the brain. Additional evidence that the parietal area is important in attention was reported by Petersen, Corbetta, Miezin, and Shulman (1994). PET scans indicated that there was much activation within the parietal area when attention shifted from one spatial location to another. Losier and Klein (2001) carried out a meta-analysis of studies focusing on disengagement of attention in brain-damaged patients. They found that problems of disengagement of attention were greater in patients suffering from neglect than in other brain-damaged patients.

Problems with disengaging attention are also found in Balint's syndrome patients suffering from simultanagnosia. In this condition (mentioned earlier), only one object (out of two or more) can be seen at any one time, even when the objects are close together. As most of these patients have full visual fields, it seems that the attended visual object exerts a "hold" on attention that makes disengagement difficult. However, neglected stimuli are processed to some extent. Coslett and Saffran (1991) observed strong effects of semantic relatedness between two briefly presented words in a patient with simultanagnosia.

Shifting of attention

Posner et al. (1985) examined problems of shifting attention by studying patients suffering from progressive supranuclear palsy. Such patients have damage to the midbrain, and find it very hard to make voluntary eye movements, especially in the vertical direction. These patients responded to visual targets, and there were sometimes cues to the locations of forthcoming targets. There was a short, intermediate, or long interval between the cue and the target. At all intervals, valid cues (cues providing accurate information about target location) speeded up responding to the targets when the targets were presented to the left or the right of the cue. However, only cues at the long interval aided responding with targets presented above or below the cues. Thus, the patients had difficulty in shifting their attention in the vertical direction.

Attentional deficits apparently associated with shifting of attention have been studied in patients with Balint's syndrome. These patients have difficulty in reaching for stimuli using visual guidance. Humphreys and Riddoch (1993) presented two Balint's patients with 32 circles in a display. The circles were either all the same colour, or half were one colour and the other half a different colour. The circles were either close together or spaced, and the task was to decide whether they were all the same colour. On trials where there were circles of two colours, one of the patients (SA) performed much better when the circles were close together than when spaced (79% vs. 62%, respectively). The other patient (SP) performed equivalently in both conditions (62% vs. 59%, respectively). Apparently some patients with Balint's syndrome (e.g., SA) find it hard to shift attention within the visual field.

Evidence that Balint's patients can only attend to one object at a time was reported by Humphreys and Riddoch (1993). When Balint's patients were presented with a mixture of red and green circles, they were generally unable to report seeing both colours. Presumably this happened because the patients could only attend to a single circle at a time. However, when the red and green circles were joined by lines (so each object contained red and green), their performance was much better.

Karnath et al. (2000) obtained evidence that the capture of attention by a specific stimulus does not entirely prevent processing of other stimuli. A patient (KB) with Balint's syndrome and simultagnosia was presented with stimuli consisting of a large letter formed from small letters which could be the same as, or different from, the large letter (see Figure 5.10). KB could identify the small letters but not the large letter. This suggests she could not shift her attention from the local level to the global level. However, KB processed some information from the global letter: when the large letter had the same identity as the small letters, the small letters were named faster than when it did not (790 vs. 806 milliseconds, respectively).

FIGURE 5.10

```
S          S
S          S
S          S
S          S
S          S
SSSSSSSSSSSS
S          S
S          S
S          S
S          S
S          S
```

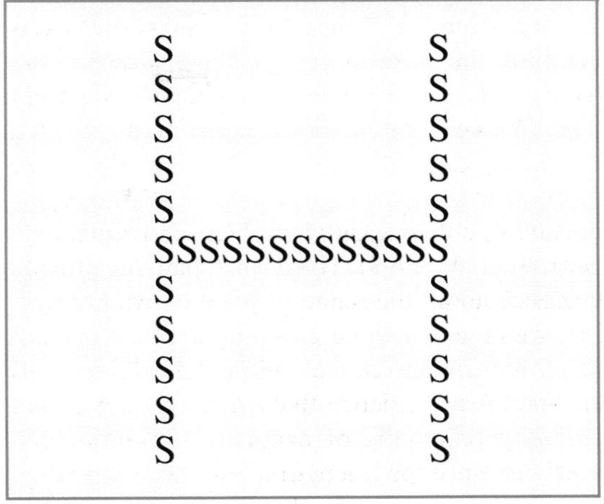

The kind of stimulus used by Karnath et al. (2000) to demonstrate the importance of global features in perception.

Engaging attention

Rafal and Posner (1987) studied problems of engaging attention in patients with damage to the pulvinar nucleus of the thalamus. These patients responded to visual targets preceded by cues. The patients responded faster when the cues were valid than when they were invalid, regardless of whether the target stimulus was presented to the same side as the brain damage or to the opposite side. However, they responded rather slowly following both kinds of cues when the target stimulus was presented to the contralesional side of the visual field. According to Rafal and Posner, these findings reflect a problem the patients have in engaging attention to such stimuli.

Additional evidence that the pulvinar nucleus of the thalamus is involved in controlling focused attention was obtained by LaBerge and Buchsbaum

(1990). PET scans indicated increased activation in the pulvinar nucleus when participants ignored a given stimulus. Thus, the pulvinar nucleus is involved in preventing attention from being focused on an unwanted stimulus as well as in directing attention to significant stimuli.

Evaluation

Several fairly specific attentional problems have been found in brain-damaged patients. As a result, it makes sense to assume that the attentional system consists of various components. At a general level, we can distinguish among disengaging of attention from a stimulus, shifting of attention, and engaging of attention on a new stimulus. However, we must be careful not to oversimplify a complex reality. The extent to which damage to one of these components impairs attention typically depends on the nature of the visual display and of the precise task given to the individual patient. We are still some way from understanding the detailed underlying processes involved in disengaging, shifting, and engaging attention.

CROSSMODAL EFFECTS

Nearly all the research discussed so far has been limited in that the visual modality has been studied on its own. In the real world, in contrast, we often need to coordinate information from two or more sense modalities at the same time (this is known as **crossmodal attention**). Crossmodal effects (although neglected by cognitive psychologists until fairly recently) are of great importance in everyday life. For example, when crossing the road, we sometimes use the sound of a car to direct visual attention. More generally, as Driver and Spence (1998b, p. 255) pointed out:

> When taken in isolation, each modality signals stimulus location with respect to its own receptor surface only (e.g., on the eye for vision . . .). Since the receptors for each modality can move freely relative to external objects (as in eye- or hand-movements), and can also move relative to each other (as when making an eye-movement but no hand-movement, or vice versa), a single modality alone cannot provide a stable representation of external space.

It is useful in considering crossmodal attention to use the distinction discussed earlier between endogenous, "voluntary", or goal-directed mechanisms of attention (influenced by expectations) and exogenous or stimulus-driven mechanisms determined in an "involuntary" way by external stimuli. The central issue is whether attention shifts to the same spatial location across different modalities of stimulation. In view of the complexity of many of the studies in this area, it is helpful to indicate beforehand what has been found. In essence, there is compelling evidence that the visual, auditory, and tactile modalities cooperate with each other. More specifically, stimulation in one modality (e.g., auditory) at a given location in space serves to direct attention in another modality (e.g., visual) to that location.

Exogenous spatial attention

Driver and Spence (1998a, 1998b) discussed several of their crossmodal studies on exogenous spatial attention. In their basic set-up, the participant fixates straight ahead with hands uncrossed, holding a small cube in each hand (see Figure 5.11). Each cube has two vibrotactile stimulators separated vertically, and there is a light source close to each stimulator. On each trial, the participant receives tactile stimulation from both stimulators on one hand. Shortly after this, one of the four light sources is illuminated briefly at random. The participant indicates whether this light is high or low regardless of which cube it comes from. The key finding was that visual judgements were significantly better when the light was on the *same* cube as the preceding tactile stimulation. Thus, the tactile cue attracted covert visual attention (note that the eyes did not move) even though it did *not* predict which light would be illuminated.

Driver and Spence (1998a, 1998b) also discussed reverse experiments in which a light cue was followed by a tactile stimulus, with the

FIGURE 5.11

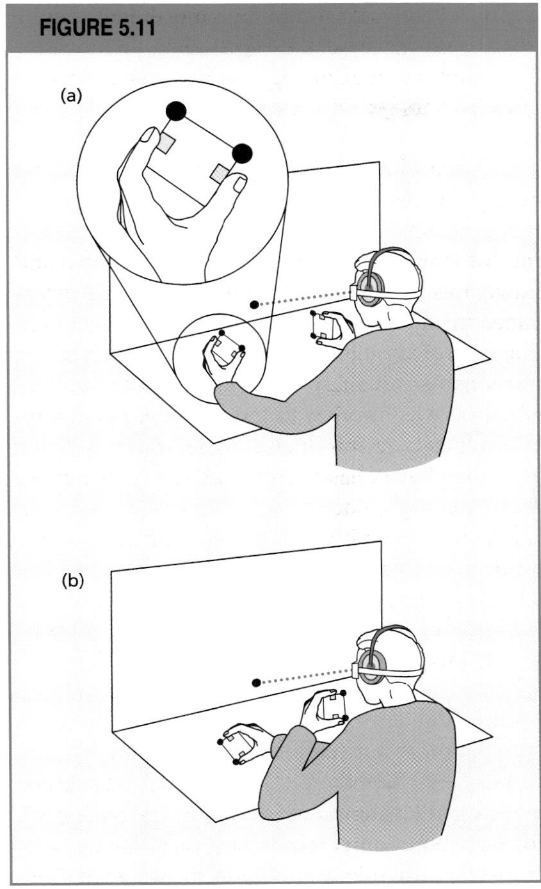

The basic set-up used by Driver and Spence (1998a). In (a), the participant is looking straight ahead and is holding a small cube in each hand. On each cube are two vibrotactile stimulators shown with shading and two visual light-emitting diodes shown as black circles. In (b), the set-up is the same except that the participant's hands are crossed. From Driver and Spence (1998b) with permission from Elsevier.

task being to indicate whether this stimulus was high or low. Tactile judgements were better when the preceding light cue was on the same cube even though it failed to predict which vibrotactile stimulator would be activated.

Spence and Driver (1996) used a similar set-up to study crossmodal effects between the visual and auditory modalities. Loudspeakers were placed directly above and below each hand, and there was a sound from one of the loudspeakers shortly before one of the four lights was illuminated. Visual judgements were more accurate when the auditory cue (which did not predict which light would be illuminated) was on the *same* side as the subsequent visual target. When the roles of the visual and auditory modalities were reversed, auditory judgements were significantly more accurate when the non-predictive visual cue was on the *same* side as the subsequent auditory target. Thus, this study provided additional evidence for crossmodal links in attention.

How can we explain these crossmodal effects? The findings discussed so far could apparently be explained by Kinsbourne's (1993) hypothesis that activation of the right hemisphere generally shifts attention to the left, whereas activation of the left hemisphere produces an attentional shift to the right. For example, a tactile cue to the right hand facilitates accurate detection of a visual target in the right visual field because stimulation from both cue and target proceeds initially to the left hemisphere. However, other evidence disproves this simple hypothesis. Driver and Spence (1998a) carried out studies using the kind of set-up previously described, but with the important difference that the participant's hands were crossed rather than uncrossed. As a result, the right hand was in the left visual field, and the left hand was in the right visual field.

What happened when the hands were crossed? Stimulation of the right hand initially activates the left hemisphere, and should cause attention to move rightwards according to Kinsbourne's hypothesis. This leads to the prediction that visual judgements should be better when the illuminated light is on the cube held by the left hand (which is in the right visual field) rather than the one held by the right hand. In fact, the findings were contrary to that prediction, and resembled those obtained when the hands were uncrossed. Thus, facilitatory effects between modalities occur in a much more flexible way than is assumed by Kinsbourne's hypothesis. More specifically, the participants' attentional processes adjusted to take account of the fact that their hands were crossed.

In sum, detecting the location of a visual stimulus can be assisted by non-predictive tactile and auditory stimulation (and vice versa), thus indicating the existence of crossmodal effects. We do not know in detail the processes underlying these effects. However, some theoretical ideas are discussed shortly.

Endogenous spatial attention

We turn now to endogenous spatial attention, in which participants *voluntarily* attend to a given spatial location in one modality because they expect that a target stimulus will be presented in that modality. Interesting evidence of crossmodal effects in endogenous spatial attention was reported by Eimer and Schröger (1998). Participants were presented with two streams of lights and two streams of sounds, with one stream in each modality being presented to the *left* and the other to the *right*. The instructions told participants to detect deviant events (e.g., longer than usual stimuli) in only one modality (vision or audition) presented to one side, while ignoring the other three streams. Event-related potentials (ERPs) were recorded to obtain information about the allocation of attention.

ERPs to deviant stimuli in the task-relevant modality were greater when presented on the to-be-attended side than when presented on the to-be-ignored side. This finding simply shows participants allocated their attention as instructed. What is of more interest is what happened to the allocation of attention on the *task-irrelevant* modality. Suppose participants were given the task of detecting *visual* stimuli on the left side. What happened was that ERPs to deviant *auditory* stimuli were greater on the left side than on the right side, although the difference was smaller than in the relevant modality. These findings indicate the allocation of attention to the left or to the right determined by the task-relevant modality also influences to a lesser extent the allocation of attention to the task-irrelevant modality.

Ventriloquist illusion

The final crossmodal effect we will discuss is based on the **ventriloquist illusion**. In this illusion, which everyone who has been to the cinema or seen a ventriloquist will have experienced, sounds are misperceived as coming from their apparent visual source. Driver (1996) studied this illusion. Two random-word messages spoken by the same voice were played from the same loudspeaker, and participants repeated back one of the messages. There was a video screen showing appropriate lip movements for the relevant auditory message. The lip movements were either at the same location as the loudspeaker or they were displaced to a different location. The key finding was that the participants' ability to select the appropriate auditory message was significantly better when the lip movements were displaced. Presumably auditory attention was directed to the apparent location of the sounds (i.e., the video screen), thus producing an illusory spatial separation of the two auditory messages.

Theoretical ideas

Crossmodal attentional effects probably depend at least in part on multimodal cells, which are responsive to stimuli in various different modalities. Multimodal cells respond strongly to multimodal stimulation at a given location, but show reduced responding when there is multimodal stimulation at different locations (see Stein & Meredith, 1993, for a review). More specifically, there are bimodal cells responsive to stimulation in two modalities and trimodal cells responsive to stimulation in the three modalities of vision, audition, and touch (Stein & Meredith, 1993).

Neurophysiological evidence may help to explain the finding that there are weaker crossmodal links in endogenous spatial attention between audition and touch than between audition and vision or between vision and touch (Lloyd, Merat, McGlone, & Spence, 2003). Stein and Meredith (1993) discussed findings showing that, in the superior colliculus of the cat, 30% of all cells are auditory–visual, 14% are visual–tactile, but only 3% are auditory–tactile.

Eimer, van Velzen, Forster, and Driver (2003) addressed an important theoretical issue relating to crossmodal effects. They pointed out that virtually all crossmodal studies on endogenous spatial attention used situations in which the locations of auditory and tactile targets were visible. As a result, it is possible that participants relied heavily on the visual modality even when crossmodal effects between audition and touch were being investigated. As Eimer et al. (2003, p. 310) pointed out, "Vision can provide better spatial acuity than other modalities, and thus might in principle allow more accurate 'anchoring' of spatial attention." An alternative view (e.g., Ward, 1994) is that endogenous spatial attention is controlled supramodally by a high-level system that influences attentional processes within each sensory modality.

How can we decide whether crossmodal effects in endogenous spatial attention are explained more adequately by the assumption that the visual modality is dominant or by the assumption that there is a supramodal attentional system? Eimer et al. (2003) compared visual–tactile crossmodal effects when the environment was illuminated and when it was dark. In essence, if visual–tactile crossmodal effects were reduced or eliminated in darkness, this would imply that visual processes and information are important in producing such effects in lit environments. In contrast, if these crossmodal effects were the same in lit and dark environments, this would be consistent with the notion that spatial attention is controlled supramodally. The findings were very similar in the lit and dark environments, thus supporting the supramodal view.

Evaluation

Studies of exogenous visual attention, endogenous visual attention, and the ventriloquist illusion indicate clearly there are numerous links between the various sense modalities. As Driver and Spence (1998b, p. 260) concluded, "The data show that attention operates on spatial representations that are subject to crossmodal influences, not merely within the receptor space of just the relevant modality." This is important progress. Until fairly recently, most research was based on the implicit assumption that attentional processes in each sensory modality operate independently from those in all other modalities. We now know that that assumption is false, and the discovery of multimodal cells sheds some light on what underlies crossmodal effects.

Some theoretical progress has been made in understanding the basis of crossmodal effects in spatial attention. For example, there is convincing neurophysiological evidence indicating the existence of bimodal and trimodal cells which presumably assist in the integration of information from different sense modalities. There is also evidence suggesting that crossmodal effects in endogenous spatial attention may depend on a supramodal attentional control system.

There are two limitations of research on crossmodal effects. First, while much has been discovered about crossmodal effects in spatial attention, little is known about crossmodal effects in the *identification* of stimuli and objects. In other words, we know little about the ways in which information from different modalities is combined to facilitate object recognition. Second, several important crossmodal effects have been discovered, but as yet we lack a detailed theoretical understanding of the processes involved. For example, it is not really possible to predict ahead of time how strong any crossmodal effects are likely to be.

VISUAL SEARCH

As Peterson et al. (2001, p. 287) pointed out, "From the time we wake in the morning until we go to bed at night, we spend a good deal of each day searching the environment . . . in the office, we may look for a coffee cup, the manuscript we were working on several days ago, or a phone number of a colleague . . . In short, much of our life is spent searching for information relevant to the task in hand." The processes involved in such activities have been examined in studies on **visual search**, in which a specified target within a visual display has to be detected as rapidly as possible. On visual search tasks, participants are typically presented with a visual display containing a variable number of items (the set or display size). A target (e.g., red G) is presented on half the trials, and the task is to decide rapidly whether the target is present in the display. Theory and research on this task are discussed below.

Feature integration theory

Feature integration theory was put forward by Treisman (e.g., 1988, 1992). She distinguished between the features of objects (e.g., colour, size, lines of particular orientation) and the objects themselves, and made the following assumptions:

- There is a rapid initial parallel process in which the visual features of objects in the environment are processed together; this is not dependent on attention.
- There is then a serial process in which features are combined to form objects.
- The serial process is slower than the initial parallel process, especially when the set size is large.
- Features can be combined by focused attending to the location of the object, in which case focused attention provides the "glue" forming unitary objects from the available features.
- Feature combination can be influenced by stored knowledge (e.g., bananas are usually yellow).
- In the absence of focused attention or relevant stored knowledge, features from different objects will be combined randomly, producing "illusory conjunctions".

Treisman and Gelade (1980) had previously obtained support for this theory. Participants searched for a target in a visual display having a set or display size of between 1 and 30 items. The target was either an object based on a conjunction of features (a green letter T), or consisted of a single feature (a blue letter or an S). When the target was a green letter T, all non-targets shared one feature with the target (i.e., they were either the brown letter T or the green letter X). The prediction was that focused attention would be needed to detect the conjunctive target (because it was defined by a combination or conjunction of features), but would not be required to detect single-feature targets.

The findings were as predicted (see Figure 5.12). Set or display size had a large effect on detection speed when the target was defined by a combination or conjunction of features (i.e., a green letter T), presumably because focused attention was required. However, there was very little effect of display size when the target was defined by a single feature (i.e., a blue letter or an S).

The notion that the binding together of an object's features requires an attention-demanding process is of fundamental importance within feature integration theory. Relevant evidence has been

FIGURE 5.12

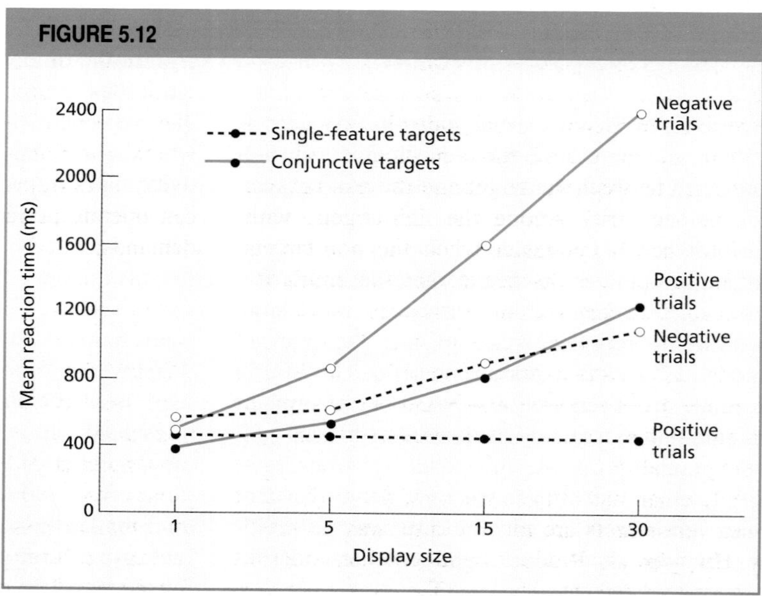

Performance speed on a detection task as a function of target definition (conjunctive vs. single feature) and display size. Adapted from Treisman and Gelade (1980).

produced in studies in which attempts have been made to identify brain areas involved in feature binding. For example, Treisman (1999) discussed a patient, RM, who had particular problems in combining the features of a stimulus, and who had damage to the parietal cortex. Independent evidence that the parietal cortex may be much involved in feature binding was reported by Ashbridge, Walsh, and Cowey (1997). They used transcranial magnetic stimulation (see Chapter 1) to produce a very brief "lesion" in parts of the parietal cortex. This disrupted performance on visual search tasks, especially when the target was defined by a conjunction of features.

According to feature integration theory, lack of focused attention can produce illusory conjunctions (random combinations of features). Treisman and Schmidt (1982) found that there were numerous illusory conjunctions when attention was widely distributed, but not when the stimuli were presented to focal attention. Balint's patients have problems with visual attention generally, especially with the accurate location of visual stimuli. Accordingly, it might be expected that they would have many illusory conjunctions. Friedman-Hill, Robertson, and Treisman (1995) studied a Balint's patient. He had numerous illusory conjunctions, combining the shape of one stimulus with the colour of another.

Duncan and Humphreys (1989, 1992) argued that Treisman's approach was limited. More specifically, they claimed that visual search times depend on two factors not included in the original version of feature integration theory: (1) the similarity between the target and the non-targets; (2) the similarity among the non-targets, with performance being faster when the non-targets are highly similar. Evidence that the similarity between the target and the non-targets is important was reported by Duncan and Humphreys (1989). There was a large effect of set on visual search times when the target was very similar to the non-targets, even when the target consisted of a single feature.

Evidence that visual search can be very rapid when non-targets are all the same was obtained by Humphreys, Riddoch, and Quinlan (1985). Participants detected inverted T targets against a background of Ts the right way up. Detection speed was hardly affected by the number of non-targets. According to feature integration theory, the fact that the target was defined by a combination or conjunction of features (i.e., a vertical line and a horizontal line) means that visual search should have been greatly affected by the number of non-targets.

Treisman and Sato (1990) developed feature integration theory, in part influenced by criticisms such as those discussed above. They argued that the degree of *similarity* between the target and the distractors influences visual search time. They found that visual search for an object target defined by more than one feature was typically limited to those distractors sharing at least one of the target's features. For example, if you were looking for a blue circle in a display containing blue triangles, red circles, and red triangles, you would ignore red triangles. This contrasts with the views of Treisman and Gelade (1980), who argued that none of the stimuli would be ignored.

Treisman (1993) put forward a more complex version of feature integration theory, in which there are four kinds of attentional selection. First, there is selection by location involving a relatively broad or narrow attention window. Second, there is selection by features. Features are divided into surface-defining features (e.g., colour, brightness, relative motion) and shape-defining features (e.g., orientation, size). Third, there is selection on the basis of object-defined locations. Fourth, there is selection at a late stage of processing which determines the object file controlling the individual's response. Thus, attentional selectivity can operate at various levels depending on task demands.

Guided search theory

Wolfe (1998) developed feature integration theory in his guided search theory. He replaced Treisman and Gelade's (1980) assumption that the initial processing is necessarily parallel and subsequent processing is serial with the notion that processes are more or less efficient. Why did he do this? "Results of visual search experiments run from flat to steep RT [reaction time] × set size functions

. . . The continuum of search slopes does make it implausible to think that the search tasks, themselves, can be neatly classified as serial or parallel" (Wolfe, 1998, p. 20). There should be no effect of set or display size on detection times if parallel processing is used, but a substantial effect of set size if serial processing is used. However, most actual findings fall between these two extremes.

According to guided search theory, the initial processing of basic features produces an activation map, with every item in the visual display having its own level of activation. Suppose someone is searching for red, horizontal targets. Feature processing would activate all red objects and all horizontal objects. Attention is then directed towards items on the basis of their level of activation, starting with those most activated. This assumption allows us to understand why search times are longer when some non-targets share one or more features with the target stimuli (e.g., Duncan & Humphreys, 1989).

A great problem with the original version of feature integration theory is that targets in large displays are typically found faster than would be predicted. The activation-map notion provides a plausible way in which visual search can be made more efficient by ignoring stimuli not sharing any features with the target stimulus.

Evaluation

Feature integration theory has influenced theoretical approaches to visual search in two ways. First, many theorists accept that two successive processes are involved. Second, those who accept the first point generally agree that the first process is fast and efficient, whereas the second process is slower and less efficient. In addition, as Quinlan (2003, p. 643) pointed out, the influence of feature integration theory goes considerably beyond that:

> FIT [feature integration theory] has influenced thinking on processes that range from the early stages of sensory encoding to higher order characteristics of attentional control. Indeed, it is no exaggeration to state that FIT was one of the most influential and important theories of visual information in the last quarter of the twentieth century.

There were four key weaknesses with early versions of feature integration theory. First, the assumption that visual search is either entirely parallel or serial is much too strong and has been disproved by the evidence (Wolfe, 1998). Second, the search for targets consisting of a conjunction or combination of features is faster than predicted by feature integration theory. Some of the factors involved (e.g., grouping of non-targets; non-targets sharing no features with targets) are incorporated into guided search theory.

Third, it was originally assumed within feature integration theory that the effect of set or display size on visual search depends mainly on the nature of the target (single feature or conjunctive feature). In fact, the nature of the non-targets (e.g., their similarity to each other) is also important.

Fourth, there is disconfirming evidence from neglect and extinction patients. According to Treisman's theory, the attentional deficits of these patients should disrupt the search for targets defined by a conjunction of features but should have no effect on the search for single features (which is allegedly not influenced by attentional processes). The evidence was reviewed by Umiltà (2001). Patients often perform more slowly than normal individuals on both conjunction and feature tasks, but the impairment is greater on conjunction tasks. According to Umiltà (2001, p. 136), "It would seem that also coding simple features requires attention and cannot take place at a preattentive stage."

Decision integration hypothesis

Palmer and his associates (e.g., Eckstein et al., 2000; Palmer, Verghese, & Pavel, 2000) proposed the decision integration hypothesis. They assumed that the processes involved in feature and conjunction searches are basically similar. More specifically, Palmer et al. assumed that parallel processing is involved in both kinds of searches. These assumptions are radically different from those incorporated into the original formulation of feature integration theory.

Palmer et al. (2000) argued that observers form internal representations of target and distractor stimuli. These representations are noisy (the internal response to any given item varies somewhat from trial to trial). Performance on a visual search task involves decision making based on the *discriminability* between target and distractor stimuli. Why is visual search less efficient with conjunction searches than feature searches? According to Eckstein et al. (2000, p. 434), "The lower search efficiency in conjunction displays is a consequence of the combination of noisy activity across the two independent feature dimensions." In other words, conjunction searches are harder than feature searches because there is less discriminability between target and distractor stimuli. Visual search is typically slower with larger set sizes because the complexity of the decision-making process is greater when there are numerous items in the visual display.

Evidence

Palmer et al. (2000) and Eckstein et al. (2000) applied the decision integration hypothesis to the findings from numerous studies on visual search. In essence, they found that their theoretical approach "can account for simple visual search without invoking mechanisms such as limited capacity or serial processing" (Palmer et al., 2000, p. 1227). In other words, mechanisms of central importance within feature integration theory may not be involved in visual search.

Convincing evidence for the general approach exemplified by the decision integration hypothesis comes from McElree and Carrasco (1999). They pointed out that assessing visual search performance only by reaction time (as is generally done) is limited, because speed of performance depends partially on the participants' willingness to accept errors. Accordingly, they used a speed–accuracy trade-off procedure. This controlled speed of performance by requiring the participants to respond rapidly when they received a signal. In one of their experiments, feature search involved a blue vertical target with blue tilted distractors, whereas conjunction search involved the same target with blue tilted and red vertical distractors. Each display contained 4, 10, or 16 items, and was presented for 150 ms.

What did McElree and Carrasco (1999) find? Maximal accuracy in both feature and conjunction search was greater with small set size than with large set size (see Figure 5.13). Overall, there was much more similarity in the performance patterns for feature and conjunction search than would be predicted by Treisman. Why did set size have more effect on conjunction search than on feature search? It might be argued that this supports Treisman's feature integration theory, with performance being slowed on conjunction search because of serial processing. However, the effects of set size were much smaller than predicted by most serial processing models. According to McEltree and Carrasco, increasing set size reduces the discriminability between target and distractor stimuli more for conjunction searches than for feature searches. Overall, the findings suggested that the processes involved in feature and conjunction searches are the same (i.e., they both involve parallel processing), and that discriminability between target and distractor stimuli is of crucial importance. McEltree and Carrasco devised various computer models. They found that those based on the notion that both types of search involve parallel processing fitted the data much better than models based on the assumption that conjunction searches involve serial processing.

A different kind of evidence suggesting that feature and conjunction searches involve very similar processes was reported in an fMRI study by Leonards, Sunaert, Van Hecke, and Orban (2000). They assessed the brain areas involved in visual search, and found that "The cerebral networks in efficient [feature] and inefficient [conjunction] search overlap almost completely." These findings provide no support for the notion that feature search depends on serial processing and conjunction search on parallel processing, but are consistent with the view that parallel processing characterises feature and conjunction search.

Overall evaluation

The processes involved in feature and conjunction searches are typically rather similar and differ less

FIGURE 5.13

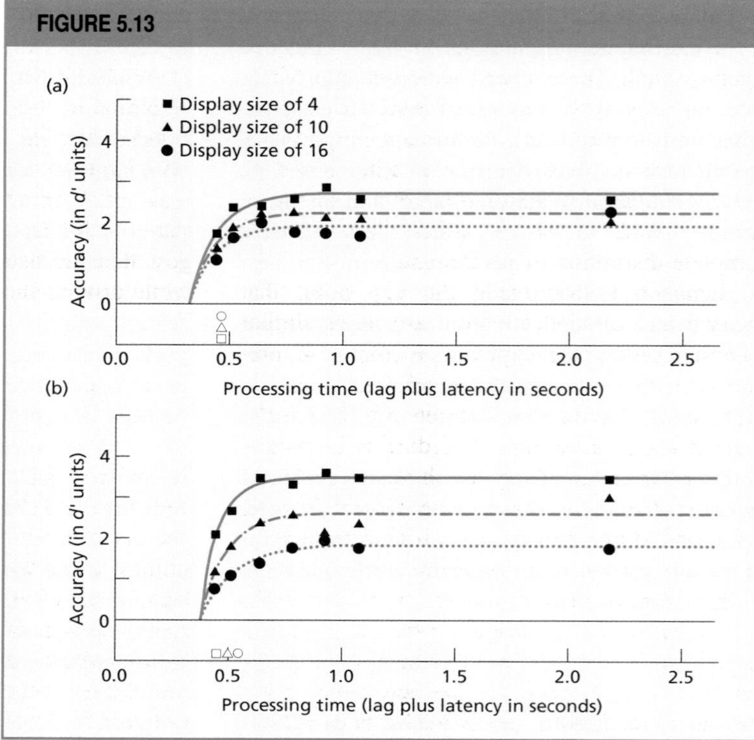

Accuracy of performance as assessed by d′ with display signs of 4, 10, or 16 items viewed for 150 ms for feature (a) and conjunction (b) searches. Open symbols at the bottom of each figure indicate when each function reached two-thirds of its final value. From McElree and Carrasco (1999). Copyright © 1999 by the American Psychological Association. Reprinted with permission.

than assumed within feature integration theory. There are grounds for arguing that discriminability between the target and distractors is the single most important factor determining performance on visual search tasks. In addition, it is reasonable to argue that parallel processing often characterises feature and conjunction searches.

There are three main limitations in research on visual search. First, we can search for an enormous range of targets defined in almost endlessly different ways. As a result, it is hard to be confident that any single theory can account for all forms of visual search. Second, most research has been based on reaction-time measures of visual search performance. This is unfortunate, because there are many ways of interpreting reaction-time data. As McElree and Carrasco (1999, p. 1532) pointed out, "RT [reaction time] data are of limited value . . . because RT can vary with either differences in discriminability, differences in processing speed, or unknown mixtures of the two effects." In that connection, the speed–accuracy trade-off procedure used by McElree and Carrasco (1999) is a definite improvement. Third, most research is of dubious relevance to our everyday lives. As Wolfe (1998, p. 56) pointed out:

> In the real world, distractors are very heterogeneous [diverse]. Stimuli exist in many size scales in a single view. Items are probably defined by conjunctions of many features. You don't get several hundred trials with the same targets and distractors . . . A truly satisfying model of visual search will need . . . to account for the range of real-world visual behaviour.

DIVIDED ATTENTION

What happens when people try to do two things at once? The answer clearly depends on the nature of the two "things". Sometimes the attempt is successful, as when an experienced motorist drives a car and holds a conversation at the same time, or a tennis player notes the position of his/her opponent while running at speed and preparing to make a stroke. At other times, as when someone tries to rub their stomach with one hand while patting their head with the other, there can be a complete disruption of performance.

Hampson (1989) made the key point that focused and divided attention are more similar than might have been expected. Factors (e.g., presenting stimuli in different modalities) that aid focused or selective attention generally also make divided attention easier. According to Hampson (1989, p. 267), "anything which minimises interference between processes, or keeps them 'further apart' will allow them to be dealt with more readily either selectively or together".

Breakdowns of performance when two tasks are combined can shed light on the limitations of the human information-processing system. Some theorists (e.g., Norman & Shallice, 1986) argue that such breakdowns reflect the limited capacity of a single multi-purpose central processor or executive sometimes described as "attention". Other theorists are more impressed by our apparent ability to perform two fairly complex tasks at the same time without disruption or interference. Such theorists favour the notion of several specific processing resources, arguing that there will be no interference between two tasks making use of different processing resources.

More progress has been made empirically than theoretically. It is possible to predict fairly accurately whether or not two tasks can be combined successfully, but the accounts offered by different theorists are very diverse. Accordingly, we will discuss the factual evidence before moving on to the murkier issue of how the data are to be explained. Before doing so, however, we will show that studying dual-task performance can have practical importance. Strayer and Johnston (2001) considered the ongoing controversy of whether driving performance is impaired when drivers are using mobile phones. They considered the ability of drivers on a simulated task to detect red lights while using a hand-held or hands-free mobile phone, or while listening to the radio. The probability of missing a red light more than doubled when the drivers were engaged in conversation on a mobile phone, and there was little difference between hand-held and hands-free mobile phones. As might be expected, the ability to detect red lights was worse when the drivers were talking rather than listening. These findings strongly suggest that the use of all types of mobile phones while driving should be banned.

Factors determining dual-task performance

Task similarity

When we think of pairs of activities performed well together, the examples that come to mind usually involve two rather dissimilar activities (e.g., driving and listening to the radio). As we have seen, when people shadow or repeat back prose passages while learning auditorily presented words, their subsequent recognition-memory performance for the words is at chance level (Allport et al., 1972). However, the same authors found that memory was excellent when the to-be-remembered material consisted of pictures.

Various kinds of similarity need to be distinguished. Similarity of stimulus modality has probably been studied most thoroughly. Treisman and Davies (1973) found that two monitoring tasks interfered with each other much more when the stimuli on both tasks were in the same sense modality (visual or auditory) rather than different modalities. Response similarity is also important. McLeod (1977) asked participants to perform a continuous tracking task with manual responding together with a tone-identification task. Some participants responded vocally to the tones, whereas others responded with the hand not involved in the tracking task. Performance on the tracking task was worse with high response similarity (manual responses on both tasks) than with low response similarity (manual responses on one task and vocal ones on the other).

It is often hard to measure similarity. How similar are piano playing and poetry writing, or driving a car and watching a football match? Only when there is a better understanding of the processes involved in the performance of such tasks will sensible answers be forthcoming.

Practice

Common sense suggests that the old saying "Practice makes perfect" is especially applicable to dual-task performance. For example, learner drivers find it almost impossible to drive and hold a conversation, whereas expert drivers often find it fairly easy. Support for this commonsensical position was obtained by Spelke, Hirst, and Neisser (1976) with two students called Diane and John. These students received five hours' training a week for 4 months on various tasks. Their first task was to read short stories for comprehension while writing down words to dictation. They found this very hard initially, and their reading speed and handwriting both suffered considerably. After 6 weeks of training, however, they could read as rapidly and with as much comprehension when taking dictation as when only reading, and the quality of their handwriting had also improved.

In spite of this impressive dual-task performance, Spelke et al. were still not satisfied. Diane and John could recall only 35 out of the thousands of words they had written down at dictation. Even when 20 successive dictated words formed a sentence or came from a single semantic category, the two students were unaware of this. With further training, however, they learned to write down the names of the categories to which the dictated words belonged while maintaining normal reading speed and comprehension.

Spelke et al. (1976, p. 229) concluded as follows: "People's ability to develop skills in specialised situations is so great that it may never be possible to define general limits on cognitive capacity." However, there are alternative interpretations. Perhaps the dictation task was performed rather automatically, and so placed few demands on cognitive capacity, or there might have been a rapid alternation of attention between reading and writing. Hirst et al. (1980) claimed writing to dictation was not done automatically, because the students understood what they were writing. They also claimed that reading and dictation could only be performed together with success by alternation of attention if the reading material were simple and highly redundant. However, most participants could still read and take dictation effectively when less redundant reading matter was used.

The studies by Spelke et al. (1976) and by Hirst et al. (1980) do not really show that two complex tasks can be performed together without disruption. One of the participants used by Hirst et al. was tested at dictation *without* reading, and made fewer than half the number of errors that occurred when reading at the same time. Furthermore, the reading task gave the participants much flexibility in terms of *when* they attended to the reading matter, and such flexibility means there may well have been some alternation of attention between tasks. However, Schumacher et al. (2001) and Hazeltine, Teague, and Ivry (2000) have recently provided evidence suggesting that two relatively simple, well-practised tasks can be performed at the same time without any impairment. These studies (and other relevant ones) are discussed later in the section headed "Cognitive bottleneck theory".

There are other cases of apparently successful performance of two complex tasks, but the requisite skills were always highly practised. Expert pianists can play from seen music while repeating back or shadowing heard speech (Allport et al., 1972), and an expert typist can type and shadow at the same time (Shaffer, 1975). These studies are often regarded as providing evidence of completely successful task combination. However, there are some signs of interference (Broadbent, 1982).

Why might practice aid dual-task performance? First, participants may develop new strategies for performing the tasks to minimise task interference. Second, the demands that a task makes on attentional or other central resources may be reduced with practice. Third, although a task initially requires the use of several specific processing resources, practice may reduce the number of resources required. These possibilities are considered in more detail below.

Task difficulty

The ability to perform two tasks together depends on their difficulty, and there are several studies showing the expected pattern of results. For example Sullivan (1976) used the tasks of shadowing an auditory message and detecting target words on a non-shadowed message at the same time. When the shadowing task was made harder by using a less redundant message, fewer targets were detected on the non-shadowed message. However, it is hard to define "task difficulty" with any precision.

The demands for resources of two tasks performed together might be thought to equal the sums of the demands of the two tasks when performed separately. However, the necessity to perform two tasks together often introduces new demands of coordination. Duncan (1979) asked participants to respond to closely successive stimuli, one requiring a left-hand response and the other a right-hand response. The relationship between each stimulus and response was either corresponding (e.g., rightmost stimulus calling for response of the rightmost finger) or crossed (e.g., leftmost stimulus calling for response of the rightmost finger). Performance was poor when the relationship was corresponding for one stimulus but crossed for the other. In these circumstances, the participants were sometimes confused, with their errors being largely those expected if the inappropriate stimulus–response relationship had been selected.

Further evidence that performing two tasks together can involve processing resources over and above those of each task performed individually was reported by D'Esposito et al. (1995). Their participants performed a semantic judgement task and a spatial rotation task either separately or at the same time. Use of fMRI revealed that there was significant activity in the prefrontal cortex and the anterior cingulate only in the dual-task condition.

Sometimes the effects of task similarity swamp those of task difficulty. For example, Segal and Fusella (1970) combined image construction (visual or auditory) with signal detection (visual or auditory). The auditory image task impaired detection of auditory signals more than the visual task did (see Figure 5.14), suggesting that the auditory image task was more demanding than the visual image task. However, the auditory image task was less disruptive than the visual image task when each task was combined with a task requiring detection of visual signals, suggesting the opposite conclusion. In this study, task similarity was clearly a much more important factor than task difficulty.

FIGURE 5.14

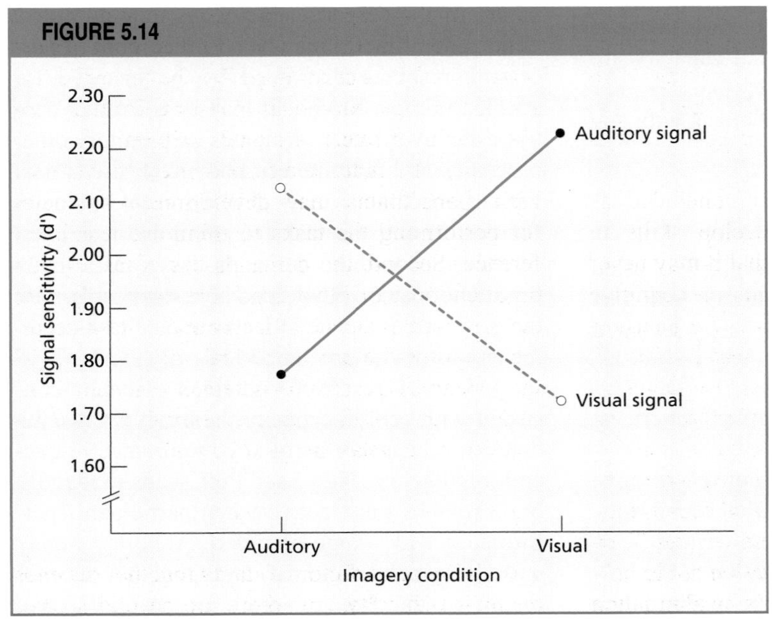

Sensitivity (d′) to auditory and visual signals as a function of concurrent imagery modality (auditory vs. visual). Adapted from Segal and Fusella (1970).

Central capacity theories

A simple way of accounting for many dual-task findings is to assume there is some central capacity (e.g. central executive) which can be used flexibly across a wide range of activities. This central processor has strictly limited resources, and is sometimes known as attention or effort. The extent to which two tasks can be performed together depends on the demands each task makes on those resources. If the combined demands of the two tasks do not exceed the total resources of the central capacity, the two tasks will not interfere with each other. However, if the resources are insufficient, then performance disruption is inevitable.

One of the best-known of the capacity theories was put forward by Kahneman (1973). He argued that attentional capacity is limited but it can vary somewhat. More specifically, it is greater when task difficulty is high than when it is low, and it increases in conditions of high effort or motivation. Increased effort tends to produce physiological arousal, and this can be assessed in various ways (e.g., pupillary dilation).

There are various problems with Kahneman's (1973) theory. He did not define his key terms very clearly, referring to a "a nonspecific input, which may be variously labelled 'effort', 'capacity', or 'attention'." Another problem is that it is assumed that effort and attentional capacity are determined in part by task difficulty, but it is very hard to determine the difficulty of a task with any precision.

Evidence

Bourke, Duncan, and Nimmo-Smith (1996) tested predictions of central capacity theory (see also Bourke, 1997). They selected four tasks designed to be as different as possible:

(1) *Random generation*: generating letters at random.
(2) *Prototype learning*: working out the features of two patterns or prototypes from seeing various exemplars.
(3) *Manual task*: screwing a nut down to the bottom of a bolt and back up to the top, and then down to the bottom of a second bolt and back up, and so on.
(4) *Tone task*: detecting the occurrence of a target tone.

The participants were given two of these tasks to perform together, with one task being identified as more important than the other. The basic argument was as follows: if there is a central or general capacity, then the task making most demands on this capacity will interfere most with all three of the other tasks. In contrast, the task making fewest demands on this capacity will interfere least with all the other tasks.

What did Bourke et al. (1996) find? First, these very different tasks interfered with each other. Second, the random generation task interfered the most overall with the performance of the other tasks, and the tone task interfered the least. Third, and of greatest importance, the random generation task consistently interfered most with the prototype, manual, and tone tasks, and it did so whether it was the primary or the secondary task (see Figure 5.15). The tone task consistently interfered least with each of the other three tasks. Thus, the findings accorded with the predictions of a general capacity theory.

Bourke et al.'s (1996) study did not clarify the nature of the central capacity. As they admitted, "The general factor may be a limited pool of processing resource that needs to be invested for a task to be performed. It may be a limited central executive that co-ordinates or monitors other processes and is limited in how much it can deal with at one time. It may also represent a general limit of the entire cognitive system on the amount of information that can be processed at a given time. The method developed here deals only with the existence of a general factor in dual-task decrements, not its nature" (p. 544).

Duncan et al. (2000) obtained evidence consistent with central capacity theory, if we assume that central capacity is of key importance in general intelligence. They used PET scans to identify brain regions most active when participants performed a wide range of tasks correlating highly with the general factor of intelligence. A specific region of the frontal cortex was highly active

FIGURE 5.15

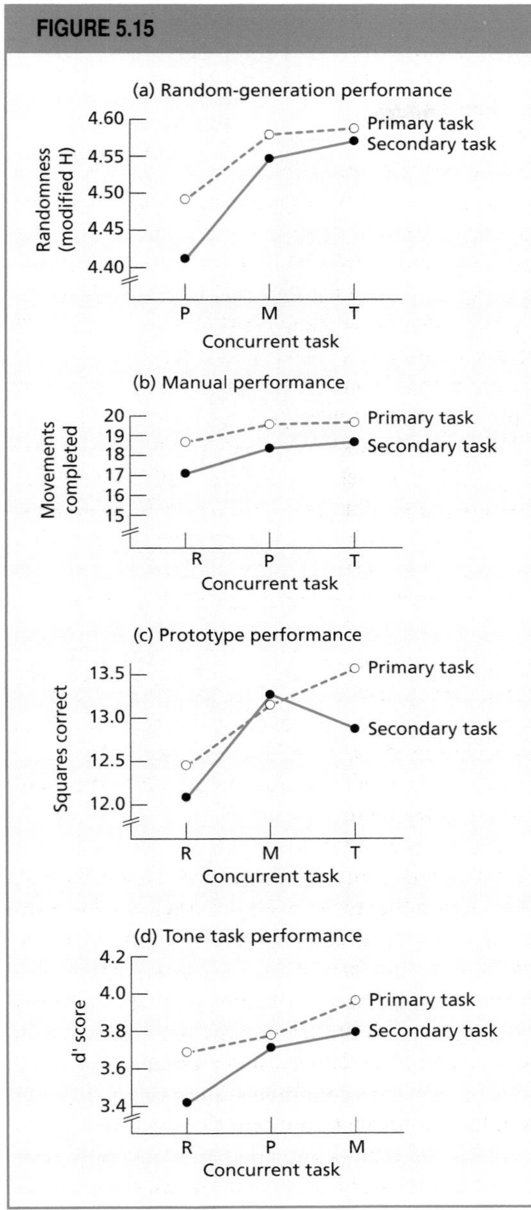

Performance on random generation (R), prototype learning (P), manual (M), and tone (T) tasks as a function of concurrent task. Adapted from Bourke et al. (1996).

during the performance of virtually all the tasks, suggesting that "'general intelligence' [central capacity?] derives from a specific frontal system important in the control of diverse forms of behaviour" (Duncan et al., 2000, p. 457).

Hegarty, Shah, and Miyake (2000) argued that dual-task performance often fails to provide support for central capacity theories. In their study, there were three primary tasks performed on their own or with a secondary task:

(1) Paper folding: the participants had to fold a piece of paper mentally, imagine a hole punched through it, and then decide what the paper would look like when unfolded.
(2) Card rotation: the participants viewed a target figure and indicated which of the test figures represented rotations of the target.
(3) Identical pictures: the participants viewed a target figure and decided which test figure was identical to it.

Two of the secondary tasks were random number generation and the two-back task (listen to a series of consonants, indicating when a consonant was identical to the one presented two items earlier).

Which primary task would we expect to be most disrupted by the secondary tasks? Hegarty et al. (2000) had evidence from previous research that the paper-folding task makes the greatest demands on central capacity and the identical-pictures task the least. Accordingly, the obvious prediction from central capacity theory is that the secondary tasks should have disrupted paper folding the most and identical pictures the least. In fact, precisely the opposite was the case (see Figure 5.16). Why was this? According to Hegarty et al. (2000), there are two reasons. First, participants found the paper-folding task to be the most difficult primary task, and so allocated more of their available processing resources to it than to the other primary tasks. Second, there is evidence that selecting a response on one task inhibits the ability to perform a second task (Pashler, 1998). The paper-folding task involved the least response selection and the identical-pictures task involved the most.

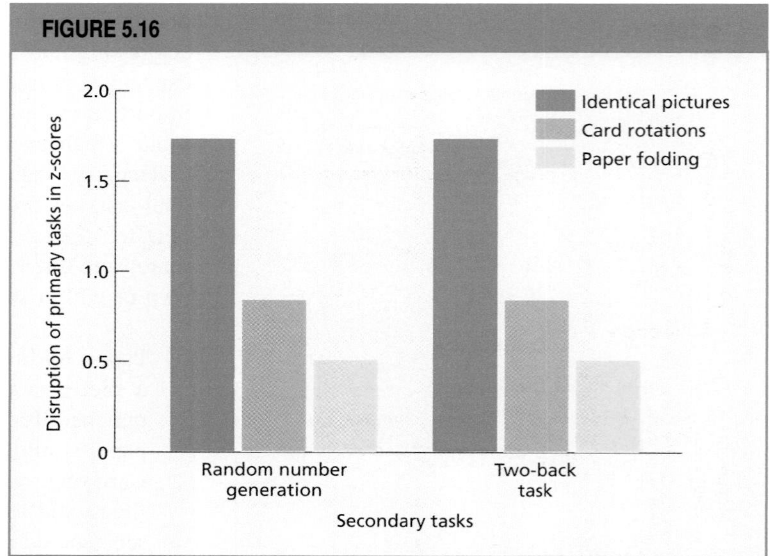

Mean disruption or decrement on three primary tasks (identical pictures; card rotations; paper folding) as a function of secondary task (random number generation; two-back task). Data from Hegarty et al. (2000).

Evaluation

We can "explain" dual-task interference by assuming that the resources of some central capacity have been exceeded, and we can account for a lack of interference by assuming that the two tasks did not exceed those resources. However, in the absence of any independent assessment of central processing capacity, this is simply a re-description of the findings rather than an explanation. The findings of Bourke et al. (1996) go some way towards addressing these issues. Specific predictions were made from central capacity theory, and these predictions were largely confirmed. In addition, recent neuroimaging research (e.g., Duncan et al., 2000) has provided suggestive evidence concerning the brain areas that might be involved in central capacity.

There are two further concerns about the evidence for central capacity. First, findings from the dual-task approach are difficult to interpret. Interference effects may reflect task demands on central capacity. However, they may also reflect additional factors such as increased allocation of resources to tasks perceived to be difficult and interference caused by response selection. Second, evidence for the existence of a central capacity does not necessarily clarify the nature of that central capacity. For example, as we saw earlier, Bourke et al. (1996) admitted that their findings were consistent with several different views on the nature of the central capacity.

Multiple-resource theories

Some theorists (e.g., Wickens, 1984) have assumed that the processing system consists of independent processing mechanisms in the form of multiple resources. If this is the case, then it is clear why the degree of similarity between two tasks is so important: similar tasks compete for the same specific resources, and thus produce interference, whereas dissimilar tasks involve different resources, and so do not interfere.

Wickens (1984) argued that we possess multiple resources. He proposed a three-dimensional structure of human processing resources (see Figure 5.17). According to his model, there are three successive stages of processing (encoding, central processing, and responding). Encoding involves the perceptual processing of stimuli, and typically involves the visual or verbal codes. Finally, responding involves manual or vocal responses. There are two key assumptions in this model:

FIGURE 5.17

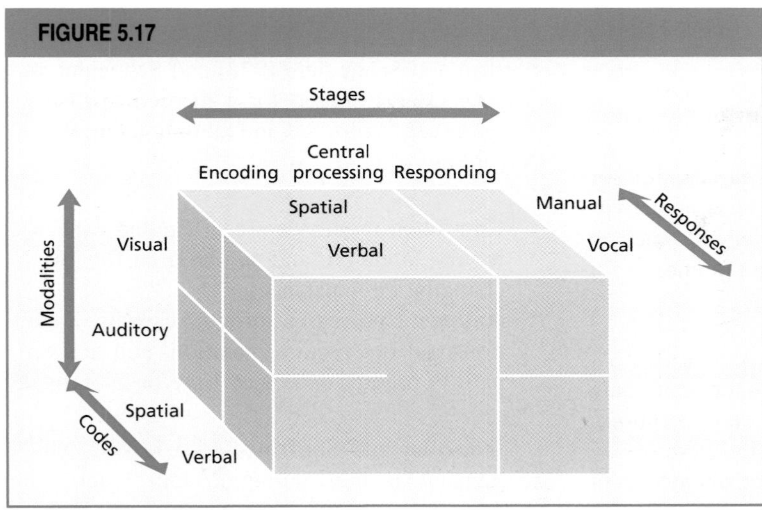

A proposed three-dimensional structure of human processing resources. From "Processing resources in attention" by Wickens, C.D. in *Varieties of Attention* edited by R. Parasuraman and D.R. Davies © 1984 by Academic Press reproduced with permission from Elsevier.

(1) There are several pools of resources based on the distinctions among stages of processing, modalities, codes, and responses.
(2) If two tasks make use of different pools of resources, then people should be able to perform both tasks without disruption.

There is much support for this multiple-resource model and its prediction that several kinds of task similarity influence dual-task performance. For example, we have seen there is more interference when two tasks share the same modality (e.g., Allport et al., 1972; Treisman & Davies, 1973), or when they share the same type of response (e.g., McLeod, 1977).

Evaluation

Most findings from dual-task studies are broadly consistent with the multiple-resource model. However, there are various limitations with it. First, the model focuses only on visual and auditory inputs, but tasks could be presented in other modalities (e.g., touch). Second, there is often some disruption to performance even when two tasks make use of different modalities. For example, Treisman and Davies (1973) found evidence of interference between two tasks presented in different modalities. Third, the model assumes that several tasks could be performed together without interference, provided each task made use of different pools of resources. This assumption seems unlikely to be correct. It minimises the problems associated with the higher-level processes of coordinating and organising the demands of tasks being carried out at the same time.

Synthesis

Baddeley (1986) favoured an approach based on a synthesis of the central capacity and multiple-resource notions (see Chapter 6). According to him, there is a hierarchical structure. The central executive is at the top of the hierarchy, and is involved in the coordination and control of behaviour. Below this level are specific processing mechanisms operating relatively independently of each other.

A problem with the notion that there are several specific processing mechanisms and one general processing mechanism is that there does not appear to be a unitary attentional system. As we saw in the earlier discussion of cognitive neuropsychological findings, it seems that somewhat separate mechanisms are involved in disengaging, shifting, and engaging attention. If there is no general processing mechanism, then it may be unrealistic to assume the processing system is hierarchical.

AUTOMATIC PROCESSING

A key phenomenon in studies of divided attention is the dramatic improvement practice often has on performance. The commonest explanation for this phenomenon is that some processing activities become automatic due to prolonged practice. There is reasonable agreement on the criteria for automatic processes:

- They are fast.
- They do not reduce the capacity for performing other tasks (i.e., they demand zero attention).
- They are unavailable to consciousness.
- They are unavoidable (i.e., they always occur when an appropriate stimulus is presented, even if that stimulus is outside the field of attention).

As Hampson (1989, p. 264) pointed out, "Criteria for automatic processes are easy to find, but hard to satisfy empirically." For example, the requirement that automatic processes should not need attention means they should have no influence on the concurrent performance of an attention-demanding task. This is rarely the case (see Pashler, 1998). There are also problems with the unavoidability criterion. The **Stroop effect**, in which the naming of the colours in which words are printed is slowed down by using colour words (e.g., the word YELLOW printed in red), seems to involve unavoidable and automatic processing of the colour words. However, Kahneman and Henik (1979) found that the Stroop effect was much larger when the distracting information (i.e., the colour name) was in the same location as the to-be-named colour rather than in an adjacent location. Thus, the processes producing the Stroop effect are not entirely unavoidable and so not completely automatic.

Few processes are fully automatic in the sense of conforming to all the criteria, with a much larger number of processes being only partially automatic. Later in this section we consider a theoretical approach (that of Norman & Shallice, 1986) which distinguishes between fully automatic and partially automatic processes.

Shiffrin and Schneider's theory

Shiffrin and Schneider (1977) and Schneider and Shiffrin (1977) argued for a theoretical distinction between controlled and automatic processes. According to them:

- Controlled processes are of limited capacity, require attention, and can be used flexibly in changing circumstances.
- Automatic processes suffer no capacity limitations, do not require attention, and are very hard to modify once they have been learned.

Schneider and Shiffrin used a task in which participants memorised up to four letters (the memory set), were then shown a visual display containing up to four letters, and finally decided rapidly whether any one of the items in the visual display was the same as any one of the items in the memory set. The crucial manipulation was the type of mapping used. With *consistent* mapping, only consonants were used as members of the memory set, and only numbers were used as distractors in the visual display (or vice versa). Thus, if a participant was given only consonants to memorise, then he/she would know that any consonant detected in the visual display *must* be an item from the memory set. With *varied* mapping, a mixture of numbers and consonants was used to form the memory set and to provide distractors in the visual display.

There were striking effects of the mapping manipulation (see Figure 5.18). The numbers of items in the memory set and visual display greatly affected decision speed only in the varied mapping conditions. According to Schneider and Shiffrin (1977), a controlled search process was used with varied mapping. This involves serial comparisons between each item in the memory set and each item in the visual display until a match is achieved or every comparison has been made. In contrast, performance with consistent mapping involved automatic processes operating independently and in parallel. According to Schneider and Shiffrin (1977), these automatic processes evolve as a result of years of practice in distinguishing between letters and numbers.

FIGURE 5.18

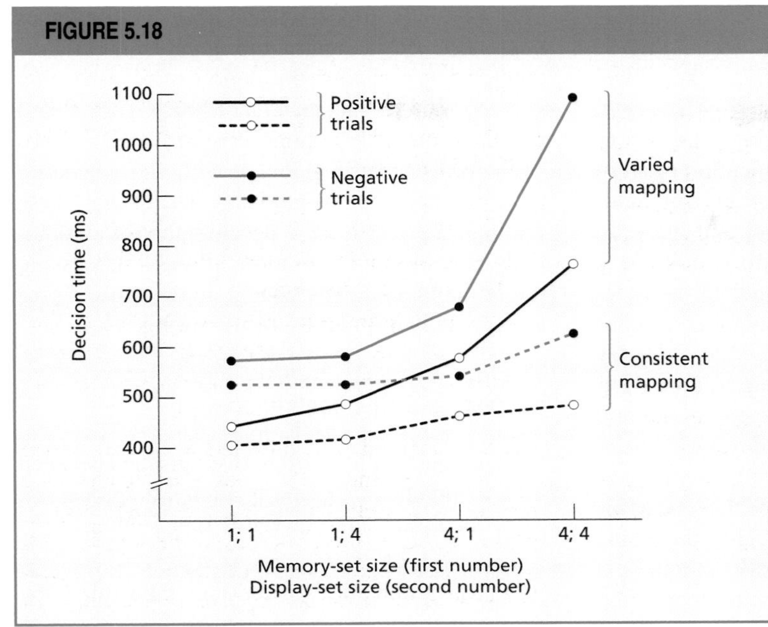

Response times on a decision task as a function of memory-set size, display-set size, and consistent vs. varied mapping. Data from Shiffrin and Schneider (1977).

The notion that automatic processes develop through practice was tested by Shiffrin and Schneider (1977). They used consistent mapping with the consonants B to L forming one set and the consonants Q to Z forming the other set. As before, items from only one set were always used in the construction of the memory set, and the distractors in the visual display were all selected from the other set. There was a great improvement in performance over 2100 trials, which seemed to reflect the growth of automatic processes.

The greatest problem with automatic processes is their *inflexibility*, which disrupts performance when the prevailing circumstances change. This was confirmed in the second part of the study. The initial 2100 trials with one consistent mapping were followed by a further 2100 trials with the reverse consistent mapping. This reversal of the mapping conditions greatly disrupted performance. Indeed, it took nearly 1000 trials before performance recovered to its level at the very start of the experiment!

Shiffrin and Schneider (1977) carried out further experiments in which participants initially tried to locate target letters anywhere in a visual display, but were then instructed to detect targets in one part of the display and to ignore targets elsewhere. Participants were less able to ignore part of the visual display when they had developed automatic processes than when they had made use of controlled search processes. As Eysenck (1982, p. 22) pointed out, "Automatic processes function rapidly and in parallel but suffer from inflexibility; controlled processes are flexible and versatile but operate relatively slowly and in a serial fashion."

Jansma, Ramsey, Slagter, and Kahn (2001) used fMRI to identify some of the changes that take place during the development of automatic processing in the consistent mapping condition. Their key finding was that the development of automatic processing was associated with reduced usage of working memory (see Chapter 6), especially its attention-like central executive component. More specifically, Jansma et al. (2001, p. 730) concluded that increased automaticity "was accompanied by a decrease in activation in regions related to working memory (bilateral but predominantly left dorsolateral prefrontal cortex, right superior frontal cortex, and right frontopolar area), and the supplementary motor area."

Evaluation

Shiffrin and Schneider's (1977) theoretical approach has been of great importance. However, there is a puzzling discrepancy between theory and data with respect to the identification of automaticity. The theoretical assumption that automatic processes operate in parallel and place no demands on capacity means there should be a slope of zero (i.e., a horizontal line) in the function relating decision speed to the number of items in the memory set and/or in the visual display when automatic processes are used. In fact, decision speed was slower when the memory set and the visual display both contained several items (see Figure 5.18).

Shiffrin and Schneider's approach is descriptive rather than explanatory. The claim that some processes become automatic with practice is uninformative about what is actually happening. However, Jansma et al. (2001) have advanced our understanding with their evidence that there is reduced usage of the central executive component of working memory as automaticity develops.

Practice may simply lead to a speeding up of the processes involved, or it may lead to a dramatic change in the nature of the processes themselves. Cheng (1985) used the term "restructuring" to refer to the latter state of affairs. For example, if you are asked to add ten twos, you could do this by adding two and two, and then two to four, and so on. Alternatively, you could short-circuit the process by simply multiplying ten by two.

Cheng (1985) argued that most of Shiffrin and Schneider's findings on automaticity were actually based on restructuring. She claimed that participants in the consistent mapping conditions did not really search systematically for a match. If, for example, they knew that any consonant in the visual display had to be an item from the memory set, then they could simply scan the visual display looking for a consonant without any regard to which consonants were actually in the memory set.

Schneider and Shiffrin (1985) pointed out that some findings could not be explained in terms of restructuring. For example, the finding that participants could not ignore part of the visual display after automatic processes had been acquired does *not* lend itself to a restructuring explanation. Further evidence against the notion of restructuring was reported by Jansma et al. (2001). They found that the same brain regions were activated as automatic processing developed, with the activation of some of the regions gradually decreasing. These findings suggest that the development of automaticity is associated with more efficient processing rather than a complete change in the type of processing as is implied by restructuring.

Norman and Shallice's theory

Norman and Shallice (1986) distinguished between fully automatic and partially automatic processes. They identified three levels of functioning:

- Fully automatic processing controlled by schemas (organised plans).
- Partially automatic processing involving contention scheduling without deliberate direction or conscious control; contention scheduling is used to resolve conflicts among schemas.
- Deliberate control by a supervisory attentional system; Baddeley (1986) argued that this system resembled the central executive of the working memory system (see Chapter 6).

According to Norman and Shallice (1986), fully automatic processes occur with very little conscious awareness of the processes involved. Such automatic processes would often disrupt behaviour if left entirely to their own devices. As a result, there is an automatic conflict resolution process known as contention scheduling. This selects one of the available schemas on the basis of environmental information and current priorities. There is generally more conscious awareness of the partially automatic processes involving contention scheduling than of fully automatic processes. Finally, there is a higher-level supervisory attentional system. This system is involved in decision making and troubleshooting, and it permits flexible responding in novel situations. The supervisory attentional system may well be located in the frontal lobes (see Chapter 6).

Shallice and Burgess (1996) argued that several different processes are carried out by the supervisory system. For example, consider how we cope with a novel situation. First of all, we need to *construct* a new schema to control behaviour. After that, it is necessary to *implement* or make use of the new schema. Finally, it is necessary to *monitor* for errors to check the appropriate schema is being used.

Evidence supporting the distinction between construction and implementation of schemas was reported by Burgess and Shallice (1996). Patients with frontal lesions were given the Brixton spatial anticipation test, which involves predicting which of various circles will be filled on each one of a series of cards. The circle that is filled is determined by various rules, and so successful performance of the task involves constructing a schema corresponding to the rule currently in operation. The errors made by the frontal patients indicated that some had problems with schema construction, whereas others had problems mainly with schema implementation. This *double dissociation* suggests that construction and implementation are separate processes.

Evaluation

The theoretical approach of Norman and Shallice (1986) includes the interesting notion that there are two separate control systems: contention scheduling and the supervisory attentional system. This contrasts with the view that there is a single control system. The approach of Norman and Shallice seems preferable, because it provides a more natural explanation for the fact that some processes are fully automatic, whereas others are only partially automatic. Another advantage of this theoretical approach is that attempts have been made to identify some of the main functions of the supervisory attentional system (e.g., construction of new schemas; implementation of new schemas; monitoring for errors).

Norman and Shallice's approach has various limitations. First, it is not always easy to decide which of the three levels of functioning is being used by people in a given situation. For example, the precise dividing line between fully and partially automatic processing is sometimes hard to establish. Second, as we have seen, there is an unresolved controversy concerning the existence of a central capacity such as the supervisory attentional system. It may be the case that there are several more specific attentional systems rather than one very general one. Third, assuming that there is a supervisory attention system, more research is needed to establish the complete list of its functions.

Instance theory

Logan (1988) pointed out that most theories do not indicate clearly how automaticity develops through prolonged practice. He tried to fill this gap by putting forward instance theory, based on these assumptions:

- Separate memory traces are stored away each time a stimulus is encountered and processed.
- Practice with the same stimulus leads to the storage of increased information about the stimulus, and about what to do with it.
- This increase in the knowledge base with practice permits rapid retrieval of relevant information when the appropriate stimulus is presented.
- "Automaticity is memory retrieval: performance is automatic when it is based on a single-step direct-access retrieval of past solutions from memory" (Logan, 1988, p. 493).
- In the absence of practice, responding to a stimulus requires thought and the application of rules. After prolonged practice, the correct response is stored in memory and can be accessed very rapidly.

These theoretical views make coherent sense of many characteristics of automaticity. Automatic processes are fast because they require only the retrieval of "past solutions" from long-term memory. Automatic processes have little effect on the processing capacity available to perform other tasks, because the retrieval of heavily over-learned information is relatively effortless. Finally, there is no conscious awareness of automatic processes, because no significant processes intervene between the presentation of a stimulus and the retrieval of the appropriate response.

Logan (1988, p. 519) summarised instance theory as follows: "Novice performance is limited by a lack of knowledge rather than by a lack of resources . . . Only the knowledge base changes with practice." Logan is probably right in his basic assumption that an understanding of automatic, expert performance will require detailed consideration of the knowledge acquired with practice, rather than simply processing changes.

Logan, Taylor, and Etherton (1996) argued that knowledge stored in memory as a result of prolonged practice may or may not be produced automatically depending on the precise conditions of retrieval. Participants were given 512 training trials during which any given word was always presented in the same colour (red or green), and the task required them to process its colour. After that, there were 32 transfer trials on which the colour of each word was *reversed* from the training trials. When the task on these transfer trials required colour processing, performance was disrupted, suggesting that there was an automatic influence of colour information.

Would we expect colour reversal to disrupt performance when the task on the transfer trials did *not* require colour processing? Information about colour had been thoroughly learned during training, and so might produce disruption via automatic processes. In fact, there was no disruption. Thus, as predicted, colour information only exerted an automatic influence on performance when this information was *relevant* to the current task.

It has often been assumed that automaticity mainly reflects processes occurring during learning or encoding. However, the findings of Logan et al. (1996) suggest that automaticity is also a memory phenomenon. More specifically, automatic performance depends on the relationship between learned information and retrieval.

Cognitive bottleneck theory

Earlier we discussed research (e.g., Hirst et al., 1980; Spelke et al., 1976) suggesting that two complex tasks could be performed very well together and with minimal disruption. Such findings might suggest that tasks can be performed automatically, given that one of the main criteria for automaticity is a lack of interference with other ongoing cognitive processes. However, the participants in these studies had considerable flexibility in terms of *when* and *how* they processed the two tasks. It is, thus, entirely possible that there were interference effects that went unnoticed because of insensitivity of measurement.

We can return to the issue of whether or not there is always some interference in dual-task studies by considering what is probably the most sensitive type of experiment for detecting such interference. In studies on the **psychological refractory period**, there are two stimuli (e.g., two lights) and two responses (e.g., button presses), and the task is to respond to each stimulus as rapidly as possible. When the second stimulus is presented very shortly after the first one, there is generally a marked slowing of the response to the second stimulus. This is known as the psychological refractory period (PRP) effect (see Pashler et al., 2001), and it has been found in numerous studies even after extensive practice.

What is the meaning of this effect? According to the central bottleneck theory of Welford (1952) and Pashler et al. (2001), there is a bottleneck in the processing system making it impossible for two decisions about the appropriate responses to two different stimuli to be made at the same time. Thus, response selection inevitably occurs in a serial fashion, and this creates a bottleneck in processing even following prolonged practice. In the words of Pashler et al. (2001, p. 642), "The PRP effect arises from postponement of central processing stages in the second task—a processing bottleneck . . . central stages in task 2 cannot commence until corresponding stages of the first task have been completed, whereas perceptual and motoric stages in the two tasks can overlap without constraint." An important implication of the psychological refractory period effect is that at least some processes (e.g., response selection) cannot occur in an automatic fashion.

Evidence

Most studies have found clear evidence of the PRP effect (see Pashler et al., 2001, for a review).

However, in most of these studies, the two tasks both involved manual responses, and it may simply be that people find it especially difficult to control their two hands separately. This issue was investigated by Van Selst, Ruthruff, and Johnston (1999). They used two tasks, one of which required a vocal response and the other of which required a manual response. The initial PRP effect was 353 ms, but this reduced to only 50 ms after extended practice over 36 sessions. There was a much greater PRP effect after practice when the experiment was repeated with both tasks requiring manual responses. Thus, most (but not all) of the PRP effect depended on manual responses being required on both tasks.

According to the central bottleneck theory, the decrease in the size of the PRP effect with practice occurs because of speed-up in several stages of processing of task 1. This assumption was tested by Ruthruff, Johnston, and Van Selst (2000). They used the well-practised participants from the study by Van Selst et al. (1999), and gave them the old, well-practised task 1 and a new task. As predicted, the PRP effect was small, because the participants could take advantage of the speed-up of processing of task 1. Ruthruff et al. (2000) also combined a new task 1 with the old, well-practised task 2. This time (as predicted), there was a large PRP effect.

Schumacher et al. (2001) seemed to destroy the notion that detailed analysis of dual-task performance will always reveal interference. They used two tasks: (1) say "one", "two", or "three" to low-, medium-, and high-pitched tones, respectively; (2) press response keys corresponding to the position of a disc on a computer screen. These two tasks were performed together for a total of 2064 trials, at the end of which some participants performed them as well together as singly. Schumacher et al. found substantial individual differences in the amount of dual-task interference. In one experiment, there was a correlation of +0.81 between dual-task interference and mean reaction time on single-task trials. Thus, those who performed each task on its own particularly well were least affected by dual-task interference.

One limitation in the study by Schumacher et al. (2001) is that their second task (pressing keys to discs) was so simple it did not require the use of central processes. However, Hazeltine et al. (2000) replicated and extended the findings of Schumacher et al. which were obtained some time previously but published in 2001. Of particular importance, they found very little dual-task interference even when the disc–key press task was made more difficult.

Evaluation

Studies on the PRP effect provide a sensitive way of assessing dual-task interference. Pashler et al. (2001, p. 646) summarised the overall findings: "In many cases, . . . practice merely reduces stage-durations, without allowing subjects to bypass the processing bottleneck . . . some new evidence suggests that under some conditions practice can eliminate the processing bottleneck entirely (Hazeltine et al., 2000; Schumacher et al., 2001)."

The evidence from (most but not all) studies of the psychological refractory period indicates that there is a bottleneck, and that some processing is serial (e.g., response selection). However, the size of the psychological refractory period is typically not very large, suggesting that most processes do *not* operate in a serial way. As Pashler and Johnston (1998, p. 184) pointed out, "The idea of obligatory serial central processing is quite consistent with a great deal of parallel processing."

Most theorists have assumed there is a *single* bottleneck. However, there may be multiple bottlenecks. Pashler and Johnston (1998, p. 175) addressed this issue: "At present, . . . a single bottleneck seems sufficient to account for the response delays observed in 'standard' PRP designs involving pairs of choice RT [response time] tasks. In fact, results from these paradigms are difficult to square with the existence of multiple bottlenecks."

The interpretation of findings on the PRP effect remains controversial. However, the evidence suggests that fully automatic processing (indicated by a total absence of interference between two tasks performed together) is rarely achievable. The jury is still out on whether such fully automatic processing is *ever* achieved.

CHAPTER SUMMARY

- Introduction
  Attention generally refers to selectivity of processing. Attention can be active and based on top-down processes or passive and based on bottom-up processes. It is important to distinguish between focused and divided attention. Most research on attention deals only with external, two-dimensional stimuli, ignoring the individual's goals and motivational states.

- Focused auditory attention
  Initial research on focused auditory attention with the shadowing task suggested very limited processing of unattended stimuli. However, there can be extensive processing of unattended stimuli. This is especially the case when the unattended stimuli are dissimilar to the attended ones. There has been a controversy between early- and late-selection theorists as to the location of a bottleneck in processing. Most evidence favours early-selection theories, but the stage at which selection occurs is somewhat flexible and depends on perceptual load.

- Focused visual attention
  There are two separate (but interacting) attentional systems, one of which is stimulus driven or exogenous and the other of which is goal directed or endogenous. According to Corbetta and Shulman (2002), the former system consists of a right-hemisphere ventral fronto-parietal network and the latter system consists of a dorsal fronto-parietal network. The two systems typically interact. For example, salient task-irrelevant stimuli are most likely to attract attention when they are similar to task-relevant stimuli. Visual attention has been compared to a spotlight or zoom lens, implying that visual attention is location based. However, visual attention can also be object based, and split attention has been demonstrated. Evidence that location-based and object-based visual attention are possible has been obtained from patients with neglect, and has also been supported in studies on inhibition of return. Unattended visual stimuli are often processed fairly thoroughly, with some of the strongest evidence coming from neglect patients. However, neuro-imaging studies indicate that attended stimuli produce much more brain activity than unattended ones. Neglect and extinction both reflect biased attention, with a strong bias towards certain objects or locations preventing other stimuli from being detected. Neglect patients typically ignore stimuli presented to the contralesional side of the visual field, but not when these stimuli can be grouped with visual stimuli on the ipsilesional side. Extinction patients process contra-lesional stimuli presented on their own more slowly than ipsilesional ones, which could explain why these stimuli do not compete effectively for attention. Neglect patients have greater problems with exogenous orienting than with endogenous orienting. Research on brain-damaged patients has provided evidence for three components of visual attention: disengagement, shifting, and engagement.

- Crossmodal effects
  In the real world, we often need to coordinate information from two or more sense modalities. Convincing evidence of crossmodal effects has been obtained in studies of exogenous and endo-genous spatial attention and the ventriloquist illusion. These studies have considered crossmodal effects involving the visual, auditory, and tactile modalities. Crossmodal effects seem to depend on bimodal and trimodal cells and on a supramodal attentional control system. Most research on crossmodal effects has been concerned with spatial attention rather than stimulus identification.

- Visual search
  According to feature integration theory, visual search often involves rapid parallel processing of features followed by a slower serial process in which features are combined to form objects. The

original theory was oversimplified, and did not take account of the similarity between the target and non-target stimuli or the similarity among non-targets. Guided search theory involved a development of some of the ideas within feature integration theory, and the assumption that visual search is either entirely parallel or serial was abandoned. According to the decision integration hypothesis, visual search involves decision making based on the discriminability between target and distractor stimuli. This theoretical approach can account for most of the findings on visual search.

- Divided attention
Dual-task performance depends on many factors, including task similarity, practice, and task difficulty. According to central capacity theory, the extent to which two tasks can be performed together depends on the demands that each task makes on the limited resources of a central processor. There is support for this theory, some of it based on neuroimaging studies. However, the notion of a multi-purpose central processor remains controversial, and dual-task performance depends in part on factors (e.g., response selection; extra allocation of resources to difficult tasks) not emphasised within central capacity theory. According to multiple-resource theories, the extent to which two tasks can be performed together depends on whether or not these tasks require the same specific processing resources. This approach de-emphasises higher-level processes such as task coordination.

- Automatic processing
Shiffrin and Schneider distinguished between controlled processes of limited capacity and automatic processes having no capacity limitations. They obtained much support for this distinction, but failed to clarify whether automatic processes based on practice involve a speeding-up of processes or a restructuring of processes. Norman and Shallice distinguished among fully automatic processes, partially automatic processes, and control by a supervisory attentional system. There is evidence that the supervisory attentional system has separate components concerned with the construction and the implementation of schemas. Logan argued that automatic processing occurs when there is direct-access retrieval of information from memory. More specifically, he claimed that automatic performance depends on the relationship between learned information and retrieval. Evidence against automatic processing has come from numerous studies on the psychological refractory period effect. The existence of this effect is consistent with the notion of a central bottleneck in processing. However, this effect is not always found, especially when participants perform each task on its own extremely well.

FURTHER READING

- Corbetta, M., & Shulman, G.L. (2002). Control of goal-directed and stimulus-driven attention in the brain. *Nature Reviews Neuroscience*, *3*, 201–215. The authors provide an interesting discussion of the brain areas involved in different attentional processes.
- Driver, J. (2001). A selective review of selective attention research from the past century. *British Journal of Psychology*, *92*, 53–78. This article contains succinct accounts of several key topics in attention.
- Lamberts, K., & Goldstone, R. (2004). *Handbook of cognition*. London: Sage. There is high-level coverage of attention in this edited book, especially in the chapter by Bundesen and Habekost.

- Logan, G.D. (2004). Cumulative progress in formal theories of attention. *Annual Review of Psychology*, *55*, 207–234. Major theoretical approaches to major phenomena in attention are considered in an authoritative way in this chapter.
- Pashler, H., Johnston, J.C., & Ruthroff, E. (2001). Attention and performance. *Annual Review of Psychology*, *52*, 629–651. This chapter discusses automatic processes and the effects of practice in detail.

Part II

Memory and Concepts

How important is memory? Imagine if we were without it. We would not recognise anyone or anything as familiar. We would be unable to talk, read, or write, because we would remember nothing about language. We would have extremely limited personalities, because we would have no recollection of the events of our own lives and, therefore, no sense of self. In sum, we would have the same lack of knowledge as newborn babies.

We use memory for numerous purposes throughout every day of our lives. It allows us to keep track of conversations, to remember telephone numbers while we dial them, to write essays in examinations, to make sense of what we read, to recognise people's faces, and to understand what we read in books or see on television or at the cinema.

The wonders of human memory are discussed in Chapters 6–9. Chapter 6 deals mainly with key issues which have been regarded as important from the very beginnings of research into memory. For example, we consider the overall architecture of the human memory system and some of the main processes operating within that architecture. We focus on the ways we use short-term memory in many of the activities of everyday life. Finally, we deal with forgetting. Why is it that we tend to forget information as time goes by? Why is recognition memory (e.g., for someone's face) often better than recall (e.g., for someone's name)?

When we think about long-term memory, it is obvious that its scope is absolutely enormous. We have long-term memories for personal information about ourselves and the people we know, knowledge about language, a huge amount of knowledge about psychology (hopefully!), knowledge about thousands of objects in the world around us, and perhaps knowledge of how to play various sports. The key issue that is addressed in Chapter 7 is how to account for the incredible richness of our long-term memories. At one time, many psychologists proposed theories in which there was a single long-term memory store. This proposal never made very much sense, and increasingly memory experts argue that there are several long-term memory systems. As we will see in Chapter 7, some of the most convincing evidence supporting that argument has come from patients whose brain damage has severely impaired their long-term memory. Alas, there is nothing like consensus among psychologists concerning the number and nature of such memory systems, but we will focus on perhaps the most influential approach. According to this approach, there are four long-term memory systems and one short-term memory system.

Memory is important in everyday life in ways that historically have not been the focus of much research. For example, autobiographical memory is of great significance to all of us. Indeed, we would lose our sense of self and life would lose much of its meaning if we lacked memory for the events and experiences that have shaped our personalities. Autobiographical memory is one of the topics discussed in Chapter 8. Other topics on everyday memory considered in that chapter are flashbulb memories, eyewitness testimony, and prospective memory. Flashbulb memories are the apparently vivid and detailed memories we have of major world events such as the horrific attack on New York on 11 September 2001. Research into eyewitness testimony is of considerable importance with respect to the legal system. It has revealed that many of the assumptions we make about the accuracy of eyewitness testimony are mistaken. This matters, because hundreds or even thousands of innocent people have been imprisoned solely on the basis of eyewitness testimony.

Finally, there is prospective memory. When we think about memory, we naturally focus on memory for what has happened in the past. However, most of us have to remember numerous commitments in the future (e.g., meeting a friend as arranged; turning up for a lecture), and such remembering involves prospective memory. We will investigate the ways in which people try to make sure they carry out their future intentions.

Chapter 9 is devoted to concepts for a very good reason. Concepts play a vital role in virtually all of our dealings with the world. We use concepts when we recognise objects in our environment, concepts are of central importance in language, and we use conceptual knowledge when we think about a problem or plan our future. Why, then, is the chapter on concepts included within the memory section of this book? The key reason is because our knowledge of concepts is stored in long-term memory, more specifically in what is often known as semantic memory.

It used to be thought that concepts are neat and tidy, consisting of a set of defining attributes that are both necessary and sufficient to define the concept in question. It also used to be conventional wisdom that concepts are stable over time. We have made progress, in that there is universal agreement that most concepts are fuzzy or untidy. In addition, there is increasing evidence that concepts are *not* stable over time, with the conceptual representations we use varying from situation to situation depending on our current goals and on the demands of the situation.

What form does our knowledge of concepts take if it does not consist of defining attributes? Various answers to that question are provided in Chapter 9. As we will see, there have been arguments about the precise nature of conceptual knowledge and about the ways in which we categorise information presented to us. These, and other issues, are discussed at length in Chapter 9.

6

Learning and Memory

INTRODUCTION

This chapter and the next three are concerned with human memory. All four chapters deal with normal human memory, but Chapter 7 also considers amnesic patients. Traditional laboratory-based research is the focus of this chapter, with more naturalistic research being considered in Chapter 8, and concepts being discussed in Chapter 9. However, there are important links among these types of research. Many theoretical issues are relevant to brain-damaged and normal individuals, whether tested in the laboratory or in the field.

Theories of memory generally consider both the *architecture* of the memory system and the *processes* operating within that structure. Architecture refers to the way in which the memory system is organised, and process refers to the activities occurring within the memory system. Architecture or structure and process are both important, but some theorists emphasise only one in their theoretical formulations.

Learning and memory involve a series of stages. Processes occurring during the presentation of the learning material are known as "encoding". This is the first stage. As a result of encoding, some information is stored within the memory system. Thus, storage is the second stage. The third, and final, stage is retrieval, which involves recovering or extracting stored information from the memory system.

We have emphasised the distinctions between architecture and process and among encoding, storage, and retrieval. However, we cannot have architecture without process, or retrieval without previous encoding and storage. It is only when processes operate on the essentially passive structures of the memory system that it becomes active and of use.

THE ARCHITECTURE OF MEMORY

Several memory theorists (e.g., Atkinson & Shiffrin, 1968) have described the basic architecture of the memory system, and it is possible to discuss the multi-store approach based on the common features of their theories. Three types of memory store were proposed:

- Sensory stores, each holding information very briefly and being modality specific (limited to one sensory modality).

FIGURE 6.1

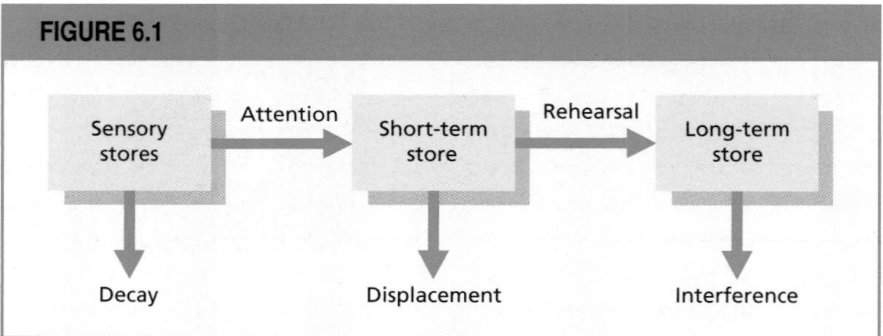

The multi-store model of memory.

- A short-term store of very limited capacity.
- A long-term store of essentially unlimited capacity holding information over extremely long periods of time.

The multi-store model is shown in Figure 6.1. Environmental information is initially received by the sensory stores. These stores are modality specific (e.g., vision; hearing). Information is held very briefly in the sensory stores, with some being attended to and processed further by the short-term store. Some information processed in the short-term store is transferred to the long-term store. Long-term storage of information often depends on rehearsal, with a direct relationship between the amount of rehearsal in the short-term store and the strength of the stored memory trace.

There is much overlap between the areas of attention and memory. Broadbent's (1958) theory of attention (see Chapter 5) was the main influence on the multi-store approach to memory (e.g., the notion of a sensory store resembles his "buffer" store).

Within the multi-store approach, the memory stores form the basic structure, and processes such as attention and rehearsal control the flow of information between them. However, the main emphasis within this approach to memory was on structure.

Sensory stores

Our senses are constantly bombarded with information, most of which does not receive any attention. If you are sitting in a chair as you read this, then tactile information from that part of your body in contact with the chair is probably available. However, you have probably been unaware of that tactile information until now. Information in every sense modality persists briefly after the end of stimulation, aiding the task of extracting its key aspects for further analysis.

Iconic store

The classic work on the visual or **iconic store** was carried out by Sperling (1960). When he presented a visual array containing three rows of four letters each for 50 milliseconds, his participants could usually report only four or five letters, but claimed to have seen many more letters. Sperling (1960) assumed that this happened because visual information had faded before most of it could be reported. He tested this by asking his participants to recall only *part* of the information presented. Sperling's (1960) findings supported his assumption, and indicated that information in iconic storage decays within about 0.5 seconds.

Iconic storage is extremely useful to us. As Coltheart (1983) pointed out, the mechanisms responsible for visual perception always operate on the icon rather than directly on the visual environment.

Echoic store

The **echoic store** is a transient auditory store holding relatively unprocessed input. For example, suppose someone reading a newspaper is asked a question. The person addressed will sometimes ask, "What did you say?", but then realise that he or she does know what has been said. This "playback" facility depends on the echoic store.

Treisman (1964) asked people to shadow (repeat back aloud) the message presented to one ear while ignoring a second identical message presented to the other ear. When the second or non-shadowed message preceded the shadowed message, the two messages were only recognised as being the same when they were within 2 seconds of each other. This suggests the temporal duration of unattended auditory information in echoic storage is about 2 seconds.

Short- and long-term stores

The distinction between a short-term and a long-term store is like the one proposed by William James (1890) between primary memory and secondary memory. Primary memory consists of information remaining in consciousness after it has been perceived and forming part of the psychological present. Secondary memory contains information about events that have left consciousness and are therefore part of the psychological past.

Trying to remember a telephone number for a few seconds is an everyday example of the use of the **short-term store**. It shows two key characteristics usually attributed to this store:

- very limited capacity (only about seven digits can be remembered);
- fragility of storage, as any distraction usually causes forgetting.

The capacity of short-term memory has been assessed by span measures and by the recency effect in free recall. Digit span involves participants repeating back random digits in the correct order when they have heard them all. The span of immediate memory is usually "seven plus or minus two" whether the units are numbers, letters, or words (Miller, 1956). Miller claimed that about seven chunks (integrated pieces or units of information) could be held in short-term memory. For example, "IBM" is one chunk for those familiar with the company name International Business Machines, but three chunks for everyone else. However, the span in chunks is less with larger chunks (e.g., eight-word phrases) than with smaller chunks (e.g., one-syllable words; Simon, 1974).

The **recency effect** in free recall (recalling the items in any order) refers to the finding that the last few items in a list are usually much better remembered in immediate recall than are the items from the middle of the list. Counting backwards for 10 seconds between the end of list presentation and the start of recall mainly affects the recency effect (Glanzer & Cunitz, 1966, see Figure 6.2). The two or three words susceptible to the recency effect may be in the short-term store at the end of list presentation, and thus especially vulnerable. However, Bjork and Whitten (1974) found that there was still a recency effect in free recall when the participants counted backwards for 12 seconds after each item in the list was presented. According to Atkinson and Shiffrin (1968) this should have eliminated the recency effect. The findings can be explained by analogy to looking along a row of telephone poles. The closer poles are more distinct than the ones further away, just as the more recent list words are more discriminable than the others (Glenberg, 1987).

Strong evidence for the distinction between short-term and long-term memory stores comes from studies with brain-damaged patients. Two tasks probably involve different processing mechanisms if there is a **double dissociation** (i.e., some patients perform normally on task A but poorly on task B, whereas others perform normally on task B but poorly on task A). Amnesic patients have generally poor long-term memory, but intact short-term memory (see Chapter 7). The reverse problem is relatively rare, but a few such cases have been reported. These cases include KF, a patient who suffered damage in the left parieto-occipital region of the brain following a motorcycle accident. KF had no problem with long-term learning and recall, but his digit span was greatly impaired, and he had a recency effect of only one item under some circumstances (Shallice & Warrington, 1970). However, KF did not perform badly on all short-term memory tasks (see next section).

Peterson and Peterson (1959) studied the duration of short-term memory by using the task

FIGURE 6.2

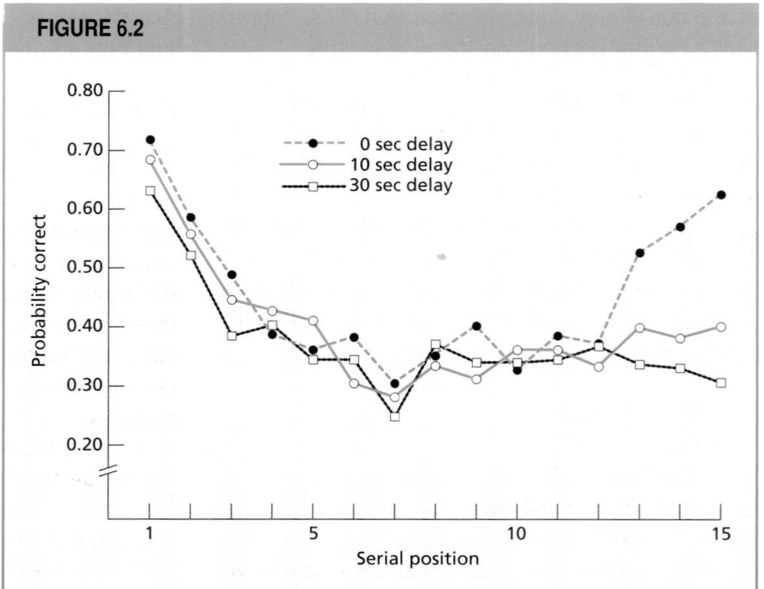

Free recall as a function of serial position and duration of the interpolated task. Adapted from Glanzer and Cunitz (1966).

FIGURE 6.3

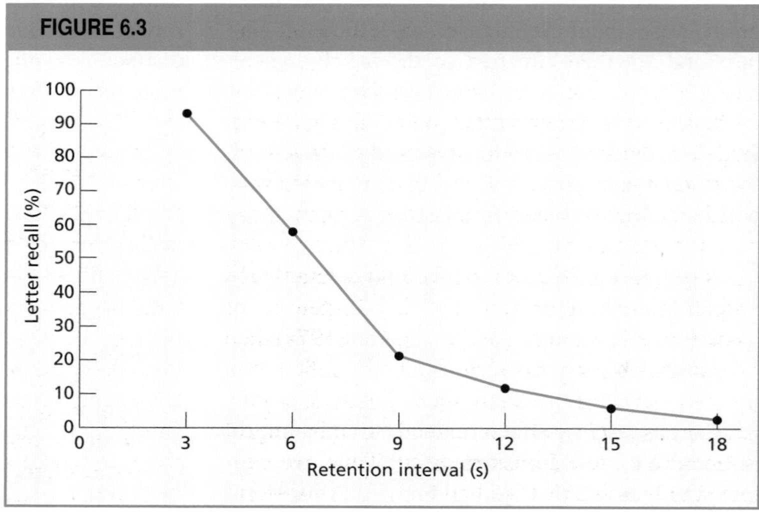

Forgetting over time in short-term memory. Data from Peterson and Peterson (1959).

of remembering a three-letter stimulus for a few seconds while counting backwards by threes. The ability to remember the three-letter stimulus declined to only about 50% after 6 seconds (see Figure 6.3), suggesting that information is lost rapidly from short-term memory.

Why does counting backwards cause forgetting from short-term memory? Counting backwards may be a source of interference, or it may divert attention away from the information in short-term memory (see below). Forgetting from the long-term store involves rather different mechanisms. As will be discussed later, it depends mainly on **cue-dependent forgetting** (i.e., the memory traces are still in the memory system, but are inaccessible).

Evaluation

The multi-store model provided a systematic account of memory structures and processes. The conceptual distinction between three kinds of memory stores (sensory stores, short-term store, and long-term store) makes sense. In order to justify the existence of three qualitatively different types of memory store, we must show major differences among them. Precisely this has been done. The memory stores differ in the following ways:

- temporal duration;
- storage capacity;
- forgetting mechanism(s);
- effects of brain damage.

Many contemporary memory theorists have used the multi-store model as the starting point of their theories. Much theoretical effort has gone into providing a more detailed account of the long-term store than that offered by Atkinson and Shiffrin (1968, 1971; see Chapter 7).

In a word, the multi-store model is oversimplified. It was assumed that both the short-term and long-term stores are unitary, i.e., that each store always operates in a single, uniform way. Evidence that the short-term store is not unitary was reported by Warrington and Shallice (1972). KF's short-term forgetting of *auditory* letters and digits was much greater than his forgetting of *visual* stimuli. Shallice and Warrington (1974) then found that KF's short-term memory deficit was limited to verbal materials such as letters, words, and digits, and did not extend to meaningful sounds (e.g., telephones ringing). Thus, we cannot simply argue that KF had impaired short-term memory. According to Shallice and Warrington (1974), his problems centred on the "auditory-verbal short-term store".

The multi-store model is also oversimplified when it comes to long-term memory. An amazing wealth of information is stored in our long-term memory, including knowledge that Russell Crowe is a film star, that 2 + 2 = 4, that we had muesli for breakfast, and perhaps information about how to ride a bicycle. It is improbable that all this knowledge is stored within a single long-term memory store (see Chapter 7).

According to the multi-store model, the short-term store acts as a gateway between the sensory stores and long-term memory (see Figure 6.1). However, the information processed in the short-term store has already made contact with information stored in long-term memory (Logie, 1999). For example, our ability to engage in verbal rehearsal of visually presented words depends on prior contact with stored information concerning pronunciation. Thus, access to long-term memory occurs *before* information is processed in short-term memory.

Finally, multi-store theorists assumed that the main way in which information is transferred to long-term memory is via rehearsal in the short-term store. However, the role of rehearsal in our everyday lives is very limited. More generally, multi-store theorists can be criticised for focusing too much on structural aspects of memory rather than on memory processes.

Short-term memory: Standard model

The central part of the multi-store model was the short-term store. More recently, several theorists (e.g., Shiffrin, 1999) have proposed a revised theoretical account of it, which we can call the standard model (Nairne, 2002a). The main assumptions of the standard model are as follows:

- Information in short-term storage is in a state of activation.
- "Permanent knowledge is activated, as a byproduct of on-line cognitive processing, and comes to reside 'in' short-term memory. Short-term memory . . . is simply defined as the collective set of this activated information in memory" (Nairne, 2002a, p. 54).
- Currently activated information can be accessed immediately and effortlessly.
- "Activation is assumed to be fragile, and it can be quickly lost—through the operation of *decay*—in the absence of rehearsal" (Nairne, 2002a, p. 54).

In sum, the standard model is very simple: activated information from long-term memory is in short-term memory, decay of that activation causes that information to leave short-term memory, and decay can be prevented by rehearsal.

Evidence

According to the standard model, short-term memory should be better for words that can be rehearsed rapidly than for words that take longer to rehearse: rapid rehearsal maintains activation and thereby prevents decay. Some evidence supports this prediction (e.g., Baddeley, Thomson, & Buchanan, 1975; see below), but other evidence does not. For example, Lovatt, Avons, and Masterson (2000) used two-syllable words varying in their spoken duration. Short-term memory was no better for short-duration words than for long-duration words, casting doubt on the assumption that short-term memory depends mainly on rehearsal.

According to the standard model, forgetting from short-term memory is due to decay. However, proactive interference (disruption of current learning and memory by previous learning) also plays an important role in forgetting from short-term memory. For example, Keppel and Underwood (1962) used the same task as Peterson and Peterson (1959). There was no forgetting over time on the very first trial, after which forgetting resembled that observed by Peterson and Peterson (1959). Why was this? The most plausible explanation is that only the items presented on the first trial avoided proactive interference.

If forgetting from short-term memory is due to decay, then there should be rapid forgetting in the absence of rehearsal. That is precisely what was observed by Peterson and Peterson (1959). However, Nairne, Whiteman, and Kelley (1999) argued that rapid forgetting is not inevitable. They presented their participants with five-item word lists, and took two steps to reduce the forgetting rate. First, memory was tested only for order information and not for the words themselves. This was done by re-presenting the five words at test, and asking participants to arrange them in order. Second, the words on each trial differed, to reduce proactive interference. There was a rehearsal-prevention task during the retention interval (reading aloud digits presented on a screen). There was remarkably little forgetting even over 96 seconds (see Figure 6.4), thus providing little support for the notion that decay causes forgetting in short-term memory.

FIGURE 6.4

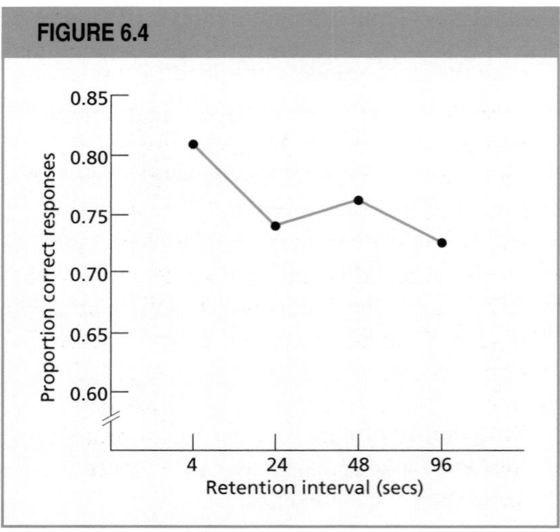

Proportion of correct responses as a function of retention interval. Data from Nairne et al. (1999).

There is evidence against the assumption of the standard model that information in short-term memory is directly accessible. Tehan and Humphreys (1996) asked their participants to remember the second of two four-item blocks. For example, the first block might be "jail silk orange peach" and the second block might be "page leap carrot witch". The participants showed better short-term memory for the word "carrot" when asked to recall the vegetable from the second block than when asked to recall the type of juice from the second block. This occurred because there was more proactive interference from the words in the first block in the latter condition (orange is a type of juice). Thus, recall from short-term memory depends on the nature of the retrieval cue (e.g., vegetable; type of juice), and information in short-term memory is *not* always directly accessible.

Evaluation

The standard model provides a simple account of short-term memory. However, most of its assumptions are incorrect or only partially correct. Nairne (2002a, p. 76) summarised its limitations:

> It leads one to the conclusion that forgetting rates are fixed, like gravity, rather than variable, as much of the data suggest. It also suggests that the main vehicle for short-term storage is rehearsal when, in fact, much of the variability in immediate retention turns out to be independent of rehearsal. Finally, it leads one to the conclusion that remembering is a direct byproduct of activation . . . It is the interpretation of that activation, through a cue-driven retrieval process, that explains how we remember over the short term.

WORKING MEMORY

Baddeley and Hitch (1974) and Baddeley (1986) replaced the concept of the short-term store with that of working memory. In the years since then, the conceptualisation of the working memory system has become increasingly complex (see also Chapter 16). According to Baddeley (2001), the working memory system has four components (see Figure 6.5):

- A modality-free **central executive** resembling attention.
- A **phonological loop** holding information in a phonological (speech-based) form.
- A **visuo-spatial sketchpad** specialised for spatial and visual coding.
- An **episodic buffer**, which is a temporary storage system that can hold and integrate information from the phonological loop, the visuo-spatial sketchpad, and long-term memory. It is controlled by the central executive. This component was added recently and is discussed later.

The key component of working memory is the central executive. It has limited capacity, resembles attention, and deals with any cognitively demanding task. The phonological loop and the visuo-spatial sketchpad are slave systems used by the central executive for specific purposes. The phonological loop preserves the order in which words are presented, and the visuo-spatial sketchpad is used for the storage and manipulation of spatial and visual information. All three components have limited capacity, and are relatively independent of the other components. Two assumptions follow:

(1) If two tasks use the same component, they cannot be performed successfully together.
(2) If two tasks use different components, it should be possible to perform them as well together as separately.

Numerous dual-task studies have been carried out on the basis of these assumptions. For example,

FIGURE 6.5

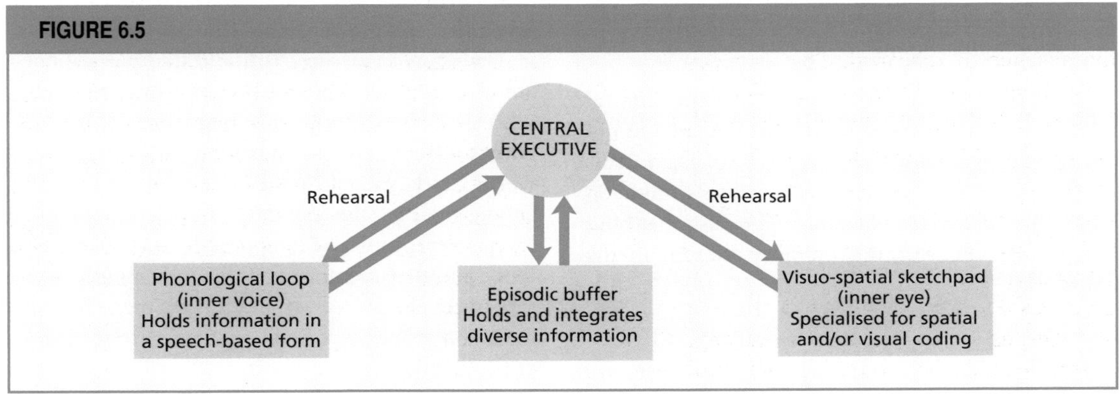

The major components of Baddeley's working memory system. Figure adapted from Baddeley (2001).

FIGURE 6.6

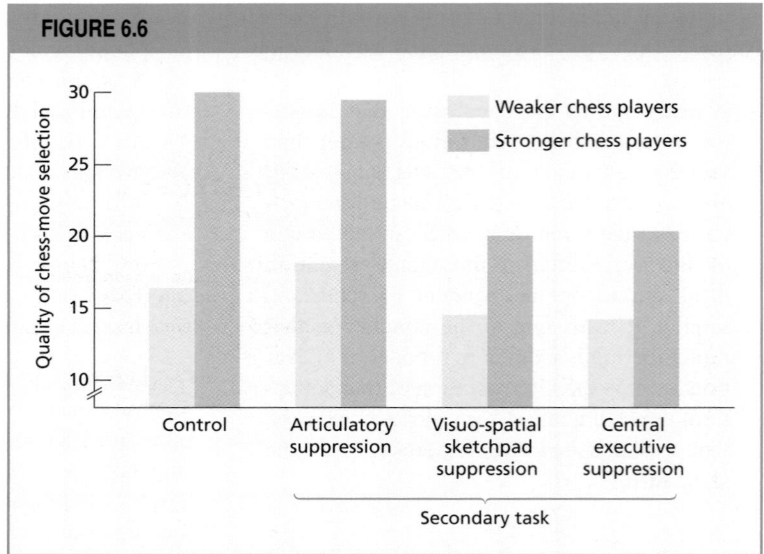

Effects of secondary tasks on quality of chess-move selection in stronger and weaker players. Adapted from Robbins et al. (1996).

Robbins et al. (1996) considered the involvement of the three original components of working memory in the selection of chess moves by weaker and stronger players. They selected continuation moves from various chess positions while performing one of the following concurrent tasks:

- Repetitive tapping: this was the control condition.
- Random number generation: this involved the central executive.
- Pressing keys on a keypad in a clockwise fashion: this used the visuo-spatial sketchpad.
- Rapid repetition of the word "see-saw": this is **articulatory suppression**, which uses the phonological loop.

Selecting chess moves involved the central executive and the visuo-spatial sketchpad, but not the phonological loop (see Figure 6.6). The effects of the various concurrent tasks were similar on stronger and weaker players, suggesting that both groups use the working memory system in the same way.

Phonological loop

Some of the most convincing evidence that we use the phonological loop on short-term memory tasks comes from the **phonological similarity effect**, in which serial recall of a short list of visually presented words is worse when the words are phonologically similar than when they are phonologically dissimilar. For example, FEE, HE, KNEE, LEE, ME, SHE form a list of phonologically similar words, whereas BAY, HOE, IT, ODD, SHY, and UP form a list of phonologically dissimilar words. Larsen, Baddeley, and Andrade (2000) used those lists, and found that serial recall was 25% worse with the phonologically similar list. This phonological similarity effect presumably reflects the use of speech-based rehearsal processes within the phonological loop.

Baddeley et al. (1975) found that participants' ability to reproduce a sequence of words was better with short words than with long words: the **word-length effect**. The participants recalled as many words as they could read out in 2 seconds. This suggested that the capacity of the phonological loop is determined by temporal duration like a tape loop, and that memory span is determined by the rate of rehearsal. As we saw earlier, these findings have sometimes not been replicated (e.g., Lovatt et al., 2000).

Baddeley et al. (1975) obtained evidence that the word-length effect depends on the phonological

FIGURE 6.7

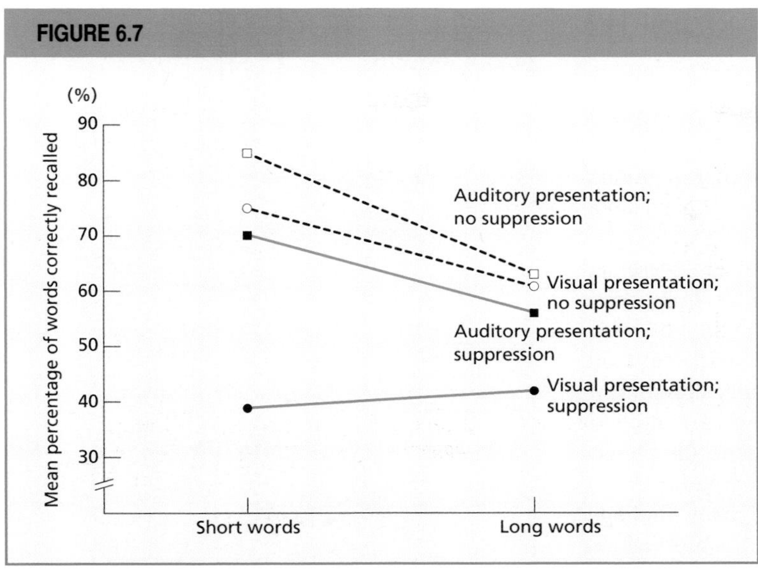

Immediate word recall as a function of modality of presentation (visual vs. auditory), presence versus absence of articulatory suppression, and word length. Adapted from Baddeley et al. (1975).

loop. The number of visually presented words (out of five) that could be recalled was assessed. Some participants were given the articulatory suppression task of repeating the digits 1 to 8 while performing the main task. The argument was that this task would involve the phonological loop and prevent it being used on the word-span task. Articulatory suppression eliminated the word-length effect (see Figure 6.7), suggesting that the effect depends on the loop.

Baddeley et al. (1975) assumed that the word-length effect occurred because of the slower rehearsal of long words at presentation, which allowed some of the information to decay. Another possibility is that it takes increased time to produce longer words during subsequent recall, and this output delay leads to decay. However, Baddeley, Chincotta, Stafford, and Turk (2002) found there was still a word-length effect even when output delay was controlled by using a recognition-memory test rather than recall. Thus, the word-length effect seems to depend mainly on the slower rehearsal time for longer words.

Baddeley (1986, 1990) drew a distinction between a phonological or speech-based store and an articulatory control process (see Figure 6.8).

FIGURE 6.8

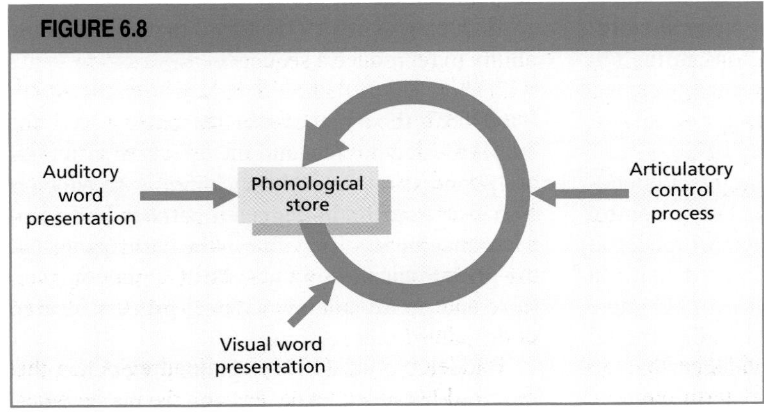

Phonological loop system as envisaged by Baddeley (1990).

According to Baddeley, the phonological loop consists of:

- a passive phonological store directly concerned with speech perception;
- an articulatory process linked to speech production that gives access to the phonological store.

According to this account, words presented auditorily are processed differently from those presented visually. Auditory presentation of words produces *direct* access to the phonological store regardless of whether the articulatory control process is used. In contrast, visual presentation of words only permits *indirect* access to the phonological store through subvocal articulation.

This account makes sense of many findings. Suppose the word-length effect observed by Baddeley et al. (1975) depends on the rate of articulatory rehearsal (see Figure 6.7). Articulatory suppression eliminates the word-length effect with visual presentation because access to the phonological store is prevented. However, it does *not* affect the word-length effect with auditory presentation, because information about the words enters the phonological store directly.

The account is supported by research on brain-damaged patients, some of whom (e.g., JB; PV) have a damaged phonological store but an intact articulatory control process (Shallice & Butterworth, 1977; Vallar & Baddeley, 1984). These patients have very poor short-term memory for auditory-verbal material, but essentially normal speech production. Similar findings were reported for another patient (LA). Which parts of the brain are involved in the phonological store? Patients JB and LA both have lesions in the left temporo-parietal cortex including the supramarginal and angular gyri (Vallar, DiBetta, & Silveri, 1997; Warrington, Logue, & Pratt, 1971).

Other patients (e.g., TO) have an intact phonological store but a damaged articulatory control process shown by a lack of evidence for rehearsal (Vallar et al., 1997). The areas of brain damage in these patients are variable. In the case of TO, there were lesions in the premotor, rolandic, frontal paraventricular and anterior insula areas of the left hemisphere.

FIGURE 6.9

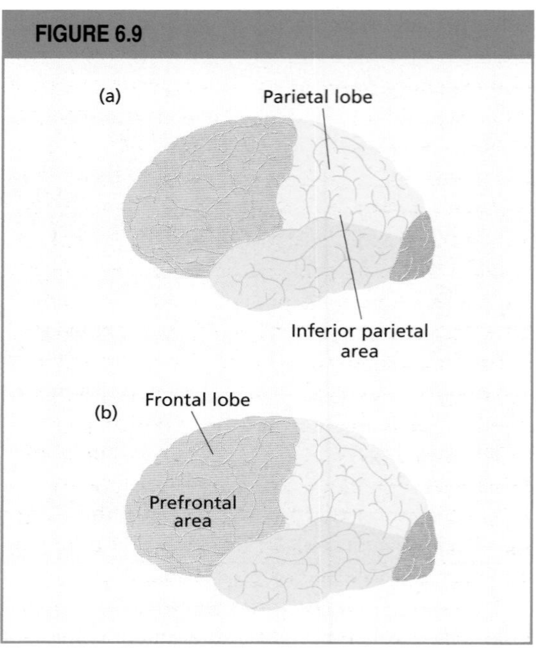

Brain areas of the phonological loop involved in (a) storage and (b) articulatory rehearsal. From Henson et al. (2000). Reproduced with permission from Elsevier.

Henson, Burgess, and Frith (2000) carried out an fMRI study on healthy volunteers to identify the brain areas associated with the phonological loop. Their findings broadly supported those from brain-damaged patients, and are shown in Figure 6.9. As Henson et al. (2000, p. 439) concluded, "Separate areas were implicated in storage and rehearsal, namely a left inferior parietal area in the former and left prefrontal areas in the latter."

Evaluation

Baddeley's theory accounts reasonably well for the word-length effect and the effects of articulatory suppression. In addition, there is convincing evidence from brain-damaged patients and from neuroimaging studies with healthy participants that the phonological loop consists of a phonological store and an articulatory control process located in different brain regions.

What is the value of the phonological loop? It increases memory span, but this is far removed from the activities of everyday life. Moreover, individuals with a severely deficient phonological loop generally cope very well, suggesting that the phonological loop has little practical significance. Baddeley, Gathercole, and Papagno (1998, p. 158) disagreed, arguing that "the phonological loop does have a very important function to fulfil, but it is one that is not readily uncovered by experimental studies of adult participants. We suggest that the function of the phonological loop is not to remember familiar words but to learn new words."

Evidence supporting the above viewpoint was reported by Papagno, Valentine, and Baddeley (1991). Native Italian speakers learned pairs of Italian words and pairs of Italian–Russian words. Articulatory suppression (which reduces use of the phonological loop) greatly slowed the learning of foreign vocabulary, but had little effect on the learning of pairs of Italian words.

Trojano and Grossi (1995) studied SC, a patient with extremely poor phonological functioning. SC showed reasonable learning ability in most situations, but was totally unable to learn auditorily presented word–nonword pairs. Presumably SC's poorly functioning phonological loop prevented the learning of the phonologically unfamiliar nonwords.

According to Baddeley et al. (1998), the phonological store is of more relevance than subvocal rehearsal in the learning of new words. Subvocal rehearsal is only used by children to maintain the contents of the phonological store from about the age of 7. However, children as young as 3 show a close link between phonological memory performance and vocabulary learning (Baddeley et al., 1998). Such evidence suggests that subvocal rehearsal is not needed for vocabulary learning.

Visuo-spatial sketchpad

The visuo-spatial sketchpad is used in the temporary storage and manipulation of spatial and visual information. In a study by Baddeley et al. (1975), participants heard the locations of digits within a matrix described by an auditory message that was either easily visualised or rather hard to visualise. They then reproduced the matrix. When this task was combined with a task called the pursuit rotor (i.e., tracking a light moving around a circular track), performance on the easily visualised message was greatly impaired, but there was no adverse effect on the non-visualisable message.

The most obvious interpretation of these findings is that the pursuit rotor involves visual perception, and thus interferes with performance on the visualisable message. However, Baddeley and Lieberman (1980; see also Chapter 3) found that a specifically visual concurrent task (making brightness judgements) actually disrupted performance *more* on the non-visualisable message. The results were very different when a spatial task with no visual input was performed while the message was being presented. This involved participants trying to point at a moving pendulum while blindfolded, with auditory feedback being provided. This spatial tracking task greatly reduced recall of the visualisable messages, but had little effect on the non-visualisable messages. Thus, recall of visualisable messages of the kind used by Baddeley et al. (1975) and by Baddeley and Lieberman (1980) is interfered with by spatial rather than by visual tasks, implying that processing of such messages relies mainly on spatial coding.

Logie (1995) argued that visuo-spatial working memory can be subdivided into two components:

- The **visual cache**, which stores information about visual form and colour.
- The **inner scribe**, which deals with spatial and movement information. It rehearses information in the visual cache, transfers information from the visual cache to the central executive, and is involved in the planning and execution of body and limb movements.

Evidence

Support for the distinction between a visual cache and an inner scribe was reported by Quinn and McConnell (1996). Their participants learned word lists in two different ways: (1) the method of loci, with each word being associated with a different familiar location; and (2) the pegword technique, in which each word was associated to easily memorised items or pegs based on the rhyme "one is a bun, two is a shoe, three is a tree, four is a door . . .". Mental images were formed by associating the first list word with a bun, the second word with a shoe, and so on. It was assumed that the method of loci mainly requires visual processing, whereas the pegword technique requires spatial and visual processing.

Quinn and McConnell (1996) obtained evidence favouring the above assumption by using two interfering tasks. One was a spatial task, in which a dot had to be monitored as it moved through a sequence of locations. The other was a visual task involving the presentation of dynamic visual noise (a meaningless display of dots that changed continuously). Memory performance based on the method of loci was disrupted by the visual task but not by the spatial task, suggesting that learning primarily depended on the visual cache rather than the inner scribe. In contrast, memory performance based on the pegword technique was adversely affected by both interference tasks, suggesting that learning with this technique required both components of the visuo-spatial sketchpad.

Evidence consistent with Logie's theory was reported by Beschin, Cocchini, Della Sala, and Logie (1997). They studied a man, NL, who had suffered a stroke. He found it very hard to describe details from the left side of scenes in visual imagery, a condition known as unilateral representational neglect. However, NL had no problems with *perceiving* the left side of scenes, so his visual perceptual system was essentially intact. He performed very poorly on tasks thought to require use of the visuo-spatial sketchpad, unless stimulus support in the form of a drawing or other physical stimulus was available. According to Beschin et al. (1997), NL may have sustained damage to the visual cache, so he could only create impoverished mental representations of objects and scenes. Stimulus support allowed him to use his intact visual perceptual skills to compensate for the deficient internal representations.

Farah et al. (1988) reported on a patient, LH. He performed much better on tasks involving spatial processing than on tasks involving the visual aspects of imagery (e.g., judging the relative sizes of animals). Presumably LH's brain damage affected the visual cache rather than the inner scribe.

Smith and Jonides (1997) carried out an ingenious study in which two visual stimuli were presented together, followed by a probe stimulus. The participants had to decide either whether the probe was in the same location as one of the initial stimuli (spatial task) or whether it had the same form (visual task). The stimuli were identical in the two tasks, but there were clear differences in brain activity as revealed by PET. Regions in the right hemisphere (prefrontal cortex, premotor cortex, occipital cortex, and parietal cortex) became active during the spatial task. In contrast, the visual task produced activation in the left hemisphere, especially the parietal cortex and the inferotemporal cortex.

Several other studies have indicated that different brain areas are activated during visual and spatial working-memory tasks (see Sala, Rämä, & Courtney, 2003, for a review). In essence, the ventral prefrontal cortex (e.g., the inferior and middle frontal gyri) is generally activated more during visual working-memory tasks than spatial working-memory tasks. In contrast, more dorsal prefrontal cortex (especially an area of the superior prefrontal sulcus) tends to be more activated during spatial working-memory tasks than visual working-memory tasks. It should be noted that this separation between visual and spatial processing is entirely consistent with evidence that rather separate pathways are involved in visual and spatial perceptual processing (see Chapter 2).

There may be important links between the visuo-spatial sketchpad and the spatial medium identified by Kosslyn (e.g., 1994). The spatial medium is used for manipulating visual images, and shares some features with Baddeley's visuo-spatial sketch pad (Brandimonte, Hitch, & Bishop, 1992; see also Chapter 3).

How useful is the visuo-spatial sketchpad in everyday life? According to Baddeley (1997, p. 82), "The spatial system is important for geographical orientation, and for planning spatial tasks. Indeed, tasks involving visuo-spatial manipulation . . . have tended to be used as selection tools for professions . . . such as engineering and architecture."

Evaluation

The notion that the visuo-spatial sketchpad consists of somewhat separate visual (visual cache) and spatial (inner scribe) components is supported by various kinds of evidence. First, when a visual task and a spatial task are performed together, there is often little interference between them (e.g., Baddeley & Lieberman, 1980; Quinn & McConnell, 1996). Second, some brain-damaged patients seem to have damage to the visual component but not to the spatial component (e.g., Beschin et al., 1997; Farah et al., 1988). Third, brain-imaging data suggest that the two components of the visuo-spatial sketchpad are located in different brain regions (e.g., Smith & Jonides, 1997; Sala et al., 2003).

In spite of the evidence for separate visual and spatial components, many tasks require both components to be used in combination. What remains for the future is to understand more fully how processing and information from the two components are combined and integrated on such tasks.

Central executive

The central executive, which resembles an attentional system, is the most important and versatile component of the working memory system. However, as Baddeley (1996, p. 6) admitted, "our initial specification of the central executive was so vague as to serve as little more than a ragbag into which could be stuffed all the complex strategy selection, planning, and retrieval checking that clearly goes on when subjects perform even the apparently simple digit span task."

Baddeley (1996) argued that damage to the frontal lobes of the cortex can cause impairments to the central executive. Rylander (1939, p. 20) described the classical frontal syndrome as involving "disturbed attention, increased distractibility, a difficulty in grasping the whole of a complicated state of affairs . . . well able to work along old routine lines . . . cannot learn to master new types of task, in new situations." Thus, patients with frontal damage sometimes behave as if they lacked a control system allowing them to direct, and to re-direct, their processing resources appropriately. Such patients are said to suffer from **dysexecutive syndrome** (Baddeley, 1996).

There have been various attempts to identify the major functions of the central executive. For example, Baddeley (1996) identified the following functions:

(1) switching of retrieval plans;
(2) timesharing in dual-task studies;
(3) selective attention to certain stimuli while ignoring others;
(4) temporary activation of long-term memory.

Smith and Jonides (1999) produced a somewhat similar list:

(1) switching attention between tasks;
(2) planning sub-tasks to achieve some goal;
(3) selective attention and inhibition;
(4) updating and checking the contents of working memory;
(5) coding representations in working memory for time and place of appearance.

Evidence

One task that Baddeley has used to study the workings of the central executive is random generation of digits or letters. The basic idea is that close attention is needed on this task to avoid producing stereotyped (and non-random) sequences. Baddeley (1996; see also Baddeley, Emslie, Kolodny, & Duncan, 1998) reported a study in which the participants held between one and eight digits in short-term memory while trying to generate a random sequence of digits. It was assumed that the demands on the central executive would be greater as the number of digits to be remembered increased. As predicted, the randomness of the sequence produced on the generation task decreased as the digit memory load increased (see Figure 6.10).

Baddeley (1996) argued that performance on the random generation task might depend on the ability to switch retrieval plans rapidly and so avoid stereotyped responses. This hypothesis was tested as follows. The random digit generation task involved pressing numbered keys. This task was done on its own, or in combination with reciting

FIGURE 6.10

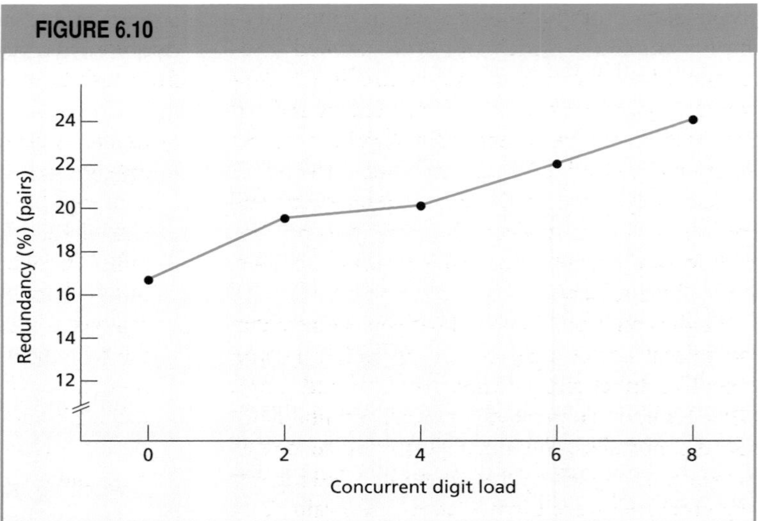

Randomness of digit generation (greater redundancy means reduced randomness) as function of concurrent digit memory load. Data from Baddeley (1996).

the alphabet, counting from 1, or alternating numbers and letters (A 1 B 2 C 3 D 4 . . .). Randomness on the random generation task was reduced by the alternation task, presumably because it required constant switching of retrieval plans. This suggests that rapid switching of retrieval plans is one of the functions of the central executive.

Towse (1998) argued that random generation is not a pure central executive task. Participants tried to produce random sequences using the numbers 1–10 or 1–15, and the relevant set of numbers was either visible in front of them or not presented. Number generation was more random when the numbers were visible. Thus, an important factor in random generation is the generation of the potential set of response alternatives, and this is easier when the alternatives are visible.

The notion that the central executive may play an important part in timesharing or distributing attention across two tasks was considered in a number of studies discussed by Baddeley (1996). One study involved patients with **Alzheimer's disease**, which involves progressive loss of mental powers and reduced central executive functioning. First of all, each participant's digit span was established. Then they were given several digit-span trials with that number of digits. Finally, they were given more digit-span trials combined with the task of placing a cross in each of a series of boxes arranged in an irregular pattern (dual-task condition). All the Alzheimer's patients showed a marked reduction in digit-span performance in the dual-task condition, but none of the normal controls did. These findings are consistent with the view that Alzheimer's patients have particular problems with the central executive function of distributing attention between two tasks.

Several researchers have argued that the central executive is located in the frontal cortex. For example, D'Esposito et al. (1995) used fMRI to identify the brain regions involved in dual-task performance. The participants carried out either a single task (deciding whether each word presented in a series was a vegetable; deciding whether two visual displays differed only in rotation) or they performed both tasks together. Areas within the dorsolateral prefrontal cortex were activated under dual-task conditions but not under single-task conditions. D'Esposito et al. (1995, p. 280) concluded as follows: "Dorsolateral prefrontal cortex is involved in the allocation and co-ordination of attentional resources, a unique process observed by the CE [central executive] component of working memory recruited through dual-task performance."

There is other evidence suggesting the involvement of the frontal cortex in the functioning of the central executive. For example, the central executive functions of attention and inhibition are involved in the **Stroop effect**, in which naming the colours in which words are printed takes longer when the words are conflicting colour words (e.g., the word BLUE printed in red). It has been found in several PET studies that the anterior one-third of cingulate cortex (which is anatomically close to the dorsolateral prefrontal cortex) is activated when the colour word conflicts with the print colour (see Smith & Jonides, 1999, for a review).

Studies on brain-damaged patients suggest that the frontal cortex may *not* be crucial to central executive functioning. Ahola, Vilkki, and Servo (1996) found that patients with focal frontal damage did not show impaired performance on the Stroop test, suggesting that attentional and inhibitory processes were unaffected by the brain damage. Andres and Van der Linden (2002) studied patients with damage to the frontal cortex. Two central executive tasks were used with these patients: (1) a directed forgetting task in which they had to inhibit information that was no longer relevant; (2) dual-task conditions, in which processing and storage operations had to be carried out at the same time. Andres and Van der Linden (2002, p. 835) obtained the following findings: "Frontal patients performed the dual task and inhibited the no-longer relevant information as well as control participants. These findings suggest that not all executive processes are exclusively sustained by the frontal cortex."

An important issue is whether the central executive is unitary in the sense that there is a single executive mechanism or whether there are several somewhat different executive mechanisms. The evidence tends to favour the latter possibility. Miyake et al. (2000) used several tasks designed to involve one of three major executive functions (i.e., shifting attention, updating information, and response inhibition). These three functions were moderately correlated with each other, but were clearly separable. The implication is that the various executive functions differ in terms of the processes involved, even though they share some common process (e.g., controlled attention).

Collette and Van der Linden (2002, p. 120) reviewed numerous brain-imaging studies involving several central executive functions. The evidence suggested that executive processes engage some common brain areas, but there are also differences from task to task:

> Some prefrontal areas (e.g., BA9/46, 10, and anterior cingulate gyrus) are systematically activated by a large range of various executive tasks, suggesting their involvement in rather general executive processes. However, other frontal areas . . . and even parietal regions . . . are also frequently found during the execution of executive tasks. Since these regions are involved less systematically in the different executive processes explored in this review, we can hypothesise that they have more specific functions.

Verbal vs. spatial working memory

Shah and Miyake (1996) disagreed with the notion that there is one central executive serving various functions. They proposed instead separate verbal and spatial working-memory systems. They obtained supporting evidence in a study in which students were presented with tests of verbal and spatial working memory. The verbal task was the reading span task (Daneman & Carpenter, 1980; see Chapter 11). In this task, the participants read a series of sentences and then recall the final word of each sentence. The reading span is the maximum number of sentences for which they can do this. There was also a spatial span task. The participants had to decide whether each of a set of letters was in normal or mirror-image orientation. After that, they had to indicate the direction in which the top of each letter had been pointing. The spatial span was the maximum number of letters for which they were able to do this.

The correlation between reading span and spatial span was a non-significant +.23, suggesting that verbal and spatial working memory are rather separate. Shah and Miyake's other findings supported this conclusion. Reading span correlated +.45 with verbal IQ, but only +.12 with spatial IQ. In contrast, spatial span correlated +.66 with spatial IQ, and only +.07 with verbal IQ.

The participants in the study by Shah and Miyake (1996) were nearly all of high intelligence, and this may have served to reduce the correlations between verbal and spatial working memory. However, Mackintosh and Bennett (2003) carried out a similar study on participants having a broader range of ability and replicated the key findings of Shah and Miyake.

Episodic buffer

According to Baddeley and Wilson (2002, p. 1738), the main characteristics of the episodic buffer are as follows:

> It is a limited capacity system that is episodic in the sense that it is capable of integrating information from a range of sources into a single complex structure or episode. It is a buffer in the sense of acting as an intermediary between the subsystems [phonological loop and visuo-spatial sketchpad] which use different codes, combining them into a unitary multi-dimensional representation. Such a process of active binding is assumed to be highly demanding of the limited capacity attentional system that constitutes the central executive.

Why did Baddeley (2000) feel it necessary to add the episodic buffer to the working memory model about 25 years after the other three components were identified? In essence, the phonological loop and the visuo-spatial sketchpad permit the processing and temporary storage of *specific* kinds of information only, and the central executive is involved in *general* processing but has no storage capacity. There seems to be something missing, since none of these three components can be regarded as a *general* storage system that can combine several kinds of information. It is precisely this gap that the episodic buffer is designed to fill.

Evidence

There are various findings that are hard to account for in terms of previous versions of the working memory model which lacked an episodic buffer. For example, Chincotta, Underwood, Abd Ghani, Papadopoulou, and Wresinksi (1999) studied memory span for Arabic numerals and digit words, finding that the participants used both verbal and visual coding while performing the task. This suggests that verbal information processed within the phonological loop and visual information processed within the visuo-spatial sketchpad must be combined and stored somewhere within working memory. It was rather mysterious where this could be within earlier versions of the working memory model, but the natural location within the current model is clearly the episodic buffer.

Additional reasons for postulating an episodic buffer can be seen if we consider the finding that immediate memory span for unrelated words is about 5 words, whereas the immediate span for sentences is about 15 or 16 words (e.g., Baddeley, Vallar, & Wilson, 1987). Before the introduction of the episodic buffer, it would have been natural to explain this difference on the basis that long-term memory plays a much larger role in recalling words within sentences. If that account were correct, then brain-damaged patients with impaired short-term phonological memory should be able to use long-term memory to produce a respectable sentence span. In fact, however, their sentence span is only about 5 words (Baddeley et al., 1987). The findings can be explained if we assume that sentence span depends on the episodic buffer, and the episodic buffer can only function effectively when the other components of working memory are intact.

Stronger evidence in support of the notion of an episodic buffer was reported by Baddeley and Wilson (2002). They argued that high levels of immediate prose recall depend on two factors: (1) the capacity of the episodic buffer; and (2) an efficiently functioning central executive which facilitates the creation and maintenance of information in the buffer. According to this argument, even severely amnesic patients (with very impaired long-term memory) should have good immediate prose recall provided that they have an efficient central executive. As predicted, immediate prose recall was much better in amnesics having little deficit in executive functioning than in those with a severe executive deficit.

There is relatively little information concerning the location of the episodic buffer within the brain, and Baddeley (2001) doubted whether it is actually located in any *single* location. Relevant evidence was reported by Prabhakaran, Narayanan, Zhao, and Gabrieli (2000, p. 89), who carried out an fMRI study and concluded that, "The present fMRI results provide evidence for another buffer, namely one that allows for temporary retention of integrated information." The brain activation associated with this (episodic) buffer was within the frontal lobes.

Evaluation

Several findings that were hard to explain within previous versions of the working memory model are relatively easy to account for by assuming that people have an episodic buffer. This suggests that the episodic buffer is a valuable addition to the model, and increases its ability to predict behaviour in many situations. It remains for future research to clarify the processes determining what information is stored in the episodic buffer and how different kinds of information are integrated within the buffer.

Overall evaluation

There are several advantages of the working memory system over the short-term store proposed by Atkinson and Shiffrin (1968). First, the working memory system is concerned with both active processing and transient storage of information, and so is involved in all complex cognitive tasks (e.g., language comprehension; see Chapter 11).

Second, the working memory model explains the partial deficits of short-term memory observed in brain-damaged patients. If brain damage affects only one of the three components of working memory, then selective deficits on short-term memory tasks would be expected.

Third, the working memory model incorporates verbal rehearsal as an optional process within the phonological loop. This is more realistic than the enormous significance of rehearsal within the multi-store model of Atkinson and Shiffrin (1968).

On the negative side, the role played by the central executive remains unclear. The central executive has limited capacity, but it has proved hard to measure that capacity. It is claimed that the central executive is "modality free" and used in numerous processing operations, but the precise constraints on its functioning are unknown. It was originally assumed that the central executive is unitary, and perhaps located in the frontal cortex. These assumptions seem increasingly implausible. It is probable that the central executive consists of several components, or that there are two or more central executives. There is some agreement on the precise functions and/or components of the central executive, but much controversy still remains. Overall, as Baddeley and Hitch (2000, p. 129) admitted, "The central executive is the least well understood component of the Baddeley and Hitch model."

Another issue requiring more research concerns the relationship between the episodic buffer and the other components of the working memory system. Some progress has been made in terms of understanding in a general way how the episodic buffer relates to other parts of the working memory system, but we still lack a detailed account of how the episodic buffer integrates information from the other components and from long-term memory.

MEMORY PROCESSES

Suppose you were interested in looking at the effects of learning processes on subsequent long-term memory. One method is to present several groups of participants with the same list of nouns, and to ask each group to perform a different activity or orienting task with the list. The tasks used range from counting the number of letters in each word to thinking of a suitable adjective for each word.

If participants were told their memory was going to be tested, they would presumably realise that a task such as simply counting the number of letters in each word would not enable them to remember much, and so they might process the words more thoroughly. As a result, the experimenter does not tell them about the memory test (incidental learning). Finally, all the participants are unexpectedly asked for recall. As the various groups of participants are presented with the same words, any differences in recall must reflect the influence of the processing tasks.

Hyde and Jenkins (1973) used the approach just described. Words were either associatively related or unrelated in meaning, and different groups of participants performed each of the following five orienting tasks:

(1) Rating the words for pleasantness.
(2) Estimating the frequency with which each word is used in the English language.
(3) Detecting the occurrence of the letters "e" and "g" in the list words.
(4) Deciding on the part of speech appropriate to each word.
(5) Deciding whether the list words fitted sentence frames.

Half the participants were told to try to learn the words (intentional learning), whereas the other half were not (incidental learning). There was a test of free recall shortly after the orienting task finished.

The findings are shown in Figure 6.11. Rating pleasantness and rating frequency of usage presumably both involve semantic processing (processing of meaning), whereas the other three orienting tasks do not. Retention was 51% higher after the semantic tasks than the non-semantic tasks on the list of associatively unrelated words, and it was 83% higher with associatively related words. Surprisingly, incidental learners recalled the same number of words as intentional learners. Thus, it is the nature of the processing activity that determines recall.

Levels-of-processing theory

Craik and Lockhart (1972) proposed a broad framework, arguing that it was too general to be regarded as a theory. However, because they made several specific predictions, it will be treated here as a theory. They assumed that attentional and perceptual processes at learning determine what information is stored in long-term memory. There are various levels of processing, ranging from shallow or physical analysis of a stimulus (e.g., detecting specific letters in words) to deep or semantic analysis. Craik (1973, p. 48) defined depth as "the meaningfulness extracted from the stimulus rather than . . . the number of analyses performed upon it."

The key theoretical assumptions made by Craik and Lockhart (1972) were as follows:

FIGURE 6.11

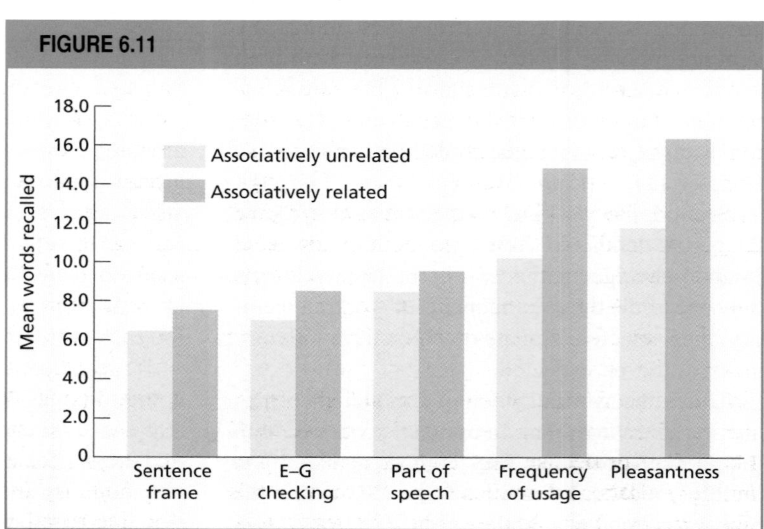

Mean words recalled as a function of list type (associatively related or unrelated) and orienting task. Data from Hyde and Jenkins (1973).

- The level or depth of processing of a stimulus has a large effect on its memorability.
- Deeper levels of analysis produce more elaborate, longer lasting, and stronger memory traces than do shallow levels of analysis.

The findings of Hyde and Jenkins (1973), as well as those of many others, accord with these assumptions.

Craik and Lockhart (1972) distinguished between maintenance and elaborative rehearsal. **Maintenance rehearsal** involves repeating previous analyses, whereas **elaborative rehearsal** involves deeper or more semantic analysis of the learning material. According to the theory, only elaborative rehearsal improves long-term memory. This contrasts with the view of Atkinson and Shiffrin (1968) that rehearsal always enhances long-term memory. In fact, maintenance rehearsal typically increases long-term memory, but by less than elaborative rehearsal. For example, Glenberg, Smith, and Green (1977) found that a nine-fold increase in the time devoted to maintenance rehearsal only increased recall by 1.5%, but increased recognition memory by 9%.

Elaboration

Craik and Tulving (1975) argued that elaboration of processing (i.e., the amount of processing of a particular kind) is important. Participants were presented on each trial with a word and a sentence containing a blank, and decided whether the word fitted into the blank space. Elaboration was manipulated by varying the complexity of the sentence frame between the simple (e.g., "She cooked the _____"), and the complex (e.g., "The great bird swooped down and carried off the struggling _____"). Cued recall was twice as high for words accompanying complex sentences, suggesting that elaboration benefits long-term memory.

Long-term memory depends on the *kind* of elaboration as well as on the *amount* of elaboration. Bransford et al. (1979) presented either minimally elaborated similes (e.g., "A mosquito is like a doctor because they both draw blood") or multiply elaborated similes (e.g., "A mosquito is like a raccoon because they both have heads, legs, jaws"). Recall was much better for the minimally elaborated similes than for the multiply elaborated ones, indicating that the nature and degree of precision of semantic elaborations need to be considered.

Distinctiveness

Eysenck (1979) argued that distinctive or unique memory traces will be more readily retrieved than those resembling other memory traces. Eysenck and Eysenck (1980) tested this theory by using nouns having irregular grapheme–phoneme correspondence (i.e., words not pronounced in line with pronunciation rules, such as "comb" with its silent "b"). Participants performed the non-semantic orienting task of pronouncing such nouns as if they had regular grapheme–phoneme correspondence, thus producing distinctive and unique memory traces (non-semantic, distinctive condition). Other nouns were simply pronounced normally (non-semantic, non-distinctive condition), and still others were processed in terms of their meaning (semantic, distinctive and semantic, non-distinctive).

Words in the non-semantic, distinctive condition were much better recognised than those in the non-semantic, non-distinctive condition (see Figure 6.12), and almost as well as the words in the semantic conditions. These findings show the importance of distinctiveness to long-term memory.

There is a further assumption of the levels-of-processing approach that deserves brief discussion. According to Craik and Lockhart (1972), memory traces can be regarded as records of analyses carried out during perception. As a result, brain areas involved in perception and storage of information should be reactivated when memory is tested. Brain-imaging research supporting that position is discussed by Nyberg (2002). For example, consider a study by Nyberg et al. (2003). Participants initially learned visually presented words paired with sounds. After that, they performed a recognition memory test on visually presented words, but were not required to remember any auditory information. In spite of that, there was increased brain activity in auditory regions

FIGURE 6.12

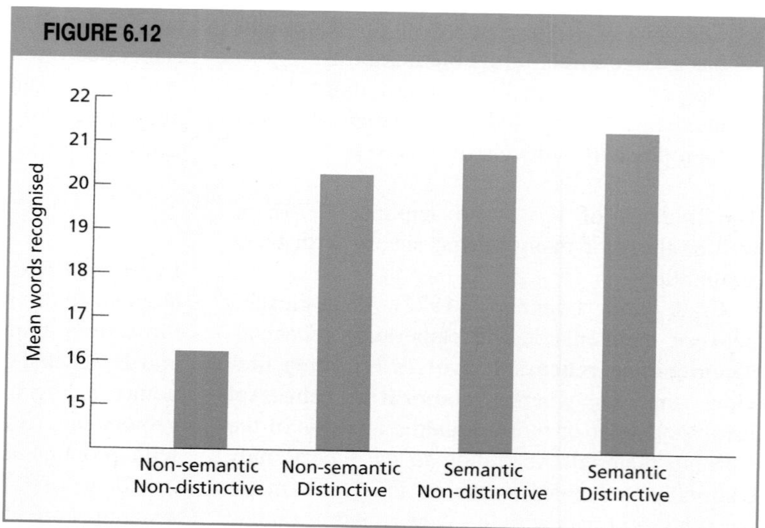

Recognition-memory performance as a function of the depth and distinctiveness of processing. Data from Eysenck and Eysenck (1980).

of the temporal lobes. As Nyberg (2002, p. 346) pointed out, this finding provides "strong evidence that perceptual information is part of memory traces".

Evaluation

Processes during learning have a major impact on subsequent long-term memory. This may sound obvious, but surprisingly little research before 1972 involved a study of learning processes and their effects on memory. Indeed, Craik (2002, p. 315) argued that, "Perhaps the most enduring legacy of the Craik and Lockhart (1972) paper is the greater emphasis on memory as processing in current theories." It is also valuable that elaboration and distinctiveness of processing have been identified as important factors in learning and memory. Another strength of the levels-of-processing approach is what Watkins (2002) called its power-to-complexity ratio: there are powerful predicted effects in some circumstances even though the basic theory is very simple.

On the negative side, it is hard to decide the level of processing being used by learners. The problem is caused by the lack of any independent measure of processing depth. This can lead to the unfortunate state of affairs described by Eysenck (1978, p. 159): "There is a danger of using retention-test performance to provide information about the depth of processing, and then using the putative [alleged] depth of processing to 'explain' the retention-test performance, a self-defeating exercise in circularity." However, it is sometimes possible to provide an independent measure of depth (e.g., Parkin, 1979). Gabrieli et al. (1996) used fMRI to identify the brain regions involved in different kinds of processing. They presented words that were to receive semantic or deep encoding (is the word concrete or abstract?), or that were to be processed perceptually or shallowly (upper- or lower-case?). Gabrieli et al. (1996, p. 282) concluded that "The fMRI found greater activation of left inferior prefrontal cortex for semantic than for perceptual encoding."

Another limitation with the levels-of-processing approach is that it fails to account for some of the findings obtained with the basic experimental method based on orienting tasks. For example, as Roediger and Gallo (2002) pointed out, the levels-of-processing construct does not explain why there is generally no difference between intentional and incidental learning, nor does it tell us why recall is higher for words given a positive response to the orienting question than for those given a negative response.

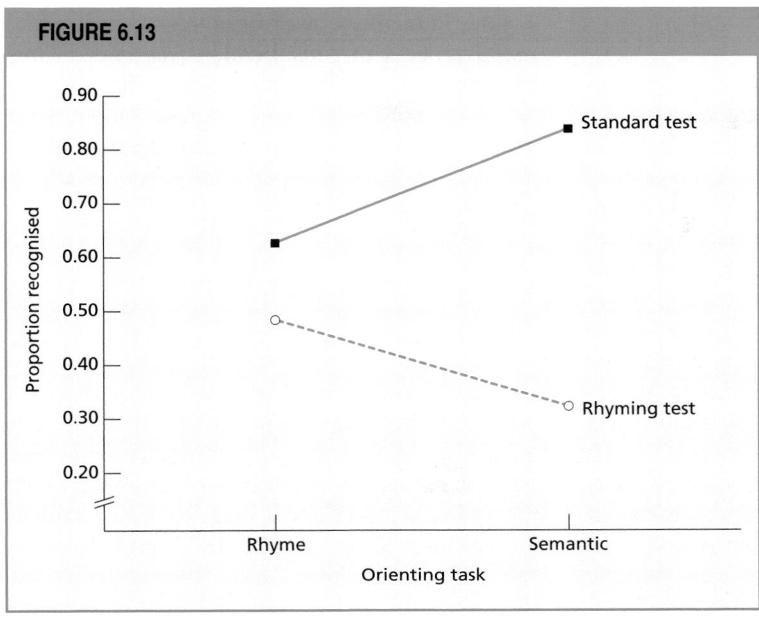

Mean proportion of words recognised as a function of orienting task (semantic or rhyme) and of the type of recognition task (standard or rhyming). Data are from Morris et al. (1977), and are from positive trials only.

Morris, Bransford, and Franks (1977) argued that stored information is remembered only if it is of *relevance* to the memory test. Their participants had to answer semantic or shallow (rhyme) questions for lists of words. Memory was tested by a standard recognition test, in which list and non-list words were presented, or it was tested by a rhyming recognition test. On this latter test, participants selected words that rhymed with list words; note that the list words themselves were not presented.

If one considers only the results obtained with the standard recognition test, then the predicted superiority of deep over shallow processing was found (see Figure 6.13). However, the opposite result was obtained with the rhyme test, and this disproves the notion that deep processing always enhances long-term memory.

Morris et al. (1977) argued that their findings supported a *transfer-appropriate processing theory*. According to this theory, different kinds of processing lead learners to acquire different kinds of information about a stimulus. Whether the stored information leads to subsequent retention depends on the relevance of that information to the memory test. For example, storing semantic information is essentially irrelevant when the memory test requires the identification of words rhyming with list words. What is required for this kind of test is shallow rhyme information.

The levels-of-processing approach was designed to account for performance on standard memory tests (e.g., recall, recognition) based on conscious and deliberate retrieval of past events. However, there is also **implicit memory** (memory not involving conscious recollection). Tests of implicit memory include **word-fragment completion** and **word-stem completion**, in which participants write down the first word they think of that completes a word fragment (e.g., _ e n _ i _, a fragment for "tennis") or a word stem (e.g., ten ___), respectively. There is only a small levels-of-processing effect in studies of implicit memory. Challis and Brodbeck (1992) reviewed the literature. They found that the levels-of-processing effect was greater than 10% in 11 out of 35 comparisons, and between 5% and 10% in 12 more comparisons.

Finally, the levels-of-processing approach describes rather than explains. Craik and Lockhart (1972) did not explain exactly *why* deep processing is so effective.

Levels-of-processing theory: Update

Lockhart and Craik (1990) updated levels-of-processing theory in three main ways. First, Lockhart and Craik (1990) accepted the notion of transfer-appropriate processing proposed by Morris et al. (1977), but argued that we can reconcile transfer-appropriate processing with the levels-of-processing approach. Transfer-appropriate theory predicts that memory performance depends on interactions between the type of processing at encoding and the type of processing at retrieval (see Figure 6.12). Levels-of-processing theory predicts a main effect of processing depth when transfer appropriateness is held constant. In the study by Morris et al. (1977), there was high transfer appropriateness when semantic processing at learning was followed by a standard recognition test, and when rhyme processing was followed by a rhyming test. In addition, memory performance was much higher in the former condition, as is predicted by levels-of-processing theory (see Figure 6.13).

Second, Lockhart and Craik (1990, pp. 97–98) accepted that their previous theoretical assumption that shallow processing always led to rapid forgetting was not correct: "Since 1972 . . . , a number of results have been reported in which sensory information persists for hours, minutes, and even months."

Third, Lockhart and Craik (1990) pointed out that they had previously implied that processing of stimuli always proceeds from shallow sensory levels to deeper semantic levels. They accepted that this was inadequate: "An adequate model will comprise complex interactions between top-down and bottom-up processes, and that processing at different levels will be temporally parallel or partially overlapping" (Lockhart & Craik, 1990, p. 95).

According to the original levels-of-processing theory, deep or semantic processing is necessary and sufficient for good long-term memory. However, Craik (2002) argued that deep processing is necessary but *not* sufficient. As he pointed out, amnesic patients typically show almost intact deep or semantic processing, but their long-term memory is often very poor (see Chapter 7). Craik argued that such findings suggest that good long-term memory involves both deep processing *and* a process of consolidation (see later in this chapter), in which the results of processing are stored securely in the brain. Amnesic patients have poor long-term memory for certain kinds of information because they have deficient consolidation processes.

IMPLICIT LEARNING

The levels-of-processing approach was concerned with the processes involved in the conscious acquisition and retrieval of information. However, some learning is apparently not like that, and the term "implicit learning" refers to such learning. According to Seger (1994, p. 163), **implicit learning** is "learning complex information without complete verbalisable knowledge of what is learned". More generally, it is assumed that implicit learning is involved when the learner lacks conscious awareness of what has been learned. There are clear similarities between implicit learning and implicit memory, which is memory not depending on conscious recollection (see Chapter 7).

The reader may wonder why implicit learning and implicit memory are not discussed together. After all, there can be no memory without prior learning, and learning necessitates the involvement of a memory system. There are two reasons. First, studies of implicit learning have typically used relatively complex, novel stimulus materials, whereas most studies of implicit memory have used simple, familiar stimulus materials. Thus, the tasks used are very different. Second, there have been surprisingly few attempts to consider the relations between implicit learning and implicit memory.

How do the systems involved in implicit learning and memory differ from those involved in explicit learning and memory? Reber (1993) proposed five such characteristics (none of which has been definitively established):

(1) Robustness: Implicit systems are relatively unaffected by disorders (e.g., amnesia) affecting explicit systems.

(2) Age independence: Implicit learning is little influenced by age or developmental level.
(3) Low variability: There are smaller individual differences in implicit learning and memory than in explicit learning and memory.
(4) IQ independence: Performance on implicit tasks is relatively unaffected by IQ.
(5) Commonality of process: Implicit systems are common to most species.

We can identify three main types of research on implicit learning. First, there are studies in which the main emphasis is to see whether healthy participants can learn fairly complex material in the absence of conscious awareness of what they have learned. Second, there are studies on brain-damaged patients with amnesia (see Chapter 7), in which the attempt is made to decide whether their implicit learning is essentially intact even though their explicit learning is seriously deficient. Third, there are brain-imaging studies, in which the main focus is to see whether the brain areas associated with implicit learning differ from those associated with explicit learning.

An important theoretical issue concerns the relationship between explicit and implicit learning. One view was expressed by Anderson (e.g., 1983, 1996) in his Adaptive Control of Thought (ACT) model (see Chapter 13). According to ACT, what happens during the development of automatic skills is that conscious representations are gradually transformed into unconscious ones. In other words, an initial process of explicit learning is followed by implicit learning. Below we discuss research that sheds some doubt on that view.

As we will see, it has proved surprisingly difficult to decide whether or not implicit learning exists. One possible reason is that the findings appear inconsistent because the extent to which implicit learning is possible varies from task to task. A key reason is that the failure of participants when questioned to indicate conscious awareness of what they have learned does *not* necessarily prove that the learning was implicit. This issue was addressed by Shanks and St. John (1994), who proposed two criteria to demonstrate implicit learning:

(1) *Information criterion*: The information participants are asked to provide on the awareness test must be the information that is responsible for the improved level of performance.
(2) *Sensitivity criterion*: "We must be able to show that our test of awareness is sensitive to all of the relevant knowledge" (Shanks & St. John, 1994, p. 374). People may be consciously aware of more task-relevant knowledge than appears on an insensitive awareness test, and this may lead us to underestimate their consciously accessible knowledge.

Evidence

We have just seen that it is important to apply the information and sensitivity criteria in order to show the existence of implicit learning. However, this was not really possible with many early studies on implicit learning. Many of these studies used very complex tasks, making it very hard for experimenters to assess accurately learners' consciously accessible knowledge. As a result, learners may have engaged in explicit learning that was not detected in questioning. An interesting study to which this problem does not seem to apply was reported by Howard and Howard (1992). They used a task in which an asterisk appeared in one of four positions on a screen, under each of which was a key. The task was to press the key corresponding to the position of the asterisk as rapidly as possible. The position of the asterisk over trials conformed to a complex pattern. The participants showed clear evidence of learning the pattern by responding faster and faster to the asterisk. However, when asked to predict where the asterisk would appear next, their performance was at chance level. Thus, the participants showed implicit learning of the pattern, but no explicit learning.

Additional evidence that implicit learning can occur in the absence of consciously accessible knowledge was reported by Shea, Wulf, Whitacre, and Park (2001). Their participants were given the task of standing on a platform, and trying to move it to mimic the movements of a line displayed on a computer screen. The participants performed the task several times. On each occasion, the middle segment was identical, but the first and third segments varied. The participants were not told that the middle segment would remain the same. Performance on the middle segment improved more than did performance on the other segments, indicating that the participants had benefited from having that segment repeated. It appeared that this learning was implicit. Two-thirds of the participants said they did not think that part of the pattern had been repeated, and they performed at chance level when trying to recognise the repeated segment on a subsequent recognition test.

In a second experiment, two of the three segments were repeated, and the participants were told explicitly about one of the repeated segments. Performance was significantly worse on this segment than on the repeated segment about which the participants had not been told. Shea et al. (2001, p. 860) concluded as follows: "The fact that providing explicit information about the repeated segment to participants produced negative effects, as compared to not providing this information, suggests that information that is not readily accessible . . . may provide important learning benefits over information that is readily available to consciousness." However, there is a potential problem of interpretation here. It is possible that the provision of explicit instructions led participants to attend to information that was not relevant for good task performance (Perruchet, Chambaron, & Ferrel-Chapus, 2003).

Wilkinson and Shanks (2004) reported an interesting study in which a black X appeared at one of four locations on each trial, and the participants' task was to respond as rapidly as possible by pressing the key corresponding to the location. There was predictability in the order of the locations over a sequence of trials (although the participants were not told this), and it has been argued that a speeding up of responses on this task indicates implicit sequence learning. After learning had occurred, there was an explicit learning test, which required participants to generate a sequence of 100 target locations. In the inclusion condition, they were told to use their sequence knowledge. In the exclusion condition, they were told to exclude from their responses any segments of the sequence they could remember.

What would we expect to find in the study by Wilkinson and Shanks (2004)? If sequence knowledge is wholly implicit, then performance should not differ between the two conditions. In contrast, if it is wholly explicit, then the sequences generated in the inclusion condition should resemble the training sequence more than the sequences generated in the exclusion condition. The findings supported the view that sequence learning was explicit: "The knowledge acquired during sequence learning is available for intentional control and is, in this sense, explicit" (Wilkinson & Shanks, 2004, p. 366).

It will be remembered that another way of showing the existence of implicit learning would be to find brain-damaged patients who showed intact implicit learning but impaired explicit learning. We should warn you that the findings here are rather inconsistent and no very clear picture emerges!

Much of the research on brain-damaged patients has used an artificial grammar learning task in which participants learn to decide whether strings of letters conform to the rules of an artificial grammar. The typical finding is that healthy participants learn to discriminate reasonably well between grammatical and ungrammatical strings even though they cannot verbalise the rules of the grammar. Knowlton, Ramus, and Squire (1992) found that amnesics' performance in artificial grammar learning was similar to that of healthy controls when they were asked to distinguish between grammatical and ungrammatical letter strings. This suggests that amnesic patients had intact implicit learning. However, the findings were different when participants were instructed to recall the specific strings used during learning, and to use these strings to aid task performance. The amnesics performed much worse than the healthy controls in this condition, presumably because performance depended more on explicit learning. Similar findings were reported by Knowlton and Squire (1996) and by other researchers (see Gooding, Mayes, & van Eijk, 2000).

There has been some controversy on the issue of precisely what it is that people learn on the artificial grammar learning task. It used to be thought that people learned abstract mental representations describing the various grammatical rules, but experts now generally believe that most of what is learned consists of small chunks or fragments consisting of two or three letters. Channon et al. (2002) devised versions of the artificial grammar learning task that allowed separate assessment of the extent to which abstract grammatical rules and fragments had been learned. Neither healthy controls nor amnesic patients showed any evidence of abstract rule learning, but both groups learned about fragments, and tended to categorise familiar two-letter fragments as grammatical. However, amnesic patients were significantly less influenced by familiar fragments than were healthy controls, leading Channon et al. (2002, p. 2195) to conclude that "The present study casts serious doubt on the assumption that grammar learning is normal in amnesia when materials of sufficient sensitivity are used."

It has generally been found that amnesic patients have essentially intact implicit learning, and so the findings of Channon et al. (2002) are out of step with previous studies. A likely reason for the difference in the findings is that Channon et al. used longer and more complex letter strings than those used in previous research. Some support for the notion that amnesic patients are at a disadvantage when an implicit learning task is complex comes in a meta-analysis reported by Gooding et al. (2000). They found that amnesic patients performed at normal levels on implicit tests with familiar material but performed worse with novel material.

The issue of whether different brain regions underlie implicit and explicit learning has been addressed in several studies. Grafton, Hazeltine, and Ivry (1995) obtained PET scans from participants engaged in learning motor sequences under implicit learning conditions or conditions making it easier for them to become consciously aware of the sequence. The motor cortex and the supplementary motor area were activated during implicit learning. In contrast, "Explicit learning and awareness of the sequences required more activations in the right premotor cortex, the dorsolateral cingulate, areas in the parietal cortex associated with working memory, the anterior cingulate, areas in the parietal cortex concerned with voluntary attention, and the lateral temporal cortical areas that store explicit memories" (Gazzaniga et al., 1998, p. 279).

Aizenstein et al. (2004) used fMRI to study implicit and explicit sequence learning. The explicit task was to learn a sequence of shapes. At the same time, the colours of the shapes formed a sequence which was used on the implicit learning task. Prefrontal and anterior cingulate cortex and early visual regions were involved during both implicit and explicit learning. However, there were some differences. Of most importance, there was greater prefrontal activation with explicit than with implicit learning, which is consistent with evidence that prefrontal activation is associated with controlled and effortful processing within working memory.

The differences between implicit learning and explicit learning in terms of brain activation are less clear in some other studies. For example, Schendan, Searl, Melrose, and Stern (2003) used fMRI to study brain activation in implicit and explicit sequence learning. In general terms, similar areas of the brain were associated with both types of learning. Schendan et al. (2003, p. 1020) concluded that "Both implicit and explicit learning of higher order sequences involve the MTL [medial temporal lobe] structures implicated in memory functions, specifically, the hippocampus and adjacent subiculum and entorhinal and parahippocampal cortex."

If we assume that there are separate implicit and explicit learning systems, it then becomes important to consider how these systems interact with each other. As mentioned earlier, Anderson (1983, 1996) assumed that what typically happens in the course of learning is that an early stage of explicit learning is followed by a subsequent stage of implicit learning. In contrast, Willingham and Goedert-Eschmann (1999) argued that explicit and implicit learning develop together in parallel. According to this theoretical position, performance is initially supported by explicit processes. After sufficient practice, implicit processes acquired at the same time as the explicit processes become strong enough to support performance on their own.

Willingham and Goedert-Eschmann (1999) obtained evidence supporting their hypothesis. They used a motor sequencing task in which participants had to respond rapidly with the appropriate responses to four different stimuli over a long series of trials. Participants in the explicit learning condition were told there was a repeating sequence, and were encouraged to memorise it. In contrast, participants in the implicit learning condition were not informed about the sequencing.

After numerous training trials, the participants were given transfer trials designed to assess implicit knowledge. The stimuli on these trials were mostly presented in a random order, and the participants who had engaged in explicit learning were told that the purpose of these trials was to see how rapidly they could respond when the stimuli were in a random order. However, the previously learned sequence or a novel sequence was introduced during the course of the trials without the participants' awareness. Those participants who had engaged in explicit learning showed as much evidence of implicit knowledge as those who had engaged in implicit learning, suggesting that they had acquired implicit knowledge at the same time as explicit knowledge.

Much more evidence is needed to clarify the relationship between explicit and implicit learning. For example, the two forms of learning may develop together on simple motor tasks such as the one used by Willingham and Goedert-Eschmann (1999). However, explicit learning may precede implicit learning on more complex or non-motor tasks.

Evaluation

There has been considerable interest in implicit learning in recent years, and much experimental evidence suggests there is an important distinction between implicit and explicit learning. Some of the most convincing evidence comes from studies (e.g., Howard & Howard, 1992; Shea et al., 2001) in which it seems that it was relatively easy to assess basic consciously accessible knowledge about the task. Amnesic patients generally show evidence of intact implicit learning (e.g., Knowlton et al., 1992; Knowlton & Squire, 1996), which contrasts with their impaired explicit learning. Finally, it is reasonable to predict that brain areas associated with working memory and attentional control should be more active during explicit learning than during implicit learning, and this prediction has been confirmed (e.g., Aizenstein et al., 2004; Grafton et al., 1995).

In spite of the range of positive findings, there are grounds for being sceptical about the existence of implicit learning. Of key importance, it is hard (or even impossible) to devise tests of awareness that can detect *all* the task-relevant knowledge of which participants have conscious awareness. Some of the evidence also stands in the way of concluding that implicit learning has been proved to exist. For example, Wilkinson and Shanks (2004) found that there was at least some explicit learning on a task generally regarded as a fairly pure measure of implicit learning. In addition, amnesic patients do not always have intact implicit learning (e.g., Channon et al., 2002), and the brain areas underlying explicit and implicit learning are not always clearly different (e.g., Schendan et al., 2003).

What conclusions can we draw about implicit learning? First, the fact that reasonable evidence for implicit learning has been obtained from three approaches suggests that implicit learning probably does exist and is clearly different from explicit learning. Second, it is probable that a mixture of implicit and explicit learning is involved in many tasks, which helps to account for some of the apparent inconsistencies in the literature. Third, we need to focus more on issues relating to possible interactions between implicit and explicit learning (see Willingham & Goedert-Eschmann, 1999). Fourth, in the future we will probably need to move away from the simple division of learning into implicit or explicit. As Kelly (2003, p. 1389) suggested, "Knowledge is not necessarily implicit or explicit per se but may be dynamic in nature, with accessibility to explicit consciousness being dependent on the quality of the underlying representation (determined by three characteristics: stability, distinctiveness, and strength)."

THEORIES OF FORGETTING

Forgetting was first studied in detail by Hermann Ebbinghaus (1885/1913). He carried out numerous studies with himself as the only participant. Ebbinghaus initially learned a list of nonsense syllables having little or no meaning. At various intervals thereafter, he recalled the nonsense syllables. He then re-learned the list. His basic measure of forgetting was the **savings method**, which involved seeing the reduction in the number of trials during re-learning compared to original learning. Forgetting was very rapid over the first hour or so after learning, with the rate of forgetting slowing considerably thereafter (see Figure 6.14). These findings suggest that the forgetting function is approximately logarithmic.

Rubin and Wenzel (1996) carried out a detailed analysis of the forgetting functions taken from 210 data sets involving numerous memory tests. Rubin and Wenzel (1996, p. 758) found (in line with Ebbinghaus, 1885), that a logarithmic function most consistently described the rate of forgetting: "We have established a law: the logarithmic-loss law." They focused on group data, but the forgetting functions from individual participants are very similar (Wixted & Ebbesen, 1997). Rubin and Wenzel found that logarithmic and similar functions fit most of the data with the exception of autobiographical memory (see Chapter 8). Thus, the rate of forgetting is generally fastest shortly after learning, and it decreases progressively after that.

According to Baddeley (1997), the forgetting rate is unusually slow for continuous motor skills (e.g., riding a bicycle), in which individuals produce an uninterrupted sequence of responses. For example, Fleishman and Parker (1962) gave participants extensive training in the continuous motor skills involved in a task resembling flying a plane. Even when they were re-tested after 2 years, there was practically no forgetting after the first trial.

Most studies of forgetting have focused on **explicit memory** (see Chapter 7), which involves conscious recollection of previously learned information. Comparisons of speed of forgetting in explicit memory and in **implicit memory** (in which conscious recollection is *not* required) have produced somewhat inconsistent findings. However, the forgetting rates are often very similar on the two types of memory test. For example, McBride, Dosher, and Gage (2001) found the

FIGURE 6.14

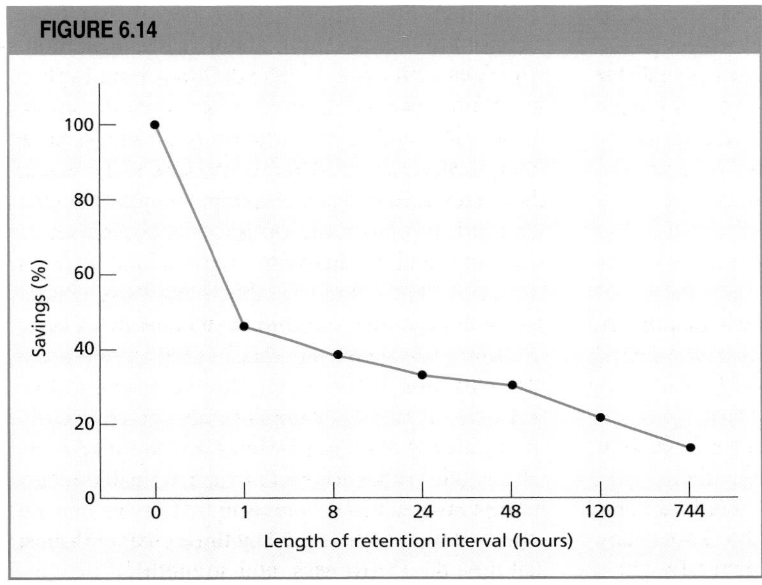

Forgetting over time as indexed by reduced savings. Data from Ebbinghaus (1885/1913).

forgetting rates over 45 minutes were essentially the same for explicit and implicit versions of a memory task.

It is often believed that forgetting is a bad thing, and that we should do everything we can to reduce forgetting. This belief is not altogether correct. We often need to update our knowledge, and it is actually helpful to forget the previous state of affairs. For example, when driving you might find it hard to remember the speed limit applying to the area through which you are driving if you had a clear recollection of different speed limits during earlier parts of the drive.

Repression

Freud (1915, 1943) argued that very threatening or anxiety-provoking material is often unable to gain access to conscious awareness, and he used the term **repression** to refer to this phenomenon. According to Freud (1915, p. 86), "The essence of repression lies simply in the function of rejecting and keeping something out of consciousness." However, Freud sometimes used the concept to refer merely to the inhibition of the capacity for emotional experience (Madison, 1956). Freud's ideas on repression emerged from his clinical experiences, with the repression he claimed to have observed mostly involving traumatic events that had happened to his patients.

It is difficult to study repression under laboratory conditions, because it would be totally unethical to expose participants to traumatic situations. However, there is non-experimental evidence of repression, with large numbers of adults apparently recovering repressed memories of sexual and/or physical abuse suffered in childhood. There has been a fierce controversy between those who believe these recovered memories are genuine and those who argue they are false. As we will see, the issues are complex, and no definitive conclusion is possible.

Those who believe in repressed memories of childhood traumatic events cite evidence such as that of Andrews et al. (1999). They obtained detailed information from 108 therapists about recovered memories from a total of 236 patients. Their evidence suggested that some recovered memories may be genuine. For example, 41% of the patients reported corroborative or supporting evidence (e.g., someone else had also reported being abused by the alleged perpetrator). Those believing most recovered memories are false typically assume that such false memories are generally produced as a result of direct pressure from the therapist. However, only 28% of the patients studied by Andrews et al. (1999) claimed that the trigger for the first recovered memory occurred during the course of a therapeutic session. In 22% of cases, the trigger occurred before therapy had even started, and so couldn't have been influenced by the therapist.

Those believing most recovered memories are false emphasise two points. First, some patients have admitted to reporting false memories of childhood abuse. For example, Lief and Fetkewicz (1995) studied 40 patients who had retracted their "memories" of childhood abuse. In about 80% of these cases, the therapist had made direct suggestions that the patient was the victim of sexual abuse. In 68% of cases, hypnosis (which can produce mistaken memories) had been used to recover memories, and in 40% of cases patients had read numerous books about sexual abuse.

Second, people can be misled into believing in the existence of events that never actually happened. For example, Ceci (1995) asked preschool children to think about real and fictitious (but plausible) events. The children found it hard to distinguish between the real and the fictitious events, with 58% of them providing detailed stories about fictitious events that they falsely believed had occurred. Experienced psychologists couldn't tell from videotapes which events were real and which were false.

There have been a few laboratory studies on patients with recovered memories. Clancy, Schacter, McNally, and Pitman (2000) used a situation known to produce false memories. What happens is that participants are given lists of semantically associated words, and are then found to falsely "recognise" other semantically related words not actually presented. They compared women with recovered memories of childhood sexual abuse with women who believed they had been sexually abused but couldn't recall the abuse,

FIGURE 6.15

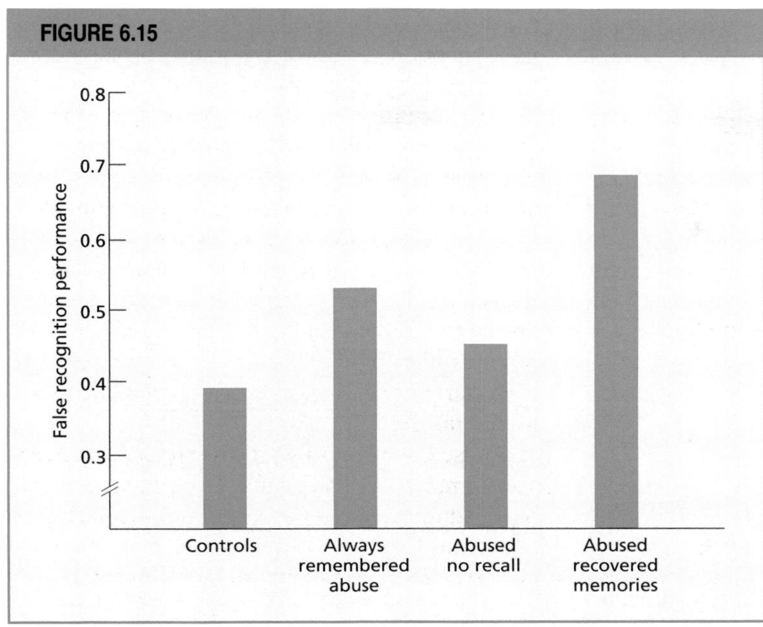

False recognition of words not presented in four groups of women with lists containing eight associates. Data from Clancy et al. (2000).

women who had always remembered being abused, and control women. Clancy et al. found that women reporting recovered memories of abuse showed the highest levels of false recognition (see Figure 6.15). As Clancy et al. (2000, p. 30) concluded, "The results are consistent with the hypothesis that women who report recovered memories of sexual abuse are more prone than others to develop certain types of illusory memories."

McNally, Clancy, and Schacter (2001) investigated whether patients with repressed or recovered memories of childhood sexual abuse were more able to forget or repress traumatic cues than women not reporting childhood sexual abuse. All participants were given directed forgetting instructions for some of the words presented to them. Women reporting either repressed or recovered memories of childhood sexual abuse did not forget trauma words (e.g., molested) to a greater extent than the control women.

Evaluation

There are reasonable arguments and evidence both for and against the genuineness of recovered memories. Clinicians tend to believe in the existence of recovered memories whereas cognitive psychologists are much more sceptical. In order to resolve the issue, we need to find more sensitive techniques for distinguishing between genuine and false recovered memories. Whatever the outcome of this controversy, it is clear that most forgetting cannot be explained in terms of repression, because only very little of what we forget concerns traumatic events.

Interference theory

The dominant approach to forgetting during much of the twentieth century was interference theory. It was assumed that our ability to remember what we are currently learning can be disrupted or interfered with by what we have previously learned or by what we learn in the future. When previous learning interferes with later learning, we have **proactive interference**. When later learning disrupts earlier learning, there is **retroactive interference** (see Figure 6.16).

Interference theory can be traced back to Hugo Munsterberg in the nineteenth century. For many years, he kept his pocket-watch in one particular pocket. When he started keeping it in a different

FIGURE 6.16

Proactive interference

Group	Learn	Learn	Test
Experimental	A–B (e.g. Cat–Tree)	A–C (e.g. Cat–Dirt)	A–C (e.g. Cat–Dirt)
Control	–	A–C (e.g. Cat–Dirt)	A–C (e.g. Cat–Dirt)

Retroactive interference

Group	Learn	Learn	Test
Experimental	A–B (e.g. Cat–Tree)	A–C (e.g. Cat–Dirt)	A–B (e.g. Cat–Tree)
Control	A–B (e.g. Cat–Tree)	–	A–B (e.g. Cat–Tree)

Note: for both proactive and retroactive interference, the experimental group exhibits interference. On the test, only the first word is supplied, and the subjects must provide the second word.

Methods of testing for proactive and retroactive interference.

pocket, he often fumbled about in confusion when asked for the time. He had learned an association between the stimulus "What time is it, Hugo?" and the response of removing the watch from his pocket. Later on, the stimulus remained the same, but a different response was now associated with it. Subsequent research using methods such as those shown in Figure 6.16 revealed that proactive and retroactive interference are both maximal when two different responses have been associated with the same stimulus, intermediate when two similar responses have been associated with the same stimulus, and minimal when two different stimuli are involved (Underwood & Postman, 1960). Strong evidence for retroactive interference has been obtained in studies of eyewitness testimony, in which memory of an event is interfered with by post-event questioning (see Chapter 8).

Jacoby, Debner, and Hay (2001) argued that proactive interference might occur for two different reasons. First, it might be due to problems in retrieving the correct response (discriminability). Second, it might be due to the great strength of the incorrect response learned initially (bias or habit). Thus, participants might show proactive interference because the correct response is very weak or because the incorrect response is very strong. Jacoby et al. carried out three experiments to distinguish between these two possibilities. Their consistent finding was that proactive interference was more due to bias or strength of initial response than to discriminability.

Nearly all the evidence for proactive and retroactive interference has come from studies on explicit memory, in which participants engage in conscious recollection of previously learned material. Evidence that implicit memory is vulnerable to interference was reported by Lustig and Hasher (2001b). They used a word-fragment completion task (e.g., A_L___GY), on which the participants wrote down the first appropriate word coming to mind. Control participants had previously been presented with the word fitting the fragment (e.g., ALLERGY), whereas those in the interference group had been presented with a word almost fitting the fragment. Implicit memory performance on the word-fragment task was worse for the interference group than the control group.

Lustig and Hasher (2001a, p. 624) concluded their review of the interference literature as

FIGURE 6.17

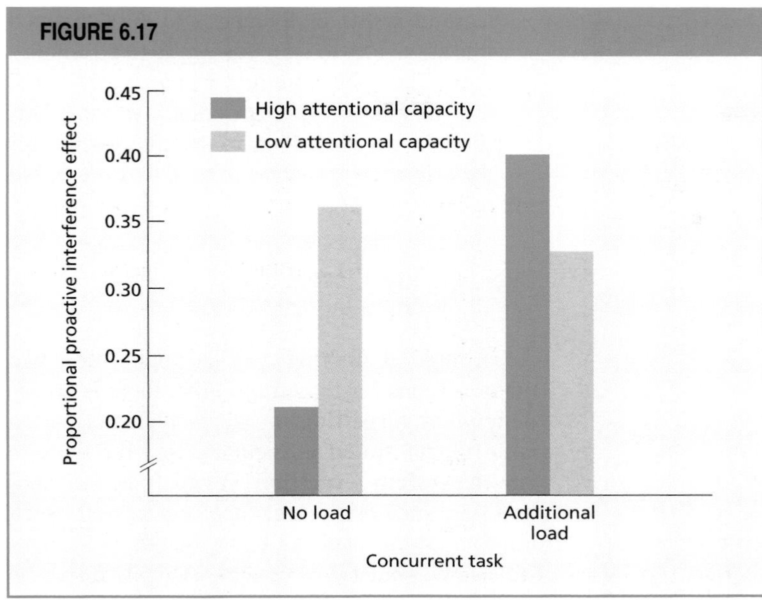

Amount of proactive interference as a function of attentional capacity (low vs. high) and concurrent task (no vs. additional load). Data from Kane and Engle (2000).

follows: "For both implicit and explicit memory, interference occurs when similar non-targets compete with the target as potential responses to the memory cue . . . the degree of interference on both implicit and explicit tests is influenced by the number of competing items and their relative strength."

Most research on interference is based on the implicit (but probably incorrect) assumption that individuals *passively* allow themselves to suffer from interference. Suppose you are learning something, but find your ability to remember it is being impaired by proactive interference from something similar learned previously. It would make sense to adopt active strategies to minimise any interference effect. Kane and Engle (2000) argued that individuals with high attentional or working-memory capacity would be better able to resist proactive interference than those with low capacity. However, even they would be unable to resist proactive interference if they had to perform an attentionally demanding task at the same time as the learning task. As predicted, the high-capacity participants with no additional task showed the least proactive interference (see Figure 6.17).

According to interference theory, forgetting is a direct consequence of acquiring and storing new memories. M.C. Anderson (2003) argued that this ignores the role played by control mechanisms that allow us to *select* certain memories while *inhibiting* others. Anderson and Green (2001) provided evidence for an inhibitory mechanism. Participants initially studied pairs of weakly associated words (e.g., flag–sword; ordeal–roach), and learned to provide the second word when presented with the first as a cue. After that, participants were told to continue to do this to most cue words (respond condition), but to avoid thinking of the response word with certain cues (suppress condition). Finally, participants were asked to recall the response words to all cues.

Some of Anderson and Green's (2001) findings are shown in Figure 6.18). Recall was much worse for words in the suppress condition than in the respond condition. In addition, recall was worse for words that had been suppressed many times as opposed to relatively few times, indicating the power of inhibitory mechanisms to cause forgetting.

Evaluation

There is strong evidence for both proactive and retroactive interference. It is probable that much

FIGURE 6.18

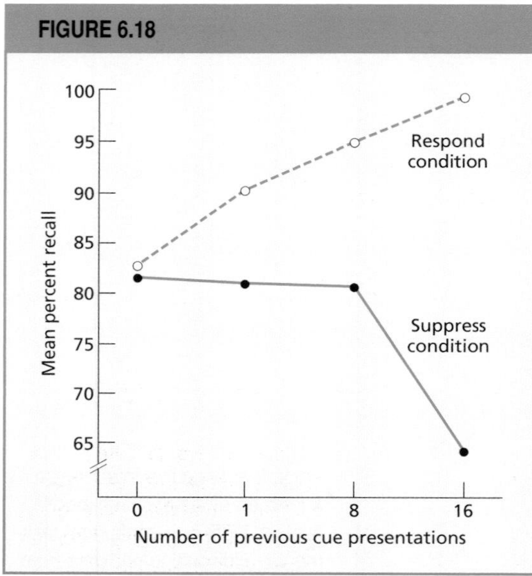

Cued recall as a function of the number of times the cues had been presented before for recall (respond condition) or for suppression (suppress condition). Data from Anderson and Green (2001).

forgetting can be attributed to both types of interference, and this is true with respect to implicit memory as well as explicit memory.

In spite of its successes, research on interference theory is limited in various ways:

(1) Only fairly recently have attempts been made to study the active processes that individuals use to minimise interference effects.
(2) Interference theory largely ignores the role of inhibitory processes in causing forgetting (M.C. Anderson, 2003).
(3) The focus has been almost exclusively on interference effects in explicit memory, and so detailed information about interference effects in implicit memory is lacking.
(4) It requires special conditions for substantial interference effects to occur (i.e., the same stimulus paired with two different responses), and these conditions may be fairly rare in everyday life.
(5) Associations learned *outside* the laboratory seem less liable to interference than those learned *inside* it. Slamecka (1966) obtained free associates to stimulus words (e.g., colour–red). Then the stimulus words were paired with new associates (e.g., colour–yellow). This should have caused retroactive interference for the original association (e.g., colour–red), but it did not.

Cue-dependent forgetting: Encoding specificity principle

According to Tulving (1974), there are two major reasons for forgetting. First, there is **trace-dependent forgetting**, in which the information is no longer stored in memory. Second, there is **cue-dependent forgetting**, in which the information is in memory, but cannot be accessed. Such information is said to be available (i.e., it is still stored) but not accessible (i.e., it cannot be retrieved).

Tulving and Psotka (1971) compared the cue-dependent approach with interference theory. There were between one and six word lists, with four words in six different categories in each list. After each list had been presented, the participants free recalled as many words as possible. That was the original learning. After all the lists had been presented, the participants recalled the words from *all* the lists that had been presented. That was total free recall. Finally, all the category names were presented, and the participants tried again to recall all the words from all the lists. That was total free cued recall.

There was strong evidence for retroactive interference in total free recall, since word recall from any given list decreased as the number of other lists intervening between learning and recall increased (see Figure 6.19). This finding would be interpreted within interference theory by assuming there had been unlearning of the earlier lists. However, this interpretation does not fit with the findings from total cued recall. There was essentially *no* retroactive interference or forgetting when the category names were available to the participants. Thus, the forgetting observed in total free recall was basically cue-dependent forgetting.

Most studies of cue-dependent forgetting have involved *external* cues (e.g., presenting category

FIGURE 6.19

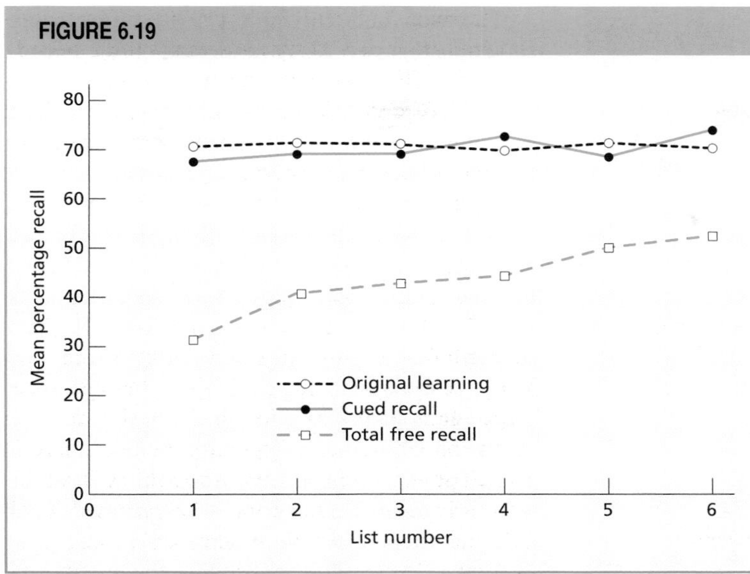

Original learning, total free recall, and total free cued recall as a function of the number of lists presented after learning. Data from Tulving and Psotka (1971).

names). However, cue-dependent forgetting has also been shown with *internal* cues (e.g., mood state). Information about current mood state is often stored in the memory trace, and there is more forgetting if the mood state at the time of retrieval is different. The notion that there should be less forgetting when the mood state at learning and at retrieval is the same is known as **mood-state-dependent memory**. Ucros (1989) reviewed 40 studies, and concluded that there is reasonable evidence for mood-state-dependent memory. The effect is stronger when the participants are in a positive than a negative mood, and is stronger when they try to remember personal events.

Kenealy (1997) provided clear evidence for mood-state-dependent memory. In one experiment, participants looked at a map and learned a set of instructions concerning a particular route until their learning performance exceeded 80%. The following day they were given tests of free recall and cued recall (the visual outline of the map). There were strong mood-state-dependent effects in free recall but not in cued recall (see Figure 6.20). Thus, mood state affects memory when no other powerful retrieval cues are available.

Encoding specificity principle

Tulving developed the notion of cue-dependent forgetting in his **encoding specificity principle** (Wiseman & Tulving, 1976, p. 349): "A to-be-remembered (TBR) item is encoded with respect to the context in which it is studied, producing a unique trace which incorporates information from both target and context. For the TBR item to be retrieved, the cue information must appropriately match the trace of the item-in-context." Tulving (1979, p. 408) put forward a more precise formulation of the encoding specificity principle: "The probability of successful retrieval of the target item is a monotonically increasing function of informational overlap between the information present at retrieval and the information stored in memory." For the benefit of puzzled readers, "monotonically increasing function" refers to a generally rising function that does not decrease at any point. Thus, memory performance depends directly on the similarity between the information in memory and the information available at retrieval.

Attempts to test the encoding specificity principle typically involve two learning conditions and two retrieval conditions. This allows the

FIGURE 6.20

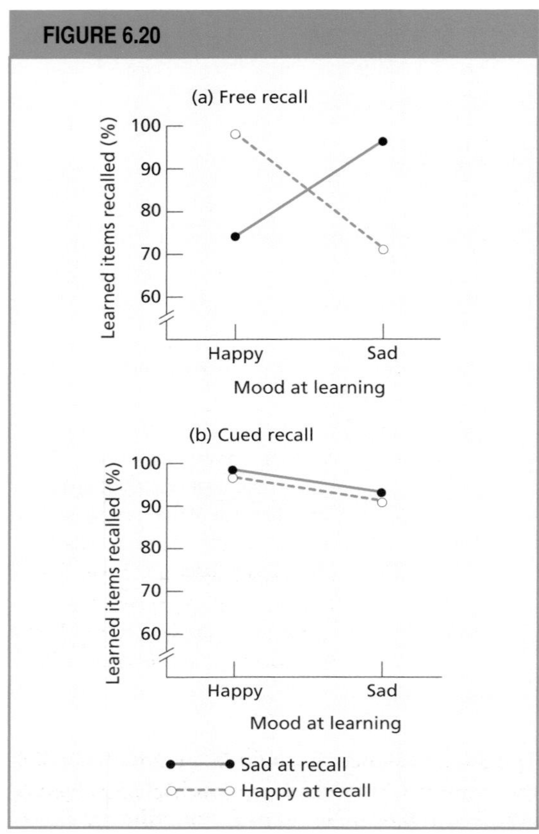

Free and cued recall as a function of mood state (happy or sad) at learning and at recall. Based on data in Kenealy (1997).

experimenter to show that memory depends on both the information in the memory trace stemming from the learning experience and the information available in the retrieval environment. The study by Kenealy (1997, discussed above) provides one example of a successful test of the encoding specificity principle. Thomson and Tulving (1970) provided another example. They presented pairs of words in which the first word was the cue and the second word was the to-be-remembered word. The cues were either weakly associated with the list words (e.g., "Train–BLACK") or were strongly associated (e.g., "White–BLACK"). Some of the to-be-remembered items were tested by weak cues (e.g., "Train–?") and others were tested by strong cues (e.g., "White–?").

Thomson and Tulving's (1970) findings are shown in Figure 6.21. As expected on the encoding specificity principle, recall performance was best when the cues provided at recall were the same as those provided at input. Any change in the cues lowered recall, even when the shift was from weak cues at input to strong cues at recall. This study by Thomson and Tulving is recognised as a classic. However, Higham (2002) has shown that the findings are limited because participants were free to withhold responses if unsure. Higham repeated the experiment, and found much less support for the encoding specificity principle when participants had to respond to all cues.

We all know that recognition memory is generally better than recall. For example, we may be unable to recall the name of an acquaintance, but if someone mentions their name we instantly recognise it. According to Tulving, the superiority of recognition over recall occurs mainly because the overlap between the information contained in the memory test and that contained in the memory trace is generally greater on a recognition test (the entire item is presented) than on a recall test.

More interestingly, it follows from the encoding specificity principle that recall can sometimes be superior to recognition memory. This should happen when the information in the recall cue overlaps more than the information in the recognition cue with the information stored in the memory trace. In a study by Muter (1978), participants were presented with names of people (e.g., DOYLE, FERGUSON, THOMAS), and asked to circle those they "recognised as a person who was famous before 1950". They were then given recall cues in the form of brief descriptions plus first names of the famous people whose surnames had appeared on the recognition test (e.g., author of the Sherlock Holmes stories: Sir Arthur Conan _______; Welsh poet: Dylan ________). Participants recognised only 29% of the names but recalled 42%.

Evaluation

There is convincing evidence that whether we remember or forget something depends on the nature of the memory trace and on the information available in the retrieval environment. The

FIGURE 6.21

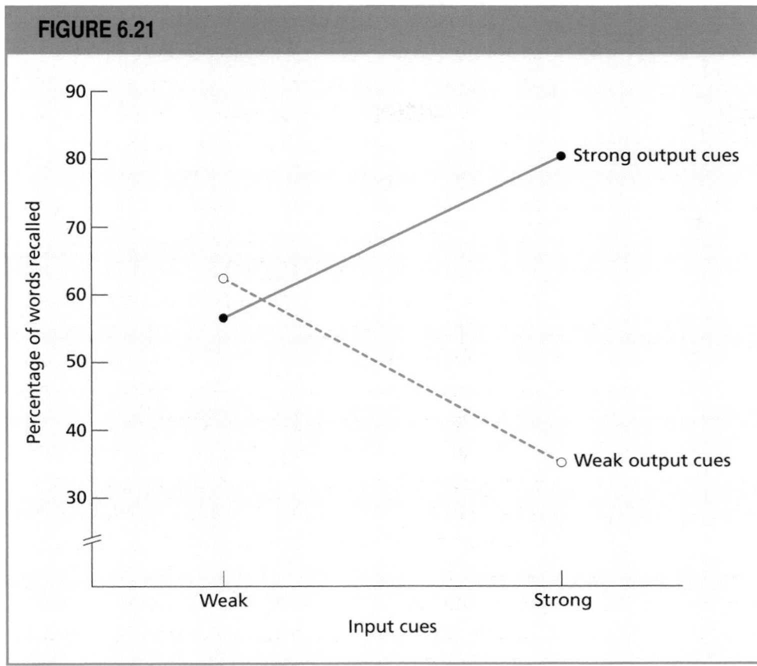

Mean word recall as a function of input cues (strong or weak) and output cues (strong or weak). Data from Thomson and Tulving (1970).

emphasis placed on the role played by contextual information in retrieval is also valuable. For example, contextual information is involved in mood-state-dependent memory (e.g., Kenealy, 1997).

The notion that memory can be accounted for by the encoding specificity principle is limited in various ways. First, there is a danger of circularity in applying the principle. Memory is said to depend on "informational overlap", but this is rarely measured. It is tempting to infer the amount of informational overlap from the level of memory performance, which produces circular reasoning.

Second, as Eysenck (1979) pointed out, what matters is not so much the informational overlap between retrieval information and stored information as the extent to which retrieval information allows us to *discriminate* the correct response from incorrect responses. We can see what that means if we consider a thought experiment (Nairne, 2002b). Suppose participants read aloud the following list of words: write, right, rite, rite, write, right. After that, participants in one condition are asked to recall the word in the third serial position (i.e., rite). In another condition, we increase the informational overlap by providing participants with the sound of the item in the third position. This additional informational overlap is of little or no use because it does not allow participants to discriminate the correct spelling of the sound from the wrong ones.

Third, another serious problem with Tulving's theoretical position is his view that the information available at the time of test is compared in a simple and direct way with the information stored in memory to assess informational overlap. This is implausible if one considers what happens if memory is tested by asking the question, "What did you do six days ago?" Most people answer such a question by engaging in a complex problem-solving strategy to reconstruct the relevant events, but Tulving's approach has little to say about such strategies.

Fourth, Tulving assumed that context influences recall and recognition in the same way, but that is not entirely true. Baddeley (1982) proposed a distinction between intrinsic context and extrinsic context. Intrinsic context has a direct impact on the

FIGURE 6.22

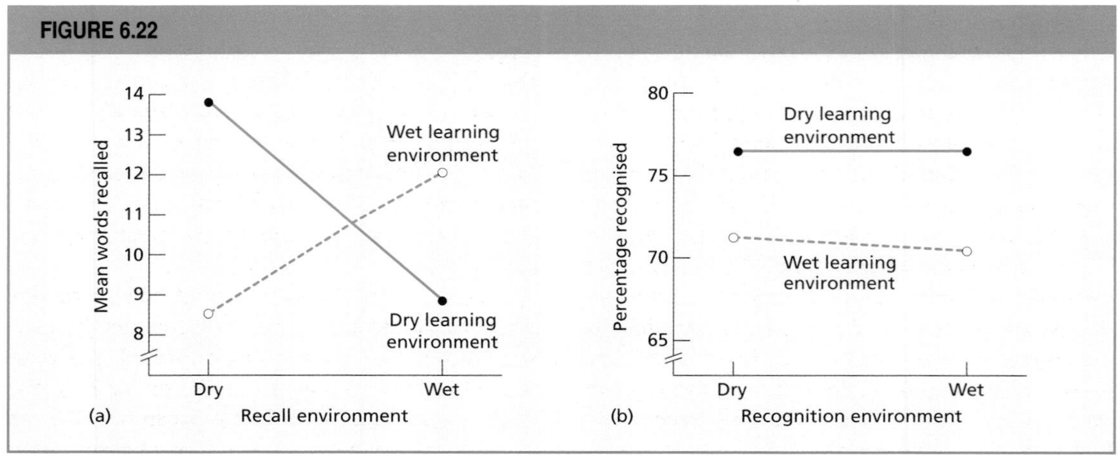

(a) Recall in the same versus different contexts, data from Godden and Baddeley (1975); (b) Recognition in the same versus different contexts. Data from Godden and Baddeley (1980).

meaning or significance of a to-be-remembered item (e.g., strawberry vs. traffic as intrinsic context for the word "jam"), whereas extrinsic context (e.g., the room in which learning takes place) does not. According to Baddeley (1982), recall is affected by both intrinsic and extrinsic context, whereas recognition memory is affected only by intrinsic context.

Godden and Baddeley (1975) asked participants to learn a list of words either on land or 20 feet underwater, and they were then given a test of free recall on land or underwater. Those who had learned on land recalled more on land, and those who learned underwater did better when tested underwater. Retention was about 50% higher when learning and recall took place in the same extrinsic context (see Figure 6.22). However, recognition memory was not influenced by extrinsic context (Godden & Baddeley, 1980; see Figure 6.22).

Context change

Studies designed to test cue-dependent forgetting and the encoding specificity principle have shown that changes in contextual information between storage and test can produce substantial reductions in memory performance. It is tempting to assume that forgetting over time can be explained in the same way. According to Bouton, Nelson, and Rosas (1999, p. 171):

> The passage of time can create a mismatch because internal and external contextual cues that were present during learning may change or fluctuate over time . . . Thus, the passage of time may change the background context and make it less likely that target material will be retrieved . . . We call this approach the *context-change account of forgetting.*

Mensink and Raaijmakers (1988) proposed a version of context-change theory based on their search of associative memory (SAM) model:

(1) Forgetting over time will occur if the contextual retrieval cues used at time 2 are less strongly associated with the correct memory trace than are the retrieval cues used at time 1.
(2) There is a contextual fluctuation process operating over time which can produce forgetting as indicated in (1).
(3) Forgetting over time will occur if the strength and number of incorrect memory traces associated with the contextual retrieval cues are greater at time 2 than time 1.

Mensink and Raaijmakers (1988) showed that a mathematical model based on the above assumptions could predict a wide range of phenomena, including proactive and retroactive interference. For example, consider proactive interference. Proactive interference is not found when List 2 learning is followed immediately by a memory test, but there is a gradual increase in such interference as the length of the retention interval increases. According to the theory, the contextual fluctuation process weakens the accessibility of the correct memory traces from List 2 over time (assumptions 1 and 2). In addition, the *relative* accessibility of the incorrect memory traces from List 1 increases (assumption 3), in part because of the decreased accessibility of the correct memory traces from List 2 over time. Thus, there is more proactive interference at long retention intervals.

Evaluation

Cue-dependent forgetting is of major importance. The relationship between the external and internal cues available at learning and at test has a great influence on memory performance. Further successes of (and limitations of) this approach are discussed in the next section of the chapter.

The notion that increased forgetting over time can be attributed to a contextual fluctuation process is more speculative, because there is little strong evidence for contextual fluctuation. Mensink and Raaijmakers (1988, p. 453) admitted they had not tested their context-change theory thoroughly: "All [mathematical] 'fits' were qualitative and it remains to be seen whether the model can predict the correct magnitude of the effects." In addition, it is not clear on context-change theory why the rate of forgetting is much faster shortly after learning than it is later on.

Consolidation

None of the theories we have discussed provides a wholly convincing account of forgetting over time. Interference theory may work very well in the laboratory, but has not been shown to account for most forgetting outside the laboratory. Context-dependent forgetting is undoubtedly important, but it is not clear that it can explain forgetting over time. Wixted (2004) argued that the secret of forgetting may lie in consolidation theory (see Dudai, 2004). **Consolidation** is a process lasting for several hours or possibly even days which fixes information in long-term memory. In spite of the fact that consolidation theory is the most popular theory of forgetting among neuroscientists, it has been largely ignored by most cognitive psychologists.

Consolidation theory's view of how memories are initially formed is that "the process [of consolidation] involves a rapidly formed and relatively long-lasting increase in the probability that postsynaptic neurons in the hippocampus will fire in response to neurotransmitters released from presynaptic neurons" (Wixted, 2004, pp. 258–259). A key assumption is that recently formed memories still being consolidated are especially vulnerable to interference and forgetting. Most of the predictions following from consolidation theory flow from this central notion: "New memories are clear but fragile and old ones are faded but robust" (Wixted, 2004, p. 265).

Evidence

There are several lines of research supporting the predictions of consolidation theory. First, consider the form of the forgetting curve. According to consolidation theory, memory traces are most vulnerable in the period of time shortly after learning, and become more resistant to interference as time goes by. It follows that forgetting over time should exhibit a pattern in which the rate of forgetting *decreases* as the length of time after learning increases. That is exactly what we find with the typical forgetting curve (see Figure 6.14).

Second, consider patients with **retrograde amnesia**, which involves impaired memory for events occurring before the onset of the amnesia. Many of these patients have suffered damage to the hippocampus as the result of an accident, and this may have a permanently adverse effect on consolidation processes. According to consolidation theory, retrograde amnesia should depend on the age of the patient's memories, with the most recently formed memories being most impaired. This pattern has been found in numerous patients with retrograde amnesia (Manns, Hopkins, & Squire, 2003).

Third, it is assumed that the process of consolidation of one memory can be disrupted by the formation of subsequent memories. Presumably fewer memories are likely to be formed (and so there will be less disruption) when people are asleep during the retention interval than when they are awake. In a classic study, Jenkins and Dallenbach (1924) tested two students who were awake or asleep during the retention interval. The students showed much less forgetting when asleep between learning and test. Hockey, Davies, and Gray (1972) pointed out a problem in the study by Jenkins and Dallenbach (1924). In the asleep condition, learning always occurred in the evening, whereas it mostly occurred in the morning in the awake condition. In their study, Hockey et al. found that the time of day at which learning took place was more important than whether or the participants slept between learning and test. However, students who slept during the retention interval remembered more than those who remained awake.

According to consolidation theory, sleep should have a greater beneficial effect on memory when it occurs early in the retention interval rather than later on. The reason is that it is only early in the retention interval that memories are very vulnerable to disruption of the consolidation process. Ekstrand (1972) found that participants who slept immediately after learning remembered more than those who slept towards the end of the retention interval (81% vs. 66%).

Fourth, consider the effects of alcohol on memory. People who drink excessive amounts of alcohol sometimes suffer from "blackout", which is an almost total loss of memory for all events occurring while they were conscious but very drunk. These blackouts probable indicate a failure to consolidate memories formed while intoxicated. An interesting (and somewhat surprising) finding is that memories formed shortly before alcohol consumption are often better remembered than memories formed by people who do not subsequently drink alcohol (Bruce & Pihl, 1997). Presumably alcohol prevents the formation of new memories that would interfere with the consolidation of the memories formed just before alcohol consumption. Thus, alcohol serves to protect previously formed memories from disruption.

Fifth, the assumption that memories are most vulnerable during the early stage of consolidation leads to a further prediction. We saw earlier that retroactive interference can cause forgetting. According to consolidation theory, retroactive interference should have a greater adverse effect on recently formed memories than on older ones. Wixted (2004) analysed the available evidence thoroughly, and found that most relevant studies obtained results in line with this prediction.

Evaluation

Unlike most other theories of forgetting, consolidation theory provides an explanation of *why* the rate of forgetting decreases over time. Other lines of evidence also show convincingly that new memories are more fragile than older ones. This greater fragility of new memories helps us to understand the finding that retrograde amnesia is greater for recently formed memories, the effects of sleep and alcohol on forgetting, and the finding that retroactive interference effects are greatest soon after learning has occurred. No other theory of forgetting comes even close to providing a plausible explanation of these effects, and so we can argue that consolidation theory currently offers the most complete account of forgetting.

Consolidation theory has various limitations. First, there are several uncertainties about the details of the consolidation process (Nadel & Moscovitch, 2001). Second, we lack strong evidence that the effects described above are all due to effects on consolidation processes. For example, there could be various reasons why newly formed memories are more easily disrupted than older ones. Third, consolidation theory, with its emphasis on the fragility of new memory traces, indicates in a general way why newly formed memory traces are very susceptible to interference effects. However, it does not directly explain why interference is greatest when two different responses are associated with the same stimulus.

CHAPTER SUMMARY

- The architecture of memory
  According to the multi-store theory, there are separate sensory, short-term, and long-term stores. There is strong evidence to support the notion of various qualitatively different memory stores, but this approach provides a very oversimplified view. For example, multi-store theorists assumed there are unitary short-term and long-term stores, but the reality is more complex. According to the standard model, activated information from long-term memory is in short-term memory, decay of that activation causes that information to leave short-term memory, and decay can be prevented by rehearsal. This account de-emphasises the roles of proactive interference and of retrieval cues in short-term memory and forgetting.

- Working memory
  Baddeley replaced the unitary short-term store with a working memory system consisting of three components: an attention-like central executive; a phonological loop holding speech-based information; and a visuo-spatial sketchpad specialised for spatial and visual coding. This working memory system is of relevance to non-memory activities such as comprehension and verbal reasoning. The phonological loop and visuo-spatial sketchpad have both been subdivided into two-component systems, one component for storage and one for processing. The central executive fulfils several functions, some of which may be mainly located in the frontal cortex. Many of the characteristics of the central executive remain unclear. Baddeley has recently added a fourth component (episodic buffer) which integrates and holds information from various sources.

- Memory processes
  Craik and Lockhart (1972) focused on learning processes in their levels-of-processing theory. They (and their followers) identified depth of processing (i.e., extent to which meaning is processed), elaboration of processing, and distinctiveness of processing as key determinants of long-term memory. Insufficient attention was paid to the relationship between the processes at learning and those at the time of test. Other problems are that the theory is not explanatory, that it is hard to assess the depth of processing, and that shallow processing can lead to very good long-term memory.

- Implicit learning
  It has been claimed that implicit learning differs from explicit learning in terms of the presence or absence of consciously accessible knowledge. Much evidence supports the distinction between implicit and explicit learning, and amnesic patients often show intact implicit learning but impaired explicit learning. In addition, brain areas involved in working memory and attention are often more active during explicit than implicit learning. However, it has proved difficult to show that claimed demonstrations of implicit learning satisfy the information and sensitivity criteria, and some brain-imaging studies and studies on amnesic patients shed doubt on the notion of implicit learning. It is likely that the distinction between implicit and explicit learning is too simple, and that more complex theoretical formulations are required.

- Theories of forgetting
  Freud argued for the importance of repression, in which threatening material in long-term memory cannot gain access to consciousness. There is controversial evidence of recovered memories in adults who claim to have suffered childhood abuse. Strong effects of proactive and retroactive interference have been shown in the laboratory. However, insufficient attention has been paid to

active strategies that individuals use to minimise interference effects. Much forgetting is probably cue-dependent, and the cues can be either external or internal (e.g., in mood-state-dependent memory). However, it is not clear that forgetting over time can be explained in cue-dependent terms. It may well be that forgetting over time depends mostly on failures of consolidation. Consolidation theory provides an explanation for the form of the forgetting curve, and for reduced forgetting rates when learning is followed by sleep or alcohol.

FURTHER READING

- Andrade, J. (2001). *Working memory in perspective*. Hove, UK: Psychology Press. The chapters in this edited book provide a good overview of theory and research on working memory.
- French, R.M., & Cleermans, A. (2002). *Implicit learning and consciousness: An empirical, philosophical and computational consensus in the making*. Hove, UK: Psychology Press. Leading researchers on implicit learning contribute their ideas on the enduring controversies surrounding implicit learning.
- Healy, A.F. (2003). *Handbook of psychology: Experimental psychology, Vol. 4*. New York: Wiley & Sons. There are good reviews of several topics in memory in this edited book, including one on working memory.
- Nairne, J.S. (2002). Remembering over the short-term: The case against the standard model. *Annual Review of Psychology, 53*, 53–81. Problems with common views of the workings of short-term memory are discussed thoroughly in this article.
- Wixted, J.T. (2004). The psychology and neuroscience of forgetting. *Annual Review of Psychology, 55*, 235–269. A convincing case is made that neuroscience has more to contribute to our understanding of forgetting than is admitted by most cognitive psychologists.

7

Long-term Memory Systems

INTRODUCTION

We have an amazing variety of information stored away in long-term memory. For example, long-term memory can contain details of our last summer holiday, the fact that Paris is the capital of France, information about how to ride a bicycle or to play the piano, and so on. In view of this variety, Atkinson and Shiffrin's (1968) notion that there is only a single long-term memory store seems improbable (see Chapter 6). Schacter and Tulving (1994) (basing themselves on the work of many other theorists) argued for a more convincing view of memory in general and long-term memory in particular. In essence, they argued that there are five major memory systems: working memory; semantic memory; episodic memory; the perceptual representation system; and procedural memory. Working memory, which was discussed in detail in Chapter 6, is of crucial importance to short-term memory. In contrast, the four other memory systems are concerned with long-term memory, and are all discussed in detail in this chapter.

Memory systems

What do we mean by a memory system? According to Schacter and Tulving (1994) and Schacter, Wagner, and Buckner (2000), three main criteria can be used to identify a memory system:

(1) Class inclusion operations: Any given memory system handles various kinds of information within a given class or domain. For example, semantic memory is concerned with general knowledge of different kinds.
(2) Properties and relations: The properties of a memory system "include types of information that fall within its domain, rules by which the system operates, neural substrates, and functions of the system (what the system is 'for')" (Schacter et al., 2000, p. 629).
(3) Convergent dissociations: Any given memory system should differ clearly in various ways from other memory systems.

As we will see, some of the most impressive evidence supporting the notion that there are several long-term memory systems comes from the study of brain-damaged patients with amnesia.

Such patients have severe problems with long-term memory. They are sometimes said to suffer from the '**amnesic syndrome**', with the following being some of the main symptoms:

- There is a marked impairment in the ability to remember new information learned after the onset of the amnesia; this is **anterograde amnesia**.
- There is often great difficulty in remembering events occurring prior to amnesia; this is known as **retrograde amnesia**.
- Patients suffering from the amnesic syndrome generally have only slightly impaired short-term memory on measures such as digit span (the ability to repeat back a random string of digits). This is also shown by the fact that it is possible to have a relatively normal conversation with an amnesic patient.
- Patients with the amnesic syndrome have some remaining learning ability after the onset of the amnesia.

Explicit and implicit memory

One of the ways in which memory systems differ from each other is in terms of their reliance on explicit or implicit memory. These terms were defined by Graf and Schacter (1985, p. 501): "**Explicit memory** is revealed when performance on a task requires conscious recollection of previous experiences . . . **Implicit memory** is revealed when performance on a task is facilitated in the absence of conscious recollection."

In terms of the definition of implicit memory, we need to ensure that effects on memory performance occur in the absence of conscious recollection. This is easier said than done. A common method is to ask the participants at the end of the study about their awareness of any conscious recollection. However, participants may forget or the questioning may be insufficiently probing. Jacoby, Toth, and Yonelinas (1993) devised the process-dissociation procedure to measure the respective contributions of explicit and implicit memory processes to performance on a test of cued recall. A list of words was presented (e.g., "mercy"), and there were two conditions at the time of the test:

- Inclusion test: participants were told to complete the cues or word stems (e.g., "mer ___") with list words they recollected, or failing that with the first word that came to mind.
- Exclusion test: participants were instructed to complete the word stems (e.g., "mer___") with words *not* presented on the list.

If conscious recollection (explicit memory) were perfect, then 100% of the completions on the inclusion test would be list words compared to 0% on the exclusion test. In contrast, a complete lack of conscious recollection would produce a situation in which participants were as likely to produce list words on the exclusion test as on the inclusion test. This would indicate that the participants could not tell the difference between list and non-list words. Jacoby et al. (1993) assessed the impact of attention on explicit and implicit memory by using full-attention and divided-attention conditions. In the full-attention condition, participants were instructed to remember the list words for a memory test; in the divided-attention condition, they had to perform a complex listening task while reading the list words, and they were not told there would be a memory test.

The findings are shown in Figure 7.1. Most studies of cued recall only use a condition resembling the inclusion test, and inspection of those findings suggests there was reasonable explicit memory performance in both attention conditions. However, the picture looks very different when the exclusion test data are also considered. Participants in the divided-attention condition produced the same level of performance on the inclusion and exclusion tests, suggesting that they were not making any use of conscious recollection or explicit memory. Participants in the full-attention condition did much better on the inclusion test than on the exclusion test, indicating considerable reliance on explicit memory.

What about implicit memory? The findings suggested that implicit memory processes were used equally in the divided-attention and full-attention conditions. Thus, attention at the time of learning may be of crucial importance to

FIGURE 7.1

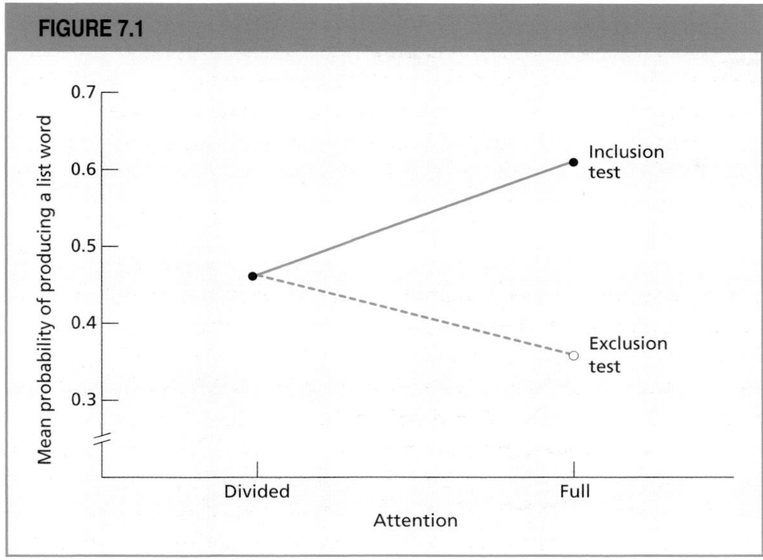

Performance on inclusion and exclusion memory tests as a function of whether attention at learning was divided or full. Adapted from Jacoby et al. (1993).

subsequent conscious recollection, but is irrelevant to implicit memory.

In sum, these findings confirm that the crucial distinction between explicit and implicit memory is in terms of the involvement of conscious recollection. This poses problems for researchers, because it is often hard to decide whether conscious recollection influences any given memory performance. In spite of this, there is now convincing evidence that the distinction between explicit and implicit memory is both valid and important. Many memory tests (e.g., cued recall; Jacoby et al., 1993) involve a mixture of explicit memory and implicit memory.

Various criticisms have been made of the process-dissociation procedure of Jacoby et al. (1993). Of particular concern is the assumption that implicit or automatic processes and explicit or controlled processes are totally *independent* of each other. If participants are instructed to complete word stems with the first word that comes to mind but to avoid words encountered previously, they are likely to use an implicit or automatic process followed by an explicit or controlled process. Such instructions are likely to lead to use of a generate–recognise strategy in which implicit and explicit processes are *not* independent of each other. Jacoby (1998, p. 10) studied the effects of such a strategy, and admitted that it produced problems: "Participants' reliance on a generate–recognise strategy violates assumptions of the estimation procedure."

Mulligan (1998) developed Jacoby et al.'s (1993) notion that attention is more important in explicit memory than in implicit memory. In one condition (full attention), the participants only had to learn the to-be-remembered material. In the other condition (divided attention), they had to learn the material *and* perform another task at the same time. Mulligan (1998) argued that divided attention at the time of learning would reduce explicit memory performance, but would have no effect on implicit memory performance. These predictions were compared against those following from an alternative viewpoint, according to which dividing attention at study reduces conceptual or semantic processing, but has little or no effect on perceptual processing. If so, then divided attention will reduce memory performance on conceptual tests, but will not affect performance on perceptual tests.

Mulligan (1998) found that there were effects of divided attention on conceptual tests involving explicit memory, but no effects on perceptual tests involving implicit memory. In order to decide between the two positions, Mulligan (1998) used

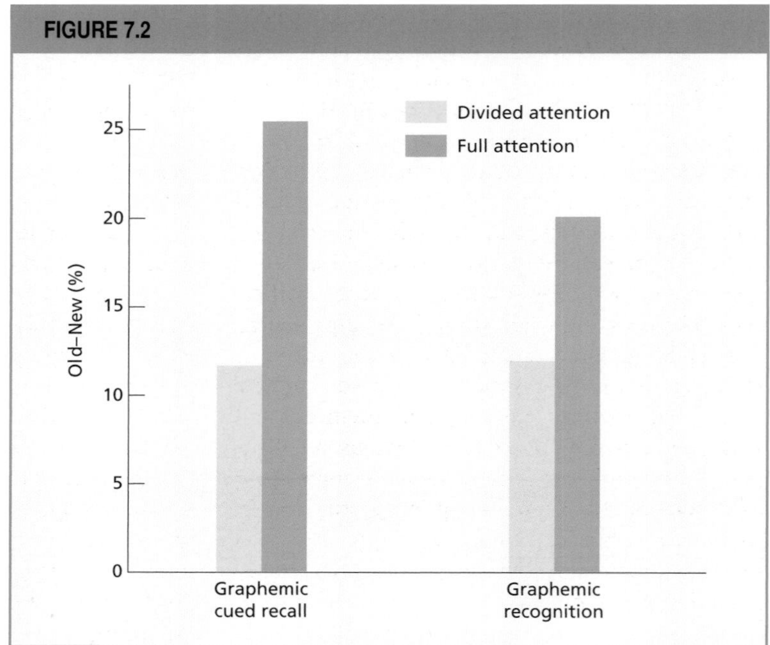

Memory performance on graphemic cued recall and graphemic recognition in full and divided attention conditions. Data from Mulligan (1998).

two explicit perceptual tests. These tests were graphemic cued recall and graphemic recognition, both of which involved nonwords resembling actual words (e.g., "cheetohs" is like "cheetahs"). In the former test, the participants had to *recall* the list words (e.g., "cheetohs" might cue the list word "cheetah"). In the latter test, the participants had to *recognise* which nonwords had a similar appearance to list words.

In spite of the fact that both tests involved perceptual processing, there was a significant effect of the attentional manipulation (see Figure 7.2). As Mulligan (1998, p. 41) concluded, the findings suggest that, "performance on explicit tests, whether perceptual or conceptual, is dependent on attention at encoding."

Evidence that different brain regions are involved in explicit and implicit memory was reported by Seger et al. (2000b). Their participants were first instructed to learn artificial grammar strings. After that, they were given additional grammar strings. Some of the participants had to perform a recognition memory test on these strings (explicit memory), whereas others had to judge whether the strings were grammatically correct (implicit memory). These two memory tasks were associated with activation in different brain areas: "Recognition activated the right frontal cortex, whereas grammatical judgement activated the left frontal cortex. Recognition led to higher activity in the precuneus and medial occipital cortex, whereas grammatical judgements led to suppression of activity in the precuneus and activation in the lateral occipital cortex" (Seger et al., 2000b, p. 283).

Explicit memory is often associated with *increased* brain activation whereas implicit memory is associated with *decreased* brain activation. For example, consider a PET study by Schacter et al. (1996). When the participants performed an explicit memory task (recall of semantically processed words), there was much activation of the hippocampus. In contrast, when they performed an implicit memory task (word-stem completion), there was reduced blood flow in the bilateral occipital cortex, but the task did not affect hippocampal activation. In similar fashion, Badgaiyan, Schacter, and Alpert (2002) found that explicit retrieval of relational information was associated with increased activation in the left prefrontal and medial temporal lobe areas, whereas Badgaiyan (2000) found that implicit memory was associated with reduced activation in various brain areas including early visual cortex (BA19).

In sum, studies of memory and of brain functioning in healthy participants have provided reasonably convincing evidence for the distinction between explicit and implicit memory. The reduced brain activation often associated with implicit memory probably reflects increased efficiency of processing when stimuli are re-presented (discussed in more detail later in the chapter). However, it remains difficult to prove that any given task assesses only implicit memory, and thus does not rely at all on conscious recollection. As we will see shortly, there is compelling evidence for the explicit–implicit distinction in studies on amnesic patients, who typically have severely impaired explicit memory but essentially intact implicit memory.

DECLARATIVE MEMORY: EPISODIC AND SEMANTIC MEMORY

We will now start to consider the four long-term memory systems identified by Schacter and Tulving (1994) and Schacter et al. (2000). We should warn the reader at this point that several experts doubt whether all of these memory systems are really *independent* of each other. In addition, just to make life more difficult, researchers differ in the terms they use to refer to the various memory systems. In order to try to minimise confusion, we will indicate the different terms used to describe essentially the same memory system as we proceed.

Schacter and Tulving (1994), following in the footsteps of Tulving (1972), argued that episodic and semantic memory form separate memory systems. However, the two memory systems are considered together here, because there has been much controversy as to whether they are clearly separate from each other. For example, episodic and semantic memory have often been regarded as two forms of **declarative memory**, which "supports explicit recollection of events and facts and is thought to rely upon the medial temporal lobe and diencephalic structures" (Poldrack & Gabrieli, 2001, p. 67). Those favouring this view generally argue that episodic and semantic memory both involve explicit memory. One of the main issues we will consider in this section is whether or not episodic and semantic memory are so different that they should be regarded as forming different memory systems.

Tulving (1972) was the first psychologist to argue persuasively for the distinction between **episodic memory** and **semantic memory**. According to Tulving, episodic memory refers to the storage (and retrieval) of specific events or episodes occurring in a particular place at a particular time. Thus, remembering what you had for breakfast this morning is an example of episodic memory. In contrast, semantic memory contains information about our stock of knowledge about the world. Tulving (1972, p. 386) defined semantic memory as follows:

> It is a mental thesaurus, organised knowledge a person possesses about words and other verbal symbols, their meanings and referents, about relations among them, and about rules, formulas, and algorithms for the manipulation of these symbols, concepts, and relations.

Wheeler, Stuss, and Tulving (1997, p. 333) defined episodic memory differently from Tulving (1972), arguing that its main distinguishing characteristic was "its dependence on a special kind of awareness that all healthy human adults can identify. It is the type of awareness experienced when one thinks back to a specific moment in one's personal past and consciously recollects some prior episode or state as it was previously experienced." They described this form of awareness as autonoetic or self-knowing. In contrast, retrieval of semantic memories lacks this sense of conscious recollection of the past. Instead it involves noetic or knowing awareness, in which we think objectively about something we know.

How do the definitions of episodic and semantic memory offered by Wheeler et al. (1997) differ from those of Tulving (1972)? According to

Wheeler et al. (1997, pp. 348–349), "The major distinction between episodic and semantic memory is no longer best described in terms of the type of information they work with. The distinction is now made in terms of the nature of subjective experience that accompanies the operations of the systems at encoding and retrieval."

What is the relationship between episodic memory and autobiographical memory (discussed in Chapter 8)? In some ways, they seem rather similar, in that both forms of memory are concerned with personal experiences from the past. However, there are important differences (see Conway, 2003). Much of the information in episodic memory is relatively trivial and is remembered for only a short period of time. In contrast, autobiographical memory stores information for long periods of time about events and experiences of some importance to the individual concerned.

Semantic memory

How is information organised in semantic memory? We will consider two of the main lines of evidence bearing on this issue (additional relevant evidence is considered in Chapter 9, which is concerned with concepts and categories). First, there is research on brain-damaged patients having problems in accessing information stored in semantic memory. Second, we will discuss brain-imaging research designed to identify the brain areas primarily associated with different kinds of knowledge.

Brain-damaged patients

Interesting findings have come from the study of brain-damaged patients showing specific problems (known as **category-specific deficits**) with certain semantic categories. For example, Warrington and Shallice (1984) studied a patient (JBR), who had much greater problems in identifying pictures of living than of non-living things, having success rates of 6% and 90%, respectively. However, JBR performed well on naming body parts (which belong to living things), and he was poor at naming objects in some inanimate categories (e.g., precious stones; musical instruments).

The general pattern shown by JBR is much more common than the opposite pattern, i.e., worse recognition of non-living than of living things. However, several patients find it harder to identify non-living things than living things. In total, over 100 patients with a category-specific deficit for living things but not for non-living things have been reported, plus more than 25 with the opposite impairment (Martin & Caramazza, 2003).

How can we account for the generally worse recognition performance on living than non-living things? Perhaps this finding simply reflects the fact that we have more familiarity with non-living than with living things (e.g., foreign animals). That may well be part of what is happening. However, contrary evidence was reported by Caramazza and Shelton (1998), who matched animate and non-animate items for frequency and familiarity. Their patient, EW, was much worse at naming animate objects than inanimate ones regardless of whether they were high in familiarity (54% versus 94%, respectively) or low in familiarity (28% versus 81%). They also found that performance on comprehension questions (e.g., "Does a giraffe live on land?") was worse for animate objects (71%) than for inanimate ones (98%).

Category-specific deficits can be more specific than simply being concerned with animate or inanimate objects. For example, Damasio et al. (1996) asked brain-damaged patients to name famous faces, animals, and tools. Different areas of the left hemisphere were associated with impaired object recognition for the three types of objects (see Figure 7.3). As Damasio et al. (1996, pp. 499–500) concluded, "Abnormal retrieval of words for persons was correlated with damage clustered in the left TP [temporal pole]; abnormal retrieval of words for animals was correlated with damage in left IT [inferotemporal region]; and abnormal retrieval of words for tools correlated with damage in posterolateral IT."

Damasio et al. (1996) then gave the same object-naming task to healthy participants. PET data showed that different areas of the left hemisphere were activated, depending on whether the participants were naming famous faces, animals, or tools. Most strikingly, the areas involved were the

FIGURE 7.3

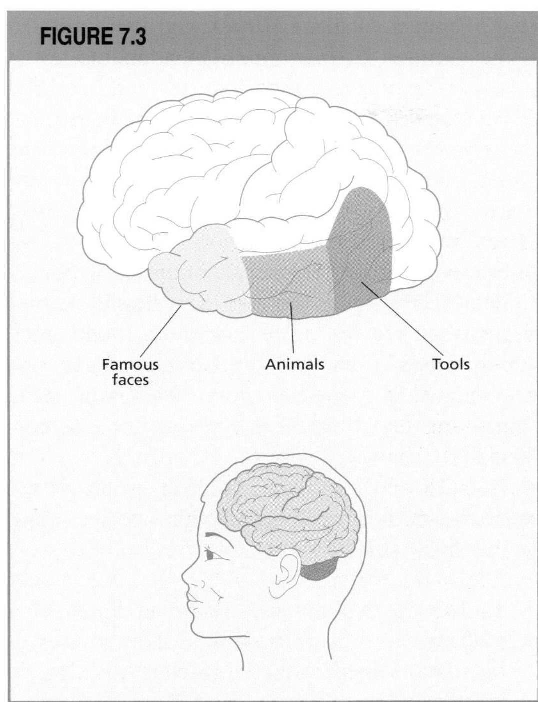

Areas of the left hemisphere associated with impaired object recognition for famous faces, animals and tools. Adapted from Damasio et al. (1996).

same as those identified from the study on brain-damaged patients.

Brain-imaging research

If different types of semantic knowledge are stored in different brain regions, then it should be possible to identify the brain regions involved by means of brain imaging. Friston and Price (2003) reviewed nine PET studies on healthy participants designed to locate brain areas associated with natural kinds (naturally occurring things) and with man-made items or artefacts. There was considerable variability from study to study, with 16 brain regions being found to be active in only a single study. However, one robust finding was obtained in nearly every study: a region in the left posterior middle temporal gyrus was more activated when man-made items were processed than when natural kinds were processed.

Devlin et al. (2002) carried out three unusually thorough experiments on healthy participants to identify brain regions selectively activated by concepts from the categories of animals, fruit, tools, and vehicles. They obtained modest evidence of selective activation: "Like previous studies, we found activation in the left antero-medial temporal pole which was specific to animals and activation in the left posterior middle temporal gyrus which was specific to tools, although in a subset of experiments and at a lowered statistical threshold" (Devlin et al., 2002, p. 70). The weakness and inconsistency of these effects led Devlin et al. (2002, p. 54) to conclude that their findings were, "most consistent with a semantic system undifferentiated by category at the neural level." Some support for this view came from the finding that there was widespread activation of temporal cortex for natural and for man-made items, suggesting that these areas may form the basis for a single semantic system.

Theoretical explanations

How should we interpret category-specific disorders and category-specific activation of certain brain areas in healthy individuals? Farah and McClelland (1991) put forward an influential sensory-functional theory based on the following key assumptions:

(1) Living things are distinguished from each other mainly on the basis of their visual or perceptual properties (i.e., what they look like).
(2) Non-living things are distinguished from each other primarily on the basis of their functional properties (i.e., what they are used for).
(3) There are three times as many visual units within the semantic system as there are functional units.

Farah and McClelland (1991) obtained some support for assumption (3) by examining the descriptors of living and non-living objects given in the dictionary. Three times more of the descriptors were classified as visual than as functional. Of particular importance, the ratio of visual to functional descriptors was 7.7:1 for living objects, but only 1.4:1 for non-living objects.

Farah and McClelland (1991) constructed a computational model based on the above assumptions. When they "lesioned" (caused structural damage to) this model by deactivating some of the semantic units, damage to the visual units impaired performance much more with object recognition of living than of non-living objects. Damage to the functional units had less effect, impairing object recognition only for non-living objects. Thus, the model simulated key findings with brain-damaged patients.

Reasonable support for the general sensory-functional approach was reported by Lee et al. (2002). Participants were PET-scanned while retrieving perceptual or non-perceptual information about living or non-living concepts when presented with the names of the concepts. Processing of perceptual information from both living and non-living concepts was associated with activation of left posterior inferior temporal lobe regions. In contrast, processing of non-perceptual information (e.g., functional attributes) from both living and non-living concepts was associated with activation of middle temporal lobe regions. Comparisons between living and non-living concepts indicated that the same brain regions were activated for both types of concepts.

Support for the notion that specific brain areas are important for functional properties of concepts was reported by Tranel, Kemmerer, Damasio, Adolphs, and Damasio (2003). They studied 26 brain-damaged patients with impairment of tool and/or action knowledge. Three areas in the left hemisphere were damaged in most of these patients: premotor and nearby frontal cortex; parietal cortex; and the posterior part of the middle temporal gyrus. All of these areas are linked to various aspects of tool use. For example, regions of ventral premotor and intraparietal cortices are involved in grasping and manipulating objects.

The sensory-functional theory of Farah and McClelland (1991) has various limitations. First, it predicts that brain-damaged patients should show *general* impairments (e.g., covering essentially all categories of living things). In fact, there is much evidence for *specific* impairments. For example, the category of plants is sometimes impaired with little or no impairment on animals (e.g., Farah & Wallace, 1992), and the ability to name pictures of plants can be impaired when naming of animals is normal, or vice versa (Hillis & Caramazza, 1991). Second, it is not totally clear exactly what qualifies as a "functional" property. Third, and related to the second point, there are many properties of living things (e.g., "carnivore", "lives in the desert"), which do not seem to be either sensory or functional. Dictionary definitions of living things are no longer heavily biased to visual or sensory properties if we divide properties into sensory and non-sensory. Thus, the notion that the properties of living and non-living things are very different in type may be exaggerated in the theory.

Shelton and Caramazza (2001) proposed the domain-specific knowledge hypothesis. According to this hypothesis:

> Knowledge is organised into broad domains (categories) reflecting evolutionarily salient distinctions in semantic knowledge; thus, we propose that there are specialised neural mechanisms for recognising and understanding certain categories of knowledge. The assumption is that the categories of animals, plant life, and conspecifics [members of the same species] are important for survival. Animals are predators and prey, plant life provides food and medicine, and the recognition of conspecifics is important for physical and social needs.

It follows from this hypothesis that some patients should show highly selective categorical deficits, provided the category in question is important for survival. Support for this prediction comes from studies by Semenza and Goodglass (1985) and by Shelton, Fouch, and Caramazza (1998). Semenza and Goodglass (1985) found some brain-damaged patients who had deficits mainly in their ability to name body parts. In contrast, Shelton et al. (1998) studied a patient, IOC, who was very good at naming body parts but was severely impaired at naming numerous other categories of objects. These various findings suggest that body parts form a specific category of knowledge within semantic memory.

Evaluation

It is premature to come to any definite conclusions about the organisation of concept-related knowledge in semantic memory. On balance, the evidence is more favourable to the sensory-functional approach than to other approaches (e.g., domain-specific knowledge hypothesis). However, there are many inconsistencies in the data (especially those based on brain imaging), and this has inhibited theoretical development.

It may well be that an adequate theory of category-specific deficits will involve a synthesis of existing views. For example, conceptual knowledge may be represented in a hierarchical fashion (Martin & Caramazza, 2003). At the highest level of the hierarchy, concepts are organised in some domain-specific way. At the lowest level of the hierarchy, the features or attributes of concepts are organised on the basis of whether they are sensory or functional in nature. What seems almost certain is that future theories based on category-specific deficits will be much more complex than existing theories.

Episodic vs. semantic memory

In spite of the major differences between episodic and semantic memory, there are also important similarities: "The manner in which information is registered in the episodic and semantic systems is highly similar – there is no known method of readily encoding information into an adult's semantic memory without putting corresponding information in episodic memory or vice versa" (Wheeler et al., 1997, p. 333). Tulving (2002, p. 5) clarified the relationship between these two memory systems: "Episodic memory . . . shares many features with semantic memory, out of which it grew, . . . but it also possesses features that semantic memory does not . . . Episodic memory is a recently evolved, late-developing, and early-deteriorating past-oriented memory system, more vulnerable than other memory systems to neuronal dysfunction."

We will shortly discuss differences between episodic and semantic memory. However, before we do so, note that there are also some major similarities between these two forms of memory. For example, most amnesic patients (especially those with widespread brain damage) have severe problems with declarative memory as a whole. Thus, they find it difficult to establish new episodic and semantic memories. For example, Spiers, Maguire, and Burgess (2001) reviewed 147 cases of amnesia involving damage to the hippocampus or fornix. There was evidence of impairment on tests of episodic memory in all cases, and many of the cases also had poor ability to form new semantic memories. For example, Gabrieli, Cohen, and Corkin (1988) found an amnesic patient with an almost complete inability to acquire new vocabulary. In similar fashion, many amnesics do not know the name of the current prime minister or president, and have very poor recognition memory for the faces of people who have become famous fairly recently (Baddeley, 1984).

Evidence

If episodic memory and semantic memory form separate memory systems, it should be possible to find various important differences between them. Several such differences have been identified in the literature (see Tulving, 2002, for a review), and we will consider three here.

First, there are numerous studies testing the ability of amnesic patients to acquire episodic and semantic memories after the onset of amnesia. The typical finding is that amnesic patients find it very difficult to acquire new episodic and semantic memories. In other words, there is anterograde amnesia for both types of memories. However, some amnesic patients have much greater anterograde amnesia for episodic memory than for semantic memory. For example, there is KC, who suffered damage to several cortical and subcortical brain regions, including the medial temporal lobes. According to Tulving (2002, p. 14), "The outstanding fact about K.C.'s mental make-up is his utter inability to remember any events, circumstances, or situations from his own life. His episodic amnesia covers his whole life, from birth to present." In contrast, Hayman, MacDonald, and Tulving (1993) found that KC could slowly acquire new semantic memories (e.g., learning to associate "toothbrush" with "performs a daily massage"). This happened even though KC could not remember having visited the laboratory in which the learning took place.

More impressive evidence that episodic and semantic memory are separate was reported by Vargha-Khadem et al. (1997). They studied three patients, two of whom had suffered bilateral hippocampal damage at an early age before they had had the opportunity to develop semantic memories. Beth suffered brain damage at birth, and Jon did so at the age of 4. Both these patients had very poor episodic memory for the day's activities, television programmes, and telephone conversations. In spite of this, Beth and Jon both attended ordinary schools, and their levels of speech and language development, literacy, and factual knowledge (e.g., vocabulary) were within the normal range.

How can we explain the ability of Beth and Jon to develop fairly normal semantic memory in spite of their grossly deficient episodic memory? According to Vargha-Khadem et al. (1997, p. 376), episodic and semantic memory depend on somewhat different regions of the brain: "Episodic memory depends primarily on the hippocampal component of the larger system [i.e., hippocampus and underlying entorhinal, perirhinal, and parahippocampal cortices], whereas semantic memory depends primarily on the underlying cortices." Why do so many amnesics have great problems with both episodic and semantic memory? According to Vargha-Khadem et al., many amnesics have damage to the hippocampus *and* to the underlying cortices. This makes sense given that the two areas are adjacent.

Vargha-Khadem et al. (1997) only studied children, and it would be valuable to show that brain damage suffered in adulthood can lead to the same pattern of good semantic memory but poor episodic memory. This issue was addressed by Verfaellie, Koseff, and Alexander (2000). They studied a 40-year-old female (PS), who as an adult suffered brain damage to the hippocampus but not the underlying cortices. In spite of severe amnesia and greatly impaired episodic memory, she showed evidence of being able to acquire new semantic memories. For example, she displayed reasonable knowledge of new vocabulary and of faces of people who only became famous after the onset of her amnesia. Verfaellie et al. (2000, p. 491) concluded as follows: "P.S.'s *pattern* of performance – severely impaired episodic learning and relatively preserved semantic learning – is similar to that reported in young children. Therefore, it appears that the subhippocampal cortices can mediate new semantic learning, not only in cases of early injury to the hippocampus, but also following hippocampal damage in adulthood." Vargha-Khadem, Gadian, and Mishkin (2002) found similar findings in a follow-up study on Jon at the age of 20. As a young adult, he had a high level of intelligence (IQ = 114), and his semantic memory continued to be markedly better than his episodic memory.

The above findings are generally regarded as important. However, there is a potential problem of interpretation, because the opportunities for learning are generally greater with respect to semantic memory (e.g., acquiring new vocabulary) than episodic memory. As Parkin (2001, p. 405) pointed out, "By definition an episode happens only once."

Second, there are several studies on amnesic patients suffering from retrograde amnesia (i.e., impaired memory for learning occurring before the onset of amnesia). If episodic and semantic memory form different systems, then one might expect to find that some patients would show retrograde amnesia for only episodic or only semantic memory. According to Tulving (2002, p. 13), "[KC's] retrograde amnesia is highly asymmetrical: He cannot recollect any personally experienced events . . . , whereas his semantic knowledge acquired before the critical accident is still reasonably intact. His knowledge of mathematics, history, geography, and other 'school subjects', as well as his general knowledge of the world is not greatly different from others' at his educational level."

The opposite pattern was reported by Yasuda, Watanabe, and Ono (1997), who studied an amnesic patient with bilateral lesions to the temporal lobe, with anterior/inferior structures being especially affected. She had very poor ability to remember public events, cultural items, historical figures, and some items of vocabulary from the time prior to the onset of amnesia. However, she was reasonably good at remembering personal experiences from episodic memory dating back to the pre-amnesia period.

Kapur (1999, p. 801) reviewed studies on retrograde amnesia in the domains of episodic and semantic memory, coming to the following conclusion: "Studies have been reported that show the selective loss of one domain of memory with relative sparing of the other [episodic and semantic memory]; taken together, the various sets of studies can be seen to yield a pattern of double dissociation between the two forms of memory disorder."

Third, if there are separate episodic and semantic memory systems, they would probably involve activation of different parts of the brain. We can consider brain activity during the original learning or *encoding* of episodic and semantic memories as well as brain activity during *retrieval* of these memories. Relevant evidence was reviewed by Wheeler et al. (1997). In 20 PET studies, attempts were made to identify those brain regions involved in episodic encoding but not in semantic encoding. In 18 out of the 20 studies, the left prefrontal cortex was more active during episodic than semantic encoding.

What about brain activation during retrieval? Wheeler et al. (1997) reported that the right prefrontal cortex was more active during episodic memory retrieval than during semantic memory retrieval in 25 out of 26 PET studies. A more detailed picture was revealed by Lepage et al. (2000). They used data from PET studies to identify six brain regions more active during episodic retrieval than during semantic retrieval, all of which were in the frontal lobes. Five of them were in the prefrontal cortex (three strong ones in the right hemisphere and two weaker ones in the left hemisphere), and the remaining one was in the medial anterior cingulate. Other evidence (reviewed by Cabeza & Nyberg, 2000) indicates that the right hemisphere is seldom involved in semantic retrieval. According to Schacter et al. (2000, p. 633), "Neuroimaging studies have consistently demonstrated activation in left prefrontal cortices during conditions thought to require extensive semantic retrieval."

Evaluation

There are several reasons for identifying separate episodic and semantic memory systems as proposed by Tulving (1972) and by Schacter et al. (2000). The relevant evidence is of various kinds, and includes studies of anterograde and retrograde amnesia as well as numerous brain-imaging studies. The fact that the great majority of amnesic patients have anterograde amnesia for *both* episodic and semantic memory may suggest some grounds for caution before concluding that they form separate memory systems. However, there is accumulating evidence that it is primarily amnesic patients with relatively widespread brain damage who show this pattern, with those having lesions only to the hippocampal system showing deficits in episodic memory but not in semantic memory.

In spite of the evidence that episodic and semantic memory are separate, these two memory systems often *combine* in their functioning. For example, suppose you form an episodic memory of an enjoyable picnic on a beach while on holiday. In order to form this memory, you must retrieve semantic information about the concepts (e.g., beach; picnic) contained in your episodic memory.

Nyberg et al. (2003) found evidence suggestive of common processes in episodic and semantic memory in a PET study. They used various episodic and semantic memory tasks, and found four regions of prefrontal cortex were activated during both types of tasks: left fronto-polar cortex; left mid-ventrolateral prefrontal cortex; left mid-dorsolateral prefrontal cortex; and dorsal anterior cingulate cortex. Nyberg et al. also found that the same areas were activated during various working-memory tasks, which raises the possibility that these regions of prefrontal cortex are involved in executive processing or cognitive control.

PROCEDURAL MEMORY AND THE PERCEPTUAL REPRESENTATION SYSTEM

Initially, we need to consider various definitions. The notion of procedural memory was first systematically explored by Cohen and Squire (1980). According to Schacter et al.'s (2000, p. 636) similar notion, **procedural memory** "refers to the learning of motor and cognitive skills, and is manifest across a wide range of situations. Learning to ride a bike and acquiring reading skills are examples of procedural memory". The term "skill learning" is often used to mean what Schacter et al. defined as procedural memory, and is shown by learning that *generalises* to a range of stimuli other than those used during training.

The **perceptual representation system** "can be viewed as a collection of domain-specific modules that operate on perceptual information about the form and structure of words and objects" (Schacter et al., 2000, pp. 635–636). As Schacter et al. (2000, p. 636) pointed out, "The main interest in the PRS [perceptual representation system] centres on its hypothesised role in the ability to identify an object as a result of a specific prior encounter with the object." More specifically, there is a **repetition priming effect**: stimulus processing occurs faster and/or more easily on the second and successive presentations of a stimulus. For example, we may *identify* a stimulus more rapidly the second time it is presented than the first time we encounter it. What we have here is learning relating to the *specific* stimuli used during training. On the face of it, this seems quite different from the more *general* learning associated with procedural memory.

Schacter et al. (2000) claimed that procedural memory and the perceptual representation system form different memory systems. However, this claim is controversial since the term "procedural memory" is often used to cover skill learning *and* priming effects. As Poldrack et al. (1999, p. 226) pointed out, "Most current accounts of memory present priming and skill learning as two forms of implicit, procedural, or non-declarative memory." Thus, some authorities draw a distinction between declarative memory (episodic + semantic memory) and procedural memory (skill learning + priming). Those who favour this approach generally assume there is a close association between declarative and explicit memory on the one hand and between procedural memory and implicit memory on the other hand.

We will first consider studies on skill learning and on priming, with an emphasis on studies involving amnesic patients. Why is this? We have seen that amnesic patients typically have impaired episodic and semantic memory, but it is generally assumed that amnesic patients have essentially intact skill learning and priming. If so, that strengthens the argument that skill learning and priming are very different from episodic and semantic memory. Finally, we will address the theoretically important issue of whether skill learning and priming involve separate memory systems, as assumed by Schacter et al. (2000).

Skill learning

What exactly is skill learning? According to Poldrack et al. (1999, p. 208), "Skill learning refers to the gradual improvement of performance with practice that generalises to a range of stimuli within a domain of processing." One of the key issues with respect to skill learning has been whether this form of learning is impaired in amnesic patients. Skill learning can be divided into sensori-motor and perceptual skills. So far as sensori-motor skills are concerned, amnesics have been shown to have normal (or nearly normal) rates of learning for the pursuit rotor, serial reaction time, and mirror tracing (see Gabrieli, 1998). Each of these skills will be considered in turn.

Corkin (1968) reported that the amnesic patient HM was able to learn mirror drawing, in which the pen used in drawing is observed in a mirror rather than directly. He also showed learning on the pursuit rotor, which involves manual tracking of a moving target. His rate of learning was slower than that of healthy individuals on the pursuit rotor. In contrast, Cermak et al. (1973) found that amnesic patients learned the pursuit rotor as quickly as healthy participants. However, the amnesic patients were slower than healthy individuals at learning a finger maze.

The typical form of the serial reaction time task involves presenting visual targets in one of four horizontal locations, with the task being to press the closest key as rapidly as possible. The sequence of targets is sometimes repeated over 10 or 12 trials, and skill learning is shown by improved performance on these repeated sequences. This skill learning is generally intact in amnesics (e.g., Nissen & Bullemer, 1987).

Mirror tracing involves tracing a figure with a stylus, with the figure to be traced being seen reflected in a mirror. Performance on this task improves with practice in healthy participants, and the same is true of amnesic patients (e.g., Milner, 1962). The rate of learning is often similar in both groups.

Which brain areas are involved in the acquisition of sensori-motor skills? Sensori-motor skill learning is often impaired in patients with damage to the basal ganglia caused by various diseases (e.g., Parkinson's disease; Huntington's disease; Gilles de la Tourette's syndrome). In addition, patients with cerebellar lesions have impaired mirror-tracing performance (e.g., Sanes et al., 1990). Gabrieli (1998, pp. 98–99) put forward a hypothesis to account for the findings: "Closed-loop skill learning, which involves continuous external, visual feedback about errors in movements, depends upon the cerebellum. In contrast, open-loop skill learning, which involves the planning of movements and delayed feedback about errors, depends upon the basal ganglia." It should be noted that these brain areas are very different from those involved in episodic and semantic memory, thereby supporting the notion that skill learning involves a different memory system from episodic and semantic memory.

The involvement of the basal ganglia and the cerebellum in sensori-motor skill learning has also been shown in brain-scanning studies. PET studies have shown that serial reaction time skill learning and other tasks involving the learning of specific manual sequences produce increased activation in the basal ganglia (e.g., Hazeltine, Grafton, & Ivry, 1997). The notion that cerebellar activity reflects error correction is supported by the finding that cerebellar activity decreased in line with a decrease in errors on a perceptual-motor task (Friston et al., 1996).

The main perceptual skill learning task studied with amnesic patients is reading mirror-reversed script, in which what is being read is seen reflected in a mirror. In these studies, we can distinguish between *general* improvement in speed of reading produced by practice and more *specific* improvement produced by re-reading the same groups of words or sentences. Cohen and Squire (1980) reported general and specific improvement in reading mirror-reversed script in amnesics, and there was evidence of improvement even after a delay of 3 months. Martone et al. (1984) also obtained evidence of general and specific improvement in amnesics. However, although the general practice effect was as great in amnesics as in healthy individuals, the specific practice effect was not. Healthy participants (but not amnesics) may use speed-reading strategies to facilitate reading of repeated groups of words.

The brain areas involved in mirror reading were studied by Poldrack et al. (1996) in a study using functional magnetic resonance imaging (fMRI). Initially, there was much activity in right parietal cortex. However, with practice, this activity decreased, and there was increasing activity in left inferior occipito-temporal cortex. According to Gabrieli (1998, p. 99), "These shifts in activity may represent a change in reliance upon visuospatial decoding of mirror-reversed words in unskilled performance to more direct reading in skilled performance."

There are several studies on skill learning in which the main brain areas involved shifted as a result of practice. For example, Van Mier, Tempel, Perlmutter, Raichle, and Petersen (1998) used PET to identify areas of brain activation during practice of a maze-tracing task. Initially, there was activation in range of brain areas including premotor and parietal cortex. After much practice, there was reduced brain activation in these brain areas, but increased activation in the supplementary motor area and primary motor cortex.

What is the significance of these changes in brain activity with practice? According to Schacter et al. (2000, p. 637), "There appears to be a tendency for tasks that require extensive prefrontal and/or premotor contributions in their naive state to shift to more automated pathways with practice, although the specific transition noted in any individual study appears highly dependent on the exact task that is performed."

In sum, amnesic patients show reasonably good learning of sensori-motor and of perceptual skills. Thus, in the terminology favoured by Schacter et al. (2000), the procedural memory system in amnesics is intact or nearly so.

Repetition priming

What exactly is repetition priming? According to Poldrack et al. (1999, p. 208), "Repetition priming (or simply priming) is a facilitation or biasing of performance occurring for the specific stimuli encountered in a task. Priming is measured as the improvement in performance (e.g., increased accuracy; decreased response times) for previously presented or repeated stimuli as compared to stimuli presented for the first time."

Evidence

In order to understand what is involved in priming, we will consider a study by Tulving, Schacter, and Stark (1982). Initially, they asked their participants to learn a list of multisyllabled and relatively rare words (e.g., "toboggan"). One hour or one week later, they were simply asked to fill in the blanks in word fragments to make a word (e.g., _ O _ O _ GA _). The solutions to half of the fragments were words from the list that had been learned, but the participants were not told this. As conscious recollection was not required on the word-fragment completion test, it can be regarded as a test of implicit memory.

There was evidence for implicit memory, with the participants completing more of the fragments correctly when the solutions matched list words. This is a repetition priming effect, which is found when stimulus processing is facilitated when it is presented on more than one occasion. A sceptical reader might argue that repetition priming occurred because the participants deliberately searched through the previously learned list, and thus the test actually reflects explicit memory. However, Tulving et al. (1982) reported an additional finding going against that possibility. Repetition priming was no greater for target words that were recognised than for those that were not. Thus, the repetition priming effect was *unrelated* to explicit memory performance as assessed by recognition memory.

This finding suggests that repetition priming and recognition memory involve different forms of memory. Tulving et al. (1982) also found that the length of the retention interval had different effects on recognition memory and fragment completion. Recognition memory was much worse after one week than after one hour, whereas fragment-completion performance was unchanged. However, there are doubts as to whether forgetting is generally slower in implicit memory than in explicit memory (see Chapter 6).

Cermak et al. (1985) compared the performance of amnesic patients and non-amnesic alcoholics on perceptual priming. The patients were presented with a list of words followed by a priming task. This task was perceptual identification, and involved presenting the words at the minimal exposure time needed to identify them correctly. The performance of the amnesic patients resembled that of the control participants, with identification times being faster for the primed list words than for the unprimed non-list words (see Figure 7.4). In other words, the amnesic patients showed as great a perceptual priming effect as the controls. Cermak et al. also used a conventional test of recognition memory (which depends mainly on episodic memory) for the list words. In line with much previous research, the Korsakoff patients did significantly worse than the controls on this task (see Figure 7.4).

Graf, Squire, and Mandler (1984) studied a different perceptual priming effect. Word lists were presented, with the participants deciding how much they liked each word. The lists were followed by one of four memory tests. Three of the tests were conventional memory tests (free recall; recognition memory; cued recall), but the fourth test (word completion) measured a priming effect. On this last test, participants were given three-letter word fragments (e.g., STR ___) and simply wrote down the first word they thought of starting with those letters (e.g., STRAP; STRIP). Priming was assessed by the extent to which the word completions corresponded to words from the list previously presented. Amnesic patients did much worse than controls on all the conventional memory tests. However, there was no difference between the two groups in the size of

FIGURE 7.4

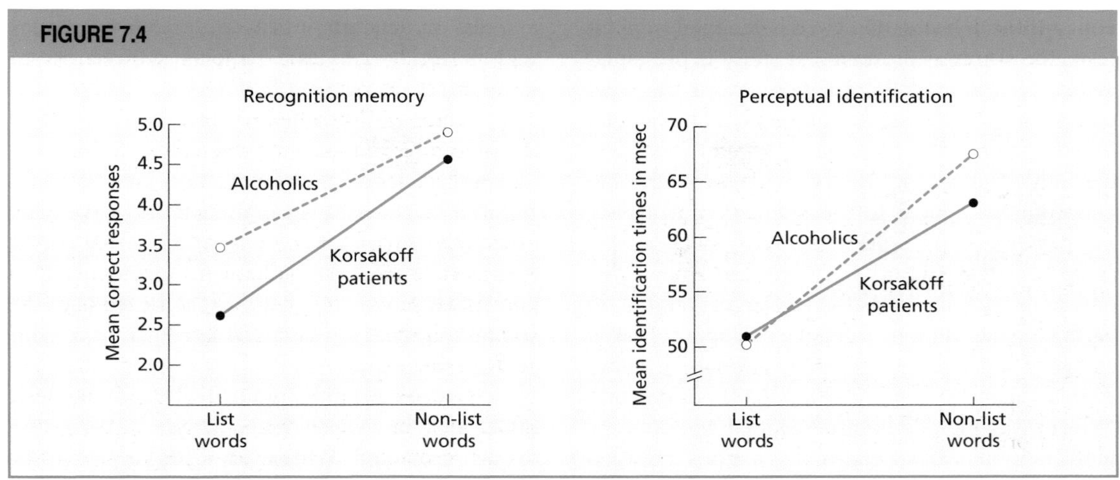

Recognition memory and perceptual identification of Korsakoff patients and non-amnesic alcoholics; delayed conditions only. Data from Cermak et al. (1985).

their priming effect on the word-completion task (see Figure 7.5).

The notion that perceptual priming depends on different brain systems from those involved in explicit memory would be strengthened if it were possible to obtain a **double dissociation**. In other words, it would be useful to find patients who had intact explicit memory but impaired perceptual priming. This was achieved by Gabrieli et al. (1995). They studied a patient, MS, who had a right occipital lobe lesion. MS had normal levels of performance on the explicit memory tests of recognition and cued recall but impaired performance on perceptual priming. Gabrieli et al. also tested amnesic patients, and confirmed that they showed the opposite pattern of impaired explicit memory but intact perceptual priming.

Several researchers (e.g., Tulving & Schacter, 1990) have suggested that there are important differences between **perceptual priming** and

FIGURE 7.5

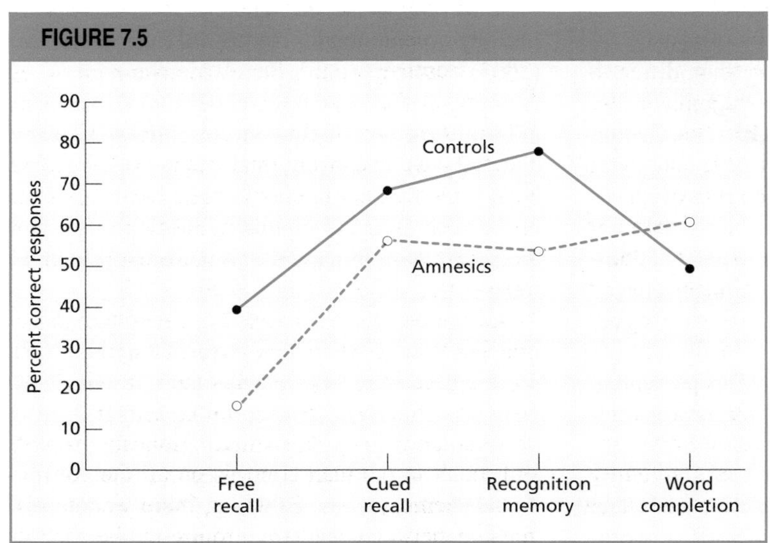

Free recall, cued recall, recognition memory, and word completion in amnesic patients and controls. Data from different experiments reported by Graf et al. (1984).

conceptual priming. On most perceptual implicit tests, the stimulus presented at study is presented at test in a degraded form (e.g., word-fragment completion; word-stem completion; perceptual identification). On conceptual implicit tests, on the other hand, the test provides information conceptually related to the studied information, but there is no perceptual similarity between the study and test stimuli (e.g., general knowledge questions such as, "What is the largest animal on earth?"; generation of category exemplars from a category such as "four-footed animals"). However, as Schacter et al. (2000, p. 627) pointed out, "Most tasks include both perceptual and conceptual components, so sharp distinctions between perceptual and conceptual priming are probably oversimplistic."

Different brain areas seem to be involved in perceptual and conceptual priming. Patients with **Alzheimer's disease** (which involves progressive dementia or loss of mental powers) typically have intact perceptual priming but impaired conceptual priming. In contrast, patients with progressive multiple sclerosis have intact conceptual priming but impaired perceptual priming (word-fragment completion) (Blum et al., 2002), and patients with right occipital lesions have no perceptual priming on visual word-identification tasks but normal conceptual priming (see Gabrieli, 1998). What we have here is a double dissociation, which is often taken as evidence that separate processes and brain areas are involved in the two types of task.

Brain-imaging studies confirm that different brain areas are involved in perceptual and conceptual priming. As we have seen, PET studies on healthy individuals indicate that perceptual priming on visual word-stem completion task produces reduced activity in bilateral occipito-temporal areas (e.g., Schacter et al., 1996). In contrast, priming on conceptual priming tasks produces reduced activity in left frontal neorcortex (e.g., Wagner et al., 1997).

In spite of the differences between perceptual and conceptual priming, there are important similarities. For example, consider a study by Vaidya et al. (1995). Perceptual priming was studied by means of a word-fragment completion task, and conceptual priming was studied with a word-association generation task (e.g., what word goes with KING?). Amnesic patients showed essentially intact priming on both tasks.

Schacter and Badgaiyan (2001, p. 1) reviewed the literature on brain-imaging studies of perceptual and conceptual priming, and concluded as follows: "Decreases [in brain activity] have been especially consistent in a part of the visual cortex (extrastriate area) that is known to be involved in perceptual processing, and in specific areas of the frontal lobe that are involved in semantic or conceptual processing."

Why does priming typically lead to reduced rather than increased brain activity? According to Schacter and Badgaiyan (2001, pp. 3–4), "Priming-related decreases in cortical activity may indicate that brain regions that are involved in initial processing of a word or picture show a kind of 'neural savings' when the entire item . . . is repeated." Thus, processing is more efficient (and so requires less brain activation) when a stimulus is re-presented than on its original presentation.

A closely related notion is that perceptual and conceptual priming are associated with reduced brain activation because the processes involved become automatic and so much less demanding of resources (see Chapter 5). For example, Gupta and Cohen (2002, p. 434) argued that, "Automaticity is merely a state in which performance on repeating stimuli has improved greatly." However, there is evidence that repetition priming is initially *not* automatic. Holbrook, Bost, and Cave (2003) studied priming involving the naming of pictures. There were three conditions of interest: (1) same pictures had been presented previously and had been task-relevant; (2) same pictures had been presented previously but had not been task-relevant; and (3) a control condition in which the pictures to be named had not been presented before.

As can be seen in Figure 7.6, perceptual priming was found when the pictures on their first presentation were task relevant but not when they were task irrelevant. Thus, priming effects depend on the significance that stimuli have for participants and do not necessarily occur automatically. As Holbrook et al. (2003, p. 380) concluded, "Priming . . . may reflect a more adaptive and

FIGURE 7.6

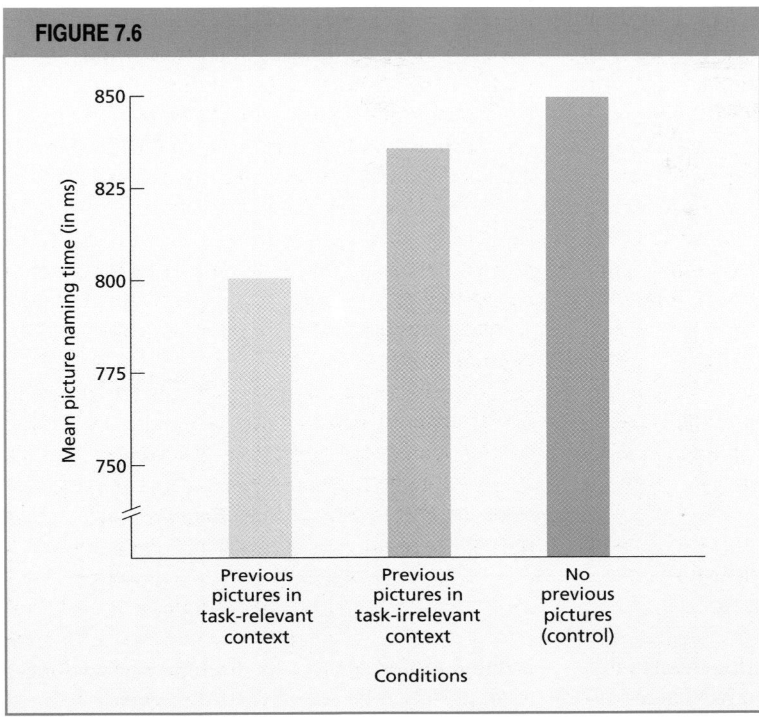

Mean times to name pictures as a function of condition (same picture presented previously in a task-relevant or task-irrelevant context; pictures not presented previously). Data from Holbrook et al. (2003).

flexible mechanism for modification of perceptual processing than previously appreciated."

How different are skill learning and priming?

Some experts (e.g., Poldrack & Gabrieli, 2001) are impressed by the *similarities* between skill learning and priming, and have argued that they both involve a single underlying memory system. In contrast, other experts (e.g., Schacter et al., 2000) are impressed by the *differences* between skill learning and priming, and argue that they involve separate memory systems. We cannot currently resolve this issue, for two main reasons. First, skill learning and priming have very rarely been considered in the same experiment. Second, it is hard to compare findings, because studies on priming typically use highly practised processes (e.g., word reading), whereas studies on skill learning mostly use processes with which the participants are initially unfamiliar. In spite of these problems, we will consider the similarities and differences between priming and skill learning.

Various arguments can be made to support the claim that skill learning and priming involve different memory systems. First, as Poldrack et al. (1999, p. 209) pointed out, skill learning and priming seem to differ in their stimulus specificity: "Priming is tied to the specific stimuli that were encountered in the experiment . . . This differs from skill learning, which is defined as applying over potentially all stimuli in the practised domain."

Second, there is some cognitive neuropsychological evidence suggesting that there is a double dissociation between skill learning and priming. Heindel et al. (1989) compared the performance of patients with Huntington's disease and with Alzheimer's disease on two tasks. One of these tasks (pursuit rotor, on which a metal stylus has to be kept in contact with a moving disc) was a test of motor skill, and the other task (word-stem completion) was a test of priming. The patients with Huntingdon's disease had impaired skill learning but intact priming, whereas the patients with Alzheimer's disease had intact motor skill learning but impaired priming (see Figure 7.7).

FIGURE 7.7

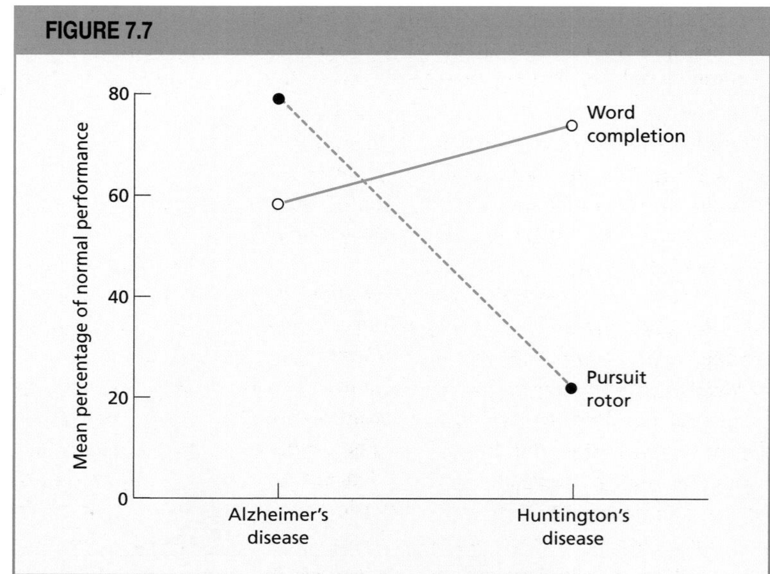

Memory performance of Alzheimer's disease and Huntington's disease patients (percentage of normal performance) on pursuit-rotor and word completion tasks. Based on data in Butters et al. (1990).

Third, if skill learning and priming involve different memory systems, there is no particular reason why individuals who are good at skill learning should be good at priming. Much of the evidence indicates that there is practically no correlation between performance on these two types of tasks. For example, Schwartz and Hashtroudi (1991), using word-identification and inverted-text reading tasks, found that the amount of skill learning and of priming were uncorrelated.

On the other hand, there are several arguments supporting the view that skill learning and priming may depend on the *same* memory system. First, as we have seen, amnesic patients have intact levels of performance on priming *and* on skill learning, in spite of their impaired performance on other kinds of memory tasks. It could be argued that priming and skill learning both depend on implicit memory. Second, there are real problems in interpreting the striking double dissociation obtained by Heindel et al. (1989). Their conclusion that patients with Huntington's disease have poor motor skill learning was *not* supported by Gabrieli et al. (1997), who found that such patients had intact skill learning on a mirror-tracing task. Heindel et al.'s other conclusion, that patients with Alzheimer's disease have poor priming performance, was disconfirmed by Keane et al. (1991), who found that Alzheimer's patients had intact priming on a perceptual identification task.

Third, the argument that a lack of correlation between skill learning and priming performance indicates that they depend on separate memory systems is relatively weak. Gupta and Cohen (2002) developed a computational model based on the notion that skill learning and priming depend on a *single* mechanism. This model accounted for zero correlations between skill learning and priming, and for various apparent dissociations between them.

What is probably of most value is to consider those very few studies in which an attempt was made to study skill learning and priming under comparable conditions. Accordingly we turn to the work of Poldrack et al. (1999) and of Poldrack and Gabrieli (2001).

Poldrack et al. (1999) compared skill learning and repetition priming within a single task. The participants were presented with five-digit numbers, which had to be entered as rapidly as possible into a computer keypad. Priming was assessed by performance on repeated digit strings, whereas skill learning was assessed by performance on non-repeated strings. A key finding was that skill learning and the increase in speed with repetition priming were both well described by a power function. Poldrack et al. (1999, p. 227) concluded that, "Priming and skill learning are . . . consequences of the same incremental learning mechanism, tied to and expressed through the operation of various neural networks at different levels of organisation in the system."

Poldrack and Gabrieli (2001) studied skill learning and repetition priming using a mirror-reading task, in which words and pronounceable nonwords presented in a mirror had to be read as fast as possible. Activity in different areas of the brain was assessed by fMRI. The findings were reasonably clear-cut: "[Skill] learning . . . was associated with increased activation in left inferior temporal, striatal, left inferior prefrontal and right cerebellar regions and with decreased activity in the left hippocampus and left cerebellum. Short-term repetition priming was associated with reduced activity in many of the regions active during mirror reading and . . . long-term repetition priming resulted in a virtual elimination of activity in those regions." The finding that very similar areas were involved in skill learning and in priming is consistent with the notion that they involve the same underlying memory system.

Evaluation

Nearly everyone accepts that skill learning and priming involve one or two memory systems very different from those underlying episodic and semantic memory. The strongest evidence for this is the consistent finding that most amnesic patients have essentially intact levels of performance on skill learning and priming, whereas they perform poorly on tests of episodic and semantic memory. The trickier issue is to decide whether skill learning and priming involve separate memory systems, as proposed by Schacter et al. (2000). The jury is still out on that issue but the limited evidence available tends to favour the view that skill learning and priming involve a single memory system. However, it could be argued that the fact that the measures of priming and of skill learning used by Poldrack et al. (1999) and by Poldrack and Gabrieli (2001) were so similar increased the probability of discovering apparent similarities between the two types of memory.

AMNESIA

We have already seen in this chapter that amnesic patients have contributed much to our understanding of human memory. One reason for this is that the study of amnesia provides a good *test-bed* for existing theories of normal memory, with data from amnesic patients strengthening or weakening the support for memory theories. For example, the notion that there is a valid distinction between short-term and long-term memory stores has been tested with amnesic patients (see Chapter 6). Some patients have severely impaired long-term memory but intact short-term memory, whereas a few patients show the opposite pattern. This is a **double dissociation**, and is good evidence that there are separate short-term and long-term stores.

The study of amnesic patients has also proved very valuable in leading to various theoretical developments. For example, important distinctions like that between explicit and implicit memory or between declarative and procedural memory were originally proposed in part because of data collected from amnesic patients. Furthermore, even though there has been much research relevant to these distinctions over the years, some of the strongest evidence supporting them comes from studies on amnesic patients.

The reasons why patients have become amnesic are very varied. Bilateral stroke is one factor causing amnesia, but closed head injury is the most common cause. However, patients with closed head injury often have a range of cognitive impairments, which makes it hard to interpret their memory deficit. As a result, most experimental work has focused on patients who have become amnesic because of chronic alcohol abuse (**Korsakoff's syndrome**). The symptoms of Korsakoff patients tend to become worse over time, whereas those of patients with closed head injury do not. It remains a matter of controversy whether there are enough similarities among these various groups to justify considering them together.

Progress in understanding amnesia has been slow. Some of the main reasons for this were identified by Hintzman (1990, p. 130):

> The ideal data base on amnesia would consist of data from thousands of patients having no other disorders, and having precisely dated lesions [injuries] of known location and extent, and would include many reliable measures spanning all types of knowledge and skills, acquired at known times ranging from the recent to the distant past. Reality falls near the opposite pole of each dimension of this description.

Many studies on amnesia have made use almost exclusively of Korsakoff patients. There are two main problems posed by Korsakoff patients. First, the amnesia usually has a gradual onset, being caused by an increasing deficiency of the vitamin thiamine associated with chronic alcoholism. As a result, it is often hard to know whether certain past events occurred before or after the onset of amnesia. Second, brain damage in Korsakoff patients is often rather widespread. Structures within the diencephalon, such as the hippocampus and amygdala, are usually damaged, and these structures seem to be of vital significance to memory. In addition, there is very often damage to the frontal lobes. This may produce a range of cognitive deficits that are not specific to the memory system, but which have indirect effects on memory performance. It would be easier to make coherent sense of findings from Korsakoff patients if the brain damage were more limited.

Brain structures

The amnesic syndrome can be produced by damage to various brain structures. The key structures are in two separate areas of the brain: a sub-cortical region called the diencephalon; and a cortical region known as the medial temporal lobe. It can be hard to locate the precise location of damage in any given patient. Attempts to do so often used to rely on post-mortem examination. However, the development of brain-imaging techniques has allowed accurate assessment of the damaged areas while the patient is alive.

Some of the brain areas producing the amnesic syndrome when damaged are shown in Figure 7.8. As was mentioned above, chronic alcoholics who develop Korsakoff's syndrome have brain damage in the diencephalon, especially the medial thalamus and the mammillary body, but typically the frontal cortex is also damaged. Harding, Halliday, Caine, and Kril (2000) compared brain damage in patients with Korsakoff's syndrome or psychosis and in alcoholics without amnesia. They found that, "neuronal loss in the anterior thalamic nuclei was found consistently only in alcoholic Korsakoff's psychosis . . . [this] supports previous evidence that degeneration of thalamic relays are important in this memory disorder."

The fact that the frontal lobes are generally damaged in Korsakoff patients means that we need to consider their role in memory functioning. Episodic memory seems to depend on the frontal lobes as well as on the diencephalon (Wheeler et al., 1997). An important aspect of episodic memory is temporal discrimination, i.e., remembering when events or episodes occurred. Shimamura, Janowsky, and Squire (1990) found that frontal lobe patients were poor at reconstructing the order in which words in a list had been presented, in spite of having normal recognition memory for those words. However, many patients without frontal lobe damage show poor temporal discrimination.

Other amnesics have damage in the medial-temporal region, in which the hippocampus is of special importance. This can happen as a result of herpes simplex encephalitis, anoxia (due to lack of oxygen), infarction, or sclerosis (involving a hardening of tissue or organs).There are other cases in which some of the temporal lobe in epileptic patients was removed to reduce the incidence of epileptic seizures. As a result, many of these patients (including the much-studied HM) became severely amnesic (Scoville & Milner, 1957). The exact extent of HM's brain damage was not known for many years. However, Corkin et al. (1997, p. 3978) used MRI on HM, finding that his brain damage was less extensive than had been believed previously. More specifically,

FIGURE 7.8

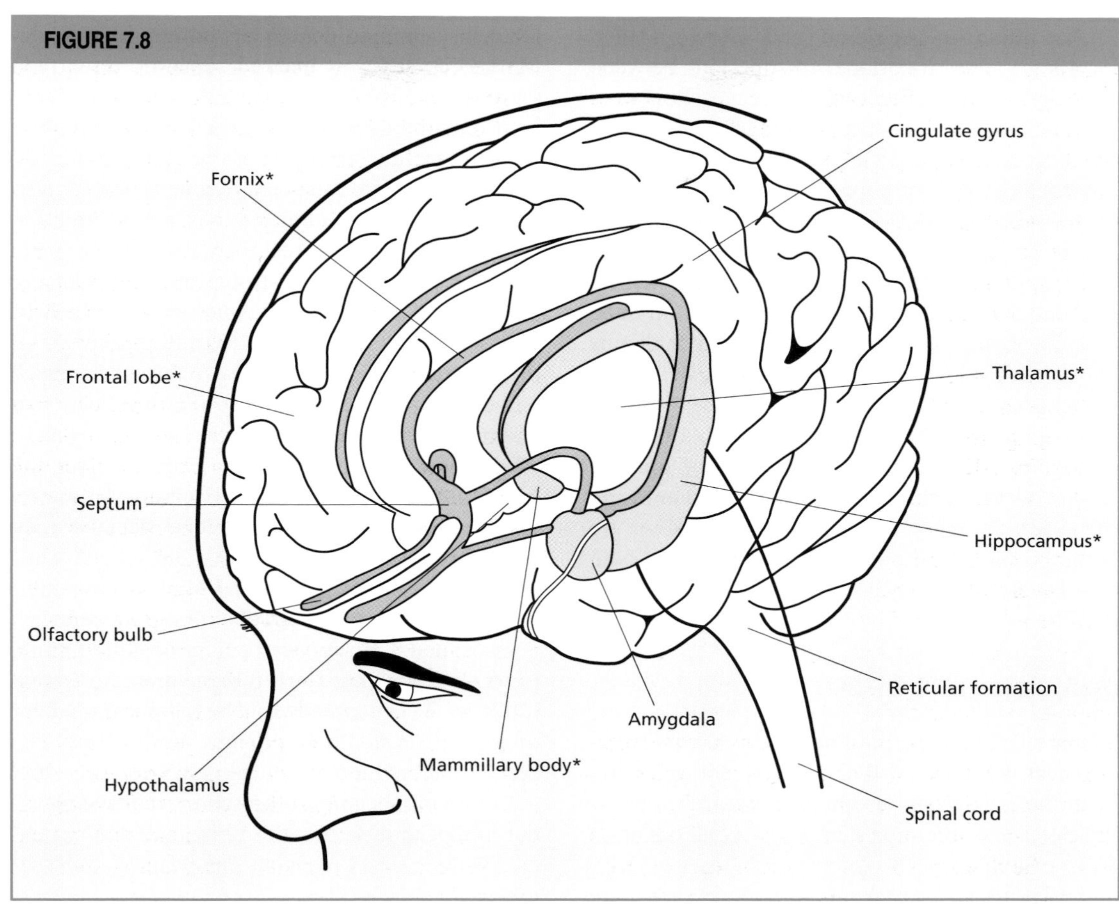

Diagram of the limbic system and related structures. Areas indicated with an asterisk are known to be associated with memory function. From Parkin (2001).

they "confirmed that the lesions responsible for the amnesic syndrome in H.M. are confined to the medial temporal lobe" (Corkin et al., 1997, p. 3978).

Theoretical considerations

Squire, Knowlton, and Musen (1993) argued that the major brain structures underlying declarative or explicit memory are located in the hippocampus and anatomically related structures in the medial temporal lobes and the diencephalon, with the neocortex being the final repository of declarative memory. McKee and Squire (1992) found that amnesics with medial temporal lobe lesions showed similar forgetting rates to amnesics with diencephalic lesions at retention intervals of between 10 minutes and 1 day. These findings led Squire et al. (1993) to argue that the diencephalon and medial lobe structures are of comparable importance to declarative or explicit memory.

Some researchers have used PET scans to study the brain structures involved in explicit memory. Squire et al. (1992) found that blood flow in the right hippocampus was much higher when participants were performing an episodic memory task (cued recall) than a priming task (word-stem completion). This supports the view that the hippocampus plays an important role in declarative memory.

According to Aggleton and Brown (1999, p. 426), "The traditional distinction between temporal lobe and diencephalic amnesics is misleading; both groups have damage to the same functional system . . . The proposed hippocampal-diencephalic system is required for the encoding of episodic information, permitting the information to be set in its spatial and temporal context." They argued that there is a second system involving the perirhinal cortex of the temporal lobe and the medial dorsal nucleus of the thalamus which is involved in making familiarity judgements on tests of recognition memory. It is difficult to find patients with damage to only one system because, "in the large majority of amnesic cases both the hippocampal-anterior thalamic and the perirhinal-medial dorsal thalamic systems are compromised, leading to severe deficits in both recall and recognition" (Aggleton & Brown, 1999, p. 426).

Retrograde amnesia

Retrograde amnesia (loss of memory for information learned prior to the onset of amnesia) has been the Cinderella of amnesia research, receiving much less attention than anterograde amnesia (loss of memory for information learned after amnesia onset). Some kinds of memory are more vulnerable than others to retrograde amnesia. Spiers et al. (2001) found in their review of 147 cases of amnesia that episodic memories are more consistently impaired than semantic memories in retrograde amnesia.

The extent of retrograde amnesia varies considerably from patient to patient, sometimes involving severe retrieval problems for memories formed several years before the onset of amnesia, and sometimes involving minor retrieval problems for memories covering a much shorter period. However, there is generally a *temporal gradient*, with retrieval problems being greater for memories acquired closer to the onset of the amnesia than those acquired longer ago. The extent of retrograde amnesia depends on the areas of brain damage. Kapur (1999, p. 800) reviewed the relevant literature, and concluded as follows: "Discrete lesions to limbic-diencephalic structures usually result in a limited degree of retrograde amnesia. Marked episodic or marked semantic retrograde amnesia is usually associated with significant involvement of cortical and neocortical structures."

The fact that retrograde amnesia is typically greater for information acquired immediately preceding the onset of amnesia than for information acquired earlier is of great theoretical importance. The establishment of strong and long-lasting memories depends on a physiological process of consolidation (see Chapter 6), and disruption of the consolidation process can cause retrograde amnesia. Studies of amnesic patients indicate that a temporal gradient of retrograde amnesia is most often observed when brain damage involves the hippocampal region (Manns, Hopkins, & Squire, 2003). Human data are imprecise because they depend on retrospective reports, but several well-controlled prospective animal studies have confirmed that temporally graded retrograde amnesia is associated with hippocampal lesions (see Squire, Clark, & Knowlton, 2001, for a review). As Wixted (2004, p. 242) concluded, "The temporal gradient of retrograde amnesia provides compelling evidence that memories consolidate over time and that the hippocampal formation (consisting of the hippocampus, dentate gyrus, subiculum, and entorhinal cortex) plays an important role in that process."

Reed and Squire (1998) confirmed the importance of the hippocampus. They studied four patients with retrograde amnesia for facts and events, and found through MRI examination that all four had hippocampal damage. Two of the patients had temporal lobe damage extending beyond the hippocampus, and they had more extensive retrograde amnesia than the other two.

Most amnesic patients show evidence of both retrograde and anterograde amnesia, which might suggest that they depend on damage to the same brain structures. The evidence from postmortem analyses indicates that the extent of both retrograde and anterograde amnesia depends on the amount of damage to medial-temporal structures in the brain. In addition, both forms of amnesia share features, such as impaired recall and recognition of factual information (e.g., public events) and of autobiographical information.

There are also important differences between retrograde and anterograde amnesia. Damage restricted to a small part of the hippocampal region known as the CA1 field produces only anterograde amnesia (Gabrieli, 1998). Perhaps as a result, the severity of retrograde amnesia often correlates poorly with the severity of anterograde amnesia. Some patients have focal retrograde amnesia, in which the main deficit is retrograde rather than anterograde. Such patients generally have damage to the anterior temporal lobe, or the posterior temporal lobe, or the frontal lobe, areas that are not thought to be directly associated with the amnesic syndrome. However, as Mayes (2002, p. 671) pointed out, "The lesions associated with it [focal retrograde amnesia] have been surprisingly heterogeneous [variable]. Some of this heterogeneity could arise because there may be several distinct kinds of focal retrograde amnesia."

Anterograde amnesia

The clearest evidence for anterograde amnesia comes from studies on episodic memory, as was discussed earlier. The extent of this impairment can be seen in the following description of a typical amnesic patient by Korsakoff (1889):

> He does not remember whether he had his dinner, whether he was out of bed. On occasion the patient forgets what happened to him just an instant ago: you came in, conversed with him, and stepped out for one minute; then you come in again and the patient has absolutely no recollection that you had already been with him.

Many amnesic patients also have severe anterograde amnesia for semantic memory. However, as we saw earlier, the evidence is somewhat inconsistent. In their review, Spiers et al. (2001, pp. 359–360) concluded as follows: "Many cases do show anterograde semantic memory deficits . . . However, a number of early-onset hypoxic [a condition caused by insufficient oxygen] patients have been reported by Vargha-Khardem et al. (1997) . . . who show relatively preserved acquisition of semantic memory in the context of severely impaired episodic memory."

Is the anterograde amnesia for episodic memory shown by amnesic patients due mainly to storage problems or to retrieval problems? Perhaps surprisingly, we still do not have a definitive answer to that question. However, most researchers assume that amnesics have a storage problem preventing episodic information being consolidated or solidly established in long-term memory. Supporting evidence was reported by Isaac and Mayes (1999). They gave amnesic patients much longer than normal controls to learn semantically related and unrelated word lists in an attempt to match the initial memory performance of the two groups. The assumption was that amnesic patients would show more rapid forgetting than the normal controls if they had a specific problem with retrieval. In fact, forgetting rates as assessed by cued recall and by recognition memory were generally comparable for both groups, suggesting that amnesics' problem occurs during storage rather than retrieval. Isaac and Mayes (1999, p. 973) concluded that "Amnesic patients are impaired at consolidating complex associations between two or more items and their study context into long-term memory."

Which aspects of memory remain intact?

We have seen that amnesic patients have intact levels of memory performance on a wide range of tasks. Much of the relevant evidence was considered by Spiers et al. (2001), who reviewed findings from numerous cases of amnesia in which there was damage to the hippocampus or fornix. There was impairment of episodic memory in every single case, and impairment of semantic memory in many (but by no means all) cases. In contrast, "None of the cases was reported to have impaired short-term memory (typically tested using digit span – the immediate recall of verbally presented digits) or to be impaired on tasks which involves learning skills or habits, priming, simple classical conditioning and simple category learning" (Spiers et al., 2001, p. 359).

There is convincing evidence that amnesic patients have good short-term memory. For example, Korsakoff patients perform almost as well as healthy individuals on the digit-span task (e.g., Butters & Cermak, 1980). Similar results have also been found in non-Korsakoff patients. NA became amnesic as a result of having a fencing foil forced up his nostril and into his brain. This caused widespread diencephalic and medial temporal damage. Teuber, Milner, and Vaughan (1968) found that he performed at the normal level on span measures. HM had an operation that damaged the temporal lobes, together with partial removal of the hippocampus and amygdala. He had intact short-term memory as indexed by immediate span (Wickelgren, 1968).

Eyeblink conditioning (a form of classical conditioning) has been studied in amnesic patients. In eyeblink conditioning, a tone is presented shortly before a puff of air is delivered to the eye, and causes an eyeblink. After the tone and puff of air have been presented together several times, the tone alone produces a conditioned eyeblink response. Many amnesic patients show intact eyeblink conditioning. However, Korsakoff patients generally have greatly impaired conditioning because the alcoholism has caused damage to the cerebellum. The involvement of the cerebellum in classical conditioning is also indicated by PET studies in which it is activated during the conditioning procedure (see Gabrieli, 1998).

Theoretical approaches to amnesia

An adequate theory of amnesia would account for the pattern of memory performance that has been found in amnesic patients. More specifically, we need to know *why* amnesic patients show intact memory performance on some tasks but severely impaired performance on other tasks. We will consider theoretical approaches that approximate to this ideal.

Explicit versus implicit memory

Several theorists have suggested that the distinction between explicit and implicit memory is of great importance for an understanding of amnesia. For example, Schacter (1987) argued that amnesic patients are at a severe disadvantage when tests of explicit memory (requiring conscious recollection) are used, but that their performance is intact on tests of implicit memory. As predicted, most amnesic patients display impaired performance on tests of recently acquired episodic and semantic memories. The majority of studies on motor skills and on the various repetition-priming effects are also consistent with Schacter's theoretical perspective, in that they are basically implicit memory tasks on which amnesic patients perform normally or nearly so (see Spiers et al., 2001, for a review).

A hackneyed anecdote related by Claparède (1911) is also consistent with Schacter's (1987) position. Claparède hid a pin in his hand before shaking hands with an amnesic patient. After that, she was understandably reluctant to shake hands with him, but was unable to explain why. The patient's *behaviour* revealed clearly that there was long-term memory for what had happened, but this occurred without any conscious recollection of the incident.

Evidence

As we saw earlier, amnesic patients generally have poor explicit memory and intact implicit memory. Another example of intact implicit memory in amnesic patients was reported by Schacter and Church (1995). Participants initially heard a series of words spoken in the same voice. After that, they tried to identify the same words passed through an auditory filter; the words were either spoken in the same voice or in an unfamiliar voice. The findings are shown in Figure 7.9a. Amnesic patients and healthy controls both showed perceptual priming, in that word-identification performance was better when the words were spoken in the same voice.

In spite of findings such as those of Schacter and Church (1995), there is increasing evidence that amnesic patients sometimes have impaired performance on tasks involving implicit memory. For example, consider a study on perceptual priming by Schacter, Church, and Bolton (1995). It resembled the study by Schacter and Church (1995), in that perceptual priming based on auditory word identification was investigated. However, it differed in that the words were initially

FIGURE 7.9

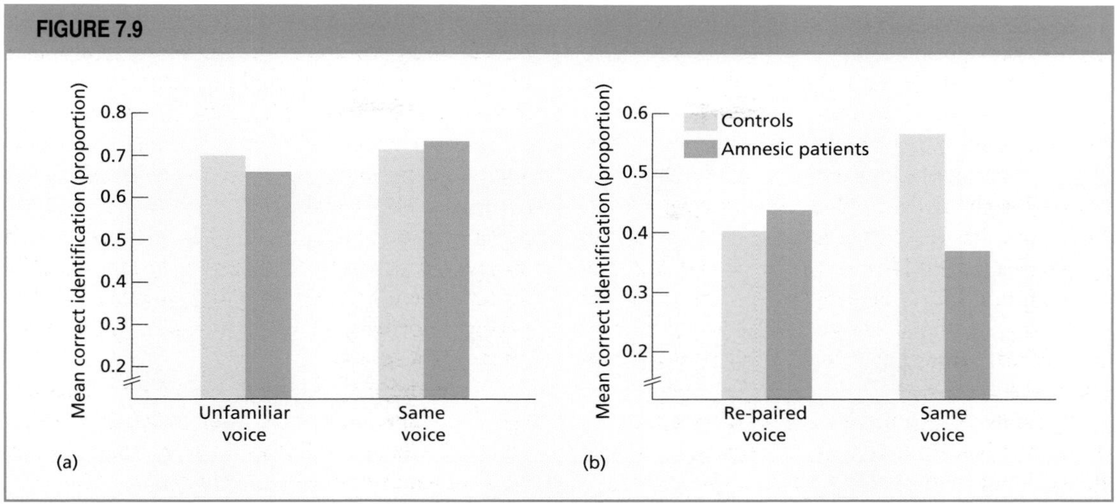

Auditory word identification for previously presented words in amnesics and controls. (a) All words originally presented in the same voice; data from Schacter and Church (1995). (b) Words originally presented in six different voices; data from Schacter et al. (1995).

presented in *six* different voices. On the word-identification test, half the words were presented in the same voice and half were spoken by one of the other voices (re-paired condition). The normal controls showed more priming for words presented in the same voice, but the amnesic patients did not (see Figure 7.9b).

How can we explain the above findings? In both the same voice and re-paired voice conditions, the participants were exposed to words and voices they had heard before. The only advantage in the same voice condition was the fact that the pairing of word and voice was the same as before. However, only those participants who had linked or associated words and voices at the original presentation would benefit from that fact. As Curran and Schacter (1997, p. 41) concluded, "Amnesics may lack the necessary ability to bind voices with specific studied words." This view of the major deficit in amnesia is discussed more fully below.

Evaluation

Most of the tasks on which amnesic patients show impaired performance involve explicit memory, and most of those on which they show intact performance involve implicit memory. However, amnesic patients do *not* always perform at normal levels on tests of implicit memory. We have already considered one such study (Schacter et al., 1995), and other examples are discussed below.

There is a second limitation with Schacter's (1987) theory. In spite of the usefulness of the explicit/implicit distinction, the notion that amnesic patients have deficient explicit memory does not provide an *explanation* of their memory impairments. As Schacter (1987, p. 501) pointed out, implicit and explicit memory "are descriptive concepts that are primarily concerned with a person's psychological experience at the time of retrieval."

Relational memory binding

Ryan et al. (2000, p. 460) put forward a different theory of amnesia: "The memory system damaged in amnesia is not the same as explicit memory or conscious memory . . . Rather, the memory system damaged in amnesia is declarative memory for relations among the constituent elements of scenes or events – relational memory binding of all manner of relations" (Ryan et al., 2000, p. 460). Thus, amnesic patients should have poor memory

FIGURE 7.10

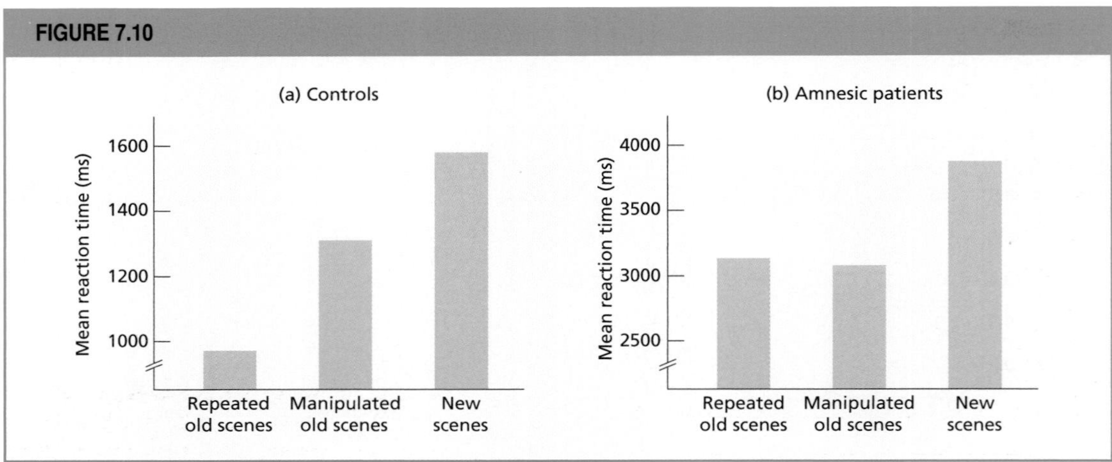

Speed of question answering in three conditions (repeated old scenes; manipulated old scenes; new scenes). Data from Whitlow et al. (1995).

on any task involving relating or integrating different pieces of information.

Two key predictions follow from this theoretical position. First, amnesic patients should have impaired performance on implicit-memory tasks requiring that different elements be related to each other. Second, amnesic patients should have essentially normal levels of performance on explicit-memory tasks *not* requiring that different elements be related to each other.

Evidence

Evidence supporting the first prediction above was reported by Whitlow, Althoff, and Cohen (1995). They presented amnesic patients and normal controls with real-world scenes, and asked them to respond as rapidly as possible to questions (e.g., "Is there a chair behind the oranges?"). After that, the participants answered questions when presented with three kinds of scenes:

(1) repeated old scenes;
(2) new scenes;
(3) manipulated old scenes, in which the positions of some of the objects had been altered.

What did Whitlow et al. (1995) find? Both groups answered faster to old scenes (whether repeated or manipulated) than to new scenes. The most plausible interpretation of these findings is that the task relies on implicit memory, which is intact in amnesic patients. However, normal controls responded faster to *repeated* old scenes than to *manipulated* old scenes, whereas the amnesic patients did not (see Figure 7.10). These findings suggest that amnesic patients did not store information about the relative positions of the objects in the scenes, and so derived no benefit from having the scene repeated. The failure of amnesics to show intact implicit memory in terms of speed of question answering to repeated old scenes is consistent with the notion that they find relational memory binding very difficult.

Ryan et al. (2000) carried out a similar study. They presented amnesic and healthy controls with colour images of real-world scenes in three conditions: novel scenes; repeated old scenes; and manipulated old scenes. The main dependent variable was the proportion of eye fixations in the critical region (i.e., the part of the scene that was systematically altered in the manipulation condition). The healthy controls had significantly more fixations in the critical region in the manipulated condition than in the other two conditions (see Figure 7.11), presumably because these participants had implicit memory for the relations among the objects in the original scene. In contrast, the amnesic patients did *not* devote more fixations to

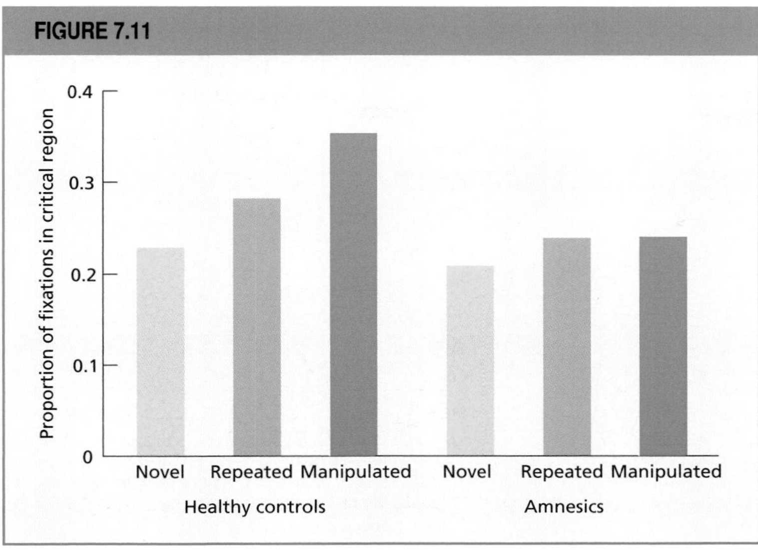

Proportion of eye fixations in the critical region in healthy controls and amnesic patients as a function of condition (novel, repeated, manipulated). Data from Ryan et al. (2000).

the critical region, presumably because they had no implicit memory for the relations among the elements of presented scenes.

Ryan et al. (2000) assumed that amnesic patients had a deficit in long-term relational memory, but their data failed to rule out the possibility that the deficit is in short-term memory. Ryan and Cohen (2004) essentially used the same paradigm as Ryan et al., but had a delay of only a few seconds between successive scenes. The amnesic patients fixated disproportionately on the critical region in the manipulated condition. Thus, their deficit in relational memory is limited to long-term memory and does not affect short-term memory.

Additional support for the notion that amnesic patients have great difficulties in storing integrated information was reported by Kroll et al. (1996). They studied conjunction errors, which occur when new objects formed out of conjunctions or combinations of objects seen previously are mistakenly recognised as old. Amnesic patients made numerous conjunction errors, presumably because they remembered having seen the elements of the new objects but did not realise that the combination of elements was novel.

How can we explain the generally poor performance of amnesic patients on tests of episodic and semantic memory by the theory being discussed here? According to Ryan et al. (2000, p. 454):

> Any direct (explicit) memory test also involves declarative memory for relations. Such tests require, by definition, the ability to gain conscious access to the prior learning episode associated with the test item, thereby requiring memory for some relation between the to-be-tested item and the context or prior learning experience in which it occurred. Thus, any deficit on a direct (explicit) memory test, as is seen in amnesia, could reflect a deficit of explicit memory or of relational memory or of both.

If the major problem of amnesics is that they have poor relational memory, then it follows that their explicit memory performance would be reasonably good if it did not depend on memory of relations. Relevant evidence was reported by Huppert and Piercy (1976). They presented a series of pictures on day 1 of their study, and a series of pictures on day 2. Some of the pictures presented on day 2 had been presented on day 1, and some had not. Ten minutes after the day 2 presentation, there was a test of recognition

FIGURE 7.12

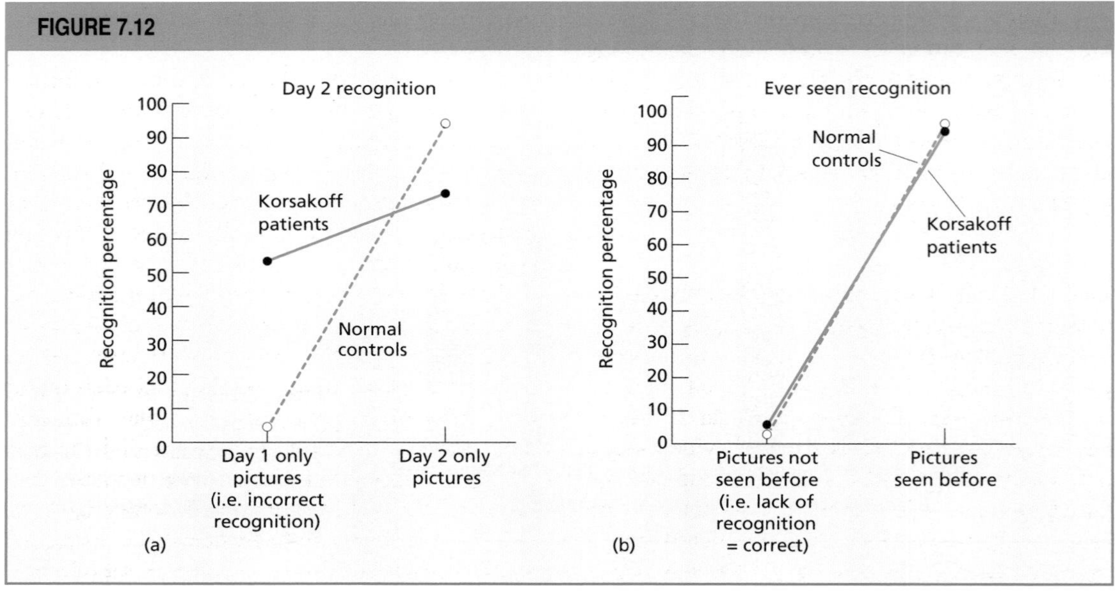

Recognition memory for pictures in Korsakoff patients and normal controls. Data from Huppert and Piercy (1976).

memory. On this test, participants were asked which pictures had been presented on day 2. The healthy controls had no problem (see Figure 7.12a). They correctly identified nearly all the pictures that had been presented on day 2, and incorrectly identified very few of the pictures presented only on day 1. Korsakoff patients did much worse, correctly identifying only 70% of the day 2 pictures, and incorrectly identifying 51% of the pictures presented only on day 1. These findings may reflect the difficulty experienced by amnesic patients in learning the relation between each picture and the context in which it was encountered.

The most important findings obtained by Huppert and Piercy (1976) arose when they asked participants whether they had *ever* seen the pictures before. With this test, it was not necessary to have stored contextual or relational information about *when* the pictures had been seen to achieve good memory performance. The Korsakoff patients and the normal controls performed this task at a very high level, with the two groups hardly differing in their performance (see Figure 7.12b). Thus, the amnesic patients had access to basic information about the pictures, and so performed well when relational memory was not required.

The notion that amnesics have particular problems with relational memory has also received support from research on **source amnesia**, in which facts are remembered but not the source of those facts. Source amnesia in amnesic patients was studied by Shimamura and Squire (1987). Amnesic patients were more impaired than normal controls in remembering the source of trivia facts they could recall. Thus, amnesic patients have particular problems in associating or relating trivia facts to their source.

Cohen et al. (1994) used fMRI to identify the brain regions involved in the integration of information. Seven healthy participants were presented with three kinds of information at the same time (faces, names, and occupations). On some trials, they were told to learn the associations among these kinds of information, a task involving integrative processes. On other trials, the participants simply made gender decisions about each face, a task not requiring the integration of information. All the participants had more activation in the hippocampus on the task requiring the integration of information, suggesting that the hippocampus plays a central role in processes of association or integration. This is of direct relevance to amnesia in view of the large numbers of amnesic patients who have suffered hippocampal damage.

Evaluation

The relational memory binding hypothesis has received reasonable support, suggesting that the central problem for amnesics may lie in information *integration* rather than in explicit memory *per se*. However, the research so far is inconclusive. What is needed is stronger evidence that implicit memory tasks involving information integration on which amnesic patients perform poorly really rely exclusively on implicit memory. In similar fashion, we need more convincing evidence that explicit tasks not involving information integration on which amnesics have intact performance genuinely involve only explicit memory.

Concluding thoughts

We can bring together some of the ideas we have been discussing. Curran and Schacter (1997) argued that the distinction between explicit and implicit memory is important, combining it with an emphasis on relational or integrative memory. However, note that they seem to have produced rather new definitions of explicit and implicit memory: "Implicit memory reflects primarily the bottom-up, non-conscious effects of prior experience on single brain subsystems, and may also involve interactions between a limited number of brain subsystems. Explicit memory reflects the top-down, simultaneous retrieval of information from multiple information-processing brain mechanisms. This massive integration of information (e.g., perceptual, semantic, temporal, spatial, etc.) may be necessary to support conscious recollection of previous experiences" (Curran & Schacter, 1997, p. 45).

According to the above viewpoint, information processing typically proceeds through two stages: (1) specific forms of processing in several brain subsystems; (2) integration of information from these brain subsystems. The processing of amnesic patients is essentially intact at the first stage, but severely impaired at the second stage.

Why are humans equipped with separate brain systems underlying different forms of memory? Squire et al. (1993, pp. 485–486) provided an answer to that question, arguing that each major brain system has its own particular function. They assumed that there is a major division into declarative/explicit memory on the one hand, and procedural/implicit memory on the other hand. As a result, their views probably need to be developed to take account of the more complex set of memory systems emerging from recent research:

> One system involves limbic/diencephalic structures, which in concert with neocortex provides the basis for conscious recollections. This system is fast, phylogenetically recent, and specialised for one-trial learning . . . The system is fallible in the sense that it is sensitive to interference and prone to retrieval failure. It is also precious . . . giving rise to the capacity for personal autobiography and the possibility of cultural evolution.
>
> Other kinds of memory have also been identified . . . Such memories can be acquired, stored, and retrieved without the participation of the limbic/diencephalon brain system. These forms of memory are phylogenetically early, they are reliable and consistent, and they provide for myriad [very numerous], non-conscious ways of responding to the world . . . they create much of the mystery of human experience.

CHAPTER SUMMARY

- Introduction
  According to Schacter et al. (2000), there are five memory systems: working memory; episodic memory; semantic memory; perceptual representation system; and procedural memory. The last four of these systems involve long-term memory. Theorists have used three criteria to identify memory systems: class inclusion operations; properties and relations; and convergent dissociations. One of the main ways in which memory systems differ from each other is in terms of their reliance on explicit versus implicit memory.

- Declarative memory: Episodic and semantic memory
  Episodic memory involves consciously recollecting personal events from the past, whereas semantic memory involves knowledge about the world. The fact that some patients have category-specific deficits suggests that different kinds of knowledge are stored in different parts of the brain, but there is little support for this view from brain-imaging studies. Many findings have been explained by the sensory-functional theory and by the domain-specific knowledge hypothesis, with the former theory attracting more empirical support. Most amnesic patients have problems with episodic and semantic memory, leading some experts to argue that episodic and semantic memory are both forms of declarative or explicit memory. However, the evidence suggests that episodic and semantic memory form separate memory systems. Some amnesics have severe anterograde amnesia for episodic memory but almost intact semantic memory. In addition, different brain areas are involved in the retrieval of episodic and semantic memories.

- Procedural memory and the perceptual representation system
  Schacter et al. (2000) argued that procedural memory is used in skill learning, whereas the perceptual representation system is used in priming. Skill learning is more general than priming, which involves learning dependent on the specific stimuli used in training. Skill learning is essentially intact in amnesic patients. The cerebellum and basal ganglia are both involved in skill learning, as has been shown in brain-scanning studies and in studies on brain-damaged patients. Amnesic patients have intact priming for both perceptual and conceptual priming. Priming leads to reduced brain activity in the extrastriate area of the visual cortex (perceptual priming) and in areas of the frontal lobe (conceptual priming), presumably because processing becomes more efficient when stimuli are repeated. Some evidence on brain-damaged patients suggests that skill learning and priming depend on different memory systems. However, it has proved difficult to replicate the key findings, and some brain-imaging studies suggest that skill learning and priming involve a single memory system.

- Amnesia
  The study of amnesia has led to new theoretical developments, and has provided a test-bed for existing theories. Amnesia can be produced by damage to the diencephalon or to the medial temporal lobe, both belonging to the same functional system. Many amnesic patients have damage to the hippocampal region, which disrupts consolidation processes and produces a temporal gradient in retrograde amnesia. The anterograde amnesia shown by amnesic patients is probably due to a storage problem preventing episodic information being consolidated in long-term memory. In general, amnesic patients have impaired explicit memory (episodic and semantic memory) but essentially intact implicit memory (procedural memory and perceptual representation system). However, the explicit/implicit distinction describes rather than explains amnesia, and fails to provide a completely accurate description. Amnesic patients have poor memory on most tasks involving relating or integrating different pieces of information regardless of whether explicit or implicit memory is involved. Thus, their central problem seems to be with relational memory binding.

FURTHER READING

- Baddeley, A., Aggleton, J.P., et al. (2002). *Episodic memory: New directions in research*. London: Oxford University Press. This book contains several interesting theoretical chapters on episodic memory by leading researchers in the field.
- Healy, A.F. (2003). *Handbook of psychology: Experimental psychology, Vol. 4*. New York: Wiley & Sons. Several topics relevant to this chapter are covered in this edited book, including semantic memory, priming, episodic memory, and procedural memory.
- Martin, A., & Caramazza, A. (Eds.) (2003). Special issue on: The organisation of conceptual knowledge in the brain: Neuropsychological and neuroimaging perspectives. *Cognitive Neuropsychology*, *20*, 195–587. This special issue consists of empirical and theoretical contributions by leading researchers in the field.
- Schacter, D.L., Wagner, A.D., & Buckner, R.L. (2000). Memory systems of 1999. In E. Tulving & F.I.M. Craik (Eds.), *The Oxford handbook of memory*. New York: Oxford University Press. This chapter provides an excellent introduction to the issue of the number of memory systems we possess.
- Tulving, E. (2002). Episodic memory: From mind to brain. *Annual Review of Psychology*, *53*, 1–25. This chapter provides a detailed account of the evidence supporting the notion that there is an episodic memory system.

8

Everyday Memory

INTRODUCTION

When most people think about memory, they consider it in terms of their own everyday experience. They wonder why their own memory is so fallible, or why some people's memories seem much better than others. Perhaps they ask themselves how they could improve their own memories. This state of affairs has led many researchers to study everyday memory. As Koriat and Goldsmith (1996) pointed out, everyday memory researchers often differ from other memory researchers in their answers to three questions:

(1) *What* memory phenomena should be studied? According to everyday memory researchers, the kinds of phenomena people experience every day should be the main focus.
(2) *How* should memory be studied? Everyday memory researchers emphasise the importance of **ecological validity** or the applicability of findings to real life, and doubt whether this is achieved in most laboratory research.
(3) *Where* should memory phenomena be studied? Some everyday memory researchers argue in favour of naturalistic settings.

Matters are actually less neat and tidy than has been suggested so far. As Koriat and Goldsmith (1996) pointed out, "Although the three dimensions—the what, how, and where dimensions—are correlated in the reality of memory research, they are not logically interdependent. For instance, many everyday memory topics can be studied in the laboratory, and memory research in naturalistic settings may be amenable to strict experimental control" (p. 168).

Koriat and Goldsmith (1996) and Koriat, Goldsmith, and Pansky 2000) argued that traditional memory research is based on the storehouse metaphor. According to this metaphor, items of information are stored in memory, and what is of interest is the *number* of items accessible at retrieval. In contrast, the correspondence metaphor is more applicable to everyday memory research. According to this metaphor, what is important is the correspondence or goodness of fit between an individual's report and the actual event. Consider eyewitness testimony of a crime. According to the storehouse metaphor, what matters is simply how many items of information can be recalled. In contrast, according to the correspondence metaphor, what matters is whether the crucial items of information (e.g., facial characteristics of the criminal) are remembered. Thus, the *content* of what is remembered is more important within the correspondence metaphor than the storehouse metaphor.

Neisser (1996) identified a crucial difference between memory as studied traditionally and memory in everyday life. Participants in traditional memory studies are generally motivated to be as accurate as possible in their memory performance. In contrast, everyday memory research should be based on the notion that "remembering is a form of purposeful action" (Neisser, 1996, p. 204). This approach involves three assumptions about everyday memory:

(1) It is purposeful.
(2) It has a personal quality about it, meaning it is influenced by the individual's personality and other characteristics.
(3) It is influenced by situational demands (e.g., the wish to impress one's audience).

Some ways in which motivation influences memory in everyday life were studied by Freud (see Chapter 6). He used the term **repression** to refer to motivated forgetting of very anxiety-provoking experiences, and claimed this was common among his patients. More generally, people's accounts of their experiences are often influenced by various motivational factors. They may be motivated to be honest in their recollections. However, they may also want to enhance their self-esteem by exaggerating their successes and minimising their failures. There are occasions in everyday life when people strive for maximal accuracy in their recall (e.g., during an examination; remembering the contents of a shopping list), but accuracy is not typically the main goal. These additional motivational factors are increasingly studied by researchers on autobiographical memory (see below).

There has been much controversy about the respective strengths and weaknesses of traditional laboratory research and everyday memory research. This is no longer the case. As Kvavilashvili and Ellis (1996) pointed out, the controversy "is in decline, probably because of the increased versatility of recent research practices, which make it difficult, if not impossible to draw clear distinctions between the ecological and laboratory approaches to the study of memory" (p. 200). The memory phenomena of everyday life need to be submitted to proper empirical test, which can be done either in naturalistic or laboratory settings.

Kvavilashvili and Ellis (in press) have developed these ideas. They argued that ecological validity consists of two aspects which are frequently confused: (1) *representativeness*; and (2) *generalisability*. Representativeness refers to the naturalness of the experimental situation, stimuli, and task, whereas generalisability refers to the extent to which the findings of a study are applicable to the real world. Generalisability is more important than representativeness.

Kvavilashvili and Ellis (in press) discussed valuable research lacking representativeness but possessing generalisability. For example, Jost (1897) used unrepresentative stimuli such as nonsense syllables, and found distributed practice produced much better learning and memory than massed practice. This effect has been repeated many times in studies possessing much more representativeness. For example, Smith and Rothkopf (1984) found distributed practice produced better memory for the material in lectures on statistics.

Before embarking on our review of research on everyday memory, we will mention a study indicating the potential relevance of such research. Conway, Cohen, and Stanhope (1991) tested how much former psychology students could remember about research methods, concepts, and names (e.g., Broadbent) in cognitive psychology. These students, who had studied psychology at periods of time up to 12 years previously, were given various memory tests (recognition, sentence verification, recall). Their memory performance was generally fairly high, which is encouraging news for students! Research methods were remembered best, probably because students were exposed to them in several different courses. Concepts were also well remembered, because students could forms schemas or packets of knowledge to connect concepts to each other. Finally, names were worst remembered, but were still remembered at better than chance over a 12-year period.

AUTOBIOGRAPHICAL MEMORY

According to Conway and Rubin (1993), "autobiographical memory is memory for the events of one's life" (p. 103). There is overlap between **autobiographical memory** and **episodic memory** (see Chapter 7), in that the recollection of personal events and episodes occurs with both types of memory. However, there can be episodic memory without autobiographical memory (Nelson, 1993, p. 357): "What I ate for lunch yesterday is today part of my episodic memory, but being unremarkable . . . will not, I am sure, become part of my autobiographical memory—it has no significance to my life story." In similar fashion, Conway (2003, p. 219) argued that episodic memories are "short-time slice records of experience". In contrast, "A uniquely human . . . memory system represents conceptually organised autobiographical knowledge that provides a context or setting for episodic memories . . . this system controls the output of the episodic system by directly inhibiting/activating it and by selecting and modifying the cues used to access it."

Why is it important to study autobiographical memory? Autobiographical memory relates to our major life goals, our most powerful emotions, and to our personal meanings. As Conway, Pleydell-Pearce, and Whitecross (2001, p. 493) pointed out, autobiographical knowledge has the function of "defining identity, linking personal history to public history, supporting a network of personal goals and projects across the life span, and ultimately in grounding the self in experience."

How can we best study autobiographical memory? Autobiographical memory is often error-prone when we are asked specific questions. For example, up to 40% of people do not report minor hospitalisations when asked only one year later! Belli (1998) recommended the use of event-history calendars. Individuals are presented with several major themes (e.g., places of residence; work), and identify the month and the year of all relevant events. A complete pattern of the individual's life over time is gradually constructed. Belli (1998, p. 403) concluded: "Traditional survey questions . . . tend to segment the various themes of respondents' pasts. Event-history calendars . . . encourage respondents to appreciate the interrelatedness of various themes which serve to cue memories both within and across these themes."

Memories across the lifetime

Suppose we ask 70-year-olds to recall personal memories suggested by cue words (e.g., nouns referring to common objects). From which parts of their lives would most of the memories come? Would they tend to think of recent experiences or the events of childhood or young adulthood? Rubin, Wetzler, and Nebes (1986) provided answers to these questions (see Figure 8.1). There are various features about the findings:

- **Infantile amnesia**, shown by the almost total lack of memories from the first 3 years of life.
- A **reminiscence bump**, consisting of a surprisingly large number of memories coming from the years between 10 and 30, and especially between 15 and 25.
- A retention function for memories up to 20 years old, with the older memories being less likely to be recalled than more recent ones.

Rubin (2000) combined data from numerous studies involving more than 11,000 autobiographical memories of the early years of life. He concluded as follows: "Childhood amnesia . . . is a robust phenomenon that is nearly identical in studies using different methods and different populations. Of the autobiographical memories reported as occurring before age 11, 1.1% occurred before age 3, with a sharp rise after that point" (Rubin, 2000, p. 268).

The reminiscence bump has not generally been found in people younger than 30 years of age, and has not often been observed in 40-year-olds. However, it is nearly always found among older people. Rubin and Schulkind (1997) used far more cue words than had been used in previous studies. They found "no evidence that any aspect of the distribution of autobiographical memories is affected by having close to 1000 as opposed to

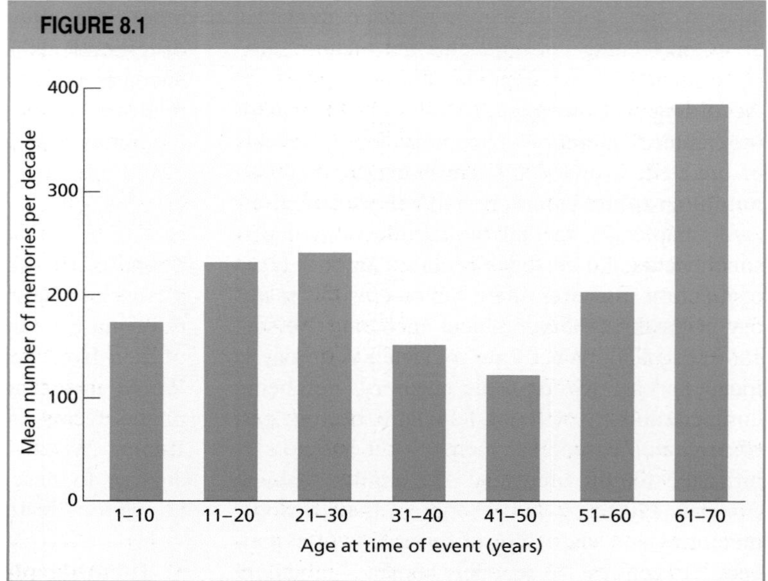

Memory for past events in the elderly as a function of the decade in which the events occurred. Based on Rubin et al. (1986).

close to 100 memories queried" (p. 863). They also found the reminiscence bump is not simply due to averaging across individuals. They studied five 70-year-olds, all of whom showed a reminiscence bump.

Rubin, Rahhal, and Poon (1998) discussed other evidence that 70-year-olds have especially good memories for early adulthood. This effect was found for the following: particularly memorable books; vivid memories; memories the participants would want included in a book about their lives; names of winners of Academy Awards; and memory for current events.

Theoretical perspectives

We will start our attempt to interpret the above findings with infantile amnesia. Howe and Courage (1997) related it to the emergence of what they called the *cognitive self* towards the end of the second year of life. Infants at about 20 months show signs of developing a sense of self in the phenomenon of visual self-recognition, which involves responding to their own image in a mirror with self-touching, shy smiling, and gaze aversion. A few months after that, infants start using words such as I, me, and you. The crucial theoretical assumption made by Howe and Courage (1997, p. 499) was as follows: "The development of the cognitive self late in the second year of life (as indexed by visual self-recognition) provides a new framework around which memories can be organised. With this cognitive advance in the development of the self, we witness the emergence of autobiographical memory and the end of infantile amnesia."

According to the above theoretical position, the lower limit for people's earliest autobiographical memories should be about 2 years of age. That is approximately in line with the findings in the literature (Rubin, 2000). However, it is hard to show that the emergence of a sense of self is the causal factor.

Howe and Courage (1997) also assumed that the processes (e.g., rehearsal) used in learning and memory develop during the years of childhood. As a result, relatively few autobiographical memories should come from the years 2 to 5. In Rubin's (2000) review of the available data, he found only 22% of memories from the first 10 years of life came from the years 2 to 5.

Other theoretical explanations of infantile amnesia have been put forward. Freud (1915/1957) famously argued that infantile amnesia occurs through repression, with threat-related experiences of infancy being consigned to the unconscious. Unfortunately, there is practically no support for this theoretical position, and it fails to explain why pleasant memories of early childhood cannot be recalled. Conway and Pleydell-Pearce (2000) were generally in agreement with Howe and Courage's (1997) approach. However, they argued that an important factor in infantile amnesia is, "the disjunction [disconnection] between the goals that originally mediated encoding (during infancy) and the goals operating at retrieval" (Conway & Pleydell-Pearce, 2000, p. 278).

Social interactionist accounts (e.g., Fivush, Haden, & Reese, 1996) have been offered to explain infantile amnesia. According to such accounts, the main purpose of autobiographical memories is to share one's personal memories with other people. In the words of Harley and Reese (1999, p. 1338), "The primary functions of autobiographical memory are to develop a life history and to tell others what one is like through relating one's past experiences." Harley and Reese (1999) argued from this perspective that the way in which parents talk to their children about the past should influence the children's autobiographical memories. More specifically, they distinguished between two maternal reminiscing styles: high elaborative (in which past events are discussed in detail) and low elaborative.

Harley and Reese (1999) assessed maternal styles of talking to their children about the past, children's self-recognition at the age of 19 months, and children's language production at the same age. They then considered children's autobiographical memories when the children were aged between 19 and 32 months. They found evidence to support the cognitive self and social interactionist positions: "Both maternal reminiscing style and children's self-recognition were strong . . . predictors of children's very early ability to talk about the past, regardless of children's linguistic or non-verbal memory skill."

There are major cultural differences in parents' interactions with their children and in the importance attached to the past. According to the social interactionist perspective, there should therefore be cultural differences in infantile amnesia. MacDonald, Uesiliana, and Hayne (2000) found that the mean age of the earliest memory was 58 months for Asian (mainly Chinese) adults, 43 months for New Zealand Europeans, and 33 months for New Zealand Maoris. MacDonald et al. argued that the Maoris had the earliest memories because of their strong cultural emphasis on the importance of the past. There was a large gender difference for age of earliest memory among the Asian participants, with females reporting much later memories than males. This may reflect a tendency for Chinese families to attach more importance to the experiences and achievements of sons than of daughters.

Reminiscence bump

We turn now to the reminiscence bump. Rubin et al. (1998, pp. 13–14) developed a theory to explain this phenomenon based on the assumption that "the best situation for memory is the beginning of a period of stability that lasts until retrieval." They argued that most adults have a period of stability starting in early adulthood, because it is then that a sense of adult identity develops. Many memories from early adulthood also have the advantage of novelty, in that they are formed shortly after the onset of adult identity. These two factors of novelty and stability produce strong memories for the following reasons:

- Novelty: This causes more effort after meaning.
- Novelty: There is a relative lack of **proactive interference** (interference from previous learning; see Chapter 6).
- Novelty: This produces distinctive memories (see Chapter 6).
- Stability: Events from a stable period of life are more likely to serve as models for future events.
- Stability: This provides a cognitive structure serving as a stable organisation to cue events.

There is evidence that novelty (e.g., first-time experiences) is an important factor in increasing the accessibility of autobiographical memories. For example, Pillemer, Goldsmith, Panter, and White (1988) carried out a study on middle-aged participants who recalled four memories from their first year at college more than 20 years previously. Their key finding was that 41% of these autobiographical memories came from the first month of the course. However, we should not exaggerate the importance of novelty. For example, Fitzgerald (1988) considered in detail the memories from the reminscence bump recalled by older adults. Fewer than 20% of these memories were of first-time experiences.

Conway and Pleydell-Pearce (2000, p. 280) argued that "the reminiscence bump reflects preferential retention of events from a period of consolidation of the self." The goals of the self are also of importance, as was shown by Holmes and Conway (1999). The kinds of autobiographical memories retrieved differed between the early years of the reminiscence bump (approximately 10–20 years) and the later years (20–30 years). Memories from the earlier period focused on external public events, and may reflect individuals' development of a social identity. In contrast, memories from the later period showed an emphasis on intimacy in personal relationships, presumably because most people in their twenties have the goal of achieving intimacy with others.

Rubin et al. (1998) and Conway and Pleydell-Pearce (2000) assumed the reminscence bump generally extends only to about the age of 30 because the self and its goals do not change much after that age. However, there should be a later reminscence bump in those individuals whose self and/or goals change dramatically after the age of 30. Support for this prediction was reported by Conway and Haque (1999). Older Bangladeshi individuals had a second reminiscence bump covering the period 35–55 years of age in addition to the typical one between the ages of 10 and 30. The main reason for this second reminiscence bump was the long-lasting conflict between Pakistan and the Bengalee people that ultimately led to the formation of an independent Bangladesh. According to Conway and Haque (1999, p. 35), "Both the reminiscence bump and later periods of unexpected rises in recall . . . [are] a product of the later privileged encoding of highly self-relevant experiences."

Finally, we turn briefly to the retention function. This has attracted relatively little interest. Presumably it simply reflects the typical phenomenon of forgetting over time.

Diary studies

It is generally hard to assess the accuracy of an individual's recollections of the events of his/her own life. Linton (1975) and Wagenaar (1986) resolved this problem by carrying out diary studies, in which they made a daily note of personal events. Both of them later tested their own memory for these events.

Linton (1975) wrote down brief descriptions of at least two events each day over a 6-year period. Every month she selected two descriptions at random, and recalled as much as possible about the events in question. Forgetting depended substantially on whether or not a given event had been tested before. For example, over 60% of events from $4\frac{1}{2}$ years previously were completely forgotten if they had not been tested, compared to under 40% of events of the same age that had been tested once before. Thus, rehearsal is important to prevent forgetting.

Events were often forgotten because they resembled other events. For example, Linton occasionally attended meetings of a distinguished committee in a distant city. The first such meeting was clearly remembered, but subsequent meetings blended into one another. Her **semantic memory** (or general knowledge) about the meetings increased over time, but her **episodic memory** (or memory for specific events) decreased (see Chapter 7). The impact of importance and event emotionality on recallability was modest, because events seeming at the time to be important and emotional often no longer seemed so with the benefit of hindsight.

What strategies do we use to remember past events? Linton (1975) considered how she recalled as many events as possible from a given month in the past. When the month in question was under 2 years previously, the main strategy involved working through events in the order in which they had occurred. In contrast, there was more use of recall by category (e.g., sporting events attended) at longer retention intervals.

Wagenaar (1986) recorded over 2000 events over a 6-year period. For each event, he noted down information about who, what, where, and when, together with the rated pleasantness, saliency or rarity, and emotionality of each event. He then tested his memory by using the who, what, where, and when information cues either one at a time or in combination. "What" information provided the most useful retrieval cue, perhaps because our autobiographical memories are organised in categories. "What" information was followed in order of declining usefulness by "where", "who", and "when" information. "When" information on its own was almost totally ineffective. The more cues presented, the higher was the resultant probability of recall. However, even with three cues almost half of the events were forgotten over a 5-year period. When these forgotten events involved another person, that person provided additional information. This typically proved sufficient for Wagenaar to remember the event. This suggests that the great majority of life events may be stored away in long-term memory.

High levels of salience, emotional involvement, and pleasantness were all associated with high levels of recall, especially high salience or rarity. The effects of salience and emotional involvement remained strong over retention intervals ranging from 1 to 5 years, whereas the effects of pleasantness decreased.

Wagenaar (1994) carried out a detailed analysis of 120 very pleasant and unpleasant memories from his 1986 study. When someone else played the major role in an event, pleasant events were much better remembered than unpleasant ones. However, the opposite was the case for events in which Wagenaar himself played the major role, which may reflect Wagenaar's self-critical personality (Groeger, 1997).

Evaluation

Diary studies have provided us with much evidence about the factors determining success or otherwise in recalling specific autobiographical memories. Of particular importance is Wagenaar's (1986) finding that his ability to access autobiographical memories depended on whether he presented himself with what, where, who, or when cues.

Burt, Kemp, and Conway (2003) identified a significant limitation with diary studies. The emphasis in such studies is on specific on-one-day events, but these may not correspond well to the autobiographical events we generally remember. For example, Barsalou (1988) asked college students to recall events that had happened during the previous summer. They recalled relatively few on-one-day memories but numerous more extended and general events. Burt et al. asked students to keep a diary over a 4-month period, with each participant producing 90 diary entries on average. When the students organised these entries into events, each event consisted on average of 6.45 diary entries. Most such events were based on content association rather than closeness in time. As Burt et al. (2003, p. 320) concluded, "Autobiographical events can be complex associations of temporally disparate episodes . . . Studies examining single on-one-day diary entries are perhaps only examining autobiographical episodes."

Dating autobiographical memories

Linton (1975) and Wagenaar (1986) both found they were fairly good at dating the events of their lives. How do we remember when past events happened? People often relate the events of their lives to major lifetime periods (Conway & Bekerian, 1987). In addition, we sometimes draw inferences about when an event happened on the basis of how much information about it we can remember: if we can remember very little about an event, we may assume it happened a long time ago. This idea was tested by Brown, Rips, and Shevell (1985). People dated several news events over a 5-year period (1977 to 1982). On average, those events about which much was known (e.g., the shooting of President Reagan) were dated as too recent by over 3 months, whereas low-knowledge events were dated as too remote by about 3 months.

In a follow-up study, Brown, Shevell, and Rips (1986) asked participants to date public events that were either political (e.g., the signing of a major treaty) or non-political (e.g., the eruption of Mount St. Helens). The participants made much use of **landmarks**, i.e., events whose dates they knew well. For example, someone might date the eruption of Mount St. Helens by relating it to the landmark of becoming engaged shortly beforehand. Landmarks were used 70% of the time to aid the dating of public events, with the landmarks being either public or personal events. However, over 60% of political events were dated with reference to other political events, compared to only 31% that were related to personal events. In contrast, two-thirds of the landmarks used to date non-political events were personal events.

Accuracy of autobiographical memories

How accurate are our memories of past personal events? This issue was addressed by Barclay (1988), who used tests of recognition memory to assess the accuracy of people's memories for personal events they had recorded in diaries. These tests were made difficult by using as distractors events resembling actual personal events. Participants made many errors, but their autobiographical memories were mostly truthful in that they corresponded to the gist of their actual experiences.

Wilson and Ross (2003) were more sceptical about the accuracy of autobiographical memories. They argued that an important function of autobiographical memory is to allow people to maintain a favourable view of themselves. This can be achieved if people regard their past self as inferior to their present self. For example, Wilson and Ross (2001) found that various groups of people including university students and middle-aged people argued that their present self was superior to their previous self. In similar fashion, Karney and Frye (2002) found that spouses often recalled their past contentment as lower than their present level of satisfaction. However, this apparent improvement over time was generally illusory, because spouses typically underestimate their past contentment.

The need for self-enhancement can also influence people's judgements of when events occurred. The key assumption is that people are motivated to place their past failures further in the past than their past achievements. Ross and Wilson (2002) asked students to remember the course in the previous semester on which they obtained their best or their worst mark. Even though the time interval was the same in both cases, students felt that previous failure was further away than previous success.

In sum, we have seen that people's autobiographical memories for *what* happened to them and *when* it happened are subject to systematic distortion. Overall, "People's constructions of themselves through time serve the function of creating a coherent—and largely favourable—view of their present selves and circumstances" (Wilson & Ross, 2003, p. 137).

Self-memory system

We will now consider a detailed theoretical account of autobiographical memory proposed by Conway and Pleydell-Pearce (2000). According to their theory, we possess a self-memory system consisting of an autobiographical knowledge base and the current goals of the working self. The autobiographical knowledge base, "contains layers of autobiographical knowledge arranged from the conceptual and abstract to highly specific details of single events" (Conway & Pleydell-Pearce, 2000, p. 264). More specifically, there are three levels of specificity:

(1) *Lifetime periods*: These typically cover substantial periods of time defined by major ongoing situations (e.g., living with someone; time as an undergraduate student). According to Conway and Pleydell-Pearce (2000, p. 262), "The content of a lifetime period represents *thematic* knowledge about common features of that period . . . , as well as *temporal* knowledge about the duration of a period."

(2) *General events*: These include repeated events (e.g., visits to a sports club) and single events (e.g., a holiday in Australia). General events are often related to each other as well as to lifetime periods.

(3) *Event-specific knowledge*: This knowledge consists of images, feelings, and other details relating to general events and spanning time periods from seconds to hours. Knowledge about a specific event is typically organised in temporal order.

We now turn to the issue of how we access information contained in the autobiographical knowledge base. According to the theory we have a working self, which is concerned with the self and what it may become in future. More specifically, the working self "refers to an individual's current set of active goals. These need not be conscious and are considered to be organised into complex goal hierarchies, each of which seeks to reduce the discrepancy between the goal and the state of the world" (Conway et al., 1999, p. 682). The currently active goals of this working self help to determine which autobiographical memories we retrieve. In addition, the goals of the working self influence the kinds of memories stored in the autobiographical knowledge base. As a result, "autobiographical memories are primary records of success or failure in goal attainment" (Conway & Pleydell-Pearce, 2000, p. 266).

Within the theory, there is a distinction between two ways in which autobiographical memories can be accessed. First, there is *generative* retrieval, in which "memories are actively and intentionally constructed through an interaction between the working self goal structure and the autobiographical memory knowledge base" (Conway et al., 2001, p. 495). According to the theory, many of the processes involved in generative retrieval (especially those relating to the goals of the working self) occur within the frontal cortex. Autobiographical knowledge that is relatively abstract is represented in frontal and anterior temporal regions of the brain, whereas sensory or perceptual details of specific autobiographical events are represented in the posterior temporal lobes and occipital lobes.

Second, there is *direct* retrieval, in which autobiographical memories "are formed outside the influence of the working self and once generated are experienced by the rememberer as spontaneously coming to mind" (Conway et al., 2001, p. 495). According to the theory, direct retrieval occurs when someone encounters a specific cue that causes activation to spread from the relevant specific autobiographical memory to more general associated memories.

Evidence

Studies of brain-damaged patients have provided evidence for the notion that there are three types of autobiographical knowledge. Of particular interest are cases of **retrograde amnesia**, in which there is widespread forgetting of events preceding the brain injury. Conway and Pleydell-Pearce (2000, p. 263) discussed several studies of patients with severe retrograde amnesia in which there was "an inability to retrieve specific memories, whereas access to knowledge of lifetime periods and general knowledge from the period covered by their amnesias remained intact." These findings suggest that event-specific knowledge is more vulnerable to loss or disruption than knowledge about lifetime periods or general events.

One of Conway and Pleydell-Pearce's (2000) main assumptions was that autobiographical memory and the self are very closely related. Support for this assumption has been obtained in several studies. For example, Woike, Gershkovich, Piorkowski, and Polo (1999) considered two types of personality: (1) agentic personality type, with an emphasis on independence, achievement, and personal power; and (2) communal personality type, with an emphasis on interdependence and similarity to others. Participants were asked to recall autobiographical memories involving different emotions (e.g., happiness, anger). Those with an agentic personality recalled more autobiographic memories concerned with agency (e.g., success, absence of failure, failure) than those with a communal personality. In contrast, individuals with a communal personality recalled more memories concerned with communion (e.g., love, friendship, betrayal of trust) than those with an agentic personality (see Figure 8.2). Thus, recall of autobiographical memories is influenced by the goals of the working self.

Another theoretical assumption made by Conway and Pleydell-Pearce (2000) was that

FIGURE 8.2

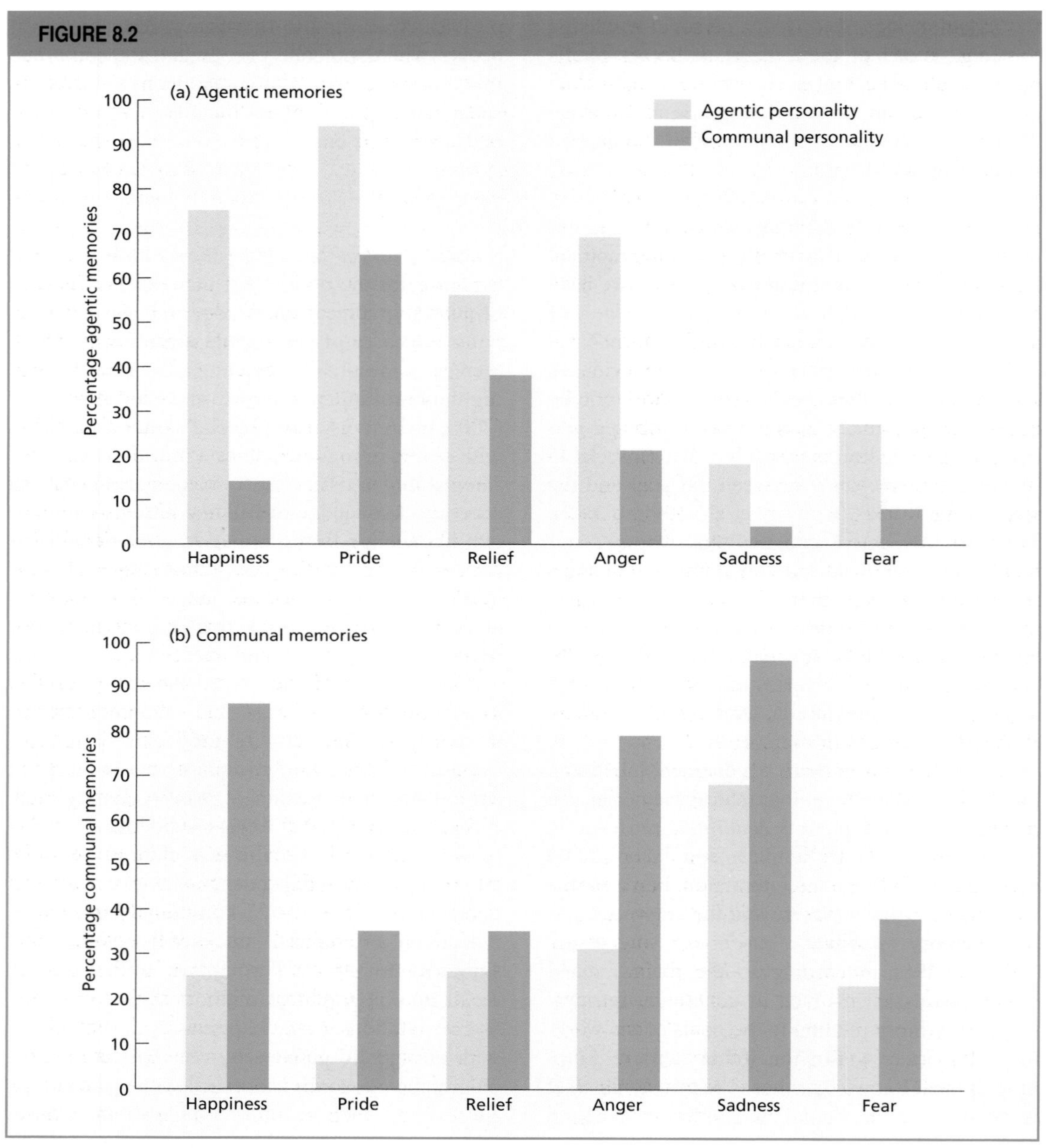

Percentages of recalled autobiographical memories that were agentic (a), or communal (b), as a function of personality type (agentic vs. communal) and type of emotion. Data from Woike et al. (1999).

autobiographical memories produced via generative retrieval are constructed rather than simply reproduced. Two pieces of evidence consistent with that assumption were reported by Conway (1996). First, it took people much longer to retrieve autobiographical memories than other kinds of information. For example, they took about 4 seconds to retrieve autobiographical memories, compared to only about 1 second to verify personal information (e.g., name of their bank). It seems likely that it would take longer to retrieve constructed memories than reproduced ones. Second, Conway (1996) found that the information contained in autobiographical memories produced on two occasions differed considerably, even when the occasions were only a few days apart. If autobiographical memories were reproduced, they would presumably be highly similar from one retrieval to another.

The distinction between generative and direct retrieval was studied by Berntsen (1998). Generative retrieval (involving voluntary memories) was assessed by presenting cues to elicit autobiographical memories, whereas direct retrieval (involving involuntary memories) was assessed by asking the participants to keep a record of autobiographical memories that came to mind without any deliberate attempt to retrieve them. A higher percentage of autobiographical memories produced by direct retrieval than by generative retrieval were of specific events (89% vs. 63%, respectively). As Berntsen (1998, p. 136) pointed out, "The results suggest that we maintain a considerable amount of specific episodes in memory which may often be inaccessible for voluntary [generative] retrieval but highly accessible for involuntary [direct] retrieval."

Berntsen and Hall (in press) replicated Berntsen's (1998) finding that involuntary memories tend to be more specific than voluntary memories. In addition, involuntary memories referred to more unusual and less positive events than did voluntary memories, and the events were associated with more bodily reaction. Conway and Pleydell-Pearce (2000) argued that direct retrieval typically involves specific cues. Berntsen and Hall found that the cues most associated with direct retrieval of autobiographical memories were being in the same place as the original event (61% of cases) or being in the same place engaged in the same activity (25% of cases).

According to the theory put forward by Conway and Pleydell-Pearce (2000), generative retrieval initially involves the control processes of the working self within the frontal lobes, followed by activation of parts of the autobiographical knowledge base in more posterior regions. Conway et al. (1999) carried out a PET study to test these theoretical assumptions. There was intense activation in the left frontal lobe during the recall of autobiographical memories, but not during the recall of paired associates. The retrieval of autobiographical memories was also associated with activation in the inferior temporal and occipital lobes in the left hemisphere. Conway et al. (1999, p. 699) concluded that autobiographical retrieval "is distinguished by activation of sites in the left cortical hemisphere and . . . this reflects an involvement of aspects of self in remembering, aspects that act to control what is remembered and how."

Conway et al. (1999) didn't provide clear evidence of the *order* in which different brain regions were activated. This issue was investigated by Conway, Pleydell-Pearce, and Whitecross (2001) using EEG. There was extensive activation in the left frontal lobe during the initial stages of generative retrieval of autobiographical memories. After that, when an autobiographical memory was being held in mind, there was activation in the temporal and occipital lobes especially in the right hemisphere. What do these findings mean? According to Conway et al. (2001, p. 517), "The working self sited in left frontal networks . . . generates a retrieval model that is subsequently used to direct searches of the knowledge base . . . The knowledge base is distributed within networks in the (right) temporal and occipital lobes, which is where a specific memory is eventually formed."

Conway, Pleydell-Pearce, Whitecross, and Sharpe (2003) replicated and extended the findings of Conway et al. (2001) by comparing memory for experienced events with memory for imagined events. What differences might we expect to find? First, if construction and maintenance are more effortful for imagined memories than for experienced ones, there should be greater activation of prefrontal cortex for imagined memories. Second, if experienced memories depend on the retrieval of more detailed and specific information, there should be more activation in occipito-temporal regions for experienced memories than for imagined ones. Both of these predictions were confirmed, thus providing support for the theory proposed by Conway and Pleydell-Pearce (2000).

Evaluation

Conway and Pleydell-Pearce (2000) have put forward the most comprehensive theory of autobiographical memory currently available. Several of their key theoretical assumptions (e.g., the hierarchical structure of autobiographical memory; the intimate relationship between autobiographical memory and the self) are well supported by the evidence. In addition, the fact that several different brain regions are involved in the generative retrieval of autobiographical memories is consistent with the general notion that such retrieval is complex. The least developed part of the theory concerns the precise ways in which the working self interacts with the autobiographical knowledge base to produce recall of specific autobiographical memories. It also remains to be seen whether there is really a clear distinction between generative and direct retrieval. It may well be that the recall of autobiographical memories often involves elements of both modes of retrieval.

MEMORABLE MEMORIES

Attempts to identify factors associated with very memorable or long-lasting memories have led to the discovery of two interesting phenomena: the self-reference effect and flashbulb memories. More generally, we also need to consider individual differences. As we will see, some individuals have trained themselves to have exceptional memories for certain kinds of information.

It seems reasonable that information about oneself should be better remembered than information of a more impersonal kind, because we are especially interested in such information. This intuition defines the **self-reference effect**. **Flashbulb memories** are produced by very important, dramatic, and surprising public or personal events, such as the death of Princess Diana or the terrorist attacks on the United States on 11 September 2001. Brown and Kulik (1977) argued that flashbulb memories are generally very accurate and immune from forgetting. The crucial issue with both phenomena is whether the processes underlying them are really different from those underlying ordinary memories. After we have discussed these phenomena, we will consider why some people have superior memories.

Self-reference effect

Rogers, Kuiper, and Kirker (1977) reported one of the first studies on the self-reference effect. They presented a series of adjectives, and asked some participants to make self-reference judgements (i.e., describes you?). Other participants made semantic judgements (i.e., means the same as ____?), phonemic judgements (i.e., rhymes with ___?), or structural judgements (i.e., capital letters?). As predicted by levels-of-processing theory (see Chapter 6), adjective recall was much higher after semantic judgements than either phonemic or structural judgements. However, the key finding was that recall was about twice as high after self-reference compared to semantic judgements (see Figure 8.3).

The self-reference effect can also be shown by comparing the effects of self-reference against those of other-reference, in which judgements are made about someone known to the participants. Bower and Gilligan (1979) found that other-reference tasks generally produced poorer levels of recall than self-reference. However, memory performance resembling that found with self-reference was obtained when a very well-known other person (e.g., one's own mother) was used as a referent.

Symons and Johnson (1997) reviewed 60 studies comparing the effects of self-reference and semantic encoding, and a further 69 comparing self-reference tasks against other-reference tasks. **Meta-analyses** (statistical analyses based on combining data from numerous studies) indicated a very clear self-reference effect. This effect was greater when self-reference was compared against semantic tasks rather than other-reference tasks. However, there was no self-reference effect when the self-reference task involved categories of nouns (e.g., parts of the body) rather than personality traits. According to Symons and Johnson (1997), "SR [Self-reference] works best to facilitate memory when certain kinds of stimuli are

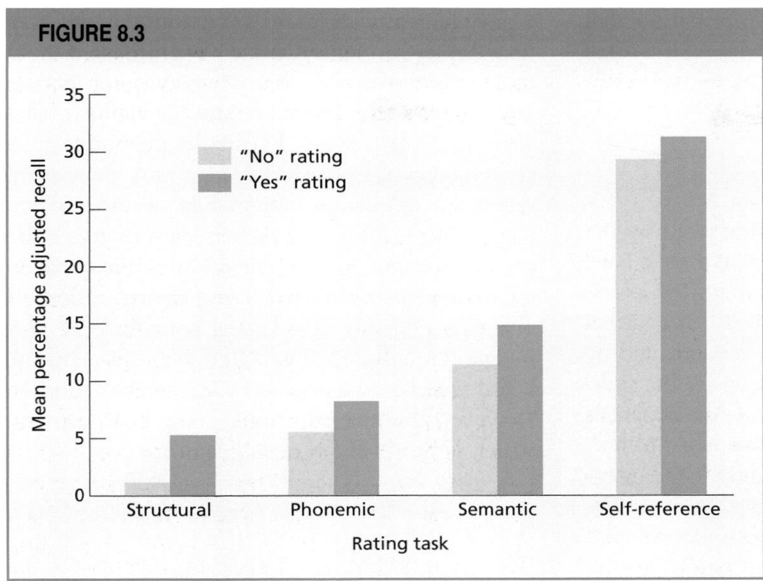

Recall performance as a function of orienting task, and "yes" versus "no" ratings. Based on data in Rogers et al. (1977).

used—stimuli that are commonly organised and elaborated on through SR" (p. 392).

Theoretical accounts

Why does the self-reference effect occur? According to Rogers et al. (1977), each individual has an extensive self-schema (an organised long-term memory structure incorporating self-knowledge). This self-schema is activated when self-referent judgements are made. At the time of recall, the self-schema activates a network of associations, and thus serves as an effective retrieval cue.

Symons and Johnson (1997) developed that theoretical approach: "The SRE [self-reference effect] results primarily because the self is a well-developed and often-used construct in memory that promotes both elaboration and organisation of encoded information" (p. 372). They reported supporting evidence. The self-reference effect was much smaller than usual in studies in which self-reference was compared against semantic encoding tasks that permitted elaboration and organisation. For example, Klein and Kihlstrom (1986) compared the importance of self-reference and organisation as factors determining memory. Participants were presented with a list of occupations, and had to perform one of four tasks on each word:

(1) Semantic, organised: Does this job require a college education?
(2) Semantic, unorganised: Different questions for each word (e.g., Does this person perform operations?).
(3) Self-reference, organised: Have you ever wanted to be a ____?
(4) Self-reference, unorganised: Yes–no decisions on different bases for each word (e.g., I place complete trust in my ____).

Organisation made a large difference to memory. However, self-reference was no more effective than ordinary semantic processing when the extent to which the information is organised was controlled. In fact, self-reference was associated with poorer recall than normal semantic processing if it failed to encourage organisation. On this line of reasoning, the self-reference effect reported by Rogers et al. (1977) and by others is found when the self-reference task encourages organisation to a greater extent than does the rival semantic task.

How unique are the effects of self-reference? According to Symons and Johnson (1997), "Our evidence suggests that SR [self-reference] is a uniquely efficient process; but it is probably unique only in the sense that, because it is a highly practised task, it results in spontaneous, efficient processing of certain kinds of information that people deal with each day—material that is often used, well organised, and exceptionally well elaborated" (p. 392).

Flashbulb memories

Brown and Kulik (1977) were impressed by the very vivid and detailed memories that people have of certain dramatic world events (e.g., the assassination of President Kennedy). They argued that a special neural mechanism may be activated by such events, provided they are seen by the individual as surprising and having real consequences for that person's life. This mechanism "prints" the details of such events permanently in the memory system. According to Brown and Kulik (1977), flashbulb memories are not only accurate and very long lasting, but also often include the following categories of information:

- Informant (person who supplied the information).
- Place where the news was heard.
- Ongoing event.
- Individual's own emotional state.
- Emotional state of others.
- Consequences of the event for the individual.

Brown and Kulik's (1977) central point was that flashbulb memories are very different from other memories in their longevity, accuracy, and reliance on a special neural mechanism. This view is controversial. Flashbulb memories may be remembered clearly because they have been rehearsed frequently, rather than because of the processing that occurred when learning about the dramatic event. Another problem is checking on the accuracy of reported flashbulb memories. At one time, Neisser (1982) was convinced he was listening to a baseball game on the radio when he heard that the Japanese had bombed Pearl Harbor. However, the bombing took place in December, which is not in the baseball season.

Evidence

Bohannon (1988) tested people's memory for the explosion of the space shuttle *Challenger* 2 weeks or 8 months afterwards. Recall fell from 77% at the short retention interval to 58% at the long retention interval, suggesting that flashbulb memories are forgotten in the same way as ordinary memories. However, long-term memory was best when the news had caused a strong emotional reaction, and the event had been rehearsed several times (see Figure 8.4).

FIGURE 8.4

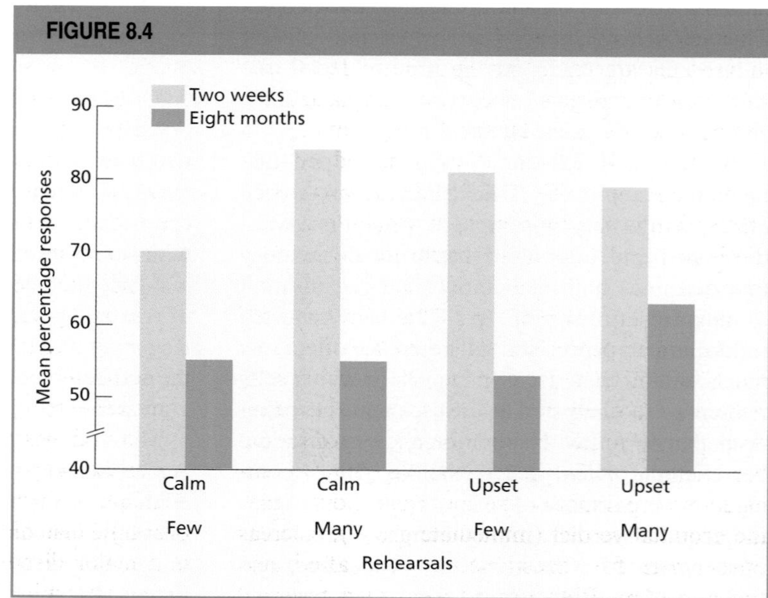

Memory for the *Challenger* explosion as a function of whether the event upset the participants, the extent of rehearsal, and the retention interval. Based on data in Bohannon (1988).

Conway et al. (1994) refused to accept that flashbulb memories are simply stronger versions of ordinary memories. According to them, the participants in the study by Bohannon (1988) may not have regarded the explosion of *Challenger* as having consequences for their lives. If so, one of the main criteria for flashbulb memories proposed by Brown and Kulik (1977) was not fulfilled.

Conway et al. (1994) studied flashbulb memories for the resignation of Mrs Thatcher in 1990. This event was regarded as surprising and consequential by most British people, and so should theoretically have produced flashbulb memories. Memory for this event was tested within a few days, after 11 months, and after 26 months. Flashbulb memories were found in 86% of British participants after 11 months, compared to 29% in other countries. Conway et al. (1994, pp. 337–338) concluded: "The striking finding of the present study was the high incidence of very detailed memory reports provided by the U.K. subjects, which remained consistent over an 11-month retention interval and, for a smaller group, over a 26-month retention interval."

Wright and Gaskell (1995, p. 70) pointed out that "The only study that has found a high percentage of subjects reporting what can realistically be considered memories that differ from ordinary memories investigated memories for Margaret Thatcher's resignation (Conway et al., 1994)". Wright, Gaskell, and Muircheartaigh (1998) carried out a large population survey in England about 18 months after Mrs Thatcher's resignation, and found that only 12% of those sampled remembered the event vividly. The fact that Conway et al. (1994) used a student sample may help to explain the high percentage of flashbulb memories they reported.

Winningham, Hyman, and Dinnel (2000) studied American people's memory for hearing about the acquittal of O.J. Simpson. He had been an American football star, and was accused of murdering his ex-wife Nicole Brown Simpson and her friend Ron Goodman in 1994. Some participants were initially questioned 5 hours after the acquittal verdict (immediate group), whereas others were first questioned 1 week afterwards (delay group). Both groups were then re-tested 8 weeks later. Winningham et al. (2000) argued that those participants whose recollections at the two testing times were highly consistent could be argued to show evidence of flashbulb memories. Their key finding was that 53% of the delay group had flashbulb memories, compared to only 23% of the immediate group.

How did Winningham et al. (2000) explain their findings? They argued that individuals' memories for a dramatic event are likely to change over the first few days for two reasons. First, there is a process of forgetting, which may be especially rapid during that time. As evidence, they found that the delay group recalled less than the immediate group at the first testing. Second, individuals often continue to learn more about dramatic events in the days after they have happened. These two factors mean that there is less consistency (and thus less evidence for flashbulb memories) in the immediate than in the delay group.

The findings of Winningham et al. (2000) are important for two reasons. First, they help to explain apparent inconsistencies in the research literature concerning the incidence of flashbulb memories. Second, their evidence that memories for dramatic events often change in the first few days thereafter undermines the entire notion of flashbulb memories being formed at the moment when individuals learn about such events.

Further problems for the view that flashbulb memories are special were provided by Talarico and Rubin (2003). They pointed out that we do not really know whether flashbulb memories are better remembered than everyday memories because very few studies have assessed retention for both kinds of memory. They rectified this omission. On 12 September 2001, they assessed students' memories for the terrorist attacks of the previous day and also their memory for a very recent everyday event. The students were then tested again 7, 42, or 224 days later. There were two main findings (see Figure 8.5). First, the reported vividness of flashbulb memories remained very high over the entire 32-week period. Second, flashbulb memories showed no more consistency over time than did everyday memories. Thus, there is a major discrepancy between people's beliefs in the strength of their flashbulb memories and

FIGURE 8.5

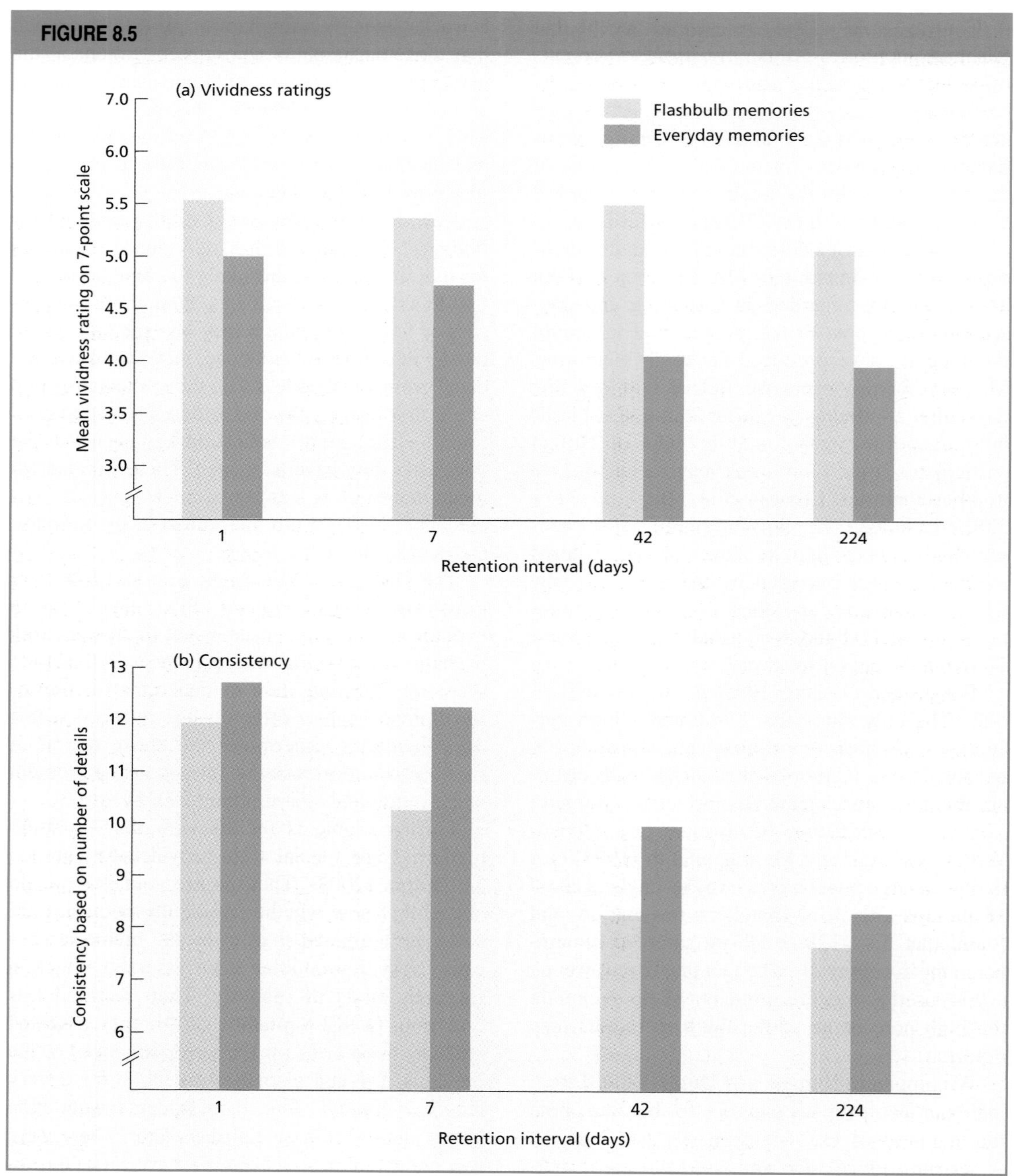

(a) Vividness ratings and (b) consistency of memory as a function of type of memory (flashbulb vs. everyday) and length of retention interval. Based on data in Talarico and Rubin (2003).

the actual accuracy of those memories. As Talarico and Rubin (2003, p. 460) concluded, "The true 'mystery' is not why flashbulb memories are so accurate for so long, . . . but why people are so confident for so long in the accuracy of their flashbulb memories."

Theory

Conway et al. (1994) argued that flashbulb memories depend on three main processes plus one optional process:

(1) *Prior knowledge*: This aids in relating the event to existing memory structures.
(2) *Personal importance*: The event should be perceived as having great personal relevance.
(3) *Surprise and emotional feeling state*: The event should produce an emotional reaction.
(4) *Overt rehearsal*: This is an optional process (some people with flashbulb memories for Mrs Thatcher's resignation had not rehearsed the event). However, rehearsal was generally strongly linked to the existence of flashbulb memories.

Finkenauer et al. (1998) put forward an emotional-integrative model. This extended Conway et al.'s (1994) model by adding the factors of novelty of the event and the individual's affective attitude towards the central person or individuals in the event. They studied flashbulb memories of the unexpected death of the Belgian King Baudouin. Those whose affective attitude towards the royal family was one of strong sympathy were most likely to experience flashbulb memories.

Finkenauer et al. (1998, p. 526) emphasised the fact that their model and that of Conway et al. (1994) agreed on many of the key variables: "(1) the reaction of surprise upon learning about the original event, (2) the appraisal of importance or consequentiality of the original event, (3) an intense emotional feeling state, and (4) rehearsal" (p. 526). However, all these factors can be involved in the formation of *any* memory, leading them to this conclusion: "FBMs [flashbulb memories] are the result of ordinary memory mechanisms. However, the great number of details constituting FBMs, their clarity, and their durability suggest that a particularly efficient encoding took place" (p. 530).

Superior memory ability

It is useful to study individuals with unusually good memories to understand the principles involved in efficient human learning. The best-known mnemonist or memory expert is Shereshevskii, usually referred to as S. His amazing powers were studied by the Russian neuropsychologist Luria (1975). After only 3 minutes' study, S learned a matrix of 50 digits perfectly, and then recalled them effortlessly in any direction. The digits were encoded in the form of visual images. He used various strategies. For example, he learned complex verbal information by linking each piece of information to a different, well-known location. This is known as the **method of loci**. S showed almost perfect retention for much of what he had learned when tested several years later.

S also made frequent use of **synaesthesia** (the tendency for one sense modality to evoke another). His usual strategy was to encode all kinds of material in vivid visual terms. For example, S once said to the psychologist Vygotsky, "What a crumbly yellow voice you have" (Luria, 1975, p. 24). Unfortunately, we do not know why S had such strong synaesthesia and such exceptional memory. He dedicated little time to improving his memory, suggesting that his abilities were innate. Perhaps S had more brain tissue than most people devoted to processing sensory information.

S was unusual among those with superior memory ability in two ways. First, his memory powers were much greater. Second, his superiority owed little to the use of highly practised memory techniques. More typical is the case of the young student (SF) studied by Ericsson and Chase (1982). He was paid to practise the digit-span task for 1 hour a day for 2 years. Digit span (the number of random digits repeated in the correct order) is typically about seven items, but SF attained a span of 80 items.

How did he do it? He reached a digit span of about 18 items by using his extensive knowledge of running times. For example, if the first few digits presented were "3594", he would note that this was Bannister's time for the mile, and so those four digits would be stored away as a single **chunk** or unit. He then increased his digit span to 80 by organising these chunks into a hierarchical structure. The fact that SF typically recalled the digits within a chunk rapidly, and then paused briefly before recalling the next chunk, fits this analysis.

SF had outstanding digit span, but his letter and word spans were only average. A similar pattern was found with Rajan Mahadevan. He produced the first 31,811 digits of *pi* (the ratio of a circle's radius to its circumference) in just under four hours, thereby gaining a place in the *Guinness Book of Records*. He also had a digit span of 59 for visually presented digits and 63 for heard digits. However, he was below average at remembering the position and orientation of images of various objects (Biederman, Cooper, Fox, & Mahadevan, 1992). Thus, exceptional memory abilities are often very specific and limited in scope.

Most research on exceptional memory has been rather artificial, in that it focuses on digit recall or memory for chess positions. However, Kalakoski and Saariluoma (2001) carried out a more naturalistic study to investigate taxi drivers' exceptional ability to remember street names. Helsinki taxi drivers and students tried to recall lists of 15 Helsinki street names in the order presented. In one condition, the streets were connected, and were presented in an order forming a spatially continuous route through the city. In this condition, the taxi drivers recalled about 87% of the street names correctly, whereas the students recalled only about 45%. In another condition, the same street names were presented in a random order. In this condition, the taxi drivers recalled 70% of the street names compared to 46% for the students. However, the two groups did not differ when non-adjacent street names were presented in a random order.

What can we conclude from the above study? According to Kalakoski and Saariluoma (2001, p. 637), "Taxi drivers' exceptional recall of street names is based on associating individual items with a spatial structure corresponding to the task environment." Thus, the taxi drivers used their extensive knowledge of the spatial layout of streets in Helsinki to facilitate learning and retrieval, and they were able to use this knowledge even when connected street names were presented in a random order.

Theoretical views

Ericsson (1988) proposed that there are three requirements to achieve very high memory skills:

- *Meaningful encoding*: The information should be processed meaningfully, relating it to pre-existing knowledge; this resembles levels-of-processing theory (see Chapter 6).
- *Retrieval structure*: Cues should be stored with the information to aid later retrieval; this resembles the **encoding specificity principle** (see Chapter 6).
- *Speed-up*: There is extensive practice so that the processes involved in encoding and retrieval function faster and faster; this produces automaticity (see Chapter 5).

This theoretical approach was developed by Ericsson and Kintsch (1995) in their long-term working memory theory. They argued that exceptional memory depends on pre-existing knowledge rather than an enlarged working memory. According to Ericsson and Kintsch (1995, p. 216), the crucial requirements for exceptional memory are as follows: "Subjects must associate the encoded information with appropriate retrieval cues. This association allows them to activate a particular retrieval cue at a later time and thus partially reinstates the conditions of encoding to retrieve the desired information from long-term memory." More specifically, Ericsson and Kintsch (1995, p. 216) claimed that experts develop appropriate retrieval structures through practice, with retrieval structures being defined as "a set of retrieval cues [that] are organised in a stable structure".

Various mnemonic techniques (see next section) provide examples of the above principles in action. In addition, SF and the taxi drivers studied by Kalakoski and Saariluoma (2001) probably made use of effective retrieval structures. The finding that the taxi drivers had much better recall than students of connected streets presented in a random order suggests that these retrieval structures provide a powerful way of organising information.

The theoretical approach of Ericsson (1988) and of Ericsson and Kintsch (1995) might lead one to conclude that those with exceptional memory rely on highly practised memory strategies. However, Wilding and Valentine (1994) found that matters are more complicated. They classified individuals with excellent memory into two groups: (1) *strategists*, who reported frequent use of memory strategies; and (2) *naturals*, who claimed naturally superior memory ability from early childhood, and who possessed a close relative exhibiting high memory ability. Wilding and Valentine used two kinds of memory tasks:

(1) Strategic tasks (e.g., recalling names to faces) that seemed to be susceptible to the use of memory strategies;
(2) Non-strategic tasks (e.g., recognition of snow crystals).

There were important differences between the strategists and the naturals (see Figure 8.6). The strategists performed much better on strategic tasks than on non-strategic tasks, whereas the naturals did well on both kinds of memory tasks. The data are plotted in percentiles, so we can see how the two groups compared against a normal control sample (50th percentile = average person's score). There was partial support for Ericsson's view of the importance of memory strategies, because easily the most impressive memory performance (surpassing that of more than 90% of the population) was obtained by strategists on strategic tasks.

Maguire, Valentine, Wilding, and Kapur (2003) used fMRI to study superior memorisers, most of whom had performed outstandingly at the World Memory Championships. These superior memorisers and control participants memorised three-digit numbers, faces, and snowflakes, with the superior memorisers outperforming the controls most with the three-digit numbers and least with the snowflakes. Maguire et al. used fMRI, and the key finding was that during learning the superior memorisers had more activity than the controls in several brain areas including the medial parietal cortex, the retrosplenial cortex, and the right posterior hippocampus (see Figure 8.7). These brain areas are involved in spatial memory and navigation. It is probably relevant that 90% of the superior memorisers reported using the method of loci

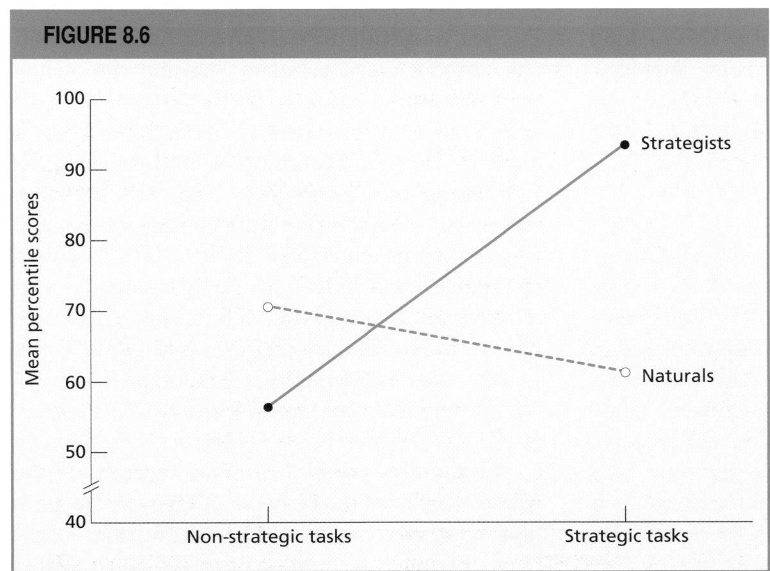

Memory performance strategists and naturals on strategic and non-strategic tasks. Based on data in Wilding and Valentine (1994).

FIGURE 8.7

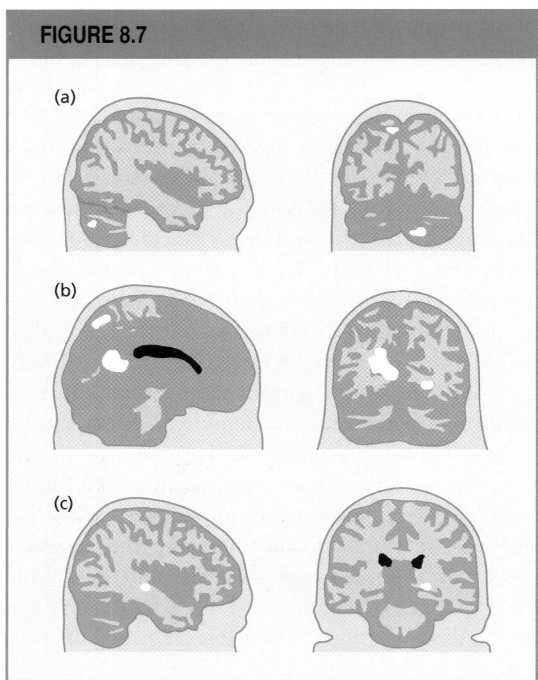

(a) Brain areas in the right cerebellum more active in superior memories than controls during learning. (b) Brain areas active only in superior memorisers in the left medial superior parietal gyrus, bilateral retrosplenial cortex, and (c) right posterior hippocampus. From Maguire et al. (2003). Copyright © 2003 by Nature Publishing Group.

for some or all of the memory tasks. This method involves visualising to-be-remembered information at various points along a known route, and so makes extensive use of spatial memory.

Mnemonic techniques

Several mnemonic techniques to increase long-term memory have been devised. Most involve the requirements for superior memory skills identified by Ericsson (1988): meaningful encoding, retrieval structure, and speed-up. There are various peg systems, in which to-be-remembered items are attached to easily memorised items or pegs. The most popular peg system is the "one-is-a-bun" mnemonic based on the rhyme, "one is a bun, two is a shoe, three is a tree, four is a door, five is a hive, six is sticks, seven is heaven . . ." One mental image is formed associating the first to-be-remembered item with a bun, a second mental image links a shoe with the second item, and so on. The seventh item can be retrieved by thinking of the image based on heaven. This mnemonic uses all of Ericsson's requirements, and doubles recall (Morris & Reid, 1970). However, we do not know which of Ericsson's three requirements is most responsible for its success.

The keyword method has been applied to the learning of foreign vocabulary. First, an association is formed between each spoken foreign word and an English word or phrase sounding like it (the keyword). Second, a mental image is created with the keyword acting as a link between the foreign word and its English equivalent. For example, the Russian word "*zvonok*" is pronounced "zvah-oak" and means bell. This can be learned by using "oak" as the keyword, and forming an image of an oak tree covered with bells.

The keyword technique is more effective when the keywords are provided than when learners provide their own. Atkinson and Raugh (1975) presented 120 Russian words and their English equivalents. The keyword method improved memory for Russian words by about 50% over a short retention interval, and by almost 75% at a long (6-week) retention interval.

Atkinson and Raugh (1975) studied receptive vocabulary learning (producing the appropriate English word to a foreign word), but didn't consider productive vocabulary learning (producing the right foreign word to an English word). Ellis and Beaton (1993) studied receptive and productive vocabulary learning of German words in four conditions: noun keyword, verb keyword, repetition (keep repeating the paired German and English words), and own strategy. The keyword technique (especially with noun keywords) was relatively more successful with receptive than with productive vocabulary learning (see Figure 8.8).

Why was the keyword technique unsuccessful with productive vocabulary learning? As Pressley et al. (1980) pointed out, "There is no mechanism in the keyword method to allow retrieval of the whole word from the keyword." Why was the repetition strategy so successful with productive vocabulary learning? Repetition involves considerable

FIGURE 8.8

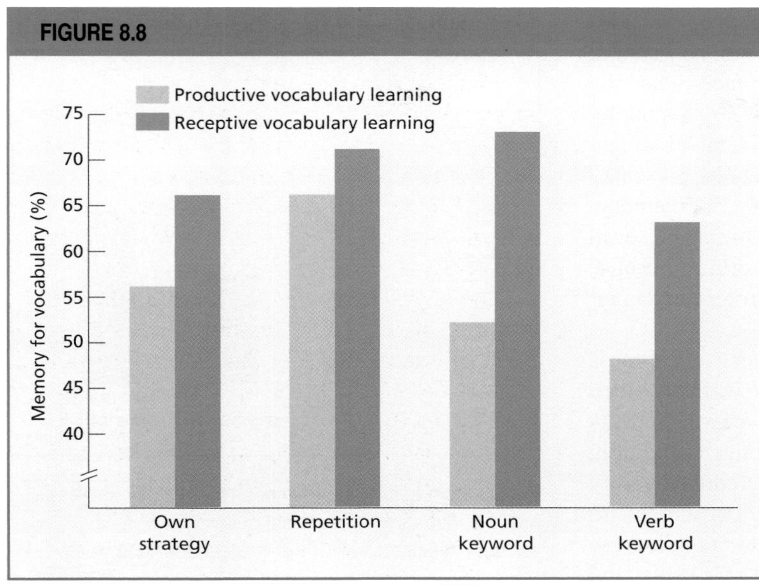

Memory for foreign vocabulary as a function of learning strategy for receptive and productive vocabulary learning. Adapted from Ellis and Beaton (1993).

use of the phonological loop, which plays a major role in language learning (Baddeley, Gathercole, & Papagno, 1998; see Chapter 6).

Evaluation

Ericsson (1988) and Ericsson and Kintsch (1995) added to our understanding of successful memory strategies. However, as Gobet (2000, p. 554) pointed out, "The concept of retrieval structure, which plays a key role in [Ericsson and Kintsch's] theory . . . is not sufficiently well specified to allow precise predictions to be made." Moreover, there are doubts about the applicability of the notion of retrieval structure to exceptional memory as found in chess or medical experts (Gobet, 2000).

Most mnemonic techniques are effective, but we generally do not know *why* in detail. However, it seems that spatial learning strategies may be important with techniques such as the method of loci (Maguire et al., 2003). Some techniques require time-consuming training, and are often of little applicability e.g., few of us need to learn the order of a list of unrelated words, which is what the one-in-a-bun mnemonic permits us to do.

EYEWITNESS TESTIMONY

Many innocent people have been found guilty of a crime and sent to prison. For example, more than 100 convicted people in the United States have been shown to be innocent by means of DNA tests. As Wells and Olson (2003) pointed out, more than 75% of these people were found guilty on the basis of mistaken eyewitness identification. It is thus a matter of considerable practical as well as theoretical importance to understand the factors making eyewitness testimony accurate or inaccurate.

One way in which eyewitness testimony can be distorted is via **confirmation bias**, i.e., event memory is influenced by the observer's expectations. For example, students from two universities in the United States (Princeton and Dartmouth) were shown a film of a football game involving both universities. The students reported that their opponents had committed many more fouls than their own team.

Does it make any difference to the memory of an eyewitness whether the crime observed by him/her is violent? A study by Loftus and Burns (1982) suggests the answer is yes. Participants saw two filmed versions of a crime. In the violent version, a young boy was shot in the face near the end of the film as the robbers were making their getaway. Inclusion of the violent incident caused impaired memory for details presented up to 2 minutes earlier. Presumably the memory-impairing effects of violence would be even greater in the case of a real-life crime, because the presence of violent criminals might endanger the life of any eyewitness.

Another factor involved in eyewitness testimony is **weapon focus**. This was described by Loftus (1979, p. 75): "The weapon appears to capture a good deal of the victim's attention, resulting in, among other things, a reduced ability to recall other details from the environment, to recall details about the assailant, and to recognise the assailant at a later time." Loftus, Loftus, and Messo (1987) asked participants to watch one of two sequences: (1) a person pointing a gun at a cashier and receiving some cash; (2) a person handing a cheque to the cashier and receiving some cash. The participants looked more at the gun than the cheque. As predicted, memory for details unrelated to the gun/cheque was poorer in the weapon condition.

Weapon focus may be less important with real line-ups (also known as "identification parades") than in the laboratory. Valentine, Pickering, and Darling (2003) found in over 300 real line-ups that the presence of a weapon had no effect on the probability of an eyewitness identifying the suspect.

Post-event and pre-event information

It is surprisingly easy to distort the memory of an incident by subsequent questioning, indicating that eyewitness memories are somewhat fragile. For example, consider a study by Loftus and Palmer (1974). Participants were shown a film of a multiple car accident. After viewing the film, they described what had happened, and then answered specific questions. Some were asked "About how fast were the cars going when they smashed into each other?", whereas for other participants the verb "hit" was substituted for "smashed into".

FIGURE 8.9

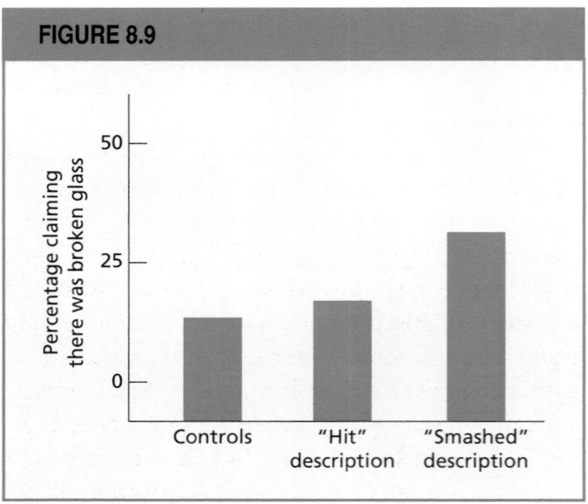

Results from Loftus and Palmer's (1974) study showing how the verb used in the initial description of a car accident affected recall of the incident after one week.

Control participants were not asked a question about car speed. The estimated speed was affected by the verb used in the question, averaging 41 mph when the verb "smashed" was used versus 34 mph when "hit" was used. Thus, the information implicit in the question affected how the accident was remembered.

One week later, all participants were asked, "Did you see any broken glass?" There was not actually any broken glass in the accident, but 32% of those who had been asked previously about speed using the verb "smashed" said they had seen broken glass (see Figure 8.9). In contrast, only 14% of the participants asked using the verb "hit" said they had seen broken glass, and the figure was 12% for the control participants. Thus, our memory for events is so fragile that it can be distorted by changing one word in one question!

Further evidence that apparently trivial differences in the way in which a question is asked can have a marked effect on the answers elicited was reported by Loftus and Zanni (1975). They showed people a short film of a car accident, and then asked them various questions. Some eyewitnesses were asked "Did you see a broken headlight?", whereas others were asked "Did you see the broken headlight?" In fact, there was no broken headlight in the film, but the latter question implied that there was. Only 7% of those asked about a broken headlight said they had seen it, compared to 1.7% of those asked about the broken headlight.

The tendency for eyewitness memory to be influenced by misleading post-event information is very strong. Eakin, Schreiber, and Sergent-Marshall (2003) showed participants slides of a maintenance man repairing a chair in an office and stealing some money and a calculator. They found that eyewitness memory was impaired by misleading post-event information. Of key importance, there was often memory impairment even when the eyewitnesses were warned immediately about the presence of misleading information.

The tendency for post-event information to distort memory depends on individual differences in susceptibility to misinformation. This issue was studied by Tomes and Katz (1997). Those who habitually accepted misinformation possessed the following characteristics:

- Poor general memory for event information *not* associated with misinformation.
- High scores on imagery vividness.
- High empathy scores, meaning they could identify with others' moods and thoughts.

Lindsay, Allen, Chan, and Dahl (2004) argued that *pre*-event information might also distort eyewitness memory. In one of their experiments, participants were shown a video of a museum burglary. On the previous day, they listened to a narrative either thematically similar (a palace burglary) or thematically dissimilar (a school field-trip to a palace) to the video. Eyewitnesses made many more errors when recalling information from the video when the narrative was thematically similar than when it was thematically dissimilar. This is potentially an important finding. In the real world, most eyewitnesses are likely to have some pre-event experiences of relevance to the questions they are asked about the event, and these experiences may serve to distort their answers.

Most studies have *only* provided evidence that eyewitness memory for peripheral details is distorted by misleading information. In fact, there is typically much less memory distortion for central details than for peripheral ones (e.g., Heath & Erickson, 1998). This reduces somewhat the practical importance of research on post-event and pre-event information.

Theoretical views

How does misleading post-event information distort what eyewitnesses report? According to Loftus (1979), information from the misleading questions permanently alters the memory representation of the incident, with the previously formed memory being "overwritten" and destroyed. Loftus (1979) supported this position in a study in which she offered participants $25 for accurate recall of an incident. This incentive totally failed to prevent their recollections being distorted by the misleading information they had heard. However, Dodson and Reisberg (1991) obtained evidence that the original information remains in long-term memory. They used an implicit memory test to show that misinformation hadn't destroyed the original memories of an event. They concluded that misinformation simply makes these memories inaccessible.

Loftus (1992) argued for a less extreme position than she had adopted previously. She emphasised the notion of *misinformation acceptance*: the participants "accept" misleading information presented to them after an event, and subsequently regard it as forming part of their memory for that event. There is a greater tendency to accept post-event information in this way as the time since the event increases.

The effects of post-event misinformation on eyewitness memory can also be understood within the source monitoring framework (Johnson, Hashtroudi, & Lindsay, 1993). A memory probe (e.g., question) activates memory traces having informational overlap with it; this memory probe may activate memories from various sources. The individual decides on the *source* of any activated memory on the basis of the information it contains, but there is a possibility of source misattribution. If the memories from one source resemble those from another source, this will increase the chances of source misattribution. If eyewitnesses falsely attribute the source of misinformation to the original event, then misinformation will form part of their recall of the event. In essence, it is assumed that separate memories are stored of the original event and the misinformation, with potential memory problems occurring at the time of retrieval.

According to the source monitoring framework, any manipulation making the memories from one source resemble those from another source increases the likelihood of source misattribution. Support for this prediction was reported by Allen and Lindsay (1998). They presented two narrative slide shows describing two different events with different people in different settings. Thus, the participants knew the post-event information contained in the second slide show was irrelevant to the event described in the first slide show. However, some details in the two events were rather similar (e.g., a can of Pepsi vs. a can of Coca-Cola). This caused source misattribution, and led the participants to substitute details from the post-event information for details of the event itself. Source misattribution occurred with an interval of 48 hours between the two events, but not when there was no time gap. Presumably the participants in the latter condition noticed the resemblances in the details incorporated in the two events, and this reduced source misattribution.

Much research in this area can be interpreted within Bartlett's (1932) schema theory (see Chapter 11). According to Bartlett, retrieval involves a process of *reconstruction*, in which all available information about an event is used to reconstruct the details of that event on the basis of "what must have been true". On that account, new information relevant to a previously experienced event can affect recollection of that event by providing a different basis for reconstruction. Such reconstructive processes may be involved in eyewitness studies on post-event information.

Eyewitness confidence and other factors

There are several factors influencing eyewitness testimony that are regarded by eyewitness experts as well established, but which differ from common sense. Kassin, Ellsworth, and Smith (1989) compiled a list of such factors (with percentages of experts believing each statement to be commonsensical in brackets):

- An eyewitness's confidence is not a good predictor of his/her identification accuracy (3%).
- Eyewitnesses overestimate the duration of events (5%).
- Eyewitness testimony about an event often reflects not only what the eyewitness actually saw but information they obtained later (7.5%).
- There is a conventional forgetting curve for eyewitness memories (24%).
- An eyewitness's testimony about an event can be affected by question wording (27%).
- The use of a one-person line-up increases the risk of misidentification (29%).

Kassin, Tubb, Hosch, and Memon (2001) carried out a similar survey to that of Kassin et al. (1989). Over 80% of eyewitness experts agreed that several phenomena are well established. These phenomena included the following: post-event information; low accuracy–confidence correlation; the forgetting curve; and weapon focus. The poor relationship between eyewitness confidence and accuracy is of particular importance, because jurors are typically more influenced by an eyewitness's confidence than any other factor when assessing his/her credibility. However, there is not always a poor relationship between eyewitness confidence and accuracy. Sporer, Penrod, Read, and Cutler (1995) carried out a meta-analysis in which they distinguished between choosers (eyewitnesses making a positive identification) and non-choosers. There was practically no correlation between confidence and accuracy among non-choosers, but the mean correlation was +.41 for choosers.

Why is an eyewitness's confidence often a poor predictor of identification accuracy? This issue was studied by Perfect and Hollins (1996). Participants were given recognition memory tests for the information contained in a film about a girl who was kidnapped, and for general knowledge questions. Accuracy of memory was not associated with confidence for questions about the film, but it was for the general knowledge questions.

Perfect and Hollins (1996, p. 379) explained the above difference as follows:

> Individuals have insight into their strengths and weaknesses in general knowledge, and tend to modify their use of the confidence scale accordingly . . . So, for example, individuals will know whether they tend to be better or worse than others at sports questions. However, eyewitnessed events are not amenable to such insight: subjects are unlikely to know whether they are better or worse . . . than others at remembering the hair colour of a participant in an event, for example.

Perfect and Hollins (1996) found eyewitnesses typically had more confidence in their accurate answers than in their inaccurate ones. Thus, they could discriminate among the quality of their own memories to some extent, even though they didn't know whether they were better or worse than others at remembering details of an event.

Perfect, Hollins, and Hunt (2000) tested the hypothesis that the very low correlation between eyewitness confidence and accuracy is due to eyewitnesses' lack of knowledge about their expertise relative to other people. In one of their studies, the participants were presented with faces followed by three recognition tests. After the first and second tests, some of them were given information about their own performance and that of other participants. As a result, the correlation between confidence and accuracy increased across trials. It was −.02 on trial 1, +.33 on trial 2, and +.50 on trial 3.

How can we explain the above findings? It seems reasonable to argue that participants discovered their relative level of ability at eyewitness memory, and this led them to have an appropriate level of confidence in the accuracy of their memory. However, participants did not display a consistent level of memory ability across trials! A more likely explanation is that eyewitnesses' mistaken beliefs about their ability at eyewitness memory influence their confidence judgements. Feedback about their relative memory performance reduces these mistaken beliefs, and thus improves the confidence–accuracy relation.

Eyewitness identification

Eyewitness identification from identification parades or line-ups is often very fallible (see Wells & Olson, 2003, for a review). For example, Valentine et al. (2003) studied the evidence from 640 eyewitnesses who tried to identify suspects in 314 real line-ups. About 20% of witnesses identified a non-suspect, 40% identified the suspect, and 40% failed to make an identification.

One of the most important reasons for inaccurate eyewitness identification is that we are often surprisingly poor at recognising unfamiliar faces. For example, consider a study by Bruce et al. (1999), who studied how easy it is to identify culprits from closed-circuit television (CCTV) images. In one experiment, participants were presented with a target face taken from a CCTV video, together with an array of 10 high-quality full-face photographs. Their task was to select the matching face or to indicate that the target face was not present in the array. Bruce et al. found that performance was relatively poor. When the target face was present in the array, it was selected only 65% of the time. When it was not present, 35% of participants nevertheless claimed that one of the faces in the array matched the target face. Allowing participants to watch a 5-second video segment of the target person as well as a photograph of their face had no effect on identification performance.

Wells and Olson (2003) distinguished between two types of variables influencing the accuracy of eyewitness identification. There are system variables (e.g., instructions given to eyewitnesses before seeing a line-up), which are under the control of the criminal justice system, and there are estimator variables (e.g., lighting conditions at the time of the event), which are not.

System variables

It is often assumed that warning eyewitnesses that the culprit may not be present in a line-up reduces the chances of mistaken identification. Steblay (1997) carried out a meta-analysis, and found that such warnings reduced mistaken identification rates in culprit-absent line-ups by 42%, while reducing accurate identification rates in culprit-present line-ups by only 2%.

Line-ups can be either simultaneous (eyewitness sees everyone at the same time) or sequential (eyewitness sees only one person at a time). Steblay, Dysart, Fulero, and Lindsay (2001) found in a meta-analysis of 25 studies that sequential line-ups reduced the chances of mistaken identification when the culprit was absent by almost 50%. However, sequential line-ups also produced a significant reduction in accurate identification rates when the culprit was present. These findings suggest that eyewitnesses adopt a more stringent criterion for identification with sequential than simultaneous line-ups.

Estimator variables

An estimator variable that has often been studied is the race or ethnicity of the eyewitness. Meissner and Brigham (2001) carried out a meta-analysis in this area. They found that eyewitnesses recognise faces of their own race or ethnic group better than faces of another race or ethnic group. One of the most interesting studies on estimator variables was carried out by Dunning and Perretta (2002). We have seen that eyewitness confidence is generally not a good predictor of accurate identification. However, Dunning and Perretta found that speed of identification is a good predictor. Eyewitnesses who made their identification decision in under 10–12 seconds were correct almost 90% of the time, whereas those who took longer to decide were correct only 50% of the time.

Evaluation

We now know much about the factors determining how accurate eyewitnesses are when trying to select the culprit from a line-up. The research on system variables is especially important, because these variables can be changed in order to reduce the chances of innocent people being identified mistakenly. The main limitation of research in this area was expressed thus by Wells and Olson (2003, p. 290): "The eyewitness identification literature has been driven much less by theoretical frameworks than by practical perspectives."

Cognitive interview

Cognitive psychologists have developed effective ways for police to interview eyewitnesses. For example, Geiselman, Fisher, MacKinnon, and Holland (1985) argued that interview techniques should be based on the following notions:

- Memory traces are usually complex and contain various kinds of information.
- The effectiveness of a retrieval cue depends on its informational overlap with information stored in the memory trace; this is the **encoding specificity principle** (see Chapter 6).
- Various retrieval cues may permit access to any given memory trace; if one retrieval cue is ineffective, find another one. For example, if you cannot think of someone's name, form an image of that person, or think of the first letter of their name.

Geiselman et al. (1985) used the above notions to develop the **basic cognitive interview**:

- The eyewitness recreates the context existing at the time of the crime, including environmental and internal (e.g., mood state) information.
- The eyewitness reports everything he/she can think of about the incident, even if the information is fragmented.
- The eyewitness reports the details of the incident in various orders.
- The eyewitness reports the events from various perspectives, an approach based on the Anderson and Pichert (1978) study (see Chapter 11).

Geiselman et al. (1985) found the average number of correct statements produced by eyewitnesses was 41.1 using the basic cognitive interview, against only 29.4 using the standard police interview (see Figure 8.10). Hypnosis produced an average of 38.0 correct statements, so it was less effective than the basic cognitive interview.

Fisher, Geiselman, Raymond, Jurkevich, and Warhaftig (1987) devised an **enhanced cognitive interview**. It incorporates key aspects of the

FIGURE 8.10

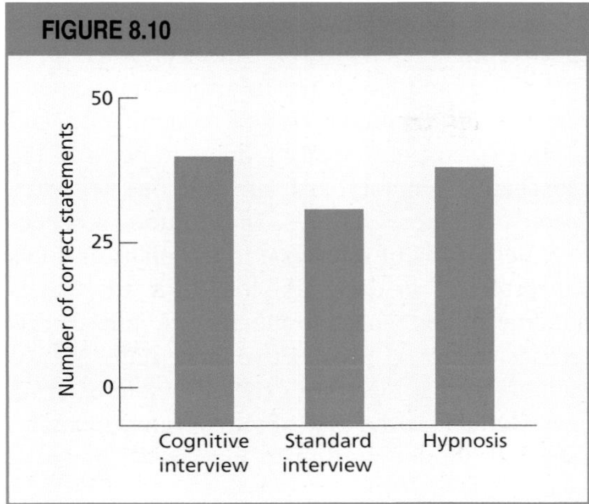

Number of correct statements using different methods of interview. Based on data in Geiselman et al. (1985).

basic cognitive interview, but adds the following recommendations (Roy, 1991, p. 399):

> Investigators should minimise distractions, induce the eyewitness to speak slowly, allow a pause between the response and next question, tailor language to suit the individual eyewitness, follow up with interpretive comment, try to reduce eyewitness anxiety, avoid judgmental and personal comments, and always review the eyewitness's description of events or people under investigation.

Fisher et al. (1987) found the enhanced cognitive interview was more effective than the basic cognitive interview. Eyewitnesses produced an average of 57.5 correct statements when given the enhanced interview, compared to 39.6 with the basic interview. However, there were 28% more incorrect statements with the enhanced interview.

Fisher et al.'s (1987) findings were obtained under artificial conditions. Fisher, Geiselman, and Amador (1990) used the enhanced cognitive interview in field conditions. Detectives working for the Robbery Division of Metro-Dade Police Department in Miami were trained in the techniques of the enhanced interview. Police interviews with eyewitnesses and the victims of crime were tape recorded and scored for the number of statements obtained, and the extent to which these statements were confirmed by a second eyewitness. Training produced an increase of 46% in the number of statements. Where confirmation was possible, over 90% of the statements proved to be accurate.

Kohnken et al. (1999) reported a meta-analysis based on over 50 studies. The cognitive interview consistently elicited more correct information than standard police interviews. Indeed, the average eyewitness given a cognitive interview produced more correct items of information than 81% of eyewitnesses given a standard interview. However, there was a small cost in terms of reduced accuracy, with the average eyewitness given a cognitive interview producing more errors than 61% of those given a standard interview.

Evaluation

In spite of its great success, the cognitive interview possesses several limitations. First, the small increase in the amount of incorrect information recalled by eyewitnesses is a cause for concern. Second, a key ingredient in the cognitive interview is the attempt to recreate the context at the time of the incident. However, context typically has more effect on recall than on recognition memory (see Chapter 6). As a result, the cognitive interview does not improve person identification from photographs or line-ups (see Fisher, 1999).

Third, the cognitive interview may be of more value in increasing recall of peripheral details than of central ones (Groeger, 1997). However, the state of high arousal experienced by many eyewitnesses to crime may prevent them from encoding such peripheral details (e.g., Loftus & Burns, 1982), and so these details will not be available for recall.

Fourth, the cognitive interview is typically less effective at enhancing recall when used at longer retention intervals (Geiselman & Fisher, 1997). Thus, eyewitnesses should be interviewed as soon after the incident or event as possible.

Fifth, as Fisher (1999, p. 551) pointed out, "Most experiments on the CI [cognitive interview] have presented the technique as a 'package' and, as a result, it is difficult to tease apart the contribution of each of the component techniques."

PROSPECTIVE MEMORY

Most studies of human memory have been on **retrospective memory**. The focus has been on the past, especially on people's ability to remember events they have experienced or knowledge they have acquired previously. We can contrast that with **prospective memory**, which involves remembering to carry out intended actions. As Burgess, Quayle, and Frith (2001, p. 545) pointed out, "Prospective memory (PM) . . . is an ability which is at the heart of competent behaviour in everyday life. Without PM functions one could not carry out an intended future action without continuous verbal rehearsal of the action until the appropriate time (or context occurred)."

Ellis and Kvavilashvili (2000) identified three key characteristics of prospective memory tasks:

(1) There is a delay between the formation of an intention and an opportunity to carry it out. This delay needs to be sufficient to prevent the individual simply focusing on the intention throughout the time period.
(2) There is often no explicit reminder to carry out the intention at an appropriate moment.
(3) There is a need to interrupt some different ongoing task to carry out the intention.

There is an important distinction between time-based and event-based prospective memory. **Time-based prospective memory** involves remembering to perform a given action at a particular time (e.g., arriving at the pub at 7.30 pm). In contrast, **event-based prospective memory** involves remembering to perform an action in the appropriate circumstances (e.g., passing on a message when you see someone).

How different are prospective and retrospective memory? As Baddeley (1997) pointed out, these two types of memory do not only differ with respect to their past versus future time orientation. Retrospective memory tends to involve remembering *what* we know about something and can be high in information content. In contrast, prospective memory typically focuses on *when* to do something, and has a low informational content. The low informational content is deliberate, and is done to ensure that any failures to perform the prospective memory task are not due to retrospective memory failures. In addition, prospective memory is of relevance to the plans or goals we form for our daily activities in a way that is not true of retrospective memory. A further difference between prospective and retrospective memory is that there are generally more external cues available in the case of retrospective memory, especially in comparison to time-based prospective memory.

Evidence

One of the relatively few attempts to study prospective memory naturalistically was reported by Marsh, Hicks, and Landau (1998). They found that people reported an average of 15 plans for the forthcoming week, of which about 25% were not completed. The main reasons for these non-completions were rescheduling and reprioritisation, with only 3% of the plans being forgotten.

Sellen, Lowie, Harris, and Wilkins (1997) compared time-based and event-based prospective memory in a work environment, with participants being equipped with badges containing buttons. They were told to press their button at pre-specified times (time-based task) or when they were in a pre-specified place (event-based task). Performance was better in the event-based task than in the time-based task (52% vs. 33% correct, respectively) although the participants thought more often about the time-based task. Sellen et al. argued that event-based prospective memory tasks are easier than time-based tasks, because the intended actions are more likely to be triggered by external cues.

Common sense indicates that motivation influences whether we remember to do things. It is easier to remember something enjoyable (e.g., visit to the theatre) than something unpleasant (e.g., visit to the dentist). According to Freud (1901, p. 157), the motive behind many of our failures of prospective memory "is an unusually large amount of unavowed contempt for other people". Freud's views (as usual) were over the top, but motivation does influence prospective memory. Meacham and Singer (1977) instructed people to post postcards at 1-weekly intervals, and performance was better when a financial incentive was offered.

Prospective memory depends more than retrospective memory on spontaneous memory retrieval. This suggests that prospective memory involves top-down or **conceptually driven processes**, a notion tested by McDaniel, Robinson-Riegler, and Einstein (1998) in a study on event-based prospective memory. They contrasted conceptually driven processes (depending on the meaning or significance of stimuli) with bottom-up or **data-driven processes** determined by the physical characteristics of stimuli.

In their first experiment, the participants had to press a key when any of three homographic words (words such as 'bat' and 'chest' having more than one distinct meaning) was presented. This prospective memory task was embedded within another ongoing task to prevent the participants from thinking continually about the prospective memory task. Performance on the prospective memory task was worse when the meaning of the homograph changed than when it remained the same. The finding that prospective memory was influenced by meaning rather than purely by the physical stimulus suggests the involvement of conceptually driven processes.

In another experiment, McDaniel et al. (1998) considered whether attentional processes are involved in prospective memory. Participants performed a prospective memory task under full or divided attention. In the latter condition, they listened for three odd numbers in a row as well as performing the prospective memory task. Prospective memory performance was much better with full attention than with divided attention, indicating that attentional processes are involved in prospective memory. This finding is consistent with everyday experience. Herrmann and Gruneberg (1993) asked people to record failures of prospective memory in their daily lives. They were most likely to forget to do things when having a conversation or when preoccupied with some other concern.

Marsh and Hicks (1998) obtained similar findings to those of McDaniel et al. (1998). Their participants had to remember three words on each trial, and the event-based prospective memory task was to respond whenever a type of fruit was presented. Participants also had to perform a third task at the same time except in the control condition, and this task involved one of the components of working memory (see Chapter 6). A task involving the attention-like **central executive** (e.g., random number generation) impaired prospective memory performance relative to the control condition, but tasks involving the **phonological loop** or the **visuo-spatial sketchpad** did not. Marsh and Hicks (1998, pp. 347–348) concluded: "Event-based prospective memory requires some optimal degree of conscious, central executive processing. This point is non-trivial given people's intuitions that event-based remembering feels spontaneous as evidenced by research participants reporting that the response 'pops to mind' on seeing a target word."

Are prospective-memory tasks attentionally demanding even during periods of time in which no target stimuli requiring response are presented? Smith (2003) addressed this issue. The main task was lexical decision, which involved deciding as rapidly as possible whether each letter string formed a word. The prospective memory task (performed by half the participants) involved pressing a button whenever a target word was presented. The key findings relate to performance on trials on which a target word was not presented. On those trials, lexical decision was much slower for those participants performing the prospective memory task than for those not doing it (1061 ms vs. 726 ms). Thus, a prospective memory task can be attentionally demanding (and so impair performance on another task) even when no target stimuli are presented.

McDaniel and Einstein (2000) argued that the extent to which attentionally demanding or strategic processes are involved in prospective memory tasks depends on various factors (e.g., the importance and simplicity of the prospective memory task). In one study, performance of an additional ongoing task was impaired by a prospective memory task being carried out at the same time only when the prospective task was perceived to be important. Thus, a prospective memory task regarded as important took processing resources away from the ongoing task, but the same task regarded as relatively unimportant did not. In another study, McDaniel and Einstein obtained evidence that a simple prospective memory task (e.g., writing down "sauce" when presented with the word "spaghetti") did not use attentional resources. However, a more complex prospective task (e.g., writing down "steeple" when presented with "spaghetti") did require the involvement of attentional resources.

Theoretical perspective

Successful performance of most prospective memory tasks requires monitoring the environment for relevant cues. The supervisory attentional system or central executive of the working memory system (see Chapter 6) may be involved in this monitoring. For example, McDaniel and Einstein (2000, p. S129) argued that "some attentional resources are voluntarily deployed for strategically considering environmental events (in regard to the prospective memory task) and/or periodically bringing the intended action to mind." Some theorists (e.g., Burgess, Veitch, De Lacy Costello, & Shallice, 2000) have argued that this attentional system is located in the frontal lobes and related structures.

Burgess et al. (2000) considered a total of 65 brain-damaged patients having problems with prospective memory, finding that various frontal regions were damaged. They argued that the right dorsolateral prefrontal cortex was involved in planning and in the creation of intentions, with Brodmann's area 10 being involved in the maintenance of intentions. In contrast, the retrospective memory component of prospective memory tasks (i.e., remembering which action needs to be carried out) was based in the anterior and posterior cingulates.

Burgess et al. (2001) carried out a PET study on prospective memory in intact individuals. They compared conditions in which an expected stimulus designed to elicit a given response either occurred or did not. In essence, they confirmed the main findings from Burgess et al. (2000), since there was increased activity in "the frontal pole (Brodmann's area 10) bilaterally, right lateral prefrontal and inferior parietal regions plus the precuneus when subjects were expecting a PM [prospective memory] stimulus regardless of whether it actually occurred" (Burgess et al., 2001, p. 545). In addition, "Further activation was seen in the thalamus when the PM stimuli occurred and were acted upon, with a corresponding . . . decrease in right lateral prefrontal cortex." These findings support the view that there is a truly significant difference between prospective and retrospective memory. Brain activation *before* the arrival of the crucial stimuli presumably reflects only processes associated with prospective memory, whereas activation after the arrival of these stimuli reflects some mixture of prospective and retrospective memory processes.

Evaluation

Evidence from cognitive neuropsychology and from cognitive neuroscience indicates that prospective memory typically involves attentional processes centred largely in the frontal areas of the brain. It also appears to be the case that somewhat different regions of the brain are involved in prospective and retrospective memory. However, the extent to which the findings of Burgess et al. (2000, 2001) generalise to other kinds of prospective memory tasks is not known. In addition, we need to know more about the time course of the various processes involved in prospective memory. Preliminary findings were reported by West, Herndon, and Ross-Munroe (2000) using ERPs. Noticing the occurrence of a crucial stimulus requiring a response was reflected in a negative wave peaking after 300 ms, and successful search for the appropriate action maintained that wave until 800–1000 ms after stimulus onset. However, these findings need replication and extension.

EVALUATION OF EVERYDAY MEMORY RESEARCH

We can draw up a balance sheet indicating the advantages and limitations of much everyday memory research. The following are some major advantages:

- Important, non-obvious phenomena have been discovered, thus enriching the study of human memory.
- There is often fairly direct applicability to everyday life.
- The functions served by memory in our lives are considered.
- It provides a test-bed for memory theories based on laboratory research.

The following are limitations of everyday memory research:

- There is often poor experimental control, especially of the learning stage.
- The *accuracy* of everyday memories often cannot be assessed, because there is incomplete knowledge of the circumstances in which learning occurred.
- Some phenomena (e.g., flashbulb memories, the self-reference effect) have produced relatively few new theoretical insights.

CHAPTER SUMMARY

- Introduction
  The views of some everyday memory researchers differ from those of more traditional memory researchers in terms of *what* should be studied, *how* memory should be studied, and *where* memory should be studied. However, the differences between these two groups of researchers have become less in recent years. According to Neisser, everyday memory is purposeful, it has a personal quality about it, and it is influenced by situational demands.

- Autobiographical memory
  Recollection of autobiographical memories by older individuals typically shows evidence of infantile amnesia, a reminiscence bump, and a retention function. Infantile amnesia occurs in part because the cognitive self only emerges towards the end of the second year of life. The reminiscence bump reflects superior memory for a period of one's life during which there is consolidation of the self. Specific autobiographical events can be accessed most readily by *what* information, followed in order of decreasing usefulness by *where*, *who*, and *when* information. Autobiographical information is stored hierarchically at three levels: lifetime periods; general-event knowledge; and event-specific knowledge. According to Conway and Pleydell-Pearce, the goals of the working self influence the storage and the retrieval of autobiographical memories. Most recall of autobiographical memories involves the control processes of the working self within the frontal lobes, followed by activation of parts of the knowledge base in more posterior regions.

- Memorable memories
  Information about oneself (the self-reference effect) and about important, dramatic, and surprising public or personal events (flashbulb memories) is generally well remembered. The self-reference effect may occur because the self-construct aids the elaboration and organisation of information. Brown and Kulik (1977) argued that flashbulb memories differ from other memories in their longevity, accuracy, and reliance on a special neural mechanism. However, the factors associated with the production of flashbulb memories (e.g., novelty, surprise, personal significance, emotional reactions, rehearsal) are also involved in forming ordinary memories. Individuals' memories for dramatic events often change over the first few days before becoming consistent. Some individuals have developed exceptional memory for digits. Such performance typically involves meaningful encoding, a retrieval structure, and speed-up through extensive practice. Most individuals with exceptional memory use deliberate strategies, but a few seem to possess outstanding natural memory ability.

- Eyewitness testimony
  Eyewitness memory is influenced by many factors, including confirmation bias, weapon focus, and post-event information. Misinformation may distort eyewitness memory because of misinformation acceptance or because of source misattribution. Eyewitness confidence often fails to correlate with accuracy, probably because many eyewitnesses have mistaken beliefs about their ability at eyewitness memory. The probability of misidentification on an identification parade is greater when the eyewitness is not warned that the culprit may not be in the line-up, or when the line-up is simultaneous rather than sequential. The cognitive interview (based on the assumptions that memory traces are complex and can be accessed in various ways) leads eyewitnesses to produce many more accurate memories at the expense of a small increase in inaccurate memories.

- Prospective memory
  Prospective memory can be time-based or event-based. Event-based prospective memory is often better, because the intended actions are more likely to be triggered by external cues. The extent to which attentionally demanding processes are involved in a prospective memory task depends on its importance and complexity. There is evidence that these attentional processes may occur in the frontal lobes and related structures. Different brain areas seem to be associated with retrospective memory, suggesting that there are truly significant differences between prospective and retrospective memory. There is preliminary evidence in event-based prospective memory that there are successive processes of detecting the occurrence of a crucial stimulus and searching for the appropriate action.

FURTHER READING

- Ellis, J., & Kvavilashvili, L. (2000). Prospective memory in 2000: Past, present, and future directions. *Applied Cognitive Psychology*, *14*, S1–S9. This article (and the ones following it in the same special issue of the journal) provide a good overview of research on prospective memory.
- Healy, A.F. (2003). *Handbook of psychology: Experimental psychology, Vol. 4*. New York: Wiley & Sons. Episodic and autobiographical memory are compared in detail in a chapter by Roediger and Marsh.
- Special issue on autobiographical memory. *Memory*, 2003, *11*, 113–224. This issue of the journal *Memory* contains several articles by leading experts on key aspects of autobiographical memory.
- Wells, G.L., & Olson, E.A. (2003). Eyewitness testimony. *Annual Review of Psychology*, *54*, 277–295. This article provides a comprehensive account of the factors influencing eyewitness identification.

9

Concepts and Categories

INTRODUCTION

The South American writer Jorge-Luis Borges (1964, pp. 93–94) described a fictional man called Funes. He had perfect memory for every second of his life, and lacked the ability to categorise his experience:

> . . . Funes remembered not only every leaf of every tree of every wood, but also every one of the times he had perceived or imagined it . . . He was, let us not forget, almost incapable of ideas of a general, Platonic sort. Not only was it difficult for him to comprehend that the generic symbol *dog* embraces so many unlike individuals of diverse size and form; it bothered him that the dog at three fourteen (seen from the side) should have the same name as the dog at three fifteen (seen from the front). His own face in the mirror, his own hands, surprised him every time he saw them.

No actual human being is like Funes, because we have to organise our knowledge. Our memory systems clearly require a certain economy in the organisation of our experience. If we were like Funes, our minds would be cluttered with many irrelevant details. In fact, we abstract away from our experience to develop general concepts. **Cognitive economy** is achieved by dividing the world into classes of things to decrease the amount of information we need to learn, perceive, remember, and recognise (Collins & Quillian, 1969).

As the quotation from Borges suggests, concepts are of vital importance in our lives, and are centrally involved in perception, learning, memory, and our use of language. Why is that the case? The answer was provided by Murphy (2002, p. 1):

> Concepts are the mental glue that holds our mental world together . . . When we walk into a room, try a new restaurant, go to the supermarket to buy groceries, meet a doctor, or read a story, we must rely on our concepts of the world to help us understand what is happening . . . Fortunately, even novel things are usually similar to things we already know, often exemplifying a category that we are familiar with . . . Concepts are a kind of mental glue in that they tie our past experiences to our present interactions with the world, and because the concepts themselves are connected to our larger knowledge structures.

This chapter is concerned with concepts and categories, and so we need to consider how these terms should be defined. **Concepts** are mental representations of classes of objects or other entities, whereas **categories** are classes of objects embodied in concepts. However, two points need to be made here. First, as Murphy (2002, p. 5) pointed out, "In both everyday speech and the literature in this field, it is often hard to keep track of which of these one is talking about, because the two [i.e., concepts and categories] go together." Second, most research on concepts has involved objects of various kinds, and this is reflected in our coverage. However, there are other kinds of concepts (e.g., verbs), which are discussed fully by Medin, Lynch, and Solomon (2000).

Types of concepts

Many concepts are organised into hierarchies. Rosch, Mervis, Gray, Johnson, and Boyes-Braem (1976) identified three levels within such hierarchies, with superordinate categories at the top, basic-level categories in the middle, and subordinate categories at the bottom. For example, "furniture" is a superordinate category, "chair" is a basic-level category, and "easy chair" is a subordinate category. Rosch et al. asked people to list all the attributes of concepts at each level. Very few attributes were listed for the superordinate categories, presumably because the categories were rather abstract. Many attributes were listed for the categories at the other two levels, but at the lowest level very similar attributes were listed for different categories. The implication is that the basic-level categories are of most general usefulness, having the best balance between informativeness and distinctiveness. Informativeness is missing at the highest level of the hierarchy, and distinctiveness is missing at the lowest level.

Rosch et al. (1976) obtained reasonable evidence that we generally use basic-level categories rather than superordinate or subordinate ones. They asked participants to name pictures of objects. Basic-level names were used 1595 times in the course of experiment, with subordinate names being used 14 times, and superordinate names only once.

As we will see, most research has focused on basic-level categories. However, we might imagine that subordinate categories would be important for experts in a given domain. For example, we would expect a botanist to refer to the various different kinds of plants in a garden rather than simply describing them all as *plants*! Tanaka and Taylor (1991) studied the concepts of birdwatchers and dog experts shown pictures of birds and dogs. Their key finding was that both groups used subordinate names much more often in their expert domain than in their novice domain. More specifically, bird experts used subordinate names 74% of the time with birds, dog experts used subordinate names 40% of the time with dogs, and the two groups used subordinate names only 24% of the time in their novice domain. Why did bird experts use subordinate names more often than dog experts in their respective areas of expertise? According to Tanaka and Taylor, this probably happened because bird experts are generally interested in most bird species, whereas dog experts typically focus on one or two breeds of dogs.

There is a sense in which some concepts are more "natural" than others. A category that included pints-of-Guinness and birds-that-fly-on-one-wing does not seem likely or natural. Human concepts cohere in certain ways, making certain groupings of entities more likely to occur than other groupings. One problem is to specify the basis for this naturalness or cohesiveness.

Functions of concepts

We have seen that concepts are useful because they provide an efficient way of representing our knowledge of the world and the objects in it. Another function of concepts is that they permit us to make accurate *predictions*. For example, if we categorise an animal as a cat, we predict that it is unlikely to do us any harm. In contrast, if we categorise an animal as a lion, we predict that it may be dangerous and so take avoiding action. Heit (1992) examined how people make predictions from learned instances or from instances similar to learned instances. Participants memorised descriptions of 30 individuals belonging to two gangs (Jets and Sharks) who had three potential traits (e.g., Larry is a Jet and liberal; Harry is a Shark and married; Ben is a Jet and unathletic). The participants learned only one trait per person, and were told that each one had two other traits. They found it reasonably easy to make predictions. For example, if asked whether Larry was likely to be unathletic, participants would say "Yes" if other members of the Jets were known to be unathletic.

A further function of categorisation is *communication*. When we have conversations with other people, we are constantly using concepts to convey information about ourselves and the world as we understand it.

In sum, it is necessary for reasons of storage and effective use to organise and categorise experience. In human memory, this organisation seems to be guided by the principles of cognitive economy, informativeness, distinctiveness, and natural coherence. One of the marvels of human memory is that it balances these principles in the acquisition of conceptual knowledge so as to allow us to predict what is going to happen and to communicate effectively with other people.

There are several key issues relating to concepts and categories, some of which are discussed in this chapter. First, we focus on the issue of concept organisation. Various approaches to concept organisation have been proposed, and we consider three of the most influential ones. Second, we move on to the issue of concept learning, with an emphasis on the ways in which such learning is influenced by prior knowledge. Third, we consider the complex issue of concept meaning. More specifically, we discuss the extent to which the meaning of any given concept depends on factors such as its relation to other concepts or relevant perceptual and motor processes. As you may imagine, these issues are actually related to each other even though we treat them somewhat separately for ease of communication.

Before proceeding, we should point out that concepts and categories are discussed in Chapters 3 and 7 as well as in this chapter. The main emphasis in those chapters is on what are known as **category-specific deficits**, in which brain-damaged patients have much greater problems in recognising members of some categories (e.g., living things) than of other categories (e.g., non-living things). Research on category-specific deficits has shed light on the ways in which conceptual information is organised in the brain, and has suggested that it is important to distinguish between objects' visual attributes and their functional attributes (i.e., their uses or functions). However, there is still much theoretical controversy concerning the most appropriate way of interpreting the evidence.

ORGANISATION OF CONCEPTS

In this section, we consider in detail three major theoretical approaches to concept organisation. We start with the defining-attribute approach because it has clear historical priority. This classical view of concepts owes its origins to the great ancient Greek philosopher and scientist Aristotle. As we will see, that approach proved itself clearly inadequate to account for the organisation of concepts. As a result, the defining-attribute approach was gradually superseded in the second half of the twentieth century by the prototype and exemplar approaches. It is generally accepted that these approaches represent significant and substantial advances on the defining-attribute approach, but both nevertheless suffer from various limitations.

Defining-attribute approach

According to the defining-attribute approach, a concept can be characterised by a set of **defining attributes**, which are those semantic features necessary and sufficient for something to be an instance of the concept (see Panel 9.1). Thus, for example, the defining attributes of the concept "bachelor" might be as follows: male; single; and adult. According to this defining-attribute view, concepts should divide up individual objects in the world into distinct classes in such a way that the boundaries between categories are well defined and rigid.

How has the defining-attribute approach fared? The short answer is, "Terribly!" According to the defining-attribute approach, everything is clear cut: any given object is very clearly a member of a

Panel 9.1: Defining-attribute theories of concepts

- The meaning of a concept can be captured by a conjunctive list of attributes (i.e., a list of attributes connected by ANDs).
- These attributes are atomic units or primitives which are the basic building blocks of concepts.
- Each of these attributes is necessary and all of them are jointly sufficient for something to be identified as an instance of the concept.
- What is and is not a member of the category is clearly defined; thus, there are clear-cut boundaries between members and non-members of the category.
- All members of the concept are equally representative.
- When concepts are organised in a hierarchy then the defining attributes of a more specific concept (e.g., sparrow) in relation to its more general relative (its superordinate; e.g., bird) include all the defining attributes of the superordinate.

given category or very clearly not a member. In fact, as we will see, many (or even most) of our concepts are nothing like that—they are fuzzy rather than neat and tidy, and we are often in doubt whether a given object is or is not a member of a given category. For example, McCloskey and Glucksberg (1978) gave 30 participants tricky questions such as, "Is a stroke a disease?" and "Is a pumpkin a fruit?" They found that 16 said a stroke is a disease, but 14 said it was not, and a pumpkin was regarded as a fruit by 16 participants but not as a fruit by the remainder. More surprisingly, when McCloskey and Glucksberg tested the same participants a month later, 11 of them had changed their minds about "stroke" being a disease, and 8 had altered their opinion about "pumpkin" being a fruit! Below we consider a range of other evidence that is inconsistent with the defining-attribute approach.

Evidence

According to the defining-attribute approach, every instance of a category is an equally strong or representative member of that category. This is simply not the case. For example, we can construct a **typicality gradient** for any category, in which members of that category are ordered in terms of their typicality as category members. There is generally a high level of agreement among people as to which category members are more or less typical. For example, a "robin" is a much more typical member of the bird category than "canary", which in turn is more typical than "penguin".

Typicality has several effects on people's use of categories. Rips, Shoben, and Smith (1973) used a verification task in which participants decided whether basic-level concepts belonged to superordinate categories. For example, they were presented with statements such as "A robin is a bird", and "A penguin is a bird". The consistent finding was that performance was faster with typical category members than with atypical ones. In other research it has been found that concept learning is faster when it involves typical category members rather than atypical category members (Mervis & Pani, 1980, discussed more fully below).

In spite of what has been said so far, some categories do possess defining attributes. For example, the category of "even numbers" consists of all numbers divisible by two, and there is no doubt whether any given number belongs to the category. However, Armstrong, Gleitman, and Gleitman (1983) obtained consistent differences in the typicality ratings given to various even numbers. For example, 22 was rated as being more typical of the concept "even number" than 18, and was also categorised faster. These findings are especially devastating for the defining-attribute approach because they are based on one of the fairly small minority of categories having defining attributes.

Typicality is also important in explaining how it is that we are sometimes unsure whether certain instances belong or do not belong to a given category (e.g., McCloskey & Glucksberg, 1978, discussed above). Instances very high in typicality are regarded as category members by virtually everyone, and instances very low in typicality are generally regarded as non-members. Between those two extremes, there is a level of typicality that is in a kind of grey area, and there is some confusion about the category membership of instances falling into that area.

According to the defining-attribute view, concepts are static and unchanging. However, Barsalou (1987, 1989) pointed out that the way people represent a concept changes as a function of the context in which it appears. For example, when people read "frog" in isolation, "eaten by humans" typically remains inactive in memory. However, "eaten by humans" becomes active when reading about frogs in a French restaurant. Thus, concepts are unstable to the extent that different information is incorporated into the representation of a concept in different situations; what Barsalou (1982) called *context-dependent information*.

Instability has also been found when the exemplars of a category are ordered from most to least typical. For example, in the bird category, American participants order the following instances as decreasing in typicality from "robin" to "pigeon" to "parrot" to "ostrich". Instability shows itself in the rearrangement of this ordering as a function of the population, the individual, or context (see Barsalou, 1989). Even though Americans consider a "robin" more typical than a "swan", they treat a "swan" as being more typical than a "robin" when asked to adopt the viewpoint of the average Chinese citizen.

Finally, and also contrary to the defining-attribute approach, some categories (known as *ad hoc* categories) seem to be formed spontaneously in certain situations. For example, if you wanted to sell off your unwanted possessions you might construct a category of "things to sell at a garage sale".

Prototype approach

The prototype approach was proposed by several theorists as an alternative to the defining-attribute approach, with the seminal research of Rosch and Mervis (1975, discussed below) being of particular importance. According to the prototype approach, categories have a central description or **prototype**, that in some sense stands for the whole category. There are various prototype-based approaches. One possibility (generally regarded as inadequate) is that the prototype is captured by a specific instance of the category, namely, the best example of the concept. For example, if "robin" is the best example for the bird category, then it would be the prototype. Another object is a member of the bird category if it shares many attributes with the best example.

A more popular theoretical view is that the prototype is a set of characteristic attributes or summary representation in which some attributes are weighted more than others. In such theories, there are *no* defining attributes, but rather only characteristic ones. For example, Hampton (1979) assessed prototypes in a fairly direct way by asking people to indicate those attributes typical of a category. For example, the characteristic attributes of "fruit" might include contains seeds, grows above ground, is edible, is sweet, and is round.

An object is a member of the concept if there is a good match between its attributes and those of the prototype. Within this approach, category members share **family resemblances**, meaning they have some features in common with other category members. We can illustrate this with reference to the concept of "games" by using a rather hackneyed quotation from Wittgenstein (1958, pp. 31–32):

> Consider for example the proceedings that we call "games". I mean board-games, card-games, ball-games, Olympic games, and so on . . . if you look at them you will not see something that is common to *all*, but similarities, relationships, and a whole series of them at that . . . Look for example at board-games, with their multifarious relationships. Now pass to card-games; here you will find many correspondences with the first group, but many common features drop out, and others appear. When we pass next to ball-games, much that is common is retained, but much is lost . . . Is there always winning and losing, or competition among players? Think of patience. In ball-games

Panel 9.2: Prototype theory of concepts

- Concepts have a prototype structure; the prototype is either a collection of characteristic attributes or the best example (or examples) of the concept.
- There is no delimiting set of necessary and sufficient attributes for determining category membership; there may be necessary attributes, but they are not jointly sufficient; indeed membership often depends on the object possessing some set of characteristic, non-necessary attributes that are considered more typical or representative of the category than others.
- Category boundaries are fuzzy or unclear; what is and is not a member of the category is ill-defined; so some members of the category may slip into other categories (e.g., tomatoes as fruit or vegetables).
- Instances of a concept can be ranged in terms of their typicality; that is, there is a typicality gradient which characterises the differential typicality of examples of the concept.
- Category membership is determined by the similarity of an object's attributes to the category's prototype.

there is winning and losing; but when a child throws his ball at the wall and catches it again, this feature has disappeared.

Why are family resemblances important? According to prototype theory, category members having the highest family resemblance scores come closer than other category members to representing the category's prototype. Accordingly, category members with high family resemblance scores are "better" or more typical category members than those having low family resemblance scores.

In sum, most prototype theories (in spite of differences among them) are based on similar sets of ideas. Some of the main assumptions within prototype theories are shown in Panel 9.2).

Evidence for the prototype approach

Reasonably direct evidence of the importance of family resemblances within categories was obtained by Rosch and Mervis (1975). They made use of six categories, with 20 members varying in their typicality representing each category (see Table 9.1). The participants' task was to list the

Table 9.1

Typicality of items belonging to six categories. From Rosch and Mervis (1975). Reproduced with permission from Elsevier.

Typicality	*Furniture*	*Fruit*	*Vehicle*	*Weapons*	*Clothing*	*Vegetables*
1	Chair	Orange	Car	Gun	Pants	Peas
2	Sofa	Apple	Truck	Knife	Shirt	Carrots
3	Table	Banana	Bus	Sword	Dress	String beans
4	Dresser	Peach	Motorcycle	Bomb	Skirt	Spinach
5	Desk	Pear	Train	Hand grenade	Jacket	Broccoli
6	Bed	Apricot	Trolley	Spear	Coat	Asparagus
7	Bookcase	Plum	Bicycle	Cannon	Sweater	Corn
8	Footstool	Grape	Aeroplane	Bow & arrow	Underpants	Cauliflower
9	Lamp	Strawberry	Boat	Club	Socks	Brussels sprouts
10	Piano	Grapefruit	Tractor	Tank	Pyjamas	Lettuce
11	Cushion	Pineapple	Cart	Tear gas	Bathing suit	Beets
12	Mirror	Blueberry	Wheelchair	Whip	Shoes	Tomato
13	Rug	Lemon	Tank	Ice pick	Vest	Lima beans
14	Radio	Watermelon	Raft	Fists	Tie	Eggplant
15	Stove	Honeydew	Sled	Rocket	Mittens	Onion
16	Clock	Pomegranate	Horse	Poison	Hat	Potato
17	Picture	Date	Blimp	Scissors	Apron	Yam
18	Closet	Coconut	Skates	Words	Purse	Mushroom
19	Vase	Tomato	Wheelbarrow	Foot	Wristwatch	Pumpkin
20	Telephone	Olive	Elevator	Screwdriver	Necklace	Rice

attributes of the category members. Most of the attributes of any given category member were shared by some other members of the same category, and this information was used to calculate family resemblance scores for each member. For example, if a category member had two attributes, one possessed by 16 category members and the other possessed by 14 category members, this would give a family resemblance score of 16 + 14 = 30.

What did Rosch and Mervis (1975) discover? Their key finding was that typical category members had much higher family resemblance scores than atypical category members. The correlation between typicality and family resemblance ranged between +.84 (for vegetables) and +.94 (for weapons). Rosch and Mervis also considered the numbers of attributes shared by the five most typical and the five least typical members of each category. We will discuss the findings from the vehicle category, but similar results were obtained with all of the categories. The five most typical members of the vehicle category had 36 attributes in common, whereas the five least typical members had only two attributes in common.

Further support for prototype theory comes from studies showing that concepts are learned better when people are initially exposed only to typical instances than when they are exposed only to atypical ones. For example, that finding was obtained by Mervis & Pani (1980) in a study in which children were initially presented with a typical or an atypical exemplar of a novel category. They made more errors in subsequent testing with other category members when they had previously seen the atypical exemplar than when they had seen the typical exemplar (7.5 vs. 1.9 errors, respectively). Such findings certainly make sense intuitively. For example, it is hard to imagine that anyone would try to teach a young child the concept of "bird" by exposing him/her only to ostriches and penguins!

Evidence against the prototype approach

Hampton (1981) argued that not all concepts have prototypic characteristics. He found that some abstract concepts (e.g., "a science"; "a crime"; "a work of art") exhibit a prototypic structure, but others (e.g., "a rule"; "a belief"; "an instinct") do not. Why do some abstract concepts seem to lack prototypes? Membership of some abstract categories seems to be almost endlessly flexible in a way that is not true of concrete categories. For example, it is not remotely possible to specify the complete set of possible rules or beliefs. This marked lack of constraint on the membership of many abstract categories may be partially responsible for their apparent absence of structure.

People seem to know about the *relations* between attributes rather than just about the attributes alone as suggested by prototype theory. Such relational information can be used in categorisation (Malt & Smith, 1983). Consider the following case (see also Holland et al., 1986). Imagine going to a strange, Galapagos-like island for the first time, accompanied by a guide. On the journey, you see a beautiful blue bird fly out of a thicket, and the guide tells you it is a "warrum". Later in the day, you meet a portly individual, and are told he is a member of the "klaatu" tribe. The next day you see another blue bird like the first, and you think it is another warrum. However, if you meet another fat native, you probably would not assume he was a member of the klaatu tribe. Why is this? We know that colour is a particularly diagnostic and invariant attribute of species of birds, but physical weight is *not* a particularly diagnostic attribute of tribal affiliations and is known to be a very variable attribute. Thus, we know some attributes vary more than others. The fact that people can make reasonable guesses about the meaning of new terms on the basis of a single exposure to an instance is an important ability ignored by prototype theory.

What makes us group certain objects together in one category rather than another? The traditional answer given by prototype theorists is that *similarity* is responsible for category cohesion. Stated simply, things form themselves into categories because they all have certain attributes in common. However, similarity cannot be the only mechanism involved: we often form categories only tenuously based on shared attributes, but which are nevertheless coherent. We saw earlier that people can create categories on the spot (so-called *ad hoc* categories). From the perspective of prototype theory, it is hard to see how such categories cohere, given the lack of overlap between the attributes of category members (e.g., things-to-sell-in-a-garage-sale). Murphy and Medin (1985) pointed to the biblical categories of clean and unclean animals: clean animals include most fish, grasshoppers, and some locusts, whereas unclean animals include camels, ostriches, crocodiles, mice, sharks, and eels.

Finally, we saw earlier that Rosch and Mervis (1975) found that family resemblance scores were very highly correlated with typicality scores, suggesting that family resemblance is important in the way suggested within prototype theories. However, Barsalou (1985) found that family resemblance scores are of little value with **goal-derived categories**, in which the members all satisfy a given goal (e.g., birthday presents that make the recipient happy). More specifically, family resemblance scores did not predict typicality scores for members of goal-derived categories (see Figure 9.1). What is going on here? In essence, typical members of goal-derived categories are those best satisfying the goal (e.g., providing pleasure to someone celebrating his/her birthday) rather than sharing attributes with other category members (Barsalou, 1991).

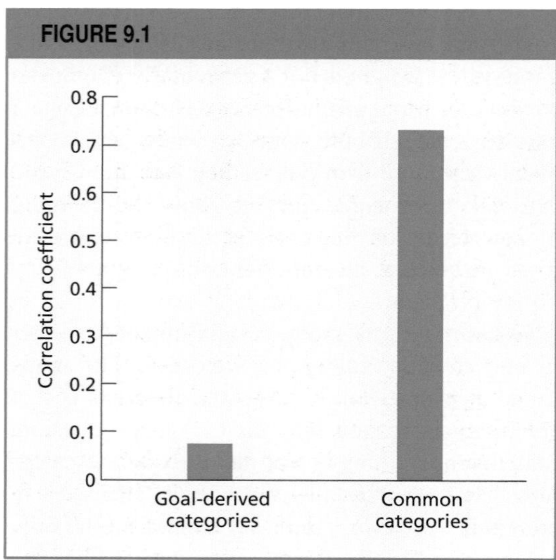

Partial correlations (removing statistically the effects of other factors) between family resemblance and typicality for two types of categories (common vs. goal-derived). Data from Barsalou (1985).

Evaluation

The prototype approach has several successes to its credit. Of particular importance, it provides a convincing account of the typicality ratings found with the members of many categories. More generally, it seems probable that summary descriptions or prototypes of most concepts are stored in long-term memory.

There are various limitations with the prototype approach. First, there is a often a lack of clarity about the precise definition of "prototype". As Murphy (2002, p. 45) pointed out, "Many statements about prototypes in the literature are somewhat vague, making it unclear exactly what the writer is referring to—a single best example? a feature list? if a feature list, determined how?"

Second, prototype approaches are more applicable to some kinds of concepts than to others. For example, some abstract concepts do not seem to have prototypes (Hampton, 1981), and family resemblances fail to predict typicality ratings for the members of goal-derived categories (Barsalou, 1985).

Third, there is compelling evidence that prior knowledge has various effects on our learning of concepts (Malt & Smith, 1983). At the very least, prototype theories would need to be developed further in order to provide an account of such knowledge effects. These issues are discussed further in the "Concept learning" section below.

Exemplar approach

Prototype theory provides a superior alternative to the failures of the classical theory. However, it has been fiercely challenged by the exemplar approach. According to this approach, we simply make use of particular instances of exemplars of a category that come to mind in a given situation (see Panel 9.3). Theorists proposing exemplar theories include Nosofsky (1991) and Kruschke (1992).

Exemplar-based theories paint a very different picture of categories from the prototype approach. Instead of there being some abstracted description

Panel 9.3: The exemplar-based view of concepts

- Categories are made up of a collection of instances or exemplars rather than any abstract description of these instances (e.g., a prototype summary description).
- Instances are grouped relative to one another by some similarity metric.
- Categorisation and other phenomena are explained by a mechanism that retrieves instances from memory given a particular cue.
- When exact matches are not found in memory the nearest neighbour to the cue is usually retrieved.

of a bird acting as a central prototype, the picture is one of a memory system storing large numbers of specific instances. Thus, instead of having a prototype for "bird" that is a list of all the characteristic features abstracted away from members of this category (e.g., *has-wings*; *flies*; etc.), we just have a store of all the instances of birds encountered in the past (e.g., the robin you see every morning). As we will see, many effects attributed to prototypes can be dealt with by this kind of account depending on which instance(s) come to mind in a specific context.

Evidence for the exemplar approach

Much evidence apparently specifically supporting prototype theories can also be explained by exemplar theories. For example, consider the effects of faster categorisation judgements for some members of a category than for others. When asked "Is a robin a bird?", you can answer "Yes" much faster than when asked "Is a penguin a bird?" Given that you have encountered many robins in the past, there are likely to be many more stored instances of robins than penguins. Therefore, a robin instance will be retrieved from memory much faster than a penguin instance, thus giving rise to the difference in judgement times. In similar fashion, typicality ratings are said to reflect the underlying pattern of instances in the category: a robin is a more typical instance of a bird than a penguin, because there are many more stored instances of robins than penguins. Typicality gradients can be accounted for in similar ways.

The exemplar-based account is more consistent than prototype theories with research on prediction and conceptual instability. Recall that the research on prediction was really all about comparing one classified target instance with other instances of the category to make appropriate predictions about features of that target instance (e.g., Heit, 1992). Similarly, effects like those involving changes in perspective and *ad hoc* categories are easier to explain in the context of a theory where one has instances that can be re-grouped in different ways to meet the demands of a specific situation. Thus, the flexibility of exemplar theories often gives them an advantage over prototype theories.

There is further evidence supporting exemplar theories over prototype ones. The exemplar view preserves the *variability* of instances in the category, whereas a prototype is a type of average over the instances of the category usually excluding this variability information. Rips and Collins (1993) showed that this variability information can influence classification. Their research involved the categories pizzas and rulers. Most pizzas in the United States are 12 inches across but can vary between about 2 and 30 inches. Most rulers are also 12 inches in size and vary in size much less than pizzas. Participants were asked to decide whether a new object 19 inches in size was a pizza or a ruler. If they had prototypes, then there should have been a 50–50 split between pizza and ruler, because the prototype average is 12 inches for each. However, if information about size variability was used (as predicted by exemplar-based theories), then participants should mostly have said the object was a pizza. The findings supported the exemplar approach over the prototype approach.

Storms, De Boeck, and Ruts (2000) compared the exemplar-based approach with the prototype approach for common categories such as "furniture", "fruit", and "birds". They assessed prototypes by using Hampton's (1979) data based on asking participants to list the characteristic attributes of these categories. They obtained exemplar measures by asking people to rate the similarity of a given category member to the 25 most frequently generated members of that category. This allowed them to identify the 10 most typical exemplars. The two theoretical approaches were then compared directly on the following four tasks:

(1) Category naming: Participants were given exemplars and had to name the category.
(2) Exemplar generation: Participants were given the category name and had to name exemplars.
(3) Typicality ratings: Participants rated the typicality of various exemplars of each category.
(4) Speeded categorisation: Participants were shown a category name followed by various words. They had to decide as rapidly as possible whether each word was or was not a member of the category.

What did Storms et al. (2000) find? As can be seen in Figure 9.2, performance on all four tasks was predicted reasonably well by the prototype and exemplar approaches. However, the predictions of the exemplar-based approach were consistently more accurate than those of the prototype approach, and that was especially the case on the exemplar-generation task. It remains to be seen whether the same findings would be obtained with different concepts and different tasks.

Evidence against the exemplar approach

The exemplar approach finds it hard to explain various effects. First, like the prototype approach, the exemplar approach depends on similarity. Thus, the difficulties that arise in the treatment of similarity in prototype theory also tend to be present in exemplar theories. For example, it would be difficult to provide an adequate exemplar-based account of *ad hoc* and goal-derived categories, since the members of such categories are generally not very similar at all.

Second, exemplar theories do not cope easily with class inclusion questions. For example, when people answer questions about the truth of a statement like "All birds are creatures", they seem to rely on general knowledge rather than specific examples. As Murphy (2002, p. 485) pointed out, "A major problem is the difficulty in coming up with any exemplar account of hierarchical structure. The fact that people know that all dogs are . . . mammals . . . is surprisingly difficult to represent in terms of exemplars."

Third, there is increasing evidence that the exemplar approach works less well with simple concepts than with complex ones. For example, Smith and Minda (2000) considered data from several studies, and obtained less support for exemplar

FIGURE 9.2

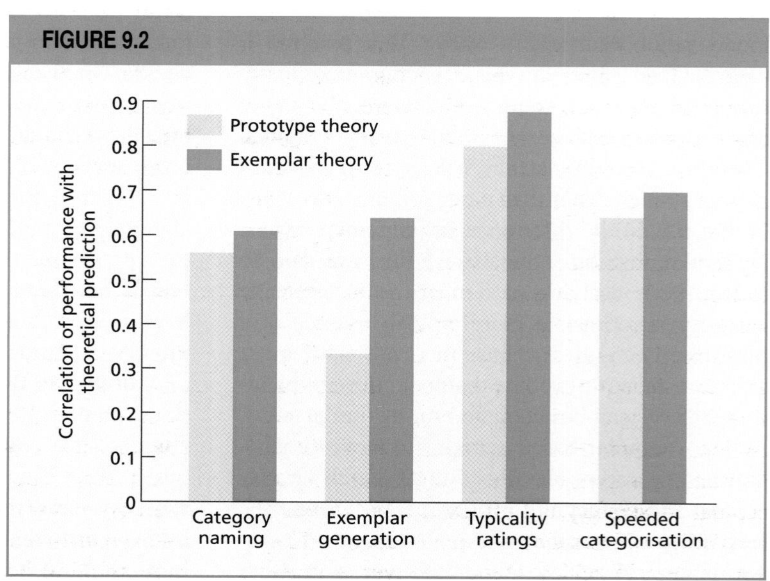

Correlations between performance on various tasks and theoretical predictions of prototype and exemplar theories. Based on data in Storms et al. (2000).

theories when relatively simple concepts were learned than when complex ones were learned. These findings suggest that there are important differences between the learning of simple and complex concepts. What are the key differences? According to Feldman (2003), simple concepts are learned by extracting their common regularities (e.g., all even numbers are divisible by 2). In contrast, it is not possible to learn more complex concepts in that way (because they lack common regularities), and so we rely on exemplars. Feldman found that exemplar theories greatly underestimated how much easier people find it to learn simple concepts than simple ones, precisely because they fail to appreciate the key role of common regularities or generalisations in the acquisition of simple concepts.

Evaluation

According to Murphy (2002, p. 114), "Exemplar models have the edge in the current battle of category-learning experiments—certainly if one just counts up the number of experiments in which exemplar models outperform prototype models." Of particular importance here is the study by Storms et al. (2000), in which it was found that the exemplar approach predicted performance better than the prototype approach on each of four tasks. However, the "victory" of the exemplar-based approach may be less decisive than it sounds. The reason for saying that is because the exemplar approach is generally more successful when applied to the learning of very complex concepts than to the learning of simpler concepts (e.g., Feldman, 2003; Smith & Minda, 2000). As Feldman (2003, p. 231) pointed out, "Many of the highly complex four-dimensional concepts studied in the 1970s and 1980s unintentionally tilted the scales in the direction of exemplar models."

Exemplar theories are potentially able to account for many of the findings in the literature. These include the effects of typicality on categorisation time, our ability to use concept knowledge to make predictions, the phenomenon of conceptual instability, and effects attributable to the variability of instances within a category. This is a considerable achievement. However, it must be borne in mind that we generally lack detailed accounts of what an exemplar-based account would look like.

It is fairly easy to see the limitations with exemplar theories. Simply ask yourself the question "Is all my knowledge of any given concept provided by the dozens or hundreds of examples of that concept and related concepts stored in long-term memory?" Hopefully, you agree that the answer must be "No!" As Murphy (2002, p. 490) pointed out, "One major problem with the [exemplar] approach is that it has been far too narrow, focusing on a small number of paradigms and not attempting to address the other conceptual phenomena that the prototype and knowledge views do." For example, it is not clear how exemplar-based accounts could explain how we work out that cats are mammals or how concept learning is influenced by prior knowledge (see below).

Is it the case that every instance of a category is stored in memory? If the answer is "Yes", then we have a huge amount of stored information about many categories, and it would seem that it would be very difficult to access most of that information. If the answer is "No", then we need a theoretical understanding of the factors determining which instances are stored in memory and which ones are not. At present, no exemplar-based account provides a convincing explanation of how we prevent information (and storage) overload.

There is a final limitation of exemplar theories. As is discussed in the next section, concept learning is typically influenced by prior knowledge. However, the role of prior knowledge is generally ignored within exemplar theories.

CONCEPT LEARNING

So far we have focused on the organisation of concepts in long-term memory. In order to understand more fully why concepts are organised as they are, it is important to consider the processes involved in concept learning. Indeed, many of the attempts to test the exemplar and prototype theories have involved studies in which the participants were asked to learn various artificial concepts.

There are several important issues related to concept learning, two of which will be discussed here. First, there is the issue of whether there is a single concept-learning mechanism or whether there are several. Second, there is the issue of the role played by prior knowledge in concept learning.

A single concept-learning mechanism?

In the great majority of laboratory experiments on concept learning (including those designed to test the exemplar and prototype theories), participants are given a classification task. They are shown numerous instances or items in sequence, and have to decide to which category (out of a small number) each instance belongs. The participants are generally provided with feedback on the accuracy of their decisions, as a result of which they gradually learn the concepts in question. Such experiments are generally based on the hidden assumptions that there is a *single* concept-learning mechanism, and that this mechanism is revealed in all its glory on the classification task.

Potential problems with the above assumptions were raised by Markham and Ross (2003). First, people performing a classification are given the *explicit* goal of learning to classify members of the various categories. In contrast, most concept learning in everyday life occurs as a by-product of our interactions with objects in the world. Second, and more importantly, when we perform a task we generally only learn what is needed to complete the task successfully. The knowledge we acquire when learning concepts in everyday life may differ from the knowledge acquired on most classification tasks, and is likely to be broader.

Chin-Parker and Ross (2004) reported findings relevant to some of the issues discussed above. Participants were shown drawings of bugs (see Figure 9.3). They learned about two categories of bugs by performing one of two tasks: (1) classification task: each of a series of bugs had to be assigned to the appropriate category; (2) inference task: bugs lacking a feature (e.g., tail) were presented and participants had to decide which of two features (e.g., two different-shaped tails) was correct. After the participants demonstrated good task learning, they were asked to draw each type of bug.

What would we expect to find? Chin-Parker and Ross (2004) argued that people performing the classification task focus on diagnostic features, i.e., those differing *between* the two categories, and pay little attention to non-diagnostic features. In contrast, those performing the inference task focus mainly on the relationship among features *within* each category. The drawings of bugs produced by the participants were in line with prediction. As can be seen in Figure 9.4, those who had performed the classification task were much less likely than those performing the inference task to include the non-diagnostic features in their drawings.

In sum, what is learned when performing a concept-learning task depends very much on the precise task requirements. In principle, participants given either task could have acquired full knowledge of the diagnostic and non-diagnostic features of each category of bug, but this did not happen. Of greatest importance, people given a typical classification task show *narrow* concept learning based mainly on diagnostic features allowing them to distinguish between categories.

FIGURE 9.3

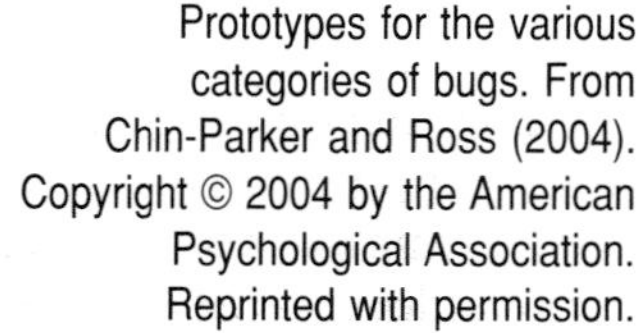
Prototypes for the various categories of bugs. From Chin-Parker and Ross (2004). Copyright © 2004 by the American Psychological Association. Reprinted with permission.

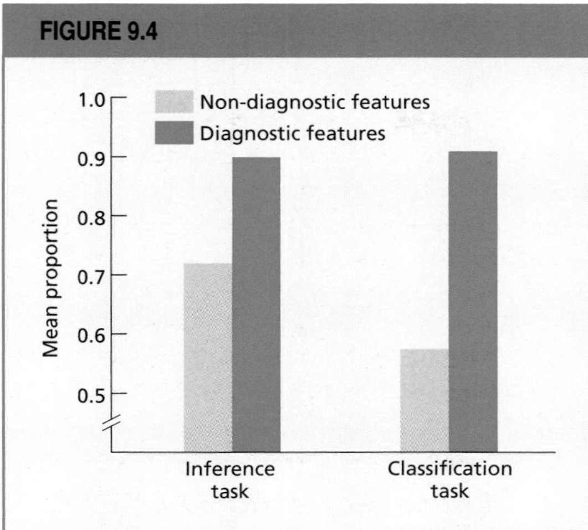

Mean proportion of diagnostic and non-diagnostic features produced in drawings following an inference or classification task. Based on data in Chin-Parker and Ross (2004).

Concrete vs. abstract processes

The processes used in a concept-learning task depend on the stage of learning and the type of concept being learned as well as on details of the task itself. For example, it could be argued that somewhat different processes are involved depending on whether we are engaged in exemplar processing or prototype processing. Speculatively, exemplar processing may be relatively concrete and specific, whereas prototype processing is more abstract. We turn now to some research of relevance to these issues.

Seger et al. (2000a) claimed that the right hemisphere is specialised for processing specific stimuli, whereas the left hemisphere is specialised for processing more abstract patterns. They tested these ideas in an fMRI study in which participants learned to classify stimuli resembling abstract paintings belonging to two categories ("Jones's" and "Smith's" art). As predicted, there was only right-hemisphere activation in the early part of learning. After that, there was increasing left-hemisphere activation, but only for those participants who succeeded at the task. Thus, left-hemisphere involvement increased as concept learning became more abstract.

Findings that may relate to those of Seger et al. (2000a) were reported by Laeng, Zarrinpar, and Kosslyn (2003). Pictures of animals, objects, and faces of famous people were presented to only one hemisphere. Immediately after each picture was presented, a category name was read out loud, and the participants' task was to decide as rapidly as possible whether the name fitted the picture. The category name was either at the basic level (e.g., "birds") or the subordinate level (e.g., falcon; parrot; robin).

What did Laeng et al. (2003) find? Performance was faster at the subordinate category level when the pictures were presented to the right hemisphere, but it was faster at the basic level when they were presented to the left hemisphere. Thus, there were processing differences between the subordinate and basic-level categories. More specifically, it appeared that specific and detailed processing at the subordinate level occurs more efficiently in the right hemisphere, whereas the more general and abstract processing at the basic level occurs more efficiently in the left hemisphere.

In sum, the research discussed in this section suggests that concept processing can be specific and concrete or general and abstract. It is tempting to assume (but we need more research) that exemplar processing is specific and concrete whereas prototype processing is general and abstract. If so, the implication would be that the right hemisphere is more involved in exemplar processing whereas the left hemisphere is more involved in prototype processing.

Knowledge-based views

Exemplar and prototype theories have been fairly successful in accounting for several effects observed in studies on concepts. However, all such theories are limited. Many of the difficulties they encounter stem from the fact that they do not take account of knowledge effects, which are "influences of prior knowledge of real objects and events that people bring to the category-learning situation" (Murphy, 2002, p. 146). The key point was made very clearly by Murphy (2002, p. 183): "Neither prototype nor exemplar models have attempted to account for knowledge effects . . . The problem is that these models start from a kind of *tabula rasa* [blank slate] representation, and concept representations are built up solely by experience with exemplars."

Why were knowledge effects largely ignored for so long? One reason is that many experimenters used materials (e.g., patterns of dots) deliberately selected to be far removed from participants' knowledge. This was done to prevent performance on concept-learning tasks from reflecting prior knowledge as well as learning occurring in the experimental situation. However, the gain in experimental control associated with the use of essentially meaningless stimuli was probably more than outweighed by the cost in terms of reduced relevance to concept learning in everyday life.

In what follows, we will first consider evidence that knowledge effects are involved in concept learning. After that, we will discuss various attempts to provide knowledge-based or explanation-based accounts of concept learning.

Evidence

One of the ways in which knowledge affects concept learning is by influencing the categorical features that are learned. For example, Palmeri and Blalock (2000) presented adult participants with children's drawings of people. Half the participants learned the two categories of drawings as Group 1 and Group 2, whereas the other half learned them as drawings by creative and uncreative children. All participants were then tested on new pictures matching the original ones in concrete features (e.g., curly hair) or abstract features (e.g., detailed). Those using neutral categories emphasised the concrete features of the drawings, whereas those using creativity categories learned more abstract features. These results presumably reflect people's belief that creativity reveals itself in abstract features rather than mundane concrete ones.

Knowledge can also influence the decisions about categorisation made after concept learning has taken place. Lin and Murphy (1997) gave participants the task of learning about objects used in a foreign country, with different participants being taught different things about each object. For example, consider the "tuk" shown in Figure 9.5.

FIGURE 9.5

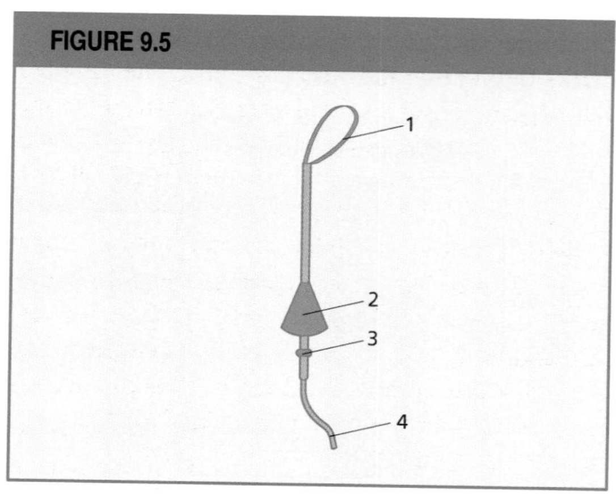

A "tuk". The numbers are used to describe its parts (see text). From Lin and Murphy (1997). Copyright © 1997 by the American Psychological Association.

One group was told that the tuk is used for hunting: the hunter slips the noose (1) over the animal's head, and pulls on the end of the rope (4), while holding the handle (3) with one hand, and having a hand guard (2) to provide protection from the animal. A second group was told that the tuk was a fertilising tool: liquid fertiliser is held in the tank (2); the knob (3) is turned to allow it to flow through the outlet pipe (4); and there is a loop (1) which is used to hand the tuk up.

After the participants had learned various concepts, Lin and Murphy (1997) created objects lacking one or more of the parts in the original objects. For example, participants might be presented with a tuk lacking the loop at the top. Those who had learned that a tuk was a hunting tool were much less likely than those who had learned it was a fertilising tool to classify this altered object as a tuk. Thus, knowledge of which parts of an object are of crucial importance influences concept learning and subsequent categorisation.

Explanation-based theories

Murphy and Medin (1985) made an influential contribution to our understanding of how knowledge can influence concept learning. As mentioned earlier, they pointed out that a distinction is drawn in the Bible between clean and unclean animals, with gazelles, grasshoppers, and frogs falling into the former category and ostriches, crocodiles, and sharks falling into the latter category. They argued that what determined the distinction was a theory or explanatory framework. The concept of clean and unclean animals rests on a theory of how the features of habitat, biological structure, and form of locomotion are correlated in various animals. Roughly speaking, creatures of the water should have fins, scales, and swim, and creatures of the land should have four legs. Creatures conforming with this theory are considered clean, whereas those not equipped for the right kind of locomotion are unclean.

Murphy and Medin's notion of a theory refers to a wide range of mental "explanations". As a consequence, it is a very general framework rather than a complete scientific account. For example, Murphy and Medin (1985, p. 290) argued that, "Causal knowledge certainly embodies a theory of certain phenomena; scripts may contain an implicit theory of entailment between mundane events; knowledge of rules embodies a theory of the relations between rule constituents; book-learning scientific knowledge certainly contains theories."

FIGURE 9.6

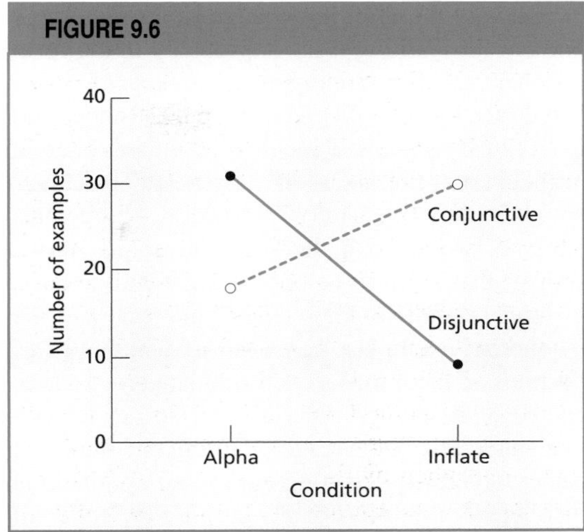

The ease of learning (measured by number of examples taken to learn a concept) either a conjunctive or disjunctive concept as a function of the instructions given (to classify as alpha, or predict inflation). The disjunctive concept is consistent with the background knowledge on the ease of inflating balloons, whereas the conjunctive concept violates this knowledge. From Pazzani (1991, Experiment 1). Copyright © 1991 by the American Psychological Association.

Evidence

One of the earliest findings in concept formation was that conjunctive concepts are generally easier to learn than disjunctive ones (Bruner, Goodnow, & Austin, 1956). Thus, for example, it is easier for people to learn a concept called DRAF consisting of the conjoined features "black *and* round *and* furry" than consisting of the disjunctive features "black *or* round *or* furry". Pazzani (1991) demonstrated a reversal of this phenomenon when the disjunctive concept was consistent with background knowledge. Groups of participants were shown pictures of people (adults or children) carrying out actions (stretching or dipping in water) on balloons of different colours and sizes. One set of instructions required participants to determine whether a given stimulus situation (e.g., a child dipping a large yellow balloon in water) was an *alpha* situation. Another set of instructions required participants to predict whether the balloon would *inflate* after the stimulus event. Groups receiving either of these instructions had to learn either a conjunctive concept (consisting of the features size-small AND balloon-yellow) or a disjunctive concept (age-adult OR action-stretching-balloon). Pazzani established that most people know that stretching a balloon makes it easier to inflate and that adults can inflate balloons more easily than children (but note that this knowledge does not correspond directly to the disjunctive definition participants had to learn).

What did Pazzani (1991) find? First, the alpha groups learned the conjunctive concept faster than the disjunctive concept (see Figure 9.6). As in previous research, this result occurred because the background knowledge about inflating balloons was irrelevant to learning the alpha categorisation. Second, the inflate groups learned the disjunctive concept faster than the conjunctive one. This was due to the fact that participants' background knowledge facilitated the formation of the disjunctive concept, but did *not* support the learning of the conjunctive-inflate concept.

Much of the prior knowledge we bring to bear on concept-learning tasks is probably in the form of schemas, which are organised packets of knowledge (see Chapter 11). For example, Rehder and Ross (2001) presented people with either coherent or incoherent exemplars of a category. The coherent exemplars consisted of features (e.g., operates on land; works to gather harmful solids; has a shovel) that seem to belong together on the basis of our schematic knowledge. In contrast, the incoherent exemplars consisted of features (e.g., operates on land; works to absorb dangerous gases; coated with spongy material) that do not fit with our schematic knowledge. Participants found it easier to classify the coherent exemplars than the incoherent ones, presumably because the coherent exemplars were consistent with their pre-existing schemas.

Ahn, Kim, Lassaline, and Dennis (2000) tested Murphy and Medin's (1985) hypothesis that people use features providing causal explanations when learning concepts. Participants were told that members of a category tend to have three features (e.g., blurred vision; headaches; insomnia). They were also told that blurred vision causes headaches and that headaches cause insomnia. After that, participants indicated the likelihood that an item belonged to the category if one of the features was absent. The rated likelihood of membership was lowest when the initial cause (i.e., blurred vision) was absent, and highest when the terminal effect (i.e., insomnia) was missing. Thus, people believe that if the cause is missing, then it is unlikely that an item is a member of the category.

How much causal knowledge about concepts do we actually possess? Keil (2003) argued that we have much less causal knowledge than we think we do; he termed this the "illusion of explanatory depth". Supporting evidence was reported by Rozenblit and Keil (2002). They initially presented participants with a list of phenomena and devices (e.g., helicopter), and asked them to rate their overall understanding of how each phenomenon or device works. Later on, they saw an expert's description of each phenomenon and device, after which they re-rated their initial level of understanding. The illusion of explanatory depth was shown by the dramatic decrease in participants' ratings of their own knowledge after seeing expert descriptions. Indeed, many participants expressed astonishment at how little they knew compared to what they thought they knew.

In spite of our deficient causal knowledge, we nevertheless have an approximate understanding of which features of an object are likely to be important. Keil (2003) carried out an experiment in which participants were presented with descriptions of an object allegedly provided by two people, and had to decide which one was the expert. For example, suppose person A says the most important properties of "phlebots" are that they are mostly black, have diagonal stripes, and have 23 parts, whereas person B says the most important properties are that they are about the size of a shoe, are crescent-shaped, and are fragile. When phlebots were said to be surgical instruments, most participants said that person B was the expert. However, when phlebots were said to be a kind of mammal, there was much less agreement on the identity of the expert. These findings indicate that we are aware that concepts differ in terms of their most important properties.

Does it matter that our causal understanding of concepts is rather limited? According to Keil (2003, p. 688), the answer is essentially "No": "The coarse level of encoding [of concepts] is powerful enough to narrow down the complexity of what one must track, but also shallow enough to allow quick and efficient processing . . . we extract the causal 'gist' to ascertain enough detail within a particular domain so that we can detect the most salient features without being overwhelmed."

Evaluation

There is compelling evidence that most (or all) aspects of concept learning are subject to knowledge effects. Progress has been made in identifying some of the kinds of knowledge that influence concept learning; these include causal knowledge and knowledge in the form of schemas. Any adequate account of everyday concept learning would have to take full account of the numerous ways in which it is affected by prior knowledge.

There are various limitations with knowledge-based and explanation-based accounts of concept learning. First, we lack a comprehensive theory applicable to all (or even most) knowledge effects. Second, we do not know in detail the factors determining the extent to which relevant prior knowledge will be used on a concept-learning task. Third, we do not have a knowledge-based theory specifying clearly the processes involved in producing knowledge effects. For example, how do we combine our schematic knowledge with the information available from presented exemplars to produce concept learning?

CONCEPT MEANING

One of the key issues in research on concepts is the following: What gives our concepts their meaning? As Goldstone and Rogosky (2002) pointed out, we can identify two main answers to the question. First, the meaning of concepts may depend on their connections to each other within semantic memory. According to this view, a concept has little or no meaning in isolation, but instead derives its meaning from forming part of a network of interconnected concepts. Goldstone and Rogosky termed this the "conceptual web" account. Second, the meaning of any given concept may depend crucially on perceptual processes, and on the connections between the concept and the external world. Some theorists (e.g., Barsalou, 2003) have gone further, and argued that there is a very close relationship between concepts and sensory-motor processes.

Both of the approaches described above may be partially correct. As Goldstone and Rogosky (2002, p. 317) argued, "To claim that all concepts in a system depend on all of the other concepts in a system is perfectly compatible with claiming that all of these concepts have a perceptual basis. These two bases of meaning are mutually reinforcing, not mutually exclusive."

Conceptual web approach

Landauer and Dumais (1997) put forward a theory based on the notion that the meaning of a concept depends on its connections to other concepts. In crude terms, what you are is determined by the company you keep. In the course of our lives, certain words often occur together (e.g., "bread" and "butter"; "politician" and "liar"), whereas other words practically never co-occur. For any given word, we can work out its pattern of co-occurrence with all other words. Landauer and Dumais's key assumption was that words with similar patterns of co-occurrence have similar meanings. This assumption was incorporated into a theory called "latent semantic analysis". At about the same time, Lund and Burgess (1996) put forward a related approach known as "hyperspace analogue to language". However, our coverage will focus mainly on latent semantic analysis.

Evidence

In order to test their approach, Landauer and Dumais (1997) input the contents of a student encyclopaedia into a computer. The encyclopaedia contained 4.6 million words, representing 60,768 different words. The computer worked out how often each word co-occurred with every other word within the same article. After that, the computer reduced the huge 60,768 × 60,768 matrix of co-occurrences to a total of 300 dimensions representing the association information from the entire encyclopaedia. This information was then used to decide the similarity of any two words across the 300 dimensions.

Landauer and Dumais (1997) tested their model by comparing its performance against that of people on the synonym test from the Test of English as a Foreign Language (TOEFL). The model was correct with 64.4% of the synonyms, which was very similar to the performance of non-native students applying to enter college in the United States. They also considered the finding that most 20-year-old university students know between 40,000 and 100,000 words, meaning that they have acquired an average of 7–15 words per day from the age of 2. This is somewhat mysterious, because attempts to mimic the learning of new words under laboratory conditions suggest a much lower rate of word acquisition. Landauer and Dumais argued that the surprisingly rapid rate of human learning could be explained in terms of *indirect* learning. If all words are interconnected to some extent, then encountering words Y and Z can alter the representation of word X even though it was not actually presented. Latent semantic analysis based on the assumption that such indirect learning is important accurately predicted the rate of vocabulary growth shown by schoolchildren.

Further support for this general approach was reported by Lund, Burgess, and Atchley (1995). They considered word-priming experiments in which participants had to decide as rapidly as possible whether a visually presented letter string forms a word (see Chapter 10). Performance on this task is faster when the letter string is preceded by a related word (e.g., DOCTOR is identified as a word faster if preceded by the word NURSE than by an unrelated word such as GROUND). Performance speed was predicted reasonably well by the latent semantic analysis approach.

Lund and Burgess (1996) worked out degrees of similarity among words on the basis of 160 million words taken from newsgroup messages. According to their computer-based analysis of these words, the words most similar to "monopoly" are "huge", "threat", "large", "gun", and "moral". You will probably agree that these words do not really tell us very much about the meaning of the word "monopoly"! As Murphy (2002, pp. 428–429) asked, "Is the monopoly a threat, or is someone threatening it? Who is it a threat to, and how does it threaten them? If one just knows that *monopoly* and *threat* are 'similar', one does not really understand what monopolies are and do."

Evaluation

The approach based on latent semantic analysis is simple in principle, although its implementation is often rather complex. The approach has various successes to its credit, especially its ability to perform as well as non-native speakers of English on a synonym test and to predict vocabulary growth in children. Thus, the contexts in which we encounter individual words undoubtedly play some part in defining their meaning.

On the negative side, the key limitation is that we cannot establish the precise meaning of a word by knowing the other words with which it is associated. Why is this? In essence, the fact that two words are associated suggests there is some important relation between them, but it does not reveal the nature of that association. Thus, word meaning must depend on factors additional to those emphasised by Landauer and Dumais (1997). Another problem is that the crucial variable of word co-occurrence is rarely manipulated experimentally, and this prevents us from assuming word co-occurrence has causal effects on acquisition of word meaning. As Barsalou (1999, p. 639) pointed out, "The human brain could work like LSA [latent semantic analysis], but . . . no evidence exists to demonstrate this, or to rule out that variables correlated with word co-occurrence are the critical causal factors."

Situated simulation theory

Barsalou (1999, 2003) argued that the nature (and meaning) of concepts is very different from what is commonly imagined to be the case. According to contemporary wisdom (including both prototype and exemplar theories), the conceptual system is rather remote from the realities of everyday life. This theoretical position was described as follows by Barsalou (2003, p. 536): "The conceptual system is a *detached database*. As categories are encountered in the world, their invariant properties are extracted and stored in descriptions, much like an encyclopaedia. The result is a database of generalised categorical knowledge that is relatively detached from the goals of specific agents." Within such a system, concepts are *amodal*, meaning they are stored in the form of abstract symbols. Concepts are also relatively *stable*: any given individual uses the same representation of a concept on different occasions, and different people have fairly similar representations of a concept.

According to Barsalou (1999, 2003), all the above theoretical assumptions about concepts are simply wrong. Within his situated simulation theory, "Conceptual representations are modal, not amodal. The same types of representations underlie perception and conception. When the conceptual system represents an object's visual properties, it uses representations in the visual system; when it represents the actions performed on an object, it uses motor representations" (Barsalou,

2003, p. 521). In contrast to the standard position, concepts are *not* stable: they are "idiosyncratic representations" which vary from situation to situation depending on the individual's current goal and the current situation.

Evidence

One of the main differences between situated simulation theory and most other theories is its emphasis on the instability of concepts. At the start of this chapter we discussed evidence showing that concepts can be unstable. Barsalou (1987, 1989) found that the specific situation influenced the properties of a concept that were considered, and also influenced typicality ratings. In another study, Barsalou (1989) obtained further evidence for concept instability when participants generated the properties of concepts. On average, pairs of participants only produced 44% of the same properties for any given concept, and the same participants only produced 66% of the same concept properties in two occasions separated by 2 weeks.

Where is the evidence that perceptual processes are involved in our use of concepts? In a study by Solomon and Barsalou (2001), participants had to decide whether concepts possessed or did not possess certain properties. The key issue was whether verification times would be speeded up when the same property was linked to two different concepts. There was a facilitation effect *only* when the shape of the property was similar in both cases, indicating that perceptual information influenced task performance. For example, verifying that "mane" is a property of "pony" was facilitated by previously verifying "mane" for "horse", but not by verifying "mane" for "lion". This did *not* happen because the general shape of ponies is much more like that of horses than that of lions. When the similarity of a given property (e.g., "belly") was high across ponies, horses, and lions, then the facilitation effect was the same.

According to situated simulation theory, we do not simply represent categories in isolation; rather, contextual and other information is associated with our concepts or categories. Wu and Barsalou (discussed in Barsalou, 2003) asked participants to produce properties of various objects. However, although not explicitly instructed to do so, they also produced other kinds of information such as background setting (e.g., the property of "picnic" for strawberries; see Figure 9.7) and other categories (e.g., the property of "cream" for strawberries). Thus, the information about object properties that was produced was richer than predicted on most theories, but entirely in line with situated simulation theory.

FIGURE 9.7

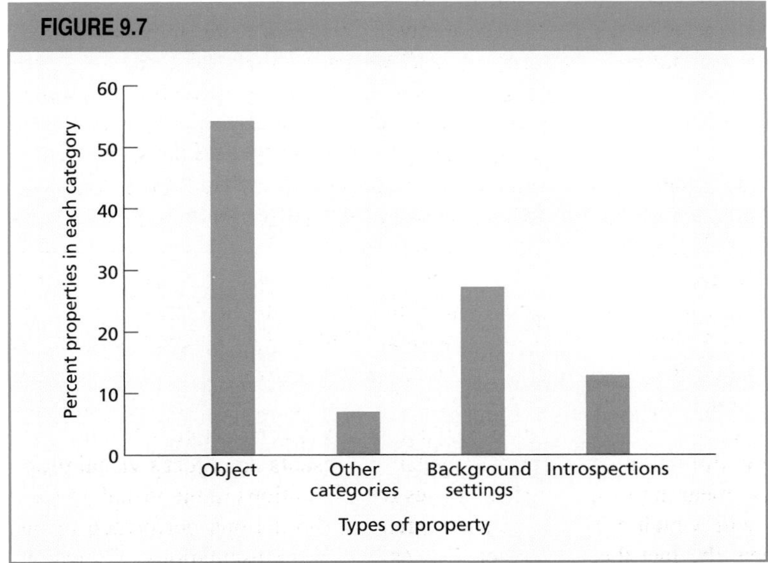

Percent of property types reported across objects. Object properties were explicitly requested, but additional property types reported were other categories, backsettings, and participants' introspections related to the object. Data from Wu and Barsalou discussed in Barsalou (2003).

What evidence indicates that the meaning we ascribe to concepts and how we use them are related directly to potential or actual actions? Relevant evidence was reported by Barsalou (2003) in a study in which the participants carried out two tasks at the same time: (1) they used their hands to imagine performing various factory operations; and (2) they identified the properties of concepts. Sometimes the actions performed by the participants were *relevant* to the property generation task. For example, they produced the properties of "dresser" while at the same time pretending to open a drawer. More internal properties (e.g., "socks", "sweater") were produced when the action revealed the inside of the drawer than when it was irrelevant.

Additional evidence that our use of concepts can be influenced by the motor system was reported by Chao and Martin (2000) in an fMRI study. Participants saw pictures and were asked to name them. There were four types of pictures: manipulable objects (e.g., hammer); animals; human faces; and dwellings. The key finding was that a circuit in the brain involving the motor system became active when the participants looked at manipulable objects, but did not become active for any of the other categories of objects.

Evaluation

Barsalou's situated simulation theory has made a refreshing contribution to our understanding of concepts. He has shown convincingly that the ways in which we actually use conceptual knowledge in everyday life are closely related to both perception and to the motor system. The theory is particularly well placed to account for the common finding that concepts show variability and instability from one situation to another. Thus, the precise meaning we assign to a concept depends on the situation and on the perceptual and motor processes engaged by the current task.

It is premature to offer a definitive view on the value of situated simulation theory. It seems to us that it probably provides an important new perspective on concepts. However, others disagree. For example, Murphy (2002, p. 480) doubts whether Barsalou's approach is all that different from previous ones: "I suspect that the argument about whether concepts and knowledge are really perceptual or symbolic will turn out not to be a substantive issue, but instead an argument about what should be called 'perceptual'." In addition, we really need to know much more about the ways in which perceptual processes influence concept learning.

CHAPTER SUMMARY

- Introduction
  Concepts are centrally involved in perception, learning, memory, and our use of language. Many concepts are organised into hierarchies with superordinate categories at the top, basic-level categories in the middle, and subordinate categories at the bottom. Concepts fulfil various functions, including providing an efficient way of representing our knowledge of the world, allowing us to make accurate predictions, and facilitating communication with other people.

- Organisation of concepts
  According to the classical view, all category members have defining attributes, which are both necessary and sufficient for category membership. That view cannot account for the findings that many concepts are fuzzy, some category members are "better" or more typical than others, and some concepts are not static and unchanging. According to the prototype approach, each concept has a prototype providing a summary description. Category members share family resemblances, and those with the greatest family resemblances are rated as being the most typical members. Prototype theories are sometimes vague about the precise definition of the "prototype", and such theories do not work very well with some abstract concepts or with goal-derived categories.

According to exemplar theories, we store numerous instances of each concept. Exemplar-based accounts can potentially account for findings on prediction and on conceptual instability. Another advantage over the prototype approach is that information about the variability of instances is retained in exemplar theories. The exemplar approach works less well with simple concepts than with complex ones, and it has difficulty in accounting for the effects of knowledge on concept learning.

- Concept learning
  We probably do not possess a *single* concept-learning mechanism, which is in contradiction to the assumptions of prototype and exemplar theories. The role of knowledge in concept learning is largely ignored within exemplar and prototype theories. In fact, there are many knowledge effects associated with concept learning, with knowledge influencing the category features that are learned and categorisation decisions made after learning. Sometimes causal knowledge is involved, or the knowledge may be in schematic form. It appears that we possess much less causal knowledge about concepts than we think we do: this is the "illusion of explanatory depth". However, we generally have sufficient causal knowledge to identify the most important features associated with a concept.
- Concept meaning
  According to Landauer and Dumais's latent semantic analysis approach, the meaning of any concept depends on its connections to other concepts. This approach accounts reasonably well for performance on synonym and word-priming tasks. However, discovering that two words are associated does not reveal the nature of that association, so concept meaning cannot be reduced to patterns of associations. According to Barsalou's situated simulation theory, conceptual representations are closely related to those involved in perception and action. As a result, conceptual representations are very flexible, and can change considerably from one situation to another. This approach is supported by much of the evidence. However, it remains unclear whether conceptual knowledge is basically perceptual rather than symbolic.

FURTHER READING

- Healy, A.F. (2003). *Handbook of psychology: Experimental psychology, Vol. 4*. New York: Wiley & Sons. Concepts and categorisation are discussed in an informative chapter by Goldstone and Kersten.
- Markham, A.B., & Ross, B.H. (2003). Category use and category learning. *Psychological Bulletin, 129*, 592–613. This important article focuses on ways of broadening research on concepts and categories so that more realistic theories can be developed.
- Moss, H., & Hampton, J. (2003). *Conceptual representations*. Hove, UK: Psychology Press. This edited book provides interesting accounts of various important theoretical approaches to concepts.
- Murphy, G.L. (2002). *The big book of concepts*. Cambridge, MA: MIT Press. This book provides a well written and comprehensive account of theory and research on concepts.

Part III

Language

Our lives would be totally different (and much more limited) without language. Our social interactions with other people rely very heavily on language, and a good command of language is vital for all students. We are considerably more knowledgeable than people of previous generations, and the main reason is that knowledge is passed on from one generation to the next in the form of language.

What is language? According to Harley (2001, p. 5), language can be defined as "a system of symbols and rules that enable us to communicate". It is true that communication is the primary function of language, but it is by no means the only one. Crystal (1997) identified a grand total of eight functions of language, of which communication was one. In addition, we can use language for thinking, to record information, to express emotion (e.g., "I love you"), to pretend to be animals (e.g., "Woof! Woof!") to express identity with a group (e.g., singing in church), and so on.

It is indisputable that language is an impressive human achievement, but are there other species that make use of language? Parrots may say certain words. However, this is not proper language, because they do not use rules and are not trying to communicate. The question becomes more interesting (and a lot more controversial) when we consider attempts to teach language to apes. There is a long history of attempts to do so. The earliest were almost farcical, because they involved trying to persuade apes to talk as we do. Countless hours of patient teaching produced the meagre outcome of three or four recognisable English words. However, such findings tell us essentially nothing about apes' ability to learn language. Our vocal apparatus has evolved to accommodate speech, whereas that of the ape has not. Therefore, the almost total lack of success of this approach should come as no surprise.

Over the past 40 years or so, rather more convincing evidence that apes can be taught the rudiments of language has been provided. For example, consider the research of Savage-Rumbaugh with a bonobo chimpanzee called Panbanisha (see Leake, 1999). Panbanisha has spent her entire life in captivity receiving training in the use of language. She uses a specially designed keypad with about 400 geometric patterns or lexigrams on it. When she presses a sequence of keys, a computer translates the sequence into a synthetic voice. Panbanisha learned a vocabulary of 3000 words by the age of 14 years, and became very good at combining a series of symbols in the grammatically correct order. For example, she can construct sentences such as "Please can I have an iced coffee?" and "I'm thinking about eating something."

Panbanisha's achievements are considerable. However, her command of language is much less than that of most fairly young children. For example, she does not produce many novel sentences, she only rarely refers to objects that are not visible, and the complexity of her sentences is generally less than that of children. As Noam Chomsky (quoted in Atkinson et al., 1993) tellingly remarked, "If animals had a capacity as biologically advantageous as language but somehow hadn't used it until now, it would be an evolutionary miracle, like finding an island of humans who could be taught to fly."

There are four main language skills (listening to speech, reading, speaking, and writing), and it is perhaps natural to assume that any given person will have generally strong or generally weak language skills. That assumption may often be correct with respect to first language acquisition, but is very frequently not so with second language acquisition. For example, the first author spent 10 years at school learning French, and he has spent his summer holidays there virtually every year over a long period of time. He can just about read newspapers and easy novels in French, and he can write reasonably coherent (if somewhat ungrammatical) letters in French. However, in common with many British people, he finds it agonisingly difficult to understand rapid spoken French, and his ability to speak French is poor.

One of the most influential ideas in theorising about language is that of modularity, which was discussed in Chapter 1. According to the notion of modularity (Fodor, 1983), the cognitive system consists of several fairly independent processors or modules. A module "is a self-contained set of processes: it converts an input to an output, without any outside help on what goes on in between" (Harley, 2001, p. 20). As we will see, many models of language processing are based to some extent on the assumption of modularity. Such models are often represented by a series of boxes connected by arrows, with some specific processing operation occurring within each box.

The next three chapters (Chapters 10–12) focus on the four main language skills. Chapter 10 deals with the basic processes involved in listening to speech and in reading. There is an emphasis in this chapter on the ways in which listeners and readers identify and make sense of individual words that they hear in speech or read on the printed page. As we will see, the study of brain-damaged patients has helped to reveal the complexity of the processes underlying speech recognition and reading.

Chapter 11 is concerned mainly with the processes involved in the comprehension of sentences and **discourse** (connected text or speech). There are some important differences between understanding text and understanding speech (e.g., it is generally easier to refer back to what has gone before with text than with speech). However, it is assumed that comprehension processes are broadly similar for text and for speech, and major theories of language comprehension are considered in detail.

Chapter 12 deals with the remaining two main language abilities: speaking and writing. Speech production takes up much more of our time than does writing. It may be no coincidence that we know much more about speech production than we do about writing. Research on writing has been somewhat neglected until recently, which is a shame given the importance of writing skills in most cultures.

One very important general issue will be discussed here before we turn to a detailed consideration of the main language skills. Philosophers and psychologists have devoted much time and energy to the relation between language and thought. There are several possible relations. Language may influence or determine thought. Thought may influence or determine language. Alternatively, there may only be a relatively weak relationship between language and thought.

THE WHORFIAN HYPOTHESIS

The best-known theory about the interrelationship between language and thought was put forward by Benjamin Lee Whorf (1956). He was a fire prevention officer for an insurance company who spent his spare time working in linguistics. According to his hypothesis of linguistic relativity (the **Whorfian hypothesis**), language determines or influences thinking. Miller and McNeill (1969) distinguished three versions of the Whorfian hypothesis. According to the strong hypothesis, language determines thinking. Thus, any given language imposes constraints on what can be thought, with those constraints varying from one language to another. The weak hypothesis states that language influences perception. Finally, the weakest hypothesis claims only that language influences memory.

Hunt and Agnoli (1991) proposed a cognitive account of the Whorfian hypothesis. The essence of their position was as follows (1991, p. 379): "Different languages lend themselves to the transmission of different types of messages. People consider the costs of computation [the mental effort likely to be involved] when they reason about a topic. The language that they use will partly determine those costs. In this sense, language does influence cognition." Thus, our native language helps to determine the computational costs or mental effort of different cognitive processes, and this may influence our ways of thinking.

Evidence

Casual inspection of the world's languages indicates significant differences among them. For example, the Hanuxoo people in the Philippines have 92 different names for various types of rice, and there are hundreds of camel-related words in Arabic. It is possible that these differences influence thought. However, it is more plausible that different environmental conditions influence the things people think about, and this in turn influences their linguistic usage. Thus, these differences occur because thought influences language rather than because language influences thought.

Much of the key research on the Whorfian hypothesis has involved studying colour categorisation and memory. According to the hypothesis, colour categorisation and memory should vary as a function of the participants' native language. In contrast, Heider (1972) argued that colour categorisation and memory are universal, and do *not* vary from language to language. She was influenced by Berlin and Kay (1969), who argued that there are 11 basic colour terms (white, black, red, yellow, blue, green, brown, purple, pink, orange, and grey), although some languages do not have words for all 11 colours. Such languages always have words corresponding to "black" and "white", but typically do not have words corresponding to "purple", "pink", "orange", and "grey". Each of the 11 basic colour terms has one generally agreed best or focal colour.

Heider (1972) claimed that English speakers find it easier to remember focal than non-focal colours, and wondered whether the same would be true of the Dani. The Dani are a "Stone-Age" agricultural people living in Indonesian New Guinea, and their language has only two basic colour terms: "mola" for bright, warm hues, and "mili" for dark, cold hues. If language influences colour perception and memory as predicted on the Whorfian hypothesis, then there should have been clear differences between the Dani and American participants. However, Heider (1972) found the Dani made confusions in memory resembling those of the American participants. In addition, the Dani and Americans showed better recognition memory for focal than non-focal colours, even though the Dani do not have terms to describe focal colours.

Roberson, Davies, and Davidoff (2000) argued that Heider (1972) had not really shown that colour categories are universal and so do not depend on language. They pointed out that there was a problem with her choice of stimuli: the focal colours were more discriminable (easier to discriminate perceptually from similar colours) than the non-focal colours. Roberson et al. (2000) tried to replicate Heider's (1972) findings comparing English participants with members of the Berinmo. The Berinmo live in Papua, New Guinea, and their language contains only five basic colour terms. Roberson et al. (2000) failed to repeat any of Heider's (1972) main findings. They concluded as follows: "When . . . the discriminability advantage for focal colours is removed, the advantage for focal colours in recognition memory disappears for both English and Berinmo speakers" (Roberson et al., 2000, p. 382).

Roberson et al. (2000) went on to obtain convincing evidence that colour perception and memory vary from language to language. In one study, they considered categorical perception, meaning that it is easier to discriminate between stimuli belonging to *different* categories than stimuli *within* the same category (see Chapter 10). In the English language, we have categories of green and blue, whereas Berinmo has categories of nol (roughly similar to green) and wor (roughly similar to yellow). Roberson et al. (2000) presented participants with three coloured stimuli, and asked them to select the two most similar. Suppose two of the stimuli would normally be described as green in English and the third one as blue. According to the notion of categorical perception, English speakers should regard the two green stimuli as being most similar. However, there is no reason to expect Berinmo speakers to do the same, because their language does not distinguish between blue and green. In similar fashion, Berinmo speakers presented with two nol stimuli and a wor stimulus should select the two nol stimuli, but there is no good reason why English-speaking participants should do the same.

What did Roberson et al. (2000) find? Language determined performance: both groups showed categorical perception based on their own language (see Figure III.1). As Roberson et al. (2000, p. 389) concluded, "Speakers of both languages make judgements in line with their own colour vocabulary more consistently than judgements relating to the other language. Indeed, both groups of participants were at chance for decisions relating to the other language's colour boundary."

FIGURE III.1

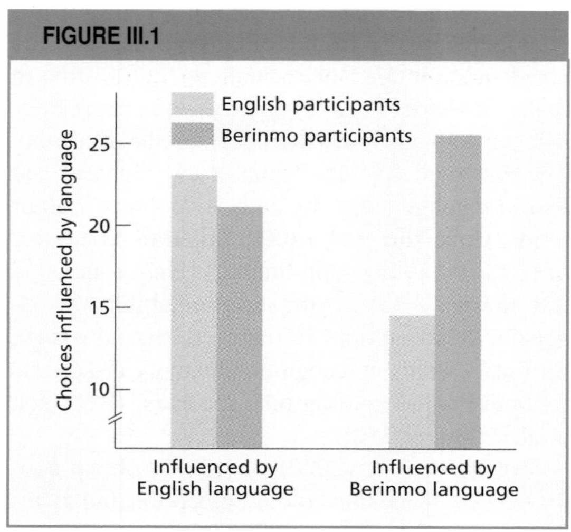

Influence of language (English vs. Berinmo) on choice of similar pairs of stimuli by English and Berinmo participants. Data from Roberson et al. (2000).

Roberson et al. (2000) also considered the effects of categorical perception on memory. The participants were first shown a target stimulus followed by two test stimuli presented together. They had to decide which of the two test stimuli matched the target stimulus. Categorical perception would be demonstrated if the participants found it easier to perform this recognition-memory task when the two test stimuli belong to *different* colour categories than when they belong to the *same* colour category. For example, English speakers should have good recognition memory when the test stimuli are on opposite sides of the green–blue colour boundary, but this should be irrelevant to the Berinmo. In contrast, Berinmo speakers should perform well when the test stimuli are on opposite sides of the nol–wor boundary, but this should be irrelevant to the English participants. That is exactly what was found.

In sum, Roberson et al. (2000, p. 396) argued that the evidence they had presented provided strong support for the Whorfian hypothesis: "The driving force behind the similarity judgements of colour is language . . . we conclude that there is an extensive influence of language on colour categorisation. The influence is deep rather than superficial, applying both to perceptual and memorial processes."

There is other evidence that language can influence thinking. In a study by Hoffman, Lau, and Johnson (1986), bilingual English–Chinese speakers read descriptions of individuals, and then provided free interpretations of the individuals described. The descriptions conformed to either Chinese or English stereotypes of personality. For example, in English there is a stereotype of the artistic type (e.g., moody and intense temperament; bohemian lifestyle), but this stereotype does not exist in Chinese. Bilinguals thinking in Chinese used Chinese stereotypes in their free interpretations, whereas those thinking in English used English stereotypes. Thus, the inferences we draw can be influenced by the language in which we are thinking.

More evidence consistent with the Whorfian hypothesis was reported by Pederson et al. (1998).

They pointed out that space can be coded in either a *relative* system (e.g., left, right, up, down) or an *absolute* system (e.g., north, south). Pederson et al. gave speakers of 13 languages various non-linguistic spatial reasoning tasks which could be solved using either system. For example, there was the animals-in-a-row task, in which three animals were presented in a row. After observing this array, participants rotated 180°, and then reconstructed the array so that it matched the first. Participants' choice of system was determined largely by the dominant system of spatial coding in their native language, showing the effect of language on spatial reasoning.

Li and Gleitman (2002) argued that whether individuals use a relative or an absolute form of spatial reasoning depends on the environmental conditions rather than features of their native language. In support of their argument, they found that American participants were more likely to use the absolute system of spatial reasoning when tested outdoors rather than indoors. Li and Gleitman (2002) suspected that those populations in the Pederson et al. (1998) study using the absolute system were tested outdoors, whereas those using the relative system were tested indoors. However, Levinson et al. (2002) pointed out that that was incorrect. They failed to replicate the findings of Li and Gleitman (2002), and concluded that spatial reasoning is strongly influenced by language.

Evaluation

Recent years have seen increased support for the Whorfian hypothesis on several kinds of tasks (e.g., colour discrimination, colour memory, reasoning). As Harley (2001, p. 87) concluded, "There is now a considerable amount of evidence suggesting that linguistic factors can affect cognitive processes. Even colour perception and memory . . . show some influence of language." Thus, the evidence supports the weak and the weakest versions of the Whorfian hypothesis. When tasks are used giving participants flexibility in the approach they adopt (e.g., Hoffman et al., 1986; Pederson et al., 1998), there is even modest evidence in favour of the strong version of the Whorfian hypothesis.

What is lacking as yet is a detailed specification of the ways in which language influences various cognitive processes. For example, Hunt and Agnoli (1991) assumed that an individual's estimate of computational costs or mental effort helps to determine whether language influences cognition. However, these costs have rarely been assessed, and so the assumption has not been tested directly.

It is important to establish whether the limiting effects of language on cognition are relatively easy to remove. Whorf (1956) assumed that it would be very hard to change the effects of language on cognition, whereas Hunt and Agnoli (1991) assumed that it would be relatively easy. Only future research will provide the answer.

10

Reading and Speech Perception

INTRODUCTION

Humanity excels in its command of language. Indeed, language is of such enormous importance to us that this chapter and the following two are devoted to it. In this chapter, we consider the basic processes involved in reading and speech perception. It often does not matter whether a message is presented to our ears or to our eyes. For example, we would understand the sentence "You have done exceptionally well in your cognitive psychology examination" in much the same way whether we heard or read it. Thus, many comprehension processes are very similar whether we are reading a text or listening to someone talking.

However, reading and speech perception differ in important ways. In reading, each word can be seen as a whole, whereas a spoken word is spread out in time and is transitory. More importantly, it is much harder to tell where one word ends and the next starts with speech than with text, in which spaces indicate word boundaries. Speech generally provides a more ambiguous and unclear signal than does printed text. For example, when words were spliced out of spoken sentences and presented on their own, they were recognised only half of the time (Lieberman, 1963).

There are other significant differences. The demands on memory are greater when listening to speech than reading a text, because the words already spoken are no longer accessible. So far we have indicated some of the ways in which listening to speech is harder than reading. However, there is one major way in which listening to speech can be easier than reading. Speech often contains **prosodic cues** (discussed in Chapter 12). Prosodic cues are hints to sentence structure and intended meaning via the speaker's pitch, intonation, stress, and timing (e.g., questions have a rising intonation on the last word in the sentence). In contrast, the main cues to sentence structure specific to text are punctuation marks (e.g., commas, semi-colons). These are sometimes regarded as having the same function as certain aspects of prosody, but are often less informative than the prosodic cues in speech.

The fact that reading and listening to speech are quite different in some ways can be shown by considering children and brain-damaged patients. Young children often have good comprehension of spoken language, but struggle to read even simple stories. Part of the reason may be that reading is a relatively recent invention in the history of the human species, and so it lacks a genetically programmed specialised processor (McCandliss et al., 2003). Some adult brain-damaged patients can understand spoken language but cannot read, and others can read perfectly well but cannot understand the spoken word.

Basic processes specific to reading are dealt with first in this chapter, followed by basic processes specific to speech. Language comprehension processes common to reading and to listening are discussed in the next chapter.

READING: INTRODUCTION

Reading is fairly effortless for most adults. However, it requires several perceptual and other cognitive processes, as well as a good knowledge of language and of grammar. Indeed, most mental activities are related to reading, and it can be regarded as "visually guided thinking".

Why is it important to study reading? Skilled reading has much value in contemporary society, and adults without effective reading skills are at a great disadvantage. Thus, we need to study reading to be able to help poor readers.

Some reading processes are concerned with identifying and extracting meaning from individual words. Other processes operate at the level of the phrase or sentence, and still others deal with the overall organisation or thematic structure of an entire story or book. However, research has focused mainly on only some of these processes: "Scanning the literature on skilled reading, one could be forgiven for thinking that the goal of reading is to turn print into speech. Of course, it is not: the goal of reading is to understand (perhaps even to enjoy) a piece of text" (Ellis, 1993, p. 35).

Research methods

Several methods are available for studying the processes involved in reading. For example, consider ways of assessing the time taken for word identification. One is the **lexical decision task** (deciding whether a string of letters forms a word), and a second is the **naming task** (saying a printed word out loud as rapidly as possible). These techniques ensure that certain processing has been performed on a given word in a given time, but possess clear limitations. Normal reading processes are disrupted by the additional task, and it is not clear precisely what processes are reflected in lexical decision or naming times.

The most generally useful method involves recording eye movements during reading. This method has two particular strengths: (1) it provides a detailed on-line record of attention-related processes, and (2) it is unobtrusive. The only important restriction on readers whose eye movements are being recorded is that they must keep their heads fairly still. The main problem is that it is hard to be sure precisely *what* processing occurs during each fixation.

Balota, Paul, and Spieler (1999) argued that reading involves several kinds of processing: **orthography** (the spelling of words); **phonology** (the sound of words); word meaning; syntax; and higher-level discourse integration. Reading tasks vary in the involvement of these kinds of processing. According to Balota et al. (1999, p. 47),

> In naming, the attentional control system would increase the influence of the computations between orthography and phonology . . . the demands of lexical decision performance might place a high priority on the computations between orthographic and meaning level modules [processors] . . . if the goal . . . is reading comprehension, then attentional control would increase the priority of computations of the syntactic-, meaning-, and discourse-level modules.

Thus, performance on naming and lexical decision tasks may not accurately reflect normal reading processes.

Phonological processes in reading

An important theoretical issue concerns the role of phonology or the sound of words in reading. This issue has been considered using various reading-related tasks including lexical decision, naming, and word-meaning tasks. Ferrand and Grainger (1993) provided a detailed account of the time course of phonological and orthographic processes in the earliest stages of visual word recognition. There was clear evidence for the build-up of phonological and orthographic information, but this occurred approximately 20 ms later for phonological than for orthographic information.

Frost (1998, p. 76) put forward an extreme theoretical position (the strong phonological model) which we will use as the basis for our discussion:

> A phonological representation is a necessary product of processing printed words, even though the explicit pronunciation of their phonological structure is not required. Thus, the strong phonological model would predict that phonological processing will be mandatory [obligatory], perhaps automatic.

Frost (1998) argued that two predictions follow from the notion that such phonological information is always involved:

(1) Phonological coding will occur even when it impairs performance.
(2) Some phonological coding occurs rapidly when a word is presented visually.

Evidence

A study supporting prediction (1) above was reported by Tzelgov et al. (1996) using a naming task. It was based on the **Stroop effect**: naming the colours in which words are printed is slowed when the words themselves are different colour names (e.g., the word RED printed in green). The participants in the study were English–Hebrew bilinguals who named the colours of nonwords in one of the two languages. Each nonword had an unfamiliar printed form, but its phonological translation was a colour name in the other language. Tzelgov et al. (1996) obtained a strong Stroop effect with these nonwords. Thus, the participants engaged in phonological coding of the nonwords even though it was disadvantageous.

A study supporting prediction (2) above was reported by Berent and Perfetti (1995). They used a backward masking technique involving the following stages: (1) a target word was presented very briefly; (2) the target word was masked by a nonword also presented very briefly; (3) a pattern mask (a mask possessing structure) was presented; and (4) the participants wrote down what they had seen. Target detection was higher when the nonwords were phonemically similar to the target words than when they were graphemically similar. It appears that basic phonological coding occurs within about 60 milliseconds of word presentation.

Is phonological processing involved in lexical decision? Positive evidence has come from studies using **heterographs** (e.g., "maid", "made") which are words with one pronunciation but two spellings. Reaction times on a lexical decision task are longer for low-frequency heterographs (e.g., "maid") than for non-heterographs (e.g., Pexman, Lupker, & Reggin, 2002). However, Pexman et al. found reaction times were not slowed for **homographs** (words with one spelling but having two meanings and sometimes two pronunciations; e.g., "wind") compared to non-homographs. Why is this? According to Pexman et al., the phonological representation of a heterograph activates both spellings, and activation of the "wrong" spelling slows down performance. In contrast, the phonological representation of a homograph activates only *one* spelling, and so there is no competition between rival spellings.

Is phonological processing necessary to access the *meaning* of words we read? The findings are mixed. Folk (1999) recorded eye movements while participants read sentences containing heterographs. Participants fixated longer on heterographs than on other words. Since heterographs are ambiguous phonologically but not orthographically, the likeliest explanation is that phonological processing slowed down reading time.

In a study on proof-reading and eye movements Jared, Levy, and Rayner (1999) found that the use of phonology depends on the nature of the words and the reading ability of the participants. Eye-movement data indicated that phonology was used in accessing the meaning of low-frequency words but not high-frequency ones. In addition, poor readers were more likely than good readers to access phonology as a way of accessing meaning.

Reasonably convincing evidence that word meaning can be accessed without access to phonology was reported by Hanley and McDonnell (1997). They studied a patient, PS, who could understand the meanings of words while reading even though he could not pronounce them accurately. PS did not even seem to have access to an internal phonological representation of words, because he could not gain access to both meanings of heterographs when he saw one of the spellings in print. The fact that PS could give accurate definitions of printed words in spite of his impairments suggests strongly he had full access to the meanings of words for which he could not supply the appropriate phonology.

Evaluation

Phonological processing is of general importance in reading. Tasks involving lexical decision, naming, assessment of word meaning, and ordinary reading of text have all been shown to involve phonological processing. As we have seen, there is evidence for phonological coding even when such coding disrupts performance (Tzelgov et al., 1996).

On the negative side, there are numerous studies on reading in which evidence of phonological processing was limited or absent (e.g., Hanley & McDonnell, 1997; Jared et al., 1999). In addition, Frost's theory has problems in accounting for phonological dyslexia. Phonological dyslexics (discussed in detail shortly) have great difficulties with phonological processing, but are nevertheless reasonably good at reading familiar words. This is puzzling if one assumes that phonological coding is of major importance in reading. As Frost (1998, p. 93) admitted, "Evidence that . . . is damaging to the strong phonological model comes from phonological dyslexia."

In sum, the strong phonological model is probably too strong, because the involvement of phonological processing in reading depends on the nature of the stimulus material, the nature of the task, and the reading ability of the participants. However, a weak phonological model (claiming only that phonological processing is often involved in reading) is consistent with most of the evidence.

WORD IDENTIFICATION

College students typically read at about 300 words per minute, thus averaging only 200 milliseconds to identify each word. It has proved hard to decide exactly how long word identification normally takes, in part because of imprecision about the meaning of "word identification". The term can refer to accessing either the name of a word or its meaning. We will see that various estimates of the time taken for word identification have been produced.

Automatic processing

Rayner and Sereno (1994) argued that word identification is generally fairly automatic. This makes intuitive sense given that most college students have read between 20 and 70 million words in their lifetimes. It has been argued that automatic processes are unavoidable and unavailable to consciousness (see Chapter 5). Evidence that word identification may be unavoidable comes from the Stroop effect (discussed above). Participants have to name the colours in which words are printed as rapidly as possible, and naming speed is slowed when the words are conflicting colour names (e.g., the word RED printed in green). The Stroop effect suggests that word meaning is extracted even when participants try not to process it. Cheesman and Merikle (1984) replicated the Stroop effect. They also found the effect could be obtained even when the colour name was presented below the level of conscious awareness. This latter finding suggests that word identification does not depend on conscious awareness.

Context effects

Is word identification influenced by context? This issue was addressed by Meyer and Schvaneveldt (1971) in a study in which the participants had to decide whether letter strings were words. On this lexical decision task, the decision time for a word (e.g., DOCTOR) was shorter when the preceding context or prime was a semantically related word (e.g., NURSE) than when it was an unrelated word (e.g., LIBRARY) or when there was no prime. This is known as the **semantic priming effect**.

Why does this semantic priming effect occur? Perhaps the context or priming word automatically activates the stored representations of all the words related to it due to massive previous learning. Alternatively, controlled processes may be involved, with a prime such as NURSE leading participants to expect that a semantically related word will follow.

Neely (1977) used an ingenious technique to distinguish between the above explanations of the semantic priming effect. The priming word was the name of a semantic category (e.g., "Bird"), and it was followed by a letter string at one of three intervals: 250, 400, or 700 milliseconds. In the key manipulation, participants expected a particular category name would usually be followed by a member of a different, pre-specified category (e.g., "Bird" followed by the name of part of a building). There were two kinds of trials with this manipulation:

(1) The category name is followed by a member of a different, but expected, category (e.g., Bird–Window).
(2) The category name is followed by a member of the same (but unexpected) category (e.g., Bird–Magpie).

FIGURE 10.1

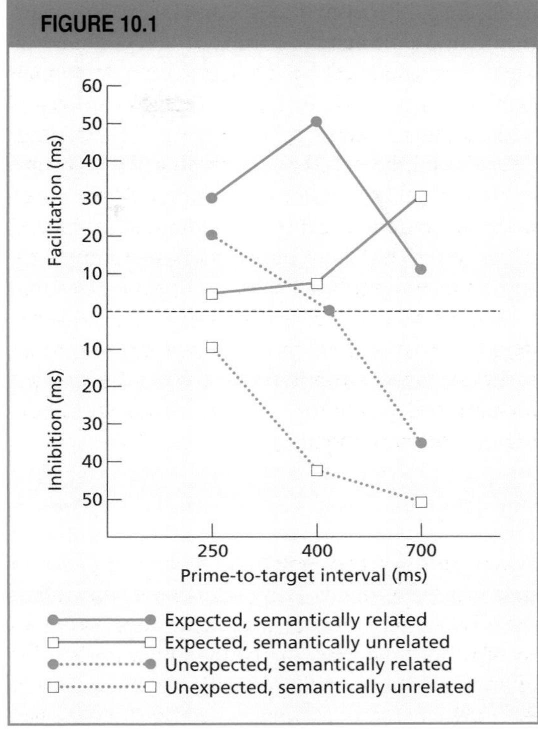

The time course of inhibitory and facilitatory effects of priming as a function of whether or not the target word was related semantically to the prime, and of whether or not the target word belonged to the expected category. Data from Neely (1977).

The findings are shown in Figure 10.1. There were two priming or context effects. First, there was a rapid, automatic effect based only on semantic relatedness. Second, there was a slower-acting attentional effect based only on expectation. Subsequent research has generally confirmed Neely's (1977) findings, except that automatic processes can cause inhibitory effects at short intervals (see Rayner & Pollatsek, 1989).

It is hard to know whether Neely's (1977) findings apply to normal reading, because the situations are so different. However, context often influences reading by producing expectations. For example, McDonald and Shillcock (2003) found that words predictable from the previous word were fixated for less time than words that were not predictable.

We have seen that word identification is affected by context. What is more controversial is whether context effects occur *before* or *after* the individual has gained **lexical access** to the stored information contained in the internal **lexicon**. Neely (1977) found that semantic or associative priming had a very rapid effect on word identification, suggesting (but not proving) that this effect of context occurs pre-lexically. He also found that the effects of participants' expectancies were slow to develop, suggesting these expectancies (and probably sentence context as well) affect post-lexical processing.

Sereno, Brewer, and O'Donnell (2003) used event-related potentials (ERPs; see Chapter 1) to investigate the effects of context on word processing. They focused on processing of ambiguous words (e.g., "bank", "feet") having a dominant and a non-dominant meaning. Each ambiguous word was preceded by a neutral context (which should activate mainly its dominant meaning) or by a context biasing its non-dominant meaning. Of central interest was an early ERP measure known as the N1 occurring within 132–192 ms of word presentation. The key finding was that the N1 for the ambiguous words differed significantly as a function of context. This finding suggests that context influenced which meaning of ambiguous words was activated at an early stage of processing.

Lucas (1999) carried out a meta-analysis of 17 studies focusing on context effects in lexical access. In most of these studies, each context sentence contained an ambiguous word (e.g., "The man spent the entire day fishing on the *bank*"). The ambiguous word was immediately followed by a target on which a naming or lexical decision task was performed. The target word was either appropriate (e.g., "river") or inappropriate (e.g., "money") to the meaning of the ambiguous word in the sentence context. Overall, the 17 studies in the meta-analysis "showed a small effect of context on lexical access of about two-tenths of a standard deviation: the appropriate interpretation of a word consistently showed greater priming than the inappropriate interpretation" (Lucas, 1999, p. 394). The findings from naming and lexical decision tasks were very similar. In view of the different limitations of these two tasks (see above), this similarity perhaps offers some reassurance that the findings are valid. However, it is likely that the processes involved in performing the naming and lexical decision tasks differ somewhat from those involved in reading a text for comprehension.

Letter and word identification

It could be argued that the recognition of a word on the printed page involves two *successive* stages:

(1) Identification of the individual letters in the word;
(2) Word identification.

In fact, however, the notion that letter identification must be complete before word identification can begin seems to be wrong. For example, consider the **word superiority effect** (Reicher, 1969). A letter string is presented very briefly followed by a pattern mask. Participants decide which of two letters was presented in a particular position (e.g., the third letter). The word superiority effect is defined by the fact that performance is better when the letter string forms a word than when it does not.

The word superiority effect suggests that information about the word presented can facilitate identification of the letters of that word. However, there is also a pseudoword superiority effect: letters are better recognised when presented in pronounceable nonwords (e.g., "MAVE") than in unpronounceable nonwords (e.g., Carr, Davidson, & Hawkins, 1978).

Interactive activation model

McClelland and Rumelhart (1981) put forward an influential interactive activation model of visual word recognition. The key assumptions of this model are as follows: "Visual word recognition involves a process of mutual constraint satisfaction between the bottom-up [stimulus-driven] information gained about the features in the words and the top-down knowledge about word and letter identities" (Ellis & Humphreys, 1999, p. 315). The more detailed theoretical assumptions made by McClelland and Rumelhart (1981) are as follows (see Figure 10.2):

- There are recognition units at three levels: the feature level at the bottom; the letter level in the middle; and the word level at the top.
- When a feature in a letter is detected (e.g., vertical line at the right-hand side of a letter), activation goes to all the letter units containing that feature (e.g., H, M, N), and inhibition goes to all other letter units.
- Letters are identified at the letter level. When a letter in a particular position within a word is identified, activation is sent to the word level for all four-letter word units containing that letter in that position, and inhibition is sent to all other word units. Note that the model focuses only on recognition of four-letter words.

FIGURE 10.2

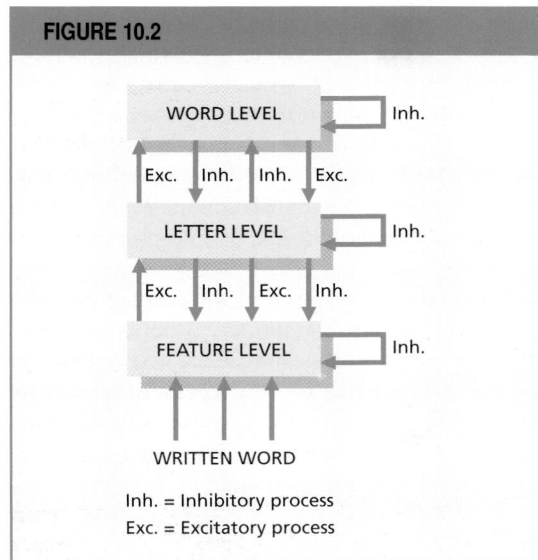

McClelland and Rumelhart's (1981) interactive activation model of visual word recognition. Adapted from Ellis (1984).

- Words are recognised at the word level. Activated word units increase the level of activation in the letter-level units for the letters forming that word (e.g., activation of the word SEAT would increase activation for the four letters S, E, A, and T at the letter level) and inhibit activity of all other letter units.
- At each level in the system, activation of one particular unit leads to suppression or inhibition of competing units.

Bottom-up processes stemming directly from the written word proceed from the feature level through the letter level to the word level by means of activation and inhibition. Top-down processing is involved in the activation and inhibition processes going from the word level to the letter level. The word superiority effect occurs because of the top-down influences of the word level on the letter level. Suppose the word SEAT is presented, and participants are asked whether the third letter is an A or an N. If the word unit for SEAT is activated at the word level, this will increase the activation of the letter A at the letter level, and inhibit the activation of the letter N.

How can the pseudoword superiority effect be explained? When letters are embedded in pronounceable nonwords, there will generally be some overlap of spelling patterns between the pseudoword and genuine words. This overlap can produce additional activation of the letters presented in the pseudoword and thus lead to the pseudoword superiority effect.

Evaluation

The interactive activation model has been very influential. It provides an interesting example of how a connectionist processing system (see Chapter 1) can be applied to visual word recognition. It accounts for various phenomena, including the word superiority effect and the pseudoword superiority effect. In addition, the common finding that context in the form of top-down lexical knowledge influences word recognition (Lucas, 1999; Sereno et al., 2003) is consistent with the notion that top-down processes are important.

There are various limitations with the interactive activation model. First, most of the directly relevant research has used artificial tasks (e.g., identifying a specific letter in a letter string) of dubious relevance to normal reading.

Second, the model was only designed to account for performance on four-letter words written in capital letters. However, it could probably be developed to apply to longer words.

Third, high-frequency or common words are more readily recognised than low-frequency or rare words. This can be explained by assuming *either* that stronger connections are formed between the letter and word units of high-frequency words, *or* that high-frequency words have a higher resting level of activation. It follows that there should be a larger word superiority effect for high-frequency words than for low-frequency words due to more top-down activation from the word level to the letter level. However, the size of the word superiority effect is unaffected by word frequency (Gunther, Gfoerer, & Weiss, 1984).

Fourth, the model assumes that lexical access is determined by *visual* information. However, as we saw earlier, there is much evidence that phonological processing often influences visual word recognition (see Frost, 1998).

Developments of the mel

The original interactive activation model predicted *accuracy* of word recognition, but could not predict the *speed* of word reading. This limitation was addressed by Grainger and Segui (1990) and Jacobs and Grainger (1992). They modified the model so responses were made when activation at the word level reached a variable threshold of activation. With this addition to the model, Jacobs and Grainger (1992) simulated the lexical decision times of human participants. Grainger and Segui assumed that high-frequency words have a lower activation threshold than low-frequency words. They focused particularly on lexical decision times to low-frequency words (e.g., BLUR) having a similar spelling to a high-frequency word (e.g., BLUE). They predicted (and found) that lexical decision times were slowed down, presumably because activation of the incorrect high-frequency word inhibited activation of the correct low-frequency word.

McClelland (1993) pointed out that the original interactive activation model was deterministic, meaning that any given input would always produce the same output. This contrasts with human performance, which is variable. Accordingly, McClelland developed the model by including variable or stochastic processes within it. This permitted the model to simulate the response distributions of human participants given various word-recognition tasks.

READING ALOUD

Read out the following list of words and nonwords:

CAT FOG COMB PINT MANTINESS FASS

Hopefully, you found it a simple task, but it involves some hidden complexities. For example, how do you know the "b" in "comb" is silent, and that "pint" does not rhyme with "hint"? Presumably you have specific information stored in long-term memory about how to pronounce these words. However, this cannot explain your ability to pronounce nonwords such as "mantiness" and "fass". Perhaps nonwords are pronounced by analogy with real words (e.g., "fass" is pronounced to rhyme with "mass"). Another possibility is that rules governing the translation of letter strings into sounds are used to generate a pronunciation for nonwords.

The above description of the reading of individual words is oversimplified. Studies on brain-damaged patients suggest there are several reading disorders, depending on which parts of the cognitive system are damaged. We turn now to theories that have considered reading aloud in unimpaired and brain-damaged individuals.

Dual-route cascaded model

Coltheart and his colleagues have proposed various theories of reading, culminating in their dual-route cascaded model (Coltheart et al., 2001; see Figure 10.3). This model is designed to account for reading aloud and for silent reading. In essence, there are three routes between the printed word and speech, all starting with orthographic analysis (used for identifying and grouping letters in printed words). Readers may be puzzled as to why a model with *three* routes is called a *dual*-route model. The explanation is that the key distinction is between a lexical or dictionary look-up route (Routes 2 and 3) and a non-lexical route (Route 1) which involves converting letters into sounds.

Coltheart et al. (2001) rejected Frost's (1998) strong phonological model (discussed earlier). They argued instead for a weak phonological model: "Reading tasks are not purely orthographic in nature and all such tasks involve both orthographic and phonological processing" (Coltheart et al., 2001, p. 235).

Evidence consistent with the existence of two separate routes was reported by Fiebach, Friederici, Müller, and von Cramon (2002) in an fMRI study. Participants decided whether letter strings (high-frequency words, low-frequency words, and pseudowords) were words (lexical decision task). High- and low-frequency words produced more activity than pseudowords in bilateral occipito-

FIGURE 10.3

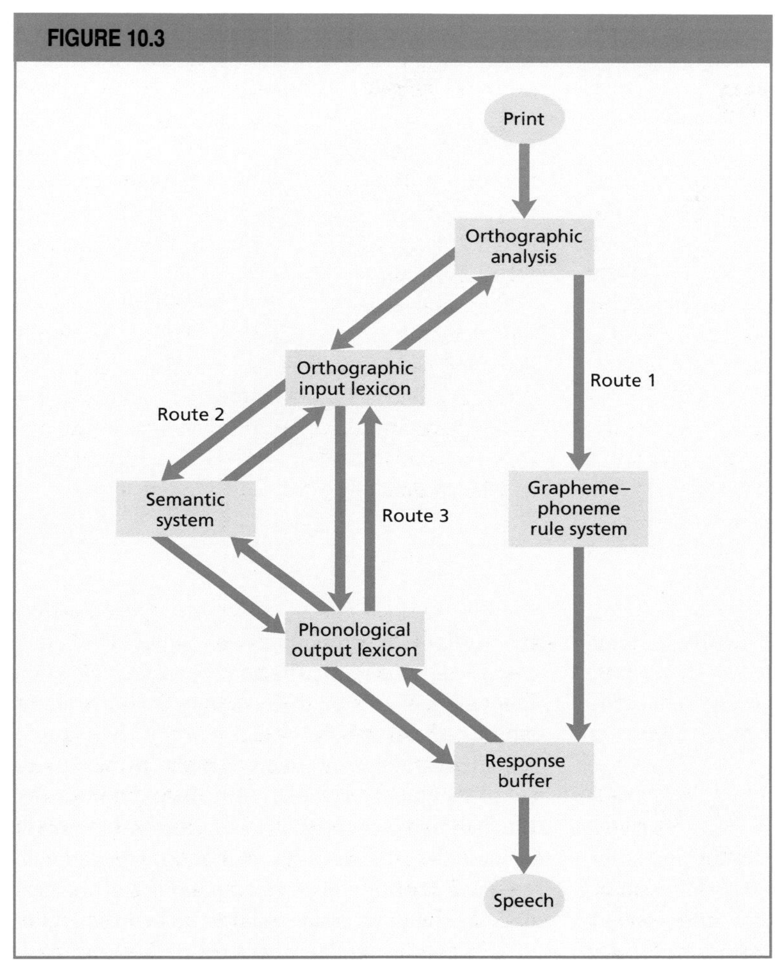

Basic architecture of the dual-route cascaded model. Adapted from Coltheart et al. (2001).

temporal brain regions and posterior left middle temporal gyrus (see Figure 10.4). In addition, low-frequency words and pseudowords produced greater activation than high-frequency words in the superior pons opercularis (BA 44) of the left inferior frontal gyrus, in the anterior insula, and in the thalamus and caudate nucleus, areas probably involved in converting spelling into sound (Route 1). As Fiebach et al. (2002, p. 11) concluded, "The results obtained strongly support dual-route models of visual word processing."

Chen et al. (2002) provided further support for dual routes in reading. They used fMRI to assess brain activity while participants read Chinese characters or read pinyin, which consists of 26 English letters and 13 letter groups developed as sound symbols for Chinese characters. Some brain areas (e.g., inferior frontal, middle, and inferior temporal gyri) were activated by reading both Chinese characters and pinyin. With reference to the dual-route model, the route involving grapheme–phoneme conversion would be much more likely to be used with pinyin than with Chinese characters. There was more activation of various areas (e.g., inferior parietal cortex; the precuneus) when reading pinyin, and more activation of other areas (e.g., bilateral cuneus; posterior middle temporal cortex) when reading Chinese

FIGURE 10.4

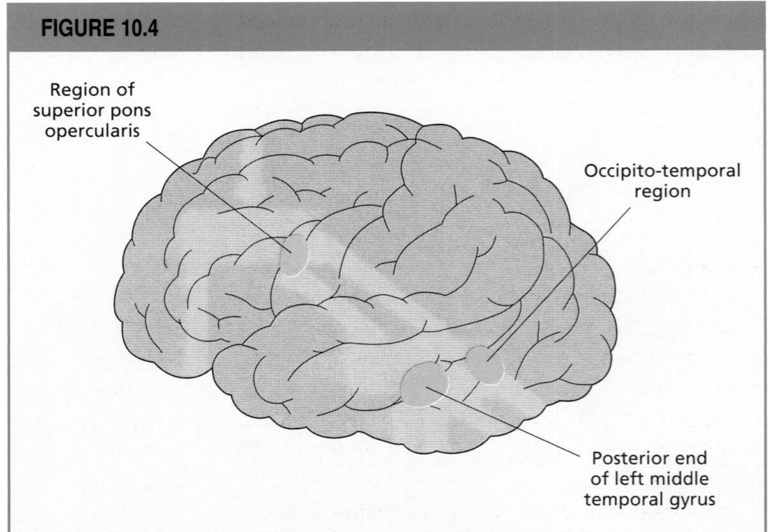

Occipito-temporal region and posterior temporal gyrus: activated most by high- and low-frequency words; superior pons opercularis: activated most by low-frequency words and pseudowords. Based on data in Fiebach et al. (2002).

characters. Processing English involves some of the areas specifically associated with reading pinyin or Chinese characters, suggesting that reading English words involves using both routes.

Route 1 (grapheme–phoneme conversion)

Route 1 differs from the other routes in using grapheme–phoneme conversion, which involves converting spelling (graphemes) into sound (phonemes). According to Coltheart et al. (2001, p. 212), "By the term 'grapheme' we mean a letter or letter sequence that corresponds to a single phoneme, such as the *i* in *pig*, the *ng* in *ping*, and the *igh* in *high*." In their computational model, "For any grapheme, the phoneme assigned to it was the phoneme most commonly associated with that grapheme in the set of English monosyllables that contain that grapheme" (Coltheart et al., 2001, p. 216).

If a brain-damaged patient used only Route 1, what would we find? The use of grapheme–phoneme conversion rules should permit accurate pronunciation of words having regular spelling–sound correspondences, but not of irregular words which do not conform to the conversion rules. For example, if an irregular word such as "pint" has grapheme–phoneme conversion rules applied to it, it should be pronounced to rhyme with "hint"; this is known as regularisation. Finally, grapheme–phoneme conversion rules can provide pronunciations of nonwords.

Patients adhering most closely to exclusive use of Route 1 were labelled surface dyslexics by Marshall and Newcombe (1973). **Surface dyslexia** is a condition involving particular problems in reading irregular words. JC, a patient with surface dyslexia, read 52% of regular words correctly, but only 32% of irregular words. More striking findings were reported by McCarthy and Warrington (1984). They studied KT, who had surface dyslexia. He read 100% of nonwords accurately, and 81% of regular words, but was successful with only 41% of irregular words. Over 70% of the errors that KT made with irregular words were due to regularisation.

Surface dyslexics such as JC and KT seem to have a strong (but not exclusive) reliance on Route 1. If they read every word by grapheme–phoneme conversion, then *all* irregular words would be mispronounced, and this simply does not happen. Presumably surface dyslexics make some use of routes other than Route 1, even though these other routes are severely damaged.

Surface dyslexics vary considerably in their specific impairments. For example, JC had no problem with understanding words he pronounced correctly, whereas other surface dylexics often fail to understand words they can pronounce. Thus, the syndrome of "surface dyslexia" has limited usefulness.

Route 2 (lexicon plus semantic system)

The basic idea behind Route 2 is that representations of thousands of familiar words are stored in an orthographic input lexicon. Visual presentation of a word leads to activation in the orthographic input lexicon. This is followed by obtaining its meaning from the semantic system, after which its sound pattern is generated in the phonological output lexicon.

How could we identify patients using Route 2 but not Route 1? Their intact orthographic input lexicon means they can pronounce familiar words whether regular or irregular. However, their inability to use grapheme–phoneme conversion should mean they find it very hard to pronounce relatively unfamiliar words and nonwords.

Phonological dyslexics fit this predicted pattern fairly well. **Phonological dyslexia** involves particular problems with reading unfamiliar words and non-words. The first case of phonological dyslexia reported systematically was RG (Beauvois & Dérouesné, 1979). In one experiment with 40 words and 40 nonwords, RG successfully read 100% of the real words but only 10% of the nonwords. Similar findings with 11 phonological dyslexic patients were reported by Berndt, Haendiges, Mitchum, and Wayland (1996).

According to the dual-route model, patients with phonological dyslexia have *specific* problems with grapheme–phoneme conversion. However, Coltheart (1996) discussed 18 patients with phonological dyslexia, all of whom had *general* phonological impairments. As Harm and Seidenberg (2001, p. 73) pointed out, this leaves the dual-route model in a tricky position: "[It] must treat this broader phonological impairment as one that happens to co-occur with the primary deficit in grapheme–phoneme conversion." As we will see later in the chapter, the notion that phonological dyslexics have a general phonological impairment is of central importance within the computational model of Plaut, McClelland, Seidenberg, and Patterson (1996).

Route 3 (lexicon only)

Route 3 resembles Route 2 in that the orthographic input lexicon and the phonological output lexicon are involved (see Figure 10.3). However, the semantic system is bypassed in Route 3, so printed words that are pronounced are not understood. Otherwise, the expectations about reading performance for users of Route 3 are the same as those for users of Route 2: familiar regular and irregular words should be pronounced correctly, whereas most unfamiliar words and nonwords should not.

Funnell (1983) studied a patient, WB, with phonological dyslexia, who seemed to be using Route 3. His ability to use Route 1 was very limited, since he could not produce the sound of any single letters or nonwords. He could read about 85% of words, but did seem to do this by using Route 2. This was shown by his poor ability to make semantic judgements about words. These findings are consistent with the view that WB was bypassing the semantic system when reading words. In similar fashion, Coslett (1991) found a patient, WT, who was reasonably good at reading irregular words, but had no understanding of them. She was extremely poor at reading nonwords, indicating that she could hardly use Route 1 at all.

Hillis and Caramazza (1995) proposed an alternative account called the summation hypothesis. According to this hypothesis, the reasonable reading performance of patients such as WB, and WT occurs because they *combine* information from their partially impaired Routes 1 and 2. Evidence against the summation hypothesis was reported by Wu, Martin, and Damian (2002). They studied a patient, ML, a phonological dyslexic with severe problems in using Route 1. According to the summation hypothesis, this patient must rely heavily on his semantic knowledge of words when reading, and so should take longer to read words for which he had relatively little semantic knowledge available. In fact this was *not* the case, indicating that ML was using the non-semantic Route 3 rather than combining information from Routes 1 and 2.

Deep dyslexia

Deep dyslexia is a condition in which there are particular problems in reading unfamiliar words, an inability to read nonwords, and semantic reading errors (e.g., "ship" read as "boat"). Deep dyslexia may occur as a result of damage to the grapheme–phoneme conversion and semantic systems. In some ways, deep dyslexia seems like a more severe form of phonological dyslexia, and deep dyslexics showing some recovery of reading skills often become phonological dyslexics (Southwood & Chatterjee, 2001).

Coltheart et al. (2001, p. 246) argued that "Deep dyslexics are reading, not with a damaged version of the normal reading system, but with a completely different reading system located in the right hemisphere." If so, then the study of deep dyslexics can tell us essentially nothing about normal reading processes, which are based primarily in the left hemisphere.

Evidence consistent with the right-hemisphere hypothesis was reported by Patterson, Vargha-Khadem, and Polkey (1989). They studied a girl, NI, whose left cerebral hemisphere was removed at the age of 13 because of a brain disease. When she was 15, NI had all the symptoms shown by deep dyslexics, leading Patterson et al. (1989, p. 56) to conclude, "Adult deep dyslexics, who may be reading with the right hemisphere, and N.I., who must be reading with the right hemisphere, are strikingly similar."

Weekes, Coltheart, and Gordon (1997) administered various reading tasks to LH (a deep dyslexic), a surface dyslexic, and two unimpaired controls. Regional cerebral blood flow during visual word recognition was greater in the right hemisphere than in the left hemisphere *only* for LH.

In spite of the above findings, there are various reasons why the right-hemisphere hypothesis has few supporters. First, deep dyslexics typically show much better reading performance than split-brain patients when presented with words to their right hemisphere (see Chapter 17). Second, split-brain patients using their right hemisphere typically have a reading advantage for concrete words over abstract ones, but that difference is not found in deep dyslexics. Third, there are the findings of Roeltgen (1987), who studied a deep dyslexic who had had a stroke in the left hemisphere. According to the right-hemisphere hypothesis, this should have caused him to use the right hemisphere for reading. However, when this patient had a second stroke in the *left* hemisphere, his reading ability disappeared. Fourth, Laine et al. (2000) used MEG (see Chapter 1), and found that HH (a 46-year-old male deep dyslexic) had activation mainly in the *left* hemisphere when performing various reading tasks. HH's pattern of brain activation while reading was generally similar to that of normal individuals, which is counter to the right-hemisphere hypothesis.

In sum, reading in deep dyslexics does *not* depend entirely on the right hemisphere. However, Coltheart (2000) argued that deep dyslexics use the left hemisphere to a limited extent. This weak version of the right-hemisphere hypothesis is hard to test, but is consistent with most of the available evidence.

Computational modelling

Coltheart et al. (2001) produced a detailed computational model to test their approach more thoroughly. They started with 7981 one-syllable words varying in length between one and eight letters. They used McClelland and Rumelhart's (1981) interactive activation model as the basis for the orthographic component of their model, and the output or response side of the model derives from the theories of Dell (1986) and of Levelt et al. (1999a) (see Chapter 12). The pronunciation most activated by processing in the lexical and non-lexical routes is the one determining the naming response: "The model is considered to have determined the pronunciation of a monosyllabic [one-syllabled] letter string when it has activated (to some criterion of satisfaction) all of the phonemes of that letter string" (Coltheart et al., 2001, p. 217). It is a **cascade model** because any activation at one level is passed on to the next level before processing at the first level is complete. Cascaded models can be contrasted with thresholded models, in which activation at one level is only passed on to other levels after a given threshold of activation is reached.

As discussed earlier, it is assumed that many brain-damaged patients rely almost exclusively on either the lexical or non-lexical route. However, unimpaired individuals typically use both routes when reading aloud, and these two routes are *not* independent in their functioning. According to Coltheart et al. (2001, p. 234):

> The lexical route and the non-lexical route share two processing components. One is the letter-identification system . . . The other is the speech (phoneme) system, because the output from both routes goes to that system . . . the derived phonology for all reading-aloud responses [words and non-words] is the result of the input from both the non-lexical (assembled) and lexical (addressed) routes to the phoneme level.

Evidence

Coltheart et al. (2001) carried out numerous simulations using their computational model to see whether the model would generate the same performance as humans. They presented the model with all 7981 words, and found 7898 (99%) were read accurately. When the model was presented with 7000 one-syllable nonwords, it read 98.9% of them correctly.

It is assumed within the model that the lexical and non-lexical routes are both involved in the naming task, and so the two routes do not operate independently. Evidence consistent with that assumption was reported by Glushko (1979), who compared naming times for two kinds of nonwords: (1) those having irregular word neighbours (e.g., "have" is an irregular word neighbour of "mave", whereas "gave" and "save" are regular word neighbours); and (2) nonwords having only regular word neighbours. Nonwords of the former type were named more slowly. This suggests that the lexical route can affect the non-lexical route in the reading of nonwords, as predicted by the model.

Some studies have focused on the effects of the regularity of words' spelling-to-sound correspondences on naming. For example, Seidenberg et al. (1984) found irregular words took longer to name than regular ones with low-frequency words but not with high-frequency ones. According to the model, the lexical route operates more slowly with low-frequency words. The naming of low-frequency irregular words is especially slow because conflicting information about their pronunciation is received from the lexical and non-lexical routes.

Many computational models are of relevance to only one task. Coltheart et al. (2001) applied the dual-route cascaded model (developed to explain performance on the word naming task) to the lexical decision task (deciding whether a string of letters forms a word). They assumed that a "Yes" response is made on the lexical decision task when the activation of any lexical item (word) exceeds a criterion level, whereas a "No" response is made when a deadline is reached without the criterion being reached. They also assumed that very common words produce greater activation than less common ones. These assumptions led to the predictions that there would be an effect of word frequency on response time, and that "Yes" responses would be faster than "No" ones. These predictions were confirmed in both human and computer simulation data. Overall, Coltheart et al. (2001) found the dual-route cascaded model accounted for five different effects on the lexical decision task.

Evaluation

The dual-route cascaded model provides an excellent account of disorders such as surface dyslexia and phonological dyslexia. It has also proved useful in accounting for the naming and lexical-decision performance of unimpaired individuals. According to Coltheart et al. (2001), the model has successfully simulated 18 effects with reading aloud or naming, plus 5 effects associated with lexical decision. In general, the theoretical assumptions contained within the model seem plausible and in line with the available evidence. The model outperforms its main rival (the model of Plaut et al., 1996), which is discussed below.

What are the model's limitations? First, it contains 31 parameters or variables, which is a very large number. It gives the modeller enormous flexibility even though not all of the parameters are free to vary, and means most sets of data could be fitted by the model. Second, as Coltheart et al. (2001, p. 249) pointed out, "All of the current computational models of reading English, including the DRC [dual route cascaded] model, are restricted to the processing of monosyllabic stimuli." Third, while the model names words and nonwords very accurately, it is much less successful in accounting for naming *times*. The model accounts for 39.4% of the variance in nonword naming times and for only 4.5% of the variance in word naming times. These figures are disappointing but higher than those based on the model of Plaut et al. (1996), which are 0.1% and 4.5%, respectively. Fourth, as Coltheart et al. (2001, p. 236) admitted, "The Chinese, Japanese, and Korean writing systems are structurally so different from the English writing system that a model like the DRC [dual route cascaded] model would simply not be applicable: for example, monosyllabic non-words cannot even be written in the Chinese script or in Japanese kanji, so the distinction between a lexical and non-lexical route for reading aloud cannot even arise."

Distributed connectionist approach: Plaut et al. (1996)

Within the dual-route model, it is assumed that pronouncing irregular words and nonwords is based mainly on different routes. This contrasts with the single-route connectionist approach of Plaut et al. (1996). Their approach "eschews [avoids] separate mechanisms for pronouncing nonwords and exception [irregular] words. Rather, all of the system's knowledge of spelling–sound correspondences is brought to bear in pronouncing all types of letter strings [words *and* nonwords]. Conflicts among possible alternative pronunciations of a letter string are resolved . . . by co-operative and competitive interactions based on how the letter string relates to all known words and their pronunciations." Thus, Plaut et al. (1996) assumed that the pronunciation of words and nonwords is based on a system that is highly *interactive* during learning.

Plaut et al. (1996) argued that words vary in consistency (the extent to which their pronunciation agrees with those of similarly spelled words). Highly consistent words can generally be pronounced faster and more accurately than inconsistent words, because more of the available knowledge supports the correct pronunciation of such words. Word naming is generally predicted well by consistency (e.g., Glushko, 1979).

Plaut et al. (1996) tried various simulations based on two crucial notions:

(1) The pronunciation of a word or nonword is influenced strongly by consistency based on the pronunciations of all words similar to it.
(2) High-frequency or common words have more influence on the pronunciation of a given word than do low-frequency or rare words: high-frequency words are encountered more often, and so contribute more to changes in the network.

A successful simulation was based on the architecture shown in Figure 10.5 (hidden units are discussed in Chapter 1). The network learns to pronounce words accurately as connections develop between the visual forms of letters and combinations of letters (grapheme units) and their corresponding phonemes (phoneme units). The network based on this architecture learned by the use of **back-propagation**, in which the actual outputs or responses of the system are compared against the correct ones. The network received

FIGURE 10.5

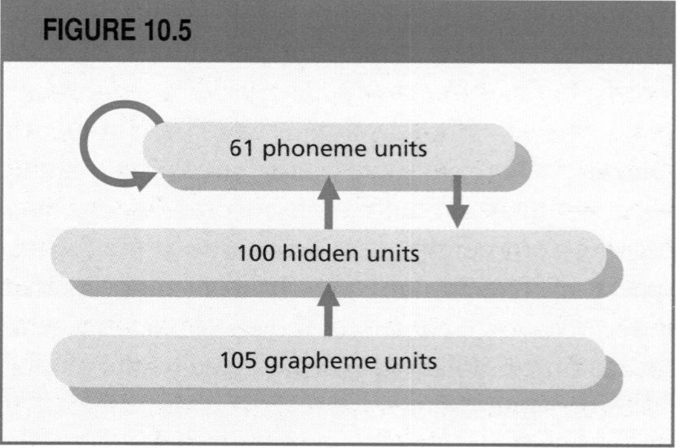

The architecture of the connectionist approach to word reading put forward by Plaut et al. (1996). Copyright © 1996 by the American Psychological Association. Reprinted with permission.

prolonged training with a set of 2998 words. At the end of training, the performance of the network closely resembled that of adult readers:

(1) Inconsistent words took longer to name than did consistent words.
(2) Rare words took longer to name than common ones.
(3) There was an interaction between word frequency and consistency, with the effects of consistency being much greater for rare words than for common ones.
(4) The network pronounced over 90% of nonwords "correctly", which is comparable with the performance of adult readers; this finding is especially impressive because the network received no direct training on nonwords.

The above simulation did not take semantic information into account. However, Plaut et al. (1996, p. 95) argued that "to the extent that the semantic pathway has learned to derive the meaning and pronunciation of a word, it affords additional input to the phoneme units, pushing them toward their correct activations." They expanded their network model to include semantic information, assuming that such information has more impact on high-frequency words. A network based on this assumption learned to read regular and exception words much faster than a network lacking semantic information.

It follows from Plaut et al.'s (1996) model that consistent nonwords (having spellings resembling those of words pronounced consistently) should be named faster than inconsistent nonwords. Support for this prediction was obtained when words and nonwords were both presented in a list. However, there was *no* consistency effect when only nonwords were presented. According to Job, Peressotti, and Cusinato (1998, p. 626), this finding can be accounted for more readily by dual-route models than by single-route models such as that of Plaut et al. (1996): "The fact that the consistency effect disappears in the pure list is explained by dual-route models by assuming that when only pseudo-words [nonwords resembling words] are presented, participants can strategically rely to a larger extent on the non-lexical route. However, current single-route models, which assume a unique pathway from print to sound, seem unable to account for these context effects."

Surface dyslexia and phonological dyslexia

Plaut et al. (1996, p. 92) argued that, "Surface dyslexia . . . seems to involve reading primarily via the phonological pathway because of an impairment of the semantic route." Plaut et al. (1996) tested this theory by making "lesions" to the network to reduce or eliminate the contribution from semantics. The network's reading performance was very good on regular high- and low-frequency words and on nonwords, worse on irregular high-frequency words, and worst on irregular low-frequency words, which matches the pattern found with surface dyslexics.

Further support for the theory comes from the study of patients suffering with **Alzheimer's disease**, which involves progressive dementia or loss of mental powers. Such patients typically have similar reading performance to surface dyslexics, and the severity of the reading impairment is correlated with the extent of semantic deterioration (Patterson, Graham, & Hodges, 1994).

What about phonological dyslexia? Plaut et al. (1996, p. 99) only considered this disorder in general terms: "In the limit of a complete lesion between orthography and phonology, non-word reading would be impossible. Thus, a lesion to the network that severely impaired the phonological pathway while leaving the contribution of semantics to phonology (relatively) intact would replicate the basic characteristics of phonological dyslexia." As we saw earlier, there is support for the notion that phonological dyslexics have a general impairment of phonological processing (e.g., Harm & Seidenberg, 2001).

Deep dyslexia

Plaut and Shallice (1993) proposed a network similar to the ones later put forward by Plaut et al. (1996) to understand deep dyslexia. This network has four key properties:

- Similar patterns of activation represent similar words in the orthographic and semantic domains.

- Learning alters the strengths of the connections between word spellings and meanings.
- The initial pattern of semantic activity produced by a visually presented word moves towards (or is attracted by) the pattern of the nearest known meaning; this is known as the operation of attractors.
- The semantic representations of most high-imageability words contain many more features than those of low-imageability words.

Plaut and Shallice (1993) studied the consequences of damage to the network, finding that virtually all the main symptoms of deep dyslexia could be simulated. The only important symptom not emerging from damage to the connectionist network was impaired writing performance. Plaut and Shallice's theory predicts about a dozen symptoms of deep dyslexia from only a few theoretical assumptions. In addition, the theory is explicit, in that the processes involved were specified in detail before the simulations proceeded.

Evaluation

The connectionist model put forward by Plaut et al. (1996) resembles the dual-route cascaded model in being interactive and cascaded. As a result, it has no difficulty in accounting for findings such as the reading of nonwords being influenced by lexical factors (Glushko, 1979). In addition, the model provides a coherent account of deep dyslexia, and its view that a general impairment in phonological processing underlies phonological dyslexia appears correct. Overall, as Harley (2001, p. 205) concluded, "Connectionist modelling has provided an explicit, single-route model that covers most of the main findings . . . At the very least, it has clarified the issues involved in reading."

Plaut et al.'s (1996) connectionist model has various limitations. First, as we saw earlier, the predictions of the dual-route cascaded model are generally more accurate than those of the Plaut et al. (1996) model (Coltheart et al., 2001). Second, as Plaut et al. (1996, p. 108) admitted, "the nature of processing within the semantic pathway has been characterised in only the coarsest way." Third, the approach provides only a sketchy account of some key issues (e.g., the nature of the impairment in phonological dyslexia). As Coltheart et al. (2001, p. 245) pointed out:

> In the DRC [dual-route cascaded] model the route on which phonological dyslexics are presumed to be relying for word reading has been implemented [specified in detail], whereas it has not been implemented in the PMSP [Plaut et al.] model. Hence the DRC model (but not the PMSP model can be used for quantitative simulation of data from phonological dyslexic patients.

Fourth, Plaut et al. (1996) argued that surface dyslexia is caused by damage to the semantic system. Thus, patients with severe damage to the semantic system should have very poor reading of irregular words (a key symptom of surface dyslexia). In fact, however, some patients with severe semantic impairments read irregular words very well (e.g., WLP studied by Schwartz, Saffran & Marin, 1980, and DRN studied by Cipolotti & Warrington, 1995).

Fifth, the model predicts that consistent nonwords should be named faster than inconsistent nonwords. As a result, it cannot readily account for the disappearance of this consistency effect when only nonwords are presented (Job et al., 1998).

Sixth, the model is limited in that its input consists of graphemes that have already been parsed or structured. According to Grainger (personal communication), "It is this prior parsing of the input that most likely determines the success of the model."

Seventh, the model has only been tested with one-syllabled words. It remains to be seen whether it could be applied successfully to multi-syllabled words.

READING: EYE-MOVEMENT STUDIES

Our eyes seem to move smoothly across the page while reading. In fact, they actually move in rapid jerks (**saccades**), as you can see if you look closely at someone else reading. Saccades are ballistic (once initiated their direction cannot be changed). There are fairly frequent regressions in which the eyes move backwards in the text, accounting for about 10% of all saccades. Saccades take 20–30 milliseconds to complete, and are separated by fixations lasting for 200–250 milliseconds. The length of each saccade is about eight letters or spaces. Information is extracted from the text only during each fixation, and not during the intervening saccades (Latour, 1962).

The amount of text from which useful information is obtained in each fixation has been studied by using the "moving window" technique (see Rayner & Sereno, 1994). Most of the text is mutilated except for an experimenter-defined area or window surrounding the reader's point of fixation. Every time the reader moves his/her eyes, different parts of the text are mutilated to permit normal reading only within the window region. The effects of different-sized windows on reading performance can be compared.

The **perceptual span** (effective field of view) is affected by the difficulty of the text and print size. It often extends 3 or 4 letters to the left of fixation and up to 15 letters to the right (see Figure 10.6). This asymmetry occurs because the most informative text lies to the right of the fixation point. The form of the asymmetry is clearly learned. Readers of Hebrew, which is read from right to left, show the opposite asymmetry (Pollatsek, Bolozky, Well, & Rayner, 1981). The size of the perceptual span is much smaller for Chinese than for English (Inhoff & Liu, 1998), presumably because Chinese characters are densely packed.

Rayner and Sereno (1994) concluded that there are three different spans:

FIGURE 10.6

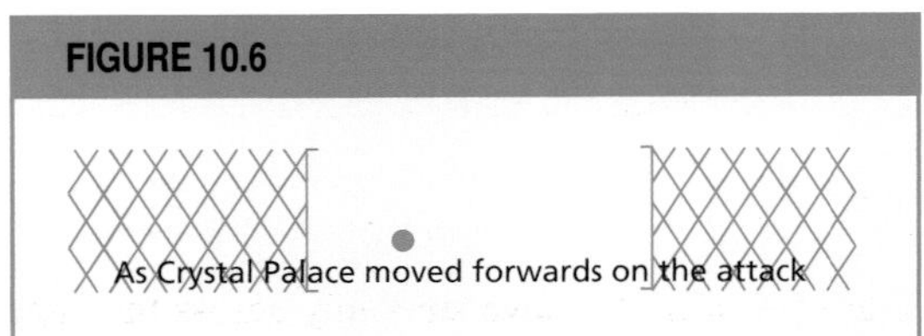

As Crystal Palace moved forwards on the attack

The perceptual span in reading.

- The *total perceptual span* (the total area from which useful information is extracted); this is the longest span.
- The *letter-identification span* (the area from which information about letters is obtained).
- The *word-identification span* (the area from which information relevant to word-identification processes is obtained); this is the shortest span.

The size of the perceptual span means that parafoveal information (surrounding the central or foveal region) is used in reading. Convincing evidence comes from use of the boundary technique, in which there is a preview word just to the right of the point of fixation. As the reader makes a saccade to this word, it changes into the target word. However, the reader is unaware of the change. The duration of fixation on the target word is less when that word is the same as the preview word than when it differs (see Reichle et al., 1998). Reading time on the target word is less when the preview word is visually or phonologically similar to the target word, suggesting that visual and phonological information can be extracted from parafoveal processing. However, the processing of information at the parafoveal level does not reach the semantic level (Rayner & Morris, 1992).

E-Z Reader model

Reichle, Pollatsek, Fisher, and Rayner (1998) and Reichle, Rayner, and Pollatsek (2003) explained the pattern of eye movements during reading in their E-Z Reader model (a spoof on the title of the film *Easy Rider*, but only obvious if you know that Z is pronounced "zee" in American English). About 80% of content words (nouns, verbs, and adjectives) are fixated, and it is important to identify the factors determining the length of fixation on such words. Only about 20% of function words (articles, conjunctions, prepositions, and pronouns) are fixated, and we need to identify the factors leading some words to be "skipped" or not fixated at all.

Here are key facts that the model was designed to explain (see Reichle et al., 1998):

- Rare words are fixated for longer than common words.
- Words that are more predictable in the sentence context are fixated for less time.
- Words not fixated tend to be common, short, or predictable.
- The fixation time on a word is longer when preceded by a rare word: the "spillover" effect.

What would be the most obvious kind of model? Perhaps readers fixate on a word until they have processed it sufficiently, after which they immediately fixate the next word. There are two major problems with such an approach. First, it takes 150–200 ms to execute an eye-movement program. If readers operated according to this simple model, they would waste time waiting for their eyes to move. Second, it is hard to see how readers could skip words, because they would know nothing about the next word until they fixated it.

How can we get round these problems? Reichle et al. (1998, 2003) argued that the next eye movement is programmed after only *part* of the processing of the currently fixated word has occurred. This greatly reduces the time between completion of processing on the current word and movement of the eyes to the next word, and is clearly an efficient way to proceed. Any spare time is used to start processing the next word. If the processing of the next word is completed rapidly enough, it is skipped. In essence, cognitive processes determine *when* to move the eyes, whereas low-level processes (e.g., length of next word) determine *where* to move the eyes.

Reichle et al. (1998, 2003) emphasised several general theoretical assumptions:

(1) Readers check the familiarity of the word they are currently fixating.
(2) Completion of frequency checking of a word (what Reichle et al., 2003, term the first stage of lexical access) is the signal to initiate an eye-movement program.
(3) Readers also engage in the second stage of **lexical access**, which involves accessing a word's semantic and phonological forms. This task takes longer to complete than the first stage.
(4) Completion of the second stage of lexical access is the signal for a shift of covert (internal) attention to the next word.
(5) Frequency checking and lexical access are completed faster for common words than rare ones, and this is more so for lexical access than for frequency checking.
(6) Frequency checking and lexical access are completed faster for predictable than for unpredictable words.

These theoretical assumptions lead to various predictions (see Figure 10.7). Assumptions (2) and (5) together predict that the time spent fixating common words will be less than rare words, which

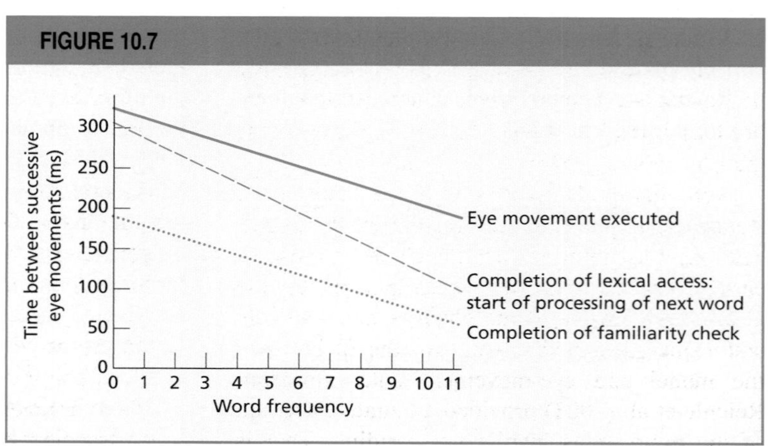

The effects of word frequency on eye movements according to the E-Z Reader model. Adapted from Reichle et al. (1998).

FIGURE 10.8

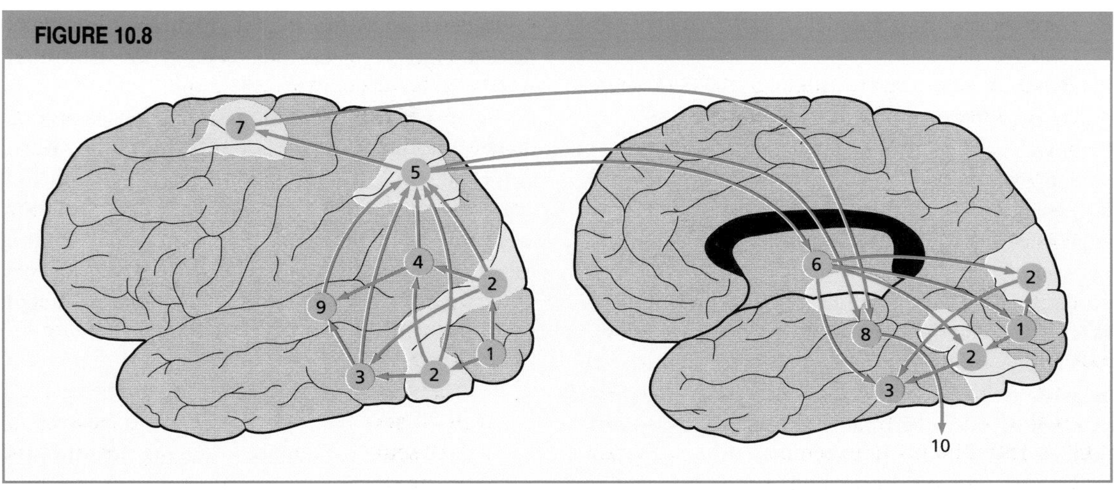

The main brain areas and pathways included in controlling eye-movements in reading according to the E-Z reader model. From Reichle et al. (2003). Reproduced with permission from Cambridge University Press.

is consistent with the evidence. According to the model, readers spend the time between completion of lexical access to a word and the next eye movement in parafoveal processing of the next word. The amount of time spent in such parafoveal processing is less when the fixated word is rare than when it is common (see Figure 10.7). Thus, the word following a rare word generally needs to be fixated for longer than the word following a common word. This is precisely the spillover effect described earlier.

Why are words that are common, predictable, or short most likely to be skipped or not fixated? According to the model, a word is skipped when its lexical access has been completed while the current word is still being fixated. This typically happens with common, predictable, or short words, because lexical access is faster for these words than for others (assumptions 5 and 6).

Note that the latest version of the model (E-Z Reader 7) is presented in Reichle et al. (2003). The basic assumptions are the same as those of earlier versions (e.g., those presented in Reichle et al., 1998). Most of the changes are relatively small ones designed to improve the fit between the model and eye-movement data. However, Reichle et al. (2003) provided a tentative account of the brain areas involved in reading. That is shown in Figure 10.8 with the numbers in brackets in the list below corresponding to numbers in the Figure:

- About 90 ms after a word is fixated, the features making up its orthographic form are processed in the primary visual cortex (1).
- The individual letters are integrated in the left extrastriate cortex (2).
- About 150–200 ms after fixation, the word's orthographic form has been assembled in the left extrastriate cortex (2) and/or the left inferior temporal gyrus (3).
- Next the word's phonological representation is accessed in the left angular gyrus (4).
- When the current word has been partly identified, the parietal fields (5) disengage visuospatial attention.
- The pulvinar nucleus of the thalamus (6) shifts the attentional focus forward, resulting in the frontal eye fields (7) and superior colliculus (8) using some information (e.g., word length) to start programming a saccade to the next word.
- At the same time, processing of the fixated word continues until its meaning is accessed via Wernicke's area (9) and various regions of associative cortex.

Evidence

Schilling, Rayner, and Chumbley (1998) carried out a computer simulation of E-Z Reader 7 to compare its performance to that of 30 college students reading 48 sentences each. The simulation predicted several aspects of reading performance very well. Of note was the finding that this version of the model was significantly better than previous versions at predicting the probabilities of fixating on individual words and gaze durations.

Various brain-imaging and other techniques can be used to shed light on the processes involved in reading. However, many processes occur very rapidly. For example, we start to plan our next eye movement within about 100–150 ms of starting to fixate any given word. As Sereno and Rayner (2000) pointed out, the speed of most reading processes means that most brain-imaging techniques are of little value. However, that is not the case with event-related potentials (ERPs; see Chapter 1), which were recorded by Sereno, Rayner, and Posner (1998). As predicted by the E-Z Reader model, they observed effects of word frequency on event-related potentials early in processing (about 150 ms). Similar findings were reported by Sereno et al. (2003).

According to the model, word frequency and word predictability are important and *independent* factors determining how long we fixate on a word during reading. These assumptions may not be altogether correct. McDonald and Shillcock (2003) studied the effects of word frequency and word predictability on eye fixations. These two factors covaried, i.e., common words tended to be more predictable than rare ones on the basis of the preceding word. Of most importance, when attempts were made to disentangle the effects of word frequency and word predictability, the effects of word frequency often disappeared. Thus, some of the apparent effects of word frequency on length of eye fixations are actually due to word predictability.

Reichle et al. (2003) admitted that factors in addition to word frequency and word probability may well influence the duration of fixations on a word. There is supporting evidence. For example, Juhasz and Rayner (2003) found a significant effect of word concreteness on gaze duration in reading.

According to the model, fixations should be fastest when eye fixations are on the centre of words rather than towards either end. This is because word identification should be easiest in those conditions. In fact, Vitu, McConkie, Kerr, and O'Regan (2001) found precisely the opposite: across a total of 153,855 eye fixations, fixations were much longer when they were at the centre of words than towards one end. It is not known why it occurs, but this large effect is not predicted by the model.

Evaluation

The model specifies the major factors determining eye movements in reading. It shows that reading occurs on a word-by-word basis, and that parafoveal processing increases the efficiency of the reading process. Computer simulations (e.g., Schilling et al., 1998) provide good support for the major assumptions of the model. Reichle et al. (2003) compared 11 models of reading including E-Z Reader 7 in terms of whether each one can account for each of eight phenomena (e.g., frequency effects; spillover effects; predictability effects; costs of skipping). They decided E-Z Reader could account for all eight phenomena, but a key finding was that eight of the other models can account for two or less of the phenomena. Finally, the model has the advantage of focusing on data obtained from reasonably natural reading situations.

What are the main limitations of the model? First, it de-emphasises the impact of higher-level cognitive processes on fixation times. For example, readers generally fixate for an unusually long time on the word "seems" when presented in the sentence "Since Jay always jogs a mile seems like a short distance" (Frazier & Rayner, 1982; see Chapter 11), but the theory does not really account for such effects. In addition, the model does not account for regressions in text. Reichle et al. (2003) defended their neglect of higher-level processes as follows: "We posit [assume] that higher-order processes intervene in eye-movement control only when 'something is wrong' and either send a message to stop moving forward or a signal to executive a regression."

Second, the emphasis of the model is perhaps too much on explaining eye-movement data rather than other findings on reading. As Sereno et al. (2003) pointed out, "The danger is that in setting out to establish a model of eye-movement control, the result may be a model of eye-movement experiments." What is needed in future is a more systematic attempt to integrate the findings from eye-movement studies more closely with general theories of reading.

Third, it may be incorrect to assume that word frequency and word predictability have independent effects on eye fixations (McDonald & Shillcock, 2003). Related to that, it may be that the impact of word frequency on the duration of eye fixation in reading is exaggerated in the model.

Fourth, the model is based on the assumption of serial processing, with only one word being processed at any given moment. There is currently much controversy on this issue. However, there is accumulating evidence (e.g., Kennedy, Pynte, & Ducrot, 2002) that the properties of two words (e.g., visual or orthographic properties) are sometimes processed in parallel.

Fifth, the finding that eye fixations at the centre of words are much longer than those towards either end (Vitu et al., 2001) is not predicted by the model.

LISTENING TO SPEECH

Understanding speech is much less straightforward than one might imagine. Some idea of the kinds of processes involved in listening to speech is provided in Figure 10.9. The first stage involves *decoding* the auditory signal. As Liberman, Cooper, Shankweiler, and Studdert-Kennedy (1967) pointed out, speech can be regarded as a

FIGURE 10.9

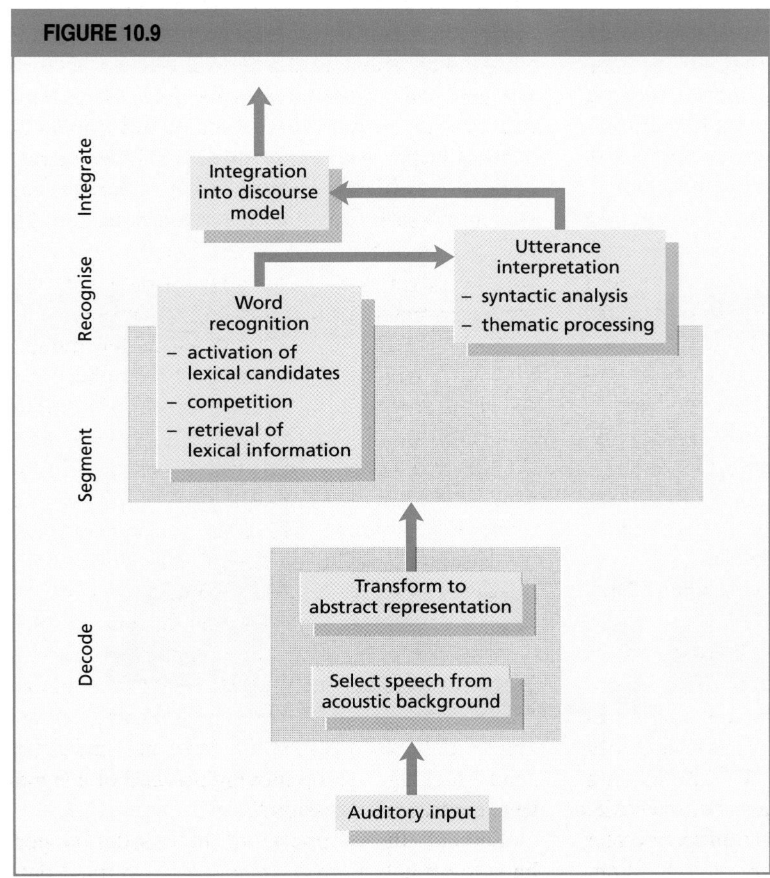

The main processes involved in speech perception and comprehension. From Cutler and Clifton (1999) by permission of Oxford University Press.

code, and we as listeners possess the key to understanding it. However, even before starting to do that, we often need to select out the speech signal from other completely irrelevant auditory input (e.g., traffic noise). Decoding itself involves extracting discrete elements from the speech signal. Cutler and Clifton (1999, p. 126) provide a good account of what is involved: "Linguists describe speech as a series of phonetic segments; a phonetic segment (**phoneme**) is simply the smallest unit in terms of which spoken language can be sequentially described. Thus, the word *key* consists of the two segments /ki/, and *sea* of the two segments /si/; they differ in the first phoneme." As we will see shortly, the acoustic information signalling a given phoneme can vary considerably, and this variability greatly complicates the task of identifying phonemes.

The second and third stages of speech perception involve identifying the constituents (i.e., syllables; words) contained in the speech signal. The third stage (that of word identification) is of particular importance. As McQueen (2004, p. 255) pointed out, "The core process in speech perception is word recognition." Some of the main problems involved in word recognition are discussed shortly. However, we will mention one problem at this point. Most people know tens of thousands of words, but these words (in English at least) are constructed out of only about 35 phonemes. The obvious consequence is that the great majority of spoken words resemble many other words at the phonemic level.

The fourth and fifth stages both emphasise speech comprehension. The focus in the fourth stage is on interpretation of the utterance. This involves constructing a coherent meaning for each sentence on the basis of information about individual words and their order in the sentence. Finally, in the fifth stage, the focus is on integrating the meaning of the current sentence with preceding speech to build up an overall model of the speaker's message.

Speech signal

Useful information about the speech signal has been obtained from the **spectrograph**. With this instrument, sound enters through a microphone, and is then converted into an electrical signal. This signal is fed to a bank of filters selecting narrow-frequency bands. Finally, the spectrograph produces a visible record of the component frequencies of sound over time; this is known as a spectrogram (see Figure 10.10). The spectrogram provides information about **formants**, which

FIGURE 10.10

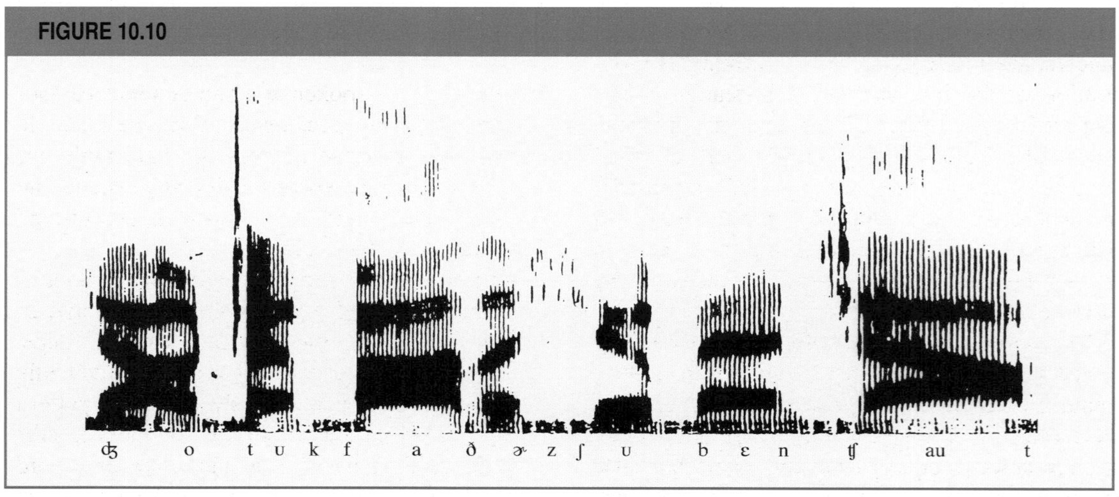

Spectrogram of the sentence "Joe took father's shoe bench out". From *Language Processes* by Vivien C. Tartter (1986, p. 210), reproduced with permission of the author.

are frequency bands emphasised by the vocal apparatus when saying a phoneme. Vowels have three formants. These are numbered first, second, and third, starting with the formant of lowest frequency. The sound frequency of vowels is generally lower than that of consonants.

Spectrograms may seem to provide an accurate picture of those aspects of the sound wave having the greatest influence on the human auditory system. However, this is not necessarily the case. For example, formants look important in a spectrogram, but this does not prove they are of value in human speech perception. Evidence that the spectrogram *is* of value has been provided by using a *pattern playback* or *vocoder*, which allows the spectrograph to be played back. Thus, the pattern of frequencies in the spectrogram was produced by speech, and pattern playback permits the spectrogram to be reconverted into speech again. Liberman, Delattre, and Cooper (1952) constructed "artificial" vowels on the spectrogram based only on the first two formants of each vowel. These vowels were easily identified when played through the vocoder, suggesting that formant information is used to recognise vowels.

Lip-reading: McGurk effect

Most deaf people use lip-reading to understand speech. However, lip-reading is also used by those whose hearing is entirely normal. McGurk and MacDonald (1976) provided a striking demonstration of the importance of lip-reading. They prepared a videotape of someone saying "ba" repeatedly. The sound channel then changed so there was a voice saying "ga" repeatedly in synchronisation with lip movements still indicating "ba". Participants reported hearing "da", a blending of the visual and the auditory information.

The so-called McGurk effect is surprisingly robust. Green, Kuhl, Meltzoff, and Stevens (1991) found the effect even with a female face and a male voice. According to them, information about pitch (relative frequency) becomes irrelevant early in speech processing. As a result, the McGurk effect is found even with a gender mismatch between vision and hearing.

Visual information from lip movements is used to make sense of speech sounds, because the information conveyed by the speech sounds is often inadequate. Of course, there are circumstances (e.g., listening to the radio) in which no relevant visual information is available. We can usually follow what is said on the radio, because broadcasters are trained to articulate clearly.

It is generally assumed that the McGurk effect depends almost entirely on bottom-up processes triggered directly by the discrepant visual and auditory signals. It follows that the McGurk effect should not be influenced by top-down processes based on participants' expectations. However, Windmann (2004) found that expectation is important. More participants produced the McGurk effect when the crucial word (based on blending the discrepant visual and auditory cues) was presented in a semantically congruent rather than a semantically incongruent sentence. These findings indicate that top-down processes help to determine the McGurk effect. However, it remains unclear whether these processes influence perceptual processes themselves or only post-perceptual processes (e.g., decision making).

Problems faced by listeners

Listeners are confronted by several problems when trying to understand speech:

(1) Language is spoken at a rate of about 10 phonemes (basic speech sounds) per second, and so requires rapid processing. Amazingly, we can understand speech artificially speeded up to 50–60 sounds or phonemes per second (Werker & Tees, 1992).

(2) There is the **segmentation problem**, which is the difficulty of separating out or distinguishing words from the pattern of speech sounds. This problem arises because speech typically consists of a continuously changing pattern of sound with few periods of silence. This can make it hard to decide when one word ends and the next word begins. Ways in which listeners cope with the segmentation problem are discussed shortly.

(3) In normal speech, there is **co-articulation**, which is defined as "the overlapping of adjacent articulations" (Ladefoged, 2001, p. 272). More specifically, the way in which a phoneme is produced depends on the phonemes preceding and following it. The existence of co-articulation means that the pronunciation of any given phoneme is not invariant, which can create problems for the listener. However, co-articulation means that listeners hearing one phoneme are provided with some information about the surrounding phonemes. For example, "The /b/ phonemes in 'bill', 'bull', and 'bell' are all slightly different acoustically, and tell us about what is coming next" (Harley, 2001, p. 221).

(4) Listeners have to contend with significant individual differences from one speaker to the next. For example, speakers vary considerably in terms of their rate of speaking. Sussman, Hoemeke, and Ahmed (1993) asked various speakers to say the same short words starting with a consonant. They found clear differences across speakers in their spectrograms. How do listeners cope with such differences? Sussman et al. (1993) focused on two aspects of the information contained in the spectrogram record: (i) the sound frequency at the transition point where the second formant starts; and (ii) the steady frequency of the second formant. There was relational invariance between these two measures: speakers having high frequencies for (i) also had high frequencies for (ii), whereas other speakers had low frequencies for both measures. Listeners probably use information about this relational invariance to identify the word being spoken.

Addressing the segmentation problem

Listeners trying to divide the speech they hear into its constituent words make use of several cues, none of which is fully reliable. First, certain sequences of speech sounds (e.g., [m, r] in English) are never found together within a syllable, and such sequences suggest a likely boundary between words. Dumay, Frauenfelder, and Content (2002) found that listeners use cues like this to separate out words in speech.

Second, Norris, McQueen, Cutler, and Butterfield (1997) argued that the segmentation of an utterance into words is influenced by the possible-word constraint (e.g., a stretch of speech lacking a vowel is not a possible word). For example, listeners found it hard to identify the word "apple" in "fapple", because the [f] could not possibly be an English word (Norris et al., 1997). In contrast, listeners found it relatively easy to detect the word "apple" in "vuffapple", because "vuff" could conceivably be an English word.

Third, there is stress. Stress within a word is relatively unimportant in many languages, but in English the initial syllable of most content words (e.g., nouns; verbs) is typically stressed. When listeners heard strings of words without the stress on the first syllable, they often misheard them. (Cutler & Butterfield, 1992). For example, many listeners who heard "conduct ascents uphill" presented very faintly misheard it, because they mistakenly assumed the words started with a stressed rather than an unstressed syllable.

Fourth, the extent of co-articulation provides a useful cue to word boundaries. As mentioned above, co-articulation can help the listener to anticipate the kind of phoneme that will occur next. Perhaps more importantly, there is generally more co-articulation within words than between them (Byrd & Saltzman, 1998).

Mattys (2004) argued that the usefulness of any given cue depends on the specific conditions and on the availability of other cues. He found that stress was more useful than co-articulation for identifying word boundaries when the speech signal was impoverished by superimposed noise. However, co-articulation was more useful than stress when the speech signal was phonetically intact. This latter finding led Mattys (2004, p. 404) to conclude that, "Stress-based segmentation is not as systematic a strategy as previously believed . . . The predominance of stress seems to be restricted to listening conditions in which few other segmentation cues are available."

Categorical perception

Speech perception differs from other kinds of auditory perception. For example, there is a definite left-hemisphere advantage for perception of speech but not other auditory stimuli. Speech perception exhibits **categorical perception** of phonemes: speech stimuli intermediate between two phonemes are typically categorised as one phoneme or the other, and there is an abrupt boundary between phoneme categories. For example, the Japanese language does not distinguish between /l/ and /r/. These sounds belong to the same category for Japanese listeners, and so they find it very hard to discriminate between them (see Massaro, 1994).

The existence of categorical perception does *not* mean we cannot distinguish at all between slightly different sounds assigned to the same phoneme category. Listeners decided faster that two syllables were the same when the sounds were acoustically identical than when they were not (Pisoni & Tash, 1974).

When in processing do listeners assign speech sounds into categories? According to Massaro (1994), there is little evidence of categorical processing at an early stage. He argued that categorical perception occurs because listeners have a bias leading them to assign all speech sounds to a given phoneme in an all-or-none way.

It used to be argued (e.g., Liberman et al., 1967) that categorical perception is unique to humans listening to speech sounds. However, studies on non-speech sounds in humans and on speech sounds in other species (e.g., Japanese quail, chinchillas) indicate that categorical perception is relatively common. Diehl, Lotto, and Holt (2004, p. 159) concluded their review as follows:

> The results of comparing speech and non-speech perception in humans and non-humans strongly indicate that general auditory mechanisms (common to human adults and infants, other mammals, and even birds) contribute to the categorical perception of speech sounds. Evidently, however, language experience is also a significant factor in categorical perception.

Context effects: Sound identification

Spoken word recognition involves a mixture of bottom-up or data-driven processes triggered by the acoustic signal, and top-down or conceptually driven processes generated from the linguistic context. In general terms, finding that the identification of a sound or a word is influenced by the context in which it is presented provides evidence for top-down effects. However, as we will see, there has been much controversy concerning the interpretation of most context effects. We will consider context effects on the identification of sounds in this section, deferring a discussion of context effects in word identification until later. There are various kinds of context. We start by considering context in the form of an adjacent sound, and then move on to discuss sentential context, i.e., the sentence within which a sound is presented. We will see that the processes underlying different kinds of context effect probably differ.

Lexical identification shift

We saw earlier that listeners show categorical perception, with speech stimuli intermediate between two phonemes being categorised as one phoneme or the other. Ganong (1980) wondered whether categorical perception of phonemes would be influenced by context. Accordingly, he presented listeners with various sounds ranging between a word (e.g., dash) and a nonword (e.g., tash). There was a contextual effect: an ambiguous initial phoneme was more likely to be assigned to a given phoneme category when that produced a word than when it did not. This phenomenon is known as the **lexical identification shift**.

Ganong (1980) showed that context influences categorical perception. There are at least two possible explanations for this effect. First, context may have a *direct* influence on perceptual processes. Second, context may influence post-perceptual processes occurring *after* the perceptual processes are completed but *before* responding. Post-perceptual processes can be influenced by providing rewards for correct responses and penalties for incorrect ones. Pitt (1995) found that rewards and penalties had *no* effect on the lexical identification shift, suggesting it depends on perceptual processes rather than post-perceptual ones.

Connine (1990) found that the identification of an ambiguous phoneme is influenced by the meaning of the sentence in which it is presented (i.e., by sentential context). However, the way in which this happened differed from the lexical identification shift observed by Ganong (1980). Sentential context did *not* influence phoneme identification during initial speech perception, but rather had a later, post-perceptual effect.

In sum, the standard lexical identification shift depends on relatively early perceptual processes. In contrast, the effects of sentence context on the identification of ambiguous phonemes involve later, post-perceptual processes.

Phonemic restoration effect

Evidence that top-down processing based on sentence context can be involved in speech perception was apparently obtained by Warren and Warren (1970). They studied the **phonemic restoration effect**. Participants heard a sentence in which a small portion had been removed and replaced with a meaningless sound. The sentences used were as follows (the asterisk indicates a deleted portion of the sentence):

- It was found that the *eel was on the axle.
- It was found that the *eel was on the shoe.
- It was found that the *eel was on the table.
- It was found that the *eel was on the orange.

The perception of the crucial element in the sentence (i.e., eel) was influenced by sentence context. Participants listening to the first sentence heard "wheel", those listening to the second sentence heard "heel", and those exposed to the third and fourth sentences heard "meal" and "peel", respectively. The crucial auditory stimulus (i.e., "*eel") was always the same, so all that differed was the contextual information.

The phonemic restoration effect has been replicated several times (e.g., Samuel, 1981, 1987). However, it has proved surprisingly hard to identify exactly how the effect is created. Samuel (1997) argued there were two possible explanations. First, listeners may restore the missing phoneme perceptually ("a true top-down creation of the missing phonemic information", Samuel, 1997, p. 98). Second, the effect may occur *after* perception, and may involve listeners simply guessing at the missing phoneme ("a matter of not really noticing that the lexical item is missing", Samuel, 1997, p. 98).

Relevant evidence was provided by Samuel (1987). Listeners heard sentences with the initial phoneme of one word deleted, with this word either fitting or not fitting the sentential context. The extent of the phonemic restoration effect did *not* depend on whether the mutilated word fitted the sentential context. This finding suggests that sentential context has no *direct* effect on speech processing but rather that it influences post-perceptual processes.

Samuel (1997) studied the phonemic restoration effect using a different paradigm in which there was *no* sentential context at all. Listeners repeatedly heard words such as "academic", "confidential", and "psychedelic", all of which have /d/ as the third syllable. The multiple presentation of these words reduces the probability of categorising subsequent sounds as /d/. This is an example of the adaptation effect, in which there is reduced responsiveness to a repeated sound. Of crucial importance is what happens when listeners are initially exposed to the same words with the key phoneme replaced by noise (e.g., aca*emic; confi*ential; psyche*elic). In essence, the *same* adaptation effect was observed in this condition as in the one in which entire words were presented. However, there was *no* adaptation effect when the /d/ phoneme in the words was replaced by silence.

What do the above findings mean? If guessing were involved, there would have been an adaptation effect in both the noise *and* silence conditions. The actual pattern of findings indicates the involvement of top-down lexical or word activation rather than guessing in the noise condition. As Samuel (1997, p. 121) concluded, "The adaptation is produced by perceptually restored phonemes, phonemes induced by lexical activation." Thus, the processes underlying the phonemic restoration effect may vary depending on the precise experimental conditions.

THEORIES OF SPOKEN WORD RECOGNITION

There are several theories of spoken word recognition, two of which will be discussed here. Both of them (the cohort model and the TRACE model) have been very influential in recent years. If you want to read about other models, McQueen (2004) compares and contrasts eight models of speech perception in addition to the cohort and TRACE models.

Cohort model

Marslen-Wilson and Tyler (1980) proposed the original version of the cohort model based on the following assumptions:

- Early in the auditory presentation of a word, words conforming to the sound sequence heard so far become active; this set of words is the "word-initial cohort".
- Words belonging to this cohort are then eliminated if they cease to match further information from the presented word, or because they are inconsistent with the semantic or other context.
- Processing of the presented word continues only until contextual information and information from the word itself are sufficient to eliminate all but one of the words in the word-initial cohort; this is known as the "recognition point" or "uniqueness point" of a word.

According to the cohort model, various knowledge sources (e.g., lexical, syntactic, semantic) are processed in parallel. These knowledge sources *interact* and combine with each other in complex ways to produce an efficient analysis of spoken language. As Harley (2001, p. 20) pointed out, "Interaction in general involves the influence of one level of processing on the operation of another." This approach can be contrasted with the notion (e.g., Forster, 1979) that processing proceeds in a serial fashion, with spoken language being analysed in a fairly fixed and invariant series of processing stages.

Marslen-Wilson and Tyler (1980) tested their theoretical notions in a word-monitoring task, in which participants had to identify pre-specified target words presented within spoken sentences. There were normal sentences, syntactic sentences (grammatically correct but meaningless), and random sentences (unrelated words), and the target was a member of a given category, a word that rhymed with a given word, or a word that was identical to a given word. The measure of interest was the speed with which the target could be detected.

According to the original version of the cohort model, sensory information from the target word and contextual information from the rest of the sentence are both used at the same time. In contrast, it is predicted by serial theories that sensory information is extracted prior to the use of contextual information. The results conformed more closely to the predictions of the cohort model. Complete sensory analysis of the longer words was not needed with adequate contextual information (see Figure 10.11). It was only necessary to listen to the entire word when the sentence context contained no useful syntactic or semantic information (i.e., random condition).

Support for the cohort model using event-related potentials (ERPs) was reported by O'Rourke and Holcomb (2002). They addressed a key assumption of the model, namely, that a spoken word is identified when the point is reached (known as the recognition or uniqueness point) at which only *one* word is consistent with the acoustic signal. They presented participants with spoken words and pseudowords, and asked them to decide as rapidly as possible whether each letter string was a word. The words were selected so that some had an early recognition point (average

FIGURE 10.11

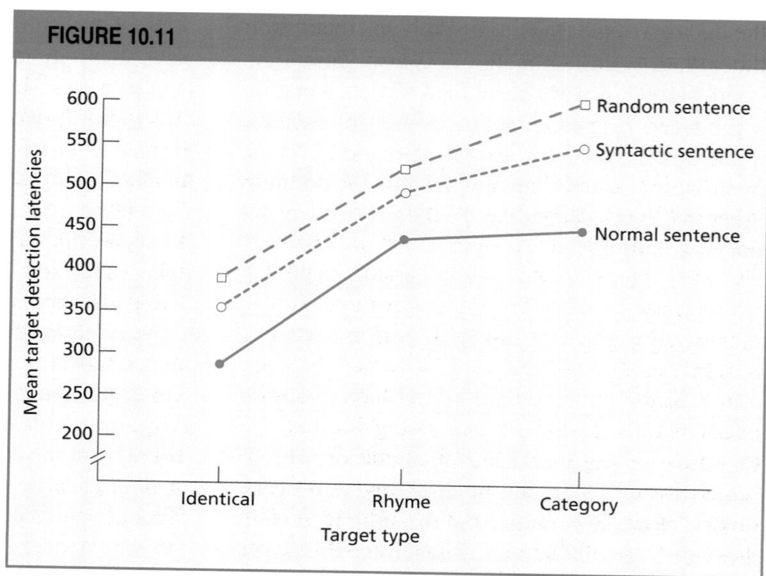

Detection times for word targets presented in sentences. Adapted from Marslen-Wilson and Tyler (1980).

of 427 ms after word onset), whereas others had a late recognition point (average of 533 ms after word onset). O'Rourke and Holcomb used the N400 (a negative-going wave assessed by ERP) as a measure of the speed of word processing.

O'Rourke and Holcomb (2002) found that the N400 occurred about 100 ms earlier for words having an early uniqueness point than for words having a late uniqueness point. This is important, because it shows the psychological reality of the uniqueness or recognition point. The further finding that N400 typically occurred shortly after the uniqueness point had been reached supports the assumption of cohort theory that spoken word processing is highly efficient.

There is considerable emphasis in the cohort model on the notion of competition among candidate words when a listener hears a word. Weber and Cutler (2004) found that such competition can include more words than one might have imagined. Dutch students with a good command of the English language had to identify a target picture corresponding to a spoken English word. Even though the task was in English, the Dutch students activated some Dutch words. More specifically, they fixated distractor pictures having Dutch names which resembled phonemically the English name of the target picture. Overall, their findings revealed that lexical competition is significantly greater in non-native than in native listening.

Undue significance was given to the initial part of the word in the original cohort model. It was assumed that a spoken word will generally not be recognised if its initial phoneme is unclear or ambiguous. Evidence against that assumption was reported by Frauenfelder, Scholten, and Content (2001) and by Allopenna, Magnuson, and Tanenhaus (1998). Frauenfelder et al. found that French-speaking listeners activated words even when the initial phoneme of spoken words was distorted (e.g., hearing "focabulaire" activated the word "vocabulaire"). However, the listeners took some time to overcome the effects of the mismatch in the initial phoneme. Allopenna et al. found that the initial phoneme of a spoken word activated other words sharing that phoneme (e.g., the initial sounds of "beaker" caused activation of "beetle"). Somewhat later in time, there was a weaker tendency for participants to activate words rhyming with the auditory input (e.g., "beaker" activated "speaker"). The key point in the studies by Frauenfelder et al. and by Allopenna et al. is that some words not sharing an initial phoneme with the auditory input were *not* totally excluded from the cohort as predicted by the cohort model.

Revised theory

Marslen-Wilson (1990) and Marslen-Wilson and Warren (1994) revised the cohort model. In the original version, words were either in or out of the word cohort. In the revised version, candidate words vary in their level of activation, and so membership of the word cohort is a matter of degree. Marslen-Wilson (1990) assumed the word-initial cohort may contain words having similar initial phonemes, rather than being limited *only* to words having the initial phoneme of the presented word. These and other changes to cohort theory allow it to account for findings such as those of Frauenfelder et al. (2001) and Allopenna et al. (1998).

There is a second major difference between the original and revised versions of cohort theory. In the original version, context influenced word recognition very early in processing. In contrast, the effects of context on word recognition are much more limited in the revised version, occurring only at a fairly late stage of processing. More specifically, context influences only the integration stage, at which a selected word is integrated into the evolving representation of the sentence. As a result of these changes, the revised cohort model has a stronger emphasis on bottom-up processing than did the original version.

Evidence supporting the revised model has come from studies on the effects of sentence context on the phonemic restoration effect (e.g., Samuel, 1987) and on the lexical identification shift (e.g., Connine, 1990). It has also come from research on cross-modal priming, in which the participants listen to speech and perform a lexical decision task (deciding whether visual letter strings form words). The key assumption is that only words activated by the speech input will produce priming in the form of faster responding on the lexical decision task. Zwitserlood (1989) considered the effects of context on cross-modal priming. Context did *not* influence the initial activation of words (i.e., contextually inappropriate words as well as appropriate ones were activated). However, it had an effect *after* the point at which a spoken word could be uniquely identified.

In spite of the above findings, sentence context can influence spoken word processing some time *before* a word's recognition point has been reached. Van Petten et al. (1999) presented participants with a spoken sentence frame (e.g., "Sir Lancelot spared the man's life when he begged for ____"), followed after 500 ms by a final word congruent (e.g., "mercy") or incongruent (e.g., "mermaid") with the sentence frame. Van Petten et al. used event-related potentials (ERPs; see Chapter 1) to assess processing of the final word. The key finding was that there were significant differences in the N400 responses to the contextually congruent and incongruent words about 200 ms *before* the recognition or uniqueness point was reached. Thus, context influenced spoken word processing earlier than expected within the revised version of the cohort model. However, the sentence context was very strong in that participants could readily predict the final word. This presumably helped them to use contextual information very early in word processing.

Evaluation

The cohort model has proved an influential approach to spoken word recognition. The revised version of the model is generally preferable to the original version for three main reasons:

(1) Its assumption that membership of the word cohort is *gradated* rather than all-or-none is more in line with the evidence;
(2) Contextual effects on spoken word recognition typically occur late rather than early in processing, as proposed within the revised theory.
(3) There is more scope for correcting errors within the revised version of the model. This is because words are less likely to be eliminated from the cohort at an early stage in the revised model.

There are various limitations with the revised version of the cohort model. First, the modifications made to the original model have made it less precise. As Massaro (1994, p. 244) pointed out, "These modifications are necessary to bring the model in line with empirical results, but they . . . make it more difficult to test against alternative models." Second, context sometimes influences relatively early stages of processing (Van Petten et al., 1999), which seems inconsistent with the model. Third, the processes assumed to be involved in processing of speech depend heavily on identification of the starting point of individual words. However, it is not clear within the theory how this is accomplished.

TRACE model

McClelland and Elman (1986) and McClelland (1991) produced a network model of speech perception based on connectionist principles (see Chapter 1). Their TRACE model of speech perception resembles the original version of cohort theory. For example, it is argued within both cohort theory and the TRACE model that several sources of information combine interactively to achieve spoken word recognition. The TRACE model also resembles the interactive activation model of visual word recognition put forward by McClelland and Rumelhart (1981; discussed earlier in the chapter). In essence, the TRACE model assumes that bottom-up and top-down processes interact flexibly in spoken word recognition. In other words, it is a matter of "All hands to the pump", meaning all sources of information are used at the same time in spoken word recognition.

The TRACE model is based on the following theoretical assumptions:

- There are individual processing units or nodes at three different levels: features (e.g., voicing, manner of production), phonemes, and words.
- Feature nodes are connected to phoneme nodes, and phoneme nodes are connected to word nodes.
- Connections between levels operate in both directions, and are only facilitatory.
- There are connections among units or nodes at the same level; these connections are inhibitory.
- Nodes influence each other in proportion to their activation levels and the strengths of their interconnections.
- As excitation and inhibition spread among nodes, a pattern of activation or trace develops.
- The word recognised or identified by the listener is determined by the activation level of the possible candidate words.

The TRACE model assumes that bottom-up and top-down processing *interact* during speech perception. Bottom-up activation proceeds upwards from the feature level to the phoneme level and on to the word level, whereas top-down activation proceeds in the opposite direction from the word level to the phoneme level and on to the feature level. Evidence that top-down processes are involved in spoken word recognition was discussed earlier in the chapter (e.g., Marslen-Wilson & Tyler, 1980; Warren & Warren, 1970).

Evidence

McClelland, Rumelhart, and The PDP Research Group (1986) applied the TRACE model to the phenomenon of categorical speech perception (discussed earlier). According to the model, the discrimination boundary between phonemes becomes sharper because of mutual inhibition between phoneme units at the phoneme level. These inhibitory processes produce a "winner takes all" situation, in which one phoneme becomes increasingly activated while other phonemes are inhibited. McClelland, Rumelhart, and The PDP Research Group (1986) carried out a simulation based on the model that successfully produced categorical speech perception.

The TRACE model can easily explain the lexical identification shift (Ganong, 1980). In this effect (discussed earlier), there is a bias towards perceiving an ambiguous phoneme in such a way that a word is formed. According to the TRACE model, top-down activation from the word level is responsible for the lexical identification shift.

Cutler et al. (1987) studied another phenomenon lending itself to explanation by the TRACE model. They used a phoneme monitoring task, in which participants responded immediately when they detected a target phoneme. Cutler et al. observed a word superiority effect: phonemes were detected faster when presented in words than in nonwords. According to the TRACE model, this phenomenon occurs because of top-down activation from the word level to the phoneme level.

According to the TRACE model, high-frequency words are processed faster than low-frequency words (e.g., because they have higher resting activation levels). Word frequency is seen as having an important role in the word-recognition process, and should influence even early stages of word processing. Support for these predictions was reported by Dahan, Magnuson, and Tanenhaus (2001) in experiments using eye fixation as a measure of the focus of attention. Participants were presented with four pictures (e.g., bench, bed, bell, lobster), three of which had names starting with the same phoneme. Their task was to click on the picture corresponding to a spoken word (e.g., "bench") while ignoring the related distractors (bed, bell) and the unrelated distractor (lobster). According to the TRACE model, more fixations should be directed to the related distractor having a high-frequency name (i.e., bed) than to the one having a low-frequency name (i.e., bell). That was precisely what Dahan et al. (2001) found. In addition, frequency influenced eye fixation very early in processing, also as predicted by the TRACE model. Finally, a computer simulation based on the TRACE model provided a very good fit to the data.

Words vary in terms of how many lexical neighbours (similar-sounding words) they have. According to the TRACE model, lexical neighbours are activated during word recognition. Words having many lexical neighbours should be harder to recognise because there is competition from those neighbours. Ziegler, Muneaux, and Grainger (2003) obtained strong support for that prediction. They also argued that the number of orthographic neighbours (a factor not considered within the TRACE model) influences auditory word recognition. On the face of it, it seems unlikely that similarities in *spelling* across words would have any effect on *auditory* word recognition. In fact, however, Ziegler et al. found that words having many orthographic neighbours (i.e., words of similar spelling) were recognised *more easily* than those with few orthographic neighbours. According to Ziegler et al., words with many orthographic neighbours are easier to recognise because the mapping between pronunciation (phonology) and spelling (orthography) is more consistent.

The TRACE model predicts that speech perception depends *interactively* on top-down and bottom-up processes. However, this was not confirmed by Massaro (1989) on a phoneme-discrimination task. Bottom-up effects stemming from stimulus discriminability and top-down effects stemming from phonological context both influenced performance. However, they did so in an *independent* rather than interactive way.

Top-down effects seem to be less important than assumed within the model. For example, Frauenfelder, Segui, and Dijkstra (1990) gave participants the task of detecting a given phoneme. The key condition was one in which a nonword closely resembling an actual word was presented (e.g. "vocabutaire" instead of "vocabulaire"). According to the model, top-down effects from the word node corresponding to "vocabulaire" should have inhibited the task of identifying the "t" in "vocabutaire". However, they did not.

Various kinds of evidence suggest that the influence of top-down processes on spoken word recognition is exaggerated in the TRACE model. This issue was examined in detail by Norris, McQueen, and Cutler (2000). Their central point was that top-down processes can impair speech processing by systematically distorting the information in the acoustic signal: "Interactive bias models [such as TRACE] run the risk of hallucinating. Particularly when the input is degraded, the information in the speech input will tend to be discarded and phonemic decisions may then be based mainly on lexical knowledge." Frauenfelder and Peeters (1998) provided evidence that top-down activation is sometimes not useful. They carried out various computer simulations based on the assumptions of the TRACE model, and found that its performance on spoken word recognition tasks was no worse when its top-down connections were removed.

The existence of top-down effects depends more on stimulus degradation than predicted by the model. For example, McQueen (1991) presented ambiguous phonemes at the end of stimuli, and asked participants to categorise these phonemes. Each ambiguous phoneme could be perceived as completing a word or a nonword. According to the model, top-down effects from the word level should have produced a preference for perceiving the phonemes as completing words. This prediction was confirmed *only* when the stimulus was degraded. It follows from the TRACE model that the effects should be greater when the stimulus is degraded. However, the absence of effects when the stimulus was not degraded is inconsistent with the model.

According to the model, spoken word recognition involves determining the phonemes in each word. Davis, Marslen-Wilson, and Gaskell (2002) reported evidence against that theoretical assumption. They focused on assessing the degree of ambiguity between short words and the onsets of longer words in which these short words are embedded (e.g., "cap" and "captain"). Participants heard only the first syllable of the target word, and had to decide which word had been presented. They heard the same phonemes whichever word had actually been presented. This task should have been very difficult (or even impossible) according to the TRACE model, because it is assumed that listeners focus on identifying phonemes. In fact, performance was good (see Figure 10.12) because participants used subtle acoustic cues (e.g., small differences in syllable duration) to discriminate between short and long words. As Davis et al. (2002, p. 239) concluded, "Models such as TRACE and Shortlist, in which input representations are phonemically categorised, . . . would require alterations to incorporate the additional non-phonemic information that appears to bias lexical activation in choosing between short and long words."

FIGURE 10.12

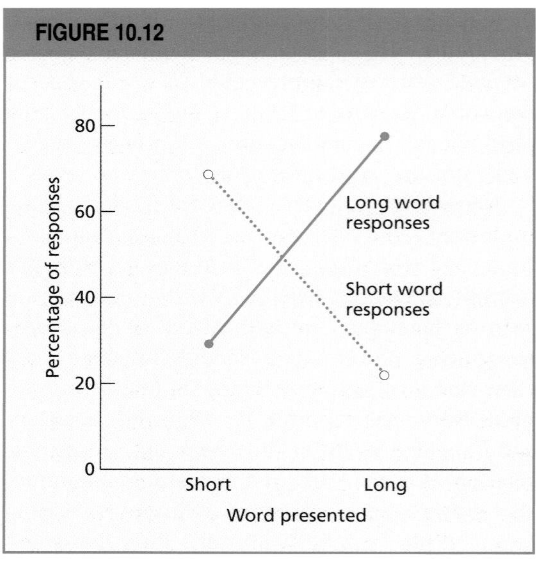

Percentage of decisions that the initial syllable of short and long words belonged to short and long words. Data from Davis et al. (2002).

Evaluation

The TRACE model has various successes to its credit. First, it provides reasonable accounts of phenomena such as categorical speech perception and the word superiority effect in phoneme monitoring. Second, a significant general strength of the TRACE model is its assumption that bottom-up and top-down processes both contribute to spoken word recognition, combined with explicit assumptions about the processes involved. Third, the model predicts with precision the effects of word frequency on auditory word processing (Dahan et al., 2001). Fourth, the model correctly predicts that words with many lexical neighbours will be harder to recognise (Ziegler et al., 2003). Fifth, as Harley (2001, p. 234) pointed out, "[TRACE] . . . copes extremely well with noisy input – which is a considerable advantage, given the noise present in natural language."

There are several problems with the TRACE model. First, the theory exaggerates the importance of top-down effects. This was shown in the studies by Frauenfelder et al. (1990) and McQueen (1991) discussed earlier. The potentially negative effects of an excessive reliance on top-down processes were discussed by Norris et al. (2000; see above). A closely related point is that the evidence suggests that speech processing is less flexible and unstructured than implied by the model.

Second, it is assumed that words phonologically similar to a presented word will be activated immediately, even though they do not match the presented word in the initial phoneme. In fact, this is often not the case (e.g., Allopenna et al., 1998; Frauenfelder et al., 2001).

Third, the model has problems in dealing with the timing of speech sounds and differences in speech rate from one speaker to another. The TRACE model assumes there are time slots, with feature, phoneme, and word units or representations being replicated across time slots to allow them to be identified. However, as Ellis and Humphreys (1999, p. 349) pointed out, "There is no guarantee that the speech signal will match the time slots set in the model. As a consequence, the model may fail to generalise its recognition across different speech rates." The consequence of this is that TRACE cannot recognise speech (Protopapas, 1999).

Fourth, tests of the model have relied heavily on computer simulations involving a small number of one-syllable words. It is not entirely clear whether the model would perform satisfactorily if applied to the vastly larger vocabularies possessed by most people.

Fifth, the model does not consider all of the factors determining auditory word recognition. For example, orthographic similarity between the presented word and other words influences word recognition (Ziegler et al., 2003), but is ignored within the model.

COGNITIVE NEUROPSYCHOLOGY

So far in this chapter we have focused mainly on the processes permitting spoken words to be identified, i.e., on word recognition. This is important, because word recognition is of vital importance on the way to understanding what the speaker is saying. In this section we consider the processes involved in the apparently very simple task of repeating a spoken word immediately after hearing it. One of the main goals of research using this task is to identify some of the main processes involved in speech perception. Performance on the task also provides useful information about speech production, which is discussed in Chapter 12.

In spite of the apparent simplicity of the above task, many brain-damaged patients experience difficulties with it even though audiometric testing reveals they are not deaf. Detailed analysis of these patients suggests various processes can be used to permit repetition of a spoken word. As we will see, the study of brain-damaged patients sheds light on various issues such as the following: Are the processes involved in repeating spoken words the same for familiar and unfamiliar words? Can spoken words be repeated without accessing their meaning?

Information from brain-damaged patients was used by Ellis and Young (1988) to propose a model of the processing of spoken words (see Figure 10.13 or Martin, 2003, for a modified version). The model has five components:

- The *auditory analysis system* is used to extract phonemes or other sounds from the speech wave.
- The *auditory input lexicon* contains information about spoken words known to the listener, but not about their meaning. The purpose of this lexicon is to recognise familiar words via activation of the appropriate word units.
- The meanings of words are stored within the *semantic system* (cf., **semantic memory**, discussed in Chapter 8).
- The *speech output lexicon* provides the spoken forms of words.
- The *phoneme response buffer* provides distinctive speech sounds.
- These components can be used in various combinations, so there are three different routes between hearing a spoken word and saying it.

The most striking feature of the model is the notion that saying a spoken word can be achieved using *three* different routes that vary in terms of which stored information about heard words is accessed. It is this feature to which we will devote the most attention. Before doing so, however, we will consider the role of the auditory analysis system in speech perception.

FIGURE 10.13

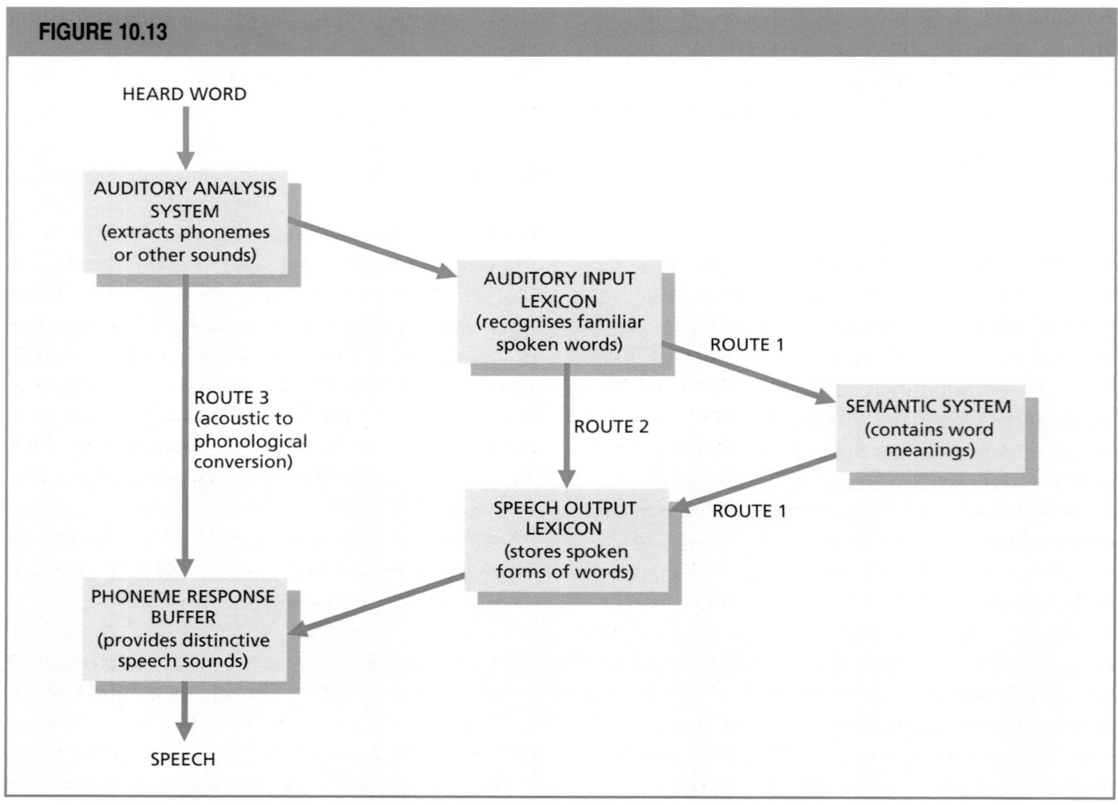

Processing and repetition of spoken words. Adapted from Ellis and Young (1988).

Auditory analysis system

Suppose a patient had damage only to the auditory analysis system, thereby producing a deficit in phonemic processing. Such a patient would have impaired speech perception for words and non-words, especially those containing phonemes that are hard to discriminate. However, such a patient would have generally intact speech production, reading, and writing, would have normal perception of nonverbal environmental sounds (e.g., coughs, whistles) not containing phonemes, and his/her hearing would be unimpaired. Several patients apparently conforming to this pattern have been identified, and the term **pure word deafness** has been used to describe their condition. The argument that there is a brain area specifically devoted to phonemic processing would be strengthened if there were some patients showing the opposite pattern (i.e., impaired perception of nonverbal sounds but intact speech perception). For example, Peretz et al. (1994) reported a patient having a functional impairment limited to perception of music and of prosody.

A crucial aspect of pure word deafness is that auditory perception problems are highly *selective*, and do not apply to non-speech sounds (see Poeppel, 2001, for a review). However, many individuals with apparent pure word deafness have problems in perceiving rapid changes in non-speech sounds with complex pitch patterns more characteristic of speech than of other common sounds (see Martin, 2003). Pinard, Chertkow, Black, and Peretz (2002) reviewed 63 cases of pure word deafness, and found normal nonverbal processing in only 5 of them. In all the other cases, there were additional impairments of music perception and/or environmental sound perception.

As Pinard et al. (2002, p. 51) concluded, "It may be that 'apparent' pure word impairment is usually an epiphenomenon [by-product] arising from the limited environmental stimuli hitherto available for testing."

Three-route model

The three-route model of repeating spoken words is shown in Figure 10.13. In essence, Routes 1 and 2 are designed to be used with familiar words, whereas Route 3 is designed to be used with unfamiliar words. When Route 1 is used, a heard word activates relevant stored information about it, including its meaning and its spoken form. Route 2 closely resembles Route 1, except that information about the meaning of heard words is not accessed. As a result, someone using Route 2 can say familiar words accurately, but does not have access to their meaning. Finally, Route 3 involves using rules about the conversion of the acoustic information contained in heard words into the appropriate spoken forms of those words. The details of what might be involved remain unclear, but it is assumed that such conversion processes must be involved to allow listeners to repeat back unfamiliar words and nonwords. The assumptions of this model would be greatly strengthened if it were possible to find brain-damaged patients who can use only one or two of these routes when repeating heard words.

Route 1

Route 1 represents the normal way in which familiar words are identified and comprehended by those with no brain damage. If a brain-damaged patient could use only this route (plus perhaps Route 2), then familiar words would be said correctly. However, there would be severe problems with saying unfamiliar words and nonwords, because they do not have entries in the auditory input lexicon, and therefore use of Route 3 would be required.

McCarthy and Warrington (1984) described a patient, ORF, who seemed to fit the bill fairly well. ORF repeated words much more accurately than nonwords (85% vs. 39%, respectively), indicating that Route 3 was severely impaired. However, the fact that he made several errors in repeating words suggests there was also some impairment to other parts of the system.

Route 2

If patients could use Route 2, but Routes 1 and 3 were severely impaired, they should be able to repeat familiar words but would often not understand their meaning (see Figure 10.13). In addition, they should have problems with unfamiliar words and nonwords, because nonwords cannot be handled through Route 2. Finally, since such patients would make use of the input lexicon, they should be able to distinguish between words and nonwords.

Patients suffering from a condition known as **word meaning deafness** fit the above description. One of the clearest cases of word meaning deafness, Dr O, was studied by Franklin et al. (1996). Dr O showed "no evidence of any impairment in written word comprehension, but auditory comprehension was impaired, particularly for abstract or low-imageability words" (Franklin et al., 1996, p. 1144). His ability to repeat words was dramatically better than his ability to repeat nonwords, 80% vs. 7%, respectively. Finally, Dr O was very good at distinguishing between words and nonwords: he was 94% correct on an auditory lexical decision task.

Dr O seems to have reasonable access to the input lexicon as shown by his greater ability to repeat words than nonwords, and by his almost perfect ability to distinguish between words and nonwords. He clearly has some problem relating to the semantic system. However, the semantic system itself does not seem to be damaged, because his ability to understand written words is intact. He probably has damage to parts of Route 1. Tyler and Moss (1997) argued that Dr O may also have problems earlier in processing (e.g., in extracting phonemic features from speech). For example, when he was asked to repeat spoken words as rapidly as possible, he made 25% errors.

Hall and Riddoch (1997) reported on KW, a man who had had a stroke, and who suffered from word meaning deafness. He showed impaired auditory comprehension of words even though his ability to understand written words was fairly intact. KW made reasonable use of the input lexicon: (1) he spelled 60% of auditorily presented words correctly, compared to only 35% of nonwords; (2) he was 89% accurate in distinguishing between auditorily presented words and nonwords.

Route 3

If a patient had damage to Route 3 only, he/she would show good ability to perceive and to understand spoken familiar words, but would be impaired at perceiving and repeating unfamiliar words and nonwords (see Figure 10.13). This is the case in patients with **auditory phonological agnosia**. Such a patient was studied by Beauvois, Dérouesné, and Bastard (1980). Their patient, JL, had almost perfect repetition and writing to dictation of spoken familiar words, but his repetition and writing of nonwords was very poor. However, he was very good at *reading* nonwords. JL had an intact ability to distinguish between words and nonwords, indicating that there were no problems with access to the input lexicon.

Deep dysphasia

Some brain-damaged patients have extensive problems with speech perception, suggesting that several parts of the speech perception system are damaged. For example, patients with **deep dysphasia** make semantic errors when asked to repeat spoken words (i.e., they say words related in meaning to those spoken). In addition, they find it harder to repeat abstract words than concrete ones, and have very poor ability to repeat nonwords. With reference to the model in Figure 10.13, it could be argued that none of the three routes between heard words and speech is intact. The presence of semantic errors can be explained by assuming some impairment in (or near) the semantic system.

Valdois et al. (1995) studied EA, a 72-year-old man who had suffered a stroke. He exhibited all the symptoms of deep dysphasia, including numerous semantic errors when trying to repeat spoken words having a synonym. In addition, EA had very poor short-term memory for auditory and visual verbal material. These latter findings led Valdois et al. (1995, p. 711) to the following conclusion: "The impairment responsible for both E.A.'s language performance and his short-term memory deficit is rooted in the inability to maintain a sufficiently activated phonological representation [in the response buffer]." They developed a connectionist model to explain the symptoms of deep dysphasia. For example, the existence of semantic errors may occur because semantic information is often activated for longer than phonological information.

Evidence consistent with the theoretical position of Valdois et al. (1995) was reported by Majerus, Lekeu, Van der Linden, and Salmon (2001). They studied a 75-year-old man, CO, who had all the main symptoms of deep dysphasia. Of particular importance, CO had a word span of under two words, leading Majerus et al. to conclude that an impairment in phonological short-term storage was a major factor in his deep dysphasia.

Which theoretical approach (damage to all three routes vs. phonological impairment) is preferable? Each approach may apply to some deep dysphasics. Valdois et al. (1995) discussed six deep dysphasics with a very severe short-term memory deficit (memory span of one or two items). These patients conformed to the theoretical expectation of Valdois et al. (1995), in that there was evidence of damage to the response buffer. They also discussed three other patients having only slightly impaired short-term memory. As Valdois et al. (1995, p. 719) concluded, "These overall data strongly suggest that different subtypes of repetition disorders of the deep dysphasia type do exist."

CHAPTER SUMMARY

- Reading: Introduction
Several methods have been used to study reading. The lexical decision and naming tasks have been used to assess word identification. These tasks ensure that certain processes have occurred, but have the disadvantage that normal reading processes are disrupted. The most generally useful method involves eye movements, because it provides detailed on-line information and is unobtrusive. Research on the role of phonological processing in reading fails to support the strong phonological model, according to which phonological processing is always involved in reading. However, such processing is often involved in various reading tasks (e.g., lexical decision, naming).

- Word identification
According to the interactive activation model, bottom-up and top-down processes are both involved in letter identification and word recognition. This model was only designed to account for performance on four-letter words written in capital letters, and makes the strong (but probably incorrect) assumption that lexical access is determined solely by visual information.

- Reading aloud
According to the dual-route cascaded model, lexical and non-lexical routes are used in naming words and nonwords. Patients with surface dyslexia rely mainly on the lexical route, whereas patients with phonological dyslexia use mostly the non-lexical route. According to the model, deep dyslexics use the right hemisphere on reading tasks, but this hypothesis is contradicted by much of the evidence. The dual-route model reads words and nonwords very accurately, and provides a good account of surface and phonological dyslexia. However, the model fares less well when predicting human naming times, and its very large number of parameters or variables means it is easy to make the model fit most data. Plaut et al. proposed a single-route connectionist model in which words and nonwords are processed by the same highly interactive system. The model accounts for most findings, and provides a good account of deep dyslexia. However, it provides sketchy accounts of some important issues (e.g., phonological dyslexia; the nature of the semantic system).

- Reading: Eye-movement studies
The least obtrusive way of studying reading is by eye-movement recordings. According to the E-Z Reader model, the next eye movement is programmed when only part of the processing of the currently fixated word has occurred. Completion of frequency checking of a word is the signal to initiate an eye-movement program, and completion of lexical access is the signal for a shift of covert attention to the next word. This model takes insufficient account of the impact of higher-level cognitive processes on fixation times, exaggerates the importance of word frequency, and has not been applied systematically to findings on reading using techniques other than eye-movement recordings.

- Listening to speech
Listeners make use of various prosodic cues. They also use lip-reading, even when the visual information conflicts with the sound presented at the same time (the McGurk effect). Among the difficulties faced by listeners are the speed of spoken language, the segmentation problem, co-articulation, and individual differences in speech patterns. Listeners cope by taking account of possible-word constraints, stress patterns within words, and the fact that co-articulation is generally greater within than between words. There is categorical perception of phonemes, but we can discriminate between sounds categorised as the same phoneme. Ambiguous phonemes are more

likely to be assigned to a given phoneme category when that produces a word than when it does not, and this lexical identification shift seems to be perceptual. The phonemic restoration effect within words involves perceptually restored phonemes produced by top-down lexical activation rather than pure guessing. Sentential context also produces a phonemic restoration effect, but here there is no direct effect on speech processing.

- Theories of spoken word recognition
  According to the original version of cohort theory, the initial sound of a word is used to construct a word-initial cohort which is reduced to one word by using additional information from the presented word and from contextual information. Cohort theory has been revised to make it more flexible and in line with the evidence. According to the TRACE model, bottom-up and top-down processes interact during speech perception. This assumption that these processes interact is probably incorrect, and the importance of top-down processes is exaggerated in the TRACE model. Non-phonemic information may be more important than assumed within the TRACE model.

- Cognitive neuropsychology
  There are three routes between sound and speech. Patients with pure word deafness have problems with speech perception, which may be due to impaired phonemic processing or may reflect a more general impairment. Patients with word meaning deafness can repeat familiar words without understanding their meaning, but have problems with nonwords. Patients with auditory phonological agnosia seem to have damage within Route 3. Deep dysphasia may reflect damage to all three routes involved in the repetition of spoken words or to the response buffer.

FURTHER READING

- Behrmann, M., & Patterson, K. (2004). *Words and things*. Hove, UK: Psychology Press. The processes involved in understanding words are discussed with reference to brain-damaged patients in several chapters in this edited book.
- Cutler, A., & Clifton, C. (1999). Comprehending spoken language: A blueprint of the listener. In C.M. Brown & P. Hagoort (Eds.), *The neurocognition of language*. Oxford: Oxford University Press. This chapter provides a very clear and informative account of the processes underlying speech perception.
- Diehl, R.L., Lotto, A.J., & Holt, L.L. (2004). Speech perception. *Annual Review of Psychology*, *55*, 149–179. The authors discuss major theoretical perspectives in terms of their ability to account for key phenomena in speech perception.
- Harley, T.A. (2001). *The psychology of language: From data to theory* (2nd Ed.). Hove, UK: Psychology Press. Chapters 6–8 of this excellent textbook provide clear accounts of the basic processes involved in speech perception and reading.
- Lamberts, K., & Goldstone, R. (2004). *Handbook of cognition*. London: Sage. There are a number of chapters on language in this edited book, and those by McQueen on speech perception and by Pollatsek and Rayner on reading are of particular relevance here.
- Reichle, E.D., Rayner, K., & Pollatsek, A. (2003). The E-Z Reader model of eye-movement control in reading: Comparisons to other models. *Behavioral and Brain Sciences*, *26*, 445–526. This article contains an updated version of an excellent theory of reading, as well as much useful discussion of major issues in reading research.

11

Language Comprehension

INTRODUCTION

The basic processes involved in the initial stages of reading and listening to speech were discussed in the previous chapter. At the end of that chapter, we had reached the point at which individual words were identified. The main objective of this chapter is to complete our account of reading and listening to speech, dealing with the ways in which phrases, sentences, and entire stories are processed and understood.

The previous chapter dealt mainly with those aspects of language processing differing between reading and listening to speech. In contrast, the higher-level processes involved in comprehension are rather similar whether a story is being listened to or read. Support for this position was reported by Chee, O'Craven, Bergida, Rosen, and Savoy (1999), in an fMRI study in which participants performed a semantic processing task on visually or auditorily presented words. Regardless of modality, similar brain areas were activated, including the inferior frontal region, the anterior prefrontal region, the left premotor region, and the cerebellum.

There has been far more research on comprehension processes in reading than in listening to speech, and so the emphasis will be on reading. However, what is true of reading is also generally true of listening to speech. Any major discrepancies between reading and listening will be discussed.

There are two main levels of analysis in the comprehension of sentences. First, there is an analysis of the syntactical (grammatical) structure of each sentence; this is known technically as **parsing**. What exactly is grammar? It is concerned with the way in which words are combined. However, as Altmann (1997, p. 84) pointed out, "It [the way in which words are combined] is important, and has meaning, only insofar as both the speaker and the hearer (or the writer and the reader) share some common knowledge regarding the significance of one combination or another. This shared knowledge is *grammar*."

Second, there is an analysis of the meaning of the sentence. The intended meaning of a sentence may not be the same as its literal meaning. The study of intended meaning is known as **pragmatics**. Cases in which the literal meaning is not the intended meaning include rhetorical devices such as irony, sarcasm, and understatement. The context in which a sentence is spoken can also influence its intended meaning in various ways. Issues concerning pragmatics are discussed later in the chapter.

The processes mentioned so far (e.g., parsing, pragmatics) are important when understanding individual sentences. Most theories of sentence processing have focused on general processes and have ignored individual differences. In fact, however, there is convincing evidence that there are important individual differences in sentence processing, and these are discussed in the third section of the chapter.

In the final two sections of the chapter, we consider processing involving larger units of language than sentences (e.g., texts or stories). When we read a text or story, we typically try to *integrate* the information contained in the sentences that comprise it. Such integration often involves drawing inferences, identifying the main themes in the text, and so on.

PARSING

This section is concerned with parsing, and the processes used by readers and listeners to comprehend the sentences they read or hear. One of the central issues deals with the relationship between syntactic and semantic analysis. There are at least four major possibilities:

(1) Syntactic analysis generally precedes (and influences) semantic analysis.
(2) Semantic analysis usually occurs *prior* to syntactic analysis.
(3) Syntactic and semantic analysis occur at the same time.
(4) Syntax and semantics are very closely associated, and have a hand-in-glove relationship (Altmann, personal communication).

The above possibilities will be addressed shortly. However, before doing so, note that most studies on parsing have considered only the English language. Does this matter? According to Harley (2001, p. 246), "English . . . is a strongly configurational [shape-based] language whose interpretation depends heavily on word order. In inflectional languages such as German, word order is less important . . . the predominance of studies that have examined parsing in English may have given a misleading view of how human parsing operates."

Grammar or syntax

An infinite number of sentences is possible in any language, but these sentences are nevertheless systematic and organised. Linguists such as Chomsky (1957, 1959) have produced rules to take account of the productivity and the regularity of language. A set of rules is commonly referred to as a grammar. Ideally, a grammar should be able to generate all the permissible sentences in a given language, while at the same time rejecting all the unacceptable ones. For example, as Harris (1990) pointed out, our knowledge of grammar allows us to be confident that "Matthew is likely to leave" is grammatically correct, whereas the similar sentence "Matthew is probable to leave" is not.

Syntactic ambiguity

It might seem that parsing or assigning grammatical structure to sentences would be fairly easy. However, numerous sentences in the English language (e.g., "They are flying planes") pose problems because their grammatical structure is ambiguous. Some sentences are syntactically ambiguous at the *global* level, in which case the whole sentence has two or more possible interpretations. For example, "They are cooking apples" is ambiguous because it may or may not mean that apples are being cooked. Other sentences are syntactically ambiguous at the *local* level, meaning that various interpretations are possible at some point during parsing.

Much research on parsing has focused on ambiguous sentences. Why is that the case? Parsing operations generally occur very rapidly, making it hard to study the processes involved. However, observing the problems encountered by readers struggling with ambiguous sentences can provide revealing information about parsing processes.

One of the ways in which listeners work out the syntactic or grammatical structure of spoken sentences is by using prosodic cues in the form of stress, intonation, and so on. For example, in the ambiguous sentence "The old men and women sat on the bench", the women may or may not be old. If the women are not old, then the spoken duration of the word "men" will be relatively long, and the stressed syllable in "women" will have a steep rise in pitch contour. Neither of these prosodic features will be present if the sentence means the women are old.

Doubts about the importance of prosodic cues were raised by Allbritton, McKoon, and Ratcliff (1996). They gave trained speakers (actors and broadcasters) and untrained speakers ambiguous sentences in a disambiguating context, and told them to read the sentences out loud. Even the trained speakers made only modest use of prosodic cues to clarify the intended meaning of the ambiguous sentences. Perhaps they largely ignored prosodic cues because the meaning of what they were saying was clear from the disambiguating context. Support for this interpretation was reported by Snedeker and Trueswell (2003), in a study in which speakers said ambiguous sentences (e.g., "Tap the frog with the flower"). Prosodic cues were used much more often when the context failed to clarify the appropriate meaning of ambiguous sentences than when it did. Listeners generally made use of these prosodic cues to produce the appropriate action.

How rapidly is prosodic information used by listeners? Snedeker and Trueswell (2003) addressed this question by recording listeners' eye movements as they heard speakers deliver ambiguous sentences. It may seem odd to record eye movements when sentences are presented auditorily. However, it was done in order to find out when participants focused attention on the relevant objects mentioned in the sentences. Listeners used information from prosodic cues at a very early stage. Indeed, listeners' interpretation of ambiguous sentences was influenced by prosodic cues even *before* the start of the ambiguous phrase. Thus, prosodic cues are used to predict information to be presented later in the sentence.

Most theoretical approaches to parsing can be divided into one-stage or two-stage models (Harley, 2001). According to one-stage models, all sources of information (syntactic and semantic) are used at the same time to construct a syntactic model of sentences. In contrast, the first stage of processing in two-stage models uses *only* syntactic information, with semantic information being used during the second stage. We will mainly consider the most influential two-stage approach (the garden-path model) and the most influential one-stage approach (the constraint-based theory of MacDonald, Pearlmutter, & Seidenberg, 1994). As you read about these theories, bear in mind that a central issue concerns *when* semantic information is used in parsing.

Garden-path model

Frazier and Rayner (1982) put forward a garden-path model. It was given that name because readers or listeners can be misled or "led up the garden path" by ambiguous sentences. The model was based on the following notions:

- Only one syntactical structure is initially considered for any sentence.
- Meaning is not involved in the selection of the initial syntactical structure.
- The simplest syntactical structure is chosen, making use of two general principles: minimal attachment and late closure.
- According to the principle of minimal attachment, the grammatical structure producing the fewest nodes (major parts of a sentence such as noun phrase and verb phrase) is preferred.
- The principle of late closure is that new words encountered in a sentence are attached to the current phrase or clause if grammatically permissible.

The principle of minimal attachment can be illustrated by the following example taken from Rayner and Pollatsek (1989). In the sentences "The girl knew the answer by heart" and "The girl knew the answer was wrong", the minimal attachment principle leads to a grammatical structure in which "the answer" is regarded as the direct object of the verb "knew". This is appropriate for the first sentence, but not for the second. So far as the principle of late closure is concerned, Rayner and Pollatsek (1989) gave an example of a sentence in which use of this principle would lead to an inaccurate syntactical structure: "Since Jay always jogs a mile seems like a short distance". The principle leads "a mile" to be placed in the preceding phrase rather than at the start of the new phrase. In contrast, the principle of late closure produces the correct grammatical structure in a sentence such as "Since Jay always jogs a mile this seems like a short distance to him".

If the sentence about Jay jogging were presented visually, you might imagine that the ambiguity would disappear if a comma were inserted after the word "jogs". One of the functions of punctuation is to reduce any ambiguity, and readers are less confused by garden-path sentences that are punctuated than by those that are not (Hills & Murray, 2000). However, some confusion still remains. In similar fashion, if the sentence were spoken with the speaker using prosodic cues (e.g., pausing after the word "jogs"), the ambiguity would be substantially reduced.

Evidence

There is plentiful evidence that readers typically follow the principles of late closure and minimal attachment (see Harley, 2001). However, what is crucial for the garden-path model is the assumption that semantic factors do *not* influence the construction of the initial syntactic structure. Ferreira and Clifton (1986) provided support for that assumption in a study in which eye movements were recorded while participants read sentences such as the following:

- The defendant examined by the lawyer turned out to be unreliable.
- The evidence examined by the lawyer turned out to be unreliable.

According to the principle of minimal attachment, readers should initially treat the verb "examined" as the main verb, and should thus experience ambiguity for both sentences. However, if readers initially make use of semantic information, they would experience ambiguity for the first sentence but not the second. The reason is that the defendant could possibly examine something, but the evidence could not. In fact, the eye-movement data suggested that readers experienced ambiguity equally for both sentences, implying that semantic information did *not* influence the formation of the initial syntactic structure. This conclusion was challenged by Trueswell, Tanenhaus, and Garnsey (1994; see below).

It may seem inefficient that readers and listeners should often construct incorrect grammatical structures for sentences. However, Frazier and Rayner (1982) claimed that the principles of minimal attachment and late closure are actually efficient because they minimise the pressure on short-term memory. They measured eye movements while participants read sentences such as those given earlier. Their crucial argument was as follows: if readers construct both (or all) possible syntactic structures, then there should be additional processing time at the point of disambiguation (e.g., "seems" in the first jogging sentence and "this" in the second jogging sentence). In contrast, according to the garden-path model, there should be increased processing time at the point of disambiguation *only* when the actual grammatical structure conflicts with the one produced by application of the principles of minimal attachment and late closure (e.g., the first jogging sentence). The eye-movement data consistently supported the predictions of the garden-path model.

More support for the garden-path model was reported by Breedin and Saffran (1999). They studied a patient (DM) who as a result of dementia had an extremely severe loss of semantic knowledge. However, he performed at essentially normal levels on tasks involving the detection of grammatical violations or deciding which was the subject and which the object in a sentence. These findings suggest that the syntactic structure of most sentences can be worked out correctly in the almost complete absence of semantic information. However, the fact that DM made very little use of semantic information when constructing syntactic structures does not necessarily mean that normal individuals do the same.

The notion that syntactic and semantic information is processed separately was supported by Osterhout and Nicol (1999) in a study using event-related potentials (ERPs; see Chapter 1). There was a negative ERP at about 400 ms (N400) when a sentence contained a semantic anomaly or incongruity, and a positive ERP at 600 ms (P600) when a sentence contained a syntactic incongruity. Of crucial importance, sentences containing a semantic *and* a syntactic incongruity produced an N400 and P600 of the same magnitude as was found when only a single incongruity was present. The implication is that syntactic and semantic processes are *independent* of each other, which is consistent with the garden-path model.

According to the garden-path model, prior context should *not* influence the initial parsing of an ambiguous sentence. However, there are several studies in which initial parsing was affected by context. For example, Tanenhaus, Spivey-Knowlton, Eberhard, and Sedivy (1995) presented participants auditorily with the ambiguous sentence "Put the apple on the towel in the box", and recorded eye movements to assess how the sentence was interpreted. According to the garden-path model, "on the towel" should initially be understood as the place where the apple should be put, because that is the simplest syntactic structure. That is what was found when the context did not remove the ambiguity. However, that did *not* happen when the visual context consisted of two apples, one on a towel and the other on a napkin. With that context, the participants rapidly interpreted "on the towel" as a way of identifying which apple was to be moved, and so they did not make the mistake of focusing on the towel presented on its own.

Spivey, Tanenhaus, Eberhard, and Sedivy (2002) reported an experiment similar to that of Tanenhaus et al. (1995) but using pre-recorded digitised speech to prevent speech intonation from influencing participants' interpretations. Context had a large effect on eye movements (see Figure 11.1). Of particular importance, there were far fewer eye movements to the incorrect object (e.g., towel on its own) when the context disambiguated the sentences than when it did not. Indeed, the pattern of eye movements was very similar for unambiguous sentences and for ambiguous sentences with a disambiguating context. As Spivey et al. (2002, p. 448) concluded, "The findings are consistent with a broad theoretical framework in which real-time language comprehension immediately takes into account a rich array of relevant non-linguistic context."

FIGURE 11.1

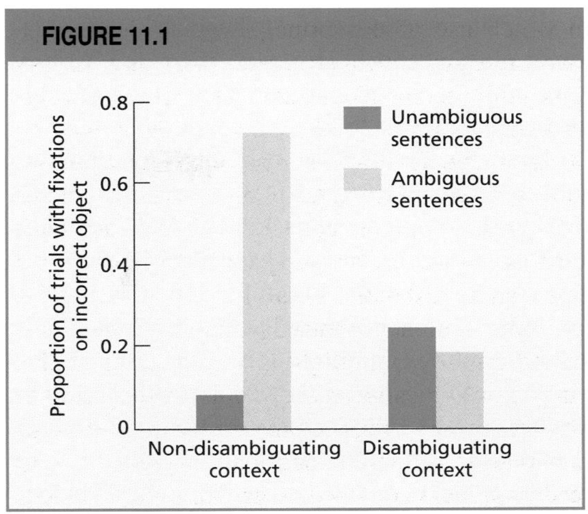

Proportion of trials with eye fixations on the incorrect object as a function of sentence type (unambiguous vs. ambiguous) and context (non-disambiguating vs. disambiguating). Based on data in Spivey et al. (2002).

Carreiras and Clifton (1993) found evidence that readers often do *not* follow the principle of late closure. They presented sentences such as "The spy shot the daughter of the colonel who was standing on the balcony". According to the principle of late closure, readers should interpret this as meaning that the colonel (rather than the daughter) was standing on the balcony. In fact, they did not strongly prefer either interpretation, which is contrary to the garden-path model. When an equivalent sentence was presented in Spanish, there was a clear preference for assuming that the daughter was standing on the balcony (early rather than late closure). This is also contrary to theoretical prediction.

Evaluation

The garden-path model has various strengths. In particular, it provides a simple and coherent account of key processes involved in sentence processing. In addition, as we have seen, there is some evidence from brain-damaged patients and from brain-imaging studies to support key assumptions of the model. However, there are various criticisms of the model, some of which are discussed below.

First, the assumption that meaning plays no part in the initial assignment of grammatical structure to a sentence seems implausible. Semantic information can clearly help readers to work out the correct syntactic structure, and it is hard to see why they would initially ignore a potentially useful source of information. This issue is discussed further below in connection with studies by Trueswell et al. (1994) and by Clifton et al. (2003).

Second, semantic information seems to be involved early in the construction of syntactic structure. Much of the relevant evidence comes from context studies (e.g., Spivey et al., 2002; Tanenhaus et al., 1995). According to Pickering (1999, p. 140), "Semantic factors can have very rapid effects on ambiguity resolution. If a restricted account [e.g., garden-path model] is correct, then the initial stage that ignores these factors must be very brief indeed."

Third, the initial choice of grammatical structure probably does not depend only on the principles of minimal attachment and late closure. For example, decisions about grammatical structure are influenced by punctuation when reading and by prosodic cues (e.g., rhythm, stress) when listening to speech (see Chapter 10).

Constraint-based theory

An alternative approach is the constraint-based theory put forward by MacDonald et al. (1994). This theory is based on a connectionist architecture, and a key assumption is that *all* relevant sources of information or constraints are available immediately to the parser. Competing analyses of the current sentence are activated at the same time, with the analyses being ranked according to the strength of their activation. The syntactic structure receiving most support from the various constraints is highly activated, with other syntactic structures being less activated. Readers become confused when reading ambiguous sentences if the correct syntactic structure is less activated than one or more incorrect structures.

According to the constraint-based theory of MacDonald et al. (1994), the processing system uses four language characteristics to resolve ambiguities in sentences:

(1) Grammatical knowledge constrains possible sentence interpretations.
(2) The various forms of information associated with any given word are typically not independent of each other.
(3) A word may be less ambiguous in some ways than in others (e.g., ambiguous for tense but not for grammatical category).
(4) The various interpretations permissible according to grammatical rules generally differ considerably in frequency and probability on the basis of past experience.

Evidence

Findings consistent with constraint-based theory were reported by Pickering and Traxler (1998). They presented their participants with sentences such as the following:

(1) As the woman edited the magazine amused all the reporters.
(2) As the woman sailed the magazine amused all the reporters.

These two sentences are identical syntactically, and both are likely to lead readers to identify the wrong syntactic structure initially. However, the semantic constraints favouring the wrong structure are greater in sentence (1) than in sentence (2). These constraints should make it harder for readers of sentence (1) to change their incorrect syntactic analysis when it needs to be abandoned (i.e., when the verb "amused" is reached). As predicted, eye-movement data indicated that eye fixations in the verb and post-verb regions were longer for those reading sentence (1), and there were more regressions (movements of the eyes backwards in the text).

Trueswell et al. (1994) carried out a modified version of the study by Ferreira and Clifton (1986) discussed earlier. They were puzzled by Ferreira and Clifton's (1986) finding that semantic information was of no use in eliminating ambiguity and allowing readers to identify the correct syntactic structure rapidly. According to Trueswell et al. (1994), the reason for this was that the semantic information was not strong enough to influence readers' initial processing. They used sentences with stronger semantic constraints, and found that semantic information was used at an early stage to permit rapid identification of the correct syntactic structure. However, the water has become muddy again. Clifton et al. (2003) used the same sentences as Trueswell et al., but analysed the resultant data more thoroughly. Their findings suggested that semantic information was of relatively little use in removing ambiguity.

According to the constraint-based theory, one factor influencing the assignment of syntactic structure to a sentence is **verb bias**. Many verbs can occur within various syntactic structures, but are more commonly found in some syntactic structures than others. For instance, Harley (2001) gave the example of the verb "read". It is most often followed by a direct object (e.g., "Susan read the book"), but it can also be used with a sentence complement (e.g., "Susan read the book had been banned"). Garnsey et al. (1997) found that readers resolved ambiguities and identified the correct syntactic structure more rapidly when the structure of a sentence was consistent with verb bias than when it was not. Thus, for example, sentences containing direct-object verbs (e.g., "read") were read more rapidly when the verb was followed by a direct object rather than by a sentence complement. This is inconsistent with the garden-path model, according to which verb bias should *not* influence the initial identification of syntactic structure.

Boland and Blodgett (2001) used noun/verb homographs (e.g., duck, train), words that can be used as either a noun or as a verb. For example, if you read a sentence that started "She saw her duck and . . .", you would not know whether the word "duck" was being used as a noun (". . . and chickens near the barn") or a verb (". . . and stumble near the barn"). According to the constraint-based approach, readers should initially try to construct a syntactic structure in which the homograph is used as its more common part of speech (e.g., "duck" is a verb more often than a noun, but "train" is more often a noun). As a result, readers should rapidly experience problems (revealed by eye movements) when a noun/verb homograph is used in its less common form. That prediction was confirmed.

Boland and Blodgett (2001) also considered the effects of previous context on syntactic processing. For example, the context is misleading in the following example:

> As they walked around, Kate looked at all of Jimmy's pets.
> She saw her duck and stumble near the barn.

It took longer to read the second sentence when the context was misleading. However, the key finding was that misleading context influenced syntactic processing *later* than predicted by constraint-based theory. Thus, the notion that *all* relevant sources of information are used immediately to influence syntactic processing was not true so far as previous context is concerned.

Evaluation

A valuable feature of the constraint-based theory is the notion that there can be varying degrees of support for different syntactic interpretations of a sentence. As someone reads a sentence, the accumulating syntactic and semantic evidence gradually leads the reader to produce a definite syntactic interpretation. It seems efficient that readers should use all the relevant information from the outset when trying to work out the syntactic structure of a sentence.

There are various limitations with constraint-based theory. First, it is not entirely correct that all relevant constraints or sources of information are used immediately (e.g., Boland & Blodgett, 2001). Second, within MacDonald et al.'s (1994) theory, little is said about the detailed processes involved in generating syntactic structures for complex sentences. Third, it is assumed within constraint-based theory that various representations are formed in parallel, with most of them subsequently being rejected. However, there is little direct evidence for the existence of these parallel representations. Fourth, many findings do not allow us to distinguish clearly between the various theories. As Harley (2001, p. 264) noted, "Proponents of the garden path model argue that the effects that are claimed to support constraint-based models arise because the second stage of parsing begins very quickly, and that many experiments that are supposed to be looking at the first stage are in fact looking at the second stage of parsing."

Unrestricted race model

Van Gompel, Pickering, and Traxler (2000) proposed a new theoretical approach to the resolution of syntactic ambiguity called the unrestricted race model. This model combines aspects of the garden-path and constraint-based models. The main assumptions of the unrestricted race model are as follows:

(1) All sources of information (semantic as well as syntactic) are used to identify a syntactic structure, as is assumed by constraint-based models.
(2) All other possible syntactic structures are ignored unless the favoured syntactic structure is disconfirmed by subsequent information.
(3) If the initially chosen syntactic structure has to be discarded, there is an extensive process of re-analysis before a different syntactic structure is chosen. This assumption makes the model similar to the garden-path model, in that parsing often involves two distinct stages.

Evidence

Van Gompel, Pickering, and Traxler (2001) tested predictions from the unrestricted race model, the garden-path model, and the constraint-based model. They presented participants with three kinds of sentence:

(1) *Ambiguous sentence*: The burglar stabbed only the guy with the dagger during the night. (This sentence is ambiguous, because it could be either the burglar or the guy who had the dagger.)
(2) *Verb-phrase attachment*: The burglar stabbed only the dog with the dagger during the night. (This sentence involves verb–phrase attachment, because it must have been the burglar who stabbed with the dagger.)
(3) *Noun-phrase attachment*: The burglar stabbed only the dog with the collar during the night. (This sentence involves noun–phrase attachment, because it must have been the dog that had the collar.)

How easy should it be to process these sentences? According to the garden-path model, the principle of minimal attachment means readers will always initially adopt the verb-phrase analysis. This leads to rapid processing of sentences such as (2) but to slow processing of sentences such as (3). It allows readers to interpret the ambiguous sentences as rapidly as verb-phrase sentences, because the verb-phrase analysis produces an acceptable interpretation. According to the constraint-based model, sentences such as (2) and (3) will be processed rapidly, because the meaning of the words supports only the correct interpretation. In contrast, there will be serious competition between the two possible interpretations of sentence (1) because both are reasonable. Thus, processing of the ambiguous sentences should be slower than for either type of unambiguous sentence.

The findings did not support either of the above models. What actually happened was that the ambiguous sentences were processed *faster* than either of the other types of sentences, which did not differ (see Figure 11.2). Why was this? According to van Gompel et al. (2001), the findings support the unrestricted race model. With the ambiguous sentences, readers rapidly use syntactic and semantic information to form a syntactic structure. Since both syntactic structures are possible, no re-analysis is necessary. In contrast, re-analysis will sometimes be required with noun-phrase and verb-phrase sentences.

Evaluation

The unrestricted race model is an interesting attempt to combine the best features of the garden-

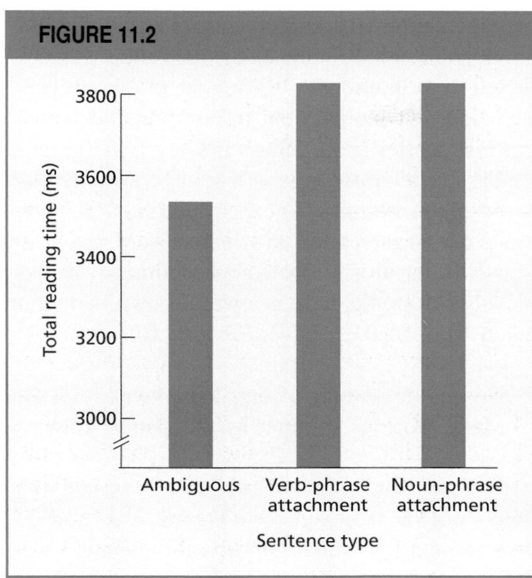

Total sentence processing time as a function of sentence type (ambiguous; verb-phrase attachment; noun-phrase attachment). Data from van Gompel et al. (2001).

path and constraint-based models. It seems reasonable that all sources of information (including world knowledge) are used from the outset to construct a syntactic structure, which is retained unless subsequent evidence is inconsistent with it. It remains for future research to specify more precisely how syntactic and semantic information are combined in the initial construction of a syntactic structure.

Good-enough representations

Ferreira, Bailey, and Ferraro (2002) identified an important limitation with nearly all theories of sentence processing including those discussed above. As they pointed out, "The language processor is believed to generate representations of the linguistic input that are complete, detailed, and accurate" (Ferreira et al., 2002, p. 11). In fact, these beliefs are often wrong. For example, consider the Moses illusion (Erickson & Mattson, 1981): when asked "How many animals of each sort did Moses put on the ark?" many people reply "Two" but the correct answer is "None" (think about it!). Ferreira et al. discussed one study in which more than 25% of readers accepted as plausible events such as the one described in the following sentence: "The dog was bitten by the man".

Wason and Reich (1979) found that most people misinterpreted the following sentence taken from a notice in a hospital casualty department: "No head injury is too trivial to be ignored". This is generally interpreted to mean "However trivial a head injury might appear, it should not be ignored". In fact, it actually means "However trivial a head injury is, it should be ignored". We can see that this is the correct meaning if we consider the following sentence: "No missile is too small to be banned", which means, "However small a missile is, it should be banned".

Ferreira (2003) presented sentences aurally, and obtained further evidence that our representations of sentences are sometimes inaccurate rather than being rich and complete. For example, a sentence such as "The mouse was eaten by the cheese", was sometimes misinterpreted as meaning the mouse ate the cheese, and a sentence such as "The man was visited by the woman" was sometimes mistakenly interpreted to mean the man visited the woman.

Why are people so prone to error when processing sentences, especially passive ones? According to Ferreira (2003), we use heuristics or rules of thumb to simplify the task of understanding sentences. A very common heuristic (called the NVN strategy) is to assume that the subject of a sentence is the agent of some action, whereas the object of the sentence is the patient or theme. It makes some sense to use this heuristic, because a substantial majority of sentences in English conform to this pattern. People are probably more concerned to construct accurate representations of what they have seen or heard in the laboratory than they are in informal situations in everyday life. It is thus very likely that language interpretation in the real world depends more on heuristics than is the case in the laboratory.

Sanford (2002) has put forward similar views. He argued that many misinterpretations of sentences occur because our processing tends to be *selective*: "Flexibility in the utilisation of processing resources is of paramount importance in resource-limited systems like the human mind . . . the problem is to determine what to analyse in detail and what to treat in a shallow fashion, to preserve economy of effort" (Sanford, 2002, p. 203).

PRAGMATICS

Pragmatics is concerned with practical language use and comprehension, especially those aspects going beyond the literal meaning of what is said and taking account of the current social context. Thus, pragmatics is concerned with *intended* rather than *literal* meaning as expressed by speakers and understood by listeners, and often involves drawing inferences. The literal meaning of a sentence is often *not* the one the writer or speaker intended to communicate. For example, we assume that someone who says "The weather's really great!" when it has been raining non-stop for several days actually thinks the weather is terrible. Entire books have been written about pragmatics, and here we will consider only a few aspects of a vast topic.

We will start by discussing a few examples in which the intended meaning of a sentence differs from the literal meaning. For example, when a speaker gives an indirect and apparently irrelevant answer to a question, the listener often tries to identify the speaker's goals to understand what he/she means. For example, consider the following (Holtgraves, 1998, p. 25):

Ken: Did Paula agree to go out with you?
Bob: She's not my type.

Holtgraves (1998) found that most people interpreted Bob's reply in a negative way as meaning that Paula had *not* agreed to go out with him. According to Holtgraves (1998), speakers give such indirect replies to save face (i.e., it would be embarrassing to give a direct reply).

Suppose Bob gave an indirect reply that did not seem to involve face saving (e.g., "She's my type"). As Holtgraves (1998, p. 17) pointed out, "Replies whose meaning contradicts a face management interpretation should be quite anomalous and very difficult to comprehend." As predicted, it took almost 50% longer to comprehend such indirect replies than to comprehend typical indirect replies (e.g., "She's not my type").

Figurative language is language not intended to be taken literally. Speakers and writers often make use of metaphor, in which a word or phrase is used figuratively to mean something it resembles. For example, here is a well-known metaphor taken from Shakespeare's *Richard III*:

Now is the winter of our discontent
Made glorious summer by this sun of York.

Cacciari and Glucksberg (1994) argued that much use of language is metaphorical, and involves intended rather than literal meanings (e.g., "My job is a jail"). We often interpret metaphorical or figurative language appropriately without being aware that we are extracting the intended rather than the literal meaning. For example, we rapidly interpret the sentence "David kicked the bucket" to mean that David has died, without considering the literal meaning at all (Gibbs et al., 1989).

Theoretical approaches

Much theorising in this area has focused on figurative language in general and metaphor in particular. The traditional theoretical approach is the standard pragmatic model originally proposed by Aristotle but endorsed more recently by Grice (1975) and Searle (1979). According to this model, three stages are involved in processing metaphors and other figurative expressions. First, the literal meaning is accessed. For example, the literal meaning of "David kicked the bucket" is that David struck a bucket with his foot. Second, the reader or listener decides whether the literal meaning makes sense in the context in which it is read or heard. If it doesn't, there is a third stage in which the reader or listener searches for a non-literal meaning of the sentence that does make sense in context.

One prediction from the standard pragmatic model is that literal meanings will be accessed faster than non-literal or figurative ones. This is because literal meanings are accessed in stage one of processing, whereas non-literal meanings are accessed only in stage three. A second prediction is that literal interpretations are accessed automatically, whereas non-literal interpretations are optional and thus not necessarily accessed.

A crucial assumption of the standard pragmatic model is that literal meanings are *always* accessed before non-literal ones. This assumption has been rejected by most other theorists. For example, Giora (1997, 2002) proposed the graded salience hypothesis, according to which initial processing is determined by salience or prominence rather than by type of meaning (literal vs. non-literal). According to this hypothesis, "Salient messages are processed initially, regardless of either literality [whether the intended meaning is the literal one] or contextual fit . . . Salience is a matter of degree, determined primarily by frequency of exposure and experiential familiarity with the meaning in question . . . Salient meanings are assumed to be accessed immediately upon encounter of the linguistic stimulus via a direct lookup in the mental lexicon. Less-salient meanings will lag behind. Non-salient meanings require extra inferential processes, and for the most part strong contextual support" (Giora, 2002, pp. 490–491).

Evidence

Most of the evidence has failed to support the standard pragmatic model. According to the model, non-literal meanings take longer to comprehend than literal ones. In fact, however, non-literal or metaphorical meanings are typically understood as rapidly as literal ones (see Glucksberg, 2003, for a review). It might be thought that we can only interpret *familiar* metaphors rapidly, but this is not the case. For example, Blasko and Connine (1993) presented participants with relatively unfamiliar metaphors (e.g., "Jerry first knew that loneliness was a desert when he was very young"). The metaphorical meanings of such sentences were understood as rapidly as the literal meanings.

According to the standard pragmatic model, figurative or metaphorical meanings are not accessed automatically. Evidence opposed to this prediction was reported by Glucksberg (2003). Participants decided as rapidly as possible whether various sentences were literally true or false. Among the sentences used were the following types: literally false (e.g., "Some fruits are tables"); metaphors (e.g., "Some surgeons are butchers"); and scrambled metaphors (e.g., "Some jobs are butchers"). If the standard pragmatic model is correct, the figurative meaning of metaphors should not be accessed (because it is not required by the task), and so there should be no problem in deciding that they are literally false. In contrast, if people automatically process the figurative meaning of metaphors, then metaphor sentences should take longer to judge as false because there is competition between the "true" non-literal meaning and the false literal meaning. The findings supported the notion that figurative meanings are accessed automatically (see Figure 11.3), thereby providing evidence against the standard pragmatic model.

We have seen that the processes involved in metaphor comprehension resemble those involved in comprehension of literal meaning in that they

FIGURE 11.3

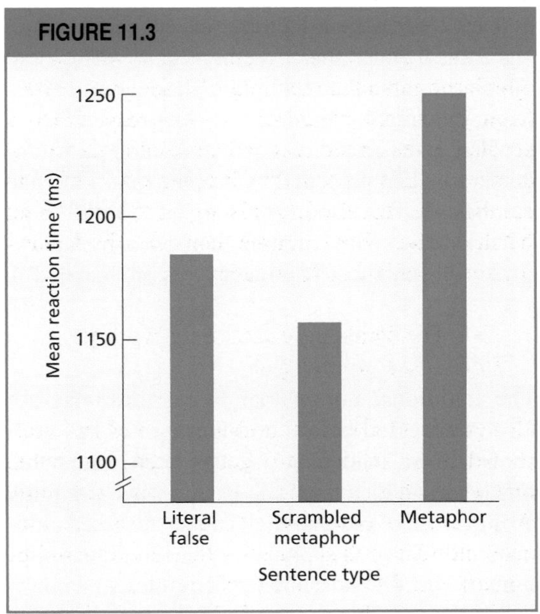

Time to decide that a sentence was literally false as a function of sentence type (literal false; scrambled metaphor; metaphor). Adapted from Glucksberg (2003).

generally occur rapidly and automatically. We now turn to a consideration of the role played by salience, a factor emphasised within the graded salience hypothesis. Giora and Fein (1999) tested this hypothesis using familiar metaphors (having salient literal and metaphorical meanings) and less-familiar metaphors (having a salient literal meaning only). These metaphors were presented in a context biasing either their metaphorical or their literal meaning. If salience is what matters, then the literal and metaphorical meanings of familiar metaphors should be activated regardless of context. In contrast, the literal meaning of less-familiar metaphors should be activated in both contexts, but the non-salient metaphorical meaning should not be activated in the literal context. The findings were exactly as predicted by the hypothesis.

As we have just seen, Giora and Fein (1999) found that context influenced the processing of metaphors. There is evidence from other studies confirming this finding. For example, consider a study by McGlone and Manfredi (2001). It seems reasonable to assume that it will take longer to understand a metaphor such as "My lawyer was a shark" when literal properties of sharks (e.g., "has fins"; "has sharp teeth"; "can swim") are more accessible than their metaphorical properties (e.g., "vicious"; "predatory"; "aggressive"). As predicted, the above metaphor took longer to understand when preceded by a contextual sentence emphasising the literal meaning of "shark" (e.g., "Sharks can swim") rather than by a metaphor-irrelevant sentence ("Some lawyers are married").

Evaluation

The traditional notion that literal meanings are always accessed before non-literal ones has been shown to be inadequate. It has been found that metaphorical meanings can be accessed as rapidly as literal ones, and that they can be accessed automatically. There is support for the central assumption of the graded salience hypothesis, namely, that salience plays a key role in the processing of metaphors and figurative language generally.

An important limitation of most theories is their neglect of individual differences. For example, the finding that it takes longer to decide that sentences are literally false with metaphors than with scrambled metaphors (Glucksberg, 2003) supports the view that metaphorical meanings are accessed automatically. Kazmerski, Blasko, and Dessalegn (2003) replicated this finding with high-IQ participants but failed to do so with low-IQ ones. The implication is that high-IQ individuals access metaphorical meanings automatically but low-IQ ones do not. It follows that theorists need to focus on individual differences in the processing of metaphors and other forms of figurative language.

Common ground

So far we have considered pragmatics mainly in situations in which listeners' comprehension of what is being said is accurate. However, there are many failures of communication between speakers and listeners. The presence or absence of **common ground** (the shared knowledge and beliefs between speaker and listener) is important in determining whether comprehension is accurate. According to Clark and Carlson (1981, p. 328), "When a listener tries to understand what a speaker means, the process he [*sic*] goes through can limit memory access to information that is common ground between the speaker and his addressees." Common ground is also important to speakers, who generally try to speak in ways that will be understood by their listeners (see Chapter 12 for a discussion of common ground from the speaker's perspective).

Keysar (e.g., Keysar et al., 2000) argued for a different theoretical approach in his perspective adjustment model. He assumed that it can be very effortful for listeners to keep working out the common ground existing between them and the speaker. Accordingly, listeners use a rapid and non-effortful **egocentric heuristic**, which is "a tendency to consider as potential referents [what is being referred to] objects that are not in the common ground, but are potential referents from one's own perspective" (Keysar et al., 2000, p. 32). Information about common ground is calculated more slowly, and can be used to correct any misunderstandings resulting from use of the egocentric heuristic.

Evidence

Keysar et al. (2000) compared the common ground and perspective adjustment approaches. A speaker and a listener were on opposite sides of a vertical array containing 16 slots arranged in a 4 × 4 pattern. Some slots contained objects (e.g., candles, toy cars), and the listener's task was to obey the speaker's instructions to move one of the objects. Of crucial importance, some slots were blocked so the listener could see the objects in them but the speaker could not. For example, in one display, the listener could see three candles of different sizes, but the speaker could see only two with the smallest candle blocked from view. What will happen when the speaker says, "Now put the small candle above it"? If the listener uses only common ground information, he/she will move the smaller of the two candles that the speaker can see. However, if the listener uses the egocentric heuristic, he/she may initially consider the candle the speaker cannot see.

The findings of Keysar et al. (2000) supported the perspective adjustment model. The initial eye movements of listeners were often directed to the object they could see but the speaker could not, indicating that they did *not* consider only the common ground. In addition, listeners reached for the object only they could see on 20% of trials, and actually picked it up on 75% of those trials.

Strong evidence of the egocentric heuristic was obtained by Barr and Keysar (2002). On each trial, two pictures were presented (e.g., car and flower), the speaker named one of them, and participants selected the appropriate picture as rapidly as possible. In the last stage of the experiment, the speaker used general terms referring to a class of objects (e.g., car). However, earlier in the experiment, participants had heard a speaker describe the pictures in more specific terms (e.g., sports car, carnation). In the last stage, the speaker was either the same as earlier in the experiment or different.

The key question was as follows: would the participants be slowed down in selecting the correct picture at the end of the experiment because they expected the speaker to use *specific* rather than *general* names? If common ground or mutual knowledge is of crucial importance, the participants should be slowed down when the speaker is the same throughout. However, they should not be slowed down if the speaker is different, because no common ground has been established with the new speaker. In fact, participants' performance was comparable in the same speaker and different speaker conditions (see Figure 11.4). Thus, listeners use the information available to them, and rely on the egocentric heuristic rather than on the common ground.

FIGURE 11.4

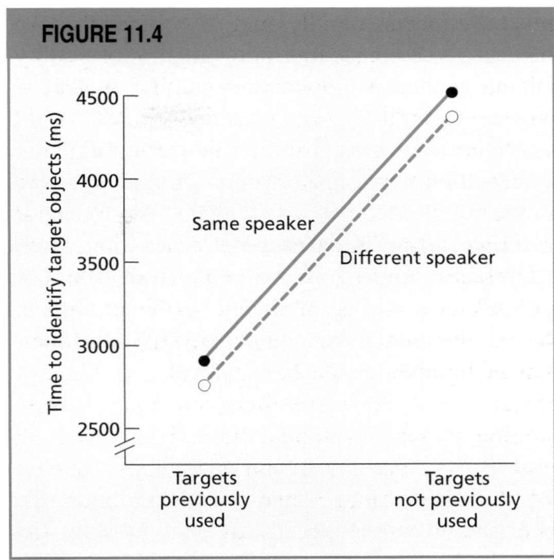

Time to identify target objects as a function of whether the speaker is the same as earlier in the experiment or different and whether or not the targets have been used previously. Data from Barr and Keysar (2002).

In some ways, the findings of Keysar et al. (2000) and of Barr and Keysar (2002) are puzzling. There is much evidence that the ability to take the perspective of the other person (e.g., focusing on the common ground) is of fundamental importance in communication (see Schober, 1998, for a review). Hanna, Tanenhaus, and Trueswell (2003) argued that the extent to which listeners take account of the common ground will depend on the strength and saliency of information about it. For example, one reason why the participants in the study by Keysar et al. (2000) made only limited use of the common ground was because it is so unusual for objects present immediately in front of a speaker and a listener to differ in their perceptual accessibility. Hanna et al. used a situation similar to that of Keysar et al. (2000), and obtained support for the egocentric heuristic. However, they also found that information about the common ground was used immediately. As they concluded, "We found no evidence for an initial stage of processing where addressees ignored information from common ground, as would be predicted by the strong version of the monitoring and perspective adjustment model" (Hanna et al., 2003, p. 59).

Evaluation

Listeners sometimes make use of the egocentric heuristic even though it can lead to error. As Keysar et al. (2000, p. 37) pointed out, "The typical benefit of egocentric interpretation outweighs the typical cost of making an error . . . [Listeners] use a strategy that is relatively effective though prone to errors, in order to accommodate a limited mental capacity." This somewhat error-prone approach works well, because common ground or mutual knowledge can be used to correct errors.

One limitation of Keysar's research is that use has been made of rather artificial situations. Thus, it is not altogether clear that the egocentric heuristic is generally used in everyday life. For example, we may make more use of the common ground and less use of the egocentric heuristic when listening to someone whose beliefs are very familiar to us (e.g., a good friend) than with a stranger in the laboratory. More generally, it is probably often the case that the common ground and the egocentric heuristic are both used at a very early stage of processing speech (Hanna et al., 2003).

INDIVIDUAL DIFFERENCES: CAPACITY THEORY

There are considerable individual differences in almost all complex cognitive activities. Accordingly, theories based on the assumption that everyone comprehends text in the same way are likely to be incorrect. The most influential theory of individual differences in comprehension was put forward by Just and Carpenter (e.g., 1992). They assumed that there are individual differences in the capacity of working memory, by which they meant a system used for both storage and processing (see Chapter 6). They also assumed that such individual differences have substantial effects on language comprehension.

How can individual differences in working memory capacity be assessed? The most common method is to use a task devised by Daneman and Carpenter (1980). Participants read a number of sentences for comprehension, and then try to recall the final word of each sentence. The largest number of sentences from which a participant can recall all the final words more than 50% of the time is his/her **reading span**, and is a measure of working memory capacity. It is assumed that the processes used in comprehending the sentences require a smaller proportion of the available working memory capacity of those with a large capacity. As a result, they have more capacity for retaining the last words of the sentences.

There is much evidence that reading span is a useful measure. For example, it correlates +.8 with the ability to answer comprehension questions about a passage and +.6 with verbal intelligence (see Just & Carpenter, 1992). In addition, those with high reading spans read hard portions of a text much faster than those with low reading spans.

Reading span is not the only measure to correlate highly with text comprehension. For example, Turner and Engle (1989) assessed the operation span. The participants were presented with a series of items such as "IS $(4 \times 2) - 3 = 5$? TABLE". They had to answer each arithmetical question and remember the last word. **Operation span** (the maximum number of items for which the participants could remember all the last words) correlated as highly with language comprehension as did reading span. This suggests that reading span and operation span both assess individual differences in general processing resources needed for text comprehension (and other cognitive tasks).

What processes underlie reading span and operation span? Just and Carpenter (1992) argued that span measures reflect a *single* cognitive resource used for processing and temporary storage. In contrast, Baddeley (e.g., 1996) assumed that *different* resources are involved in processing and in storage. Duff and Logie (2001) obtained relevant evidence from a study on the operation span. There were three conditions: (1) arithmetic verification (e.g., 8 + 7 = 17: correct or incorrect?), which emphasises processing; (2) memory span: serial recall of words presented individually, which emphasises storage; (3) operation span or combined condition: arithmetic verification and memory span performed at the same time, which requires processing *and* storage.

Suppose arithmetic verification and memory span both depend on a single processing resource. If so, there would presumably be a substantial impairment of performance on both tasks when performed together (Condition 3). In contrast, if the two tasks involve separate processing resources, then combining both tasks should *not* severely impair performance. The findings are shown in Figure 11.5. They support the notion that processing and storage involve separate resources. For example, arithmetic verification may require the central executive component of working memory, whereas memory span requires the phonological loop (see Chapter 6).

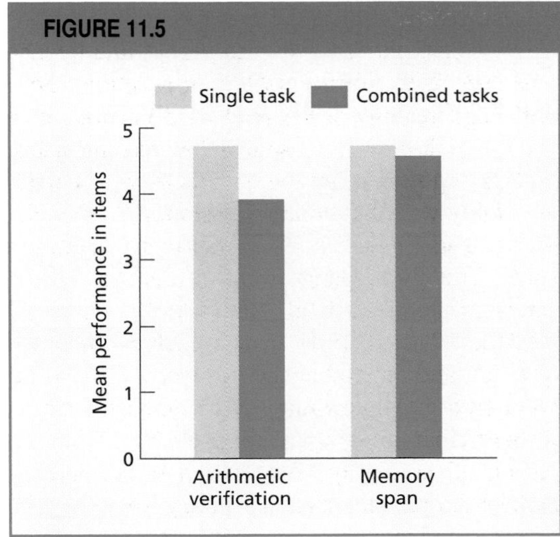

Performance on the arithmetic verification and memory-span tasks as a function of whether the tasks were carried out singly or were combined. Data from Duff and Logie (2001).

Whitney, Arnett, Driver, and Budd (2001) considered the processes underlying Daneman and Carpenter's (1980) reading span measure. They found clear evidence that reading span does *not* depend on a single process. Instead, "There are two independent contributions to RST (Reading Span Test) performance: efficiency of manipulation of information and susceptibility to interference" (Whitney et al., 2001, p. 9).

Most research involving reading span and operation span has been based on the implicit assumption that these span measures assess a single processing resource. We have discussed reading span and operation span at some length to show that this assumption is incorrect. Thus, the correct interpretation of research using span measures is more complex than is generally assumed.

Evidence

Capacity theory has been applied to issues considered earlier in the chapter, such as whether the initial syntactic parsing of a sentence is affected by meaning. Just and Carpenter (1992) examined reading times for sentences such as "The evidence examined by the lawyer shocked the jury" and "The defendant examined by the lawyer shocked the jury". "The evidence" (an inanimate noun) is unlikely to be doing the examining, whereas "the defendant" (an animate noun) might well be. Accordingly, the actual syntactic structure of the sentence should come as more of a surprise to readers given the second sentence. However, if meaning does not influence initial syntactic parsing, then the gaze duration on the critical phrase "by the lawyer" should be the same for both sentences.

Just and Carpenter (1992) found that the reading times of participants with a low reading span were unaffected by the animate/inanimate noun manipulation (see Figure 11.6). In contrast, participants with a high reading span used the cue of inanimacy, and so their initial parsing was affected by meaning. Presumably only those participants

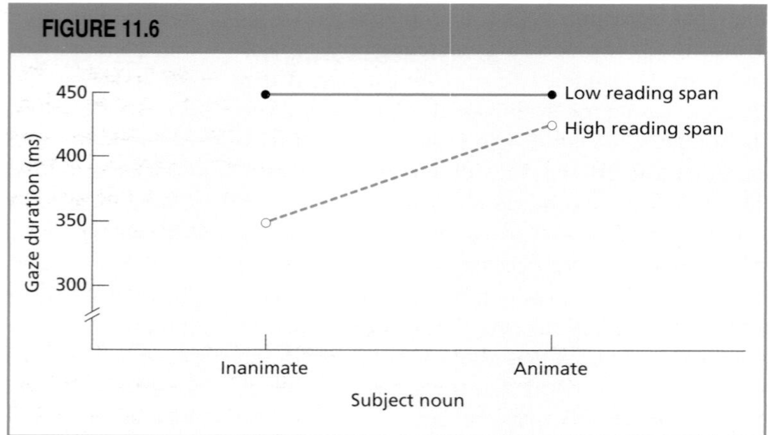

Gaze duration as a function of whether the subject noun was inanimate or animate. Adapted from Just and Carpenter (1992).

with a high reading span had sufficient working memory capacity available to take the animacy/inanimacy of the subject noun into account. Thus, individual differences influence whether meaning affects initial syntactic parsing.

Another area of controversy relates to the processing of sentences containing syntactic ambiguity. One possibility is that those encountering such ambiguity try to retain both (or all) interpretations until disambiguating information is provided. Alternatively, people might select a single interpretation, and retain it unless (or until) there is invalidating information. Just and Carpenter (1992) discussed a study in which sentences were presented in a self-paced, word-by-word moving window paradigm. Some sentences were syntactically ambiguous until the end (e.g., "The experienced soldiers warned about the dangers before the midnight raid"), but were finally given the more predictable resolution. This sentence is ambiguous, because it might have been the case that the experienced soldiers were warned about the dangers by someone else. Other sentences were unambiguous (e.g., "The experienced soldiers spoke about the dangers before the midnight raid").

Participants with a high reading span processed the ambiguous sentences more slowly than the unambiguous ones, especially close to the part of the sentence in which the ambiguity was resolved (see Figure 11.7). These participants incurred a

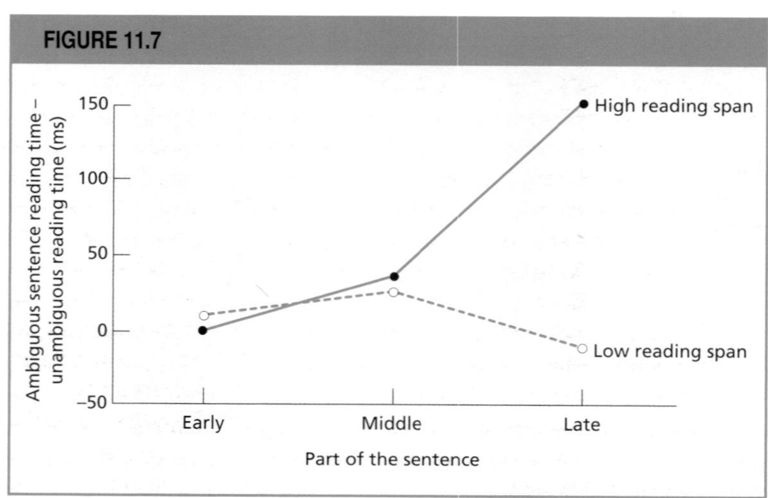

Differences in reading time per word between ambiguous and unambiguous sentences as a function of part of the sentence. Adapted from Just and Carpenter (1992).

FIGURE 11.8

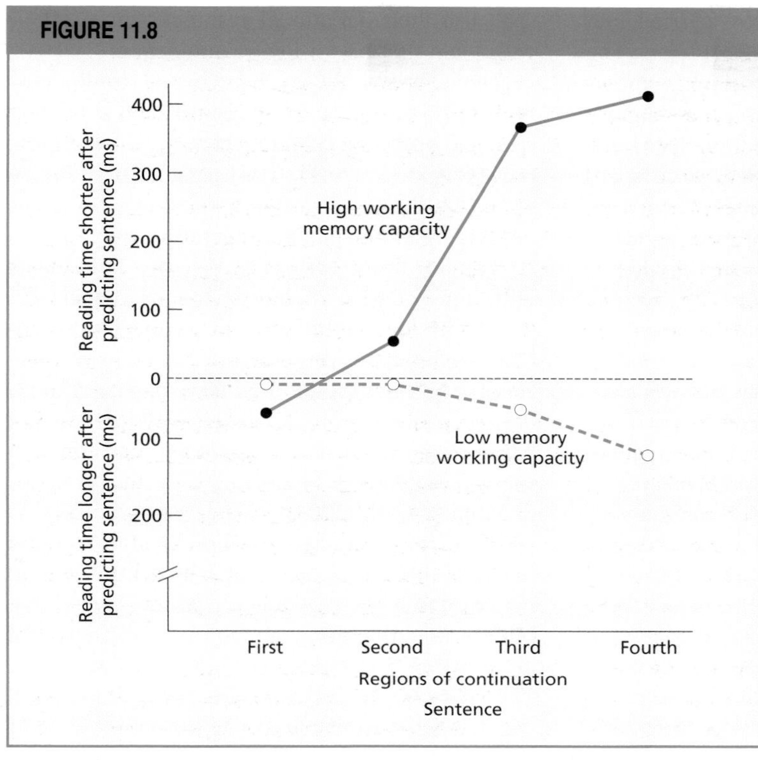

Effect of a preceding predicting sentence on reading time of a continuation sentence. Data from Calvo (2001).

cost in terms of processing time because they maintained two different syntactic interpretations of the ambiguous sentences. In contrast, those with a low reading span did *not* differ in their processing times for ambiguous and unambiguous sentences, presumably because they treated such sentences as if they were unambiguous.

There has been some controversy (discussed later in the chapter) about the extent to which readers draw elaborative inferences (inferences that add details not contained in the text). Calvo (2001) considered this from the perspective of individual differences in working memory capacity as assessed by reading span. We will consider an example of the materials he used. In one condition, a continuation sentence (e.g., "The pupil studied for an hour approximately") was preceded by a predicting sentence (e.g., "Three days before the examination the pupil went to the library, looked for a separate table and opened his notebook"). In a second condition, the same continuation sentence was preceded by a control sentence (e.g., "The pupil, who was a little tired after finishing his examination, forgot his notebook and left it on a table in the library"). Participants who formed elaborative inferences should have found it easier to process the continuation sentence when it followed the predicting sentence than when it followed the control sentence, because the former sentence is directly relevant to it. Ease of processing was assessed by recording eye movements.

What did Calvo (2001) find? Individuals with high working memory capacity spent less time on integrating information from the continuation sentence when preceded by a predicting sentence, whereas those with low working memory capacity did not (see Figure 11.8). The implication of these findings is that high-capacity individuals rapidly drew elaborative inferences, but low-capacity individuals did not. This may help to explain why somewhat inconsistent findings have been obtained in other studies on elaborative inferences.

Daneman and Merikle (1996) carried out a meta-analysis of data from 77 studies. The emphasis in this meta-analysis was on comparing the ability of measures of working memory capacity (e.g., reading span, operation span) and of storage capacity (e.g., digit span, word span) to predict comprehension performance. There were two key findings. First, measures of working memory capacity consistently had greater predictive power than measures of storage capacity. Second, comprehension performance was predicted as well by operation span as by reading span. This finding is important, because it means that the ability of reading span to predict comprehension performance is not simply due to the fact that reading span itself involves sentence comprehension.

Why do individuals with high working memory capacity have superior language comprehension to those with low working memory capacity? Kaakinen, Hyönä, and Keenan (2003) shed some light on the question. Participants read a text on rare diseases containing a mixture of relevant and irrelevant information. Those with high working memory capacity allocated extra time to reading the relevant information during the *initial* reading of the text. In contrast, those with low working memory capacity only devoted extra attention to the relevant information later on. As Kaakinen et al. (2003, p. 456) concluded, "High-span readers are better at allocating their attentional resources to relevant information than low-span readers."

Evaluation

Probably the greatest strength of the capacity theory put forward by Just and Carpenter (e.g., 1992) is the assumption that there are substantial individual differences in the processes used in language comprehension. That assumption is undoubtedly correct, and yet most theorists have studiously avoided incorporating it into their theories. Some individuals have more processing resources available than others, and so can carry out forms of processing that those with fewer processing resources cannot. This approach has shed important new light on some major controversies (e.g., the role of meaning in the initial parsing of sentences). There is evidence (Kaakinen et al., 2003) that individuals with high reading span use their attentional resources more efficiently than those with low reading span.

The capacity theory has several limitations. First, the assumption that measures such as reading span and operation span reflect a *single* underlying process is incorrect (Duff & Logie, 2001; Whitney et al., 2001). It seems that at least two resources underlie reading span and operation span.

Second, the precise reasons *why* individuals with high working memory capacity outperform those with low working memory capacity on sentence comprehension tasks are not entirely clear. However, MacDonald and Christiansen (2002) have provided a more detailed theoretical account based on a connectionist approach, and efficient use of attentional resources is a likely factor (Kaakinen et al., 2003).

Third, the theory ignores individual differences in the ability to *suppress* unwanted information. For example, Gernsbacher, Varner, and Faust (1990) asked participants to decide whether a given word was related to a previous sentence. The crucial condition was one in which the word was related to an inappropriate meaning of one of the words in the sentence (e.g., "ace" following "He dug with the spade"). When the word followed the sentence by 850 ms, only individuals with low comprehension skills showed an interference effect. Thus, individuals with high comprehension skills can suppress irrelevant information more efficiently than those with low comprehension skills.

Fourth, the theory emphasises working memory capacity rather than the specific processes involved in comprehension. Thus, Just and Carpenter (1992) failed to provide a comprehensive account of the complex processes underlying language comprehension.

DISCOURSE PROCESSING

So far we have focused mainly on the processes involved in understanding individual sentences. However, in real life we are generally presented with connected **discourse** (written text or speech at least several sentences in length). What are the main differences? "A sentence out of context is nearly always ambiguous, whereas a sentence in a discourse context is rarely ambiguous . . . Both stories and everyday experiences include people performing actions in pursuit of goals, events that present obstacles to these goals, conflicts between people, and emotional reactions" (Graesser, Millis, & Zwaan, 1997, p. 164).

Most research on discourse comprehension has used written texts. Some researchers have used published texts written by professional writers, whereas others have used specially constructed texts. The former approach has the advantage of **ecological validity** (applicability to real life), but poor control over many variables affecting comprehension. The latter approach has the advantage that textual variables can be manipulated systematically, but the resulting texts tend to be artificial. How should researchers proceed? Ideally, hypotheses should be confirmed with both types of text.

Inference drawing

Comprehension of discourse would be impossible without the process of drawing inferences or filling in gaps. For example, consider the following story taken from Rumelhart and Ortony (1977):

(1) Mary heard the ice-cream van coming.
(2) She remembered the pocket money.
(3) She rushed into the house.

You probably made various assumptions or inferences while reading the story: Mary wanted to buy some ice-cream; buying ice-cream costs money; Mary had some pocket money in the house; and Mary had only a limited amount of time to get hold of some money before the ice-cream van arrived. None of these assumptions is explicitly stated in the three sentences. It is so natural for us to draw inferences that we are often unaware that we are doing so.

Distinctions can be drawn among logical inferences, bridging inferences, and elaborative inferences. **Logical inferences** depend only on the meanings of words. For example, we can infer that anyone who is a widow is female. **Bridging inferences** need to be made to establish coherence between the current part of the text and the preceding text, whereas **elaborative inferences** serve to embellish or add details to the text.

Most theorists accept that readers generally draw logical and bridging inferences, because they are essential for understanding. What is more controversial is the extent to which non-essential or elaborative inferences are drawn automatically. Singer (1994) compared the time taken to verify a test sentence (e.g., "A dentist pulled a tooth") following one of three contexts: (1) the information had already been explicitly presented; (2) a bridging inference was needed to understand the test sentence; and (3) an elaborative inference was needed. Verification times in conditions (1) and (2) were fast and the same, suggesting that the bridging inference was drawn automatically during comprehension. However, verification times were significantly slower in condition (3), presumably because the elaborative inference was *not* drawn automatically.

Anaphor resolution

Perhaps the simplest form of bridging inference is involved in **anaphor resolution**, in which a pronoun or noun has to be identified with a previously mentioned noun or noun phrase (e.g., "Fred sold John his lawn mower, and then he sold him his garden hose"). It requires a bridging inference to realise that "he" refers to Fred rather than to John. How do people make the appropriate anaphoric inference? Sometimes gender makes the task very easy (e.g., "Juliet sold John her lawn mower, and then she sold him her garden hose"). Sometimes the number of the noun provides a useful cue (e.g., "Juliet and her friends sold John their lawn mower, and then they sold him their garden hose").

Evidence that gender information can make anaphor resolution easier was reported by Arnold, Eisenband, Brown-Schmit, and Trueswell (2000). Participants looked at pictures while listening to text. Gender information ("he" or "she") was used more rapidly to look at the appropriate picture when it contained a male and a female character than when it contained two same-sex characters.

Anaphor resolution is also easier when pronouns are in the expected order. Harley (2001) provided the following example:

(1) Vlad sold Dirk his broomstick because he hated it.
(2) Vlad sold Dirk his broomstick because he needed it.

The first sentence is easy to understand, because "he" refers to the first-named man (i.e., Vlad). In contrast, the second sentence is relatively hard to understand, because "he" refers to the second-named man (i.e., Dirk).

It seems reasonable to assume that ease of anaphor resolution should depend on the distance between the pronoun and the noun to which it refers. Some support for that assumption was found in children's text comprehension by Yuill and Oakhill (1991). However, Clifton and Ferreira (1987) showed that distance was *not* important. What mattered was whether the relevant noun was still the topic of discourse.

Suppose a listener has to decide who "she" is when asked the question "Is she asleep?" by their wife. As Keysar, Barr, Balin, and Paek (1998) pointed out, it is generally assumed (restricted search hypothesis) that listeners will restrict their search to females known to the speaker. However, they proposed an unrestricted search hypothesis, according to which listeners' search is *not* restricted. The wife was referring to their daughter. However, the husband has a secret lover, and had just been thinking she was probably asleep. According to the unrestricted search hypothesis, the existence of the secret lover should slow down the listener's attempt to verify that the "she" in the question is the daughter. However, this should not happen according to the restricted search hypothesis. The findings strongly supported the unrestricted search hypothesis when participants imagined themselves in the role of the husband.

When are inferences drawn?

Consider the following passage (O'Brien et al., 1988):

> All the mugger wanted was to steal the woman's money. But when she screamed, he stabbed her with his weapon in an attempt to quiet her. He looked to see if anyone had seen him. He threw the knife into the bushes, took her money, and ran away.

O'Brien et al. (1988) were interested in seeing *when* readers drew the inference that the "weapon" referred to in the second sentence was in fact a knife. They compared reading time on the last sentence in the passage quoted here, and in an almost identical passage in which the word "weapon" was replaced by "knife". There was no difference in the reading time, suggesting the inference that the weapon was a knife had been drawn *immediately* by readers.

O'Brien et al. (1988) also considered reading time for the last sentence when the second sentence was altered so the inference that the weapon was a knife was less clear ("But when she screamed, he assaulted her with his weapon in an attempt to quiet her"). This time, the last sentence took longer to read, presumably because the inference that the weapon was a knife was drawn only while the last sentence was being read. Overall, these findings suggest that obvious inferences are drawn immediately, whereas non-obvious ones are not.

Singer (1979) also found that only strong and obvious inferences are drawn immediately. He asked participants to read pairs of sentences. In some cases, the subject noun of the second sentence had been explicitly mentioned in the first sentence (e.g., "The boy cleared the snow with a shovel. The shovel was heavy."). In other cases, the subject noun had not been specifically referred to before (e.g., "The boy cleared the snow from the stairs. The shovel was heavy."). Singer (1979) found that the time taken to read the second sentence in the pair was greater when the subject noun of the sentence had not been explicitly mentioned before. This suggests that the inference that a shovel was used to clear the snow was not drawn while the first sentence was being read, but was drawn subsequently.

How are inferences drawn?

Suppose you are asked to read the following two sentences:

> Keith drove to London yesterday.
> The car kept overheating.

You have no trouble (hopefully!) in linking these sentences based on the assumption that Keith drove to London in a car, and that car kept overheating. Garrod and Terras (2000) argued there are two possible explanations for the way in which the bridging inference could be made. First, reading the verb "drove" in the first sentence may activate concepts relating to driving (especially "car"). Second, readers may form a representation of the entire situation described in the first sentence, and then relate information in the second sentence to that representation. The crucial difference is that the sentential context is irrelevant in the first explanation but is highly relevant in the second explanation.

Garrod and Terras (2000) tried to distinguish between these two possibilities. They recorded eye movements while participants read a sentence such as "However, she was disturbed by a loud scream from the back of the class and the pen dropped on the floor". This sentence was preceded by a sentence about a teacher writing a letter or writing on a blackboard. If context is important, then participants should have found it harder to process the word "pen" when the previous sentence was about writing on a blackboard rather than writing a letter. In fact, the initial fixation on the word "pen" was uninfluenced by context. However, participants spent longer going back over the sentence containing the word "pen" when the preceding context was inappropriate.

What do the above findings mean? According to Garrod and Terras (2000), there are two stages in forming bridging inferences. The first stage is *bonding*, which is a low-level process involving the automatic activation of words from the preceding sentence. The second stage is *resolution*, which involves making sure that the overall interpretation is consistent with the contextual information. Resolution is influenced by context, but bonding is not.

Which inferences are drawn?

Everyone agrees that various inferences are made while people are reading text or listening to speech. What is of interest theoretically is to understand *why* inferences are made, and to predict which inferences are likely to be made. The constructionist approach originally proposed by Bransford (e.g., Bransford, Barclay, & Franks, 1972) and later developed by others (e.g., Johnson-Laird, 1980; van Dijk & Kintsch, 1983) represents one very influential theoretical position. Bransford argued that comprehension typically requires our active involvement to supply information not explicitly contained in the text. Johnson-Laird (1980) argued that readers typically construct a relatively complete "mental model" of the situation and events referred to in the text (see Chapter 16). A key implication of the constructionist approach is that numerous elaborative inferences are typically drawn while reading a text.

Most early research supporting the constructionist position involved using memory tests to assess inference drawing. For example, Bransford et al. (1972) presented their participants with sentences such as "Three turtles rested on a floating log, and a fish swam beneath them". They argued that the inference would be drawn that the fish swam under the log. To test this, some participants on a subsequent recognition-memory test were given the sentence "Three turtles rested on a floating log, and a fish swam beneath it". Most participants were confident this inference was the original sentence. Indeed, the level of confidence was as high as it was when the original sentence was re-presented on the memory test! Bransford et al. (1972) concluded that inferences from text are typically stored in memory just like information actually presented in the text.

Memory tests provide only an *indirect* measure of inferential processes. The potential problem is that any inferences found on a memory test may be made at the time of test rather than during reading. In fact, many (or most) inferences found on memory tests reflect reconstructive processes occurring during retrieval.

Minimalist hypothesis

The constructionist position has increasingly come under attack. According to McKoon and Ratcliff (1992, p. 442), "The widely accepted constructionist view of text processing has almost no unassailable empirical support . . . it is difficult to point to a single, unequivocal [definite] piece of evidence in favour of the automatic generation of constructionist inferences." McKoon and Ratcliff (1992, p. 440) proposed an alternative view known as the *minimalist hypothesis*: "In the absence of specific, goal-directed strategic processes, inferences of only two kinds are constructed: those that establish locally coherent representations of the parts of a text that are processed concurrently and those that rely on information that is quickly and easily available."

Here are the main assumptions made by McKoon and Ratcliff (1992):

- Inferences are either automatic or strategic (goal directed).
- Some automatic inferences establish local coherence (two or three sentences making sense on their own or in combination with easily available general knowledge); these inferences involve parts of the text in working memory at the same time (this is working memory in the sense of a general-purpose capacity rather than the Baddeley multiple-component working memory system discussed in Chapter 6).
- Other automatic inferences rely on information readily available because it is explicitly stated in the text.
- Strategic inferences are formed in pursuit of the reader's goals; they sometimes serve to produce local coherence.

The greatest difference between the minimalist hypothesis and the constructionist position concerns the number of automatic inferences formed. Constructionists claim that numerous automatic inferences are drawn in reading, whereas those who favour the minimalist hypothesis argue that there are very definite constraints on the number of inferences generated automatically.

Evidence

McKoon and Ratcliff (1986) argued that a sentence such as "The actress fell from the fourteenth storey" would automatically lead to the inference that she died according to the constructionist viewpoint but not according to the minimalist hypothesis. Participants read several short texts containing such sentences, followed by a recognition memory test on which they had to decide very rapidly whether or not certain words had been presented in any of the texts. There were critical test words representing inferences from a presented sentence (e.g., "dead" for the sentence about the actress). The correct response to this critical test word was "No". However, if participants had formed the inference that falling from the fourteenth storey inevitably causes death, then this would presumably lead to errors. Errors should not occur if the inference had not been formed.

McKoon and Ratcliff (1986) found that the number of errors on critical test words was no higher than on control words when immediately preceded on the recognition memory test by the neutral word "ready". However, when preceded by a word from the relevant sentence (e.g., "actress"), there were more errors to the critical test words. These findings suggest that the inferences were not generated fully, which is in line with the minimalist hypothesis. However, the fact that they were formed to a limited extent provides some support for the constructionists.

Evidence opposing the constructionist position and indicating the importance of the distinction between automatic and strategic inferences was obtained by Dosher and Corbett (1982). They used instrumental inferences (e.g., "Mary stirred her coffee" has "spoon" as its instrumental inference). In order to decide whether participants generated these instrumental inferences during reading, Dosher and Corbett used an unusual procedure. The time taken to name the colour in which a word is printed is slowed down if the word has recently been activated. Thus, if presentation of the sentence "Mary stirred her coffee" activates the word "spoon", this should slow the time taken to name the colour in which the word "spoon" is printed. In a control condition, the words presented bore no relationship to the preceding sentences. The predicted findings were obtained when the participants were instructed to guess the instrument in each sentence as it was presented. However, there was no evidence that the instrumental inferences had been formed with normal reading instructions.

What do the above findings mean? First, whether an inference is drawn can depend on the reader's intentions or goals, which is one of the central assumptions made by McKoon and Ratcliff (1992). Second, the findings go against the constructionist position. We need to infer the instrument used in stirring coffee to attain full understanding, but such instrumental inferences are *not* normally drawn.

McKoon and Ratcliff (1992) assumed that automatic inferences are drawn to establish local coherence for information contained in working memory, but that global inferences (inferences connecting widely separated pieces of textual information) are not drawn automatically. They tested these assumptions with short texts containing a global goal (e.g., assassinating a president) and one or two local or subordinate goals (e.g., using a rifle; using hand grenades). Active use of global and local inferences was tested by presenting a test word after each text, and instructing the participants to decide rapidly whether the word had appeared in the text.

Local inferences were drawn automatically, but global inferences were not. These findings are more consistent with the minimalist hypothesis than with the constructionist position, in which no distinction is drawn between local and global inferences.

Some of the available evidence suggests that people often draw more inferences than is implied by the minimalist hypothesis. For example, Suh and Trabasso (1993) used texts in which a character's initial goal was satisfied or was not satisfied. For example, Jimmy wanted a bicycle, and his mother either bought him one immediately or did not. Later on, Jimmy has earned a lot of money, and sets off for a department store. In the condition in which Jimmy has not satisfied his goal of having a bicycle, it could be inferred that his intention was to buy one in the store, and that is precisely what readers of the goal-unsatisfied version of the story did. This was shown by the finding that Jimmy's bicycle goal was much more available at the end of the story to readers of the goal-unsatisfied version of the story. The assumptions of the minimalist hypothesis would not seem to predict that such readers would draw inferences about Jimmy's intentions when he reaches the department store.

Individual differences have been ignored in most of the research even though they are likely to be important. Murray and Burke (2003) considered inference drawing in participants with high, moderate, or low reading skill. Participants were tested on predictive inferences (e.g., inferring "break" when presented with a sentence such as "The angry husband threw the fragile vase against the wall"). All three groups showed evidence of drawing these predictive inferences. However, these inferences were only drawn automatically by participants with high reading skill. The existence of such individual differences points to a limitation of the minimalist and constructionist approaches.

Evaluation

The minimalist hypothesis clarifies which inferences are automatically drawn when someone is reading a text. In contrast, constructionist theorists often argue that inferences needed to understand fully the situation described in a text are drawn automatically. This is rather vague, as there could be differences of opinion over exactly what information needs to be encoded for full understanding.

Another strength of the minimalist hypothesis is that it emphasises the distinction between automatic and strategic inferences. The notion that many inferences will be drawn only if they are consistent with the reader's goals in reading is an important one.

On the negative side, we cannot always predict accurately from the hypothesis *which* inferences will be drawn. For example, automatic inferences are drawn if the necessary information is "readily available", but it can be problematic to establish the precise degree of availability of some piece of information. There is also evidence that the minimalist hypothesis is too minimalist, and often underestimates the inferences drawn from text (e.g., Suh & Trabasso, 1993). Finally, neither the minimalist nor the constructionist approach provides an adequate account of individual differences in inference drawing (e.g., Murray & Burke, 2003).

Search-after-meaning theory

Graesser, Singer, and Trabasso (1994) agreed with McKoon and Ratcliff (1992) that constructionist theories often fail to specify which inferences are drawn during comprehension. They tried to eliminate this omission in their search-after-meaning theory, according to which readers engage in a search after meaning based on the following:

- The reader goal assumption: the reader constructs a meaning for the text that addresses his/her goals.
- The coherence assumption: the reader tries to construct a meaning for the text that is coherent locally and globally.
- The explanation assumption: the reader tries to explain the actions, events, and states referred to in the text.

Graesser et al. (1994) pointed out that readers will not search after meaning if their goals do not require the meaning of the text to be constructed (e.g., proof reading); if the text appears to lack coherence; or if they do not possess the necessary background knowledge to make sense of the text. Even if readers do search after meaning, several kinds of inference are not normally drawn according to the search-after-meaning theory. As can be seen in Figure 11.9, these undrawn inferences include ones about future developments (causal consequence); the precise way in which actions are accomplished (subordinate goal-actions); and the author's intent.

Nine different types of inference are described in Figure 11.9. According to Graesser et al. (1994), it is assumed within search-after-meaning theory that six of these types of inference are generally drawn, whereas only three are drawn on the minimalist hypothesis. The evidence seems to be

FIGURE 11.9

	Type of inference	Answers query	Predicted by search-after-meaning theory	Predicted by minimalist perspective	Normally found
1.	Referential	To what previous word does this apply? (e.g., anaphora)	✓	✓	✓
2.	Case structure role assignment	What is the role? (e.g., agent, object) of this noun	✓	✓	✓
3.	Causal antecedent	What caused this?	✓	✓	✓
4.	Supraordinate goal	What is the main goal?	✓		✓
5.	Thematic	What is the overall theme?	✓		?
6.	Character emotional reaction	How does the character feel?	✓		✓
7.	Causal consequence	What happens next?			×
8.	Instrument	What was used to do this?			×
9.	Subordinate goal-action	How was the action achieved?			×

The types of inferences normally drawn, together with the predictions from the constructionist and minimalist perspectives. Adapted from Graesser et al. (1994).

more in line with the predictions of the search-after-meaning theory than those of the minimalist hypothesis (see Figure 11.9). For example, it is assumed within search-after-meaning theory that the main goals are inferred, whereas the main goals are not inferred according to the minimalist hypothesis. Poynor and Morris (2003) compared texts in which the goal of the protagonist [principal character] was explicitly stated or was only implied. Later in the text there was a sentence in which the protagonist carried out an action consistent or inconsistent with his/her goal. Readers took longer to read a sentence describing an inconsistent action than one describing a consistent action, and this was the case regardless of whether the goal was explicit or implied. Thus, readers inferred the protagonist's goal even when it was only implied, and so they noticed when his/her actions were inconsistent with that goal.

Concluding thoughts

Graesser et al. (1997, p. 183) came to the following reasonable conclusion: "We suspect that each of the . . . models is correct in certain conditions. The minimalist hypothesis is probably correct when the reader is very quickly reading the text, when the text lacks global coherence, and when the reader has very little background knowledge. The constructionist [or search-after-meaning] theory is on the mark when the reader is attempting to comprehend the text for enjoyment or mastery at a more leisurely pace." We might add that the likelihood of certain inferences being drawn also depends on individual differences in reading skill (Murray & Burke, 2003) and in working memory capacity (Calvo, 2001, discussed earlier in the chapter).

Some theorists (e.g., van Dijk & Kintsch, 1983) have argued that readers often construct a mental model or representation of the situation described by the text. The information contained in mental models can go well beyond the information contained in a text, and such information is based on inferences. The notion of situational representations plays an important part in the theory of story processing proposed by van Dijk and Kintsch (1983), which is discussed later in the chapter.

STORY PROCESSING

If someone asks us to describe a story or book we have read recently, we discuss the major events and themes of the story, and leave out the minor details. Thus, our description of the story is highly *selective*, depending on the meaning extracted from the story while reading it and on selective processes operating at the time of retrieval. Imagine the questioner's reaction if our description were not selective, but simply involved recalling sentences taken at random from the story!

Gomulicki (1956) showed the selective way in which stories are comprehended and remembered. One group of participants wrote a précis (abstract or summary) of a story visible in front of them, and a second group recalled the story from memory. A third group of participants given each précis and each recall found it very hard to tell them apart. Thus, story memory resembles a précis in that people focus mainly on important information.

At a very general level, it seems undeniable that our processing of stories or other texts involves relating the information contained in the text to relevant structured knowledge stored in long-term memory. More specifically, it is probable that *what* we process in stories, *how* we process information in stories, and *what* we remember from stories we have read all depend in part on such stored information. We will initially consider theories emphasising the importance of **schemas**, which are well-integrated chunks of knowledge about the world, events, people, and actions. After that, we will turn to theories that attempt to identify in more detail the processes occurring when someone reads or listens to a story.

Schema theories

The schemas stored in long-term memory include what are often referred to as *scripts* and *frames*. Scripts deal with knowledge about events and consequences of events. Thus, for example, Schank and Abelson (1977) referred to a restaurant script, which contains information about the usual sequence of events involved in having a restaurant meal. In contrast, frames are knowledge structures relating to some aspect of the world (e.g., building) containing fixed structural information (e.g., has floors and walls) and slots for variable information (e.g., material or materials from which the building is constructed). Schemas are important in language processing, because they contain much of the knowledge used to facilitate understanding of what we hear and read.

Schemas allow us to form *expectations*. In a restaurant, for example, we expect to be shown to a table, to be given a menu by the waiter or waitress, to order food and drink, and so on. If any of these expectations is violated, we usually take appropriate action. For example, if no menu is forthcoming, we try to catch the eye of the waiter or waitress. Schemas help us to make the world a more predictable place than it would otherwise be, because our expectations are generally confirmed.

Evidence that schemas can influence story comprehension was reported by Bransford and Johnson (1972, p. 722). They presented a passage in which it was hard to work out which schemas were relevant. Part of it was as follows:

> The procedure is quite simple. First, you arrange items into different groups. Of course one pile may be sufficient depending on how much there is to do. If you have to go somewhere else due to lack of facilities that is the next step; otherwise, you are pretty well set. It is important not to overdo things. That is, it is better to do too few things at once than too many. In the short run this may not seem important but complications can easily arise.

What on earth was that all about? Participants hearing the passage in the absence of a title rated it as incomprehensible and recalled an average of only 2.8 idea units. In contrast, those supplied beforehand with the title "Washing clothes" found it easy to understand and recalled 5.8 idea units on average. This effect of relevant schema knowledge occurred because it helped comprehension of the passage rather than because the title acted as a useful retrieval cue. We know this because participants receiving the title *after* hearing the passage but *before* recall recalled only 2.6 idea units on average. As we will see, it does not follow that schematic knowledge cannot influence retrieval processes. Indeed, Bartlett (whose theory is discussed next) believed that the main impact of schematic knowledge was at the time of retrieval rather than during initial comprehension of a story.

Bartlett's theory

Bartlett (1932) was the first psychologist to argue persuasively that schemas play an important role in determining what we remember from stories. According to him, memory is affected not only by the presented story, but also by the participant's store of relevant prior schematic knowledge. Bartlett had the ingenious idea of presenting participants with stories producing a *conflict* between what was presented to them and their prior knowledge. If, for example, people read a story taken from a different culture, then prior knowledge might produce distortions in the remembered version of the story, rendering it more conventional and acceptable from the standpoint of their own cultural background. Bartlett's (1932) findings supported his predictions. A substantial proportion of the recall errors were in the direction of making the story read more like a conventional English story. He used the term **rationalisation** to refer to this type of error.

Bartlett (1932) assumed that memory for the precise material presented is forgotten over time, whereas memory for the underlying schemas is not. As a result, rationalisation errors (which depend on schematic knowledge) should increase in number at longer retention intervals. Bartlett (1932) obtained evidence for this prediction. However, his studies were not as tightly controlled as recommended in textbooks on research methods. For example, he did not give very specific instructions to his participants (Bartlett, 1932, p. 78): "I thought it best, for the purposes of these experiments, to try to influence the subjects' procedure as little as possible." As a result, some distortions observed by Bartlett may have been due to conscious guessing rather than deficient memory. There is some force in this criticism. Instructions stressing the need for accurate recall (and thus presumably reducing deliberate guessing) eliminated almost half the errors usually obtained (Gauld & Stephenson, 1967).

In spite of these problems with Bartlett's procedures, evidence from well-controlled studies has confirmed his major findings. For example, Sulin and Dooling (1974) presented some participants with a story about Gerald Martin: "Gerald Martin strove to undermine the existing government to satisfy his political ambitions . . . He became a ruthless, uncontrollable dictator. The ultimate effect of his rule was the downfall of his country" (Sulin & Dooling, 1974, p. 256). Other participants were given the same story, but the main actor was called Adolf Hitler. Those participants told the story about Adolf Hitler were much more likely than the other participants to believe incorrectly that they had read the sentence "He hated the Jews particularly and so persecuted them". Their schematic knowledge about Hitler distorted their recollections of what they had read (see Figure 11.10). As Bartlett (1932) predicted, this type of distortion was more frequent at a long than a short retention interval, because schematic information is more long lasting than information contained in the text itself.

There are doubts as to whether some of Bartlett's main findings can be replicated under more naturalistic conditions. Wynn and Logie (1998) tested students' recall of "real-life" events experienced during their first week at university at various intervals of time ranging from 2 weeks to 6 months. What they found was as follows: "The initial accuracy sustained throughout the time period, together with the relative lack of change over time, suggests very limited use of reconstructive processes" (Wynn & Logie, 1998, p. 1).

Bartlett (1932) assumed that memorial distortions occur mainly because of schema-driven reconstructive processes operating at the time of retrieval. However, as we have seen, schemas often influence *comprehension* processes rather than *retrieval* processes (e.g., Bransford & Johnson, 1972). In addition, as Bartlett predicted, schemas can influence the retrieval of information from long-term memory. Anderson and Pichert (1978) asked participants to read a story from the perspective of a burglar or of someone interested in buying a home. After they had recalled the story, they were asked to shift to the alternative perspective, and then to recall the story again. On the second recall, participants recalled more information that was important only to the second perspective or schema than they had done on the first recall (see Figure 11.11).

Altering the perspective produced a shift in the schematic knowledge accessed by the participants (e.g., from knowledge of what burglars are interested in to knowledge of what potential house buyers are interested in). Accessing different schematic knowledge enhanced recall, and thus provides support for the notion of schema-driven retrieval.

FIGURE 11.10

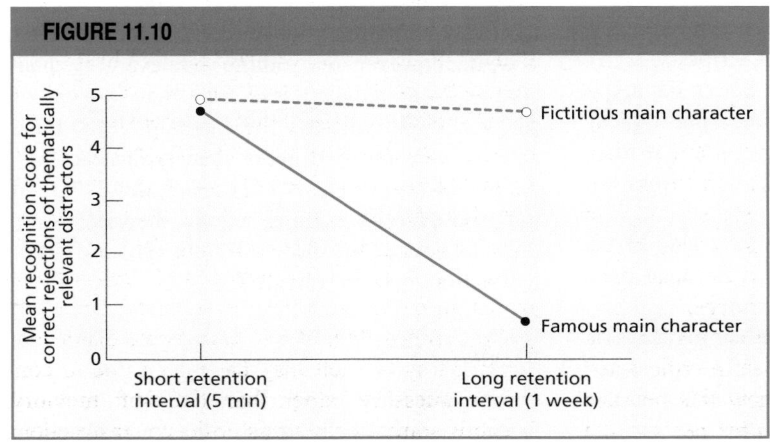

Correct rejection of thematic distractor as a function of main actor (Gerald Martin or Adolf Hitler) and retention interval. Data from Sulin and Dooling (1974).

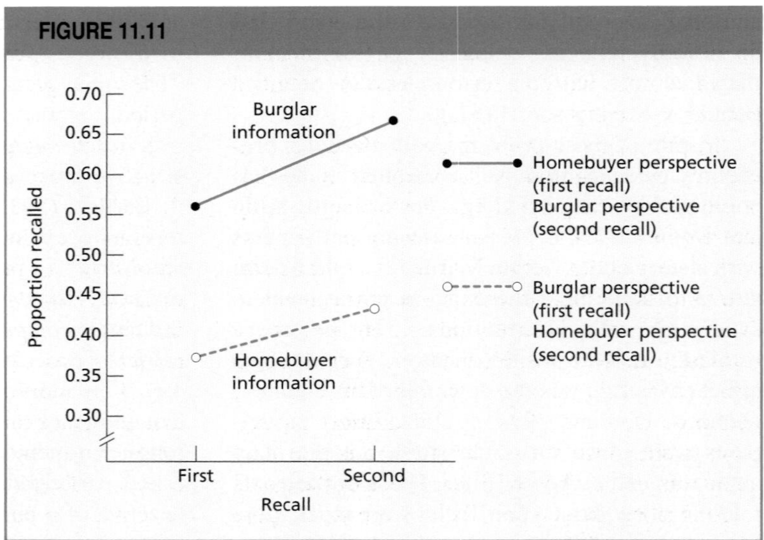

Recall as a function of perspective at the time of retrieval. Based on data from Anderson and Pichert (1978).

Script-pointer-plus-tag hypothesis

The script-pointer-plus-tag hypothesis was put forward by Schank and Abelson (1977). It represents a development of some of Bartlett's ideas, and consists of various assumptions about memory for script-based or schema-based stories:

- Information from the story is combined with information from the underlying script or schema in memory.
- Story actions are either typical (consistent with the underlying script or schema) or atypical (inconsistent with the underlying script).
- Information about atypical actions is tagged individually to the underlying script.
- Recognition memory will be better for atypical than for typical actions, because typical actions present in the story are hard to discriminate from typical actions absent from the story.
- Initial recall for atypical actions should be better than for typical actions, because they are tagged individually in memory.
- Recall for atypical actions at long retention intervals should be worse than for typical actions, because recall increasingly relies on the underlying script or schema.

As predicted, recognition memory for atypical actions is generally better than for typical ones at all retention intervals (Davidson, 1994). However, recall findings are more inconsistent. Davidson (1994) shed light on these inconsistencies. She used routine atypical actions irrelevant to the story and atypical actions interrupting the story. For example, in a story about going to the cinema, "Sarah mentions to Sam that the screen is big" belongs to the former category and "Another couple, both of whom are very tall, sits in front of them and blocks their view" belongs to the latter category. As predicted, both kinds of atypical actions were better recalled than typical ones at a relatively short retention interval (1 hour). After 1 week, however, the routine, irrelevant atypical actions were recalled less well than typical or script actions, whereas the interruptive atypical actions were recalled better than typical actions. As Davidson (1994, p. 772) concluded, "Part of the problem with existing schema theories is that they do not specify how different types of atypical actions will be recalled."

Evaluation

Our organised schematic knowledge of the world is used systematically to help text comprehension and recall. In addition, many of the errors and distortions that occur when we try to remember texts or stories we have read are due to the influence of schematic information.

On the negative side, it has proved hard to identify the characteristics of schemas. More importantly, most versions of schema theory are sadly lacking in testability. If we want to explain text comprehension and memory in terms of the activation of certain schemas, then we need independent evidence of the existence (and appropriate activation) of those schemas. However, such evidence is generally not available. As Harley (2001, p. 331) pointed out, "The primary accusation against schema and script-based approaches is that they are nothing more than re-descriptions of the data."

According to schema theory, top-down processes lead to the generation of numerous inferences during story comprehension. However, the evidence discussed earlier in the chapter (e.g., McKoon & Ratcliff, 1992) suggests that the number of inferences generated by the average reader is less than implied by schema theory.

Finally, the reader may have noticed that memory rather than comprehension was the primary focus of the research discussed in this section. Real-world knowledge manifestly affects comprehension processes, but schema theory does not indicate in detail how this happens.

Kintsch's construction–integration model

Kintsch (1988, 1998) put forward a construction–integration model based on an earlier model of Kintsch and van Dijk (1978). Both models are intended to specify in some detail the processes involved in comprehending and storing information from stories. We will start by considering the original model, in which there were two basic units of analysis: the *argument* (the representation of the meaning of a word) and the **proposition** (a statement making an assertion or denial and which can be true or false). The text of a story is processed to form structures at two main levels:

- The *micro-structure*: the level at which the propositions extracted from the text are formed into a connected structure.
- The *macro-structure*: the level at which an edited version of the micro-structure (resembling the gist of the story) is formed.

Kintsch and van Dijk (1978) argued that story propositions enter a short-term working buffer of limited capacity similar to the working memory system (see Chapter 6). Additional propositions are formed from bridging inferences, and added to those formed directly from the text itself. When the buffer contains a number of propositions, the reader tries to link them together in a coherent way. For example, two propositions referring to the same concept would be linked. Linking of propositions is limited by short-term memory capacity. There is a *processing cycle*: at regular intervals, the buffer is emptied of everything but a few key propositions that are high-level or central in the evolving structure of the story.

The macro-structure of a story combines schematic information with an abbreviated version of the micro-structure. Various rules are applied to the propositions of the micro-structure:

- *Deletion*: any proposition not required to interpret a later proposition is deleted.
- *Generalisation*: a sequence of propositions may be replaced by a more general proposition.
- *Construction*: a sequence of propositions may be replaced by a single proposition that is a necessary consequence of the sequence.

Memory for the text depends on both the micro-structure and the macro-structure. Higher-level or more central propositions are remembered better than low-level propositions, because they are held longer in the working buffer and are more likely to be included in the macro-structure. This prediction has been confirmed several times (e.g., Kintsch et al., 1975).

Evidence for the importance of propositions was obtained by Kintsch and Keenan (1973). They varied the number of propositions in sentences, but equated the number of words. An example of a sentence with four propositions is: "Romulus, the legendary founder of Rome, took the women of the Sabine by force", whereas the following sentence contains eight propositions: "Cleopatra's downfall lay in her foolish trust of the fickle political figures of the Roman world". The reading time increased by about one second for each additional proposition.

Ratcliff and McKoon (1978) also provided evidence for the existence of propositions. They presented sentences (e.g., "The mausoleum that enshrined the tsar overlooked the square"). This was followed by a recognition test in which participants decided whether test words had been presented before. For the example given, the test word "square" was recognised faster when the preceding test word was from the same proposition (e.g., "mausoleum") than when it was closer in the sentence but from a different proposition (e.g., "tsar").

McKoon and Ratcliff (1980) presented participants with a paragraph. This was followed by tests of recognition memory, with participants deciding whether the ideas contained in sentences had been presented in the paragraph. The response times to perform this recognition-memory task were speeded up when a sentence was preceded by another sentence from the paragraph. This speeding up or priming effect was determined more by closeness of the two sentences within the propositional structure of the micro-structure than by closeness in the text, thus providing evidence for the reality of the micro-structure.

Kintsch (1974) used a verification task to distinguish between effects of the micro-structure and of the macro-structure on memory for text. Participants decided whether explicit and implicit inferences were consistent with a text that they had either just read or had read about 15 minutes earlier. Explicitly stated propositions were verified faster than implicitly stated propositions on the immediate test, but there was no difference in verification time after 15 minutes. According to the theory, explicit propositions are better represented than implicit propositions in the micro-structure, but both are equally well represented in the macro-structure. Information in the micro-structure is much more available immediately than after a delay, and this explains the different pattern of results at the two time intervals.

Why was the model of Kintsch and van Dijk (1978) replaced? First, the details of how propositions are formed were not spelled out. Second, it was not clear how bridging inferences are formed or how schematic knowledge interacts with textual information. Third, Kintsch and van Dijk (1978) were wrong to claim that the coherence of a text depends very largely on the same argument or concept being repeated several times. For example, a series of essentially unrelated statements about the same individual would not be coherent, but would be deemed to be so within the model.

Kintsch's (1988, 1998) construction–integration model developed and extended his previous model. It provided more information about the ways in which inferences are formed and stored knowledge interacts with textual information to form the macro-structure. The basic structure of the construction–integration model is shown in Figure 11.12. According to the model, the following stages occur during the comprehension process:

- Sentences in the text are turned into propositions representing the meaning of the text.
- These propositions are entered into a short-term buffer and form a *propositional net*.
- Each proposition constructed from the text retrieves a few associatively related propositions (including inferences) from long-term memory.
- The propositions constructed from the text plus those retrieved from *long-term memory* jointly form the *elaborated propositional net*; this net will usually contain many irrelevant propositions.
- A spreading activation process is then used to select propositions for the text representation; clusters of highly interconnected propositions attract most activation and have the greatest probability of inclusion in the text representation, whereas irrelevant propositions are discarded. This is the *integration process*.
- The *text representation* is an organised structure stored in *episodic text memory*; information about the relationship between any two propositions is included if they were processed together in the short-term buffer.
- As a result of these processes, three levels of representation are constructed:

FIGURE 11.12

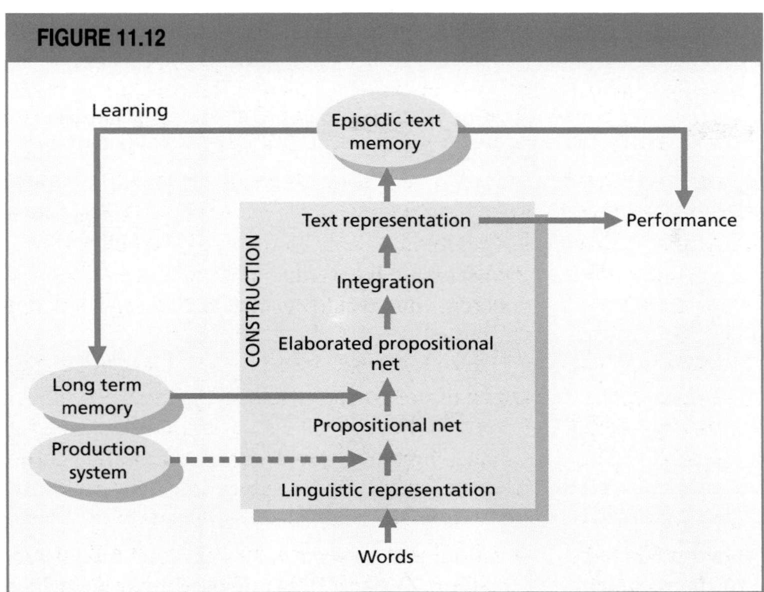

The construction–integration model. Adapted from Kintsch (1992).

(1) Surface representation (the text itself).
(2) Propositional representation or textbase (propositions formed from the text).
(3) Situation representation (a mental model describing the situation referred to in the text). Schemas can be used as building blocks for the construction of situational representations or models.

A distinctive feature of this model is the assumption that the processes involved in the construction of the elaborated propositional net are relatively *inefficient*, with many irrelevant propositions being included. This is basically a bottom-up approach, in that the elaborated propositional net is constructed without taking account of the context provided by the overall theme of the text. In contrast, "Most other models of comprehension attempt to specify strong, 'smart' rules which, guided by schemata, arrive at just the right interpretations, activate just the right knowledge, and generate just the right inferences" (Kintsch et al., 1990, p. 136). According to Kintsch et al. (1990), such strong rules would need to be very complex, and might prove insufficiently flexible across different situations. In contrast, the weak rules incorporated into the construction–integration model are much more robust and can be used in virtually all situations.

Evidence

Kintsch et al. (1990) tested the assumption that text processing produces three levels of representation ranging from the surface level based directly on the text itself, through the propositional level, to the situation or mental model level (providing a representation similar to the one that would result from directly experiencing the situation described in the text). Participants were presented with brief descriptions of very stereotyped situations (e.g., going to see a film), and then their recognition memory was tested immediately or at times ranging up to 4 days later.

The forgetting functions for the surface, propositional, and situational representations were distinctively different (see Figure 11.13). There was rapid and complete forgetting of the surface representation, whereas information from the situational representation showed no forgetting over 4 days. Propositional information differed from situational information in that there was forgetting over time, and it differed from surface information in that there was only partial

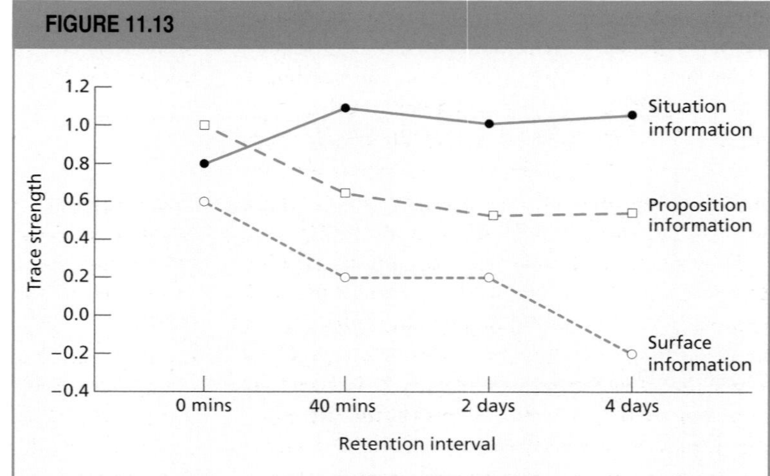

Forgetting functions for situation, proposition, and surface information over a four-day period. Adapted from Kintsch et al. (1990).

forgetting. As Kintsch et al. (1990) had predicted, the most complete representation of the meaning of the text (i.e., the situation representation) was best remembered, and the least complete representation (i.e., the surface representation) was the worst remembered.

Zwaan (1994) tested the psychological reality of the levels of representation identified in the construction–integration model. He argued that the reader's goals influence the extent to which different representational levels are constructed. For example, someone reading an excerpt from a novel might be expected to focus on the text itself (e.g., the wording; stylistic devices), and so form a strong surface representation. In contrast, someone reading a newspaper article may focus on updating his/her representation of a real-world situation, and so form a strong situational representation. Zwaan (1994) devised texts described as literary extracts or news stories. As predicted, memory for surface representations was better for stories described as literary, whereas memory for situation representations was better for stories described as newspaper reports (see Figure 11.14).

According to the model, the more relevant knowledge about the content of a text that a reader possesses, the better he/she should be able to construct deeper levels of representation (propositional and situational). This prediction was supported by Caillies, Denhière, and Kintsch (2002) who presented texts describing the use of software packages to participants whose relevant knowledge ranged from non-existent to advanced. As predicted, intermediate and advanced participants

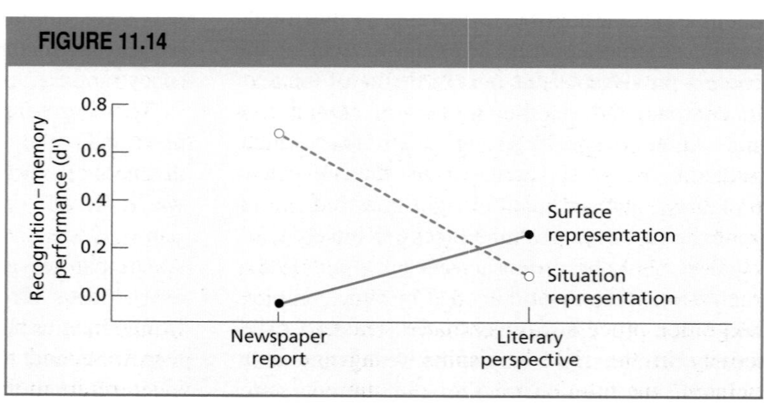

Memory for surface and situation representations for stories described as literary or as newspaper reports. Data from Zwaan (1994).

showed superior text comprehension to the beginner participants. On another memory test (recognition memory for parts of the text), the beginners actually performed better than the other two groups. Why was this? The beginners had focused mainly on forming a surface representation, and the information contained in that representation was perfectly adequate for good recognition memory.

How do propositional representations of sentences differ from situational representations? Propositional representations contain information about *all* the key entities in a sentence regardless of whether they are present or absent. In contrast, situational representations only (or primarily) contain information about entities that are *present*. For example, consider the following sentence: "Sam was relieved that Laura was not wearing her pink dress". Information about the absent pink dress would be included in the propositional representation of this sentence but not in the situational representation. According to the construction–integration model, information about absent objects should be as accessible as information about present objects for some time after the presentation of a sentence. However, Kaup and Zwaan (2003) found that information about absent objects was less accessible than information about present objects only 1.5 seconds after a sentence had been read. They suggested people may simply generate a situational representation without previously constructing a propositional representation.

According to the construction–integration model, inference processing involves two successive stages. First, there is a process of *generation*, in which several possible inferences are produced. Second, there is a process of *integration*, in which the inference that seems most appropriate is incorporated into the text representation. Mason and Just (2004) obtained support for this part of the model in an fMRI study. When the generation process was more demanding, there was increased activity in the dorsolateral frontal cortex, suggesting that this brain area is involved in generating inferences. In contrast, increased difficulty in the integration process was associated with increased activity in the right-hemisphere language area including the inferior, middle, and superior temporal gyri and the angular gyrus. Thus, different brain areas are associated with the generation and integration processes.

Evaluation

The construction–integration model has the advantage over previous theories that the ways in which information in the text combines with the reader's related knowledge are spelled out in much more detail. In particular, the notion that propositions for the text representation are selected on the basis of a spreading activation process operating on propositions drawn from the text and from stored knowledge is an interesting one. Another great strength of the model is that there is reasonably convincing evidence for the three levels of representation (surface, propositional, and situational) specified in the model. Overall, as Harley (2001, p. 335) concluded, "Kintsch's model is the most detailed and promising, and as a consequence has recently received the most attention."

On the negative side, situation representations of texts are not *always* constructed, even by individuals possessing enough relevant knowledge to do so. Zwaan and van Oostendop (1993) asked participants to read part of an edited mystery novel describing the details of a murder scene, including the locations of the body and various clues. Most participants did *not* construct a situational or spatial representation when they read normally. However, such representations were constructed (at the cost of a marked increase in reading time) when the initial instructions emphasised the importance of constructing a spatial representation. Thus, limited processing capacity may often restrict the formation of situational representations or mental models.

Graesser et al. (1997) argued that Kintsch (1988, 1998) ignored two levels of discourse representation. First, there is the *text genre* level, which is concerned with the nature of the text (e.g., narration, description, jokes, exposition). The kinds of information presented, how the information is presented, and the ways in which the information is to be interpreted differ greatly across genres. Second, there is the *communication level*, which refers to the ways in which the writer tries to communicate with his/her readers. However, some readers may not form a representation at the communication level. As Graesser et al. (1997, p. 169) pointed out, "The reader of a novel may not construct an invisible, virtual writer or story-teller that communicates with the reader, unless there are explicit features in the text that signal that communication level."

There are three other problems with the construction–integration model. First, it is assumed that numerous inferences are considered initially, with most being discarded before the reader becomes aware of them. This key theoretical assumption has not been tested systematically. Second, there are doubts as to whether propositional representations are always formed. Propositional representations would contain information about absent objects, but such information is somewhat inaccessible very soon after a sentence has been read (Kaup & Zwaan, 2003). Third, the model is not specific about the processes involved in the construction of situational models. This omission was remedied in the event-indexing model, to which we turn next.

Event-indexing model

According to the event-indexing model (Zwaan & Radvansky, 1998), readers monitor five aspects or indexes of the evolving situation model at the same time when they read stories:

(1) The protagonist: the central character or actor in the present event compared to the previous event.
(2) Temporality: the relationship between the times at which the present and previous events occurred.
(3) Causality: the causal relationship of the current event to the previous event.
(4) Spatiality: the relationship between the spatial setting of the current event and that of the previous event.
(5) Intentionality: the relationship between the character's goals and the present event.

As readers work their way through a text, they are continually updating the situation model so that it accurately reflects the information presented with respect to all five aspects or indexes. It is assumed that discontinuity (unexpected change) in any of the five aspects of a situation (e.g., a change in the spatial setting; a flashback in time) requires more processing effort than when all five aspects or aspects remain the same. Another assumption is that the five aspects or indexes are monitored *independently* of each other. A prediction that follows from that assumption is that the processing effort should be greater when *two* aspects change at the same time than when only *one* aspect changes.

Evidence

Support for the prediction that reading a sentence involving discontinuity in one aspect takes longer than one with no discontinuity was reported by Zwaan, Magliano, and Graesser (1995, p. 387). They argued that "*Temporal* continuity occurs when an incoming sentence in a story describes an event, state, or action that occurs within the same time interval as the previous sentence . . . *Causal* continuity occurs when there is a direct causal link between the current sentence and prior story information." It took 297 ms longer to read a sentence involving temporal discontinuity rather than temporal continuity, and it took 201 ms longer to read a sentence involving causal discontinuity rather than causal continuity.

Rinck and Weber (2003) replicated some of the findings of Zwaan et al. (1995). They considered shifts (versus continuity) in the protagonist, temporality, and spatiality. Overall, there was a progressive increase in reading time as the number of indexes or aspects shifted. More specifically, the reading time per syllable was 164 ms when there were no shifts, 220 ms with one shift, 231 ms with two shifts, and 248 ms with three shifts. These findings are precisely in line with theoretical prediction. However, one finding was contrary to the theory. When the protagonist and the spatial location both changed, this should have made reading times longer than when only the protagonist or only the spatial location changed. In fact, however, reading time was no longer when both indexes changed than when only one did (see Figure 11.15).

FIGURE 11.5

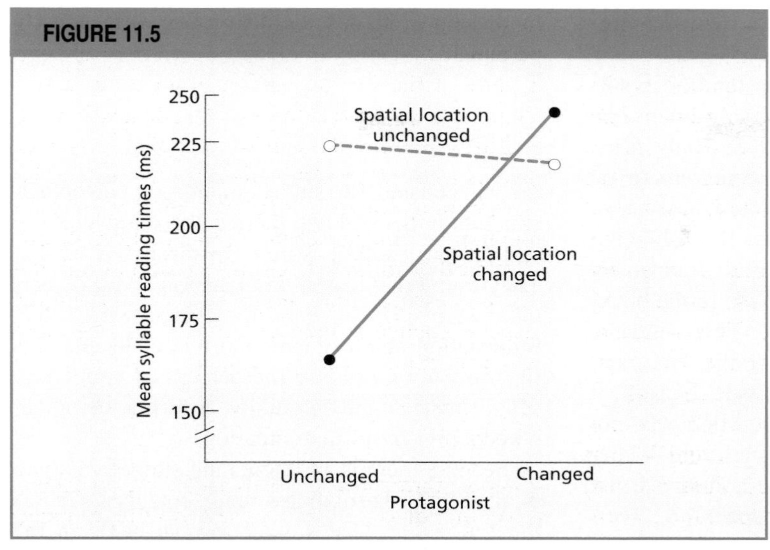

Mean reading time per syllable as a function of changed vs. unchanged spatial location and protagonist. Data from Rinck and Weber (2003).

According to the model, readers frequently update their situational model to take account of the fact that the situations described in a text typically change over time. As a result, information *not* relevant to the current situational model should be less accessible than relevant information. Radvansky and Copeland (2001) tested this prediction by presenting their participants with short stories such as the following, with some having the words "picked up" in the second sentence and others having "set down":

> Warren spent the afternoon shopping at the store.
> He *picked up/set down* his bag and went over to look at some scarves.
> He had been shopping all day.
> He thought it was getting too heavy to carry.

The above short story was followed by the word "bag", with the participants having to decide whether it had appeared in the story. It was argued that the bag still formed part of the situational model at the end of the story when the words "picked up" were used in the second sentence but did not when the words "set down" were used. As predicted, the participants given "set down" were less likely to recognise the word "bag".

Rinck and Bower (2000) drew a distinction between story time (time passing within the story) and discourse time (time spent on reading a text). Would the accessibility in memory of information be more affected by story time or by discourse time? They found that story time was important but discourse time was not. This indicates the importance of the situational model formed by readers, and led Rinck and Bower (2000, p. 1317) to the following conclusion: "Readers use quite sophisticated focusing strategies during narrative comprehension: Rather than rely on external features such as time passing while they are reading, they focus attention within the situation model by using clues to critical features of the story world itself."

Evaluation

The greatest strength of the event-indexing model is that it identifies key processes involved in creating and updating situational models. In general, reading times increase when readers have to cope with changes in any of the five indexes or aspects. The emphasis of the model on the construction of situational models is probably well placed. As Zwaan and Radvansky (1998, p. 177) argued, "Language can be regarded as a set of processing instructions on how to construct a mental representation of the described situation."

On the negative side is the fact that the event-indexing model "treats the individual dimensions as independent entities" (Zwaan & Radvansky, 1998, p. 180). This approach is unlikely to be correct, because the various situational dimensions *interact* in various ways. Consider the following sentence provided by Zwaan and Radvansky (1998): "Someone was making noise in the backyard; Mike had left hours ago". This sentence provides information about temporality. However, it has relevance to the causality issue, because it permits the causal inference that Mike was not the person making the noise. Rinck and Weber (2003) cast further doubts on the notion that the five indexes are monitored independently.

Another problem is that readers often fail to construct situational models (e.g., Zwaan & van Oostendop, 1993, discussed above). This is especially likely to be the case if readers lack adequate motivation, if they possess poor reading skills, or if they do not have good background knowledge relating to the text they are reading.

Perceptual-simulation theory

The construction–integration model and the event-indexing model both emphasise the importance of situational representations or models. A related approach is perceptual-simulation theory (Barsalou, 1999; Zwaan, Stanfield, & Yaxley, 2002), according to which the only meaning-related representation that is formed is a perceptual simulation resembling a situational representation or model. However, there are two important differences between perceptual-simulation theory and the other two models. First, it is assumed that propositional representations are not formed, so the theory is more economical than the construction–integration model in particular. Second, the theory makes the notion of a situation model more precise by assuming that it consists of a perceptual simulation of the situation described by the text. Thus, situation models contain many of the perceptual details that would be present if the described situation were actually perceived.

Evidence

We will consider two studies supporting perceptual-simulation theory. First, there is the study by Kaup and Zwaan (2003), which we discussed earlier. They found that textual information about objects that were present was more accessible than information about objects that were absent. This fits the theory, because the perceptual simulation of a situation only contains information about objects present in that situation.

Second, there is an interesting study by Zwaan et al. (2002). Participants read sentences such as the following: "The ranger saw an eagle in the sky" or "The ranger saw an eagle in the nest". They were then presented with a picture, and decided as rapidly as possible whether the object in the picture had been mentioned in the sentence. On "Yes" trials, the picture was either a match for the implied shape of the object (e.g., an eagle with outstretched wings after the "in the sky" sentence) or was not a match (e.g., an eagle with folded wings after the "in the sky" sentence). Participants responded much faster when the object's shape in the picture matched that implied by the sentence than when it did not. This suggests that people construct a perceptual simulation of the situation described by sentences.

Evaluation

Perceptual-simulation theory represents an interesting development of previous theories. As such, it provides a more detailed account of the situational models formed by readers as they understand text. According to the theory, propositional representations are not constructed when people read text. It may be that propositional representations are less important than assumed within the construction–integration model. However, it is hard to dismiss other evidence (e.g., Kintsch & Keenan, 1973; Ratcliff & McKoon, 1978) pointing to the existence of such representations.

CHAPTER SUMMARY

- Parsing
  Sentence processing involves parsing and the assignment of meaning. The garden-path model is a two-stage model in which the simplest syntactic structure is selected at the first stage using the principles of minimal attachment and late closure. Semantic processing occurs only during the second stage. In fact, semantic information is often used earlier in sentence processing than proposed by the model. According to the constraint-based theory, all relevant sources of information are available immediately to someone processing a sentence. Competing analyses of a sentence are activated at the same time, with several language characteristics (e.g., verb bias) being used to resolve ambiguities. In fact, all sources of information are not always used immediately, and there is little direct evidence that several possible syntactic structures are constructed at the same time. According to the unrestricted race model, all sources of information are used to identify a single syntactic structure for a sentence. If this structure is disconfirmed, there is extensive re-analysis. Nearly all theories assume that sentences are eventually interpreted correctly, but the evidence suggests we use heuristics and are prone to error.

- Pragmatics
  It used to be assumed that the literal meaning of figurative language (e.g., metaphors) is always accessed before the non-literal meaning. That assumption is incorrect, as is shown by evidence that non-literal meanings are often accessed as rapidly as literal ones, and are accessed automatically. There is reasonable support for the graded salience hypothesis, according to which salient messages (whether literal or non-literal) are processed initially. The processing of metaphors is also influenced by context and by individual differences in IQ. It has been claimed that listeners use their knowledge of the common ground when trying to understand a speaker. However, listeners sometimes use the egocentric heuristic, only utilising the common ground to correct any misunderstandings. Use of the egocentric heuristic may be more frequent in artificial laboratory settings than in everyday life.

- Individual differences capacity theory
  Reading span and operation span have been used as measures of working memory capacity. However, there is increasing evidence that these measures do not assess a single underlying cognitive resource, and that at least two resources are involved (processing and storage or manipulation of information and susceptibility to interference). According to Just and Carpenter's capacity theory, individual differences in working memory capacity have substantial effects on language comprehension. Individuals with high working memory capacity are better able than those with low capacity to allocate resources to relevant information and to suppress unwanted information.

- Discourse processing
  There is general agreement that we typically make logical and bridging inferences, with anaphor resolution being a very common type of bridging inference. However, there is more controversy concerning the extent to which elaborative inferences are drawn. According to the minimalist hypothesis, only a few inferences are drawn automatically; additional strategic inferences depend on the reader's goals. This contrasts with the constructionist viewpoint, according to which numerous automatic inferences are drawn. A reasonable compromise is provided by the search-after-meaning theory. This assumes that readers try to construct coherent meaning for texts based on their goals, and they try to explain actions and events in those texts.

- Story processing
  According to schema theory, schemas or organised packets of knowledge help to determine what we remember of stories. Recall of texts often includes schematic information that was not presented. Schemas influence comprehension and retrieval processes. There is some support for a specific form of schema theory known as the script-pointer-plus-tag hypothesis. According to Kintsch and van Dijk's model, texts are processed to produce a micro-structure and a macro-structure. According to Kintsch's construction–integration model, three levels of representation of a text are constructed, with the surface representation being forgotten most rapidly and the situation representation most slowly. Processes involved in the formation of situational models were identified in the event-indexing model. According to this model, readers monitor five aspects of the evolving situational model. Discontinuity in any of these aspects creates difficulties in situation-model construction and increases reading times. According to perceptual-simulation theory, people construct a single meaning-related representation consisting of a perceptual simulation of the situation described by the text.

FURTHER READING

- Balota, D.A., & Marsh, E.J. (2004). *Cognitive psychology*. Hove, UK: Psychology Press. This edited book of key readings contains various important papers on language including language comprehension.
- Behrmann, M., & Patterson, K. (2004). *Words and things*. Hove, UK: Psychology Press. Several of the contributors to this edited book consider issues relating to language comprehension in brain-damaged patients.
- Clifton, C., & Duffy, S.A. (2001). Sentence and text comprehension: Roles of linguistic structure. *Annual Review of Psychology*, *52*, 167–196. This chapter provides a good overview of the literature on comprehension processes.
- Garnham, A. (2004). Language comprehension. In K. Lamberts & R. Goldstone (Eds.), *Handbook of cognition*. London: Sage. Alan Garnham discusses in detail theory and research in the area of language comprehension.
- Gernsbacher, M.A., & Kashak, M.P. (2003). Neuroimaging studies of language production and comprehension. *Annual Review of Psychology*, *54*, 91–114. As the title indicates, this chapter provides an overview of the brain-imaging approach to language.
- Giora, R. (2003). *On our mind: Salience, context and figurative language*. New York: Oxford University Press. Key issues in language (especially in pragmatics) are discussed thoroughly in this book.
- Harley, T. (2001). *The psychology of language from data to theory* (2nd. Ed.). Hove, UK: Psychology Press. Chapters 9 and 11 of this excellent textbook contain detailed coverage of many of the topics discussed in this chapter.

12

Language Production

INTRODUCTION

We know more about language comprehension than language production. Why is this so? We can control the material to be comprehended, but it is harder to constrain an individual's production of language. A further problem in accounting for language production (shared with language comprehension) is that more than a theory of language is needed. Language production is basically a goal-directed activity having communication as its main purpose. People speak and write to impart information, to be friendly, and so on. Thus, motivational and social factors need to be considered.

The two major topics considered in this chapter are speech production and writing, including coverage of the effects of brain damage on these language processes. More is known about speech production than about writing. Nearly everyone spends more time talking than writing, and so it is of more practical use to understand the processes involved in talking. However, writing is an important skill in most societies.

Spoken and written language both have as their central function the communication of information about people and the world. However, children and adults often find writing much harder than speaking, suggesting that there are major differences between the production of spoken and written language. The similarities and differences between speaking and writing will now be considered.

Similarities

The view that speaking and writing are similar receives some support if we consider theoretical approaches to speech production and to writing. It is generally assumed that there is an initial attempt to decide on the overall meaning to be communicated (e.g., Dell, Schwartz, Martin, Saffran, & Gagnon, 1997, on speech production; Hayes & Flower, 1986, on writing). At this stage, the actual words to be spoken or written are not considered. This is followed by the production of language, which often proceeds on a clause-by-clause basis.

Evidence that speaking and writing or typing are similar was reported by Hartley, Sotto, and Pennebaker (2003). They studied one individual (Eric Sotto) who either dictated word-processed academic letters using a voice-recognition system or simply word processed them. Eric Sotto had much less experience of dictating word-processed letters than word processing them, but the letters produced did not differ in readability or in typographical and grammatical errors. One of the few differences was that there were significantly fewer long sentences when dictation was used, because Eric Sotto found it harder to change the structure of a sentence when dictating it rather than word processing it.

Gould (1978) compared dictated and written business letters. Even those highly practised at dictation rarely dictated more than 35% faster than they wrote. This is noteworthy, given that people can speak five or six times faster than they can write. Gould (1980) divided the time taken to dictate and to write letters into various component times. His participants were videotaped while composing letters, and the generating, reviewing, accessing, editing, and planning times were calculated. Planning took up two-thirds of the total composition time for both dictated and written letters, which explains why dictation was only slightly faster than writing.

Gould (1978) compared the quality of letter writing across three different response modes: writing, dictating, and speaking. Those who wrote very good letters generally dictated and spoke very good letters. The quality of letter writing is determined mainly by internal planning processes, and these processes are similar regardless of the type of response. In addition, the knowledge someone possesses (e.g., vocabulary, relevant information) is available for use whether that person is writing, speaking, or dictating. However, some findings may be specific to business letters. The absence of visual feedback with dictation might be a real disadvantage when composing essays or longer pieces of writing.

Differences

How do speaking and writing differ? Spoken language makes use of prosody (rhythm, intonation, and so on, discussed shortly) to convey meaning and grammatical information, and gesture is also used for emphasis. In contrast, writers rely heavily on punctuation to supply the information provided by prosody in spoken language. Writers also make more use than speakers of words or phrases signalling what is coming next (e.g., but, on the other hand). This helps to compensate for the lack of prosody in written language.

Five differences between speaking and writing are as follows:

- Speakers typically know precisely who is receiving their message.
- Speakers generally receive moment-by-moment feedback from the listener or listeners (e.g., expressions of bewilderment). This is a key difference. As we will see shortly, speakers often adapt what they are saying in response to verbal and non-verbal feedback from listeners (e.g., Clark & Krych, 2004).
- Speakers generally have much less time than writers to plan their language production.
- Writers typically have direct access to what they have written so far, whereas speakers do not have direct access to what they have said earlier. However, this difference may not be of major importance. Olive and Piolat (2002) compared writers who did or did not have access to visual feedback of what they had already written. The two groups did not differ in the quality of the texts they produced, and the high-level cognitive processes involved in text composition seemed unaffected by the absence of visual feedback.
- "Writing is in essence a more conscious process than speaking . . . spontaneous discourse is usually spoken, self-monitored discourse is usually written" (Halliday, 1987, pp. 67–69).

As a result, spoken language is generally fairly informal and simple in structure, with information often being communicated rapidly. In contrast, written language is more formal and complex in structure. Writers need to write clearly because they do not receive immediate feedback, and this slows down the communication rate.

Some brain-damaged patients have writing skills that are largely intact in spite of an almost total inability to speak and a lack of inner speech. For example, this pattern was observed in EB, who had suffered a stroke (Levine, Calvanio, & Popovics, 1982). Others can speak fluently, but find writing very difficult. In addition, there are other patients whose patterns of errors in speaking and in writing differ so much that it is hard to believe that a single system could underlie both language activities. However, these findings do *not* mean that the higher-level processes involved in language production (e.g., planning, use of knowledge) differ between speaking and writing.

BASIC ASPECTS OF SPOKEN LANGUAGE

In this section, we consider some of the basic characteristics of spoken language, leaving theoretical accounts of the processes involved in speech production for the next section. For most people (unless there is something seriously wrong with them!), overt speech nearly always occurs within a social context. In other words, when we speak we are addressing one or more listeners. Our central theme is that the primary goal when speaking is to communicate with other people, and so most aspects of spoken language are designed to facilitate communication. According to Grice (1967), the key to successful communication is the cooperative principle, according to which speakers and listeners must try to be cooperative.

As we all know to our cost, we do not always manage to communicate as successfully as we would wish. At the end of this section, we discuss some of the most common errors that occur in speech, followed in the next section by theoretical approaches to understanding the processes underlying these errors.

Discourse markers

There are important differences between our spontaneous conversational speech and prepared speech (e.g., a public talk). As Fox Tree (2000) pointed out, several words and phrases (e.g., well; you know; oh; but anyway) are far more common in spontaneous than prepared speech. These **discourse markers** do not contribute directly to the content of utterances, but are nevertheless of value. Flowerdew and Tauroza (1995) found their participants understood a videotaped lecture better when the discourse markers were left in compared to the same lecture with markers edited out. However, it should be noted that the lecture was in the participants' second language, and so the findings may not generalise to first-language listening.

Why do we use discourse markers? Fox Tree (2000, pp. 392–393) argued that they are used "to show politeness, . . . to play down interpersonal difficulty, and to identify with a social group . . . Discourse markers like *oh*, *then*, *now*, and *well* can help listeners deal with speakers' shifts of topic and focus by indicating when a topic shift will occur . . . *Anyway* and *anyway be that as it may* can be used to mark the end of a digression and the return to the prior topic." Evidence that different discourse markers vary in their function was reported by Fuller (2003). She found that the discourse markers "oh" and "well" were used more often in casual conversations than in interviews, whereas "you know", "like", "yeah", and "I mean" were not. The increased use of "oh" and "well" in conversations probably occurred because speakers need to respond more to what the other person has said in conversations than in interviews.

Prosody

An important aspect of speech production is the provision of **prosodic cues**. These cues include rhythm, stress, and intonation, and they make it easier for listeners to understand what speakers are trying to say (see Chapter 10). Allbritton, McKoon, and Ratcliff (1996) studied the extent to which speakers provide prosodic cues. Their participants read short passages containing ambiguous sentences (e.g., "So, for lunch today he is having either pork or chicken and fries") disambiguated by the passage context. Very few speakers (even trained actors and broadcasters) consistently produced prosodic cues. However, prosodic cues are used in the real world. Lea (1973) analysed hundreds of naturally occurring spoken sentences, and found that syntactic boundaries (e.g., ends of sentences) were generally signalled by prosodic cues.

Keysar and Henly (2002) asked participants to read ambiguous sentences to convey a specific meaning, with listeners deciding which of two meanings was intended. The speakers did not use prosodic cues (or used them ineffectively), because the listeners only guessed correctly 61% of the time. Why didn't the speakers make their meaning clearer? One reason is that the speakers overestimated their effectiveness. They believed the listeners understood the intended meaning 72% of the time, which was significantly higher than the actual figure.

Snedeker and Trueswell (2003; see Chapter 11) identified a major factor determining whether speakers provide prosodic cues. They argued that such cues are much more likely to be provided when the context fails to clarify the meaning of an ambiguous sentence. Speakers said ambiguous sentences (e.g., "Tap the frog with the flower"), and provided many more prosodic cues when the context was consistent with both interpretations of the sentence.

Common ground

We have seen that speakers often provide prosodic cues and discourse markers in order to facilitate effective communication. However, speakers often go much further than that to ensure that their message is understood. According to Clark (e.g., Clark & Carlson, 1981; Clark & Krych, 2004), speakers and listeners typically work together to maximise **common ground**, i.e., mutual beliefs, expectations, and knowledge. Common ground (also known as grounding) is probably especially likely to occur in the context of a dialogue involving two or more people, a situation that is extremely common in the real world.

There has been some controversy concerning the extent to which speakers focus on the common ground or grounding in what they say. Horton and Keysar (1996) distinguished between two theoretical positions:

(1) The initial design model: this is based on the principle of optimal design, in which "the speaker intends each addressee to base his/her inferences not on just *any* knowledge or beliefs he may have, but only on their *mutual* knowledge or beliefs—their common ground" (Clark, 1992, p. 81).Thus, the initial plan for an utterance takes account of the common ground with the listener.

(2) The monitoring and adjustment model: according to this model, speakers plan their utterances initially on the basis of information available to them *without* considering the listener's perspective. These plans are then monitored and corrected to take account of the common ground.

Horton and Keysar (1996) tested these models. Their participants described moving objects so the listener could identify them. These descriptions had to be produced either rapidly (speeded condition) or slowly (unspeeded condition). There was a shared-context condition in which the participants knew the listener could see the same additional objects that they could see. There was also a non-shared-context condition, in which the participants knew the listener could *not* see the other objects. If participants made use of the common ground, they should have used contextual information in their descriptions only in the shared-context condition.

The key findings are shown in Figure 12.1. Participants in the unspeeded condition incorporated common ground in their descriptions. However, participants in the speeded condition were as likely to include contextual information in their descriptions when it was inappropriate (non-shared-context condition) as when it was appropriate (shared-context condition). These findings fit the predictions of the monitoring and adjustment model better than those of the initial design model. Presumably the common ground was not used properly in the speeded condition because there was insufficient time for the monitoring process to operate.

Would it not be better if we operated on the basis of the initial design model rather than the monitoring and adjustment model? One obvious advantage is that we would communicate more effectively with other people. However, the processing demands involved in always taking account of the listener's knowledge when planning utterances could be excessive.

The findings of Horton and Keysar (1996) probably underestimate speakers' normal use of the common ground. For example, speakers take more account of the common ground as they gain

FIGURE 12.1

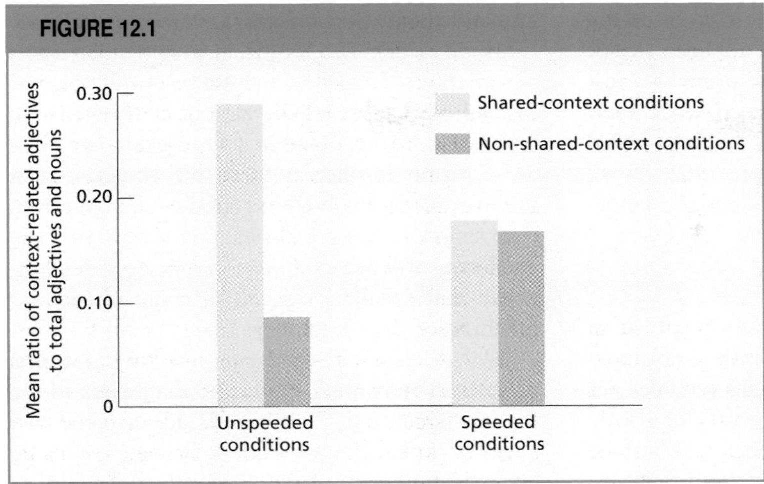

Mean ratio of context-related adjectives to adjectives plus nouns in speeded vs. unspeeded conditions and shared vs. non-shared-context conditions. Adapted from Horton and Keysar (1996).

more experience in a given situation (Horton & Gerrig, 2002). More importantly, the listeners in the Horton and Keysar study simply listened to what the speaker had to say, and so there was no dialogue. Very clear evidence that grounding is much more readily achieved in a situation involving interaction and dialogue than in one not permitting interaction was reported by Clark and Krych (2004). They had pairs of participants, with one member of the pair being a director who instructed the other member (the builder) how to construct 10 Lego models. There were various conditions, three of which were as follows: (1) a non-interactive condition in which the director recorded instructions for use by a future builder; (2) an interactive condition in which the director could not see the builder's blocks, hands, or model in progress; and (3) an interactive condition in which the director and builder were free to talk as much as they needed and they could observe each other closely.

We will discuss three of the main findings from the study by Clark and Krych (2004). First, the opportunity to interact greatly increased the accuracy of the builder's performance. There were errors in the constructed model on 39% of trials in the non-interactive condition compared to only 5% when the participants could interact but the director could not see the builder's blocks or model. Second, directors often very rapidly altered what they said to maximise the common ground between them and the builders. For example, when Ken (one of the builders) holds a block over the right location while Jane (one of the directors) is speaking, she almost instantly takes advantage by interrupting herself to say "Yes": "and put it on the right hand half of the—yes—of the green rectangle." Third, the builders produced a considerable amount of non-verbal behaviour (e.g., pointing, nodding) which influenced the directors' spoken language. As Clark and Krych (2004, p. 79) concluded, "The participants . . . rely not only on each other's vocal signals, but on each other's gestural signals such as exhibiting, poising, pointing at and placing physical objects, nodding and shaking heads, and directing eye gaze . . . They use the signals . . . to ground what they are currently saying."

Evaluation

There is convincing evidence that people engaged in dialogue communicate verbally and non-verbally so as to produce grounding or a common understanding between them. This emphasis on grounding is of fundamental importance in everyday life, but has not been studied extensively in the laboratory. Indeed, as we will see, most theories are not designed to account for the ways in which monitoring one's listener or listeners influences speech production.

The conditions in which speakers do or do not focus on the common ground have not been clearly established. However, speakers are probably most likely to try to ground their speech when their listener provides them with verbal and non-verbal feedback, and when they have some time to work out the listener's current beliefs and understanding.

Speech errors

It is hard to identify the processes involved in speech production, partly because they normally occur so rapidly (we produce several syllables per second on average, with the figure varying somewhat from one language to another). One way of discovering how people normally produce fluent speech is by focusing on speech errors. As Dell (1986, p. 284) pointed out, "The inner workings of a highly complex system are often revealed by the way in which the system breaks down."

There are various collections of speech errors (e.g., Garrett, 1975; Stemberger, 1982), consisting of those personally heard by the researchers concerned. This procedure poses some problems. For example, some kinds of error are more readily detectable than others. Thus, we should be sceptical about percentage figures for the different kinds of speech errors. It is less clear there are any major problems with the main categories of speech errors that have been identified. The existence of some types of speech errors has been confirmed by experimentation in which errors have been created under laboratory conditions (see Dell, 1986).

Several forms of speech error involve problems with selecting the correct word (lexical selection). A simple kind of lexical selection error is *semantic substitution* (the correct word is replaced by a word of similar meaning, e.g., "Where is my tennis bat?" instead of "Where is my tennis racquet?"). In 99% of cases, the substituted word is of the same form class as the correct word (e.g., nouns substitute for nouns). Verbs are much less likely than nouns, adjectives, or adverbs to undergo semantic substitution (Hotopf, 1980).

Blending is another kind of lexical selection error (e.g., "The sky is shining" instead of "The sky is blue" or "The sun is shining"). A further kind of lexical selection error is the *word-exchange error*, in which two words in a sentence switch places (e.g., "I must let the house out of the cat" instead of "I must let the cat out of the house"). The two words involved in a word-exchange error are typically further apart in the sentence than the two words involved in sound-exchange errors (two sounds switching places) (Garrett, 1980). The existence of word-exchange errors provides evidence that speakers typically engage in forward planning of their utterances.

Morpheme-exchange errors involve inflections or suffixes remaining in place but attached to the wrong words (e.g., "He has already trunked two packs"). An implication from morpheme-exchange errors is that the positioning of inflections is dealt with by a rather separate process from the one responsible for positioning word stems (e.g., "trunk", "pack"). The word stems may be worked out *before* the inflections are added. Smyth et al. (1987) pointed out that inflections are generally altered to fit in with the new word stems to which they are linked. For example, the "s" sound in the phrase "the forks of a prong" is pronounced in a way appropriate within the word "forks", but this is different to the "s" sound in the original word "prongs".

A *spoonerism* occurs when the initial letter or letters of two or more words are switched. The Rev. William Archibald Spooner, after whom the spoonerism is named, is credited with several memorable examples (e.g., "You have hissed all my mystery lectures"; "The Lord is a shoving leopard to his flock"). Alas, most of the Rev. Spooner's gems were the result of much painstaking effort. The study of genuine spoonerisms reveals that consonants always exchange with consonants and vowels with vowels, and that the exchanging phonemes are generally similar in sound (see Fromkin, 1993). Garrett (1976) reported that 93% of the spoonerisms in his collection involved a switching of letters between two words within the same clause, suggesting that the clause is an important unit in speech production.

What we have done here is to identify some of the main kinds of speech errors. How these errors can be accounted for theoretically is discussed shortly.

THEORIES OF SPEECH PRODUCTION

There is agreement among theorists that speech production involves various general processes. For example, Levelt (1989) argued that there are three main processes:

- *Conceptualisation*: planning the message that is to be communicated.
- *Formulation*: transforming the intended message into a specific sentence, and working out the sounds of the words in the sentence.
- *Articulation*: this is the final stage, in which the words are turned into speech.

Most theoretical interest has focused on the formulation stage. However, we will start with the earlier process of conceptualisation or planning. After discussing planning processes, we will focus mainly on two theoretical approaches. First, the spreading-activation theory of Dell (1986) and Dell, Burger, and Svec (1997a) will be discussed. It emphasises a psychological process (spreading activation) of general significance within language processing (see Chapter 10). Second, the theoretical approach of Levelt, Roelofs, and Meyer (1999a) is discussed. This approach (known as WEAVER++) is based mainly on findings from experimental studies of speech production rather than on speech errors. As we will see, these two theories are designed to account for rather different aspects of speech production. Spreading-activation theory focuses on the processes involved in producing sentences, whereas WEAVER++ is more narrowly focused, and deals with the processes involved in producing individual words.

Speech planning

A consideration of hesitations and pauses in speech production suggests that speech is planned in clauses. Pauses in spontaneous speech occur more often at grammatical junctures (e.g., the ends of clauses) than anywhere else. Boomer (1965) found that such pauses last longer on average than those at other locations (1.03 seconds vs. 0.75 seconds, respectively). Pauses coinciding with clause boundaries are often filled with sounds such as "um", "er", or "ah", whereas those occurring within a clause tend to be silent (Maclay & Osgood, 1959). These longish pauses at the end of clauses permit forward planning of the next utterance. However, as Harley (2001, p. 376) pointed out, "Although the early work was originally interpreted as showing that pausing reflected semantic planning, this is far from clear."

Smith (2000) identified two ways in which speakers reduce processing demands when planning an utterance: preformulation and underspecification. Preformulation involves reducing processing costs by producing phrases used before. About 70% of the speech we produce consists of word combinations that we use repeatedly (Altenberg, 1990). Underspecification involves using simplified expressions. Smith (2000) gives this example: "Wash and core six cooking apples. Put them in an oven." In this example, the word "them" underspecifies the complex phrase "six cooking apples". As Smith (2000, p. 342) concluded, "Speakers try to minimise their own formulation costs and shift as much of the processing burden onto the listener as possible."

Can speakers engage in planning while they are speaking, or must these two activities occur one at a time? This issue was addressed by Ferreira and Swets (2002) in two experiments in which the participants were given mathematical problems (e.g., 62 + 23) and had to respond "The answer is X". The problems ranged in difficulty, and the participants were told to respond rapidly.

The two key measures obtained by Ferreira and Swets (2002) were latency (time taken to start responding) and duration (length of time spent speaking the answer). Suppose the participants always planned their responses before starting to speak. If so, latencies would be longer for more difficult problems than for easy ones, but the duration should not vary. If participants started speaking before planning their responses, latencies would not vary across changes in problem difficulty, but durations would vary.

Ferreira and Swets (2002) found in their Experiment 1 that task difficulty affected latencies but not durations. Thus, the participants fully planned their responses before speaking. In contrast, task difficulty affected latencies *and* durations in Experiment 2, which differed from the first experiment in that participants had to respond very rapidly for their responses to count. These findings indicate that some planning occurred prior to speaking, with further planning taking place while speaking. In general, speakers operate flexibly: "A decision that every speaker must make is how to strike the appropriate balance between planning and initiating speech quickly" (Ferreira & Swets, 2002, p. 77).

Spreading-activation theory

Dell (1986) and Dell and O'Seaghdha (1991) put forward a spreading-activation theory. We will start by considering the central notion of **spreading activation**. It is assumed that the nodes within a network (many of which correspond to words) vary in their activation or energy. When a node or word is activated, activation or energy spreads from it to other related nodes. For example, strong activation of the node corresponding to "tree" may cause some activation of the node corresponding to "plant". According to the theory, spreading activation can occur for sounds as well as for words.

Spreading-activation theory is based on connectionist principles, and consists of four levels:

- *Semantic level*: the meaning of what is to be said; this level is not considered in detail within the theory.
- *Syntactic level*: the grammatical structure of the words in the planned utterance.
- *Morphological level*: the **morphemes** (basic units of meaning or word forms) in the planned sentence.
- *Phonological level*: the **phonemes** or basic units of sound within the sentence.
- A representation is formed at each level.
- Processing during speech planning occurs at the same time at all four levels, and is both parallel and interactive; however, it is typically more advanced at higher levels (e.g., semantic) than lower ones (e.g., phonological).

According to spreading-activation theory, there are *categorical rules* at each level. These rules are constraints on the categories of items and combinations of categories that are acceptable. The rules at each level define categories appropriate to that level. For example, the categorical rules at the syntactic level specify the syntactic categories of items within the sentence.

In addition to the categorical rules, there is a *lexicon* (dictionary) in the form of a constructionist network. It contains nodes for concepts, words, morphemes, and phonemes. When a node is activated, it sends activation to all the nodes connected to it (see Chapter 1). Finally, *insertion rules* select the items for inclusion in the representation at each level according to the following criterion: the most highly activated node belonging to the appropriate category is chosen. For example, if the categorical rules at the syntactic level dictate that a verb is required at a particular point within the syntactic representation, then the verb whose node is most activated will be selected. After an item has been selected, its activation level immediately reduces to zero, preventing it from being selected repeatedly.

According to spreading-activation theory, speech errors occur because an incorrect item is sometimes more activated than the correct item. The existence of spreading activation means that numerous nodes are *all* activated at the same time, which increases the likelihood of errors being made in speech.

Evidence

What kinds of errors are predicted by the theory? First, errors should belong to the appropriate category (e.g., an incorrect noun replacing the correct noun), because of the operation of the categorical rules. As expected, most errors do belong to the appropriate category (Dell, 1986).

Second, many errors should be anticipation errors, in which a word is spoken earlier in the sentence than is appropriate (e.g., "The sky is in the sky"). This happens because all of the words in the sentence tend to become activated during the planning for speech.

Third, anticipation errors should often turn into exchange errors, in which two words within a sentence are swapped (e.g., "I must write a wife to my letter"). Remember that the activation level of a selected item immediately reduces to zero. Therefore, if "wife" has been selected too early, it is unlikely to be selected in its correct place in the sentence. This allows a previously unselected and highly activated item such as "letter" to appear in the wrong place. Many speech errors are of the exchange variety.

Fourth, anticipation and exchange errors generally involve words moving only a relatively short distance within the sentence. Those words relevant to the part of the sentence under current consideration will tend to be more activated than those words relevant to more distant parts of the sentence. As a result, the findings are in line with the predictions of spreading-activation theory.

Fifth, speech errors should tend to consist of actual words (the **lexical bias effect**). This effect was demonstrated by Baars, Motley, and MacKay (1975). Word pairs were presented briefly, and participants had to say both words as rapidly as possible. The error rate was twice as great when the word pair could be re-formed to create two new words (e.g., "lewd rip" can be turned into "rude lip") than when it could not (e.g., "Luke risk" turns into "ruke lisk"). Gagnon et al. (1997) found that patients with **aphasia** (impaired language abilities as a result of brain damage) also showed the lexical bias effect.

Sixth, the notion that the various levels of processing interact flexibly with each other means that speech errors can be multiply determined. This is known as the **mixed error effect**, and occurs when a spoken word is both semantically and phonemically related to the correct word. Dell (1986) quoted the example of someone saying "Let's stop" instead of "Let's start". The error is both semantic and phonemic, because the substitute word shares a common sound with the appropriate word. Detailed investigation of word-substitution errors in unimpaired individuals reveals that the spoken word and the intended word are more similar in sound than would be expected by chance alone (Dell & O'Seaghdha, 1991). The mixed error effect has also been found in aphasic patients (Blanken, 1998).

According to spreading-activation theory, speech errors occur when the wrong word is more highly activated than the correct one, and so is selected. Thus, there should be numerous errors when incorrect words are readily available. For example, Glaser (1992) studied the time taken to name pictures (e.g., a table). Theoretically, there should have been a large increase in the number of errors made when each picture was accompanied by a semantically related distractor word (e.g., chair). In fact, there was only a modest increase in the error rate. According to Roelofs (2000, p. 82), "When multiple words are activated under experimental conditions, . . . almost no errors are made. Yet, the Dell model predicts massive amounts of errors."

Evaluation

Spreading-activation theory makes testable predictions about the kinds of errors that should occur most often in speech production, most of which have been confirmed. Examples include the lexical bias and mixed error effects. The theory's emphasis on spreading activation provides links between speech production and other cognitive activities (e.g., word recognition: McClelland & Rumelhart, 1981). It has also been argued (e.g., Dell, 1986) that the widespread activation assumed within the theory facilitates the production of novel sentences.

There are various limitations with the theory. First, the focus of spreading-activation theory is mainly on individual words or concepts, with broader issues relating to the construction of a message and its intended meaning being de-emphasised. Second, the theory predicts the errors produced in speech, but not the *time* taken to produce spoken words. Third, the theory predicts too many errors in situations in which two or more words are all activated at the same time (e.g., Glaser, 1992).

Anticipation and perseveration errors

Dell et al. (1997a) developed and extended spreading-activation theory, arguing that most speech errors belong to the following two categories:

(1) *Anticipatory*: Sounds or words are spoken ahead of their time (e.g., "cuff of coffee"

FIGURE 12.2

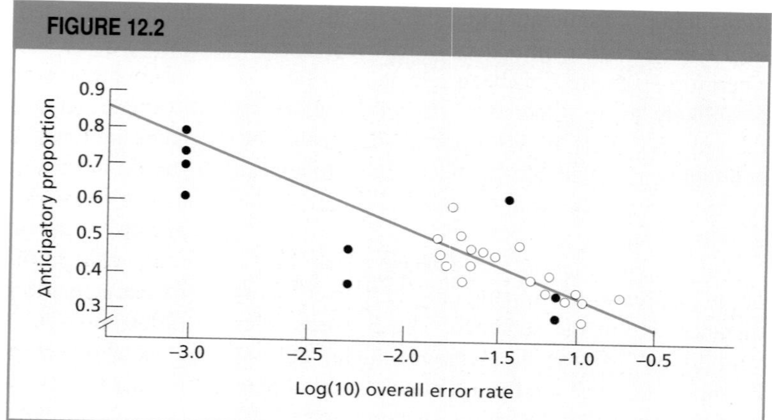

The relationship between overall error rate and the anticipatory proportion. The filled circles come from studies reported by Dell et al. (1997a) and unfilled circles come from other studies. Adapted from Dell et al. (1997a).

instead of "cup of coffee"). These errors mainly reflect inexpert planning.

(2) *Perseverated*: Sounds or words are spoken later than they should have been (e.g., "beef needle" instead of "beef noodle"). These errors reflect either failure to monitor what one is about to say or planning failure. Note that their theory was concerned *only* with these speech errors.

The key assumption was that expert speakers plan ahead more than non-expert speakers, and so a higher proportion of their speech errors will be anticipatory. According to Dell et al. (1997a, p. 140), "Practice enhances the activation of the present and future at the expense of the past. So, as performance gets better, perseverations become relatively less common." Thus, the activation levels of sounds and words that have already been spoken are little affected by practice. However, the increasing activation levels of present and future sounds and words increasingly prevent the past from intruding into present speech.

Dell et al. (1997a) assessed the effects of practice on the anticipatory proportion (the proportion of total errors [anticipation + perseveration errors] that is anticipatory). In one study, the participants were given extensive practice at saying several tongue twisters (e.g., five frantic fat frogs; thirty-three throbbing thumbs). As expected, the number of errors decreased as a function of practice. However, the anticipatory proportion increased from .37 early in practice to .59 at the end of practice in line with prediction.

Dell et al. (1997a) argued that speech errors are most likely when the individual speaker has not formed a coherent speech plan. In such circumstances, there will be relatively few anticipatory errors, and so the anticipatory proportion will be low. Thus, the overall error rate (anticipatory + perseverative) should correlate *negatively* with the anticipatory proportion. Dell et al. (1997a) worked out the overall error rate and the anticipatory proportion for several sets of published data. The anticipatory proportion decreased from about .75 with low overall error rates to about .4 with high overall error rates (see Figure 12.2).

The above theory has implications for clinical patients having problems with speech production. Patients whose speech is error prone should tend to make relatively more perseverative errors than normals. Schwartz et al. (1994) tested a patient, FL, who was classified as suffering from **jargon aphasia** (discussed later). This patient had an anticipatory proportion of .32 (compared to the normal adult figure of about .75), indicating that FL was especially prone to perseverative errors. In addition, Helm-Estabrooks, Bayles, and Bryant (1994) found that patients whose speech was moderately impaired made many more perseverative errors than did those with mild impairment.

Levelt's theoretical approach and WEAVER++

The main focus in this section is on the computational model WEAVER++ proposed by Levelt et al. (1999a). However, many of the ideas contained within this computational model derive from Levelt (1989). The model is called WEAVER to stand for Word-form Encoding by Activation and VERification, and as mentioned earlier focuses primarily on the processes involved in producing individual spoken words. The model is based on the following major assumptions:

- There is a feedforward activation-spreading network, meaning that activation proceeds forwards through the network but not backwards.
- There are three main levels within the network: at the highest level are nodes representing lexical concepts; at the second level are nodes representing **lemmas** or abstract words from the mental lexicon; at the lowest level are nodes representing word forms in terms of morphemes (basic units of meaning) and their phonemic segments.
- The network does not contain any inhibitory links.
- Speech production involves a series of processing stages following each other in *serial* fashion.
- Speech errors are avoided by means of a checking mechanism.

A more detailed account of the theory is given in Figure 12.3. There are six stages of processing:

(1) Conceptual preparation: potential lexical concepts are activated on the basis of meaning.

FIGURE 12.3

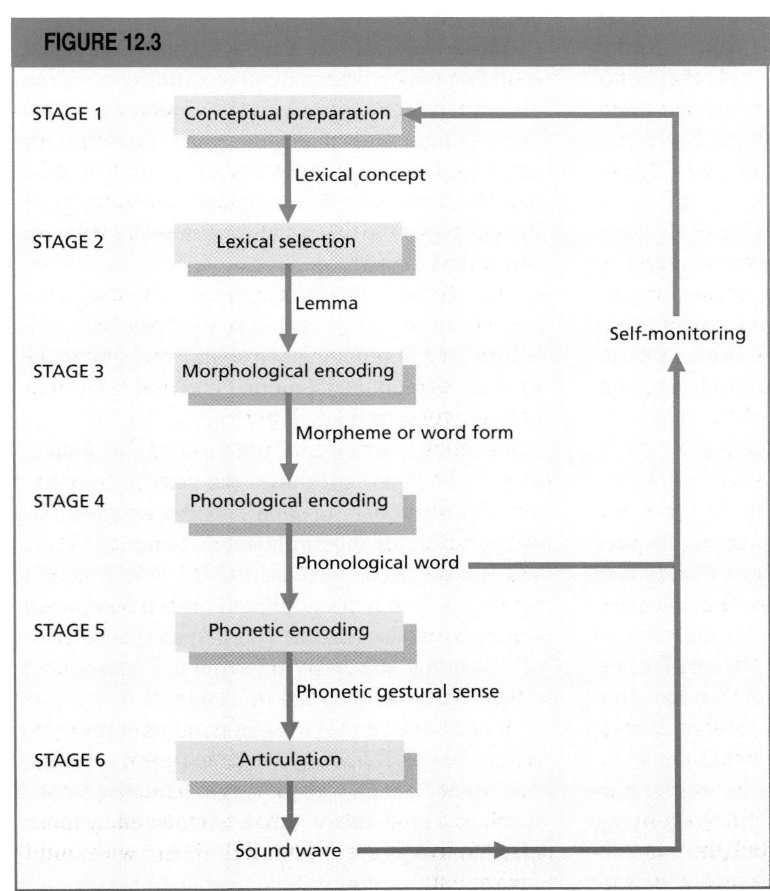

The WEAVER++ computational model. Adapted from Levelt et al. (1999a).

(2) Lexical selection: an abstract word or lemma is selected, together with its syntactic features; a given lemma is generally selected because it is more activated than any other lemma.
(3) Morphological encoding: the basic word form of the selected lemma is activated.
(4) Phonological encoding: during this stage, the syllables of the word are computed (syllabification).
(5) Phonetic encoding: speech sounds are prepared using a syllabary, "a repository of gestural scores for the frequently used syllables of the language" (Levelt et al., 1999a, p. 5).
(6) Articulation: the actual production of the word by the speech musculature.

In addition, there is a self-monitoring process checking the speaker's overt and internal speech.

It is easy to get lost in the complexities of this theory. However, it is mainly designed to show how word production proceeds from meaning (lexical concepts and lemmas) to sound (phonological words, phonetic gestural scores, and sound waves). Indeed, Levelt et al. (1999a, p. 2) referred to "the major rift" between a word's meaning and its sound. WEAVER++ is a discrete feedforward theory (Rapp & Goldrick, 2000). It is discrete, because the speech-production system completes its task of identifying the correct lemma or abstract word before starting to work out the sound of the selected word. It is feedforward, because processing proceeds in a strictly forward (from meaning to sound) direction.

Experimental evidence

According to the model, speakers construct a word they are going to say syllable by syllable, and only begin to say it when it has been fully planned. It follows that the time for speech onset should be greater for long than for short words. Participants named or categorised objects having one- or two-syllabled names, and (as predicted) took longer to start saying the two-syllabled names.

Lexicalisation is "the process in speech production whereby we turn the thoughts underlying words into sounds: we translate a semantic representation (the meaning) of a content word into its phonological representation or form (its sound)" (Harley, 2001, p. 359). According to Levelt et al. (1999a), lexicalisation occurs when the lemma is translated into its word form in terms of morphemes, phonological encoding, and so on. We can see the distinction between a lemma and the word itself in the "tip-of-the-tongue" state. We all know the experience of having a concept or idea in mind, but searching in vain for the right word to describe it. This frustrating situation defines the tip-of-the-tongue state. Brown and McNeill (1966, p. 325) stated that a participant in this state "would appear to be in a mild torment, something like the brink of a sneeze". They presented participants with dictionary definitions of rare words, and asked them to identify the words defined. The reason for doing this was to produce the tip-of-the-tongue state. This state probably occurs when the lemma or abstract word has been activated, but the actual word cannot be accessed.

Harley and Bown (1998) found that words sounding unlike nearly all other words (e.g., apron, vineyard) were much more susceptible to the tip-of-the-tongue state than were words sounding like several other words (e.g., litter, pawn). Why is this? The unusual phonological forms of words susceptible to the tip-of-the-tongue state may make them hard to retrieve.

According to WEAVER++, a word's semantic and syntactic properties (stage 2) are activated before its phonological or sound features (stage 4). Van Turennout, Hagoort, and Brown (1998) measured event-related potentials (ERPs) while their Dutch participants produced noun phrases (e.g., "*rode tafel*" meaning "red table"). Syntactic information about the noun's gender was available 40 ms before its initial phoneme. Schmitt, Münte, and Kutas (2000) also used ERPs. On a picture-naming task they found that the N200 component peaked 89 ms earlier when participants could make decisions on the basis of semantic information rather than phonological information.

Studies on brain-damaged patients support the theoretical assumptions of Levelt et al. (1999a). According to their theory, the lemma contains syntactic information. Brain-damaged patients who can access the relevant lemma but not the subsequent stages of morphological and phonological encoding should possess syntactic information about words they cannot produce. Badecker, Miozzo, and Zanuttini (1995) studied an Italian patient with **anomia** (an inability to name objects). This patient found it virtually impossible to name pictures, but was almost perfect at deciding whether the correct word was masculine or feminine (a syntactic feature).

According to Levelt et al. (1999a), morphological encoding precedes phonological encoding. As a result, some brain-damaged patients might possess morphological information about a word (e.g., whether it is a compound word) without being able to gain access to its phonological form. Semenza, Luzzatti, and Mondini (1999) discussed studies on aphasic patients having this pattern of impairment.

Neuroimaging evidence supports the sequence of processes identified by Levelt et al. (1999a). Idefrey and Levelt (2000) carried out a meta-analysis of 58 brain-imaging studies. As expected, most processing occurred in the left hemisphere. What Idefrey and Levelt (2000) found was as follows: "Visual and conceptual processing appears to involve the occipital, ventro-temporal, and anterior frontal regions of the brain; the middle part of the middle temporal gyrus seems to be involve with lemma retrieval . . . Next, activation spreads to Wernicke's area, where the phonological code of the word appears to be retrieved; activation is then transmitted to Broca's area and the left mid superior temporal lobe for phonological processing such as syllabification [producing syllables]" (Roelofs, 2000, p. 75).

We turn now to the self-monitoring process. It is clear that we possess a reasonably effective mechanism for detecting our speech errors, because most people correct at least 50% of them (see Postma, 2000, for a review). According to Levelt (1989), speakers use their speech comprehension system to monitor their own current overt speech and inner speech plan. There is much evidence that speakers monitor their own inner speech plan. Motley, Camden, and Baars (1982) presented participants with pairs of words (e.g., "mad back") which form new pairs of words (e.g., "bad mac") if the initial consonants are exchanged. Participants were more likely to say the wrong words when they were innocuous than when they were slightly vulgar (e.g., "cool tits" when "tool kits" was presented). This suggests that participants monitored (and sometimes censored) what they were planning to say.

According to the model, the same monitoring process is involved in checking inner and overt speech. Support for this assumption was reported by Dell and Repka (1992). They asked participants to recite tongue twisters in overt or inner speech, and to report any speech errors. The types of errors that were reported (e.g., in terms of position of phoneme in the word) were similar in both conditions, suggesting that the same mechanism detected errors in inner and overt speech.

Some findings seem inconsistent with the proposed self-monitoring process, especially the notion that the speech comprehension system monitors an individual's own speech. The implication is that the ability to detect errors in one's own speech should correlate highly with the ability to detect errors in the speech of others. However, Marshall, Robson, Pring, and Chiat (1998) found that jargon aphasics sometimes fail to detect errors in their own speech but can detect them in others' speech (discussed in more detail later). In similar fashion, Nickels and Howard (1995) found in aphasic patients that there was no relationship between their auditory comprehension and their ability to correct their own speech errors.

Some evidence is inconsistent with other assumptions of Levelt et al.'s (1999a) model. For example, the notion that abstract word or lemma selection is *completed* before phonological information about the word is accessed is an important part of their serial processing model. In contrast, other theorists (e.g., Dell et al., 1997a) have proposed cascade models based on the assumption that phonological processing can start *before* lemma or word selection is completed.

How can we compare these models? Suppose participants were presented with pictures having a dominant name (e.g., rocket) and a non-dominant name (e.g., missile). They have to name the picture as rapidly as possible. The stage of lemma selection typically produces the dominant name (e.g., rocket). According to the serial processing model, there should be very little phonological processing of the non-dominant name (e.g., missile). According to the cascade model, however, this is not necessarily the case.

Peterson and Savoy (1998) tested the above predictions. Sometimes a word appeared in the middle of the picture (e.g., of a rocket or missile), and the participants had to name that word out loud rather than name the picture. As both models would predict, word naming was speeded up, or primed, when the word was phonologically related to the dominant picture name (e.g., racket). More importantly, word naming was also speeded up when the word was phonologically related to the non-dominant picture name (e.g., muscle). As Peterson and Savoy (1998, p. 552) concluded, "We obtained clear evidence for phonological activation of both dominant and secondary picture names during early moments of picture lexicalisation. Thus, in contrast to the serial model's central claim, it appears that multiple lexical candidates do undergo phonological encoding . . . the cascade model provides the best account."

Similar findings were reported by Morsella and Miozzo (2002). Two coloured pictures were presented, one superimposed on the other. The participants' task was to name the pictures of a given colour (target pictures) and ignore pictures in a different colour (distractor pictures). Some distractor pictures were phonologically related to the target pictures (e.g., bell as a distractor presented with bed), whereas others were not phonologically related (e.g., hat as a distractor presented with bed). According to Levelt et al.'s model, the phonological features of the names for distractor pictures should not be activated. Thus, speed of naming target pictures should not be influenced by whether or not the names of the two pictures are phonologically related. In contrast, cascade models (e.g., Dell, 1986) predict that the phonological features of distractors are often activated. As a result, target pictures should be named more rapidly when accompanied by phonologically related distractors rather than by unrelated distractors. The findings were as predicted by cascade models, but provide evidence against the model of Levelt et al. (1999a).

Evaluation

WEAVER++ has some advantages over the theoretical approach of Dell (1986) and Dell et al. (1997a), which is unsurprising given that it focuses in much more detail on the processes involved in production of individual words. First, it makes detailed predictions about the speed with which words are produced in different situations, whereas Dell has focused on predicting error rates. Second, WEAVER++ (with its emphasis on serial processing) can be regarded as simpler in some ways than Dell's approach based on highly interactive processing. Third, Levelt et al. (1999a) relied much less than Dell (e.g., 1986) on data about speech errors. As Levelt et al. (1991, p. 615) pointed out, "an exclusively error-based approach to . . . speech production is as ill-conceived as an exclusively illusion-based approach in vision research."

There are several limitations with WEAVER++. First, and most importantly, it does not consider most of the processes involved in planning and producing sentences. Second, interactive theories such as that of Dell (1986) account for some findings much better than discrete feedforward theories such as WEAVER++. For example, WEAVER++ has problems explaining the finding that there can be phonological processing of more than one word at a time (Morsella & Miozzo, 2002; Peterson & Savoy, 1998). Interactive theories are also better at accounting for the lexical bias and mixed error effects discussed earlier. As Rapp and Goldrick (2000, p. 467) pointed out with respect to the lexical bias effect, "According to a discrete account, the phoneme level 'knows' nothing about words . . . , and thus there is no reason why disruptions at the phoneme level should preferentially result in word responses." Rapp and Goldrick (2000, p. 478) carried out a computer simulation, and found that "A simulation incorporating the key assumptions of a discrete feedforward theory of spoken naming did not exhibit either mixed error or lexical bias effects."

Third, as Levelt, Roelofs, and Meyer (1999b, p. 63) admitted, "WEAVER++ has been designed to account primarily for latency data, not for speech errors . . . in further development of WEAVER++, its error mechanism deserves much more attention." For example, Levelt et al. (1999a) compared the numbers of word-exchange errors produced by human participants against those produced by WEAVER++. The model produced far fewer than humans.

Fourth, most of Levelt et al.'s research has involved the production of single words. According to Roberts et al. (1999, p. 54):

> Implementation of naming and lexical decision experiments involving isolated words can only yield evidence about the way in which isolated words are produced in response to impoverished experimental conditions. If the way in which a given word is accessed and uttered is sensitive to . . . contextual variables, single-word test procedures will not reveal this.

COGNITIVE NEUROPSYCHOLOGY: SPEECH PRODUCTION

The cognitive neuropsychological approach to speech production started in the nineteenth century. Our initial focus will be on the historically important research on aphasia or language disorder in brain-damaged patients. After that, we will consider recent research involving the study of more specific language disorders. In general terms, it has been argued that some aphasic or language-disordered patients have relatively intact access to syntactic information but impaired access to content words (e.g., nouns, verbs), whereas other aphasic patients have the opposite pattern. The existence of such patterns provides support for the notion that speech production involves separable stages of syntactic processing and word finding. Such patterns are consistent with theories of speech production such as those discussed earlier in the chapter (e.g., spreading-activation theory, WEAVER++). However, as we will see, the data are not clear-cut.

Broca's and Wernicke's aphasia

For many years, it was claimed that there is an important distinction between Broca's and Wernicke's aphasia. In essence, patients with **Broca's aphasia** have slow, non-fluent speech. They also have a poor ability to produce syntactically correct sentences although their speech comprehension is relatively intact. In contrast, patients with **Wernicke's aphasia** have fluent and apparently grammatical speech which often lacks meaning, and they have severe problems with speech comprehension.

According to the classical view, these two forms of aphasia involve different brain regions within the left hemisphere (see Figure 12.4). More specifically, Broca's aphasia arises because of damage within a small area of the frontal lobe (Broca's area), whereas Wernicke's aphasia involves damage within a small area of the posterior temporal lobe (Wernicke's area). As we will see, the classical view (which was very influential) has been shown to be very oversimplified and inaccurate in many ways.

FIGURE 12.4

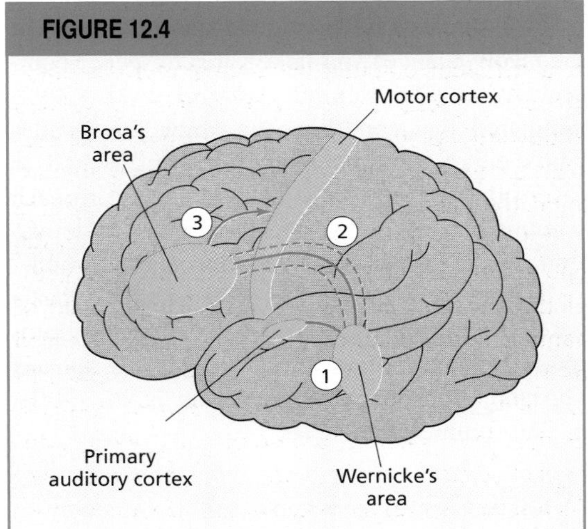

The locations of Wernicke's area (1) and Broca's area (3) are shown. When someone speaks a heard word, activation proceeds from Wernicke's area through the arcuate fasciculus (2) to Broca's area.

Evidence

Research has provided only partial support for the classical view. Willmes and Poeck (1993) found only 59% of patients with non-fluent aphasia had lesions or damage in Broca's area, and 35% of patients with lesions involving Broca's area had non-fluent aphasia. Various PET studies on normal individuals indicate that Broca's area is involved in speech production. For example, Chertkow et al. (1993) used the task of silent picture naming, and observed activation of Broca's area.

De Bleser (1988) studied six very clear cases of fluent or Wernicke's aphasia and seven very clear cases of non-fluent or Broca's aphasia. The sites of brain damage were assessed by computerised tomography (CT) scans, which allowed the patients to be put into three groups: (1) damage to frontal areas including Broca's area; (2) damage to temporo-parietal areas including Wernicke's area; and (3) large lesions including both Broca's and Wernicke's areas. Four of the six patients with fluent aphasia had damage only to Wernicke's area, but the other two had lesions in Broca's area as well as in Wernicke's area. Of the seven non-fluent aphasic patients, four had damage to Broca's area, but the others had damage to Wernicke's area.

PET studies have provided clearer evidence of the involvement of Wernicke's area in speech comprehension. For example, Howard et al. (1992) compared two conditions in which the participants either repeated real words or listened to reversed words and said the same word to each stimulus. As predicted, there was greater activation of Wernicke's area in the former condition.

The notion that patients with Broca's aphasia have much greater problems in speaking grammatically than patients with Wernicke's aphasia appears to be incorrect. As Dick et al. (2001, p. 764) pointed out:

> Studies of speech production in richly inflected languages show that Wernicke's aphasic patients make grammatical errors similar in quantity and severity to the errors produced by Broca's aphasic patients . . . The English system of grammatical morphology is so impoverished that it offers few opportunities for grammatical substitution errors [and so the grammatical limitations of patients with Wernicke's aphasia are not very obvious]. This is not the case in languages such as Italian, German, Turkish, Hungarian, or Serbo-Croatian, where the substitution errors observed in Wernicke's aphasia are . . . obvious.

Evaluation

Why is there more evidence for localisation of language functions in brain-scanning (e.g., PET) studies on normals than in studies of brain-damaged patients? Individual differences in localisation are clear with brain-damaged patients, but are less apparent when information about brain activation is averaged across many people. According to Howard (1997, p. 288), "Language functions, while localised in individual subjects, are not consistently localised in different individuals . . . higher cortical functions such as language may have a certain amount of freedom in the areas of cortex devoted to them."

The distinction between Broca's aphasia and Wernicke's aphasia has become blurred, in part because grammatical errors are common in both forms of aphasia. The terms Broca's aphasia and Wernicke's aphasia imply that numerous brain-damaged patients all have very similar patterns of language impairment. In fact, patients exhibit a wide range of different symptoms, which undermines the usefulness of syndromes such as Broca's aphasia and Wernicke's aphasia.

Anomia

Some patients suffer from anomia, which is an impaired ability to name objects. According to Levelt et al.'s (1999a) WEAVER++ model (discussed earlier), there are two main reasons why such patients might have difficulties in naming. First, there could be a problem in lemma or abstract word selection, in which case errors in naming would be similar in meaning to the correct word. Second, there could be a problem in word-form selection, in which case patients would be unable to find the appropriate phonological form of the word. As we will see, the evidence supports these predictions.

A case of anomia involving a semantic impairment (deficient lemma selection) was reported by Howard and Orchard-Lisle (1984). The patient, JCU, had good object recognition and reasonable comprehension. However, she was very poor at naming the objects shown in pictures unless given the first phoneme or sound as a cue. If the cue was the first phoneme of a word closely related to the object shown in the picture, then JCU would often be misled into producing the wrong answer. This wrong answer she accepted as correct 76% of the time. In contrast, if she produced a name very different in meaning from the object depicted, she rejected it 86% of the time. JCU had access to *some* semantic information, but this was often insufficient to specify precisely what she was looking at.

Problems in lemma selection are especially clear in patients who have difficulty in naming objects belonging to some categories (e.g., living objects) but not others (e.g., non-living objects). Some of the evidence on such category-specific deficits is discussed in Chapters 7 and 9.

Kay and Ellis (1987) studied a patient, EST, who could select the right lemma but not the phonological form of the word. His performance on several tasks (e.g., object recognition) revealed no significant impairment to his semantic system, and thus no real problem with lemma selection. However, he had a very definite anomia, as can be seen from his description of a picture (Kay & Ellis, 1987): "Er . . . two children, one girl one male . . . the . . . the girl, they're in a . . . and their, their mother was behind them in in, they're in the kitchen . . . the boy is trying to get . . . a . . . er, a part of a cooking . . . jar."

EST's speech is reasonably grammatical, and his greatest problem lies in finding words other than very common ones. Kay and Ellis (1987) argued that his condition resembles in greatly magnified form that of the rest of us when in the "tip-of-the-tongue" state. The difference is that, with EST, the problem is present with all but the most common words. However, word frequency correlates highly with age of acquisition, with more common words being acquired earlier in life. Hirsh and Funnell (1995) found that age of acquisition seemed to be the main determinant of anomia, with word frequency also playing a role.

Lambon Ralph, Sage, and Roberts (2000) studied a patient, GM, who had anomia. He could apparently select the correct lemma but had problems finding the correct phonological forms of words. When he could not name a picture, he nevertheless guessed accurately whether the name was a compound word (84% correct) and also the number of syllables (88% correct). However, there was evidence that GM also had problems with lemma selection. For example, when a related word was presented immediately before each picture (e.g., the word "ladder" before a picture of stilts), GM's naming performance fell from 63% to 40%. Lambon Ralph et al. (2000) concluded that GM's data do not fit neatly into two-stage models such as that of Levelt et al. (1999a). More specifically, "The naming system is not characterised by discrete [separate] stages, but sound encoding can begin before lemma selection has finished" (Lambon Ralph et al., 2000, p. 196).

Agrammatism

It has been assumed within most theories of speech production that there are separate stages for working out the syntax or grammatical structure of utterances and for producing the content words to fit that grammatical structure (e.g., Dell, 1986). Thus, some brain-damaged patients should be able to find the appropriate words, but not to order them grammatically. Such patients are said to suffer from **agrammatism** or non-fluent aphasia, a condition traditionally associated with Broca's area. Patients with agrammatism tend to produce short sentences containing content words (e.g., nouns, verbs), but lacking function words (e.g., the, in, and) and word endings. This makes good sense, because function words play a key role in producing a grammatical structure for sentences. Finally, it has often been assumed that patients with agrammatism have problems with the comprehension of sentences that are syntactically complex.

Evidence

Saffran, Schwartz, and Marin (1980a, 1980b) studied patients suffering from grammatical impairments. For example, one patient produced the following description of a picture of a woman kissing a man: "The kiss . . . the lady kissed . . . the lady is . . . the lady and the man and the lady . . . kissing." In addition, Saffran et al. found that agrammatic aphasics had great difficulty in putting the two nouns in the correct order when asked to describe pictures containing two living creatures in interaction.

An important problem in agrammatism revolves around difficulties in processing function words. Evidence that agrammatic patients have particular problems with function words was reported by Biassou et al. (1997). Agrammatic patients given the task of reading words made significantly more phonological errors on function words than on content words.

Guasti and Luzzatti (2002) provided a detailed analysis of the spontaneous speech of agrammatic patients. Their patients showed much evidence of deficient syntactic processing, especially in their inappropriate use of verbs. For example, they often failed to adjust the form of verbs to take account of person or number, mostly used only the present tense of verbs, and omitted many verbs altogether. In addition, they rarely used a **subordinate clause**, a minor clause that cannot stand on its own to form a sentence. For example, in the sentence "The pop star who had taken drugs was arrested at his hotel", "who had taken drugs" is the subordinate clause.

The greatest problem in studying agrammatism is the existence of large individual differences in symptoms. For example, Miceli et al. (1989) studied the speech productions of 20 patients classified as agrammatic. Some patients omitted many more prepositions than definite articles from their speech, whereas other patients showed the opposite pattern.

Do the syntactic deficiencies of agrammatic aphasics extend to language comprehension? Berndt, Mitchum, and Haendiges (1996) reported a meta-analysis of studies on comprehension of active and passive sentences by agrammatic aphasics. In 34% of the data sets, comprehension performance on both active and passive sentences was at, or close to, chance level. In 30% of the data sets, comprehension was better than chance on both kinds of sentences. In the remaining 36% of data sets, there was good performance on active sentences but chance performance on passive sentences. These findings led to two conclusions: (1) agrammatic aphasics do not necessarily have major problems with language comprehension; (2) "Selection of patients for study on the basis of features of aphasic sentence production does not assure a homogeneous [similar] grouping of patients" (Berndt et al., 1996, p. 298).

Evaluation

Research on agrammatism provides general support for the notion (e.g., Dell, 1986) that speech production involves a syntactic level at which the grammatical structure of an utterance is formed. Most of the problems of agrammatic patients, including the difficulties they experience with function words and with using verbs appropriately, could revolve around this level of processing. However, the various symptoms of agrammatism are often not all present in any given patient (e.g., Berndt et al., 1996; Miceli et al., 1989). Thus, it is dangerous to assume there is a single explanation equally applicable to all patients with agrammatism. Harley (2001, p. 379) doubted the value of identifying a syndrome of agrammatism: "If it is a meaningful syndrome, we should find that the sentence construction deficit, grammatical element loss, and a syntactic comprehension deficit should always co-occur. Recent reports of single case studies have found dissociations between these impairments."

Jargon aphasia

As we have seen, grammatic aphasics can find the content words they want to say, but cannot produce grammatically correct sentences. Patients suffering from jargon aphasia apparently show the opposite pattern. They seem to speak fairly grammatically, leading many experts to assume that they have a largely intact syntactic level of processing.

However, this assumption may well be incorrect. Patients with jargon aphasia would often have been diagnosed as having Wernicke's aphasia in the past, and we have seen that such patients often have severe problems with grammatical processing (Dick et al., 2001).

Unlike agrammatic aphasics, jargon aphasics experience great difficulty in finding the right words. They frequently substitute one word for another, and often produce **neologisms**, which are made-up words (see below). In addition, most jargon aphasics have very severe problems with comprehension. Finally, jargon aphasics are typically not aware that their speech contains numerous errors, indicating that they are very poor at self-monitoring (Marshall et al., 1998).

Evidence

Ellis, Miller, and Sin (1983) studied a jargon aphasic, RD. He provided the following description of a picture of a scout camp (the words he seemed to be searching for are given in brackets): "A b-boy is swi'ing (SWINGING) on the bank with his hand (FEET) in the stringt (STREAM). A table with orstrum (SAUCEPAN?) and . . . I don't know . . . and a three-legged stroe (STOOL) and a strane (PAIL)—table, table . . . near the water." RD, in common with most jargon aphasics, produced more neologisms (invented words) when the word he wanted was not a common one.

Robson, Pring, Marshall, and Chiat (2003) asked LT, a jargon aphasic whose speech consisted almost entirely of neologisms, to name pictures. Even though most of his answers were unintelligible, the phonemes he used were generally related to those in the correct answer. The key finding was that LT had a strong tendency to produce consonants common in the English language regardless of whether they were correct or not (see Figure 12.5). This finding can be explained on Dell's spreading-activation theory (discussed earlier). In essence, it is assumed that the resting activation of frequently used consonants is greater than that of rarely used consonants, thus increasing the probability of producing frequently used consonants correctly and incorrectly.

FIGURE 12.5

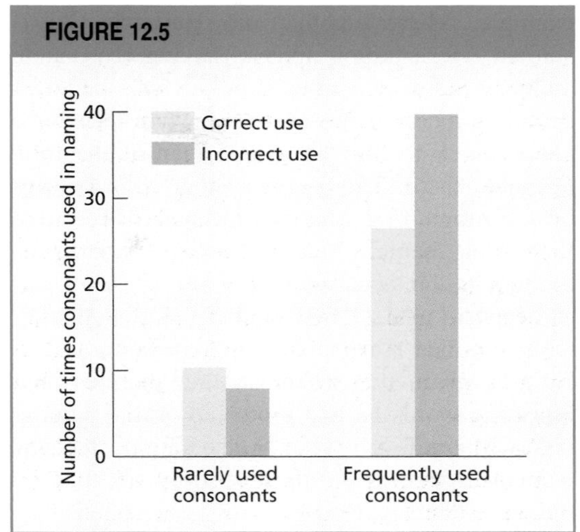

Mean number of times rarely used and frequently used consonants were produced correctly and incorrectly on a picture-naming task. Based on data in Robson et al. (2003).

It is generally assumed that jargon aphasics have some ability to engage in syntactic processing. If so, their neologisms or made-up words might possess appropriate prefixes or suffixes to fit into the syntactic structure of the sentence. For example, if the neologism refers to the past participle of a verb, then it might end in -ed. Evidence that jargon aphasics do modify their neologisms to make them fit syntactically was reported by Butterworth (1985).

Most jargon aphasics are largely unaware of the fact that they are producing neologisms and so do not try to correct them. For example, Robson et al. (2003, p. 112) pointed out that "LT seems unable to detect the disordered nature of his speech. He repeatedly expresses surprise when misunderstood and continues to rely on speech for communication." Why do jargon aphasics have a lack of self-monitoring? It has been claimed that unimpaired individuals use their speech comprehension system to monitor their own speech, but this claim is controversial (see Postma, 2000). It follows that the problem with jargon aphasics' self-monitoring might stem from their severe comprehension impairments. However, that explanation does not apply to all jargon aphasics. For example, Maher, Rothi, and Heilman (1994) studied AS, a jargon aphasic having reasonable auditory word comprehension. AS was better at detecting his own speech errors when they were played back to him on a tape than at the time he made them. This suggests that AS's failures of self-monitoring occurred because of resource limitations, namely, he could not speak and self-monitor at the same time.

Marshall et al. (1998) studied a jargon aphasic, CM, who had reasonable comprehension ability. He was given two tasks: naming pictures, and repeating words he had produced on the naming task. CM was much better at detecting neologisms or made-up words on the repetition task than on the naming task (95% vs. 55%, respectively). According to Marshall et al. (1998, p. 79), "His monitoring difficulties arise when he is accessing phonology from semantics." More generally, CM's inferior error-detection performance on the naming task may reflect the greater cognitive demands associated with performing that task than simple word repetition.

WRITING: THE MAIN PROCESSES

Writing involves the retrieval and organisation of information stored in long-term memory. In addition, it involves complex thought processes. As Kellogg (1994, p. 13) expressed it, "I regard thinking and writing as twins of mental life. The study of the more expressive twin, writing, can offer insights into the psychology of thinking, the more reserved member of the pair." Thus, although writing is an important topic in its own right (no pun intended!), it is not separate from other cognitive activities.

Key processes

Hayes and Flower (1986) identified three key processes in writing:

- The *planning process* involves producing ideas and organising them into a writing plan to satisfy the writer's goals.
- The *sentence-generation process* involves turning the writing plan into the actual writing of sentences.
- The *revision process* involves evaluating what has been written, and ranges between individual words and the overall structural coherence of the writing.
- The "natural" sequence is planning, sentence generation, and revision, but writers often deviate from this sequence.

Evidence

We can identify the processes involved in writing by using **directed retrospection**. Writers are stopped at various times during the writing process and categorise what they were just doing (e.g., planning, sentence generation, revision). Kellogg (1994) discussed studies involving directed retrospection. On average, writers devoted about 30% of their time to planning, 50% to sentence generation, and 20% to revision.

Levy and Ransdell (1995) analysed systematically the processes involved in writing. As well as asking their participants to verbalise what they were doing, they also obtained video recordings as the participants wrote essays on computers. The study lasted 12 weeks, with the participants producing an essay on a different topic each week. There was a practice effect, with the percentage of the time devoted to planning decreasing from 40% in the first week to about 30% in the last week. The most surprising finding reported by Levy and Ransdell (1995) was that the amount of time spent on each process before moving on to another process was often very short. In the case of text generation, the median time was 7.5 seconds, and it was only about 2.5 seconds for planning, reviewing, and revising. Consistent individual differences in writing style were revealed by looking at the typical sequence in which the various processes were used.

Levy and Ransdell (1995) reported a final interesting finding, namely that writers were not fully aware of how they allocated their time. Most overestimated the amount of time spent on revising and reviewing, and underestimated the time spent on generating text. In the case of revising and reviewing, the writers estimated they spent just over 30% of their time on those processes but actually only devoted about 5% of their time to them.

Kellogg (1988) considered the effects of producing an outline (focus on main themes) on subsequent letter writing. Outline producers spent more time in sentence generation than did the no-outline participants, but less in planning and reviewing or revising. Producing an outline increased the quality of the letter. Why was this? Outline producers did not have to devote so much time to planning, which is the hardest process in writing.

Planning

Writing plans depend heavily on the writer's knowledge. Alexander, Schallert, and Hare (1991) identified three kinds of relevant knowledge:

(1) *Conceptual knowledge*: information about concepts and schemas stored in long-term memory.
(2) *Socio-cultural knowledge*: information about the social background or context.
(3) *Metacognitive knowledge*: knowledge about what one knows.

According to Hayes and Flower (1986), strategic knowledge also plays a major role in the construction of a writing plan. Strategic knowledge concerns ways of organising the goals and sub-goals of writing to construct a coherent writing plan. Hayes and Flower (1986) found that good writers use strategic knowledge very flexibly, which often leads to changes in the structure of the writing plan.

Sentence generation

The gap between the writing plan and the actual writing of sentences is usually large. Kaufer, Hayes, and Flower (1986) found that essays were always at least eight times longer than outlines. The technique of asking writers to think aloud permitted Kaufer et al. (1986) to explore the process of sentence generation. They compared the sentence-generation styles of expert and average writers. Both groups accepted about 75% of the sentence parts they verbalised. The length of the average sentence part was 11.2 words for the expert writers compared with 7.3 words for the average writers. Thus, good writers use larger units or "building blocks".

Revision

Revision is a key process in writing. Expert writers devote more of their writing time to revision than do non-expert ones (Hayes & Flower, 1986), in part because they focus on more complex issues such as the coherence and structure of the arguments expressed. Faigley and Witte (1983) found that 34% of revisions by experienced adult writers involved a change of meaning, against only 12% of the revisions of inexperienced college writers. This difference probably occurred because experienced writers are more concerned with coherence and meaning.

Evaluation

Planning, sentence generation, and revision are all important processes in writing, with some theorists distinguishing between revision and reviewing. Techniques such as directed retrospection and video recording have shed important light on the processes involved in writing. However, they cannot reveal details of processes of which the writer has no conscious awareness.

The three processes of planning, sentence generation, and revision cannot be neatly separated. In particular, planning and sentence generation are often almost inextricably bound up with each other. Kellogg (1990, p. 376) argued that writing is more of a social act than proposed by Hayes and Flower (1986): "Instead of focusing on the cognitive processes of an individual, the social approach studies the writer as an agent in a literate community of discourse." This idea was developed by Hayes (2000). He argued that the most important part of the social environment of which writers need to take full account is the intended audience of the texts they produce. This is a complex matter, especially when they lack personal knowledge of that audience.

Writing expertise

Why are some writers more skilful than others? As expected, writers possessing more relevant knowledge produce better essays. For example, Kellogg (2001) asked students with much or little relevant knowledge to write an essay about baseball. The rated quality of the essays was much higher for those students who knew a lot about baseball.

Individual differences in writing ability probably depend most on planning processes. Bereiter and Scardamalia (1987) identified two major strategies used in the planning stage:

- a knowledge-telling strategy;
- a knowledge-transforming strategy.

The knowledge-telling strategy involves writers simply writing down everything they know about a topic with no planning. The text already generated provides retrieval cues for generating the rest of the text. In the words of a 12-year-old child who used the knowledge-telling strategy (Bereiter & Scardamalia, 1987, p. 9), "I have a whole bunch of ideas and write them down until my supply of ideas is exhausted."

The knowledge-transforming strategy involves use of a *rhetorical problem space* and a *content problem space*. Rhetorical problems relate to the achievement of the goals of the writing task (e.g., "Can I strengthen the argument?"), and content problems relate to the specific information to be written down (e.g., "The case of Smith vs. Jones strengthens the argument"). There should be movement of information in *both* directions between the content space and the rhetorical space. This happens more often with skilled writers using a knowledge-transforming strategy. According to Bereiter and Scardamalia (1987, p. 303), "The novice possesses productions for transferring information from the content space to the rhetorical space, but lacks productions for the return trip."

Bereiter, Burtis, and Scardamalia (1988) hypothesised that knowledge-transforming strategists would be more likely than knowledge-telling strategists to produce high-level main points capturing important themes. Children and adults wrote an essay, and thought aloud while planning what to write. Those producing a high-level main point used on average 4.75 different knowledge-transforming processes during planning. In contrast, those producing a low-level main point used only 0.23 knowledge-transforming processes.

Successful use of the planning process also depends on the writer's relevant knowledge. Adults possessing either a lot of knowledge or relatively little on a topic were compared by Hayes and Flower (1986). The experts produced more goals and sub-goals, and so constructed a more complex overall writing plan. In addition, the various goals of the experts were much more interconnected.

Expert writers also differ from non-expert ones in their ability to use the revision process. For example, Hayes et al. (1985) found that expert writers detected 60% more problems in a text than did non-experts. The expert writers correctly identified the nature of the problem in 74% of cases, against only 42% for the non-expert writers.

In a study already discussed, Levy and Ransdell (1995) found that those writers who produced the essays of highest quality spent 40% more of their time revising and reviewing than did those producing the poorest quality essays. More specifically, "It is the revising that occurs late in a writing session . . . that contributes most to the differences among documents varying widely in quality" (Levy & Ransdell, 1995, p. 777).

Developing expertise

It is important for writers trying to develop their expertise to focus on ensuring that any text they produce can be readily understood by its intended audience. This is a problem in writing a textbook such as this, where the readers vary considerably in their relevant knowledge. An interesting way of teaching writers to be more alert to the reader's needs was used by Schriver (1984). Students read an imperfect text, and predicted the comprehension problems a reader would have with it. Then the students read a reader's verbal protocol produced while he/she tried to understand that text. After the students had been given various texts plus readers' protocols, they became better at predicting the kinds of problems readers would have with new texts.

Carvalho (2002) adopted a somewhat different approach, using a technique known as procedural facilitation. In this technique, writers evaluate what they have written for relevance, repetition, missing details, and clarity to readers after writing each sentence. They also decide what changes should be made. The student participants (most of whom were either 11 or 15 years old) wrote more effectively and were more responsive to the needs of the audience following use of procedural facilitation.

Working memory

Most people find writing difficult and effortful. Kellogg has argued for many years that this is because writing makes much use of working memory (discussed in Chapter 6). According to Kellogg (2001, p. 43), "Many kinds of writing tasks impose considerable demands on working memory, the system responsible for processing and storing information on a short-term basis." The key component of the working memory system is the central executive, which is an attention-like process involved in organising and coordinating cognitive activities. Other components of the working memory system are the visuo-spatial sketchpad (involved in visual and spatial processing) and the phonological loop (involved in verbal rehearsal). Note that all of these components have limited capacity. As we will see, there is evidence that writing can involve any or all of these components of working memory (see Olive, 2004, for a review).

We can test Kellogg's hypothesis by measuring reaction times to auditory signals presented either in isolation (control condition) or while participants are engaged on a writing task. It follows from the hypothesis that reaction times will be longer in the writing condition, because writing uses much of the available capacity of working memory. As a result, participants will have less working memory capacity available for responding to the auditory signal in the writing than in the control condition.

Evidence

Much of the evidence using the reaction-time approach was discussed by Kellogg (1994). He concluded that all of the main processes in writing are highly demanding of working memory capacity. Indeed, the evidence suggests that writing is more effortful than most learning and reading tasks.

Olive and Kellogg (2002) used the reaction-time approach to assess the involvement of working memory in the following conditions:

(1) Transcription: A prepared text was simply copied, so no planning was required.
(2) Composition: A text had to be composed, i.e., the writer had to plan and produce a coherent text. There was a pause in writing at the time the auditory signal was presented.
(3) Composition + transcription: A text had to be composed, and the participant was writing when the auditory signal was presented.

Olive and Kellogg (2002) found that composition was more demanding than transcription (see Figure 12.6), because composition involves planning and sentence generation. They also found

FIGURE 12.6

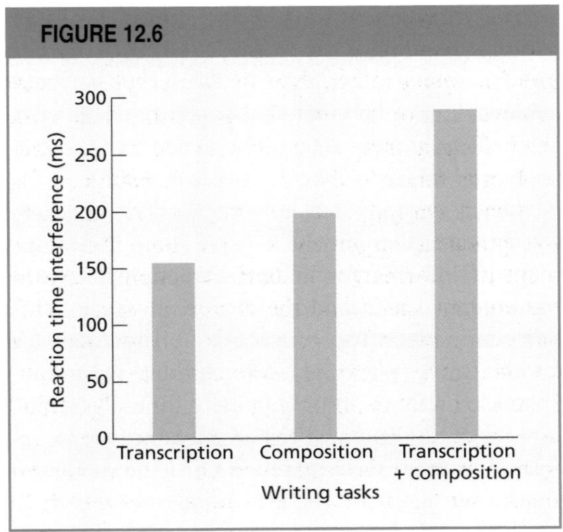

Interfering effects of writing tasks (transcription; composition; transcription + composition) on reaction time to an auditory signal. Adapted from Olive and Kellogg (2002).

that composition + transcription was more demanding than composition. This finding indicates that writers can engage in higher-level processes (e.g., planning) *and* lower-level processes (writing words) at the same time.

Kellogg (2001) tested his workload hypothesis in a study already discussed. Students had to write an essay about baseball, and the key assumption was that those possessing much knowledge about baseball should find writing less effortful and demanding of working memory resources than those possessing little knowledge. It was assumed that writers with much relevant knowledge would have large amounts of well-organised information stored in long-term memory, thus reducing the effort involved in essay writing. Kellogg (2001) used the reaction-time method, and found that the writing task increased reaction times to auditory signals less among writers possessing considerable relevant knowledge. This finding provides support for the hypothesis.

According to Kellogg's working memory theory, all of the main processes involved in writing depend on the central executive component of working memory. As a result, writing quality is likely to suffer if *any* one of the writing processes is made more difficult. For example, the physical act of writing words in a text would be much more demanding if the words had to be written in capital letters rather than in the writer's normal handwriting. As predicted, the quality of the written texts was lower when the text had to be written in capital letters (Olive & Kellogg, 2002).

Other components of the working-memory system are also involved in writing. Levy and Ransdell (2001) found that involvement of the visuo-spatial sketchpad with a visuo-spatial task (detecting when two consecutive characters were in the same place or were similar in colour) increased writers' initial planning time. Passerault and Dinet (2000) found that overloading the visuo-spatial sketchpad increased the time taken to produce a written text. The effect was stronger when the writing task was relatively concrete (i.e., producing descriptions) rather than when it was rather abstract (i.e., producing arguments).

Marek and Levy (1999) studied the involvement of the phonological loop (a verbal rehearsal system) on writing processes by observing the effects of unattended speech. Unattended speech impaired performance on a sentence-generation task, but had no effect when writers copied a text or revised a text. Thus, it is mainly the planning process that involves use of the phonological loop. Additional evidence that the phonological loop is involved in writing was reported by Chenoweth and Hayes (2003), in a study in which participants typed sentences describing cartoons. This task was carried out either on its own or while repeating a syllable continuously (syllable repetition uses the phonological loop and is known as articulatory suppression). Articulatory suppression slowed the rate of writing and increased the number of mechanical errors in typing.

Evaluation

As predicted, the main writing processes are highly demanding or effortful. There is also good evidence that the central executive is involved in most processes concerned with writing. Since the central executive has limited processing capacity, writing quality is typically reduced when the demands on it are increased (e.g., by requiring text to be written in capital letters). The visuo-spatial sketchpad and the phonological loop also both play a part in the writing process, but the involvement of the visuo-spatial sketchpad depends in part on the type of text being produced (Passerault & Dinet, 2000).

The main limitation of Kellogg's theoretical approach is that it does not indicate clearly *why* processes such as planning or sentence generation are so demanding. What is needed is a more fine-grain analysis of the strategies used by writers engaged in the planning process. The theory focuses on the effects of writing processes on working memory. However, it is also likely that working-memory limitations influence *how* we allocate our limited resources during writing. For example, we may shift rapidly from one writing process to another (Levy & Ransdell, 1995) when our processing capacity is in danger of being exceeded. Finally, it would be useful to go beyond demonstrations that the central executive, phonological loop, and visuo-spatial sketchpad are involved in writing to reveal the ways in which these components of the working memory system combine and interact in the writing process.

Word processing

There has been a large increase in the use of word processors in recent years. Is this a good thing? Kellogg and Mueller (1993) compared text produced by word processor and by writing in longhand. For highly experienced users of word processors, the rate at which text was produced and its quality did not differ between the two conditions. However, word processing impaired production rate and quality of text for less experienced users of word processors.

Kellogg and Mueller (1993) assessed effortfulness of writing by measuring reaction time to an occasional probe stimulus. Word processing produced more effortful planning and revision than writing in longhand as indicated by longer reaction times to probe stimuli, but there was no difference for sentence generation. Those using word processors were much less likely than those writing in longhand to make notes (12% vs. 69%, respectively), which may explain the findings.

According to Kellogg (1994, p. 160), "Studies on writing fluency [speed] and quality generally show no difference between composing on a computer or with pen and paper . . . a writer should select whatever tool he or she finds comfortable and useful." However, the finding that the outcomes (speed and quality) are approximately the same for word processing and writing does not, of course, prove that the underlying processes are the same. According to Kellogg, what matters is that the writer has access to all the relevant knowledge needed for the particular writing task. The method of writing is unlikely to have much effect on knowledge accessibility, and so should have only minor effects on writing performance.

SPELLING

Spelling is an aspect of writing that has been the subject of considerable research interest (see Tainturier & Rapp, 2001, for a review). As we will see, much of this research has focused on brain-damaged patients having severe spelling impairments. Note that the cognitive neuropsychological approach has been dominant in the field of spelling research, but has contributed little to our understanding of writing processes such as planning and revision. Thus, it provides us with a detailed picture of a small fraction of the processes involved in writing.

FIGURE 12.7

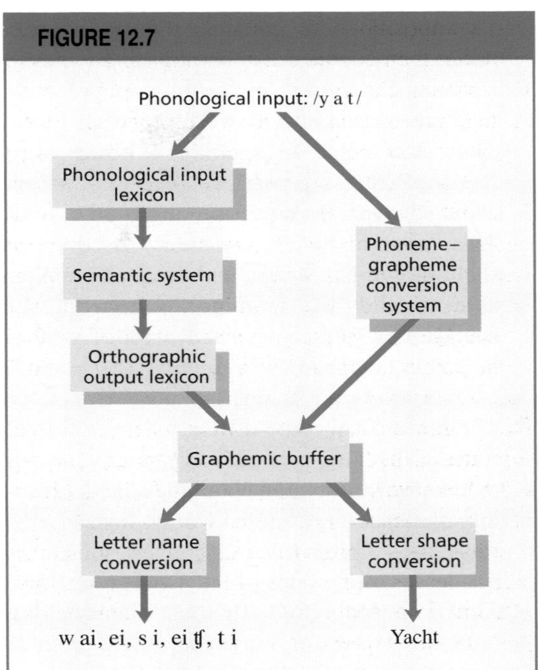

Two routes between learning a word and spelling it. From Rapp et al. (2002).

We will base our discussion on a theoretical sketch map of the main processes involved in spelling heard words proposed by Rapp, Epstein, and Tainturier (2002; see Figure 12.7):

- There are two main routes between hearing a word and spelling it: the lexical route (left-hand side of Figure 12.7) and the non-lexical route (right-hand side). There are some similarities here with the dual-route cascaded model of reading (Coltheart et al., 2001; see Chapter 10).

- The lexical route contains the information needed to relate phonological (sound), semantic (meaning), and orthographic (spelling) representations of words to each other. Thus, this route to spelling a heard word involves accessing much detailed information about all characteristics or features of the word. This route is the one normally used when spelling familiar words, and is equally applicable whether the relationship between the sound units (phonemes) and units of written language (graphemes) is regular (e.g., "cat") or irregular (e.g., "yacht").
- The non-lexical route differs from the lexical route in that it does not involve gaining access to detailed information about the sound, meaning, and spelling of heard words. Instead, this route uses stored rules to convert sounds or phonemes into groups of letters or graphemes. This is the route normally used when spelling unfamiliar words or nonwords. It will produce correct spellings when the relationship between phonemes and graphemes is regular or common (e.g., "cat"), but will produce systematic spelling errors when the relationship is irregular or uncommon (e.g., "yacht").
- Both routes make use of a graphemic buffer, which briefly holds graphemic representations consisting of abstract letters or letter groups.

Below we consider evidence relating to the major assumptions incorporated in the model.

Lexical route: Phonological dysgraphia

What would we expect to find if a brain-damaged patient could make little or no use of the non-lexical route, but the lexical route was essentially intact? He/she would spell known words accurately, because their spellings would be available in the orthographic output lexicon. However, there would be great problems with unfamiliar words and nonwords, for which relevant information is *not* contained in the orthographic output lexicon. The term **phonological dysgraphia** is applied to patients with these symptoms.

A patient fitting the above description is PR (Shallice, 1981). PR wrote over 90% of common words correctly to dictation, and was only slightly worse in his spelling of relatively uncommon words. However, he spelled only 18% of nonwords appropriately. Even when he did spell a nonword accurately, he often reported using a real word to assist him.

Evidence that accurate spelling can occur with no use of the non-lexical route was reported by Shelton and Weinrich (1997). Their patient, EA, could not write correctly any of 55 nonwords to dictation, but wrote 50% of regular words and 45% of irregular words correctly. As Shelton and Weinrich (1997, p. 126) concluded, "E.A. does not appear to be able to do any phoneme-to-grapheme conversion [involving the non-lexical route], yet he can write single words accurately. Thus, his data suggest that writing can be carried out completely independently of sublexical [non-lexical] phonological generation."

Non-lexical route: Surface dysgraphia

If a patient had damage to the lexical route and so relied largely on the phoneme–grapheme conversion system in spelling, what pattern of performance would we expect to see? Apart from producing misspellings sounding like the relevant word, such a patient would have some success in generating appropriate spellings of nonwords. In addition, he/she would be more accurate at spelling regular words (i.e., words where the spelling can be worked out from the sound) than irregular words. Patients with these symptoms suffer from **surface dysgraphia**.

All of the above features characterised the spelling of patient TP, who was studied by Hatfield and Patterson (1983). For example, she wrote "flud" instead of "flood" and "neffue" instead of "nephew". However, she spelled various irregular words correctly (e.g., "sign", "cough"), suggesting some use of the orthographic output lexicon.

According to the model, the semantic system forms part of the lexical route. Evidence of the involvement of the semantic system in surface dysgraphia was reported by Macoir and Bernier (2002). Their patient, MK, spelled 92% of regular words correctly but only 52% of irregular words. Of particular importance, her overall word spelling was much better for words about which she could access semantic information than those about which she could not (85% vs. 19%, respectively).

Are the two routes independent?

Do the lexical and non-lexical routes typically operate independently of each other? According to Tainturier and Rapp (2001, p. 270), "It is commonly assumed that . . . the output of one of these 'routes' will ultimately be selected (and the other suppressed if needed) and then 'transferred' to the graphemic buffer." In other words, lexical and non-lexical processes are independent. However, as we will see, there is increasing evidence that this is *not* always the case.

Suppose we ask normal participants to spell various words and nonwords. On the independence view, we would expect the spelling of nonwords to involve *only* the phoneme–grapheme conversion system within the non-lexical route. However, there is evidence for lexical influences on nonword spelling. For example, Campbell (1983) found that the spoken nonword (pri:t) tended to be spelled PREAT when it followed the word "meat", but to be spelled PREET when it followed the word "sweet". Thus, the participants' knowledge of the spellings of real words (information associated with the lexical route) influenced their spelling of nonwords. More specifically, nonwords were spelled by analogy to real words heard immediately beforehand.

Convincing evidence that the lexical and non-lexical routes are sometimes not independent was reported by Rapp et al. (2002). They studied LAT, a patient with **Alzheimer's disease**. He made many errors in spelling, but used the phoneme–grapheme conversion system reasonably well. For example, he showed good spelling for nonwords and most of his spelling errors on real words were phonologically plausible (e.g., "pursuit" spelled PERSUTE; "leopard" spelled LEPERD). Such findings indicated clearly that LAT was using the non-lexical route.

Rapp et al. (2002) found that LAT made other errors that suggested he was using the lexical route. For example, he spelled "bouquet" as BOUKET and "knowledge" as KNOLIGE. These spellings suggest some use of the non-lexical route. However, there are features of these spellings that could *not* have come directly from the sounds of the words. LAT could only have known that "bouquet" ends in "t" and "knowledge" starts with "k" by using information contained in the orthographic output lexicon, which forms part of the lexical route. Thus, LAT sometimes integrated information from lexical and non-lexical processes when spelling familiar words.

Deep dysgraphia

If, for some reason, only partial semantic information about a heard word was passed on from the semantic system to the orthographic output lexicon, then a word similar in meaning to the correct word might be written down. Precisely this has been observed in patients with **deep dysgraphia**. For example, Bub and Kertesz (1982) studied a young woman, JC. She made numerous semantic errors, writing "sun" when the word "sky" was spoken, writing "chair" when "desk" was spoken, and so on. However, her reading aloud was very good, and did not contain semantic errors. Thus, the semantic system itself was probably *not* damaged, but rather the connection between the semantic system and the orthographic output lexicon.

Graphemic buffer

The lexical and non-lexical routes both lead to the graphemic buffer (see Figure 12.7). It is a memory store in which graphemic information about the letters in a word is held briefly prior to spelling it. Suppose a brain-damaged patient had damage to the graphemic buffer so that information in it decayed unusually rapidly. What would be the effects in terms of his/her spelling ability? According to Schiller et al. (2001), such a patient would spell short words better than long words, because letter information needs to be stored in the graphemic buffer for less time with short words. In addition, the errors made in spelling long words should occur mainly towards the end of the word, by which time letter information would have decayed in the graphemic buffer.

Schiller et al. (2001) studied two patients (TH and PB), both of whom showed the above predicted pattern of spelling impairments. Schiller et al. (2001) also obtained evidence that these patients could access the complete spelling of long words when they used tasks not requiring them to keep information in the graphemic buffer for several seconds. Schiller et al. (2001, p. 13) concluded as follows: "This pattern of performance locates their [the patients'] deficit to the mechanism that keeps graphemic representations active for further processing."

Evaluation

There is reasonably convincing evidence that the spelling of heard words can be based either on a lexical route or a non-lexical route. Some of the strongest support comes from studies on patients with surface dysgraphia having a severely impaired lexical route, and from those with phonological dysgraphia having a severely impaired non-lexical route. The lexical route with its phonological input lexicon, its semantic system, and its orthographic output lexicon is much more complex than the non-lexical route, and it is no surprise that some patients (e.g., those with deep dysgraphia) have a partially intact and partially impaired lexical route. Some of the characteristics of the graphemic buffer have been identified (Schiller et al., 2001).

There are various issues relating to the two-route model that will only be resolved by further research. First, there is still controversy as to whether the two routes are independent or interactive in their functioning. Second, the precise rules used in phoneme–grapheme conversion have not been clearly identified. Third, much remains to be discovered about the ways in which the three components of the lexical route combine to produce spellings of heard words.

One or two orthographic lexicons?

Knowledge of word spellings (orthography) is important in reading and in spelling. The simplest theoretical assumption (the *shared-components position*) is that a *single* orthographic lexicon is used in both reading and spelling. The alternative position (the *distinct-components position*) is that one orthographic input lexicon is used in reading *and* a separate orthographic output lexicon is used in spelling. We turn now to some of the relevant evidence.

Evidence

There are numerous brain-damaged patients whose spelling is impaired much more than their reading, and some whose reading is impaired more than their spelling (see Tainturier & Rapp, 2001). On the face of it, that provides support for the distinct-components position and the notion that there are separate orthographic lexicons for reading and for spelling. However, *full* knowledge of the letters in a word is essential for spelling, but is often not needed for accurate reading. Thus, there may be numerous patients with poorer spelling than reading simply because spelling is a harder task.

Evidence supporting the above argument comes from the case of MLB, a French woman with severe surface dysgraphia (Tainturier, 1996). She spelled correctly only 8% of irregular words, but read aloud correctly 69% of irregular words. Her reading performance suggests that her orthographic input lexicon was reasonably intact. However, MLB was then given a more difficult reading task, in which she was presented with words and with nonwords pronounced the same as actual words (examples in English are BOATH and SKOOL). MLB performed at chance level when deciding which of the letter strings were words. Thus, her reading ability was shown to be severely impaired when she was given a difficult reading task.

Brain-damaged patients with a reading impairment (dyslexia) generally also have a spelling impairment (dysgraphia), and the reverse is also often the case. Such evidence is consistent with the shared-components position. Stronger support for that position comes from studies on brain-damaged patients with more specific impairments (see Tainturier & Rapp, 2001). For example, patients having particular problems with reading nonwords typically also have specific problems

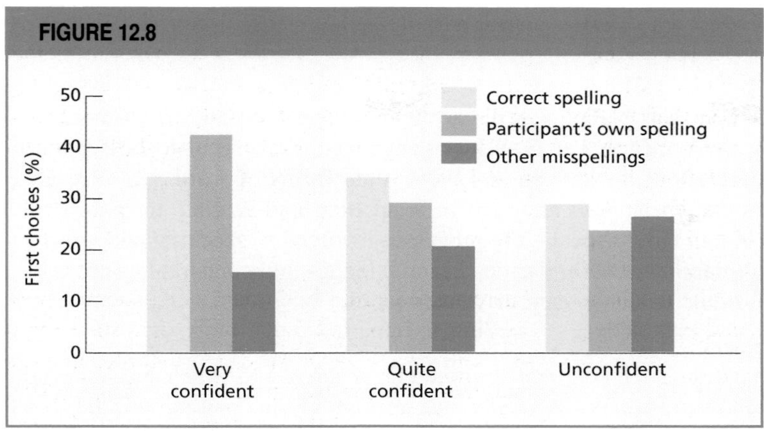

Ability to select the correct spelling of a word from various misspellings as a function of confidence in correctness of decision. Based on data in Holmes and Carruthers (1998).

in spelling nonwords. In addition, patients who find it especially hard to read irregular words also generally have a selective spelling deficit for irregular words. Some patients even show great similarity between the specific words they can read and those they can spell (e.g., Behrmann & Bub, 1992).

Holmes and Carruthers (1998) obtained evidence from normal participants that the same orthographic lexicon is used in reading and spelling. In essence, they wanted to show that the errors made in reading can resemble the errors made in spelling. In order to do this, they presented their participants with five versions of words they could not spell: the correct version; their own misspelling; the most popular misspelling (if that differed from their own misspelling); and two or three other misspellings. The participants showed *no* ability to select the correct spelling over their own misspelling (see Figure 12.8). As Holmes and Carruthers (1998, p. 284) concluded, "Normal adult readers access the same orthographic representation for both reading and spelling."

Additional evidence supporting the notion that there is a single orthographic lexicon serving reading and spelling was reported by Burt and Tate (2002). University students performed a reading task (lexical decision—deciding whether letter strings formed words) and a spelling task. Reading performance in terms of the speed and accuracy of lexical decisions was worse for words that participants had misspelled previously than for words they had spelled correctly. This similarity between reading and spelling is as predicted from the single-lexicon position.

Evaluation

It is very hard to obtain definitive evidence on the issue of one vs. two orthographic lexicons. However, we have considered research evidence from normal and from brain-damaged individuals which provides reasonable support for the assumption that there is a single orthographic lexicon. That assumption makes sense in that it would presumably be more efficient for us to have one orthographic lexicon rather than two. It is also hard to think of any real advantages associated with having separate orthographic lexicons for reading and for spelling.

CHAPTER SUMMARY

- Introduction
  The same knowledge base and similar planning skills are used in speaking and in writing, but spoken language is typically more informal than written language. There seem to be separate lexicons containing information about the spoken and the written forms of words. As a result, some brain-damaged patients can speak well although their spelling and writing are poor, and others can write accurately but can hardly speak. The processes involved in speaking and writing are most similar during initial planning. Dissimilarities become increasingly apparent as processing moves towards the end-product of the spoken or written word.
- Basic aspects of spoken language
  A key to successful communication is the cooperative principle, according to which speakers and listeners must try to be cooperative. Speakers generally take account of the common ground they share with their listener(s), and are responsive to the verbal and non-verbal reactions of any listeners. Discourse markers (commonly found in spontaneous speech) indicate shifts of topic and can show politeness. Prosodic cues can help listeners but are often omitted by speakers unless the context fails to clarify the meaning of what they are saying. Speech errors, many of which involve problems with selecting the correct word, can shed light on the processes involved in speech production.
- Theories of speech production
  Speakers reduce their processing effort by means of preformulation and underspecification. Sometimes planning occurs while the individual is speaking. According to Dell's spreading-activation theory, speech production involves semantic, syntactic, morphological, and phonological levels, with processing being parallel and interactive. The theory accounts for most speech errors, but predicts more errors than are actually found. According to the WEAVER++ model, the production of individual words is serial and involves six processes. Neuroimaging and other evidence supports the processing sequence assumed within the model. However, the assumption that lemma selection is completed before activation of phonological information is incorrect. In addition, WEAVER++ is not designed to account for the processes involved in producing sentences, and cannot account for the lexical bias and mixed error effects.
- Cognitive neuropsychology: Speech production
  A distinction used to be drawn between Broca's aphasia and Wernicke's aphasia, based in part on the brain regions involved. No rigid distinction is possible, and there are doubts about the precise brain areas involved. Patients with anomia have an impaired ability to name objects. Some anomic patients have problems with lemma selection, whereas others have problems with word-form selection. Patients with agrammatism generally produce the appropriate words when speaking, but cannot order them grammatically. The syntactic deficiencies of agrammatic aphasics sometimes extend to language comprehension. Patients with jargon aphasia sometimes speak fairly grammatically (with numerous exceptions). They have severe problems with word finding, and produce made-up words that often resemble the correct word phonemically. Jargon aphasics are generally unaware they are producing made-up words. Agrammatic aphasics and jargon aphasics show some evidence for a double dissociation between syntactic planning and content-word retrieval, but the evidence is less strong than used to be believed.
- Writing: The main processes
  Writing involves planning, sentence-generation, and revision processes, but these processes cannot be separated neatly. On average, writers devote about 30% of their time to planning, 50% to

sentence generation, and 20% (or less) to revision. Planning makes use of conceptual, socio-cultural, and strategic knowledge. Good writers use a knowledge-transforming rather than knowledge-telling strategy, and this helps them to produce high-level main points. Good writers also spend more time revising than do other writers, and are better at detecting problems in a text. The processes involved in writing typically make large demands on working memory, especially its central executive component. Composition places more demands on working memory than does transcription, and the demands are even greater when writers engage in composition and transcription at the same time. It is not entirely clear why composition is so demanding. For highly experienced users of word processors, the rate at which text is produced and its quality are the same whether they write in longhand or use a word processor.

- Spelling
  It is generally assumed that there are separate lexical and non-lexical routes in spelling, with the former being used to spell familiar words and the latter being used to spell unfamiliar words and nonwords. Both routes make use of a graphemic buffer that briefly holds graphemic representations. Patients with phonological dysgraphia have damage to the lexical route, whereas those with surface dysgraphia have damage to the non-lexical route. There is evidence from unimpaired individuals and from brain-damaged patients that information from the two routes is sometimes integrated. There has been controversy as to whether the same orthographic lexicon is used in reading and spelling. Most of the evidence is consistent with the single-lexicon position. Some patients with damage to the graphemic buffer find it hard to spell long words.

FURTHER READING

- Altmann, G. (2002). *Psycholinguistics: Critical concepts in psychology*. London: Routledge. Volume 5 of this six-volume set contains key articles on spoken language production.
- Balota, D.A., & Marsh, E.J. (2004). *Cognitive psychology*. Hove, UK: Psychology Press. Some of the readings in this edited book (especially the one by Fromkin) are relevant to language production.
- Berhrmann, M., & Patterson, K. (2004). *Words and things*. Hove, UK: Psychology Press. In this edited book, there are various contributions dealing with the processes of language production in brain-damaged patients.
- Harley, T.A. (2001). *The psychology of language: From data to theory* (2nd Ed.). Hove, UK: Psychology Press. Chapter 12 in this book provides a very clear introduction to language production, including the relevant cognitive neuropsychological evidence.
- Indrisano, R., & Squire, J. (2000). *Perspectives on writing: Research, theory, and practice*. Newark, NJ: I.R.A. This edited book contains several interesting chapters on the processes involved in writing.
- Olive, T. (2004). Working memory in writing: Empirical evidence from the dual-task technique. *European Psychologist*, *9*, 32–42. This article represents an impressive attempt to identify the role played by the working memory system in writing.
- Vigliocco, G., & Hartsuiker, R.J. (2002). The interplay of meaning, sound, and syntax in sentence production. *Psychological Bulletin*, *128*, 442–472. The authors of this article provide a comprehensive analysis of the strengths and weaknesses of major theories of speech production.
- Wheeldon, L.R. (2000). *Aspects of language production*. Hove, UK: Psychology Press. The various chapters in this edited book deal with all of the main issues relating to speech production in an authoritative and well-informed way.

Part IV

Thinking and Reasoning

Our ability to reflect in a complex way on our lives, to plan and solve problems that arise on a daily basis, is the bedrock of thinking behaviour. However, as in all things humans, the ways in which we think (and reason and make decisions) are many and varied, from solving puzzles in the newspaper to troubleshooting when our car breaks down to developing a new theory of the universe. Consider a sample of the sorts of things to which we apply the term "thinking".

First, a fragment of Molly Bloom's sleepy thoughts from James Joyce's Ulysses (1922/1960, pp. 871–872), about Mrs Riordan:

> . . . God help the world if all the women in the world were her sort down on bathingsuits and lownecks of course nobody wanted her to wear I suppose she was pious because no man would look at her twice I hope I'll never be like her a wonder she didn't want us to cover our faces but she was a welleducated woman certainly and her gabby talk about Mr. Riordan here and Mr. Riordan there I suppose he was glad to get shut of her . . .

Next, a person (S) answering an experimenter's (E) question about regulating the thermostat on a home-heating system (Kempton, 1986, p. 83):

> E: Let's say you're in the house and you're cold . . . Let's say it's a cold day, you want to do something about it.
>
> S: Oh, what I might do is, I might turn the thing up high to get out, to get a lot of air out fast, then after a little while turn it off or turn it down.
>
> E: Uh-huh.
>
> S: So there are also, you know, these issues about, um, the rate at which the thing produces heat, the higher the setting is, the more heat that's produced per unit of time, so if you're cold, you want to get warm fast, um, so you turn it up high.

Finally, a protocol of the first author trying to use Powerpoint:

> Why has the Artwork put the title in the wrong part of the slide? Suppose I try to put a frame around it so I can drag it up to where I want it. Ah-ha, now if I just summon up the arrows I can move the top bit up, and then I can do the same with the bottom bit. If I move the bottom bit up more than the top bit, then the title will fit in OK.

These three samples illustrate several general aspects of thinking. First, all the pieces involve individuals being *conscious* of their thoughts. Clearly, thinking must involve conscious awareness. However, we tend to be conscious of the products of thinking rather than the processes themselves (see Chapter 17). Furthermore, even when we can introspect on our thoughts, our recollections of them are often inaccurate. Joyce does a good job of reconstructing the character of idle, associative thought in Molly Bloom's internal monologue. However, if we interrupted her and asked her to tell us her thoughts from the previous five minutes, little of it would be recalled.

Second, thinking varies in the extent to which it is directed. At one end of the scale, it can be relatively undirected, as in the case of Molly Bloom letting one thought slide into another as she is on the point of slipping into a dream. In the other two cases, the goal is much clearer and well defined. As we will see, most research on thinking has dealt with relatively well-defined, goal-driven situations.

Third, the amount and nature of the knowledge used in different thinking tasks can vary enormously. For example, the knowledge required in the Powerpoint case is quite limited, even though it took the author concerned a fair amount of time to acquire it! On the other hand, Molly Bloom is using a vast amount of knowledge about the mores of old widows, expectations about what she herself will be like when old, general knowledge about the irony of those who criticise that which they cannot do themselves, and much more besides. As we will see, the tasks used in research on thinking and reasoning range all the way from those requiring little knowledge to those depending heavily on previous knowledge (e.g., chess playing).

The next four chapters are concerned with the higher-level cognitive processes involved in thinking and reasoning. The topics covered include problem solving, expertise, creativity, hypothesis testing, scientific discovery; deductive reasoning, inductive reasoning, judgement, and decision making. Bear in mind that we use the *same* cognitive system to deal with all these types of task. As a result, many distinctions among different forms of thinking and reasoning are rather arbitrary and camouflage underlying similarities in cognitive processes.

There are two other reasons for assuming that the underlying processes may be rather similar on most of the types of task itemised above. First, the same (or at least similar) brain areas are typically involved in most problem-solving and reasoning tasks (see Chapter 16). Second, individuals with high intelligence (as assessed by IQ tests) perform a wide range of problems involving thinking and reasoning much better than those with less intelligence (Mackintosh, 1998). More specifically, Stanovich and West (1998) found significant positive correlations between intelligence and performance on a range of tests of deductive and inductive reasoning.

In spite of what has been said so far, some distinctions among types of task *are* important and worth making (see Panel IV.1). For example, problem solving involves generating various possibilities and then choosing among them to make

Panel IV.1: Forms of thinking

Problem solving:	Cognitive activity which involves moving from the recognition that there is a problem through a series of steps to the solution or goal state. Most other forms of thinking involve some problem solving.
Decision making:	Selecting one out of a number of presented options or possibilities, with the decision having consequences for the individual concerned.
Judgement:	The component of decision making that involves calculating the likelihood of various possible events; what is of most concern is the accuracy (or inaccuracy) of the judgements that are made.
Deductive reasoning:	Deciding what conclusions follow necessarily provided that various statements are assumed to be true; the form of thinking most closely associated with logic.
Inductive reasoning:	Deciding whether certain statements or hypotheses are true on the basis of the available information; a form of thinking used by scientists and detectives, but not guaranteed to produce valid conclusions.

progress towards a goal. Expertise involves highly skilled problem solving based on a considerable amount of relevant knowledge. In contrast, in decision making the possibilities are presented, and the task involves choosing one of them. Judgement is that part of decision making concerned with working out the probability of occurrence of one or more events. Finally, reasoning involves calculating which inferences or conclusions follow from a given set of information. As shown in Panel IV.1, there is a distinction (sometimes clearer in principle than in practice) between deductive reasoning and inductive reasoning. We can draw conclusions in deductive reasoning that are 100% certain to be valid, whereas no such certainty is possible with inductive reasoning.

We will briefly describe the structure of this section of the book, which covers Chapters 13–16. Chapter 13 is concerned primarily with problem solving. One line of research has had as its focus the identification of the processes used to solve problems that do not require specialised knowledge for their solution. Another line of research has concentrated on the role of learning in problem solving, with a particular emphasis on the knowledge and skills possessed by experts but not by novices.

Chapter 14 is also concerned with problem solving, especially those aspects of relevance to hypothesis testing. Of particular importance in this chapter is the discussion of advanced forms of problem solving (e.g., scientific discovery). Several different types of research are considered: laboratory-based tasks involving hypothesis testing; simulated research environments; analysis of actual scientific achievement; and studies on creativity. As we will see, much of interest has been discovered, even if we do not as yet understand all the mysteries of creativity.

Chapter 15 deals with the important topics of judgement and decision making, which have attracted a substantial increase in research interest in recent years. Among the questions posed (and answered!) in this chapter are the following: What are the factors (cognitive and social) that influence the decisions that we make? Why do we sometimes ignore relevant information? What kinds of biases impair our judgements and our decision making? One of the central themes of this chapter is that we often use heuristics or rules of thumb. Heuristics have the advantage of being simple to use but the disadvantage that they typically only allow us to make approximately accurate judgements and decisions.

Chapter 16 is mainly concerned with the important topic of deductive reasoning. The original focus of research in this area was on the issue of the extent to which people are able to think logically. However, it has been clear for many years that research on deductive-reasoning tasks illuminates a range of other important issues. We conclude our coverage of deductive reasoning by discussing and evaluating leading theories of deductive reasoning. We end Chapter 16 by addressing broader issues that span the four chapters in this section. First, we consider the extent to which the same brain areas are involved in various forms of higher-level cognition. Second, we provide a provisional answer to the key question, "Are humans rational?" As you can probably guess, the essence of the answer is, "Yes and no", rather than a definite "Yes" or "No"!

13

Problem Solving and Expertise

INTRODUCTION

We often find ourselves in situations in which we need to solve a problem. We will consider three examples here. First, you have an urgent meeting in another city and so must get there as soon as possible. However, the trains generally run late or are cancelled, your car is old and unreliable, and the buses are slow. Second, you are struggling to work out the correct sequence of operations to make your new computer do what you want to do. You try to remember what you needed to do with your previous computer. Third, you are an expert chess player in the middle of a competitive match against a strong opponent. The time clock is ticking away, and you have to decide on your move in a complicated position.

We chose the above examples because they relate to the three main topics of this chapter. The first topic is problem solving, which Mayer (1990, p. 284) defined as, "cognitive processing directed at transforming a given situation into a goal situation when no obvious method of solution is available to the problem solver." As we will see, most of the problems studied by psychologists are such that it is clear when the goal has been reached.

The second topic is transfer, which is concerned with the beneficial (or adverse) effects of previous learning and problem solving on some current task or problem. This topic is of great importance, because we constantly make use of past experience and knowledge to assist us in whatever happens to be our current task. There is reasonable overlap between the areas of problem solving and transfer. However, transfer is more concerned with the effects of learning than is most research on problem solving, and the knowledge that is transferred from the past to the present extends beyond that directly relevant to problem solving.

The third topic is expertise. There are overlaps between expertise and problem solving, in that experts are very efficient at solving numerous problems in their area of expertise. However, there are important differences between the two areas. First, most traditional research on problem solving involved problems requiring no special training or knowledge for their solution. In contrast, studies on expertise have typically involved problems requiring considerable knowledge beyond that presented in the problem itself. Second, there is more focus on individual differences in research on expertise than in research on problem solving. Indeed, a central issue in expertise research is to identify the main differences (e.g., in knowledge; in strategic processing) between experts and novices.

There is also overlap between the areas of transfer and expertise. One of the key reasons why experts perform at a much higher level than novices is because they are able to transfer or make use of their huge stock of relevant knowledge. What is of fundamental importance to both areas is an emphasis on understanding the processes involved in learning.

In sum, there are important similarities among the areas of problem solving, transfer, and expertise. For example, participants in all three areas are often presented with a problem requiring them to generate their own options (possible answers). In all three areas, participants then need to use their ability and knowledge to select the best choice from those options. In addition, issues relating to improved performance with practice are of importance, especially in the areas of transfer and expertise. However, it is important to strike a balance. In spite of some similarities, there are good reasons why rather separate bodies of theory and research have built up around the three areas.

PROBLEM SOLVING

There are three major aspects to problem solving:

(1) It is purposeful (i.e., goal-directed).
(2) It involves cognitive rather than automatic processes.
(3) A problem only exists when someone lacks the relevant knowledge to produce an immediate solution. Thus, a problem for most people (e.g., a mathematical calculation) may not be so for someone with relevant expertise (e.g., a professional mathematician).

There is an important distinction between well-defined and ill-defined problems. **Well-defined problems** are ones in which all aspects of the problem are clearly specified: these include the initial state or situation, the range of possible moves or strategies, and the goal or solution. The goal is well specified in the sense that it is clear when the goal has been reached. For example, a maze is a well-defined problem, in which escape from it (or reaching the centre as in the Hampton Court maze) is the goal. Mind you, one of the authors has managed to get completely lost on the way out from the centre of the Hampton Court maze on more than one occasion!

In contrast, **ill-defined problems** are underspecified. Suppose you have locked your keys inside your car, and want to get into it without causing any damage. However, you have urgent business to attend to elsewhere, and there is no-one around to help you. In such circumstances, it may be very hard to identify the best solution to the problem. For example, breaking a window will solve the immediate problem, but will obviously create additional problems.

Most everyday problems are ill-defined problems. In contrast, psychologists have focused mainly on well-defined problems. Why is this? One important reason is that well-defined problems have a best strategy for their solution. As a result, we can identify the errors and deficiencies in the strategies adopted by human problem solvers.

There is a further important distinction between knowledge-rich and knowledge-lean problems. **Knowledge-rich problems** can only be solved by individuals possessing a considerable amount of specific knowledge. In contrast, **knowledge-lean problems** do not require the possession of such knowledge, because most of the information required is given in the problem statement. Most traditional research on problem solving has involved the use of knowledge-lean problems. In contrast, research on expertise (discussed later in the chapter) has typically involved knowledge-rich problems.

Gestalt approach

Some of the earliest research on problem solving was carried out by Thorndike (1898). Hungry cats in closed cages could see a dish of food outside the cage. The cage doors could be opened when a pole inside the cage was hit. Initially, the cats thrashed about and clawed the sides of the cages. However, after some time, the cat hit the pole inside the cage and opened the door. On repeated trials, the cats gradually learned what was required. Eventually they would hit the pole almost immediately, and so gain access to the food. Thorndike (1898) was unimpressed by the cats' performance, referring to their apparently almost random behaviour as **trial-and-error learning**.

There was a reaction against the above view by German psychologists known as the Gestaltists during the 1920s and 1930s. They argued that Thorndike's problem situation was unfair, because there was a purely arbitrary relationship between the cats' behaviour (hitting the pole) and the desired consequence (the opening of the cage door). As we will see, the Gestaltists showed how limited Thorndike's approach had been by studying several problems which seemed very different from the one Thorndike had used.

A key difference between Thorndike's approach and that of the Gestaltists is captured in the distinction between reproductive and productive problem solving. **Reproductive thinking** involves the re-use of previous experiences, and was the focus of Thorndike's research. In contrast, **productive thinking** involves a novel restructuring of the problem. It is more complex than reproductive problem solving, but the Gestaltists argued that several species are capable of this higher-level form of problem solving.

Insight

Köhler (1925) showed that animals can engage in productive problem solving. In one of his studies, an ape called Sultan was inside a cage, and could only reach a banana outside the cage by joining two sticks together. The ape seemed lost at first. However, Sultan then seemed to realise how to solve the problem, and rapidly joined the sticks together. According to Köhler, the ape had suddenly restructured the problem. By so doing, it had shown **insight**, which is often accompanied by the "ah-ha experience".

There is at least one potential difficulty with Köhler's claimed demonstrations of insight in apes. The apes had spent the early months of their lives in the wild, and so could have acquired useful information about sticks and how they can be combined. Birch (1945) found that apes raised in captivity showed little evidence of the kind of insightful problem solving observed by Köhler (1925). Thus, the apparent insight shown by Sultan may have been due to a slow learning process rather than a sudden flash of insight.

What about studies on problem solving in humans? Maier (1931) carried out a famous study on restructuring. The participants were given the "pendulum problem", and superficially their performance was not as good as that of Köhler's apes on insight problems! The participants were brought into a room containing various objects (e.g., poles, pliers, extension cords), plus two strings hanging from the ceiling (see Figure 13.1). The task was to tie together the two strings hanging from the ceiling, but the strings were too far apart for the participants to reach one string while holding the other. The most "insightful" (but rarely produced) solution was the pendulum solution. This involved taking the pliers, tying them to one of the strings, and then swinging the string like a pendulum. In this way, it was possible to hold one string and to catch the other on its upswing.

Maier (1931) found it was possible to facilitate problem restructuring or insight by having the experimenter apparently accidentally brush against the string to set it swinging. Soon afterwards, many participants produced the pendulum solution, but few reported having noticed the experimenter brush against the string. This finding is sometimes known as the unconscious cue effect.

In spite of its fame, Maier's (1931) study was fairly slipshod, and the *unconscious* cue effect was not replicated for many years (Jonathan Evans, personal communication). However, Knoblich and Wartenberg (1998) found evidence that subtle hints not consciously noticed by participants led to problem restructuring and solution. In addition, there is evidence for a *conscious* cue effect. Battersby et al. (1953) found the experimenter could greatly speed up solution times on the pendulum problem by highlighting objects that might be relevant to the problem.

The Gestaltists claimed that insight involves special processes, and so is very different from normal problem solving. Relevant findings were reported by Metcalfe and Weibe (1987). They recorded participants' feelings of "warmth"

FIGURE 13.1

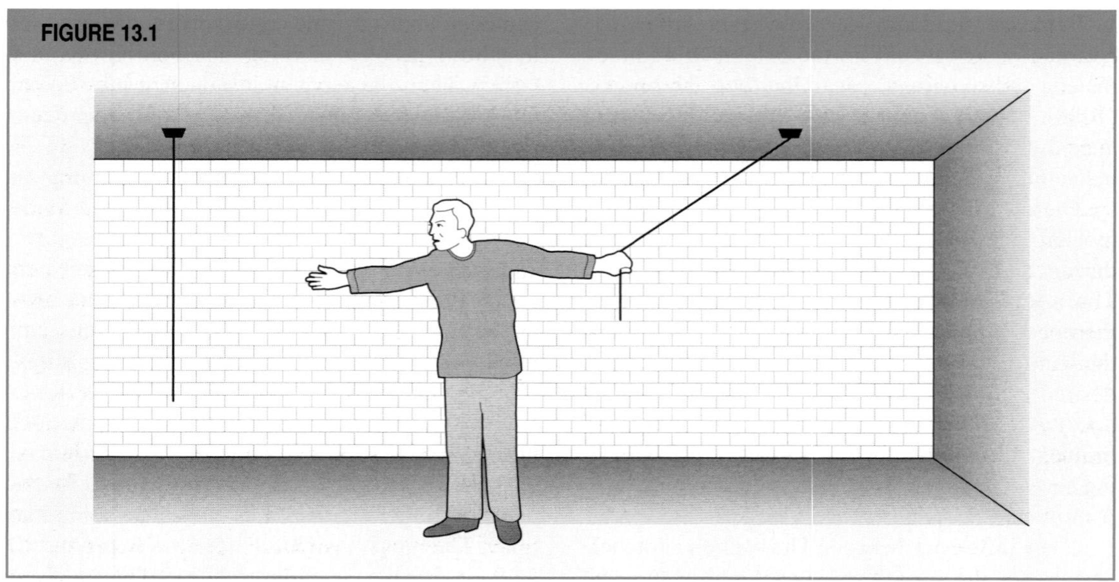

The two-string problem in which it is not possible to reach one string while holding the other.

(closeness to solution) while engaged in solving insight and non-insight problems. There was a progressive increase in warmth during non-insight problems. With insight problems, in contrast, the warmth ratings remained at the same low level until suddenly increasing dramatically shortly before the solution was reached. These findings suggest (but do not prove) that insight *is* special, and occurs in an all-or-none fashion.

Novick and Sherman (2003) argued that we need to distinguish between our subjective experience and the underlying processes. They presented expert and non-expert anagram solvers with five-letter anagrams, and asked them to indicate which out of various statements best described how they arrived at the answer. One statement referred to insight or "pop-out" solutions: "The solution came to mind suddenly, seemingly out of nowhere. I have no awareness of having done anything to try to get the answer." The percentages of pop-out solutions were 41% for the expert solvers and 22% for the non-experts. Most of these solutions were produced very rapidly (within 2–3 seconds of anagram presentation).

The above findings apparently indicate that insight occurs suddenly and does not involve the gradual accumulation of information. However, Novick and Sherman (2003) obtained conflicting evidence in a further experiment. Anagrams and non-anagrams were presented very briefly (469 or 953 ms), after which the participants had to indicate very rapidly whether each letter string could be rearranged to form an English word. Expert anagram solvers performed this task better than non-experts, but both groups had above-chance levels of performance. Thus, partial information was available to the participants at times much shorter than those needed to produce pop-out or insight solutions. The implication is that relevant processing occurs prior to "insight" anagram solutions, even though people have no conscious awareness of such processing. How, then, can we account for the fact that pop-out solutions differ from other anagram solutions in speed and subjective experience? According to Novick and Sherman (2003, p. 378), "Pop-out solutions, which are more often obtained by highly skilled solvers, may result from parallel processing of the constraints on the rearranged order of the anagram letters . . . there may be a transition from primarily serial to greater parallel processing with increasing expertise in the domain of anagram solution."

Evidence suggesting an important difference between insightful and non-insightful problem solving was reported by Jung-Beeman et al. (2004). Participants were given three words (e.g., "fence", "card", "master"), and had to think of a word (e.g., "post") that would go with each of them to form a compound word. Participants indicated whether they solved each problem in a rapid, insightful way or in a more methodical way. The right anterior superior temporal gyrus was activated (as assessed by fMRI) only when solutions involved insight. In another experiment using EEG, there was a burst of high-frequency brain activity one-third of a second prior to insightful problem solving.

Past experience

Past experience usually benefits our ability to solve problems. However, Duncker (1945) argued this is not always the case. He studied **functional fixedness**, in which we fail to solve problems because we assume from past experience that any given object only has a limited number of uses. We may note in passing that Maier's (1931) pendulum problem can be seen as a case of functional fixedness, because participants failed to realise that pliers can be used as a pendulum weight (see Keane, 1989).

Duncker (1945) gave his participants a candle, a box of nails, and several other objects. Their task was to attach the candle to a wall next to a table so it didn't drip onto the table below. Most participants tried to nail the candle directly to the wall or to glue it to the wall by melting it. Only a few decided to use the inside of the nail-box as a candle holder, and then nail it to the wall. According to Duncker, the participants "fixated" on the box's function as a container rather than as a platform. More correct solutions were produced when the nail-box was empty at the start of the experiment, presumably because that made the box appear less like a container. Similar results in a better-controlled experiment were reported by Adamson (1952).

Weisberg and Suls (1973) argued that many participants given Duncker's candle problem failed to solve it because they hardly noticed the box had been present. When non-solvers of the problem were asked to recall all the objects that had been available to solve the problem, 54% of them did not recall the box. Thus, it seems as if many participants failed to consider the box at all, rather than that they considered it and then rejected it.

Duncker (1945) assumed that functional fixedness occurred in his study because of the participants' past experience with boxes. However, he had no direct evidence that past experience was the key factor. Luchins (1942) and Luchins and Luchins (1959) adopted the superior approach of *controlling* participants' relevant past experience by providing it within the experiment. They used water-jar problems involving three water jars of varying capacity. The participants' task was to imagine pouring water from one jar to another to finish up with a specified amount of water in one of the jars. As we will see, they found striking evidence for **Einstellung** or mental set, in which a well-practised strategy is used on a problem when it is inappropriate or sub-optimal.

The most striking finding obtained by Luchins can be illustrated by considering one of his studies in detail. One problem was as follows: Jar A can hold 28 quarts of water, Jar B 76 quarts, and Jar C 3 quarts. The task is to end up with exactly 25 quarts in one of the jars. The solution is not difficult: Jar A is filled, and then Jar C is filled from it, leaving 25 quarts in Jar A. Of participants who had previously been given similar problems, 95% solved it. Other participants were trained on a series of problems, all having the same complex three-jar solution. Of these participants, only 36% managed to solve this relatively simple problem. These findings led Luchins (1942, p. 15) to conclude: "Einstellung—habituation—creates a mechanised state of mind, a blind attitude towards problems; one does not look at the problem on its own merits but is led by a mechanical application of a used method."

Evaluation

On the positive side, the Gestaltists showed that problem solving often involves productive thinking as well as reproductive thinking. They emphasised the notions of problem restructuring and of insight, both of which remain influential concepts. In addition, their research findings provided suggestive evidence for both restructuring and insight. Another important contribution they made was to show that past experience can disrupt (rather than benefit) current problem solving, with their research on functional fixedness.

On the negative side, the Gestalt concepts such as "insight" and "restructuring" are rather vague and hard to measure. We are also left with no clear idea of the *processes* underlying insight and restructuring. Subjectively, insightful solutions seem to occur suddenly out of nowhere, but insight may depend on the gradual accumulation of partial information (Novick & Sherman, 2003). Furthermore, the Gestaltists focused on a limited range of problems, tending to ignore those (e.g., chess playing) in which the systematic accumulation of knowledge has primarily beneficial effects.

Representational change theory

There have been various attempts to incorporate key aspects of the Gestalt approach into an information-processing theory of problem solving. According to Ohlsson (1992, p. 4), "insight occurs in the context of an impasse [block], which is unmerited in the sense that the thinker is, in fact, competent to solve the problem." The key assumptions of Ohlsson's representational change theory are as follows:

- The way in which a problem is currently represented or structured in the problem-solver's mind serves as a memory probe to retrieve related knowledge from long-term memory (e.g., operators or possible actions).
- The retrieval process is based on spreading activation among concepts or items of knowledge in long-term memory.
- An impasse or block occurs when the way a problem is represented does not permit retrieval of the necessary operators or possible actions.
- The impasse is broken when the problem representation is changed. The new mental representation acts as a memory probe for relevant operators in long-term memory. Thus, it extends the information available to the problem solver.
- Changing the representation of a problem can occur in various ways: (1) Elaboration or addition of new problem information; (2) Constraint relaxation, in which inhibitions on what is regarded as permissible are removed; (3) Re-encoding, in which some aspect of the problem representation is reinterpreted (e.g., a pair of pliers is reinterpreted as a weight in the pendulum problem).
- Insight occurs when an impasse is broken, and the retrieved knowledge operators are sufficient to solve the problem.

Ohlsson's theory is based squarely on Gestalt theory. Changing the problem representation in Ohlsson's theory is essentially the same as restructuring in the Gestaltist approach, and both theories emphasise the role of insight in producing problem solution. The main difference is that Ohlsson specified in more detail the processes leading to insight.

Evidence

Changing the representation of a problem often leads to solution. For example, consider the mutilated draughtboard problem (see Figure 13.2). Initially the board is completely covered by 32 dominoes occupying two squares each. Then two squares from diagonally opposite corners are removed. Can the remaining 62 squares be filled by

FIGURE 13.2

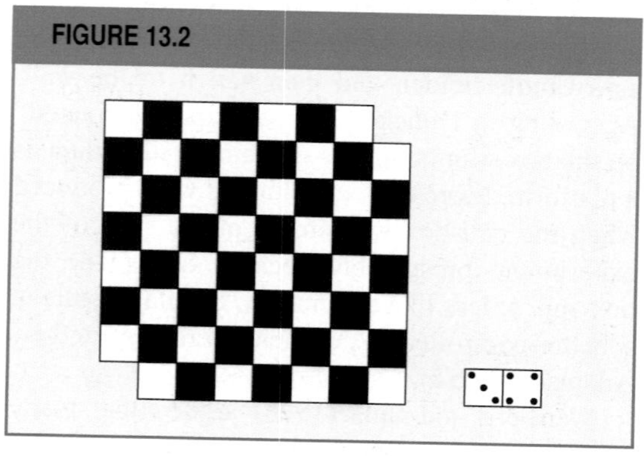

The mutilated draughtboard problem.

31 dominoes? Kaplan and Simon (1990) asked participants to think aloud while trying to solve the problem. They all started by mentally covering squares with dominoes. However, this strategy is not terribly effective, because there are 758,148 permutations of the dominoes!

In order to solve the mutilated draughtboard problem, you have to form a new representation of the problem involving elaboration and re-encoding. If you represent each domino as an object covering one white and one black square (re-encoding), and represent the draughtboard as having lost two white (or two black) squares (elaboration), then it becomes clear that the 31 dominoes cannot cover the mutilated board.

Yaniv and Meyer (1987) found that their participants' initial efforts to access relevant stored information were often unsuccessful. However, these unsuccessful efforts produced spreading activation to other concepts stored in long-term memory. As a result, the participants were more likely to recognise relevant information when it was presented to them (e.g., hints; noticing that the swinging string in the pendulum problem provides a solution). These findings are consistent with Ohlsson's theory.

Knoblich, Ohlsson, Haider, and Rhenius (1999) showed the importance of constraints in reducing the likelihood of insight. They presented participants with problems such as those shown in Figure 13.3. As you can see, you would need to know all about Roman numerals to solve the problems! The task involved moving a *single* stick to produce a true statement in place of the initial false one. Some problems (Type A) only required changing two of the values in the equation (e.g., VI = VII + I becomes VII = VI + I). In contrast, other problems (Type B problems) involved a more fundamental change in the representation of the equation (e.g., IV = III – I becomes IV – III = I).

Knoblich et al. (1999) argued that our experience of arithmetic tells us that many operations change the *values* (numbers) in an equation (as is the case with Type A problems). In contrast, relatively few operations change the *operators* (i.e., plus, minus, and equal signs), as is required in Type B problems. As predicted, they found it was much harder for participants to relax the normal constraints of arithmetic (and thus to show insight) for Type B problems than for Type A ones (see Figure 13.3).

Knoblich et al.'s (1999) study does not provide *direct* evidence about the underlying *processes* causing difficulties with Type B problems. This issue was addressed by Knoblich, Ohlsson, and Raney (2001). As Knoblich et al. (1999) had done, they used matchstick arithmetic problems. However, they also recorded eye movements while participants were solving the problems. Participants initially spent much more time fixating the values than the operators for both types of problem. Thus, participants' initial representation was based on the assumption that values rather than operators needed to be changed.

FIGURE 13.3

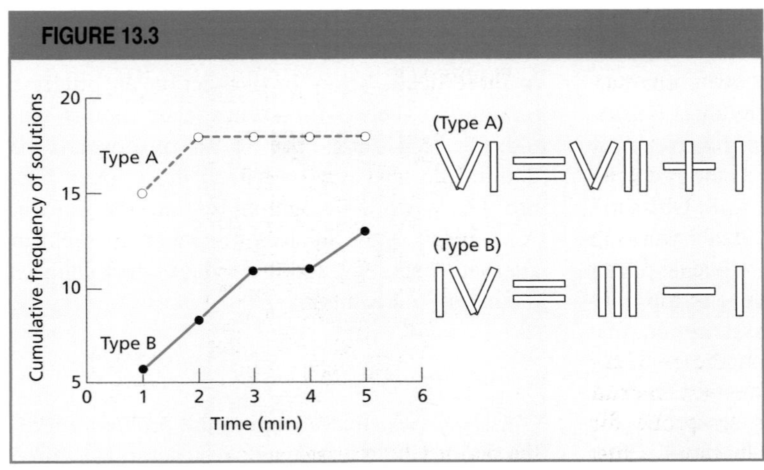

Two of the matchstick problems used by Knoblich et al. (1999), and the cumulative solution rates produced to these types of problems in their study. Copyright © 1999 by the American Psychological Association. Reprinted with permission.

FIGURE 13.4

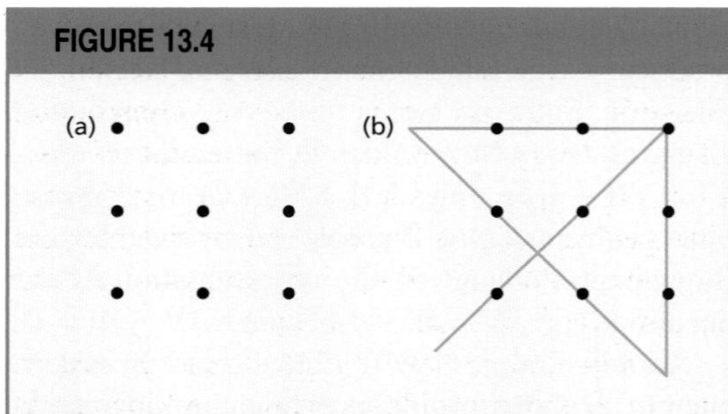

The nine-dot problem (a) and its solution (b).

FIGURE 13.5

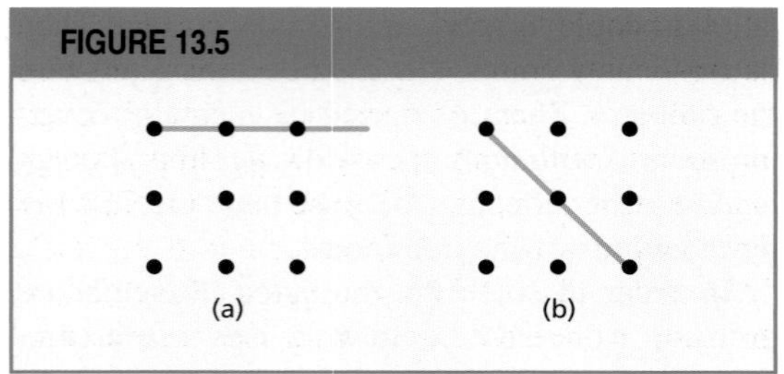

Two variants of the nine-dot problem presented in MacGregor et al. (2001). Copyright © 2001 by the American Psychological Association.

The other key finding reported by Knoblich et al. (2001) was that individuals who solved the Type B problem showed a progressive increase in the proportion of the time they fixated the operators, whereas non-solvers showed no systematic changes over time. Presumably this happened because only those who solved the problem realised that changes to operators might be required.

What factors lead to constraint relaxation and problem solution on insight problems? Consider the well-known nine-dot problem, in which you have to draw four straight lines connecting all nine dots without taking your pen or pencil from the paper. The standard answer is shown in Figure 13.4 (but see Adams, 1979, for several wild but valid alternatives). According to the Gestalt psychologists (e.g., Scheerer, 1963), the square formed by the dots constitutes a "good" figure (see Chapter 3). As a result, participants mistakenly assume they must stay within the square. That is certainly one of the factors leading most people to fail to solve the problem. However, it is not a complete explanation. Weisberg and Alba (1981) gave some participants a hint that they could draw lines outside the square formed by the nine dots. However, only 20% of those given this hint solved the problem.

The most plausible assumption from Ohlsson's theoretical approach is that individuals who fail to solve the nine-dot problem do so because their initial representation of the problem is too constrained (i.e., is based on the assumption that they should not go outside the boundaries of the square). However, a study by MacGregor, Ormerod, and Chronicle (2001) shows this assumption is inadequate. Their participants were given a first correct line on the nine-dot problem. For some of them, the correct line did not remain within the confines of the square (Figure 13.5a), whereas for the others it did (Figure 13.5b). Everyone failing to solve the problem within 10 trials was told explicitly to move outside the figure, and then given 10 more trials.

As predicted by Ohlsson's theory, using instructions to produce constraint relaxation (i.e., go outside the figure) led to a substantial improvement in performance. However, according to Ohlsson's theory, we would expect performance to be better when the given line goes outside the square than when it does not. The reason for making this prediction is that it should be easier for participants to change their initial, wrong representation of the problem when the line goes beyond the boundaries of the square. In fact, precisely the opposite was the case: only 31% of those given Figure 13.5a solved the nine-dot problem, compared to 53% of those given Figure 13.5b. MacGregor et al.'s (2001) explanation is discussed in more detail below in the section on progress monitoring theory. In essence, they argued that individuals given Figure 13.5a can cover more dots in the next two lines than those given Figure 13.5b while remaining within the square. As a result, they are less motivated to seek an alternative strategy, and this reduces their chances of finding the solution.

Evaluation

Ohlsson's view that changing the problem representation (the Gestaltists' restructuring) often allows people to solve problems is correct. There is reasonably convincing evidence that constraint relaxation is of major importance in solving insight problems. Ohlsson's theory is an improvement on the Gestalt approach because the mechanisms underlying insight are specified more precisely. More generally, the theory involves a fruitful combination of Gestalt ideas with the information-processing approach.

There are several limitations with representational change theory. First, it is often not possible to predict when (or in what way) the representation of a problem will change. For example, Ohlsson's approach does not seem very successful when applied to the nine-dot problem. More specifically, Ohlsson predicts that instructions removing participant-imposed constraints will typically lead to problem solution, but this is not always the case (MacGregor et al., 2001).

Second, the theory is basically a single-factor theory, in that it is assumed that constraint relaxation is crucial to successful solution of insight problems. However, Kershaw and Ohlsson (2004) found with the nine-dot problem that multiple factors are involved, and that hints to produce constraint relaxation had only a modestly beneficial effect.

Third, Ohlsson paid little attention to individual differences in problem-solving skills and the ability to attain insight. For example, it seems probable that highly intelligent individuals are more likely to show insight and solve complex problems than less intelligent ones.

Fourth, the theory is more applicable to some problems than to others. For example, changing the problem representation is probably more important in the kinds of problems studied by Ohlsson and the Gestaltists than in other kinds of problems (e.g., solving a simple problem in mathematics) which are best approached in a systematic and methodical way.

Computational approach: Newell and Simon

Allen Newell and Herb Simon (1972) argued that it is possible to produce systematic computer simulations of human problem solving. They achieved this with their General Problem Solver, which is a computer program designed to solve a wide range of well-defined problems. Newell and Simon's starting assumptions in the construction of the General Problem Solver were that information processing is serial (one process at a time), that people possess limited short-term memory capacity, and that they can retrieve relevant information from long-term memory.

Newell and Simon (1972) started by asking people to solve problems while thinking aloud. They then used these verbal reports to decide what general strategy was used on each problem. Finally, Newell and Simon (1972) specified the problem-solving strategy in sufficient detail for it to be programmed in their General Problem Solver. In the General Problem Solver, problems are represented as a **problem space**. This problem space consists of the initial state of the problem, the goal state, all of the possible mental operators (e.g., moves) that can be applied to any state to change it into a different state, and all of the intermediate states of the problem. Thus, the process of problem solving involves a sequence of different knowledge states. These knowledge states intervene between the initial state and the goal state, with mental operators producing the shift from one knowledge state to the next.

The above notions can be illustrated by considering the Tower of Hanoi problem (see Figure 13.6). The initial state of the problem consists of up to five discs piled in decreasing size on the first of three pegs. When all the discs are piled in the same order on the last peg, the goal state has been reached. The rules specify that only one disc can be moved at a time, and a larger disc cannot be

FIGURE 13.6

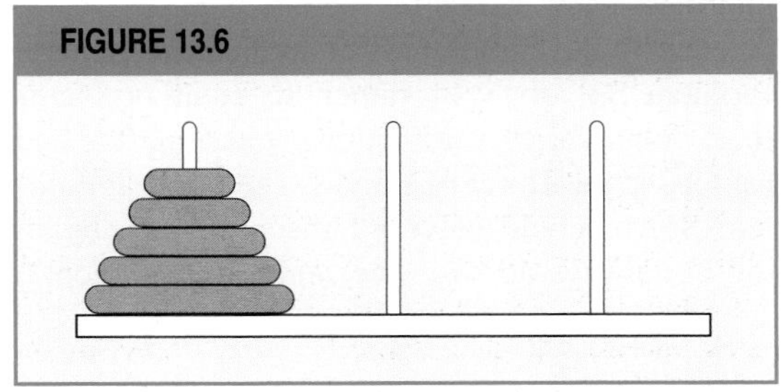

The initial state of the five-disc version of the Tower of Hanoi problem.

placed on top of a smaller disc. These rules restrict the possible mental operators on each move.

How do people select mental operators or moves as they proceed through a problem? According to Newell and Simon (1972), the complexity of most problems means that we rely heavily on **heuristics** or rules of thumb. Heuristics can be contrasted with **algorithms**, which are generally complex methods or procedures guaranteed to lead to problem solution. The most important of the various heuristic methods is **means–ends analysis**:

- Note the difference between the current state of the problem and the goal state.
- Form a subgoal that will reduce the difference between the current and goals states.
- Select a mental operator that will permit attainment of the subgoal.

Means–ends analysis is a heuristic rather than an algorithm because, while useful, it is not guaranteed to lead to problem solution.

Another important heuristic is hill climbing. **Hill climbing** involves changing the present state within the problem into one that is closer to the goal or problem solution. As Robertson (2001, p. 38) pointed out, "Hill climbing is a metaphor for problem solving in the dark", in that it is used when the problem solver has no clear understanding of the structure of a problem.

The way in which means–ends analysis is used can be illustrated with the Tower of Hanoi problem. A reasonable subgoal in the early stages of the problem is to try to place the largest disc on the last peg. If a situation arises in which the largest disc must be placed on either the middle or the last peg, then means–ends analysis will lead to that disc being placed on the last peg.

Newell and Simon (1972) applied the General Problem Solver to 11 rather different problems (e.g., letter-series completions; missionaries and cannibals; the Tower of Hanoi). The General Problem Solver could solve all the problems, but it did not always do so in the same way as people.

Evidence

Thomas (1974) argued that people should experience difficulties in solving a problem at those points at which it is necessary to make a move that temporarily *increases* the distance between the current state and the goal state. In other words, problem solvers should struggle when heuristics are inadequate. He used a variant of the missionaries and cannibals problem based on hobbits and orcs. In the standard form of this problem, three missionaries and three cannibals need to be transported across a river in a boat which can hold only two people. The number of cannibals on either bank of the river must never exceed the number of missionaries, because then the cannibals would eat the missionaries. One move involves transferring one cannibal and one missionary back to the starting point. This move seems to be going away from the goal or solution, and so is inconsistent with the hill-climbing heuristics. As predicted, it was at this point that the participants experienced severe difficulties. However, General Problem Solver did *not* find this move especially difficult.

Thomas (1974) also obtained evidence that participants set up subgoals. They would often carry out a block of several moves at increasing speed, followed by a long pause before embarking on another rapid sequence of moves. This suggested that participants were dividing up the problem into three or four major subgoals.

Simon and Reed (1976) studied a more complex version of the missionaries and cannibals problem. It can be solved in 11 moves, but on average participants took 30 moves to solve it. There was evidence that the participants initially adopted a *balancing strategy*, in which they simply tried to ensure there were equal numbers of missionaries and cannibals on each side of the river. After a while, the participants shifted to the *means–ends strategy*, in which the focus was on moving more people to the goal side of the river. Finally, the participants used an *anti-looping heuristic* designed to avoid any moves reversing the immediately preceding move.

Anzai and Simon (1979) studies the strategies used by a single participant in four successive attempts to solve a five-disc version of the Tower of Hanoi (see Figure 13.6). On each of the four attempts, the participant used a different strategy, becoming progressively more efficient at solving the problem. Initially, the participant explored the problem space without much planning of moves. Search at this stage seemed to be guided by avoidance of certain states rather than moves towards definite goal/subgoal states. Anzai and Simon argued the participant was using general *domain-independent strategies*. These strategies included a *loop-avoidance strategy* to avoid returning to previously visited states and a heuristic strategy preferring shorter over longer sequences of moves to achieve a goal. These general strategies allowed the participant to learn better sequences of moves, and these sequences were carried forward to be used in later attempts to solve the problem. Anzai and Simon (1979) developed an adaptive production system model that learned in the same manner. This model could create new production rules that were used to solve the problem on a later attempt. From Anzai and Simon's research, learning on the Tower of Hanoi initially involves general, domain-independent heuristics or rules of thumb, which then allow one to learn domain-dependent or domain-specific heuristics.

Evaluation

The relevant experimental evidence indicates that the Newell and Simon approach works well with several well-defined problems. Their theory also has the advantage that it allows us to specify the shortest sequence of moves from the initial state to the goal state. Thus, we can see exactly *when* and *how* an individual participant's performance deviates from the ideal.

In general terms, the theoretical approach is consistent with our knowledge of human information processing. For example, we have limited working memory capacity (see Chapter 6), and that helps to explain why we typically use heuristics or rules of thumb such as means–ends analysis and hill climbing rather than algorithms.

In spite of its successes, there are some limitations with Newell and Simon's approach. First, the General Problem Solver is better than humans at remembering what has happened on a problem. However, it is inferior to humans at planning future moves: it focuses on only a single move whereas humans often plan small sequences of moves (Greeno, 1974).

Second, most problems in everyday life are ill defined, and so are very different from those studied by Newell and Simon. Solving the ill-defined problems of real life typically depends much more on possessing relevant specific knowledge and expertise.

Third, the theoretical approach is best suited to multiple-move problems requiring serial processing. As a result, it is not well equipped to account for performance on insight problems.

Fourth, Newell and Simon paid little attention to individual differences in strategy and speed of problem solving. For example, Handley, Capon, Copp, and Harper (2002) found that individual differences in spatial working memory capacity predicted solution on the Tower of Hanoi task, whereas verbal working memory capacity did not. The greater relevance of spatial ability than verbal ability on this task is not predicted by General Problem Solver.

Progress monitoring theory

MacGregor, Ormerod, and Chronicle (2001) have proposed a progress monitoring theory resembling Newell and Simon's (1972) theoretical approach. Two general problem-solving heuristics are of central importance within progress monitoring theory:

(1) Maximisation heuristic: Problem solvers try to make as much headway as possible towards goal attainment on each move; this is a form of means–ends analysis.
(2) Progress monitoring: Problem solvers assess their rate of progress towards the goal. Criterion failure occurs if the rate of progress seems to be too slow to solve the problem within the maximum permissible number of moves.

What happens when problem solvers experience criterion failure? According to MacGregor et al. (2001), criterion failure leads problem solvers to seek an alternative strategy, and this in turn sometimes leads to insight. Thus, criterion failure acts as a "wake-up call". Suppose participants are given a task on which they nearly all initially adopt an inappropriate strategy. Conditions in which criterion failure is experienced rapidly should lead to faster problem solution than conditions in which criterion failure is only experienced later on.

According to Ohlsson's (1992) representational change theory (discussed earlier), the key to developing insight on many problems is constraint relaxation. In other words, problem solvers need to realise that the range of permissible moves is greater than they had imagined. According to progress monitoring theory, constraint relaxation is often necessary but is not sufficient. More specifically, constraint relaxation will facilitate problem solution much more for individuals experiencing criterion failure than for those who do not.

Evidence

In an earlier section on representational change theory, we discussed a study by MacGregor et al. (2001) on the nine-dot problem (see Figure 13.4). The task is to draw four connecting lines to cover all the dots without lifting the pen or pencil from the paper. It has generally been assumed that the main difficulty people have with this problem is that they impose the constraint on themselves of keeping all the lines within the confines of the square. MacGregor et al. found that telling participants to go outside the boundaries of the square improved performance. However, of crucial relevance to progress monitoring theory, those constraint-removing instructions were much more effective when given to participants who had experienced criterion failure than to those who had not. Thus, criterion failure was important in making people receptive to the constraint-removing instructions.

Ormerod, MacGregor, and Chronicle (2002) obtained similar findings using the eight-coin problem (see Figure 13.7). The task is to move two coins so that each coin touches exactly three others, but be warned that this problem is harder than it looks! The key insight required to solve the problem is to think in three-dimensional terms (i.e., putting coins on top of other coins) rather than two-dimensional ones. Anyone who failed to solve the problem after several minutes was provided with hints (e.g., "The solution requires the use of three dimensions").

As you can see in Figure 13.7, four versions of the eight-coin problem were used. In two versions, one coin was presented on top of another coin, thus presumably making it much easier to gain the key insight into the problem. There was another important difference between the various versions: there were a number of ways of moving a coin in two dimensions to touch exactly three others for the versions on the right-hand side of

FIGURE 13.7

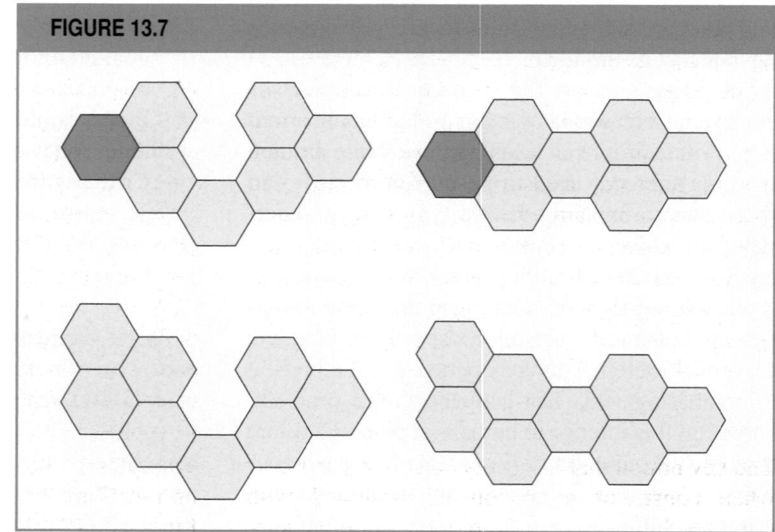

Four versions of the eight-coin problem. The dark shading indicates that one coin was on top of another coin. The figures on the right have valid two-dimensional moves, whereas those on the left do not. From Ormerod et al. (2002). Copyright © 2002 by the American Psychological Association. Reprinted with permission.

Figure 13.7, but there were no legitimate ways of doing that with the versions on the left-hand side. According to progress monitoring theory, participants given the no-move-available versions should have experienced much more criterion failure than those given the move-available versions, and so should have found it easier to solve the problem. That is exactly what was found. Surprisingly, the strong visual hint of having one coin on top of another at the start of the problem did not help participants to solve the problem.

Jones (2003) carried out an experiment on the car-park game, in which the crucial problem involved manoeuvring a taxi out of a car park when the way to the exit is obstructed by other cars. Most people find this problem difficult because it is necessary to move the taxi *before* an exit route has been created. The crucial problem was preceded by practice problems, none of which required problem solvers to move the taxi to create an exit route. There were various conditions designed to maximise (or minimise) the probability that knowledge gained from the practice problems would be applied to the crucial car-park problem.

Jones (2003) argued that progress monitoring theory and representational change theory (discussed earlier) would make different predictions. According to the progress monitoring theory, performance is governed by the attempt to reduce the difference between the current state of the problem and the final state. As a result, the nature of the practice problems should have no effect on the crucial problem. From the perspective of the representational change theory, performance on the crucial problem will suffer if experience with the practice problems leads participants to assume the taxi does not need to be moved to create an exit. There were large differences across conditions in the percentages of participants solving the car-park problem, thus supporting representational change theory rather than progress monitoring theory.

Evaluation

The key notion that insight is most likely to occur when constraint relaxation is combined with criterion failure has received good empirical support (e.g., MacGregor et al., 2001; Ormerod et al., 2002). Thus, problem solvers who realise that means–ends analysis is proving unsuccessful are more responsive to changing their strategy than are those for whom means–ends analysis is at least partially successful. To oversimplify a little, you need to experience real failure to maximise the chances that you will alter your approach to a problem. Progress monitoring theory resembles the General Problem Solver (e.g., with its maximisation heuristic), but has the advantage of considering motivational factors triggering strategy change in some detail.

In spite of the fact that criterion failure is an important factor in problem solving, it is clear that several other factors are important. The findings of Jones (2003) indicate that problem solvers' previous experience with related problems influences the kinds of problem representations they produce. These representations in turn affect problem-solving performance.

It may prove fruitful to combine elements of the progress monitoring theory and the representational change theory (see Jones, 2003). More specifically, progressive monitoring theory predicts *when* problem solvers will seek insight, and representational change theory predicts *how* insight is achieved.

TRANSFER OF TRAINING

Suppose you have solved a particular problem in the past, and are now confronted by a similar problem. You would probably assume your previous experience would permit you to solve the current problem faster and more easily than would otherwise have been the case. In the jargon of psychologists, this is known as **positive transfer**. However, learning to solve a given problem in the past sometimes disrupts and slows down our ability to solve a similar current problem. As you have probably guessed, this state of affairs is known as **negative transfer**. We encountered examples of negative transfer earlier in studies on functional fixedness (e.g., Duncker, 1945) and Luchins' (1942) water-jar problems.

Panel 13.1: Content: What is transferred
1. Learned skill (specific vs. general)
2. Performance change (e.g., speed vs. accuracy)
3. Memory demands (e.g., recognition vs. recall of key information)
Context: Comparison between learning and transfer
1. Knowledge domain (similar vs. dissimilar knowledge base)
2. Physical context (similar vs. dissimilar learning environment)
3. Temporal context (short vs. long time between learning and transfer)
4. Functional context (similar vs. dissimilar purpose of learned behaviour)
5. Social context (e.g., both individual vs. one individual and one social)
6. Modality (e.g., both visual vs. one visual and one auditory)

The content and context factors determine the extent to which positive transfer is found. It is assumed that transfer will be greater when the training and transfer contexts are similar rather than dissimilar. Based on Barnett and Ceci (2002).

It may seem as if transfer of training is of little practical interest and importance. In fact, nothing could be further from the truth! Consider, for example, the value of education. Nearly everyone involved in education firmly believes that what students learn at school and at university facilitates learning in their future lives. In other words, educators assume that there is considerable positive transfer from the classroom or lecture theatre to subsequent forms of learning (e.g., work-related skills). Educationalists are especially interested in **far transfer** (positive transfer to a dissimilar context), because that is of direct relevance to everyday life.

In spite of the importance of far transfer, most research has focused on **near transfer** (positive transfer to a similar context). In such research, what has been studied is the immediate application of knowledge and skills from one situation to a similar one. This approach (which Bransford & Schwartz, 1999, labelled the direct-application theory of transfer) differs from most real-life situations in that participants on the transfer task are not permitted to make use of external support (e.g., texts; friends; feedback from others). Bransford and Schwartz (1999) argued that a preferable approach is preparation for future learning, in which the emphasis is on participants' ability to learn in new, support-rich situations. Within this approach, learning is regarded as an active and constructive process, and the importance of **metacognition** (beliefs and knowledge about one's own cognitive processes) is emphasised.

Barnett and Ceci (2002) argued that two major factors are involved in transfer studies: (1) content (i.e., what is transferred from one task to another); and (2) context (i.e., when and where knowledge is transferred from and to). They also identified various dimensions relevant to each of these factors (see Panel 13.1). There has been relatively little systematic research with respect to several of these dimensions. As mentioned above, it is especially unfortunate that most studies have tested transfer soon after training (temporal context), given that what matters most for education is transfer lasting for several years.

We will first of all consider far transfer (including whether it actually exists) with reference to the theoretical approach of Barnett and Ceci (2002). After that, we will move on to a discussion of analogical problem solving. Research in this area has proved a rich source of information on the factors increasing or decreasing near transfer.

Far transfer

Some of the strongest evidence that there can be large far transfer effects was reported in a study by Chen and Klahr (1999). Children aged between 7 and 10 years of age were given training in designing and evaluating experiments in the domain of physical science. Of central importance in the children's learning was the control of variables strategy, involving the ability to create sound experiments and to distinguish between confounded and unconfounded experiments.

Chen and Klahr (1999) carried out a test of far transfer 7 months after the training, including a control group of children who had not received training. This test assessed mastery of the control of variables strategy in five new domains (plant growth; biscuit making; model aeroplanes; drink sales; running speed). The children who had received the previous training were much more likely than control children to perform well on the test (see Figure 13.8).

Evidence that metacognition is useful in producing far transfer was reported by De Corte (2003). Students studying business economics were provided with training over a 7-month period in two metacognitive skills: orienting and self-judging. Orienting involves preparing oneself to solve problems by thinking about possible goals and cognitive activities, and self-judging is a motivational activity designed to assist students to assess accurately the effort required for successful task completion.

De Corte (2003) found on the subsequent learning of statistics that students who had received the training performed better than those who had not. Within the group that had been trained, orienting and self-judging behaviour were both positively correlated with academic performance in statistics.

Barnett and Ceci (2002) reviewed the evidence on the efforts on transfer of the six contextual factors they identified as important (see Panel 13.1). In general, the findings provide support for their theoretical framework. For example, Spencer and Weisberg (1986) studied the effects of physical context on transfer by arranging for the experimenter to be the same or different during training and transfer. This apparently small change in the physical context significantly reduced the amount of transfer.

Herrnstein, Nickerson, de Sanchez, and Swets (1986) considered modality effects by assessing

FIGURE 13.8

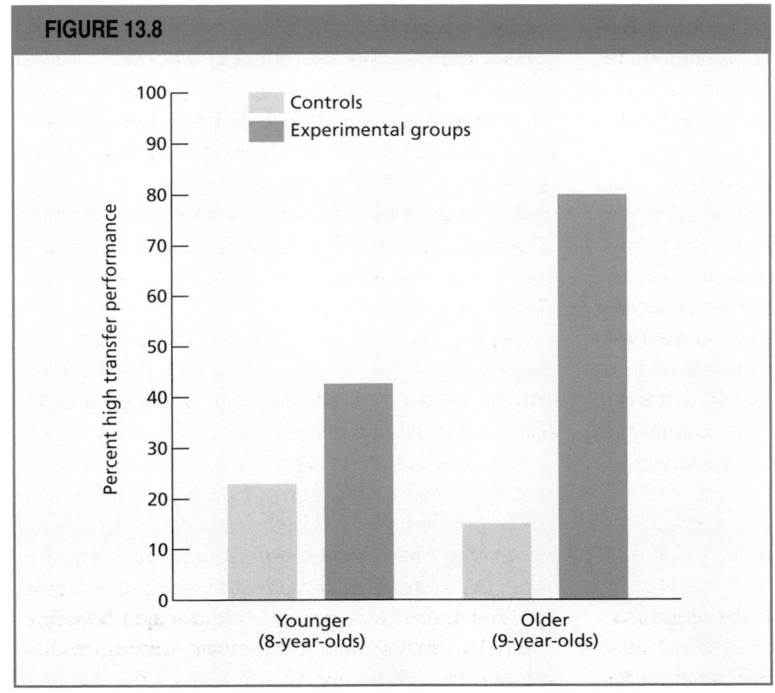

Percentage of children performing at a high level on the transfer test (13 or more out of 15) as a function of age (8 vs. 9) and previous relevant training (control vs. experimental). Based on data from Chen and Klahr (1999).

transfer using various measures such as multiple-choice tests, open-ended written questions, questions read out by the teacher, a practical design task, and an oral argumentation task. Transfer effects were obtained with most of the tests, but the greatest transfer was generally obtained on tests most resembling the original training.

As predicted by Barnett and Ceci (2002), the specificity–generality of learned skills influences the amount of transfer. Bassok and Holyoak (1989) found that the same algebraic formula was generally learned in a general form when acquired in the context of algebra but in a specific form when acquired in the context of physics. There was greater transfer to new situations when the initial learning was general rather than specific.

The most obvious omission from Barnett and Ceci's (2002) theoretical approach is a full consideration of individual differences. However, while they did not explicitly include intelligence as a factor determining the extent of transfer, they did suggest that its effects might manifest themselves via their various content and contextual factors. For example, more intelligent learners may acquire more general learned skills than less intelligent ones in a given training environment. Evidence that individual differences in intelligence are important in determining the amount of transfer was reported by Davidson and Sternberg (1984). Children of high intelligence performed at the same level as those of average intelligence on logical-mathematical problems when they had not been given any prior examples. However, gifted children showed substantial positive transfer when exposed to a single prior example. In contrast, average children required several prior examples and fully explicit information about the relevance of those examples in order to show significant positive transfer. In a study discussed above, De Corte (2003) found that training in metacognitive skills produced more transfer among the most intelligent students.

Evaluation

There is reasonable support for the major assumptions made by Barnett and Ceci (2002). First, as they concluded, "Instances of far transfer, although not frequent, are documentable and may even be predictable once the relevant dimensions are specified" (Barnett & Ceci, 2002, p. 634). Second, the extent of positive transfer depends on several of the content and contextual factors suggested by Barnett and Ceci. More generally, Barnett and Ceci have made an impressive attempt to provide a coherent framework within which transfer effects can be understood.

We will consider three limitations of this theoretical approach. First, the available evidence does not provide a searching test of whether far transfer can generally be obtained. As Barnett and Ceci (2002, p. 631) admitted, "None of the studies to date has tested for transfer that would be classified as far along *all* of the dimensions described, and indeed none tested transfer that was far on even a majority of the dimensions."

Second, Barnett and Ceci de-emphasised *interactions* between the various content and contextual factors. For example, Chen (1996) studied the effects of similarity of knowledge domain on children's transfer in analogical problem solving. The key finding was that knowledge domain similarity interacted with the generality of learned skills: transfer depended on similarity of knowledge domain for children whose initial learning was concrete and specific but not for children whose learning was abstract and general.

Third, there is evidence that intelligence influences transfer (e.g., Davidson & Sternberg, 1984; De Corte, 2003). There is an urgent need to consider more fully the effects of intelligence on transfer, and the ways in which these effects are produced.

Analogical problem solving

Much research on positive and negative transfer (especially near transfer) has involved analogical problem solving, in which the solver uses similarities between the current problem and one or more problems solved in the past. Problem solving by analogy has proved important in the history of science. Examples include the computer model of human information processing, the billiard-ball model of gases, and the hydraulic model of the blood circulation system.

Under what circumstances do people make successful use of previous problems in order to solve a current problem? What is crucial is that they notice (and make use of) *similarities* between the current problem and a previous one. According to Chen (2002), there are three main types of similarity between problems:

(1) Superficial similarity: Solution-irrelevant details (e.g., specific objects) are common to both problems.
(2) Structural similarity: Causal relations among some of the main components are shared by both problems.
(3) Procedural similarity: Procedures for turning the solution principle into concrete operations are common to both problems.

As we will see, these forms of similarity all influence analogical reasoning.

Evidence

Needham and Begg (1991) addressed the issue of how to increase the chances that people would use analogies when appropriate. Initially, they presented participants with a series of training problems. Some participants were told to adopt a problem-oriented approach towards the problems, focusing on understanding the solution to each problem. Other participants were told to take a memory-oriented approach, focusing on remembering the problems. After that, the participants were given several further test problems related to the original problems. Participants who had adopted the problem-oriented approach solved 90% of the test problems, whereas those who had adopted the memory-oriented approach solved only 69%. Thus, understanding is much more important than memory in producing effective analogical reasoning.

Gick and Holyoak (1980) used Duncker's radiation problem, in which a patient with a malignant tumour in his stomach can only be saved by a special kind of ray. However, a ray of sufficient strength to destroy the tumour will also destroy the healthy tissue, whereas a ray that will not harm healthy tissue will be too weak to destroy the tumour.

Only about 10% of the participants given the problem on its own managed to solve it. The answer is to direct several low-intensity rays at the tumour from different directions. However, other participants were given three stories to memorise, one of which was structurally similar to the radiation problem. This story was about a general capturing a fortress by having his army converge at the same time on the fortress along several different roads. When the participants were told that this story was relevant to solving the radiation problem, about 80% of them solved it (see Figure 13.9). When the hint was not offered, however, only about 40% solved the problem, suggesting that they tended not to make use of the analogy

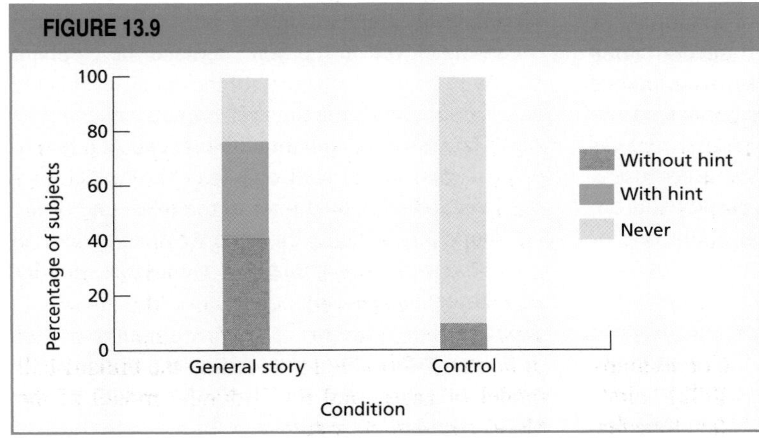

Some of the results from Gick and Holyoak (1980, Experiment 4) showing the percentage of subjects who solved the radiation problem when they were given an analogy (general-story condition) or were just asked to solve the problem (control condition). Note that just under half of the subjects in the general-story condition had to be given a hint to use the story analogue before they solved the problem.

provided by the story. Thus, the fact that relevant information is stored in long-term memory is no guarantee that it will be used.

Why did most participants in the Gick and Holyoak (1980) study fail to make spontaneous use of the relevant story they had memorised? Keane (1987) hypothesised that it might be because of the lack of superficial similarities between the story and the problem. He presented participants with either a semantically close story (about a surgeon using rays on a cancer) or a semantically remote story (the general-and-fortress story). They were given this story during a lecture, and were then asked to take part in an experiment several days later. Of those participants given the close analogy, 88% spontaneously retrieved it when given the radiation problem. In contrast, only 12% of those who had been given the remote analogy spontaneously retrieved it.

Evidence that even experienced problem solvers are influenced by superficial problem features was reported by Blessing and Ross (1996). They presented various problems in which the superficial features or content were either *consistent* or *inconsistent* with the underlying structure. The participants took longer to solve problems and made more errors with inconsistent problems than with consistent ones. This happened because the experienced problem solvers were unable to focus only on a problem's structure, but were also influenced by its superficial features. This may well have been advantageous in evolutionary terms. As Gentner, Ratterman, and Forbus (1993, p. 567) pointed out, "If something looks like a tiger, it probably is a tiger."

Blanchette and Dunbar (2000) argued that it would be wrong to conclude that most people focus on the superficial similarities between problems at the expense of structural similarities. As they pointed out, most laboratory studies use a "reception paradigm" in which the participants are provided with detailed information about one or more possible analogies before being presented with a current problem. In contrast, what typically happens in real life is that people produce their own analogies rather than being given them. Blanchette and Dunbar compared performance using the standard reception paradigm and the more realistic "production paradigm", in which participants generated their own analogies. As in previous research, participants in the reception paradigm often selected analogies based on superficial similarities. However, those in the production paradigm tended to produce analogies sharing structural features with the current problem. Blanchette and Dunbar (2000, p. 109) concluded that, "The reception paradigm may constrain the search for structural relations and provide a picture of analogical reasoning that underestimates the subjects' abilities to use deep structural features in the retrieval of source analogues. In real world contexts, people generate their own analogies."

It has often been assumed that individuals who realise that a current problem has important similarities with a previous problem are almost bound to solve it. However, Chen (2002) disputed that assumption. He argued that people may use a previous problem to gain insight into the type of solution needed on a current problem, but may still be unable to solve it if the two problems do not share procedural similarity.

Chen (2002) supported the above argument by studying the weigh-the-elephant problem: a boy needs to weigh an elephant, but only has access to scales weighing objects up to 200 pounds. The general solution is based on weight equivalence, and involves using smaller objects to equal the weight of the elephant, and then weighing the smaller objects separately on the scales. This solution can be implemented by using two different sets of procedures or operations:

(1) Put the elephant into a boat and mark the water level on the boat; replace the elephant with smaller objects until the water level is the same; weigh the smaller objects separately.
(2) Harness the elephant with one end of a length of rope which is thrown over the branch of a tree; attach a container to the other end of the rope and balance the rope by placing several objects in the container; weigh the smaller objects separately.

Participants provided with an initial story resembling the weigh-the-elephant problem in both structural and procedural similarity performed much better on the problem than did those provided with an initial story containing only structural similarity to the problem. Many participants in the latter condition grasped the general solution based on weight equivalence, but could not find appropriate procedures to solve the problem. Thus, effective analogies often need to possess procedural as well as structural similarity to a current problem.

Evaluation

Much progress has been made in identifying the factors determining whether people will use relevant past knowledge when engaged in analogical problem solving. There is reasonable evidence that superficial, structural, and procedural similarity between past problems and a current problem are all important.

There are at least three major limitations with most research on analogical problem solving in the laboratory. First, analogical problems can often be solved simply by using an appropriate analogy provided earlier in the experiment. In everyday life, in contrast, the fit or match between previous knowledge and the current problem is typically imprecise. Second, the finding that many laboratory participants choose analogies based on superficial rather than structural similarities may *not* generalise to more realistic situations. As Blanchette and Dunbar (2000) found, people who have to generate their own analogies (as typically happens in real life) tend to produce ones sharing structural rather than superficial similarities with the current problem. Third, some people are much better than others at finding and using analogies. However, as yet little research has focused on individual differences in performance in analogical problem solving.

EXPERTISE

So far in this chapter we have mostly discussed studies in which the time available for learning has been short, the tasks involved relatively limited, and prior specific knowledge is not required. In the real world, however, people sometimes spend several years acquiring knowledge and skills in a given area (e.g., psychology; law; medicine). The end point of such long-term learning is the development of **expertise**, which is, "highly skilled, competent performance in one or more task domains [areas]" (Sternberg & Ben-Zeev, 2001, p. 365). We can, of course, study the processes involved on the road to achieving expertise. This involves the investigation of **skill acquisition**, defined as follows by Rosenbaum et al. (2001, p. 454):

> When we speak of a "skill" we mean an ability that allows a goal to be achieved within some domain with increasing likelihood as a result of practice. When we speak of "acquisition of skill" we refer to the attainment of those practice-related capabilities that contribute to the increased likelihood of goal achievement.

The development of expertise resembles problem solving, in that experts are extremely efficient at solving numerous problems in their area of expertise. However, as mentioned in the Introduction, most traditional research on problem solving involved "knowledge-lean" problems, meaning no special training or knowledge is required for the solution. In contrast, studies on expertise have typically used "knowledge-rich" problems, requiring much knowledge beyond that presented in the problem itself.

In this section of the chapter, we will first consider in detail one specific domain of expertise, namely, chess expertise. After that, we turn to two major theories of expertise. First, we discuss Anderson's Adaptive Control of Thought (ACT) theory, which deals with the processes involved in skill acquisition. Second, we analyse Ericsson's theoretical approach, according to which deliberate practice is the main requirement for the development of expertise.

Chess expertise

Why are some people much better than others at playing chess? Solso (1994) provided the obvious answer:

> Several years ago the late Bill Chase gave a talk on experts in which he promised to tell the audience what it would take to become a grand master chess player. His answer: "Practice." After the talk, I asked Chase how much practice. "Did I forget to say how much?" he asked quizzically. "Ten thousand hours."

What benefits occur as a result of practice? Expert chess players have very detailed information about chess positions stored in long-term memory, and this allows them to relate the position in the current game to previous games. This notion was first tested by DeGroot (1965), and then more thoroughly by Chase and Simon (1973a). DeGroot argued that if expert chess players have stored previous board positions, then this knowledge should be reflected in tasks measuring memory. He gave participants brief presentations (between 2 and 15 seconds) of board positions from actual games. After removing the board, he asked them to reconstruct the positions. Chess masters recalled the positions very accurately (91% correct), whereas less expert players made many more errors (41% correct). Thus, chess masters were better at recognising and encoding the various configurations of pieces than less expert players.

Chase and Simon (1973a) argued that chess players asked to memorise board positions would break them down into about seven **chunks** or units. Their key assumption was that the chunks formed by expert players contain more information than those of other players, because they can bring more chess knowledge to bear on the memory task. They asked three chess players to look at the position of the pieces on one board, and to reconstruct it on a second board with the first board still visible. Chase and Simon (1973a) calculated the size of the chunks being formed by taking account of the number of pieces placed on the second board after each glance at the first board. The most expert player (a master) had chunks averaging 2.5 pieces, whereas the novice had chunks averaging only 1.9 pieces. Subsequent evidence from Gobet and Simon (1998) suggests that Chase and Simon (1973a) substantially underestimated the chunk size of masters.

Two points need to be made here. First, the ability of expert chess players to reconstruct board positions might occur simply because they have generally better memories than non-experts. However, there is very little evidence that this is the case (see Gobet & Waters, 2003). Second, experts' good ability to remember board positions strongly suggests that they have relevant stored knowledge in long-term memory. However, it is hard to use such evidence to discover in detail what knowledge they possess.

Chase and Simon (1973b) argued in their chunking theory that a major advantage held by chess experts is that they have very large numbers of chess chunks stored in long-term memory. However, we should not assume the *only* advantage that chess experts have over novices is that they have stored information about tens of thousands of chess pieces. That would be like arguing that the only advantage that Shakespeare had over other writers was a larger vocabulary! As many researchers have argued (e.g., Holding & Reynolds, 1982), expert players also possess superior strategic processing skills to non-expert players.

Do the strategies used by human expert chess players resemble those used by computers? The answer is clearly no, because computer programs search through vastly more possible moves than human players. For example, Newell and Simon (1972) discussed a program called MANIAC which explored nearly one million moves at each turn. It considered each move to a depth of four turns (an initial move, an opponent's reply, a reply to this move, and the opponent's counter move). Even with this brute-force computation, it did not play chess well, and occasionally made serious mistakes.

Recent chess programs do almost unimaginable amounts of search. For example, Deep Blue considers 90 billion moves at each turn, at a rate of 9 billion per second! This vast amount of search allowed it to beat the then World Chess Champion, Garry Kasparov, in May 1997. All the evidence indicates the strategies of human chess players have nothing in common with the approach of Deep Blue. We turn now to template theory, which is a prominent account of human chess playing.

Template theory

Template theory represents a development and extension of chunk theory. As Gobet and Waters (2003) pointed out, there are two major weaknesses with chunking theory. First, the theory fails to relate mechanisms at the chunk level with the various higher-level representations used by expert chess players. Second, the theory predicts that it will take longer than is actually the case to encode chess positions.

Template theory overcomes the above weaknesses with chunking theory. According to template theory, chunks that are used frequently by chess players develop into more complex data structures known as templates. A **template** is a schematic structure more general than an actual board position. Each template consists of a *core* (very similar to the fixed information stored in chunks) plus *slots* (which contain variable information about pieces and locations). A template is larger than a chunk. It typically stores information relating to about 10 pieces, although it can be larger than that. The fact that templates contain slots means that templates are more flexible and adaptable than chunks.

According to template theory, outstanding chess players owe their excellence mostly to their superior template-based knowledge of chess. This knowledge can be accessed rapidly, and allows them to narrow down the possible moves they need to consider. In contrast, Holding and Reynolds (1982) emphasised the importance of strategic thinking and considering numerous possible moves. These theories can be tested by comparing the performance of an outstanding chess player when playing a single opponent and when playing simultaneously against up to eight opponents with very little time to make each move. According to template theory (but not more strategy-focused theories such as that of Holding & Reynolds, 1982), the greatly reduced time to search for future moves in the multiple-opponent situation should have little effect on an outstanding player's performance.

We will be considering two further predictions of template theory. First, it is assumed that expert chess players generally store away the precise board locations of pieces after studying a board position (Gobet & Simon, 2000). It is also assumed that chess pieces close together are more likely to be found in the same template than pieces further apart. Second, the theory predicts that expert chess players will have better recall of random chess positions than non-experts. The reason is that some patterns occur by chance even in random positions, and these patterns relate to template-based information.

Evidence

As predicted by template theory, expert chess players assess chess positions very rapidly. Charness et al. (2001) asked expert and intermediate chess players to study chess positions and identify the best move. Their first five eye fixations (lasting in total only about 1 second) were recorded. Even at this early stage in considering each board position, the experts were more likely than the intermediate players to fixate on tactically relevant pieces (80% vs. 64% of fixations).

What happens when an outstanding player plays simultaneous chess against several opponents? Gobet and Simon (1996c) considered the performance of Garry Kasparov, the ex-World Champion. As predicted by template theory, Gobet and Simon reported that his performance was only slightly affected by playing several games at the same time. However, Lassiter (2000) disputed Gobet and Simon's arguments. He pointed out that Kasparov's playing strength was reduced by about 100 Elo points (a measure of playing strength) when he was engaged in simultaneous chess rather than playing a single opponent. This reduction is most plausibly attributed to reduced opportunities to search for (and to evaluate) future moves.

Lassiter (2000) also discussed matches in which expert players competed against chess-playing computers. When the game must be completed in 25 minutes, computers gain about 100 Elo points relative to their human opponents. More strikingly, computers gain 200 or more Elo points when the game is limited to 5 minutes. According to Lassiter (2000, p. 172), "The tendency for chess-playing computers to become relatively stronger at shorter time controls is most likely due to the

FIGURE 13.10

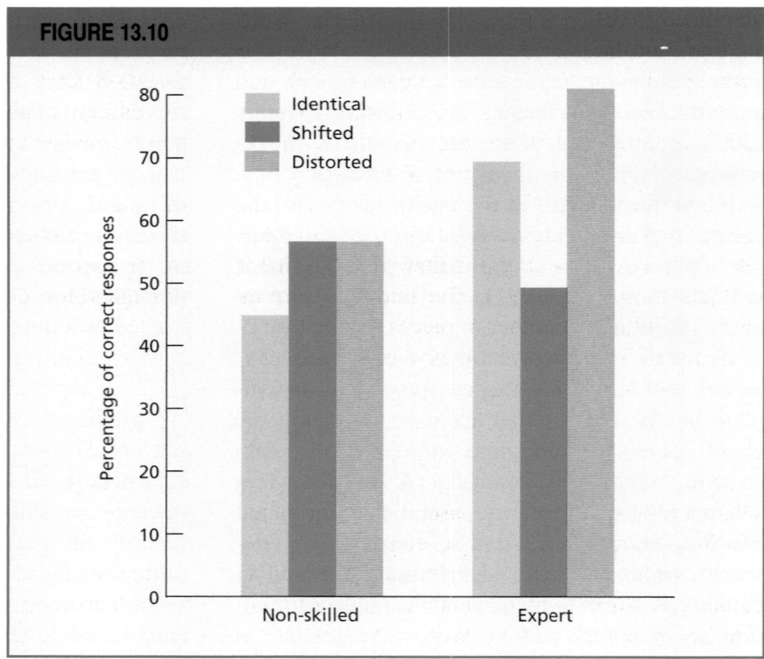

Percentage of correct responses on a recognition test as a function of skill group (non-skilled vs. expert) and condition (identical, shifted, or distorted). Data from McGregor and Howes (2002).

fact that a human's ability to engage in search-evaluation is more hampered by increasingly higher time constraints than is a computer's."

According to template theory, chess players who study a board position typically recall the precise squares on the board occupied by given pieces, and the pieces contained within a template tend to be those close together on the board. In general, the findings support these two predictions (e.g., Chase & Simon, 1973a; Gobet & Simon, 1996a). However, McGregor and Howes (2002) identified an important limitation with these findings. They pointed out that the participants in most studies were asked to *memorise* board positions, whereas actual chess playing focuses much more on the need to *evaluate* board positions. McGregor and Howes argued that chess players evaluating a board position would probably remember the attack/defence relations among pieces rather than their precise location.

McGregor and Howes (2002) asked expert and non-skilled chess players to evaluate 30 chess positions (decide which colour was winning or if there was no advantage). After that, there was a test of recognition memory on which the chess players had to decide whether or not they had seen each board position before. Some board positions were *identical* to those presented previously, others were *shifted* (all pieces moved one square horizontally), and others were *distorted* (only one piece was moved one square, but this changed the attack/defence relations among the pieces). The findings are shown in Figure 13.10. Expert chess players had much better memory for attack/defence relations than for the precise board locations of pieces. In another experiment, McGregor and Howes found the structure of chunks is determined more by attack/defence relations among pieces than by proximity of pieces.

We turn now to recall of random chess positions. It will be remembered that template theory predicts that expert players will have better recall than non-experts of such positions. Support for this position was reported by Gobet and Simon (1996b). They carried out a meta-analysis combining the findings from several studies, and found there was a small effect of skill on random board positions. However, Gobet and Waters (2003) pointed out that the random board positions used in these studies were not totally random. More specifically, the positions of the pieces were random, but the pieces placed on the board were not selected at random (e.g., two kings were always present). Gobet and Waters used truly random positions (i.e., random pieces as well as piece locations), and argued, "TT [template theory] predicts a skill effect on the . . . truly random stimuli because low-level patterns arise by chance in these stimuli, and these patterns facilitate recall" (Gobet & Waters, 2003, p. 1091). The findings were as predicted, with the number of pieces recalled varying from 14.8 for the most expert players to 12.0 for the least expert.

Evaluation

Outstanding chess players possess much more template-based knowledge of chess positions than non-experts, and this gives them a substantial advantage when playing chess. For example, template-based knowledge may explain how it is that expert chess players can identify key pieces in a board position in under 1 second (Charness et al., 2001). It also helps to explain how outstanding chess players can play effectively under considerable time pressure or when playing several opponents at the same time (e.g., Gobet & Simon, 1996c). While template theory evolved out of chunking theory, it is easier to account for outstanding chess-playing ability with reference to templates (large, flexible structures) than with reference to chunks (smaller, rigid structures). Template theory also successfully predicts that template knowledge allows expert players to recall even truly random chess positions better than non-experts (Gobet & Waters, 2003).

There are at least two limitations with template theory. First, the precise information stored in long-term memory remains controversial. For example, it is assumed within the theory that chunks consist mainly of pieces that were close together on the board, and that the precise locations of individual pieces are stored. However, attack/defence relations seem to be more important (McGregor & Howes, 2002).

Second, the finding that the performance of even experts and the ex-World Champion suffers when they play under time pressure or against several opponents at the same time (Lassiter, 2000) suggests that outstanding chess performance depends on more than rapid access to relevant stored templates. Hatano and Inagaki's (1986) distinction between routine and adaptive expertise may be relevant here. **Routine expertise** is involved when a chess player can solve familiar problems rapidly and efficiently, whereas **adaptive expertise** is involved when a player has to develop strategies for deciding what to do when confronted by a novel board position. Template theory may be more relevant to routine expertise than to adaptive expertise.

THEORIES OF EXPERTISE

Several theories on the development of expertise have been proposed over the years. In this section, we will concern ourselves with two of the most influential of such theories. First, we discuss Anderson's ACT theory, which is a computational approach to learning and expertise. Second, we consider Ericsson's theoretical ideas on deliberate practice. We all know practice plays an important role in the development of expertise, but Ericsson has tried to clarify the conditions that are necessary in order for practice to produce expertise.

Anderson's ACT theory

Anderson (e.g., 1983, 1990, 1993, 1996) has produced various models designed to account for the development of expertise. All these models are based on a rather similar cognitive architecture known as the Adaptive Control of Thought (ACT), and so they are called ACTE, ACT*, and ACT-R. In ACT-R, the "R" stands for Rational. According to Anderson's (1990, p. 28) General Principle of Rationality, "The cognitive system operates at all times to optimise the adaptation of the behaviour of the organism."

At the heart of the ACT approach are three interconnected systems (see Figure 13.11):

- Declarative memory: This consists of a semantic network of interconnected concepts.

FIGURE 13.11

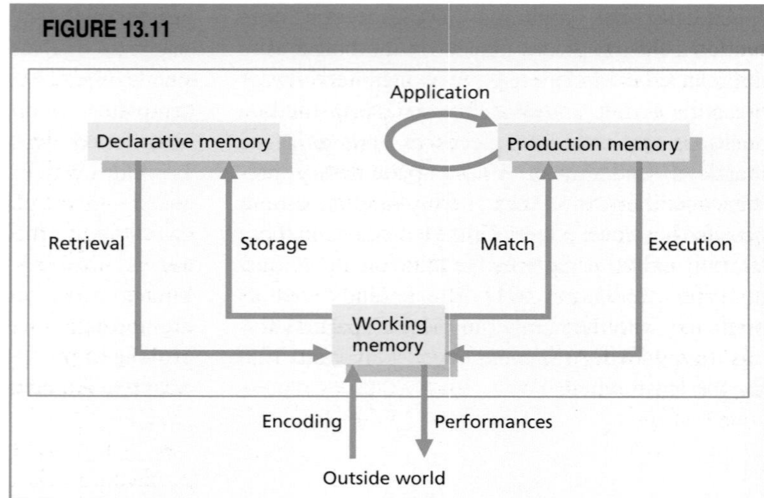

A schematic diagram of the major components and interlinking processes used in Anderson's (1983, 1993) ACT models. Reprinted by permission of the author.

- Procedural or production memory: This consists of production rules. **Production rules** are "if . . . then" or condition–action rules: whenever the initial condition is satisfied, the appropriate action follows (e.g., "If you see a friend, then you smile").
- Working memory: This contains information that is currently active (see Chapter 6).

There are important differences between declarative and procedural knowledge. Declarative knowledge is stored in chunks or small packets of knowledge, and is consciously accessible. It can be used across a wide range of situations. For example, suppose you have acquired a considerable amount of declarative knowledge about attention. You can use this information flexibly in a seminar group, in an essay, or in an examination essay. In contrast, it is often not possible to gain conscious access to procedural knowledge, which is used automatically whenever a production rule matches the current contents of working memory. The use of production rules is tied to specific situations (e.g., we only use production rules about subtraction when given a suitable mathematical problem), which makes it less flexible.

Anderson's crucial assumption is that skill acquisition typically involves knowledge compilation. What happens with **knowledge compilation** is a progressive shift from the use of declarative knowledge to that of procedural knowledge, and an increase in automaticity. A clear example of knowledge compilation is the development of touch-typing skills. Typing speed increases greatly with practice, with a fairly skilled typist making one keystroke every 60 milliseconds. The *nature* as well as the *speed* of the processes involved change with practice. As Fitts and Posner (1967) pointed out, typists initially rely on rules of which they are consciously aware (e.g., move the index finger of the left hand to the right to type the letter g). These rules are stored in what we would now call declarative memory. Eventually, typing becomes fast, accurate, and automatic, and depends only on procedural memory. For example, one of the authors has typed about four million words in his life, but finds it very hard to tell anyone where any given letter is on the keyboard!

What processes are involved in knowledge compilation? First, there is **proceduralisation**, which involves the creation of specific production rules. Production rules reduce or eliminate the necessity to search through long-term memory during skilled performance. For example, as a result of proceduralisation, and the development of production rules, typists do not need to ask themselves where the letters are on the keyboard. Second, there is **composition**, which improves performance by reducing a repeated sequence of actions to a more efficient single sequence.

Anderson has emphasised two aspects of production rules. First, there is an important asymmetry in production rules: the conditions of rules cause the actions to occur, but the actions do not cause the conditions to fire. Thus, the direction of causality is from condition to action rather than the reverse. Second, there is the **principle of use specificity** (Anderson, 1993): practice leads to the creation of rather specific production rules, and any given production rule will only lead to action when its condition (i.e., the "if . . ." part of the rule) is satisfied. As a result, there is little positive transfer from one task to another when the conditions change.

Evidence

Much research suggests that extended practice on most tasks leads to increased use of automatic processes (Chapter 5). For example, consider a study by Zbrodoff (1995), in which participants solved alphabet arithmetic problems. A sample problem is S + 3 = ?, which involves working three letters through the alphabet to produce "V" as the answer. The number of letters needed to be added on (the addendum) varied between 2 and 4. Initially, performance was fastest when the addendum was 2 and slowest when it was 4 (see Figure 13.12), because the participants were working through the alphabet letter by letter. After prolonged practice, the participants produced the answers "automatically" based on their past experience, and there was then no effect of addendum size. Thus, participants had switched to use of production rules.

Some neuroimaging evidence is consistent with the general ACT approach. Raichle (1998) used PET and fMRI to assess brain activity while

FIGURE 13.12

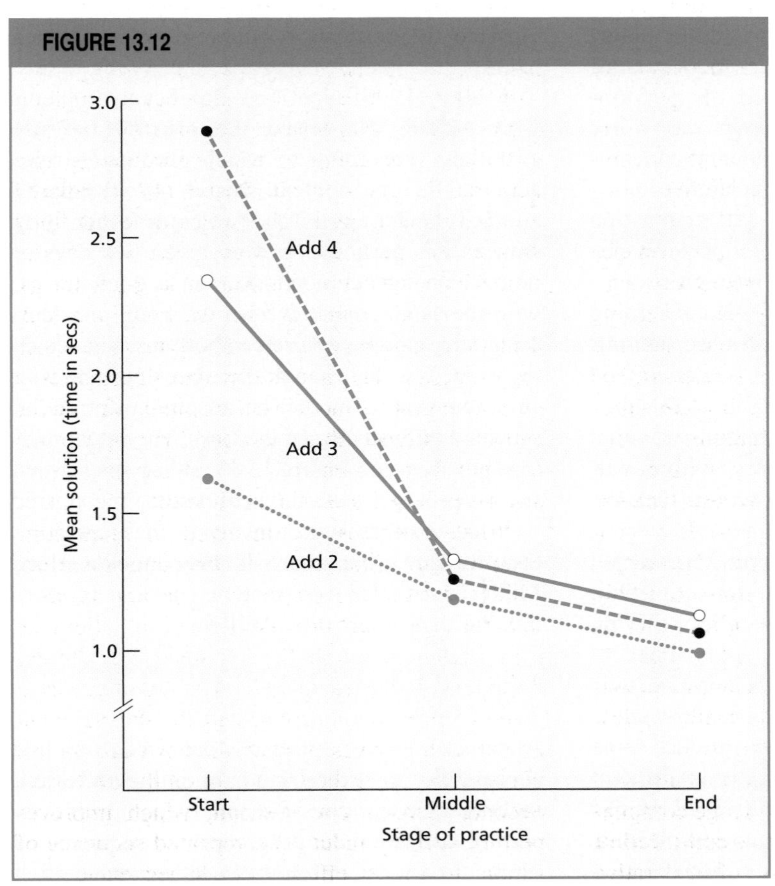

Speed of solution of alphabet arithmetic problems as a function of stage of practice and size of addendum (add 2, 3, or 4). Data from Zbrodoff (1995).

participants gained practice in performing various tasks. Initially there was much activity in brain areas involved in planning (e.g., left prefrontal cortex; left temporal cortex; anterior cingulate cortex). However, far fewer areas were active after practice, perhaps because of the increased usage of procedural memory.

According to ACT theory, skilled performance depends on procedural rather than declarative knowledge. Might skilled performance be disrupted more in individuals who access declarative knowledge than in those who do not? This prediction was tested by Masters (1992), who gave participants considerable practice in putting (400 putts). Some of them (explicit learning) were encouraged to acquire much declarative knowledge about putting by reading detailed instructions on putting before starting to practice. In contrast, other participants (implicit learning) were given no special instructions. Both groups were then put under pressure by being told the money they received would depend on their performance in a final test session. As predicted, the performance of the explicit learning group was worse than it had been, whereas that of the implicit learning group improved. Presumably declarative knowledge from an earlier stage of skill acquisition was responsible for the much poorer performance of the explicit group than of the implicit group.

One of the assumptions of ACT-R concerning production rules is that conditions fire actions, but actions do not fire conditions. Anderson and Fincham (1994) tested this using the LISP programming language. Their key finding was that there was the predicted asymmetry, with conditions being much better at firing actions than the opposite.

Some limitations of the ACT approach emerged in a study by Koedinger and Anderson (1990). They focused on experts given the task of solving proofs in geometry. The experts spent much of their time planning at a rather abstract or schematic level, and tended to skip the same steps while performing the task. These findings produce some problems for ACT theory. First, it is difficult within the theory to understand *why* the schemas formed by experts are so well organised. Second, as Koedinger and Anderson (1990, p. 545) pointed out with reference to ACT theory, "We would not expect any regularity in the kinds of steps that would be skipped . . . However, such a regularity is exactly what we observed of subjects." The problem solving of the experts was more systematic and at a higher level of abstraction than would have been predicted by ACT theory.

Another limitation with the ACT approach emerged in a study by Anderson (1993). Anderson presented participants with maps on a computer screen. These maps included a road system, a starting point, a destination point, and various intermediate locations. The participants could "walk", "drive", or a mixture of both. There were some similarities in the performance of the human participants and the ACT-R model of navigation. However, ACT-R reached the destination in fewer moves than the human participants. This was in part because ACT-R was less inclined to use means–ends analysis to follow routes that went close to the destination but were not connected to it.

Müller (1999) identified significant problems with ACT-R. He tested the principle of use specificity, according to which production rules acquired in one context should not transfer to another context, even if the two contexts are fairly similar. His participants were given two days of practice on a generation task or an evaluation task, with the same concepts from the LISP programming language being used in both tasks. According to ACT-R, there should have been poor transfer from one task to another because the information provided differs between the tasks. The actual findings are shown in Figure 13.13. What was learned on one task (generation or evaluation) transferred well to the other, with transfer to the generation task from the evaluation task being almost perfect. Müller concluded that human learning is more flexible than implied by ACT-R.

Evaluation

Anderson's ACT approach has been applied successfully to several kinds of skill acquisition, including the learning of geometry, computer text-editing, and computer programming. As predicted by the theory, the development of expertise often

FIGURE 13.13

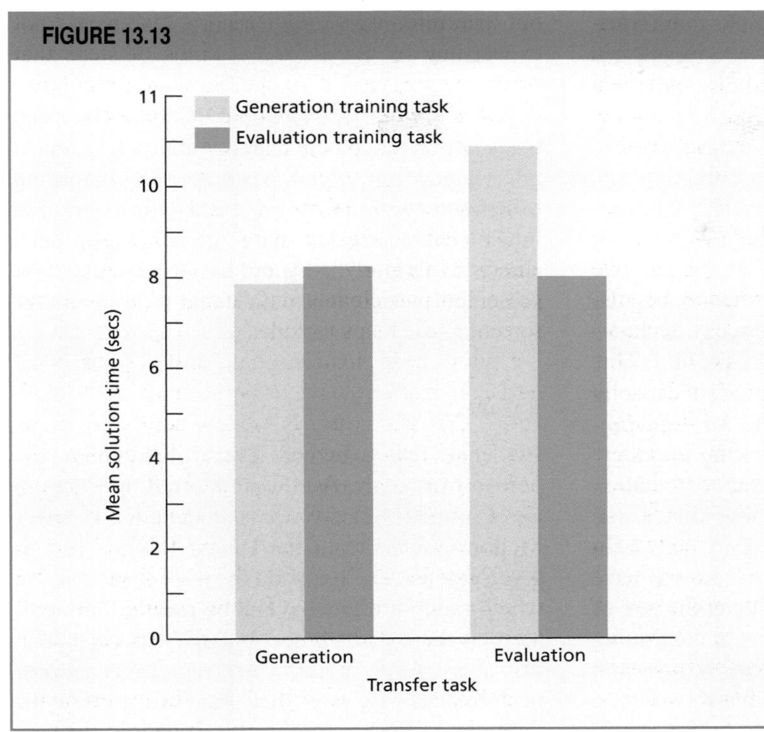

Solution speed as a function of training task (generation vs. evaluation) and transfer task (generation vs. evaluation). Data from Müller (1999).

involves a progressive shift from use of declarative knowledge to use of procedural knowledge. In general, theories based on production rules provide reasonably powerful accounts of the learning process.

On the negative side, there are some differences in performance between ACT-R and humans. For example, people sometimes make more use of means–ends analysis than does ACT-R (Anderson, 1993), and they often think in ways that are more abstract than ACT-R (Koedinger & Anderson, 1990). There are problems with the principle of use specificity, because human experts (and non-experts) are typically less rigid than is assumed by the principle (e.g., Müller, 1999). In general, the ACT approach is most applicable to the development of routine expertise requiring unvarying procedures (e.g., touch-typing), and is less relevant when *flexibility* of approach is important. Thus, the model has little to say about expertise that is creative and/or adaptive (e.g., constructing scientific theories). Finally, the notion that we use production rules may be no more than a convenient fiction. As Copeland (1993, p. 101) argued, "My actions [when making an omelette] can be described by means of if-then sentences: if the mixture sticks then I flick the pan, and so on. But it doesn't follow from this that my actions are produced by some device in my brain scanning through lists of if-then rules of this sort."

Ericsson: Deliberate practice

Nearly everyone agrees that prolonged and carefully structured practice is essential in the development of expertise. However, Ericsson (1988) went further. He claimed that practice of the right sort is not only necessary but also sufficient for memory expertise to develop. He argued that there are three requirements for someone to develop very high memory skills:

- Meaningful encoding: the information should be processed meaningfully, relating it to previous knowledge; this resembles levels-of-processing theory (see Chapter 6).

- Retrieval structure: cues should be stored with the information to aid later retrieval; this resembles the encoding specificity principle (see Chapter 6).
- Speed-up: there is extensive practice so that the processes involved in encoding and retrieval function faster and faster; this produces automaticity (see Chapter 5).

This theoretical approach was developed by Ericsson and Kintsch (1995). They argued that a substantial advantage enjoyed by experts is that they manage to get round the limited capacity of working memory. Ericsson and Kintsch proposed the notion of **long-term working memory**: experts learn how to store relevant information in long-term memory in such a way that it can be accessed readily through retrieval cues held in working memory. Thus, experts do *not* have greater working memory capacity than the rest of us. However, they are more efficient at combining efficiently the resources of long-term memory and working memory. Ericsson and Kintsch assumed that long-term working memory is useful for all kinds of expertise, not just those directly involving memory.

Note that the development of long-term working memory is a slow business and *only* provides benefits for specific kinds of information directly relevant to someone's area of expertise. As Ericsson and Delaney (1998, pp. 104–105) pointed out, "The expanded working-memory capacity provided by LT-WM [long-term working memory] is domain-specific and its structure reflects an adaptation to the storage and retrieval demands of the corresponding task domain."

Ericsson and Lehmann (1996) developed Ericsson's earlier ideas into a general theory of expertise. They emphasised that a wide range of expertise can be developed through **deliberate practice**, which has four aspects:

(1) The task is at an appropriate level of difficulty (not too easy or hard).
(2) The learner is provided with informative feedback about his/her performance.
(3) The learner has sufficient opportunities for repetition;
(4) It is possible for the learner to correct his/her errors.

What is controversial about Ericsson's position is the notion that innate talent or ability has almost *no* influence on expert performance. According to Ericsson et al. (1993) it is only for height that innate characteristics have convincingly been shown to matter: being tall is an advantage for some sports (e.g., basketball) and a disadvantage for others (e.g., gymnastics).

Evidence

Evidence that amazing levels of memory expertise can be acquired was reported by Ericsson and Chase (1982). SF was a student at Carnegie-Mellon University in the United States. He was given extensive practice on the digit-span task, on which random digits have to be recalled immediately in the correct order. Initially, his digit span was about seven digits, which represents average performance. He was then paid to practise the digit-span task for one hour a day for two years. At the end of that time, he reached a digit span of 80 digits. This is very impressive, because hardly anyone in the normal population has a digit span or more than about 10 or 11 items. Sadly, the beneficial effects of practice were very limited, because his letter and word spans at the end of the study were no greater than those of most other people!

How did SF do it? He reached a digit span of about 18 items by using his extensive knowledge of running times. For example, if the first few digits presented were "3594", he would note that this was Banister's world-record time for the mile, and so those four digits would be stored as a single unit or chunk. He then increased his digit span by organising these chunks into a hierarchical retrieval structure. The strategy used by SF conforms to Ericsson's (1988) assumptions that the development of memory expertise involves meaningful encoding, retrieval structure, and speed-up as a result of extensive practice.

It will be remembered that Ericsson and Kintsch (1995) argued that experts' superior memory for information in their area of expertise depends very much on the use of long-term memory. As a result, experts' memory for specific information should not be affected much by interruptions. Ericsson and Kintsch discussed several studies showing that the major impact of interruptions on experts was to increase the time they took to activate relevant retrieval cues rather than to cause them to forget information. For example, there is the famous waiter, JC, who could memorise dinner orders for up to 16 people while engaging in unrelated conversation (Ericsson & Polson, 1988).

Experts in many areas appear to have excellent long-term working memory (see Ericsson & Kintsch, 1995). For example, the first author is constantly surprised how expert bridge players can recall nearly every detail of hands that have just been played. Norman, Brooks, and Allen (1989) found that medical experts were much better than novices when unexpectedly asked to recall medical information, which is consistent with the notion that they had superior long-term working memory.

What evidence is there that experts organise information into retrieval structures? Ericsson and Chase (1982) asked highly practised participants to learn digit matrices consisting of 25 digits in 5×5 displays. They set up retrieval structures so they could recall the digits rapidly row by row. The most convincing evidence that they had constructed these specific retrieval structures came when they were asked to recall the digits column by column. Their performance was very much slower, because their retrieval structures did not fit well with the requirements of the task.

According to Ericsson and Lehmann (1996), what is important in acquiring expertise is the amount of *deliberate* practice rather than simply the sheer amount of practice. Charness, Krampe, and Mayr (1996) found that amount of chess playing failed to predict chess skill when they controlled statistically for the amount of chess study or deliberate practice. The best players were those who had engaged in the most deliberate practice, for example, by using published games to try to predict the moves made by chess masters.

Deliberate practice has been shown to be of crucial importance in the development of expertise in other contexts. Ericsson et al. (1993) reported a study on violinists in a German music academy. The key difference between 18-year-old students having varying levels of expertise on the violin was the amount of deliberate practice they had had over the years. The most expert violinists had spent on average nearly 7500 hours engaged in deliberate practice, compared to the 5300 hours clocked up by the good violinists.

What we have in the above study is essentially a correlation or association between amount of deliberate practice and level of performance. Perhaps those musicians with the greatest innate talent and/or musical success decide to spend more time practising than do those with less talent or previous success. Evidence tending to go against that interpretation was reported by Sloboda, Davidson, Howe, and Moore (1996). They compared highly successful young musicians with less successful ones. The two groups did not differ in terms of the amount of practice time they required to achieve a given level of performance. This suggests that the advantage possessed by the very successful musicians is not due to their greater level of natural musical ability.

We turn now to evidence relating to the controversial notion that innate ability or intelligence is unimportant in the development of expertise. Ceci and Liker (1986) considered individuals with considerable expertise concerning harness racing. For those unfamiliar with harness racing, it involves horses pulling a sulky (a light two-wheeled cart) holding one person. They identified 14 experts and 16 non-experts. However, even the non-experts knew a vast amount about harness racing, since nearly all of them attended horse races virtually every day. The IQs of the experts ranged from 81 to 128, and those of the non-experts from 80 to 130. Four of the experts had IQs in the low 80s, which is well below the population mean of 100.

The two groups were given information about 50 unnamed horses and an unnamed standard horse. There were 14 pieces of information (e.g., each horse's lifetime record; speed, race driver's ability; track size). The participants worked out the probable odds for 50 comparisons with each horse in turn being compared against the standard horse. Not surprisingly, the experts performed better than the non-experts. The performance of the experts indicated that they took account of complex interactions among up to seven variables at the same time. The key finding was that the experts' high level of performance did not depend at all on a high IQ. Thus, experts with low IQs were very successful at combining information in extremely complex ways. Indeed, experts with low IQs used more complex cognitive models than non-experts with high IQs when processing information about horses and horse racing.

What conclusions follow from the above study? According to Ceci and Liker (1986, p. 255), the findings mean that "IQ is unrelated to real-world forms of cognitive complexity that would appear to conform to some of those that scientists regard as the hallmarks of intelligent behaviour." However, it should be noted that Ceci and Liker were concerned with a very narrow form of expertise. There is strong evidence that intelligence is an important factor with broader forms of learning and expertise (see Mackintosh, 1998).

Hulin, Henry, and Noon (1990) carried out various meta-analyses to investigate the relationship between IQ and performance. The key findings were as follows: (1) the correlation between IQ and performance decreased steadily over time; (2) the correlation was only slightly greater than zero among individuals with more than five years of professional experience. These findings led them to conclude that innate talent in the form of intelligence was relatively unimportant at high levels of expertise. However, many of the studies included in their meta-analyses were concerned with relatively narrow types of learning, and so this conclusion may not have general applicability.

Relatively few studies have assessed both the amount of deliberate practice *and* innate talent or genetically-determined ability. One such study was reported by Horgan and Morgan (1990), who focused on the progress made by elite child chess players. Improvement in chess-playing performance was determined mainly by deliberate practice, motivation, and the degree of parental support. However, individual differences in non-verbal intelligence were of some importance as well, accounting for 12% of the variation in performance.

Evaluation

There is much support for the notion that memory expertise can be developed via the use of meaningful encoding, formation of retrieval structures, and speed-up. As predicted, most (or all) experts seem to develop superior long-term working memory, which serves to reduce limitations on processing capacity. The evidence indicates that deliberate practice is *necessary* for the achievement of an outstanding level of expertise. There is also some support for the notion that deliberate practice may be *sufficient* for the development of expertise. However, the evidence here is somewhat inconsistent.

There are several limitations with Ericsson's emphasis on deliberate practice. First, much evidence indicates that deliberate practice is *not* the only important factor in the development of expertise. For example, innate ability (at least as assessed by IQ) predicts long-term career success in many occupations, especially those involving complex skills. Gottfredson (1997) discussed the literature on intelligence and occupational success. The correlation between intelligence and work performance was only +.23 with low-complexity jobs (e.g., shrimp picker; corn-husking machine operator), but rose to +.58 for high-complexity jobs (e.g., biologist; city circulation manager). There is also considerable evidence that the mean IQ of those in very complex occupations (e.g., accountants; lawyers; doctors) is approximately 120–130, which is much higher than the population mean of 100 (see Mackintosh, 1998). Thus, high intelligence seems to be especially important for obtaining (and succeeding in) occupations of high complexity.

Second, the notion that innate talent is unimportant seems implausible. As Sternberg and Ben-Zeev (2001, p. 302) argued, "Is one to believe that anyone could become a Mozart if only he or she put in the time? . . . Or that becoming an Einstein is just a matter of deliberate practice?"

Third, there is another possibility that deserves consideration. Perhaps it is mainly those individuals possessing high levels of intelligence or talent who are willing to put in thousands of hours of deliberate practice. If that is the case, then the amount of deliberate practice reflects talent as well as practice itself. This would make it very hard to interpret most of the evidence.

Fourth, if nearly all experts in a given field have enormous talent, then it is not surprising that individual differences in talent do not predict levels of expertise. This resembles the situation in professional basketball, in which virtually all players are so tall that height does not predict performance (Detterman et al., 1998).

Fifth, much more remains to be discovered about the precise ways in which deliberate practice translates into expert performance. It is probable that the processes involved vary as a function of the task or domain in which the expertise is developed.

CHAPTER SUMMARY

- Introduction
This chapter is devoted to problem solving, transfer of training, and expertise. Most research on problem solving focuses on problems requiring no special training or knowledge. In contrast, research on expertise typically involves problems requiring a considerable amount of relevant background knowledge and experience. The topics of transfer and expertise both focus on learning processes. Transfer research is concerned with the beneficial (or adverse) effects of previous learning on current performance, whereas expertise research is concerned with the issue of what it is (e.g., knowledge; strategies) that differentiates experts from novices in a given domain or area.

- Problem solving
Problem solving is goal directed and involves cognitive rather than automatic processes. The problems studied by psychologists tend to be well defined, whereas those encountered in everyday life are typically ill defined. There is a further important distinction between knowledge-rich problems (requiring much specific knowledge for their solution) and knowledge-lean problems (not requiring specific knowledge). The Gestalt psychologists argued that problems often require insight, and past experience sometimes disrupts current problem solving (e.g., functional fixedness; Einstellung). Insight solutions seem subjectively to emerge out of nowhere, but probably depend on previous non-conscious processing. Ohlsson's representational change theory is a neo-Gestalt theory emphasising the importance of changing representations through elaboration, constraint relaxation, and re-encoding for insight to occur. The precise factors triggering representation change are not altogether clear. Newell and Simon's General Problem Solver is a computer program based on the assumptions that processing is serial and that people have limited short-term memory capacity. According to the theory, problem solvers make extensive use of heuristics (e.g., means–ends analysis; hill climbing). The General Problem Solver has better memory than (but inferior planning ability to) humans. According to progress monitoring theory, when means–ends analysis is unsuccessful, this produces criterion failure and the search for alternative strategies. As predicted, problem solvers experiencing criterion failure are more likely to alter their problem representation and solve the problem. The theory predicts *when* insight will be sought, but not *how* insight is achieved.

- Transfer of training
Transfer of training depends on content (what is transferred from one task to another) and on context (when and where knowledge is transferred from and to). Far transfer is of great importance for education. It has been obtained in several studies, and can be facilitated by the development of metacognitive skills. Transfer in analogical problem solving depends on three kinds of similarity: superficial, structural, and procedural. Even experts are influenced by superficial similarities in laboratory studies, but this finding does not always generalise to more realistic situations.

- Expertise
  Expertise is typically assessed by using knowledge-rich problems. Computers consider hugely more possibilities than outstanding chess players before making a move. Expert chess players differ from non-expert players in possessing far more templates containing knowledge of chess positions. These templates allow expert players to identify good moves rapidly and to remember even random chess positions better than non-experts. The precise information contained in templates remains unclear, and template theory may not fully account for the adaptive expertise shown by outstanding players.

- Theories of expertise
  According to Anderson's ACT-R theory, declarative memory, procedural memory, and working memory form three interconnected systems. Skill acquisition involves knowledge compilation, in which there is a progressive shift from the use of declarative knowledge to the use of procedural knowledge in the form of "if . . . then" production rules. There is evidence for this process of proceduralisation, but there are various differences between ACT-R and human performance (e.g., ACT-R makes less use of means–ends analysis). The theory assumes that skilled performance is less flexible than is actually the case. According to Ericsson, the development of expertise depends on deliberate practice involving informative feedback and the opportunity to correct errors. Deliberate practice is necessary for the development of expertise, but it is rarely sufficient. Individual differences in innate ability are also important, and it may be mainly individuals of high innate ability who are willing to devote hundreds or thousands of hours to deliberate practice.

FURTHER READING

- Barnett, S.M., & Ceci, S.J. (2002). When and where do we apply what we learn? A taxonomy for far transfer. *Psychological Bulletin*, *128*, 612–637. The authors provide a very useful framework for transfer research, including a preliminary identification of the key factors.
- Robertson, S.I. (2001). *Problem solving*. Hove, UK: Psychology Press. This book provides comprehensive and up-to-date accounts of several topics in problem solving and the development of expertise.
- Sternberg, R.J., & Ben-Zeev, T. (2001). *Complex cognition: The psychology of human thought*. Oxford: Oxford University Press. Chapters 7 and 8 in this textbook provide good coverage of key issues in problem solving and expertise.

14

Creativity and discovery

INTRODUCTION

In the previous chapter, we focused on relatively mundane forms of thinking mainly associated with problem solving. In this chapter, we move on to the allegedly more exceptional and valuable forms of thinking associated with creativity, hypothesis testing, and scientific discovery. There are various reasons for addressing these issues. First, the advance of science has transformed our world, bringing us increased longevity, fast forms of transport, computers, the internet, and email. It is thus of considerable practical importance to understand the processes involved in creativity, and how research scientists test hypotheses and make scientific discoveries. Second, psychologists have carried out much interesting research in these areas, and the fruits of their labour will be considered shortly. As will become apparent, Albert Einstein was probably wrong when (considering his own cognitive processes leading to the theory of relativity), he said, "I am not sure there can be a way of really understanding the miracle of thinking" (Wertheimer, 1945, p. 227).

One of the central themes of the chapter is that there is much wrong with the traditional view. According to this view, there are a few "great" individuals who are responsible for what we call "creative thoughts"; these are people of talent, the Einsteins and Mozarts of this world, who have intellectual and creative abilities stretching far beyond those of the mass of humanity (otherwise known as *us*). In contrast to this view, we will be focusing on the notion that we are all a bit creative, and that the cognitive processes used to produce Nobel prize ideas may not differ radically from those used to produce a joke over coffee.

CREATIVITY

At the outset, it is worth distinguishing between originality and creativity. **Originality** involves producing ideas that are novel or different with no regard for whether they are useful or worthwhile. Originality can be assessed by tests such as the Uses of a Brick test, in which participants simply list as many uses of a brick as they can think of. Someone who thinks of uses of a brick that differ from those of other people is deemed to be high in originality. In contrast, **creativity** involves producing ideas that are original, but there is the additional requirement that the ideas are useful or worthwhile. Creativity is more important than mere originality, but unfortunately it is easier for psychologists to assess originality than creativity. There is a detailed discussion of creativity as it relates to scientific discoveries in a later section of the chapter.

In the past, accounts of creativity were often descriptive rather than explanatory. The classic example of this descriptive approach is Wallas's (1926) classification of the broad stages of the creative process:

- Preparation: The problem under consideration is formulated and preliminary attempts are made to solve it.
- **Incubation**: The problem is put aside to work on other tasks, which nevertheless allows relevant processing to occur below the conscious level.
- Illumination: The solution comes to the problem solver as a sudden insight.
- Verification: The problem solver makes sure the solution actually works.

There appears to be some support for this classification from the reports of creative scientists. For example, there is the account of the French mathematician Henri Poincaré (1913), who reported working intensively on the development of Fuchsian functions for 15 days. At the end of this time, he reported as follows:

> I left Caen, where I was living, to go on a geologic excursion under the auspices of the school of mines. The changes in travel made me forget my mathematical work. Having reached Coutances, we entered an omnibus to go some place or other. At the moment when I put my foot on the step the idea came to me, without anything in my former thoughts seeming to have paved the way for it, that the transformations I had used to define Fuchsian functions were identical to those of non-Euclidean geometry . . . I felt a perfect certainty.

Poincaré's report fits Wallas's framework perfectly, with illumination following an incubation period after extensive preparation. However, even though Wallas's analysis provides us with a broad framework, it is too general and descriptive. Some attempts have been made to specify these stages. For example, incubation and illumination have been treated in Gestalt research on insight (see Chapter 13).

Simon (1966) explained incubation as a special type of forgetting. He distinguished between control information about a problem (e.g., a record of the subgoals tried in a problem) and factual information (e.g., some property of an object or substantive aspect of the problem). For example, in Maier's (1931) two-string problem (see Chapter 13), control knowledge might include the subgoal "try to reach something that is far away", and substantive information would be that "the string is a flexible object". Factual knowledge discovered in the context of one subgoal will not be available to other goals. However, during incubation control information decays faster than factual information. Therefore, after the problem has been set aside for a time, subgoal information will be lost but the factual information will still be present. This factual information will thus be available to newly generated subgoals of the problem, increasing the likelihood of the problem being solved.

Evidence for the existence of incubation was reported by Smith and Blankenship (1991). They used the Remote Associates Test in which participants had to find a word that linked three other words. For example, the words "wheel", "electric", and "high" are all linked by the word "chair". In one condition, differences in the meanings of the three words were emphasised (e.g., indicating that "high" is the opposite of "low"). The key comparison was between participants given a 5-minute break and those not given a break. Participants in the 5-minute break or incubation condition solved 57% of the problems compared to only 27% in the no-break condition.

There is little empirical support for illumination. If we are to relate the phenomenon to any research, it is that on the use of hints in problem solving. Much of this work has been carried out within the Gestalt tradition (see Chapter 13). The current favoured account is that any new information introduced into the problem or encountered in the environment may activate related concepts in memory and result in the sudden emergence of a solution. For example, in the case of the two-string problem, Maier reported that when the experimenter brushed against the string, setting it swinging in the line of sight of participants, many of them suddenly produced the solution of swinging the string and catching it on the upswing while holding the other string.

Evaluation

Wallas (1926) provided a useful framework within which to consider creativity. As we have seen, there is evidence for the key notion of incubation (e.g., Smith & Blankenship, 1991). In addition, some real-life examples of scientific breakthroughs (e.g., the case of Poincaré) seem to fit the framework.

There are various limitations with Wallas's approach. First, as mentioned already, his account is descriptive rather than explanatory. For example, we are left with no clear sense of the precise processes producing incubation. Second, there is little support for the notion of illumination. Third, Wallas probably made creativity seem more mysterious than is actually the case. As Weisberg (1993, p. 10) pointed out, "It is often assumed that if a creative product has extraordinary effects, it must have come about in extraordinary ways, but that does not necessarily follow. The creative achievement can be extraordinary because of the effect it produces, rather than because of the way in which it was brought about."

Geneplore model

Finke, Ward, and Smith (1992) proposed the Geneplore model of creativity (the name comes from combining generation and exploration). This model divides creativity into a generative phase and an exploratory phase (Ward, Smith, & Finke, 1995). In the generative phase, people are said to construct mental representations, called **preinventive structures**, which have properties promoting creative discovery and which can be formed before determining the use to which they will be put. In the exploratory phase, these properties are exploited to make sense of the preinventive structures. If these explorations are successful, then a creative product might result. If the explorations are unsuccessful, one cycles back to the generative phase to produce either new preinventive structures or to modify the original structure. In this cycling process, various constraints are applied to (or even discovered on) the creative product, gradually refining and improving it.

One of the main assumptions of the Geneplore model is that people find it hard to be very creative because their ideas are constrained by their existing knowledge. This assumption was developed in the path-of-least-resistance model (e.g., Ward, Patterson, Sifonis, Dodds, & Saunders, 2002). According to this model, people trying to generate novel entities will tend to make extensive use of readily accessible information. There will be a reliance on such information even when people are explicitly instructed to be as creative as possible.

Evidence

One of the Geneplore model's best-known applications has been in the area of structured imagination. The preinventive structures built during the generative processes should be based on people's prior knowledge. As a result, people given imaginative tasks should generate products structured in various ways. Ward (1992) asked participants to draw imaginary creatures on a planet somewhere else in the galaxy. More specifically, they were asked to draw their initially imagined animal, another animal of the same species, and a member of a different species (see Figure 14.1). Ward found that "the majority of imagined creatures were structured by properties that are typical of animals on earth: bilateral symmetry, sensory receptors and appendages" (see Figure 14.2).

In a similar study, Bredart (1998) found that when a feature was not included (e.g., an eye), a novel structure with the same function was included (e.g., some sensor for extracting sensory information). Ward and Sifonis (1997) asked some participants to produce "wildly different" animals. Their drawings resembled those of controls given the standard instructions in that their drawings

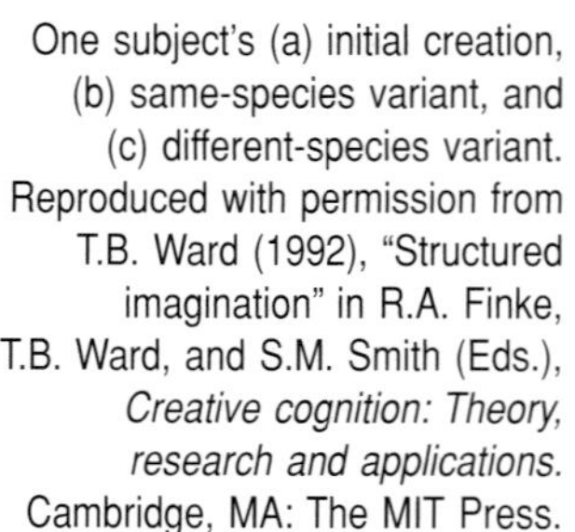

One subject's (a) initial creation, (b) same-species variant, and (c) different-species variant. Reproduced with permission from T.B. Ward (1992), "Structured imagination" in R.A. Finke, T.B. Ward, and S.M. Smith (Eds.), *Creative cognition: Theory, research and applications.* Cambridge, MA: The MIT Press.

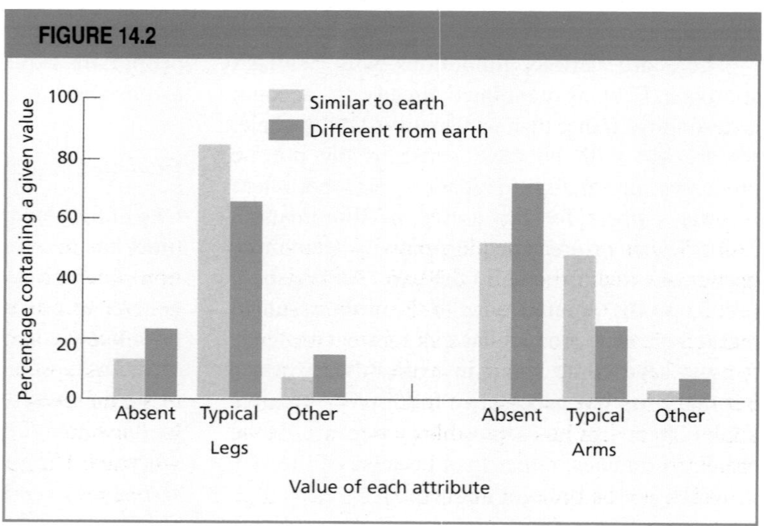

The percentages of imaginary creatures with no legs, two or four legs, or some other number of legs, no arms, two arms, or some other number of arms, when people imagined a planet similar to or completely unlike earth. Reproduced with permission from T.B. Ward (1992), "Structured imagination" in R.A. Finke, T.B. Ward, and S.M. Smith (Eds.), *Creative cognition: Theory, research and applications.* Cambridge, MA: The MIT Press.

retained symmetry and other properties. However, they tended to produce more novel variations (e.g., in the number of eyes or limbs).

Ward et al. (2002) tested predictions of the path-of-least-resistance model, according to which people trying to be creative nevertheless rely heavily on easily accessible prior knowledge. In one experiment, some participants were asked to imagine, draw, and describe fruit which might be found on a planet very different from Earth, and to identify the factors influencing their creations. This was the control condition. Other groups were told to be as creative as they could be (creative group) or to use their wildest imagination and not "feel bound by what fruit is like on earth" (not bound group).

There were three key findings in Ward et al.'s (2002) experiment. First, many participants in all conditions used at least one Earth fruit as a source of information for their imagined fruit (see Figure 14.3). Second, participants who relied on Earth fruit produced imaginary fruits that were

FIGURE 14.3

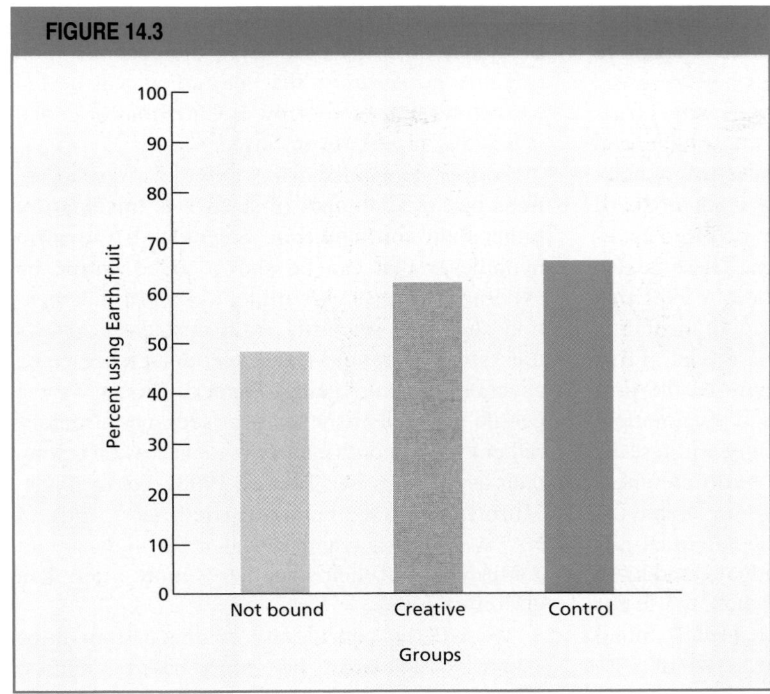

Percent of participants using Earth fruit as a source of information for imaging an extraterrestrial fruit as a function of initial instructions (not bound; creative; control). Data from Ward et al. (2002).

less original or creative than those produced by participants who did not (2.50 vs. 3.40 on a 7-point scale). Third, as predicted by the path-of-least-resistance model, there was a strong tendency for participants who relied on Earth fruit to use very common or accessible fruit (e.g., orange; apple) rather than less accessible ones (e.g., apricot; cranberry).

What can be done to make people more creative? According to the model, one useful approach would be to generate preinventive structures *before* thinking of possible uses for them. Support for this prediction was reported by Finke (1990). Participants were presented with basic forms such as a sphere, cube, cylinder, wire, hook, wheels, handle, and so on. Three of these forms were then selected, and participants had to close their eyes and combine them to make a useful object. This object had to belong to one out of eight categories (e.g., furniture; appliances; weapons). In the key condition, participants were only told the appropriate category *after* they had assembled the object. As predicted, the objects produced were more creative in this condition than in a condition in which the category was announced *before* the object was assembled.

There is some evidence that the Geneplore model is applicable to real-world creativity. For example, consider the creative approach adopted by Hirshberg (1998), the director of Nissan Design America. He noticed that a drawing of a car produced by one of his designers had a very thick line separating the upper rear quadrant of the car from the rest of the car. This led Hirshberg to engage in a process of exploration based on the notion that cars can be regarded as consisting of constituent panels which can be removed and replaced with other panels. This led to the development of the Pulsar NX, which was the first modular production car in the world.

Evaluation

There is reasonable evidence that the processes of generation and exploration emphasised within the Geneplore model are important in the production of creative solutions to problems. In addition, various predictions following from the Geneplore and path-of-least-resistance models have received empirical support. For example, preinventive structures are typically rooted in prior knowledge, and people typically use readily accessible prior knowledge. In addition, preinventive structures produced with no clear goal in mind tend to be more creative than those that are goal-driven. There is also suggestive evidence (e.g., Hirshberg, 1998) that the Geneplore model has real-world applicability.

What are the limitations of the model? First, we are not given a detailed account of the processes involved in generation and exploration. Second, much of the research designed to test the model has focused on originality or differentness of responses rather than directly on creativity. Third, there has been a neglect of individual differences. Highly intelligent individuals tend to be more original and creative than those of lesser intelligence. For example, Barron (1969) found that creative architects had a mean IQ of 130. In addition, individuals high in psychoticism (a personality dimension involving coldness, aggression, and lack of concern for others) exhibit more originality than those low in psychoticism. For example, Rawlings and Toogood (1997) found that psychoticism correlated about +.30 with originality as assessed by tests such as making circles into unusual objects and finding unusual uses of objects.

HYPOTHESIS TESTING

Hypothesis testing is a form of **inductive reasoning**, which involves making a generalised conclusion from premises that refer to particular instances. One of the key features of inductive reasoning is that the conclusions of inductively valid arguments are probably (but not necessarily) true. More specifically, Karl Popper (1968) argued that hypotheses can never be shown to be logically true by simply generalising from *confirming* instances (i.e., induction). As the philosopher Bertrand Russell pointed out, a scientist turkey might form the generalisation, "Each day I am fed", because this hypothesis has been confirmed every day of his life. However, the generalisation provides no *certainty* that the turkey will be fed tomorrow, and if tomorrow is Christmas Eve then it is likely to be proven false.

Popper concluded from the above considerations that the hallmark of science is **falsification** rather than **confirmation**. Scientists try to form hypotheses that can be shown to be untrue by experimental tests. According to Popper, falsification separates scientific from unscientific activities such as religion and pseudo-science (e.g., psychoanalysis). Against Popper's dictates, most people and scientists seem to seek confirmatory rather than disconfirmatory evidence when testing their hypotheses (see Tweney, 1998). For example, Mitroff (1974; see below) carried out a study of NASA scientists which revealed that they sought confirmation of their hypotheses more often than disconfirmation.

We will be considering evidence from three sources: standard, laboratory-based studies; laboratory-based simulated research environments; and studies of real scientific discoveries (this is discussed in the next section). The strengths and limitations of each approach were discussed by Klahr and Simon (1999). In general terms, laboratory-based studies have good rigour and precision, but only limited relevance to scientific discovery, although this is less so with studies in simulated research environments. The opposite is the case with studies of real scientific discoveries, since they typically have low levels of rigour and precision.

2-4-6 task

A hypothesis-testing task that has attracted much interest was devised by Peter Wason (1960). Participants were told that three numbers 2-4-6 conformed to a simple relational rule. Their task was to generate sets of three numbers, and to provide reasons for each choice. After each choice, the experimenter indicated whether or not the set of numbers conformed to the rule the experimenter had in mind. The task was to discover the rule. The rule itself was apparently very simple: "Three numbers in ascending order of magnitude."

However, it took most participants a long time to produce the rule. Only 21% of them were correct with their first attempt, and 28% never discovered the rule at all.

It may seem to you that the 2-4-6 task is trivial and of no relevance to real life. However, that is not the case, and Manktelow (1999) gave the following example which is conceptually the same as the 2-4-6 task. Suppose you have been given the task of setting up an anti-smoking publicity campaign. Your initial hypothesis is that it will be most effective to use television to promote your campaign, but you need to test this hypothesis. In fact, your hypothesis is too narrow, because advertisements in any medium will be equally effective. In similar fashion, the incorrect hypotheses on the 2-4-6 task are almost invariably narrower than the correct rule.

Why was performance so poor on Wason's 2-4-6 problem? According to Wason (1960), people show **confirmation bias**, i.e., they try to generate numbers confirming their original hypothesis. For example, participants whose original hypothesis or rule was that the second number is twice the first, and the third number is three times the first number tended to generate sets of numbers consistent with that hypothesis (e.g., 6-12-18; 50-100-150). Wason argued that confirmation bias and failure to try hypothesis disconfirmation prevented the participants from replacing their initial hypothesis (which was too narrow and specific) with the correct general rule.

Before discussing the relevant evidence, we will consider Wason's ideas in more detail. As Wetherick (1962) pointed out, we need to distinguish between confirmation and positivity. A positive test means that the numbers you produce are an instance of your hypothesis, but it is only confirmatory if you believe your hypothesis to be correct. It is perhaps easier to see the point here if we consider negative tests, in which the numbers you produce do *not* conform to your hypothesis. In that case, discovering that your set of numbers does not conform to the rule actually confirms your hypothesis!

Poletiek (1996, p. 455) carried this line of argument a little further. She argued that your hypothesis is your best guess, and so disconfirmatory testing makes little sense: "Subjects expect their best guess to be confirmed, regardless of the tests they propose." Thus, confirmatory testing is the obvious approach to take, and it is not sensible to call it a confirmation bias.

Evidence

The main prediction following from Wason's position is that participants should perform better when instructed to engage in disconfirmatory testing. The evidence is rather inconsistent. Gorman (1996) reviewed several relevant studies, and found that instructions to disconfirm sometimes improved performance and sometimes did not. There was some evidence that disconfirming instructions improved performance when feedback was only given at the end of the experiment (e.g., some of Gorman's own studies), but did not do so when feedback was given after each rule announcement (e.g., Tweney et al., 1980). A potential problem with much of the research here is that there was a failure to distinguish clearly between disconfirmation and negative testing. Poletiek (1996) found that instructions to disconfirm produce more negative tests. However, participants generally expected these negative tests to receive a "No" response, and so they actually involved confirmation.

Klayman and Ha (1987, p. 212) argued that the participants in Wason's studies were producing positive tests of their hypotheses: "You test an hypothesis by examining instances in which the property or event is expected to occur (to see if it does occur), or by examining instances in which it is known to have occurred (to see if the hypothesised conditions prevail)." The difficulty with the 2-4-6 task is that it possesses the unusual characteristics that the correct rule is much more general than any of the initial hypotheses that participants are likely to form. As a result, positive testing cannot lead to discovery of the correct rule, and negative testing is required. However, positive testing is often more likely than negative testing to lead to falsification of incorrect hypotheses, provided that the numbers of instances confirming to the hypothesis are approximately equal to those conforming to the actual rule. For example, if the rule is "ascending by two", then positive testing will generally lead to hypothesis falsification and rule discovery.

The importance of negative evidence on a version of the 2-4-6 task was shown by Rossi, Caverni, and Girotto (2001). They used the reverse rule to Wason (1960), namely, "descending numbers", and the participants were presented initially with the number triple 2-4-6 or 6-4-2. There was a dramatic difference in first-attempt solvers between the two conditions: 54% of those receiving 2-4-6 versus only 16% of those receiving 6-4-2. Why was there this large difference? Those presented with 2-4-6 experienced much more negative evidence via producing triples not conforming to the rule. This negative evidence forced them to revise their hypotheses and this promoted discovery of the rule.

Tweney et al. (1980) discovered perhaps the most effective way of improving performance on the 2-4-6 task. Participants were told that the experimenter had *two* rules in mind, and it was their task to identify these rules. One of these rules generated DAX triples, whereas the other rule generated MED triples. They were also told that 2-4-6 was a DAX triple. Whenever the participants generated a set of three numbers, they were informed whether the set fitted the DAX rule or the MED rule. The correct answer was that the DAX rule was any three numbers in ascending order, and the MED rule covered all other sets of numbers.

Over 50% of the participants produced the correct answer on their first attempt, which was much higher than when the 2-4-6 problem was presented in its standard version. An important reason for this high level of success was that participants could use positive testing and did not have to focus on disconfirmation of hypotheses. They could identify the DAX rule by confirming the MED rule, and so they did not have to try to disconfirm the DAX rule.

There has been some controversy as to whether it is crucial for the two rules to be complementary, i.e., to cover all possibilities. Vallée-Tourangeau, Austin, and Rankin (1995) found that complementarity is *not* essential. For example, the success rate was greater than on the standard 2-4-6 task when there was a possibility of a third kind of triple that was both DAX and MED. Thus, it seems that people are more likely to discover a rule if there is more than one hypothesis to consider.

Vartanian, Martindale, and Kwiatkowski (2003) addressed the issue of the differences between those who succeed on the 2-4-6 task and those who do not. They argued that those who discover the rule think more flexibly than those who do not. Accordingly, Vartanian et al. predicted (and found) that individuals high in **divergent thinking** (the ability to generate numerous solutions to a given problem) would be more likely to discover the rule than those low in divergent thinking. An implication is that a failure to think in flexible and original ways may lie behind failure on the 2-4-6 task.

Evaluation

The 2-4-6 task has generated much interesting and important research. Of particular importance, accounts of participants' behaviour on this task have become increasingly revealing over time. As Manktelow (1999, p. 140) concluded, "Early work seemed to indicate a bias towards confirming hypotheses, but later experiment and theory have shown that this has a cognitive rather than a motivational basis." Thus, we should regard a confirmatory strategy as being an appropriate way of testing people's best-guess hypotheses (Poletiek, 1996) rather than as a worrying indication of bias.

To what extent can we generalise the findings from the 2-4-6 task? There are two main reasons for having some concerns on this score. First, as was emphasised by Klayman and Ha (1987), the 2-4-6 task differs from most other hypothesis-testing tasks in that the rule is much broader than is initially expected by participants. Admittedly, this makes it easier to show the limitations of positive testing, but may also limit the generality of the findings. Second, additional factors may come into play in the real world. For example, professional scientists often focus their research on trying to disconfirm the theories of other scientists. In 1977 the first author took part in a conference on the levels-of-processing approach to memory (see Chapter 6). Almost without exception, the research presented was designed to identify limitations and problems with that approach.

Simulated research environments

Mynatt, Doherty, and Tweney (1977) found evidence of confirmation bias in a simulation world that was apparently closer to real scientific testing than the 2-4-6 task. In this computer world, participants fired particles at circles and triangles presented at two brightness levels (low and high). The world had other features, but all of them were irrelevant to the task (see Figure 14.4). Participants were not told that the lower-brightness shapes had a 4.2 cm invisible boundary around them that deflected particles. At the start of the experiment, they were shown arrangements of shapes suggesting the initial hypothesis that "triangles deflect particles".

Subsequently, participants were divided into three groups instructed to adopt either a confirmatory strategy, a disconfirmatory strategy, or no particular strategy (i.e., a control group). They had to choose to continue the experiment on one of two screens:

(1) A screen containing similar features to those that deflected particles; on this screen, participants' observations would probably confirm their initial incorrect hypothesis.
(2) A screen containing novel features; on this screen, other hypotheses could be tested.

Mynatt et al. (1977) found that 71% of the participants chose the first screen, thus providing some evidence for a confirmation bias. Furthermore, the strategy instructions (i.e., use a disconfirmatory strategy) did not deflect participants from this confirmation bias.

Mynatt, Doherty, and Tweney (1978) found similar results using an interactive version of this simulation world. They also found that participants tended to ignore falsificatory evidence when it occurred. Garavan, Doherty, and Mynatt (1997) argued that attempts to falsify in such complex environments are just too hard for people to do. More generally, they argued that falsification and confirmation may each be appropriate at different times. For example, Chalmers (1982) pointed out that established theories should be falsifiable. However, it will often be more beneficial to a scientist to seek confirmatory evidence during the development of a new theory.

Dunbar (1993) also used a simulated research environment. Participants were given the difficult task of providing an explanation for the ways genes are controlled by other genes using a computer-based molecular genetics laboratory. The difficulty of the task can be seen in the fact that solving this problem in real life had led to the award of the Nobel prize! The participants were led to focus on the hypothesis that the gene control was by activation, whereas it was actually by inhibition.

Dunbar (1993) found that those participants who simply tried to find data consistent with their activation hypothesis failed to solve the problem. In contrast, the 20% of participants who did solve the problem set themselves the goal of trying to

FIGURE 14.4

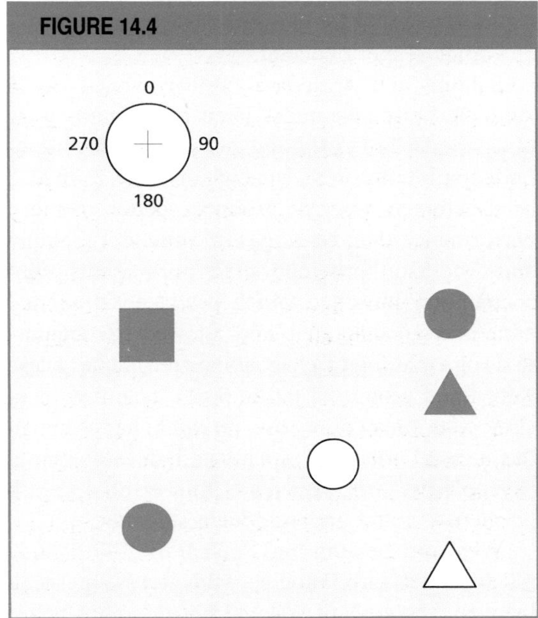

The type of display used by Mynatt et al. (1977) to study confirmation bias. Subjects had to direct a particle that was fired from the upper left part of the screen, by selecting the direction of its path. The relative shading of the objects indicates the two levels of brightness at which objects were presented.

explain the discrepant findings. According to the participants' own reports, most of them started with the general hypothesis that activation was the key controlling process. They then applied this hypothesis in specific ways, focusing on one gene after another as the potential activator. It was typically only when all the various specific activation hypotheses had been disconfirmed that some participants focused on explaining the data that did not fit the general activation hypothesis.

How closely do the above findings resemble those in real research environments? Mitroff (1974) studied geologists involved in the Apollo space programme as experts in lunar geology. They devoted most of their time to trying to confirm rather than falsify their hypotheses, but they were not opposed to the notion of falsifying the hypotheses of other scientists. Their focus on confirmation rather than falsification resembles that found in participants in simulated research environments. However, the real scientists seemed more reluctant than the participants in simulated research studies to abandon their hypotheses. There are probably two main reasons for this:

(1) The real scientists emphasised the value of commitment to a given position as a motivating factor.
(2) Real scientists are more likely than participants in an experiment to attribute contrary findings to deficiencies in the measuring instruments.

The issue of whether real scientists focus on confirmation or disconfirmation was considered by Gorman (1995) in an analysis of Alexander Graham Bell's research on the development of the telephone. Bell showed evidence of confirmatory bias in that he continued to focus on undulating current and electromagnets even after he and others had obtained good results with liquid devices. For example, a liquid device was used to produce the first intelligible telephone call to Bell from his assistant Watson on 12 March 1876. More generally, it appears that some research groups focus on confirmation, whereas others attach more importance to disconfirmation (Tweney & Chitwood, 1995).

Most of the laboratory studies discussed so far were based on individual hypothesis testing. However, Okada and Simon (1997) pointed out that real-life research is generally a collaborative effort involving teams of researchers. They compared pairs of participants and single participants on Dunbar's (1993) genetic control task (discussed earlier). They scored performance on a scale ranging from 1 to 4. Pairs scored an average of 2.89, which was significantly greater than the singles' average score of 1.67. Why did the pairs perform better than the singles? The key reason was that pairs engaged in more explanatory activities such as entertaining hypotheses more frequently, considering alternative ideas more often, and discussing ways of justifying ideas more of the time. According to Okada and Simon (1997, p. 130), these activities are important for the following reason: "In a collaborative situation, subjects must often be more explicit than in an individual learning situation, to make partners understand their ideas and to convince them. This can prompt subjects to entertain requests for explanation and construct deeper explanations."

Schunn and Anderson (1999) carried out a simulated research study. Their participants were given the task of designing and interpreting memory experiments on the spacing effect (i.e., spaced or distributed practice produces better memory performance than does massed practice). Schunn and Anderson provided their participants with a computer interface which produced simulated experimental outcomes and allowed participants to design and interpret several experiments. There were three groups of participants: cognitive psychologists most of whose research had been in the area of memory; social and developmental psychologists who had done little or no research on memory; and undergraduate students.

What did Schunn and Anderson (1999) find? As expected, psychologists who were experts in memory research performed considerably better than the undergraduate students in every aspect of the simulated research. The research skills possessed by the memory experts can be divided into domain-specific skills (those only of use in memory experiments) and domain-general skills (those of use generally in psychology). The overall research performance of the memory experts was superior to that of the social and developmental psychologists primarily with respect to domain-specific skills (e.g., experimental design), with the two groups having comparable levels of domain-general skills (e.g., interpretation of findings). These results led Schunn and Anderson (1999, p. 362) to conclude as follows: "Contrary to a general reasoning ability model or a model in which expertise is highly domain-specific, it appears that expertise in scientific reasoning consists of both domain-specific and domain-general skills."

Evaluation

Studies on simulated research environments have produced similar findings to those on hypothesis testing on the 2-4-6 task. In particular, participants in simulated research environments tend to seek information consistent with their hypothesis and to avoid seeking falsificatory evidence. Thus, there appears to be some generality to the findings. However, observations of real scientists indicate that while some research groups focus on confirmation, there are other groups that emphasise disconfirmation (especially of other researchers' theories).

Research in simulated research environments has various limitations. First, the commitment that motivates real researchers to defend their own theories and try to disprove those of other researchers is lacking. Second, performance on a hypothesis-testing task varies depending on whether it is performed by one person or by two (Okada & Simon, 1997), and so we cannot safely generalise from studies using individual participants. Third, the processes involved in hypothesis testing (e.g., domain-specific skills; domain-general skills) need to be studied in more detail if we are to understand fully the factors determining success and failure on hypothesis-testing tasks.

SCIENTIFIC DISCOVERY

Klahr and Dunbar (1988; Klahr, Fay, & Dunbar, 1993) have considered scientific discovery in various situations. In one task, they asked participants to discover the function of a mystery button (labelled "RPT") for controlling a toy vehicle called Big Trak. Participants tested the function of the button by including it in brief sets of instructions they had to write to make the toy move. Thus, participants adopted a positive test strategy, reasoning, "If Big Trak does X, then my hypothesis is correct", although they were often forced to revise their theories by taking account of negative evidence.

Klahr and Dunbar (1988) made use of Newell and Simon's notion of **problem space**, which is a description of all the possible states of affairs within a given problem situation (see Chapter 13). However, the problem space considered by scientists is typically much less clearly defined than the problem space used by participants solving problems in the laboratory.

Dual-space search

Klahr and Dunbar (1988) characterised scientific discovery as a **dual-space search**: one space contains the experimental possibilities in the situation, and the other contains a space of possible hypotheses. Note that these ideas are very similar to those put forward by Ohlsson (1992) to explain insight in problem solving (see Chapter 13). In searching the hypothesis space, the initial state is some knowledge of the domain [specific area], and the goal state is a hypothesis that can account for that knowledge in a more concise, universal form. Hypothesis generation in this space may involve various mechanisms (e.g., memory search; analogical mapping; reminding).

Search in the experiment space is directed towards experiments that will discriminate between rival hypotheses and yield interpretable outcomes. On the basis of **protocol analysis** (analysis of participants' verbalisations while performing a task), Klahr and Dunbar (1988) distinguished two groups of participants:

(1) Theorists who prefer to search the space of hypotheses.
(2) Experimenters who prefer to search the space of experiments.

Van Joolingen and DeJong (1997) provided an elaboration of this approach.

Gorman (1992) argued that much previous research had concentrated on the experiment space while ignoring the hypothesis space. The latter is important, as is illustrated by the DAX-MED study by Tweney et al. (1980; discussed earlier). This study showed that the representation of hypothesis goals can be very important in determining participants' subsequent success on a task.

Thagard (1998) argued that the number of search spaces varies across scientific problems. He used as an example the discovery of the bacterial origins of stomach ulcers. The scientists involved in this discovery made use of three search spaces: experiment space, hypothesis space, and instrumentation space. Schuun and Klahr (1995) went one better as a result of research in a complex micro-world laboratory. They identified four problem spaces in science: in addition to an experiment space and a hypothesis space, there was also a paradigm space and a representation space (see Figure 14.5). The paradigm space is an offshoot of the experiment space, and consists of various classes of experiments. The data-representation space is an offshoot of the hypothesis space, and consists of ways of representing phenomena.

Most scientific discoveries are collaborative efforts, as in Crick and Watson's discovery of the double helix in biology. Okada et al. (1995) found in a study of cognitive scientists in Japan that successful scientific collaboration requires four features to be present:

(1) Frequent and intense interaction among the scientists.
(2) An exploratory style of discussion in which all the scientists are treated as equals.
(3) A shared interest in the research issues.
(4) Diversity in skills and experience.

Scientists' methods: Strong and weak

Klahr and Simon (1999, 2001) considered evidence on scientific discovery from several different types of study, including historical studies, various kinds of laboratory studies, and computational modelling. As a result, they developed some of their earlier ideas on the search processes involved in scientific discovery. They accepted that scientists

FIGURE 14.5

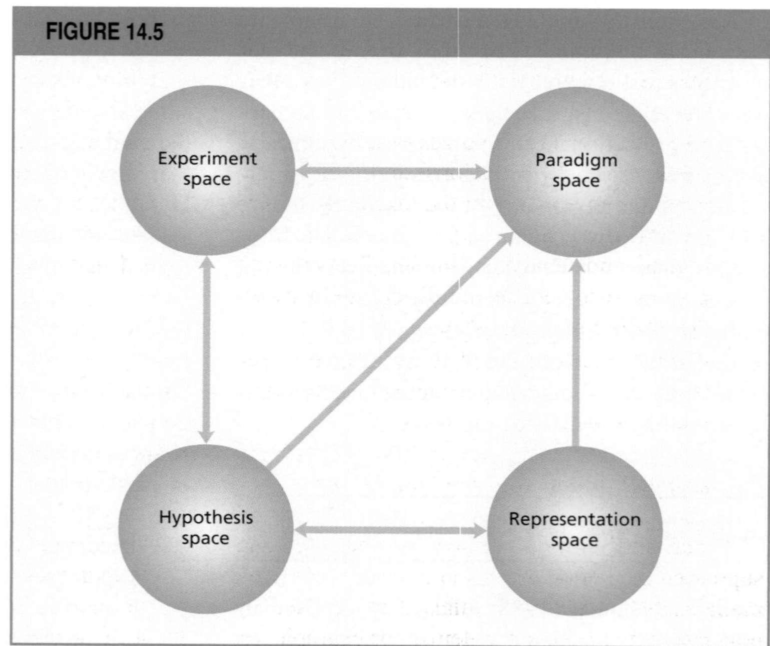

A four-space model of scientific discovery with arrows indicating the direction of information flow between the spaces. From Schunn and Klahr (1995). Copyright © 1995 by Lawrence Erlbaum Associates, Inc. Reprinted with permission.

use various problem spaces (e.g., experiment space; hypothesis space), but were concerned to identify the processes used within these spaces. They drew a distinction between two kinds of methods used by scientists:

(1) **Strong methods**: These methods are acquired through a lengthy process of acquiring huge amounts of **domain-specific knowledge** (knowledge in a limited area) about scientific phenomena, theories, procedures, experimental paradigms, and so on. When a scientific problem is relatively simple, scientists can often solve it rapidly by using strong methods. However, domain-specific knowledge on its own is insufficient to permit creative scientific discoveries.

(2) **Weak methods**: These methods are very general, and can be applied to almost any scientific problem. Indeed, they are so general that, "The weak methods invoked by scientists as they ply their trade are the same ones that underlie all human cognition" (Klahr & Simon, 1999, p. 532). Weak methods are especially important in scientific discovery, because the knowledge contained within strong methods is not sufficient on its own to produce scientific breakthroughs. Here are some of the main weak methods (some of which were discussed in Chapter 13):

(i) Generate and test or trial and error: this involves trying various solutions in a fairly random way.
(ii) Hill climbing: this involves making tentative steps in several directions, and then selecting the one apparently moving most clearly towards the goal.
(iii) Means–ends analysis: this involves creating a subgoal to reduce the difference between the current and goal states.
(iv) Planning: solving an abstract version of the problem and then applying the solution to the actual problem.
(v) Analogy: applying ideas from a different scientific problem to the current one.

Klahr and Simon's review of the literature supported the notion that scientists often use weak methods that are very similar to those used by non-scientists to solve problems. For example, let us return once more to Dunbar's (1993) study simulating important research on genetic control. What is of interest here is the degree of similarity between the approach taken by the participants and by the scientists (Monod and Jacob) who carried out the original research and won the Nobel Prize. As predicted by Klahr and Simon's theory, there were very clear similarities:

> The subjects generated a new concept of mutually interacting genes that regulate enzyme production by inhibition. These subjects behaved just like Monod and Jacob. Furthermore, just like the subjects in the experiments reported in this article, Monod and Jacob had difficulty in formulating the concept of inhibitory control due to their belief in activation.
>
> (Dunbar, 1993, p. 431)

In sum, the process of scientific discovery may be much less mysterious than might have been imagined. The essence of what is currently believed about the processes involved was expressed clearly by Klahr and Simon (2001, pp. 78–79):

> A painter is not a scientist; nor is a scientist a lawyer or a cook. But they all use the same weak methods to help solve their respective problems. When their activity is described as search in a problem space, each can understand the rationale of the other's activity . . . At the outer boundaries of creativity . . . recognition becomes less able to evoke pre-learned solutions . . . , and more reliance has to be placed on weak methods.

Evaluation

The approach adopted by Klahr and Simon is a refreshing one. There has been too much of a tendency to regard the processes involved in scientific discovery as being almost incomprehensible to non-scientists because they were so different from those used by people in their everyday lives. It is much more plausible that scientists entering the unknown rely on the same weak methods that most of us use to cope with our daily problems.

The main limitation of Klahr and Simon's approach is that it is more descriptive than explanatory. For example, they identify several weak methods, but it is not possible to predict beforehand which of these methods will be used by a given scientist confronting a particular scientific problem. The approach is also not totally explicit about the ways in which scientists combine the scientific knowledge incorporated in strong methods with the range of weak methods at their disposal.

Variation-selection model

Simonton (e.g., 1997, 2003) developed the notion that there is nothing very special about scientific and other forms of creativity. According to his variation-selection model, creative contributions involve two stages:

(1) *Ideation*, in which ideas are combined in unpredictable and fairly random ways.
(2) *Elaboration*, in which a small fraction of the most promising ideational combinations from the first stage are worked on and turned into finished products (e.g., experiments).

Of central importance is the notion of a *random* element in making creative contributions: "The individual has no a priori way of foreseeing which ideational combinations will prove most fruitful . . . useful and useless variations are more or less randomly distributed both (a) across individual creators and (b) within individual careers . . . for significant acts of creativity, . . . the creator has minimal guidance from logic or past experience and thus must rely on effectively non-directed search for new ideational variations among the population of relevant concepts" (Simonton, 1997, p. 67).

We can test the model by considering the actual major contributions of numerous scientists and other creative individuals. The central prediction is that quantity predicts quality. Thus, those generating numerous ideas and publications (high quantity) are more likely than those generating relatively few to make creative contributions (high quality). Quality can be assessed in several ways (e.g., expert ratings; citations of research in the scientific literature), but fortunately the main measures correlate highly with each other.

Evidence

Quantity of publications predicts quality, since the correlation between quantity and quality is typically between +.50 and +.70. Stronger support for the model comes from studies showing the *ratio* of high-impact publications to total publications is uncorrelated with the total number of publications (see Simonton, 2003). This is known as the equal-odds rule, and means that those producing the greatest number of influential publications also tend to produce the greatest number of ignored publications. This is exactly what we would expect if there is a random element in creative contributions.

What happens when we consider creative contributions *within* individuals? According to the equal-odds rule, the ratio of high-impact contributions to total contributions should remain fairly constant throughout an entire career. That is precisely what the evidence indicates (Simonton, 2003). It also follows from the equal-odds rule that an individual's single most important creative contribution should be most likely to occur when they are most productive. In most fields, people are most productive in mid-career, and it is at that time that they have the highest probability of making their most important contribution. There are also predictable differences between groups of creative individuals. For example, poets on average are most productive 20 years into their career, whereas novelists are most productive 27 years into theirs. As predicted, the age at which the greatest contribution is made is younger for poets than for novelists.

Scientists with similar knowledge working in the same field sometimes independently make the same discovery (e.g., Darwin and Wallace proposing theories of evolution by natural selection). According to the model, such multiple discoveries are expected when scientists with very similar knowledge are working in the same field. However, since scientists generate ideas fairly randomly and the probability of any given idea being successful is very low, it is expected that the great majority of multiple discoveries would typically involve only two scientists. As predicted, 77% of multiple discoveries involve two scientists, and only 1.5% involve five or more (Simonton, 2003).

Evaluation

The notion that there is a random element in creativity in scientists and other creative individuals has received much support. Of particular importance, the single most important factor predicting the number of important creative contributions a scientist or other creative person will make is simply his/her total number of contributions. Such evidence lends credence to the view that even highly intelligent and motivated scientists struggle to move beyond what is already known. As Simonton (2003, p. 487) pointed out, "If it was easy to acquire inferential tools that lead inevitably to breakthrough discoveries, then scientists should improve their hit rates [ratio of successes to total efforts] over the course of their careers."

The model possesses various limitations. First, even though it includes processes such as ideation and elaboration, the model contributes little to our understanding of the cognitive processes underlying creative behaviour. Second, the model is in danger of exaggerating the importance of random elements or chance and underestimating individual differences. As Simonton (1997) admitted, some people (perfectionists) have a much higher ratio of successes to total output than the norm, and perhaps we need to consider such individuals in detail. Third, there is a need to integrate the insights of the variation-selection model with those of more cognitive approaches (e.g., the Geneplore model discussed earlier).

CHAPTER SUMMARY

- Introduction
  The chapter is concerned with issues relating to creativity, hypothesis testing, and scientific discovery. The traditional view that most major creative contributions are made by a few individuals possessing exceptional intellectual and creative abilities is very oversimplified. Instead, it appears that the cognitive processes involved in creative thinking may resemble those used in everyday life.

- Creativity
  Wallas identified separate stages of preparation, incubation, illumination, and verification. There is more support for incubation than for illumination, but this approach is limited because it is mainly descriptive. According to the Geneplore model, we generate ideas and then explore them in detail. The generation process typically relies heavily on prior knowledge, especially on readily accessible knowledge. According to the model, people are more creative if they generate ideas *before* thinking of possible uses for them. The model does not provide a detailed account of the generation and exploration processes, and de-emphasises individual differences.

- Hypothesis testing
  Hypothesis testing has often been studied with Wason's 2-4-6 task. Performance on this task is generally poor. Wason attributed this to confirmation bias, and argued that performance would improve if people engaged in disconfirmatory testing. The evidence is inconsistent, and does not support the notion of a bias towards confirmation. The 2-4-6 task may lack generality because the correct rule is much more general than any of the initial hypotheses participants are likely to form. Performance on the 2-4-6 task is much better when participants have to consider more than one hypothesis. Studies in simulated research environments have found similar evidence that most participants prefer to seek confirmatory evidence for their hypotheses. However, studies of real scientists indicate that research groups vary in their focus on confirmation or disconfirmation.

- Scientific discovery
  According to the dual-search approach, there is one space containing the experimental possibilities and another containing possible hypotheses. Theorists prefer to search the space of hypotheses, whereas experimenters prefer to search the space of experiments. This approach has been expanded to include a paradigm space and a data-representation space. According to Klahr and Simon, scientists use weak methods based on heuristics to produce scientific discoveries. These weak methods resemble those used by non-scientists in everyday life. According to the variation-selection model, creative contributions involve combining ideas in a fairly random way. This is supported by the finding that the probability of producing a significant creative contribution depends much more on the total number of contributions than on the individual concerned or the stage of career.

FURTHER READING

- Klahr, D., & Simon, H.A. (1999). Studies of scientific discovery: Complementary approaches and convergent findings. *Psychological Bulletin*, *125*, 524–543. The authors provide a fascinating account of the main processes and strategies used by scientists.
- Poletiek, F.H. (2001). *Hypothesis-testing behavior*. Philadelphia, PA: Psychology Press. This book contains interesting views on several aspects of hypothesis testing, including Wason's 2-4-6 task.
- Runco, M.A. (2004). Creativity. *Annual Review of Psychology*, *55*, 657–687. The approaches of different disciplines (e.g., cognitive; biological; developmental) to creativity are discussed in this chapter.
- Simonton, D.K. (2003). Scientific creativity as constrained stochastic behaviour: The integration of product, person, and process perspectives. *Psychological Bulletin*, *129*, 475–494. What is special about this article is the way in which theoretical ideas are constructed on the basis of rich data on the scientific contributions of thousands of scientists.
- Sternberg, R.J. (2003). *Wisdom, intelligence, and creativity synthesised*. New York: Cambridge University Press. Bob Sternberg focuses on ways of incorporating creativity into theories of intelligence.

15

Judgement and Decision Making

INTRODUCTION

In this chapter, we consider the overlapping areas of judgement and decision making. In spite of some disagreements about the precise relationship between these two areas, there is a reasonable amount of consensus (Maule, 2001). Judgement researchers address the question, "How do people integrate multiple, incomplete, and sometimes conflicting cues to infer what is happening in the external world?" (Hastie, 2001, p. 657). In contrast, decision making involves choosing among various options. Decision-making researchers address the question, "How do people choose what action to take to achieve labile [changeable], sometimes conflicting goals in an uncertain world?" (Hastie, 2001, p. 657).

There are other differences between judgement and decision making. For example, as Harvey (2001, p. 104) pointed out, "Judgements are assessed in terms of how accurate they are whereas decisions are assessed in terms of their potential consequences . . . judgements have no direct consequences but they can have indirect ones via the decisions that they inform . . . all one has to do to change judgements into decisions is to add consequences to different types of outcome."

Decision making involves some problem solving, since individuals try to make the best possible choice from a range of options. However, there is a difference, in that the options are generally presented in decision making, whereas problem solvers have to generate their own options (Gilhooly, 1996). Another possible difference between decision making and problem solving is that we make decisions in unpredictable environments, whereas we solve problems in predictable ones (Harvey, 2001). However, there are many exceptions to that generalisation.

Finally, we turn to the issue of the relationship between the areas of judgement and of decision making: "Decision making refers to the entire process of choosing a course of action. Judgement refers to the components of the larger decision-making process that are concerned with assessing, estimating, and inferring what events will occur and what the decision-maker's evaluative reactions to those outcomes will be" (Hastie, 2001, p. 657).

There has been heated controversy about what research on judgement and decision making tells us about human rationality. However, that issue is part of a broader one concerning human rationality and logicality in general. That broader issue (which includes consideration of research on judgement and decision making) is discussed at some length at the end of Chapter 16.

JUDGEMENT RESEARCH

We often change our opinion of the likelihood of something in the light of new information. For example, suppose you are 90% confident someone has lied to you. However, their version of events is later confirmed by another person, leading you to believe there is only a 60% probability you have been lied to. Everyday life is full of cases in which the strength of our beliefs is increased or decreased by fresh information.

The Rev. Thomas Bayes provided a more precise way of thinking about such cases. Bayes focused on situations in which there are two possible beliefs or hypotheses (e.g., X is lying vs. X is not lying), and he showed how new information or data change the probabilities of each hypothesis being correct.

According to Bayes' theorem, we need to assess the relative probabilities of the two hypotheses *before* the data are obtained (the prior odds). We also need to calculate the relative probabilities of obtaining the observed data under each hypothesis (the posterior odds). Bayesian methods evaluate the probability of observing the data, D, if hypothesis A is correct, written $p(D/H_A)$, and if hypothesis B is correct, written $p(D/H_B)$. Bayes' theorem is expressed in the form of an odds ratio as follows:

$$\frac{p(H_A/D)}{p(H_B/D)} = \frac{p(H_A)}{p(H_B)} \times \frac{p(D/H_A)}{p(D/H_B)}$$

The above formula may look intimidating and offputting, but is not really so (honest!). On the left side of the equation are the relative probabilities of hypotheses A and B in the light of the new data. These are the probabilities we want to work out. On the right side of the equation, we have the prior odds of each hypothesis being correct *before* the data were collected, multiplied by the posterior odds based on the probability of the data given each hypothesis.

We can clarify Bayes' theorem by considering the taxi-cab problem used by Tversky and Kahneman (1982). In this problem, a taxi-cab was involved in a hit-and-run accident one night. Of the taxi-cabs in the city, 85% belonged to the Green company and 15% to the Blue company. An eyewitness identified the cab as a Blue cab. However, when her ability to identify cabs under appropriate visibility conditions was tested, she was wrong 20% of the time. The participants had to decide the probability that the cab involved in the accident was Blue.

The hypothesis that the cab was Blue is H_A and the hypothesis that it was Green is H_B. The prior probability for H_A is .15, and for H_B it is .85, because 15% of the cabs are blue and 85% are green. The probability of the eyewitness identifying the cab as Blue when it was Blue, $p(D/H_a)$, is .80. Finally, the probability of the eyewitness saying the cab was Blue when it was Green, $p(D/H_b)$ is .20. According to the formula:

$$\frac{.15}{.85} \times \frac{.80}{.20} = \frac{.12}{.17}$$

That means that the odds ratio is 12:17. Thus, there is a 41% (12/29) probability that the taxi-cab was Blue compared to a 59% (17/29) probability that it was Green.

Neglecting base rates

The available evidence indicates that people often take less account of the prior odds (base-rate information) than they should from Bayes' theorem. **Base-rate information** was defined by Koehler (1996, p. 1) as "the relative frequency with which an event occurs or an attribute is present in the population." People often fail to take base rates fully into account. For example, consider the taxi-cab problem discussed earlier. Tversky and Kahneman (1982) found that most participants ignored the base-rate information about the relative numbers of Green and Blue cabs. They concentrated only on the evidence of the witness, and maintained there was an 80% likelihood that the

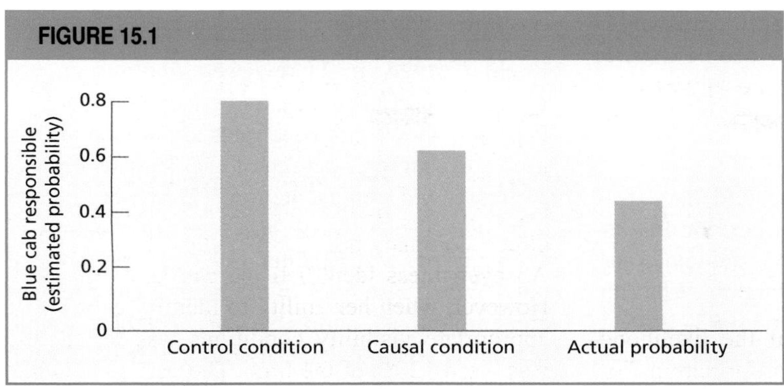

Estimated probability in the taxi-cab problem that a Blue cab was responsible for the accident in causal and control conditions. Data from Tversky and Kahneman, (1982).

taxi was Blue rather than Green (see Figure 15.1). In fact, as we have seen, the correct answer based on Bayes' theorem is 41%.

Tversky and Kahneman (1982) also used a second condition in which people *did* take base-rate information into account. They changed the first part of the problem to:

> Although the two companies are roughly equal in size, 85% of cab accidents in the city involve Green cabs, and 15% involve Blue cabs.

In this version, a clear *causal* relation is drawn between the accident record of a cab company and the likelihood of there being an accident. With this version, base-rate information was used to some extent, with the average estimated probability that a Blue cab was responsible for the accident being 60% (see Figure 15.1).

Some insight into factors determining the extent to which base-rate information is used can be gained by considering the related studies of Casscells, Schoenberger, and Graboys (1978) and of Cosmides and Tooby (1996). The problem used by Casscells et al. (1978) was as follows:

> If a test to detect a disease whose prevalence is 1/1000 has a false positive rate of 5%, what is the chance that a person found to have a positive result actually has the disease, assuming that you know nothing about the person's symptoms or signs?

You may want to pit your wits against the staff and students at Harvard Medical School given this problem, 45% of whom ignored the base-rate information, and so produced the wrong answer of 95%. The correct answer (which is 2%) was given by only 18% of the participants. Why is 2% correct? According to the base-rate information, 999 people out of 1000 do not suffer from the disease. The fact that the false positive rate is 5% means that 50 out of every 1000 people tested would give a misleading positive finding. Thus, 50 times as many people give a false positive result as give a true positive result (the one person in 1000 who actually has the disease), and so there is only a 2% chance that a person testing positive has the disease.

Cosmides and Tooby (1996) expressed the same problem differently by emphasising the *frequencies* of individuals in the various categories:

> One out of 1000 Americans has disease X. A test has been developed to detect when a person has disease X. Every time the test is given to a person who has the disease, the test comes out positive. But sometimes the test also comes out positive when it is given to a person who is completely healthy. Specifically, out of every 1000 people who are perfectly healthy, 50 of them test positive for the disease. Imagine that we have assembled a random sample of 1000 Americans. They were selected by a lottery. Those who conducted the lottery had

no information about the health status of any of these people. How many people who test positive for the disease will actually have the disease? (___ out of ___).

Cosmides and Tooby (1996) found that 76% of the participants produced the correct answer with this frequency version of the problem compared to 12% with the original version. What do these findings mean? Gigerenzer (1993) argued that our experience of the world typically comes in the form of frequencies rather than probabilities. This theoretical approach is discussed shortly. However, note here that the frequency version makes it much easier to make the appropriate calculations. All that has to be done is to relate the figure of 1 per 1000 (those having the disease and testing positive) to the 50 per 1000 (those not having the disease but testing positive).

Further evidence that even experts often fail to use base-rate information when dealing with probabilities was reported by Hoffrage, Lindsey, Hertwig, and Gigerenzer (2000). They gave advanced medical students four realistic diagnostic tasks containing base-rate information presented in either a probability version or a frequency version. These experts paid little attention to base-rate information in the probability versions, but performed much better when given the frequency versions (see Figure 15.2).

Evaluation

Koehler (1996, p. 1) reviewed findings on use of base-rate information, and concluded that "the literature shows that base rates are almost always used and that their degree of use depends on task structure and representation." However, people may make less use of base-rate information in everyday life. As Koehler (1996, p. 14) pointed out, "When base rates in the natural environment are ambiguous, unreliable, or unstable, simple normative rules for their use do not exist. In such cases, the diagnostic value of base rates may be substantially less than that associated with many laboratory experiments."

There are often several competing base rates in the real world. Suppose you want to calculate the probability that a particular professional golfer will score under 70 in her next round on a given course. What is the relevant base rate? Is it her previous scores on that course during her career, or her general level of performance that season, or her performance over her entire career, or the average performance of other professionals on that course?

Natural sampling

We have seen that judgements are often more accurate when based on frequency information rather than on probabilities (Cosmides & Tooby, 1996;

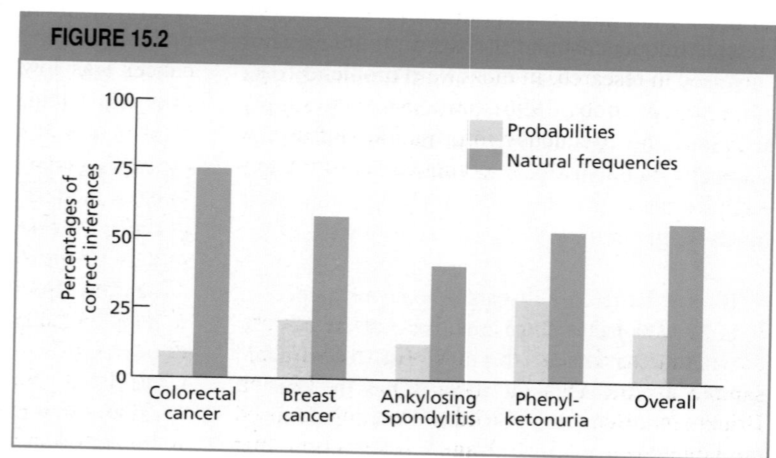

Percentage correct inferences by advanced medical students given four realistic diagnostic tasks expressed in probabilities or frequencies. Reprinted with permission from Hoffrage, U., Lindsey, S., Hertwig, R., & Gigerenzer, G. (2000). Communicating statistical information. *Science, 290,* 2261–2262. Copyright 2000 AAAS.

Hoffrage et al., 2000). Gigerenzer and Hoffrage (1995, 1999) have provided an influential theoretical approach designed to account for such findings. The approach is evolutionary in emphasis and relies heavily on the notion of *natural sampling*, which is "the process of encountering instances in a population sequentially" (Gigerenzer & Hoffrage, 1999, p. 425). Natural sampling is what generally happens in everyday life, and it is assumed that as a result of our evolutionary history we find it easy to work out the frequencies of different kinds of events. According to Gigerenzer and Hoffrage (1999, p. 430), "Humans seem to be developmentally and evolutionarily prepared to handle natural frequencies. In contrast, many of us go through a considerable amount of mental agony to think in terms of fractions, percentages and other forms of normalised counts."

It is important to draw some distinctions which are blurred or unclear in this theoretical approach. For example, the emphasis in the theory is on the "natural" or objective frequencies of certain kinds of events, and it is indisputable that such frequencies can provide potentially valuable information when making judgements. However, in the real world we actually encounter only a sample of events, and the frequencies of various events in this sample may be selective and very different from natural or objective samples (Sloman & Over, 2003). For example, the frequencies of highly intelligent and less intelligent people encountered by most university students are likely to be very different from the frequencies in the population at large. It is also important to distinguish between natural frequencies and the word problems actually used in research. In most word problems (e.g., Cosmides & Tooby, 1996), participants are simply provided with frequency information and do not have to grapple with the complexities of natural sampling.

Evidence

In view of our analysis so far, it is clearly important to address the issue of how effectively people sample events. This has been done by Fiedler, Brinkmann, Betsch, and Wild (2000), who focused on Gigerenzer and Hoffrage's assumption that base-rate fallacies are eliminated when frequencies are sampled. The underlying problem they used is one in which there is an 80% probability that a woman with breast cancer will have a positive mammogram, compared to a 9.6% probability that a woman without breast cancer will have a positive mammogram. The base rate of breast cancer in women is 1%. The task is to decide the probability that a woman has breast cancer given a positive mammogram. The correct answer is 7.8%.

Participants in the experiments of Fiedler et al. (2000) were not given the problem in the form described above. Instead they were provided with index card files and sampled from them. For participants in the criterion-sampling condition, the file was organised into the categories of women with breast cancer versus those without, and each card selected informed them whether the woman in question had breast cancer. The key finding was that the participants' frequency sampling was very biased. The average probability that a woman had breast cancer given a positive mammogram was 85% in the cards they selected, even though the actual probability across all of the cards was only 17%. It was this biased sampling that led the participants to produce an average estimate of 63% that a woman had breast cancer given a positive mammogram.

Other participants were in the predictor-sampling condition, in which the card file was organised into the categories of positive versus negative mammograms. Frequency sampling in this condition typically revealed more clearly than did criterion sampling that the percentage of positive mammograms produced by women with breast cancer was low. As a result, judgements of the probability that a woman has breast cancer given a positive mammogram were much more accurate with predictor sampling than with criterion sampling. However, many people are unaware of the advantages of predictor sampling over criterion sampling with this type of problem. When participants were given the choice, 35% opted for criterion sampling, presumably not realising that this would lead to great oversampling of the rare event (i.e., positive mammogram + breast cancer).

The notion that judgements are more accurate when information is presented in frequencies rather than probabilities has not always been supported. For example, Griffin and Buehler (1999) studied the **planning fallacy**, which is the tendency to underestimate how long it will take to complete a given task even though it is known that similar tasks in the past have taken longer than expected. Most students have found to their cost the problems that can result from the planning fallacy! Griffin and Buehler asked students to list 10 projects, estimate a "best-guess" completion date for each task, estimate the probability that each project would be completed in time, and estimate the number of tasks that would meet the deadline.

Griffin and Buehler (1999) converted the estimates into percentages. Students expected 73% of the projects to be finished on time when using probabilities compared to 65% when using frequencies. In fact, only 48% of the projects were actually completed on time, so there was convincing evidence of a planning fallacy in both cases. As Griffin and Buehler (1999, p. 75) concluded, "Under most real-life circumstances, intuitive judgements are equally biased regardless of . . . whether frequency or probability is used."

Evaluation

There are two major apparent strengths of the theoretical approach advocated by Gigerenzer and Hoffrage (1995, 1999). First, it makes sense to argue that use of natural or objective sampling could enhance the accuracy of many of our judgements. Second, we have seen that judgements based on frequency information are often superior to those based on probability information, and we will discuss further examples shortly (e.g., Fiedler, 1988).

The natural sampling approach has several limitations. First, there is often a yawning chasm between people's actual sampling behaviour and the neat-and-tidy frequency data provided in laboratory experiments. As we saw in the experiments of Fiedler et al. (2000), the samples selected by participants can provide biased and complex information which is very hard to interpret. As Fiedler (2000, p. 670) pointed out in an excellent analysis of the perils of sampling, "On the one hand, the density and distribution of information in the environment varies strongly. On the other hand, the individual's attention and information search are selective. The result of this cognitive-ecological interaction is a sampling product that is very unlikely to conserve all properties of the world."

Second, it is simply not the case that the frequency data magically eliminate all (or even most) cognitive biases. For example, we saw that the use of frequencies failed to remove the planning fallacy (Griffin & Buehler, 1999).

Third, even when judgements are significantly more accurate when based on frequencies rather than probabilities, the findings do not require an explanation in evolutionary terms. Sloman and Over (2003) have reviewed the evidence, and shown convincingly that frequency versions of problems nearly always make their underlying structure much easier to grasp (see also Girotto & Gonzalez, 2001). For example, in the frequency version of the diagnosis problem (Cosmides & Tooby, 1996), participants could ignore base rates and focus only on the absolute frequencies of (1) patients with the disease testing positive and (2) patients without the disease testing positive. At the risk of being facetious, note that our evolutionary ancestors did not have to solve the kinds of judgement problems used in laboratory research in order to survive (Over, personal communication)! More seriously, we cannot test directly the notion that success for our ancestors only required an ability to work with frequencies.

Representativeness heuristic

Why do we fail to make proper use of base-rate information? According to Kahneman and Tversky, we often use a simple heuristic or rule of thumb known as the **representativeness heuristic**. When people use this heuristic, "events that are representative or typical of a class are assigned a high probability of occurrence. If an event is highly similar to most of the others in a population or class of events, then it is considered representative" (Kellogg, 1995, p. 385). The representativeness heuristic is used when people judge the probability that an object or event A belongs to a class or process B. Suppose you are given the description of an individual, and estimate the probability he/she has a certain occupation. You would probably estimate the probability mostly in terms of the *similarity* between that individual's description and your stereotype of that occupation.

Kahneman and Tversky (1973, p. 241) studied people's use of the representativeness heuristic. Their participants were given the following description:

> Jack is a 45-year-old man. He is married and has four children. He is generally conservative, careful, and ambitious. He shows no interest in political and social issues and spends most of his free time on his many hobbies which include home carpentry, sailing, and mathematical puzzles.

The participants had to decide the probability that Jack was an engineer or a lawyer. They were all told the description had been selected at random from a total of 100 descriptions. Half of the participants were told there were descriptions of 70 engineers and 30 lawyers, whereas the other half were told there were descriptions of 70 lawyers and 30 engineers.

The participants decided on average that there was a .90 probability that Jack was an engineer, regardless of whether most of the 100 descriptions were of lawyers or of engineers. Thus, the participants did not take account of the base-rate information (i.e., the 70:30 split of the 100 descriptions).

Slugoski and Wilson (1998) related Kahneman and Tversky's (1973) findings to Grice's Co-operative Principle (discussed in Chapter 12). Grice (1967) argued that we expect a speaker to focus on things relevant to the situation. Thus, participants given the engineers/lawyers problem assume the description of Jack is directly relevant to the problem. This leads them to concentrate on the description rather than the base-rate information. Slugoski and Wilson (1998) argued that individuals with good conversational skills would be most likely to be led astray in this way. As predicted, their performance on the engineers/lawyer was *worse* than that of individuals with poor conversational skills. Thus, one of the reasons why people ignore base-rate information on this problem is because of a simple misinterpretation.

Griffin and Buehler (1999) took various steps in the attempt to make participants focus more on base-rate information. They used a large transparent plastic box containing 100 balls, 70 of which were white and 30 of which were green, with white indicating either the descriptions of engineers or of lawyers. Participants guessed the relative numbers of white and green balls (base-rate information) and then chose a ball at random with their eyes closed. They then received the description of Jack. Finally, they estimated either the probability that Jack was an engineer or how many descriptions out of 10 resembling the one of Jack would be engineers. Base-rate information had much more effect on frequency judgements than on probability judgements, showing that frequency formats are sometimes useful in improving judgemental accuracy.

The representativeness fallacy is also involved in the **conjunction fallacy**. This is the mistaken belief that the conjunction or combination of two events (A and B) is more likely than one of the two events alone. Tversky and Kahneman (1983) obtained evidence of the conjunction fallacy using the following description:

> Linda is 31 years old, single, outspoken, and very bright. She majored in philosophy. As a student, she was deeply concerned with issues of discrimination and social justice, and also participated in anti-nuclear demonstrations.

They were then asked to rank-order eight possible categories in terms of the probability that Linda belonged to each one. Three of the categories were bank teller, feminist, and feminist bank teller. Most participants ranked feminist bank teller as more probable than either bank teller or feminist. This is incorrect, because all feminist bank tellers belong to the larger categories of bank tellers and of feminists!

Fiedler (1988) compared performance on the original version of the Linda problem with that on a frequency version, in which the participants indicated how many of 100 people fitting Linda's

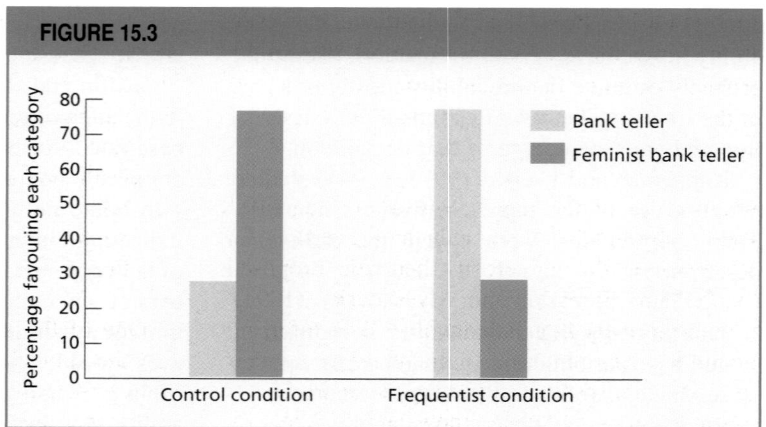

Performance on the Linda problem in the frequentist and control conditions. Data from Fiedler (1988).

description were bank tellers, and how many were bank tellers and active feminists. The percentage of participants showing the conjunction fallacy dropped dramatically with the frequency version (see Figure 15.3). Performance may have been better with the frequency version because people are more used to dealing with frequencies than with probabilities or because it makes the structure of the problem more obvious. (In the interests of historical accuracy, it should be noted that Tversky & Kahneman, 1983, were the first to use a frequency version of the Linda problem.)

Availability heuristic

Tversky and Kahneman (1974) studied another heuristic or rule of thumb. This was the **availability heuristic**, which involves estimating the frequencies of events on the basis of how easy or difficult it is to retrieve relevant information from long-term memory. Tversky and Kahneman (1974) asked their participants the following question:

> If a word of three letters or more is sampled at random from an English text, is it more likely that the word starts with "r" or has "r" as its third letter?

Most participants argued that a word starting with "r" was more likely to be picked out at random than a word with "r" as its third letter. There are actually more words with "r" as the third letter, but words starting with "r" can be retrieved more easily from memory (i.e., are more available). That is why the participants made the wrong decision.

Tversky and Kahneman (1983) reported a more striking case in which use of the availability heuristic led to error. Their participants rated the frequency of seven-letter words ending in "ing" and "-n-" out of 2000 words taken from a novel. Most of them claimed that there would be many more words ending in "ing". This claim resulted from use of the availability heuristic. However, it is wrong, because all words ending in "ing" also end in "-n-"!

Use of the availability heuristic often produces errors in everyday life. Lichtenstein et al. (1978) asked people to judge the relative likelihood of different causes of death. Those causes of death attracting considerable publicity (e.g., murder) were judged more likely than those that do not (e.g., suicide), even when the opposite is actually the case.

People do not always use the availability heuristic to judge the frequency of events. For example, Brown (1995) presented category–exemplar pairs (e.g., Country–France), with each category being presented several times. The category name was always accompanied by the same exemplar (same context) or a different exemplar (different context). The task was to decide how frequently each category name had been presented. In the different-context condition, about 60% of the participants reported using the availability heuristic. However, in the same-context condition, almost 70% of the participants did not use any clear strategy.

Numerosity heuristic

Most of the heuristics involved in judgement were proposed by Kahneman and Tversky. An exception is the numerosity heuristic proposed by Pelham, Sumarta, and Myaskovsky (1994). The **numerosity heuristic** involves over-inferring quantity or amount from numerosity or number of units into which something is divided. For example, as many dieters know, people generally eat less when food is divided into small pieces, in part because that makes it seem as if there is more food present than is actually the case. Participants asked to estimate the value of sets of coins gave higher estimates when there were many coins. In general, there is more evidence for the numerosity heuristic when the judging task is difficult. For example, the amount of pizza present is judged to be greater when pieces of pizza are arranged in a straight line rather than in a circular pattern.

Support theory

Tversky and Koehler (1994) put forward their support theory, based in part on the availability heuristic. The key assumption is that any given event will appear more or less likely depending on how it is described. Thus, we need to distinguish between events themselves and the descriptions of those events. For example, you would almost certainly assume that the probability that you will die on your next summer holiday is extremely low. However, it would seem more likely if you were asked the following question: "What is the probability that you will die on your next summer holiday from a disease, a car accident, a plane crash, or from any other cause?"

Why would the subjective probability of death on holiday be greater in the second case than the first? According to support theory, a more explicit description of an event will typically be regarded as having greater subjective probability than the same event described in less explicit terms. There are two main reasons (related to the availability heuristic) behind this theoretical assumption:

(1) An explicit description may draw attention to aspects of the event that are less obvious in the non-explicit description.
(2) Memory limitations may mean that people do not remember all of the relevant information if it is not supplied.

One of the assumptions of support theory is that the subjective probability of any given possibility increases when it is mentioned explicitly and so becomes salient or conspicuous. Suppose there are three possible events (A, B, and C), and that the probability of each is assessed in turn. The prediction is that the probability of each event will tend to be exaggerated when it is made explicit. As a result, the total subjective probability of A + B + C will exceed 1.

Rottenstreich and Tversky (1997) developed support theory, adding a counterintuitive prediction to it. Suppose we ask some individuals to estimate the probability of event A and then separately to estimate the probability of event B. We can then add them together (event A + event B) to give a combined probability. We ask other individuals to estimate a *single* probability, namely, that either event A or event B will occur (event A or event B). Common sense would suggest that the overall probability estimate would be the same for both groups. However, Rottenstreich and Tversky (1997) argued that the estimated probability (event A or event B) will often be *less* than that for event A + event B. This prediction is based on the assumption that there is a more thorough consideration of the two events when each one has to be assigned its own probability.

Evidence

Johnson et al. (1993) reported evidence consistent with support theory. Some participants were offered hypothetical health insurance covering hospitalisation for any reason, whereas others were offered health insurance covering hospitalisation for any disease or accident. These offers are the same, but participants were willing to pay a higher premium in the latter case. Presumably the explicit references to disease and accident made it seem more likely that hospitalisation would be required, and so increased the value of being insured.

We might imagine that it would be harder to obtain evidence favouring support theory if experts were studied. After all, experts provided with a non-explicit description can presumably fill in the missing details from their own knowledge. However, the phenomenon of higher subjective probability for an explicitly described event has been found in experts as well as non-experts. Redelmeier et al. (1995) presented expert doctors with a description of a woman with abdominal pain. Half of them assessed the probabilities of two specified diagnoses (gastroenteritis and ectopic pregnancy) and of a residual category of everything else. The other half assigned probabilities to five specified diagnoses (including gastroenteritis and ectopic pregnancy) and the residual category of everything else. The key comparison was between the subjective probability of the residual category for the former group and the combined probabilities of the three additional diagnoses plus the residual category in the latter group. Since both subjective probabilities cover the same range of diagnoses, they should have been the same. However, the former probability was .50, whereas the latter probability was .69, indicating that subjective probabilities are higher for explicit descriptions even with experts.

The prediction that the sum of the judged probabilities of a complete set of possibilities will be greater than 1 has been confirmed several times, even with experts. For example, Fox, Rogers, and Tversky (1996) asked options traders to estimate the probabilities of each of four hypotheses concerning the closing price of Microsoft stock. These hypotheses covered all possibilities and so the sum of the probabilities must actually be 1. In fact, the sum of the probabilities assigned to the four hypotheses by the expert traders was substantially greater than 1. Furthermore, the traders were willing to bet on the accuracy of their inflated probability estimates!

Rottenstreich and Tversky (1997) tested the prediction that the combined probability of one out of two events (A and B) occurring will be greater when the probability of each event is assessed separately rather than jointly. For some of the participants, event A was daytime murder and event B was night-time murder. For other participants, event A was murder by an acquaintance and event B was murder by a stranger. The estimated probabilities in the various conditions that a random death is due to murder rather than being an accidental death are shown in Figure 15.4. As can be seen, the prediction was confirmed.

Evaluation

The main predictions of support theory have often been confirmed with a range of tasks. Another strength of support theory is that it helps us to understand more clearly how the availability heuristic can lead to errors in judgement. It is also impressive (and somewhat surprising) that experts' judgements are influenced by the explicitness of the information provided. On the negative side, it is not very clear *why* people often overlook information that is well known to them. It is also not entirely clear *why* focusing on a given possibility typically increases its perceived support.

Overall evaluation

Kahneman and Tversky have shown that several general heuristics or rules of thumb (e.g., representativeness heuristic; availability heuristic) underlie judgements in many different contexts. These biases may well be of great practical importance, and also help us to understand aspects of human reasoning (see Chapter 16). The importance of this research is shown in the award of the Nobel Prize to Daniel Kahneman.

There are various limitations of the approach advocated by Kahneman and Tversky. First, as Gigerenzer (1996) pointed out, Kahneman and Tversky have failed to provide process models specifying in detail when and how the various heuristics are used. According to Gigerenzer (1996, p. 594), "The two major surrogates [substitutes] for modelling cognitive processes have been (a) one-word labels such as representativeness that seem to be traded as explanations, and (b) explanations by redescription." Thus, we have

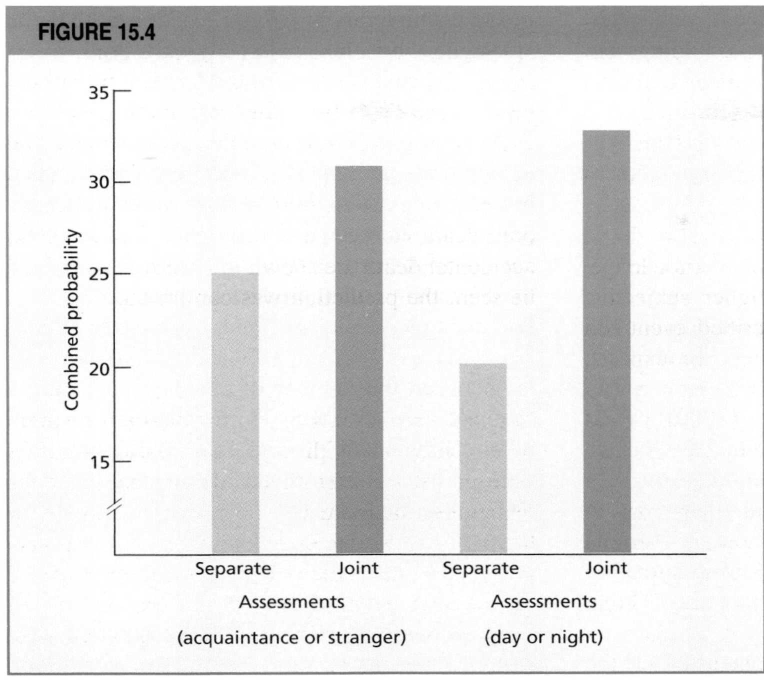

The subjective probability that an accidental death is due to murder as a function of categories used (acquaintance vs. stranger; day vs. night) and whether probabilities were assessed separately or jointly. Data from Rottenstreich and Tversky (1997).

a very limited understanding of what is involved in the use of these heuristics.

Second, some errors of judgement in the various studies occurred because the participants misunderstood parts of the problem presented to them. For example, it has been found in studies on the Linda problem that between 20% and 50% of participants interpret "Linda is a bank teller" as implying that she is not active in the feminist movement (see Gigerenzer, 1996). However, there is still significant evidence of the conjunction fallacy even when almost everything possible is done to ensure that participants do not misinterpret the problem (Sides, Osherson, Bonini, & Viale, 2002).

Third, much research on heuristics and biases is rather detached from the realities of everyday life. Our judgements are often influenced by a range of emotional and motivational factors rarely studied in the laboratory. For example, Hewstone, Benn, and Wilson (1988) carried out a study using the same numbers as in the taxi-cab problem (Tversky & Kahneman, 1982), but they changed the problem into one about a burglary said by a witness to have been committed by a white or black youth. In the causal version of this problem, base-rate information about the numbers of white and black youths committing burglaries was provided. The participants (all of whom were white) made use of the base-rate information, but did so in a prejudiced way. When the base-rate probability was .41 that the burglary was committed by a black youth, the actual reported probability was .60. However, when the base-rate probability was .41 that it was committed by a white youth, the reported probability was only .21.

Fourth, Kahneman and Tversky have paid relatively little attention to individual differences, and this may be an important omission. Stanovich and West (1998a) considered individual differences when they studied accuracy on the non-causal version of the taxi-cab problem (Tversky & Kahneman, 1982) and on an AIDS testing problem based on the diagnosis problem used by Casscells et al. (1978). Performance on the taxi-cab problem was unrelated to intelligence and performance on the AIDS problem was *negatively* related to intelligence! These findings are surprising given that intelligence nearly always correlates positively with performance on cognitively demanding tasks. The reasons why this typical relationship does not apply on two judgement tasks remain to be identified.

Fast and frugal heuristics

We have seen that heuristics or rules of thumb often lead us to make errors of judgement. In contrast, Gigerenzer, Todd, and the ABC Research Group (1999) and Todd and Gigerenzer (2000) argued that heuristics are often very valuable. Indeed, they entitled their 1999 book *Simple heuristics that make us smart*. Their central focus was on fast and frugal heuristics, defined as "simple rules in the mind's adaptive toolbox for making decisions with realistic mental resources" (Todd & Gigerenzer, 2000, p. 727).

One of the key fast-and-frugal heuristics is the take-the-best heuristic or strategy, which involves "take the best, ignore the rest". We can illustrate the use of this strategy with the concrete example of deciding whether Herne or Cologne has the larger population. Suppose you start by assuming the most valid cue to city size is that cities whose names you recognise typically have larger populations than those whose names you do not recognise. However, you recognise both names. Then you think of another valid cue to city size, namely that cities with cathedrals tend to be larger than those without. Accordingly, since you know that Cologne has a cathedral but are unsure about Herne, you produce the answer "Cologne". In essence, then, the take-the-best strategy has three components: (1) Search rule: search cues (e.g., name recognition; cathedral) in order of validity; (2) Stopping rule: stop after finding a discriminatory cue; (3) Decision rule: choose outcome.

The most researched example of the take-the-best strategy is the **recognition heuristic**, which is as follows: "If one of two objects is recognised and the other is not, then infer that the recognised object has the higher value with respect to the criterion" (Goldstein & Gigerenzer, 2002, p. 76). In the example above, if you recognise the name "Cologne" but not "Herne", then you guess (correctly) that Cologne is the larger city without taking account of any other information.

Why might people use the take-the-best and recognition heuristics? There are three main reasons. First, it is claimed from an evolutionary perspective that humans have learned to use valid cues to make certain kinds of decisions. Second, these heuristics often produce accurate predictions. For example, Goldstein and Gigerenzer (2002) reported correlations of +.60 and +.66 in two studies between the number of people recognising a city and its population. Third, it is hard to think of any judgement process that would take less time or be less cognitively demanding than the recognition heuristic.

Evidence

Goldstein and Gigerenzer (2002) carried out several experiments to study use of the recognition heuristic. In one experiment, students from the University of Chicago were given numerous pairs of German cities and were asked to decide which was the larger city in each case. When only one city name was recognised, the participants used the recognition heuristic in their judgements 90% of the time.

It could be argued that the above finding is fairly trivial, because participants may often have had no other useful information other than recognition to guide their judgement. More impressive evidence was reported by Goldstein and Gigerenzer (2002) in another experiment. The task was as before, but this time the participants were told at the outset that German cities with football teams tend to be larger than those without. They were also told the names of well-known cities with and without football teams. Of key importance were the judgements when participants decided whether a recognised city without a football team was larger or smaller than an unrecognised city. In spite of the conflicting information about the absence of a football team, participants used the recognition heuristic 92% of the time.

Suppose we presented American and German students with pairs of American cities and pairs of German cities, and asked them to select the larger city in each pair. Common sense would suggest that performance would be better when the participants were judging cities in their own country, because they would obviously have much more information about such cities. However, the disadvantage is that you cannot apply the recognition heuristic when you recognise both cities in a pair. The findings were impressive: American and German students performed less well on cities in their own country than on those in the other country. Thus, the recognition heuristic can be more useful than a substantial amount of additional knowledge.

There are potential interpretive problems with some of the findings reported by Goldstein and Gigerenzer (2002). Consider the finding that participants typically decide that a recognised city is larger than an unrecognised one. The decision could be due solely to the recognition heuristic, but could also be due to participants' knowledge that the recognised city is large. Oppenheimer (2003) carried out a study to unconfound the effects of recognition and knowledge of size. In the crucial condition, participants had to decide whether recognised cities that were known to be small were larger than unrecognised cities. The small cities were relatively local to Stanford University where the study took place and the unrecognised cities were fictitious but sounded plausible (e.g., Las Besas; Rio Del Sol). The recognition heuristic failed to predict the results: the recognised city was judged to be larger on only 37% of trials. Thus, knowledge of city size can override the recognition heuristic.

There is accumulating evidence that the take-the-best strategy is used less often than assumed by Gigerenzer et al. (1999). For example, Newell, Weston, and Shanks (2003) asked participants to choose between the shares of two fictitious companies (Share A and Share B) on the basis of various cues. When the data were pooled across two experiments, it emerged that only 33% of the participants conformed to all three components of the take-the-best strategy. The most common deviation from that strategy was to fail to stop searching for information after finding a discriminatory cue. Participants who used more cue information than predicted by the take-the-best strategy were said to be using a weight-of-evidence strategy. As Newell et al. (2003, p. 92) concluded, "The description of TTB [take-the-best] as it stands is too restrictive to encompass the wide variability in the behaviour we observed."

Newell and Shanks (2003) considered various versions of the share-choosing task used by Newell et al. (2003) in an attempt to discover factors influencing use or non-use of the take-the-best strategy. The take-the-best strategy was most likely to be used when the cost of obtaining information was high and when the validities of the cues were known. However, there were no circumstances in which all participants used the take-the-best strategy, even though on average those who used that strategy outperformed those who did not.

Bröder (2003) also employed the task of choosing between shares, setting up two conditions in which the take-the-best strategy was or was not the best strategy to use. He found that 77% of the participants used the take-the-best strategy when it was the best one to use, compared to only 15% when it was not. In the former condition, it was mainly the more intelligent participants who used the take-the-best strategy. These findings raise the issue of how people decide which strategy to adopt, an issue that has not been considered systematically by advocates of fast-and-frugal heuristics.

Evaluation

There is good evidence that people often use fast-and-frugal heuristics such as the recognition heuristic and the take-the-best strategy. These heuristics can be surprisingly effective in spite of their simplicity, and it is especially impressive that individuals with little knowledge who use simple heuristics sometimes outperform those with greater knowledge. In general, the notion that we frequently make choices by focusing on a very small number of valid sources of information is an attractive one.

In spite of its various successes, the approach based on fast-and-frugal heuristics has several important limitations. First, as we have seen, the major fast-and-frugal heuristics are used much less frequently than predicted theoretically (e.g., Newell & Shanks, 2003; Newell et al., 2003; Oppenheimer, 2003).

Second, fast-and-frugal heuristics are clearly of relevance only in certain circumstances. As Todd and Gigerenzer (2000, p. 776) admitted, "Some higher-order processes, such as the creative processes involved in the development of scientific theories or the design of sophisticated artefacts, are most likely beyond the purview [scope] of fast and frugal heuristics."

Third, far too little attention has been paid to the issue of the importance of the decision that has to be made. Compare deciding which of two cities is larger with a woman deciding which of two men to marry. Decision making may well stop after a single discriminatory cue has been found with the city-size decision, but most women want to consider *all* of the relevant evidence before getting married!

Fourth, the theoretical approach of Gigerenzer et al. (1999) lacks an adequate account of the sheer *variety* of strategies used depending on the situation and on individual differences. As Newell et al. (2003, p. 92) argued, "Unless we can *a priori* specify the conditions under which certain heuristics will be selected over others—and provide human data consistent with these predictions—the predictive and explanatory power of the fast-and-frugal approach remains questionable."

Fifth, Gigerenzer et al. (1999) emphasised the differences between their theoretical approach and that of Kahneman and Tversky. However, the similarities seem more apparent than the differences. Both approaches are based squarely on heuristics, and their take-the-best strategy clearly resembles the availability heuristic of Kahneman and Tversky.

DECISION MAKING

When we are faced by a choice affecting us personally (e.g., going to France or to Spain for a holiday), there are typically benefits and costs associated with each option. How do we decide what to do? At one time, it was assumed that people behave rationally, and so select the best option. This assumption was built into **normative theories**, which focused on how people should make decisions while de-emphasising how they actually make them. For example, according to the utility theory put forward by von Neumann and Morgenstern (1947), we try to maximise *utility*, which is the subjective value we attach to an outcome. When we need to choose between simple options, we assess the expected utility or expected value of each one by means of the following formula:

$$\text{Expected utility} = (\text{probability of a given outcome}) \times (\text{utility of the outcome})$$

One of the important contributions of von Neumann and Morgenstern (1947) was to treat decisions as if they were gambles. As Manktelow (1999) pointed out, this approach was subsequently coupled with Savage's (1954) mathematical approach based on using information from people's preference to combine subjective utilities and subjective probabilities. This led to the development of subjective expected utility theory.

In the real world, there will typically be various factors associated with each option. For example, one holiday option may be preferable to another because it is in a more interesting area and the weather is likely to be better. However, the first holiday is more expensive and more of your valuable holiday time would be spent in travelling. In such circumstances, people are supposed to calculate the expected utility or disutility (cost) of each factor to work out the overall expected value or utility of each option. In fact, people's choices and decisions are often decided by factors other than simply utility.

There is a key limitation of theory and research on decision making. As Hastie (2001, p. 665) pointed out, "Most current decision theories are designed to account for the choice of one action at one point in time. The image of a decision maker standing at a choice point like a fork in a road and choosing one direction or the other is probably much less appropriate for major everyday decisions than the image of a boat navigating a rough sea with a sequence of many embedded choices and decisions to maintain a meandering course toward the ultimate goal." Thus, decision making in everyday life is typically much more complex than it is under laboratory conditions.

Prospect theory

We can distinguish between risky and risk-free decision making. In the former case, there is uncertainty about the consequences of making a decision, whereas in the latter case there is not. Kahneman and Tversky (1979, 1984) developed an approach to risky decision making known as prospect theory. Prospect theory has its origins in subjective expected utility theory. However, there are important differences between the two theories. As we will see, prospect theory can account for several findings that are inconsistent with predictions from subjective expected utility theory.

The major assumptions of the theory are contained in the value function shown in Figure 15.5. Value or utility forms the vertical axis, and money value in terms of gains and losses forms the horizontal axis. There is a reference point (where the two axes cross), which typically represents an individual's current state. Of most importance, it follows from the theory that risky decisions depend very much on whether decision making concerns possible gains or losses. According to the value function, people show **loss aversion**, i.e., they are much more sensitive to potential losses than potential gains.

According to prospect theory, people give too much weight to very small probabilities. This helps to explain (Jonathan Evans, personal communication) the human tendency for risk seeking with gains (e.g., gambling on remote events) and for risk avoidance with losses (e.g., buying insurance).

FIGURE 15.5

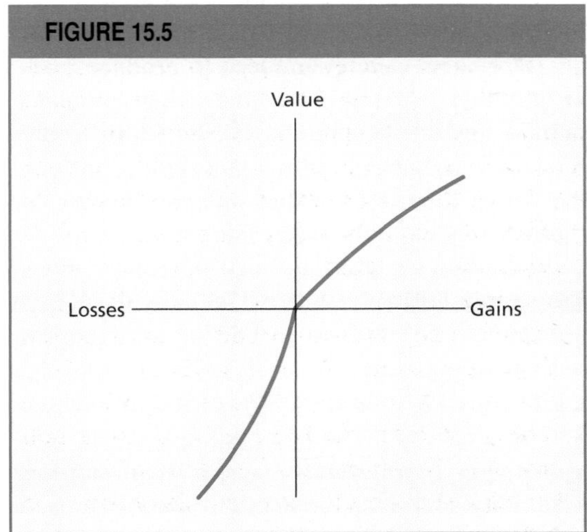

A hypothetical value function. From Kahneman and Tversky (1984). Copyright © 1984 by the American Psychological Association. Reprinted with permission.

Evidence

There is substantial evidence for the existence of loss aversion. For example, Kahneman and Tversky (1984) found that most of their participants refused to bet when offered \$20 if a tossed coin came up heads and a loss of \$10 if it came up tails. This showed clear sensitivity to loss, because the bet provides an average expected gain of \$5 per toss.

A phenomenon resembling loss aversion is the **sunk-cost effect**, in which additional resources are expended to justify some previous commitment. Dawes (1988) discussed a study in which participants were told that two people had paid a \$100 non-refundable deposit for a weekend at a resort. On the way to the resort, both of them became slightly unwell, and felt they would probably have a more pleasurable time at home than at the resort. Should they drive on or turn back? Many participants argued the two people should drive on to avoid wasting the \$100: this is the sunk-cost effect. This decision involves extra expenditure (money spent at the resort vs. staying at home), even though it is less preferred than being at home!

It follows from prospect theory that a sure gain should be chosen over a risky but potentially greater gain. Kahneman and Tversky (1984) found that most people preferred a sure gain of \$800 to an 85% probability of gaining \$1000 and a 15% probability of gaining nothing. This is known as **risk aversion**, and occurs in spite of the fact that the expected value of the risky decision is greater than that of the sure gain (\$850 versus \$800, respectively).

Prospect theory does *not* lead to the prediction that people will *always* seek to avoid risky decisions. Suppose people were offered the choice between a sure loss of $800 or an 85% probability of losing $1000 with a 15% probability of not incurring any loss. When Kahneman and Tversky (1984) offered their participants that choice, most of them engaged in **risk seeking**. They took a chance on avoiding loss, in spite of the fact that this increased the average expected loss from $800 to $850. This is as predicted by prospect theory, according to which people are very sensitive about potential losses.

Some research has compared predictions from prospect theory against those from subjective expected utility theory or other normative theories. A clear prediction from the latter theories is that individuals should adhere to the **dominance principle**. According to this principle, "if Option A is at least as good as Option B in all respects and better than B in at least one aspect, then A should be preferred to B" (Gilhooly, 1996, p. 178). As we will see, the dominance principle is sometimes violated.

Kahneman and Tversky (1984) asked their participants to make two decisions. The first decision involved choosing between:

(A) a sure gain of $240;
(B) a 25% probability of gaining $1000 and a 75% probability of gaining nothing.

The second decision involved choosing between:

(C) a sure loss of $750;
(D) a 76% probability of losing $1000 and a 24% probability of losing nothing.

According to the dominance principle, the participants should have chosen B and C over A and D. Options B and C together offer a 25% probability of gaining $250 and a 75% probability of losing $750, whereas options A and D together offer a 24% probability of gaining $240 and a 76% probability of losing $760. In fact, 73% of the participants chose A and D, whereas only 3% chose B and C. Kahneman and Tversky (1984) argued that the participants showed risk aversion in the domain of gains and risk seeking in the domain of losses.

Prospect theory is of relevance in real-world decision making. Banks et al. (1995) studied the effectiveness of two videotapes in persuading women to undergo a mammogram or breast examination. Both videotapes contained the same medical facts, but one emphasised the gains of mammography whereas the other focused on the risks of not undergoing a mammogram. As predicted by prospect theory, more of the women watching the risk-focused videotape obtained a mammogram within the following 12-month period.

Little research has considered individual differences. This is strange, given that some people are much more willing than others to engage in risky decision making. An exception was a study by Lopes (1987), who used a short questionnaire to identify risk-averse and risk-seeking participants. According to Lopes (1987, pp. 274–275), "Risk-averse people appear to be motivated by a desire for *security*, whereas risk-seeking people appear to be motivated by a desire for *potential gain* . . . Risk-averse people look more at the downside and risk seekers more at the upside."

Lopes (1987) asked her participants to choose between various lotteries having 100 tickets, all of which had an expected value of about $100. The lotteries varied in terms of risk: at one extreme, all 100 tickets were guaranteed to produce $100; at the other extreme, 31 of the tickets produced nothing and 6 tickets produced over $300. As predicted, the risk-averse participants tended to avoid the riskier lotteries, but that was not the case for the risk-seeking ones (see Figure 15.6).

Self-esteem is also important. Josephs, Larrick, Steele, and Nisbett (1992) asked individuals high and low in self-esteem to choose between two options of equal utility but differing in risk (e.g., a sure win of $10 versus a 50% chance of winning $20 on a gamble). The key finding was that individuals low in self-esteem were 50% more likely than those high in self-esteem to choose the sure gain. People with low self-esteem seem to focus on self-protection, and are concerned that negative or threatening events will reduce still further their self-esteem.

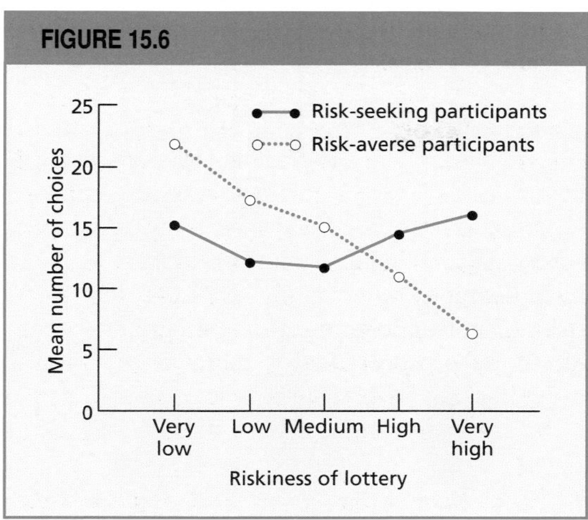

Mean riskiness of lotteries chosen by risk-seeking and by risk-averse participants. Based on data in Lopes (1987).

Framing effect

One of the main lines of research on prospect theory has involved the **framing effect**, in which decisions are influenced by irrelevant aspects of the situation. For example, Tversky and Kahneman (1987) used the Asian disease problem. Their participants were told that there was likely to be an outbreak of an Asian disease in the United States, and it was expected to kill 600 people. Two programmes of action had been proposed: Programme A would allow 200 people to be saved; programme B would have a 1/3 probability that 600 people would be saved, and a 2/3 probability that none of the 600 would be saved. When the issue was expressed in this form, 72% of the participants favoured programme A, although the two programmes (if implemented several times) would on average both lead to the saving of 200 lives.

Other participants in the study by Tversky and Kahneman (1987) were given the same problem, but this time it was negatively framed. They were told that programme A would lead to 400 people dying, whereas programme B carried a 1/3 probability that nobody would die and a 2/3 probability that 600 would die. In spite of the fact that the problem was the same, 78% chose programme B. The various findings obtained by Tversky and Kahneman (1987) can be accounted for in terms of loss aversion in the sense of avoiding certain losses. However, since the problem was identical whether framed positively or negatively, the prediction from subjective expected utility theory is that framing would have no effect.

Wang (1996) carried out a series of studies using different versions of the Asian disease problem in which the total number of people in the patient group varied between 600 and 6. He replicated the findings of Tversky and Kahneman (1987) when the group size was 600. However, the key findings were as follows:

(1) There was no framing effect when the size of the patient group was 60 or 6.
(2) With the smaller patient groups, there was a clear preference for the probabilistic outcome (1/3 probability that nobody would die, and a 2/3 probability that everyone would die).

What do these findings mean? The participants who chose the probabilistic outcome said they wanted to give everyone an equal chance to survive. Thus, they were concerned about fairness, and this concern was greater in a small-group than in a large-group context.

Wang (1996) then asked participants to choose between two options: (1) one-third of the group is saved; (2) one-third of the group is selected to be saved. When the group size was 600, 60% of the participants chose the option with the non-selected survivors; this rose to 80% when the group size was 6. Thus, concerns about fairness are greater when dealing with small groups than with large ones.

In a final study, Wang (1996) asked participants to choose between definite survival of two-thirds of the patients (deterministic option) or a one-third probability of all patients surviving and a two-thirds probability of none surviving (probabilistic option). They were told that the group size was 600, 6, or 3 patients unknown to them, or 6 patients who were close relatives of the participant. Wang (1996) found that the decision was greatly influenced by group size and by the relationship between the participants and the group members (see Figure 15.7). Presumably the increased percentage of participants choosing

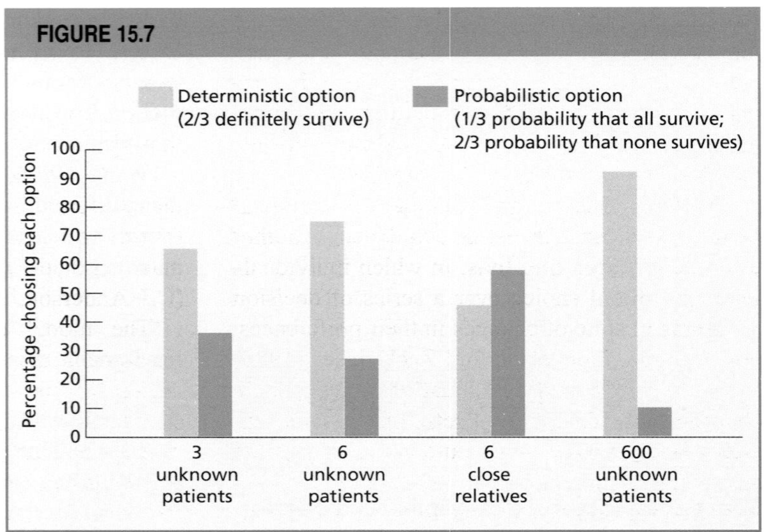

Effects of fairness manipulation on choice of the option with selected or with non-selected survivors. Data from Wang (1996).

the probabilistic option with small group size (especially for relatives) occurred because the social context and psychological factors relating to fairness were regarded as more important in those conditions. Of course, these are self-report data, and so some participants may simply have given what seemed to be socially desirable responses.

The above findings are hard to explain within prospect theory, because they indicate that decision making can be influenced by social and moral considerations not included in the theory. In addition, the findings are totally inconsistent with utility theory, especially those from the final study. According to utility theory, the participants should always have chosen the definite survival of two-thirds of the patients rather than a one-third probability of all patients surviving. However, this was not what happened.

Omission bias and decision avoidance

There is other evidence that emotional and social factors not included within prospect theory influence decision making. Ritov and Baron (1990) carried out a study in which their participants were told to assume that their child had 10 chances in 10,000 of dying from flu during an epidemic if he/she was not vaccinated. They were told that the vaccine was certain to prevent the child from catching flu, but had potentially fatal side effects. The participants had to indicate the maximum death rate from the vaccine they were willing to tolerate in order to decide to have their child vaccinated. Ritov and Baron (1990) found that the average maximum acceptable risk was 5 deaths per 10,000. Thus, people would choose not to have their child vaccinated when the likelihood of the vaccine causing death was much lower than the death rate from the disease against which the vaccine protects! This is puzzling from the perspective of prospect theory, which would predict that people would make the decision minimising the risk of loss.

What was going on in the study by Ritov and Baron (1990)? The participants argued that they would feel more responsible for the death of their child if it resulted from their own actions rather than from their inaction. This is an example of **omission bias**, in which individuals prefer inaction to action. An important factor in omission bias is anticipated regret, with the level of anticipated regret being greater when an unwanted outcome has been caused by an individual's own actions. It should be noted that evidence for omission bias with vaccination decisions has not always been found. For example, Connolly and Reb (2003) found that a majority of students and non-student adults chose to vaccinate when the risks from vaccination equalled those from the disease. However, omission bias and anticipated regret influence many real-life decisions, including those involving choices between consumer products, sexual practices, and medical decisions (see Mellers, Schwartz, & Cooke, 1998).

Omission bias is an example of emotional factors producing decision avoidance. Another example is **status quo bias**, in which individuals repeat an initial choice over a series of decision situations in spite of changes in their preferences. For example, Samuelson and Zeckhauser (1988) found that in a real-life situation many people kept the same allocation of retirement funds year after year even when they would not have incurred any costs by changing.

C.J. Anderson (2003) put forward a rational-emotional model to account for the impact of emotions on decision making in (Figure 15.8). Decision making is determined by rational factors based on inferences and outcome information as well as experienced and anticipated emotion. The two key emotions within the model are regret (as in omission bias) and fear. Fear can be reduced when an individual chooses not to make a decision for the time being. The essence of the model is as follows: "It is reasonable to assume that people make choices that reduce negative emotions" (C.J. Anderson, 2003, p. 142).

The model can account for some of the phenomena discussed earlier. For example, one reason for loss aversion is because of the effects of anticipated regret at the possibility of making a decision that might produce losses. C.J. Anderson (2003) discussed studies showing that decisions are more likely to be avoided when the situation is complex than when it is straight-forward. Complex decisions produce more fear than easy ones,

FIGURE 15.8

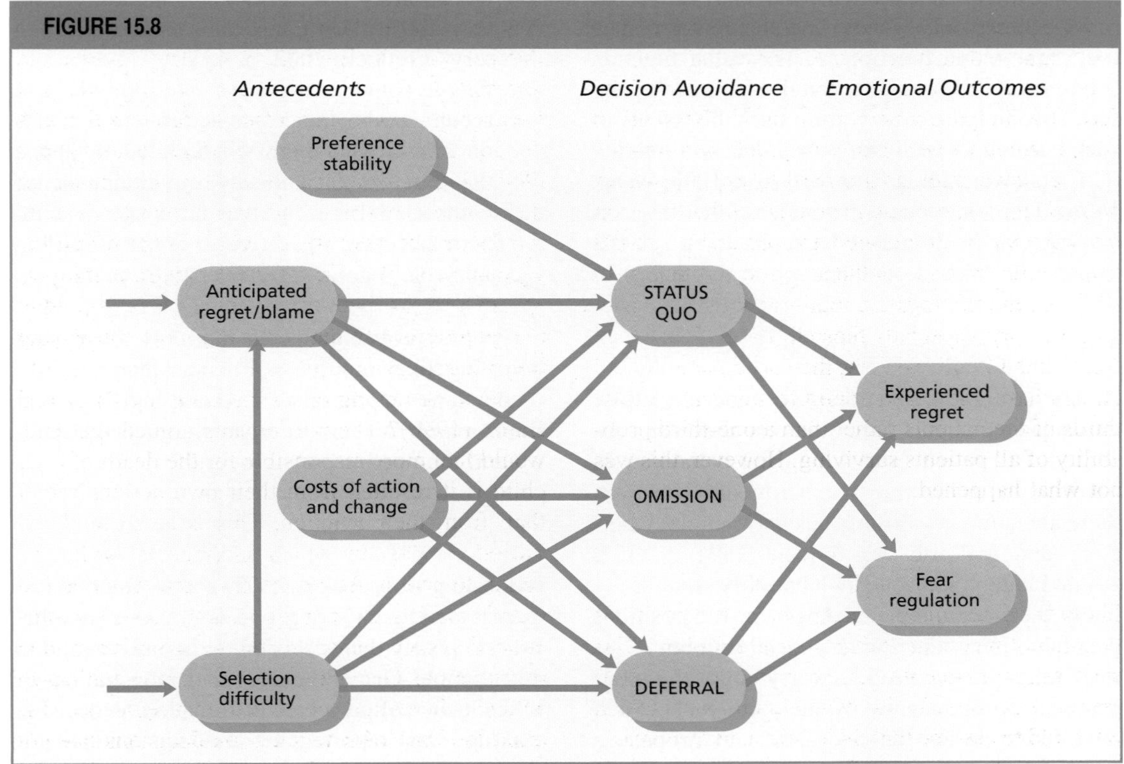

Anderson's rational-emotional model identifying factors associated with decision avoidance. From C.J. Anderson (2003). Copyright © 2003 by the American Psychological Association. Reprinted with permission.

and so fear regulation via decision avoidance is more likely to occur in the former case.

Evaluation

There is no doubt that prospect theory provides a more adequate account of decision making than previous normative approaches such as subjective expected utility theory. The value function (especially the assumption that people attach more weight to losses than to gains) allows us to account for many phenomena (e.g., risk aversion; risk seeking; sunk-cost effect; framing effect) that are not readily explicable by subjective expected utility theory. Even clearer evidence supporting prospect theory and disproving subjective expected utility theory has come from demonstrations that people's behaviour does not always conform to the dominance principle.

What are the main limitations of prospect theory? First, as Hardman and Harries (2002, p. 76) pointed out, "There is no apparent rationale for . . . the value function . . . The value function is descriptive of behaviour but does not go beyond this." Second, the theory minimises the effects of social and emotional factors on decision making (C.J. Anderson, 2003; Ritov & Baron, 1990; Wang, 1996). Third, individual differences in willingness to make risky decisions (Josephs et al., 1992; Lopes, 1987) are de-emphasised in the theory.

Social functionalist approach

A key limitation of subjective expected utility theory and prospect theory is that they are concerned mainly with explaining the behaviour of participants in laboratory experiments. However, there are some key differences between the laboratory and real life. As Tetlock (1991, p. 453) pointed out, "Subjects in laboratory studies . . . rarely feel accountable to others for the positions they take. They function in a social vacuum . . . in which they do not need to worry about the interpersonal consequences of their conduct." Such considerations led Tetlock (2002) to propose a social functionalist approach, in which the social context of decision making was taken fully into account.

Tetlock (2002) argued that social and cultural context can influence people's decision making in three main ways:

(1) People sometimes behave like intuitive politicians, in that, "they are accountable to a variety of constituencies, they suffer consequences when they fail to create desired impressions on key constituencies, and their long-term success at managing impressions hinges on their skill at anticipating objections that others are likely to raise to alternative courses of action and at crafting accounts that pre-empt those objections" (Tetlock, 2002, p. 454). Thus, people acting as intuitive politicians need to be able to justify their decisions to other people.
(2) People sometimes behave like intuitive theologians, who "believe that the prevailing accountability and social control regime is not arbitrary but rather flows naturally from an authority that transcends accidents of history" (Tetlock, 2002, p. 453).
(3) People sometimes behave like intuitive prosecutors, who "place accountability demands on others who might be tempted to derive the benefits of collective interdependence without contributing their fair share or without respecting other aspects of the prevailing role-rule regime" (Tetlock, 2002, p. 453).

People probably spend more of their time behaving like intuitive politicians than intuitive theologians or prosecutors. Accordingly, we will focus mainly on studies focusing on accountability and the need to justify oneself.

Evidence

According to Tetlock's (2002) social functionalist theory, people choosing one option over another want to justify their decision to themselves and to other people. One of the clearest demonstrations of the influence of perceived justification on decision making was reported by Tversky and Shafir (1992). Their participants were asked to imagine they had the chance to buy a very cheap holiday in Hawaii, but the special offer expired the next

FIGURE 15.9

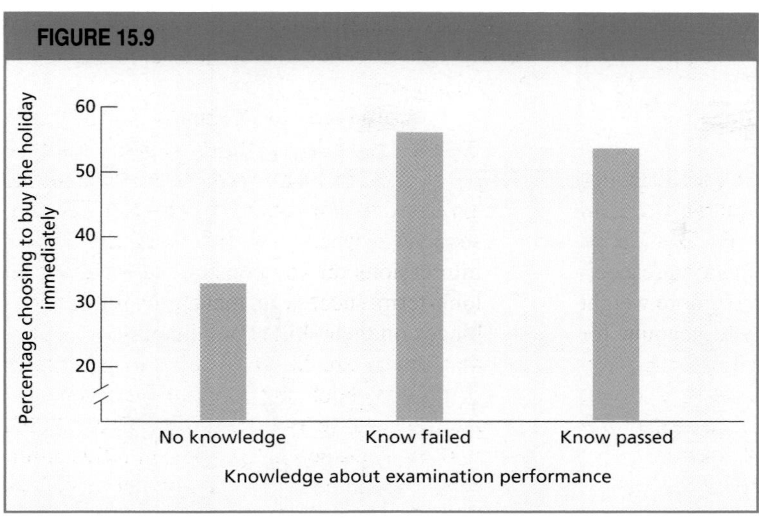

Percentage choosing to buy a holiday immediately as a function of having passed an examination, failed an examination, or not knowing whether the examination has been passed or failed. Data from Tversky and Shafir (1992).

day. They had three choices: (1) buy the holiday; (2) decide not to buy the holiday; (3) pay a $5 non-refundable fee to retain the opportunity to buy the holiday in two days' time. All of the participants were asked to assume that they had just taken a difficult examination. In one version of the problem, they knew they had passed the examination. In a second version, they knew they had failed. In the third version, they would find out the next day whether they had passed or failed.

What do you think the three groups of participants decided to do? Of those who had passed the exam, a majority decided to buy the holiday, as did most of those who had failed (see Figure 15.9). However, only 32% of those who did not know their examination result decided to buy the holiday immediately. These findings can be explained in terms of perceived justification. Those who have passed an examination "deserve" a holiday, and those who have failed "deserve" some kind of consolation. If someone does not know whether they have passed an examination, there is no compelling justification for going on holiday. The participants' use of perceived justification sounds rational. However, it violates subjective expected utility theory, because it costs more to delay buying the holiday.

We can test Tetlock's theory more directly by manipulating individuals' need to justify their decisions to other people. This was done by Simonson and Staw (1992) in a study on the sunk-cost effect. Their participants were given information about a beer company selling light beer and non-alcoholic beer. They were asked to recommend which product should receive an additional $3 million for marketing support (e.g., advertising). They were then told that the president of the company had made the same decision as the participants, but this had produced disappointing results. Finally, they were told that the company had decided to allocate $10 million of additional marketing support which could be divided between the two products. In a high-accountability condition, participants were told that information about their decisions might be shared with other students and instructors, and they were asked to give permission to record an interview about their decisions. In the low-accountability condition, participants were told that their decisions would be confidential and that there was no connection between participants' performance on the task and their managerial effectiveness or intelligence. In the medium-accountability condition, participants were told that the amount of information provided should be sufficient to allow a good decision to be made.

The findings from the study by Simonson and Staw (1992) are shown in Figure 15.10. The tendency towards a sunk-cost effect was strongest in the high-accountability condition and lowest in

FIGURE 15.10

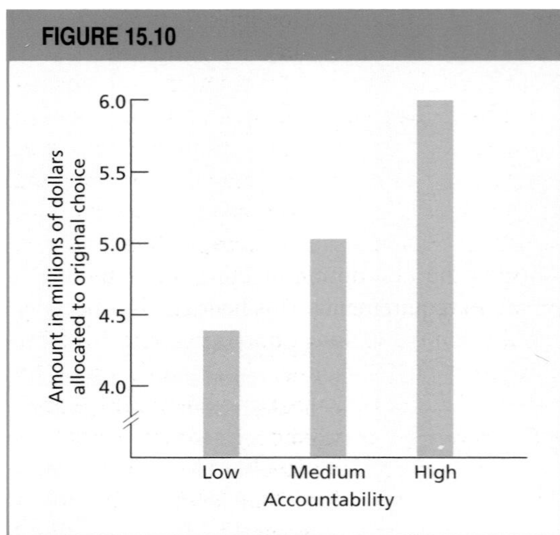

Millions of dollars allocated to original choice (sunk-cost effect) as a function of accountability. Data from Simonson and Staw (1992).

FIGURE 15.11

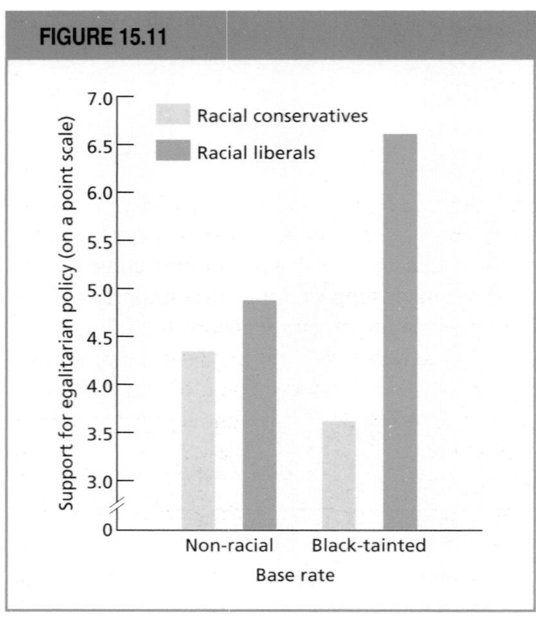

Support for an egalitarian policy as a function of base rate (non-racial vs. black-tainted) and participants' racial views (racial conservatives vs. racial liberals). Data from Tetlock et al. (2000).

the low-accountability condition. Presumably the participants in the high-accountability condition experienced the greatest need to justify their previously ineffective course of action (i.e., fruitless investment in one type of beer) by increasing their commitment to it.

It seems likely that human adults experience more need to justify themselves than do children or the members of other species (e.g., apes). If that is the case, then we would expect on Tetlock's (2002) theory to find a much smaller sunk-cost effect in children and other species such as apes than in human adults. This is precisely what has been found (see Arkes & Ayton, 1999, for a review). What is striking about these findings is that adults do not typically commit more errors than children or members of other species.

A study by Tetlock et al. (2000) showed that people sometimes make decisions as if they were intuitive theologians. The participants were told that Dave Johnson is an insurance executive who has to decide whether his company should write home-insurance policies in six different towns. Three of the towns are high-risk (10% of houses suffer damage each year) and the other three are low-risk (only 1% of houses suffer damage each year). Some participants were told that 85% of the population in the high-risk towns was black (black-tainted base rate), whereas others were given no information about racial composition (non-racial base rate). Participants were characterised as racial liberals or racial conservatives on the basis of their responses to a questionnaire.

Some participants were told that Dave Johnson decided to write policies at the same price for all six towns (egalitarian policy), a decision that involved ignoring the base-rate differences in risk between the two types of towns. The extent of agreement with Dave Johnson's decision on a 9-point scale is shown in Figure 15.11. Racial liberals felt more strongly than racial conservatives that base-rate information about differing levels of risk in different towns should be ignored, and this was especially the case when the high-risk towns were identified as predominantly inhabited by black people. These findings show a moral dimension to decision making: liberals insisted that, "base rates became 'off limits' once the linkage with race was revealed. Their overriding concern was to ensure that a group that had historically suffered from discriminatory practices . . . would not, once again, be victimised" (Tetlock et al., 2000, p. 863).

Evaluation

The central assumption of the social functionalist approach, namely that most decision making is influenced by social and cultural context, has attracted much support. Of central importance, we feel a need to justify our decisions to other people as well as to ourselves, and this leads us to behave like intuitive politicians, theologians, or prosecutors. Overall, the social functionalist approach emphasises important factors de-emphasised within prospect theory.

We turn now to some of the limitations of the social functionalist approach. First, it is often not clear exactly what would be predicted from this approach. For example, what determines whether people will behave as intuitive politicians rather than intuitive theologians or prosecutors? Second, the focus on social and cultural determinants may be excessive, with more general factors (e.g., greater sensitivity to losses than to gains) not receiving enough attention. Third, advocates of the social functionalist approach are critical of other researchers for using laboratory tasks on which there are no real gains and losses, and where the participants have no proper social responsibility. Ironically, much the same can be said of their own research!

Complex decisions: Bounded rationality

So far we have focused mainly on decision making applied to relatively simple problems. In real life, however, we are often confronted by very complex problems. How do we deal with such problems? According to the multi-attribute utility approach, the decision maker should identify dimensions relevant to the decision, decide how to weight these dimensions, obtain a total utility (i.e., usefulness) for each option by summing its weighted dimensional values, and then select the option with the highest weighted total. In practice, this approach is so complex that it is rarely adopted.

A more realistic approach to complex decision making owes its origins to Simon (1957). He argued that human decision making typically possesses **bounded rationality**, meaning that we produce reasonable or workable solutions to problems by using various short-cut strategies. Some of the heuristics or rules of thumb discussed earlier in the chapter can be seen as elements of bounded rationality. Simon (1978) emphasised one particular heuristic known as **satisficing**, which involves choosing the first option meeting the individual's minimum requirements. This heuristic is especially useful when the various options become available at different points in time. An example would be the vexed issue of choosing someone to marry. Someone using the satisficing heuristic would set a minimum acceptable level, and the first person reaching (or exceeding) that level is chosen. If the initial level of acceptability is set too high, then the level is adjusted downwards.

We can distinguish between individuals who are satisficers (content with making reasonable decisions) and those who are maximisers (perfectionists). Is it preferable to be a satisficer or a maximiser? This issue was addressed by Schwartz et al. (2002). They found that there are various advantages associated with being a satisficer. Satisficers are happier and more optimistic than maximisers, they have greater life satisfaction, and they experience less regret and self-blame.

Tverksy (1972) put forward a theory of complex decision making resembling Simon's approach. According to Tversky's elimination-by-aspects theory, decision makers eliminate options by considering one relevant attribute after another. For example, someone buying a house may first of all consider the attribute of geographical location, eliminating from consideration all those houses not lying within a given area. They may then consider the attribute of price, eliminating all properties costing above a certain figure. This process continues attribute by attribute until there is only one option remaining. This is a reasonably undemanding strategy, but it suffers from the limitation that the option selected can vary as a function of the order in which the attributes are considered. This means that often the best choice will not be made.

Payne (1976) studied the ways in which participants chose a flat or apartment from information presented on cards. Most participants initially used techniques such as elimination by aspects or satisficing to reduce the possibilities to manageable proportions. After that, they considered the remaining possibilities in a more thorough way corresponding to the assumptions of multi-attribute utility theory.

Finally, we will consider what happens in the real world. Frisch and Jones (1993) asked their participants to answer numerous questions relating to a recent decision that had proved to be very successful or unsuccessful. The most important difference between decisions that turned out well and those that turned out badly was that participants were much more likely to have considered alternative courses of action before making the former decisions.

CHAPTER SUMMARY

- Introduction
  There are close relationships between the areas of judgement and decision making. More specifically, decision-making research covers all of the processes involved in deciding on a course of action. In contrast, judgement research focuses mainly on those aspects of decision making concerned with estimating the likelihood of various events. In addition, judgements are evaluated in terms of their accuracy, whereas decisions are evaluated on the basis of their consequences.

- Judgement research
  There are numerous cases in everyday life in which our estimates of the probability of something change in the light of new evidence. In making such estimates, people often fail to take full account of base-rate information, and this is true even of experts. Base-rate information is more likely to be used if its causal relevance is clear. Gigerenzer and Hoffrage argue that judgements are more accurate when based on natural sampling and frequencies rather than probabilities. However, people often adopt biased sampling strategies, and are inaccurate even when using frequency data. One reason why people fail to make proper use of base-rate information is because of their reliance on the representativeness heuristic. This heuristic underlies the conjunction fallacy, which is the mistaken belief that the combination of two events is more likely than one of the events. Another commonly used rule of thumb is the availability heuristic. According to support theory, the subjective probability of an event increases as the description of the event becomes more explicit and detailed. The take-the-best and recognition heuristics are very simple rules of thumb which are often surprisingly accurate but are used less often than predicted theoretically by Gigerenzer. People frequently use heuristics, but the factors determining when and how they are used are not well understood.

- Decision making
  According to prospect theory, people are typically much more sensitive to potential losses than to potential gains. As a result, they are much more willing to take risks to avoid losses. An example of this is the sunk-cost effect. There is support for prospect theory in the framing effect, in which decisions are influenced by irrelevant aspects of the situation. However, decision making is sometimes influenced by social, emotional, and moral considerations that are not included in the prospect theory, as in omission bias. It is not clear within prospect theory why people are more sensitive to losses than to gains, nor why some people are more sensitive than others to losses. According to Tetlock's social functionalist approach, decision making is strongly influenced by the social context. More specifically, when making decisions we often focus on accountability and on the need to justify ourselves to others. However, it is not possible within this approach to predict precisely which information will be used by individuals when making decisions.

FURTHER READING

- Anderson, C.J. (2003). The psychology of doing nothing: Forms of decision avoidance result from reason and emotion. *Psychological Bulletin*, *129*, 139–167. The role of emotional factors in decision making (and avoiding making decisions) is discussed within the context of a theoretical model.
- Gigerenzer, G. (2002). *Reckoning with risk*. London: Penguin Books. One of the leading theorists on judgement provides an accessible account of his controversial views.
- Gilovich, T., Griffin, D., & Kahneman, D. (2002). *Heuristics and biases: The psychology of intuitive judgement*. Cambridge: Cambridge University Press. This edited book contains chapters covering all the main issues in judgement research.
- Hastie, R. (2001). Problems for judgement and decision making. *Annual Review of Psychology*, *52*, 653–683. This article identifies the main issues that are currently the focus of research in the areas of judgement and decision making.
- Over, D.E. (2003). *Evolution and the psychology of thinking*. Hove, UK: Psychology Press. This edited book contains several very relevant chapters (e.g., those by Sloman and Over on probability judgement and by Stanovich and West on the evolutionary psychology approach).

16

Reasoning and Deduction

INTRODUCTION

Reasoning is related to problem solving, because people trying to solve a reasoning task have a definite goal and the solution is not obvious. However, problem solving and reasoning are typically treated separately. Reasoning problems differ from other kinds of problems in that they often owe their origins to systems of formal logic. However, as we will see, there are clear overlaps between the two areas, which may differ less than one might initially suppose.

Deductive reasoning allows us to draw conclusions that are definitely valid provided that other statements are assumed to be true. For example, if we assume that Tom is taller than Dick, and Dick is taller than Harry, the conclusion that Tom is taller than Harry is necessarily true.

DEDUCTIVE REASONING

Researchers have used numerous deductive reasoning problems. However, we will focus on conditional reasoning and syllogistic reasoning problems. After we have discussed the relevant research, theoretical explanations of the findings will be considered. Before we proceed, we will issue a warning: do NOT assume that participants given a deductive-reasoning problem to solve necessarily use logical reasoning processes. As we will see, there is increasing evidence that the cognitive processes used by people solving deductive-reasoning problems resemble the processes used on other types of thinking problem.

Conditional reasoning

Conditional reasoning (basically, reasoning with "if") has been studied to decide whether human reasoning is logical. It has its origins in propositional logic, in which logical operators such as *or*, *and*, *if*. . . *then*, *if and only if* are included in sentences or propositions. In this logical system, symbols are used to stand for sentences, and logical operators are applied to them to reach conclusions. Thus, in propositional logic, we might use P to stand for the proposition "It is raining" and Q to stand for "Alicia gets wet", and then use the logical operator *if*. . . *then* to relate these two propositions: *if P then Q*.

The meanings of words and propositions in propositional logic differ from their meanings in natural language. For example, in this logical system, propositions can only have one of two truth-values: they are either true or false. If *P* stands for "It is raining", then *P* is either true (in which case it is raining) or *P* is false (it is not raining). Propositional logic does not admit any uncertainty about the truth of *P* (where it is not really raining, but is so misty you could almost call it raining).

Differences of meaning between propositional logic and ordinary language are especially great with respect to "*if . . . then*". Consider the following, which involves *affirmation of the consequent*:

Premises
If Susan is angry, then I am upset.
I am upset.
Conclusion
Therefore, Susan is angry.

Do you accept the above conclusion as valid? Many people would, but it is *not* valid according to propositional logic. The explanation is as follows: I may be upset for some other reason (e.g., I have lost my job).

We will now consider other concrete problems in conditional reasoning, starting with the following one:

Premises
If it is raining, then Alicia gets wet
It is raining.
Conclusion
Alicia gets wet.

This conclusion is valid. It illustrates an important rule of inference known as *modus ponens*: "If A, then B", and also given "A", we can validly infer B.

Another major rule of inference is *modus tollens*: from the premise "If A, then B", and the premise "B is false", the conclusion "A is false" necessarily follows. This rule of inference is shown in the following example:

Premises
If it is raining, then Alicia gets wet.
Alicia does not get wet.
Conclusion
It is not raining.

People consistently perform much better with modus ponens than modus tollens.

Another inference in conditional reasoning is known as *denial of the antecedent*:

Premises
If it is raining, then Alicia gets wet.
It is not raining.
Conclusion
Therefore, Alicia does not get wet.

Many people argue the above conclusion is valid, but it is invalid. It does not have to be raining for Alicia to get wet (e.g., she might have jumped into a swimming pool).

We have considered four types of inference in conditional reasoning. There have been many studies on these types of inference, but we will consider a study by Marcus and Rips (1979, Experiment 2). Nearly 100% of the participants made the valid modus ponens inference, but far fewer made the valid modus tollens inference (see Figure 16.1). On the other hand, many people accept the invalid inferences. In the study by Marcus and Rips, 21% of participants made the invalid denial of the antecedent inference and 33% made the affirmation of the consequent inference. However, the difference is not always in this direction; see Evans (1993b), and Evans, Newstead, and Byrne (1993, p. 36) for a composite table showing the results from several different experiments.

Context effects

The evidence discussed so far indicates that we often make mistakes in conditional reasoning. Even stronger evidence that we have only limited ability to reason logically comes from studies in which additional contextual information in the form of an additional premise is presented. Context effects sometimes greatly impair (or improve) performance on conditional reasoning tasks. For example, consider a study by Byrne (1989), in which she compared conditional reasoning performance under standard conditions with two other conditions:

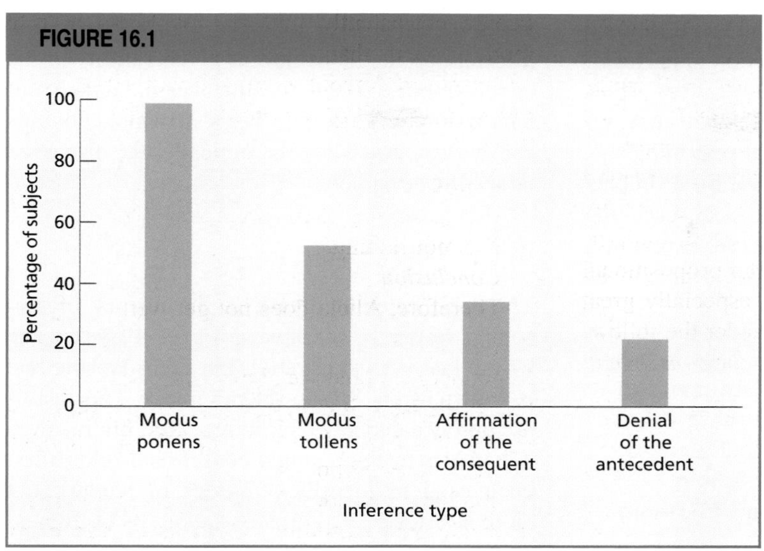

The percentage of subjects endorsing the various conditional inferences from Marcus and Rips (1979, Experiment 2).

(1) Alternative argument (in brackets):
If it is raining, then she will get wet.
(If it is snowing, then she will get wet.)
She got wet.
Therefore, ?

(2) Additional argument or requirement (in brackets):
If she has an essay to write, then she will study late in the library.
(If the library stays open, then she will study late in the library.)
She has an essay to write.
Therefore, ?

Byrne found that alternative arguments improved performance with affirmation of the consequent and denial of the antecedent (see Figure 16.2), because they made people more reluctant to

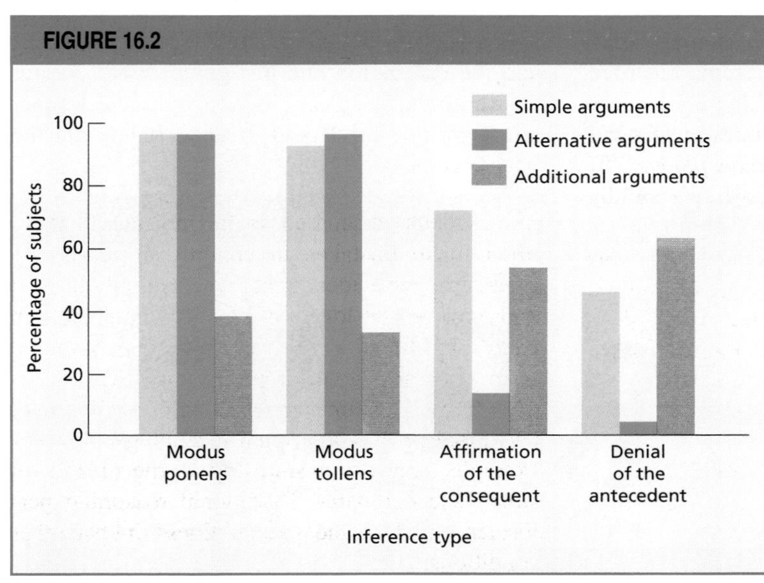

The percentage of subjects endorsing the various conditional inferences from Byrne (1989) when they are given simple (standard conditional) arguments, alternative arguments, and additional arguments.

endorse invalid inferences. In contrast, additional arguments led to a dramatic reduction in performance with modus ponens and modus tollens. Thus, we are greatly influenced by contextual information not strictly relevant to logical reasoning.

Stevenson and Over (1995) found the impact of an additional premise on conditional reasoning depends on the degree of certainty (or uncertainty) regarding this additional premise. Here is an example taken from their study:

> If John goes fishing, he will have a fish supper. (standard premise)
> If John catches a fish, he will have a fish supper. (additional premise)
> John is * lucky when he goes fishing. (qualification)
> John goes fishing.
> Therefore, ?
> [* One of the following words was used: *always*; *usually*; *rarely*; *never*]

What did Stevenson and Over (1995) find? When *always* was used in the qualifying sentence, the suppression of the valid modus ponens disappeared. However, it gradually increased as the insert word moved from *always* to *never*.

Summary

Various findings suggest that many people fail to think logically on conditional reasoning tasks. First, modus tollens is valid but is often regarded as invalid. Second, affirmation of the consequent and denial of the antecedent are both invalid but are sometimes seen as valid. Third, contextual information that is irrelevant to the validity of the conclusion nevertheless influences judgements of conclusion validity. The ways in which findings can be accounted for theoretically are discussed later in the chapter.

Wason selection task

The most celebrated task in the history of reasoning research was invented over 40 years ago by the late British psychologist Peter Wason, and is known as the Wason selection task. This task is *not* purely a deductive reasoning task, but involves hypothesis testing using a conditional rule. It has been used in literally hundreds of studies, but there is still some controversy about its usefulness as an instrument to examine human reasoning (Evans, 2002).

In the standard version of the Wason task, there are four cards lying on a table. Each card has a letter on one side and a number on the other. The participant is told that a rule applies to the four cards (e.g., "If there is an R on one side of the card, then there is a 2 on the other side of the card"). The task is to select *only* those cards that would need to be turned over to decide whether or not the rule is correct.

In one of the most used versions of this selection task, the four cards have the following symbols visible: R, G, 2, and 7 (see Figure 16.3), and the rule is the one just given. What is your answer to this problem? Most people select either the R card or the R and 2 cards. If you did the

FIGURE 16.3

Rule: If there is an R on one side of the card, then there is a 2 on the other.

same, you got the answer wrong! You need to see whether any of the cards *fail* to obey the rule. From this perspective, the 2 card is irrelevant. If there is an R on the other side of it, then this only tells us the rule might be correct. If there is any other letter on the other side, then we have also discovered nothing about the validity of the rule.

The correct answer is to select the cards with R and 7 on them, an answer given by only about 5–10% of university students. The 7 is necessary because it would definitely disprove the rule if it had an R on the other side. There are clear similarities between Wason's selection task and conditional reasoning. The selection of the 7 card resembles the modus tollens rule of inference: from the premises "If there is an R on one side of the card, then there is a 2 on the other side" and "The 7 card does not have a 2 on it", it follows logically that the 7 card should not have an R on the other side. If it does, then the premise specifying the rule must be incorrect. Thus, incorrect performance on the Wason selection task may reflect the general difficulty people have with the modus tollens inference.

Several researchers have argued that the abstract nature of the Wason task makes it hard to solve. Wason and Shapiro (1971) used four cards (Manchester, Leeds, car, and train) and the rule "Every time I go to Manchester I travel by car." The task was to select only those cards needing to be turned over to prove or disprove the rule. The correct answer that the Manchester and train cards need to be turned over was given by 62% of the participants, against only 12% when the Wason selection task was given in its abstract form.

The findings of Wason and Shapiro (1971) suggest the use of concrete and meaningful material facilitates performance on the Wason task. However, Griggs and Cox (1982) used the same tasks as Wason and Shapiro with American students in Florida. They failed to find a greater success rate for the meaningful task, presumably because most American students have no direct experience of Manchester or Leeds (or because they have little experience of trains!). In general, there is inconsistent evidence that concrete material leads to better performance than abstract material on the Wason task (Evans, 2002).

Some findings from the Wason task can be interpreted within social contract theory (Cosmides, 1989), which is based on an evolutionary approach to cognition. According to this theory, people have rules maximising their ability to achieve their goals in social situations. Cosmides emphasised situations involving social exchange, in which two people must cooperate for mutual benefit. Of particular importance are social contracts based on an agreement that someone will only receive a benefit (e.g., travelling by train) provided they have incurred the appropriate cost (e.g., buying a ticket). Allegedly, people possess a "cheat-detecting algorithm" (computational procedure) allowing them to identify cases of cheating (e.g., travelling by train without having bought a ticket).

The main prediction from social contract theory as applied to Wason's selection task is that people should perform especially well when the task is phrased so that showing the rule is false involves detecting cheaters. For example, consider a study by Sperber and Girotto (2002). Some of their participants were given a version of the selection task in which Paolo buys things through the Internet but is concerned he will be cheated. For each order, he fills out a card. On one side of the card, he indicates whether he has received the item ordered, and on the other side he indicates whether he has paid for the items ordered. He places four orders, and what is visible on the four cards is as follows: "item paid for"; "item not paid for", "item received", and "item not received". Which cards does he need to turn over to decide whether he has been cheated? Sperber and Girotto found that 68% of their participants made the correct choices (i.e., "item paid for"; "item not received").

The high success rate reported by Sperber and Girotto (2002) apparently supports social contract theory. However, we need to distinguish between two types of rules on the Wason task:

- Indicative type: If there is a p then there is a q.
- Deontic type: If you do p then you *must* do q.

Standard versions of the Wason task use indicative rules, whereas cheating-detection versions use deontic rules. With deontic rules, the crucial issue is whether what matters for successful performance is specifically detection of cheating (as predicted by social contract theory) or more generally detection of rule violation. Sperber and Girotto (2002) found that detection of rule violation is of vital importance. Some of their participants had to decide which of the following cards needed to be turned over to decide whether Paolo has bought any non-Italian food items through the Internet: "food item"; "non-food item"; "Italian item"; and "non-Italian item". On this version, 91% of the participants correctly selected the food item and non-Italian item cards even though the task had nothing to do with cheating.

Deontic versions of Wason's selection task are much easier than standard indicative versions at least in part because the structure of the problem is made more explicit. For example, cheating means we have fulfilled our side of the bargain but failed to receive the agreed benefit. Social contract theory may account for some findings involving cheating. However, it does not account for performance on most deontic and indicative versions of the task, and it has not been developed to explain reasoning on other tasks.

Sperber and Girotto (2002) argued that findings on Wason's selection task can be explained by their relevance theory. According to this theory, participants simply engage in a comprehension process in which they evaluate the *relevance* of the four cards to the conditional rule. This comprehension process often produces an incorrect interpretation of the problem. Worryingly for those who regard the Wason selection task as an important measure of deductive reasoning, Sperber and Girotto argued that participants generally do not engage in reasoning at all. In their own words, "The selection task is not a standard reasoning problem. Participants are not . . . even told that the question they are asked can best be answered by making use of deductive reasoning . . . there is no incentive to engage in active reasoning" (Sperber & Girotto, 2002, p. 280).

Syllogistic reasoning

Syllogistic reasoning has been studied for over 2000 years. A **syllogism** consists of two premises or statements followed by a conclusion. Here is an example of a syllogism: "All A are B. All B are C. Therefore, all A are C." A syllogism contains three terms (A, B, and C), with one of them (B) occurring in both premises. The premises and the conclusion each contain one of the following quantifiers: *all*; *some*; *no*; and *some . . . not*. Altogether there are 64 different possible sets of premises. Each pair of premises can be combined with 8 possible conclusions to give a grand total of 512 possible syllogisms, most of which are invalid.

When you are presented with a syllogism, you have to decide whether the conclusion is valid in the light of the premises. The validity (or otherwise) of the conclusion depends *only* on whether it follows logically from the premises. Thus, the truth or falsity of the conclusion in the real world is irrelevant. Consider the following example:

> *Premises*
> All children are obedient.
> All girl guides are children.
> *Conclusion*
> Therefore, all girl guides are obedient.

The conclusion follows logically from the premises. Thus, it is valid regardless of your views about the obedience of children.

Biases

People often make errors in syllogistic reasoning, in part because of the existence of various biases. For example, there is **belief bias**, in which people accept believable conclusions and reject unbelievable conclusions irrespective of their logical validity or invalidity (see Evans, Barston, & Pollard, 1983). For example, Oakhill, Garnham, and Johnson-Laird (1990) presented syllogisms such as the following:

> All of the Frenchmen are wine drinkers.
> Some of the wine drinkers are gourmets.
> Therefore, some of the Frenchmen are gourmets.

The conclusion is very believable, and is endorsed by many people. However, it is actually invalid, and does *not* follow logically from the premises.

Klauer, Musch, and Naumer (2000) found various biases in syllogistic reasoning. Participants were all told the syllogisms they would see were sampled at random from a large pool of syllogisms. Some participants were told only one-sixth of the syllogisms in the pool were valid, whereas other participants were told that five-sixths of them were valid. In fact, half of the syllogisms were valid and half were invalid. In addition, half the conclusions were believable (e.g., "Some fish are not trout"), whereas others were unbelievable (e.g., "Some trout are not fish").

What did Klauer et al. (2000) find? First, they discovered a **base-rate effect**: syllogistic reasoning performance was influenced by the perceived probability of syllogisms being valid (see Figure 16.4). Second, Klauer et al. obtained evidence for belief bias: valid and invalid conclusions were more likely to be endorsed as valid when believable than when they were unbelievable (see Figure 16.4). Both of these findings indicate that participants' decisions on the validity of syllogism conclusions were influenced by factors having nothing to do with logic.

Another factor in producing poor performance on reasoning tasks is the **atmosphere effect** (Woodworth & Sells, 1935), in which the form of the premises of a syllogism influences our expectations about the form of the conclusion. For example, if both premises include the word "all", then we expect the conclusion to include it as well. There is good support for the atmosphere effect, and Chater and Oaksford (1999) have incorporated it in their probability heuristics model (see below).

Another factor leading to poor performance is **conversion error**, in which a statement in one form is mistakenly converted into a statement with a different form. As Chapman and Chapman (1959) found, participants often assume that "All As are Bs" means that "All Bs are As", and that "Some As are not Bs" means that "Some Bs are not As". Ceraso and Provitera (1971) tried to prevent conversion errors from occurring by spelling out the premises more unambiguously (e.g., "All As are Bs" was stated as "All As are Bs, but some Bs are not As"). This produced a substantial improvement in performance. Begg and Denny (1969) considered the findings from several studies in which the atmosphere effect and conversion errors had been investigated. Their key finding was that many apparent conversion errors can simply be regarded as examples of the atmosphere effect.

FIGURE 16.4

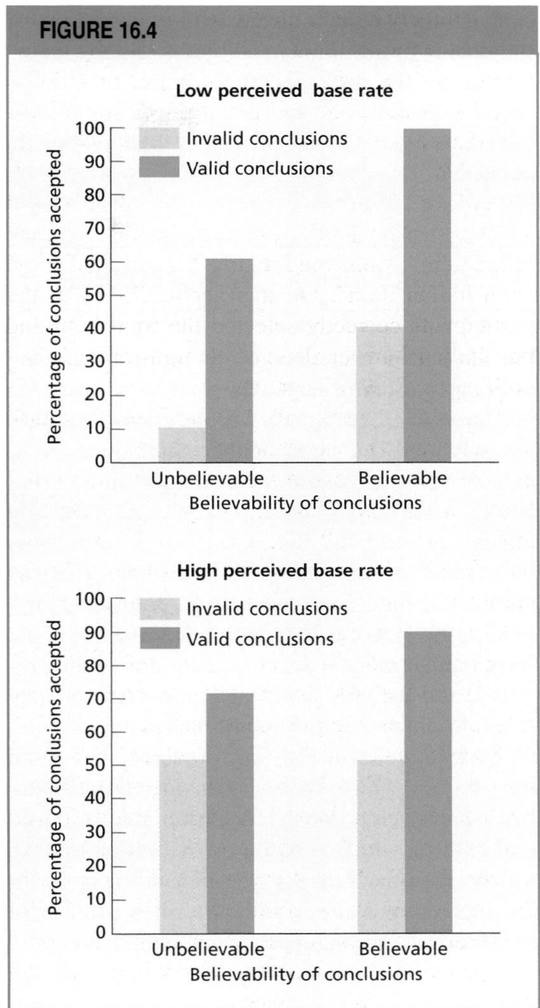

Percent acceptance of conclusions as a function of perceived base rate (low vs. high), believability of conclusions, and validity of conclusions. Based on data in Klauer et al. (2000).

In sum, many people are prone to biases in syllogistic reasoning which undermine the accuracy of our reasoning processes. Most accounts focusing on biases and errors provide a *description* rather than an *explanation*. For example, a full explanation would indicate *why* people convert statements or are influenced by the "atmosphere" created by the premises. In addition, most bias-based approaches do not explain *why* some individuals avoid biases and errors in their syllogistic reasoning.

THEORIES OF DEDUCTIVE REASONING

We have seen that people are prone to making errors on reasoning tasks. Many theories have been put forward to account for these errors, but here we will focus on three of the major ones. First, there are abstract-rule theories (e.g., Braine, 1994, 1998), according to which people are basically logical, but can be led into error if they misunderstand the reasoning task. Second, there is the mental model approach (e.g., Johnson-Laird, 1983, 1999). According to this approach, people form mental models or representations of the premises, and use these mental models (rather than rules) to draw conclusions. Mental models sometimes lead to error-free performance, but often they do not. Third, we will consider the probabilistic approach proposed by Chater and Oaksford (e.g., 2001), which is based on the notion that we use the cognitive processes developed to cope with the uncertainties of everyday life when confronted by deductive reasoning problems in the laboratory.

Abstract-rule theories

According to abstract-rule theories, people use mental logic when confronted by a reasoning task. Invalid inferences are made when people misunderstand or misrepresent the reasoning task (e.g., conversion errors discussed above). However, after their initial misunderstanding, people engage in a logical reasoning process.

We will focus on the abstract-rule theory originally proposed by Braine (1978), and subsequently developed and extended by various theorists (e.g., Braine, 1994, 1998; Braine, Reiser, & Rumain, 1984; Rips, 1994). According to the theory, the following processes occur when people are confronted by a deductive reasoning problem:

(1) The premises of the problem are encoded by comprehension mechanisms into a mental representation in working memory.
(2) Abstract-rule schemas are applied to these premises to derive a conclusion. *Core schemas* encode fundamental reasoning rules (e.g., modus ponens).
(3) *Feeder schemas* are additional schemas that are applied to produce intermediate conclusions for core schemas.
(4) *Incompatibility rules* examine the contents of working memory for incompatible inferences (e.g., contradictions such as inferring both P and not-P).

Braine et al. (1984) argued there are three main reasons why people make errors in reasoning:

(1) Comprehension errors: The premises of a reasoning problem (or the conclusion) are interpreted incorrectly (e.g., conversion error).
(2) Heuristic inadequacy: The participant's reasoning process fails to locate the correct line of reasoning.
(3) Processing errors: The participant fails to attend fully to the task in hand or suffers from memory overload.

In sum, it is assumed within abstract-rule theory that people are natural logicians who are slightly fallible at the edges. When reasoning, people always reason validly, except for extraneous influences from the comprehension of premises or the inherent limitations of working memory. Why, then, do so many people make mistakes on reasoning problems? According to the theory, modus tollens is a hard inference to make because no single rule can be applied to it. Instead, a proof involving several rules has to be formed to reach a conclusion, and this increases the likelihood that errors will occur. People make mistaken inferences such as denial of the antecedent and affirmation of the consequent because they use the conversational assumptions used in everyday life to reinterpret the premises (Braine, 1994). Thus, people apply their logically valid rules, but make errors when the input to the rules is wrong.

Evidence

We will show how this theory works by considering its account of a reasoning error known as affirmation of the consequent. Earlier we considered an example of this error, in which it is mistakenly assumed that the premises "If it is raining, then Alicia gets wet" and "Alicia gets wet" lead to the valid conclusion "Therefore, it is raining". According to Braine et al. (1984), this error occurs because of a conversion error: "If it is raining, then Alicia gets wet" is interpreted to mean "If Alicia gets wet, then it has been raining." Why should this be so? According to Braine et al. (1984), we assume other people will provide us with the information we need to know. If someone says "If it is raining, then Alicia gets wet" it is reasonable to assume that rain is the *only* event likely to make Alicia wet. We can easily see what Braine et al. (1984) had in mind if we consider the statement "If you mow the lawn, I will give you five dollars." This statement invites the inference "If you don't mow the lawn, I won't give you five dollars" (Geis & Zwicky, 1971).

Braine et al. (1984) tried to prevent participants from misinterpreting the premises in affirmation of the consequent syllogisms by providing an additional, clarifying premise:

Premises
If it is raining, then Alicia gets wet.
If it is snowing, then Alicia gets wet.
Alicia gets wet
Conclusion
?

Participants were much more likely to argue correctly that there is no valid conclusion when the additional premise was used.

Additional evidence in support of abstract-rule theory was obtained by Braine et al. (1984). In one experiment, participants were given a simple reasoning task about the presence or absence of letters on an imaginary blackboard. For example, participants were given a problem such as the following:

If there is a T, there is an L.
There is a T.
?There is an L?

They had to decide whether the provided conclusion was true. These problems were designed to be solved in a single step by one of the 16 rules proposed by the theory. As predicted, reasoning on these problems was essentially error-free.

According to Braine et al. (1984) people have a mental rule corresponding to modus ponens. Thus, syllogisms based on modus ponens are easy to handle, and pose no comprehension problems. However, Byrne (1989) showed that this is not always true. As we saw earlier, she found that including an additional argument in a syllogism meant that participants were much less likely to draw the valid modus ponens conclusion. Thus, the processes involved in reasoning can be more complex (and less logical) than assumed by the theory.

Evaluation

Abstract-rule theory accounts for many experimental findings with relatively few reasoning rules (e.g., Braine et al., 1984). As predicted, comprehension errors (e.g., conversion errors) and misunderstandings cause many problems in deductive reasoning, as we saw in our earlier discussion of the errors and biases associated with conditional and syllogistic reasoning.

There are several limitations with abstract-rule theory. First, the comprehension component of the theory is under-specified. As a result, it is not always clear *what* theoretical predictions should be made. Second, abstract-rule theory has only been applied to a limited range of problems. For example, O'Brien (1995) claimed that abstract versions of the Wason selection task are not reasoning problems proper, and so the theory is not of direct relevance to performance on that task. Third, as we have seen, the theory does not provide an adequate account of context effects (e.g., Byrne, 1989). Fourth, individual differences are de-emphasised. For example, Ford (1995) found that some people solving syllogisms used mainly spatial processes whereas others used verbal processes. It is unclear how such findings could be explained within abstract-rule theory. Fifth, and most importantly, there is little convincing evidence that people actually use mental logic when presented with deductive reasoning problems.

Mental models

One of the most influential approaches to deductive reasoning is the mental model theory of Johnson-Laird (e.g., 1983, 1999). What is a **mental model**? According to Johnson-Laird (1999, p. 116), "Each mental model represents a *possibility*, and its structure and content capture what is common to the different ways in which the possibility might occur." More simply, a mental model represents a possible state-of-affairs in the world. Let's consider a concrete example:

Premises
The lamp is on the right of the pad.
The book is on the left of the pad.
The clock is in front of the book.
The vase is in front of the lamp.
Conclusion
The clock is to the left of the vase.

According to Johnson-Laird (1983), people use the information contained in the premises to construct a mental model like this:

book	pad	lamp
clock		vase

The conclusion that the clock is to the left of the vase clearly follows from the mental model. The fact that we cannot construct a mental model consistent with the premises but inconsistent with the conclusion indicates that it is valid.

Johnson-Laird has developed and extended mental model theory over the years. Here are some of the main assumptions incorporated into the theory:

- A mental model describing the given situation is constructed, and the conclusions following from the model are generated.
- An attempt is made to construct alternative models that will falsify the conclusion.
- If a counterexample model is not found, the conclusion is assumed to be valid.
- The construction of mental models involves the limited processing resources of working memory (see Chapter 6).
- The **principle of truth**: "Individuals minimise the load on working memory by tending to construct mental models that represent explicitly only what is true, and not what is false" (Johnson-Laird, 1999, p. 116).
- Deductive reasoning problems requiring the construction of several mental models are harder to solve than problems requiring the construction of only one mental model, because of the increasing demands on working memory.

In sum, Johnson-Laird (1999, p. 130) argued, "Reasoning is just the continuation of comprehension by other means." This view has important implications, because we do not normally use logical processes when understanding sentences. Successful thinking results from the use of appropriate mental models and unsuccessful thinking occurs when we use inappropriate mental models. Thus, deductive reasoning can apparently be achieved without using any logical rules. However, some experts (e.g., Chater & Oaksford, 2001) argue that the search for counterexamples that will falsify the conclusion involves a form of logic.

Evidence

The notion that people's ability to construct mental models is constrained by the limited capacity of working memory was tested by Johnson-Laird (1983). Participants indicated what conclusions followed validly from sets of premises. The demands on working memory were varied by manipulating the number of mental models consistent with the premises. When the premises only allowed the generation of one mental model 78% of participants drew the valid conclusion. This figure dropped to 29% when two mental models were possible, and to 13% with three mental models. The finding that performance is much worse with multiple-model syllogisms than with single-model ones has been replicated several times (e.g., Newstead, Handley, & Buck, 1999).

According to the theory, it takes time to construct a mental model. Thus, reasoning problems requiring the generation of several mental models should take longer than those requiring the generation of only one model. Bell and Johnson-Laird (1998) argued that a single mental model can establish that something is possible, but *all* models must be constructed to show that something is not possible. In contrast, all mental models must be constructed to show that something is necessary, but *one* model can show that something is not necessary. Bell and Johnson-Laird (1998) used reasoning problems consisting of premises followed by a question about a possibility (e.g., "Can Betsy be in the game?") or a question about a necessity (e.g., "Must Betsy be in the game?").

According to the theory, people should respond faster to *possibility* questions when the correct answer is "Yes" rather than "No". However, they should respond faster to *necessity* questions when the answer is "No" rather than "Yes". That is precisely what Bell and Johnson-Laird (1998) found (see Figure 16.5).

Johnson-Laird et al. (1999) discussed the principle of truth, according to which most mental models represent what is true and ignore what is false. It follows that most people should make systematic and predictable errors when given a reasoning problem requiring active consideration of falsity. This prediction was tested by Johnson-Laird and Goldvarg (1997). The participants received the following problem (be warned it is VERY difficult!):

> Only one of the following premises is true about a particular hand of cards:
> (1) There is a king in the hand or there is an ace, or both.
> (2) There is a queen in the hand or there is an ace, or both.
> (3) There is a jack in the hand or there is a 10, or both.
> Is it possible that there is an ace in the hand?

What is the correct answer? Johnson-Laird and Goldvarg (1997) found that 99% of their participants gave the answer "Yes", which is amazingly high given that the correct answer is "No". According to Johnson-Laird and Goldvarg (1997), the participants formed mental models of the premises. Thus, for example, the first premise generates the following mental models:

King	
	Ace
King	Ace

These mental models suggest an ace is possible, as do the mental models formed from the second premise. However, this is the wrong answer, because it ignores issues of falsity revolving around the fact that only *one* of the premises is true. If there were an ace in the hand, then premises (1) and (2) would both be true, which is inconsistent with the requirement that only one premise is true. Thus, the participants' over-emphasis on the principle of truth caused nearly all of them to produce faulty reasoning.

Legrenzi, Girotto, and Johnson-Laird (2003) carried out further studies to test the principle of truth. The participants had to decide whether descriptions of everyday objects (e.g., a chair) were consistent or inconsistent. Some of the descriptions were constructed so that participants would be lured into error (illusory inferences) if they adhered to the principle of truth. These illusory inferences were either that a description was consistent when it was inconsistent or inconsistent

FIGURE 16.5

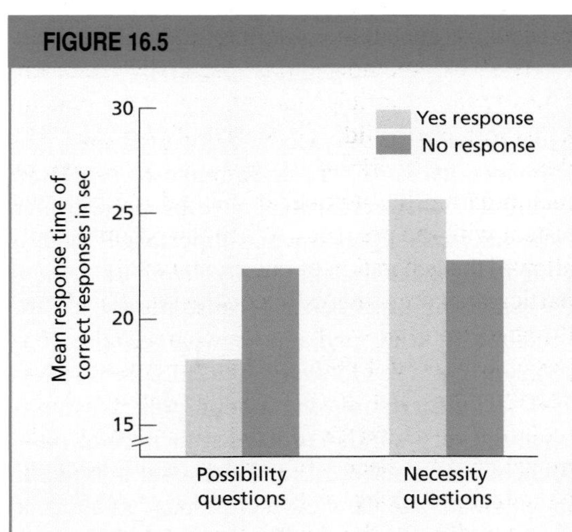

Mean response times (in seconds) for correct responses (yes and no) to possibility and necessity questions. Based on data in Bell and Johnson-Laird (1998).

FIGURE 16.6

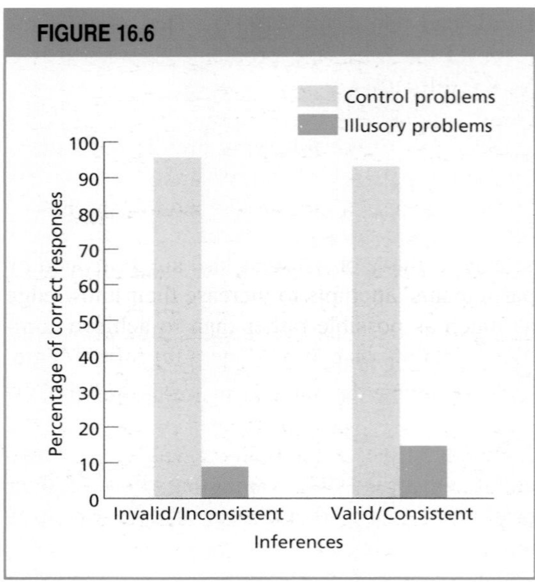

Percentage correct responses to reasoning problems as a function of validity of inferences (invalid vs. valid) and type of problem (control vs. illusory). Based on data in Legrenzi et al. (2003).

when it was consistent. Here is an example of an inference that was typically interpreted as consistent (valid) when it is actually inconsistent (invalid):

Only one of the following assertions is true:
The tray is heavy or elegant, or both.
The tray is elegant and portable.
The following assertion is definitely true:
The tray is elegant and portable.

Legrenzi et al. also used other problems (control) which were supposed to be much simpler because the correct inferences could be drawn simply by using the principle of truth (e.g., the above problem with the valid assertion: The tray is heavy and elegant).

There was convincing evidence for the predicted illusory inferences (see Figure 16.6) when the principle of truth did not permit the correct inferences to be drawn. In contrast, performance was very high on control problems where adherence to the principle of truth was sufficient. The systematic errors in thinking found by Legrenzi et al. and by Johnson-Laird and Goldvarg (1997) cannot be predicted within the abstract-rule approach.

One of the central assumptions of mental model theory is that people will search for counterexamples after having constructed an initial mental model and generated a conclusion. However, this assumption is often incorrect. For example, Newstead et al. (1999) compared syllogisms permitting either one or multiple mental models. In their first experiment, participants indicated immediately after each syllogism how many conclusions they had considered. The prediction from mental model theory is that more conclusions should have been considered with the multiple-model than with the single-model syllogisms. In fact, there was no difference: 1.12 and 1.05 conclusions were considered on average with multiple- and single-model syllogisms, respectively.

In the above experiment, participants may have forgotten some of the conclusions they considered by the time they tried to recall them. Accordingly, Newstead et al. (1999) carried out further experiments in which participants drew diagrams of the mental models they were forming while working on syllogisms. The participants consistently failed to produce more mental models for multiple-model syllogisms than for single-model ones.

Evaluation

Mental model theory accounts for reasoning performance across a very wide range of problems, and most of its predictions have been confirmed experimentally. Of particular importance, there is convincing evidence that many errors on deductive reasoning tasks occur because people use the principle of truth and ignore what is false (e.g. Johnson-Laird & Goldvarg, 1997; Legrenzi et al., 2003). Furthermore, the notion that reasoning involves very similar processes to normal comprehension is powerful, and provides a convincing alternative to the view that we possess a mental logic. An important implication is that the artificial problems used in most reasoning studies may be more relevant to everyday life than is generally supposed.

On the negative side, the processes involved in forming mental models are under-specified. Johnson-Laird and Byrne (1991) argued that people make use of background knowledge when forming mental models. However, the theory does not spell out how we decide *which* pieces of information should be included in a mental model. The theory also tends to ignore individual differences. For example, in a study mentioned earlier, Ford (1995) asked people solving syllogisms to say aloud what they were thinking while working on each problem. About 40% of the participants used spatial reasoning, and a further 35% used verbal reasoning. Ford (1995, p. 69) concluded that "Neither the spatial nor the verbal reasoners could be said to provide evidence of developing mental models that are structural analogues of the world [as predicted by Johnson-Laird]."

Finally, it is assumed within the theory that people will attempt to produce mental models to falsify conclusions generated from their initial mental model. However, most of the evidence indicates that people typically produce only a single mental model, and so systematic attempts at falsification are generally absent (e.g., Newstead et al., 1999).

Probabilistic approach

Chater and Oaksford (e.g., 2001) have put forward a probabilistic approach to explain performance on deductive-reasoning problems. The central insight motivating this approach is as follows: "Everyday rationality is founded on uncertain rather than certain reasoning . . . , and so probability provides a better starting point for an account of human reasoning than logic" (Chater & Oaksford, 2001, p. 204). How do people deal with deductive reasoning problems presented in the laboratory? In the words of Chater and Oaksford (2001, p. 204), "Much of the experimental research in the 'psychology of deductive reasoning' does not engage people in deductive reasoning at all but rather engages strategies suitable for probabilistic reasoning. According to this viewpoint, the field of research appears crucially to be misnamed!" Thus, people learn to think in probabilistic ways as a result of their everyday experience, and these habitual ways of thinking continue to be used under laboratory conditions even when in some ways they seem inappropriate.

The probabilistic approach has been applied to the Wason selection task and to syllogistic reasoning tasks. So far as Wason's task is concerned, Oaksford and Chater (1994) proposed the optimal data selection model. According to this model, the selections made on Wason's task are motivated by participants' attempts to increase their knowledge as much as possible rather than to achieve complete certainty as can be done with formal logic.

Some of the basic ideas of the model can be seen in Oaksford's (1997) example of testing the rule "All swans are white". According to formal logic, people should try to find swans and non-white birds. However, there is a problem with formal logic when applied to the real world: only a few birds are swans, and the overwhelming majority of birds are non-white. Thus, the pursuit of non-white birds may take up enormous amounts of time and effort and would be very inefficient. In the real world, it makes more sense (and is more informative) to look for white birds to see whether they are swans. From this perspective, the choices made by most participants on Wason's selection task may be very sensible rather than illogical.

How does all this talk of swans relate directly to the Wason task? In essence, the task has the form "If p, then q" (e.g., "If there is an R on one side of the card, then there is a 2 on the other side of the card"). All theories predict that participants should select the p card, so that is of little relevance at this point. The most distinctive predictions of the model are that people should tend to choose q cards (e.g., 2) when the expected probability of q is low, but should choose not-q cards (e.g., 7) when the expected probability of q is high. These predictions are made on the assumption that people try to maximise information gain, and those card choices achieve that goal.

Why do most people given the Wason selection task select the q card rather than the not-q card? According to Oaksford and Chater (1994), the answer lies in the rarity assumption. According to the **rarity assumption**, the properties or categories described by p (e.g., swans) and by q (e.g., white birds) are generally fairly rare in our experience of the world, and so we can usually maximise information gain by selecting q instead of not-q.

Chater and Oaksford (1999) have developed a probability heuristics model to account for performance on syllogistic reasoning problems. The premises in a syllogism contain quantifiers (e.g., all; some), and these quantifiers can be ordered in terms of how informative they are (All > Some > None > Some . . . not). According to the theory, when people are presented with a syllogism, they use the informativeness of the quantifiers to select what they take to be a valid conclusion. More specifically, when asked to produce a valid conclusion, participants use a heuristic or rule of thumb known as the ***min*-heuristic**, which states that the form of a syllogism's conclusion should have the same form as that of the less informative premise (a notion resembling the atmosphere effect discussed earlier). For example, consider the following syllogism:

Premises
All B are A
Some B are not C
Conclusion
Some A are not C

As you can see, the quantifier for the conclusion (i.e., Some) is the same as that of the less informative premise (Some B are not C).

What are the advantages of using the *min*-heuristic? First, it is very easy to use. Second, in spite of its simplicity, the min-heuristic captures the form of the conclusion for most syllogisms having a valid conclusion. The downside of the *min*-heuristic is that it sometimes leads people to draw invalid conclusions.

Evidence

We will start by considering evidence relating to the optimal data selection model and performance on the Wason selection task. As we have seen, the model predicts that people should choose q cards (e.g., 2) when the expected probability of q is low, but should choose not-q cards (e.g., 7) when the expected probability of q is high. Oaksford et al. (1997) carried out an experiment in which the percentage of q cards was 17%, 50%, or 83%, and the participants were invited to select as many cards as they needed to decide whether the rule "All the triangles are blue" was true or false. As can be seen in Figure 16.7, both predictions from the model were supported.

Oaksford and Chater (2003) compared the performance of the optimal data selection and the mental model models in accounting for performance on the Wason selection task. They considered 34 studies, and found that each theory or model fitted the data better for 17 studies. However, there was a marginal advantage for the optimal data selection model: "On average the mental models model accounted for 93.1% of the variance in each study whereas the optimal data selection model accounted for 95.5%" (Oaksford & Chater, 2003, pp. 371–372).

There is some research relating to the probability heuristics model of syllogistic reasoning. Chater and Oaksford (1999) carried out a meta-analysis of five studies in which the full possible range of syllogisms had been presented. Overall, their model accounted for over 80% of the variance, and thus provided a good fit to the data. However, we must distinguish between syllogisms where there is a valid conclusion and those where there is not. There are various reasons why participants might produce the correct conclusion on logically valid syllogisms, and use of the *min*-heuristic is only one possibility. However, of particular importance, the model was also very good at predicting participants' conclusions on syllogisms having no valid conclusion, and it is unlikely that such accurate predictions would follow from other theoretical positions.

Evaluation

The probabilistic approach provides an interesting explanation of why we cope so well with the problems of everyday life but so poorly with deductive reasoning problems. In essence, we use the same cognitive processes in everyday life and in the laboratory, and these processes were developed to allow us to cope successfully with

FIGURE 16.7

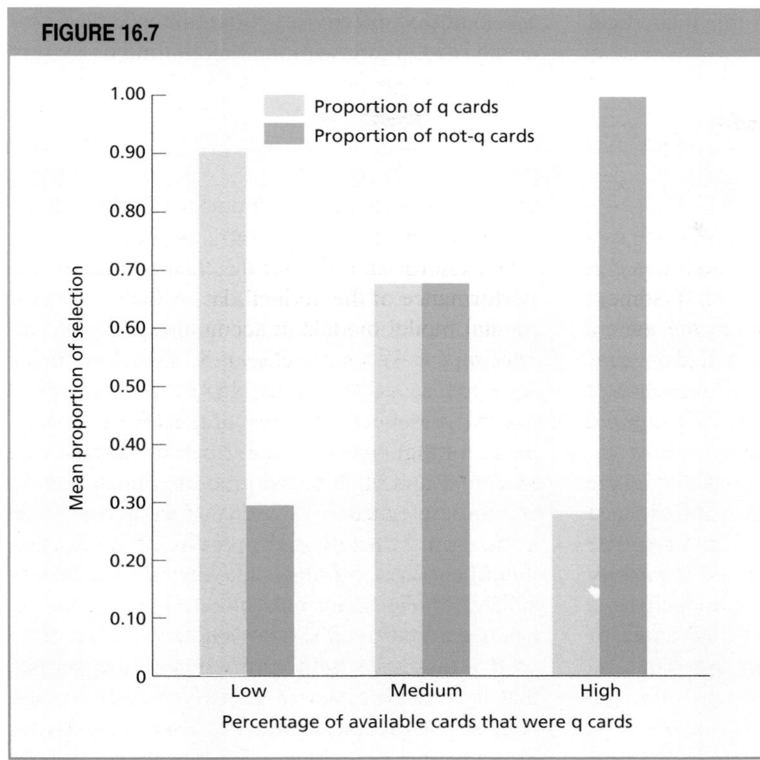

Mean proportion of q and not-q cards selected as a function of the percentage of available cards that were q cards. Based on data in Oaksford et al. (1997).

day-to-day problems. There is reasonable empirical evidence that the probabilistic approach is applicable to both conditional reasoning and to syllogistic reasoning. The notion that we use rules of thumb like the *min*-heuristic on syllogistic reasoning is consistent with evidence that we use rules of thumb or heuristics when engaged in problem solving (see Chapter 13) and judgement and decision making (see Chapter 15).

What are the main limitations of the probabilistic approach? First, the theory lacks a performance component (Johnson-Laird, 1999). More specifically, the theory specifies what needs to be computed in a reasoning task (e.g., information gain), but it does not indicate the processing mechanisms involved. As Oaksford and Chater (2003, p. 376) admitted, "We need an account of how people can recruit the relevant probabilities from world knowledge."

Second, Chater and Oaksford have produced very complex mathematical formulae to predict the kinds of performance shown by people on deductive reasoning problems. However, according to Oaksford and Chater (2003, p. 364), "We doubt that people make these actual calculations." More generally, you may feel it seems unlikely that people given, say, an abstract version of the Wason selection task think in terms of probabilities at all.

Third, we are not provided with an **algorithm** (well-defined computational procedure providing a specified set of steps to a solution) to indicate what is happening. In the words of Oaksford and Chater (2003, p. 376), "There is no explicit algorithmic level account that shows how the theory is implemented in the mind/brain." As a result, the theory has little to say about reasoning *per se* (i.e., how specific conclusions are generated from premises).

Fourth, and possibly most importantly, most of the successes of the probabilistic approach have involved reinterpretations of existing data. What we need are more studies in which novel predictions of the probabilistic approach are tested.

That would provide an acid test of this theoretical approach.

DUAL-SYSTEM THEORIES

It is increasingly argued that there are two major limitations with most theory and research on human reasoning. First, as Evans (2003) and Stanovich and West (1998a, 2000) among others have pointed out, there are important individual differences in reasoning performance, even though they have generally been ignored. For example, Stanovich and West (1998a) reported a correlation of +.50 between intelligence and syllogistic reasoning, and one of +.36 between intelligence and performance on the Wason selection task. The participants in these studies were all university students, and the correlations would probably have been higher if there had been a wider range of intelligence among the participants. Second, and related to the first point, individuals differ in the processes they use on reasoning tasks. It is important to consider such variations in the processes used rather than simply to assume that there are universal processes.

Several theorists have proposed dual-system theories shedding light on individual differences in reasoning ability. There is some agreement on the nature of the two systems involved, but there are some differences from theorist to theorist (see Newstead, 2000). Here we will focus on the reasonably representative views of Evans (2003). He distinguished between what he and Stanovich and West (2000) have termed System 1 and System 2: "System 1 processes are rapid, parallel and automatic in nature; only their final product is posted in consciousness . . . System 2 thinking is slow and sequential in nature and makes use of the central working memory system . . . Despite its limited capacity and slower speed of operation, System 2 permits abstract hypothetical thinking that cannot be achieved by System 1" (Evans, 2003, p. 454).

Evans (2003) and Stanovich and West (2000) have related their two-system theories to individual differences in intelligence. In essence, it is assumed that differences in intelligence are associated much more with the functioning of System 2 than of System 1.

Evidence

One of the most useful phenomena for distinguishing between Systems 1 and 2 is the belief-bias effect discussed earlier in the chapter. This effect occurs when a conclusion that is logically valid but not believable is rejected as invalid, or a conclusion that is logically invalid but believable is accepted as valid (Evans, 1983). It is assumed that the presence or absence of this effect depends on a conflict between belief-based processes in System 1 and logic-based processes in System 2. If more intelligent individuals make more use of System 2 logic-based processes than do less intelligent ones, it follows that they should be less subject to the belief-bias effect. This prediction has been confirmed (Stanovich & West, 1998b).

It is assumed within two-system approaches that it is much easier to alter System 2 thinking than the more automatic processes underlying System 1 thinking. Support for this position comes in studies in which the instructions given to participants are varied (see Evans, 2000). When instructions stress the importance of logical necessity, this leads to an increase in System 2 thinking and thus to a reduction in belief bias. In similar fashion, instructions that do not stress logical reasoning lead to an increase in belief bias.

Goel and Dolan (2003) used fMRI to provide additional evidence for the existence of two systems in thinking. They presented participants with syllogisms, and asked them to decide whether the conclusion followed validly from the premises. Of most importance was what happened when the conclusion was valid but unbelievable or invalid but believable. When participants made the logically correct decision, there was activation of the right inferior prefrontal cortex (see Figure 16.8a), presumably reflecting the involvement of System 2 processes. According to Goel and Dolan (2003, p. B19), "We conjecture that right prefrontal cortex involvement in correct response trials is detecting and/or resolving the conflict between belief and logic."

FIGURE 16.8

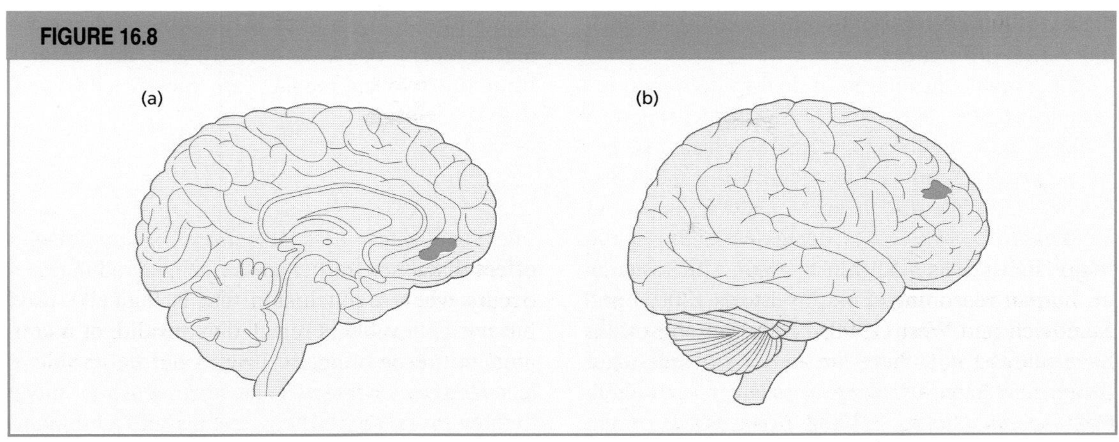

Brain activation when there was a conflict between conclusion validity and belief. Brain areas more activated when responses were correct than incorrect are shown in (a), and brain areas more activated when responses were incorrect than correct are shown in (b). Based on data in Goel and Dolan (2003).

When participants made the incorrect decision (and so showed belief bias), there was activation of the ventral medial prefrontal cortex (see Figure 16.8b). Such activation presumably reflects the use of System 1 belief-based processes. The notion that the ventral medial prefrontal cortex is involved in belief-based processing is also supported by the findings of Adolphs, Tranel, Bechara, Damasio, and Damasio (1996). As we saw earlier in the chapter, it has typically been found that performance on the Wason selection task is better with concrete or belief-laden content than with abstract content. However, Adolphs et al. found that patients with lesions in the ventral medial prefrontal cortex performed equally poorly with concrete and abstract versions of the task.

We mentioned earlier that Stanovich and West (1998a) found that intelligence was associated with performance on syllogistic reasoning and on the Wason selection task. This is consistent with predictions from dual-system theories, but is also consistent with several other theoretical positions. Clearer evidence that intelligence is associated with greater use of System 2 processes but not System 1 processes was reported by Stanovich and West (1998b). They used a realistic, deontic version of the Wason selection task and the original abstract version. They assumed that successful performance on the deontic version of the task is typically based on relevant prior knowledge and reflects System 1 processes. In contrast, success on the abstract version requires System 2 abstract logical reasoning. As a result, Stanovich and West predicted that intelligence would predict performance better on the abstract version of the task than on the realistic deontic version. This prediction was supported. However, subsequent research by Newstead, Handley, Harley, Wright, and Farrelly (2004) only replicated those findings when the participants were of relatively high intellectual ability.

Evaluation

There is convincing evidence for a distinction between relatively automatic, knowledge- or belief-based processes and more abstract, logic-based processes. Some of this evidence is based on reasoning performance (e.g., Evans, 2000; Stanovich & West, 1998a), and some is based on brain imaging (e.g., Goel & Dolan, 2003). Another significant strength of dual-system theories is their emphasis on individual differences in reasoning. There are moderately strong associations between intelligence and reasoning performance (e.g., Stanovich & West, 1998a, 2000), and an adequate theory of human reasoning must account for such individual differences.

The greatest limitation of dual-system theories is their relative vagueness. For example, theorists differ in how they describe the two systems, but we do not know as yet how significant these differences are. We also need to know more about the kinds of *interactions* occurring between the two systems. It is plausible to assume that intelligence is related to superior reasoning performance because of individual differences in System 2 processes rather than System 1 processes, but strong evidence is lacking. Finally, it is unlikely that we can capture all the richness of human reasoning simply by assuming the existence of two cognitive systems.

BRAIN SYSTEMS IN THINKING AND REASONING

Which parts of the brain are of the most importance for problem solving, reasoning, and other forms of thinking? It has often been argued that the frontal lobes (one in each cerebral hemisphere) play a key role. The frontal lobes are located (unsurprisingly) in the front part of the brain. They form about one-third of the cerebral cortex in humans. The posterior border of the frontal lobe with the parietal lobe is marked by the central sulcus [groove or furrow], and the frontal and temporal lobes are separated by the lateral fissure.

It has often been argued that the prefrontal cortex, which lies within the frontal lobes, is of special significance for various cognitive activities including problem solving. In humans, 50% of the entire frontal cortex consists of the prefrontal cortex. One fact suggesting that it may be of great importance for complex cognitive processing is that the prefrontal cortex is considerably larger in humans than in other mammalian species.

Most attempts to specify brain areas involved in thinking have either used brain-damaged patients or brain imaging with healthy participants. Historically, the former approach was the main one. However, there has been a rapid increase in brain-imaging studies of thinking and reasoning in recent years. As we will see, the findings from the two approaches are mostly consistent with each other.

Evidence

There is much evidence from brain-damaged patients that the frontal cortex is involved in problem solving. For example, Owen et al. (1990) used a computerised version of the Tower of London problem, resembling the Tower of Hanoi problem discussed in Chapter 13. This problem was given to three groups of participants: patients with damage to the left frontal lobe; patients with damage to the right frontal lobe; and normal controls. The three groups did not differ in time to plan the first move. After that, however, both groups of frontal patients were much slower than the normal controls. In addition, they required more moves to solve the problem. There were no differences between the left and right frontal patients.

Goel and Grafman (1995) used a five-disc version of the Tower of Hanoi. Patients with damage to the prefrontal cortex performed significantly worse than normal controls, even though both groups used basically the same strategy. The patients were especially at a disadvantage compared to the controls with respect to a difficult move that involves moving away from the goal (see Chapter 13). This finding suggests that patients with prefrontal damage find it more difficult than normal individuals to plan ahead.

The notion that problem solving and reasoning both involve extensive use of the prefrontal cortex has been supported by brain-imaging studies. Dagher et al. (1999) used PET scans while healthy participants performed the Tower of London task in various versions varying in complexity. The more complex versions of the task were associated with increased activity in several brain areas compared to simpler versions. Of particular note, the dorsolateral prefrontal cortex was more active when participants were engaged in solving complex versions of the Tower of London task. Baker et al. (1996) obtained PET scans while normal individuals performed a reasoning task (transitive inference). There was increased activation in the dorsolateral prefrontal cortex during task performance.

The frontal cortex seems to be involved in most higher-level cognitive processing. For example, Duncan et al. (2000) used PET scans to identify brain regions most active when participants performed a wide range of tasks (e.g., spatial; verbal) correlating highly with the general factor of intelligence. A specific region of the lateral frontal cortex was highly active during the performance of virtually all the tasks. Duncan et al. (2000, p. 457) concluded that, "The results suggest that 'general intelligence' derives from a specific frontal system important in the control of diverse forms of behaviour." In similar fashion, Probhakaran et al. (1997) used fMRI while normal individuals performed the Raven's Progressive Matrices Test, which is a measure of intelligence. Brain activation levels were greatest in the dorsolateral prefrontal cortex and other associated areas.

Ackerman, Beier, and Boyle (2002) found that working memory capacity correlated +.57 with general intelligence, so we might imagine that tasks involving working memory would also be associated with activation of prefrontal cortex. Sylvester et al. (2003) recorded fMRI while participants carried out tasks involving either switching of attention or resolving interference, both of which are processes associated with the central executive component of the working memory system (see Chapter 6). Intriguingly, among the brain areas activated during both processes was our old friend the dorsolateral prefrontal cortex. Thus, brain-imaging research substantiates the notion that common processes may be involved across a wide range of cognitively demanding tasks.

The working memory system is heavily involved when someone processes one kind of information while temporarily storing another kind of information. Accordingly, we might expect much prefrontal activation when people have to combine processing and temporary storage of information. Koechlin, Basso, Pietrini, Panzer, and Grafman (1999) found that areas in the frontopolar prefrontal cortex were activated when people held a goal in mind *and* explored and processed other goals, but not when only one of these tasks had to be performed.

So far we have emphasised the notion that similar regions within the frontal cortex (and especially the prefrontal cortex) are involved in numerous forms of higher-level cognitive processing including problem solving, reasoning, solving intelligence-test items, and performing tasks making substantial demands on the working memory system. As yet, there has been little systematic research designed to identify brain areas associated with *specific* cognitive processes. However, an exception is a study by Newman et al. (2003). They recorded fMRI while participants performed easy, moderate, and difficult versions of the Tower of London task, and found that prefrontal cortex was active during performance of all versions. However, their main findings were as follows: the *right* prefrontal area (especially the right dorsolateral prefrontal cortex) was more involved in plan generation, whereas the *left* prefrontal area (especially the left dorsolateral frontal cortex) was more involved in plan execution.

Similar findings have been reported in other studies. Braver and Bongiolatti (2002) carried out an fMRI study involving goal management, which is an important aspect of plan generation. There was more activation in the right prefrontal cortex than in the left prefrontal cortex. Burgess et al. (2000) asked frontal lobe patients to carry out a multi-tasking experiment requiring plan generation. Patients with lesions in the right dorsolateral prefrontal cortex found it especially difficult to formulate plans.

Theoretical developments

Waltz et al. (1999) argued that the prefrontal region of the brain is of crucial importance in relational integration. By "relational integration" they meant activities involving the manipulation and combination of the relations between objects and events. For example, consider a form of deductive reasoning known as transitive inference. Here is an example of a transitive inference problem requiring only modest relational integration: Tom taller than William; William taller than Richard. The following transitive inference problem involves more complex relational integration: Bert taller than Matthew; Fred taller than Bert.

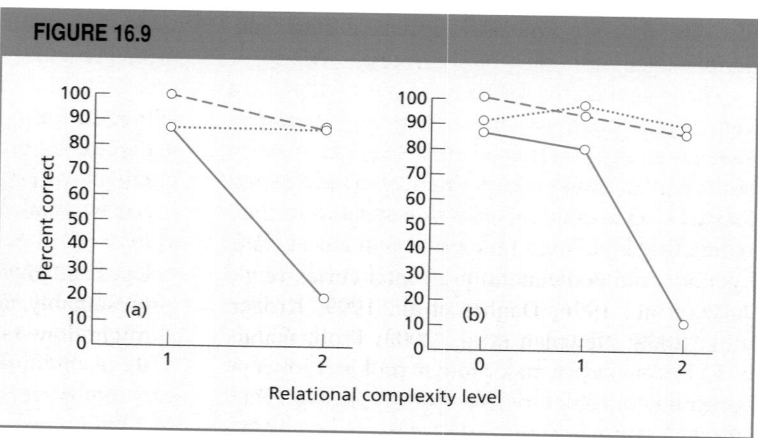

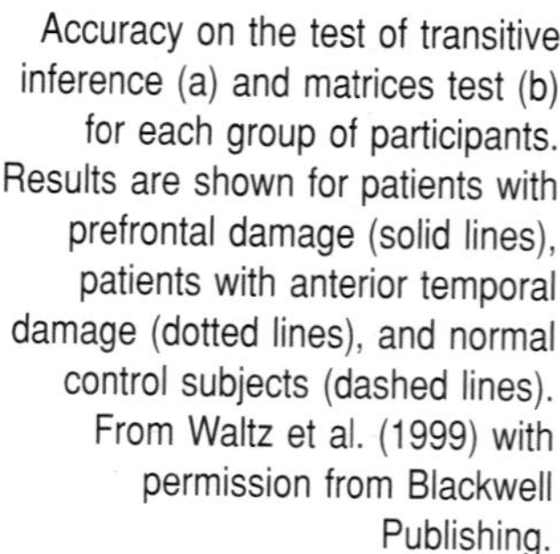
Accuracy on the test of transitive inference (a) and matrices test (b) for each group of participants. Results are shown for patients with prefrontal damage (solid lines), patients with anterior temporal damage (dotted lines), and normal control subjects (dashed lines). From Waltz et al. (1999) with permission from Blackwell Publishing.

Waltz et al. (1999) tested groups of patients of similar IQs with prefrontal damage and patients with anterior temporal lobe damage. The two groups performed comparably on the simple version of the transitive inference task discussed above, but the prefrontal patients were at a massive disadvantage on the more complex version (see Figure 16.9a).

Waltz et al. (1999) also tested the same groups of patients on a test of inductive reasoning involving matrix problems (Figure 16.9b), in which the appropriate stimulus to complete each pattern had to be selected. The extent to which relational integration was necessary for problem solution was manipulated. The pattern of findings was the same as with deductive reasoning: the two groups performed comparably when little relational integration was required. However, the prefrontal patients were dramatically worse than the anterior temporal patients when the task required substantial relational integration. Waltz et al. (1999, p. 122) concluded as follows: "Our findings indicate that the human prefrontal cortex plays an essential role in relational reasoning —specifically, in the integration of multiple relations."

Kroger et al. (2002) proposed a similar (but more specific) theory, according to which tasks of high relational complexity are associated with activation of the dorsolateral prefrontal cortex. They gave healthy participants reasoning problems varying in relational complexity adapted from an intelligence test. They also manipulated task difficulty by varying the number of distracting stimuli presented. There was a progressive increase in activation of the dorsolateral prefrontal cortex with increases in relational complexity (see Figure 16.10). In contrast, increasing the amount of distraction had little effect on such activation, indicating that increased activation of the

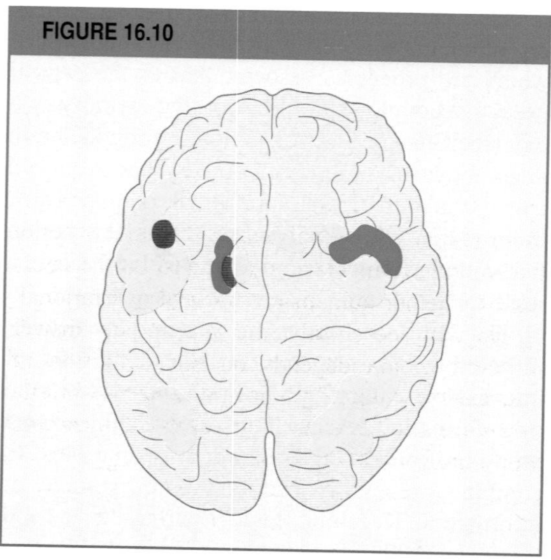

Brain areas showing increased activation with increases in relational complexity (light blue), increases in distortion (dark blue), and increases in both complexity and distortion (grey). Based on Kroger et al. (2002).

dorsolateral prefrontal cortex was due to relational complexity rather than simply to task difficulty.

Evaluation

There is considerable evidence from brain-damaged patients and from brain-imaging studies on healthy individuals that the frontal cortex, and especially the dorsolateral prefrontal cortex (e.g., Baker et al., 1996; Dagher et al., 1999; Kroger et al., 2002; Newman et al., 2003; Probhakaran et al., 1997), plays a major role in problem solving, reasoning, and thinking. In future, brain-imaging research may prove to be very useful in clarifying the similarities and differences in processing among numerous tasks involving higher-level cognition.

What is needed for the future is to identify more precisely the cognitive processes associated with activation within the prefrontal cortex. Waltz et al. (1999) suggested that relational integration is of crucial importance, Kroger et al. (2002) emphasised relational complexity, and Koechlin et al. (1999) focused on processing plus temporary storage. The factors emphasised by different theorists are probably rather similar to each other, but we cannot be sure on the basis of the available evidence.

ARE HUMANS RATIONAL?

Theorists working in the areas of thinking and reasoning have increasingly focused on the question of whether humans are rational or irrational. As we will see shortly, the appropriate answer to that question depends on our definition of "rationality". First of all, however, we will briefly review the evidence discussed in this chapter and the three previous ones.

Evidence

At first glance, much of the available evidence seems to indicate that our thinking and reasoning are often inadequate, suggesting that we are not rational. For example, Reisberg (1997, pp. 469–470) concluded his discussion of research on various heuristics or rules of thumb as follows:

> We have discussed several sources of error, and we have suggested that these errors are rather widespread. These studies have been run on many different campuses, including some of the world's most prestigious colleges and universities. Thus, the subjects are, presumably, talented and intelligent . . . One might draw rather cynical conclusions from these findings: Human reasoning is fundamentally flawed.

In similar fashion, human performance on deductive reasoning tasks seems very prone to error. That was certainly the view of Wason (1983, p. 59), who argued as follows: "The selection task reflects [a tendency toward irrationality in argument] to the extent that the subjects got it *wrong* . . . It could be argued that irrationality rather than rationality is the norm. People all too readily succumb to logical fallacies." Note that most psychologists nowadays argue that it is possible for people to be rational even though they make logical errors.

If we take the above findings at face value, they reveal a paradox. Most people apparently cope reasonably well with the problems and challenges of everyday life, and yet seem irrational and illogical when given thinking and reasoning problems in the laboratory. However, this probably overstates the differences between everyday life and the laboratory. It may well be that our everyday thinking is less rational than we believe and that our thinking and reasoning in the laboratory are less inadequate than is often supposed. So far as everyday thinking is concerned, for example, most British people argue that transport safety is so important that it is worth spending billions of pounds to improve the safety of the rail system. However, the same people habitually travel by car rather than by train, even though travelling by car is approximately 30 times more dangerous than travelling by train!

What about laboratory research? There are several reasons why many of the apparent inadequacies and limitations of human thinking and reasoning under laboratory conditions should *not* be taken at face value. We will start by considering judgement and decision making. First, it may make a lot of sense for people to make extensive use of heuristics (e.g., the representativeness heuristic; the recognition heuristic) in everyday life. Heuristics are cost-efficient, allowing us to make reasonably accurate, rapid judgements and decisions. Another argument in favour of the use of heuristics in everyday life was advanced by Maule and Hodgkinson (2002, p. 71): "Often . . . people have to judge situations or objects that change over time, making it inappropriate to expend a good deal of effort to make a precise judgement at any particular point in time. Under these circumstances, an approximate judgement based on a simpler, less effortful heuristic may be much more appropriate."

Second, even in laboratory research, there are many cases in which human judgement and decision making appear rational and relatively free from error. For example, in Chapter 15 we considered several studies in which performance was substantially more accurate when problems were presented in the form of frequencies rather than probabilities. Such findings suggest that people can think rationally when problems are presented in a readily understandable form not requiring extensive calculations.

Third, many of the so-called "errors" in human judgement and decision making only appear as such when we think of people as operating in a social vacuum. As Tetlock and Mellers (2002, p. 98) pointed out, "Many effects that look like biases from a strictly individual level of analysis may be sensible responses to interpersonal and institutional pressures for accountability."

Many of the apparent "errors" on deductive-reasoning tasks may also be less serious than they seem. For example, Evans (1993a) identified three major problems with the conclusion that poor performance on deductive reasoning tasks means that people are both illogical and irrational. First, there is the normative system problem: the system (e.g., propositional logic) used by the experimenter may differ from that used by participants. This is especially likely to occur when participants are unfamiliar with that system.

Second, there is the interpretation problem: the participants' understanding of the problem may differ from that of the experimenter. Indeed, some participants who produce the "wrong" answer may actually be reasoning logically based on their interpretation of the problem! We can see the interpretation problem clearly in problems using the word "if". In propositional logic, "If a, then b", is valid except in the case of a and not-b. However, the word "if" is often ambiguous in natural language, with "If a, then b" meaning "*If and only if* a, then b". Examples of this misunderstanding were discussed earlier. When people are told to assume "If a, then b" and "b", the conclusion that "a occurs" is invalid according to propositional logic (this is the fallacy of affirmation of the consequent). However, the conclusion is perfectly valid given the way the word "if" is normally interpreted in everyday life.

Third, there is the external validity problem: the tasks used in psychology experiments are artificial, and tell us little about reasoning in the real world. In other words, failure in the laboratory does not necessarily translate into failure in everyday life.

Evans (2002, p. 991) provided an excellent summary of the reasons why most people seem illogical and error-prone on deductive-reasoning tasks:

> To pass muster, participants are required not only to disregard the problem content but also any prior beliefs they may have relevant to it. They must also translate the problem into a logical representation using the interpretations of key terms that accord with a textbook (not supplied) of standard logic (but not contemporary philosophical logic), while disregarding the meaning of the same terms in everyday natural discourse.

Evans (1993a, 2003) has made a strong case for the argument that performance on most deductive-reasoning problems may *underestimate* people's ability to think logically or rationally. However, we must beware of the temptation to go further and claim that *all* our difficulties with such problems stem from inadequacies in the problems themselves. Convincing evidence that other factors are also involved comes from the research of Stanovich and West (1998a, 2000) discussed above. Their central finding that highly intelligent individuals perform better than less intelligent ones on various deductive-reasoning problems suggests that poor performance on such problems is due in part to processing limitations.

Shafir and LeBoeuf (2002, p. 509) argued forcefully that attempts to explain away poor human performance on tasks involving thinking and reasoning have gone too far:

> Various arguments have been made disputing the accumulation of findings that show people systematically violating fundamental normative principles of reasoning, judgement, and decision . . . the violations cannot be dismissed as either random or trivial, nor can can they be attributed to experimenters' misinterpretation of answers that are actually appropriate to alternative, valid interpretations of the problems. The systematic and well-documented findings cannot be attributed to simple computational limitations, nor does it appear that inappropriate types of questions are being asked or inappropriate norms applied.

There is reasonable support for the notion that factors such as participants' misinterpretation of problems or lack of motivation explain only a fraction of errors in thinking and reasoning. We will briefly discuss three types of evidence providing such support.

First, Camerer and Hogarth (1999) reviewed 74 studies concerned with the effects of motivation on thinking and reasoning. They found across several tasks that the provision of incentives rarely led to improved performance.

Second, some researchers have found inadequacies in performance even when steps are taken to ensure that participants fully understand the problem. For example, Tversky and Kahneman (1983) studied the conjunction fallacy (see Chapter 15), in which many participants decided from a description of Linda that it was more likely that she was a feminist bank teller than that she was a bank teller. There was still a strong (although somewhat reduced) conjunction fallacy when the category of bank teller was made completely explicit: "Linda is a bank teller whether or not she is active in the feminist movement."

Third, it seems probable that experts would be much less likely than non-experts to misinterpret problems. However, Shafir and LeBoeuf (2002) discussed several studies in which experts were prone to error. For example, Redelmeier, Koehler, Liberman, and Tversky (1995; see Chapter 15) found that medical experts deciding on the probabilities of various diagnoses were biased by irrelevant information.

Theoretical considerations

We have made some headway in explaining how it is that most people seem to cope reasonably well with everyday problems but often fail miserably to solve reasoning and other problems in the laboratory. It is now time to consider in more detail the meaning of "rationality". Evans and Over (1996, 1997) made an important contribution by distinguishing between two types of rationality: rationality$_1$ and rationality$_2$. According to Evans and Over (1997, p. 4), people have personal rationality or rationality$_1$, "when they are generally successful in achieving their basic goals, keeping themselves alive, finding their way in the world, and communicating with each other." This form of rationality depends on an implicit cognitive system operating at an unconscious level. Rationality$_1$ permits us to cope effectively with everyday life.

In contrast, people display impersonal rationality or rationality$_2$ when "they act with good reasons sanctioned by a normative theory such as formal logic or probability theory" (Evans & Over, 1997, p. 2). This form of rationality depends on an explicit cognitive system operating at a conscious level; it also differs from rationality$_1$ in that it allows us to think in a hypothetical way about the future. Evans (2000) clarified the essence of rationality$_2$: "Rationality$_2$ involves individual differences in g [general factor of intelligence] . . . Hence intelligence—in the sense of g—depends upon the effective use of the explicitly thinking system." Laboratory research has focused on rationality$_2$, which can be error-prone even when rationality$_1$ is not.

The distinction between rationality$_1$ and rationality$_2$ appears useful, and resembles fairly closely that between two systems in dual-process theories. However, it is unlikely that all the cognitive processes used in thinking and decision making can appropriately be seen as involving one or other form of rationality. There is probably more diversity in cognitive processes than is implied by this approach. Finally, it can be argued that Evans and Over (1997) have described two forms of rationality, but have not provided an explanatory account of human rationality.

We will now consider where some major theorists stand on the rationality debate. Advocates of the probabilistic approach (e.g., Chater & Oaksford, 2001) argue that people do not make use of logic-based systems at all. Instead, what they are doing is searching for the most useful information, with their thinking being more rational than might initially appear to be the case. People often make everyday decisions on the basis of very incomplete information, but this is not typically the case in laboratory studies. There are other situations in the real world in which people are exposed to much redundant or unnecessary information, and this is also not true of most laboratory studies. People's reasoning strategies work reasonably well in everyday life, but may not do so in the laboratory. As Oaksford (1997, p. 260) argued, "Many of the errors and biases seen in people's reasoning are likely to be the result of importing their everyday probabilistic strategies into the lab." However, as we have seen, the ultimate value of the probabilistic approach is in doubt given the relatively few novel predictions it has produced.

Johnson-Laird's mental model theory is another example of an approach based on the assumption that processes used in everyday life are applied to laboratory reasoning problems. More specifically, Johnson-Laird assumed that the processes typically involved in language comprehension are used on reasoning problems, and that these processes often fail to provide a complete representation of such problems. The success of this theoretical approach suggests that people often import their everyday thinking and reasoning strategies into the laboratory.

In sum, most people can be regarded as showing **bounded rationality** (Simon, 1955), meaning they behave rationally within their processing limitations, and thereby produce workable (but not ideal) solutions to problems. According to Simon (1990, p. 7), bounded rationality is the norm, because "Human rational behaviour is shaped by a scissors whose two blades are the structure of task environments and the computational capabilities of the actor." The plentiful evidence that people make extensive use of heuristics or rules of thumb in problem solving, judgement, and decision making is entirely consistent with the bounded rationality approach.

CHAPTER SUMMARY

- Deductive reasoning
  Conditional reasoning has its origins in a system of logic known as propositional logic. Performance on conditional reasoning problems is typically better for the modus ponens inference than for other inferences (e.g., modus tollens). Conditional reasoning is influenced by context effects (e.g., the inclusion of additional premises). Performance on the Wason selection task is generally very poor, but is markedly better when the rule is deontic rather than indicative. Performance on syllogistic reasoning tasks is affected by various biases including belief bias, the base-rate effect, the atmosphere effect, and conversion errors. The fact that performance on deductive reasoning tasks is prone to error and bias suggests that people often fail to reason logically.

- Theories of deductive reasoning
  According to abstract-rule theory, people use mental logic when confronted by a reasoning task. Invalid inferences are drawn when people misunderstand or misrepresent the reasoning task. The theory accounts for many errors in reasoning. However, the comprehension component of the theory is under-specified, and it is not clear that people actually use mental logic when presented with a deductive reasoning problem. According to mental models theory, people construct one or more mental models, mainly representing explicitly what is true. They then try to find a counterexample model that will falsify the conclusion. Performance is constrained by the limited capacity of working memory and by the tendency when constructing mental models to ignore what is false. Mental model theory fails to specify in detail how the initial mental models are constructed, and people often form fewer mental models than expected. According to the probabilistic approach, people have developed various strategies (e.g., heuristics) for dealing with the uncertainties of everyday life, and these strategies are applied to deductive reasoning tasks. This approach accounts for many findings. However, it has not identified clearly the processes underlying performance on reasoning tasks, and the approach has failed to generate many novel predictions.

- Dual-system theories
  Various dual-system theories of reasoning have been proposed. In essence, one system uses processes that are rapid and relatively automatic whereas the second system uses the working memory system and is slow in its functioning. Individual differences in intelligence are associated mainly with the functioning of the second system, there is support for dual-process theories, but we need to know more about the detailed functioning of each system as well as the ways in which the two systems interact with each other.

- Brain systems in thinking and reasoning
  Brain-imaging studies and those on brain-damaged patients have indicated that the frontal cortex (especially the prefrontal cortex) is of major importance in numerous tasks involving higher-level cognitive processes. Similar brain areas are also active when people do an intelligence test. There is some empirical support for the notion that the right prefrontal area is more involved in plan generation, whereas the left prefrontal area is more involved in plan execution. Neuroimaging findings suggest that some common cognitive processes may underlie performance on problem-solving and reasoning tasks, intelligence tests, and working memory tasks. What is common may be relational integration, relational complexity, or the combination of active processing and temporary storage of information.

- Are humans rational?
  Apparently poor performance by most people on deductive reasoning tasks does not mean we are illogical and irrational because of the existence of the normative system problem, the interpretation problem, and the external validity problem. One way of explaining the discrepancy between the relatively successful nature of our reasoning in everyday life but unsuccessful reasoning in the laboratory is to distinguish between rationality$_1$ (an implicit cognitive system allowing us to cope with real-life problems) and rationality$_2$ (an explicit cognitive system resembling intelligence) which is required on laboratory deductive reasoning tasks. An alternative view is that our everyday comprehension processes and probabilistic strategies are simply imported into the laboratory. It is probably appropriate to argue that most people possess bounded rationality.

FURTHER READING

- Chater, N., & Oaksford, M. (2001). Human rationality and the psychology of reasoning: Where do we go from here? *British Journal of Psychology*, *92*, 193–216. The authors give a very useful overview of theory and research on reasoning.
- Evans, J.St.B.T. (2002). Logic and human reasoning: An assessment of the deduction paradigm. *Psychological Bulletin*, *128*, 978–996. This article contains a detailed evaluation of research on deductive reasoning.
- Evans, J.St.B.T. (2003). In two minds: Dual-process accounts of reasoning. *Trends in Cognitive Sciences*, *7*, 454–459. Jonathan Evans provides an excellent review of dual-system theories of deductive reasoning.
- Fiddick, L. (2003). Is there a faculty of deontic reasoning? A critical re-evaluation of abstract deontic versions of the Wason selection task. In D.E. Over (Ed.), *Evolution and the psychology of thinking: The debate*. Hove, UK: Psychology Press. This chapter provides an informed analysis of the strengths and weaknesses of social contract theory.
- Markman, A.B., & Gentner, D. (2001). Thinking. *Annual Review of Psychology*, *52*, 223–247. The authors consider the relationship between reasoning and other forms of higher-level cognition.
- Oaksford, M., & Chater, N. (2001). The probabilistic approach to human reasoning. *Trends in Cognitive Sciences*, *5*, 349–357. This article provides a succinct account of the main assumptions of the authors' influential probabilistic approach.
- Shafir, E., & LeBoef, R.A. (2002). Rationality. *Annual Review of Psychology*, *53*, 491–517. The authors make a strong case that much of our thinking and reasoning is not rational.

Part V

Present and Future

INTRODUCTION

One of the two main themes pursued in this chapter is that of consciousness. The first author remembers clearly a conversation with the distinguished cognitive psychologist Endel Tulving in the late 1980s. Endel Tulving said one criterion he used when evaluating a textbook on cognitive psychology was the amount of coverage of consciousness. Reference back to the fourth edition of this textbook reveals that consciousness was only discussed on two pages out of 525 pages of text. Accordingly, that edition clearly failed the Tulving test! There has been a marked increase in the amount of research on consciousness in recent years. As a result, it has been decided to devote a major section of the chapter to a discussion of our present state of knowledge about consciousness.

The second main theme explored in this chapter concerns the future of brain-imaging research. There has been much progress in our understanding of human cognition since the fourth edition of this textbook was published in 2000. All four approaches to human cognition (experimental cognitive psychology; cognitive neuropsychology; computational cognitive science; and cognitive neuroscience) have contributed fully to this progress, and there are encouraging signs that more research involves combining two or even three of the approaches within a single study. However, brain-imaging research within the cognitive neuroscience approach deserves to be singled out for special consideration, and will be discussed at length later in the chapter. The various reasons for this are addressed below.

First, there has been a huge increase percentage-wise in the number of brain-imaging studies on cognition. Second, technological developments have improved brain-imaging techniques by increasing sensitivity of measurement, temporal resolution, and spatial resolution. Third, and most important, there has been a substantial increase in the percentage of brain-imaging studies carefully designed to provide answers to theoretically interesting and important questions. In the past, there were too many brain-imaging studies for which the main aim was simply to find out which parts of the brain were most active when a certain task was performed. Savoy (2001, p. 32) had such mindless studies in mind when he referred to "vast quantities of 'here it is activated, here it is not' data."

CONSCIOUSNESS: NATURE AND FUNCTIONS

We all know that consciousness is an extremely difficult topic. As a result, progress in understanding the nature of consciousness has been relatively slow. However, Sutherland (1989) minimised our understanding when claiming, "Nothing worth reading has ever been written on it [consciousness]." What is **consciousness**? According to Velmans (2000, p. 6), "A person is conscious if they experience *something*; conversely, if a person or entity experiences nothing, they are not conscious. Elaborating slightly, we can say that when consciousness is present, phenomenal content [experience of seeing, hearing, and so on] is present. Conversely when *phenomenal content* is absent, consciousness is absent." In similar fashion, consciousness is defined in the *Oxford Dictionary of Psychology* (2001) as "the normal mental condition of the waking state of humans, characterised by the experience of perceptions, thoughts, feelings, awareness of the external world, and often in humans . . . self-awareness."

Functions

What functions are served by consciousness? There are more answers to that question than you can shake a stick at. One common answer was expressed as follows by Dehaene and Naccache (2001, p. 31): "By allowing more sources of knowledge to bear on the internal decision process, the neuronal workspace [strongly associated with consciousness] may represent an additional step in a general trend towards an increasing internalisation of representation in the course of evolution, whose main advantage is the freeing of the organism from its immediate environment." In other words, consciousness allows us to deal more flexibly and effectively with the complexities of the environment than would be possible in its absence. The issue of whether consciousness is present in other species is important and interesting, but lies beyond the scope of this book (see Velmans, 2000, for a relevant discussion).

Another common (and related) view about the functions of consciousness was provided by Baars (1997a, p. 7), who argued that consciousness "is a facility for *accessing, disseminating, and exchanging information*, and for *exercising global co-ordination and control*." This view seems similar to the impression we have that our conscious intentions cause our actions. It follows that conscious awareness should be present *early* in processing and *before* we engage in action. However, there are controversial findings to suggest that may not be the case. For example, evidence that conscious awareness can occur surprisingly late in processing was reported by Frith, Perry, and Lumer (1999). There were three rods near the participants, and they had to grasp the illuminated one. On some trials, the rod that was illuminated changed *after* participants had started to move their hand. They made a vocal response to indicate their conscious awareness of the target switch. The key finding was that the participants often grasped the new target rod about 300 ms *before* making the vocal response.

More dramatic findings were reported by Libet et al. (1983), who instructed participants to perform a rapid flexion (bending) of their wrist and fingers at a time of their choosing. Three key measures were obtained:

(1) Event-related potentials (ERPs; see Chapter 1), which revealed a consistent pattern (the readiness potential) occurring prior to the movement of the wrist and fingers.
(2) Time at which participants were consciously aware of the intention to move their wrist and fingers.
(3) The moment at which the hand muscles were activated (assessed with an electromyograph, an instrument used to measure the electrical activity of a muscle).

The findings were surprising (but consistent with other findings obtained by Libet). The readiness potential in the brain occurred 350 ms *before* conscious awareness of the intention to bend the wrist and fingers. This apparently means that "Initiation of the voluntary process is developed unconsciously, well before there is any awareness of the intention to act" (Libet, 1996, p. 112). However, conscious awareness occurred about 200 ms before the actual hand movement started, and this "provides time in which the conscious process could interfere with or 'veto' the consummation of the voluntary act" (Libet, 1996, p. 112). Gregory (cited in Blackmore, 2003) summarised the findings neatly: "We don't have free will, but we do have free won't!"

Several psychologists have challenged Libet's findings. For example, Trevena and Miller (2002, p. 163) argued that "RP [readiness potential] actually reflects non-motor as well as motor activity, and its early onset reflects general anticipatory processes rather than cortical movement preparation." They carried out an experiment in which participants decided which hand to move on each trial. Trevena and Miller used ERPs to compute the lateralised readiness potential, which assesses hand-specific movement preparation. In other words, the lateralised readiness potential differs according to whether it is the right or the left hand that moves. Thus, it is more clearly a measure of movement preparation than the readiness potential, which they also measured.

What did Trevena and Miller (2002) find? First, in line with what Libet et al. (1983) reported, the readiness potential typically occurred several hundred milliseconds before the decision of which hand to use was reported (see Figure 17.1). Second, the lateralised readiness potential occurred some time *after* the readiness potential. Third, the mean onset of the lateralised readiness potential was significantly earlier than the mean reported decision time. Fourth, "About 20% of the decisions [about which hand to move] were reported before the start of the LRP [lateralised readiness potential]." Overall, these findings confirm Libet et al.'s (1983) findings, but suggest that voluntary initiation of a hand movement generally precedes conscious awareness by less time than claimed by Libet et al.

Where do the findings of Frith et al. (1999), Libet et al. (1983), and Trevena and Miller (2002) leave us? According to Velmans (2000, p. 219), such findings leave us with a causal paradox (otherwise known as a headache): "Viewed from a first-person perspective, consciousness appears to be necessary for most forms of complex or novel processing. But viewed from a third-person perspective, consciousness does not appear to be necessary for any form of processing."

FIGURE 17.1

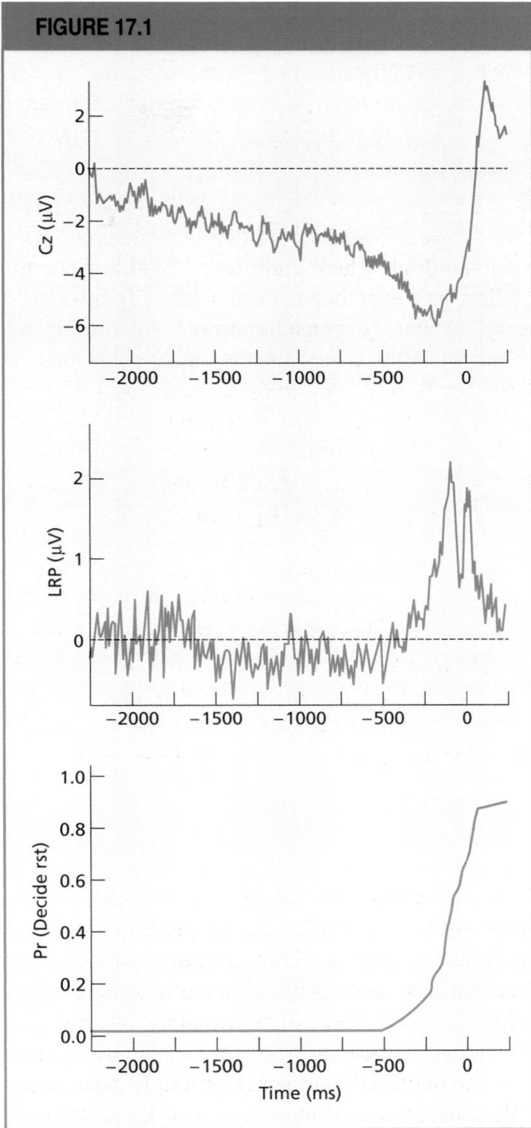

Readiness potential (top panel), lateralised readiness potential (middle panel), and probability of a conscious decision to move the hand (bottom panel) as a function of time in ms before a voluntary hand movement (shown as 0 ms). From Trevena and Miller (2002) with permission from Elsevier.

Why are we fooled into exaggerating the role of consciousness in determining our behaviour? Wegner and Wheatley (1999) provided one answer. A small square board was mounted on a computer mouse, and movements of the board moved a cursor over a screen showing pictures of about 50 objects. Two participants (one genuine, one the experimenter's confederate) placed their fingers on the board and moved the cursor over the objects. They were told to stop the cursor roughly every 30 seconds, and then indicate how strongly they had intended to make that particular stop. Both participants wore headphones. On four trials, the confederate was instructed over headphones to stop on a given object (e.g., swan). The real participant heard the object's name (e.g., "swan") over headphones 30 seconds, 5 seconds, or 1 second before the confederate stopped the cursor, or 1 second afterwards, having been led to believe that the other person was hearing different words through their headphones.

Wegner and Wheatley (1999) found the participants believed much more strongly that they had intended to stop the cursor when they heard the object's name 1 or 5 seconds before the cursor stopped than when it was 30 seconds before or 1 second afterwards. In the 5-second and 1-second before conditions, the participants were thinking about an object (e.g., swan) shortly before the cursor stopped on that object. They wanted to make sense of that thought–action sequence, and the simplest way of doing so was to assume (mistakenly) that they had willed the action. As Wegner and Wheatley (1999, p. 490) concluded, "Believing that our conscious thoughts cause our actions is an error based on the illusory experience of will—much like believing that a rabbit has indeed popped out of an empty hat."

We have by no means exhausted the possible functions for consciousness. However, we will consider only one more such function. According to Humphrey (1983), the function of consciousness is social. Humans have for a long time lived in social groups and so have needed to predict, understand, and manipulate the behaviour of other people. Thus, people had to become natural psychologists. Humphrey argued that the ability to put yourself in the position of someone else and consider what you would do in their position allows you to be more effective in group situations. This led to the development of self-reflexive insight and consciousness. Expressed differently, "Imagine that a new form of sense organ evolves, an 'inner eye', whose field of view is not the outside world but the brain itself" (Humphrey, 2002, p. 75). The extent to which these developments have occurred in other species of social animals is unknown.

Key issues

According to Pinker (1997), we must consider three somewhat different issues when trying to understand consciousness:

(1) *Sentience*: This is our subjective experience or phenomenal awareness, which is only available to the individual having the experience.
(2) *Access to information*: This relates to our ability to report the *content* of our subjective experience but without the ability to report on the *processes* producing that experience.
(3) *Self-knowledge*: Of particular importance to us as individuals is the ability to have conscious awareness of ourselves. In the words of Pinker (1997), "I cannot only feel pain and see red, but think to myself, 'Hey, here I am, Steve Pinker, feeling pain and seeing red!'"

You may be disappointed to learn that cognitive neuroscientists and cognitive psychologists have shed little light on the issue of sentience and the origins of our subjective experience. This is what Chalmers (1995b, p. 63) famously called the "hard problem", which is "the question of how physical processes in the brain give rise to subjective experience." Chalmers (1995a, pp. 201–203) spelled out in more detail the essence of the hard problem:

> If any problem qualifies as *the* problem of consciousness, it is this one . . . even when we have explained the performance of all the cognitive and behavioural functions in the vicinity of experience—perceptual discriminations, categorisations, internal

> access, verbal report—there may still remain a further unanswered question: Why is the performance of these functions accompanied by experience? . . . Why doesn't all this information processing go on "in the dark", free of any feel?

The good news is that much progress has been made with what Chalmers (1995a, 1995b) described as "easy problems". These problems (which are only relatively easy!) relate to Pinker's (1997) access-to-information issue, and involve understanding the processes involved in discriminating and categorising stimuli, integrating information, focal attention, control of behaviour, and so on. Theoretical approaches clarifying the relationship between these processes and consciousness are discussed shortly.

THEORIES OF CONSCIOUSNESS

Most theories have focused on the "easy problems" of consciousness. However, there have been various attempts to grapple with key philosophical issues raised by consciousness. We will start our discussion of theoretical approaches with one such attempt before proceeding to discuss other theories.

Dual-aspect theory

One of the most influential approaches to consciousness owes its origins to the Dutch philosopher Baruch Spinoza (1632–1677). In his double aspect theory, Spinoza (1677, p. 131) argued that mind and body are simply different aspects of a single underlying reality: "Mind and body are one and the same thing . . . the order of states of activity or passivity in our bodies is simultaneous in nature with the order of states of activity and passivity in the mind." Velmans (e.g., 2000) developed the above approach in his dual-aspect theory by claiming that consciousness and aspects of brain activity are *one* process with *two* sides. What are the practical implications of this position? Velmans (2000, p. 247) considered a situation in which he has access to your brain activity (e.g., via neuroimaging): "I know something about your mental states that you do not know (their physical embodiment). But you know something about them that I do not know (their manifestation in experience). Such first- and third-person information is complementary. We need your first-person story and my third-person story for a complete account of what is going on."

What functions are served by consciousness according to dual-aspect theory? First, as Velmans (2000, p. 257) pointed out, "Conscious representations of inner body and external events . . . generally represent those events and their causal interactions sufficiently well to allow a fairly accurate understanding of what is happening in our lives. Although they are only representations of events and their causal interactions, for everyday purposes we can take them to *be* those events and their causal interactions." Second, "From a first-person view, it is obvious how this [i.e., consciousness] affects our life and survival. Without it, life would be like nothing. So without it, there would be no point to survival" (Velmans, 2000, p. 278).

According to dual-aspect theory, the mental state of consciousness and physical brain activity form two sides of a single underlying process. If there is a single underlying process, we might expect that physical states can cause mental states, and that mental states can cause physical states. Plentiful evidence (e.g., from the use of drugs in therapy) suggests that physical states can cause mental states. However, the notion that mental states can cause physical states remains controversial in spite of much supporting evidence. For example, consider what happens when patients are given a salt tablet but told it contains active ingredients. This often improves the physical health of the patients (this is known as a placebo effect). Hashish, Finman, and Harvey (1988) provided evidence of a placebo effect. There was less jaw swelling and tightness after the removal of wisdom teeth when an ultrasound machine was used. Of relevance here, the same beneficial effects were obtained when the patients were misleadingly told they were exposed to ultrasound. Thus, as predicted by dual-aspect theory, mental states can apparently influence subsequent physical states.

Global workspace and working memory

Several theories of consciousness (e.g., Baars, 1988, 1997a; Baars & Franklin, 2003; Dehaene & Naccache, 2001) are based on similar assumptions. One such assumption is that we are only consciously aware of a small fraction of the information processing going on in our brain at any given moment. The information of which we become aware is usually that of most importance (e.g., in connection to our current goals). For example, Baars (1988, p. 31) argued in his global workspace theory that conscious events occur "in the theatre of consciousness", which is the global workspace. This metaphor is based on the notion that focal consciousness is like a "bright spot" on the stage. It is surrounded by several events that are only vaguely conscious and numerous events that are not conscious at all.

Another assumption is that conscious awareness depends on focal attention (see Chapter 5). For example, Baars (1997b) invited us to consider sentences such as "We look in order to see" or "We listen in order to hear". According to Baars (1997b, p. 364), "The distinction is between selecting an experience and being conscious of the selected event. In everyday language, the first word of each pair ['look', 'listen'] involves attention; the second word ['see', 'hear'] involves consciousness." Thus, attention resembles choosing a television channel and consciousness resembles the picture on the screen.

According to the global workspace theory, "Consciousness is associated with a global workspace in the brain—a fleeting memory capacity whose focal contents are widely distributed . . . to many unconscious specialised networks . . . a global workspace can serve to integrate many competing and co-operating input networks" (Baars & Franklin, 2003, p. 166). This limited-capacity global workspace is involved in "conscious perception, imagery, inner speech, and reportable goals" (Baars & Franklin, 2003, p. 167). There is some similarity between this global workspace and the central executive of Baddeley's (e.g., 2001) working memory system (see Chapter 6). The central executive is a modality-free, limited-capacity component of the working memory system, and there is conscious awareness of its contents.

In addition, information from "a collection of distributed specialised networks (processors)" (Baars & Franklin, 2003, p. 166) influences the content of the global workspace. Something similar is assumed to occur within the working memory system (e.g., Baddeley, 2001), according to which information from its various components (visuo-spatial sketchpad, phonological loop, and episodic buffer) influences the content of the central executive.

Evidence for the involvement of working memory in conscious experience was reported by Baddeley and Andrade (2000; see Chapter 4). Their starting point was that the conscious experience of vivid visual imagery depends on a rich representation in the visuo-spatial sketchpad component of the working memory system. In contrast, vivid auditory imagery requires a rich representation in the phonological loop component of the working memory system. As predicted, requiring participants to perform a visuo-spatial task (tapping) at the same time selectively reduced the vividness of visual images, whereas doing counting (which involves the phonological loop) mainly reduced the vividness of auditory images. Andrade (2001) found that a task requiring use of the central executive (logical reasoning) greatly reduced the vividness of both visual and auditory images.

There are some important differences between the two theories. People have at least potential conscious awareness of information in all of the components of the working memory system. In contrast, most of the information in the specialised networks of global workspace theory is not accessible to consciousness.

Evaluation

As we will see shortly, some of the key assumptions of global workspace theory have received much empirical support. For example, we are typically consciously aware of only a small fraction of the information processing occurring in the brain. It is also probable that attentional processes play an important role in determining access to conscious awareness. On the negative side, it is sometimes suggested that consciousness has a causal role in information processing: "Actions that are performed consciously are shaped by conscious feedback while unconscious actions are not. For example, you might unconsciously make a speech error but when you consciously hear the mistake you can put it right because consciousness creates global access to further unconscious resources" (Baars, 1997a, p. 165). In fact, however, there is a dearth of evidence that consciousness has a *causal* influence. In addition, the global workspace theory does not try to explain our first-person conscious experience.

The working memory model shares most of the strengths of the global workspace theory. In addition, there is great potential in using dual-task methods (as in Baddeley & Andrade, 2000) to study conscious experience. However, there are some problems of interpretation. As Andrade (2001, p. 72) pointed out, "Finding that manipulations of working memory alter consciousness does not imply that working memory is consciousness. Working memory processes may simply contribute to conscious processing occurring elsewhere, just as opening one's eyes causes consciousness of daylight because of mediating cognitive processes, and not because the eyes are the seat of consciousness." For example, it may well be that "the central executive controls which of the potentially conscious representations in the slave systems of working memory becomes conscious, but it is not consciousness itself" (Andrade, 2001, p. 73).

Dehaene and Naccache's theory

So far we have focused mainly on Baars' global workspace theory. Baars was one of the first psychologists to propose a coherent theory of consciousness based on the notion of a global workspace, and he remains a central figure in its development. However, in what follows we will focus primarily on Dehaene and Naccache's (2001) global workspace theory, and our reasons for doing this need to be indicated. First, the basic assumptions made by Dehaene and Naccache are very similar to those made by Baars, and so our discussion of Baars' theoretical views is of direct relevance to Dehaene and Naccache's theory. Second, Dehaene and Naccache have gone further than Baars in identifying the main brain areas associated with conscious awareness. Third, Dehaene and Naccache took many of Baars' ideas as the basis for their theory, but have subsequently developed and extended those ideas.

Three research findings played an important part in the initial development of Dehaene and Naccache's global workspace theory. First, most information processing occurs without conscious awareness. This has been shown in studies on brain-damaged patients suffering from several different disorders (see below). For example, evidence that perceptual and semantic processing can occur below the conscious level has been found in patients with achromatopsia and blindsight (see Chapter 2), with prosopagnosia (see Chapter 4), with neglect and extinction (see Chapter 5), and with amnesia (see Chapter 7). In normal individuals, there is similar evidence for extensive non-conscious processing in phenomena such as subliminal perception (see Chapter 2) and insight (see Chapter 13).

Second, Dehaene and Naccache (2001) assumed that attention is a necessary precondition for consciousness. Evidence for that assumption comes from extinction, in which brain-damaged patients presented with two visual stimuli at the same time report seeing only the one on the right. In fact, they seem not to attend to the stimulus on the left, which is why they do not perceive it consciously even though it is processed to some extent (see Driver & Vuilleumier, 2001).

A similar phenomenon in normal individuals was reported by Mack and Rock (1998) in a study on inattentional blindness (see Chapter 4). Participants performed a demanding visual discrimination task at a given location in their visual field. On one trial, a second visual stimulus was presented briefly (typically for 200 ms) and unexpectedly. Most participants did not report detecting this second stimulus, and denied having seen it even when explicitly questioned about it. More striking findings were reported by Simons and Chabris (1999; see Chapter 4), who showed participants a short film called "Gorillas in our

Midst". In this film, two teams of students throw balls to each other. Some participants were told to watch the white team very carefully and to count the number of passes made. When the film ended, they were asked whether they had seen anything unusual. In fact, a woman dressed in a gorilla suit walked right into shot, turned to the camera, and thumped her chest before walking off. About 50% of the participants did not notice the gorilla!

Third, Dehaene and Naccache (2001, p. 11) assumed that several specific mental operations require conscious awareness: "The strategic operations which are associated with planning a novel strategy, evaluating it, controlling its execution, and correcting possible errors cannot be accomplished unconsciously." In similar fashion, Baars and McGovern (1996, p. 92) assumed that "Information in the global workspace corresponds to conscious contents . . . Consciousness appears to be the major way in which the central nervous system adapts to novel, challenging and informative events in the world."

According to global workspace theory, automatic or unconscious processing involves numerous specific dedicated processors or modules. These processors typically operate in parallel. We now come to the central theoretical assumption of the theory: "Besides specialised processors, the architecture of the human brain also comprises *a distributed neural system or 'workspace' with long-distance connectivity that can potentially interconnect multiple specialised brain areas in a co-ordinated, though variable manner*" (Dehaene & Naccache, 2001, p. 13). Thus, there is a control system making conscious some of the information from specialised processors, and using it in a flexible way to perform complex tasks. The control system as envisaged by Dehaene and Naccache is very similar to Baddeley's (1986) notion of a central executive (see Chapter 6) or Baars' (1988) global workspace. For example, Baars (2002, p. 47) argued that the central hypothesis of his global workspace theory is that "consciousness facilitates widespread access between otherwise independent brain functions".

How does the above system function? According to Dehaene and Naccache (2001, p. 14), "*Top-down attentional amplification is the mechanism by which modular processes can be temporarily mobilised and made available to the global workspace, and therefore to consciousness.*" Thus, any given brain process may or may not contribute to the content of consciousness depending on whether or not it is connected to brain areas involved in attentional processes. An implication of this assumption is that conscious awareness can be associated with activity in numerous different brain areas.

Dennett (2001, p. 225) clarified what is involved by providing a useful metaphor: "Consciousness is . . . political influence—a good slang term is *clout*. When processes compete for ongoing control of the body, the one with the greatest clout dominates the scene until a process with even greater clout displaces it . . . there are plenty of quite sharp differences in political clout exercised by contents over time."

Where is consciousness in the brain?

According to Dehaene and Naccache (2001), conscious awareness depends on simultaneous activation of several distant areas of the brain. The specific brain areas involved depend in part on the content of the conscious experience. As Gazzaniga et al. (2002, p. 109) pointed out, "Neural correlates of the contents of perceptual awareness can be found in many different cortical areas, from V1 to MT and the face area . . . the contents of awareness are not represented in a single unitary consciousness system, but rather each conscious perceptual content is represented in the same set of neurons that analyse that perceptual information in the first place." For example, conscious experience of a face involves sufficient activation in the so-called fusiform face area (Kanwisher, 2001), whereas conscious experience of motion involves MT+ within the middle temporal area. Using transcranial magnetic stimulation (TMS) to produce a temporary lesion in that area prevented the conscious perception of motion (Walsh, Ellison, Battelli, & Cowey, 1998). Dehaene and Naccache (2001) assumed that the brain areas involved in the global workspace and conscious experience include the prefrontal cortex (e.g., BA46) and the anterior cingulate as well as various content-specific areas (see Figure 17.2).

FIGURE 17.2

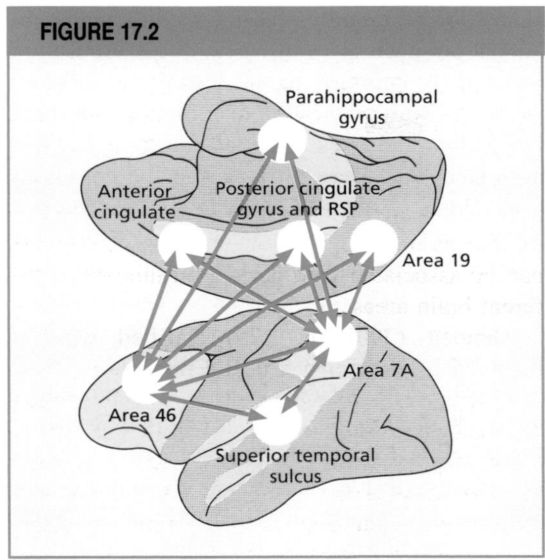

Proposed brain areas involved in the global workspace in which there are associations between the prefrontal cortex, the anterior cingulate, the parietal area, and the temporal area. From Goldman-Rakic (1988). Reprinted, with permission, from the *Annual Review of Neuroscience, Volume 11* © 1988 by Annual Reviews www.annualreviews.org.

Numerous studies have indicated that the prefrontal cortex and anterior cingulate are active when people are performing activities thought to involve consciousness (e.g., dividing attention; processing novel stimuli; performing complex processes). Corbetta, Miezin, Dobmeyer, and Shulman (1990) found using PET that dividing attention among three visual features (colour, shape, motion) was associated with increased activity of the anterior cingulate. Raichle et al. (1994) found that prefrontal cortex and the anterior cingulate were both active during initial task performance on a verb-generation task. Such activation disappeared when the task became automatised (and so no longer involved conscious processes), but reappeared when novel items were presented. Chochon, Cohen, van de Moortele, and Dehaene (1999) gave their participants the task of performing complex mental calculations. Prefrontal cortex and the anterior cingulate were both active throughout each calculation.

Interesting findings were reported by Lumer, Friston, and Rees (1998) from a study on **binocular rivalry**. Binocular rivalry occurs when two visual stimuli are presented (one to each eye), and the observer perceives only one of them. It provides a good way of assessing brain activity associated with consciousness, because there are shifts in conscious content as the stimulus being perceived varies, without any change in the stimuli themselves. Lumer et al. presented a red drifting grating to one eye and a green face to the other, and the participants pressed keys to indicate which stimulus they were consciously perceiving. Lumer et al. used fMRI to identify the brain areas especially active immediately prior to a switch in conscious perception from one stimulus to the other. As you have probably guessed, the anterior cingulate and the prefrontal cortex were among the several areas showing increased activation during shifts in conscious perception.

According to the theory, conscious awareness is typically associated with activation across several brain regions (see Figure 17.2). Some of the most relevant brain-imaging research has involved presenting all participants with the same stimuli and the same task. The brain activation data are then analysed separately for those participants who did or did not become consciously aware of some aspect of the experimental situation. For example, McIntosh, Rajah, and Lobaugh (1999) carried out a PET study on associate learning. There were two visual stimuli, and the task was to respond to one of them (the target) but not to the other. There were also two tones, one predicting that a visual stimulus would be presented and the other predicting the absence of a visual stimulus. The participants were divided into those who noticed the association between the auditory and visual stimuli (the aware group) and those who did not (unaware group).

McIntosh et al. (1999) found that the greatest difference between the two groups in the brain activity produced by the tones was in the left prefrontal cortex (Brodmann Area 9; see Chapter 1), suggesting that this area was associated with conscious awareness of the significance of the tones. In addition, they found evidence that the left prefrontal cortex forms part of a much larger neural system associated with conscious awareness including the right prefrontal cortex, bilateral superior temporal cortices, medial cerebellum, and occipital cortex. McIntosh et al. (1999, p. 1531) concluded that "These results suggest cerebral processes underlying awareness are mediated through interactions of large-scale neuro-cognitive systems."

Similar findings were reported by Rodriguez et al. (1999). Participants saw pictures that are easily perceived as faces when presented upright but which are seen as meaningless black-and-white shapes when presented upside down. EEGs were recorded from 30 electrodes, and the resultant data were then analysed to work out the extent to which electrical activity was in synchrony across electrodes (phase synchrony). The key findings related to brain activity at the time after picture presentation (180–360 ms) at which faces were perceived in the upright condition. There was considerable phase synchrony in this condition, especially in the area between the left parieto-occipital and frontotemporal regions (see Figure 17.3). In contrast, there was phase desynchrony rather than synchrony when no face was seen. As Rodriguez et al. (1999, p. 431) concluded, "Only face perception induces a long-distance pattern of synchronisation, correlating to the moment of [conscious] perception itself."

There is additional evidence that conscious awareness is associated with activation of several brain areas. For example, Dehaene et al. (2001) compared brain activation during conscious

FIGURE 17.3

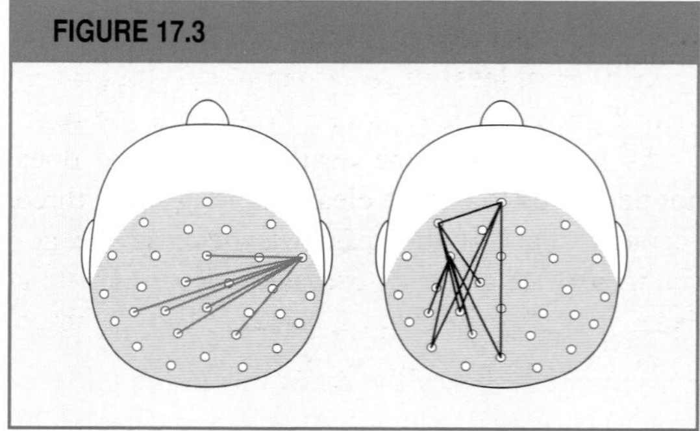

Phase synchrony (black lines) and phase desynchrony (blue lines) in EEG 180–360 ms. After stimulus presentation in the no face perception (left side) and face perception (right side) conditions. From Rodriguez et al. (1999). Copyright © 1999 by the Nature Publishing Group. Reproduced with permission.

perception of visually presented words with subliminal presentation of the same words. Activation was largely confined to the visual cortex when the words were presented subliminally, but there was widespread visual, parietal, and frontal activation when they were presented at the conscious level. Baars (2002, p. 47) reviewed 13 studies in which conscious and non-conscious conditions were compared, and came to the following conclusion: "Conscious perception . . . enables access to widespread brain sources, whereas unconscious input processing is limited to sensory regions."

Finally, evidence that most of the brain plays some role in consciousness was reported by Alkire, Haier, and Fallon (2000). They used PET to study the effects of two anaesthetics (propofol and isoflurane) on the brain. There was no evidence of any "consciousness circuits"; instead, there was a progressive general reduction in neuronal functioning with increasing doses of anaesthetic.

Evaluation

Many of the theoretical assumptions made by Dehaene and Naccache (2001) are plausible and in line with the available evidence. For example, most information processing occurs below the level of conscious awareness, and attentional processes seem to play a major role in determining which fraction of the information being processed at any given moment enters consciousness. Several brain areas are associated with conscious experience, with the prefrontal cortex and the anterior cingulate often being involved. What is of particular importance is the accumulating evidence in favour of the notion that integrated, large-scale brain activity underlies much conscious awareness (e.g., Baars, 2002; McIntosh et al., 1999; Rodriguez et al., 1999). Thus, the theory (which builds on several previous theories) provides us with a good overview of many aspects of consciousness.

The theories put forward by Dehaene and Naccache (2001), Baars (1997a), and others can be regarded as functionalist theories, in that consciousness plays an important role in information processing, especially in the integration and dissemination (distribution) of information. However, there are various difficulties with functionalist theories. A relatively frequent problem is that conscious awareness typically occurs only *after* the crucial processing has already occurred. Consider, for example, Velmans' (2000, p. 209) account of what happens when you read: "You are conscious of what is written, but not conscious of the complex input analysis involved. Nor are you aware of *consciously carrying* out any system-wide integration and dissemination of information . . . Rather, information that enters consciousness has *already been integrated*."

Velmans (2000) also identified a much more serious problem with the functionalist approach. Consciousness is indisputably a "first-person" phenomenon: we have detailed knowledge of our own conscious experience, but cannot observe directly anyone else's conscious experience. However, accounts of consciousness by functionalist theorists are "third-person" accounts describing various processes of relevance to consciousness. Why is this a problem? According to Velmans (2000, p. 66):

> [Functionalist] theories typically move, without blinking, from relatively well-justified claims about the forms of information processing with which consciousness is *associated*, to entirely unjustified claims about what consciousness is or what it *does*. Baars and McGovern (1996), for example, move without any discussion . . . to the claim that consciousness actually *carries out the functions of the global workspace*.

We can see the limitations of the functionalist approach if we consider the views of computational functionalists such as Sloman and Logan (1998). According to such theorists, "There is nothing to prevent mind and consciousness in non-human systems, for the reason that mental operations are nothing more than computations" (Velmans, 2000, p. 73). Thus, a computer programmed carefully to mimic the attentional and other processes of human beings would have conscious experiences! That seems wildly improbable to me (and to you?), and certainly has not been shown to be the case. However, it follows from the functionalist position.

PERCEPTION WITHOUT AWARENESS

One way of increasing our understanding of consciousness is to study brain-damaged patients having a partial lack of conscious awareness. For example, several categories of patients lack conscious perception of stimuli that they nevertheless process to some extent. These include patients with blindsight (Chapter 2), with apperceptive agnosia, associative visual agnosia, and prosopagnosia (Chapter 4), and with neglect and extinction (Chapter 5). Farah (2001, p.159) posed an important question with respect to such patients: "What is different, or missing, in a patient who perceives without awareness, compared to a normal person who perceives with awareness?"

Farah (2001) argued that three main answers have been proposed to the above question. First, there are privileged role accounts (e.g., Schacter, McAndrews, & Moscovitch, 1988), according to which only certain brain systems are involved in mediating conscious awareness. Second, there are integration accounts (e.g., Crick & Koch, 1990), according to which conscious perception involves binding together the various properties of a stimulus (e.g., shape, colour, motion). Third, there are quality-of-representation accounts (e.g., Farah, O'Reilly, & Vecera, 1993), according to which conscious experience requires reasonably high-quality perceptual representations. The quality of such perceptual representations may be related to the activation level of their neural substrate or to their capacity to be activated by a given stimulus.

As we will see, the available evidence does not permit us to decide clearly among these three accounts. Part of the reason is because the accounts are not mutually exclusive. To anticipate a little, it is probably safe to assume that all three accounts possess some validity.

Evidence

Even though our primary focus is on brain-damaged patients, it is worth considering briefly studies of subliminal perception in normal individuals (see Chapter 2). In these studies, the participants lack conscious awareness of certain visual stimuli in spite of sometimes processing these stimuli fairly thoroughly (e.g., Dehaene et al., 1998). What invariably happens is that subliminal perception is produced by reducing the quality of perceptual representations (e.g., by presenting visual stimuli very briefly). Thus, such studies support the quality-of-representation account.

Brain-imaging studies have also provided some support for the quality-of-representation account. For example, consider a study on extinction (a condition in which one out of two visual stimuli presented simultaneously is not detected). Rees et al. (2000) presented pictures of faces and of houses either singly or in pairs to a patient suffering from extinction. When the pictures were presented singly, some brain areas responded selectively to faces, whereas others responded selectively to houses. When two stimuli were presented together, there was reduced activation in the face area for extinguished (non-consciously detected) faces and in the house area for extinguished houses. These reduced levels of activation may well reflect reduced quality of representation of presented stimuli.

Hadjikhani and de Gelder (2002) reporting findings consistent with the quality-of-representation account in a study on patients with prosopagnosia (selective impairment of face recognition). They found with fMRI that normal individuals showed more activity to faces than objects in the mid-fusiform gyrus and the inferior occipital gyrus. However, patients with prosopagnosia had the same low levels of activity in those areas to faces and objects. These findings suggest that patients with prosopagnosia formed low-quality perceptual representations of faces in the so-called face area of the brain.

Other findings suggest the quality-of-representation account may be inadequate. For example, Luck, Vogel, and Shapiro (1996) measured a neural correlate of gaining access to word meaning (N400) using event-related potentials (ERPs). Their key finding was that N400 was the same regardless of whether the word was consciously perceived. With respect to the Rees et al. (2000) study discussed above, activation in the face area was nearly as great when faces were not consciously perceived as when they were. According to Kanwisher (2001), such findings suggest that conscious awareness of a visual stimulus depends on two factors: (1) a reasonably strong neural representation of that stimulus; and (2) making information about that representation accessible to other parts of the brain. Thus, some combination of the quality-of-representation and integration accounts may be necessary to explain conscious perception.

We turn now to blindsight. Patients with blindsight have no conscious experience of visual stimuli in part of the visual field but can nevertheless indicate through their behaviour that some processing has occurred (see Chapter 2). Patients with blindsight have damage to the ventral pathway (concerned with object recognition and associated with conscious perception). However, they have a partially intact dorsal pathway (concerned with motion detection and less associated with conscious perception). For example, Morland (1999) found that GY, a patient with blindsight, could match the speed of moving stimuli in his blind field to those in his seeing field. In terms of theoretical accounts, blindsight patients have severe reduction in the quality of the representations formed using the ventral pathway. In addition, they cannot integrate different kinds of information from objects. For example, they show evidence of detecting motion without being consciously aware of the moving object itself.

There is relatively little experimental support for the privileged role account, according to which conscious perception depends crucially on certain brain systems. This can be seen if we consider the brain areas associated with conditions such as blindsight, prosopagnosia, extinction, and neglect. Blindsight can involve damage to various areas, but is typically centred on primary visual cortex (V1; see Weiskrantz, 1997). So far as prosopagnosia is concerned, a key area is the fusiform gyrus and surrounding areas (Pelphrey et al., 2003). Still other areas are associated with other disorders. The temporo-parietal junction is generally damaged in cases of extinction (Karnath, Himmelbach, & Küker, 2003), and visual neglect is associated with damage to the superior temporal gyri and planum temporale (Karnath et al., 2003).

The fact that diverse sites of brain damage are associated with different disorders suggests that there is no set of brain regions *always* responsible for failures of conscious perception. However, it is likely that some areas are much more important than others. As we saw earlier, Dehaene and Naccache (2001) argued with supporting evidence that brain areas such as the prefrontal cortex and the anterior cingulate are of particular significance with respect to conscious perception.

Evaluation

Research on brain-damaged patients with attentional and/or perceptual impairments who process some information about stimuli they cannot consciously perceive has proved of value. The privileged role approach has the least direct evidence in its favour. Kanwisher (2001, p. 109) concluded her review of the relevant evidence as follows: "Neural correlates of the contents of perceptual awareness can be found in many different cortical areas, from V1 to MT and the face area . . . the contents of consciousness are not represented in a single unitary consciousness system." That conclusion is in line with our earlier discussion, and suggests that privileged role accounts can be no more than partially correct.

There is probably more evidence supporting the quality-of-representation account than the other accounts. However, as was mentioned earlier, the various theoretical approaches are not incompatible with each other. It may well be that the perceptual impairments of many brain-damaged patients can best be explained by combining the quality-of-representation and integration accounts.

IS CONSCIOUSNESS UNITARY?

Most people believe they have a single, unitary consciousness, although some are in two minds on the issue. However, consider **split-brain patients**, who have very few connections between the two brain hemispheres as a result of surgery. In the great majority of cases, the corpus callosum (bridge) between the two brain hemispheres was cut surgically to contain epileptic seizures within one hemisphere. The corpus callosum is a collection of 250 million axons connecting sites in one hemisphere with those in the other (see Figure 17.4). Thus, split-brain patients potentially provide an exciting opportunity to decide whether it is possible to have two consciousnesses, one based in each hemisphere.

Roger Sperry (1913–1994) carried out much of the early work on split-brain patients, for which he received the Nobel Prize. He argued that these patients had two consciousnesses: "Each hemisphere seemed to have its own separate and private sensations . . . the minor hemisphere [the right one] constitutes a second conscious entity that is characteristically human and runs along in parallel with the more dominant stream of consciousness in the major hemisphere [the left hemisphere]" (Sperry, 1968, p. 723). As we will see, it is doubtful whether this view is correct.

Gazzaniga et al. (2002) argued for an alternative position. According to them, conscious awareness depends on a conscious system in the left hemisphere which tries to make sense of the information available to it. This system is called the **interpreter**, defined as "A left-brain system that seeks explanation for internal and external events in order to produce appropriate response behaviour" (Gazzaniga et al., 2002, p. G-5). This theoretical position was developed by Cooney and Gazzaniga (2003). They argued that the interpretive process continues to function even when provided with very limited information, as is the case with many brain-damaged patients. In their own words, "This [system] generates a causal understanding of events that is subjectively complete and seemingly self-evident, even when that understanding is incomplete" (Cooney & Gazzaniga, 2003, p. 162).

Evidence

In order to understand the findings from split-brain patients, note that information from the left visual field goes to the right hemisphere, whereas information from the right visual field goes to the left hemisphere (see Chapter 2). More generally, the left half of the body is controlled by the right

FIGURE 17.4

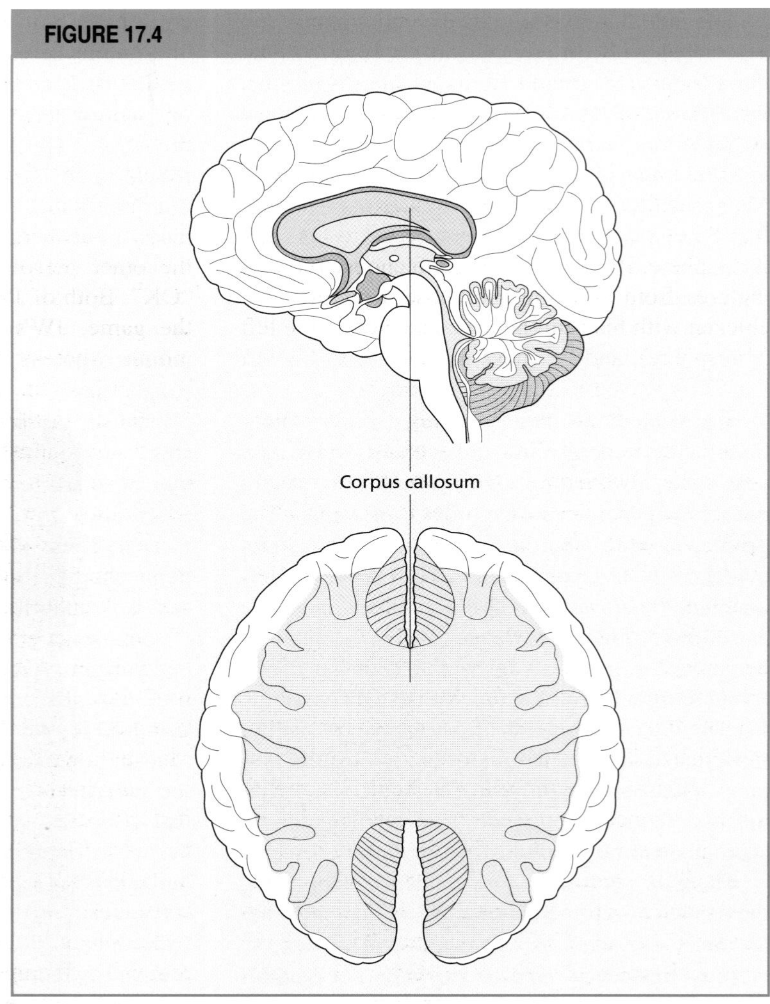

The corpus callosum.

hemisphere, and the right half of the body is controlled by the left hemisphere. It is often thought that split-brain patients have great difficulty in functioning effectively. This is NOT the case. Indeed, it was not realised initially that cutting the corpus callosum caused any problems for split-brain patients. In fact, split-brain patients ensure that information about the environment reaches both hemispheres simply by moving their eyes around. Researchers who have found impaired performance in split-brain patients have typically done so by presenting visual stimuli *briefly* to only one hemisphere so there are no eye movements while the stimuli are visible.

The language abilities of most people (including split-brain patients) are located mainly in the left hemisphere. The lack of language ability in the right hemisphere makes it hard to decide whether the right hemispheres of most split-brain patients have conscious experiences. Accordingly, it is important to study split-brain patients with reasonable language abilities in the right hemisphere.

Gazzaniga and LeDoux (1978) reported findings from PS, a split-brain patient with unusually well-developed right-hemisphere language abilities. The left hand is connected to the right hemisphere, and PS showed limited evidence of consciousness in his right hemisphere by responding appropriately to questions using his left hand. For example, PS could spell out his own name, that of his girlfriend, his hobbies, his current mood, and so on.

Gazzaniga (1992) discussed other studies on PS. For example, a chicken claw was presented to his left hemisphere and a snow scene to his right hemisphere. PS was then asked to choose relevant pictures from an array. He chose a picture of a chicken with his right hand (connected to the left hemisphere), and he chose a shovel with his left hand (connected to the right hemisphere).

Superficially, the above findings are consistent with the notion that PS had a separate consciousness in each hemisphere. However, this seems less likely when we take into account PS's explanation of his choices: "Oh, that's simple. The chicken claw goes with the chicken, and you need a shovel to clean out the chicken shed" (Gazzaniga, 1992, p. 124). According to Gazzaniga (1992), PS's left hemisphere was interpreting actions initiated by the right hemisphere, with the right hemisphere contributing relatively little to the interpretation. In similar fashion, when PS's right hemisphere was given the command to walk, PS obeyed. However, his left hemisphere explained his behaviour by saying something such as that he wanted a Coke.

Findings indicating that PS's left hemisphere often over-ruled his right hemisphere led Gazzaniga et al. (2002) to argue that PS (and other split-brain patients) have very limited right-hemisphere consciousness. For example, these patients find it hard to make inferences from information presented to the right hemisphere. Consider the task of deciding which of six possible answers best describes the causal relationship between two words (e.g., "bleed" describes the relation between "pin" and "finger"). The split-brain patients understood the meanings of the words, but their task performance was poor. Gazzaniga et al. (2002, p. 680) concluded as follows: "[The right hemisphere] deals mainly with raw experience in an unembellished [unadorned] way. The left hemisphere, though, is constantly . . . labelling experiences, making inferences as to cause, and carrying out a host of other cognitive activities. The right hemisphere is simply monitoring the world." This is consistent with the notion that the left hemisphere contains an interpreter.

If split-brain patients have two minds, it might be possible to produce a dialogue between these minds. Mackay (1987) tried to achieve this. For example, he asked a split-brain patient called JW to play a game in which another person chose a number between 0 and 9. When JW made a guess, the other person responded "Up", "Down", or "OK". Both of JW's hemispheres learned to play the game. JW's left hemisphere responded by mouth, whereas the right hemisphere responded by pointing with the left hand.

Mackay (1987) found that the two hemispheres could play against each other, and they could even cooperate with each other and pay each other winnings in the form of tokens.

However, Mackay (1987) was unconvinced that these findings provided evidence for a proper dialogue between two consciousnesses: "Despite all encouragements we found no sign at all of recognition of the other 'half' as a separate person." One of the patients even asked Mackay, "Are you guys trying to make two people out of me?" Mackay argued that our consciousness involves a self-supervisory system that determines our current priorities. Split-brain patients (like the rest of us) have a single self-supervisory system based in the left hemisphere, and thus have only a single consciousness.

Subsequent research has produced more promising findings. Baynes and Gazzaniga (2000) discussed the case of VJ, whose writing and speech are controlled by different hemispheres. According to Baynes and Gazzaniga (2000, p. 1362), "She [VJ] is the first split . . . who is frequently dismayed by the independent performance of her right and left hands. She is discomfited by the fluent writing of her left hand to unseen stimuli and distressed by the inability of her right hand to write out words she can read out loud and spell." Speculatively, we could interpret the evidence from VJ as suggesting limited dual consciousness.

Finally, we consider evidence for Cooney and Gazzaniga's (2003) hypothesis that the left-hemisphere interpretive system often continues to function in brain-damaged patients even when it lacks access to important information. They claimed support for this hypothesis from patients with neglect (lack of conscious perception of the left side of visual space; see Chapter 5), with **anosognosia for hemiplegia** (inability to recognise paralysis in the paralysed side of the body), and with **reduplicative paramnesia** (believing there are multiple copies of places and people). For example, Halligan and Marshall (1998) quoted a patient with neglect: "I knew the word 'neglect' was a sort of medical term for whatever was wrong but the word bothered me because you only neglect something that is actually there, don't you? If it's not there, how can you neglect it?"

Damage to the right parietal cortex in patients with anosognosia for hemiplegia deprives them of the ability to monitor or represent the existence of limbs on the left side of the body. When such patients look at their own paralysed left hand, they say things such as "That's not my hand" (Ramachandran, 1995). Gazzaniga (2000) studied a female patient with reduplicative paramnesia. She was being studied at a New York Hospital, but was convinced she was at home in Freeport, Maine. When asked to explain why there were several lifts outside the door, she replied, "Do you know how much it cost me to have those put in?"

Evaluation

Research on split-brain patients is undeniably fascinating, and has produced several interesting findings. However, it has not fully resolved the issue of whether it is possible to have two separate consciousnesses. The commonest view is that the left hemisphere in split-brain patients plays the dominant role in consciousness, because it is the location of an interpreter or self-supervisory system. In contrast, the right hemisphere can engage in various relatively low-level processing activities, but probably lacks its own consciousness. This view is supported by findings showing the left hemisphere over-ruling the right hemisphere. It is also supported by the persistent failure to observe anything approaching a genuine dialogue between the two hemispheres. However, we still lack definitive evidence.

There is reasonable evidence that many brain-damaged patients are unaware of their cognitive impairments, leading the left-hemisphere interpreter to provide coherent (but inaccurate) interpretations of events. However, many brain-damaged patients are well aware of the impairments in their cognitive functioning, and so do not produce misleading interpretations of events. The processes determining whether there is conscious awareness of the adverse effects of brain damage remain unclear.

WHITHER BRAIN IMAGING?

There has been a dramatic increase in the number of brain-imaging studies in the past 10–15 years, and the quality of such studies has increased in line with their quantity. The increased quality is most obvious in the greater emphasis on designing brain-imaging studies of direct relevance to theoretical issues. In the past, there were many studies in which no specific predictions were made about the brain areas expected to be active when people performed a given task.

One of the key brain-imaging techniques is fMRI (see Chapter 1), a technique that has been associated with two major developments in recent years. First, MRI scanners have become more powerful. In 1998, it was estimated that there were 2200 MRI scanners in the world, of which about 99% were 1.5-T (tesla) machines, with only 1% being more powerful (Fitzpatrick & Rothman, 2002). In the years since then, there has been a dramatic increase in the number of 3-T machines, which are twice as powerful as 1.5-T machines. Note, however, that artefacts of measurement are more likely to occur with more powerful machines. Second, an increasing number of researchers have used **event-related fMRI**, in which the pattern of brain activity following some specific event is measured by presenting the event several times and averaging.

We can see the usefulness of event-related fMRI by considering a study by Wagner et al. (1998). They recorded fMRI while participants learned a list of words. About 20 minutes later, the participants were given a test of recognition memory, on which they failed to recognise 12%

of the words. Did these recognition failures occur because of problems during *learning* or because of problems at *retrieval*? Wagner et al. answered this question by using event-related fMRI, comparing brain activity during learning for words subsequently recognised with that for words subsequently not recognised. There was more brain activity in the prefrontal cortex and the hippocampus during learning for words subsequently remembered than for those not remembered, suggesting that forgotten words were processed less thoroughly than remembered words at the time of learning.

The growing maturity of brain-imaging research is also shown in the increasing number of meta-analyses in which the findings from numerous studies are combined (e.g., Fox, Parsons, & Lancaster, 1998; Kosslyn & Thompson, 2003). Such meta-analyses have indicated that there is increasingly good agreement concerning the brain areas involved in a wide range of cognitive activities. An important reason for this increased agreement is greater reliance on stereotactic instruments to provide precise three-dimensional localisation of brain activity (Fox et al., 1998). In the past, there was more reliance on less precise structural measures based on lobe, sulcus (groove or furrow), gyrus (ridge), or Brodmann area (see Chapter 1).

Posner and DiGirolamo (2000) provided an overview of the impact of brain-imaging research on our understanding of human cognition. They pointed out that such research has transformed our knowledge in several areas, including visual imagery; the effects of practice; attentional selection; and the central executive component of working memory. Posner and DiGirolamo (2000, p. 885) concluded as follows: "The progress made in mapping cognitive functions in the human brain has been swift and startling . . . The future of cognitive neuroscience provides a means of understanding human cognition . . . in terms of the neural basis of mental events."

Why has brain imaging proved valuable? Much of the behavioural evidence obtained by cognitive psychologists is *ambiguous*, i.e., the behaviour is consistent with various possible interpretations. Brain-imaging research provides detailed information about *where* and *when* cognitive processes occur, and such information helps to identify the most appropriate interpretation of the behavioural evidence.

In the course of this book, we have considered many cases in which brain-imaging studies have helped to resolve theoretical controversies, and brief reference will be made to a few of them here. First, there has been a long-running battle concerning the nature of visual imagery (see Chapter 4). On the one hand, Kosslyn (e.g., 1994) has consistently argued that visual imagery makes use of the same processes as visual perception, whereas Pylyshyn (e.g., 2000) claims that visual imagery involves making use of propositional knowledge about what things would look like in the imagined situation. Most of the behavioural evidence has proved inconclusive, because it is consistent with both theoretical positions. However, the issue has now been resolved, in large part through brain-imaging studies. Visual imagery is often associated with activation in the primary visual cortex or BA17 (Kosslyn & Thompson, 2003). This is convincing evidence that there are major similarities between visual imagery and visual perception.

Second, one of the great controversies in the area of attention concerned the processing of unattended stimuli (see Chapter 5). Early-selection theorists (e.g., Broadbent, 1958) argued that unattended stimuli generally receive very little processing, whereas late-selection theorists (e.g., Deutsch & Deutsch, 1967) claimed that they are thoroughly processed. Again, most of the behavioural evidence failed to distinguish clearly between the rival positions. Brain-imaging studies using event-related potentials showed that unattended stimuli (visual and auditory) were less thoroughly processed than attended stimuli even very shortly after stimulus presentation (see Luck, 1998, for a review). These findings provide strong support for early-selection theories over late-selection ones.

Third, there is the vexed issue of how knowledge is organised in semantic memory (see Chapter 7). According to Farah and McClelland (1991) it is organised by semantic attributes (e.g., information about perceptual attributes stored in one brain region and information about functional attributes stored elsewhere). In contrast, Shelton and Caramazza (2001) argued that knowledge is organised in categories or domains (e.g., information about living things stored in one region and information about non-living things stored in another region). Most findings in this area have been rather inconsistent (Harley, 2001).

In contrast to previous findings, a brain-imaging study by Lee et al. (2002) has provided clear evidence relevant to the above theoretical issue. PET scans were taken while participants retrieved perceptual or non-perceptual information about living or non-living things. There was no evidence that different brain regions were associated with the retrieval of information about living and non-living things. However, retrieval of perceptual information about both categories of things was associated with activation of BA37, and retrieval of non-perceptual information about both categories involved activation of BA21 and BA37. Thus, these brain-imaging findings support the attribute-based approach over the category-based approach.

In what follows, we will consider other ways in which brain-imaging techniques have contributed to our understanding of human behaviour. The emphasis will be on identifying those types of brain-imaging research offering the greatest potential for the future.

Combining brain-imaging techniques

As we saw in Chapter 1, brain-imaging techniques vary in the precision with which they identify the brain areas active during the performance of a task: this is a measure of their spatial resolution. They also vary in the precision with which they measure the timing of brain activity: this is a measure of their temporal resolution. Unfortunately, no single technique combines excellent spatial resolution with outstanding temporal resolution. One way of making progress is to collect information from two or more brain-imaging techniques to obtain a more detailed understanding of the where and the when of brain activity. Two examples of this approach are discussed below.

Heinze et al. (1994) carried out a study on visual selective attention using PET and event-related potentials (ERP). Participants were presented with a mixture of attended and unattended stimuli. PET revealed that there was increased brain activity in the visual areas close to primary visual cortex when the participants were attending to the stimuli. However, PET has poor temporal resolution, and so shed no light on the detailed timing of participants' attentional processes. Here is where ERP came to the rescue, because it has excellent temporal resolution. ERP data obtained in the same study indicated that attended stimuli received more processing than unattended stimuli within about 100 ms of stimulus onset. Thus, PET and ERP in combination provided a fuller account of how the brain responds to attended stimuli than was available from either technique on its own.

Our second example concerns what happens when people with their eyes closed identify objects by touch alone. Deibert, Kraut, Kremen, and Hart (1999) used fMRI, and found this task produced activation of the visual cortex, even though the participants could not see the objects they were touching. This is an interesting finding, but its interpretation is unclear. It is possible that visual imagery plays an active role in tactile object recognition, but it is also possible that visual imagery only occurs *after* an object has been recognised by touch.

Zangaladze, Epstein, Grafton, and Sathian (1999) applied transcranial magnetic stimulation (TMS) to the visual cortex to decide between the two above possibilities. What is the logic here? If visual imagery is necessary for tactile object recognition, then TMS (which creates a temporary lesion) will impair task performance; if visual imagery only follows object recognition, then TMS should *not* affect object recognition. The findings were clear-cut: TMS did impair performance on the tactile object recognition task provided it was applied about 180 ms after the participant's hand touched the object. Thus, visual imagery facilitates the task of identifying objects by touch.

Brain imaging and brain damage

One of the most exciting developments in brain imaging (and one likely to prove increasingly important) is its application to brain-damaged patients (see Humphreys & Price, 2001). Of particular importance, neuroimaging can assist in the task of interpreting the findings obtained from brain-damaged patients in various ways. Why is this the case? Humphreys and Price (2001, p. 119) provided a succinct answer: "Functional imaging complements cognitive neuropsychology by: (i) not being reliant on accidents of nature and by enabling effects of lesions on 'distant' neural areas to be measured, (ii) revealing the brain systems necessary and sufficient for a given task, (iii) providing tests of neural-level models of cognition, and by (iv) providing novel evidence on the mechanisms of functional recovery in patients." We consider some of these points below.

A study by Price et al. (2001) is relevant to the first point above. They gave four patients with damage to the left posterior inferior frontal cortex (i.e., Broca's area) the task of deciding whether a visually presented letter string contained an ascender, in which part of the letter rises above its body (e.g., b, d, f, h). Each letter string was either a word or simply a set of consonants. Previous brain-imaging studies on normal participants indicated greater activation in several areas (e.g., posterior inferior frontal cortex; posterior inferior temporal cortex) on word trials than on nonword trials. In contrast, the patients failed to show activation of the posterior inferior frontal cortex or the left posterior inferior temporal cortex. Absence of activation in the former area is unsurprising given that it was damaged in the patients. However, the lack of activation in the left posterior inferior temporal cortex suggests that disruption of language processing may have occurred in part because this area no longer received input from the damaged area. Thus, fMRI permitted a fuller account of the patients' processing impairments than could be obtained from the site of the brain damage on its own.

A study discussed by Humphreys and Price (2001) is relevant to the second point listed earlier. A patient, SW, with damage to the left inferior frontal cortex performed normally on a semantic judgement task that involved deciding which of two words was more similar to a third word. From the perspective of cognitive neuropsychology, it would be natural to conclude that the left inferior frontal cortex is not necessary for the performance of this task. However, it is possible that neurons remaining in the damaged area were sufficient for SW to perform the task. This possibility was excluded when fMRI revealed there was no activation of the damaged area during task performance (see Humphreys & Price, 2001). This strengthens the argument that the left inferior frontal cortex is *not* necessary for making semantic judgements.

Transcranial magnetic stimulation

In spite of the numerous exciting findings obtained in brain-imaging studies, one major problem has proved stubbornly resistant to resolution. The essence of this problem is as follows: "Mapping techniques record brain activity which is correlated with some behavioural event. But the correlations do not show that an area is necessary for a particular function" (Walsh & Rushworth, 1999, p. 126). The implications were spelled out more explicitly by Robertson, Théoret, and Pascual-Leone (2003, p. 948): "These methods [of assessing brain activity] offer little or no insight into whether a brain region has a pivotal or merely subsidiary role in shaping behaviour."

In principle, we can resolve the above problem by using transcranial magnetic stimulation (TMS; discussed in Chapter 1). TMS briefly disrupts organised cortical activity in a small brain area, thus providing a "virtual lesion" method (Stewart et al., 2001) of studying the functions of various brain areas. The great advantage of TMS over brain-imaging techniques is that it can reveal whether a particular brain region is *necessary* for the performance of any given task. In other words, TMS allows us to move some of the way to establishing that certain brain areas are *causally* involved in performing a given task.

Evidence

TMS has already been shown to be useful in answering various different kinds of questions. Most frequently, TMS has been used to establish whether a given brain area is necessary for the performance of some cognitive task. For example,

Kosslyn et al. (1999) found that performance on a visual imagery task was significantly impaired when TMS pulses were applied to the primary visual cortex (BA17).

TMS can also provide insights into *when* any given brain area is most involved in performance of a task. For example, Cracco, Cracco, Maccabee, and Amassian (1999) gave participants the task of detecting letters. Performance was maximally impaired when TMS was applied to occipital cortex 80–100 ms after the presentation of the letters rather than at shorter or longer delays.

TMS is also of value when trying to understand dynamic interactions between different brain areas. We take a study by Pascual-Leone and Walsh (2001) to illustrate the point. A TMS pulse applied to the motion area MT+ produced **phosphenes**, which involve the perception of flashes of light *not* dependent on retinal stimulation. Their key finding was that a second TMS pulse applied to the primary visual cortex (BA 17) 10–40 ms after the pulse to MT+ suppressed the phosphenes. Thus, conscious awareness of phosphenes involves the primary visual cortex as well as MT+, with the involvement of the primary visual cortex occurring shortly after that of MT+.

Evaluation

Is TMS the answer to all our prayers? In spite of its potential importance to cognitive neuroscience, TMS has various problematical aspects (see Chapter 1). Robertson et al. (2003) have identified several such problems, but we will just briefly discuss four. First, "Little is known about the duration of the effects, neurophysiological or behavioural, of single TMS pulses or rTMS [repetitive] trains" (Robertson et al., 2003, p. 955). It is typically assumed that the effects of a single TMS pulse last for 500 ms or less, but they may last longer. Second, while the main effects of TMS are confined to a relatively small brain area, some effects have been detected over much larger areas. For example, Bohning et al. (1999) used both TMS and fMRI, and found that TMS pulses caused activity changes in brain areas distant from the area of stimulation. Third, it may be hard to show that TMS applied to any brain area has adverse effects on relatively simple tasks: "With the inherent redundancy of the brain and its resulting high capacity to compensate for disruption caused by TMS, it is perhaps only through straining the available neuronal resources with a reasonably complex task that it becomes possible to observe behavioural impairment" (Robertson et al., 2003, p. 955). Fourth, TMS cannot be applied to brain areas in which there is overlying muscle. That means that use of TMS is limited largely to some of the parietal cortex and a smaller amount of occipital cortex.

Conclusions

In the nineteenth century there was much enthusiasm for an approach known as **phrenology**. According to advocates of phrenology (of whom there are now very few), various mental faculties are located in specific parts of the brain and are identifiable by bumps on the external skull. It has sometimes been suggested that brain imaging is the new phrenology, and fMRI has been described jokingly as "phrenology with magnets" (Steve Hammett, personal communication). Those sceptical about the value of brain imaging often argue that we only need behavioural evidence to test theories in psychology. However, the history of psychology is full of examples of competing theories based on very different assumptions which nevertheless manage to account for the available behavioural data. This state of affairs strongly suggests that behavioural data often impose insufficient constraints on theorising. In our opinion, evidence about the pattern of brain activity during the performance of cognitive tasks can potentially play a valuable role in adjudicating between competing theories. Indeed, we have provided various examples showing that that is already the case. We predict that progress in understanding human cognition over the next few years will depend in part on the ever-increasing sophistication of brain-imaging techniques.

CHAPTER SUMMARY

- Consciousness: Nature and functions
  It is claimed that consciousness has evolved to permit us to deal flexibly and effectively with the environment. Consciousness is also claimed to be used in disseminating information, adapting to novel events, and exercising global control. However, we can apparently plan or even execute movements before being consciously aware of that intention. Another proposed function of consciousness is social: our possession of consciousness makes it easier for us to predict and understand other people. In order to understand consciousness, we need to consider the nature of conscious experience, access to information in consciousness, and self-knowledge.

- Theories of consciousness
  According to Velmans' dual-aspect theory, consciousness and aspects of brain activity are two sides of a single underlying process. According to several theorists (e.g., Baars; Baddeley; Dehaene & Naccache), we are aware of only a small fraction of our information processing, with attentional processes determining the contents of consciousness. According to Dehaene and Naccache's global workspace theory, information in conscious awareness is distributed widely throughout the brain. Many brain areas are associated with conscious experience, but Dehaene and Naccache argued that the prefrontal cortex and the anterior cingulate are of particular importance. This global workspace theory seems to exaggerate the importance of consciousness and fails to provide a first-person account of conscious experience.

- Perception without awareness
  Some research has considered brain-damaged patients lacking conscious perception of stimuli that nevertheless receive some processing. Various theoretical accounts have been proposed to explain their impairments. According to the quality-of-representation account, conscious perception depends on reasonably high-quality representations. According to integration accounts, conscious perception requires that various stimulus properties are bound or combined together. According to privileged role accounts, conscious perception depends on certain crucial brain regions. Much of the evidence is consistent with the quality-of-representation and integration accounts, which are not incompatible with each other. In contrast, the evidence fails to support privileged role accounts, because patients with various attentional and perceptual deficits have brain damage in diverse areas.

- Is consciousness unitary?
  Evidence from split-brain patients indicates that behaviour can be controlled to some extent by each hemisphere. However, the left hemisphere of split-brain patients is clearly dominant in determining conscious awareness and behaviour. Thus, the left hemisphere can be regarded as acting as an interpreter of internal and external events. In contrast, the right hemisphere of split-brain patients engages in low-level processing activities, but probably lacks consciousness. The interpreter in the left hemisphere often continues to function even when deprived of important relevant information.

- Whither brain imaging?
  Brain imaging is likely to become more important in the future than it is already. Brain imaging provides valuable information about *where* and *when* cognitive processes occur, although some dismiss this approach as the new phrenology. Information obtained from brain imaging has helped to resolve several theoretical issues such as the nature of visual imagery, the extent to which unattended stimuli are processed, and the organisation of knowledge in semantic memory.

Our understanding of human cognition has already been enhanced by the following: combining different brain-imaging techniques in a single study; using brain imaging with brain-damaged patients; and the introduction of transcranial magnetic stimulation to produce temporary lesions.

FURTHER READING

- Baars, B.J., Banks, W.P., & Newman, J.B. (2003). *Essential sources in the scientific study of consciousness*. Cambridge, MA: MIT Press. This edited book addresses the key scientific issues in the study of consciousness.
- Blackmore, S. (2003). *Consciousness: An introduction*. London: Hodder & Stoughton. If you want an accessible and well-informed introduction to the topic of consciousness, you will find it in this interesting book.
- Dehaene, S., & Naccache, L. (2001). Towards a cognitive neuroscience of consciousness: Basic evidence and a workspace framework. *Cognition*, *79*, 1–37. This article provides a good account of behavioural and brain-imaging research on consciousness, together with a coherent theoretical framework.
- Gazzaniga, M.S., Ivry, R.B., & Mangun, G.R. (2002). *Cognitive neuroscience: The biology of the mind* (2nd Ed.). New York: Norton. This textbook covers the whole of cognitive neuroscience including brain-imaging techniques and research findings based on their use. It also has a chapter dealing with consciousness.
- Humphreys, G.W., & Price, C.J. (2001). Cognitive neuropsychology and functional brain imaging: Implications for functional and anatomical models of cognition. *Acta Psychologica*, *107*, 119–153. This article illustrates exciting developments in neuroimaging research, including the application of neuroimaging techniques to brain-damaged patients.
- Koch, C. (2003). *The quest for consciousness: A neurobiological approach*. New York: Roberts & Co. The author of this book emphasises the progress made in understanding consciousness from a biological perspective.

Glossary

accommodation: one of the **binocular cues** to depth, based on the variation in optical power produced by a thickening of the lens of the eye when focusing on a close object.

achromatopsia: this is a brain-damaged condition in which there is little or no colour perception, but form and motion perception are sometimes intact.

adaptive expertise: using acquired knowledge to solve familiar problems efficiently; see **routine expertise**.

affordances: the potential uses of an object, which Gibson claimed are directly perceived.

agrammatism: a condition in which speech productions lack grammatical structure, and many function words and word endings are omitted.

akinetopsia: this is a brain-damaged condition in which objects in motion cannot be perceived, whereas stationary objects are perceived fairly normally.

alexia: a condition in which there are great problems with reading even though speech is understood.

algorithm: a computational procedure providing a specified set of steps to a solution.

Alzheimer's disease: a disease involving progressive dementia or loss of mental powers.

amnesic syndrome: a condition in which there is substantial impairment of long-term memory; the condition includes both **anterograde amnesia** and **retrograde amnesia**.

anaphor resolution: working out the referent of a pronoun or noun by relating it to some previously mentioned noun or noun phrase.

anomia: a condition caused by brain damage in which there is an impaired ability to name objects.

anosognosia for hemiplegia: lack of recognition of the existence of paralysis on one side of the body.

anterograde amnesia: reduced ability to remember information acquired after the onset of amnesia.

aphasia: impaired language abilities as a result of brain damage.

apperceptive agnosia: this is a form of **visual agnosia** in which there is impaired perceptual analysis of familiar objects.

articulatory suppression: rapid repetition of some simple sound (e.g., "the the the") which uses the articulatory control process of the **phonological loop**.

artificial intelligence: this involves developing computer programs that produce intelligent outcomes; see **computational modelling**.

association: concerning brain damage, the finding that certain symptoms or performance impairments are consistently found together in numerous brain-damaged patients.

associative agnosia: this is a form of **visual agnosia** in which perceptual processing is fairly normal but there is an impaired ability to derive the meaning of objects.

atmosphere effect: the tendency to accept a conclusion if its form is consistent with the form of the premises (e.g., use of the word "all").

Aubert–Fleischl effect: the perceived speed of a moving object is less when it is tracked by the eyes than when they remain stationary.

auditory phonological agnosia: a condition in which there is poor perception of unfamiliar words and nonwords, but not familiar words.

autobiographical memory: memory for the events of one's own life.

availability heuristic: the assumption that the frequencies of events can be estimated accurately by the accessibility in memory.

back-propagation: a learning mechanism in **connectionist networks** based on comparing actual responses to correct ones.

Balint's syndrome: a brain-damaged condition in which some patients find it hard to shift visual attention.

base-rate effect: influence of perceived probability of a **syllogism** being valid on judgements of its validity.

base-rate information: the relative frequency of an event within a population.

basic cognitive interview: an approach to improving the memory of eyewitnesses based on the assumption that memory traces contain many features.

belief bias: the tendency to decide whether the conclusion of a syllogism is valid on the basis of whether or not it is believable.

binding problem: issues arising when different kinds of information need to be integrated to produce object recognition.

binocular cues: cues to depth that require both eyes to be used together.

binocular rivalry: this occurs when an observer perceives only one visual stimulus when two are presented, one to each eye.

blindsight: the ability to respond appropriately to visual stimuli in the absence of conscious vision in patients with damage to the primary visual cortex.

blobs: areas in the primary visual cortex forming part of the P pathway and responding strongly to contrast and to colour; see **interblobs**.

bottom-up processing: processing that is directly influenced by environmental stimuli; see **top-down processing**.

bounded rationality: the notion that people are as rational as their processing limitations permit.

bridging inferences: inferences that are drawn to increase the coherence between the current and preceding parts of a text.

Broca's aphasia: a form of **aphasia** involving non-fluent speech and grammatical errors.

Capgras delusion: the belief that extremely familiar people have been replaced by impostors, doubles, or aliens.

cascade model/processing: a model in which information passes from one level to the next before processing is complete at the first level.

categorical perception: perceiving stimuli as belonging to a given category.

categories: sets or classes of objects or items; see **concepts**.

category-specific disorders/deficits: disorders caused by brain damage in which **semantic memory** is disrupted for certain semantic categories.

central executive: a modality-free, limited capacity, component of **working memory**.

centre of moment: the reference point in the upper body around which the shoulders and hips swing.

change blindness: failure to detect changes in the visual environment.

chromatic adaptation: reduced sensitivity to light of a given colour after lengthy exposure.

chunk: a stored unit formed from integrating smaller pieces of information.

co-articulation: the finding that the production of a phoneme in one speech segment is influenced (and distorted) by the production of the previous sound and preparations for the next sound.

cognitive economy: the principle (mainly applied in categorisation theory) that human knowledge is organised to maximise the distinctions between categories while minimising the number of knowledge items to be stored.

cognitive neuropsychology: an approach that involves studying cognitive functioning in brain-damaged patients to increase our understanding of normal human cognition.

cognitive neuroscience: an approach based on using brain-imaging techniques to study human cognition (narrow definition); an approach that involves trying to understand human cognition by combining behavioural data with information about the structure and functioning of the brain (broad definition).

colour constancy: the tendency for any given object to be perceived as having the same colour under widely varying viewing conditions.

common ground: the mutual knowledge and beliefs shared by a speaker and listener.

composition: in the ACT theory, a process in which a repeated sequence of actions is reduced to a more efficient single sequence.

computational cognitive science: an approach that involves constructing computational models to understand human cognition.

computational modelling: this involves constructing computer programs that will simulate or mimic some aspects of human cognitive functioning; see **artificial intelligence**.

concepts: mental representations of **categories** of objects or items.

conceptual priming: a form of **repetition priming** in which there is a conceptual relationship between the information at study and at test.

conceptually driven processes: processes initiated by the individual in a top-down way; see **data-driven processes**.

confirmation: the attempt to find supportive evidence for one's hypotheses; this approach is logically incorrect according to Popper (1968); see **falsification**.

confirmation bias: memory that is distorted by being influenced by the individual's expectations rather than what actually happened; in reasoning, it refers to a greater focus on evidence confirming one's hypothesis than on disconfirming evidence.

conjunction fallacy: the mistaken belief that the probability of a conjunction of two events (A and B) is greater than the probability of one of them (A or B).

connectionist networks: these consist of elementary units or nodes, which are connected; each network has various structures or layers (e.g., input; intermediate or hidden; output).

consciousness: a state in which something is experienced; what is experienced can include perceptions, thoughts, and self-awareness.

consolidation: a process lasting several hours or more which fixes information in **long-term memory**.

convergence: one of the **binocular cues**, based on the inward focus of the eyes with a close object.

conversion error: a mistake in syllogistic reasoning occurring because a statement is invalidly converted from one form into another.

covert attention: attention to an object or sound in the absence of overt movements of the relevant receptors (e.g., looking at an object out of the corner of one's eye).

creativity: producing ideas that are both novel or different and useful or worthwhile; see **originality**.

crossmodal attention: the coordination of attention across two or more modalities (e.g., vision and audition).

cytoarchitectonic map: a map of the brain based on variations in the cellular structure of tissues.

cue-dependent forgetting: forgetting in which the information is stored in memory but cannot be retrieved because of inadequate retrieval cues; see **trace-dependent forgetting**.

data-driven processes: processes triggered directly by external stimuli in a bottom-up way; see **conceptually driven processes**.

declarative knowledge/memory: it is concerned with knowing that something is the case (e.g., that London is the capital of England); it covers **episodic memory** and **semantic memory**; see **procedural knowledge**.

deductive reasoning: reasoning to a conclusion from some set of premises, where that conclusion follows necessarily from the assumption that the premises are true; see **inductive reasoning**.

deep dysgraphia: a condition in which there are semantic errors in spelling and nonwords are incorrectly spelled.

deep dyslexia: a condition in which reading of unfamiliar words is impaired, and there are semantic reading errors (e.g., reading "missile" as "rocket").

deep dysphasia: a condition in which there is poor ability to repeat spoken nonwords and there are semantic errors in repeating spoken words.

defining attributes: semantic features of a concept that are necessary and sufficient to instances of the concept.

deliberate practice: this involves the learner being provided with informative feedback during practice and having the opportunity to correct his/her errors.

directed retrospection: a method of studying writing in which writers are asked to categorise their immediately preceding thoughts while writing.

discourse: connected text or speech, at least several sentences in length.

discourse markers: spoken words and phrases that do not contribute directly to the content of what is being said but still serve various functions (e.g., clarification of the speaker's intentions).

dissociation: as applied to brain-damaged patients, normal performance on one task combined with severely impaired performance on another task.

divergent thinking: the ability to generate numerous answers when presented with a problem (e.g., different uses for a brick).

divided attention: a situation in which two tasks are performed at the same time.

domain-specific knowledge: a relatively self-contained collection of knowledge about a particular topic (e.g., knowledge of car engines or of the solar system would be distinct domains of knowledge).

dominance principle: in decision making, the notion that the better of two similar options will be preferred.

dorsal: superior or on top.

double dissociation: the finding that some individuals (often brain-damaged) do well on task A and poorly on task B, whereas others show the opposite pattern.

dual-space search: the theoretical notion that in scientific discovery there are two distinct **problem spaces**: one is searched for hypotheses and the other is searched for experiments.

dysexecutive syndrome: a condition in which damage to the frontal lobes causes impairments to the **central executive** component of **working memory**.

echoic store: a sensory store in which auditory information is briefly held.

ecological validity: the extent to which the findings of laboratory studies are applicable to everyday settings.

egocentric heuristic: a comprehension strategy in which listeners interpret what they hear based on their own knowledge rather than on knowledge they share with the speaker.

Einstellung: mental set, in which people use a familiar strategy even when there is a simpler alternative or the problem cannot be solved using it.

elaborative inferences: inferences that add details to a text being read.

elaborative rehearsal: processing that involves a deeper or more semantic analysis of the learning material; see **maintenance rehearsal**.

Emmert's law: the size of an afterimage appears larger when viewed against a far surface than when viewed against a near surface.

encoding specificity principle: the notion that retrieval depends on the overlap between the information available at retrieval and the information within the memory trace.

enhanced cognitive interview: an approach to improving the memory of eyewitnesses based on developing the **basic cognitive interview** to improve its effectiveness.

episodic buffer: a component of **working memory** that can hold information from the **phonological loop**, the **visuo-spatial sketchpad**, and **long-term memory**.

episodic memory: a form of long-term memory concerned with personal experiences or episodes that happened in a given place at a specific time; see **semantic memory**.

event-based prospective memory: remembering to perform some action when the circumstances are suitable; see **time-based prospective memory**.

event-related fMRI: using **functional magnetic resonance imaging** to assess patterns of brain activity following specific events.

event-related potentials (ERPs): the pattern of electroencephalograph (EEG) activity obtained by averaging the brain responses to the same stimulus presented repeatedly.

experimental cognitive psychology: this involves carrying out traditional experiments on normal human participants, generally under laboratory conditions.

expertise: the specific knowledge an expert has about a given domain (e.g., that an engineer may have about bridges).

explicit memory: memory that involves conscious recollection; see **implicit memory**.

extinction: a disorder of visual attention in which a stimulus presented to the side opposite the brain damage is not detected when another stimulus is presented at the same time.

falsification: proposing hypotheses and then trying to falsify them by experimental tests; the logically correct means by which science should work according to Popper (1968); see **confirmation**.

family resemblance: the notion that members of a category share some features or attributes with other category members.

far transfer: beneficial effects of previous learning on current learning in a dissimilar context; a form of **positive transfer**.

figurative language: forms of language (e.g., metaphor) that are not intended to be taken literally.

figure–ground segregation: the perceptual organisation of the visual field into a figure (object of central interest) and a ground (less important background).

Filehne illusion: a stationary background object is perceived to move in the opposite direction to a moving object tracked by the eyes.

flashbulb memories: vivid and detailed memories of dramatic events.

functional magnetic resonance imaging (fMRI): a technique based on detecting magnetic changes in the brain; it provides information about the location and time course of brain processes.

focus of expansion: this is the point towards which someone who is in motion is moving; it is the only part of the visual field that does not appear to move; synonymous with **pole**.

focused attention: a situation in which individuals try to attend to only one source of stimulation while ignoring other stimuli.

formants: frequency bands within **phonemes** emphasised by the vocal apparatus.

framing: the influence of irrelevant aspects of a situation on decision making.

functional fixedness: the **Gestalt School's** term for the inflexible use of the usual functions of an object in problem solving.

generalised cone: in Marr's theory, the surface formed by moving a cross-section of constant shape but varying in size along an axis.

Gestalt school: a largely German school of perception and thinking researchers from the early 20th century, who proposed theories that stressed the active, productive nature of cognition rather than its passive associationist nature.

goal-derived categories: categories in which the members all satisfy a given goal.

gyri: ridges in the brain ("gyrus" is the singular).

heterographs: words having the same pronunciation but different spellings (e.g., "maid", "made").

heuristics: rules of thumb that often (but not invariably) solve any given problem.

hill climbing: a **heuristic** involving changing the present state of a problem into one apparently closer to the goal.

homographs: words having one spelling but two different meanings and sometimes also different pronunciation (e.g., "wind").

iconic store: a sensory store in which visual information is held very briefly.

ideomotor apraxia: a condition caused by brain damage in which patients find it hard to carry out learned movements.

ill-defined problems: problems in which the definition of the problem statement is imprecisely specified; the initial state, goal state, and methods to be used to solve the problem may be unclear; see **well-defined problems**.

implicit learning: learning complex information without the ability to provide conscious recollection of what has been learned.

implicit memory: memory that does not depend on conscious recollection; see **explicit memory**.

inattentional blindness: failure to detect an unexpected object appearing in a visual display; see **change blindness**.

incubation: the notion that putting a problem aside for a while can facilitate solving it by allowing relevant non-conscious processes to operate.

inductive reasoning: forming generalisations (which may be probable but are not certain) from examples or sample phenomena, see **deductive reasoning**.

infantile amnesia: the inability of adults to recall autobiographical memories from early childhood.

inhibition of return: a reduced probability of visual attention returning to a previously attended location.

inner scribe: according to Logie, the part of the **visuo-spatial sketchpad** that deals with spatial and movement information.

insight: the experience of suddenly realising how to solve a problem.

integrative agnosia: a form of **visual agnosia** in which the patient has difficulty combining or integrating features of an object in the process of recognition.

interblobs: areas in the primary visual cortex forming part of the P pathway and responding strongly to contrast, location, and orientation; see **blobs**.

interpreter: the notion that only the left side of the brain is involved in seeking explanations for events occurring externally and internally.

introspection: examination or observation of one's own mental processes.

invariants: in Gibson's theory, properties of the **optic array** that remain constant even though other aspects vary.

isomorphism: the assumption that the organisation of the mind closely matches that of the physical brain.

jargon aphasia: a brain-damaged condition in which speech is reasonably correct grammatically, but there are great problems in finding the right words.

knowledge compilation: the shift from **declarative knowledge** to **procedural knowledge** during skill acquisition.

knowledge-lean problems: problems that can be solved without the use of much prior knowledge, with most of the necessary information being provided by the problem statement; see **knowledge-rich problems**.

knowledge-rich problems: problems that can only be solved through the use of considerable amounts of prior knowledge; see **knowledge-lean problems**.

Korsakoff's syndrome: amnesia (impaired long-term memory) caused by chronic alcoholism.

landmarks: key public or personal events that can be used to date less significant political or personal events.

lateral: situated at the side.

lateral inhibition: reduction of activity in one neuron caused by activity in a neighbouring neuron.

lemmas: abstract words possessing syntactic features but not phonological ones.

lexical access: entering the **lexicon** with its store of detailed information about words.

lexical bias effect: the tendency for speech errors to consist of words rather than nonwords.

lexical decision task: a task in which participants have to decide as rapidly as possible whether a letter string forms a word.

lexical identification shift: the finding that an ambiguous **phoneme** tends to be perceived so as to form a word rather than a nonword.

lexicalisation: the process of translating the meaning of a word into its sound representation during speech production.

lexicon: a store of detailed information about words, including orthographic, phonological, semantic, and syntactic knowledge.

logical inferences: inferences depending solely on the meaning of words.

long-term working memory: this is used by experts to store relevant information in long-term memory and to access it through retrieval cues in **working memory**.

loss aversion: the tendency to be more sensitive to potential losses than to potential gains.

magnetic resonance imaging (MRI and fMRI): an imaging technique based on the detection of magnetic changes within the brain; MRI provides information about the structure of the brain, and fMRI provides information about brain activity and processes.

magneto-encephalography (MEG): a non-invasive brain-scanning technique based on recording the magnetic fields generated by brain activity.

maintenance rehearsal: processing that involves simply repeating analyses which have already been carried out.

means–ends analysis: a **heuristic** method for solving problems based on noting the difference between a current and a goal state, and creating a subgoal to overcome this difference.

medial: situated in the middle.

mental model: a representation of a possible state-of-affairs in the world.

meta-analyses: statistical analyses based on data from numerous studies on a given issue.

metacognition: an individual's beliefs and knowledge about his/her own cognitive processes and strategies.

method of loci: a mnemonic technique in which the to-be-remembered items are associated with locations (e.g., places along a walk).

microspectrophotometry: a technique that allows measurement of the amount of light absorbed at various wavelengths by individual cone receptors.

***min*-heuristic**: a rule of thumb used when drawing a conclusion from a **syllogism**; it states that the conclusion of the syllogism will have the same form as the less informative premise.

mixed error effect: speech errors that are semantically and phonologically related to the intended word.

modularity: the assumption that the cognitive system consists of several fairly independent processors or modules.

monocular cues: cues to depth that can be used with one eye, but can also be used with both eyes.

mood-state-dependent memory: the finding that memory is better when the mood state at retrieval is the same as that at learning than when the two mood states differ.

morphemes: the smallest units of meaning within words.

motion aftereffect: illusory perception of motion in one direction caused by prolonged observation of actual motion in the opposite direction.

motion parallax: movement of an object's image across the retina due to movements of the observer's head.

naming task: a task in which visually presented words have to be pronounced aloud as rapidly as possible.

near transfer: beneficial effects of previous learning on current learning in a similar context; a form of **positive transfer**.

negative afterimage: the illusory perception of the complementary colour to the one that has just been fixated for several seconds; green is the complementary colour to red, and blue is complementary to yellow.

negative transfer: past experience in solving one problem disrupts the ability to solve a similar current problem.

neglect: a disorder of visual attention in which stimuli or parts of stimuli presented to the side opposite the brain damage are undetected and not responded to; the condition resembles **extinction**, but is more severe.

neologisms: made-up words produced by individuals suffering from **jargon aphasia**.

normative theories: as applied to decision making, theories focusing on how people should make decisions.

numerosity heuristic: exaggerating the quantity or amount of something when it is divided into numerous parts.

oculomotor cues: kinaesthetic cues to depth produced by muscular contraction of the muscles around the eye.

omission bias: the tendency to prefer inaction over action when engaged in decision making.

operation span: the maximum number of items (arithmetical questions + words) from which an individual can recall all the last words.

optic array: the structured pattern of light falling on the retina.

optic ataxia: a condition in which there are problems with making visually guided limb movements in spite of reasonably intact visual perception.

optic flow: the changes in light intensity reaching an observer, created when there is movement of the observer and/or aspects of the environment.

originality: producing ideas that are novel or different without consideration of whether they are useful or worthwhile; see **creativity**.

orthography: information about the spellings of words.

parallel processing: processing in which two or more cognitive processes occur at the same time; see **serial processing**.

parsing: an analysis of the syntactical or grammatical structure of sentences.

perceived causality: the impression that one object has caused movement of a second object.

perceptual implicit tests: memory tests on which the stimuli that are presented are degraded versions of the stimuli presented at study and on which conscious recollection is not required.

perceptual priming: a form of **repetition priming effect** in which the stimulus presented at test is the same as (or a degraded version of) the stimulus presented at study.

perceptual representation system: an implicit memory system thought to be involved in the faster processing of previously presented stimuli as in the repetition priming effect.

perceptual segregation: human ability to work out accurately which parts of presented visual information belong together and thus form separate objects.

perceptual span: the effective field of view in reading, often measured in terms of the number of letters to the left and to the right of fixation that can be processed.

phoneme: a basic speech sound conveying meaning.

phonemic restoration effect: the finding that listeners are unaware that a phoneme has been deleted from an auditorily presented sentence.

phonological dysgraphia: a condition in which familiar words can be spelled reasonably well but nonwords cannot.

phonological dyslexia: a condition in which familiar words can be read but there is impaired ability to read unfamiliar words and nonwords; see **surface dyslexia**.

phonological loop: a component of **working memory**, in which speech-based information is held and subvocal articulation occurs.

phonological similarity effect: the finding that serial recall of visually presented words is worse when the words are phonologically similar rather than phonologically dissimilar.

phonology: information about the sounds of words and parts of words.

phosphenes: perceived flashes of light in the absence of retinal stimulation.

phrenology: the (discredited) notion that the bumps on an individual's skull provide useful information about his/her mental abilities.

planning fallacy: underestimating how long a given task will require for completion in spite of information about how long similar tasks have taken in the past.

pole: the point towards which someone who is in motion is moving; it is the only part of the visual field not appearing to move; synonymous with **focus of expansion**.

positive transfer: past experience of solving one problem makes it easier to solve a similar current problem.

positron emission tomography (PET): a brain-scanning technique based on the detection of positrons; it has reasonable spatial resolution but poor temporal resolution.

pragmatics: the study of the ways in which language is used and understood in the real world, including a consideration of its intended meaning.

preinventive structures: structures that are formed in the initial stage of creative thinking and before the use to which they will be put is clear.

principle of truth: the notion that we represent assertions by constructing **mental models** containing what is true but not what is false.

principle of use specificity: in the ACT theory, the assumption that **production rules** will only lead to action when their specific conditions are fulfilled.

proactive interference: disruption of memory by previous learning, often of similar material; see **retroactive interference**.

problem space: an abstract description of all the possible states-of-affairs that can occur in a problem situation.

procedural knowledge/memory: this is concerned with knowing how, and includes the ability to perform skilled actions; see **declarative knowledge**.

proceduralisation: the process of creating specific **production rules**.

production rules: "IF . . . THEN" or condition–action rules in which the action is carried out whenever the appropriate condition is present.

production systems: these consist of numerous "IF . . . THEN" **production rules** and a working memory containing information.

productive thinking: solving a problem by developing an understanding of the problem's underlying structure; see **insight** and **reproductive thinking**.

proposition: a statement which makes an assertion or denial and which can be true or false.

prosodic cues: features of spoken language such as stress and intonation.

prosopagnosia: a condition caused by brain damage in which the patient cannot recognise familiar faces but can recognise familiar objects.

prospective memory: remembering to carry out intended actions.

protocol analysis: a method of studying writing or problem-solving processes in which tape recordings are made of participants' verbalisations while engaged in a task.

prototype: a central description or abstraction that represents a category.

psychological refractory period: the slowing of response to the second of two stimuli when they are presented close together in time.

pure word deafness: a condition in which there is severely impaired speech perception combined with good speech production, reading, writing, and perception of non-speech sounds.

rarity assumption: the assumption on Wason's selection task that p and q are both relatively rare compared to not-p and not-q.

rationalisation: in Bartlett's theory, the tendency in recall of stories to produce errors that conform to the cultural expectations of the rememberer.

raw primal sketch: in Marr's theory, a representation containing information about intensity changes in the image.

reading span: the largest number of sentences read for comprehension from which an individual can recall all the final words more than 50% of the time.

recency effect: the finding that the last few items in a list are much better remembered than other items in immediate free recall.

receptive field: the region of the retina within which light influences the activity of a particular neuron.

recognition heuristic: using the knowledge that only one out of two objects is recognised to make a judgement.

reduplicative paramnesia: a memory disorder in which the person believes that multiple copies of people and places exist.

reminiscence bump: the tendency of older people to recall a disproportionate number of autobiographical memories from the years of adolescence and early adulthood.

repetition priming effect: the finding that stimulus processing is faster and easier on the second and successive presentations.

representativeness heuristic: the assumption that representative or typical members of a category are encountered most frequently.

repression: motivated forgetting of traumatic or other threatening events.

reproductive thinking: re-use of previous knowledge to solve a current problem; see **productive thinking**.

resonance: the process of automatic pick-up of visual information from the environment in Gibson's theory.

retinal flow field: the changing pattern of light on the retina produced by movement of the observer relative to the environment as well as by eye and head movements.

retinotopic map: nerve cells occupying the same positions relative to each other as their respective **receptive fields** have on the retina.

retroactive interference: disruption of memory by learning other material during the retention interval; see **proactive interference**.

retrograde amnesia: impaired memory for events occurring before the onset of amnesia.

retrospective memory: memory for events, words, people, and so on encountered or experienced in the past; see **prospective memory**.

risk aversion: a tendency to prefer a sure gain over a potentially greater gain involving risk.

risk seeking: a tendency to prefer to accept a risk if it offers the possibility of avoiding loss rather than to accept a sure loss.

routine expertise: using acquired knowledge to develop strategies for dealing with novel problems; see **adaptive expertise**.

saccades: fast eye movements that cannot be altered after being initiated.

satisficing: a rule of thumb in which the first option meeting an individual's minimum requirements is selected; this leads to rapid (but sometimes deficient) decision making.

savings method: a measure of forgetting introduced by Ebbinghaus, in which the number of trials for re-learning is compared against the number for original learning.

schemas: organised packets of information about the world, events, or people, stored in long-term memory.

segmentation problem: the listener's problem of dividing the almost continuous sounds of speech into separate **phonemes** and words.

self-reference effect: the finding that memory is especially good after self-reference judgements.

semantic memory: a form of long-term memory consisting of general knowledge about the world, language, and so on; see **episodic memory**.

semantic priming effect: the finding that word identification is facilitated when there is priming by a semantically related word.

serial processing: processing in which one process is completed before the next one starts; see **parallel processing**.

short-term store: a limited-capacity store holding a few items for a period of several seconds.

simultanagnosia: a brain-damaged condition in which only one object can be seen at a time.

single-unit recording: an invasive technique for studying brain function, permitting the study of activity in single neurons.

size constancy: objects are perceived to have a given size regardless of the size of the retinal image.

skill acquisition: developing abilities through practice so as to increase the probability of goal achievement.

source amnesia: retention of a fact combined with an inability to remember where or how the fact was learned.

spectrograph: an instrument used to produce visible records of the sound frequencies in speech.

split attention: allocation of attention to two non-adjacent regions of visual space.

split-brain patients: these are patients in whom most of the direct links between the two hemispheres have been severed; as a result, they can experience problems in coordinating their processing and behaviour.

spreading activation: the notion that activation of a given node (often a word) in long-term memory leads to activation or energy spreading to other related nodes or words.

status quo bias: a tendency for individuals to repeat a choice several times in spite of changes in their preferences.

stereopsis: one of the **binocular cues**, based on the disparity or discrepancy in the retinal images of the two eyes.

strong methods: methods used in science based on **domain-specific knowledge**; see **weak methods**.

Stroop effect: the finding that naming of the colours in which words are printed is slower when the words are conflicting colour words (e.g., the word RED printed in green).

subliminal perception: perception occurring below the level of conscious awareness.

subordinate clause: a minor clause that differs from a main clause in that it cannot form a sentence on its own; it generally begins with a word such as "that", "which", or "who".

sulcus: a groove or furrow in the brain.

sunk-cost effect: expending additional resources to justify some previous commitment (as in "throwing good money after bad").

surface dysgraphia: a condition in which there is poor spelling of irregular words and non-words, but not of regular words.

surface dyslexia: a condition in which regular words can be read but there is impaired ability to read irregular words; see **phonological dyslexia**.

syllogism: a logical argument consisting of two premises (e.g., ("All X are Y") and a conclusion; syllogisms formed the basis for the first logical system attributed to Aristotle.

synaesthesia: the tendency for one sense modality to evoke another.

syndromes: labels used to categorise patients on the basis of co-occurring symptoms.

template: as applied to chess, an abstract, schematic structure consisting of a mixture of fixed and variable information about chess pieces.

texture gradient: the rate of change of texture density from the front to the back of a slanting object.

time-based prospective memory: remembering to carry out a future action at the right time; see **event-based prospective memory**.

top-down processing: stimulus processing that is affected by factors such as the individual's past experience and expectations.

trace-dependent forgetting: forgetting that occurs because the information contained in memory traces has been lost; see **cue-dependent forgetting**.

transcranial magnetic stimulation (TMS): a technique in which magnetic pulses temporarily disrupt the functioning of a given brain area, thus creating a short-lived "lesion".

trial-and-error learning: a type of problem solving in which the solution is reached by producing fairly random responses rather than by a process of thought.

typicality gradient: the ordering of the members of a category in terms of their typicality ratings (e.g., "robin" is a more typical instance of the "bird" category than is "canary").

uniform connectedness: the notion that adjacent regions in the visual environment possessing uniform visual properties (e.g., colour) are perceived as a single perceptual unit.

unilateral visual neglect: a condition in brain-damaged patients in which half of the visual field is neglected or ignored.

ventral: inferior, or at the bottom.

ventriloquist illusion: the mistaken perception that sounds are coming from their apparent visual source, as in ventriloquism.

verb bias: the notion that some verbs are found more often in some syntactic structures than in others.

visual agnosia: a condition in which there are great problems in recognising objects presented visually even though visual information reaches the visual cortex.

visual cache: according to Logie, the part of the **visuo-spatial sketchpad** that stores information about visual form and colour.

visual direction: the angle between a visual object or target and the front–back body axis.

visual search: a task involving the rapid detection of a specified target stimulus within a visual display.

visuo-spatial sketchpad: a component of **working memory** that is involved in visual and spatial processing of information.

weak methods: general rules of thumb or **heuristics** which can be used to solve numerous problems (e.g., scientific ones).

weapon focus: the finding that eyewitnesses pay so much attention to some crucial aspect of the situation (e.g., the weapon) that they tend to ignore other details.

well-defined problems: problems in which the initial state, goal, and methods available for solving them are clearly laid out; see **ill-defined problems**.

Wernicke's aphasia: a form of **aphasia** involving impaired comprehension and fluent speech with many content words missing.

Whorfian hypothesis: the notion that language determines or at least influences thinking.

word-fragment completion: a task on which participants try to think of a word based on a few letters (e.g., f _ ag _ _ t); a **perceptual implicit test**.

word-length effect: the finding that word span is greater for short words than for long words.

word meaning deafness: a condition in which there is a selective impairment of the ability to understand spoken (but not written) language.

word-stem completion: a task on which participants try to think of a word based on its first few letters (e.g., fra ____); a **perceptual implicit test**.

word superiority effect: a target letter is more readily detected in a letter string when the string forms a word than when it does not.

References

Abramov, I., & Gordon, J. (1994). Colour appearance: On seeing red, or yellow, or green, or blue. *Annual Review of Psychology, 36*, 715–729.

Ackerman, P.L., Beier, M.E., & Boyle, M.O. (2002). Individual differences in working memory within a nomological network of cognitive and perceptual speed abilities. *Journal of Experimental Psychology: General, 131*, 567–589.

Adams, J.L. (1979). *Conceptual blockbusting: A guide to better ideas* (2nd Ed.). New York: W.W. Norton.

Adamson, R.E. (1952). Functional fixedness as related to problem-solving. *Journal of Experimental Psychology, 44*, 288–291.

Adolphs, R., Tranel, D., Bechara, A., Damasio, H., & Damasio, A.R. (1996). Neuropsychological approaches to reasoning and decision-making. In A.R. Damasio (Ed.), *Neurobiology of decision-making*. Berlin: Springer-Verlag.

Aggleton, J.P., & Brown, M.W. (1999). Episodic memory, amnesia, and the hippocampal-anterior thalamic axis. *Behavioral & Brain Sciences, 22*, 425–489.

Ahn, W., Kim, N.S., Lassaline, M.E., & Dennis, M. (2000). Causal status as a determinant of feature centrality. *Cognitive Psychology, 41*, 361–416.

Ahola, K., Vilkki, J., & Servo, A. (1996). Frontal tests do not detect frontal infarctions after ruptured intracranial aneurysm. *Brain & Cognition, 31*, 1–16.

Aizenstein, H.J., Stenger, V.A., Cochran, J., Clark, K., Johnson, M., Nebes, R.D. et al. (2004). Regional brain activation during concurrent implicit and explicit sequence learning. *Cerebral Cortex, 14*, 199–208.

Aleman, A., Schutter, D.L.G., Ramsey, N.F., van Honk, J., Kessels, R.P.C., Hoogduin, J.M. et al. (2002). Functional anatomy of top-down visuo-spatial processing in the human brain: Evidence from rTMS. *Cognitive Brain Research, 14*, 300–302.

Alexander, P.A., Schallert, D.L., & Hare, U.C. (1991). Coming to terms: How researchers in learning and literacy talk about knowledge. *Review of Educational Research, 61*, 315–343.

Alkire, M.T., Haier, R.J., & Fallon, J.H. (2000). Toward a unified theory of narcosis: Brain imaging evidence for a thalamocortical switch as the neurophysiologic basis of anesthetic-induced unconsciousness. *Conscious Cognition, 9*, 370–386.

Allbritton, D.W., McKoon, G., & Ratcliff, R. (1996). Reliability of prosodic cues for resolving syntactic ambiguity. *Journal of Experimental Psychology: Learning, Memory, & Cognition, 22*, 714–735.

Allen, B.P., & Lindsay, D.S. (1998). Amalgamations of memories: Intrusion of information from one event into reports of another. *Applied Cognitive Psychology, 12*, 277–285.

Allison, T., Puce, A., & McCarthy, G. (2000). Social perception from visual cues: Role of the STS region. *Trends in Cognitive Sciences, 4*, 267–278.

Allopenna, P.D., Magnuson, J.S., & Tanenhaus, M.K. (1998). Tracking the time course of spoken word recognition using eye movements: Evidence for continuous mapping models. *Journal of Memory and Language, 38*, 419–439.

Allport, D.A. (1989). Visual attention. In M.I. Posner (Ed.), *Foundations of cognitive science*. Cambridge, MA: MIT Press.

Allport, D.A., Antonis, B., & Reynolds, P. (1972). On the division of attention: A disproof of the single channel hypothesis. *Quarterly Journal of Experimental Psychology, 24*, 225–235.

Alonso, J.M., & Martinez, L.M. (1998). Functional connectivity between simple cells and complex cells in cat striate cortex. *Nature Neuroscience, 1*, 395–403.

Altenberg, B. (1990). Speech as linear composition. In G. Caie, K. Haastrup, A.L. Jakobsen, J.E. Nielsen,

J. Sevaldsen, H. Sprecht et al. (Eds.), *Proceedings from the Fourth Nordic Conference for English Studies*. Copenhagen, Denmark: Copenhagen University Press.

Altmann, G. (2002). *Psycholinguistics: Critical concepts in psychology*. London: Routledge.

Altmann, G.T.M. (1997). *The ascent of Babel: An exploration of language, mind, and understanding.* Oxford: Oxford University Press.

Andersen, R.A., Snyder, L.H., Bradley, D.C., & Xing, J. (1997). Multimodal representation of space in the posterior parietal cortex and its use in planning movements. *Annual Review of Neuroscience, 20*, 303–330.

Anderson, C.J. (2003). The psychology of doing nothing: Forms of decision avoidance result from reason and emotion. *Psychological Bulletin, 129*, 139–167.

Anderson, J.R. (1983). *The architecture of cognition.* Harvard, MA: Harvard University Press.

Anderson, J.R. (1990). *The adaptive character of thought.* Hillsdale, NJ: Lawrence Erlbaum Associates Inc.

Anderson, J.R. (1993). *Rules of the mind.* Hillsdale, NJ: Lawrence Erlbaum Associates Inc.

Anderson, J.R. (1996). ACT: A simple theory of complex cognition. *American Psychologist, 51*, 355–365.

Anderson, J.R., & Fincham, J.M. (1994). Acquisition of procedural skills from examples. *Journal of Experimental Psychology: Learning, Memory, and Cognition, 20*, 1322–1340.

Anderson, J.R., & Lebiere, C. (1998). *The atomic components of thought.* Hillsdale, NJ: Lawrence Erlbaum Associates Inc.

Anderson, J.R., & Lebiere, C. (2003). The Newell Test for a theory of cognition. *Behavioral and Brain Sciences, 26*, 587–640.

Anderson, M.C. (2003). Rethinking interference theory: Executive control and the mechanisms of forgetting. *Journal of Memory and Language, 49*, 415–445.

Anderson, M.C., & Green, C. (2001). Suppressing unwanted memories by executive control. *Nature, 410*, 131–134.

Anderson, R.C., & Pichert, J.W. (1978). Recall of previously unrecallable information following a shift in perspective. *Journal of Verbal Learning & Verbal Behavior, 17*, 1–12.

Anderson, S.J., Holliday, I.E., Singh, K.D., & Harding, G.F.A. (1996). Localisation and functional analysis of human cortical area V5 using magnetoencephalography. *Proceedings of the Royal Society London B, 263*, 423–431.

Andrade, J. (2001). *Working memory in perspective.* Hove, UK: Psychology Press.

Andres, P., & Van der Linden, M. (2002). Are central executive functions working in patients with focal frontal lesions? *Neuropsychologia, 40*, 835–845.

Andrews, B., Brewin, C.R., Ochera, J., Morton, J., Bekerian, D.A., Davies, G.M. et al. (1999). The timing, triggers and quality of recovered memories in therapy. *British Journal of Psychiatry, 175*, 141–146.

Anzai, Y., & Simon, H.A. (1979). The theory of learning by doing. *Psychological Review, 86*, 124–180.

Arkes, H.R., & Ayton, P. (1999). The sunk cost and Concorde effects: Are humans less rational than lower animals? *Psychological Bulletin, 125*, 591–600.

Armstrong, S.L., Gleitman, L.R., & Gleitman, H. (1983). What some concepts might not be. *Cognition, 13*, 263–308.

Arnold, J.E., Eisenband, J.G., Brown-Schmidt, S., & Trueswell, J.C. (2000). The immediate use of gender information: Eyetracking evidence of the time-course of pronoun resolution. *Cognition, 76*, B13–B26.

Ashbridge, E., Walsh, V., & Cowey, A. (1997). Temporal aspects of visual search studied by transcranial magnetic stimulation. *Neuropsychologia, 35*, 1121–1131.

Atkinson, R.C., & Raugh, M.R. (1975). An application of the mnemonic keyword method to the acquisition of a Russian vocabulary. *Journal of Experimental Psychology: Human Learning and Memory, 104*, 126–133.

Atkinson, R.C., & Shiffrin, R.M. (1968). Human memory: A proposed system and its control processes. In K.W. Spence & J.T. Spence (Eds.), *The psychology of learning and motivation, Vol. 2.* London: Academic Press.

Atkinson, R.C., & Shiffrin, R.M. (1971). The control of short-term memory. *Scientific American, 225*, 82–90.

Atkinson, R.L., Atkinson, R.C., Smith, E.E., & Bem, D.J. (1993). *Introduction to psychology* (11th Ed.). New York: Harcourt Brace.

Awh, E., & Pashler, H. (2000). Evidence for split attentional foci. *Journal of Experimental Psychology: Human Perception and Performance, 26*, 834–846.

Baars, B.J. (1988). *A cognitive theory of consciousness.* Cambridge: Cambridge University Press.

Baars, B.J. (1997a). *In the theatre of consciousness: The workspace of the mind.* New York: Oxford University Press.

Baars, B.J. (1997b). Consciousness versus attention, perception, and working memory. *Consciousness and Cognition, 6*, 363–371.

Baars, B.J. (2002). The conscious access hypothesis: Origins and recent evidence. *Trends in Cognitive Sciences, 6*, 47–52.

Baars, B.J., Banks, W.P., & Newman, J.B. (Eds.) (2003). *Essential sources in the scientific study of consciousness.* Cambridge, MA: MIT Press.

Baars, B.J., & Franklin, S. (2003). How conscious experience and working memory interact. *Trends in Cognitive Sciences*, *7*, 166–172.

Baars, B.J., & McGovern, K. (1996). Cognitive views of consciousness: What are the facts? How can we explain them? In M. Velmans (Ed.), *The science of consciousness: Psychological, neuropsychological, and clinical reviews.* London: Routledge.

Baars, B.J., Motley, M.T., & MacKay, D.G. (1975). Output editing for lexical status from artificially elicited slips of the tongue. *Journal of Verbal Learning & Verbal Behavior*, *14*, 382–391.

Backus, B., Fleet, D.J., Parker, A.J., & Heeger, D.J. (2001). Human cortical activity correlates with stereoscopic depth perception. *Journal of Neurophysiology*, *86*, 2054–2068.

Baddeley, A.D. (1982). Domains of recollection. *Psychological Review*, *89*, 708–729.

Baddeley, A.D. (1984). Neuropsychological evidence and the semantic/episodic distinction. *Behavioral & Brain Sciences*, *7*, 238–239.

Baddeley, A.D. (1986). *Working memory.* Oxford: Clarendon Press.

Baddeley, A.D. (1990). *Human memory: Theory and practice*. Hove, UK: Psychology Press.

Baddeley, A.D. (1996). Exploring the central executive. *Quarterly Journal of Experimental Psychology*, *49*A, 5–28.

Baddeley, A.D. (1997). *Human memory: Theory and practice (revised edition).* Hove, UK: Psychology Press.

Baddeley, A.D. (2000). The episodic buffer: A new component of working memory? *Trends in Cognitive Science*, *4*, 417–423.

Baddeley, A.D. (2001). Is working memory still working? *American Psychologist*, *56*, 851–64.

Baddeley, A.D. (2003). Double dissociations: Not magic, but still useful. *Cortex*, *39*, 129–131.

Baddeley, A., Aggleton, J.P., & Conway, M. (2002). *Episodic memory: New directions in research.* London: Oxford University Press.

Baddeley, A., Chincotta, D., Stafford, L., & Turk, D. (2002). Is the word length effect in STM entirely attributable to output delay? Evidence from serial recognition. *Quarterly Journal of Experimental Psychology*, *55*A, 353–369.

Baddeley, A.D., & Andrade, J. (2000). Working memory and the vividness of imagery. *Journal of Experimental Psychology: General*, *129*, 126–145.

Baddeley, A.D., Emslie, H., Kolodny, J., & Duncan, J. (1998). Random generation and the executive control of working memory. *Quarterly Journal of Experimental Psychology*, *51*A, 819–852.

Baddeley, A.D., Gathercole, S., & Papagno, C. (1998). The phonological loop as a language learning device. *Psychological Review*, *105*, 158–173.

Baddeley, A.D., & Hitch, G.J. (1974). Working memory. In G.H. Bower (Ed.), *The psychology of learning and motivation*, *Vol. 8*. London: Academic Press.

Baddeley, A.D., & Hitch, G.J. (2000). Development of working memory: Should the Pascual-Leone and the Baddeley and Hitch models be merged? *Journal of Experimental Child Psychology*, *77*, 128–137.

Baddeley, A.D., & Lieberman, K. (1980). Spatial working memory. In R.S. Nickerson (Ed.), *Attention & performance, Vol. VIII.* Hillsdale, NJ: Lawrence Erlbaum Associates Inc.

Baddeley, A.D., Thomson, N., & Buchanan, M. (1975). Word length and the structure of short-term memory. *Journal of Verbal Learning and Verbal Behavior*, *14*, 575–589.

Baddeley, A.D., Vallar, G., & Wilson, B.A. (1987). Sentence comprehension and phonological memory: Some neuropsychological evidence. In M. Coltheart (Ed.), *Attention and performance XII: The psychology of reading* (pp. 509–529). Hove, UK: Lawrence Erlbaum Associates Inc.

Baddeley, A.D., & Wilson, B. (2002). Prose recall and amnesia: Implications for the structure of working memory. *Neuropsychologia*, *40*, 1737–1743.

Badecker, W., Miozzo, M., & Zanuttini, R. (1995). The two-stage model of lexical retrieval: Evidence from a case of anomia with selective preservation of gender. *Cognition*, *57*, 193–216.

Badgaiyan, R.D. (2000). Executive control, willed actions, and nonconscious processing. *Human Brain Mapping*, *9*, 38–41.

Badgaiyan, R.D., Schacter, D.L., & Alpert, N.M. (2002). Retrieval of relational information: A role for left inferior prefrontal cortex. *NeuroImage*, *17*, 393–400.

Baizer, J.S., Ungerleider, L.G., & Desimone, R. (1991). Organisation of visual inputs to the inferior temporal and posterior parietal cortex in macaques. *Journal of Neuroscience*, *11*, 168–190.

Baker, S.C., Rogers, R.D., Owen, A.M., Frith, C.D., Dolan, R.J., Frackowiak, R.S.J. et al. (1996). Neural systems engaged by planning: A PET study of the Tower of London task. *Neuropsychologia*, *34*, 515–524.

Balota, D.A., & Marsh, E.J. (2004). *Cognitive psychology.* Hove, UK: Psychology Press.

Balota, D.A., Paul, S., & Spieler, D. (1999). Attentional control of lexical processing pathways during word recognition and reading. In S. Garrod & M.J. Pickering (Eds.), *Language processing*. Hove, UK: Psychology Press.

Banich, M.T. (1997). *Neuropsychology: The neural bases of mental function*. New York: Houghton Mifflin.

Banks, S.M., Salovey, P., Greener, S., Rothman, A.J., Moyer, A., Beauvais, J., & Epel, E. (1995). The effects of message framing on mammography utilisation. *Health Psychology*, *14*, 178–184.

Bar, M., & Biederman, I. (1998). Subliminal visual priming. *Psychological Science*, *9*, 464–469.

Barclay, C.R. (1988). Truth and accuracy in autobiographical memory. In M.M. Gruneberg, P.E. Morris, & R.N. Sykes (Eds.), *Practical aspects of memory: Current research and issues: Vol. 1. Memory in everyday life*. Chichester, UK: John Wiley.

Barnett, S.M., & Ceci, S.J. (2002). When and where do we apply what we learn? A taxonomy for far transfer. *Psychological Bulletin*, *128*, 612–637.

Barr, D.J., & Keysar, B. (2002). Anchoring comprehension in linguistic precedents. *Journal of Memory and Language*, *46*, 391–418.

Barron, F. (1969). *Creative person and creative process*. New York: Holt, Rinehart & Winston, Inc.

Barsalou, L.W. (1982). Context-independent and context-dependent information in concepts. *Memory & Cognition*, *10*, 82–93.

Barsalou, L.W. (1985). Ideals, central tendency, and frequency of instantiation as determinants of graded structure in categories. *Journal of Experimental Psychology: Learning, Memory, & Cognition*, *11*, 629–654.

Barsalou, L.W. (1987). The instability of graded structure: Implications for the nature of concepts. In U. Neisser (Ed.), *Concepts and conceptual development: Ecological and intellectual factors in categorisation*. Cambridge: Cambridge University Press.

Barsalou, L.W. (1988). The content and organization of autobiographical memories. In U. Neisser & E. Winograd (Eds.), *Remembering reconsidered: Ecological and traditional approaches to the study of memory*. New York: Cambridge University Press.

Barsalou, L.W. (1989). Intra-concept similarity and its implications for inter-concept similarity. In S. Vosniadou & A. Ortony (Eds.), *Similarity and analogical reasoning*. Cambridge: Cambridge University Press.

Barsalou, L.W. (1991). Deriving categories to achieve goals. In G.H. Bower (Ed.), *The psychology of learning and motivation, Vol. 27*, (pp. 1–64). New York: Academic Press.

Barsalou, L.W. (1999). Perceptual control systems. *Behavioral and Brain Sciences*, *22*, 577–660.

Barsalou, L.W. (2003). Situated simulation in the human conceptual system. *Language and Cognitive Processes*, *18*, 513–562.

Bartlett, F.C. (1932). *Remembering*. Cambridge: Cambridge University Press.

Bartolomeo, P. (2002). The relationship between visual perception and visual mental imagery: A re-appraisal of the neuropsychological evidence. *Cortex*, *38*, 357–378.

Bartolomeo, P., Bachoud-Lévi, A.C., De gelder, B., Denes, G., Dalla Barba, G., Brugieres, P. et al. (1998). Multiple-domain dissociation between impaired visual perception and preserved mental imagery in a patient with bilateral extrastriate lesions. *Neuropsychologia*, *36*, 239–249.

Bartolomeo, P., & Chokron, S. (2002). Orienting of attention in left unilateral neglect. *Neuroscience and Biobehavioral Reviews*, *26*, 217–234.

Bartolomeo, P., Siéroff, E., Decaix, C., & Chokron, S. (2001). Modulating the attentional bias in unilateral neglect: The effect of the strategic set. *Experimental Brain Research*, *137*, 432–444.

Bassok, M., & Holyoak, J.J. (1989). Interdomain transfer between isomorphic topics in algebra and physics. *Journal of Experimental Psychology: Learning, Memory, and Cognition*, *15*, 153–166.

Battersby, W.S., Teuber, H.L., & Bender, M.B. (1953). Problem solving behavior in men with frontal or occipital brain injuries. *Journal of Psychology*, *35*, 329–351.

Baynes, K., & Gazzaniga, M. (2000). Consciousness, introspection, and the split-brain: The two minds/one body problem. In M.S. Gazzaniga (Ed.), *The new cognitive neurosciences*. Cambridge, MA: MIT Press.

Beauvois, M.-F., & Dérouesné, J. (1979). Phonological alexia: Three dissociations. *Journal of Neurology, Neurosurgery & Psychiatry*, *42*, 1115–1124.

Beauvois, M.-F., Dérouesné, J., & Bastard, V. (1980, June). *Auditory parallel to phonological alexia*. Paper presented at the Third European Conference of the International Neuropsychological Society, Chianciano, Italy.

Beck, D., Rees, G., Frith, C.D., & Lavie, N. (2001). Change blindness and change awareness. *Nature Neuroscience*, *4*, 645–650.

Beckers, G., & Zeki, S. (1995). The consequences of inactivating areas V1 and V5 on visual motion perception. *Brain*, *118*, 49–60.

Begg, I., & Denny, J.P. (1969). Empirical reconciliation of atmosphere and conversion interpretations of syllogistic reasoning errors. *Journal of Experimental Psychology*, *81*, 351–354.

Behrmann, M., & Bub, D. (1992). Surface dyslexia and dysgraphia: Dual routes, single lexicon. *Cognitive Neuropsychology*, *9*, 209–251.

Behrmann, M., & Kimchi, R. (2003). What does visual agnosia tell us about perceptual organisation and its relationship to object perception? *Journal of Experimental Psychology: Human Perception and Performance*, *29*, 19–42.

Behrmann, M., Nelson, J., & Sekuler, E.B. (1998). Visual complexity in letter-by-letter reading: "Pure" alexia is not pure. *Neuropsychologia*, *36*, 1115–1132.

Behrmann, M., & Patterson, K. (2004). *Words and things*. Hove, UK: Psychology Press.

Bell, V.A., & Johnson-Laird, P.N. (1998). A model theory of model reasoning. *Cognitive Science*, *22*, 25–51.

Belli, R.F. (1998). The structure of autobiographical memory and the event history calendar: Potential improvements in the quality of retrospective reports in surveys. *Memory*, *6*, 383–406.

Benguigui, N., Ripoli, H., & Broderick, M.P. (2003). Time-to-contact estimation of accelerated stimuli is based on first-order information. *Journal of Experimental Psychology: Human Perception and Performance*, *29*, 1083–1101.

Bereiter, C., Burtis, P.J., & Scardamalia, M. (1988). Cognitive operations in constructing main points in written composition. *Journal of Memory & Language*, *27*, 261–278.

Bereiter, C., & Scardamalia, M. (1987). *The psychology of written composition*. Hillsdale, NJ: Lawrence Erlbaum Associates Inc.

Berent, I., & Perfetti, C.A. (1995). A rose is a REEZ: The two-cycles model of phonology assembly in reading English. *Psychological Review*, *102*, 146–184.

Berlin, B., & Kay, P. (1969). *Basic colour terms: Their universality and evolution.* Berkeley & Los Angeles: University of California Press.

Berndt, R.S., Haendiges, A.N., Mitchum, C.C., & Wayland, S.C. (1996). An investigation of non-lexical reading impairments. *Cognitive Neuropsychology*, *13*, 763–801.

Berndt, R.S., Mitchum, C.C., & Haendiges, A.N. (1996). Comprehension of reversible sentences in "agrammatism": A meta-analysis. *Cognition*, *58*, 289–308.

Berntsen, D. (1998). Voluntary and involuntary access to autobiographical memory. *Memory*, *6*, 113–141.

Berntsen, D., & Hall, N.M. (in press). The episodic nature of involuntary autobiographical memories. *Memory and Cognition*.

Bertamini, M., Yang, T.L., & Proffitt, D.R. (1998). Relative size perception at a distance is best at eye level. *Perception & Psychophysics*, *60*, 673–682.

Beschin, N., Cocchini, G., Della Sala, S., & Logie, R.H. (1997). What the eyes perceive, the brain ignores: A case of pure unilateral representational neglect. *Cortex*, *33*, 3–26.

Best, C.J., Crassini, B., & Day, R.H. (2002). The roles of static depth information and object–image relative motion in perception of heading. *Journal of Experimental Psychology: Human Perception and Performance*, *28*, 884–901.

Best, C.J., Day, R.H., & Crassini, B. (2003). The influence of object–image velocity change on perceived heading in minimal environments. *Perception & Psychophysics*, *65*, 1273–1284.

Beusmans, J.M.H. (1998). Optic flow and the metric of the visual ground plane. *Vision Research*, *38*, 1153–1170.

Biassou, N., Obler, L.K., Nespoulous, J.-L., Dordain, M., & Harris, K.S. (1997). Dual processing of open- and closed-class words. *Brain & Language*, *57*, 360–373.

Biederman, I. (1987). Recognition-by-components: A theory of human image understanding. *Psychological Review*, *94*, 115–147.

Biederman, I. (1990). Higher-level vision. In D.N. Osherson, S. Kosslyn, & J. Hollerbach (Eds.), *An invitation to cognitive science: Visual cognition and action.* Cambridge, MA: MIT Press.

Biederman, I., Cooper, E.E., Fox, P.W., & Mahadevan, R.S. (1992). Unexceptional spatial memory in an exceptional memorist. *Journal of Experimental Psychology: Human Perception and Performance*, *19*, 1162–1182.

Biederman, I., & Gerhardstein, P.C. (1993). Recognising depth-rotated objects: Evidence for 3-D viewpoint invariance. *Journal of Experimental Psychology: Human Perception & Performance*, *19*, 1162–1182.

Biederman, I., & Ju, G. (1988). Surface versus edge-based determinants of visual recognition. *Cognitive Psychology*, *20*, 38–64.

Biederman, I., Subramaniam, S., Bar, M., Kalocsai, P., & Fiser, J. (1999). Subordinate-level object classification re-examined. *Psychological Research*, *62*, 131–153.

Binkofski, F., Dohle, C., Posse, S., Stephan, K.M., Hefter, H., Seitz, R.J. et al. (1998). Human anterior intraparietal area subserves prehension: A combined lesion and functional MRI activation study. *Neurology*, *50*, 1253–1259.

Birch, H.G. (1945). The relationship of previous experience to insightful problem solving. *Journal of Comparative Psychology*, *38*, 267–383.

Bjork, R.A., & Whitten, W.B. (1974). Recency-sensitive retrieval processes in long-term free recall. *Cognitive Psychology*, *6*, 173–189.

Blackmore, S. (2003). *Consciousness: An introduction.* London: Hodder & Stoughton.

Blakemore, C. (1976). The conditions required for the maintenance of binocularity in the kitten's visual cortex. *Journal of Physiology*, *261*, 423–444.

Blakemore, S.-J., Fonlupt, P., Pachot-Clouard, M., Darmon, C., Boyer, P., Meltzoff, A.N. et al. (2001). How the brain perceives causality: An event-related fMRI study. *NeuroReport*, *12*, 3741–3746.

Blanchette, I., & Dunbar, K. (2000). How analogies are generated: The roles of structural and superficial similarity. *Memory & Cognition*, *28*, 108–124.

Blanken, G. (1998). Lexicalisation in speech production: Evidence from form-related word substitutions in aphasia. *Cognitive Neuropsychology*, *15*, 321–360.

Blasko, D., & Connine, C. (1993). Effects of familiarity and aptness on metaphor processing. *Journal of Experimental Psychology: Learning, Memory, & Cognition*, 19, 295–308.

Blessing, S.B., & Ross, B.H. (1996). Content effects in problem categorisation and problem solving.

Journal of Experimental Psychology: Learning, Memory, and Cognition, *22*, 792–810.

Bloj, M.G., Kersten, D., & Hurlbert, A.C. (1999). Perception of three-dimensional shape influences colour perception through mutual illumination. *Nature*, *402*, 877–879.

Blum, D., Yonelinas, A.P., Luks, T., Newitt, D., Oh, J., Lu, Y. et al. (2002). Dissociating perceptual and conceptual implicit memory in multiple sclerosis patients. *Brain and Cognition*, *50*, 51–61.

Bohannon, J.N. (1988). Flashbulb memories for the space shuttle disaster: A tale of two theories. *Cognition*, *29*, 179–196.

Bohning, D.E., Shastri, A., McConnell, K.A., Nahar, Z., Lorberbaum, J.P., Roberts, D.R. et al. (1999). A combined TMS/fMRI study of intensity-dependent TMS over motor cortex. *Biological Psychiatry*, *45*, 385–394.

Boland, J.E., & Blodgett, A. (2001). Understanding the constraints on syntactic generation: Lexical bias and discourse congruency effects on eye movements. *Journal of Memory and Language*, *45*, 391–411.

Boomer, D. (1965). Hesitation and grammatical encoding. *Language & Speech*, *8*, 145–158.

Borges, J.-L. (1964). *Labyrinths*. London: Penguin.

Bourke, P.A. (1997). Measuring attentional demand in continuous dual-task performance. *Quarterly Journal of Experimental Psychology*, *50A*, 821–840.

Bourke, P.A., Duncan, J., & Nimmo-Smith, I. (1996). A general factor involved in dual-task performance decrement. *Quarterly Journal of Experimental Psychology*, *49*A, 525–545.

Bouton, M.E., Nelson, J.B., & Rosas, J.M. (1999). Stimulus generalisation, context change, and forgetting. *Psychological Bulletin*, *125*, 171–186.

Bower, G.H., & Gilligan, S.G. (1979). Remembering information related to one's self. *Journal of Research in Personality*, *13*, 420–432.

Bowers, J.S. (2002). Challenging the widespread assumption that connectionism and distributed representations go hand-in-hand. *Cognitive Psychology*, *45*, 413–445.

Bowmaker, J.K., & Dartnall, H.J.A. (1980). Visual pigments of rods and cones in a human retina. *Journal of Physiology*, *298*, 501–511.

Bradley, D.C., Maxwell, M., Andersen, R.A., Banks, M.S., & Shenoy, K.V. (1996). Mechanisms of heading perception in primate visual cortex. *Science*, *273*, 1544–1547.

Bradshaw, M.F., & Rogers, B.J. (1996). The interaction of binocular disparity and motion parallax in the computation of depth. *Vision Research*, *36*, 3457–3468.

Braine, M.D.S. (1978). On the relationship between the natural logic of reasoning and standard logic. *Psychological Review*, *85*, 1–21.

Braine, M.D.S. (1994). Mental logic and how to discover it. In J. Macnamara & G.E. Reyes (Eds.), *The logical foundations of cognition*. Oxford: Oxford University Press.

Braine, M.D.S. (1998). Steps towards a mental predicate logic. In M.D.S. Braine & D.P. O'Brien (Eds.), *Mental logic*. Mahwah, NJ: Lawrence Erlbaum Associates Inc.

Braine, M.D.S., Reiser, B.J., & Rumain, B. (1984). Some empirical justification for a theory of natural propositional logic. In G.H. Bower (Ed.), *The psychology of learning and motivation, Vol. 18*. New York: Academic Press.

Bramwell, D.I., & Hurlbert, A.C. (1996). Measurements of colour constancy by using a forced-choice matching technique. *Perception*, *25*, 229–241.

Brandimonte, M.A., Hitch, G.J., & Bishop, D.V. (1992). Mental image reversal and verbal recoding. *Memory & Cognition*, *20*, 449–455.

Bransford, J.D., Barclay, J.R., & Franks, J.J. (1972). Sentence memory: A constructive versus interpretive approach. *Cognitive Psychology*, *3*, 193–209.

Bransford, J.D., Franks, J.J., Morris, C.D., & Stein, B.S. (1979). Some general constraints on learning and memory research. In L.S. Cermak & F.I.M. Craik (Eds.), *Levels of processing in human memory*. Hillsdale, NJ: Lawrence Erlbaum Associates Inc.

Bransford, J.D., & Johnson, M.K. (1972). Contextual prerequisites for understanding. *Journal of Verbal Learning and Verbal Behavior*, *11*, 717–726.

Bransford, J.D., & Schwartz, D.L. (1999). Rethinking transfer: A simple proposal with multiple implications. In A. Iran-Nejad & P.D. Pearson (Eds.), *Review of Research in Education*, *24*, 61–101. Washington DC: American Educational Research Association.

Braver, T.S., & Bongiolatti, S.R. (2002). The role of frontopolar cortex in subgoal processing during working memory. *NeuroImage*, *15*, 523–536.

Bredart, S. (1998). Structured imagination of novel creatures' faces. *American Journal of Psychology*, *111*, 607–626.

Breedin, S.D., & Saffran, E.M. (1999). Sentence processing in the face of semantic loss: A case study. *Journal of Experimental Psychology: General*, *128*, 547–562.

Britten, K.H., & van Wezel, R.J.A. (1998). Electrical microstimulation of cortical area MST biases heading perception in monkeys. *Nature Neuroscience*, *1*, 59–63.

Broadbent, D.E. (1958). *Perception and communication*. Oxford: Pergamon.

Broadbent, D.E. (1982). Task combination and selective intake of information. *Acta Psychologica*, *50*, 253–290.

Bröder A. (2003). Decision making with the adaptive toolbox: Influence of environmental structure, personality, intelligence, and working memory load.

Journal of Experimental Psychology: Learning, Memory, and Cognition, *29*, 611–625.

Brown, N.R. (1995). Estimation strategies and the judgement of event frequency. *Journal of Experimental Psychology: Learning, Memory, & Cognition*, *21*, 1539–1553.

Brown, N.R., Rips, L.J., & Shevell, S.K. (1985). The subjective dates of news events in very-long-term memory. *Cognitive Psychology*, *17*, 139–177.

Brown, N.R., Shevell, S.K., & Rips, L.J. (1986). Public memories and their personal context. In D.C. Rubin (Ed.), *Autobiographical memory*. Cambridge: Cambridge University Press.

Brown, R., & Kulik, J. (1977). Flashbulb memories. *Cognition*, *5*, 73–99.

Brown, R., & McNeill, D. (1966). The "tip of the tongue" phenomenon. *Journal of Verbal Learning and Verbal Behavior*, *5*, 325–337.

Bruce, K.R., & Pihl, R.O. (1997). Forget drinking to forget: Enhanced consolidation of emotionally charged memory by alcohol. *Experimental and Clinical Psychopharmacology*, *5*, 242–250.

Bruce, V., Green, P.R., & Georgeson, M.A. (2003). *Visual perception* (4th Ed.). Hove, UK: Psychology Press.

Bruce, V., Henderson, Z., Greenwood, K., Hancock, P., Burton, A.M., & Miller, P. (1999). Verification of face identities from images captured on video. *Journal of Experimental Psychology: Applied*, *5*, 339–360.

Bruce, V., & Valentine, T. (1986). Semantic priming of familiar faces. *Quarterly Journal of Experimental Psychology*, *38*A, 125–150.

Bruce, V., & Young, A.W. (1986). Understanding face recognition. *British Journal of Psychology*, *77*, 305–327.

Bruner, J.S., Goodnow, J.J., & Austin, G.A. (1956). *A study of thinking*. New York: John Wiley.

Bruner, J.S., Postman, L., & Rodrigues, J. (1951). Expectations and the perception of colour. *American Journal of Psychology*, *64*, 216–227.

Bruno, N., & Cutting, J.E. (1988). Mini-modularity and the perception of layout. *Journal of Experimental Psychology: General*, *117*, 161–170.

Brunswik, E. (1956). *Perception and the representative design of psychological experiments*. Berkeley, CA: University of California Press.

Bub, D., & Kertesz, A. (1982). Deep agraphia. *Brain and Language*, *17*, 146–165.

Bülthoff, I., Bülthoff, H., & Sinha, P. (1998). Top-down influences on stereoscopic depth-perception. *Nature Neuroscience*, *1*, 254–257.

Burgess, P.W., Quayle, A., & Frith, C.D. (2001). Brain regions involved in prospective memory as determined by positron emission tomography. *Neuropsychologia*, *39*, 545–555.

Burgess, P.W., & Shallice, T. (1996). Bizarre responses, rule detection and frontal lobe lesions. *Cortex*, *32*, 241–259.

Burgess, P.W., Veitch, E., De Lacy Costello, A., & Shallice, T. (2000). The cognitive and neuroanatomical correlates of multi-tasking. *Neuropsychologia*, *38*, 848–863.

Burt, C.D.B., Kemp, S., & Conway, M.A. (2003). themes, events, and episodes in autobiographical memory. *Memory & Cognition*, *31*, 317–325.

Burt, J.S., & Tate, H. (2002). Does a reading lexicon provide orthographic representations for spelling? *Journal of Memory and Language*, *46*, 518–543.

Burton, A.M., & Bruce, V. (1993). Naming faces and naming names: Exploring an interactive activation model of person recognition. *Memory*, *1*, 457–480.

Burton, A.M., Bruce, V., & Hancock, P.J.B. (1999). From pixels to people: A model of familiar face recognition. *Cognitive Science*, *23*, 1–31.

Butters, N., & Cermak, L.S. (1980). *Alcoholic Korsakoff's syndrome: An information-processing approach*. London: Academic Press.

Butters, N., Heindel, W.C., & Salmon, D.P. (1990). Dissociation of implicit memory in dementia: Neurological implications. *Bulletin of the Psychonomic Society*, *28*, 359–366.

Butterworth, B. (1985). Jargon aphasia: Processes and strategies. In S. Newman & R. Epstein (Eds.), *Current perspectives in dysphasia*. Edinburgh: Churchill Livingstone.

Buxbaum, L.J., Glosser, G., & Coslett, H.B. (1999). Impaired face and word recognition without object agnosia. *Neuropsychologia*, *37*, 41–50.

Byrd, D., & Saltzman, E. (1998). Intragestural dynamics of multiple phrasal boundaries. *Journal of Phonetics*, *26*, 173–199.

Byrne, R.M.J. (1989). Suppressing valid inferences with conditionals. *Cognition*, *31*, 61–83.

Cabeza, R., & Nyberg, L. (2000). Imaging cognition. II. An empirical review of 275 PET and fMRI studies. *Journal of Cognitive Neuroscience*, *12*, 1–47.

Cacciari, C., & Glucksberg, S. (1994). Understanding figurative language. In M.A. Gernsbacher (Ed.), *Handbook of psycholinguistics*. San Diego, CA: Academic Press.

Caillies, S., Denhière, G. & Kintsch, W. (2002). The effect of prior knowledge on understanding from text: Evidence from primed recognition. *European Journal of Cognitive Psychology*, *14*, 267–286.

Calvo, M.G. (2001). Working memory and inferences: Evidence from eye fixations during reading. *Memory*, *9*, 365–381.

Camerer, C., & Hogarth, R.B. (1999). The effects of financial incentives in experiments: A review and capital-labor-production framework. *Journal of Risk and Uncertainty*, *19*, 7–42.

Campbell, R. (1983). Writing non-words to dictation. *Brain and Language*, *19*, 153–178.

Caramazza, A. (1984). The logic of neuropsychological research and the problem of patient classification in aphasia. *Brain and Language*, *21*, 9–20.

Caramazza, A., & Shelton, J.R. (1998). Domain specific knowledge systems in the brain: The animate–inanimate distinction. *Journal of Cognitive Neuroscience*, *10*, 1–34.

Carey, D.P., Harvey, M., & Milner, A.D. (1996). Visuomotor sensitivity for shape and orientation in a patient with visual form agnosia. *Neuropsychologia*, *34*, 329–338.

Carey, D.P., & Milner, A.D. (1994). Casting one's net too widely? *Behavioral & Brain Sciences*, *17*, 65–66.

Carr, T.H., Davidson, B.J., & Hawkins, H.L. (1978). Perceptual flexibility in word recognition: Strategies affect orthographic computation but not lexical access. *Journal of Experimental Psychology: Human Perception & Performance*, *4*, 674–690.

Carreiras, M., & Clifton, C. (1993). Relative clause interpretation preferences in Spanish and English. *Language & Speech*, *36*, 353–372.

Carvalho, J.B. (2002). Developing audience awareness in writing. *Journal of Research in Reading*, *25*, 271–282.

Casscells, W., Schoenberger, A., & Graboys, T.B. (1978). Interpretation by physicians of clinical laboratory results. *New England Journal of Medicine*, *299*, 999–1001.

Ceci, S.J. (1995). False beliefs: Some developmental and clinical considerations. In D.L. Schacter (Ed.), *Memory distortions*. Cambridge, MA: Harvard University Press.

Ceci, S.J., & Liker, J.K. (1986). A day at the races: A study of IQ, expertise, and cognitive complexity. *Journal of Experimental Psychology: General*, *115*, 255–266.

Ceraso, J., & Provitera, A. (1971). Sources of error in syllogistic reasoning. *Cognitive Psychology*, *2*, 400–410.

Cermak, L.S., Lewis, R., Butters, N., & Goodglass, H. (1973). Role of verbal mediation in performance of motor tasks by Korsakoff patients. *Perceptual & Motor Skills*, *37*, 259–262.

Cermak, L.S., Talbot, N., Chandler, K., & Wolbarst, L.R. (1985). The perceptual priming phenomenon in amnesia. *Neuropsychologia*, *23*, 615–622.

Challis, B.H., & Brodbeck, D.R. (1992). Level of processing affects priming in word fragment completion. *Journal of Experimental Psychology: Learning, Memory, & Cognition*, *18*, 595–607.

Chalmers, A.F. (1982). *What is this thing called science?* Milton Keynes, UK: Open University Press.

Chalmers, D.J. (1995a). Facing up to the problem of consciousness. *Journal of Consciousness Studies*, *3*, 200–219.

Chalmers, D.J. (1995b). The puzzle of conscious experience. *Scientific American*, December, 62–68.

Channon, S., Shanks, D., Johnstone, T., Vakili, K., Chin, J., & Sinclair, E. (2002). Is implicit learning spared in amnesia? Rule abstraction and item familiarity in artificial grammar learning. *Neuropsychologia*, *40*, 2185–2197.

Chao, L.L., & Martin, A. (2000). Representation of manipulable man-made objects in the dorsal stream. *NeuroImage*, *12*, 478–484.

Chapman, L.J., & Chapman, J.P. (1959). Atmosphere effects re-examined. *Journal of Experimental Psychology*, *58*, 220–226.

Charness, N., Krampe, R.Th., & Mayr, U. (1996). The role of practice and coaching in entrepreneurial skill domains: An international comparison of life-span chess skill acquisition. In K.A. Ericsson (Ed.), *The road to excellence: The acquisition of expert performance in the arts and sciences, sports, and games*. Mahwah, NJ: Lawrence Erlbaum Associates Inc.

Charness, N., Reingold, E.M., Pomplun, M., & Stampe, D.M. (2001). The perceptual aspect of skilled performance in chess: Evidence from eye movements. *Memory & Cognition*, *29*, 1146–1152.

Chase, W.G., & Simon, H.A. (1973a). Perception in chess. *Cognitive Psychology*, *4*, 55–81.

Chase, W.G., & Simon, H.A. (1973b). The mind's eye in chess. In W.G. Chase (Ed.), *Visual information processing*. London: Academic Press.

Chater, N., & Oaksford, M. (1999). The probability heuristics model of syllogistic reasoning. *Cognitive Psychology*, *38*, 191–258.

Chater, N., & Oaksford, M. (2001). Human rationality and the psychology of reasoning: Where do we go from here? *British Journal of Psychology*, *92*, 193–216.

Chee, M.W.L., O'Craven, K.M., Bergida, R., Rosen, B.R., & Savoy, R.L. (1999). Auditory and visual word processing studied with fMRI. *Human Brain Mapping*, *7*, 15–28.

Cheesman, J., & Merikle, P.M. (1984). Priming with and without awareness. *Perception & Psychophysics*, *36*, 387–395.

Chen, Y., Fu, S., Iversen, S.D., Smith, S.M., & Matthews, P.M. (2002). Testing for dual brain processing routes in reading: A direct contrast of Chinese characters and pinyin reading using fMRI. *Journal of Cognitive Neuroscience*, *14*, 1088–1098.

Chen, Z. (1996). Children's analogical problem solving: The effects of superficial, structural, and procedural similarity. *Journal of Experimental Child Psychology*, *62*, 410–431.

Chen, Z. (2002). Analogical problem solving: A hierarchical analysis of procedural similarity. *Journal of Experimental Psychology: Learning, Memory, and Cognition*, *28*, 81–98.

Chen, Z., & Klahr, D. (1999). All other things being equal: Children's acquisition of the control of variables strategy. *Child Development*, *70*, 1098–1120.

Cheng, P.W. (1985). Restructuring versus automaticity: Alternative accounts of skills acquisition. *Psychological Review*, *92*, 414–423.

Chenoweth, N.A., & Hayes, J.R. (2003). The inner voice in writing. *Written Communication*, *20*, 99–118.

Cherry, E.C. (1953). Some experiments on the recognition of speech with one and two ears. *Journal of the Acoustical Society of America*, *25*, 975–979.

Chertkow, H., Bub, D., Evans, E., Meyer, S., & Marrett, S. (1993). Neural correlates of picture processing studied with positron emission tomography. *Brain & Language*, *44*, 460.

Chincotta, D., Underwood, G., Abd Ghani, K., Papadopoulou, E., & Wresinksi, M. (1999). Memory span for Arabic numerals and digit words: Evidence for a limited-capacity visuo-spatial storage system. *Quarterly Journal of Experimental Psychology*, *2*A, 325–351.

Chin-Parker, S., & Ross, B.H. (2004). Diagnosticity and prototypicality in category learning: A comparison of inference learning and classification learning. *Journal of Experimental Psychology: Learning, Memory, and Cognition*, *30*, 216–226.

Chochon, F., Cohen, L., van de Moortele, P.F., & Dehaene, S. (1999). Differential contributions of the left and right inferior parietal lobules to number processing. *Journal of Cognitive Neuroscience*, *11*, 617–630.

Chomsky, N. (1957). *Syntactic structures*. The Hague: Mouton.

Chomsky, N. (1959). Review of Skinner's "Verbal behaviour". *Language*, *35*, 26–58.

Churchland, P.S., & Sejnowski, T.J. (1991). Perspectives on cognitive neuroscience. In R.G. Lister & H.J. Weingarter (Eds.), *Perspectives on cognitive neuroscience*. Oxford: Oxford University Press.

Churchland, P.S., & Sejnowski, T. (1994). *The computational brain*. Cambridge, MA: MIT Press.

Cicerone, C.M., & Nerger, J.L. (1989). The relative number of long-wavelength-sensitive to middle-wavelength-sensitive cones in the human fovea centralis. *Vision Research*, *29*, 115–128.

Cipolotti, L., & Warrington, E.K. (1995). Towards a unitary account of access dysphasia: A single case study. *Memory*, *3*, 309–332.

Clancy, S.A., Schacter, D.L., McNally, R.J., & Pitman, R.K. (2000). False recognition in women reporting recovered memories of sexual abuse. *Psychological Science*, *11*, 26–31.

Claparède, E. (1911). Recognition et moitié. *Archives de Psychologie*, *11*, 75–90.

Clark, H.H. (1992). *Arenas of language use*. Chicago: University of Chicago Press.

Clark, H.H., & Carlson, T.B. (1981). Context for comprehension. In J. Long & Baddeley (Eds.), *Attention and performance, Vol. IX*. Hillsdale, NJ: Lawrence Erlbaum Associates Inc.

Clark, H.H., & Krych, M.A. (2004). Speaking while monitoring addressees for understanding. *Journal of Memory and Language*, *50*, 62–81.

Clark, M.A., Merians, A.S., Kothari, A., Poizner, H., Macauley, B., Rothi, L.J.G. et al. (1994). Spatial planning deficits in limb apraxia. *Brain*, *117*, 1093–1106.

Clifton, C., & Duffy, S.A. (2001). Sentence and text comprehension: Roles of linguistic structure. *Annual Review of Psychology*, *52*, 167–196.

Clifton, C., & Ferreira, F. (1987). Discourse structure and anaphora: Some experimental results. In M. Coltheart (Ed.), *Attention and performance, Vol. XII*. Hove, UK: Psychology Press.

Clifton, C., Traxler, M.J., Mohamed, M.T., Williams, R.S., Morris, R.K., & Rayner, K. (2003). The use of thematic role information in parsing: Syntactic processing autonomy revisited. *Journal of Memory and Language*, *49*, 317–334.

Cohen, G. (1990). Why is it difficult to put names to faces? *British Journal of Psychology*, *81*, 287–297.

Cohen, N.J., Ramzy, C., Hut, Z., Tomaso, H., Strupp, J., Erhard, P. et al. (1994). Hippocampal activation in fMRI evoked by demand for declarative memory-based bindings of multiple streams of information. *Society for Neuroscience Abstracts*, *20*, 1290.

Cohen, N.J., & Squire, L.R. (1980). Preserved learning and retention of pattern-analysing skill in amnesia using perceptual learning. *Cortex*, *17*, 273–278.

Cole, G.G, Heywood, C.A., Kentridge, R.W., Fairholm, I., & Cowey, A. (2003). Attentional capture by colour and motion in cerebral achromatopsia. *Neuropsychologia*, *41*(3), 1837–1846.

Collette F., & Van Der Linden M. (2002). Brain imaging of the central executive component of working memory. *Neuroscience & Biobehavioral Reviews*, *26*, 105–125.

Collins, A.M., & Quillian, M.R. (1969). Retrieval time from semantic memory. *Journal of Verbal Learning & Verbal Behavior*, *8*, 240–248.

Coltheart, M. (1980). Deep dyslexia: A review of the syndrome. In M. Coltheart, K.E. Patterson, & J.C. Marshall (Eds.), *Deep dyslexia*. London: Routledge & Kegan Paul.

Coltheart, M. (1983). Ecological necessity of iconic memory. *Behavioral and Brain Sciences*, *6*, 17–18.

Coltheart, M. (1984). Acquired dyslexias and normal reading. In R.N. Malatesha & H.A. Whitaker (Eds.), *Dyslexia: A global issue*. The Hague: Martinus Nijhoff.

Coltheart, M. (Ed.) (1996). *Phonological dyslexia*. Hove, UK: Lawrence Erlbaum Associates Ltd. [A special issue of *The Journal of Cognitive Neuropsychology* (1996, September).]

Coltheart, M. (1999). Modularity and cognition. *Trends in Cognitive Sciences*, *3*, 115–120.

Coltheart, M. (2000). Deep dyslexia is right-hemisphere reading. *Brain and Language*, *71*, 299–309.

Coltheart, M. (2001). *Assumptions and methods in cognitive neuropsychology.* Hove, UK: Psychology Press.

Coltheart, M. (2004). Brain imaging, connectionism, and cognitive neuropsychology. *Cognitive Neuropsychology*, 21, 21–25.

Coltheart, M., Inglis, L., Cupples, L., Michie, P., Bates, A., & Budd, B. (1998). A semantic subsystem specific to the storage of information about visual attributes of animate and inanimate objects. *Neurocase*, *4*, 353–370.

Coltheart, M., Rastle, K., Perry, C., Langdon, R., & Ziegler, J. (2001). The DRC model: A model of visual word recognition and reading aloud. *Psychological Review*, *108*, 204–258.

Connine, C.M. (1990). Effects of sentence context and lexical knowledge in speech processing. In G.T.M. Altmann (Ed.), *Cognitive models of speech processing.* Cambridge, MA: MIT Press.

Connolly, T., & Reb, J. (2003). Omission bias in vaccination decisions: Where's the "omission"? Where's the "bias"? *Organizational Behavior and Human Decision Processes*, *91*, 186–202.

Conway, A.R.A., Cowan, N., & Bunting, M.F. (2001). The cocktail party phenomenon revisited: The importance of working memory capacity. *Psychonomic Bulletin and Review*, *8*, 331–335.

Conway, M.A. (1996). Autobiographical knowledge and autobiographical memories. In D.C. Rubin (Ed.), *Remembering our past: Studies in autobiographical memory.* Cambridge: Cambridge University Press.

Conway, M.A. (2003). Commentary: Cognitive-affective mechanisms and processes in autobiographical memory. *Memory*, *11*, 217–224.

Conway, M.A., Anderson, S.J., Larsen, S.F., Donnelly, C.M., McDaniel, M.A., McClelland, A.G.R. et al. (1994). The function of flashbulb memories. *Memory & Cognition*, *22*, 326–343.

Conway, M.A., & Bekerian, D.A. (1987). Organisation in autobiographical memory. In A.F. Collins, S.E. Gathercole, M.A. Conway, & P.E. Morris (Eds.), *Theories of memory*. Hove, UK: Psychology Press.

Conway, M.A., Cohen, G., & Stanhope, N. (1991). On the very long-term retention of knowledge acquired through formal education: Twelve years of cognitive psychology. *Journal of Experimental Psychology: General*, *120*, 395–409.

Conway, M.A., & Haque, S. (1999). Overshadowing the reminiscence bump: Memories of a struggle for independence. *Journal of Adult Development*, *6*, 35–44.

Conway, M.A., & Pleydell-Pearce, C.W. (2000). The construction of autobiographical memories in the self-memory system. *Psychological Review*, *107*, 261–288.

Conway, M.A., Pleydell-Pearce, C.W., & Whitecross, S.E. (2001). The neuroanatomy of autobiographical memory: A slow cortical potential study of autobiographical memory retrieval. *Journal of Memory and Language*, *45*, 493–524.

Conway, M.A., Pleydell-Pearce, C.W., Whitecross, S.E., & Sharpe, H. (2003). Neurophysiological correlates of memory for experienced and imagined events. *Neuropsychologia*, *41*, 334–340.

Conway, M.A., & Rubin, D.C. (1993). The structure of autobiographical memory. In A.F. Collins, S.E. Gathercole, M.A. Conway, & P.E. Morris (Eds.), *Theories of memory.* Hove, UK: Psychology Press.

Conway, M.A., Turk, D.J., Miller, S.L., Logan, J., Nebes, R.D., Meltzer, C.C. et al. (1999). A positron emission tomography (PET) study of autobiographical memory retrieval. *Memory*, *7*, 679–702.

Cooney, J.W., & Gazzaniga, M.S. (2003). Neurological disorders and the structure of human consciousness. *Trends in Cognitive Sciences*, *7*, 161–165.

Cooper, E.E., & Biederman, I. (1993, May). *Metric versus viewpoint-invariant shape differences in visual object recognition.* Poster presented at the Annual Meeting of the Association for Research in Vision and Ophthalmology, Sarasota, Florida.

Cooper, L.A., & Shepard, R.N. (1973). Chronometric studies of the rotation of mental images. In W.G. Chase (Ed.), *Visual information processing.* New York: Academic Press.

Cooper, R., & Shallice, T. (1995). SOAR and the case for unified theories of cognition. *Cognition*, *55*, 115–149.

Cooper, R.P., Fox, J., Farringdon, J., & Shallice, T. (1996). A systematic methodology for cognitive modelling. *Artificial Intelligence*, *85*, 3–44.

Copeland, B.J. (1993). *Artificial intelligence: A philosophical introduction.* Oxford: Blackwell.

Corbetta, M., Miezin, F.M., Dobmeyer, S., Shulman, G.L. et al. (1990). Attentional modulation of neural processing of shape, colour, and velocity in humans. *Science*, *248*, 1556–1559.

Corbetta, M., & Shulman, G.L. (2002). Control of goal-directed and stimulus-driven attention in the brain. *Nature Reviews Neuroscience*, *3*, 201–215.

Corkin, S. (1968). Acquisition of motor skill after bilateral medial temporal-lobe excision. *Neuropsychologia*, *6*, 255–265.

Corkin, S., Amaral, D.G., Gonzalez, R.G., Johnson, K.A., & Hyman, B.T. (1997). H.M.'s medial temporal lobe lesion: Findings from magnetic resonance imaging. *Journal of Neuroscience*, *17*, 3964–3979.

Coslett, H.B. (1991). Read but not write "idea": Evidence for a third reading mechanism. *Brain and Language*, *40*, 425–443.

Coslett, H.B., & Saffran, E. (1991). Simultagnosia: To see but two see. *Brain*, *113*, 475–486.

Cosmides, L. (1989). The logic of social exchange: Has natural selection shaped how humans reason? Studies with the Wason selection task. *Cognition*, *31*, 187–276.

Cosmides, L., & Tooby, J. (1996). Are humans good intuitive statisticians after all? Rethinking some conclusions from the literature on judgement under uncertainty. *Cognition*, *58*, 1–73.

Costello, F.J., & Keane, M.T. (2000). Efficient creativity: Constraint-guided conceptual combination. *Cognitive Science*, *24*, 299–349.

Cowey, A., & Stoerig, P. (1989). Projection patterns of surviving neurons in the dorsal lateral geniculate nucleus following discrete lesions of striate cortex: Implications for residual vision. *Experimental Brain Research*, *75*, 631–638.

Cracco, R.Q., Cracco, J.B., Maccabee, P.J., & Amassian, V.E. (1999). Cerebral function revealed by transcranial magnetic stimulation. *Journal of Neuroscience Methods*, *86*, 209–219.

Craik, F.I.M. (1973). A "levels of analysis" view of memory. In P. Pliner, L. Krames, & T.M. Alloway (Eds.), *Communication and affect: Language and thought*. London: Academic Press.

Craik, F.I.M. (2002). Levels of processing: Past, present . . . and future? *Memory*, *10*, 305–318.

Craik, F.I.M, & Lockhart, R.S. (1972). Levels of processing: A framework for memory research. *Journal of Verbal Learning and Verbal Behavior*, *11*, 671–684.

Craik, F.I.M., & Tulving, E. (1975). Depth of processing and the retention of words in episodic memory. *Journal of Experimental Psychology: General*, *104*, 268–294.

Creem, S.H., & Proffitt, D.R. (2001a). Defining the cortical visual systems: "What", "Where", and "How". *Acta Psychologica*, *107*, 43–68.

Creem, S.H., & Proffitt, D.R. (2001b). Grasping objects by their handles: A necessary interaction between cognition and action. *Journal of Experimental Psychology: Human Perception and Performance*, *27*, 218–228.

Crick, F., & Koch, S. (1990). Some reflections on visual awareness. *Cold Spring Harbor Symposia on Quantitative Biology*, *55*, 953–962.

Crystal, D. (1997). *A dictionary of linguistics and phonetics* (4th Ed.). Cambridge, MA: Blackwell.

Curran, T., & Schacter, D.L. (1997). Implicit memory: What must theories of memory explain? *Memory*, *5*, 37–47.

Cutler, A., & Butterfield, S. (1992). Rhythmic cues to speech segmentation: Evidence from juncture misperception. *Journal of Memory and Language*, *31*, 218–236.

Cutler, A., & Clifton, C. (1999). Comprehending spoken language: A blueprint of the listener. In C.M. Brown & P. Hagoort (Eds.), *The neurocognition of language*. Oxford: Oxford University Press.

Cutler, A., Mehler, J., Norris, D., & Segui, J. (1987). Phoneme identification and the lexicon. *Cognitive Psychology*, *19*, 141–177.

Cutting, J.E. (1978). Generation of synthetic male and female walkers through manipulation of a biomechanical invariant. *Perception*, *7*, 393–405.

Cutting, J.E., & Kozlowski, L.T. (1977). Recognising friends by their walk: Gait perception without familiarity cues. *Bulletin of the Psychonomic Society*, *9*, 353–356.

Cutting, J.E., Proffitt, D.R., & Kozlowski, L.T. (1978). A biomechanical invariant for gait perception. *Journal of Experimental Psychology: Human Perception & Performance*, *4*, 357–372.

Cutting, J.E., & Readinger, W.O. (2002). Perceiving motion while moving: How pairwise nominal invariants make optical flow cohere. *Journal of Experimental Psychology: Human Perception and Performance*, *28*, 731–747.

Cutting, J.E., Wang, R.F., Fluckiger, M., & Baumberger, B. (1999). Human heading judgments and object-based motion information. *Vision Research*, *39*, 1079–1105.

Dagher, A., Owen, A.M., Boecker, H., & Brooks, D.J. (1999). Mapping the network for planning: A correlational PET activation study with the Tower of London task. *Brain*, *122*, 1973–1987.

Dahan, D., Magnuson, J.S., & Tanenhaus, M.K. (2001). Time course of frequency effects in spoken-word recognition: Evidence from eye movements. *Cognitive Psychology*, *42*, 317–367.

Damasio, H., Grabowski, T.J., Tranel, D., Hichwa, R.D., & Damasio, A.R. (1996). A semantic subsystem of visual attributes. *Neurocase*, *4*, 499–505.

Daneman, M., & Carpenter, P.A. (1980). Individual differences in working memory and reading. *Journal of Verbal Learning and Verbal Behavior*, *19*, 450–466.

Daneman, M., & Merikle, P.M. (1996). Working memory and language comprehension: A meta-analysis. *Psychonomic Bulletin & Review*, *3*, 422–433.

Dartnall, H.J.A., Bowmaker, J.K., & Mollon, J.D. (1983). Human visual pigments: Microspectrophotometric results from the eyes of seven persons. *Proceedings of the Royal Society of London Series B*, *220*, 115–130.

Davidson, D. (1994). Recognition and recall of irrelevant and interruptive atypical actions in script-based stories. *Journal of Memory & Language*, *33*, 757–775.

Davidson, J.E., & Sternberg, R.J. (1984). The role of insight in intellectual giftedness. *Gifted Child Quarterly*, *28*, 58–64.

Davis, M.H., Marslen-Wilson, W.D., & Gaskell, M.G. (2002). Leading up the lexical garden path: Segmentation and ambiguity in spoken word recognition. *Journal of Experimental Psychology: Perception and Performance*, *28*, 218–244.

Dawes, R.M. (1988). *Rational choice in an uncertain world.* San Diego, CA: Harcourt Brace Jovanovich.

DeAngelis, G.C., Cumming, B.G., & Newsome, W.T. (1998). A new role for cortical area MT: The perception of stereoscopic depth. *Nature, 394*, 677–680.

De Bleser, R. (1988). Localisation of aphasia: Science or fiction? In G. Denese, C. Semenza, & P. Bisiacchi (Eds.), *Perspectives on cognitive neuropsychology.* Hove, UK: Psychology Press.

Debner, J.A., & Jacoby, L.L. (1994). Unconscious perception: Attention, awareness and control. *Journal of Experimental Psychology: Learning, Memory, and Cognition, 20*, 304–317.

De Corte, E. (2003). Transfer as the productive use of acquired knowledge, skills, and motivations. *Current Directions in Psychological Science, 12*, 142–146.

DeGroot, A.D. (1965). *Thought and choice in chess.* The Hague: Mouton.

De Haan, E.H.F., Young, A.W., & Newcombe, F. (1991). A dissociation between the sense of familiarity and access to semantic information concerning familiar people. *European Journal of Cognitive Psychology, 3*, 51–67.

Dehaene, S., & Naccache, L. (2001). Towards a cognitive neuroscience of consciousness: Basic evidence and a workspace framework. *Cognition, 79*, 1–37.

Dehaene, S., Naccache, L., Cohen, L., Le Bihan, D., Mangin, J., Poline, J. et al. (2001). Cerebral mechanisms of word masking and unconscious repetition priming. *Nature Neuroscience, 4*, 752–758.

Dehaene, S., Naccache, L., Le Cle, H.G., Koechlin, E., Mueller, M., Dehaene-Lambertz, G. et al. (1998). Imaging unconscious semantic priming. *Nature, 395*, 597–600.

Deibert, E., Kraut, M., Kremen, S., & Hart, J. Jr. (1999). Neural pathways in tactile object recognition. *Neurology, 52*, 1413.

Delk, J.L., & Fillenbaum, S. (1965). Differences in perceived colour as a function of characteristic colour. *American Journal of Psychology, 78*, 290–293.

Dell, G.S. (1986). A spreading-activation theory of retrieval in sentence production. *Psychological Review, 93*, 283–321.

Dell, G.S., Burger, L.K., & Svec, W.R. (1997a). Language production and serial order: A functional analysis and a model. *Psychological Review, 104*, 123–147.

Dell, G.S., & O'Seaghdha, P.G. (1991). Mediated and convergent lexical priming in language production: A comment on Levelt et al. (1991). *Psychological Review, 98*, 604–614.

Dell, G.S., & Repka, R.J. (1992). Errors in inner speech. In B.J. Baars (Ed.), *Experimental slips and human error: Exploring the architecture of volition.* New York: Plenum Press.

Dell, G.S., Schwartz, M.F., Martin, N., Saffran, E.M., & Gagnon, D.A. (1997b). Lexical access in aphasic and nonaphasic speakers. *Psychological Review, 104*, 801–838.

Dennett, D. (2001). Are we explaining consciousness yet? *Cognition, 79*, 221–237.

Desmurget, M., Gréa, H., Grethe, J.S., Prablanc, C., Alexander, G.E., & Grafton, S.T. (1999). Functional anatomy of nonvisual feedback loops during reaching: A positron emission tomography study. *Journal of Neuroscience, 21*, 2919–2928.

D'Esposito, M. (2003). *Neurological foundations of cognitive neuroscience.* Cambridge, MA: MIT Press.

D'Esposito, M., Detre, J.A., Alsop, D.C., Shin, R.K., Atlas, S., & Grossman, M. (1995). The neural basis of the central executive of working memory. *Nature, 378*, 279–281.

Detterman, D.K., Gabrieli, T., & Ruthsatz, J.M. (1998). Absurd environmentalism. *Behavioural and Brain Sciences, 21*, 411–412.

Deutsch, J.A., & Deutsch, D. (1963). Attention: Some theoretical considerations. *Psychological Review, 93*, 283–321.

Deutsch, J.A., & Deutsch, D. (1967). Comments on "Selective attention: Perception or response?" *Quarterly Journal of Experimental Psychology, 19*, 362–363.

DeValois, R.L., & DeValois, K.K. (1975). Neural coding of colour. In E.C. Carterette & M.P. Friedman (Eds.), *Handbook of perception, Vol. 5.* New York: Academic Press.

Devlin, J.T., Russell, R.P., Davis, M.H., Price, C.J., Moss, H.E., Fadili, M.J. et al. (2002). Is there an anatomical basis for category-specificity? Semantic memory studies in PET and fMRI. *Neuropsychologia, 40*, 54–75.

Dick, F., Bates, E., Wulfeck, B., Utman, J.A., Dronkers, N., & Gernsbacher, M.A. (2001). Language deficits, localisation, and grammar: Evidence for a distributive model of language breakdown in aphasic patients and neurologically intact individuals. *Psychological Review, 108*, 759–788.

Diehl, R.L., Lotto, A.J., & Holt, L.L. (2004). Speech perception. *Annual Review of Psychology, 55*, 149–179.

Dijkerman, H.C., Milner, A.D., & Carey, D.F. (1998). Grasping spatial relationships: Failure to demonstrate allocentric visual coding in a patient with visual form agnosia. *Consciousness and Cognition, 7*, 424–437.

Dodson, C., & Reisberg, D. (1991). Indirect testing of eyewitness memory: The (non) effect of misinformation. *Bulletin of the Psychonomic Society, 29*, 333–336.

Dosher, B.A., & Corbett, A.T. (1982). Instrument inferences and verb schemata. *Memory & Cognition, 10*, 531–539.

Driver, J. (1996). Enhancement of selective listening by illusory mislocation of speech sounds due to lipreading. *Nature*, *381*, 66–68.

Driver, J. (1998). The neuropsychology of spatial attention. In H. Pashler (Ed.), *Attention*. Hove, UK: Psychology Press.

Driver, J. (2001). A selective review of selective attention research from the past century. *British Journal of Psychology*, *92*, 53–78.

Driver, J., & Spence, C. (1998a). Crossmodal links in spatial attention. *Proceedings of the Royal Society London Series B*, *353*, 1–13.

Driver, J., & Spence, C. (1998b). Attention and the crossmodal construction of space. *Trends in Cognitive Sciences*, *2*, 254–262.

Driver, J., & Vuilleumier, P. (2001). Perceptual awareness and its loss in unilateral neglect and extinction. *Cognition*, *79*, 39–88.

Dudai, Y. (2004). The neurobiology of consolidations, or how stable is the engram? *Annual Review of Psychology*, *55*, 51–86.

Duff, S.C., & Logie, R.H. (2001). Processing and storage in working memory span. *Quarterly Journal of Experimental Psychology*, *54*A, 31–48.

Dumay, N., Frauenfelder, U.H., & Content, A. (2002). The role of the syllable in lexical segmentation in French: Word-spotting data. *Brain and Language*, *81*, 144–161.

Dunbar, K. (1993). Concept discovery in a scientific domain, *Cognitive Science, 17*, 397–434.

Duncan, J. (1979). Divided attention: The whole is more than the sum of its parts. *Journal of Experimental Psychology: Human Perception*, *5*, 216–228.

Duncan, J. (1980). The locus of interference in the perception of simultaneous stimuli. *Psychological Review*, *87*, 272–300.

Duncan, J. (1984). Selective attention and the organisation of visual information. *Journal of Experimental Psychology: General*, *113*, 501–517.

Duncan, J., Bundesen, C., Olson, A., Humphreys, G., Chavda, S., & Shibuya, H. (1999). Systematic analysis of deficits in visual attention. *Journal of Experimental Psychology: General*, *128*, 450–478.

Duncan, J., & Humphreys, G.W. (1989). A resemblance theory of visual search. *Psychological Review*, *96*, 433–458.

Duncan, J., & Humphreys, G.W. (1992). Beyond the search surface: Visual search and attentional engagement. *Journal of Experimental Psychology: Human Perception & Performance*, *18*, 578–588.

Duncan, J., & Owen, A.M. (2000). Consistent response of the human frontal lobe to diverse cognitive demands. *Trends in Neurosciences*, 23, 475–483.

Duncan, J., Seitz, R.J., Kolodny, J., Bor, D., Herzog, H., Ahmed, A. et al. (2000). A neural basis for general intelligence. *Science*, *289*, 457–460.

Duncker, K. (1945). On problem solving. *Psychological Monographs*, *58* (Whole No. 270).

Dunning, D., & Perretta, S. (2002). Automaticity and eyewitness accuracy: A 10-to-12-second rule for distinguishing accurate from inaccurate positive identifications. *Journal of Applied Psychology*, *87*(5), 951–962.

Eakin, D.K., Schreiber, T.A., & Sergent-Marshall, S. (2003). Misinformation effects in eyewitness memory: The presence and absence of memory impairment as a function of warning and misinformation accessibility. *Journal of Experimental Psychology: Learning, Memory, and Cognition*, *29*, 813–825.

Ebbinghaus, H. (1885/1913). *Uber das Gedächtnis* (Leipzig: Dunker) [translated by H. Ruyer & C.E. Bussenius]. New York: Teacher College, Columbus University.

Eckstein, M.P., Thomas, J.P., Palmer, J., & Shimozaki, S.S. (2000). A signal detection model predicts the effects of set size on visual search accuracy for feature, conjunction, triple conjunction, and disjunction displays. *Perception and Psychophysics*, *62*, 425–451.

Egly, R., Driver, J., & Rafal, R.D. (1994). Shifting visual attention between objects and locations: Evidence from normal and parietal lesion subjects. *Journal of Experimental Psychology: General*, *123*, 161–177.

Eimer, M., & Schröger, E. (1998). ERP effects of intermodal attention and crossmodal links in spatial attention. *Psychophysiology*, *35*, 317–328.

Eimer, M., van Velzen, J., Forster, B., & Driver, J. (2003). Shifts of attention in light and in darkness: An ERP study of supramodal attentional control and crossmodal links in spatial attention. *Cognitive Brain Research*, *15*, 308–323.

Ekstrand, B.R. (1972). To sleep, perchance to dream: About why we forget. In C.P. Duncan, L. Sechrest, & A.W. Melton (Eds.), *Human memory: Festschrift in honor of Benton J. Underwood*. New York: Appleton-Century-Crofts.

Ellis, A.W. (1984). *Reading, writing and dyslexia: A cognitive analysis*. London: Lawrence Erlbaum Associates Ltd.

Ellis, A.W. (1993). *Reading, writing and dyslexia* (2nd Ed.). Hove, UK: Psychology Press.

Ellis, A.W., Miller, D., & Sin, G. (1983). Wernicke's aphasia and normal language processing: A case study in cognitive neuropsychology. *Cognition*, *15*, 111–144.

Ellis, A.W., & Young, A.W. (1988). *Human cognitive neuropsychology*. Hove, UK: Psychology Press.

Ellis, H.D., Lewis, M.B., Moselhy, H.F., & Young, A.W. (2000). Automatic without autonomic responses to familiar faces: Capgras delusion differentiates components of face recognition. *Cognitive Neuropsychiatry*, *5*, 255–269.

Ellis, J., & Kvavilashvili, L. (2000). Prospective memory in 2000: Past, present, and future directions. *Applied Cognitive Psychology*, 14, S1–S9.

Ellis, N., & Beaton, A. (1993). Factors affecting the learning of foreign language vocabulary: Imagery keyword mediators and phonological short-term memory. *Quarterly Journal of Experimental Psychology*, *46*A, 522–558.

Ellis, R., & Humphreys, G. (1999). *Connectionist psychology: A text with readings*. Hove, UK: Psychology Press.

Enns, J.T., & Rensick, R.A. (1990). Sensitivity to three-dimensional orientation from line drawings. *Psychological Review*, *98*, 335–351.

Erickson, T.A., & Mattson, M.E. (1981). From words to meaning: A semantic illusion. *Journal of Verbal Learning and Verbal Behavior*, *20*, 540–552.

Ericsson, K.A. (1988). Analysis of memory performance in terms of memory skill. In R.J. Sternberg (Ed.), *Advances in the psychology of human intelligence, Vol. 4*. Hillsdale, NJ: Lawrence Erlbaum Associates Inc.

Ericsson, K.A., & Chase, W.G. (1982). Exceptional memory. *American Scientist*, *70*, 607–615.

Ericsson, K.A., & Delaney, P.F. (1998). Working memory and expert performance. In R.H. Logie & K.J. Gilhooly (Eds.), *Working memory and thinking*. Hove, UK: Psychology Press.

Ericsson, K.A., & Kintsch, W. (1995). Long-term working memory. *Psychological Review*, *102*, 211–245.

Ericsson, K.A., Krampe, R.T., & Tesch-Römer, C. (1993). The role of deliberate practice in the acquisition of expert performance. *Psychological Review*, *100*, 363–406.

Ericsson, K.A., & Lehmann, A.C. (1996). Expert and exceptional performance: Evidence on maximal adaptations on task constraints. *Annual Review of Psychology*, *47*, 273–305.

Ericsson, K.A., & Polson, P.G. (1988). Experimental analysis of the mechanisms of a memory skill. *Journal of Experimental Psychology: Learning, Memory, and Cognition*, *14*, 305–316.

Eriksen, C.W., & St. James, J.D. (1986). Visual attention within and around the field of focal attention: A zoom lens model. *Perception & Psychophysics*, *40*, 225–240.

Evans, J.St.B.T. (1983). Linguistic determinants of bias in conditional reasoning. *Quarterly Journal of Experimental Psychology*, *35*A, 635–644.

Evans, J.St.B.T. (1993a). Bias and rationality. In K.I. Manktelow & D.E. Over (Eds.), *Rationality: Psychological and philosophical perspectives*. London: Routledge.

Evans, J.St.B.T. (1993b). The mental model theory of conditional reasoning: Critical appraisal and revision. *Cognition*, *48*, 1–20.

Evans, J.St.B.T. (2000). What could and could not be a strategy in reasoning. In W. Schaeken, G. de Vooght, A. Vandierendonck, & G. d'Ydewalle (Eds.), *Deductive reasoning and strategies*. Hove, UK: Laurence Erlbaum Associates Ltd.

Evans, J.St.B.T. (2002). Logic and human reasoning: An assessment of the deduction paradigm. *Psychological Bulletin*, *128*, 978–996.

Evans, J.St.B.T. (2003). In two minds: Dual-process accounts of reasoning. *Trends in Cognitive Sciences*, *7*, 454–459.

Evans, J.St.B.T., Barston, J.L. & Pollard, P. (1983). On the conflict between logic and belief in syllogistic reasoning. *Memory & Cognition*, *11*, 295–306.

Evans, J.St.B.T., Newstead, S.E., & Byrne, R.M.J. (1993). *Human reasoning: The psychology of deduction*. Hove, UK: Psychology Press.

Evans, J.St.B.T., & Over, D.E. (1996). Rationality in the selection tesk: Epistemic utility versus uncertainty reduction. *Psychological Review*, *103*, 356–363.

Evans, J.St.B.T., & Over, D.E. (1997). Rationality in reasoning: The problem of deductive competence. *Current Psychology of Cognition*, *16*, 3–38.

Eysenck, M.W. (1978). Verbal remembering. In B.M. Foss (Ed.), *Psychology survey, No. 1*. London: Allen & Unwin.

Eysenck, M.W. (1979). Depth, elaboration, and distinctiveness. In L.S. Cermak & F.I.M. Craik (Eds.), *Levels of processing in human memory*. Hillsdale, NJ: Lawrence Erlbaum Associates Inc.

Eysenck, M.W. (1982). *Attention and arousal: Cognition and performance*. Berlin: Springer.

Eysenck, M.W., & Eysenck, M.C. (1980). Effects of processing depth, distinctiveness, and word frequency on retention. *British Journal of Psychology*, *71*, 263–274.

Faigley, L., & Witte, S. (1983). Analysing revision. *College Composition and Communication*, *32*, 400–414.

Farah, M.J. (1990). *Visual agnosia: Disorders of object recognition and what they tell us about normal vision*. Cambridge, MA: MIT Press.

Farah, M.J. (1994a). Specialisation within visual object recognition: Clues from prosopagnosia and alexia. In M.J. Farah & G. Ratcliff (Eds.), *The neuropsychology of high-level vision: Collected tutorial essays*. Hillsdale, NJ: Lawrence Erlbaum Associates Inc.

Farah, M.J. (1994b). Neuropsychological inference with an interactive brain: A critique of the "locality" assumption. *Behavioral and Brain Sciences*, *17*, 43–104.

Farah, M.J. (1999). Relations among the agnosias. In G.W. Humphreys (Ed.), *Case studies in the neuropsychology of vision*. Hove, UK: Psychology Press.

Farah, M.J. (2001). Consciousness. In B. Rapp (Ed.), *The handbook of cognitive neuropsychology*. Hove, UK: Psychology Press.

Farah, M.J., & Aguirre, G.K. (1999). Imaging visual recognition: PET and fMRI studies of the functional anatomy of human visual recognition. *Trends in Cognitive Sciences*, *3*, 179–186.

Farah, M.J., Hammond, K.M., Levine, D.N., & Calvanio, R. (1988). Visual and spatial mental imagery: Dissociable systems of representation. *Cognitive Psychology*, *20*, 439–462.

Farah, M.J., & McClelland, J.L. (1991). A computational model of semantic memory impairment: Modality-specificity and emergent category-specificity. *Journal of Experimental Psychology: General*, *120*, 339–357.

Farah, M.J., O'Reilly, R.C., & Vecera, S.P. (1993). Dissociated overt and covert recognition as an emergent property of a lesioned neural network. *Psychological Review*, *100*, 571–588.

Farah, M.J., & Wallace, M.A. (1992). Semantically-bounded anomia: Implications for the neural implementation of naming. *Neuropsychologia*, *30*, 609–621.

Farah, M.J., Wilson, K.D., Drain, M., & Tanaka, J.N. (1998). What is "special" about face perception? *Psychological Review*, *105*, 482–498.

Feldman, J. (2003). The simplicity principle in human concept learning. *Current Directions in Psychological Science*, *12*, 227–232.

Fernandez-Duque, D., & Thornton, I.M. (2000). Change detection without awareness: Do explicit reports underestimate the representation of change in the visual system? *Visual Cognition*, *7*, 323–344.

Ferrand, L., & Grainger, J. (1993). The time course of orthographic and phonological code activation in the early phases of visual word recognition. *Bulletin of the Psychonomic Society*, *31*, 119–122.

Ferreira, F. (2003). The misinterpretation of noncanonical sentences. *Cognitive Psychology*, *47*, 164–203.

Ferreira, F., Bailey, K.G.D., & Ferraro, V. (2002). Good-enough representations in language comprehension. *Current Directions in Psychological Science*, *11*, 11–15.

Ferreira, F., & Clifton, C. (1986). The independence of syntactic processing. *Journal of Memory and Language*, *25*, 348–368.

Ferreira, F., & Swets, B. (2002). How incremental is language production? Evidence from the production of utterances requiring the computation of arithmetic sums. *Journal of Memory and Language*, *46*, 57–84.

Fery, P., & Morais, J. (2003). A case study of visual agnosia without perceptual processing or structural descriptions' impairment. *Cognitive Neuropsychology*, *20*, 595–618.

ffytche, M.J., Howard, R.J., Brammer, M.J., David, A., Woodruff, P., & Williams, S. (1998). The anatomy of conscious vision: An fMRI study of visual hallucinations. *Nature Neuroscience*, *1*, 738–742.

Fiddick, L. (2003). Is there a faculty of deontic reasoning? A critical re-evaluation of abstract deontic versions of the Wason selection task. In D.E. Over (Ed.), *Evolution and the psychology of thinking: The debate*. Hove, UK: Psychology Press.

Fiebach, C.J., Friederici, A.D., Müller, K., & von Cramon, D.Y. (2002). fMRI evidence for dual routes to the mental lexicon in visual word recognition. *Journal of Cognitive Neuroscience*, *14*, 11–23.

Fiedler, K. (1988). The dependence of the conjunction fallacy on subtle linguistic factors. *Psychological Research*, *50*, 123–129.

Fiedler, K. (2000). Beware of samples! A cognitive-ecological sampling approach to judgment biases. *Psychological Review*, *107*, 659–676.

Fiedler, K., Brinkmann, B., Betsch, T., & Wild, B. (2000). A sampling approach to biases in conditional probability judgements: Beyond base-rate neglect and statistical format. *Journal of Experimental Psychology: General*, *129*, 1–20.

Finke, R.A. (1980). Levels of equivalence in imagery and perception. *Psychological Review*, *87*, 113–132.

Finke, R.A. (1990). *Creative imagery: Discoveries and inventions in visualization*. Hillsdale, NJ: Lawrence Erlbaum Associates Inc.

Finke, R.A., & Kosslyn, S.M. (1980). Mental imagery acuity in the peripheral visual field. *Journal of Experimental Psychology: Human Perception and Performance*, *6*, 126–139.

Finke, R.A., Ward, T.B., & Smith, S.M. (1992). *Creative cognition: Theory, research and applications*. Cambridge, MA: MIT Press.

Finkenauer, C., Luminet, O., Gisle, L., El-Ahmadi, A., & van der Linden, M. (1998). Flashbulb memories and the underlying mechanisms of their formation: Toward an emotional-integrative model. *Memory & Cognition*, *26*, 516–531.

Fisher, R.P. (1999). Probing knowledge structures. In D. Gopher & A. Koriat (Eds.), *Attention and performance XVII: Cognitive regulation of performance: Interaction of theory and application*. Cambridge, MA: MIT Press.

Fisher, R.P., Geiselman, R.E., & Amador, M. (1990). A field test of the cognitive interview: Enhancing the recollections of actual victims and witnesses of crime. *Journal of Applied Psychology*, *74*, 722–727.

Fisher, R.P., Geiselman, R.E., Raymond, D.S., Jurkevich, L.M., & Warhaftig, M.L. (1987). Enhancing enhanced eyewitness memory: Refining the cognitive interview. *Journal of Police Science and Administration*, *15*, 291–297.

Fitts, P.M., & Posner, M.I. (1967). *Human performance*. London: Prentice Hall.

Fitzgerald, J.M. (1988). Vivid memories and the remiscence phenomenon: The role of a self narrative. *Human Development*, *31*, 261–273.

Fitzpatrick, S.M., & Rothman, D.L. (2002). Meeting report: Choosing the right MR tools for the job. *Cognitive Neuroscience*, *14*, 806–815.

Fivush, R., Haden, C.A., & Reese, E. (1996). Remembering, recounting, and reminiscing: The development of autobiographical memory in social context.

In D.C. Rubin (Ed.), *Remembering our past: Studies in autobiographical memory.* Dordrecht, the Netherlands: Kluwer Academic.

Fleishman, E.A., & Parker, J.F. (1962). Factors in the retention of perceptual-motor skill. *Journal of Experimental Psychology, 64,* 215–226.

Flowerdew, J., & Tauroza, S. (1995). The effect of discourse markers on second language lecture comprehension. *Studies in Second Language Acquisition, 17,* 455–458.

Flude, B.M., Ellis, A.W., & Kay, J. (1989). Face processing and name retrieval in an anomic aphasia: Names are stored separately from semantic information about people. *Brain & Cognition, 11,* 60–72.

Fodor, J.A. (1983). *The modularity of mind.* Cambridge, MA: MIT Press.

Fodor, J. (2000). *The mind doesn't work that way: The scope and limits of computational psychology.* Cambridge, MA: MIT Press.

Fodor, J.A., & Pylyshyn, Z.W. (1981). How direct is visual perception? Some reflections on Gibson's "ecological approach". *Cognition, 9,* 139–196.

Folk, C.L., Remington, R.W., & Johnston, J.C. (1992). Involuntary covert orienting is contingent on attentional control settings. *Journal of Experimental Psychology: Human Perception and Performance, 18,* 1030–1044.

Folk, J.R. (1999). Phonological codes are used to access the lexicon during silent reading. *Journal of Experimental Psychology: Learning, Memory, and Cognition, 25,* 892–906.

Ford, M. (1995). Two modes of mental representation and problem solution in syllogistic reasoning. *Cognition, 54,* 1–71.

Forster, K. (1979). Levels of processing and the structure of the language processor. In W.E. Cooper & E.C.T. Walker (Eds.), *Sentence processing: Psycholinguistic studies presented to Merrill Garrett.* Hillsdale, NJ: Lawrence Erlbaum Associates Inc.

Fox, C.R., Rogers, B.A., & Tversky, A. (1996). Options traders exhibit subadditive decision weights. *Journal of Risk and Uncertainty, 13,* 5–19.

Fox, P.T., Parsons, L.M., & Lancaster, J.L. (1998). Beyond the single study: Function/location meta-analysis in cognitive neuroimaging. *Current Opinion in Neurobiology, 8,* 178–187.

Fox, R., & McDaniel, C. (1982). The perception of biological motion by human infants. *Science, 218,* 486–487.

Fox Tree, J.E. (2000). Co-ordinating spontaneous talk. In L. Wheeldon (Ed.), *Aspects of language production.* Hove, UK: Psychology Press.

Franklin, S., Turner, J., Ralph, M.A.L., Morris, J., & Bailey, P.J. (1996). A distinctive case of word meaning deafness? *Cognitive Neuropsychology, 13,* 1139–1162.

Frauenfelder, U.H., & Peeters, G. (1998). Simulating the time-course of spoken word recognition: An analysis of lexical competition in TRACE. In J. Grainger & A.M. Jacobs (Eds.), *Localist connectionist approaches to human cognition.* Hillsdale, NJ: Lawrence Erlbaum Associates Inc.

Frauenfelder, U.H., Scholten, M., & Content, A. (2001). Bottom-up inhibition in lexical selection: Phonological mismatch effects in spoken word recognition. *Language and Cognitive Processes, 16,* 583–607.

Frauenfelder, U.H., Segui, J., & Dijkstra, T. (1990). Lexical effects in phonemic processing: Facilitatory or inhibitory? *Journal of Experimental Psychology: Human Perception & Performance, 16,* 77–91.

Frazier, L., & Rayner, K. (1982). Making and correcting errors in the analysis of structurally ambiguous sentences. *Cognitive Psychology, 14,* 178–210.

Freeman, T.C.A., & Banks, M.S. (1998). Perceived head-centric speed is affected by both extra-retinal and retinal errors. *Vision Research, 38,* 941–945.

French, R.M., & Cleermans, A. (2002). *Implicit learning and consciousness: An empirical, philosophical and comutational consensus in the making.* Hove, UK: Psychology Press.

Freud, S. (1901). *The psychopathology of everyday life.* New York: W.W. Norton.

Freud, S. (1915). Repression. In *Freud's collected papers, Vol. IV.* London: Hogarth.

Freud, S. (1943). *A general introduction to psychoanalysis.* New York: Garden City.

Friedman-Hill, S.R., Robertson, L.C., & Treisman, A. (1995). Parietal contributions to visual feature binding: Evidence from a patient with bilateral lesions. *Science, 269,* 853–855.

Frisby, J.P. (1986). The computational approach to vision. In I. Roth & J.P. Frisby (Eds.), *Perception and representation: A cognitive approach.* Milton Keynes, UK: Open University Press.

Frisch, D., & Jones, S.K. (1993). Assessing the accuracy of decisions. *Theory and Psychology, 3,* 115–135.

Friston, K.J., Frith, C.D., Passingham, R.E., Liddle, P.F., & Frackowiak, R.S.J. (1996). Motor practice and neurophysiological adaptation in the cerebellum: A positron tomography study. *Proceedings of the Royal Society of London, Series B Biological Sciences, 248,* 223–228.

Friston, K.J., & Price, C.J. (2003). Degeneracy and redundancy in cognitive anatomy. *Trends in Cognitive Science, 7,* 151–152.

Frith, C.D., Perry, R., & Lumer, E. (1999). The neural correlates of conscious experience: An experimental framework. *Trends in Cognitive Sciences, 3,* 105–114.

Fromkin, V.A. (1993). Speech production. In J.B. Gleason & N.B. Ratner (Eds.), *Psycholinguistics.* Orlando, FL: Harcourt Brace.

Frost, R. (1998). Toward a strong phonological theory of visual word recognition: True issues and false trails. *Psychological Bulletin, 123,* 71–99.

Fuller, J.M. (2003). The influence of speaker roles on discourse marker use. *Journal of Pragmatics*, *35*, 23–45.

Funnell, E. (1983). Phonological processes in reading: New evidence from acquired dyslexia. *British Journal of Psychology*, *74*, 159–180.

Gabrieli, J., Fleischman, D., Keane, M., Reminger, S., & Morell, F. (1995). Double dissociation between memory systems underlying explicit and implicit memory in the human brain. *Psychological Science*, *6*, 76–82.

Gabrieli, J.D., Stebbins, G.T., Singh, J., Willingham, D.B., & Goetz, C.G. (1997). Intact mirror-tracing and impaired rotary pursuit skill learning in patients with Huntington's disease: Evidence for dissociable memory systems in skill learning. *Neuropsychology*, *2*, 272–281.

Gabrieli, J.D.E. (1998). Cognitive neuroscience of human memory. *Annual Review of Psychology*, *49*, 87–115.

Gabrieli, J.D.E., Cohen, N.J., & Corkin, S. (1988). The impaired learning of semantic knowledge following bilateral medial temporal-lobe resection. *Brain*, *7*, 157–177.

Gabrieli, J.D.E., Desmond, J.E., Demb, J.B., Wagner, A.D., Stone, M.V., Vaidya, C.J. et al. (1996). Functional magnetic resonance imaging of semantic memory processes in the frontal lobes. *Psychological Science*, *7*, 278–283.

Gaffan, D., & Heywood, C.A. (1993). A spurious category-specific visual agnosia for living things in normal human and nonhuman primates. *Journal of Cognitive Neuroscience*, *5*, 118–128.

Gagnon, D.A., Schwartz, M.F., Martin, N., Dell, G.S., & Saffran, E.M. (1997). The origins of formal paraphasias in aphasics' picture naming. *Brain and Language*, *59*, 450–472.

Galton, F. (1883). *Inquiries into the human faculty and its development.* London: Macmillan.

Ganis, G., & Kutas, M. (2003). An electrophysiological study of scene effects on object identification. *Cognitive Brain Research*, *16*, 123–144.

Ganong, W.F. (1980). Phonetic categorisation in auditory word perception. *Journal of Experimental Psychology: Human Perception and Performance*, *6*, 110–125.

Garavan, H., Doherty, M.E., & Mynatt, C.R. (1997). When falsification fails. *Irish Journal of Psychology*, *18*, 267–292.

Gardner, H. (1985). *The mind's new science*. New York: Basic Books.

Garnham, A. (2004). Language comprehension. In K. Lamberts & R. Goldstone (Eds.), *Handbook of cognition.* London: Sage.

Garnsey, S.M., Pearlmutter, N.J., Myers, E., & Lotocky, M.A. (1997). The contributions of verb bias and plausibility to the comprehension of temporarily ambiguous sentences. *Journal of Memory and Language*, *37*, 58–93.

Garrett, M.F. (1975). The analysis of sentence production. In G.H. Bower (Ed.), *The psychology of learning and motivation, Vol. 9.* San Diego, CA: Academic Press.

Garrett, M.F. (1976). Syntactic processes in sentence production. In R.J. Wales & E. Walker (Eds.), *New approaches to language mechanisms.* Amsterdam: North-Holland.

Garrett, M.F. (1980). Levels of processing in sentence production. In B. Butterworth (Ed.), *Language production: Vol. 1. Speech and talk.* San Diego, CA: Academic Press.

Garrod, S., & Terras, M. (2000). The contribution of lexical and situational knowledge to resolving discourse roles: Bonding and resolution. *Journal of Memory and Language*, *42*, 526–544.

Garson, J. (2002). Connectionism. In E.N. Zalta (Ed.), *The Stanford encyclopaedia of philosophy (winter 2002 edition)* http://plato.stanford.edu/archives/win2002/entries/connectionism

Gauld, A., & Stephenson, G.M. (1967). Some experiments relating to Bartlett's theory of remembering. *British Journal of Psychology*, *58*, 39–50.

Gauthier, I., Behrmann, M., & Tarr, M.J. (1999). Can face recognition really be dissociated from object recognition? *Journal of Cognitive Neuroscience*, *11*, 349–370.

Gauthier, I., Skudlarski, P., Gore, J.C., & Anderson, A.W. (2000). Expertise for cars and birds recruits brain areas involved in face recognition. *Nature Neuroscience*, *3*, 191–197.

Gauthier, I., & Tarr, M.J. (2002). Unravelling mechanisms for expert object recognition: Bridging brain activity and behaviour. *Journal of Experimental Psychology: Human Perception and Performance*, *28*, 431–446.

Gauthier, I., Tarr, M.J., Anderson, A.W., Skudlarski, P., & Gore, J.C. (1999). Activation of the fusiform "face area" increases with expertise in recognising novel objects. *Nature Neuroscience*, *2*, 568–573.

Gazzaniga, M.S. (1992). *Nature's mind.* London: Basic Books.

Gazzaniga, M.S. (2000). Cerebral specialisation and interhemispheric communication: Does the corpus callosum enable the human condition? *Brain*, *123*, 1293–1328.

Gazzaniga, M.S., Ivry, R.B., & Mangun, G.R. (1998). *Cognitive neuroscience: The biology of the mind.* New York: Norton.

Gazzaniga, M.S., Ivry, R.B., & Mangun, G.R. (2002). *Cognitive neuroscience: The biology of the mind* (2nd Ed.). New York: Norton.

Gazzaniga, M.S., & Ledoux, J.E. (1978). *The integrated mind.* New York: Plenum Press.

Geis, M., & Zwicky, A.M. (1971). On invited inferences. *Linguistic Inquiry*, *2*, 561–566.

Geiselman, R.E., & Fisher, R.P. (1997). Ten years of cognitive interviewing. In D.G. Payne & F.G. Conrad

(Eds.), *Intersections in basic and applied memory research*. Mahwah, NJ: Lawrence Erlbaum Associates Inc.

Geiselman, R.E., Fisher, R.P., MacKinnon, D.P., & Holland, H.L. (1985). Eyewitness memory enhancement in police interview: Cognitive retrieval mnemonics versus hypnosis. *Journal of Applied Psychology*, *70*, 401–412.

Geisler, W.S., Perry, J.S., Super, B.J., & Gallogly, D.P. (2001). Edge co-occurrence in natural images predicts contour grouping performance. *Vision Research*, *41*, 711–724.

Gentner, D. Rattermann, M.J., & Forbus, K.D. (1993). The roles of similarity in transfer: Separating retrievability from inferential soundness. *Cognitive Psychology*, *25*, 524–575.

Georgeson, M.A., & Freeman, T.C.A. (1997). Perceived location of bars and edges in 1-D images: Computational models and human vision. *Vision Research*, *37*, 127–142.

Georgopoulos, A.P. (1997). Voluntary movement: Computational principles and neural mechanisms. In M.D. Rugg (Ed.), *Cognitive neuroscience*. Hove, UK: Psychology Press.

Gernsbacher, M.A., & Kashak, M.P. (2003). Neuroimaging studies of language production and comprehension. *Annual Review of Psychology*, *54*, 91–114.

Gernsbacher, M.A., Varner, K.R., & Faust, M.E. (1990). Investigating differences in general comprehension skill. *Journal of Experimental Psychology: Learning, Memory, and Cognition*, *16*, 430–445.

Gibbs, R.W., Nayak, N.P., & Cutting, C. (1989). How to kick the bucket and not decompose: Analysability and idiom processing. *Journal of Memory and Language*, *28*, 576–593.

Gibson, J.J. (1950). *The perception of the visual world.* Boston: Houghton Mifflin.

Gibson, J.J. (1966). *The senses considered as perceptual systems.* Boston: Houghton Mifflin.

Gibson, J.J. (1979). *The ecological approach to visual perception*. Boston: Houghton Mifflin.

Gick, M.L., & Holyoak, K.J. (1980). Analogical problem solving. *Cognitive Psychology*, *12*, 306–355.

Giersch, A., Humphreys, G., Boucart, M., & Kovacs, I. (2000). The computation of contours in visual agnosia: Evidence for early computation prior to shape binding and figure–ground coding. *Cognitive Neuropsychology*, *17*, 731–759.

Gigerenzer, G. (1993). The bounded rationality of probabilistic mental models. In K.I. Manktelow & D.E. Over (Eds.), *Rationality: Psychological and philosophical perspectives.* London: Routledge.

Gigerenzer, G. (1996). On narrow norms and vague heuristics: A reply to Kahneman and Tversky (1996). *Psychological Review*, *103*, 592–596.

Gigerenzer, G. (2002). *Reckoning with risk*. London: Penguin.

Gigerenzer, G., & Hoffrage, U. (1995). How to improve Bayesian reasoning without instruction: Frequency formats. *Psychological Review*, *102*, 684–704.

Gigerenzer, G., & Hoffrage, U. (1999). Overcoming difficulties in Bayesian reasoning: A reply to Lewis and Keren (1999) and Mellers and McGraw (1999). *Psychological Review*, *106*, 425–430.

Gigerenzer, G., Todd, P.N., & the ABC Research Group (1999). *Simple heuristics that make us smart.* Oxford: Oxford University Press.

Gilhooly, K.J. (1996). *Thinking: Directed, undirected and creative* (3rd Ed.). London: Academic Press.

Gilovich, T., Griffin, D., & Kahneman, D. (2002). *Heuristics and biases: The psychology of intuitive judgement*. Cambridge: Cambridge University Press.

Giora, R. (1997). Understanding figurative and literal language: The graded salience hypothesis. *Cognitive Linguistics*, *7*, 183–206.

Giora, R. (2002). Literal vs. figurative language: Different or equal? *Journal of Pragmatics*, *34*, 487–506.

Giora, R., & Fein, O. (1999). On understanding familiar and less-familiar figurative language. *Journal of Pragmatics*, *31*, 1601–1618.

Girotto, V., & Gonzalez, M. (2001). Solving probabilistic and statistical problems: A matter of information structure and question form. *Cognition*, *78*, 247–276.

Glanzer, M., & Cunitz, A.R. (1966). Two storage mechanisms in free recall. *Journal of Verbal Learning and Verbal Behavior*, *5*, 351–360.

Glaser, W.R. (1992). Picture naming. *Cognition*, *42*, 61–105.

Glenberg, A.M. (1987). Temporal context and recency. In D.S. Gorfein & R.R. Hoffman (Eds.), *Memory and learning: The Ebbinghaus centennial conference.* Hillsdale, NJ: Lawrence Erlbaum Associates Inc.

Glenberg, A.M., Smith, S.M., & Green, C. (1977). Type I rehearsal: Maintenance and more. *Journal of Verbal Learning & Verbal Behavior*, *16*, 339–352.

Glover, S. (2004). Separate visual representations in the planning and control of action. *Behavioral and Brain Sciences*, *27*, 3–78.

Glover, S., & Dixon, P. (2001). Dynamic illusion effects in a reaching task: Evidence for separate visual representations in the planning and control of reaching. *Journal of Experimental Psychology: Human Perception and Performance*, *27*, 560–572.

Glover, S., & Dixon, P. (2002a). Dynamic effects of the Ebbinghaus illusion in grasping: Support for a planning–control model of action. *Perception and Psychophysics*, *64*, 266–278.

Glover, S., & Dixon, P. (2002b). Semantics affect the planning but not control of grasping. *Experimental Brain Research*, *146*, 383–387.

Glucksberg, S. (2003). The psycholinguistics of metaphor. *Trends in Cognitive Sciences*, *7*, 92–96.

Glushko, R.J. (1979). The organisation and activation of orthographic knowledge in reading aloud. *Journal of Experimental Psychology: Human Perception and Performance*, *5*, 674–691.

Gobet, F. (2000). Some shortcomings of long-term working memory. *British Journal of Psychology*, *91*, 551–570.

Gobet, F., & Simon, H.A. (1996a). Templates in chess memory: A mechanism for recalling several boards. *Cognitive Psychology*, *31*, 1–40.

Gobet, F., & Simon, H.A. (1996b). Recall of rapidly presented random chess positions is a function of skill. *Psychonomic Bulletin & Review*, *3*, 159–163.

Gobet, F., & Simon, H.A. (1996c). The roles of recognition processes and look-ahead search in time-constrained expert problem-solving: Evidence from grandmaster level chess. *Psychological Science*, *7*, 52–55.

Gobet, F., & Simon, H.A. (1998). Expert chess memory: Revisiting the chunking hypothesis. *Memory*, *6*, 225–255.

Gobet, F., & Simon, H.A. (2000). Five seconds or sixty? Presentation time in expert memory. *Cognitive Science*, *24*, 651–682.

Gobet, F., & Waters, A.J. (2003). The role of constraints in expert memory. *Journal of Experimental Psychology: Learning, Memory & Cognition*, *29*, 1082–1094.

Godden, D.R., & Baddeley, A.D. (1975). Context-dependent memory in two natural environments: On land and under water. *British Journal of Psychology*, *66*, 325–331.

Godden, D.R., & Baddeley, A.D. (1980). When does context influence recognition memory? *British Journal of Psychology*, *71*, 99–104.

Goel, V., & Dolan, R.J. (2003). Explaining modulation of reasoning by belief. *Cognition*, *87*, B11–22.

Goel, V., & Grafman, J. (1995). Are the frontal lobes implicated in "planning" functions? Interpreting data from the Tower of Hanoi. *Neuropsychologia*, *33*, 623–642.

Goldman-Rakic, P.S. (1988). Topography of cognition: Parallel distributed networks in primate association cortex. *Annual Review of Neuroscience*, *11*, 137–156.

Goldstein, D.G., & Gigerenzer, G. (2002). Models of ecological rationality: The recognition heuristic. *Psychological Review*, *109*, 75–90.

Goldstein, E.B. (1996). *Sensation and perception* (4th Ed.). New York: Brooks/Cole.

Goldstone, R.L., & Rogosky, B.J. (2002). Using relations within conceptual systems to translate across conceptual systems. *Cognition*, *84*, 295–320.

Gomulicki, B.R. (1956). Recall as an abstractive process. *Acta Psychologica*, *12*, 77–94.

Goodale, M.A., & Milner, A.D. (1992). Separate visual pathways for perception and action. *Trends in Neuroscience*, *15*, 22–25.

Gooding, P.A., Mayes, A.R., & van Eijk, R. (2000). A meta-analysis of indirect memory tests for novel material in organic amnesia. *Neuropsychologia*, *38*, 666–676.

Gordon, I.E. (1989). *Theories of visual perception*. Chichester, UK: John Wiley & Sons.

Gorman, M.E. (1992). Experimental simulations of falsification. In M.T. Keane & K.J. Gilhooly (Eds.), *Advances in the psychology of thinking*. London: Harvester Wheatsheaf.

Gorman, M.E. (1995). Hypothesis testing. In S.E. Newstead & J.St.B.T. Evans (Eds.), *Perspectives on thinking and reasoning. Essays in honour of Peter Wason*. Hove, UK: Lawrence Erlbaum Associates Ltd.

Gorman (1996). Psychology of science. In R.F. Kitchener & W. O'Donohue (Eds.), *The philosophy of psychology*. Thousand Oaks, CA: Sage.

Gottfredson L.S. (1997). Why g matters? The complexities of everyday life. *Intelligence*, *24*, 79–132.

Gould, J.D. (1978). An experimental study of writing, dictating, and speaking. In J. Requin (Ed.), *Attention and performance, Vol. VII*. Hillsdale, NJ: Lawrence Erlbaum Associates Inc.

Gould, J.D. (1980). Experiments on composing letters: Some facts, some myths, and some observations. In L.W. Gregg & E.R. Sternberg (Eds.), *Cognitive processes in writing*. Hillsdale, NJ: Lawrence Erlbaum Associates Inc.

Graesser, A.C., Millis, K.K., & Zwaan, R.A. (1997). Discourse comprehension. *Annual Review of Psychology*, *48*, 163–189.

Graesser, A.C., Singer, M., & Trabasso, T. (1994). Constructing inferences during narrative text comprehension. *Psychological Review*, *101*, 371–395.

Graf, P., & Schacter, D.L. (1985). Implicit and explicit memory for new associations in normal and amnesic subjects. *Journal of Experimental Psychology: Learning, Memory, & Cognition*, *11*, 501–518.

Graf, P., Squire, L.R., & Mandler, G. (1984). The information that amnesic patients do not forget. *Journal of Experimental Psychology: Learning, Memory, & Cognition*, *10*, 164–178.

Grafton, S., Hazeltine, E., & Ivry, R. (1995). Functional mapping of sequence learning in normal humans. *Journal of Cognitive Neuroscience*, 7B, 497–510.

Grainger, J., & Segui, J. (1990). Neighbourhood frequency effects in visual word recognition: A comparison of lexical decision and masked identification latencies. *Perception & Psychophysics*, *47*, 191–198.

Gray, J.A., & Wedderburn, A.A. (1960). Grouping strategies with simultaneous stimuli. *Quarterly Journal of Experimental Psychology*, *12*, 180–184.

Gray, R., & Regan, D. (1998). Accuracy of estimating time to collision using binocular and monocular information. *Vision Research*, *38*, 499–512.

Gray, R., & Regan, D. (2000). Estimating the time to collision with a rotating non-spherical object. *Vision Research*, *40*, 49–63.

Grea, H., Pisella, L., Rossetti, Y., Desmurget, M., Tilikete, C., Grafton, S. et al. (2002). A lesion of the posterior parietal cortex disrupts on-line adjustments during aiming movements. *Neuropsychologia*, *40*, 2471–2480.

Green, K.P., Kuhl, P.K., Meltzoff, A.N., & Stevens, E.B. (1991). Integrating speech information across talkers, gender, and sensory modality: Female faces and male voices in the McGurk effect. *Perception & Psychophysics*, *50*, 524–536.

Greeno, J.G. (1974). Hobbits and orcs: Acquisition of a sequential concept. *Cognitive Psychology*, *6*, 270–292.

Gregory, R.L. (1973). The confounded eye. In R.L. Gregory & E.H. Gombrich (Eds.), *Illusion in nature and art.* London: Duckworth.

Grice, H.P. (1967). Logic and conversation. In P. Cole & J.L. Morgan (Eds.), *Studies in syntax, Vol. III.* New York: Seminar Press.

Grice, H.P. (1975). Logic and conversation. In P. Cole & J.L. Morgan (Eds.), *Syntax and semantics, III: Speech acts*. New York: Seminar Press.

Griffin, D., & Buehler, R. (1999). Frequency, probability, and prediction: Easy solutions to cognitive illusions? *Cognitive Psychology*, *38*, 48–78.

Griggs, R.A., & Cox, J.R. (1982). The elusive thematic-materials effect in Wason's selection task. *British Journal of Psychology*, *73*, 407–420.

Groeger, J.A. (1997). *Memory and remembering.* Harlow, UK: Addison Wesley Longman.

Grossman, E.D., Donnelly, R., Price, R., Pickens, D., Morgan, V., Neighbor, G. et al. (2000). Brain areas involved in perception of biological motion. *Journal of Cognitive Neuroscience*, *12*, 711–720.

Guasti, M.T., & Luzzatti, C. (2002). Syntactic breakdown and recovery of clausal structure in agrammatism. *Brain and Cognition*, *48*, 385–391.

Gunther, H., Gfoerer, S., & Weiss, L. (1984). Inflection, frequency, and the word superiority effect. *Psychological Research*, *46*, 261–281.

Gupta, P., & Cohen, N.J. (2002). Theoretical and computational analysis of skill learning, repetition priming, and procedural memory. *Psychological Review*, *109*, 401–448.

Haarmeier, T., Thier, P., Repnow, M., & Petersen, D. (1997). False perception of motion in a patient who cannot compensate for eye movements. *Nature*, *389*, 849–852.

Haart, E.G.O.-de, Carey, D.P., & Milne, A.B. (1999). More thoughts on perceiving and grasping the Müller-Lyer illusion. *Neuropsychologia*, *37*, 1437–1444.

Haber, R.N., & Levin, C.A. (2001). The independence of size perception and distance perception. *Perception & Psychophysics*, *63*, 1140–1152.

Hadjikhani, N., & de Gelder, B. (2002). Neural basis of prosopagnosia: An fMRI study. *Human Brain Mapping*, *16*, 176–182.

Hadjikhani, N., Liu, A.K., Dale, A.M., Cavanagh, P., & Tootell, R.B.H. (1998). Retinotopy and colour sensitivity in human visual cortical area V8. *Nature Neuroscience*, *1*, 235–241.

Hahn, S., Andersen, G.J., & Saidpour, A. (2003). Static scene analysis for the perception of heading. *Psychological Science*, *14*, 543–548.

Hall, D.A., & Riddoch, M.J. (1997). Word meaning deafness: Spelling words that are not understood. *Cognitive Neuropsychology*, *14*, 1131–1164.

Halliday, M.A.K. (1987). Spoken and written modes of meaning. In R. Horowitz & S.J. Samuels (Eds.), *Comprehending oral and written language*. New York: Academic Press.

Halligan, P.W., & Marshall, J.C. (1993). When two is one: A case study of spatial parsing in visual neglect. *Perception*, *22*, 309–312.

Halligan, P.W., & Marshall, J.C. (1998). Neglect of awareness. *Consciousness and Cognition*, *7*, 356–380.

Hampson, P.J. (1989). Aspects of attention and cognitive science. *The Irish Journal of Psychology*, *10*, 261–275.

Hampton, J.A. (1979). Polymorphous concepts in semantic memory. *Journal of Verbal Learning & Verbal Behavior*, *18*, 441–461.

Hampton, J.A. (1981). An investigation of the nature of abstract concepts. *Memory & Cognition*, *9*, 149–156.

Han, S., Humphreys, G.W., & Chen, L. (1999). Uniform connectedness and classical Gestalt principles of perceptual grouping. *Perception & Psychophysics*, *61*, 661–674.

Handley, S.J., Capon, A., Copp, C., & Harper, C. (2002). Conditional reasoning and the Tower of Hanoi: The role of verbal and spatial working memory. *British Journal of Psychology*, *93*, 501–518.

Hanley, J.R., & McDonnell, V. (1997). Are reading and spelling phonologically mediated? Evidence from a patient with a speech production impairment. *Cognitive Neuropsychology*, *14*, 3–33.

Hanna, J.E., Tanenhaus, M.K., & Trueswell, J.C. (2003). The effects of common ground and perspective on domains of referential interpretation. *Journal of Memory and Language*, *49*, 43–61.

Harding, A., Halliday, G., Caine, D., & Kril, J. (2000). Degeneration of anterior thalamic nuclei differentiates alcoholics with amnesia. *Brain*, *123*, 141–154.

Hardman, D., & Harries, C. (2002). How rational are we? *The Psychologist*, *15*, 76–79.

Harley, K., & Reese, E. (1999). Origins of autobiographical memory. *Developmental Psychology*, *35*, 1338–1348.

Harley, T.A. (2001). *The psychology of language: From data to theory* (2nd Ed.). Hove, UK: Psychology Press.

Harley, T.A. (2004). Does cognitive neuropsychology have a future? *Cognitive Neuropsychology*, *21*, 3–16.

Harley, T.A., & Bown, H.E. (1998). What causes a tip-of-the-tongue state? Evidence for lexical neighbourhood effects in speech production. *British Journal of Psychology*, *89*, 151–174.

Harm, M.W., & Seidenberg, M.S. (2001). Are there orthographic impairments in phonological dyslexia? *Cognitive Neuropsychology*, *18*, 71–92.

Harris, I.M., & Miniussi, C. (2003). Parietal lobe contribution to mental rotation demonstrated with rTMS. *Journal of Cognitive Neuroscience*, *15*, 315–323.

Harris, M. (1990). Language and thought. In M.W. Eysenck (Ed.), *The Blackwell dictionary of cognitive psychology.* Oxford: Blackwell.

Harris, M.G., & Carré, G. (2001). Is optic flow used to guide walking while wearing a displacing prism? *Perception*, *30*, 811–818.

Hartley, J., Sotto, E., & Pennebaker, J. (2003). Speaking versus typing: A case-study of the effects of using voice-recognition software on academic correspondence. *British Journal of Educational Technology*, *34*, 5–16.

Harvey, N. (2001). Studying judgement: General issues. *Thinking and Reasoning*, *7*, 103–118.

Hashish, I., Finman, C., & Harvey, W. (1988). Reduction of postoperative pain and swelling by ultrasound: A placebo effect. *Pain*, *83*, 303–311.

Hastie, R. (2001). Problems for judgement and decision making. *Annual Review of Psychology*, *52*, 653–683.

Hatano, G., & Inagaki, K. (1986). Two courses of expertise. In H. Stevenson, H. Azuma, & K. Hatuka (Eds.), *Child development in Japan.* San Francisco, CA: Freeman.

Hatfield, F.M., & Patterson, K.E. (1983). Phonological spelling. *Quarterly Journal of Experimental Psychology*, *35*A, 451–468.

Haxby, J.V., Horwitz, B., Ungerleider, L.G., Maisog, J.M., Pietrini, P., & Grady, C.L. (1994). The functional organization of human extrastriate cortex: A PET-rCBF study of selective attention to faces and locations. *Journal of Neuroscience*, *14*, 6336–6353.

Hayes, J.R. (2000). A new framework for understanding cognition and affect in writing. In R. Indrisano & J. Squire (Eds.), *Perspectives on writing: Research, theory, and practice*. Newark, NJ: I.R.A.

Hayes, J.R., & Flower, L.S. (1986). Writing research and the writer. *American Psychologist*, *41*, 1106–1113.

Hayes, J.R., Flower, L.S., Schriver, K., Stratman, J., & Carey, L. (1985). *Cognitive processes in revision* (Technical Report No. 12). Pittsburgh, PA: Carnegie Mellon University.

Hayman, C.A., MacDonald, C.A., & Tulving, E. (1993). The role of repetition and associative interference in new semantic learning in amnesia: A case experiment. *Journal of Cognitive Neuroscience*, *5*, 375–389.

Hazeltine, E., Grafton, S.T., & Ivry, R. (1997). Attention and stimulus characteristics determine the locus of motor-sequence encoding: A PET study. *Brain*, *120*, 123–140.

Hazeltine, E., Teague, D., & Ivry, R. (2000). *Dual-task performance during simultaneous execution: Evidence for concurrent response selection processes.* Presented at the Annual Meeting of the Cognitive Neuroscience Society, San Francisco.

Healy, A.F. (2003). *Handbook of psychology: Experimental psychology, Vol. 4*. New York: Wiley.

Heath, W.P., & Erickson, J.R. (1998). Memory for central and peripheral actions and props after varied post-event presentation. *Legal and Criminal Psychology*, *3*, 321–346.

Hegarty, M., Shah, P., & Miyake, A. (2000). Constraints on using the dual-task methodology to specify the degree of central executive involvement in cognitive tasks. *Memory & Cognition*, *28*, 376–385.

Hegde, J., & Van Essen, D.C. (2000). Selectivity for complex shapes in primate visual area V2. *Journal of Neuroscience*, *20*, RC61.

Heider, E. (1972). Universals in colour naming and memory. *Journal of Experimental Psychology*, *93*, 10–20.

Heindel, W.C., Salmon, D.P., Shults, C.W., Walicke, P.A., & Butters, N. (1989). Neuropsychological evidence for multiple implicit memory systems: A comparison of Alzheimer's, Huntington's, and Parkinson's disease patients. *Journal of Neuroscience*, 9, 582–587.

Heinze, H.J., Mangun, G.R., Burchert, W., Hinrichs, H., Scholz, M., Münte, T.F. et al. (1994). Combined spatial and temporal imaging of brain activity during visual selective attention in humans. *Nature*, *372*, 543–546.

Heit, E. (1992). Categorisation using chains of examples. *Cognitive Psychology*, *24*, 341–380.

Helm-Estabrooks, N., Bayles, K., & Bryant, S. (1994). Four forms of perseveration in dementia and aphasia patients and normal elders. *Brain and Language*, *47*, 457–460.

Helmholtz, H. von (1866). *Treatise on physiological optics, Vol. III.* New York: Dover [translation published 1962].

Henderson, J.M., & Hollingworth, A. (2003). Global transsaccadic change blindness during scene perception. *Psychological Science*, *14*, 493–497.

Henke, K., Schweinberger, S.R., Grigo, A., Klos, T., & Sommer, W. (1998). Specificity of face recognition: Recognition of exemplars of non-face objects in prosopagnosia. *Cortex*, *34*, 289–296.

Henson, R.N.A., Burgess, N., & Frith, C.D. (2000). Recoding, storage, rehearsal and grouping in verbal short-term memory: An fMRI study. *Neuropsychologia*, *38*, 426–440.

Hering, E. (1878). *Zur Lehre vom Lichtsinn*. Vienna: Gerold.

Herrmann, D., & Gruneberg, M. (1993). The need to expand the horizons of the practical aspects of memory movement. *Applied Cognitive Psychology*, *7*, 553–565.

Herrnstein, R., Nickerson, R., de Sanchez, M., & Swets, J. (1986). Teaching thinking skills. *American Psychologist*, *41*, 1279–1289.

Hewstone, M., Benn, W., & Wilson, A. (1988). Bias in the use of base rates: Racial prejudice in decision making. *European Journal of Psychology*, *18*, 161–176.

Heywood, C.A., & Cowey, A. (1999). Cerebral achromatopsia. In G.W. Humphreys (Ed.), *Case studies in the neuropsychology of vision*. Hove, UK: Psychology Press.

Heywood, C.A., Cowey, A., & Newcombe, F. (1994). On the role of parvocellular P and magnocellular M pathways in cerebral achromatopsia. *Brain*, *117*, 245–254.

Higham, P.A. (2002). Strong cues are not necessarily weak: Thomson and Tulving (1970) and the encoding specificity principle revisited. *Memory & Cognition*, *30*, 67–80.

Hill, H., & Bruce V. (1993). Independent effects of lighting, orientation and stereopsis on the hollow face illusion. *Perception*, *22*, 887–897.

Hillis, A.E., & Caramazza, A. (1991). Category-specific naming and comprehension impairment: A double dissociation. *Brain*, *114*, 2081–2094.

Hillis, A.E., & Caramazza, A. (1995). Converging evidence for the interaction of semantic and sublexical phonological information in accessing lexical representations for spoken output. *Cognitive Neuropsychology*, *12*, 187–227.

Hills, R.L., & Murray, W.S. (2000). Commas and spaces: Effects of punctuation on eye movements and sentence parsing. In A. Kennedy, R. Radach, D. Heller, & J. Pynte (Eds.), *Reading as a perceptual process*. Oxford: Elsevier.

Hintzman, D.L. (1990). Human learning and memory: Connections and dissociations. *Annual Review of Psychology*, *41*, 109–139.

Hirsh, K.W., & Funnell, E. (1995). Those old, familiar things: Age of acquisition, familiarity and lexical access in progressive aphasia. *Journal of Neurolinguistics*, *9*, 23–32.

Hirshberg, J. (1998). *The creative priority driving innovative business in the real world.* London: HarperCollins.

Hirst, W., Spelke, E.S., Reaves, C.C., Caharack, G., & Neisser, U. (1980). Dividing attention without alternation or automaticity. *Journal of Experimental Psychology: General*, *109*, 98–117.

Hirstein, W., & Ramachandran, V.S. (1997). Capgras syndrome: A novel probe for understanding the neural representation of the identity and familiarity of persons. *Proceedings of the Royal Society of London B*, *264*, 437–444.

Hockey, G.R.J., Davies, S., & Gray, M.M. (1972). Forgetting as a function of sleep at different times of day. *Quarterly Journal of Experimental Psychology*, *24*, 386–393.

Hoffman, C., Lau, I., & Johnson, D.R. (1986). The linguistic relativity of person cognition. *Journal of Personality & Social Psychology*, *51*, 1097–1105.

Hoffman, D.D., & Richards, W.A. (1984). Parts of recognition. *Cognition*, *18*, 65–96.

Hoffrage, U., Lindsey, S., Hertwig, R., & Gigerenzer, G. (2000). Communicating statistical information. *Science*, *290*, 2261–2262.

Holbrook, J.B., Bost, P.R., Cave, C.B. (2003). The effects of study-task relevance on perceptual repetition priming. *Memory & Cognition*, 31, 380–392.

Holding, D.H., & Reynolds, J.R. (1982). Recall or evaluation of chess positions as determinants of chess skill. *Memory & Cognition*, *10*, 237–242.

Holland, J.H., Holyoak, K.J., Nisbett, R.E., & Thagard, P. (1986). *Induction: Processes in inference, learning and discovery*. Cambridge, MA: MIT Press.

Hollingworth, A., & Henderson, J.M. (2002). Accurate visual memory for previously attended objects in natural scenes. *Journal of Experimental Psychology: Human Perception and Performance*, *28*, 113–136.

Hollingworth, A., Williams, C.C., & Henderson, J.M. (2001). To see and remember: Visually specific information is retained in memory from previously attended objects in natural scenes. *Psychonomic Bulletin & Review*, *8*, 761–768.

Holmes, A., & Conway, M.A. (1999). Generation identity and the reminiscence bump: Memories for public and private events. *Journal of Adult Development*, *6*, 21–34.

Holmes, V.M., & Carruthers, J. (1998). The relation between reading and spelling in skilled adult readers. *Journal of Memory and Language*, *39*, 264–289.

Holtgraves, T. (1998). Interpreting indirect replies. *Cognitive Psychology*, *37*, 1–27.

Holway, A.F., & Boring, E.G. (1941). Determinants of apparent visual size with distance variant. *American Journal of Psychology*, *54*, 21–37.

Horgan, D.D., & Morgan, D. (1990). Chess expertise in children. *Applied Cognitive Psychology*, *4*, 109–128.

Horton, W.S., & Gerrig, R.J. (2002). Speakers' experiences and audience design: Knowing *when* and knowing *how* to adjust utterances to addressees. *Journal of Memory and Language*, *47*, 589–606.

Horton, W.S., & Keysar, B. (1996). When do speakers take into account common ground? *Cognition*, *59*, 91–117.

Hotopf, W.H.N. (1980). Slips of the pen. In U. Frith (Ed.), *Cognitive processes in spelling.* London: Academic Press.

Howard, D. (1997). Language in the human brain. In M.D. Rugg (Ed.), *Cognitive neuroscience*. Hove, UK: Psychology Press.

Howard, D., & Orchard-Lisle, V. (1984). On the origin of semantic errors in naming: Evidence from the case of a global aphasic. *Cognitive Neuropsychology, 1*, 163–190.

Howard, D., Patterson, K.E., Wise, R.J.S., Brown, W.D., Friston, K., Weiller, C. et al. (1992). The cortical localisation of the lexicons: Positron emission tomography evidence. *Brain, 115*, 1769–1782.

Howard, D.V., & Howard, J.H. (1992). Adult age differences in the rate of learning serial patterns: Evidence from direct and indirect tests. *Psychology & Aging, 7*, 232–241.

Howard, I.P., Bergstrom, S.S., & Masao, O. (1990). Shape from shading in different frames of reference. *Perception, 19*, 523–530.

Howe. M.L., & Courage, M.L. (1997). The emergence and early development of autobiographical memory. *Psychological Review, 104*, 499–523.

Hubel, D.H., & Wiesel, T.N. (1962). Receptive fields, binocular interaction and functional architecture in the cat's visual cortex. *Journal of Physiology, 160*, 106–154.

Hubel, D.H., & Wiesel, T.N. (1968). Receptive fields and functional architecture of monkey striate cortex. *Journal of Physiology, 148*, 574–591.

Hubel, D.H., & Wiesel, T.N. (1979). Brain mechanisms of vision. *Scientific American, 249*, 150–162.

Hulin, C.L., Henry, R.A., & Noon, S.L. (1990). Adding a dimension: Time as a factor in the generalisability of predictive relationships. *Psychological Bulletin, 107*, 328–340.

Hummel, J.E., & Biederman, I. (1992). Dynamic binding in a neural network for shape recognition. *Psychological Review, 99*, 480–517.

Hummel, J.E., & Holyoak, K.J. (1997). Distributed representations of structure: A theory of analogical access and mapping. *Psychological Review, 104*, 427–466.

Humphrey, N. (1983). *Consciousness regained: Chapters in the development of mind.* Oxford: Oxford University Press.

Humphrey, N. (2002). *The mind made flesh: Frontiers of psychology and evolution.* Oxford: Oxford University Press.

Humphreys, G.W. (1999). *Case studies in the neuropsychology of vision*. Hove, UK: Psychology Press.

Humphreys, G.W., & Bruce, V. (1989). *Visual cognition: Computational, experimental and neuropsychological perspectives*. Hove, UK: Psychology Press.

Humphreys, G.W., & Forde, E.M.E. (2001). Hierarchies, similarity and interactivity in object recognition: On the multiplicity of "category-specific" deficits in neuropsychological populations. *Behavioural and Brain Sciences, 24*, 453–509.

Humphreys, G.W., & Price, C.J. (2001). Cognitive neuropsychology and functional brain imaging: Implications for functional and anatomical models of cognition. *Acta Psychologica, 107*, 119–153.

Humphreys, G.W., & Riddoch, M.J. (1984). Routes to object constancy: Implications from neurological impairments of object constancy. *Quarterly Journal of Experimental Psychology, 36*A, 385–415.

Humphreys, G.W., & Riddoch, M.J. (1985). Author corrections to "Routes to object constancy". *Quarterly Journal of Experimental Psychology, 37*A, 493–495.

Humphreys, G.W., & Riddoch, M.J. (1987). *To see but not to see: A case study of visual agnosia*. Hove, UK: Psychology Press.

Humphreys, G.W., & Riddoch, M.J. (1993). Interactions between object and space systems revealed through neuropsychology. In D.E. Meyer & S.M. Kornblum (Eds.), *Attention and performance, Vol. XIV*. London: MIT Press.

Humphreys, G.W., Riddoch, M.J., & Quinlan, P.T. (1985). Interactive processes in perceptual organization: Evidence from visual agnosia. In M.I. Posner & O.S.M. Morin (Eds.), *Attention and performance, Vol. XI*. Hillsdale, NJ: Lawrence Erlbaum Associates Inc.

Humphreys, G.W., Riddoch, M.J., Quinlan, P.T., Price, C.J., & Donnelly, N. (1992). Parallel pattern processing in visual agnosia. *Canadian Journal of Psychology, 46*, 377–416.

Humphreys, G.W., & Rumiati, R.I. (1998). Agnosia without prosopagnosia or alexia: Evidence for stored visual memories specific to objects. *Cognitive Neuropsychology, 15*, 243–277.

Hunt, E., & Agnoli, F. (1991). The Whorfian hypothesis: A cognitive psychological perspective. *Psychological Review, 98*, 377–389.

Huppert, F.A., & Piercy, M. (1976). Recognition memory in amnesic patients: Effect of temporal context and familiarity of material. *Cortex, 4*, 3–20.

Hurlbert, A. (1999). Colour vision: Is colour constancy real? *Current Biology, 9*, R558–R561.

Hyde, T.S., & Jenkins, J.J. (1973). Recall for words as a function of semantic, graphic, and syntactic orienting tasks. *Journal of Verbal Learning & Verbal Behavior, 12*, 471–480.

Idefrey, P., & Levelt, W.J.M. (2000). The neural correlates of language production. In M. Gazzaniga (Ed.), *The new cognitive neurosciences* (2nd Ed.). Cambridge, MA: MIT Press.

Indrisano, R., & Squire, J. (2000). *Perspectives on writing: Research, theory, and practice.* Newark, NJ: I.R.A.

Inhoff, A.W., & Liu, W. (1998). The perceptual span and oculo-motor activity during the reading of Chinese sentences. *Journal of Experimental Psychology: Human Perception and Performance, 24*, 20–34.

Isaac, C.L., & Mayes, A.R. (1999). Rate of forgetting in amnesia: II. Recall and recognition of word lists at different levels of organisation. *Journal of Experimental Psychology: Learning, Memory, and Cognition, 25*, 963–977.

Ittelson, W.H. (1951). Size as a cue to distance: Static localisation. *American Journal of Psychology*, *64*, 54–67.

Jackson, S.R., & Shaw, A. (2000). The Ponzo illusion affects grip force but not grip aperture scaling during prehension movements. *Journal of Experimental Psychology: Human Perception and Performance*, *26*, 418–423.

Jacobs, A.M., & Grainger, J. (1992). Testing a semistochastic variant of the interactive activation model in different word recognition experiments. *Journal of Experimental Psychology: Human Perception & Performance*, *18*, 1174–1188.

Jacoby, L.L. (1998). Invariance in automatic influences of memory: Toward a user's guide for the process-dissociation procedure. *Journal of Experimental Psychology: Learning, Memory, & Cognition*, *24*, 3–26.

Jacoby, L.L., Debner, J.A., & Hay, J.F. (2001). Proactive interference, accessibility bias, and process dissociations: Valid subjective reports of memory. *Journal of Experimental Psychology: Learning, Memory, & Cognition*, *27*, 686–700.

Jacoby, L.L., Toth, J.P., & Yonelinas, A.P. (1993). Separating conscious and unconscious influences on memory: Measuring recollection. *Journal of Experimental Psychology: General*, *122*, 139–154.

Jakobson, L.S., Archibald, Y.M., Carey, D.P., & Goodale, M.A. (1991). A kinematic analysis of reaching and grasping movements in a patient recovering from optic ataxia. *Neuropsychologia*, *29*, 803–809.

James, W. (1890). *Principles of psychology.* New York: Holt.

Jankowiak, J., & Albert, M.L. (1994). Lesion localisation in visual agnosia. In A. Kertesz (Ed.), *Localisation and neuroimaging in neuropsychology*. London: Academic Press.

Jansma, J.M., Ramsey, N.F., Slagter, H.A., & Kahn, R.S. (2001). Functional anatomical correlates of controlled and automatic processing. *Journal of Cognitive Neuroscience*, *13*, 730–743.

Jared, D., Levy, B.A., & Rayner, K. (1999). The role of phonology in the activation of word meanings during reading: Evidence from proof-reading and eye movements. *Journal of Experimental Psychology: General*, *128*, 219–264.

Jenkins, J.G., & Dallenbach, K.M. (1924). Obliviscence during sleep and waking. *American Journal of Psychology*, *35*, 605–612.

Job, R., Peressotti, F., & Cusinato, A. (1998). Lexical effects in naming pseudowords in shallow orthographies: Further empirical data. *Journal of Experimental Psychology: Human Perception and Performance*, *24*, 622–630.

Johansson, G. (1973). Visual perception of biological motion and a model for its analysis. *Perception & Psychophysics*, *14*, 201–211.

Johansson, G. (1975). Visual motion perception. *Scientific American*, *232*, 76–89.

Johansson, G., von Hofsten, C., & Jansson, G. (1980). Event perception. *Annual Review of Psychology*, *31*, 27–64.

Johnson, E.J., Hershey, J., Meszaros, J., & Kunreuther, H. (1993). Framing, probability distortions, and insurance decisions. *Journal of Risk & Uncertainty*, *7*, 5–51.

Johnson, M.K., Hashtroudi, S., & Lindsay, D.S. (1993). Source monitoring. *Psychological Bulletin*, *114*, 3–28.

Johnson-Laird, P.N. (1980). Mental models in cognitive science. *Cognitive Science*, *4*, 71–115.

Johnson-Laird, P.N. (1983). *Mental models.* Cambridge: Cambridge University Press.

Johnson-Laird, P.N. (1999). Deductive reasoning. *Annual Review of Psychology*, *50*, 109–135.

Johnson-Laird, P.N., & Byrne, R.M.J. (1991). *Deduction.* London: Psychology Press.

Johnson-Laird, P.N., & Goldvarg, Y. (1997). How to make the impossible seem possible. In *Proceedings of the 19th Annual Conference of the Cognitive Science Society.* Mahwah, NJ: Lawrence Erlbaum Associates Inc.

Johnson-Laird, P.N., Legrenzi, P., Girotto, V., Legrenzi, M.S., & Caverni, J.-P. (1999). Naive probability: A mental model theory of extensional reasoning. *Psychological Review*, *106*, 62–88.

Johnston, E.B., Cumming, B.G., & Parker, A.J. (1993). Integration of depth modules: Stereo and texture. *Vision Research*, *33*, 813–882.

Jones, G. (2003). Testing two cognitive theories of insight. *Journal of Experimental Psychology: Learning, Memory, and Cognition*, *29*, 1017–1027.

Joseph, J.E., & Proffitt, D.R. (1996). Semantic versus perceptual influences of colour in object recognition. *Journal of Experimental Psychology: Learning, Memory, & Cognition*, *22*, 407–429.

Josephs, R.A., Larrick, R.P., Steele, C.M., & Nisbett, R.E. (1992). Protecting the self from the negative consequences of risky decisions. *Journal of Personality & Social Psychology*, *62*, 26–37.

Jost, A. (1897). Die Assoziationsfestigkeit in ihrer Abhängigheit von der Verteiling der Wiederholungen. *Zeitschrift für Psychologie*, *14*, 436–472.

Joyce, J. (1922/1960). *Ulysses.* London: Bodley Head.

Juhasz, B.J., & Rayner, K. (2003). Investigating the effects of a set of intercorrelated variables on eye fixation durations in reading. *Journal of Experimental Psychology: Learning, Memory and Cognition*, *29*, 1312–1318.

Julesz, B. (1971). *Foundations of cyclopean perception*. Chicago: University of Chicago Press.

Jung-Beeman, M., Bowden, E.M., Haberman, J., Frymiare, J.L., Arambel-Liu, S., Greenblatt, R. et al. (2004). Neural activity observed in people solving verbal problems with insight. *Public Library of Science—Biology*, *2*, 500–510.

Just, M.A., & Carpenter, P.A. (1992). A capacity theory of comprehension. *Psychological Review*, *99*, 122–149.

Kaakinen, J.K., Hyönä, J., & Keenan, J.M. (2003). How prior knowledge, WMC, and relevance of information affect eye fixations in expository text. *Journal of Experimental Psychology: Learning, Memory, and Cognition*, *29*, 447–457.

Kahneman, D. (1973). *Attention and effort*. Englewood Cliffs, NJ: Prentice Hall.

Kahneman, D., & Henik, A. (1979). Perceptual organisation and attention. In M. Kubovy & J.R. Pomerantz (Eds.), *Perceptual organisation*. Hillsdale, NJ: Lawrence Erlbaum Associates Inc.

Kahneman, D., & Tversky, A. (1973). On the psychology of prediction. *Psychological Review*, *80*, 237–251.

Kahneman, D., & Tversky, A. (1979). Prospect theory: An analysis of decision under risk. *Econometrica*, *47*, 263–291.

Kahneman, D., & Tversky, A. (1984). Choices, values and frames. *American Psychologist*, *39*, 341–350.

Kaiser, M.K., & Phatak, A.V. (1993). Things that go bump in the light: On the optical specification of contact severity. *Journal of Experimental Psychology: Human Perception and Performance*, *19*, 194–202.

Kalakoski, V., & Saariluoma, P. (2001). Taxi drivers' exceptional memory of street names. *Memory & Cognition*, *29*, 634–638.

Kalat, J.W. (2001). *Biological psychology* (7th Ed.). Pacific Grove: Brooks/Cole.

Kane, M.J., & Engle, R.W. (2000). Working-memory capacity, proactive interference, divided attention: Limits on long-term memory retrieval. *Journal of Experimental Psychology: Learning, Memory, and Cognition*, *26*, 336–358.

Kaneko, H., & Uchikawa, K. (1997). Perceived angular and linear size: The role of binocular disparity and visual surround. *Perception*, *26*, 17–27.

Kanizsa, G. (1976). Subjective contours. Scientific American, *234*, 48–52.

Kanwisher, N. (2001). Neural events and perceptual awareness. *Cognition*, *79*, 89–113.

Kanwisher, N., McDermott, J., & Chun, M.M. (1997). The fusiform face area: A module in human extrastriate cortex specialised for face perception. *Journal of Neuroscience*, *9*, 605–610.

Kaplan, G.A., & Simon, H.A. (1990). In search of insight. *Cognitive Psychology*, *22*, 374–419.

Kapur, N. (1999). Syndromes of retrograde amnesia: A conceptual and empirical synthesis. *Psychological Bulletin*, *125*, 800–825.

Karnath, H.O., Ferber, S., Rorden, C., & Driver, J. (2000). The fate of global information in dorsal simultagnosia. *Neurocase*, *6*, 295–306.

Karnath, H.O., Himmelbach, M., & Küker, W. (2003). The cortical substrate of visual extinction. *NeuroReport*, *14*, 437–442.

Karney, B.R., & Frye, N.E. (2002). But we've been getting better lately: Comparing prospective and retrospective views of relationship development. *Journal of Personality and Social Psychology*, *82*, 222–238.

Kassin, S.M., Ellsworth, P.C., & Smith, U.L. (1989). The "general acceptance" of psychological research on eyewitness testimony. *American Psychologist*, *44*, 1089–1098.

Kassin, S.M., Tubb, V.A., Hosch, H.M., & Memon, A. (2001). On the "general acceptance" of eyewitness testimony research. *American Psychologist*, *56*, 405–416.

Kaufer, D., Hayes, J.R., & Flower, L.S. (1986). Composing written sentences. *Research in the Teaching of English*, *20*, 121–140.

Kaup, B., & Zwaan, R.A. (2003). Effects of negation and situational presence on the accessibility of text information. *Journal of Experimental Psychology: Learning, Memory, and Cognition*, *29*, 439–446.

Kay, J., & Ellis, A.W. (1987). A cognitive neuropsychological case study of anomia: Implications for psychological models of word retrieval. *Brain*, *110*, 613–629.

Kazmerski, V.A., Blasko, D.G., & Dessalegn, B.G. (2003). ERP and behavioural evidence of individual differences in metaphor comprehension. *Memory & Cognition*, *31*, 673–689.

Keane, M. (1987). On retrieving analogues when solving problems. *Quarterly Journal of Experimental Psychology*, *39*A, 29–41.

Keane, M.M., Gabrieli, J.D.E., Fennema, A.C., Growdon, J.H., & Corkin, S. (1991). Evidence for a dissociation between perceptual and conceptual priming in Alzheimer's disease. *Behavioural Neuroscience*, *105*, 326–342.

Keane, M.T. (1989). Modelling "insight" in practical construction problems. *Irish Journal of Psychology*, *11*, 201–215.

Keane, M.T. (1997). What makes an analogy difficult?: The effects of order and causal structure in analogical mapping. *Journal of Experimental Psychology: Language, Memory, & Cognition*, *23*, 946–967.

Keane, M.T., Ledgeway, T., & Duff, S. (1994). Constraints on analogical mapping: A comparison of three models. *Cognitive Science*, *18*, 287–334.

Keil, F.C. (2003). Categorisation, causation, and the limits of understanding. *Language and Cognitive Processes*, *18*, 663–692.

Kellogg, R.T. (1988). Attentional overload and writing performance: Effects of rough draft and outline strategies. *Journal of Experimental Psychology: Learning, Memory, & Cognition*, *14*, 355–365.

Kellogg, R.T. (1990). Writing. In M.W. Eysenck (Ed.), The *Blackwell dictionary of cognitive psychology*. Oxford: Blackwell.

Kellogg, R.T. (1994). *The psychology of writing.* Oxford: Oxford University Press.

Kellogg, R.T. (1995). *Cognitive psychology.* Thousand Oaks, CA: Sage.

Kellogg, R.T. (2001). Long-term working memory in text production. *Memory & Cognition*, *29*, 43–52.

Kellogg, R.T., & Mueller, S. (1993). Performance amplification and process restructuring in computer-based writing. *International Journal of Man–Machine Studies*, *39*, 33–49.

Kelly, S.W. (2003). A consensus in implicit learning? *Quarterly Journal of Experimental Psychology*, *56*A, 1389–1391.

Kempton, W. (1986). Two theories of home heat control. *Cognitive Science*, *10*, 75–91.

Kenealy, P.M. (1997). Mood-state-dependent retrieval: The effects of induced mood on memory reconsidered. *Quarterly Journal of Experimental Psychology*, *50*A, 290–317.

Kennedy, A., Pynte, J., & Ducrot, S. (2002). Parafoveal-on-foveal interactions in word recognition. *Quarterly Journal of Experimental Psychology*, *55*A, 1307–1338.

Kentridge, R.W., Heywood, C.A., & Weiskrantz, L. (1999). Effects of temporal cueing on residual visual discrimination in blindsight. *Neuropsychologia*, *37*, 479–483.

Keppel, G., & Underwood, B.J. (1962). Proactive inhibition in short-term retention of single items. *Journal of Verbal Learning and Verbal Behavior*, *1*, 153–161.

Kershaw T.C., & Ohlsson, S. (2004). Multiple causes of difficulty in insight: The case of the nine-dot problem. *Journal of Experimental Psychology: Learning, Memory, & Cognition*, *30*, 3–13.

Kersten, D., Mamassian, P., & Knill, D.C. (1997). Moving cast shadows induce apparent motion in depth. *Perception*, *26*, 171–192.

Keysar, B., Barr, D.J., Balin, J.A., & Brauner, J.S. (2000). Taking perspective in conversation: The role of mutual knowledge in comprehension. *Psychological Science*, *11*, 32–38.

Keysar, B., Barr, D.J., Balin, J.A., & Paek, T.S. (1998). Definite reference and mutual knowledge: Process models of common ground in comprehension. *Journal of Memory and Language*, *39*, 1–20.

Keysar, B., & Henly, A.S. (2002). Speakers' overestimation of their effectiveness. *Psychological Science*, *13*, 207–212.

Kilpatrick, F.P., & Ittelson, W.H. (1953). The size–distance invariance hypothesis. *Psychological Review*, *60*, 223–231.

Kimchi, R., Behrmann, M., & Olson, C. (Eds.) (2003). *Perceptual organisation in vision: Behavioural and neural perspectives*. Mahwah, NJ: Lawrence Erlbaum Associates Inc.

Kinsbourne, M. (1993). Orientational bias model of unilateral neglect: Evidence from attentional gradients within hemispace. In I.H. Robertson & J.C. Marshall (Eds.), *Unilateral neglect: Clinical and experimental studies*. Hillsdale, NJ: Lawrence Erlbaum Associates Inc.

Kintsch, W. (1974). *The representation of meaning in memory.* Hillsdale, NJ: Lawrence Erlbaum Associates Inc.

Kintsch, W. (1988). The role of knowledge in discourse comprehension: A construction–integration model. *Psychological Review*, *95*, 163–182.

Kintsch, W. (1992). A cognitive architecture for comprehension. In H.L. Pick, P. van den Broek, & D.C. Knill (Eds.), Cognition: Conceptual and methodological issues. Washington, DC. American Psychological Association.

Kintsch, W. (1998). *Comprehension: A paradigm for cognition.* New York: Cambridge University Press.

Kintsch, W., & Keenan, J.M. (1973). Reading rate and retention as a function of the number of propositions in the base structure of sentences. *Cognitive Psychology*, *5*, 257–274.

Kintsch, W., Kozminsky, E., Streby, W.J., McKorn, G., & Keenan, J.M. (1975). Comprehension and recall of text as a function of content variables. *Journal of Verbal Learning & Verbal Behavior*, *14*, 196–214.

Kintsch, W., & van Dijk, T.A. (1978). Toward a model of text comprehension and production. *Psychological Review*, *85*, 363–394.

Kintsch, W., Welsch, D., Schmalhofer, F., & Zimny, S. (1990). Sentence memory: A theoretical analysis. *Journal of Memory & Language*, *29*, 133–159.

Klahr, D., & Dunbar, K. (1988). Dual space search during scientific reasoning. *Cognitive Science*, *12*, 1–55.

Klahr, D., Fay, A.L., & Dunbar, K. (1993). Heuristics for scientific experimentation: A developmental study. *Cognitive Psychology*, *25*, 111–146.

Klahr, D., & Simon, H.A. (1999). Studies of scientific discovery: Complementary approaches and convergent findings. *Psychological Bulletin*, *125*, 524–543.

Klahr, D., & Simon, H.A. (2001). What have psychologists (and others) discovered about the process of scientific discovery? *Current Directions in Psychological Science*, *10*, 75–79.

Klauer, K.C., Musch, J., & Naumer, B. (2000). On belief bias in syllogistic reasoning. *Psychological Review*, *107*, 852–884.

Klayman, J., & Ha, Y.-W. (1987). Confirmation, disconfirmation, and information in hypothesis testing. *Psychological Review*, *94*, 211–228.

Klein, S.B., & Kihlstrom, J.F. (1986). Elaboration, organization, and the self-reference effect in memory. *Journal of Experimental Psychology*, *115*, 26–38.

Knoblich, G., Ohlsson, S., Haider, H., & Rhenius, D. (1999). Constraint relaxation and chunk decomposition in insight. *Journal of Experimental Psychology: Learning, Memory, & Cognition*, *25*, 1534–1555.

Knoblich, G., Ohlsson, S., & Raney, G.E. (2001). An eye movement study of insight problem solving. *Memory & Cognition*, *29*, 1000–1009.

Knoblich, G., & Wartenberg, F. (1998). Unnoticed hints facilitate representational change in problem solving. *Zeitschrift für Psychologie*, *206*, 207–234.

Knowlton, B.J., Ramus, S.J., & Squire, L.R. (1992). Intact artificial grammar learning in amnesia: Dissociation of category-level knowledge and explicit memory for specific instances. *Psychological Science*, *3*, 172–179.

Knowlton, B.J., & Squire, L.R. (1996). Artificial grammar learning depends on implicit acquisition of both rule-based and exemplar-based information. *Journal of Experimental Psychology: Learning, Memory, and Cognition*, *22*, 169–181.

Kobatake, E., & Tanaka, K. (1994). Neuronal selectivities to complex object features in the ventral visual pathway of the macaque cerebral cortex. *Journal of Neurophysiology*, *71*, 856–867.

Koch, C. (2003). *The quest for consciousness: A neurobiological approach.* New York: Roberts & Co.

Koechlin, E., Basso, G., Pietrini, P., Panzer, S., & Grafman, J. (1999). The role of the anterior prefrontal cortex in human cognition. *Nature*, *399*, 148–151.

Koedinger, K.R., & Anderson, J.R. (1990). Abstract planning and perceptual chunks: Elements of expertise in geometry. *Cognitive Science*, *14*, 511–550.

Koehler, J.J. (1996). The base rate fallacy reconsidered: Descriptive, normative, and methodological challenges. *Behavioral & Brain Sciences*, *19*, 1–17.

Koffka, K. (1935). *Principles of Gestalt psychology.* New York: Harcourt Brace.

Kohler, I. (1962). Experiments with goggles. *Scientific American*, *206*, 62–72.

Köhler, S., & Moscovitch, M. (1997). Unconscious visual processing in neuropsychological syndromes: A survey of the literature and evaluation of models of consciousness. In M.D. Rugg (Ed.), *Cognitive neuroscience.* Hove, UK: Psychology Press.

Köhler, W. (1925). *The mentality of apes*. New York: Harcourt Brace & World.

Kohnken, G., Milne, R., Memon, A., & Bull, R. (1999). The cognitive interview: A meta-analysis. *Psychology of Crime Law*, *5*, 3–27.

Koriat, A., & Goldsmith, M. (1996). Memory metaphors and the real-life/laboratory controversy: Correspondence versus storehouse conceptions of memory. *Behavioral & Brain Sciences*, *19*, 167–188.

Koriat, A., Goldsmith, M., & Pansky, A. (2000). Toward a psychology of memory accuracy. *Annual Review of Psychology*, *51*, 481–537.

Korsakoff, S.S. (1889). Uber eine besondere Form psychischer Störung, kombiniert mit multiplen Neuritis. *Archiv für Psychiatrie und Nervenkrankheiten*, *21*, 669–704.

Kosslyn, S.M. (1980). *Image and mind.* Cambridge, MA: Harvard University Press.

Kosslyn, S.M. (1994). *Image and brain: The resolution of the imagery debate.* Cambridge, MA: MIT Press.

Kosslyn, S.M., Pascual-Leone, A., Felician, O., Camposano, S., Keenan, J.P., Thompson, W.L. et al. (1999). The role of Area 17 in visual imagery: Convergent evidence from PET and rTMS. *Science*, *284*, 167–170.

Kosslyn, S.M., & Thompson, W.L. (2003). When is early visual cortex activated during visual mental imagery? *Psychological Bulletin*, *129*, 723–746.

Kozlowski, L.T., & Cutting, J.E. (1978). Recognising the gender of walkers from point-lights mounted on ankles: Some second thoughts. *Perception & Psychophysics*, *23*, 459.

Kraft, J.M., & Brainard, D.H. (1999). Mechanisms of colour constancy under nearly natural viewing. *Proceedings of the National Academy of Sciences, USA*, *96*, 307–312.

Krams, M., Rusthworth, M., Deiber, M.P., Frackowiak, R., & Passingham, R. (1998). The preparation, execution, and suppression of copied movements in the human brain. *Experimental Brain Research*, *120*, 386–398.

Kroger, J.K., Sabb, F.W., Fales, C.L., Bookheimer, S.Y., Cohen, M.S., & Holyoak, K.J. (2002). Recruitment of anterior dorsolateral prefrontal cortex in human reasoning: A parametric study of relational complexity. *Cerebral Cortex*, *12*, 477–485.

Kroll, N.E., Knight, R.T., Metcalfe, J., Wolf, E.S., & Tulving, E. (1996). Cohesion failure as a source of memory illusions. *Journal of Memory & Language*, *35*, 176–196.

Kruschke, J. (1992). ALCOVE: An exemplar-based connectionist model of category learning. *Psychological Review*, *99*, 22–44.

Künnapas, T.M. (1968). Distance perception as a function of available visual cues. *Journal of Experimental Psychology*, *77*, 523–529.

Kvavilashvili, L., & Ellis, J. (1996). Let's forget the everyday/laboratory controversy. *Behavioral & Brain Sciences*, *19*, 199–200.

Kvavilashvili, L., & Ellis, J. (in press). Ecological validity and twenty years of real-life/laboratory controversy in memory research: A critical (and historical) review. *History and Philosophy of Psychology*.

LaBerge, D. (1983). The spatial extent of attention to letters and words. *Journal of Experimental Psychology: Human Perception & Performance*, *9*, 371–379.

LaBerge, D., & Buchsbaum, J.L. (1990). Positron emission tomography measurements of pulvinar activity during an attention task. *Journal of Neuroscience, 10*, 613–619.

Lacquaniti, F., Carozzo, M., & Borghese, N. (1993). The role of vision in tuning anticipatory motor responses of the limbs. In A. Berthoz (Ed.), *Multisensory control of movement.* Oxford: Oxford University Press.

Ladefoged, P. (2001). *Vowels and consonants: An introduction to the sounds of languages.* Oxford: Blackwell.

Laeng, B., Zarrinpar, A., & Kosslyn, S.M. (2003). Do separate processes identify objects as exemplars versus members of basic-level categories? Evidence from hemispheric specialisation. *Brain and Cognition, 53*, 15–27.

Laine, M., Salmelin, R., Helenius, P., & Marttila, R. (2000). Brain activation during reading in deep dyslexia: An MEG study. *Journal of Cognitive Neuroscience, 12*, 622–634.

Lamberts, K., & Goldstone, R. (2004). *Handbook of cognition.* London: Sage.

Lambon Ralph, M.A., Sage, K., & Roberts, J. (2000). Classical anomia: A neuropsychological perspective on speech production. *Neuropsychologia, 38*, 186–202.

Lamme, V.A.F., & Roelfsema, P.R. (2000). The distinct modes of vision offered by feedforward and recurrent processing. *Trends in Neuroscience, 23*, 571–579.

Land, E.H. (1977). The retinex theory of colour vision. *Scientific American, 237*, 108–128.

Land, E.H. (1986). Recent advances in retinex theory. *Vision Research, 26*, 7–21.

Landauer, T.K., & Dumais, S.T. (1997). A solution to Plato's problem: The latent semantic analysis theory of the acquisition, induction, and representation of knowledge. *Psychological Review, 104*, 211–240.

Lappe, M., Bremmer, F., & van den Berg, A.V. (1999). Perception of self-motion from visual flow. *Trends in Cognitive Sciences, 3*, 329–336.

Larsen, J.D., Baddeley, A., & Andrade, J. (2000). Phonological similarity and the irrelevant speech effect: Implications for models of short-term memory. *Memory, 8*, 145–157.

Lashley, K.S., Chow, K.L., & Semmes, J. (1951). An examination of the electrical field theory of cerebral integration. *Psychological Review, 58*, 123–136.

Lassiter, G.D. (2000). The relative contributions of recognition and search-evaluation processes to high-level chess performance: Comment on Gobet and Simon. *Psychological Science, 11*, 172–173.

Latour, P.L. (1962). Visual threshold during eye movements. *Vision Research, 2*, 261–262.

Lavie, N. (1995). Perceptual load as a necessary condition for selective attention. *Journal of Experimental Psychology: Human Perception and Performance, 21*, 451–648.

Lavie, N. (2000). Selective attention and cognitive control: Dissociating attentional functions through different types of load. In S. Monsell & J. Driver (Eds.), *Control of cognitive processes, Attention and performance XVIII* (pp. 175–194). Cambridge, MA: MIT Press.

Lavie, N., & Tsal, Y. (1994). Perceptual load as a major determinant of the locus of selection in visual attention. *Perception & Psychophysics, 56*, 183–197.

Lawson, R., & Humphreys, G.W. (1996). View-specificity in object processing: Evidence from picture matching. *Journal of Experimental Psychology: Human Perception & Performance, 22*, 395–416.

Lea, W.A. (1973). An approach to syntactic recognition without phonemics. *IEEE Transactions on Audio & Electroacoustics, AU-21*, 249–258.

Leake, J. (1999). Scientists teach chimpanzees to speak English. *Sunday Times.*

Lee, A.C.H., Graham, K.S., Simons, J.S., Hodges, J.R., Owen, A.M., & Patterson, K. (2002). Regional brain activations differ for semantic features but not for categories. *NeuroReport, 13*, 1497–1501.

Lee, D.N. (1976). A theory of visual control of braking based on information about time-to-collision. *Perception, 5*, 437–459.

Lee, D.N. (1980). Visuo-motor coordination in space–time. In G.E. Stelmach & J. Requin (Eds.), *Tutorials in motor behaviour.* Amsterdam: North-Holland.

Lee, H.W., Hong, S.B., Seo, D.W., Tae, W.S., & Hong, S.C. (2000). Mapping of functional organisation in human visual cortex: Electrical cortical stimulation. *Neurology, 54*, 849–854.

Lee, T.S., Mumford, D., Romero, R., & Lamme, V.A.F. (1998). The role of the primary visual cortex in higher level vision. *Vision Research, 38*, 2429–2454.

Leek, E.C., Reppa, I., & Tipper, S.P. (2003). Inhibition of return for objects and locations in static displays. *Perception & Psychophysics, 65*, 388–395.

Legrenzi, P., Girotto, V., & Johnson-Laird, P.N. (2003). Models of consistency. *Psychological Science, 14*, 131–137.

Lennie, P. (1998). Single units and visual cortical organisation. *Perception, 27*, 889–935.

Leonards, U., Sunaert, S., Van Hecke, P., & Orban, G.A. (2000). Attention mechanisms in visual search—an fMRI study. *Journal of Cognitive NeuroScience, 12*, 61–75.

Lepage, M., Ghaffar, O., Nyberg, L., & Tulving, E. (2000). Prefrontal cortex and episodic memory retrieval mode. *Proceedings of the National Academy of Science USA, 97*, 506–511.

Leslie, A.M., & Keeble, S. (1987). Do six-month-old infants perceive causality? *Cognition, 25*, 265–288.

Levelt, W.J.M. (1989). *Speaking: From intention to articulation.* Cambridge, MA: MIT Press.

Levelt, W.J.M., Roelofs, A., & Meyer, A.S. (1999a). A theory of lexical access in speech production. *Behavioral and Brain Sciences*, *22*, 1–38.

Levelt, W.J.M., Roelofs, A., & Meyer, A.S. (1999b). Multiple perspectives on word production. *Behavioral and Brain Sciences*, *22*, 61–75.

Levelt, W.J.M., Schriefers, H., Vorberg, D., Meyer, A.S., Pechmann, T., & Havinga, J. (1991). Normal and deviant lexical processing: Reply to Dell and O'Seaghda (1991). *Psychological Review*, *98*, 615–618.

Levin, D.T., Momen, N., Drivdahl, S.B., & Simons, D.J. (2000). Change blindness blindness: The meta-cognitive error of overestimating change-detection ability. *Visual Cognition*, *7*, 397–412.

Levine, D.N., Calvanio, R., & Popovics, A. (1982). Language in the absence of inner speech. *Word*, *15*, 19–44.

Levinson, S.C., Kita, S., Haun, D.B.M., & Rasch, B.H. (2002). Returning the tables: Language affects spatial reasoning. *Cognition*, *84*, 155–188.

Levy, C.M., & Ransdell, S.E. (1995). Is writing as difficult as it seems? *Memory & Cognition*, *23*, 767–779.

Levy, C.M., & Ransdell, S. (2001). Writing with concurrent memory loads. In T. Olive & C.M. Levy (Eds.), *Contemporary tools and techniques for studying writing.* Dordrecht: Kluwer Academic Publishers.

Li, P.W., & Gleitman, L.R. (2002). Turning the tables: Language and spatial reasoning. *Cognition*, *83*, 265–294.

Liberman, A.M., Cooper, F.S., Shankweiler, D.S., & Studdert-Kennedy, M. (1967). Perception of the speech code. *Psychological Review*, *74*, 431–461.

Liberman, A.M., Delattre, P.C., & Cooper, F.S. (1952). The role of selected stimulus variables in the perception of the unvoiced stop consonants. *American Journal of Psychology*, *65*, 497–516.

Libet, B. (1996). Neural processes in the production of conscious experience. In M. Velmans (Ed.), *The science of consciousness: Psychological, neuropsychological and clinical reviews.* London: Routledge.

Libet, B., Gleason, C.A., Wright, E.W., & Pearl, D.K. (1983). Time of conscious intention to act in relation to onset of cerebral activity (readiness potential): The unconscious initiation of a freely voluntary act. *Brain*, *106*, 623–642.

Lichten, W., & Lurie, S. (1950). A new technique for the study of perceived size. *American Journal of Psychology*, *63*, 280–282.

Lichtenstein, S., Slovic, P., Fischhoff, B., Layman, M., & Coombs, J. (1978). Judged frequency of lethal events. *Journal of Experimental Psychology: Human Learning and Memory*, *4*, 551–578.

Lieberman, P. (1963). Some effects of semantic and grammatical context on the production and perception of speech. *Language & Speech*, *6*, 172–187.

Lief, H., & Fetkewicz, J. (1995). Retractors of false memories: The evolution of pseudo-memories. *The Journal of Psychiatry & Law*, *23*, 411–436.

Lin, E.L., & Murphy, G.L. (1997). Effects of background knowledge on object categorisation and part detection. *Journal of Experimental Psychology: Human Perception & Performance*, *23*, 1153–1169.

Lindsay, D.S., Allen, B.P., Chan, J.C.K., & Dahl, L.C. (2004). Eyewitness suggestibility and source similarity: Intrusions of details from one event into memory reports of another event. *Journal of Memory and Language*, *50*, 96–111.

Linton, M. (1975). Memory for real-world events. In D.A. Norman & D.E. Rumelhart (Eds.), *Explorations in cognition*. San Francisco, CA: Freeman.

Lloyd, D.M., Merat, N., McGlone, F., & Spence, C. (2003). Crossmodal links between audition and touch in covert endogenous spatial attention. *Perception & Psychophysics*, *65*, 901–924.

Lockhart, R.S., & Craik, F.I.M. (1990). Levels of processing: A retrospective commentary on a framework for memory research. *Canadian Journal of Psychology*, *44*, 87–112.

Loftus, E.F. (1979). *Eyewitness testimony*. Cambridge, MA: Harvard University Press.

Loftus, E.F. (1992). When a lie becomes memory's truth: Memory distortion after exposure to misinformation. *Current Directions in Psychological Science*, *1*, 121–123.

Loftus, E.F., & Burns, H.J. (1982). Mental shock can produce retrograde amnesia. *Memory & Cognition*, *10*, 318–323.

Loftus, E.F., Loftus, G.R., & Messo, J. (1987). Some facts about "weapons focus". *Law and Human Behavior*, *11*, 55–62.

Loftus, E.F., & Palmer, J.C. (1974). Reconstruction of automobile destruction: An example of the interaction between language and memory. *Journal of Verbal Learning & Verbal Behavior*, *13*, 585–589.

Loftus, E.F., & Zanni, G. (1975). Eyewitness testimony: The influence of the wording of a question. *Bulletin of the Psychonomic Society*, *5*, 86–88.

Logan, G.D. (1988). Toward an instance theory of automatization. *Psychological Review*, *95*, 492–527.

Logan, G.D. (2004). Cumulative progress in formal theories of attention. *Annual Review of Psychology*, *55*, 207–234.

Logan, G.D., Taylor, S.E., & Etherton, J.L. (1996). Attention in the acquisition and expression of automaticity. *Journal of Experimental Psychology: Learning, Memory, & Cognition*, *22*, 620–638.

Logie, R.H. (1995). *Visuo-spatial working memory*. Hove, UK: Psychology Press.

Logie, R.H. (1999). State of the art: Working memory. *The Psychologist*, *12*, 174–178.

Lopes, L.L. (1987). Between hope and fear: The psychology of fear. In L. Berkowitz (Ed.), *Advances in experimental social psychology*, *Vol. 20*. San Diego, CA: Academic Press.

Losier, B.J.W., & Klein, R.M. (2001). A review of the evidence for a disengagement deficit following parietal lobe damage. *Neuroscience and Biobehavioral Reviews*, *25*, 1–13.

Lovatt, P., Avons, S.E., & Masterson, J. (2000). The word-length effect and disyllabic words. *Quarterly Journal of Experimental Psychology*, *53*A, 1–22.

Lucas, M. (1999). Context effects in lexical access: A meta-analysis. *Memory & Cognition*, *27*, 385–398.

Luchins, A.S. (1942). Mechanisation in problem solving. The effect of Einstellung. *Psychological Monographs*, *54*, 248.

Luchins, A.S., & Luchins, E.H. (1959). *Rigidity of behaviour.* Eugene, OR: University of Oregon Press.

Luck, S.J. (1998). Neurophysiology of selective attention. In H. Pashler (Ed.), *Attention*. Hove, UK: Psychology Press.

Luck, S.J., Vogel, E.K., & Shapiro, K.L. (1996). Word meanings are accessed but cannot be reported during the attentional blink. *Nature*, *383*, 616–618.

Lueck, C.J., Zeki, S., Friston, K.J., Deiber, M.-P., Cope, P., Cunningham, V.J. et al. (1989). The colour centre in the cerebral cortex of man. *Nature*, *340*, 386–389.

Lumer, E.D., Friston, K.J., & Rees, G. (1998). Neural correlates of perceptual rivalry in the human brain. *Science*, *280*, 1930–1934.

Lund, K., & Burgess, C. (1996). Producing high-dimensional semantic spaces from lexical co-occurrence. *Behavior Research Methods, Instruments and Computers*, *28*, 203–208.

Lund, K., Burgess, C., & Atchley, R. (1995). Semantic and associative priming in high-dimensional semantic space. In *Proceedings of the 17th Annual Conference of the Cognitive Science Society* (pp. 660–665). Mahwah, NJ: Lawrence Erlbaum Associates Inc.

Luria, A.R. (1975). *The mind of a mnemonist.* New York: Basic Books.

Lustig, C., & Hasher, L. (2001a). Implicit memory is not immune to interference. *Psychological Bulletin*, *127*, 618–628.

Lustig, C., & Hasher, L. (2001b). Implicit memory is vulnerable to proactive interference. *Psychological Science*, *12*, 408–412.

MacDonald, M.C., & Christiansen, M.H. (2002). Reassessing working memory: Comment on Just and Carpenter (1992) and Waters and Caplan (1996). *Psychological Review*, *109*, 36–54.

MacDonald, M.C., Pearlmutter, N.J., & Seidenberg, M.S. (1994). Lexical nature of syntactic ambiguity resolution. *Psychological Review*, *101*, 676–703.

MacDonald, S., Uesiliana, K., & Hayne, H. (2000). Cross-cultural and gender differences in childhood amnesia. *Memory*, *8*, 365–376.

MacGregor, J.N., Ormerod, T.C., & Chronicle, E.P. (2001). Information processing and insight: A process model of performance on the nine-dot and related problems. *Journal of Experimental Psychology: Learning, Memory, and Cognition*, *27*, 176–201.

Mack, A. (2003). Inattentional blindness: Looking without seeing. *Current Directions in Psychological Science*, *12*, 180–184.

Mack, A., & Rock, I. (1998). *Inattentional blindness*. Cambridge, MA: MIT Press.

MacKay, D. (1987). Divided brains—divided minds. In C. Blakemore & S. Greenfield (Eds.), *Mindwaves: Thoughts, identity and consciousness*. Oxford: Blackwell.

Mackintosh, N.J. (1998). *IQ and human intelligence*. Oxford: Oxford University Press.

Mackintosh, N.J., & Bennett, E.S. (2003). The fractionation of working memory maps onto different components of intelligence. *Intelligence*, *31*, 519–531.

Maclay, H., & Osgood, C.E. (1959). Hesitation phenomena in spontaneous English speech. *Word*, *15*, 19–44.

Macoir, J., & Bernier, J. (2002). Is surface dysgraphia tied to semantic impairment? Evidence from a case of semantic dementia. *Brain and Cognition*, *48*, 452–457.

Madison, P. (1956). Freud's repression concept: A survey and attempted clarification. *International Journal of Psychoanalysis*, *37*, 75–81.

Maguire, E.A., Valentine, E.R., Wilding, J.M., & Kapur, N. (2003). Routes to remembering: The brains behind superior memory. *Nature Neuroscience*, *6*, 90–95.

Maher, L., Rothi, L., & Heilman, K. (1994). Lack of awareness in an aphasic patient with relatively preserved auditory comprehension. *Brain and Language*, *46*, 402–418.

Maier, N.R.F. (1931). Reasoning in humans II: The solution of a problem and its appearance in consciousness. *Journal of Comparative Psychology*, *12*, 181–194.

Majerus, S., Lekeu, F., Van der Linden, M., & Salmon, E. (2001). Deep dysphasia: Further evidence on the relationship between phonological short-term memory and language processing impairments. *Cognitive Neuropsychology*, *18*, 385–410.

Malone, D.R., Morris, H.H., Kay, M.C., & Levin, H.S. (1982). Prosopagnosia: A double dissocation between the recognition of familiar and unfamiliar faces. *Journal of Neurology, Neurosurgery, & Psychiatry*, *45*, 820–822.

Malt, B.C., & Smith, E.E. (1983). Correlated properties in natural categories. *Journal of Verbal Learning & Verbal Behavior*, *23*, 250–269.

Manktelow, K.I. (1999). *Reasoning and thinking.* Hove, UK: Psychology Press.

Manns, J.R., Hopkins, R.O., & Squire, L.R. (2003). Semantic memory and the human hippocampus. *Neuron*, *38*, 127–133.

Marcus, S.L., & Rips, L.J. (1979). Conditional reasoning. *Journal of Verbal Learning & Verbal Behavior*, *18*, 199–233.

Marek, J.P., & Levy, C.M. (1999). Testing the role of the phonological loop in writing. In M. Torrance & G. Jeffery (Eds.), *Cognitive demands of writing*. Amsterdam: Amsterdam University Press.

Markham, A.B., & Ross, B.H. (2003). Category use and category learning. *Psychological Bulletin*, *129*, 592–613.

Markman, A.B., & Gentner, D. (2001). Thinking. *Annual Review of Psychology*, *52*, 223–247.

Marr, D. (1976). Early processing of visual information. *Philosophical Transactions of the Royal Society (London)*, *B275*, 483–524.

Marr, D. (1982). *Vision: A computational investigation into the human representation and processing of visual information*. San Francisco, CA: W.H. Freeman.

Marr, D., & Hildreth, E. (1980). Theory of edge detection. *Proceedings of the Royal Society of London*, *B207*, 187–217.

Marr, D., & Nishihara, K. (1978). Representation and recognition of the spatial organisation of three-dimensional shapes. *Philosophical Transactions of the Royal Society, Series B*, 269–294.

Marsh, R.L., & Hicks, J.L. (1998). Event-based prospective memory and executive control of working memory. *Journal of Experimental Psychology: Learning, Memory & Cognition*, *24*, 336–349.

Marsh, R.L., Hicks, J.L., & Landau, J.D. (1998). An investigation of everyday prospective memory. *Memory & Cognition*, *26*, 633–643.

Marshall, J., Robson, J., Pring, T., & Chiat, S. (1998). Why does monitoring fail in jargon aphasia? *Brain and Language*, *63*, 79–107.

Marshall, J.C., & Halligan, P.W. (1988). Blindsight and insight in visuo-spatial neglect. *Nature*, *336*, 766–767.

Marshall, J.C., & Halligan, P.W. (1994). The yin and yang of visuo-spatial neglect: A case study. *Neuropsychologia*, *32*, 1037–1057.

Marshall, J.C., & Newcombe, F. (1973). Patterns of paralexia: A psycholinguistic approach. *Journal of Psycholinguistic Research*, *2*, 175–199.

Marslen-Wilson, W.D. (1990). Activation, competition, and frequency in lexical access. In G.T.M. Altmann (Ed.), *Cognitive models of speech processing: Psycholinguistics and computational perspectives*. Cambridge, MA: MIT Press.

Marslen-Wilson, W.D., & Tyler, L.K. (1980). The temporal structure of spoken language comprehension. *Cognition*, *6*, 1–71.

Marslen-Wilson, W.D., & Warren, P. (1994). Levels of perceptual representation and process in lexical access: Words, phonemes, and features. *Psychological Review*, *101*, 653–675.

Martin, A., & Caramazza, A. (2003). Neuropsychological and neuroimaging perspectives on conceptual knowledge: An introduction. *Cognitive Neuropsychology*, *20*, 195–221.

Martin, G.N. (1998). *Human neuropsychology*. London: Prentice Hall.

Martin, R.C. (2003). Language processing: Functional organisation and neuroanatomical basis. *Annual Review of Psychology*, *54*, 55–89.

Martinez, A., Anllo-Vento, L., Sereno, M.I., Frank, L.R., Buxton, R.B., Dubowitz, D.J. et al. (1999). Involvement of striate and extrastriate visual cortical areas in spatial attention. *Nature Neuroscience*, *4*, 364–369.

Martone, M., Butters, N., Payne, M., Becker, J.T., & Sax, D.S. (1984). Dissociations between skill learning and verbal recognition in amnesia and dementia. *Archives of Neurology*, *41*, 965–970.

Marzi, C.A., Girelli, M., Natale, E., & Miniussi, C. (2001). What exactly is extinguished in unilateral visual extinction? *Neuropsychologia*, *39*, 1354–1366.

Marzi, C.A., Smania, N., Martini, M.C., Gambina, G., Tomelleri, G., Palamara, A. et al. (1997). Implicit redundant-targets effect in visual extinction. *Neuropsychologia*, *34*, 9–22.

Mason, R.A., & Just, M.A. (2004). How the brain processes causal inferences in text. *Psychological Science*, *15*, 1–7.

Massaro, D.W. (1989). Testing between the TRACE model and the fuzzy logical model of speech perception. *Cognitive Psychology*, *21*, 398–421.

Massaro, D.W. (1994). Psychological aspects of speech perception: Implications for research and theory. In M.A. Gernsbacher (Ed.), *Handbook of psycholinguistics*. San Diego, CA: Academic Press.

Masters, R.S.W. (1992). Knowledge, nerves and know-how: The role of explicit versus implicit knowledge in the breakdown of a complex skill under pressure. *British Journal of Psychology*, *83*, 343–358.

Mather, G. (1997). The use of image blur as a depth cue. *Perception*, *26*, 1147–1158.

Mather, G., & Murdoch, L. (1994). Gender discrimination in biological motion displays based on dynamic cues. *Proceedings of the Royal Society of London*, *B*, 273–279.

Mather, G., Radford, K., & West, S. (1992). Low-level visual processing of biological motion. *Proceedings of the Royal Society of London B*, *249*, 149–155.

Mattingley, J.B., Davis, G., & Driver, J. (1997). Pre-attentive filling-in of visual surfaces in parietal extinction. *Science*, *275*, 671–674.

Mattys, S.L. (2004). Stress versus coarticulation: Toward an integrated approach to explicit speech segmentation. *Journal of Experimental Psychology: Human Perception and Performance*, *30*, 397–408.

Maule, A.J. (2001). Studying judgement: Some comments and suggestions for future research. *Thinking and Reasoning*, *7*, 91–102.

Maule, A.J., & Hodgkinson, G.P. (2002). Heuristics, biases and strategic decision making. *The Psychologist*, *15*, 69–71.

Mayer, R.E. (1990). Problem solving. In M.W. Eysenck (Ed.), *The Blackwell dictionary of cognitive psychology.* Oxford, UK: Blackwell.

Mayes, A.R. (2002). Does focal retrograde amnesia exist and if so, what causes it? *Cortex*, *38*, 670–673.

McBride, D.M., Dosher, B.A., & Gage, N. (2001). A comparison of forgetting for conscious and automatic memory processes in word fragment completion tasks. *Journal of Memory and Language*, *45*, 585–615.

McCandliss, B.D., Cohen, L., & Dehaene, S. (2003). The visual word form area: Expertise for reading in the fusiform gyrus. *Trends in Cognitive Sciences*, *7*, 293–299.

McCarthy, R., & Warrington, E.K. (1984). A two-route model of speech production. *Brain*, *107*, 463–485.

McClelland, J.L. (1991). Stochastic interactive processes and the effect of context on perception. *Cognitive Psychology*, *23*, 1–44.

McClelland, J.L. (1993). The GRAIN model: A framework for modelling the dynamics of information processing. In D.E. Meyer & S. Kornblum (Eds.), *Attention and performance, Vol. XIV*. Hillsdale, NJ: Lawrence Erlbaum Associates Inc.

McClelland, J.L., & Elman, J.L. (1986). The TRACE model of speech perception. *Cognitive Psychology*, *18*, 1–86.

McClelland, J.L., & Rumelhart, D.E. (1981). An interactive activation model of context effects in letter perception. Part 1. An account of basic findings. *Psychological Review*, *88*, 375–407.

McClelland, J.L., Rumelhart, D.E., & The PDP Research Group (1986). *Parallel distributed processing: Vol. 2. Psychological and biological models*. Cambridge, MA: MIT Press.

McCloskey, M. (2001). The future of cognitive neuropsychology. In B. Rapp (Ed.), *The handbook of cognitive neuropsychology: What deficits reveal about the human mind* (pp. 593–610). Philadelphia: Psychology Press.

McCloskey, M.E., & Glucksberg, S. (1978). Natural categories: Well defined or fuzzy sets? *Memory & Cognition*, *6*, 462–472.

McDaniel, M.A., & Einstein, G.O. (2000). Strategic and automatic processes in prospective memory retrieval: A multiprocess framework. *Applied Cognitive Psychology*, *14*, S127–S144.

McDaniel, M.A., Robinson-Riegler, B., & Einstein, G.O. (1998). Prospective remembering: Perceptually driven or conceptually driven processes? *Memory & Cognition*, *26*, 121–134.

McDermott, K.B., & Roediger, H.L. (1994). Effects of imagery on perceptual implicit memory tests. *Journal of Experimental Psychology: Learning, Memory, and Cognition*, *20*, 1379–1390.

McDonald, S.A., & Shillcock, R.C. (2003). Eye movements reveal the on-line computation of lexical probabilities during reading. *Psychological Science*, *14*, 648–652.

McElree, B., & Carrasco, M. (1999). Temporal dynamics of visual search: A speed–accuracy analysis of feature and conjunction searches. *Journal of Experimental Psychology: Human Perception & Performance*, *25*, 1517–1539.

McGlinchey-Berroth, R., Milber, W.P., Verfaellie, M., Alexander, M., & Kilduff, P.T. (1993). Semantic processing in the neglected visual field: Evidence from a lexical decision task. *Cognitive Neuropsychology*, *10*, 79–108.

McGlone, M.S., & Manfredi, D. (2001). Topic–vehicle interaction in metaphor comprehension. *Memory & Cognition*, *29*, 1209–1219.

McGregor, S.J., & Howes, A. (2002). The role of attack and defence semantics in skilled players' memory for chess positions. *Memory & Cognition*, *30*, 707–717.

McGurk, H., & MacDonald, J. (1976). Hearing lips and seeing voices. *Nature*, *264*, 746–748.

McIntosh, A.R., Rajah, M.N., & Lobaugh, N.J. (1999). Interactions of prefrontal cortex in relation to awareness in sensory learning. *Science*, *284*, 1531–1533.

McIntyre, J., Zago, M., Berthoz, A., & Lacquaniti, F. (2001). Does the brain model Newton's laws? *Nature Neurosciences*, *4*, 693–694.

McKee, R., & Squire, L.R. (1992). Equivalent forgetting rates in long-term memory for diencephalon and medial temporal lobe amnesia. *Journal of Neuroscience*, *12*, 3765–3772.

McKoon, G., & Ratcliff, R. (1980). Priming in item recognition: The organization of propositions in memory for text. *Journal of Verbal Learning & Verbal Behavior*, *19*, 369–386.

McKoon, G., & Ratcliff, R. (1986). Inferences about predictable events. *Journal of Experimental Psychology: Learning, Memory, & Cognition*, *12*, 82–91.

McKoon, G., & Ratcliff, R. (1992). Inference during reading. *Psychological Review*, *99*, 440–466.

McLeod, P. (1977). A dual-task response modality effect: Support for multiprocessor models of attention. *Quarterly Journal of Experimental Psychology*, *29*, 651–667.

McLeod, P., Dittrich, W., Driver, J., Perrett, D., & Zihl, J. (1996). Preserved and impaired detection of structure from motion by a "motion-blind" patient. *Visual Cognition*, *3*, 363–391.

McLeod, P., Plunkett, K., & Rolls, E.T. (1998). *Introduction to connectionist modelling of cognitive processes*. Oxford: Oxford University Press.

McNally, R.J., Clancy, S.A., & Schacter, D.L. (2001). Directed forgetting of trauma cues in adults reporting repressed or recovered memories of childhood sexual abuse. *Journal of Abnormal Psychology, 110*, 151–156.

McQueen, J.M. (1991). The influence of the lexicon on phonetic categorisation: Stimulus quality in word-final ambiguity. *Journal of Experimental Psychology: Human Perception & Performance, 17*, 433–443.

McQueen, J.M. (2004). Speech perception. In K. Lamberts & R. Goldstone (Eds.), *The handbook of cognition*. London: Sage Publications.

Meacham, J.A., & Singer, J. (1977). Incentive in prospective remembering. *Journal of Psychology, 97*, 191–197.

Medin, D.L., Lynch, E.B., & Solomon, K.O. (2000). Are there kinds of concepts? *Annual Review of Psychology, 51*, 121–147.

Meissner, C., & Brigham, J.C. (2001). Twenty years of investigating the own-race bias in memory for faces: A meta-analytic review. *Psychology and Public Policy Law, 7*, 3–35.

Mellers, B.A., Schwartz, A., & Cooke, A.D.J. (1998). Judgement and decision making. *Annual Review of Psychology, 49*, 447–477.

Mensink, G.-J., & Raaijmakers, J.G.W. (1988). A model for interference and forgetting. *Psychological Review, 95*, 434–455.

Merikle, P.M., Smilek, D., & Eastwood, J.D. (2001). Perception without awareness: Perspectives from cognitive psychology. *Cognition, 79*, 115–134.

Mervis, C.B., & Pani, J.R. (1980). Acquisition of basic object categories. *Cognitive Psychology, 12*, 496–522.

Metcalfe, J., & Weibe, D. (1987). Intuition in insight and noninsight problem solving. *Memory & Cognition, 15*, 238–246.

Meyer, D.E., & Schvaneveldt, R.W. (1971). Facilitation in recognising pairs of words: Evidence of a dependence between retrieval operations. *Journal of Experimental Psychology, 90*, 227–234.

Miceli, G., Silveri, M.C., Romani, C., & Caramazza, A. (1989). Variation in the pattern of omissions and substitutions of grammatical morphemes in the spontaneous speech of so-called agrammatic patients. *Brain & Language, 36*, 447–492.

Michotte, A. (1946). *The perception of causality* [1963 translation by T. & E. Miles]. London: Methuen.

Miller, G.A. (1956). The magic number seven, plus or minus two: Some limits on our capacity for processing information. *Psychological Review, 63*, 81–93.

Miller, G.A., & McNeill, D. (1969). Psycholinguistics. In G. Lindzey & E. Aronson (Eds.), *The handbook of social psychology, Vol. 3*. Reading, MA: Addison-Wesley.

Milner, A.D., & Goodale, M.A. (1995). *The visual brain in action*. Oxford: Oxford University Press.

Milner, A.D., & Goodale, M.A. (1998). The visual brain in action. *Psyche, 4*, 1–14.

Milner, A.D., Perrett, D.I., Johnston, R.S., Benson, P.J., Jordan, T.R., Heeley, D.W. et al. (1991). Perception and action in "visual form agnosia". *Brain, 114*, 405–428.

Milner, B. (1962). Les troubles de la mémoire accompagnant des lésions hippocampiques bilaterales. In P. Passouant (Ed.), *Physiologie de l'hippocampe*. Paris: Centre des Recherches Scientifiques.

Mishkin, M., & Ungerleider, L.G. (1982). Contribution of striate inputs to the visuospatial functions of parieto-preoccipital cortex in monkeys. *Behavioral Brain Research, 6*, 57–77.

Mitroff, I. (1974). *The subjective side of science*. Amsterdam: Elsevier.

Miyake, A., Friedman, N.P., Emerson, M.J., Witzki, A.H., Howerter, A., & Wager, T. (2000). The unity and diversity of executive functions and their contributions to complex "frontal lobe" tasks: A latent variable analysis. *Cognitive Psychology, 41*, 49–100.

Moore, C.J., & Price, C.J. (1999). A functional neuroimaging study of the variables that generate category-specific object processing differences. *Brain, 122*, 943–962.

Moray, N. (1959). Attention in dichotic listening: Affective cues and the influence of instructions. *Quarterly Journal of Experimental Psychology, 11*, 56–60.

Morgan, M. (2003). *The space between our ears: How the brain represents visual space*. London: Weidenfeld & Nicolson.

Morland, A.B. (1999). Conscious and veridical motion perception in a human hemianope. *Journal of Consciousness Studies, 6*, 43–53.

Morris, C.D., Bransford, J.D., & Franks, J.J. (1977). Levels of processing versus transfer appropriate processing. *Journal of Verbal Learning & Verbal Behavior, 16*, 519–533.

Morris, P.E., & Reid, R.L. (1970). The repeated use of mnemonic imagery. *Psychonomic Science, 20*, 337–338.

Morrison, D.J., Bruce, V., & Burton, A.M. (2003). Understanding provoked overt recognition in prosopagnosia. *Visual Cognition, 8*, 47–65.

Morrone, M.C., Tosetti, M., Montanaro, D., Fiorentini, A., Cioni, G., & Burr, D.C. (2000). A cortical area that responds specifically to optic flow, revealed by fMRI. *Nature Neuroscience, 3*, 1322–1328.

Morsella, E., & Miozzo, M. (2002). Evidence for a cascade model of lexical access in speech production. *Journal of Experimental Psychology: Learning, Memory, and Cognition, 28*, 555–563.

Morton, N., & Morris, R.G. (1995). Imagine transformation dissociated from visuo-spatial working memory. *Cognitive Neuropsychology, 12*, 769–791.

Moss, H., & Hampton, J. (2003). *Conceptual representations*. Hove, UK: Psychology Press.

Most, S.B., Simons, D.J., Scholl, B.J., Jimenez, R., Clifford, E., & Chabris, C.F. (2001). How not to be seen: The contribution of similarity and selective ignoring to sustained inattentional blindness. *Psychological Science*, *12*, 9–17.

Motley, M.T., Camden, C.T., & Baars, B.J. (1982). Covert formulation and editing of anomalies in speech production: Evidence from experimentally elicited slips of the tongue. *Journal of Verbal Learning and Verbal Behavior*, *21*, 578–594.

Mozer, M.C., & Sitton, M. (1998). *Computational modeling of spatial attention*. In H. Pashler (Ed.), *Attention* (pp. 341–388). Hove, UK: Psychology Press.

Müller, B. (1999). Use specificity of cognitive skills: Evidence for production rules? *Journal of Experimental Psychology: Learning, Memory, and Cognition*, *25*, 191–207.

Mulligan, N.W. (1998). The role of attention during encoding in implicit and explicit memory. *Journal of Experimental Psychology: Learning, Memory, & Cognition*, *24*, 27–47.

Murphy, G.L. (2002). *The big book of concepts*. Cambridge, MA: MIT Press.

Murphy, G.L., & Medin, D.L. (1985). The role of theories in conceptual coherence. *Psychological Review*, *92*, 289–316.

Murray, J.D., & Burke, K.A. (2003). Activation and encoding of predictive inferences: The role of reading skill. *Discourse Processes*, *35*, 81–102.

Muter, P. (1978). Recognition failure of recallable words in semantic memory. *Memory & Cognition*, *6*, 9–12.

Muthukumaraswamy, S.D., Johnson, B.W., & Hamm, J.P. (2003). A high density ERP comparison of mental rotation and mental size transformation. *Brain and Cognition*, *52*, 271–280.

Mynatt, C.R., Doherty, M.E., & Tweney, R.D. (1977). Confirmation bias in a simulated research environment. *Quarterly Journal of Experimental Psychology*, *29*, 85–95.

Mynatt, C.R., Doherty, M.E., & Tweney, R.D. (1978). Consequences of confirmation and disconfirmation in a simulated research environment. *Quarterly Journal of Experimental Psychology*, *30*, 395–406.

Nadel, M., & Moscovitch, M. (2001). The hippocampal complex and long-term memory revisited. *Trends in Cognitive Neuroscience*, *5*, 228–230.

Nairne, J.S. (2002a). Remembering over the short-term: The case against the standard model. *Annual Review of Psychology*, *53*, 53–81.

Nairne, J.S. (2002b). The myth of the encoding–retrieval match. *Memory*, *10*, 389–395.

Nairne, J.S., Whiteman, H.L., & Kelley, M.R. (1999). Short-term forgetting of order under conditions of reduced interference. *Quarterly Journal of Experimental Psychology*, *52*A, 241–251.

Nealey, T.A., & Maunsell, J.H.R. (1994). Magnocellular and parvocellular contributions to the responses of neurons in macaque striate cortex. *Journal of Neuroscience*, *14*, 2069–2079.

Needham, D.R., & Begg, I.M. (1991). Problem-oriented training promotes spontaneous analogical transfer, memory-oriented training promoted memory for training. *Memory and Cognition*, *19*, 5453–5570.

Neely, J.H. (1977). Semantic priming and retrieval from lexical memory: Roles of inhibitionless spreading activation and limited capacity attention. *Journal of Experimental Psychology: General*, *106*, 226–254.

Neisser, U. (1967). *Cognitive psychology*. New York: Appleton-Century-Crofts.

Neisser, U. (1982). *Memory observed*. San Francisco, CA: Freeman.

Neisser, U. (1996). Remembering as doing. *Behavioral & Brain Sciences*, *19*, 203–204.

Nelson, K. (1993). Explaining the emergence of autobiographical memory in early childhood. In A.F. Collins, S.E. Gathercole, M.A. Conway, & P.E. Morris (Eds.), *Theories of memory*. Hove, UK: Psychology Press.

Newell, A. (1980). Physical symbol systems. *Cognitive Science*, *4*, 135–183.

Newell, A., Shaw, J.C., & Simon, H.A. (1958). Elements of a theory of human problem solving. *Psychological Review*, *65*, 151–166.

Newell, A., & Simon, H.A. (1972). *Human problem solving*. Englewood Cliffs, NJ: Prentice Hall.

Newell, B.R., & Shanks, D.R. (2003). Take-the-best or look at the rest? Factors influencing "one-reason" decision making. *Journal of Experimental Psychology: Learning, Memory, and Cognition*, *29*, 53–65.

Newell, B.R., Weston, N.J., & Shanks, D.R. (2003). Empirical tests of a fast and frugal heuristic: Not everyone "takes-the-best". *Organizational Behavior and Human Decision Processes*, *91*, 82–96.

Newman, S.D., Carpenter, P.A., Varma, S., & Just, M.A. (2003). Frontal and parietal participation in problem solving in the Tower of London: fMRI and computational modelling of planning and high-level perception. *Neuropsychologia*, *41*, 1668–1682.

Newsome, W.T., & Paré, E.B. (1988). A selective impairment of motion perception following lesions of the middle temporal visual area (MT). *Journal of Neuroscience*, *8*, 2201–2211.

Newstead, S. (2000). What is an ecologically rational heuristic? *Behavioural and Brain Sciences*, *23*, 759–760.

Newstead, S.E., Handley, S.J., & Buck, E. (1999). Falsifying mental models: Testing the predictions of theories of syllogistic reasoning. *Memory & Cognition*, *27*, 344–354.

Newstead, S.E., Handley, S.J., Harley, C., Wright, H., & Farrelly, D. (2004). Individual differences in deductive reasoning. *Quarterly Journal of Experimental Psychology*, *57*, 33–60.

Nickels, L., & Howard, D. (1995). Phonological errors in aphasic naming: Comprehension, monitoring and lexicality. *Cortex*, *31*, 209–237.

Nishitani, N., & Hari, R. (2000). Free in PMC, temporal dynamics of cortical representation for action. *Proceedings of the National Academy of Sciences USA*, *97*, 913–918.

Nissen, M.J., & Bullemer, P. (1987). Attentional requirements of learning: Evidence from performance measures. *Cognitive Psychology*, *19*, 1–32.

Norman, D.A. (1980). Twelve issues for cognitive science. *Cognitive Science*, *4*, 1–32.

Norman, D.A., & Shallice, T. (1986). Attention to action: Willed and automatic control of behaviour. In R.J. Davidson, G.E. Schwartz, & D. Shapiro (Eds.), *The design of everyday things*. New York: Doubleday.

Norman, G.R., Brooks, L.R., & Allen, S.W. (1989). Recall by expert medical practitioners and novices as a record of processing attention. *Journal of Experimental Psychology: Learning, Memory, and Cognition*, *15*, 1166–1174.

Norman, J. (2002). Two visual system and two theories of perception: An attempt to reconcile the constructivist and ecological approaches. *Behavioral and Brain Sciences*, *25*, 73–144.

Norris, D., McQueen, J.M., & Cutler, A. (2000). Merging information in speech recognition: Feedback is never necessary. *Behavioral and Brain Sciences*, *23*, 299–370.

Norris, D., McQueen, J.M., Cutler, A., & Butterfield, S. (1997). The possible-word constraint in the segmentation of continuous speech. *Cognitive Psychology*, *34*, 191–243.

Nosofsky, R.M. (1988). Exemplar-based accounts of relations between classification, recognition and typicality. *Journal of Experimental Psychology: Learning, Memory, and Cognition*, *14*, 700–708.

Nosofsky, R.M. (1991). Tests of an exemplar model for relating perceptual classification and recognition memory. *Journal of Experimental Psychology: Human Perception and Performance*, *17*, 3–27.

Novick, L.R., & Sherman, S.J. (2003). On the nature of insight solutions: Evidence from skill differences in anagram solution. *Quarterly Journal of Experimental Psychology*, *56*A, 351–382.

Nyberg, L. (2002). Levels of processing: A view from functional brain imaging. *Memory*, *10*, 345–348.

Nyberg, L., Marklund, P., Persson, J., Cabeza, R., Forkstam, C., Petersson, K.M., & Ingvar, M. (2003). Common prefrontal activations during working memory, episodic memory, and semantic memory. *Neuropsychologia*, *41*, 371–377.

Oakes, L.M. (1994). Development of infants' use of continuity cues in their perception of causality. *Developmental Psychology*, *30*, 869–879.

Oakhill, J., Garnham, A., & Johnson-Laird, P.N. (1990). Belief bias effects in syllogistic reasoning. In J.J. Gilhooly, R.H. Logie, & G. Erdos (Eds.), *Lines of thinking, Vol. 1*. New York: Wiley.

Oaksford, M. (1997). Thinking and the rational analysis of human reasoning. *The Psychologist*, *10*, 257–260.

Oaksford, M., & Chater, N. (1994). A rational analysis of the selection task as optimal data selection. *Psychological Review*, *101*, 608–631.

Oaksford, M., & Chater, N. (2003). Conditional probability and the cognitive science of conditional reasoning. *Mind & Language*, *18*, 359–379.

Oaksford, M., Chater, N., Grainger, B., & Larkin, J. (1997). Optimal data selection in the Reduced Array Selection Test (RAST). *Journal of Experimental Psychology: Learning, Memory, and Cognition*, *23*, 441–458.

O'Brien, D.P. (1995). Finding logic in human reasoning requires looking in the right places. In S.E. Newstead & J.St.B.T. Evans (Eds.), *Perspectives on thinking and reasoning: Essays in honour of Peter Wason*. Hove, UK: Psychology Press.

O'Brien, E.J., Shank, D.M., Myers, J.L., & Rayner, K. (1988). Elaborative inferences during reading: Do they occur on-line? *Journal of Experimental Psychology: Learning, Memory, & Cognition*, *14*, 410–420.

O'Craven, K., Downing, P., & Kanwisher, N. (1999). fMRI evidence for objects as the units of attentional selection. *Nature*, *401*, 584–587.

O'Craven, K., Downing, P., & Kanwisher, N. (2000). fMRI evidence for objects as the units of attentional selection. *Nature*, *401*, 584–587.

Ohlsson, S. (1992). Information processing explanations of insight and related phenomena. In M.T. Keane & K.J. Gilhooly (Eds.), *Advances in the psychology of thinking*. London: Harvester Wheatsheaf.

Okada, T., Schunn, C.D., Crowley, K., Oshima, J., Miwa, K., Aoki, T. et al. (1995). *Collaborative scientific research: Analyses of historical and interview data*. Paper presented at the 1995 Meeting of the Japanese Cognitive Science Society.

Okada, T., & Simon, H.A. (1997). Collaborative discovery in a scientific domain. *Cognitive Science*, *21*, 109–146.

Olive, T. (2004). Working memory in writing: Empirical evidence from the dual-task technique. *European Psychologist*, *9*, 32–42.

Olive, T., & Kellogg, R.T. (2002). Concurrent activation of high- and low-level production processes in written composition. *Memory & Cognition*, *30*, 594–600.

Olive, T., & Piolat, A. (2002). Suppressing visual feedback in written composition: Effects on processing demands and co-ordination of the writing processes. *International Journal of Psychology*, *37*, 209–218.

Oppenheimer, D.M. (2003). Not so fast! (and not so frugal!): Re-thinking the recognition heuristic. *Cognition*, *90*, B1–B9.

Orban, G.A., Fize, D., Peuskens, H., Denys, K., Nelissen, K., Sunaert, S. et al. (2003). Similarities and differences in motion processing between the human and macaque brain: Evidence from fMRI. *Neuropsychologia*, *41*, 1757–1768.

Ormerod, T.C., MacGregor, J.N., & Chronicle, E.P. (2002). Dynamics and constraints in insight problem solving. *Journal of Experimental Psychology: Learning, Memory, and Cognition*, *28*, 791–799.

O'Rourke, T.B., & Holcomb, P.J. (2002). Electrophysiological evidence for the efficiency of spoken word processing. *Biological Psychology*, *60*, 121–150.

O'Shea, R.P., Blackburn, S.G., & Ono, H. (1994). Contrast as a depth cue. *Vision Research*, *34*, 1595–1604.

Osterhout, L., & Nicol, J. (1999). On the distinctiveness, independence, and time course of the brain responses to syntactic and semantic anomalies. *Language and Cognitive Processes*, *14*, 283–317.

Over, D.E. (2003). *Evolution and the psychology of thinking*. Hove, UK: Psychology Press.

Owen, A.M., Downes, J.J., Sahakian, B.J., Polkey, C.E., & Robbins, T.W. (1990). Planning and spatial working memory following frontal lobe lesions in man. *Neuropsychologia*, *28*, 1021–1034.

Page, M. (2000). Connectionist modelling in psychology: A localist manifesto. *Behavioral and Brain Sciences*, *23*, 443–512.

Palmer, S., & Rock, I. (1994). Rethinking perceptual organisation: The role of uniform connectedness. *Psychonomic Bulletin & Review*, *1*, 29–55.

Palmer, S.E. (1975). The effects of contextual scenes on the identification of objects. *Memory & Cognition*, *3*, 519–526.

Palmer, S.E., & Kimchi, R. (1986). The information processing approach to cognition. In T. Knapp & L.C. Robertson (Eds.), *Approaches to cognition: Contrasts and controversies*. Hillsdale, NJ: Lawrence Erlbaum Associates Inc.

Palmer, J., Verghese, P., & Pavel, M. (2000). The psychophysics of visual search. *Vision Research*, *40*, 1227–1268.

Palmeri, T.J., & Blalock, C. (2000). The role of background knowledge in speeded perceptual categorisation. *Cognition*, *77*, B45–B57.

Papagno, C., Valentine, T., & Baddeley, A.D. (1991). Phonological short-term memory and foreign-language learning. *Journal of Memory & Language*, *30*, 331–347.

Parkin, A.J. (1979). Specifying levels of processing. *Quarterly Journal of Experimental Psychology*, *31*, 175–195.

Parkin, A.J. (2001). The structure and mechanisms of memory. In B. Rapp (Ed.), *The handbook of cognitive neuropsychology: What deficits reveal about the human mind.* Hove, UK: Psychology Press.

Pascual-Leone, A., Bartres-Faz, D., & Keenan, J.P. (1999). Transcranial magnetic stimulation: Studying the brain–behaviour relationship by induction of "virtual lesions". *Philosophical Transactions of the Royal Society of London B*, *354*, 1229–1238.

Pascual-Leone, A., & Walsh, V. (2001). Fast backprojections from the motion to the primary visual necessary for visual awareness. *Science*, *292*, 510–512.

Pashler, H. (1998). *Attention*. Hove, UK: Psychology Press.

Pashler, H. (2001). Involuntary orienting to flashing distrators in delayed search? In B.S. Gibson & C.L. Fox (Eds.), Attention, distraction and action: Multiple perspectives on attentional capture. New York, NY: Elsevier Science.

Pashler, H., & Johnston, J.C. (1998). Attentional limitations in dual-task performance. In H. Pashler (Ed.), *Attention*. Hove, UK: Psychology Press.

Pashler, H., Johnston, J.C., & Ruthroff, E. (2001). Attention and performance. *Annual Review of Psychology*, *52*, 629–651.

Passerault, J.-M., & Dinet, J. (2000). The role of visuospatial sketchpad in the written production of descriptive and argumentative texts. *Current Psychology Letters: Behavior, Brain, & Cognition*, *3*, 31–42.

Patterson, K., Graham, N., & Hodges, J.R. (1994). Reading in Alzheimer's type dementia: A preserved ability? *Neuropsychology*, *8*, 395–412.

Patterson, K., Vargha-Khadem, F., & Polkey, C. (1989). Reading with one hemisphere. *Brain*, *112*, 39–63.

Payne, J. (1976). Task complexity and contingent processing in decision making: An information search and protocol analysis. *Organizational Behavior and Human Performance*, *16*, 366–387.

Pazzani, M.J. (1991). Influence of prior knowledge on concept acquisition: Experimental and computational results. *Journal of Experimental Psychology: Learning, Memory, & Cognition*, *15*, 416–432.

Pederson, E., Danziger, E., Wilkins, D., Levinson, S. Kita, S., & Senft, G. (1998). Semantic typology and spatial conceptualisation. *Language*, *74*, 557–589.

Pelham, B.W., Sumarta, T.T., & Myaskovsky, L. (1994). The easy path from many to much: The numerosity heuristic. *Cognitive Psychology*, *26*, 103–133.

Pelphrey, K.A., Mack, P.B., Song, A., Guzeldere, G., & McCarthy, G. (2003). Faces evoke spatially differentiated patterns of BOLD activation and deactivation. *NeuroReport*, *14*, 955–959.

Pelz, J., & Hayhoe, M. (1995). Influence of the visual scene in visual direction constancy. *Vision Research*, *35*, 2267–2275.

Peper, C.E., Bootsma, R.J., Mestre, D.R., & Bakker, F.C. (1994). Catching balls: How to get the hand to the right place at the right time. *Journal of Experimental Psychology: Human Perception & Performance*, *20*, 591–612.

Perenin, M.-T. (1997). Optic ataxia and unilateral neglect: Clinical evidence for dissociable spatial functions in posterior parietal cortex. In P. Thier &

H.-O. Karnath (Eds.), *Parietal lobe contributions to orientation in 3D space*. Berlin: Springer.

Perenin, M.-T., & Vighetto, A. (1988). Optic ataxia: A specific disruption in visuomotor mechanisms. 1. Different aspects of the deficit in reaching for objects. *Brain*, *111*, 643–674.

Peretz, I., Kolinsky, R., Trano, M., et al. (1994). Functional dissociations following bilateral lesions of auditory cortex. *Brain*, *117*, 1283–1301.

Perfect, T.J., & Hollins, T.S. (1996). Predictive feeling of knowing judgements and postdictive confidence judgements in eyewitness memory and general knowledge. *Applied Cognitive Psychology*, *10*, 371–382.

Perfect, T.J., Hollins, T.S., & Hunt, A.L.R. (2000). Practice and feedback effects on the confidence–accuracy relation in eyewitness memory. *Memory*, *8*, 235–244.

Perruchet, P., Chambaron, S., & Ferrel-Chapus, C. (2003). Learning from implicit learning literature: Comment on Shea, Wulf, Whitacre, and Park (2001). *Quarterly Journal of Experimental Psychology*, *56*A, 769–778.

Petersen, S.E., Corbetta, M., Miezin, F.M., & Shulman, G.L. (1994). PET studies of parietal involvement in spatial attention: Comparison of different task types. *Canadian Journal of Experimental Psychology*, *48*, 319–338.

Peterson, L.R., & Peterson, M.J. (1959). Short-term retention of individual verbal items. *Journal of Experimental Psychology*, *58*, 193–198.

Peterson, M.S., Kramer, A.F., Wang, R.F., Irwin, D.E., & McCarley, J.S. (2001). Visual search has memory. *Psychological Science*, *12*, 287–292.

Peterson, R.R., & Savoy, P. (1998). Lexical selection and phonological encoding during language production: Evidence for cascaded processing. *Journal of Experimental Psychology: Learning, Memory, & Cognition*, *24*, 539–557.

Pexman, P.M., Lupker, S.J., & Reggin, L.D. (2002). Phonological effects in visual word recognition: Investigating the impact of feedback activation. *Journal of Experimental Psychology: Learning, Memory, and Cognition*, *28*, 572–584.

Pickering, M.J. (1999). Sentence comprehension. In S. Garrod & M.J. Pickering (Eds.), *Language processing*. Hove, UK: Psychology Press.

Pickering, M.J., & Traxler, M.J. (1998). Plausibility and recovery from garden paths: An eye-tracking study. *Journal of Experimental Psychology: Learning, Memory, & Cognition*, *24*, 940–961.

Pillemer, D.B., Goldsmith, L.R., Panter, A.T., & White, S.H. (1988). Very long-term memories of the first year in college. *Journal of Experimental Psychology: Learning, Memory, & Cognition*, *14*, 709–715.

Pinard, M., Chertkow, H., Black, S., & Peretz, I. (2002). A case study of pure word deafness: Modularity in auditory processing? *Neurocase*, *8*, 40–55.

Pinker, S. (1997). *How the mind works*. New York: W.W. Norton.

Pinker, S. (1999). *How the mind works*. London: Penguin Books.

Pisella, L., Grea, H., Tilikete, C., Vighetto, A., Desmurget, M., Rode, G. et al. (2000). An "automatic pilot" for the hand in human posterior parietal cortex: Towards reinterpreting optic ataxia. *Nature Neuroscience*, *3*, 729–736.

Pisoni, D.B., & Tash, J. (1974). Reaction times to comparisons within and across phonetic categories. *Perception & Psychophysics*, *15*, 285–290.

Pitt, M.A. (1995). The locus of the lexical shift in phoneme identification. *Journal of Experimental Psychology: Learning, Memory, and Cognition*, *21*, 1037–1052.

Plaut, D.C., McClelland, J.L., Seidenberg, M.S., & Patterson, K. (1996). Understanding normal and impaired word reading: Computational principles in quasi-regular domains. *Psychological Review*, *103*, 56–115.

Plaut, D.C., & Shallice, T. (1993). Deep dyslexia: A case study of connectionist neuropsychology. *Cognitive Neuropsychology*, *10*, 377–500.

Poeppel, D. (2001). Pure word deafness and the bilateral processing of the speech code. *Cognitive Science*, *21*, 679–693.

Poincaré, H. (1913). Mathematical creation. In H. Poincaré (Ed.), *The foundations of science*. New York: Science Press.

Poldrack, R.A., Desmond, J.E., Glover, G.H., & Gabrieli, J.D.E. (1996). The neural bases of visual skill: An fMRI study of mirror reading. *Society of Neuroscience*, *22*, 719.

Poldrack, R.A., & Gabrieli, J.D.E. (2001). Characterising the neural mechanisms of skill learning and repetition priming: Evidence from mirror reading. *Brain*, *124*, 67–82.

Poldrack, R.A., Selco, S.L., Field, J.E., & Cohen, N.J. (1999). The relationship between skill learning and repetition priming: Experimental and computational analyses. *Journal of Experimental Psychology: Learning, Memory, and Cognition*, *25*, 208–235.

Poletiek, F.H. (1996). Paradoxes of falsification. *Quarterly Journal of Experimental Psychology*, *49*A, 447–462.

Poletiek, F.H. (2001). *Hypothesis-testing behaviour*. Philadelphia, PA: Psychology Press.

Pollatsek, A., Bolozky, S., Well, A.D., & Rayner, K. (1981). Asymmetries in the perceptual span for Israeli readers. *Brain & Language*, *14*, 174–180.

Pomerantz, J.R. (1981). Perceptual organisation in information processing. In M. Kubovy & J.R. Pomerantz (Eds.), *Perceptual organisation*. Hillsdale, NJ: Lawrence Erlbaum Associates Inc.

Popper, K.R. (1968). *The logic of scientific discovery*. London: Hutchinson.

Posner, M.I. (1980). Orienting of attention. The VIIth Sir Frederic Bartlett lecture. *Quarterly Journal of Experimental Psychology*, *32*A, 3–25.

Posner, M.I. (1995). Attention in cognitive neuroscience: An overview. In M.S. Gazzaniga (Ed.), *The cognitive neurosciences*. Cambridge, MA: MIT Press.

Posner, M., & Cohen, Y. (1984). Components of visual orientating. In H. Bouma & D.G. Bouwhuis (Eds.), *Attention and performance X* (pp. 531–556). Hillsdale, NJ: Lawrence Erlbaum Associates Inc.

Posner, M.I., & DiGirolamo, G.J. (2000). Cognitive neuroscience: Origins and promise. *Psychological Bulletin*, *126*, 873–889.

Posner, M.I., & Petersen, S.E. (1990). The attention system of the human brain. *Annual Review of Neuroscience*, *13*, 25–42.

Posner, M.I., Rafal, R.D., Choate, L.S., & Vaughan, J. (1985). Inhibition of return: Neural basis and function. *Cognitive Neuropsychology*, *2*, 211–228.

Postma, A. (2000). Detection of errors during speech production: A review of speech monitoring models. *Cognition*, *77*, 97–131.

Poynor, D.V., & Morris, R.K. (2003). Inferred goals in narratives: Evidence from self-paced reading, recall, and eye movements. *Journal of Experimental Psychology: Learning, Memory, and Cognition*, *29*, 3–9.

Prabhakaran, V., Narayanan, K., Zhao, Z., & Gabrieli, J.D. (2000). Integration of diverse information in working memory within the frontal lobe. *Nature Neuroscience*, 3, 85–90.

Prabhakaran, V., Smith, J.A.L., Desmond, J.E., Glover, G., & Gabrieli, J.D.E. (1997). Neural substrates of fluid reasoning: A fMRI study of neocortical activation during performance of the Raven's Progressive Matrices Test. *Cognitive Psychology*, *33*, 43–63.

Pratkanis, A.R., & Aronson, E. (1992). *Age of propaganda: The everyday use and abuse of persuasion.* New York: W.H. Freeman.

Pressley, M., Levin, J.R., Hall, J.W., Miller, G.E., & Berry, J.K. (1980). The keyword method and foreign word acquisition. *Journal of Experimental Psychology: Human Learning and Memory*, *6*, 163–173.

Preuss, T.M., Qi, H., & Kaas, J.H. (1999). Distinctive compartmental organisation of human primary visual cortex. *Proceedings of the National Academy of Science USA*, *96*, 11601–11606.

Price, C.J., & Friston, K.J. (2002). What has neuroimaging contributed to category-specificity? In G. Humphreys & E. Forde (Eds.), *Category specificity in mind and brain*. Hove, UK: Psychology Press.

Price, C.J., Howard, D., Patterson, K., Warburton, E.A., Friston, K.J., & Frackowiak, R.S.J. (1998). Functional neuroimaging description of two deep dyslexic patients. *The Journal of Cognitive Neuroscience*, *10*, 303–315.

Price. C.J., Warburton, E.A., Moore, C.J., Frackowiak, R.S.J., & Friston, K.J. (2001). Dynamic diaschisis: Anatomically remote and context-sensitive human brain lesions. *Journal of Cognitive Neuroscience*, *13*, 419–429.

Prime, D.J., & Ward, L.M. (2004). Inhibition of return from stimulus to response. *Psychological Science*, *15*, 272–276.

Protopapas, A. (1999). Connectionist modeling of speech perception. *Psychological Bulletin*, *125*, 410–436.

Purves, D., & Lotto, R.B. (2003). *Why we see what we do.* Sunderland, MA: Sinauer Associates Inc.

Pylyshyn, Z.W. (2000). Situating vision in the world. *Trends in Cognitive Science*, *4*, 197–207.

Pylyshyn, Z.W. (2002). Mental imagery: In search of a theory. *Behavioral and Brain Sciences*, *25*, 157–238.

Pylyshyn, Z. (2003). *Seeing and visualizing: It's not what you think*, Cambridge, MA: The MIT Press.

Quinlan, P.T. (2003). Visual feature integration theory: Past, present, and future. *Psychological Bulletin*, *129*, 643–673.

Quinlan, P.T., & Wilton, R.N. (1998). Grouping by proximity or similarity? Competition between the Gestalt principles in vision. *Perception*, *27*, 417–430.

Quinn, J.G., & McConnell, J. (1996). Irrelevant pictures in visual working memory. *Quarterly Journal of Experimental Psychology*, *49*A, 200–215.

Radvansky, G.A., & Copeland, D.E. (2001). Working memory and situation model updating. *Memory & Cognition*, *29*, 1073–1080.

Rafal, R., Smith, J., Krantz, A., Cohen, A., & Brennan, C. (1990). Extrageniculate vision in hemianopic humans: Saccade inhibition by signals in the blind field. *Science*, *250*, 118–121.

Rafal, R.D., & Posner, M.I. (1987). Deficits in human visual spatial attention following thalamic lesions. *Proceedings of the National Academy of Science*, *84*, 7349–7353.

Raichle, M.E. (1994a). Images of the mind: Studies with modern imaging techniques. *Annual Review of Psychology*, 45, 333–356.

Raichle, M.E. (1994b). Visualizing the mind. *Scientific American*, *270*, 36–42.

Raichle, M.E. (1998a). The neural correlates of consciousness: An analysis of cognitive skill learning. *Philosophical Transactions of the Royal Society, London B: Biological Sciences*, *353*, 1889–1901.

Raichle, M.E., Fiez, J.A., Videen, T.O., MacLeod, A-M.K., Pardo, J.V., Fox, P.T. et al. (1994). Practice-related changes in human brain functional anatomy during nonmotor learning. *Cerebral Cortex*, *4*, 8–26.

Ramachandran, V.S. (1988). Perception of shape from shading. *Nature*, *331*, 163–166.

Ramachandran, V.S. (1995). Anosognosia in parietal lobe syndrome. *Conscious Cognition*, *4*, 22–51.

Rapp, B. (Ed.). (2001). *The handbook of cognitive neuropsychology*. New York: Psychology Press.

Rapp, B., Epstein, C., & Tainturier, M.-J. (2002). The integration of information across lexical and sub-lexical processes in spelling. *Cognitive Neuropsychology, 19*, 1–29.

Rapp, B., & Goldrick, M. (2000). Discreteness and interactivity in spoken word production. *Psychological Review, 107*, 460–499.

Ratcliff, R., & McKoon, G. (1978). Priming in item recognition: Evidence for the propositional structure of sentences. *Journal of Verbal Learning & Verbal Behavior, 20*, 204–215.

Rawlings, D., & Toogood, A. (1997). Using a "Taboo Response" measure to examine the relationship between divergent thinking and psychoticism. *Personality and Individual Differences, 22*, 61–68.

Rayner, K., & Morris, R.K. (1992). Eye movement control in reading: Evidence against semantic pre-processing. *Journal of Experimental Psychology: Human Perception & Performance, 18*, 163–172.

Rayner, K., & Pollatsek, A. (1989). *The psychology of reading.* London: Prentice Hall.

Rayner, K., & Sereno, S.C. (1994). Eye movements in reading: Psycholinguistic studies. In M.A. Gernsbacher (Ed.), *Handbook of psycholinguistics*. New York: Academic Press.

Reber, A.S. (1993). *Implicit learning and tacit knowledge: An essay on the cognitive unconscious.* Oxford, UK: Oxford University Press.

Redelmeier, D., Koehler, D.J., Liberman, V., & Tversky, A. (1995). Probability judgement in medicine: Discounting unspecified alternatives. *Medical Decision Making, 15*, 227–230.

Reed, J.M., & Squire, L.R. (1998). Retrograde amnesia for facts and events: Findings from four new cases. *Journal of Neuroscience, 18*, 3943–3954.

Rees, G., Wojciulik, E., Clarke, K., Husain, M., Frith, C., & Driver, J. (2000). Unconscious activation of visual cortex in the damaged right hemisphere of a parietal patient with extinction. *Brain, 123*, 82–92.

Rehder, B., & Ross, B.H. (2001). Abstract coherent concepts. *Journal of Experimental Psychology: Learning, Memory, and Cognition, 27*, 1261–1275.

Reicher, G.M. (1969). Perceptual recognition as a function of meaningfulness of stimulus material. *Journal of Experimental Psychology, 81*, 274–280.

Reichle, E.D., Pollatsek, A., Fisher, D.L., & Rayner, K. (1998). Toward a model of eye movement control in reading. *Psychological Review, 105*, 125–157.

Reichle, E.D., Rayner, K., & Pollatsek, A. (2003). The E-Z Reader model of eye-movement control in reading: Comparisons to other models. *Behavioral and Brain Sciences, 26*, 445–526.

Reisberg, D. (1997). *Cognition: Exploring the science of the mind*. New York: W.W. Norton.

Remington, R.W., Johnston, J.C., & Yantis, S. (1992). Involuntary attentional capture by abrupt onsets. *Perception & Psychophysics, 51*, 279–290.

Rensink, R.A. (2000). When good observers go bad: Change blindness, inattentional blindness, and visual experience. *Psyche, 6*.

Rensink, R.A. (2002). Change detection. *Annual Review of Psychology, 53*, 245–277.

Riddoch, M.J., & Humphreys, G.W. (1987). Visual object processing in optic aphasia: A case of semantic access agnosia. *Cognitive Neuropsychology, 4*, 131–185.

Riddoch, M.J., & Humphreys, G.W. (2001). Object recognition. In B. Rapp (Ed.), *The handbook of cognitive neuropsychology: What deficits reveal about the human mind.* Hove, UK: Psychology Press.

Rinck, M., & Bower, G.H. (2000). Temporal and spatial distance in situation models. *Memory & Cognition, 28*, 1310–1320.

Rinck, M., & Weber, U. (2003). Who when where: An experimental test of the event-indexing model. *Memory & Cognition, 31*, 1284–1292.

Rips, L.J. (1994). *The psychology of proof: Deductive reasoning in human thinking.* Cambridge, MA: MIT Press.

Rips, L.J., & Collins, A. (1993). Categories and resemblance. *Journal of Experimental Psychology: General, 122*, 468–486.

Rips, L.J., Shoben, E.J., & Smith, E.E. (1973). Semantic distance and the verification of semantic relations. *Journal of Verbal Learning and Verbal Behavior, 12*, 1–20.

Ritov, J., & Baron, J. (1990). Reluctance to vaccinate: Omission bias and ambiguity. *Journal of Behavioral Decision Making, 3*, 263–277.

Robbins, T.W., Anderson, E.J., Barker, D.R., Bradley, A.C., Fearnyhough, C., Henson, R., Hudson, S.R., & Baddeley, A. (1996). Working memory in chess. *Memory & Cognition, 24*, 83–93.

Roberson, D., Davies, I., & Davidoff, J. (2000). Colour categories are not universal: Replications and new evidence from a stone-age culture. *Journal of Experimental Psychology: General, 129*, 369–398.

Roberts, B., Kalish, M., Hird, K., & Kirsner, K. (1999). Decontextualised data in, decontextualised theory out. *Behavioral and Brain Sciences, 22*, 54–55.

Robertson, E.M., Théoret, H., & Pascual-Leone, A. (2003). Studies in cognition: The problems solved and created by transcranial magnetic stimulation. *Journal of Cognitive Neuroscience, 15*, 948–960.

Robertson, S.I. (2001). *Problem solving*. Hove, UK: Psychology Press.

Robson, J., Pring, T., Marshall, J., & Chiat, S. (2003). Phoneme frequency effects in jargon aphasia: A phonological investigation of non-word errors. *Brain and Language, 85*, 109–124.

Rock, I. (1973). *Orientation and form.* New York: Academic Press.

Rock, I., & Palmer, S. (1990). The legacy of Gestalt psychology. *Scientific American*, December, 48–61.

Rodriguez, E., George, N., Lachaux, J., Martinerie, J., Renault, B., & Varela, F.J. (1999). Perception's shadow: Long-distance synchronization of human brain activity. *Nature*, *397*, 430–433.

Roediger, H.L. III, & Gallo, D.A. (2002). Levels of processing: Some unanswered questions. In M. Naveh-Benjamin, M. Moscovitch, & H.L. Roediger (Eds.), *Perspectives on human memory and cognitive aging: Essays in honour of Fergus Craik* (pp. 28–47). Philadelphia: Psychology Press.

Roelofs, A. (2000). WEAVER++ and other computational models of lemma retrieval and word-form encoding. In L. Wheeldon (Ed.), *Aspects of language production*. Hove, UK: Psychology Press.

Roeltgen, D.P. (1987). Loss of deep dyslexic reading ability from a second left-hemisphere lesion. *Archives of Neurology*, *44*, 346–348.

Rogers, B.J., & Collett, T.S. (1989). The appearance of surfaces specified by motion parallax and binocular disparity. *Quarterly Journal of Experimental Psychology*, *41*A, 697–717.

Rogers, B.J., & Graham, M.E. (1979). Motion parallax as an independent cue for depth perception. *Perception*, *8*, 125–134.

Rogers, T.B., Kuiper, N.A., & Kirker, W.S. (1977). Self-reference and the encoding of personal information. *Journal of Personality & Social Psychology*, *35*, 677–688.

Roorda, A., & Williams, D.R. (1999). The arrangement of the three cone classes in the living human eye. *Nature*, *397*, 520–522.

Rosch, E., & Mervis, C.B. (1975). Family resemblances: Studies in the internal structure of categories. *Cognitive Psychology*, *7*, 573–605.

Rosch, E., Mervis, C.B., Gray, W.D., Johnson, D.M., & Boyes-Braem, P. (1976). Basic objects in natural categories. *Cognitive Psychology*, *8*, 382–439.

Rosen, A.C., Rao, S.M., Caffarra, P., Scaglioni, A., Bobholz, J.A., Wordley, S.J. et al. (1999). Neural basis of endogenous and exogenous orienting: A functional MRI study. *Journal of Cognitive Neuroscience*, *11*, 135–152.

Rosenbaum, D.A., Carlson, R.A., & Gilmore, R.O. (2001). Acquisition of intellectual and perceptual-motor skills. *Annual Review of Psychology*, *52*, 453–470.

Ross, M., & Wilson, A.E. (2002). It feels like yesterday: Self-esteem, valence of personal past experiences, and judgements of subjective distance. *Journal of Personality and Social Psychology*, *82*, 792–803.

Rossi, S., Caverni, J.P., & Girotto, V. (2001). Hypothesis testing in a rule discovery problem: When a focused procedure is effective. *Quarterly Journal of Experimental Psychology*, *54*A, 263–267.

Rottenstreich, Y., & Tversky, A. (1997). Unpacking, repacking, and anchoring: Advances in support theory. *Psychological Review*, *104*, 406–415.

Roy, D.F. (1991). Improving recall by eyewitnesses through the cognitive interview: Practical applications and implications for the police service. *The Psychologist*, *4*, 398–400.

Rozenblit, L.R., & Keil, F.C. (2002). The missunderstood limits of folk science: An illusion of explanatory depth. *Cognitive Science*, *26*, 521–562.

Rubin, D.C. (2000). The distribution of early childhood memories. *Memory*, *8*, 265–269.

Rubin, D.C., Rahhal, T.A., & Poon, L.W. (1998). Things learned in early childhood are remembered best. *Memory & Cognition*, *26*, 3–19.

Rubin, D.C., & Schulkind, M.D. (1997). The distribution of autobiographical memories across the lifespan. *Memory & Cognition*, *25*, 859–866.

Rubin, D.C., & Wenzel, A.E. (1996). One hundred years of forgetting: A quantitative description of retention. *Psychological Bulletin*, *103*, 734–760.

Rubin, D.C., Wetzler, S.E., & Nebes, R.D. (1986). Autobiographical memory across the life span. In D.C. Rubin (Ed.), *Autobiographical memory*. Cambridge: Cambridge University Press.

Rudge, P., & Warrington, E.K. (1991). Selective impairment of memory and visual perception in splenial tumours. *Brain*, *114*, 349–360.

Rugg, M.D. (1997). *Cognitive neuroscience*. Hove, UK: Psychology Press.

Rumelhart, D.E., & McClelland, J.L. (1986). On learning the past tenses of English verbs. In D.E. Rumelhart, J.L. McClelland, & The PDP Research Group (Eds.), *Parallel distributed processing, Vol. 2* (pp. 216–271). Cambridge, MA: MIT Press.

Rumelhart, D.E., McClelland, J.L., & The PDP Research Group (Eds.) (1986). *Parallel distributed processing, Vol. 1: Foundations*. Cambridge, MA: MIT Press.

Rumelhart, D.E., & Ortony, A. (1977). The representation of knowledge in memory. In R.C. Anderson, R.J. Spiro, & W.E. Montague (Eds.), *Schooling and the acquisition of knowledge*. Hillsdale, NJ: Lawrence Erlbaum Associates Inc.

Runco, M.A. (2004). Creativity. *Annual Review of Psychology*, *55*, 657–687.

Runeson, S., & Frykholm, G. (1983). Kinematic specifications of dynamics as an informational basis for person-and-action perception: Expectation, gender recognition, and deceptive intention. *Journal of Experimental Psychology: General*, *112*, 585–615.

Rushton, S.K., Harris, J.M., Lloyd, M.R., & Wann, J.P. (1998). Guidance of locomotion on foot uses perceived target direction rather than optic flow. *Current Biology*, *8*, 1191–1194.

Rushton, S.K., & Wann, J.P. (1999). Weighted combination of size and disparity: A computational model for timing a ball catch. *Nature Neuroscience*, *2*, 186–190.

Rushworth, M.F.S., Ellison, A., & Walsh, V. (2001). Complementary localization and lateralization of orienting and motor attention. *Nature Neuroscience*, *4*, 656–661.

Ruthruff, E., Johnston, J.C., & Van Selst, M.V. (2000). Why practice reduces dual-task interference. *Journal of Experimental Psychology: Human Perception and Performance*, *27*, 3–21.

Ryan, J.D., Althoff, R.R., Whitlow, S., & Cohen, N.J. (2000). Amnesia is a deficit in relational memory. *Psychological Science*, *11*, 454–461.

Ryan, J.D., & Cohen, N.J. (2004). Processing and short-term retention of relational information in amnesia. *Neuropsychologia*, *42*, 497–511.

Rylander, G. (1939). Personality changes after operations on the frontal lobes. *Acta Psychiatrica Neurologica* (Supplement No 30).

Saffran, E.M., Schwartz, M.F., & Marin, O.S.M. (1980a). Evidence from aphasia: Isolating the components of a production model. In B. Butterword (Ed.), *Language production, Vol. 1*. London: Academic Press.

Saffran, E.M., Schwartz, M.F., & Marin, O.S.M. (1980b). The word order problem in agrammatism: II. Production. *Brain & Language*, *10*, 249–262.

Sala, J.B., Rämä, P., & Courtney, S.M. (2003). Functional topography of a distributed neural system for spatial and nonspatial information maintenance in working memory. *Neuropsychologia*, *41*, 341–356.

Salzman, C.D., Britten, K.H., & Newsome, W.T. (1990). Cortical microstimulation influences perceptual judgments of motion direction. *Nature*, *346*, 174–177.

Salzman, C.D., Murasugi, C.M., Britten, K.H., & Newsome, W.T. (1992). Microstimulation in visual area MT: Effects on direction discrimination performance. *Journal of Neuroscience*, *12*, 2331–2355.

Samuel, A.G. (1981). Phonemic restoration: Insights from a new methodology. *Journal of Experimental Psychology: General*, *110*, 474–494.

Samuel, A.G. (1987). The effect of lexical uniqueness on phonemic restoration. *Journal of Memory and Language*, *26*, 36–56.

Samuel, A.G. (1997). Lexical activation produces potent phonemic percepts. *Cognitive Psychology*, *32*, 97–127.

Samuel, A.G., & Kat, D. (2003). Inhibition of return: A graphical meta-analysis of its time course and an empirical test of its temporal and spatial properties. *Psychonomic Bulletin & Review*, *10*, 897–906.

Samuelson, W., & Zeckhauser, R.J. (1988). Status quo bias in decision making. *Journal of Risk and Uncertainty*, *1*, 7–59.

Sanes, J.N., Dimitrov, B., & Hallett, M. (1990). Motor learning in patients with cerebellar dysfunction. *Brain*, *113*, 103–120.

Sanford, A.J. (2002). Context, attention and depth of processing during interpretation. *Mind & Language*, *17*, 188–206.

Sanocki, T., Bowyer, K.W., Heath, M.D., & Sarkar, S. (1998). Are edges sufficient for object recognition? *Journal of Experimental Psychology: Human Perception & Performance*, *24*, 340–349.

Savage, L.J. (1954). *The foundations of statistics*. New York: Dover.

Savelsbergh, G.J.P., Pijpers, J.R., & van Santvoord, A.A.M. (1993). The visual guidance of catching. *Experimental Brain Research*, *93*, 148–156.

Savelsbergh, G.J.P., Whiting, H.T.A., & Bootsma, R.J. (1991). Grasping tau. *Journal of Experimental Psychology: Human Perception & Performance*, *17*, 315–322.

Savoy, R.L. (2001). History and future directions of human brain mapping and functional neuroimaging. *Acta Psychologica*, *107*, 9–42.

Schacter, D.L. (1987). Implicit memory: History and current status. *Journal of Experimental Psychology: Learning, Memory, and Cognition*, *13*, 501–518.

Schacter, D.L., Alpert, N.M., Savage, C.R., Rauch, S.L., & Albert, M.S. (1996). Conscious recollection and the human hippocampal formation: Evidence from positron emission tomography. *Proceedings of the National Academy of Science, USA*, *93*, 321–325.

Schacter, D.L., & Badgaiyan, R.D. (2001). Neuroimaging of priming: New perspectives on implicit and explicit memory. *Current Directions in Psychological Science*, *10*, 1–4.

Schacter, D.L., & Church, B.A. (1995). Implicit memory in amnesic patients: When is auditory priming spared? *Journal of the International Neuropsychological Society*, *1*, 434–442.

Schacter, D.L., Church, B.A., & Bolton, E. (1995). Implicit memory in amnesic patients: Impairment of voice-specific impairment priming. *Psychological Science*, *6*, 20–25.

Schacter, D.L., McAndrews, M.P., & Moscovitch, M. (1988). Access to consciousness: Dissociations between implicit and explicit knowledge in neuropsychological syndromes. In L. Weiskrantz (Ed.), *Thought without language.* Oxford: Oxford University Press.

Schacter, D.L., & Tulving, E. (1994). What are the memory systems of 1994? In D.L. Schacter & E. Tulving (Eds.), *Memory systems.* Cambridge, MA: MIT Press.

Schacter, D.L., Wagner, A.D., & Buckner, R.L. (2000). Memory systems of 1999. In E. Tulving & F.I.M. Craik (Eds.), *The Oxford handbook of memory*. New York: Oxford University Press.

Schank, R.C., & Abelson, R.P. (1977). *Scripts, plans, goals and understanding.* Hillsdale, NJ: Lawrence Erlbaum Associates Inc.

Scheerer, M. (1963). Problem-solving. *Scientific American, 208*(4), 118–128.

Schendan, H.E., Searl, M.M., Melrose, R.J., & Stern, C.E. (2003). An fMRI study of the role of the medial temporal lobe in implicit and explicit sequence learning. *Neuron, 37*, 1013–1025.

Schiff, W., & Detwiler, M.L. (1979). Information used in judging impending collision. *Perception, 8*, 647–658.

Schiller, N.O., Greenhall, J.A., Shelton, J.R., & Caramazza, A. (2001). Serial order effects in spelling errors: Evidence from two dysgraphic patients. *Neurocase, 7*, 1–14.

Schilling, H.E.H., Rayner, K., & Chumbley, J.I. (1998). Comparing naming, lexical decision, and eye fixation times: Word frequency effects and individual differences. *Memory & Cognition, 26*, 1270–1281.

Schlottmann, A., & Anderson, N.H. (1993). An information integration approach to phenomenal causality. *Memory & Cognition, 21*, 785–801.

Schlottmann, A., & Shanks, D.R. (1992). Evidence for a distinction between judged and perceived causality. *Quarterly Journal of Experimental Psychology, 44*A, 321–342.

Schmitt, B.M., Münte, T.F., & Kutas, M. (2000). Electrophysiological estimates of the time course of semantic and phonological encoding during implicit picture naming. *Psychophysiology, 37*, 473–484.

Schneider, W., & Oliver, W.L. (1991). An instructable connectionist/control architecture: Using rule-based instructions to accomplish connectionist learning in a human time scale. In K. Van Lehn (Ed.), *Architecture for intelligence: The 22nd Carnegie Mellon symposium on cognition*. Hillsdale, NJ: Lawrence Erlbaum Associates Inc.

Schneider, W., & Shiffrin, R.M. (1977). Controlled and automatic human information processing: 1. Detection, search, and attention. *Psychological Review, 84*, 1–66.

Schneider, W., & Shiffrin, R.M. (1985). Categorisation (restructuring) and automatisation: Two separable factors. *Psychological Review, 92*, 424–428.

Schober, M.F. (1998). Different kinds of conversational perspective-taking. In S.R. Fussell & R.J. Kreuz (Eds.), *Social and cognitive psychological approaches to interpersonal communication*. Mahwah, NJ: Lawrence Erlbaum Associates Inc.

Schrater, P.R., Knill, D.C., & Simoncelli, E.P. (2001). Perceiving visual expansion without optic flow. *Nature, 410*, 816–819.

Schriver, K. (1984). *Revised computer documentation for comprehension: Ten lessons in protocol-aided revision* (Tech. Rep. No. 14). Pittsburgh, PA: Carnegie Mellon University.

Schumacher, E.H., Seymour, T.L., Glass, J.M., Fencsik, D.E., Lauber, E.J., Kieras, D.E. et al. (2001). Virtually perfect time sharing in dual-task performance: Uncorking the central cognitive bottleneck. *Psychological Science, 12*, 101–108.

Schunn, C.D., & Anderson, J.R. (1999). The generality/specificity of expertise in scientific reasoning. *Cognitive Science, 23*, 337–370.

Schunn, C.D., & Klahr, D. (1995). A 4-space model of scientific discovery. *Proceedings of the 15th. Annual Conference of the Cognitive Science Society.* Hillsdale, NJ: Lawrence Erlbaum Associates Inc.

Schwartz, B., Ward, A., Monterosso, J., Lyubomirsky, S., White, K., & Lehman, D.R. (2002). Maximising versus satisficing: Happiness is a matter of choice. *Journal of Personality and Social Psychology, 83*, 1178–1197.

Schwartz, B.L., & Hashtroudi, S. (1991). Priming is independent of skill learning. *Journal of Experimental Psychology: Learning, Memory, and Cognition, 17*, 1177–1187.

Schwartz, M.F., Saffran, E.M., Bloch, D.E., & Dell, G.S. (1994). Disordered speech production in aphasic and normal speakers. *Brain and Language, 47*, 52–88.

Schwartz, M.F., Saffran, E.M., & Marin, O.S.M. (1980). Fractionating the reading process in dementia: Evidence for word-specific print-to-sound associations. In M. Coltheart, K.E. Patterson, & J.C. Marshall (Eds.), *Deep dyslexia*. London: Routledge & Kegan Paul.

Schweinberger, S.R., & Burton, A.M. (2003). Covert recognition and the neural system for face processing. *Cortex, 39*, 9–30.

Scoville, W.B., & Milner, B. (1957). Loss of recent memory after bilateral hippocampal lesions. *Journal of Neurology, Neurosurgery, & Psychiatry, 20*, 11–21.

Searle, J. (1979). Metaphor. In A. Ortony (Ed.), *Metaphor and thought*. Cambridge: Cambridge University Press.

Segal, S.J., & Fusella, V. (1970). Influence of imaged pictures and sounds on detection of visual and auditory signals. *Journal of Experimental Psychology, 83*, 458–464.

Seger, C.A. (1994). Implicit learning. *Psychological Bulletin, 115*, 163–196.

Seger, C.A., Poldrack, R.A., Prabhakaran, V., Zhao, M., Glover, G.H., & Gabrieli, J.D.E. (2000a). Hemispheric asymmetries and individual differences in visual concept learning as measured by functional MRI. *Neuropsychologia, 38*, 1316–1324.

Seger, C.A., Prabhakaran, V., Poldrack, R.A., & Gabrieli, J.D.E. (2000b). Neural activity differs between explicit and implicit learning of artificial grammar strings: An fMRI study. *Psychobiology, 28*, 283–292.

Seidenberg, M.S., Waters, G.S., Barnes, M.A., & Tanenhaus, M. (1984). When does irregular spelling or pronunciation influence word recognition? *Journal of Verbal Learning & Verbal Behavior, 23*, 383–404.

Sejnowski, T.J., & Rosenberg, C.R. (1987). Parallel networks that learn to pronounce English text. *Complex Systems*, *1*, 145–168.

Sekuler, R., & Blake, R. (2002). *Perception* (4th Ed.). New York: McGraw-Hill.

Sellen, A.J., Lowie, G., Harris, J.E., & Wilkins, A.J. (1997). What brings intentions to mind? An *in situ* study of prospective memory. *Memory*, *5*, 483–507.

Semenza, C., & Goodglass, H. (1985). Localization of body parts in brain injured subjects. *Neuropsychologia*, *23*, 161–175.

Semenza, C., Luzzatti, C., & Mondini, S. (1999). Lemma theory and aphasiology. *Behavioral & Brain Sciences*, *22*, 56.

Sereno, S.C., Brewer, C.C., & O'Donnell, P.J. (2003). Context effects in word recognition: Evidence for early interactive processing. *Psychological Science*, *14*, 328–333.

Sereno, S.C., & Rayner, K. (2000). The when and where of reading in the brain. *Brain and Cognition*, *42*, 78–81.

Sereno, S.C., Rayner, K., & Posner, M.I. (1998). Establishing a time-line of word recognition: Evidence from eye movements and event-related potentials. *NeuroReport*, *9*, 2195–2200.

Servos, P., & Goodale, M.A. (1995). Preserved visual imagery in visual form agnosia. *Neuropsychologia*, *33*, 1383–1394.

Servos, P., Osu, R., Santi, A., & Kawato, M. (2002). The neural substrates of biological motion perception: An fMRI study. *Cerebral Cortex*, *12*, 772–782.

Shaffer, L.H. (1975). Multiple attention in continuous verbal tasks. In P.M.A. Rabbitt & S. Dornic (Eds.), *Attention and performance, Vol. V.* London: Academic Press.

Shafir, E., & LeBoeuf, R.A. (2002). Rationality. *Annual Review of Psychology*, *53*, 491–517.

Shah, P., & Miyake, A. (1996). The separability of working memory resources for spatial thinking and language processing: An individual differences approach. *Journal of Experimental Psychology: General*, *125*, 4–27.

Shallice, T. (1981). Phonological agraphia and the lexical route in writing. *Brain*, *104*, 413–429.

Shallice, T. (1991). From neuropsychology to mental structure. *Behavioral & Brain Sciences*, *14*, 429–439.

Shallice, T. (2004). On Harley on Rapp. *Cognitive Neuropsychology*, *21*, 41–43.

Shallice, T., & Burgess, P. (1996). The domain of supervisory processes and temporal organisation of behaviour. *Philosophical Transactions of the Royal Society of London B*, *351*, 1405–1412.

Shallice, T. & Butterworth, B. (1977). Short-term memory impairment and spontaneous speech. *Neuropsychologia*, *15*, 729–735.

Shallice, T., & Warrington, E.K. (1970). Independent functioning of verbal memory stores: A neuropsychological study. *Quarterly Journal of Experimental Psychology*, *22*, 261–273.

Shallice, T., & Warrington, E.K. (1974). The dissociation between long-term retention of meaningful sounds and verbal material. *Neuropsychologia*, *12*, 553–555.

Shanks, D.R., & St. John, M.F. (1994). Characteristics of dissociable human learning systems. *Behavioral & Brain Sciences*, *17*, 367–394.

Shea, C.H., Wulf, G., Whitacre, C.A., & Park, J.-H. (2001). Surfing the implicit wave. *Quarterly Journal of Experimental Psychology*, *54*A, 841–862.

Shelton, J.R., & Caramazza, A. (2001). The organisation of semantic memory. In B. Rapp (Ed.), *The handbook of cognitive neuropsychology.* Hove, UK: Psychology Press.

Shelton, J.R., Fouch, E., & Caramazza, A. (1998). The selective sparing of body part knowledge: A case study. *Neurocase*, *4*, 343–345.

Shelton, J.R., & Weinrich, M. (1997). Further evidence of a dissociation between output phonological and orthographic lexicons: A case study. *Cognitive Neuropsychology*, *14*, 105–129.

Shepard, R.N. (1978). The mental image. *American Psychologist*, *33*, 125–137.

Sherrington, Sir C.S., (1906). *The integrative action of the nervous system.* New York: Scribner's Sons.

Shiffrin, R.M. (1999). 30 years of memory. In C. Izawa (Ed.), *On human memory: Evolution progress and reflections of the 30th anniversary of the Atkinson-Shiffrin model.* Mahwah, NJ: Lawrence Erlbaum Associates Inc.

Shiffrin, R.M., & Schneider, W. (1977). Controlled and automatic human information processing: II. Perceptual learning, automatic attending, and a general theory. *Psychological Review*, *84*, 127–190.

Shimamura, A.P., Janowsky, J., & Squire, L.R. (1990). Memory for temporal order of events in patients with frontal lobe lesions and amnesic patients. *Neuropsychologia*, *28*, 803–813.

Shimamura, A.P., & Squire, L.R. (1987). A neuropsychological study of fact memory and source amnesia. *Journal of Experimental Psychology: Learning, Memory, and Cognition*, *13*, 464–473.

Shipp, S., de Jong, B.M., Zihl, J., Frackowiak, R.S.J., & Zeki, S. (1994). The brain activity related to residual activity in a patient with bilateral lesions of V5. *Brain*, *117*, 1023–1038.

Shotter, J. (1991). The rhetorical-responsive nature of mind: A social constructionist account. In A. Still & A. Costall (Eds.), *Against cognitivism: Alternative foundations for cognitive psychology*. Hemel Hempstead, UK: Harvester Wheatsheaf.

Sides, A., Osherson, D., Bonini, N., & Viale, R. (2002). On the reality of the conjunction fallacy. *Memory & Cognition*, *30*, 191–198.

Simon, H.A. (1955). A behavioural model of rational choice. *Quarterly Journal of Economics*, *69*, 99–118.

Simon, H.A. (1957). *Models of man: Social and rational.* New York: Wiley.

Simon, H.A. (1966). Scientific discovery and the psychology of problem solving. In H.A. Simon (Ed.), *Mind and Cosmos: Essays in contemporary science and philosophy.* Pittsburgh, PA: University of Pittsburgh Press.

Simon, H.A. (1974). How big is a chunk? *Science, 183*, 482–488.

Simon, H.A. (1978). Rationality as process and product of thought. *American Economic Association, 68*, 1–16.

Simon, H.A. (1990). Invariants of human behaviour. *Annual Review of Psychology, 41*, 1–19.

Simon, H.A., & Reed, S.K. (1976). Modelling strategy shifts on a problem solving task. *Cognitive Psychology, 8*, 86–97.

Simons, D.J. (2000). Current approaches to change blindness. *Visual Cognition, 7*, 1–16.

Simons, D.J., & Chabris, F. (1999). Gorillas in our midst: Sustained inattentional blindness for dynamic events. *Perception, 28*, 1059–1074.

Simons, D.J., & Levin, D.T. (1998). Failure to detect changes to people during a real-world interaction. *Psychonomic Bulletin and Review, 5*, 644–649.

Simonson, I., & Staw, B.M. (1992). De-escalation strategies: A comparison of techniques for reducing commitment to losing courses of action. *Journal of Applied Psychology, 77*, 419–426.

Simonton, D.K. (1997). Creative productivity: A predictive and explanatory model of career trajectories and landmarks. *Psychological Review, 104*, 66–89.

Simonton, D.K. (2003). Scientific creativity as constrained stochastic behaviour: The integration of product, person, and process perspectives. *Psychological Bulletin, 129*, 475–494.

Sinai, M.J., Ooi, T.L., & He, Z.H. (1998). Terrain influences the accurate judgement of distance. *Nature, 395*, 497–500.

Singer, M. (1979). Processes of inference during sentence encoding. *Memory & Cognition, 7*, 192–200.

Singer, M. (1994). Discourse inference processes. In M.A. Gernsbacher (Ed.), *Handbook of psycholinguistics.* San Diego, CA: Academic Press.

Sirigu, A., & Duhamel, J.R. (2001). Motor and visual imagery as two complementary but neurally dissociable mental processes. *Journal of Cognitive Neuroscience, 13*, 910–919.

Slamecka, N.J. (1966). Differentiation versus unlearning of verbal associations. *Journal of Experimental Psychology, 71*, 822–828.

Sloboda, J.A., Davidson, J.W., Howe, M.J.A., & Moore, D.G. (1996). The role of practice in the development of performing musicians. *British Journal of Psychology, 87*, 287–309.

Sloman, A., & Logan, B. (1998, April). *Architectures for human-like agents.* Paper presented at the European conference on Cognitive Modelling, Nottingham, UK.

Sloman, S.A., & Over, D.E. (2003). Probability judgment: From the inside and out. In D.E. Over, *Evolution and the psychology of thinking.* Hove, UK: Psychology Press.

Slotnick, S.D., Hopfinger, J.B., Klein, S.A., & Sutter, E.E. (2002). Darkness beyond the light: Attentional inhibition surrounding the classic spotlight. *NeuroReport, 13*, 773–778.

Slugoski, B.R., & Wilson, A.E. (1998). Contribution of conversation skills to the production of judgmental errors. *European Journal of Social Psychology, 28*, 575–601.

Smallman, H.S., MacLeod, D.I.A., He, S., & Kentridge, R.W. (1996). Fine grain of the neural representation of human spatial vision. *Journal of Neuroscience, 16*, 1852–1859.

Smania, N., Martini, M.C., Gambina, G., Tomelleri, G., Palamara, A., Natale, E. et al. (1998). The spatial distribution of visual attention in hemineglect and extinction patients. *Brain, 121*, 1759–1770.

Smith, E.E., & Jonides, J. (1997). Working memory: A view from neuroimaging. *Cognitive Psychology, 33*, 5–42.

Smith, E.E., & Jonides, J. (1999). Storage and executive processes in the frontal lobes. *Science, 283*, 1657–1661.

Smith, J.D., & Minda, J.P. (2000). Thirty categorisation results in search of a model. *Journal of Experimental Psychology: Learning, Memory, and Cognition, 26*, 3–27.

Smith, M. (2000). Conceptual structures in language production. In L. Wheeldon (Ed.), *Aspects of language production.* Hove, UK: Psychology Press.

Smith, R.E. (2003). The cost of remembering to remember in event-based prospective memory: Investigating the capacity demands of delayed intention performance. *Journal of Experimental Psychology: Learning, Memory, and Cognition, 29*, 347–361.

Smith, S.D., & Merikle, P.M. (1999). *Assessing the duration of memory for information perceived without awareness.* Poster presented at the 3rd annual meeting of the Association for the Scientific Study of Consciousness, London, Canada.

Smith, S.M., & Blankenship, S.E. (1991). Incubation and the persistence of fixation in problem solving. *American Journal of Psychology, 104*, 61–87.

Smith, S.M., & Rothkopf, E.Z. (1984). Contextual enhancement and distribution of practice in the classroom. *Cognition & Instruction, 1*, 341–358.

Smyth, M.M., Morris, P.E., Levy, P., & Ellis, A.W. (1987). *Cognition in action.* Hove, UK: Psychology Press.

Snedeker, J., & Trueswell, J. (2003). Using prosody to avoid ambiguity: Effects of speaker awareness and referential context. *Journal of Memory and Language*, *48*, 103–130.

Solomon, K.O., & Barsalou, L.W. (2001). Representing properties locally. *Cognitive Psychology*, *43*, 129–169.

Solso, R.L. (1994). *Cognition and the visual arts*. Cambridge, MA: MIT Press.

Southwood, M.H., & Chatterjee, A. (2001). The simultaneous activation hypothesis: Explaining recovery from deep to phonological dyslexia. *Brain and Language*, *76*, 18–34.

Spelke, E.S., Breinlinger, K., Jacobson, K., & Phillips, A. (1993). Gestalt relations and object perception: A developmental study. *Vision Research*, *22*, 531–544.

Spelke, E.S., Hirst, W.C., & Neisser, U. (1976). Skills of divided attention. *Cognition*, *4*, 215–230.

Spence, C., & Driver, J. (1996). Audiovisual links in endogenous covert spatial attention. *Journal of Experimental Psychology: Human Perception and Performance*, *22*, 1005–1030.

Spencer, R.M., & Weisberg, R.W. (1986). Context-dependent effects on analogical transfer during problem solving. *Memory & Cognition*, *14*, 442–449.

Sperber, D., & Girotto, V. (2002). Use or misuse of the selection task? Rejoinder to Fiddick, Cosmides, and Tooby. *Cognition*, *85*, 277–290.

Sperling, G. (1960). The information that is available in brief visual presentations. *Psychological Monographs*, *74* (Whole No. 498), 1–29.

Sperry, R.W. (1968). Hemisphere deconnection and unity in conscious awareness. *American Psychologist*, *23*, 723–733.

Spiers, H.J., Maguire, E.A., & Burgess, N. (2001). Hippocampal amnesia. *Neurocase*, *7*, 357–382.

Spinoza, B. (1677). *On the improvement of the understanding, the ethics, correspondence*. [Translation by R.H.M. Elwes, 1955, New York: Dover Publications Ltd.]

Spivey, M.J., Tanenhaus, M.K., Eberhard, K.M., & Sedivy, J.C. (2002). Eye movements and spoken language comprehension: Effects of visual context on syntactic ambiguity resolution. *Cognitive Psychology*, *45*, 447–481.

Sporer, S.L., Penrod, S., Read, D., & Cutler, B. (1995). Choosing, confidence, and accuracy: A meta-analysis of the confidence–accuracy relation in eyewitness identification studies. *Psychological Bulletin*, *118*, 315–327.

Squire, L.R., Clark, R.E., & Knowlton, B.J. (2001). Retrograde amnesia. *Hippocampus*, *11*, 50–55.

Squire, L.R., Knowlton, B., & Musen, G. (1993). The structure and organisation of memory. *Annual Review of Psychology*, *44*, 453–495.

Squire, L.R., Ojemann, J.G., Miezin, F.M., Petersen, S.E., Videen, T.O., & Raichle, M.E. (1992). Activation of the hippocampus in normal humans: A functional anatomical study of memory. *Proceedings of the National Academy of Science, USA*, *89*, 1837–1841.

Stanovich, K.E., & West, R.F. (1998a). Individual differences in rational thought. *Journal of Experimental Psychology: General*, *127*, 161–188.

Stanovich, K.E., & West, R.F. (1998b). Evaluating principles of rational indifference: Individual differences in framing and conjunction effects. *Thinking & Reasoning*, *4*, 289–317.

Stanovich, K.E., & West, R.F. (2000). Individual differences in reasoning: Implications for the rationality debate? *Behavioral and Brain Sciences*, *23*, 645–665.

Steblay, N.M. (1997). Social influence in eyewitness recall: A meta-analytic review of line-up instruction effects. *Law and Human Behavior*, *21*, 283–298.

Steblay, N.M., Dysart, J., Fulero, S., & Lindsay, R.C.L. (2001). Eyewitness accuracy rates in sequential and simultaneous line-up presentations: A meta-analytic comparison. *Law and Human Behavior*, *25*, 459–474.

Stein, B.E., & Meredith, M.A. (1993). *The merging of the senses*. Cambridge, MA: MIT Press.

Stemberger, J.P. (1982). The nature of segments in the lexicon: Evidence from speech errors. *Lingua*, *56*, 235–259.

Sternberg, R.J., & Ben-Zeev, T. (2001). *Complex cognition: The psychology of human thought*. Oxford: Oxford University Press.

Stevens, J.K., Emerson, R.C., Gerstein, G.L., Kallos, T., Neufield, G.R., Nichols, C.W. et al. (1976). Paralysis of the awake human: Visual perceptions. *Vision Research*, *16*, 93–98.

Stevenson, R., & Over, D. (1995). Deduction from uncertain premises. *Quarterly Journal of Experimental Psychology*, *48*A, 613–643.

Stewart, L., Ellison, A., Walsh, V., & Cowey, A. (2001). The role of transcranial magnetic stimulation (TMS) in studies of vision, attention and cognition. *Acta Psychologica*, *107*, 275–291.

Stoerig, P., & Cowey, A. (1997). Blindsight in man and monkey. *Brain*, *120*, 535–559.

Stoerig, P., Kleinschmidt, A., & Frahm, J. (1998). No visual responses in denervated V1: High-resolution functional magnetic resonance imaging of a blindsight patient. *NeuroReport*, *9*, 21–25.

Storms, G., De Boeck, P., & Ruts, W. (2000). Prototype and exemplar-based information in natural language categories. *Journal of Memory and Language*, *42*, 51–73.

Strayer, D.L., & Johnston, W.A. (2001). Driven to distraction: Dual-task studies of simulated driving and conversing on a cellular telephone. *Psychological Science*, *12*, 462–466.

Styles, E.A. (1997). *The psychology of attention*. Hove, UK: Psychology Press.

Sugase, Y., Yamane, S., Ueno, S., & Kawano, K. (1999). Global and fine information coded by single neurons in the temporal visual cortex. *Nature*, *400*, 869–872.

Suh, S., & Trabasso, T. (1993). Inferences during reading: Converging evidence from discourse analysis, talk-aloud protocols, and recognition priming. *Journal of Memory and Language*, *32*, 279–300.

Sulin, R.A., & Dooling, D.J. (1974). Intrusion of a thematic idea in retention of prose. *Journal of Experimental Psychology*, *103*, 255–262.

Sullivan, L. (1976). Selective attention and secondary message analysis: A reconsideration of Broadbent's filter model of selective attention. *Quarterly Journal of Experimental Psychology*, *28*, 167–178.

Sussman, H.M., Hoemeke, K.A., & Ahmed, F.S. (1993). A cross-linguistic investigation of locus equations as a phonetic descriptor for place of articulation. *Journal of the Acoustical Society of America*, *94*, 1256–1268.

Sutherland, N.S. (Ed.) (1989). *Macmillan dictionary of psychology*. London: Macmillan.

Sylvester, C.-Y. C., Wager, T.D., Lacey, S.C., Hernandez, L., Nichols, T.E., Smith, E.E. et al. (2003). Switching attention and resolving interference: fMRI measures of executive functions. *Neuropsychologia*, *41*, 357–370.

Symons, C.S., & Johnson, B.T. (1997). The self-reference effect in memory: A meta-analysis. *Psychological Bulletin*, *121*, 371–394.

Tainturier, M.J. (1996). Phonologically-based errors and their implications in the specification of phonology to orthography conversion processes. *Brain And Cognition*, *32*, 148–151.

Tainturier, M.-J., & Rapp, B. (2001). The spelling process. In B. Rapp (Ed.), *The handbook of cognitive neuropsychology*. Hove, UK: Psychology Press.

Talarico, J.M., & Rubin, D.C. (2003). Confidence, not consistency, characterises flashbulb memories. *Psychological Science*, *14*, 455–461.

Tanaka, J.W., & Taylor, M.E. (1991). Object categories and expertise: Is the basic level in the eye of the beholder? *Cognitive Psychology*, *15*, 121–149.

Tanenhaus, M.K., Spivey-Knowlton, M.J., Eberhard, K.M., & Sedivy, J.C. (1995). Integration of visual and linguistic information in spoken language comprehension. *Science*, *268*, 1632–1634.

Tarr, M.J. (1995). Rotating objects to recognise them: A case study of the role of viewpoint dependency in the recognition of three-dimensional objects. *Psychonomic Bulletin & Review*, *2*, 55–82.

Tarr, M.J., & Bülthoff, H.H. (1995). Is human object recognition better described by geon structural descriptions or by multiple views? Comment on Biederman and Gerhardstein (1993). *Journal of Experimental Psychology: Human Perception & Performance*, *21*, 1494–1505.

Tarr, M.J., & Bülthoff, H.H. (1998). Image-based object recognition in man, monkey and machine. *Cognition*, *67*, 1–20.

Tarr, M.J., Williams, P., Hayward, W.G., & Gauthier, I. (1998). Three-dimensional object recognition is viewpoint-dependent. *Nature Neuroscience*, *1*, 195–206.

Tartter, V. (1986). *Language processes*. New York: Holt, Rinehart & Winston.

Taylor, T.L., & Klein, R.M. (1998). On the causes and effects of inhibition of return. *Psychonomic Bulletin & Review*, *5*, 625–643.

Tehan, G., & Humphreys, M.S. (1996). Cueing effects in short-term recall. *Memory & Cognition*, *24*, 719–732.

Tetlock, P.E. (1991). An alternative metaphor in the study of judgement and choice: People as politicians. *Theory and Psychology*, *1*, 451–475.

Tetlock, P.E. (2002). Social functionalist frameworks for judgement and choice: Intuitive politicians, theologians, and prosecutors. *Psychological Review*, *109*, 451–471.

Tetlock, P.E., Kristel, O.V., Elson, B., Green, M.C., & Lerner, J.S. (2000). The psychology of the unthinkable: Taboo trade-offs, forbidden base rates, and heretical counterfactuals. *Journal of Personality and Social Psychology*, *78*, 853–870.

Tetlock, P.E., & Mellers, B.A. (2002). The great rationality debate. *Psychological Science*, *13*, 94–99.

Teuber, H.-L., Milner, B., & Vaughan, H.G. (1968). Persistent anterograde amnesia after stab wound of the basal brain. *Neuropsychologia*, *6*, 267–282.

Thagard, P. (1998). Ulcers and bacteria I: Discovery and acceptance. *Studies in History and Philosophy of Science. Part C: Studies in History and Philosophy of Biology and Biomedical Sciences*, *29*, 107–136.

Thomas, J.C. (1974). An analysis of behaviour in the hobbits–orcs problem. *Cognitive Psychology*, *6*, 257–269.

Thomson, D.M., & Tulving, E. (1970). Associative encoding and retrieval: Weak and strong cues. *Journal of Experimental Psychology*, *86*, 255–262.

Thorndike, E.L. (1898). Animal intelligence: An experimental study of the associative processes in animals. *The Psychological Review Monograph Supplements*, *2*, No. 4 (Whole No. 8).

Tipper, S.P., Lortie, C., & Baylis, G.C. (1992). Selective reaching: Evidence for action-centred attention. *Journal of Experimental Psychology: Human Perception & Performance*, *18*, 891–905.

Todd, P.N., & Gigerenzer, G. (2000). Precis of simple heuristics that make us smart. *Behavioral and Brain Sciences*, *23*, 727–780.

Tolhurst, D.J. (1973). Separate channels for the analysis of the shape and the movement of a moving visual stimulus. *Journal of Physiology*, *231*, 385–402.

Tomes, J.L., & Katz, A.N. (1997). Habitual susceptibility to misinformation and individual differences in eyewitness memory. *Applied Cognitive Psychology*, *11*, 233–251.

Tootell, R.B.H., Reppas, J.B., Dale, A.M., Look, R.B., Sereno, M.I., Malach, R. et al. (1995b). Visual motion aftereffect in human cortical area MT revealed by functional magnetic resonance imaging. *Nature*, *375*, 139–141.

Tootell, R.B.H., Reppas, J.B., Kwong, K.K., Malach, R., Born, R.T., Brady, T.J. et al. (1995a). Functional analysis of human MT and related visual cortical areas using magnetic-resonance-imaging. *Journal of Neuroscience*, *15*, 3215–3230.

Towse, J.N. (1998). On random generation and the central executive of working memory. *British Journal of Psychology*, *89*, 77–101.

Tranel, D., & Damasio, A.R. (1988). Non-conscious face recognition in patients with face agnosia. *Behavioural Brain Research*, *30*, 235–249.

Tranel, D., Kemmerer, D., Damasio, H., Adolphs, R., & Damasio, A.R. (2003). Neural correlates of conceptual knowledge for actions. *Cognitive Neuropsychology*, *20*, 409–432.

Tranel, D., Logan, C.G., Frank, R.J., & Damasio, A.R. (1997). Explaining category-related effects in the retrieval of conceptual and lexical knowledge for concrete entities. *Neuropsychologia*, *35*, 1329–1339.

Treisman, A.M. (1960). Contextual cues in selective listening. *Quarterly Journal of Experimental Psychology*, *12*, 242–248.

Treisman, A.M. (1964). Verbal cues, language, and meaning in selective attention. *American Journal of Psychology*, *77*, 206–219.

Treisman, A.M. (1988). Features and objects: The fourteenth Bartlett memorial lecture. *Quarterly Journal of Experimental Psychology*, *40*A, 201–237.

Treisman, A.M. (1992). Spreading suppression or feature integration? A reply to Duncan and Humphreys (1992). *Journal of Experimental Psychology: Human Perception & Performance*, *18*, 589–593.

Treisman, A.M. (1993). The perception of features and objects. In A. Baddeley & L. Weiskrantz (Eds.), *Attention: Selection, awareness, and control*. Oxford: Clarendon Press.

Treisman, A.M. (1999). Feature binding, attention and object perception. In G.W. Humphreys, J. Duncan, & A. Treisman (Eds), *Attention, space and action*. Oxford: Oxford University Press.

Treisman, A.M., & Davies, A. (1973). Divided attention to ear and eye. In S. Kornblum (Ed.), *Attention and performance, Vol. IV.* London: Academic Press.

Treisman, A.M., & Geffen, G. (1967). Selective attention: Perception or response? *Quarterly Journal of Experimental Psychology*, *19*, 1–18.

Treisman, A.M., & Gelade, G. (1980). A feature integration theory of attention. *Cognitive Psychology*, *12*, 97–136.

Treisman, A.M., & Riley, J.G.A. (1969). Is selective attention selective perception or selective response: A further test. *Journal of Experimental Psychology*, *79*, 27–34.

Treisman, A.M., & Sato, S. (1990). Conjunction search revisited. *Journal of Experimental Psychology: Human Perception & Performance*, *16*, 459–478.

Treisman, A.M., & Schmidt, H. (1982). Illusory conjunctions in the perception of objects. *Cognitive Psychology*, *14*, 107–141.

Tresilian, J.R. (1994). Two straw men stay silent when asked about the "direct" versus "inferential" controversy. *Behavioural & Brain Sciences*, *17*, 335–336.

Tresilian, J.R. (1999). Visually timed action: Time out for "tau"? Trends in Cognitive Sciences, *3*, 301–310.

Trevena, J.A., & Miller, J. (2002). Cortical movement preparation before and after a conscious decision to move. *Consciousness and Cognition*, *11*, 162–190.

Trojano, L., & Grossi, D. (1995). Phonological and lexical coding in verbal short-term memory and learning. *Brain & Cognition*, *21*, 336–354.

Trueswell, J.C., Tanenhaus, M.K., & Garnsey, S.M. (1994). Semantic influences on parsing: Use of thematic role information in syntactic disambiguation. *Journal of Memory and Language*, *33*, 285–318.

Tulving, E. (1972). Episodic and semantic memory. In E. Tulving & W. Donaldson (Eds.), *Organisation of memory.* London: Academic Press.

Tulving, E. (1974). Cue-dependent forgetting. *American Scientist*, *62*, 74–82.

Tulving, E. (1979). Relation between encoding specifity and levels of processing. In L.S. Cermak & F.I.M. Craik (Eds.), *Levels of processing in human memory*. Hillsdale, NJ: Lawrence Erlbaum Associates Inc.

Tulving, E. (1998). An interview with Endel Tulving. In M.S. Gazzaniga, R.B. Ivry, & G.R. Mangun (Eds.), *Cognitive neuroscience: The biology of the mind.* New York: W.W. Norton.

Tulving, E. (2002). Episodic memory: From mind to brain. *Annual Review of Psychology*, *53*, 1–25.

Tulving, E., & Psotka, J. (1971). Retroactive inhibition in free recall: Inaccessibility of information available in the memory trace. *Journal of Experimental Psychology*, *87*, 1–8.

Tulving, E., & Schacter, D.L. (1990). Priming and human memory. *Science*, *247*, 301–306.

Tulving, E., Schacter, D.L., & Stark, H.A. (1982). Priming effects in word-fragment completion are independent of recognition memory. *Journal of Experimental Psychology: Learning, Memory, & Cognition*, *17*, 595–617.

Turatto, M., Angrilli, A., Mazza, V., Umiltà, C., & Driver, J. (2002). Looking without seeing the background change: Electrophysiological correlates of change detection versus change blindness. *Cognition, 84*, B1–B10.

Turner, M.L., & Engle, R.W. (1989). Is working-memory capacity task dependent? *Journal of Memory & Language, 28*, 127–154.

Tversky, A. (1972). Elimination by aspects: A theory of choice. *Psychological Review, 79*, 281–299.

Tversky, A., & Kahneman, D. (1974). Judgement under uncertainty: Heuristics and biases. *Science, 185*, 1124–1131.

Tversky, A., & Kahneman, D. (1982). Evidential impact of base rates. In D. Kahneman, P. Slovic, & A. Tversky (Ed.), *Judgment under uncertainty: Heuristics and biases*. Cambridge: Cambridge University Press.

Tversky, A., & Kahneman, D. (1983). Extensional versus intuitive reasoning: The conjunction fallacy in probability judgement. *Psychological Review, 91*, 293–315.

Tversky, A., & Kahneman, D. (1987). Rational choice and the framing of decisions. In R. Hogarth & M. Reder (Eds.), *Rational choice: The contrast between economics and psychology*. Chicago: University of Chicago Press.

Tversky, A., & Koehler, D.J. (1994). Support theory: A nonextensional representation of subjective probability. *Psychological Review, 101*, 547–567.

Tversky, A., & Shafir, E. (1992). The disjunction effect in choice under uncertainty. *Psychological Science, 3*, 305–309.

Tweney, R.D. (1998). Toward a cognitive psychology of science: Recent research and its implications. *Current Directions in Psychological Science, 7*, 150–154.

Tweney, R.D., & Chitwood, S.C. (1995). Scientific reasoning. In S. Newstead & J.St.B.T. Evans (Eds.), *Perspectives on thinking and reasoning: Essays in honour of Peter Wason,* (pp. 241–260). Hove, UK: Lawrence Erlbaum Associates Ltd.

Tweney, R.D., Doherty, M.E., Worner, W.J., Pliske, D.B., Mynatt, C.R., Gross, K.A. et al. (1980). Strategies for rule discovery in an inference task. *Quarterly Journal of Experimental Psychology, 32*, 109–123.

Tyler, L.K., & Moss, H.E. (1997). Imageability and category-specificity. *Cognitive Neuropsychology, 14*, 293–318.

Tzelgov, J., Henik, A., Sneg, R., & Baruch, O. (1996). Unintentional reading via the phonological route: The Stroop effect with cross-script homophones. *Journal of Experimental Psychology: Learning, Memory, and Cognition, 22*, 336–339.

Ucros, C.G. (1989). Mood state-dependent memory: A meta-analysis. *Cognition & Emotion, 3*, 139–167.

Umiltà, C. (2001). Mechanisms of attention. In B. Rapp (Ed.), *The handbook of cognitive neuropsychology*. Hove, UK: Psychology Press.

Underwood, B.J., & Postman, L. (1960). Extra-experimental sources of interference in forgetting. *Psychological Review, 67*, 73–95.

Underwood, G. (1974). Moray vs. the rest: The effect of extended shadowing practice. *Quarterly Journal of Experimental Psychology, 26*, 368–372.

Ungerleider, L.G., & Mishkin, M. (1982). Two cortical visual systems. In D.J. Ingle, M.A. Goodale, & R.J.W. Mansfield (Eds.), *Analysis of visual behavior*. Cambridge, MA: MIT Press, 549–586.

Vaidya, C.J., Gabrieli, J.D.E., Keane, M.M., & Monti, L.A. (1995). Perceptual and conceptual memory processes in global amnesia. *Neuropsychology, 10*, 529–537.

Vaina, L.M. (1998). Complex motion perception and its deficits. *Current Opinion in Neurobiology, 8*, 494–502.

Vaina, L.M., Cowey, A., LeMay, M., Bienfang, D.C., & Kinkinis, R. (2002). Visual deficits in a patient with "kaleidoscopic disintegration of the visual world". *European Journal of Neurology, 9*, 463–477.

Vaina, L.M., Soloviev, S., Bienfang, D.C., & Cowey, A. (2000). A lesion of cortical area V2 selectively impairs the perception of the direction of first-order visual motion. *NeuroReport: For Rapid Communication of Neuroscience Research, 11*, 1039–1044.

Valdois, S., Carbonnel, S., David, D., Rousset, S., & Pellat, J. (1995). Confrontation of PDP models and dual-route models through the analysis of a case of deep dysphasia. *Cognitive Neuropsychology, 12*, 681–724.

Valentine, T., Bredart, S., Lawson, R., & Ward, G. (1991). What's in a name? Access to information from people's names. *European Journal of Cognitive Psychology, 3*, 147–176.

Valentine, T., Pickering, A., & Darling, S. (2003). Characteristics of eyewitness identification that predict the outcome of real line-ups. *Applied Cognitive Psychology, 17*, 969–993.

Vallar, G., & Baddeley, A.D. (1984). Phonological short-term store, phonological processing and sentence comprehension: A neuropsychological case study. *Cognitive Neuropsychology, 1*, 121–141.

Vallar, G., Di Betta, A. M., & Silveri, M. C. (1997). The phonological short-term store-rehearsal system: Patterns of impairment and neural correlates. *Neuropsychologia, 35*, 795–812.

Vallar, G., & Perani, D. (1987). The anatomy of spatial neglect in humans. In M. Jeannerodd (Ed.), *Neurophysiological and neuropsychological aspects of spatial neglect* (pp. 235–258). Amsterdam: Elsevier.

Vallée-Tourangeau, F., Austin, N.G., & Rankin, S. (1995). Inducing a rule in Wason 2-4-6 task: A test of the information quantity and goal-complementarity hypotheses. *Quarterly Journal of Experimental Psychology, 48*A, 895–914.

Van den Berg, A.V., & Brenner, E. (1994). Why two eyes are better than one for judgements of heading. *Nature*, *371*, 700–702.

Van Dijk, T.A., & Kintsch, W. (1983). *Strategies of discourse comprehension.* New York: Academic Press.

Van Gompel, R.P.G., Pickering, M.J., & Traxler, M.J. (2000). Unrestricted race: A new model of syntactic ambiguity resolution. In A. Kennedy, R. Radach, D. Heller, & J. Pynte (Eds.), *Reading as a perceptual process*. Oxford: Elsevier.

Van Gompel, R.P.G., Pickering, M.J., & Traxler, M.J. (2001). Reanalysis in sentence processing: Evidence against current constraint-based and two-stage models. *Journal of Memory and Language*, *45*, 225–258.

Van Joolingen, W.R., & DeJong, T. (1997). An extended dual space search model of scientific discovery learning. *Instructional Science*, *25*, 306–346.

Van Mier, H., Tempel, L.W., Perlmutter, J.S., Raichle, M.E., & Petersen, S.E. (1998). Changes in brain activity during motor learning measured with PET: Effects of hand of performance and practice. *Journal of Neurophysiology*, *80*, 2177–2199.

Van Petten, C., Coulson, S., Rubin, S., Plante, E., & Parks, M. (1999). Time course of word identification and semantic integration in spoken language. *Journal of Experimental Psychology: Learning, Memory, and Cognition*, *25*, 394–417.

Van Selst, M.V., Ruthruff, E., & Johnston, J.C. (1999). Can practice eliminate the Psychological Refractory Period effect? *Journal of Experimental Psychology: Human Perception and Performance*, *25*, 1268–1283.

Van Turennout, M., Hagoort, P., & Brown, C.M. (1998). Brain activity during speaking: From syntax to phonology in 40 milliseconds. *Science*, *280*, 572–574.

Vanrie, J., Béatse, E., Wagemans, J., Sunaert, S., & van Hecke, P. (2002). Mental rotation versus invariant features in object perception from different viewpoints: An fMRI study. *Neuropsychologia*, *40*, 917–930.

Vargha-Khadem F., Gadian, D.G., & Mishkin, M. (2002). Dissociations in cognitive memory: The syndrome of developmental amnesia. In *Episodic memory: new directions in research* 2002 (pp.153–163). New York: Oxford University Press.

Vargha-Khadem, F., Gadian, D.G., Watkins, K.E., Connelly, A., Van Paesschen, W., & Mishkin, M. (1997). Differential effects of early hippocampal pathology on episodic and semantic memory. *Science*, *277*, 376–380.

Vartanian, O., Martindale, C., & Kwiatkowski, J. (2003). Creativity and inductive reasoning: The relationship between divergent thinking and performance on Wason's 2-4-6 task. *Quarterly Journal of Experimental Psychology*, *56*A, 641–655.

Veale, T., & Keane, M.T. (1994). Belief modelling, intentionality, and perlocution in metaphor comprehension. *Proceedings of the sixteenth annual meeting of the cognitive science society*. Hillsdale, NJ: Lawrence Erlbaum Associates Inc.

Vecera, S.P., & Farah, M.J. (1997). Is visual image segmentation a bottom-up of an interactive process? *Perception & Psychophysics*, *59*, 1280–1296.

Velmans, M. (2000). *Understanding consciousness*. London: Routledge.

Verfaellie, M., Koseff, P., & Alexander, M.P. (2000). Acquisition of novel semantic information in amnesia: Effects of lesion location. *Neuropsychologia*, *38*, 484–492.

Vigliocco, G., & Hartsuiker, R.J. (2002). The interplay of meaning, sound, and syntax in sentence production. *Psychological Bulletin*, *128*, 442–472.

Vishton, P.M., Rea, J.G., Cutting, J.E., & Nuñez, L.N. (1999). Comparing effects of the horizontal–vertical illusion on grip scaling and judgement: Relative versus absolute, not perception versus action. *Journal of Experimental Psychology: Human Perception and Performance*, *25*, 1659–1672.

Vitu, F., McConkie, G.W., Kerr, P., & O'Regan, J.K. (2001). Fixation location effects on fixation durations during reading: An inverted optimal viewing position effect. *Vision Research*, *41*, 3511–3531.

Vogels, R., Biederman, I., Bar, M., & Lorincz, A. (2001). Inferior temporal neurons show greater sensitivity to non-accidental than to metric shape differences. *Journal of Cognitive Neuroscience*, *13*, 444–453.

Von Neumann, J., & Morgenstern, O. (1947). *Theory of games and economic behaviour.* Princeton, NJ: Princeton University Press.

Von Wright, J.M., Anderson, K., & Stenman, U. (1975). Generalisation of conditioned G.S.R.s in dichotic listening. In P.M.A. Rabbitt & S. Dornic (Eds.), *Attention and performance, Vol. V.* London: Academic Press.

Vuilleumier, P., & Landis, T. (1998). Illusory contours and spatial neglect. *NeuroReport*, *9*, 2481–2484.

Vuilleumier, P., & Rafal, R. (1999). Both means more than two: Localising and counting in patients with visuospatial neglect. *Nature Neuroscience*, *2*, 783–784.

Wachtel, P. (1973). Psychodynamics, behaviour therapy and the implacable experimenter: An inquiry into the consistency of personality. *Journal of Abnormal Psychology*, *82*, 324–334.

Wade, A.R., Brewer, A.A., Rieger, J.W., & Wandell, B.A. (2002). Functional measurements of human ventral occipital cortex: Retinopy and colour. *Philosophical Transactions: Biological Sciences*, *357*, *963–973.*

Wade, N.J., & Swanston, M.T. (2001). *Visual perception: An introduction* (2nd Ed.). Hove, UK: Psychology Press.

Wagenaar, W.A. (1986). My memory: A study of autobiographical memory over six years. *Cognitive Psychology*, *18*, 225–252.

Wagenaar, W.A. (1994). Is memory self-serving? In U. Neisser & R. Fivush (Eds.), *The remembering self: Construction and accuracy in the self-narrative*. Cambridge: Cambridge University Press.

Wagner, A.D., Desmond, J.E., Demb, J.B., Glover, G.H., & Gabrieli, J.D.E. (1997). Semantic repetition priming for verbal and pictorial knowledge: A functional MRI study of left inferior prefrontal cortex. *Journal of Cognitive Neuroscience*, *9*, 714–726.

Wagner, A.D., Schacter, D.L., Rotte, M., Koutstaal, W., Maril, A., Dale, A.M., Rosen, B.R., & Buckner, R.L. (1998). Building memories: Remembering and forgetting of verbal experiences as predicted by brain activity. *Science*, *281*, 188–191.

Wallas, G. (1926). *The art of thought*. London: Cape.

Walsh, V., Ellison, A., Battelli, L., & Cowey, A. (1998). Task-specific impairment and enhancement induced by magnetic stimulation of human visual area V5. *Proceedings of the Royal Society of London: Biological Sciences*, *265*, 537–543.

Walsh, V., & Rushworth, M. (1999). A primer of magnetic stimulation as a tool for neuropsychology. [Review]. *Neuropsychologia*, *37*, 125–135.

Waltz, J.A., Knowlton, B.J., Holyoak, K.J., Boone, K.B., Mishkin, F.S., de Menezes Santos, M. et al. (1999). A system for relational reasoning in human prefrontal cortex. *Psychological Science*, *10*, 119–125.

Wang, R.F., & Cutting, J.E. (1999). Where we go with a little good information. *Psychological Science*, *10*, 71–75.

Wang, X.T. (1996). Domain-specific rationality in human choices: Violations of utility axioms and social contexts. *Cognition*, *60*, 31–63.

Wann, J.P. (1996). Anticipating arrival: Is the tau margin a specious theory? *Journal of Experimental Psychology: Human Perception & Performance, 22*, 1031–1048.

Wann, J.P., & Rushton, S.K. (1995). Grasping the impossible: Stereoscopic virtual balls. In B.G. Bardy, R.J. Bootsma, & Y. Guiard (Eds.), *Studies in perception and action, Vol. III*. Hillsdale, NJ: Lawrence Erlbaum Associates Inc.

Ward, L.M. (1994). Supramodal and modality-specific mechanisms for stimulus-driven shifts of auditory and visual attention. *Canadian Journal of Experimental Psychology*, *48*, 242–259.

Ward, T.B. (1992). Structured imagination. In R.A. Finke, T.B. Ward, & S.M. Smith (Eds.), *Creative cognition: Theory, research and applications*. Cambridge, MA: MIT Press.

Ward, T.B., Patterson, M.J., Sifonis, C.M., Dodds, R.A., & Saunders, K.N. (2002). The role of graded category structure in imaginative thought. *Memory & Cognition*, *30*, 199–216.

Ward, T.B., & Sifonis, C.M. (1997). Task demands and generative thinking: What changes and what remains the same? *Journal of Creative Behaviour*, *31*, 245–259.

Ward, T.B., Smith, S.M., & Finke, R.A. (1995). *The creative cognition approach*. Cambridge, MA: MIT Press.

Warren, R.M., & Warren, R.P. (1970). Auditory illusions and confusions. *Scientific American*, *223*, 30–36.

Warren, W.H., & Hannon, D.J. (1988). Direction of self-motion is perceived from optical flow. *Nature*, *336*, 162–163.

Warrington, E.K., & James, M. (1988). Visual apperceptive agnosia: A clinico-anatomical study of three cases. *Cortex*, *24*, 13–32.

Warrington, E.K., Logue, V.F., & Pratt, R.T.C. (1971). The anatomical localization of selective impairment of auditory verbal short-term memory. *Neuropsychologica*, *9*, 377–387.

Warrington, E.K., & Shallice, T. (1972). Neuropsychological evidence of visual storage in short-term memory tasks. *Quarterly Journal of Experimental Psychology*, *24*, 30–40.

Warrington, E.K., & Shallice, T. (1984). Category-specific semantic impairments. *Brain*, *107*, 829–853.

Warrington, E.K., & Taylor, A.M. (1978). Two categorical stages of object recognition. *Perception*, *7*, 695–705.

Wason, P.C. (1960). On the failure to eliminate hypotheses in a conceptual task. *Quarterly Journal of Experimental Psychology*, *12*, 129–140.

Wason, P.C. (1983). Realism and rationality in the selection task. In J.St.B.T. Evans (Ed.), *Thinking and reasoning*. London: Routledge & Kegan Paul.

Wason, P.C., & Reich, S.S. (1979). A verbal illusion. *Quarterly Journal of Experimental Psychology*, *31*, 591–597.

Wason, P.C., & Shapiro, D. (1971). Natural and contrived experience in reasoning problems. *Quarterly Journal of Experimental Psychology*, *23*, 63–71.

Watkins, M. (2002). Limits and province of levels of processing: Considerations of a construct. *Memory*, *10*, 339–343.

Weber, A., & Cutler, A. (2004). Lexical competition in non-native spoken-word recognition. *Journal of Memory and Language*, *50*, 1–25.

Weekes, B., Coltheart, M., & Gordon, E. (1997). Deep dyslexia and right-hemisphere reading—A regional cerebral blood flow study. *Aphasiology*, *11*, 1139–1158.

Wegner, D.M., & Wheatley, T. (1999). Apparent mental causation: Sources of the experience of will. *American Psychologist*, *54*, 480–492.

Weisberg, R.W. (1993). *Creativity: Beyond the myth of genius*. San Francisco, CA: W.H. Freeman.

Weisberg, R.W., & Alba, J.W. (1981). An examination of the alleged role of "fixation" in the solution of several insight problems. *Journal of Experimental Psychology: General*, *110*, 169–192.

Weisberg, R.W., & Suls, J. (1973). An information-processing model of Duncker's candle problem. *Cognitive Psychology*, *4*, 255–276.

Weiskrantz, L. (1980). Varieties of residual experience. *Quarterly Journal of Experimental Psychology*, *32*, 365–386.

Weiskrantz, L. (1986). *Blindsight: A case study and implications.* Oxford: Oxford University Press.

Weiskrantz, L. (1995). Blindsight—not an island unto itself. *Current Directions in Psychological Science*, *4*, 146–151.

Weiskrantz, L. (1997). *Consciousness lost and found.* Oxford: Oxford University Press.

Weiskrantz, L. (2002). Prime-sight and blindsight. *Consciousness and Cognition*, *11*, 568–581.

Weiskrantz, L., Barbur, J.L., & Sahraie, A. (1995). Parameters affecting conscious versus unconscious visual discrimination with damage to the visual cortex V1. *Proceedings of the National Academy of Sciences, USA*, *92*, 6122–6126.

Weiskrantz, L., Warrington, E.K., Sanders, M.D., & Marshall, J. (1974). Visual capacity in the hemianopic field following a restricted occipital ablation. *Brain*, *97*, 709–728.

Weisstein, N., & Wong, E. (1986). Figure–ground organisation and the spatial and temporal responses of the visual system. In E.C. Schwab & H.C. Nusbaum (Eds.), *Pattern recognition by humans and machines, Vol. 2.* New York: Academic Press.

Welford, A.T. (1952). The psychological refractory period and the timing of high speed performance. *British Journal of Psychology*, *43*, 2–19.

Wells, G.L., & Olson, E.A. (2003). Eyewitness testimony. *Annual Review of Psychology*, *54*, 277–295.

Werker, J.F., & Tees, R.C. (1992). The organisation and reorganisation of human speech perception. *Annual Review of Neuroscience*, *15*, 377–402.

Wertheimer, M. (1945). *Productive thinking.* New York: Harper & Row.

Wessinger, C.M., Fendrich, R., & Gazzaniga, M.S. (1997). Islands of residual vision in hemianopic patients. *Journal of Cognitive Neuroscience*, *9*, 203–221.

West, R., Herndon, R.W., & Ross-Munroe, K. (2000). Event-related neural activity associated with prospective remembering. *Applied Cognitive Psychology*, *14*, S115–S126.

Wetherick, N.E. (1962). Eliminative and enumerative behaviour in a conceptual task. *Quarterly Journal of Experimental Psychology*, *14*, 246–249.

Wheatstone, C. (1838). Contributions to the physiology of vision. Part 1: On some remarkable and hitherto unobserved phenomena of binocular vision. *Philosophical Transactions of the Royal Society of London*, *128*, 371–394.

Wheeldon, L.R. (Ed.) (2000). *Aspects of language production.* Hove, UK: Psychology Press.

Wheeler, M.A., Stuss, D.T., & Tulving, E. (1997). Toward a theory of episodic memory: The frontal lobes and autonoetic consciousness. *Psychological Bulletin*, *121*, 331–354.

Whitlow, S.D., Althoff, R.R., & Cohen, N.J. (1995). Deficit in relational (declarative) memory in amnesia. *Society for Neuroscience Abstracts*, *21*, 754.

Whitney, P., Arnett, P.A., Driver, A., & Budd, D. (2001). Measuring central executive funcitioning: What's in a reading span? *Brain and Cognition*, *45*, 1–14.

Whorf, B.L. (1956). *Language, thought, and reality: Selected writings of Benjamin Lee Whorf.* New York: Wiley.

Wickelgren, W.A. (1968). Sparing of short-term memory in an amnesic patient: Implications for strength theory of memory. *Neuropsychologia*, *6*, 235–244.

Wickens, C.D. (1984). Processing resources in attention. In R. Parasuraman & D.R. Davies (Eds.), *Varieties of attention*. London: Academic Press.

Wilding, J., & Valentine, E. (1991). Superior memory ability. In J. Weinman & J. Hunter (Eds.), *Memory: Neurochemical and abnormal perspectives.* London: Harwood.

Wilkie, R.M., & Wann, J.P. (2002). Driving as night falls: The contribution of retinal flow and visual direction to the control of steering. *Current Biology*, *12*, 2014–2017.

Wilkie, R., & Wann, J. (2003), Controlling steering and judging heading: Retinal flow, visual direction, and extraretinal information. *Journal of Experimental Psychology: Human Perception and Performance*, *29*, 363–378.

Wilkinson, L., & Shanks, D.R. (2004). Intentional control and implicit sequence learning. *Journal of Experimental Psychology: Learning, Memory, & Cognition*, *30*, 354–369.

Willingham, D.B., & Goedert-Eschmann, K. (1999). The relation between implicit and explicit learning: Evidence for parallel development. *Psychological Science*, *10*, 531–534.

Willmes, K., & Poeck, K. (1993). To what extent can aphasic syndromes be localised? *Brain*, *116*, 1527–1540.

Wilson, A.E., & Ross, M. (2001). From chump to champ: People's appraisals of their earlier and present selves. *Journal of Personality and Social Psychology*, *80*, 572–584.

Wilson, A.E., & Ross, M. (2003). The identity function of autobiographical memory: Time is on our side. *Memory*, *11*, 137–149.

Windmann, S. (2004). Effects of sentence context and expectation on the McGurk illusion. *Journal of Memory and Language*, *50*, 212–230.

Winningham R.G., Hyman I.E. Jr, & Dinnel, D.L. (2000). Flashbulb memories? The effects of when the initial memory report was obtained. *Memory, 8*, 209–216.

Wiseman, S., & Tulving, E. (1976). Encoding specificity: Relations between recall superiority and recognition failure. *Journal of Experimental Psychology: Human Learning & Memory, 2*, 349–361.

Wittgenstein, L. (1958). *Philosophical investigations*. New York: Macmillan

Wixted, J.T. (2004). The psychology and neuroscience of forgetting. *Annual Review of Psychology, 55*, 235–269.

Wixted, J.T., & Ebbesen, E.B. (1997). Genuine power curves in forgetting: A quantitative analysis of individual subject forgetting functions. *Memory & Cognition, 25*, 731–739.

Woike, B., Gershkovich, I., Piorkowski, R., & Polo, M. (1999). The role of motives in the content and structure of autobiographical memory. *Journal of Personality and Social Psychology, 76*, 600–612.

Wojciulik, E., Kanwisher, N., & Driver, J. (1998). Modulation of activity in the fusiform face area by covert attention: An fMRI study. *Journal of Neuropsysiology, 79*, 1574–1579.

Woldorff, M.G., Gallen, C.C., Hampson, S.A., Hillyard, S.A., Pantev, C., Sobel, D. et al. (1993). Modulation of early sensory processing in human auditory cortex during auditory selective attention. *Proceedings of the National Academy of Sciences, 90*, 8722–8726.

Wolfe, J.M. (1998). Visual search. In H. Pashler (Ed.), *Attention*. Hove, UK: Psychology Press.

Woodworth, R.S., & Sells, S.B. (1935). An atmosphere effect in formal syllogistic reasoning. *Journal of Experimental Psychology, 18*, 451–460.

Wright, D.B., & Gaskell, G.D. (1995). Flashbulb memories: Conceptual and methodological issues. *Memory, 3*, 67–80.

Wright, D.B., Gaskell, G.D., & O'Muircheartaigh, C.A. (1998). Flashbulb memory assumptions: Using national surveys to explore cognitive phenomena. *British Journal of Psychology, 89*, 103–121.

Wu, D.H., Martin, R.C., & Damian, M.F. (2002). A third route for reading? Implications from a case of phonological dyslexia. *Neurocase, 8*, 274–295.

Wynn, V.E., & Logie, R.H. (1998). The veracity of long-term memories—Did Bartlett get it right? *Applied Cognitive Psychology, 12*, 1–20.

Yaniv, I., & Meyer, D.E. (1987). Activation and metacognition of inaccessible information. Potential bases for incubation effects in problem solving. *Journal of Experimental Psychology: Learning, Memory and Cognition, 13*, 187–205.

Yantis, S., & Jonides, J. (1990). Abrupt visual onsets and selective attention: Voluntary versus automatic allocation. *Journal of Experimental Psychology: Human Perception and Performance, 16*, 121–134.

Yasuda, K., Watanabe, O., & Ono, Y. (1997). Dissociation between semantic and autobiographic memory: A case report. *Cortex, 33*, 623–638.

Yates, F.A. (1966). *The art of memory*. London: Routledge & Kegan Paul.

Yilmaz, E.H., & Warren, W.H. (1995). Visual control of braking: A test of the "tau-dot" hypothesis. *Journal of Experimental Psychology: Human Perception and Performance, 21*, 996–1014.

Young, A.W., Hay, D.C., & Ellis, A.W. (1985). The faces that launched a thousand slips: Everyday difficulties and errors in recognising people. *British Journal of Psychology, 76*, 495–523.

Young, A., Hellawell, D., & de Haan, E. (1988). Cross-domain semantic priming in normal subjects and a prosopagnosic patient. *Quarterly Journal of Experimental Psychology, 40*, 561–580.

Young, A.W., McWeeny, K.H., Hay, D.C., & Ellis, A.W. (1986a). Naming and categorisation latencies for faces and written names. *Quarterly Journal of Experimental Psychology, 38*A, 297–318.

Young, A.W., McWeeny, K.H., Hay, D.C., & Ellis, A.W. (1986b). Matching familiar and unfamilar faces on identity and expression. *Psychological Research, 48*, 63–68.

Young, A.W., Newcombe, F., de Haan, E.H.F., Small, M., & Hay, D.C. (1993). Face perception after brain injury: Selective impairments affecting identity and expression. *Brain, 116*, 941–959.

Young. M.P., & Yamane, S. (1992). Sparse population coding of faces in the inferotemporal cortex. *Science, 256*, 1327–1331.

Yuill, N.M., & Oakhill, J. V. (1991). *Children's problems in text comprehension*. Cambridge: Cambridge University Press.

Zajonc, R.B. (1984). On the primacy of affect. *American Psychologist, 39*, 117–123.

Zangaladze, A., Epstein, C.M., Grafton, S.T., & Sathian, K. (1999). Involvment of visual cortex in tactile discrimination of orientation. *Nature, 401*, 587–590.

Zbrodoff, N.J. (1995). Why is 9 + 7 harder than 2 + 3? Strength and interference as explanations of the problem-size effect. *Memory and Cognition, 23*, 689–700.

Zeki, S. (1983). Colour coding in the cerebral cortex: The reaction of cells in monkey visual cortex to wavelengths and colour. *Neuroscience, 9*, 741–756.

Zeki, S. (1992). The visual image in mind and brain. *Scientific American, 267*, 43–50.

Zeki, S. (1993). *A vision of the brain*. Oxford: Blackwell.

Zeki, S., & ffytche, D.H. (1998). The Riddoch Syndrome: Insights into the neurobiology of conscious vision, *Brain, 121*, 25–45.

Zeki, S., Watson, J.D.G., Lueck, C.J., Friston, K.J., Kennard, C., & Frackowiak, R.S.J. (1991). A direct demonstration of functional specialisation in human visual cortex. *Journal of Neuroscience, 11*, 641–649.

Ziegler, J.C., Muneaux, M., & Grainger, J. (2003). Neighbourhood effects in auditory word recognition: Phonological competition and orthographic facilitation. *Journal of Memory and Language*, *48*, 779–793.

Zihl, J., von Cramon, D., & Mai, N. (1983). Selective disturbance of movement vision after bilateral brain damage. *Brain*, *106*, 313–340.

Zihl, J., von Cramon, D., Mai, N., & Schmid, C. (1991). Disturbance of movement vision after bilateral posterior brain damage, further evidence and follow up observations. *Brain*, *114*, 2235–2252.

Zwaan, R.A. (1994). Effects of genre expectations on text comprehension. *Journal of Experimental Psychology: Learning, Memory, & Cognition*, *20*, 920–933.

Zwaan, R.A., Magliano, J.P., & Graesser, A.C. (1995). Dimensions of situation-model construction in narrative comprehension. *Journal of Experimental Psychology: Learning, Memory, and Cognition*, *21*, 386–397.

Zwaan, R.A., & Radvansky, G.A. (1998). Situation models in language comprehension and memory. *Psychological Bulletin*, *123*, 162–185.

Zwaan, R.A., Stanfield, R.A., & Yaxley, R.H. (2002). Language comprehenders mentally represent the shapes of objects. *Psychological Science*, *13*, 168–171.

Zwaan, R.A., & van Oostendop, U. (1993). Do readers construct spatial representations in naturalistic story comprehension? *Discourse Processes*, *16*, 125–143.

Zwitserlood, P. (1989). The locus of the effects of sentential–semantic context in spoken-word processing. *Cognition*, *32*, 25–64.

Author index

Subject index

Entries given in **bold** indicate glossary terms.